Japanese Patent Law – Cases and Comments

Max Planck Series on Asian Intellectual Property Law

Volume 17

The Institution

The Max Planck Institute for Innovation and Competition has pioneered intellectual property research and education in Asia since the late 1960s and in 1975 set up a Department for Japan and East Asia. The Institute has not only been involved in fundamental research on Asian intellectual property law, but also in drafting legislation for various Asian countries both on the Institute's own account, and in cooperation with projects funded by the European Union, WIPO, the World Bank, UNDP, the German GTZ and others. In order to foster academic exchange, cooperation agreements were concluded with institutions in Japan, Korea, Taiwan, China and Thailand. The Max Planck Institute regularly receives guest researchers from Asian countries and conducts conferences and workshops on Asian intellectual property law.

Contents/Issues addressed

Spurred by the TRIPS Agreement and an increasing number of bilateral or multilateral free-trade agreements, most Asian countries have completely overhauled their intellectual property systems in the past twenty years. Extension systems for patents, protection of geographical indications or general fair use provisions have been added, enforcement structures have been improved and specialised IP courts been set up in China, Taiwan, Japan, Thailand and Korea.

These developments are reflected in the Max Planck Institute's Asian IP series that includes both country-specific reports and comparative studies on current problems of interest. Particular attention in this respect is given to the non-English speaking countries of Asia where reliable information is often difficult to come by.

Objective & Readership

The Max Planck Series on Asian Intellectual Property Law aims at providing expert coverage of intellectual property rights, their administration and enforcement in Asian jurisdictions for both academic and practicing lawyers. Since the year 2000, more than fifteen volumes have been published.

The titles published in this series are listed in the back of this volume.

Japanese Patent Law – Cases and Comments

Edited by

Christopher Heath

Atsuhiro Furuta

Max Planck Institute
for Innovation and Competition

Wolters Kluwer

Published by:
Kluwer Law International B.V.
PO Box 316
2400 AH Alphen aan den Rijn
The Netherlands
E-mail: international-sales@wolterskluwer.com
Website: lrus.wolterskluwer.com

Sold and distributed in North, Central and South America by:
Wolters Kluwer Legal & Regulatory U.S.
7201 McKinney Circle
Frederick, MD 21704
United States of America
Email: customer.service@wolterskluwer.com

Sold and distributed in all other countries by:
Air Business Subscriptions
Rockwood House
Haywards Heath
West Sussex
RH16 3DH
United Kingdom
Email: international-customerservice@wolterskluwer.com

ISBN 978-90-411-9419-0

e-Book: ISBN 978-90-411-9420-6
web-PDF: ISBN 978-90-411-9421-3

List of Authors and Editors

Prof. Dr. Marc Dernauer is an associate professor of law at Chuo University.

Jinzō Fujino is a former professor at Tokyo University of Science. e-mail: ren3fujino@gmail.com

Atsuhiro Furuta is an administrative judge at the Japanese Patent Office. e-mail: furuta.atsuhiro@gmail.com

Miki Gotō is a Japanese attorney at law at Anderson Mōri & Tomotsune.

Nobuyuki Hamanaka is an administrative judge at the Japanese Patent Office.

Makoto Hattori is a Japanese attorney at law at Abe, Ikubo & Katayama.

Dr. Christopher Heath is a judge at the European Patent Office and former head of the Max Planck Institute's Asian Department. e-mail: blitzblitzblau@web.de

Dr. Klaus Hinkelmann is a German and European patent attorney at Patentanwaltskanzlei Hinkelmann. e-mail: khinkelmann@hinkelmann-ip.com

Yūsuke Ichikawa is a Japanese patent attorney at Anderson Mori & Tomotsune.

Takuya Iizuka is a Japanese attorney at law at Mori Hamada & Matsumoto.

Masahito Imai is a Japanese attorney at law at KUBOTA.

Yasuhiko Irinoda is a Japanese attorney at law.

Hirotsugu Ishikawa is an attorney at the Ministry of Justice and Ministry of Foreign Affairs.

Yūichiro Kaburaki is a judge at the Nagoya District Court.

Kumiko Katsumata is a judge at the Nagano District Court.

Hiroaki Kikuchi is a judge at the Osaka District Court.

Masakazu Kobayashi is a Japanese attorney at law at Nakamura & Partners.

Teru Koide is an examiner at the Japanese Patent Office.

Prof. Toshiyuki Kōno is a professor of law at Kyushu University.

Dr. Mineko Mohri is a legal officer at the World Intellectual Property Organization and licensed attorney in Japan and New York State.

Motoyuki Nakashima is a judge at the Sendai District Court.

Prof. Dr. Yuko Nishitani is a professor at Kyoto University.

Hirotaka Nonaka is a Japanese attorney at law and patent attorney at Yodoyabashi & Yamagami LPC. e-mail: h-nonaka@yglpc.com

Prof. Dr. Luke Nottage is a professor of law at University of Sydney Law School.

Asayo Ohyori is a judge, Judicial Resesarch Official at the Supreme Court.

Dr. Shōichi Okuyama is a Japanese patent attorney at Okuyama & Sasajima.

Ryoko Oshikamo is a Japanese patent attorney and researcher at the Max-Planck Institute for Innovation and Competition in Munich.

Dr. Anja Petersen-Padberg is a German attorney at law at TDK Europe.

Kengo Sakai is a Japanese attorney at law at Sonderhoff & Einsel.

Yasuhiro Sato is a Japanese attorney at law at STW & Partners.

Kazuo Shibata is a principal examiner at the Japanese Patent Office. e-mail: kaz-xmas@cpost.plala.or.jp

Yumiko Shirahase is a Japanese attorney at law at Anderson Mōri & Tomotsune.

Ryōta Shitamichi is a professor and government attorney at the International Cooperation Department of the Research and Training Institute, Ministry of Justice.

Wataru Sueyoshi is a Japanese attorney at law at STW & Partners.

Prof. Dr. Toshiko Takenaka is a professor at the University of Washington & Keio University.

Shinichiro Tanaka is a Japanese attorney at Nakamura & Partners.

Kōichi Tanaka is a judge at the Tokyo High Court.

Takeshi Tsuru is an examiner at the Japanese Patent Office.

Masashi Yasui works at NGK INSULATORS LTD.

Prof. Hisayoshi Yokoyama is a professor of law at Gakushuin University.

Tetsutaro Yukutake is an examiner at the Japanese Patent Office.

All opinions expressed in this volume the personal views of the authors and cannot be attributed to the institutions or organisations the authors are affiliated with.

Table of Contents

PART IV: PROCEDURES BEFORE THE PATENT OFFICE

3. The Scope of Protection: Interpreting Patent Claims

PART VI: THE ENFORCEMENT OF PATENT RIGHTS

1. Jurisdiction, Procedure and Applicable Law

Preface

On Contributors and Decisions

The contributors to this volume are part of the "Max Planck Connection". Since the Max Planck Institute for Foreign and International Patent, Copyright and Competition Law was founded in Munich in 1966, Japanese visitors have come to study at the Institute, be it as researchers or, since 2003, also as master students of the MIPLC. The first visitors were Professors *Keiko* and *Yoshinobu Someno* in 1967 and *Kōe Toyosaki* in 1971. A list of Japanese visitors up to 1996 can be found in the *Festschrift für Friedrich-Karl Beier* (*Chiteki zaisan to kyōsōhō no riron*, Tokyo 1996). In the early 2000s, the monthly case law discussion (*Hanrei Kenkyūkai*) was started when *Mineko Mohri* and *Makoto Hattori* were at the Institute. Over the years, most contributors have participated in this monthly *hanrei kenkyukai* and made presentations and translations.

Most of the decisions selected for this volume date from the two decades after 1995, the time when *Ryōichi Mimura* and *Toshiaki Iimura* were active as judges in the IP field, be it in the Tokyo District Court, the IP High Court or as assistants in the Supreme Court. The decisions they prepared or rendered were bold, well-reasoned and often questioned established practice. They were read and commented amongst the international patent community, and they were taken into account by courts abroad. The personality of these two judges, as their decisions, make a case not only for specialised courts, but also for a specialised judiciary where judges are not continuously transferred, but can obtain an experience equal to their peers in the English Patents Court, the Düsseldorf courts or the U.S. CAFC.

When the Max Planck Institute's Asian IP series was conceived back in 1997, a publication on Japanese Patent Law was already planned, but life came in between. *Gut Ding will Weile haben.*

The preface to this book was supposed to be written by *Dr. Shōen Ono*. Lamentably, he passed away in August 2018 at the age of 86. His generosity towards foreign students, his intellectual depth, his humanity and humour will not be forgotten.

The Editors

Introduction

History and Economic Importance of the Patent System for Japan

Christopher Heath and Atsuhiro Furuta

1. INVENTIVE JAPAN IN ANCIENT REGIME

The Japanese word *tokkyo*, which means patent, was itself invented or introduced in the *Meiji*-era (1868-1912), while the inventive nature of Japan goes back to old ages. There are inventions which originated in Japan, such as Japanese style *kimono* (clothes), *orimono* (textiles), *shōyu* (soy sauce), etc., but we do not know when and by whom these were invented.[1] Even if products as such were imported from or originated in foreign countries, Japanese always made significant efforts to produce and adapt them in Japanese style. *Hinawajū* (matchlock rifles), which were first imported in 1543, were soon mass-produced in Japan with immense effort by analysing their mechanism. They were widely used in the latter half of *Sengoku*-era (1467-1603).

After the *Sengoku*-era, *Ieyasu Tokugawa* (1543-1616) seized governmental power over the whole nation, became *shōgun* and started the *bakufu* (regime) of his dynasty in *Edo* (current Tokyo) in 1603. During this feudal regime, Japan enjoyed a long and durable peace with its exotic and self-contained culture that became a closed nation (*sakoku*) between 1630 to 1852.[2] The *Tokugawa* regime in general was very conservative and often prohibited the manufacture of new things. A typical ruling of July 1721 read as follows:

> "1. All new things, such as utensils or textiles, are prohibited.
>
> 2. The new publishing of books is also prohibited. If it is difficult to do so, one shall ask the governmental office. But for the time being also woodcut picture print business is prohibited ..."

---

1. For Japanese inventions in old times, see, for example, N. SUGIBAYASHI, Shin kōgyo shoyūken hō gairon dai ni hen jō *(New general studies of industrial property rights 2nd part 1st volume)*, 1962, 11; M. KUROKAWA, Zōtei kōgei siryō *(History of Craftworks in Japan, supplementarily edited)*; 1974, 3, series Mono to ningen no bunkashi *(Cultural History of Human and Things)*, including K. UEMURA, Orimono *(Textiles)*, 2014, H. YOSHIDA, shōyu *(soy sauce)*, etc.
2. The closed nation system was established step by step over the years in relation to a prohibition of Christianity in Japan. In 1630, the import of Chinese books for Christianity or Western studies was prohibited, in 1633, trade with Western countries was prohibited with a few exceptions and the travel of Japanese people to foreign countries was also severely punished, In 1634, the construction of Dejima *(separated island)* started in Nagasaki for separate housing of foreigners in Japan, etc. See, e.g., J. ŌTSUKI/E. SATŌ, Nihon yōgaku hennenshi *(Chronological History of Western Study in Japan)*, 1995, 74, 77, 78.

But it would not be correct to say that during the long *Edo*-era, Japan was completely closed from the outside world and prohibited new things in general. The *Tokugawa* regime decreed the Japanese or Chinese traditional science as the authorised one and subsidised it with its governmental budget. But the stance of the regime towards science and technology varied over the times.

Yoshimune Tokugawa (1684-1751), 8th *shōgun* (1716-1745), was a governmental reformer within the limits of a feudal system. The above ruling of prohibiting new things went in parallel with the official allowance of commercial monopoly guilds, and the main purpose of the ruling was to supress economic luxury and to put commerce under the governance of the regime, and was also accompanied by the promotion of special regional products.[3]

Even when limiting import and export, the regime continued contacts with one European country, the Netherlands, through one designated port, *Dejima*, an island off Nagasaki in Kyushu. Prohibition of western (Dutch) books was loosened especially for science and technology from 1720 onwards. *Rangaku/Yōgaku* (Dutch/Western studies) were eagerly continued mainly by private scholars in the later *Edo* period, and in 1811 the regime set up the governmental institute for the translation of European languages, one of precursors of Tokyo University.[4] *Gennai Hiraga* (1728-1779), one of most famous inventors of the *Edo*-era, in 1776 reinvented a static electricity producing machine, *Erekiteru*, which had been imported from Holland, yet was broken upon arrival. *Genpaku Sugita* (1733-1817) and *Ryōtaku Maeno* (1723-1803) in 1774 published *Kaitaishinsho*, the first full translation of a European anatomy book. However, many private or official scholars in this sector were arrested and punished in 1828 after the German scholar *Philipp Franz von Siebold* was secretly given maps of Japan under prohibition of export. Further arrests of followers of Western studies followed in 1839 for criticism against the regime.[5] By rulings between 1840 and 1850, the import, translation and publication of Dutch books became more difficult under strict censorship, because it was considered important for the stability of the feudal regime to suppress criticism, which in the long run was impossible. The continuous interest in Western studies in Japan along with the traditional science was a base for the rapid introduction and adoption of modern Western science and technology during the *Meiji*-era.

---

3. JPO, Kōgyō shoyūken seido hyakunenshi *(100 year history of industrial property right system)*, 1984, 7. For monopoly policy and promotion of special products in *Edo*-era, see also, A. YOSHINAGA, Kinsei no senbai seido *(Monopoly system in middle age)*, 1973, 209.
4. For a history of Western studies in the Edo-era, see, for example, JAPAN-NETHERLANDS INSTITUTE (ed.) Yōgakushi jiten *(Dictionary of history of western study)*, 1984, 7; J. NUMATA, Yōgaku *(Western study)*, 1996, 234.
5. *Philipp Franz von Siebold* (1796-1876) was a famous German physician who stayed in Japan from 1823 to 1829 and taught Western science to many Japanese disciples, but he was expelled from Japan because he tried to export a detailed map of Japan. More than 50 Japanese officials and disciples were arrested and punished. In the incident of 1839, so called Bansha no goku *(Arrest for Western Study)*, *Chōei Takano* (1804-1850) and *Kazan Watanabe* (1793-1841), who criticised the policy of closing off Japan, and their followers were arrested and punished. *Takano* was a disciple scholar of *Siebold*, and *Watanabe* was a high ranking official and regarded as a big supporter of Western studies. Such incidents also afterwards influenced the regime's policy of suppressing Western ideas.

Up until the end of the *Edo*-era, there existed some monopolies, primitive trade marks, censorship and a control of publications. While Japanese were diligent and inventive, there certainly was no modern concept or idea of intellectual property.[6]

2. INTRODUCTION OF THE PATENT SYSTEM IN JAPAN

After US admiral Perry arrived with his *kurofune* (black ships) in 1853, Japan had to open the nation to foreign countries and - after 1858 - to conclude what is referred to in Japan as 'Unequal Treaties'. This event troubled the whole nation and after a civil war, the *Tokugawa* regime handed over its governmental power to the new movement, which had the *Meiji* emperor in its centre. Starting with the *Meiji Ishin* (Restoration) of 1868, the new government made constant efforts to build a modern imperial nation with a constitution, to import and emulate modern Western science and technology, and to revise the Unequal Treaties. For the latter, it was made a precondition to become a member to the 1883 Paris Convention and thus mandatory to introduce a concept of intellectual property protection comparable to Western standards.

The first attempt to introduce a patent system through the *senbai ryaku kisoku* (Monopoly Ruling) of 6 April 1871 was soon abandoned, as industry was unprepared and there was no mechanism for enforcement. No patent had been granted. The real modern patent was first established by the *senbai tokkyo jōrei* (Monopoly Patent Ordinance) of 18 April 1885. This Monopoly Patent Ordinance stipulated the requirements for patentability such as utility, novelty and the exclusion of medicines, and a protection period of 5, 10 or 15 years.

In drafting this law, *Korekiyo Takahashi* (1854-1936),[7] the first commissioner of the Japanese Patent Office (JPO), played a central role as an employee of the Ministry of Agriculture and Commerce (precursor of the Ministry of Economics, Trade and Industry (METI)), which was first established in 1881. A great adventurer in the *Meiji*-era, as a teenager he secretly travelled to the US without a penny in his pocket, narrowly escaped from slavery, returned to Japan, became a teacher, official, entrepreneur, official of the central bank, minister of finance and prime minister. He was murdered by right wing military in a coup d'état on 26 February 1936 because he had opposed a further increase of the military budget. After drafting the above first patent law (which required some convincing of the Japanese government that IP laws were important), in 1885 and 1886 he travelled to the United States, United Kingdom, France and Germany for further research of Western patent systems. Thereafter, he drafted an amendment to the Patent Ordinance, the *tokkyo jōrei* that was promulgated on 18 December 1888 and reflected the conclusions Takahashi drew from his study visit, namely that the US patent system at that time was the world's

---

6. For treatment of inventions etc. in the *Edo*-era, see also, N. SUGIBAYASHI (above); Y. FUSE, Edojidai ni okeru mukeizaisan *(Immaterial property in the Edo-era)*, in: Y. SOMENO et al. (eds.), Chitekishoyūken ronkō *(Study of intellectual property)*, 1985, 117; S. KOBAYASHI, Edo jidai ni okeru hatsumei/sōsaku to kenri hogo *(Invention/creation in the Edo-era and protection of right)*, 61-5 Patent 48 (2008).
7. For a bibliography of *Korekiyo Takahashi* in English, see: R. SMETHURST, Takahashi Korekiyo, Japan's Keynes, Cambridge (Mass.), 2007.

the most advanced. In accordance with the US system,[8] the *tokkyo jōrei* provided for a modern patent right, a first-to-invent principle, and a system of examination and appeal/invalidation trial.[9]

The law amendment of 1 March 1899, renaming the *tokkyo jōrei* to *tokkyo hō* (Patent Act), reflected Japan's ratification of the Paris Convention on 18 April 1899 and provided for a recognition of an international priority, method inventions, 15 years protection period, an appeal to the *daishin'in* (the old Supreme Court, subsequently referred to in this book as the Imperial Supreme Court) against an invalidation trial decision of the JPO,[10] etc. As an important step for the foreign affairs policy of Japan in the *Meiji*-era, the Unequal Treaties were abolished.

While a new utility model system was introduced in 1905 (an idea adopted from Germany), the Patent Act was amended in 1909, 1921, 1929 and 1938. The law amendment of 1909 provided a limitation of publicly known prior art in Japan, an employee's invention scheme, in which the right over the invention in principle belonged to the employee, *kōkoku shimpan* (appeal proceedings) in the JPO, etc. The amendment of 30 April 1921 was of major importance because it meant a change towards the first-to-file system. The amendment also introduced a reasoned notice of rejection and a pre-grant opposition system.[11] The Japanese patent system had

---

8. *Korekiyo Takahashi* wrote in his autobiography (first published in 1936) the impression that the US patent system was most developed at that time. He wrote also many episodes about the research such as that he got the US patent documents by promising an exchange of future publishing Japanese patent documents. See also, Research Office of Industrial Property Training Institute of the JPO (ed.), Takahashi Korekiyo ikō (1) – wagakuni tokkyo seido no kiin kōen *(Postumous worls of Korekiyo Takahashi (1) – lecture on the origin of the Japanese Patent System)*, 27 Tokkyo Kenkyū 43 (1999); Reserch Office of Industrial Property Training Institute of the JPO (ed.), Takahashi Korekiyo ikō (2) – tokkyokyoku no omoide *(Postumous works of Korekiyo Takahashi (2), lecture on memory of the Japanese Patent Office)*, 28 Tokkyo Kenkyū 59 (1999).
9. At that time, the appeal/trial system was yet primitive. There was a re-examination procedure against a decision of examination, and an internal appeal could be filed in the JPO against a decision of re-examination. There was also an invalidation trial in the JPO. But such appeal or trial procedure in the JPO acted as final instance and a further appeal to judicial courts was impossible. The old trial system in the German Patent Office had influenced the early patent law legislation in Japan. For the history of appeal and trial system in Japan, see, e.g., M. Amino, Wagakuni no kōgyō shoyūkenhō ni okeru shinpan seido no enkaku *(Histrory of appeal and trial system in the industrial property laws of Japan)*, 5 Nihon Kōgyō Shōyūken Hōgakkai Nenpō 119 (1982).
10. This administrative side to the law may very well have been emulated from Germany where appeals from the invalidation board of the Patent Office went directly to the German Imperial Supreme Court, and where the validity of patents could not be challenged before ordinary courts (see Case No. 49 for further details).
11. Japan adopted at first US like patent system, but by the amendment of 1921 a continental or German-like system was introduced. *Ichirō Kiyose* (1884-1967) stated that the Patent Act of 1921 was based on the inventor's right like under continental law, based on a granting procedure through examination like under US law, while the effects and scope of a patent by trial within the Patent Office was based on the German system, and the pre-grant opposition system on UK law. See I. Kiyose, Tokkyohō Genri *(Principle of Patent)*, 1922, 57. *I. Kiyose* studied patent law directly under *Josef Kohler* in Germany in 1913 and his Tokkyohō Genri and his doctoral thesis, Hatumei Tokkyo Seido no Kigen oyobi Hattatsu *(Origin and Development of Invention Patent System)* which was published in 1918, were the earliest works in Japan for patent law with a comparative view including an introduction of *J. Kohler*'s legal thinking. *Kiyose* also contributed

almost been completed by that time.[12] In 1929, the Patent Act was amended regarding provisions for introducing evidence in the JPO trial etc. because of the amendment of the Code of Civil Procedure, and in 1938 because of the ratification of the 1934 London Revision of the Paris Convention.

The patent attorney system was developed in parallel with the intellectual property laws in Japan. Already in 1887 or 1889, representation for the patent procedure was provided in the ordnances of the Ministry of Agriculture and Commerce, yet anyone could become a representative without restriction. The patent attorney system where only persons who passed a test could became patent attorneys started by the ordinances of 1899, and the Utility Model Act of 1905 first provided that only patent attorneys could represent before the JPO. The Patent Attorney's Act was first introduced in 1921 and the Association of Patent Attorneys was founded in 1922. Different from many other countries, patent attorneys can qualify not only by passing an exam, but also by working as a patent examiner at the JPO for a minimum of seven years.

Although the patent system as envisaged by the Paris Convention had initially been introduced in order to abolish the Unequal Treaties, by studying foreign patent systems, the importance of patents for economic or industrial development through promoting inventions was soon recognised in Japan.

3. AFTER THE SECOND WORLD WAR (1945–2002)

After the Second World War, Japan restarted the nation with the new constitution under the strong influence of the United States. The JPO started the internal consideration for the amendment of IP laws in 1945, and the Cabinet order of 2 December 1949 decided to commission a fundamental study to this end. On 31 July 1950, the Ministry of Trade and Industry decided the foundation of the *Kogyōshoyūken seido kaisei shingikai* (Council for Amendment of Industrial Properties System), which is currently the *Sangyōkōzō shingikai Chitekizaisan seisaku bukai* (Intellectual Property Policy Sub-Council under Council for Structure of Industries).[13]

---

as a member of the Diet to the important amendments of the Patent Act of 1921 and of 1959, and was very famous for works on patent law. But as a prominent lawyer and politician in the turbulent *Meiji- Taishō- and Shōwa*-eras, his activities were of course not limited to the patent field.

12. By the law amendment of 1921, the old 3 instance examination/trial/court system was also established in Japan: for *ex parte* procedure, (i) an examination *(shinsa)*, (ii) appeal proceedings *(kōkoku shimpan)* in the JPO; (iii) an appeal to the old Supreme Court; for *inter parte* procedure, (i) an invalidation trial *(mukō shimpan)*, (ii) appeal proceedings *(kōkoku shimpan)* in the JPO; (iii) an appeal to the old Supreme Court. In 1909, *kōkoku shimpan* was introduced but there was a re-examination procedure as second instance against a decision of examination, *kōkoku shimpan* in the JPO was regarded as last instance for *ex parte* procedure and before the law amendment of 1921 no further appeal to judicial courts was not allowed for *ex parte* procedure. Under the old three instance system, an appeal procedure before the JPO was regarded as a fact finding court instance and appeal grounds to the old Supreme Court were limited to legal ones. See, M. AMINO (above).
13. In the IP field and other many fields, such law amendments are first deliberated through a council, committee or study group, which consists of academics, practitioners and other interested parties (users). These study groups are convened by the responsible ministries already with a

The Council started its studies and on 21 December 1956 submitted its final report to the Minister.[14] After its publication, the Diet passed the JPO-drafted law amendments (amongst which was the current Patent Act[15]) on 28 March 1959, which then came into force on 1 April 1960 and continue to be in force with numerous amendments. The Patent Act 1959 has the following features:

- Extension of novelty-destroying prior art to documents published in foreign countries;
- Introduction of a provision about inventive step;[16]
- Introduction of a provision defining an invention;
- Prohibition of change of the essence of the invention by amendment before grant or correction after grant;
- Strengthening the position of employees for employees' inventions;
- Limitation of the patent right to acts of commercial use;
- Introduction of a system of exclusive and non-exclusive licences;
- Introduction of a clear provision about infringement and remedies, such as injunctive relief, indirect infringement, damage calculation;
- Abolishment of *kōkoku shimpan* (additional tier of appeals) in the JPO and establishment of appeal/trial/court proceedings in the current scheme, etc.[17]

---

certain outcome in mind, which is standard law-making process in Japan. Law amendments are considered at first in such councils or committees, reports of these are published, offices draft the amendment bills, the Cabinet decides to pass them to the Diet, and the Diet passes the bills and they become law. For the current structure of the Intellectual Property Policy Sub-Council, see, the website of the JPO <http://www.jpo.go.jp/resources/shingikai/sangyo-kouzou/shousai/index.html>. Amendments to the Patent Act are usually first deliberated in the Patent System Committee under the Intellectual Property Policy Sub-Council.

14. This report was published in 125 Jurist 37 (1957) with comment by *Y. Kōgyoku*. It was stated in the introduction to the report that after WWII, there was a general tendency in Japan to take the legal systems of the US or UK as model, and the view that also for the patent system, legal ideas of the US and UK should be introduced, while the 1921 Patent Act was considered to be based on the German system. *H. Kaneko* also indicated in his comment on the law amendment in 174 Jurist 2 (1959) that the deliberation for the amendment was initiated by the direction of the General Head Quarters of the United Nations, but the idea differed from the original one because of a change of international and domestic circumstances and some compromise should be also made with the existing patent practice.
15. Law No. 121/1959 of 13 April 1959.
16. In practice, examination of inventive step was already established at this time, based on an interpretation of the novelty provision of the Patent Act of 1921.
17. The current scheme: for *ex parte* procedure, (i) appeal proceedings in the JPO after an examination; (ii) an appeal to the IP (Tokyo) High Court; (iii) an appeal to the Supreme Court; for *inter partes* procedure, (i) an invalidation trial, (ii) an appeal to the IP (Tokyo) High Court; (iii) an appeal to the Supreme Court. Before the current Patent Act of 1959, the law amendment of 1948 changed the appeal instance against a decision of *kōkoku shimpan* in the JPO simply from the old Supreme Court to the Tokyo High Court which could act as fact finding court, because the new Constitution of Japan allowed no special courts and a decision of appeal/trial proceedings of the JPO should be regarded also as an administrative disposition. See, M. AMINO (above). The change of the legal position of judicial courts also made case law more important for patent cases in Japan. *H. Kaneko* stated: "After the Second World War, an appeal against an appeal/trial decision of the Patent Office became a case under the special jurisdiction of the Tokyo High Court and the High Court engages in the fact finding of cases, which increases the role of case law for the practice of the Patent Act. Because appropriateness of fact finding of the

After the workload and delay of the JPO examination became problem, the law amendment of 1970 introduced a publication of the application after 18 months and a deferred examination on request, a re-examination before appeal proceedings and a time limitation for amendments, a system of divisional applications etc.[18] By the law amendment of 1975, a multiple claim system was introduced and patent protection was extended to drinks, foods, medicines and chemically produced substances.[19] After the introduction of the multiple claim system, Japan ratified the Patent Cooperation Treaty in 1978.[20] The law amendment of 1985 introduced an internal priority system.[21] By the law amendment of 1987, the multiple claim system was improved in that independent multiple claims became possible without a restriction to dependent embodiments, and at the same time the system of patent term extension for medicines was introduced.[22]

By amendment of 1993, addition of new subject matter by amendment was prohibited and the utility model system was changed to a registration without examination, which seriously weakened this legal instrument and led to a drop in the number of utility model filings.[23] By the law amendment of 1994, the pre-grant opposition system changed to post-grant, and the original filing of applications in English was allowed.[24] In order to implement the WTO/TRIPs agreement, the provisions for the patent term (hitherto 15 year from publication of the patent gazette up to 20 years from the application date towards 20 years from the application date), and the acts of infringing use (addition of offering for sale or rent) were aligned. By the law amendment of 1998, improvements in the presumption of damages for patent infringements were introduced.[25] By the law amendment of 1999, the period to file a request for examination was shortened (from 7 years to 3 years), and an invention

---

Patent Office can be directly disputed in court proceedings and the scope of determination of court goes beyond a simple application of law." See H. KANEKO, Tokkyo hō wo meguru hanrei no yakuwari, *(Role of case law for patent law)*, in: S. WAGATSUMA et al. (eds.), Tokkyo Hanrei Hyakusen *(Hundred Selected Patent Cases)*, 1st ed. 1966, 6. *Y. Someno* stated also that this change of 1948 became a factor for later reform of the patent system. See Y. SOMENO, Kōgyō shoyūken seido *(Industrial property system)*, 361 Jurist 292 (1967).

18. Law No. 91/1970 of 22 May 1970. The corresponding report of the Committee of the JPO was published in 415 Jurist 67 (1969).
19. The corresponding report of the Committee of the JPO was published in 576 Jurist 39 (1974). In the old Patent Act, in principle, only one single claim was allowed, and patent protection for drinks etc. was denied.
20. Law No. 30/1978 of 26 April 1978.
21. Law No. 41/1985 of 28 May 1985.
22. Law No. 27/1987 of 25 May 1987.
23. Law No. 26/1993 of 23 April 1993. The documents about the law amendments from 1993 to 2006 are available at the website of the JPO <https://www.jpo.go.jp/system/laws/rule/kaisetu/sangyozaisan/sangyou_zaisanhou.html> and <https://www.jpo.go.jp/system/laws/rule/kaisetu/sangyozaisan/sangyou_zaisanhou_hyou.html>.
24. Law No. 116/1994 of 14 December 1994. Japanese translation is needed for such application filed in English, but in the case of an amendment or correction of claims etc. the original English application can be referred to. Such law amendment was based on an agreement between the Japanese and US patent offices. See JPO, Kōgyō shoyūken seido kono jūnen no ayumi – Kōgyō shoyūken seido hyakujūsshūnenkinen *(Recent 10 year steps of the industrial property right system – 110th anniversary of the industrial property right system)*, 1995, 75.
25. Law No. 51/1998 of 6 May 1998.

disclosed on the Internet was recognised as novelty destroying prior art.[26] By the law amendment of 2002, "program" (software) was clearly stipulated as a product and thus became patentable subject matter under the Patent Act.[27]

The current Code of Civil Procedure which included a modernisation of provision statements, preparative procedure for oral proceedings, obligation of submission of documents, adjustment of appeal grounds to the Supreme Court, etc. was enacted in 1996 and set in force in 1998.[28]

4. RECENT PRO-PATENT POLICY (2002–)

In 2002, Prime Minister Junichiro Koizumi declared the *Chiteki Zaisan Rikkoku* (Project of Nation Built on Intellectual Property), thereby starting the recent pro-patent approach of Japan. After the Intellectual Property Basic Act of 2003, government established an Intellectual Property Strategy Headquarters and has devised Intellectual Property Strategy Plans from 2003 onwards. Under this scheme, the JPO also decreed the plan of "First Action within 11 Months" as a 10 years plan in 2004.[29]

From 2003 onwards, all IP laws have been frequently amended, the Patent Act almost every year. Major amendments during this period are as follows:

- 2003: Abolition of the post-grant opposition system and integration of opposition and invalidation trial systems;[30] centralisation of IP jurisdiction to the Tokyo and Osaka District Courts;[31]

---

26. Law No. 41/1999 of 6 May 1999.
27. Law No. 24/2002 of 17 April 2002. The documents about the law amendments of 2002 are available on the website of the JPO <https://www.jpo.go.jp/system/laws/rule/hokaisei/tokkyo/houkaisei_h140417/index.html> and also the corresponding report of the Committee of the JPO at <http://www.jpo.go.jp/resources/shingikai/sangyo-kouzou/shousai/housei-shoi/h13houkokusho.html>.
28. Before and after 1996 there were many minor changes in the Code of Civil Procedure (CCP) in Japan, but the current CCP was completely modernised by Law No. 109 of 26 June 1996, and the old CCP of 1890 was applied with amendments up to 1997 (the major amendment in this period was made in 1926). For a history of the CCP, see, e.g., H. MATSUMOTO/Y. UENO, Minji soshō hō *(Code of Civil Procedure)*, 8th ed. 2015, 25.
29. For the recent pro-patent policy in Japan, see also, M. MORISHIMA, Japan: Success and Setbacks of the "Nation Built on IP" Problems and Expectations, Mitteilungen der deutschen Patentanwälte 2017, 110; T. TAKENAKA/I. NAKAYAMA, Will Intellectual Property Policy Save Japan from Recession? Japan's Basic Intellectual Property Law and Its Implementation Through the Strategic Program, 35 IIC 877 (2004).
30. Law No. 47/2003 of 23 May 2003. The documents about the law amendments of 2003 are available at the website of the JPO <https://www.jpo.go.jp/system/laws/rule/hokaisei/tokkyo/tokkyo_kaiei47gou.html> and <https://www.jpo.go.jp/system/laws/rule/kaisetu/sangyozaisan/sangyou_zaisanhou.html> and also the corresponding report of the Committee of the JPO <https://www.jpo.go.jp/resources/shingikai/sangyo-kouzou/shousai/hunsou-shoi/document/index/fun_report.pdf>. In retrospect, abolishing the opposition system was not a good move.
31. Law No. 108/2003 of 16 July 2003. The corresponding report of the Council of the Cabinet is available at the website of the Cabinet Secretariat <https://www.kantei.go.jp/jp/sihouseido/report-dex.html> and also the corresponding report of the Council of the Ministry of Justice (MOJ) at the website of the MOJ <http://www.moj.go.jp/shingi1/shingi_030205-7.html>

- 2004: Revision of the rules for remunerating employees for their inventions by encouraging company-based remuneration schemes;[32] Setting up of the IP High Court, introducing protective orders, *in camera* proceedings and the statute-based invalidity defence in infringement proceedings;[33]
- 2006: Addition of 'export' to working of patent;[34]
- 2008: Introduction of a registration system for provisional non-exclusive licences;[35]
- 2011: Protection of non-exclusive licences without registration against good-faith purchases of the IP right, limitation of retrial after patent invalidation;[36]
- 2014: Introduction of a new post-grant opposition system;[37]
- 2015: Ownership of employees' inventions now vested in the employer, ratification of the Patent Law Treaty;[38]

---

32. Law No. 79/2004 of 4 June 2004. The documents about the law amendments of 2004 are available at the website of the JPO <https://www.jpo.go.jp/system/laws/rule/hokaisei/tokkyo/sinsa_jinsoku79.html> and <https://www.jpo.go.jp/system/laws/rule/kaisetu/sangyozaisan/sangyou_zaisanhou.html> also the corresponding report of the Committee of the JPO at <http://www.jpo.go.jp/resources/shingikai/sangyo-kouzou/shousai/tokkyo_shoi/h15houkokusho.html>.
33. Law No. 119&120/2004 of 18 June 2004. The documents about the law amendments of 2004 related to the courts system are available at the website of the Cabinet Secretariat <https://www.kantei.go.jp/jp/singi/sihou/hourei/index.html> and also the corresponding report of the Committee of the Cabinet Secretariat at <https://www.kantei.go.jp/jp/singi/sihou/kentoukai/titeki/dai15/15siryou_list.html>.
34. Law No. 55/2006 of 7 June 2006. The documents about the law amendments of 2006 are available at the website of the JPO <https://www.jpo.go.jp/system/laws/rule/hokaisei/isho-shohyo/ishou_houkaisei.html> and <https://www.jpo.go.jp/system/laws/rule/kaisetu/h18/tokkyo_kaisei18_55.html> and also the corresponding report of the Committee of the JPO at <https://www.jpo.go.jp/resources/shingikai/sangyo-kouzou/shousai/tokkyo_shoi/document/index/tokkyo.pdf>.
35. Law No. 16/2008 of 18 April 2008. The documents about the law amendments of 2008 are available at the website of the JPO <https://www.jpo.go.jp/system/laws/rule/hokaisei/tokkyo/tokkyohoutou_kaiei_200201.html> and <https://www.jpo.go.jp/system/laws/rule/kaisetu/h20/tokkyo_kaisei20_16.html> and also the corresponding report of the Committee of the JPO at <https://www.jpo.go.jp/resources/shingikai/sangyo-kouzou/shousai/jisshiken_wg/document/index/wg_tourokuseido.pdf>.
36. Law No. 63/2011 of 8 June 2011. The documents about the law amendments of 2011 are available at the website of the JPO <https://www.jpo.go.jp/system/laws/rule/hokaisei/tokkyo/tokkyohoutou_kaiei_230608.html> and <https://www.jpo.go.jp/system/laws/rule/kaisetu/h23/tokkyo_kaisei23_63.html> and also the corresponding report of the Committee of the JPO at <https://www.jpo.go.jp/resources/shingikai/sangyo-kouzou/shousai/tokkyo_shoi/document/index/housei_kadai.pdf>.
37. Law No. 36/2014 of 14 May of 2014. The documents about the law amendments of 2014 are available at the website of the JPO <https://www.jpo.go.jp/system/laws/rule/hokaisei/tokkyo/tokkyohoutou_kaiei_260514.html> and <https://www.jpo.go.jp/system/laws/rule/kaisetu/h26/tokkyo_kaisei26_36.html> and also the corresponding report of the Committee of the JPO at <http://www.jpo.go.jp/resources/shingikai/sangyo-kouzou/shousai/tokkyo_shoi/h25houkokusho.html>.
38. Law No. 55/2015 of 10 July 2015. The documents about the law amendments of 2015 are available at the website of the JPO <https://www.jpo.go.jp/system/laws/rule/hokaisei/tokkyo/tokkyohoutou_kaiei_270710.html> and <https://www.jpo.go.jp/system/laws/rule/kaisetu/h27/tokkyo_kaisei27_55.html> and also the corresponding report of the Committee of

- 2016: Ratification of the TPP (the Trans Pacific Partnership Agreement, a regional free trade agreement) by 12 countries[39] (not in force);
- 2018: Prolongation of the grace period;[40] Ratification of the TPP by 11 countries[41] (in force);
- 2019: Introduction of German like expert inspection after filing a infringement lawsuit in a court (a new bill).[42]

During the last 15 years, Japan's pro-patent policy resulted in continuous efforts to improve the intellectual property system, but these not always proved sure-footed and at times looked rather confused (e.g. for the opposition system, the employee's invention).

One notable change during this period was the role and the qualification of patent attorneys. While the major service of patent attorneys lies in the application and prosecution of industrial property rights before the JPO, the need for qualified IP experts with broader qualifications has increased. To this end, the Patent Attorneys Act was amended many times. By the amendment of 2000,[43] licensing, consultation, arbitration etc. were added to the list of services that patent attorneys could provide. By the law amendment of 2002,[44] patent attorneys became eligible to represent clients in infringement cases in courts together with attorneys at law. By the amendments of 2007, the scope of the services was further extended.[45]

---

the JPO at <http://www.jpo.go.jp/resources/shingikai/sangyo-kouzou/shousai/tokkyo_shoi/h26houkokusho.html>.

39. Law No. 108/2016 of 16 December 2016. The documents about the law amendments of 2016 are available at the website of the Cabinet Secretariat <http://www.cas.go.jp/jp/tpp/torikumi/index.html>.
40. Law No. 33/2018 of 30 May 2018. The documents about the law amendment of 2018 are available at the website of the JPO <https://www.jpo.go.jp/system/laws/rule/hokaisei/sangyozaisan/fuseikyousou_h300530.html> and the corresponding report of the Committee of the JPO <http://www.jpo.go.jp/resources/shingikai/sangyo-kouzou/shousai/tokkyo_shoi/180215_tokkyo_houkoku.html> and the documents about patent, etc. related part at the website of the JPO <https://www.jpo.go.jp/system/laws/rule/hokaisei/sangyozaisan/tpp_houritu_seibi_h281228.html>.
41. Law No. 70/2018 of 6 July of 2018. The documents about the law amendments of 2018 related to TPP11 are available at the website of the Cabinet Secretariat <https://www.cas.go.jp/jp/tpp/tpp11/index.html>.
42. The new bill is approved by the Govorment and sent to the Diet in March 2019. See the document at the website of the METI <http://www.meti.go.jp/press/2018/03/20190301004/20190301004.html> and the corresponding report of the Committee of the JPO at the website of the JPO <https://www.jpo.go.jp/resources/shingikai/sangyo-kouzou/shousai/tokkyo_shoi/190215_tokkyo_houkoku.html>.
43. Law No. 49/2000 of 26 April 2000. The documents about the law amendment are available at the website of the JPO <https://www.jpo.go.jp/system/laws/rule/hokaisei/benrishi/benrihouan0321/index.html> and also the corresponding abstract report of the Committee of the JPO at <https://www.jpo.go.jp/system/laws/rule/hokaisei/benrishi/benrihouan0321/38_34_1222.html>.
44. Law No. 25/2002 of 17 April 2002. The documents about the law amendment are available at the website of the JPO <https://www.jpo.go.jp/system/laws/rule/hokaisei/benrishi/benrishihou_kaisei_h140418/index.html> and also the corresponding report of the Committee of the JPO at <https://www.jpo.go.jp/shiryou/toushin/toushintou/pdf/agent.pdf>.
45. Law No. 91/2007 of 20 June 2007. The documents about the law amendment are available at the website of the JPO <https://www.jpo.go.jp/system/laws/rule/hokaisei/benrishi/

5. PARALLEL DEVELOPMENT OF CASE LAW

Parallel to many law amendments, the Japanese courts developed its case law in the field of intellectual property law. In this respect, one can identify two epoch making events in the last 20 years. One of them was the *Kilby* decision of 2000, the other the foundation of a specialised IP jurisdiction, in particular the IP High Court.

For the details of the *Kilby* decision, the reader is referred to Case No. 50 in this book. This decision overturned a couple of almost century-old precedents and gave jurisdiction of the infringement courts to determine the validity of a patent and thereby shifted the authoritative power over this issue from the JPO to the courts.[46]

The discussion about the establishment of an IP High Court was waged from 2002 to 2004 in parallel by the Judicial System Reform Headquarters and the Intellectual Property Strategy Headquarters. After a long deliberation, the IP High Court was set up on 1 April 2005 as a separate appeal court within the Tokyo High Court. By amending the Code of Civil Procedure in 2003, the jurisdiction over IP cases had already been centralised in Tokyo and Osaka, but the foundation of the IP High Court was of great symbolic significance in the "Project of a Nation Built on Intellectual Property", and strongly influenced subsequent case law.[47]

Until now, the *daigōgi* (Grand Panel), which consists of 5 judges of the IP High Court[48] decided twelve cases, all of which dealt with issues of patent law:

(i) 30 September 2005, Case No. 10040 (Ne) of 2005 – *Ichitarō*[49]

---

benrishi_kaisei_h190620/index.html> and also the corresponding report of the Committee of the JPO at <http://www.jpo.go.jp/resources/shingikai/sangyo-kouzou/shousai/benrishi_shoi/document/index/01.pdf>. The above Law No. 36/2014 of 14 May of 2014 and Law No. 33/2018 of 30 May 2018 include also amendments to the Patent Attorney Act. For the amendments of 2014 and 2018 to the Patent Attorney Act, the corresponding reports of the Committee of the JPO is available at the website of the JPO <http://www.jpo.go.jp/resources/shingikai/sangyo-kouzou/shousai/benrishi_shoi/h26houkokusho.html> and <http://www.jpo.go.jp/resources/shingikai/sangyo-kouzou/shousai/benrishi_shoi/h30houkokusho.html>.

46. Prior to the *Kilby* decision and the law amendment of 2004 (Law No. 120/2004 of 18 June 2004, set in force in 2005), the validity of a patent could not be disputed in the infringement courts. To invalidate a patent, it was necessary to request an invalidation trial before the JPO, and any decision could be appealed to the Tokyo High Court and the Supreme Court as final instance. Such strict double-track or bifurcated patent system by separating invalidation and infringement procedures is still standard practice in Germany with little exception until now (see the comparative remarks for Case No. 49).
47. The documents of the deliberation are available at the website of the Judicial System Reform Headquarters <https://www.kantei.go.jp/jp/singi/sihou/kentoukai/11titeki.html> and the website of the Intellectual Property Strategy Headquarters <https://www.kantei.go.jp/jp/singi/titeki2/tyousakai/kenrihogo/index.html>. For comments or an analysis of the IP High Court, see also, N. NAKAYAMA, Chitekizaisan kōtosaibansho e no michinori *(Road to the Intellectual Property High Court)*, 1293 Jurist 6 (2005); W. SUEYOSHI, Chitekizaisan kōtosaibansho ni tsuite *(About the Intellectual Property High Court)*, in: N. NAKAYAMA et al. (ed.), Chizairikkoku no hatten e *(For the development of an IP nation)*, 2013, 493; ZADANKAI *(Group Meeting of the IP High Court judges)*, Shinka suru chitekizaisan soshō ni mukete no kentō to kadai *(Consideration and problem for developing intellectual property lawsuit)*, 50 L&T 10 (2011); T. NAKANO, Chizaikōsai 5 nen no kaiko to tenbō *(5 years history of the IP High Court and its future)*, 50 L&T 30 (2011).
48. Website of the IP High Court <http://www.ip.courts.go.jp/hanrei/g_panel/index.html>.
49. Published in 1904 Hanrei Jihō 47 = 1188 Hanrei Times 191. This case is an early case of indirect infringement. The issue of indirect infringement is discussed in Case No. 30.

(ii) 11 November 2005, Case No. 10042 (Gyō-Ke) 2005 – *Method for Producing Polarizer Film*[50]
(iii) 31 January 2006, Case No. 10021 (Ne) of 2005 – *Canon Ink Cartridge*[51]
(iv) 22 March 2007, Case No. 10039 (Ne) of 2006 – *Semiconductor Memory Device* (withdrawn)
(v) 30 May 2008, Case No. 10563 (Gyō-Ke) of 2006 – *Solder Resist*[52]
(vi) 27 January 2012, Case No. 10043 (Ne) of 2010 – *Pravastatin*[53]
(vii) 1 February 2013, Case No. 10015 (Ne) of 2012 – *Container for Disposing Paper Diapers*[54]
(viii) 16 May 2014, Case No. 10043 (Ne) of 2013, No. 10007&10008 (Ra) of 2013 – *FRAND Declaration*[55]
(ix) 30 May 2014, Case No. 10195&10196&10197&10198 (Gyō-Ke) of 2013 – *Bevacizmab*[56]
(x) 25 March 2016, Case No. 10014 (Ne) of 2005 – *Maxacaltitol*[57]
(xi) 20 January 2017, Case No. 10046 (Ne) of 2016 – *Oxaliplatinum*[58]
(xii) 13 April 2018, Case No. 10182&10184 of 2016 – *Pyrimidine Derivative*[59]

Four of these decisions, namely (iii), (vi), (ix) and (x) were amended by the Supreme Court, but this does not diminish the Grand Panel's achievements in developing the law on (i) indirect infringement, (ii) support requirement for parameter inventions, (iii) exhaustion and reconstruction, (v) disclaimers, (vi) product-by-process claims, (vii) presumption of damages, (viii) standard essential patents and FRAND, (ix) patent term extension, (x) doctrine of equivalents, (xi) scope of an extended patent, (xii) *locus standi* / inventive step).[60]

For the development of case law, judges specialised in intellectual property have become increasingly important. Some of these, such as *Ryōichi Mimura*, *Toshiaki Iimura* and *Makiko Takabe*, have become well-known far beyond Japan. While they have worked mainly in IP related district courts or the IP High Court, it

50. For details, see, Case No. 10 in this book.
51. For details, see, Case No. 31 in this book.
52. For details, see, Case No. 22 in this book.
53. For details, see, Case No. 37 in this book.
54. For details, see, Case No. 55 in this book.
55. For details, see, Case No. 52 in this book.
56. For details, see, Case No. 59 in this book.
57. For details, see, Case No. 40 in this book.
58. For details, see, Case No. 60 in this book.
59. Published on the website of the courts <http://www.courts.go.jp/app/files/hanrei_jp/667/087667_hanrei.pdf>. The IP High Court decided in this case there was still a *locus standi* in an appeal against an invalidation trial decision after the expiration of the patent right. Further, that novelty and inventive step could be acknowledged as a selection invention compared to a prior art document that mentioned the chemical together with many others. The result in this case appears quite common sensical.
60. Problems on how to appropriately choose cases for a decision by the Grand Panel with the purpose of a harmonisation of diverging case law remain pertinent, though. See, for example, T. Kudō, Chitekizaisan soshō no genjō to kadai *(Current situation and problem of intellectual property lawsuit)*, 24 Quarterly Jurist 65 (2018); Y. Tamura, Chizaikōsai daigōgi no un'yō to saikōsai no kankei ni kansuru seidoronteki kōsatsu *(Systematic considerations about the relationship between the operation of the IP High Court Grand Panel and the Supreme Court)*, 69-5 Hōsō Jihō 1231 (2017).

should be noted that there is no clear career path to become an IP judge in Japan, and it is common that appointed judges are rotated every couple of years, making a specialisation in certain areas very difficult.[61]

6. STATISTICS

The statistics of patent and utility model applications in Japan from 1885 to 2017 are as follows:[62]

Year	Patent			Utility Model	
	Domestic Applications	PCT Applications	Registered	Applications	Registered
1885	425		99		
1886	1,384		205		
1887	906		109		
1888	778		183		
1889	1,064		209		
1890	1,180		240		
1900	2,006		586		
1910	5,964		1,769	12,545	3,302
1920	11,017		2,161	19,717	3,942
1930	15,430		4,976	38,487	12,236
1940	19,827		6,716	31,833	15,703
1950	16,896		4,272	24,324	8,021
1960	43,484		11,252	63,077	22,102
1970	130,831		30,879	142,066	27,718
1980	191,020		46,106	197,785	50,001
1990	367,590		59,401	138,294	43,300
2000	436,865	9,447	125,880	9,587	5,372
2001	439,175	11,688	121,742	8,806	9,441

61. See, for example, ZADANKAI (above); Y. TAMURA (above); T. IIMURA (interview), Chizaisaibankan ga umarete kara sodatsu made *(Birth and upbringing of an IP Judge)*, 66-1 Patent 31 (2013). All judges are legally qualified, and *chōsakan* (technical researchers) are dispatched from the JPO to support judges in technical fields (currently, for example, 11 researchers from the JPO work in the IP High Court). There is also an appointment system of *senmon iin* (technical experts) in the IP High Court.
62. JPO, Hyakunenshi (above); Hyakujūsshūnenkinen (above); Sangyōzaisanken seido 125 shūnenkinenshi – sanōgyōzaisanken seido kono jūgonen no ayumi – *(125th anniversary of the industrial property right system – the most recent 15 years)*, 2010, available at the website of the JPO <https://www.jpo.go.jp/introduction/rekishi/125th_kinenshi.html>; Annual reports, available at the website of the JPO <https://www.jpo.go.jp/resources/report/nenji/index.html>. These numbers represent the Japanese fiscal year (from 1 April of the indicated year to 31 March of the next year).

	Patent			Utility Model	
Year	Domestic Applications	PCT Applications	Registered	Applications	Registered
2002	421,044	13,879	120,018	8,602	7,793
2003	413,092	17,097	122,511	8,169	7,694
2004	423,081	19,850	124,192	7,986	7,363
2005	427,078	24,290	122,944	11,386	10,573
2006	408,674	26,422	141,399	10,965	10,593
2007	396,291	26,935	164,954	10,315	10,080
2008	391,002	28,027	176,950	9,452	8,917
2009	348,596	29,291	193,349	9,507	9,019
2010	344,598	31,524	222,693	8,679	8,571
2011	342,610	37,974	238,323	7,984	7,595
2012	342,796	42,787	274,791	8,112	8,054
2ß13	328,436	43,075	277,079	7,622	7,363
2014	325,989	41,292	227,142	7,095	7,017
2015	318,721	43,097	189,358	6,860	6,695
2016	318,381	44,495	203,087	6,480	6,297
2017	318,479	47,425	199,577	6,105	6,024

The number of patent applications almost continuously increased along with the economic growth of Japan up to around 2005. After the financial crisis of 2007, the trend changed towards a decline and until now has not completely recovered (which is also in line with the GDP of Japan.[63] And while it can be said that the patent system may influence a countries' economic growth, the number of patents and patent applications in a developed country certainly depends on the countries' economy). In recent years, the number of patent filings has been almost stable at around 320 thousand. But the number of PCT applications has been continuously rising even during recession. This shows that Japanese industry strategically selects inventions that will also be filed in foreign markets.

The following table shows the number of lawsuits on patents and utility models at the District Court and High Court level between 1993 and 2017:[64]

63. GDP Statistics of Japan are available at the website of the Cabinet Office <http://www.esri.cao.go.jp/jp/sna/data/data.html>.
64. Recent statistics of IP court cases are annually published in *Hōsō Jihō*, For the most recent ones, see, GENERAL SECRETARIAT OF THE SUPREME COURT, Heisei 29 nendo chitekizaisanken kankei minji/gyōsei jiken no gaikyō *(General report on intellectual property civil and administrative cases in fiscal year 2017)*, 70-10 Hōsō Jihō 2705 (2018).

Year	District Court Level		High Court Level		
	Patent	Utility Model	Patent	Utility Model	Appeal cases to JPO decisions (total)
1993	91	130	38	14	196
1994	106	98	28	12	285
1995	111	61	18	17	280
1996	157	77	23	14	279
1997	167	70	40	16	328
1998	156	58	50	23	393
1999	191	72	62	22	429
2000	176	59	69	30	478
2001	153	34	58	23	575
2002	165	38	77	13	636
2003	189	27	66	14	534
2004	217	35	68	6	527
2005	196	13	51	3	589
2006	139	16	41	5	566
2007	156	12	58	4	437
2008	147	3	57	2	496
2009	174	1	55	2	443
2010	122	9	57	5	413
2011	207	7	47	4	453
2012	155	3	58	1	457
2013	164	8	61	4	353
2014	182	5	71	2	278
2015	154	6	68	3	263
2016	142	3	62	3	279
2017	158	5	67	1	236

The statistics of court cases mirror the trend in the number of patent applications and may also be influenced by the economic situation of Japan. The number of patent infringement cases at the District Court level exceeded 200 only in 2004 and 2011, and has otherwise been stable at around 150, which may be less than in other countries of a comparable economy, such as Germany or South Korea. It is sometimes said that the Japanese are somewhat averse to dispute resolution through the courts and rather prefer to settle disputes in a different manner, e.g. by way of cross licensing.[65]

65. G. RAHN, Patentstrategien in Japan *(Patent Strategies in Japan)*, GRUR Int. 1994, 377.

7. ASSOCIATIONS AND PUBLICATIONS

a) Associations

- The Association of Patent Attorneys was founded in 1922. The association published the Journal of the Association of Patent Attorneys, which between 1921 and 1934 was renamed *Tokkyo to Shōhyō* (Patents and Trademarks). This journal was again renamed to *Patento* (Patent) in 1946 and continues up to this day.
- The *Kogyō shoyūken hogo kyōkai* (Association for Protection of Industrial Property), renamed *Hatsumei kyōkai* (Association for Invention) and the *Hatsumei suishin kyōkai* (Association for Promotion of Invention), were both founded in 1904. In 1905, these started to publish the *Kogyō shoyūken zasshi* (Journal of Industrial Property) which in 1910 was renamed *Hatsumei* (The Invention), a monthly journal that continues up to this day.
- The ten major Japanese electronics companies in 1938 founded the *Jūyōkai*, the association of Japanese patent companies. Subsequently, other industries such as metals, mechanics, chemicals etc. joined, and the *Jūyōkai* became the most important IP user company group in Japan. The name of the association changed to *Jigyōsha kogyōshōyuken kyōkai* (Company Association of Industrial Property) in 1956, *Nihon tokkyo kyōkai* (Japan Patent Association) in 1959, Nihon chitekizaisan kyōkai (Japan Intellectual Property Association) in 1994. This association publishes the Journal *Chizai Kanri* (Intellectual Property Management), which was formerly named *Tokkyo Kanri* (Patent Management).
- AIPPI (Association of Internationale pour la Proproприété Industrielle) is an international association for cooperation in the field of IP that was founded in 1897. Although Japanese government officials had participated in the general congresses of AIPPI as early as 1905, the Japanese group of AIPPI was founded only in 1956. AIPPI Japan publishes the AIPPI Journals in both Japanese and English (with different content).
- One of most important academic IP institutions, *Kōgyō shōyūken hōgakkai* (Japan Association of Industrial Property Law) was founded in 1974. The academic studies of IP, initiated by professor *Kōe Toyosaki*, played a central role in the foundation.[66]

---

66. *K. Toyosaki* (1908-1980) was a famous professor of trade law and intellectual property law at Gakushūin University and the first president of the Japan Association of Industrial Property Law (JAIPL). See, K. Toyosaki, Nihon kōgyō shōyūken hōgakkai no setsuritsu *(Foundation of Japan Association of Industrial Property Law)*, 576 Jurist 44 (1974). *Yoshinobu Someno* (1918-2007) was a successor president of the JAIPL after *K. Toyosaki*. *Y. Someno* was known as professor of the Nihon University for civil procedure law, but he was an official of the JPO from 1943 to 1955 (interrupted by military service and detention from 1943 to 1949) and as expert of patent law wrote textbooks for patent and trade marks with *Hajime Kaneko* (1906-1973), who was a famous professor of the Tokyo University for civil procedure law, and continued to contribute to Japanese patent law. *Y. Someno* together with his wife *Keiko* in 1967 were the first Japanese researchers of the newly founded Max Planck Institute (MPI) for Intellectual Property and Competition Law in Munich. Between 1967 and 1997, more than 30 academics made research studies at the MPI in Munich, see: Kentei no ji *(Dedication)*, in: Y. SOMENO et al. (eds.), Chiteki zaisan to kyōsōhō

- Another important institution, *Chitekizaisan kenkyūjo* (Intellectual Property Institute) was founded in 1989 and mainly conducts researches in IP field. The IIP also publishes the journal *Chizaiken Fōramu* (IIP Forum) which was renamed in 2017 to IP Journal and provides an exchange study program for IP scholars.

b) Publications

Between 1969 and 1999, the General Secretariat of the Supreme Court published a collection of decisions especially focused on intellectual property cases, *Mutaizaisanken kankei minji gyōsei saibanreishū* (*Mutaishū*, Collection of decisions in civil and administrative cases related to immaterial rights). This collection in 1991 was renamed to *Chitekiizaisanken Kankei Minji Gyōsei Saibanreishū* (*Chitekisaishū*, Collection of decisions in civil and administrative cases related to immaterial rights). Currently almost all court decisions in the IP field can be found on the website of the courts or the IP High Court.[67]

Around the 1970s, the reception of foreign academic works also became important.[68] *Kōe Toyosaki* and *Nobuhiro Nakayama*[69] as supervisors translated *Stephan P. Ladas*' seminal work "The International Protection of Industrial Property" (1975) into Japanese and published the first volume in 1980 and the second in 1985 (the third volume remained untranslated).

As a spin-off, the popular legal journal *Jurist* has been publishing the series *Hanrei Hyakusen* (Hundred Selected Cases) in almost all fields of laws. Such

---

no riron - Theorien zum Recht des geistiges Eigentums und Wettbewerbsrechts -Festschrift zum 70. Geburtstag von Professor Friedrich-Karl Beier - *(Theories for Intellectual Property and Competition Law -Anniversary Publication for 70th Birthday of Professor Friedrich-Karl Beier-)*, Tokyo 1996, iii. Such relationship between Japan and the MPI in Munich (including its law school founded in 2003), the Munich Intellectual Property Law Center (MIPLC) continues until this day with participants who come from the JPO, the judiciary, the bar or the patent bar.

67. The website of the courts <http://www.courts.go.jp/> or the website of the IP High Court <http://www.ip.courts.go.jp/index.html>. Such publication of IP decisions through the websites of the courts started in 1999, but some decisions before 1999, e.g. of the Supreme Court or famous cases, can be found on this website as well. For reference of official publication of decisions, there are also: Saikō saibansho minji hanreishū *(Minshū, collection of decisions of the Supreme Court in civil cases)*, Saikō saibansho saibanshū minjihen *(Shūmin, collection of cases of the Supreme Court civil part)*, Dishin'in minji hanreishū *(Minshū, collection of decisions of the old Supreme Court in civil cases)*, Dishin'in minji hanketsuroku *(Minroku, record of decisions of the old Supreme Court in civil cases)*, Kakyū saibansho minji saibanreishū *(Kaminshū, collection of cases of lower courts in civil cases)*, Gyōsei jiken saibanreishū *(Gyōsaishū, collection of cases in administrative cases)*, etc.
68. In 1920, the library of *Josef Kohler* was acquired by Japan and kept at the University of Tokyo, yet was unfortunately destroyed by fire in the Great Kantō Earthquake in 1923.
69. *K. Toyosaki* held a patent law seminar at the University of Tokyo from 1967 onwards as a non-permanent lecturer. In 1974, *N. Nakayama* (1945-) became the first IP professor of the University of Tokyo and held his seminar from 1974 onwards until his retirement in 2003. See, N. NAKAYAMA, Chitekizaisanhō kenkyū no kaiko to shōrai e no kadai *(History and problems for the future study of intellectual property laws)*, 877 NBL 5 (2008). There was also some history of making IP a specialised subject matter in each university, see, for example, S. OGAWA, Nihondaigaku chitekizaisanshi *(Nihon University's intellectual property study history)*, 4 Nihon Daigaku Chizai Journal 7 (2011).

publication of cases with commentaries first started in 1960 in an anniversary volume No. 200 as a general volume, and soon continued as *bessatsu* (special volumes). The 1st edition of *Tokkyo Hanrei Hyakusen* (Hundred Selected Patent Cases) was published in 1966 as *Bessatsu Jurist* No. 8, the 2nd edition in 1985, the 3rd edition in 2004 and the current 4th edition in 2012.[70]

8. OUTLOOK

While the promotion of intellectual property protection, or a so-called pro-patent policy may be able to boost the development of industry of a nation in a certain stage of development. But in a developed, complex economy such as Japan, it becomes patent policy becomes one of many tools, and the economic impact of patent policy must be considered relatively small and not a *passepartout* remedy for economic development.

Apart from the IP provisions of the - controversial - TPP, Japanese pro-patent policy is currently almost at a standstill, because the Japanese government in the last 15 years has taken almost all possible steps for improving the patent system. If Japan wants to go further, amendments to the patent system would be blocked by fundamental principles of civil law, the law of civil procedure (e.g. further-reaching rights of inspection), organisation of the judiciary (conventional rotation of judges, absence of technical judges) etc. As such interconnection between different fields of law becomes more and more important to solve complicated problems in the intellectual property field, a better cooperation between different ministries and disciplines is of vital importance. The same holds true for comparative studies and international efforts to calibrate the patent system in accordance with its historical objectives so as to confer on the inventor a reward that is commensurate to the invention's contribution to society, and to promote progress in accordance with the interests of society at large.

Also case law in the area of patents seems to have been influenced by the governmental pro-patent policy, sometimes on the side of patentees, sometimes not, depending on the case. Although a country of civil law tradition, case law has played a major role in shaping the Japanese patent system, be it as a starting point for changes in legislation or the practice of the Patent Office. Not least this fact justifies a decision-based approach to patent law as is undertaken by this book.

70. Japanese *Hanrei Hyakusen* series publication is one of the sources of the editors' inspiration to publish this book. As related *Hanrei Hyakusen* in the IP field, one should mention: N. NAKAYAMA et al. (eds.), Shōhyō/Ishō/Fuseikyosō Hanrei Hyakusen *(Hundred Selected Trademark/Design/ Unfair Competition Cases)*, 2007, N. KOIZUMI et al. (eds.), Chosakuken Hanrei Hyakusen *(Hundred Selected Copyright Cases)*, 5th ed. 2016, etc. No. 1 of *Jurist* itself was published in 1952. As to legal journals reporting cases in Japan, this book uses also *Hanrei Jihō* of which No. 1 was published in 1953 and *Hanrei Times* of which No. 1 was published in 1948, etc.

Appendix: Flowchart of Patent Procedure in Japan

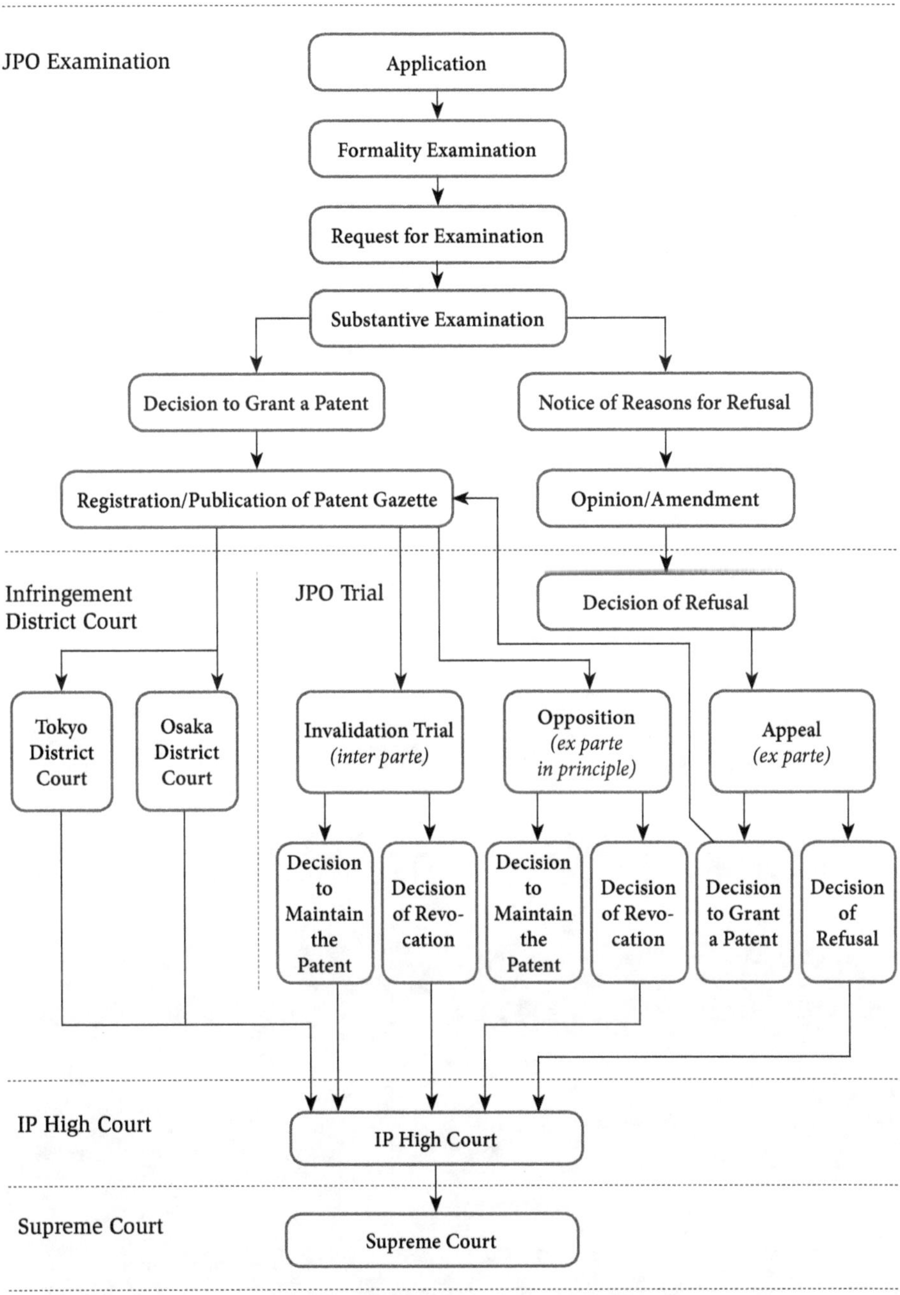

(Editors simplified flowcharts in the JPO Annual/Status Reports, available at the website of the JPO <https://www.jpo.go.jp/e/resources/report/statusreport/2018/index.html> and <https://www.jpo.go.jp/resources/report/nenji/2018/index.html>.)

Case No. 1

Definition of an Invention – Mental Activity

Atsuhiro Furuta

1. While a mental activity as such is not an invention, an invention is not excluded from patentability merely because it contains or is related to mental activities.

2. A computer-based dental network can qualify as an invention where the claims are not exclusively directed towards mental activities as such.

Intellectual Property High Court, 24 June 2008,
Case No. 10369 (Gyō-Ke) of 2007 – *Dental Network*

Shade Analysing Technologies v. Japanese Patent Office

1. BACKGROUND

What is a patentable invention? That is the first question of patent law. Sec. 2(1) Japanese Patent Act provides the definition of an invention in that "'invention' in this Act means the high-level creation of technical ideas using the laws of nature". So the second question under Japanese patent law should be what is considered a "creation", "technical idea" or "using the natural law"?[1]

The Examination Guidelines of the Japanese Patent Office state that one of requirement of an "invention" is creation. The simple discovery of natural things (for example: mineral ore) or natural phenomena, which have not been created as a technical idea in the inventor's mind, is not an "invention", as natural things and phenomena itself are neither "creations" nor "inventions". The Guidelines list also (a) technical ability, (b) simple presentation of information (which is characterised only in shown information and has as its purpose mainly to present information) and (c) simple aesthetic creation as "not a technical idea". In Japan an aesthetic creation or display of information is also not patentable, as it is not considered a "technical idea". It is also stated that as an "invention" should use the laws of nature, a law of nature itself such as the energy conservation law or the law of gravity is not "invention". Because a law of nature itself such as science theory is not using the

1. There may be another question for "high-level", but in the view of the author, such words are too ambiguous to derive some criteria for definition of invention. It is inserted to make difference in definition provision of the Patent Act and the Utility Model Act. The definition of the later Act lacks the words "high-level". See N. Nakayama, Tokkyohō *(Patent Law)*, 3rd ed. 2016, 106.

laws of nature" and is thus not an "invention". Further, when the claimed invention is a law rather than law of nature (for example: economic law), a human rule (for example: rule of game itself), a mathematical formula, a human mental act, or the use thereof (for example: a business method itself), this invention is not using the laws of nature and is not an "invention". Mathematical methods, mental activities, games and business methods, etc. are also not using the "laws of nature" and are not regarded as an "invention".[2]

There is also developed case law for the definition of an invention or for patent eligibility. The *Dental Network* decision of 24 June 2008 is a leading case where such problem of the definition of an invention is discussed.

2. DECISION[3]

a) Facts

The plaintiff, a US company, has applied for a patent for an invention with the title "Interactive Dental Network". The application was refused by the Patent Office, and the applicant has appealed before the court.

b) Reasons

a. The Japanese Patent Office has refused the application. The latter in claim 1 refers to "means for determining the relevant dental prosthesis", and "means for setting up a treatment plan with criteria as to the shape for fitting the dental prosthesis". As the person deciding on the "necessary dental prosthesis" or the "first treatment plan with criteria as to shape for fitting the dental prosthesis" is the dentist as the person to decide about the treatment of patients by a mental act, or the person to draft a treatment plan, for which reason the "means" in claim 1 relates to the mental activities of deciding and drafting. Any definition that would exclude the dentist or his mental activities as a subject of the claim could not be found in either the description or the drawings. Even the fact that the applicant amended "interactive dental process" to "computer-based dental system", "to decide" to "means for decision" and "to draw up" to "means for drawing up", changed nothing in the fact that the means for a decision and drafting should be considered mental activities of the dentist and that the invention therefore could not be considered the creation of a technical idea using the laws of nature and therefore not in compliance with the definition of sec. 2(1) Patent Act that required a high-level creation of a technical idea using the laws of nature.

In reviewing the above decision, we hold as follows:

b. α. Claim 1 of the patent reads as follows:

2. The Japanese Patent Examination Guidelines, Part III Chapter 1, at the website of the JPO <https://www.jpo.go.jp/e/system/laws/rule/guideline/patent/tukujitu_kijun/index.html>.
3. Published in 2026 Hanrei Jihō 123 = N. Nakayama et al. (eds.), Tokkyo Hanrei Hyakusen *(Hundred Selected Patent Cases)*, 4th ed. 2012, 6. German translation in GRUR Int. 2011, 177.

"A computer-based dental system characterised in that it consists of: A network server that contains an information, a communication network generated by access to a network server, one or more computers in at least one dental practice that can access and display information from a database in a human-readable format, one means in order to decide about the necessary dental prosthesis, and one means with shape criteria for fitting the dental prosthesis, whereby the communication network sends a first treatment plan, and, where necessary, a second modified last treatment plan to the dental laboratory."

β. Claim 1 shows a connection to a "dental system" and as components contains "a network server with a database", a "communication network", "one or more computers", "means for determining dental prosthesis" and "means for a first treatment plan with shape criteria for fitting dental prosthesis". All this is realised in a computer.

A "system" is defined as "a cluster of components that have an organic relationship with each other and realise an organised function" ("Kōjien" dictionary, 4th edition). Thus, claim 1 is a cluster of components that in relationship with each other and via a computer realise a dental function.

c. According to the legal definition, "inventions" are "high-level creations of technical ideas using the laws of nature" and are completed by way of identifying a problem, the use of technical means for its solution and the ascertainment that the means employed for the solution of such problem are effective.

Mere mental activities are not an "invention" and thus not patentable. But it is incorrect that an "invention" does not qualify as such only because it employs mental activities or relates to such mental activities. Every man-made technical means serves, assists or replaces human activity, including mental activity, and is thus related to human activity.

On the one hand, a claim containing technical means does not qualify as an "invention" according to sec. 2(1) Patent Act when the essence of the invention as expressed in the claims is directed towards a mental activity as such.

On the other hand, patentability is not excluded by the fact that technical means that assist or replace human activities feature prominently, even if they contain mental activities or relate thereto ...

d. In the case at issue, the wording of claim 1 requires "means to decide about dental prosthesis", or "means to draft a first treatment plan with shape criteria for fitting the dental prosthesis", and thus not only computer-implemented activities, but also human activities. Thus, the "means to decide" and "means to draft" are human or intellectual activities. Furthermore, it is a human being who decides about the necessary dental prosthesis and drafts a treatment plan. Claim 1 thus has a connection to a mental activity.

As mentioned under above c., patentability is not per se excluded where the patent claims contain a mental activity or are related thereto.

e. As mentioned under above d., "the means in order to determine the necessary dental prosthesis" or the "means to draft a first treatment plan with shape criteria for the fitting of dental prosthesis" are not entirely clear in their technical meaning. In such case, the description should be consulted for interpretation.

...

β. Based on the above-cited description, the problem appears to be that an increase in possible treatments with new materials and new technologies has led to the situation that the dentist has a lot of information for choosing the best materials and treatment at his disposal. In this respect, the invention offers a process to help the dentist or dental assistant to make the best choice of a treatment plan and gives him the means thereto. And the database saves the information regarding materials, procedures and types of dental prosthesis. The network server in this respect contains a program that allows requests regarding materials or procedures for dental prosthesis. To this end, there is a computer in the dental clinic or laboratory that provides such information in a readable format. The materials and procedures will be confirmed, determined or modified by the computer. The computer receives its answers from the database. In addition, means for analysing coloured tooth images and digital images to determine the colour of the tooth will be provided.

δ. Paragraphs (10), (12), (13) and (15) of the description indicate that only the treatment plan will be transformed into a digital image. The materials, the procedure and the models will be chosen according to such digital image. The selected file will be saved in the database. The first treatment plan that is drafted will be communicated between the dental clinic and the dental laboratory via a network, and the actions of a dentist, namely the taking of photos, and choosing the images and the material will be undertaken by an image-displaying computer that is connected to a network.

From paragraphs (20), (21) and (22) it becomes apparent that the invention described in the application contains a scanner that allows to scan a tooth or its mounting. The scanner allows an analysis as to whether a treatment plan needs to be amended based on a comparison between the scanned data and the file saved in the database. The decision in this respect is made by a person.

f. "Means for determining the relevant tooth prosthesis" and "means for drafting a first treatment plan with the shape criteria for fitting the prosthesis" contain human actions that are necessary for carrying out claim 1 in regard of evaluation etc. But due to the reasons mentioned above, claim 1 or the description are not directed to a mental act as such for achieving the purpose of the invention. Rather, the claim also refers to "a network server with a database", "a communication network", a "computer set up in a dental practice" and an "installation showing images", and all this relates to computer-based technical means in order to assist dental treatment.

g. For the above reasons, claim 1 is the "creation of a technical idea using the laws of nature", and the decision under appeal is erroneous and must be set aside.

3. ANALYSIS

In this case, the wording of claim 1 (as above) became the issue of the lawsuit. The JPO decided that this claim was not patentable because it was a mental activity and not an "invention" according to sec. 2(1) PA. On appeal, the IP High Court did not agree with the view of the JPO and decided that the claim at issue was not directed to a mental activity as such and qualified as an "invention" under the PA. The IP High Court indicated in this case that a mental activity as such was in fact not patentable where the essence of the invention, which should be determined by the claim as whole, was directed at a mental activity as such. But even if an invention included or was related to some mental activity, and the essence of the invention supported a mental activity or provided technical means for replacing a mental activity, such invention could was not excluded from patentable subject matter and could still be considered an "invention".

In the author's opinion, this conclusion of the IP High Court is reasonable, because an invention should be considered based in the claim as whole, and an application should not be rejected merely because the claim also includes some mental activity.

There is no list of unpatentable subject matter in the Patent Act, yet the JPO sometimes took a rather rigid stance in the definition of the PA. But as indicated in this case, it is preferable in each case, even where certain subject matter "as such" should be excluded from patentable subject matter, an invention as a whole should not automatically become unpatentable by partially including some unpatentable subject matter. So, e.g. laws of nature as such or human rules as such, which do not use the laws of nature, should be not patentable, but if part of claim includes such unpatentable subject matter, the claim as whole may still be regarded as an "invention" on the Patent Act and thus be patentable.

In another case decided by the IP High Court on 26 August 2008,[4] patentability of an invention directed to the use of a dictionary was acknowledged although it contained some mental activity. There was in fact some repeatable effect such as identifying the meaning of English words without knowledge of their correct spelling. While the decision recognised patentability of using a dictionary, an activity, which is completed in human brain, it may not be appropriate under the principles of patent law to extend the effect of the patent to activities completed in the human brain.

In the case of IP High Court, 5 December 2012,[5] in which the applicant claimed a sheet describing ecological action, the IP High Court decided that the creation of technical ideas, which did not use the laws of nature at all, could not be considered an "invention" under sec. 2(1) PA and denied the utility of the claim under the laws of nature.

The decision of IP High Court, 6 March 2013,[6] held that the patent application should indicate whether some technical idea using the laws of nature was used as a principal means for the solution of the problem or not, and denied the utility requirement by the use of the laws of nature of a claim which was directed to a calendar wherein the birth dates of great personalities were arranged.

On the other hand, of course, it should be noted also that the addition of some formal features to a claim which look like technical features or those using the laws of nature does not make the invention patentable as whole. For example, in the decision of Tokyo High Court of 21 December 2004,[7] it was held that "it is clear

---

4. IP High Court, 26 August 2008, Case No. 10001 (Gyō-Ke) of 2008, 2041 Hanrei Jihō 124 – *Parallel Translation Dictionary.*
5. IP High Court, 5 December 2012, Case No. 10134 (Gyō-Ke) of 2012, 2181 Hanrei Jihō 127 – *Ecology Action Sheet.*
6. IP High Court, 6 March 2013, Case No. 10043 (Gyō-Ke) of 2012, 2187 Hanrei Jihō 71 – *Great Personalities Calendar.*
7. Tokyo High Court, 21 December 2004, Case No. 188 (Gyō-Ke) of 2004, 1891 Hanrei Jihō 139 – *Method of Circuit Simulation.*

that an analytical method of a mathematical problem or a calculation process itself is not a 'creation of a technical idea using the laws of nature'", and merely adding "which shows the characteristics of a circuit" to the claim of a simple mathematical method, which was the solution of a non-linear equation did not make the invention patentable.[8]

In the author's view, the above Japanese jurisprudence on patentability based on the definition of an invention under sec. 2(1) PA is appropriate in clarifying that human mental activities as such, etc. do not become patentable merely by adding some limitation to the claim which is unclear in its technical meaning. Japan has interpreted the current definition in a consistent manner. It is said that such definition originates in the ideas of Josef Kohler,[9] and we should pay tribute to him in this point.

4. COMPARATIVE REMARKS

a) In the **US**, and it is sometimes said that everything under the sun can be patentable, but a law of nature, a natural phenomenon, or an abstract idea is excluded from patentable subject matter as a judicial exception by case law about the patent eligibility. And as to counter the trend of the pro-patent policy, the recent US Supreme Court decisions *Mayo*[10] case of 30 March 2012 and *Alice*[11] case of 19 March 2014, set the new test for patent eligibility as follows:[12]

---

8. For other example cases, see also R. HIRASHIMA, Tokkyohō no yakuwari kino kara mita hatsumei hogo no taishō han'i (*Scope of patentable invention from the viewpoint of role and function of patent law*), 40 Nihon Kōgyōshōyuken Hōgakkai Nenpō 97 (2016).). As a recent example case (opposition case), there is, IP High Court, 17 October 2018, Case No. 10232 (Gyō-Ke) of 2017, the website of the courts <http://www.courts.go.jp/app/files/hanrei_jp/058/088058_hanrei.pdf> – *Ikinari Steak*. In this case, patentability of a system for serving steak was disputed and the IP High Court held that, even though the claim at issue included human steps for serving steak in a steak shop, it adopted also technical means such as a table number tag, a weighing machine which weights cut meat according to a customer order and outputs a seal with the weight of the meat and the table number of the tag, and therefore the claimed invention solved a technical problem by such means with technical meaning to distinguish meat to distinguish the meat for the customer from other meat for other customers and the patented claim as whole was patentable.
9. The current definition of invention was at first stipulated by the Law No. 121/1959 of 13 April 1959. There was no statutory definition of an invention before that time, but only a simple list of unpatentable subject matter such as foods, drinks, aesthetic goods, medicines and chemically produced products, Under the previous Patent Act 1921, inventions were said to be similarly interpreted with the requirement of natural forces under the influence of German legal theory or Josef Kohler. For this point, see N. NAKAYAMA et al. (eds.), Shin Chūkai Tokkyohō *(New Commentary on Japanese Patent Act)*, 2nd ed. 2017, 13; H. SAKAI et al., Hatsumei gainen no kenkyū *(Study on concept of invention)*, 58-10 Patent 16 (2005); K. TAMAI, Hatumei no gainen *(Concept of Invention)* in: K. MORIOKA et al. (eds.), Chitekizaisanhō to kyōsōhō no gendaiteki tenkai *(Modern Development of the Intellectual Property Law and the Competition Law)*, 2006, 139. J. KOHLER, Deutsches Patentrecht *(German Patent Law)*, 1900, 106 states that inventions which relate to a methods of mental activity are not patentable, and on p. 111–114 elaborates this with words that the IP High Court in the case at issue repeats almost verbatim.
10. US Supreme Court, *Mayo v. Prometheus*, 132 S. Ct. 1289 (2012).
11. US Supreme Court, *Alice Corp. v. CLS Bank International*, 134 S. Ct. 2347 (2014).
12. For case law in the US, see, e.g., L. M. SUNG et al., Patent Law Handbook 2017-2018 Edition, 2017, 216.

(Step 1) Is the claim to a process, machine, manufacture or composition of matter? If no, the claim is not eligible subject matter under sec. 101 U.S.C. 35. If yes, proceed to step 2A.

(Step 2A) Is the claim directed to a law of nature, a natural phenomenon, or an abstract idea (judicial exceptions)? If no, the claim qualifies as eligible subject matter. If yes, proceed to step 2B.

(Step 2B) Does the claim recite additional elements that amount to significantly more than the judicial exception? If yes, the claim qualifies as eligible subject matter. If no, the claim is not eligible subject matter.

This *Mayo/Alice* test has confused US patent practice, because the addition "significantly more than the judicial exception" of Step 2B is quite a steep requirement for patent eligibility. The USPTO has published some guidance following the above case law and also in July 2017 issued a report that includes criticism about the case law and a policy proposal for patent eligibility, in January 2019 a revised guidance.[13]

b) Under the **European** Patent Convention, the technical character on an invention is considered an implicit requirement of patentability under Art. 52 EPC. In this respect, there appears to be no big difference between Japan and the EPC in this respect, namely that a simple discovery is not an invention, and a claim as a whole directed to a mental act is not patentable. But when we consider the requirement of using the laws of nature in Japan, and the technical character under the EPC, an assessment based mainly on technical character might pose some delicate problem. For example, in the case **T 931/95**[14] regarding a method of administration of interest with computer, it is stated that all the features of this claim are steps of processing and producing information having purely administrative, actuarial and/or financial character ... the invention as claimed does not go beyond a method of doing business as such and, therefore, is excluded from patentability under Article 52(2)(c) in combination with Article 52(3) EPC; the claim does not define an invention within the meaning of Article 52(1) EPC ... the feature of using technical means for a purely non-technical purpose and/or for processing purely non-technical information does not necessarily confer technical character to any such individual steps of use or to the method as a whole. What is of technical character is a difficult question, but it may be regarded as a business method itself if it concerns only the daily business administration. How to avoid an exclusion sometimes becomes a very difficult question, but case law such as **T 1161/04**[15] or **T 1284/04**[16] acknowledged the technical character of an invention simply by using hardware. The decision **G 3/08**[17] of the Enlarged Board of Appeal confirmed such practice.[18]

13. See documents at the websites of the USPTO <https://www.uspto.gov/patent/laws-and-regulations/examination-policy/subject-matter-eligibility> and <https://www.uspto.gov/blog/director/entry/new_report_presents_viewpoints_on>.
14. Decision **T 931/95** of 8 September 2000 – *Controlling pension benefits system/PBS Partnership.*
15. Decision **T 1161/04** of 6 December 2006 – *Stock Index/NASDAQ.*
16. Decision **T 1284/04** of 7 March 2007 – *Loan System/KNG.*
17. Decision **G 3/08** of 12 March 2010 – *Programs for Computers.*
18. For case law of the EPO about unpatentable subject matters such as mental activity, see also SINGER/STAUDER, Europäisches Patentübereinkommen *(Commentary on European Patent Convention)*, 7th ed. 2016, 180.

c) In **Germany**, the *Red Dove* case of the Federal Supreme Court of 1969[19] is a leading case regarding patent eligibility and there are also many more recent cases of the Federal Supreme Court on this point, such as *Logic Verification* (1999), *Method of Showing Topographic Information* (2010) and *Method of Showing Website* (2011),[20] etc. The German case law indicates that for patent eligibility, an invention should use natural forces directly or indirectly and solve a technical problem by technical means. The German requirement of natural forces is thus similar to the Japanese case law on this point.

d) In the **UK**, in the *Aerostel & Macrossan* case,[21] the Court of Appeal proposed a four part test on patentability: (i) Properly construe the claim; (ii) identify the actual contribution; (iii) ask whether it falls solely within the excluded subject matter; (iv) check whether the actual or alleged contribution is actually technical in nature. But the approach of the EPO is also followed in some other cases, especially regarding European patent validated in the UK.

e) In **France**, the Court of Appeal of Paris in 2016 denied the patentability of a European patent, holding that the claimed invention of a procedure of search in a database, which was only defined by abstract steps without any technical means, lacked the technical character.[22] The High Court of Paris held in the case of 2015 that the patent claims to program products were excluded from the patentability as programs for computers as such in Art. 52 EPC.[23] The High Court of Paris held also in the other case of 2016 that the simplification of the claimed invention of application management system, which consisted in the adaptation of an abstract model in order to personalise an application, belonged to the activity of programming without technical character and was unpatentable.[24]

f) In **China**, as stated in the Examination Guidelines of the SIPO, "'Invention' under patent law refers to any new technical solution concerning a product, a process or improvement thereof. ... A technical solution is an aggregation of technical means applying the laws of nature to solve a technical problem".[25] Such reference to the laws of nature may have been influenced by the Japanese Patent Act. In addition,

19. German Federal Supreme Court, 27 March 1969, GRUR 1969, 674 = 1 IIC 136 (1970) - *Rote Taube*. For this case see also the comparative remarks of Case No. 2 of this book.
20. German Federal Supreme Court, 13 December 1999, GRUR 2000, 498 - *Logikverifikation*; German Federal Supreme Court, 11 May 2000, 33 IIC 343 (2002) - *Speech Analysis Apparatus*; German Federal Supreme Court, 26 October 2010, GRUR 2011, 125 - *Wiedergabe topographischer Informationen*; German Federal Supreme Court, 24 February 2011, GRUR 2011, 610 - *Webseitenanzeige*. For German case law on this point, see also F. RUMMLER, Computer Program Inventions Before the German Courts, 36 IIC 225 (2005); BENKARD, Patentgesetz *(Commentary on German Patent Act)*, 11th ed. 2015, 132.
21. UK Court of Appeal, *Aerotel Limited v. Telco Limited, Macrossan's Application* [2007] R.P.C.7; [2006] EWCA Civ 1371. See also the Manual of the UKIPO, Section 1, and the cited decisions, at the website of the UK government <https://www.gov.uk/guidance/manual-of-patent-practice-mopp/section-1-patentability>; C. BIRSS et al. (eds.), Terrell on the Law of Patents, 18th ed. 2016, 41.
22. Paris Court of Appeal, 16 December 2016, Case No. 14/06444, PIBD 2017, 1065-IIIB-74.
23. Tribunal de Grande Instance Paris *(Paris District Court)*, 18 June 2015, Case No. 14/05735.
24. Tribunal de Grande Instance Paris *(Paris District Court)*, 18 November 2016, Case No. 13/11351.
25. The Examination Guidelines of the SIPO, Part II Chapter 1, at the website of CNIPA <http://english.cnipa.gov.cn/docs/20180131104843547234.pdf>. (The Chinese Patent Office, SIPO

sec. 25 Chinese Patent Act lists unpatentable subject matter. The Patent Reexamination Board (Appeal Board) of the SIPO decided in 2009 against the decision of refusal of the Examination Department that the claim of method for sending a message to programs, which had an element of rule and method of intellectual activity, included also technical means to obtain technical effect and solve technical problem, and therefore it was patentable as whole.[26]

g) In **Korea**, the provision regarding the definition of an invention is same as in Japan, and the Examination Guidelines of the Korean Intellectual Property Office describe almost the same as the Japanese ones.[27] The Korean Supreme Court held in a case of 2008 that whether or not the laws of nature was used should be determined by the claim as whole, and decided to maintain the decision of the Korean Patent Court that the core process of the claimed invention of providing consulting information should be carried out by a human and include human intellectual determination and therefore it was unpatentable as whole not using the laws of nature.[28]

(State Intellectual Property Office) was renamed to Chinese National Intellectual Property Administration in 2018.)

26. Patent Reexamination Board of the SIPO, 26 December 2009, Case No. 20084.
27. The Examination Guidelines of the KIPO, Part III Chapter 1, at the website of the KIPO <http://www.kipo.go.kr/upload/en/download/patent_examination_guidelines_2013_07.pdf>.
28. Korean Supreme Court, 24 December 2008, Case No. 265 (Hu) of 2007. See also Korean Supreme Court, 23 December 2010, Case No. 436 (Hu) of 2009, in which it acknowledged the patentability of the patentability of the claimed invention of method of mutual key authenticating and exchanging, which included possibly a part of human intellectual determination, as whole could not be regarded as human mental activity as such.

Case No. 2

Definition of an Invention – Repeatability

Takeshi Tsuru

The invention should be concrete and objective to the extent that a person skilled in the art can carry out the invention and repeat the intended technical effect. With respect to the repeatability of a "method of breeding and propagating a new plant variety," it should be enough that the person skilled in the art can scientifically reproduce the plant, and a high probability for such reproduction should not be required.

Supreme Court, 29 February 2000, Case No. 19 (Gyō-Tsu) of 1998 – *Method of Yellow Peach Breeding and Propagating*

Japan Fruit Growers Cooperative Association v. Kurakata

---

1. BACKGROUND

According to sec. 29(1) Patent Act, "an inventor of an invention that is industrially applicable may be entitled to obtain a patent for said invention". Sec. 2(1) Patent Act defines "an invention under this Act" as "the highly advanced creation of technical ideas using the laws of nature". Being a statutory invention is, therefore, a prerequisite for a patent, and an invention which does not comply with the definition provided in the sec. 2(1) of the Japan Patent Act shall not be granted a patent.[1] In accordance with the definition, use of the laws of nature leads to a notion of "repeatability" as a requirement of an invention which must not require any extraordinary skills and/or personal talents; rather, it must be possible for any person with ordinary skills and knowledge in the relevant field of technology to repeatedly carry out the invention and to obtain the same result.

Repeatability of an invention often becomes an issue when the claimed invention relates to life phenomena in general and traditional plant breeding in particular, where the probability of repeating these kinds of phenomena is generally very low. As regards the repeatability of traditional plant breeding, there had been

---

1. Neither the provision of the Patent Act for an examiner's decision of refusal (sec. 49) nor that for patent invalidation (sec. 123) stipulates sec. 2 as a ground for refusal or invalidation, respectively. However, if the claimed subject matter does not comply with the definition of the invention in sec. 2, a patent application shall be refused and a patent shall be invalidated under sec. 29, since the subject matter is not *an invention* within the meaning of sec. 29.

conflicting opinions in Japan. Those who denied repeatability argued for example that the traditional plant breeding generally requires personal skills or extraordinary experience,[2] or that it is practically quite difficult to reproduce the same plants by repeating the same process.[3] On the other hand, there had also been an opinion that when a new plant is created by e.g. crossing and/or grafting, the creation is governed by certain laws and its repeatability cannot be ruled out.[4] The Japanese Patent Office (JPO) had historically refused patent applications for a new plant variety or its breeding method at least partly following the former opinions.[5] However, in 1975, the JPO, in response to the needs from industry that had asked for better protection of plant technologies, revised its Examination Guidelines for "New Plant Varieties" and started to allow claims for new plant varieties or their breeding methods. The patent at issue was granted by the JPO according to this new practice.

There were two main issues in the present case: first, whether repeatability can be affirmed for a breeding method essentially comprising crossings and selections where reproduction of a plant created by the method occurs with extremely low probability, and second, whether repeatability of the breeding method is impaired in a case where the parent plant used for the method was lost and became unavailable during the patent term.

2. DECISION[6]

a) Facts

(1) Original defendant was the owner of the patent No. 1459061 entitled "Method of Breeding and Propagating a New Yellow Peach Variety," which was filed on 24 October 1977 and registered on 28 September 1988.

(2) The patent is for a method of breeding a new yellow peach and of propagating it asexually, wherein the breeding process is comprising crossing a seed parent peach variety Tusberta and a pollen parent peach variety Ban-ōtō and selection among plants sprouted from the seeds obtained in said crossing, and wherein the new yellow peach resulting from the breeding process has such characteristics as described in the claim.[7]

---

2. N. MONYA, Shokubutsu shin hinshu no ikusei zōshoku hoho no hatsumei *(Invention of breeding and propagating method of new plant variety)*, 1202 Jurist 268 (2001).
3. S. MITSUISHI, Tokkyohō shōsetsu [shinban] *(Detailed commentary of Japan Patent Act [new edition])*, 1976, 135.
4. S. MITSUISHI, *supra* note 2, 137.
5. Y. HIRAKI, Momo no shin hinshu ōtō no ikushu zoushoku hou no tokkyosei ni tsuite *(Patentability of breeding and propagating methods for a new yellow peach variety)*, 51 Chizai Kanri 576 (2001).
6. Published in 54-2 Minshū 709 = 1796 Hanrei Jihō 112 = 1028 Haneri Times 173 = N. NAKAYAMA et al. (eds.), Tokkyo Hanrei Hyakusen *(Hundred Selected Patent Cases)*, 4th ed. 2012, 16 = T. ŌBUCHI et al. (eds.), Chitekizaisan hō hanrei shū *(Intellectual Property Law Case Book)*, 2nd ed. 2015, 8.
7. A literal translation of the patent claim read as follows: "Method of breeding of a new yellow peach and of propagating it asexually by a conventional method, wherein a peach variety Tusberta, which is bred and improved by the inventor through crossing a well-known can peach variety Tuscan as a seed parent and a peach variety Tusberta as a pollen parent, is used as a

(3) The plaintiff on 18 September 1989 requested an invalidation trial before the Japanese Patent Office mainly because the invention at issue lacks repeatability and thus is not patentable. The JPO proceeded with this case under No. H1-15082 and on 16 December 1991 decided to reject the request for invalidation. The plaintiff appealed.

(4) At the time of the patent application, a person skilled in the art could obtain the parent variety of the yellow peach at issue, Ban-ōtō, but the original plant of the Ban-ōtō subsequently got lost in 1995.

(5) "In fruit trees, each of their characteristics is governed by multiple genetic factors that affect with each other, and some of its aspects are not completely explained by Mendel's law of heredity. Reproduction of a genetically identical fruit tree by crossing occurs at a very low probability. However, since the same characteristics can be expressed even when there are genetic differences, it is possible to reproduce a fruit tree with the same characteristics by repeatedly carrying out the breeding process."

(6) "The essence of the invention at issue lies in the acquisition of the characteristics which are targets of breeding, irrespective of presence or absence of differences in genes that are the basis for such characteristics. Each characteristic of the yellow peach of the invention at issue contains various aspects: some being the characteristics of either of the parent varieties Tusberta or Ban-ōtō, the others being intermediate of them. However, from the viewpoint of identity of the characteristics themselves, even if in the light of genetics or breeding science there is not a high probability of reproduction, it is possible to reproduce the yellow peach with the same characteristics as the invention by repeatedly carrying out the breeding processes of the yellow peach at issue and to reproduce peaches which have the same characteristics as the invention."

(7) "The specification of this patent describes that the selection should be performed based on the criteria of the characteristics in between those of the parent variety. Such selecting criteria are objectively recognizable and clear."

b) Reasons

(1) "An invention is a creative idea related to a certain technology and based on use of the laws of nature, and the created technical subject matter should be concrete and objective to the extent that any person with ordinary knowledge and experience in the relevant technical field can carry out the invention and repeatedly achieve the intended technical effect. Technical subject matter that is not concrete and objective

seed parent and crossbred with a peach variety Ban-ōtō, which is an incidental seedling with a yellow pulp; selection is performed among plants sprouted from seeds that are obtained in the above crossbreeding; and, as shown in the specification and the figures, the resulting new yellow peach has big lanceolate leaves with slightly wavy edges not to the extent of those in the seed parent Tusberta, staminoid petaled pink flower with many pollen and self-fertilisation nature, well sphere shaped fruits, tough pericarp, reddish colour with sunshine on yellow, very beautiful appearance, yellow pulp, very thick quality of the pulp with few filaments, sticky core, few colours around the core, a little sour sweet taste, no taste difference between top and bottom of the fruit, and good fragrance."

to that extent is an incomplete invention and should not qualify as an "invention" under sec. 2(1) of the Japanese Patent Act (see Supreme Court, 28 January 1969, 92 (Gyō-Tsu) of 1964, 23-1 Minshū 54). Therefore, for an invention that uses the laws of nature within the meaning of sec. 2 of the Patent Act, it is necessary that the person skilled in the art can repeatedly carry out the invention and obtain the same result; namely, repeatability is necessary."

(2) "With respect to the repeatability, when it comes to the breeding process in an invention of a 'method of breeding and propagating a new plant variety' and when the nature of this kind of invention is taken into account, it should be enough if the person skilled in the art can scientifically reproduce the plant, and a high probability of the reproduction should not be required. This is because for such an invention, once the new plant variety is bred, it can be reproduced by a conventional propagating method, and if the breeding of the new plant variety is possible, even if its probability is low, the technical effect intended by the invention can be realised."

(3) "In the present case, considering the above facts, a person can repeatedly carry out the breeding process of the invention at issue and scientifically reproduce peaches that have the same characteristics as those claimed in the invention, though the probability is not high. It thus should be affirmed that this invention is repeatable."

(4) "Moreover, with respect to repeatability, it is enough that the invention could be repeated at the time the application was filed. The fact that the parent variety of the yellow peach Ban-ōtō subsequently got lost does not influence the above findings."

(5) "The decision of the former instance is consistent with the above consideration, is appropriate, does not contain legal errors and can be affirmed. ..."

3. ANALYSIS

This is the first decision rendered by the Supreme Court of Japan about the patent eligibility of inventions for traditional plant breeding methods that essentially comprise crossing and selection.

In case of sexually reproduced plants such as peaches of the present case, a new plant variety can be created by a breeding process comprising crossing of parent plants and subsequent selection of specific offspring. Once the offspring with intended characteristics is obtained, it can be proliferated by well-known techniques such as grafting without altering the characteristics. Among these lines of processes, repeatability of the breeding process often become an issue, while in the proliferation process the characteristics of the plants are usually maintained and repeatable.

Point (1) of the reasons is a general ruling about the requirement of repeatability. The Supreme Court of Japan confirmed its precedent (Supreme Court, 28 January 1969, 92 (Gyō-Tsu) of 1964, 23-1 Minshū 54) that repeatability is necessary, and further held that this is so because sec. 2(1) of the Patent Act requires use of the laws of nature. From an analytical point of view, repeatability is required in two respects. For one, the requirement of repeatability is derived from the *use of the laws of nature*. This is because if an invention uses the laws of nature, the intended effects of the invention shall be inevitably obtained provided that certain conditions are met.[8] On the other hand, the requirement of repeatability can be derived from the statutory invention being a *technical idea*. As it is held in the above-mentioned case law of the Supreme Court of Japan,[9] the *technology* of the *technical idea* has been interpreted as meaning "concrete means to achieve a certain goal that can be actually utilized", and that *technology* should be "objective so as to be transferred to any other person". This nature of the *technical idea* leads to the consequence that an invention needs to be enough concrete and objective so that any other person can utilise the invention and, by doing so, repeat the intended effects of the invention. Otherwise, such an invention is called an "incomplete invention" and does not qualify as a statutory invention. Although some arguments can be made about the relationship of these two,[10] after all, if an invention cannot be implemented by a person skilled in the art, namely because it lacks repeatability, the invention does not qualify as an invention within the meaning of sec. 2(1) Japan Patent Act and is thus not patentable.

The necessity of repeatability leads to several questions. First, whether the invention shall always be repeatable or how much certainty or success rate is required for the repeatability. In this respect, the commonly accepted theory in Japan was that a high success rate is not always necessary, and even if the success rate is very low, the invention meets the requirement of repeatability so long as the intended technical effects can be realised under given conditions with certain amount of certainty.[11] In the first part of the point (2) of the reasons, the Supreme Court in line with the commonly accepted theory held that a high success rate is not necessary *inter alia* in the case of a plant breeding process. One should note that the Supreme Court mentioned the nature of the relevant technical field, and the standard may thus vary according to the field of technology. For example, as one scholar argued, when an invention exclusively uses well-known laws of physics or chemistry, while the success rate of the invention is very low, it may not be patentable because of being an "incomplete invention."[12]

When considering that the probability of reproducing a plant of the invention is very low, the next question would be whether repeatability in a practical sense would be required, or whether theoretical repeatability should be sufficient? According to the present decision, the Supreme Court of Japan seemed to take the position that theoretical repeatability was enough. In this respect, some factual findings by the Tokyo High Court and affirmed by the Supreme Court of Japan appear confusing. From point (5) of the facts it appears that the Courts found reproduction of a plant with the same characteristics was possible, while reproduction of a genetically identical plant was not. Technically speaking, however, the probability of reproducing plants with the same characteristics is still so low so that it can be considered as

8. R. Hirashima, in: N. Nakayama/N. Koizumi (eds.), Shin Chūkai Tokkyohō [Jō-kan] *(New commentary of Japan Patent Act [first volume])*, 2011, 16.
9. Supreme Court, 28 January 1969, 92 (Gyō-Tsu) of 1964, 23-1 Minshū 54.
10. R. Hirashima, *supra* note 10, 24. It is discussed that the requirement for repeatability derived from a *technical idea* and that from use of the laws of nature partially overlap each other.
11. See e.g. N. Nakayama, Kōgyōshoyūkenhō jō *(Industrial property law, first volume)*, 2nd ed. 1998, 98; K. Yoshifuji, Tokkyohō gaisetsu *(Commentary of the Japan Patent Act)*, 10th ed. 1994, 55; H. Aizawa, Baio tekunorojī to Tokkyohō *(Biotechnology and patent law)*, 1994, 57.
12. R. Hirashima, *supra* note 10, 17.

practically impossible.[13] For the reason of the present holding, the Supreme Court of Japan explained that the intended technical effect of the invention at issue can be realised by the propagating process. Some might find this contradictory, too; while the repeatability at issue should relate to the breeding process, and deficiencies thereof in the breeding process should not be compensated by the subsequent propagating process, because these two processes are different and independent from each other. Despite several ambiguous findings, the Supreme Court seemed to base its rulings on (i) whether repeating the invention is theoretically possible and (ii) whether the description is sufficiently objective to repeat the invention. On balance, this appears reasonable.

The second main issue of the present case was whether repeatability of a breeding method is impaired when one of the parent plants used for the method was lost and became unavailable during the patent term. The present decision in point (4) of the reasons discussed this issue in the context of repeatability of the statutory invention and held that the extinction of the parental plant did not affect the eligibility of the invention. This is reasonable because whether the invention was completed or not should be assessed at the time of filing and the subsequent loss of the parental tree would not be problematic. However, one should note that if this issue was dealt with in the context of sufficient disclosure or enablement (sec. 36 of the Japanese Patent Act), the conclusion may not be so clear. If a parental plant is indispensable for the person skilled in the art to carry out the invention, the parental plant should be available after the grant of a patent just like microorganisms deposited to certain depository institutions. Indeed, the JPO revised its Examination Guidelines in 1993 and a section for "completion of an invention" was deleted. Since then, repeatability of the plant breeding process has been dealt with as a matter of disclosure. Therefore, the current practitioners who are to file an application for plant breeding methods are advised to assure availability of the parental plants by deposition or alternative means.

4. COMPARATIVE REMARKS

a) Repeatability of an invention for breeding methods of plants or animals has long been discussed in **Germany**. There were various different positions, which can be categorised as follows:

Tetzner, Lindenmaier, Benkard and others had argued that, because the essence of an invention of breeding methods lies in the breeding process of a genetically new organism, the breeding process should be actually reproduceable by the person skilled in the art.[14]

Schade had argued that the repeatability of a breeding method could be affirmed by prima facie proof from applicants.[15]

---

13. See. Y. HIRAKI, *supra* note 5, 580-581. It is pointed outed that, when considering that the claim contains as many as 15 characteristics and that the parental peaches are mostly unlikely to be homozygotes, the probability of reproducing a peach with the same characteristics as the patent at issue is very low.
14. Arguments listed in German Federal Patent Court, 30 July 1965, BPatGE 8, 121.
15. H. SCHADE, BlPMZ 1959, 70-71.

Kirchner, Wuesthoff, Marx and others argued that problems with the repeatability of a breeding process can be compensated by propagation ability of the product obtained by the process.[16]

Heydt thought that patentability should be decided by categories in that a method claim for a breeding process requires repeatability of the process, while a product claim does not require the repeatability of process to produce it.[17]

The decision by the Supreme Court of Japan seems to be based upon theories (B) and/or (C).

In 1969, the German Federal Supreme Court for the first time affirmed the patent eligibility of breeding methods (X ZB 15/67 - *Rote Taube/Red Dove*[18]). The claim at issue was directed to a method for breeding a dove with specific characteristics that comprises multiple crossing and selection steps. The German Federal Supreme Court held that "a method for breeding animals can represent a teaching to utilise natural biological forces and phenomena and therefore be patentable". However, the Court denied the patent eligibility of the claim at issue, because disclosure was insufficient to make repetition of the breeding procedure plausible. The German Federal Supreme Court, therefore, seemed to take a position similar to (A) above. Subsequent decisions rendered by the German courts were based on the same idea.[19]

b) A very similar discussion was waged in Switzerland more than 10 years before the German *Red Dove* decision. In 1953, the **Swiss** Federal Court denied the patentability of a claim directed to a newly created red rose, because the breeding method was not feasible, rendering the claimed invention unpatentable.[20]

c) In the **European** Patent Office (EPO) practice, the repeatability in biotechnology invention is also sometimes discussed in relation to the sufficient disclosure requirement. On this point, it has been clarified by the EPO case law that the identical exact repeatability is not required and that an invention may rely on chance event unless it leads to an undue burden for success: E.g., in the case **T 281/86**,[21] the Board of

16. BENKARD, Patentgesetz *(Patent Law)*, 4th ed. 1963, 115.
17. German Federal Supreme Court, 27 March 1969, GRUR 1969, 674 - *Rote Taube* w. comment HEYDT.
18. German Federal Supreme Court, 27 March 1969, GRUR 1969, 674 = 1 IIC 136 (1970) - *Rote Taube*.
19. E.g., German Federal Supreme Court, 30 March 1993, GRUR 1993, 651 - *Tetraploide Kamille*. There is also a case of invention in chance, not related to biotechnology, German Federal Supreme Court, 4 October 1979, GRUR 1980, 166 - *Doppelachsaggregat*. In this case, the German Federal Supreme Court held: "A proposal, which a person skilled in the art can realise practically only with great difficulty or only through chance without prior mistakes, when he will reach at it from a patent motivated success, is not sufficiently disclosed technical idea."
20. Swiss Federal Court, 27 January 1953, BGE 79 I 77. See also JPO/APIC/Y. HIRAKI/T. FUJITA, Bio Patent, 2010, 4, available at the website of the JPO <https://www.jpo.go.jp/e/news/kokusai/developing/training/textbook/document/index/Bio_Patent.pdf>.
21. Decision **T 281/86** of 27 January 1988 - *Preprothaumatin/UNILEVER*. See also, Decision **T 299/86** of 17 August 1989. Decision **T 727/95** of 21 May 1999 - *Cellulose/WEYERSHAEUSER* held: "In the Board's judgment, finding other stable, cellulose high-producing Acetobacter in nature is indeed a chance event and relying on chance for reproducibility amounts to undue burden in the absence of evidence that such chance events occur and can be identified frequently enough to guarantee success. There must exist other stable means for producing such strains for sufficiency of disclosure to be acknowledged." The Board suggested that an invention may

Appeal held: "There is no requirement under Article 83 EPC to the effect that a specifically described example of a process must be exactly repeatable."

not rely on chance events unless they occur frequently enough to guarantee success and do not provide and undue burden to reproduce (it is noted here that repeatability and reproducibility are similar but different concepts.)

Case No. 3

Novelty – Novelty Destroying Prior Application – Double Patenting

Christopher Heath and Atsuhiro Furuta

A comparison of a patent with prior art for the purposes of novelty and double patenting should disregard those elements of the claim that cannot serve as a distinction from prior art.

Supreme Court, 30 March 1993, Case No. 98 (Gyō-Tsu) of 1991 – *Numerical Control Energization Processing Device*

Mitsubishi Electric Corp. v. Sodick Co., Ltd.

1. BACKGROUND

In the Patent Act of Japan, specific provisions exist which prohibit double patenting[1] and prescribe what should be done if two overlapping inventions are filed: If on different dates, the application first filed takes precedence (first-to-file principle), sec. 39(1)). If on the same day, the issue has to be resolved by mutual consent, or, in the absence thereof, all the conflicting applications are refused, sec. 39(2). Sec. 39 corresponds to the original sec. 39 of the Patent Act of 1959 despite the fact that significant changes have been made meanwhile including the introduction of an 18-month period for publication in 1970. Sec. 29bis provides for the novelty-destroying effect of the entire disclosure of an earlier-filed, yet later-published application (corresponding to Art. 54(3) European Patent Convention, see below). Sec. 29bis includes a safeguard provision for cases where the applicant or the inventor of the present and cited applications are identical in order to avoid self-collision. This makes sec. 39 still necessary. The present case relates to two patents that were filed close to each other by different applicants and directed to very similar subject matter. The inventors of the two patents were entirely different.

Since the time of filing the application for the disputed patent, two notable changes to the Patent Act occurred.

First, the version of the Patent Act which was applicable to the two patents involved in this case required that a patent claim set forth only the features

1. Only the prior application with an earlier filing date is patented. There is also sec. 29(1) which provides that a publicly disclosed or used invention cannot be patented.

indispensable for the constitution of the invention (old sec. 36(4)(ii)). Under such provision, the applicant was expected to claim structural features of a product patent without relying on functional or product-by-process limitations. In order to allow for more flexibility in the claim language, this provision in 1994 was replaced by the current requirement that each claim "set forth all matters necessary to specify the invention", sec. 36(5).

Second, when the two relevant patents were filed, the 18-month period for publication and sec. Sec. 29bis did not exist. The two patents were published for pre-grant opposition purposes after substantive examination without early publication, and subsequently registered as patents.

Against this background, the main issue in dispute was whether the present invention was identical to the cited invention with an earlier filing date (called "prior invention" in the Supreme Court's decision). The present invention was published for opposition purposes as JP S48-3720 A (filed on 12 September 1968 and published on 10 November 1973), and the cited invention was published for opposition purposes as JP S53-13838 A (filed as No. S43-41029 on 15 June 1968 and published on 12 May 1978). The cited invention was filed about three months earlier than the filing date for the present invention. If the two inventions were identical, only the prior invention should have been patented under sec. 39(1), yet both inventions were patented. Subsequently, a request for invalidating the disputed patent was filed before the JPO on double patenting grounds. The Trial and Appeal Board of the JPO invalidated the disputed patent based on sec. 39(1). The JPO noted in its decision that the feature of "in the event of the short circuit, the workpiece or the machining electrode can follow a trajectory of tracking in a reverse direction" found in the present invention was essential to the cited invention, although the patent claim of the prior invention did not include this feature. Effectively, the JPO interpreted the disputed claim in such a way as to introduce a feature taken from the description into the claim and found that the cited and present inventions were substantially identical.

On appeal, the Tokyo High Court reversed the JPO trial decision and found the patent valid. The reason for this was simple: the prior invention did not have a feature the disputed claim had, and the disputed claim was found narrower than the prior invention. Because the technical scopes of the disputed and prior inventions were different, sec. 39 did not apply.

2. DECISION[2]

III. ... According to the facts established by the lower court, the patent claim of the prior invention was amended more than once during prosecution, and the language corresponding to the feature of reverse-direction trajectory existed prior to an amendment to the claim. A notice of reasons for refusal was issued during the appeal proceedings for the prior invention, stating that "the language is merely a statement of an action and such action is not a feature that is indispensable for the constitution of the invention," and the applicant responded with an amendment that deleted the objected language, i.e., the feature of reverse-direction trajectory.

2. Published in 168 Shūmin 571 = 1461 Hanrei Jihō 150 = 820 Hanrei Times 194 = N. Nakayama et al. (eds.), Tokkyo Hanrei Hyakusen *(Hundred Selected Patent Cases)*, 4th ed. 2012, 74.

Accordingly, it might be possible for us to regard that the feature of reverse-direction trajectory merely represents an action that results from other features, and, therefore, that the feature of reverse-direction trajectory of the present invention may not be a feature that is indispensable for the constitution of the invention. The lower court, however, did not discuss this point and looked only whether or not the language as to the feature of reverse-direction trajectory existed when it found the present invention different from the prior invention, and the original judgement is therefore deficient in its reasoning and not in conformity with the law.

Furthermore, the feature of "a control device that moves the tape in a reverse direction when a short circuit occurs" found in the patent claim of the prior invention clearly encompasses the feature of reverse-direction trajectory, and if we assume that this feature is indispensable for the constitution of the invention, the present invention of the appellee should be said to have adapted only the feature of reverse-direction trajectory. In addition to this point, if we assume that the present invention is the same as the prior invention in all other features, the present invention is considered to have a further limitation added to the prior invention. The appellee does not dispute the findings of the trial decision by the JPO with respect to the identity of all features except the feature of reverse-direction trajectory and, even if the constitution of the present invention is assumed to be encompassed by the prior invention, presents no arguments as to the existence of special circumstances that would deny the identity between the present invention and the prior invention. Therefore, the present invention is covered by the prior invention and is the same as the prior invention. On the other hand, according to the above analysis, if the feature of reverse-direction trajectory is merely an action that results from other features as discussed above, it would be safe to say that the present invention is identical to the prior invention. When the present case is analysed further, both inventions are concerned with energisation processing devices, while a liner electrode is used for creating an arbitrary continuous shape. If the feature of "a control device that moves the tape in a reverse direction when a short circuit occurs" of the prior invention is adapted, the processing electrode would not take any other action than tracing the tracking trajectory in the reverse direction, and it is clear that the feature of reverse-direction trajectory is included also in the prior invention. In the case of such energisation processing devices, there is no room for doubt that the present invention has an identical constitution as the prior invention. It therefore has to be said that after all the present invention is encompassed by the prior invention and identical to the prior invention.

The first instance decision erroneously interpreted and applied sec. 39(1) of the Patent Act and is therefore not in accordance with the law. This deficiency clearly affects the conclusion of the decision, and the appellant's arguments are reasonable, and the original judgement has to be vacated. The main reason for cancellation of the trial decision the appellee put forward by arguing that the trial decision is erroneous and illegal because it found the present invention identical to the prior invention does not have any basis.

IV. The appellee advances an auxiliary ground for the cancellation of the trial decision by arguing that the essence of the prior invention was changed by an amendment made prior to the decision for publication for opposition purposes, and the filing date of the prior invention should effectively be considered to fall after the filing date of the present invention. Thus, the trial decision that was made based on the fact that the prior invention was filed prior to the filing date of the present invention is not in conformity with the law. This ground has not been clearly discussed in the trial decision. The trial decision finds that the prior invention was filed prior to the filing date of the present invention, and based on such finding it is clear that the trial decision implicitly indicates that the essence of the prior invention was not changed by the amendment. In the present case, the first instance court should review this auxiliary ground. For this review by the first instance court, the present case is remanded.

3. ANALYSIS

a) Historical Meaning of the Decision

The Supreme Court essentially found the disputed patent invalid and vacated the judgement of the Tokyo High Court. Instead of rendering its own judgement as to the validity, it remanded the case to the original court because the auxiliary ground that the appellee had asserted required additional consideration.[3]

The Supreme Court noted that one feature that existed in the present invention was literally missing in the cited invention. That is to say, the feature of "in the event of the short circuit, the workpiece or the machining electrode can follow a trajectory of tracking in a reverse direction" found in the present invention existed in the patent claim of the cited invention during prosecution, but that feature was removed because the appeal examiners during the appeal proceedings pointed out that such feature was an action that resulted from other claimed features and that might not be "indispensable for the constitution of the invention." According to the Supreme Court, the previous instance court erred because it did not pay sufficient attention to this file history and because it did not find the present invention identical to the prior invention. The Supreme Court did not determine whether the feature of "in the event of the short circuit, the workpiece or the machining electrode can follow a trajectory of tracking in a reverse direction" in fact contravened the requirement of sec. 36(4) (ii) Patent Act, which existed at the time of the decision.

On a number of occasions, the Supreme Court has emphasised the importance of public notice function of patent claims and has not accepted reading some features from the description into patent claims.[4] In the present case, however, the Supreme Court gave some weight to the examination history beyond what was recited in the patent claim of the previously filed patent (the "prior invention" according to the Supreme Court). The main issue in dispute was overlapping patent protection under sec. 39 Patent Act, and normally, the focal point is the identity of scope of the two patented claims. The Supreme Court held that a feature missing in the claim of the previously filed patent was substantially recited in the claim because such feature

---

3. Subsequently, in 1991, another request for invalidating the disputed patent was filed by the same party, *Mitsubishi Electric*, on the ground of two prior art publications and the disputed patent was invalidated for the lack of inventive step by another JPO decision on 29 August 1996 (Invalidation Case No. 6140 of 1991).
4. See, for example, Case Nos. 35 and 37 in this book.

represented an action that automatically resulted from other claimed features and therefore added no further technical information that could distinguish the claim from prior art. The approach and conclusion the Supreme Court presented seem very well reasoned and correct. The authors believe that the present decision does not contradict other Supreme Court decisions that emphasise the importance of the public notice function of patent claims. Even today, this decision remains applicable to the question of double patenting or novelty destroying with regard to a prior application unpublished at the filing date.[5]

b) Current JPO Practice

The following is a quotation from Part III, Chapter 4 "Prior Application (Patent Act sec. 39)" of the current Examination Guidelines of the JPO (the authors revised the English translation prepared by the JPO):

> "As a result of a comparison between the claimed invention and a prior invention claimed in the prior application, the examiner shall interpret that the two inventions are same,
>
> (i) when no difference exists between the claimed invention and the prior invention; or
> (ii) when the claimed invention and the prior invention are substantially same.
>
> 'Substantially the same' herein means a case,
>
> (ii-1) where the difference is a very minor difference (an addition, deletion, conversion, etc., of common general knowledge or commonly used art, which does not have any new effect) in embodying means for resolving a problem;
> (ii-2) where the difference is resulted from that the subject matter of the prior invention is expressed by a generic concept in the claimed invention; or

5. We have to carefully consider the applicability, because this case was before the above-mentioned law amendment and there were different provisions for "novelty destroying" prior art existed. Sec 39 for the prohibition of double patenting of claims, sec. 29bis due to unpublished prior art based on the whole contents approach, sec. 29(1)(i) for publicly known prior art, ii) for publicly worked prior art, and (iii) for published prior art. As stated in a commentary of this case, T. IWATSUBO, Sengan hatsume to no dōitsusei *(Identity of an invention to a prior application)*, in N. NAKAYAMA et al. (eds.), Tokkyo Hanrei Hyakusen *(Hundred Selected Patent Cases)*, 4th ed. 2012, 74, under the current Patent Act, it may very well be that the Supreme Court would not have reversed the original decision only because the statement at issue concerned the effect of the invention(at the time, a statement concerning the effect of an invention was not considered as indispensable and might be inappropriate under the old sec. 36) and the case would be treated more flexibly for whole contents approach based on sec. 29bis. T. IWATSUBO for the current Patent Act cites Tokyo High Court, 29 January 2004, Case No. 239 (Gyō-Ke) of 2002, the website of the court <http://www.courts.go.jp/app/files/hanrei_jp/551/010551_hanrei.pdf>, which acknowledged a substantial identity between inventions beyond a formal comparison of the claim statement and the publicly worked prior art (sec. 29(1)(i)), an approach that can be used both for the question of double patenting and novelty destroying prior art.

(ii-3) where the difference is a mere difference in categorical expressions (for example, a difference between expression forms, or an invention of 'product' to an invention of 'method')."[6]

Almost the same statement about the comparison of two inventions exists in Part III, Chapter 3 "Unpublished Prior Art (Patent Act sec. 29bis)".

And while not directly related to the present Supreme Court decision, the JPO examination practice on preventing double patenting between divisional applications, which have the same filing date in the name of the same applicant, should also be discussed, because it is different from the above mentioned practice for the same inventions with other filing dates or practices found outside Japan:

> "When an invention A and an invention B have the same filing date, the examiner shall consider them 'same', if the two inventions can be considered to be same in either of two scenarios (i) and (ii) provided below:
>
> (i) The invention A is assumed to be an earlier application and the invention B is assumed to be a later application;
> (ii) The invention B is assumed to be an earlier application and the invention A is assumed to be a later application.
>
> On the other hand, the examiner shall not consider 'same' the two inventions with the same filing date, if the inventions A and B are not considered same assuming that the invention B has an earlier filing date and the invention A has a later filing date, even if the inventions A and B are considered same assuming that the invention A has an earlier filing date and the invention B has a later filing date (e.g., the invention A states a 'spring,' and the invention B states an 'elastic member' as corresponding subject matter)."[7]

What this portion of the Examination Guidelines says may not be easy to understand, but the message is that when two applications have the same filing date in the name of the same applicant, sec. 39 should not be invoked if the two claimed inventions are somewhat different in scope.[8]

In regard of foreign applications, the Examination Guidelines for sec. 29bis state the following:

> "With regard to a foreign application claiming priority under the Paris Convention, an invention stated commonly in (i) and (ii) below shall be handled as filed to Japan on the filing date of the first foreign application:
>
> (i) Entire filing documents of the first foreign application.
> (ii) Originally filed description, etc., of an application to Japan."[9]

6. The Examination Guideline of the JPO, Part III, Chapter 4, at the website of the JPO <https://www.jpo.go.jp/e/system/laws/rule/guideline/patent/tukujitu_kijun/index.html>
7. The Examination Guideline of the JPO, Part III, Chapter 4, *supra* note 6.
8. The reason is that in such case the claims of the two applications should be treated as if they ere claims of one application, even they are in fact two divisional applications.
9. The Examination Guideline of the JPO, Part III, Chapter 3, at the website of the JPO <https://www.jpo.go.jp/e/system/laws/rule/guideline/patent/tukujitu_kijun/index.html>

4. COMPARATIVE REMARKS

a) First to file, double patenting and the definition of novelty – the EPC

While there is no explicit provision that would stipulate the first to file rule under the EPC, Art. 54(3) in connection with Arts. 80, 87-89 EPC clarify that the requirements of patentability are not fulfilled for an application that at the filing or priority date is not novel. An invention shall not be considered new also in regard of "the content of European patent applications as filed, the dates of filing of which are prior to the date referred to in paragraph 2 [filing or priority date of the application at issue] and which were published on or after that date."

This means:

1) There are no rules that are applicable to two overlapping applications (be it by the same[10] or different applicants) made on the same day, and
2) Yet unpublished EP applications will only be perceived as conflicting where the one filed earlier destroys the novelty of the later.

In order to determine which applications are "conflicting" according to Art. 54(3) EPC, the provision applies the "whole contents approach" that does not compare the claims, but (for the earlier application) rather the application as whole. While this approach is broader than the approach taken by the Japanese Supreme Court, Art. 56 EPC 2nd sentence clarifies that prior, yet unpublished EP application do not count as prior art for determining inventive step. So as not to obfuscate the difference between novelty and inventive step, an Art. 54(3) comparison would not include obvious equivalents[11] or implicit disclosures[12] of the prior application. In particular, all features, not just the essential ones, must be contained in the earlier application[13]

In the case of foreign applications filed with priory, Art. 89 EPC clarifies that for Art. 54(2) EPC, the priority date is considered as the EP filing date. However, foreign applications that are not subsequently filed before the EPC do not become prior art under Art. 54(3) EPC because this provision only wants to avoid conflicting patents within the jurisdiction of the EPC.

b) First to file, double patenting and the definition of novelty – the US

Prior to the America Invents Act 2013, priority in the domestic context was established by the first-to-invent rather than the first to file principle. Correspondingly, conflicts

10. There is case law that has refused one of two identical applications made on the same date by the same applicant: Case **T 307/03** of 3 July 2007, OJ 2009, 422. This approach, however, was not followed by a later decision (**T 1423/07** of 19 April 2010) that indicated lack of a justifiable legal interest as a possible reason for refusal (based on Art. 125 EPC), yet ultimately denied this.
11. Decision **T 167/84**, OJ 1987, 369.
12. Decision **T 572/88** of 27 February 1991.
13. Decision **T 411/98** of 11 January 2000:"A claimed subject matter would lack novelty only if it were derivable as a whole directly and unambiguously from a prior art disclosure and if a clear and unmistakable teaching of the combination of all claimed features (and not only the essential ones) could be found in said disclosure."

between two applications were not merely resolved by the filing dates, but rather by the date when an invention was reduced to practice. This became particularly clear in the pre-2013 version of 35 USC sec. 102(g): The provision clarified that an invention made in the US that was not abandoned, suppressed or concealed served as prior art against a subsequent patent application even where the invention had never been made public. The provision both served the conflict between different inventions covering the same subject matter (interference proceedings under 35 USC sec. 135), and establishing prior art.[14] Under the America Invents Act, only a prior user right under sec. 273 is now recognised for this scenario.

The definition of novelty under US law is rather narrow, as each and every element of the claim must be present in the prior art document.[15] Mechanical equivalents are also considered as novelty destroying prior art.[16]

As to unpublished patent applications (and until the American Inventors Protection Act 1999, patent applications were not regularly published after 18 months (as is the case now), but only after grant, thereby creating a rather lengthy interval of secret prior art for patent applications), 35 USC sec. 102(a)(2) creates the same rule as Art. 54(3) EPC, namely a novelty-destroying effect of an unpublished US application vis-a-vis subsequently filed applications.[17] The controversial provision[18] of sec. 102(e)(2) that gave prior art effect to US applications that eventually matured into a patent retroactively from the filing date yet excluded foreign applications,[19] was replaced by sec. 102(d)(2) that recognised a first filing date world-wide.

c) Korea

A Korean patent application filed prior to but published after the filing of another person's patent application can be used as a prior art for the purpose of defeating the novelty of the later-filed patent application in accordance with the "expanded earlier application" rule, sec. 29(3) Patent Act. Therefore, a patent application may be rejected on the ground of lack of novelty if the invention claimed in the application is substantially identical to the one stated in the description, claims and/or drawing(s) of an earlier filed, but later published patent application, unless the inventors or the applicants of such two applications at the time of filing the applications are the same. However, such a patent application cannot be used as a prior art reference for the purpose of determining the requirement of inventive step.

---

14. US CAFC *Thomson SA v. Quixote Corp.*, 166 F. 3d 1172 (Fed. Cir. 1999).
15. US CAFC, *Titanium Metals v. Banner*, 778 F2d 775 (Fed. Cir. 1985).
16. US Court of Claims, *Straussler v. United States*, 339 F2d 670 (Ct. Cl. 1964).
17. Also here, the whole contents of the application is decisive, to the extent that the subject matter of the subsequent application has been reduced to practice in the earlier one: US Supreme Court, *Alexander Milburn v. Davis-Bournonville*, 270 US 390 (1926).
18. The provision was widely held to contravene the Paris Convention provision of national treatment: C. Heath, National Treatment under the Paris Convention, in: K. Sanders (ed.), The Principle of National Treatment in International Economic Law, Edward Elgar 2014, 223 - 247.
19. US Court of Claims, *In re Hilmer*, 359 F.2d 859 (1966).

Case No. 4

Novelty – Grace Period – Combination with Priority

Christopher Heath

A patent applicant can only avail himself of the grace period of six months when the domestic application is filed within this period of time. The filing of the first international application within six months after publication and the subsequent combination with the right of priority is not foreseen by Japanese law.

Tokyo High Court, 13 March 1997, Case No. 148 of (Gyō-Ke) of 1995 – *Therapeutic Agent Inducted from Blood Sludging*

Sanofi v. Ohara Pharmaceutical

---

1. BACKGROUND

Sec. 30 of the Patent Act makes an exception to the standard of absolute novelty as provided for in section 29 under two circumstances. Either where an invention has been published by the person who has a right to obtain by way of a presentation,[1] experiment, etc. (paragraph 1), or where the invention has been made public against the intention of the person who has a right to obtain a patent (paragraph 2). Sec. 30(3) provides for a grace period in regard of exhibitions in conformity with Art. 11 Paris Convention. The grace period allowed under the above circumstances can be invoked up six months (one year as of 6 September 2018)[2] from the date on which the

---

1. The presentation or publication has to be in the name of the inventor, otherwise sec. 30(1) does not apply: Tokyo High Court, 16 March 1992, Case No. 158 (Gyō-Ke) of 1991, the website of the courts <http://www.courts.go.jp/app/files/hanrei_jp/754/014754_hanrei.pdf>; Commentary on this case: S. NEMOTO, Hatsumeisha wo meiki sezu kenkyūshūkai de bunsho happyō shita hatsumei ni taisuru tokkyohō 30 jō no tekiyō ni kansuru handan *(Applicability of sec. 30 Patent Act to an invention which is disclosed documentary in a research meeting without statement of inventor's name)*, 43-7 Tokkyo Kanri 869 (1993); German translation in 1994 GRUR Int. 257 – *Betonverstärkung*.
2. As agreed under the Trans-Pacific Partnership Agreement (TPP), Japan in 2018 has extended the grace period to one year under Law No. 108 of 28 December 2017 implementing the TPP. See documents at the website of the JPO <https://www.jpo.go.jp/system/laws/rule/hokaisei/sangyozaisan/tpp_houritu_seibi_h281228.html>.

   Although this law has not come into force (because the TPP is not yet operative), the revision of sec. 30 was implemented by Law no. 33 of 30 May 2018 amending the Unfair Competition Prevention Act. See documents at the website of the JPO <https://www.jpo.go.jp/system/laws/rule/hokaisei/sangyozaisan/fuseikyousou_h300530.html>.

invention was published. It is immaterial in this respect where the publication has taken place.[3] In other words, the patent application for such invention must be made within six months from the date on which the invention became public. In the case at issue, the patent application was filed within six months from the occurrence of publication, but it was filed in France and not in Japan. Based on the French filing, the applicant then used the right of priority under the Paris Convention and filed the Japanese application within one year from the date of the French filing. The applicant could thus rely on the grace period for filing the French application, and the Paris Convention priority period for filing the Japanese application. Yet could the applicant also rely on the grace period under Japanese law by filing the application in France?

2. DECISION[4]

a) Facts

The plaintiff applied for a patent in France on 2 January 1976. He subsequently used this application under the priority rules of the Paris Convention to apply for a patent in Japan on 28 December 1976. The patent was granted on 30 November 1981, but subsequently attacked on 14 October 1992 by the defendants for the reason that the patented invention had been published already before the patent application in France in a journal that was received by a Japanese university on 11 December 1975. The plaintiff had asserted that the contents of the invention were published against his intention in the above-mentioned journal that was issued in France on 13 September 1975. The Japanese Patent Office invalidated the patent nevertheless, arguing that the publication against the will of the inventor had not been effected within the period of time prescribed in sec. 30(2) Japanese Patent Act that reads as follows:

> "In the case of an invention which has fallen under any of the paragraphs of sec. 29(1) against the intention of the person having the right to obtain a patent, the preceding subsection shall also apply, provided that such person has filed a patent application within six months from the date on which the invention first fell under those paragraphs."

b) Reasons

According to Art. 2(1) Paris Convention, nationals of each of the countries of the Union shall enjoy in all the other countries of the Union the advantages that their respective laws grant. When applying this to sec. 30(2) Patent Act regardless of a publication within Japan or abroad, the person entitled to file for a patent shall have

---

The amendment came into force on 6 September 2018. See documents at the website of the JPO <https://www.jpo.go.jp/system/laws/rule/guideline/patent/hatumei_reigai_encho.html>.

3. Tokyo High Court, 29 May 1986, Case No. 285 (Gyō-Ke) of 1984, 1215 Hanrei Jihō 118 = 18-2 Mutaishū 192 (in the case where the invention was published in the Netherlands and Germany); Supreme Court, 10 November 1989, Case No. 160 (Gyō-Tsu) of 1986, 1337 Hanrei Jihō 117 (publication in the US).

4. Published in 1611 Hanrei Jihō 122. English translation in IIC 1999, 449 w. critical comment HINKELMANN.

the right to do so within six months from the date the invention has been published against his intention. The priority application was made in France on 2 January 1976, and subsequently in Japan on 28 December 1976. While under French law, novelty may not have been lost under these circumstances, the respective provision of Japanese law cannot apply in this case, since Japanese and foreign nationals are treated in absolutely the same way. With regard to the application in Japan, the plaintiff is treated exactly in the same way as a national of Japan, and therefore the Patent Office's interpretation of sec. 30(2) Patent Act does not contravene Art. 2 Paris Convention. ... While it is not explicitly stated to what extent sec. 30(2) Patent Act refers to an application on which a priority right is based, Art. 4(B) Paris Convention requires that any sort of publication between the first and the subsequent filing shall not invalidate the patent right. However, sec. 30(2) Patent Act is a special provision that cannot be understood in the sense that it would refer to the first application with the consequence that any subsequent application could still be filed until 18 months after the publication against the will of the patentee.

3. COMPARATIVE ANALYSIS

a) A **grace period** refers to an exception of the absolute novelty standard in that the publication of an invention even prior to patent filing is not considered prior art for this very invention. Some countries such as the US[5] and Canada[6] allow for a grace period of twelve months, while Art. 55 EPC and the corresponding provisions under the domestic laws of Germany,[7] France,[8] the United Kingdom,[9] and Italy[10] only grant a grace period of six months in very limited circumstances, namely if the invention was published with the intention to harm the inventor or applicant.

From a historical perspective, sec. 6 of the **English** Statute of Monopolies 1624 granted patents for "the sole working or making of any manner of new manufacture within this realm, to the true and first inventor and inventors of such manufactures which others at the time of making such letters patent and grants shall not use". The novelty requirement expressed therein should ensure that "a patent takes absolutely nothing away from the public which it had the right to use before the grant of the absolute rights conferred upon the patentee."[11] For that reason, it was held immaterial by whom the patented invention was made public prior to the application for a patent:

> "If the public once becomes possessed of an invention by any means whatever, no subsequent patent can be granted for it, either to the true and first inventor himself, or to any other person, for the public cannot be deprived of the right to use the invention and a patentee of the invention could not give any

5. Two years until 1940 under sec. 4886 of the US Patents Act 1870. Current rules under sec. 102(b) and (d) of the US Patents Act 1952.
6. Sec. 28(2)1(a) Canadian 1952 Patents Act.
7. Sec. 3(4) German Patent Act 1981.
8. Sec. 9 French Patent Act 1968.
9. Sec. 2(4) UK Patents Act 1977.
10. Sec. 15 Italian Law on Patents for Inventions of 1939.
11. G. AMDUR, Patent Fundamentals, New York 1956, 50.

> consideration to the public for the grant, the public already possessing everything that he could give."[12]

In a later case, it was held:

> "Public use ... means a use in public, not by the public, I think there is no room for doubt that the use by the defender of his own paint was of this character. It is quite true that, in order to obtain letters patent, the inventor must disclose his secret to the public in return for the monopoly conferred upon him. But such a disclosure as that is not necessary to the prior use, which will anticipate and so avoid a patent."[13]

Subsequently, however, a number of circumstances would allow for a certain grace period, e.g., necessary public use for experimental purposes,[14] and use of a provisional specification similar to the US instrument of a provisional filing.[15] The provisional filing preserved novelty if a proper specification was made within 12 months, yet initially allowed the inventor to file only a rough sketch of the invention. This instrument was scrapped and the novelty requirements harmonised in accordance with the EPC in the UK Patents Act 1977.

The **French** position under the Patent Act 1844 was also hostile to a grace period, yet for different reasons. Under Sec. 31 of this Act, any form of publicité antérieure" was novelty destroying. While some French academics argued that publication by the inventor was, strictly speaking, not "*antériorité*" but rather "*divulgation*",[16] this distinction was widely rejected, as the fact of publication could not be made subject to the question of who had published due to the principle under Roman law that "*protestatio non valit contra factum*".[17]

As a starting point, the **US** patent system took the English position that publication by the inventor would amount to an "abandonment" of the patent right.[18] Yet this stance was soon modified in favour of publications due to misappropriation or other unlawful acts by third parties.[19] The U.S. Patent Acts of 1836 and 1839 broadened this exception to a grace period of two years in cases of acts of prior use by the inventor or third parties.[20] The revisions of 1870 and 1897 dropped any limiting requirements of the grace period.

Finally, the **Canadian** grace period of originally two years was introduced under the Canadian Patent Act 1935 in an apparent wish to harmonise its system with that of the United States.[21]

---

12. English Court of Appeal, *Patterson v. Gaslight & Coke*, 3 Appeal Cases 244 [1875].
13. Scottish Court of Session, *Gill v. Coutts*, [1896] RPC125.
14. Sec. 51(3) UK Patents Act 1949.
15. Sec. 52 UK Patents Act 1949.
16. ROUBIER, Le Droit de la Propriété Industrielle *(Industrial Property Rights)*, Vol. 2, Paris 1954, 141.
17. E.g., French Cour de Cassation *(French Supreme Court)*, Annales 1866, 289; French Cour de Cassation, Annales 1885, 59; French Cour de Cassation, Annales 1967, 3.
18. US Supreme Court, *Pennock v. Dialogue*, 7L.Ed.326 (u.s. 1829).
19. US Supreme Court, *Shaw v. Cooper*, 8L.Ed.699 (u.s. 1833).
20. Sec. 6 Patent Act 1836, sec. 7 Patent Act 1839 and *Andrews v. Hovey*, 31L.Ed.163.
21. VOJÁČEK, A Survey of the Principal National Patent Systems, London 1936, 133.

The **German** Patent Act of 1877 also did not provide for any grace period.[22] Some academics found this lamentable, in particular in cases of publications against the inventor's will.[23] This was amended in 1891 to allow for a three month grace period in case of publications and on condition of reciprocity.[24] This provision, of course, was no longer relevant after Germany joined the Paris Convention. A general grace period of six months was introduced in Sec. 2 (2) German Patent Act 1936, which just as the US Patent Revision one hundred years earlier, was the result of an inventor friendly climate.[25] This general grace period of six months was maintained until the Patent Act 1981 was harmonised with the EPC.

b) In the past, numerous attempts for **international harmonisation** of the grace period were made, two at revision conferences of the Paris Convention. At the revision conference in London, some of the discussion focussed on improving the position of the inventor. Under the heading "*nouveau droit morale de l'inventeur*", the right of the inventor's nomination in the patent was discussed together with aspects of employees' inventions and a grace period for publications prior to the first filing. The Italian and Dutch delegates proposed a grace period of 12 months for presentations before an academic forum (Italy) and six months in general (the Netherlands). The Dutch delegation highlighted the problem of hastily drafted patent applications, legally untrained inventors and the necessity of a grace period for academia.[26] While this proposal apparently fizzled out in the course of several committee meetings, a similar proposal made at the Lisbon Conference was supported by the US and Germany. The proposal was particularly aimed at clarifying the relationship between a grace period and a priority filing. It should be clarified that the grace period should not only become generally available for a period of six months but that this grace period could also be combined with the priority period of 12 months, thus covering publications up to six months prior to the first filing as non-novelty destroying. The discussions concerned two scenarios: first, a third-party publication against the inventor's intentions, and, second, a publication by the inventor himself. The proposal

---

22. Sec. 2 of the German Patent Act 1877 merely stated that "An invention is not considered as new if at the date of filing the application according the provisions of this present law, the same has been so described in public prints, or so publicly employed in the country that the use of the same by other competent persons appears possible."
23. Criticism particularly by *J. Kohler*, who had done so much to interpret patent law as a proper protection for the inventor's rights. He criticised in particular that "the inventor loses unaccountable wealth without deeper justification" if a law did not come to the inventor's rescue in case of such unauthorised publications: J. KOHLER, Handbuch des deutschen Patentrechts *(Handbook of German Patent Law)*, Mannheim 1900, 199.
24. Sec. 2(2) German Patent Act 1891. Comparable provisions could be found in a number of national laws before these countries joined the Paris Convention. Grace periods in cases of foreign publications were contained in the German-Austrian Trade Agreement of 1881, in the Austrian Patent Act of 1899 (Sec. 3), in the Finnish Patent Act of 1898 and the Mexican Patent Act of 1890.
25. Glorification of inventors had become fashionable in the Third Reich, not least because Hitler had mentioned them in his book, *Mein Kampf*, as some academics of that period were anxious to point out: RISTOW, Die Praxis und das neue Patentgesetz *(Practice and the new Patent Act)*, Juristische Wochenschrift 1936, 1492.
26. Actes de la Conference de Londres (1935), 260.

was ultimately defeated by Austria, France and the Netherlands.[27] Within AIPPI the problem was discussed at a number of annual meetings: so in Prague 1938,[28] and in particular in Vienna in 1952.[29] The Vienna congress came out in favour of a grace period in the case of publications against the inventor's will. The last attempt to harmonise the grace period to date was made within the framework of the proposed Patent Law Treaty of 21 December 1990. According to Art. 12, disclosure by a third party, who obtained information directly or indirectly from the inventor, would not affect patentability during the 12 months preceding the filing date or, where priority is claimed, the priority of the application. However, agreement on the overall framework of the Patent Law Treaty has not yet been reached. A grace period in case of public display at a recognised exhibition is contained in Art. 11 Paris Convention, yet as an optional provision ("If later the right of priority is invoked, each country may provide that the period shall start from the date of introduction of the goods into the exhibition" – in effect allowing for the priority period to run from the exhibition date; whether this implicitly means that the grace period is the extended to one year in such case is unclear. It seems that no country has introduced such rule. Some countries, however, regard the public display at a recognised exhibition as a case for which the grace period can be invoked, e.g. Art. 55(1)b EPC).[30]

c) In a scenario where the applicant relies on the grace period for the subsequent filing of the (first) patent application, and subsequently makes use of the priority right in order to file also in other countries, the question arises whether for the subsequent filings, the grace period is calculated as the interval between the publication and the first (priority) filing, or the interval between the publication and the subsequent filing.

One could think of three different possibilities of how **a grace period can be combined with the right to priority**.

- The country of subsequent filing does not treat the publication prior to the priority filing as novelty destroying if the country of the priority filing does not do so, either. In this case, the grace period for the country of the subsequent filing is determined by the law of the country of first filing. With a first filing in the US or Canada, an applicant could thus "export" the generous grace period of one year also to countries that are less generous. If the invention was published on 1 February 2000, and the first filing was made in the US on 1 December 2000, the applicant could successfully rely on the grace period of one year stipulated by US law. A subsequent filing before the EPO on 1 December 2001 could rely on the rules in the US in order to avoid that the publication on 1 February would be used as prior art for the EP patent.

27. Actes de la Conference de Lisbonne (1963), 349-364.
28. AIPPI Annuaire 1938, 188.
29. AIPPI Annuaire 1952, 133.
30. Art. 11 Paris Convention is not very satisfactory, and during the Hague Revision Conference 1925, a proposal was made to combine the public display of an invention during an exhibition with the right of priority: S. LADAS, Patents, Trademarks and Related Rights, Cambridge Mass. 1975, vol. 1 p. 552. However, there were vastly differing views on this provision, and no agreement could be reached about the combination of public use (and a corresponding grade period), and the right of priority.

Such a solution is not mandated by the rules of national treatment and may even run counter to the principle of independence of rights as stipulation in Art. 4bis Paris Convention. No country therefore applies such a rule.

- The country of subsequent filing applies its domestic rules for the grace period also to filings using the right of priority, yet calculates the grace period as the interval between publication and priority filing. For the above example, the applicant could thus succeed with its application in countries that allow for a one-year grace period (e.g. Canada and Thailand), while for countries with a grace period of six months, the publication would count as prior art. Where the grace period depends on certain conditions (e.g. publication by the inventor himself, or against his intentions, etc.), the applicant for the subsequent filing would have to demonstrate that these conditions are met even in cases where the time period as such is complied with (e.g. in Malaysia, the grace period is one year, but limited to certain circumstances). Some countries have explicit provisions in their patent law that allow a combination of grace period and priority period, e.g. sec. 7b Swiss Patent Act.

- The country of subsequent filing applies its domestic rules for the grace period and calculates the latter from the actual filing date in that country rather than the priority application. Examples are sec. 30 Japanese Patent Act, Sec. 28 Canadian Patent Act and Art. 55 EPC that refer to the filing date, rather than the priority date.

d) The question is whether the last solution would not run counter to the principle of **national treatment.** This was particularly argued by one of Board of Appeal of the EPO that referred the issue to the Enlarged Board,[31]

> "because calculating the period from the date of the subsequent application might produce unsatisfactory results. Subsequent developments had to be taken into account, such as the frequency with which priorities are claimed for European patent applications or the duration of grant and opposition proceedings. Another significant factor was the right of the parties to a case to be treated equally, as recognised in the practice relating to Article 6(1) of the European Convention on Human Rights (ECHR). That included the right to defend oneself by presenting facts and evidence in order to contest the opposing party's claims. In patent literature, opinions on calculating the six-month period were divided. Proponents of the priority date as reference point could rely on the argument that Article 89 EPC implicitly referred to Article 55 EPC by way of Article 54(2) and (3) EPC. Moreover, the narrower interpretation of Article 55(1) EPC did not guarantee the right of priority arising from the first application. That contravened not only Article 4A(1) of the Paris Convention for the Protection of Industrial Property (PC) but also Article 87 EPC. Nor was it reasonable that the fate of a patent application should depend on whether it was filed with a national office or with an international authority like the EPO. With regard to balancing the interests

31. Referral decision **T 377/95**, cited in the Enlarged Board decision **G 2/99**, 12 July 2000, OJ EPO 2001, 83 – "Six-months period/Dewert", point X of the decision.

of the applicant against those of the public, the facts of the case showed that applicants were not in a position to prepare for an abusive disclosure and file a subsequent application in time, i.e within six months after the disclosure, because as a rule they did not find out about abusive disclosures until later."

In fact, the Dutch Supreme Court found that a broad interpretation of Art. 55 EPC was correct:[32]

> "It follows from Article 89 EPC that the right of priority has the effect that, inter alia for Article 54(2) EPC – a provision which lays down the relevant state of the art in terms of time and hence is closely linked to Article 55(1) EPC – to be applied, the date of priority must be taken as being the date of filing of the European patent application. Article 55(1) EPC would not serve its purpose – to protect the applicant – if this provision were to be interpreted literally in cases of a pre-existing priority right. The system underlying the Convention thus justifies an interpretation according to which the date of priority also takes the place of the date of filing when calculating the rime limit under Article 55(1) EPC."

The German[33] and Swiss Supreme Courts[34] came to a different conclusion, though, as did the Enlarged Board of Appeal in case **G 2/99:**[35]

> "2.1 According to Article 55 EPC, the starting point for calculating the period for non-prejudicial disclosures is the filing of the European patent application. Hence the reference point for the provision is the filing of the application which is to be examined, not the filing of an application from which priority is claimed. According to Article 89 EPC, which governs the effects of the right of priority, the date of priority counts as the date of filing of the European patent application for the purposes of Article 54(2) and (3) EPC and Article 60(2) EPC; there is no reference to Article 55 EPC. Thus neither the wording of Article 55 EPC nor that of Article 89 EPC provides for the period for non-prejudicial disclosures to be calculated from the priority date ...
>
> 2.5.1 The referral T 377/95 (Reasons point 27) cites Loth (Münchner Gemeinschaftskommentar, Article 55 EPC, point 65), who, referring to the high percentage of European applications claiming priority, takes the view that the non-cumulation of the six-month period with the priority year would make Article 55 EPC more or less meaningless and undermine the right of priority.
>
> It may be true that the legislator did not foresee the scale on which European applications would claim priorities. It was certainly to be expected, however, that at least applicants from non-member States would generally claim priority from their own country. Thus, abusive disclosure arising before the priority date was not a possibility that the legislator would have seen as being in any way exceptional. Moreover, in assessing the conflict of interests between the applicant affected by the abusive disclosure and the public, especially competitors, the

32. Dutch Supreme Court, 23 June 1995, OJ EPO 1998, 278.
33. German Federal Supreme Court, 5 December 1995, OJ EPO 1998, 263 – *Coriolskraft*.
34. Swiss Federal Supreme Court, 19 August 1991, GRUR Int. 1992, 293 – *Stapelvorrichtung*.
35. EPO Enlarged Board of Appeal case **G 2/99,** 12 July 2000, OJ EPO 2001, 83 – *Six-months period/ Dewert*.

> frequency with which this conflict arises is not a crucial factor: the interests to be balanced, in particular individual justice and legal certainty, are always the same. Changing this balance in the applicant's favour on account of a large number of cases necessarily means changing it just as frequently to the public's disadvantage."

Finally, also the Tokyo High Court (as above) saw no problem in disallowing the combination of grace and priority period because the provision under domestic law did not specifically provide for this combination, because foreigners and domestic applicants were treated alike and because the right of priority only referred to the period between the first and the subsequent filing.[36]

e) Despite these decisions, one could take a closer look at the question of a **de facto discrimination of foreigners**. *Loth*[37] has indeed made the point that the more the instrument of priority is used in a given domestic patent system, the more de facto discrimination there actually is. Where 90% of all patent filings are based on a priority, these 90% cannot use the right of priority to its proper extent when publication has occurred prior to the first filing, a hugely unsatisfactory result. This de facto discrimination does not result from a lack of harmonisation in the field of grace periods, but from an insufficient recognition of the right of priority in respect of cases where publication occurred prior to the first filing. The Enlarged Board of Appeal correctly mentioned the fact that the right of priority only starts with the first filing, and is thus not concerned with occurrences before this date. This is certainly correct, but does not necessarily mean that a rule in conformity with the right of priority also complies with the obligations under national treatment. On the other hand, the discussion in connection with Art. 11 Paris Convention (above) may indicate that the Member States to the Paris Convention were aware of the issue, but did not find it necessary to introduce an explicit rule whereby acts preceding the first filing should be connected to the one year priority period. The position of applicants that rely on a foreign priority for a subsequent filing in Europe and Japan is thus not entirely satisfactory to the extent that the invention has been published prior to the first filing.

---

36. The decision is referred to with approval by N. Nakayama, Tokkyohō *(Patent Law)*, 3rd ed. 2016, 129. Sec. 30 is applicable, though, where the priority application is a domestic application that was made within six months from the publication and the applicant subsequently files a domestic application based on the domestic priority filing, see sec. 41 Japanese Patent Act. Both applications in this case have to make explicit reference to sec. 30, though: IP High Court, 30 November 2017, Case No. 10279 (Gyō-Ke) of 2016, the website of the courts <http://www.courts.go.jp/app/files/hanrei_jp/285/087285_hanrei.pdf>.
37. Loth, in: Münchener Gemeinschaftskommentar zum EPÜ *(Munich Commentary to the EPC)*, 13th instalment 1990, Art. 55 note 65.

Case No. 5

Inventive Step – Problem Solution Approach and Ex Post Analysis

Atsuhiro Furuta

For objectively assessing the involvement of an inventive step, it is necessary to properly understand the problem of the invention. An illogical or ex post analysis must be avoided.

Intellectual Property High Court, 28 January 2009,
Case No. 10096 (Gyō-Ke) of 2008 – *Adhesive for Electric Circuits*

Hitachi Kasei v. Japanese Patent Office

1. BACKGROUND

According to sec. 29(2), "where, prior to the filing of the patent application, a person skilled in the art would have been able to easily make the invention based on an invention prescribed in any of the items of the preceding paragraph, a patent shall not be granted for the invention notwithstanding the preceding paragraph."

As a principle of patent law, an invention which is easy to invent based on prior art is not patentable.

The prior art which is taken into consideration for considering inventive step is same as for the assessment of novelty. As stated in the Examination Guideline of the Japanese Patent Office (JPO), "a person skilled in the art" means a hypothetical person (also possible to be a team of experts) who meets all the following conditions:[1]

i) A person who has the common general knowledge in the technical field of the claimed invention at the time of filing;
ii) A person who is able to use ordinary technical means for research and development (including document analysis, experiment, technical analysis, manufacture, etc.);
iii) A person who is able to exercise ordinary creativity in selecting materials and modifying designs;
iv) A person who is able to comprehend all the subject matter contained in the state of the art.

1. The Examination Guideline of the JPO, Part III, Chapter 2, at the website of the JPO <https://www.jpo.go.jp/e/system/laws/rule/guideline/patent/tukujitu_kijun/index.html>

The Guidelines further state: "The examiner selects the prior art most suitable for its reasoning, and determines whether it is possible to reason that a person skilled in the art would easily arrive at the claimed invention from the primary prior art."

While such practice about determining inventive step has a long history in Japan, in this case of 28 January 2009, the IP High Court suggested to apply a problem-solution like approach in Japan, and established that an *ex post* analysis (hindsight) must be avoided. In the opinion of the author, this had a huge influence on the patent practice concerning inventive step in Japan.

2. DECISION[2]

a) Facts

1. Procedure before the Patent Office

The invention at issue bears the title "Adhesive for Electric Circuits". The plaintiff filed the patent application on 16 May 1995 and amended the description on 27 April 2004. The examination division of the Japanese Patent Office refused the application on 27 April 2004. The plaintiff filed an appeal against this refusal on 4 July 2004 and on 3 August 2004 filed a new set of claims. On 29 January 2008, the Patent Office rejected the appeal. The plaintiff was notified of this decision on 12 February 2008.

...

3. Claim after the amendment

The amended claim 1 reads as follows:

> "Claim 1:
>
> Adhesive for integrated circuits characterised in that the adhesive is composed of the following adhesive components (1), (2) and (3) plus conducting particles in the amount of 0.1 up to 10% of the volume of the adhesive composition, and that the adhesive is film-like:
>
> (1) Bisphenol F phenoxide resin
> (2) Bisphenol epoxide resin
> (3) Latent hardener"

...

b) Reasons

The decision under appeal is based on the opinion that for a person skilled in the art the use of bisphenol F phenoxide resin instead of the phenoxide resin as known

2. Published in 2043 Hanrei Jihō = 1299 Hanrei Times 272 = N. NAKAYAMA et al. (eds.), Tokkyo Hanrei Hyakusen *(Hundred Selected Patent Cases)*, 4th ed. 2012, 34. German translation in GRUR Int. 2011, 179.

in the prior art would be obvious. Regardless of whether the decision is otherwise correct or not, this assessment is incorrect ...

2. Assessment of the State of the Art

(1) Sec. 29(2) Patent Act makes it determinative whether a person skilled in the art could have easily conceived the invention from the state of the art. In other words, whether the inventive features (features that differ from the state of the art) could have been easily conceived from the state of the art. The problem of the invention must be defined according to these features (features that differ from the state of the art). For objectively assessing the inventive step it is necessary to properly grasp the inventive features, that is, to understand the problem of the invention. An illogical or *ex post* analysis must be avoided. This requires an assessment that does not subconsciously take into account the "means for solving the problem", or the "result of solution."

For the assessment of an inventive step it is furthermore not necessary that there was an assumption for coming across the inventive features. But of course some hint how the relevant features can be achieved is necessary.

(2) The appealed decision must be judged in the light of the above considerations.

a. According to the description of the application, especially a comparison between executive example and comparative example 1, the patent claim requires the application of phenoxide resin bisphenol F. The problem to be solved is the improvement of the adhesive properties (initially and after 500 hours) and the adhesive strength in comparison with phenoxide resin bisphenol A.

The state of the art is described as follows: "Phenoxide resin is a composition similar to other epoxide resins and has the advantage of compatibility and adhesive strength." Yet there is no description of the problem concerning compatibility and adhesive strength. And other elements that need to be considered in the manufacture of the adhesive and the circuit concern the thermostability, hardness, viscosity, etc. Thus, there is no mention of the application of phenoxide resin bisphenol F only for the concerns of compatibility and adhesive strength. Even if phenoxide resin bisphenol F as such was known at the application date, there is no sufficient evidence of the knowledge of such improvement regarding adhesive properties and compatibility by the use of phenoxide resin bisphenol F.

There is the additional problem that bisphenol F epoxide resin has a lower thermostability than phenoxide resin bisphenol A. Such lower thermostability was known, e.g. from the "Journal of Applied Polymer Science Vol. 7, pp. 2135-2144 (1963)" according to which the glass transition temperature of bisphenol F was 80 degrees and that of bisphenol A was 100 degrees. With such a property of bisphenol F and the lower thermostability thereof it is not apparent for the person skilled in the art that this substance is advantageous over bisphenol A with its better thermostability that is normally considered an important property of the required adhesive.

b. As to the reasons why the use of phenoxide resin bisphenol F would not involve an inventive step, the decision under appeal sets out that PKHA (an epoxide resin made from bisphenol A manufactured by the company Union Carbide) was described in the relevant document as a working example. Yet the use of PKHA was described in the publication of the patent application H9-279121, and PKHA (a phenoxide resin made from bisphenol A manufactured by the company Union Carbide) in the US Patent Bulletin 4343841, here defined as follows: "These resins are commercially available from the company Union Carbide" as "PKHA, a Bakelite phenoxide resin made from bisphenol A and epichlorohydrin and classified as a thermoplastically high molecular polymer." The cited PKHA is thus not phenoxide resin F, but rather phenoxide resin A, and from the mention of PKHA in the relevant document we cannot see any hint for the application of phenoxide resin bisphenol F.

(3) Summary

For the reasons explained above, based on the above document, the use of phenoxide resin bisphenol F as a phenoxide resin was not obvious for the person skilled in the art. The decision and the refusal of the patent application based on sec. 29(2) Patent Act is thus incorrect and must be set aside.

3. ANALYSIS

a) Japanese Case Law and Examination Practice

First, it appears appropriate to cite some other cases about assessing inventive step and the assessment factors in Japanese patent practice.

There are many cases about the relationship between the technical field of the invention at issue and prior art, for example, in the case of IP High Court, 20 August 2009 – *Separated Boots*, the court held that the technology of attaching a bicycle tube is applicable to the attachment of boots.[3] On the other hand, in the case of Tokyo High Court, 19 September 1989 – *Chaff Collection Support Tube*, it was held that the incinerator technology for human bodies is not applicable in order to determine inventive step for a chaff collection machine.[4]

About the proper formulation of the problem, there is the case of the Tokyo High Court, 21 May 2001 – *Gradation Drive Apparatus for Flat Display*, in which a combination of prior art documents is difficult because of a lack of sufficient disclosure of this problem in the prior art document: "The prior art document discloses a method of addressing in line, and its problem is only the upgrading of addressing, and lacks any teaching to make a gradation display. Yet such teaching is necessary to apply a well-known technology in question to the prior art. The prior art document lacks a concrete description of a gradation display system. So it is not easy for a person skilled in the art to apply the well-known technology in question to the prior art."[5]

These are general factors taken into consideration in the Japanese patent practice, and the Examination Guidelines of the JPO list factors for denying an

3. IP High Court, 20 August 2009, Case No. 10291 (Gyō-Ke) of 2008, the website of the courts <http://www.courts.go.jp/hanrei/pdf/20090821133801.pdf> – *Separated Boots*.
4. Tokyo High Court, 19 September 1989, Case No. 62 (Gyō-Ke) of 1987, 1349 Hanrei Jihō 140 – *Chaff Collection Support Tube*.
5. Tokyo High Court, 21 May 2001, Case No. 38 (Gyō-Ke) of 1999, the website of the courts <http://www.courts.go.jp/hanrei/pdf/8E0EF17111633F0F49256A920027709C.pdf> – *Gradation Drive Apparatus for Flat Display*.

inventive step such as close relationship of technical fields, similarity of problems to be solved, operations or functions, or suggestions in the prior art, and also positive factors such as an advantageous effect or prejudice against a combination.[6]

In Japanese patent practice, the difference between the claimed invention at issue and the prior art document is determined and for the inventive step analysis it needs to be considered whether such difference is easy to conceive for a person skilled in the art. And of course the problem to be solved in the invention is also a factor of consideration, but it is one of several factors and not always to be determined through the difference between the invention and prior art.

b) Problem Solution Approach

But the reasoning of the above decision requires first and foremost to determine the problem through the difference between the invention at issue and the prior art in order to avoid an *ex post* analysis, and holds that "the problem of the invention must be defined according to these features that differ from the state of the art ... so as to understand the problem of the invention." Such reasoning for determining inventive step was epoch making in Japan, and in the author's view was strongly influenced by the European Patent Office's problem-solution approach.

The problem-solution approach of the European Patent Office (EPO) consists of three main steps, (i) determining the "closest prior art," (ii) establishing the "objective technical problem" to be solved, and (iii) considering whether or not the claimed invention, starting from the closest prior art and the objective technical problem, would have been obvious to the skilled person.

This approach is very famous, but sometimes misleadingly explained in Japan, especially regarding step (i), such as that he prior art which is least different from the invention at issue is automatically chosen as the closest prior art.[7] If such choice was practically possible in every case, an *ex post* analysis might be excluded in all three steps of the approach. But in the practical application of the approach, it is said that the closest prior art is sometimes chosen as the most appropriate starting point for the assessment of inventive step: If, for example, the claimed invention has the features A + B + C + D, document D1 A + B + C and D2 A + D, D1 is not always chosen as the closest prior art, and D2 may also become the closest prior art if it is reasonably seen as the most appropriate starting point for assessing inventive step, e.g. where there is difficult for some reason to combine D1 with another prior art, even if the featured differences to the claimed invention are smallest in D1.[8]

---

6. The Examination Guideline of the JPO, Part III, Chapter 2, at the website of the JPO <https://www.jpo.go.jp/e/system/laws/rule/guideline/patent/tukujitu_kijun/index.html>
7. For example, Japan Patent Attorneys Association, Central Research Institute of IP the 20th Anniversary Open Forum, Shinposei ni tsuite saranaru kenkyū *(Further analysis about inventive step)*, 69-14 Patent 195 (2016); Y. Aida, Shinposei handan no kokusai hikaku *(International comparison of consideration of inventive step)*, 1413 Hanrei Times 58.
8. For example, case **T 540/07** of 23 February 2010; see also, A. Furuta, Nichiō ni okeru shinposei handan shuhō no hikaku kadai kaiketsu apurōchi wo chūshin ni *(Inventive step assessment methods in European and Japanese patent practice about the utility of the problem/solution approach)*, 60-11 Chizai Kanri 1807 (2010).

In the author's view, the main difference between the assessment method of the EPO and the JPO is step (ii) establishing the "objective technical problem" to be solved. For step (ii), the non-technical features are not taken into account for the establishment of the objective technical problem. The analysis of the technical character of an invention is not the issue in this case and this may be not be the place to mention it. But in Japan, if a claimed invention as a whole is regarded as a technical and patentable invention, then all features of the claimed invention should find reflection in prior art documents in order to prove a lack of inventive step. This may very well make a difference in the assessment of inventive step between the JPO and the EPO.

It is agreed that the problem-solution approach is only one method for countries to assess inventive step and useful to apply a unified assessment in a multitude of cases, but the author agrees with the critics that establishing an objective technical problem sometimes leads to construing an artificial problem even in the case that a problem is already mentioned in the application at issue or prior art documents. And there may be yet some risk that the adoption of the EPO's approach in Japan may lead to some artificial or rigid practice because of some misunderstandings. In the author's view, the application of the EPO-like problem-solution approach in this case did not find broad acceptance in Japan.

But of course it is very important to avoid an *ex post* analysis at any time, and it is very reasonable to note that the Examination Guidelines after this decision require the examiner to avoid hindsight by misconstruing the evidence which discloses the prior art in light of the description, claims or drawings of the application, in other words to read prior art after obtaining knowledge of the claimed invention. Nevertheless, it is very difficult to completely avoid an *ex post* analysis in any assessment method.

Another strong indication in this case is that there should be some indication or suggestion for the combination of features in two prior art documents in the relevant technical fields. The IP High Court recently has put more and more emphasis on this point, for which reason the indication or suggestion for a combination of features is now more often taken into consideration and has great influence on the outcome of a case.[9] The variation in the cancellation rate of JPO *ex parte* decisions by the IP High Court give some indication as to differences in approach between these two bodies:[10]

9. About the influence and trend about the assessment of inventive step in relation with this decision, see also, M. SHIMIZU, Kono 10 nen no shinposei no handan ni tsuite *(About assesment of inventive step in recent 10 years)*, 1413 Hanrei Times 5 (2015); THE THIRD SUBCOMMITTEE OF THE FIRST PATENT COMMITTEE OF THE JIPA, Chizaikōsai no shinposei handan no henka ni taiou shita chizaikatsudō no suishin *(Promotion of IP activity corresponding to the change of assessment of inventive step in the IP High Court)*, 62-4 Chizai Kanri 519 (2012).

10. The numbers are taken from the annual report of the JPO, at the website of the JPO <https://www.jpo.go.jp/resources/report/nenji/index.html>.

	Cancellation Rate (%)	Number of the IP High Court Decisions in ex parte Cases		
		Cancellation	Maintenance	Total
2005	7.5	11	136	147
2006	14.2	23	139	162
2007	13.2	25	163	188
2008	17.5	30	141	171
2009	33.1	42	85	127
2010	22.0	28	99	137
2011	20.3	27	106	133
2012	24.3	37	115	152
2013	25.1	35	104	139
2014	20.0	21	84	105
2015	26.9	18	49	67
2016	18.6	11	48	59
2017	16.0	8	42	50

Sometimes it is argued that the level of inventive step became lower after the above decision of the IP High Court, but the decision is perhaps rather a reminder for examiners to carefully consider the motivation behind a possible combination in the assessment of inventive step, and a reasoning only based on the relevance of technical fields should be avoided.

c) Unexpected technical effect

Last but not least, another important factor should be mentioned, namely an unexpected advantageous effect. In Japanese patent practice, it is sometimes said that an invention lacks inventive step because it is possible to easily conceive the invention from prior art, which is as much as to say "a person skilled in the art could invent."[11] But in Japan, an unexpected advantageous effect or a prejudice against a certain combination is also taken into consideration in the assessment of inventive step, and thus not only "could", but also "would" is considered in the assessment. The step (iii) of the problem-solution approach of the EPO comprises the so-called "could/would" approach, and there is no big difference between the JPO and EPO in this respect.[12]

For example, in the IP High Court decision of 24 July 2013, the Court decided that a racemate of a certain known compound is novel and inventive because of the surprising bio medical effect, even if the compound itself was known and the

11. In Japanese "hatsumei wa tōgyōsha ga yōi ni sōtō dekita mono de aru".
12. See, A. FURUTA (above).

racemate in the claim was one of only two possible racemates (optical isomer).[13] It is needless to say that such advantageous effect is also carefully considered.

d) Two easy steps

The author would also like to mention another approach for inventive step in Japan, the "two easy steps" (*yōi no yōi*) approach. In a recent example case *Friction Ball* regarding the claim for a ballpoint pen whose ink was erasable by frictional heat ("FriXion", very popular with school children), the IP High Court held that the claimed invention which could be made from the cited invention in two obvious steps, namely (i) providing friction tool to erase ink with pen and (ii) attaching the friction tool to the pen itself or cap of the pen after (i), should *not* be considered easy to invent.[14] As in this example case, inventive step is sometimes affirmed when arriving at the invention from prior art requires two easy steps in one direction. Still, such assessment should be considered carefully and does not automatically lead by itself to the acknowledgement of an inventive step.[15]

13. IP High Court, 24 July 2013, Case No. 10207 (Gyō-Ke) of 2012, 2226 Hanrei Jihō 93 – *Optically Active Piperidine*. For theories on the effect of invention and inventive step assessment, see, e.g., T. Maeda, Sinposei handan ni okeru kōka no igi (*Meaning of an effect in inventive step assessment*), 82 L&T 33 (2019).
14. IP High Court, 21 March 2017, Case No. 10186 (Gyō-Ke) of 2016, the website of the courts <http://www.courts.go.jp/app/files/hanrei_jp/616/086616_hanrei.pdf> – *Friction Ball*. As commentary of this case, see also, K. Ueki, Shuinrei to fukuinrei tono kumiawase no tekisetsusei to yōi no yōi ga arasowareta jirei *(Case where the appropriateness of combination of main and sub prior arts and the easiness on easiness were disputed)*, 68-3 Chizai Kanri 371 (2018); T. Ikuta/M Chūsho, Shuinyō hatsumei kara 2 tsu no dankai wo hete sōiten no kōsei ni itaru koto wa kakubetsu na doryoku wo ysuru to sareta jirei *(Case where special effort was needed for the 2 steps from the main prior art for the difference point)*, 114-7 Hatsumei 37 (2017).
15. On the "two easy steps" approach, see also, T. Tamai, Iwayuru yōi no yōi ni tsuite no ichi kōsatsu *(An analysis to inventive step assessment on so called two easy steps)*, 66-12 Chizai Kanri 1567 (2016); M. Fukazawa, Iwayuru yōi no yōi ga mondai to natta jirei *(Case where "two easy steps" was disputed)*, 239 Tokugikon 85 (2005). The author does not know correctly when "two easy steps" was at first argued in Japan, but the JPO decision of 2001 (Opposition Case No. 2000-73885) already mentioned two easy steps, so it should have been discussed before 2000. The notion of two easy steps in Japan corresponds to "multiple steps" in the German or EPO case law, e.g., German Federal Supreme Court, 3 May 2006, GRUR 2006, 903 – *Mikrotom*; German Federal Supreme Court, 22 November 1984, GRUR 1985,369 – *Körperstativ*; EPO Board of Appeal, 22 June 1986, case **T 113/82** – *Recording apparatus*. The following indication of the German Supreme Court in the *Mikrotom* case is very suggestive: "Inventive step may be affirmed when the person skilled in the art must carry out multiple steps for which no suggestion was found in the prior art to reach the object of the invention; but one must determine whether as whole, this can be considered routine work or whether there is difficulty in the way for the person in the art for some reason such as that there were alternatives to lead to different results in one or multiple steps." See also, Schulte, Patentgesetz mit EPÜ *(Commentary on the German Patent Act and the EPC)*, 10th ed. 2017, 362.

4. COMPARATIVE REMARKS

In the **US**, the US Supreme Court Graham case of 1966 as an assessment test of obviousness (inventive step) required the following steps:[16]

i) Determining the scope and content of the prior art;
ii) Ascertaining the differences between the claimed invention and the prior art; and
iii) Resolving the level of ordinary skill in the pertinent art.

In the Graham test, "secondary considerations" such as evidence of commercial success, long-felt but unsolved needs, failure of others, and unexpected results could be taken into consideration.

After the Graham test, the Court of Appeals for the Federal Circuit (CAFC) developed the so-called TSM (Teaching-Suggestion-Motivation) test, where some statement of teaching, suggestion or motivation in a prior art document is required for proving the obviousness of the invention in question. But in the famous KSR decision of 2007, the Supreme Court referred to the Graham case and rejected a rigid application of the TSM test.[17] After the KSR decision, the examination manual (MPEP) of the USPTO lists the following exemplary considerations for obviousness:

A) Combining prior art elements according to known methods to yield predictable results;
B) Simple substitution of one known element for another to obtain predictable results;
C) Use of known techniques to improve similar devices (methods, or products) in the same way;
D) Applying a known technique to a known device (method, or product) ready for improvement to yield predictable results;
E) "Obvious to try" – choosing from a finite number of identified, predictable solutions, with a reasonable expectation of success;
F) Known work in one field of endeavour may prompt variations of it for use in either the same field or a different one based on design incentives or other market forces if the variations are predictable to one of ordinary skill in the art;
G) Some teaching, suggestion, or motivation in the prior art that would have led one of ordinary skill to modify the prior art reference or to combine prior art reference teachings to arrive at the claimed invention.

Such change of case law about the obviousness test in the US away from the rigid, motivation-based TSM test towards a more flexible rule of reason approach is very interesting from a comparative perspective. In the author's view, such change in US law is also important for the international harmonisation in assessing inventive step.[18]

16. US Supreme Court, *Graham v. John Deere Co.*, 383 U.S. 1, 148 USPQ 459 (1966).
17. US Supreme Court, *KSR International Co. v. Teleflex Inc.*, 550 U.S. 398, 82 USPQ2d 1385 (2007).
18. For the assessment of obviousness in the US, see also, MPEP, 2141, at the website of the USPTO <https://www.uspto.gov/web/offices/pac/mpep/s2141.html>; Y. AIDA (above).

In the **EPO**, for the assessment of inventive step the problem-solution approach is used.[19] This approach is explained in the Examination Guidelines of the EPO as follows:

> "In order to assess inventive step in an objective and predictable manner, the so-called 'problem-and-solution approach' should be applied. Thus, deviation from this approach should be exceptional.
>
> In the problem-and-solution approach, there are three main stages:
>
> (i) determining the 'closest prior art',
> (ii) establishing the 'objective technical problem' to be solved, and
> (iii) considering whether or not the claimed invention, starting from the closest prior art and the objective technical problem, would have been obvious to the skilled person."

The biggest difference between the JPO and EPO in the assessment of inventive step is the approach. The JPO takes the one document most appropriate to start with, and it is not necessary to specify the technical problem objectively. Under this approach, it is possible to make a reasoning with problem and solution described in the application in question. Under the European approach, it is necessary to objectively specify the problem of the invention from one prior art document. In the opinion of the author, the European problem-solution approach is suitable for excluding an *ex post* analysis in many cases, but the assessment of inventive step should always be a case-by-case assessment.[20]

In **Germany**, the problem-solution approach is generally not adopted in patent cases, but sometimes the technical problem is determined from the claimed invention.[21] Suggestion or motivation are also emphasised in the assessment of inventive step.[22] Thereby, the German approach is very similar to the Japanese one, yet in Germany, as the EPO, the non-technical features are not taken into consideration in the assessment of inventive step.[23]

In the **UK**, the *Pozzoli* decision of 2007 elaborated the following steps for the assessment of inventive step: [24]

> (1) (a) Identify the notional "person skilled in the art"

19. This approach is mandated by Rule 42(1) c) EPC (formerly Rule 27 (1) d) and was first applied in decision **T 26/81** of 28 October 1981. See G. SZABO, The Problem and Solution Approach to the Inventive Step, EIPR 1986, 293. See also G. SZABO, The Problem and Solution Approach in the European Patent Office, 26 IIC 457 (1995).
20. But of course, there should be other considerations under the EPC, a treaty that is applied in many countries and that perhaps thereby attaches more importance to objectivity than to convince the applicant.
21. German Federal Supreme Court, 11 November 2014, GRUR 2015, 356 – *Repaglinid*; German Federal Supreme Court, 1 March 2011, GRUR 2011, 607 – *Kosmetisches Sonnenschutzmittel III.*
22. German Federal Supreme Court, 30 April 2009, GRUR 2009, 746 – *Betrieb einer Sicherheitseinrichtung.*
23. German Federal Supreme Court, 26 October 2010, GRUR 2011, 125 – *Wiedergabe topografischer Informationen.* For the German approach to the assessment of inventive step, see also, Y. AIDA (above).
24. UK Court of Appeal, 22 June 2007, *Pozzoli SPA v. BDMO SA* [2007] EWCA Civ 588.

(1) (b) Identify the relevant common general knowledge of that person;
(2) Identify the inventive concept of the claim in question or if that cannot readily be done, construe it;
(3) Identify what, if any, differences exist between the matter cited as forming part of the "state of the art" and the inventive concept of the claim or the claim as construed;
(4) Viewed without any knowledge of the alleged invention as claimed, do those differences constitute steps which would have been obvious to the person skilled in the art or do they require any degree of invention?

Some decisions of the UK courts have expressed a rather negative view about the general adoption of the EPO's problem-solution approach for the UK patent practice.[25]

In **China**, a three-step assessment similar to the problem-solution approach of the EPO is adopted:[26]

i) Determining the closest prior art;
ii) Determining the distinguishing features of the invention and the technical problem actually solved by the invention;
iii) Determining whether or not the claimed invention is obvious to a person skilled in the art.

In the author's view, the Chinese three step assessment is strongly influenced by the EPO approach.

In **Korea**, the Korean Supreme Court indicated in a decision of 6 September 2007 that the inventive step of a claimed invention can be denied when some implication or motivation is indicated in the prior art documents for combining the cited technologies and arriving at the claimed invention, or otherwise when a person skilled in the art could easily arrive at such combination with regard to the technical level, technical common knowledge, fundamental problem in the technical field, trend of development etc. at the filing date of the application.[27] The Korean Supreme Court decision of 24 August 2007 clarified the principle of prohibition of *ex post* analysis.[28] In Korean patent practice, the problem-solution approach is not adopted, and in the author's view, such general assessment of inventive step in Korea is close to Japan.[29]

---

25. UK Court of Appeal, 17 February 2010, *Actavis UK Ltd v. Novartis AG* [2010] EWCA Civ 82. For the UK approach in the assessment of inventive step, see also, the Manual of the UKIPO, Section 3, and the cited decisions, at the website of the UK government <https://www.gov.uk/guidance/manual-of-patent-practice-mopp/section-3-inventive-step>; Y. Aida (above).
26. Examination Guidelines of the SIPO, Part II Chapter 4, at the website of CNIPA <http://english.cnipa.gov.cn/docs/20180131104843547234.pdf>. (The Chinese Patent Office, SIPO (State Intellectual Property Office) was renamed to Chinese National Intellectual Property Administration in 2018.)
27. Korean Supreme Court, 6 September 2007, Case No. 3277 (Hu) of 2015 – *Probe Card Assembly*.
28. Korean Supreme Court, 24 August 2007, Case No. 138 (Hu) of 2006 – *Emergency Call Sending Device and Method Using Mobile Network*.
29. See also, the Examination Guideline of the KIPO, Part III Chapter 3, at the website of the KIPO <http://www.kipo.go.kr/upload/en/download/patent_examination_guidelines_2013_07.pdf>; C. JUNG, Inventive Step, in: B.-I. KIM/C. HEATH (eds.), Intellectual Property Law in Korea, 2nd ed. 2015, 24-26.

Case No. 6

Inventive Step – Assessment of Prior Art

Teru Koide

In order to deny an inventive step by choosing a particular prior art document as the closest state of the art and combining it with another document, the suggestion or motivation for the person skilled in the art to combine both documents should be clarified.

Intellectual Property High Court, 8 March 2011,
Case No. 10273 (Gyō-Ke) of 2010 – *Aluminium Foil*

Nippon Foil v. Japanese Patent Office

---

1. BACKGROUND

Sec. 29(2) provides that a patent shall not be granted for an invention where a person of ordinary skill in the art in the technical field of the invention (hereinafter referred to as "a person skilled in the art") would have been able to easily make the invention based on the prior art.

In the Examination Guidelines of the JPO, it is stated that the examiner conducts the examination in accordance with the following procedures:[1]

> "The examiner selects the prior art most suitable for his reasoning (hereinafter referred to as 'the closest prior art'), and determine whether it is possible to reason that a person skilled in the art would easily arrive at the claimed invention from the closest prior art. The examiner determines whether or not his reasoning is coherent based on the various factors such as factors in support of a lack of an inventive step for the differences between the claimed invention and the closest prior art by adopting other pieces of prior art (hereinafter referred to as 'other or secondary prior art'), or considering common general knowledge. Then, if the examiner determines that the reasoning is coherent, the examiner decides that the claimed invention does not involve an inventive step."

Among the above-mentioned factors in support of a lack of inventive step, the existence of a motivation for combining the secondary prior art with the closest prior art must be considered, i.e. whether the secondary prior art (B) when applied to the

1. The Examination Guideline of the JPO, Part III, Chapter 2, at the website of the JPO <https://www.jpo.go.jp/e/system/laws/rule/guideline/patent/tukujitu_kijun/index.html>.

closest prior art (A) is not only equivalent to the claimed invention, but whether there was a motivation to make such combination. The latter is a factor in support of the lack of an inventive step.

In determining whether or not there is a motivation for combining the secondary prior art with the primary prior art, the following should be considered:

1) Similarity of technical fields;
2) Similarity of problems to be solved;
3) Similarity of operations or functions;
4) Suggestions (pointers) shown in the content of prior art;

In practice, an inventive step analysis can often hinge on whether or not there was a motivation to combine two prior art documents. Also in the case at issue, it was the determinative issue.

Following this case, in October 2015 (approximately four years after the decision), the Examination Guidelines were reformed and an inventive step analysis must now "comprehensively" consider the above points (1) to (4), while the examiner should note that "it is not always possible to determine whether there is motivation by paying attention to only one of these points of view (1) to (4)."[2]

2. DECISION[3]

a) Facts

1. Procedure before the JPO

The plaintiff on 31 October 2003 filed a patent application (application No. 2003-372727, published on 26 May 2005, publication No. 2005-132462) with the title "Aluminium Foil with Good Infrared Transparency Print for Packaging". The examination division of the Japanese Patent Office rejected the application on 23 October 2009, and the plaintiff appealed. The JPO handled the request as Case No. 2010-1866, notified the grounds for the rejection on 22 February 2010, and the plaintiff thereupon filed an amendment on 22 April 2010. The JPO on 7 July 2010 decided to reject the request because the invention at issue was easy to conceive by a person skilled in the art based on the cited document (invention) 1 (JP 2003-215047 A) and the cited document (invention) 2 (JP H9-249821 A), and was therefore not patentable under Sec. 29 (2) Patent Act. This decision was notified to the plaintiff on 21 July 2010.

2. Claim 1 of the invention after the amendment of 22 April 2010 reads as follows:

> [Claim 1] "Aluminium foil with good infrared transparency print for packaging which is used when aluminium foil packaging is produced by an appearance inspection apparatus which at least following means and apparatus, characterized in that the aluminium foil has on its body surface a print such as letters or

---

2. JPO, Revision History of the Examination Guidelines for Patent and Utility Model in Japan, October 2015, at the website of the JPO <https://www.jpo.go.jp/e/system/laws/rule/guideline/patent/kaitei/document/index/point_of_update.pdf>.
3. Published in 1375 Hanrei Times 195.

a design, the print is formed by the printing using printing ink which is made by pigment added resin varnish, while the pigment body surface is coated by synthetic resin:

(1) an illuminating means which irradiate light including infrared light to the aluminium foil;
(2) an imaging means which has sensitivity in infrared and images the surface irradiated by the said illuminating means; and
(3) an imaging processing apparatus which processes the imaging signal output by the imaging means."

3. Cited invention 1 and 2 and difference between the cited invention 1 and the invention at issue

[Cited invention 1]

> "PTP sheet which is produced by a PTP packaging machine with an appearance inspection apparatus, in that the PTP sheet comprises a packaging film 3 in which plural pocket parts are formed to accept tablets and aluminium made cover film 4, the cover film has print part 9 as identification information consisting of mark etc. with using infrared transparent ink, the appearance inspection apparatus comprises an illuminating means 21 which can irradiate infrared light, an imaging means 22 which has sensitivity in the wavelength range irradiated by the illuminating means 21 and an imaging processing apparatus 23 which can process the imaging signal outputted by the imaging means 22, it detects extraneous material on the cover film 4 with using a threshold δ2 which is lower than the brightness of the print parts 9 and higher than the brightness of the extraneous material bases on the image of reflected light from the irradiation of infrared light to the PTP sheet."

[Cited invention 2]

> "Oil based paint in which good dispersibility pigment coated by reactive water soluble resin is added to resin varnish."

[Difference between the cited invention 1 and the invention at issue]

The printing ink of the invention at issue is pigment added resin varnish and the pigment body surface is coated by synthetic resin, but the ink of the invention 1 is not.

b) Reasons

1. About the combination of the cited invention 1 and the cited invention 2

(1) The difference between the cited invention 1 and the invention at issue is, as in the facts, that "the printing ink of the invention at issue is pigment added resin varnish and the pigment body surface is coated by synthetic resin, but the ink of the invention 1 is not." The decision of the JPO reasoned about this point that "the cited invention 1 uses the small difference of the brightness between the print parts 9 and the cover film 4 itself through the use of the infrared transparent ink to the print parts 9, but it is clear that if the threshold δ2 is appropriately chosen, the extraneous material on the cover film 4 can be distinguished from the print part 9

and detected without especially good infrared transparent ink. On the other hand, the cited invention is 'paint', but 'paint' and 'ink' are originally not distinguished. For example the substance is called 'paint' when adhered to metal plate, but 'ink' when impregnated in paper. But there are many cases where the materials themselves have no substantial difference, and it is easy to guess that the paint of the cited invention 2 can be used for printing on the surface of aluminium foil. Therefore, the use of the paint of the cited invention 2 instead of the ink of the cited invention 1, identified above as a difference, is easy to invent by the person skilled in the art." The JPO thus denied an inventive step of the invention at issue.

But for the following reasons, the above considerations wrongly assume that the person skilled in the art would apply the cited invention to the cited invention 1. There is no motivation to apply the feature of the cited invention 2, "Oil based paint in which good dispersibility pigment coated by reactive water soluble resin is added to resin varnish".

(2) At first it can be affirmed, as in the facts, that the technical purpose of the cited invention 1 is to detect extraneous material also on aluminium made cover film by the radiation of infrared light, whereby the print parts as identification information consisting of marks etc. are formed by the infrared transparent ink, and the brightness difference becomes extremely small, further the second threshold δ2 is set a little under the brightness of the cover film. Through such features, the effect of the detection of only the extraneous material on the cover film is achieved, regardless of the presence of the print parts, and not detecting only the print parts. On the other hand, as mentioned above, the decision of the JPO indicated that "it is clear that, if the threshold δ2 is appropriately chosen, the extraneous material on the cover film 4 can be distinguished from the print part 9 and detected without especially good infrared transparent ink.", but when infrared transparent ink is not used, the brightness of the print parts decrease to a certain degree and the extraneous material cannot be detected if the extraneous material of the same brightness as the print parts exists on the print parts (If the brightness of the extraneous material is already known and the threshold δ2 is set under the brightness of the print parts, the detecting of the extraneous material may be possible. But such case is not to be generally understood).

Therefore, the above indication of the decision of the JPO shows only the prior art which cannot solve the technical problem of the cited invention 1, and does not clarify the motivation for applying the feature of the cited invention 2 to the cited invention 1.

(3) And the decision of the JPO, as mentioned above, indicated that "the cited invention is 'paint', but 'paint' and 'ink' is originally not distinguished. For example, the material is called 'paint' when it is adhered to a metal plate, and called 'ink' when it is impregnated in paper, but there are many cases in which materials themselves have no substantial difference, and it is easy to guess that the paint of the cited invention 2 can be used for printing the surface of an aluminium foil". But this reasoning only shows that "paint" and "ink" are not strictly distinguished and that there is no substantial difference between them. And even if "paint" and "ink" were not distinguished and the paint of the invention 2 might be used on aluminium foil, document 2 discloses only ink that might be used on aluminium foil. Document

2 does not disclose that the paint has good infrared transparency, and the use of "paint" of the cited invention 2 as the "ink" of the cited invention 1 is not suggested.

In the first place, known technologies about "paint" or "ink" exist in abundance, and in order to deny an inventive step by choosing a particular technical idea as an invention and combining it with another invention, the suggestion or motivation for the combination should be clarified. But the decision of the JPO does not show the motivation for applying the feature of the cited invention 2 which uses a coated pigment to the cited invention 1, and from what technical point of view the combination could be made. Where the technology is only a commonly used technology for the person skilled in the art, demonstrating motivation etc. is not always necessary, but here the feature of the cited invention 2 is no commonly used technology, and the defendant does not argue this.

(4) About this point the defendant argued, based on the description of the paragraph [0006] of the cited document 2, that good hue, colouring strength or dispersibility is generally preferable in ink or paint, and this is also applicable to the ink of the cited invention 1, so the person skilled in the art can easily conceive to use the oil based paint of the cited invention 2 as the ink of the cited invention 1.

Certainly, good hue, colouring strength or dispersibility is generally preferable in ink or paint, but there exist many inks or paints which demonstrate good characteristics in either hue or colouring strength or dispersibility, and choosing the cited invention 2 only based on the above generality is not easy to conceive for the person skilled in the art.

Therefore, the above argument of the defendant is fallacious.

2. As mentioned above, the considerations in the decision of the JPO did not properly evaluate the technical difference, and the decision of the JPO which denied an inventive step of the invention at issue by applying the feature of the cited invention 2 to the cited invention 1 based on this premise, should be set aside.

3. ANALYSIS

As mentioned above, determining whether there was a motivation for the person skilled in the art to combine different documents of prior art is often of critical importance. In this case, it became a point of contention whether the decision of the JPO explained the motivation for applying a certain feature of the cited invention 2 (coated pigment) to the cited invention 1. In this case, the court held that even if "paint" and "ink" were not distinguished as indicated in the decision under appeal, this reasoning only showed that document 2 disclosed only ink that might be used on aluminium foil. However, the decision of the JPO did not explain the motivation for applying the feature of the cited invention 2 to the cited invention 1, and from which technical point of view the combination could be made.

In the Examination Guidelines, the above-mentioned four aspects should be considered when determining whether or not there is a motivation for combining two documents. However, in this case, the court suggested that even if the technical fields were strongly related to each other, it was not possible to determine whether there was a motivation by paying attention to this aspect only.

In this analysis, the author would like to present two theories relevant to this issue, together with case law on this issue and an assessment of this case. One theory is the "Same Technical Field Theory", the other the "Suggestion/Motivation Theory".

According to several published reports,[4] the Same Technical Field Theory has been applied since around 1999 in order to determine whether the claimed invention involves an inventive step for the examination, appeal or litigation stages. This theory is not clearly defined and its details differ slightly in each report, but can be generally described as follows. If the secondary prior art (B) is applied to the primary prior art (A) and the result (A + B) is equivalent to the claimed invention and moreover the technical fields of each invention are the same or strongly related to each other, it is generally considered that the claimed invention does not involve an inventive step.

For example, in the case of Tokyo High Court, 22 June 2004, Case No. 534 (Gyō-Ke) of 2003 – *Half-Split Polishing Roller And Core Metal Fitting Therefor,*[5] it is stated that if the secondary prior art is applied to the primary prior art and moreover the technical fields of each invention are the same, it is generally considered that there is a motivation for applying the secondary prior art to the primary prior art bar special circumstances such as obstruction factors.

This theory tends to deny an inventive step more often and is considered less advantageous to patent applicants.

For the "Suggestion/Motivation Theory", decisions in order to deny an inventive step not only require related technical fields but also a suggestion or motivation for the combination of documents. This theory was voiced around 2006. Especially the case of IP High Court, 29 June 2006, Case No. 10490 (Gyō-Ke) of 2005 – *Optical Detection Part For Paper Sheet Discriminating Device*[6] was pioneering this theory[7] and worth mention. In this case it was held that even though the sheet paper-layer sensing device as the primary prior art and the sheet paper identification device as the secondary prior art belong to closely-related technical fields, an appropriate motivation needs to exist in order to justify the argument that a person skilled in the art could easily arrive at the idea that such constituent features of the primary prior art could be applied to the secondary prior art.

4. For example, T. TSUKAHARA, Dōitsu gijutsubunya ron wa shuuen wo mukaeruka *(The End of the Same Technical Field Theory in Patent Litigation)*, 51 Tokkyo Kenkyū 2 (2011); S. NAGANO, Tokkyoken shimposei handan kijun no taikei to hanrei riron *(System and theory of the courts in determining an inventive step for patent)*, 2013, 156; K. MAEDA, Saibanrei ni miru shimposei handan to arubeki handan shuhō *(Determinations in court for the inventive step and their reasonable theory)*, in: R. SHITARA et al. (ed.), Gendai chitekizaisan hō, riron to jitsumu *(Modern intellectual property law, theory and practice)*, 2015, 353.
5. Published at the website of the courts <http://www.courts.go.jp/app/files/hanrei_jp/222/010222_hanrei.pdf>.
6. Published at the website of the courts <http://www.courts.go.jp/app/files/hanrei_jp/268/033268_hanrei.pdf>. English translation is available at the website of the IP High Court <http://www.ip.courts.go.jp/app/files/hanrei_en/357/000357.pdf>.
7. As is explained in analysis by several published reports. For example, T. SHINOHARA et al., [Tēma betsu] jūyō tokkyo hanrei kaisetsu *([Thematic] Important case law analysis on patent)*, 2013, 49-54; Y. HORIGOME, Hatsumei no kadai to shimposei handan (Problems in inventions and decision of inventive step), 14544 Tokkyo News (2017).

The case of IP High Court, 11 October 2006, Case No. 10717 (Gyō-Ke) of 2005 – *Siloxane and Siloxane Derivatives as Encapsulants for Organic Light-Emitting Devices*[8] is also remarkable and relevant for the latter theory. In this case, it was held that even if both in the primary prior art and the secondary prior art the light-emitting part was coated by a covering layer (an overcoat layer in the case of the primary prior art and a siloxane layer in the case of the secondary prior art) and both the primary prior art and the secondary prior art belonged to the same technical field of organic light-emitting element, it was impossible to logically conclude that a person skilled in the art could easily come up with the idea of replacing the siloxane of the secondary prior art with the overcoat layer of the primary prior art.

On the basis of above mentioned discussion, the author concludes that the approach in the *Aluminium Foil* case is consistent with the latter theory.

In addition, Case No. 5 of this book (IP High Court, 28 January 2009, Case No. 10096 (Gyō-Ke) of 2008 – *Adhesive for Electric Circuit*) and IP High Court, 31 January 2012, Case No. 10121 (Gyō-Ke) of 2011 – *Method for Producing Semiconductor Device*[9] are also highly remarkable cases and proponents of the latter theory in the sense that the motivation for the combination should be clarified in order to deny an inventive step.

As to the Examination Guidelines of the JPO, as above mentioned, the word "comprehensively" for consideration of an inventive step was introduced in October 2015. This means that prior to the reform, the Examination Guidelines did not clearly require that the examiner should always determine whether there was motivation by paying attention by "comprehensively" considering the four points as above. This point is also mentioned in the document published by the Working Group on the Patent Examination Standards supervised by the Patent System Subcommittee under the Intellectual Property Committee of the Industrial Structure Council.[10] It is expected that this working group will have a positive influence on the patent practice as to whether or not, and how motivation should be properly considered in determining inventive step.

At last, the author concludes that *Aluminium Foil* case is one of the remarkable cases to highlight when the question of motivation becomes a point of contention, and we should pay close attention to the future trends of motivation in the analysis of inventive step.

4. COMPARATIVE REMARKS

a) In order to determine whether starting from the closest prior art (see Case No. 6 regarding the problem-solution approach in order to determine the closest prior art)

---

8. Published at the website of the courts <http://www.courts.go.jp/app/files/hanrei_jp/644/033644_hanrei.pdf>. English translation is available at the website of the IP High Court <http://www.ip.courts.go.jp/app/files/hanrei_en/379/000379.pdf>.
9. Published at the website of the courts <http://www.courts.go.jp/app/files/hanrei_jp/960/081960_hanrei.pdf>. English translation is available at the website of the IP High Court <http://www.ip.courts.go.jp/app/files/hanrei_en/665/000665.pdf>.
10. JPO, Shinposei no shinsakijun no tenken pointo *(Points for reviewing the Examination Guidelines on the inventive step)*, at the website of the JPO <https://www.jpo.go.jp/resources/shingikai/sangyo-kouzou/shousai/kijun_wg/document/03-shiryou/03.pdf>.

the claimed invention would have been obvious to a person skilled in the art, the **EPO** uses the so-called could-would approach. According to this approach, it is not enough that the person skilled in the art **could** have combined two (or more) prior art documents in order to arrive at the claimed invention, but it is actually necessary to ascertain whether the person skilled in the art **would** actually have done so.[11] This requires an indication of conclusive reasons for such a combination, while idle curiosity would not be enough. Good reasons for adducing further prior art must therefore be identified.

As a general guideline, the following applies:

- It is not necessary that the closest prior art contains a pointer towards the solution, or even indicates that there is still a problem to be solved;
- A person skilled in the art would generally be prompted to look into the same technical field, or a neighbouring technical field where similar problems arise;[12]
- The necessity to combine two or more prior art documents would be an indication of non-obviousness, unless the claimed invention consists of aggregate partial problems without a synergistic effect;
- In the field of biotechnology in particular, a reasonable expectation of success is sufficient to establish that the skilled person would have followed the teaching of the prior art;[13]
- In rare cases, inventive step can be demonstrated where the claimed invention either has an unexpected effect, or, even stronger, goes against a technical prejudice in the prior art.

b) In the **US**, the Federal Circuit's corresponding approach to could/would was the so-called "teaching, suggestion or motivation test" under which a patent claim is only obvious if some motivation or suggestion to combine the prior art teachings could be found.[14] The court thereby explicitly rejected the notion of "obvious to try". The Supreme Court overturned this rather rigid test: "A patent composed of several elements is not proved obvious merely by demonstrating that each of its elements was, independently, known in the prior art ... it can be important to identify a reason that would have prompted a person of ordinary skill in the relevant field to combine the elements in the way the claimed invention does ... Helpful insights, however, need not become rigid and mandatory formulas ... Under the correct analysis, any need or problem known in the field of endeavour at the time of invention and addressed by the patent can provide a reason for combining the elements in the manner claimed ... When there is a design need or market pressure to solve a problem and there are a finite number of identified, predictable solutions, a person of ordinary skill has good reason to pursue the known options within his or her technical grasp."[15] This suggests a more common sense approach towards assessing inventive step.[16]

---

11. E.g. EPO Boards of Appeal, cases **T 2/83**, OJ 1984, 265; **T 7/86**, OJ 1988, 381.
12. EPO Boards of Appeal, case **T 176/84**, OJ 1986, 50.
13. EPO Boards of Appeal, case **T 149/93**.
14. US CAFC, *Al-Site Corp. v. VSI Int'l*, 174 F.3d 1308.
15. US Supreme Court, *KSR v. Teleflex*, 550 US 398 (2007).
16. In this regard, it is noticed that the current Manual of Patent Examining Procedure (MPEP) of the USPTO, 2141, mentions that "Although the Supreme Court in KSR cautioned against

In assessing inventive step, a prejudice in prior art can lead to a finding of non-obviousness and secondary considerations such as commercial success, long felt needs or failure of others can be taken into account.[17]

c) In **Germany**, the so-called TSM test or could-would approach is not generally adopted, but suggestion or motivation is sometimes argued as a factor in the assessment of inventive step. For example, in the decision of 8 December 2009,[18] the Federal Supreme Court indicated that "the finding of a new idea about technical act does not lack a inventive step already because no grounds explicitly appear that would prevent the person skilled in the art from reaching the object of the teaching from the matter known in the state of the art, but this assessment presupposes that the known prior art gives motivation or suggestion to the person skilled in the art to arrive at the proposed idea". The case was then back to the German Patent Court for further action.

d) In the **UK**, the motivation in the prior art is neither considered as an essential requirement for obviousness. But, of course, the motivation is sometimes taken into account in relation to the assessment of obviousness.[19]

---

an overly rigid application of TSM, it also recognized that TSM was one of a number of valid rationales that could be used to determine obviousness", and 2143 lists "teaching, suggestion, or motivation in the prior art" as an exemplary rationale in a prima facie case of obviousness.

17. US Supreme Court, *United States v. Adams*, 383 US 39 (1966).
18. German Federal Court, 8, December 2009, GRUR 2010, 407 – *Einteilige Öse*
19. England and Wales Court of Appeal, *Napp v. Ratiopharm*, [2009] EWCA Civ 252; *Asahi Medical v. Macopharma*, [2002] EWCA Civ 466; *Actavis v. Novartis*, [2010] EWCA Civ 82. See also, C. Birss et al. (ed.), Terrell on the Law of Patents, 18th Ed., 2018, 387.

Case No. 7

Inventive Step of New Medical Indications and Dosage Regimes

Yūichiro Kaburaki

The invention of a medicine, which is characterised in the dosage regime and differs from the prior art only in the claimed dosage, may be patentable in relation to novelty and inventive step, when the invention is not easy to conceive by a person skilled in the art.

IP High Court, 24 December 2014, Case No. 10045 (Gyō-Ke) of 2014 – *Zoledronate*

Novartis v. Japanese Patent Office

---

1. BACKGROUND

Until April 2005, the Japanese Patent Office (JPO) had taken the view that a patent could not be granted to medicinal inventions characterised in dosage and administration. This interpretation was based on the ground that if such inventions were described as a process, they could not fulfil one of the requirements of patentability – industrial applicability (sec. 29 (1) Patent Act) – since such methods were regarded as methods of surgery, therapy or diagnosis of humans and therefore, as monopolising such methods.[1] Furthermore, even if such inventions were described as a product, they could not fulfil the requirement of novelty since their compounds were not different from the prior art.[2]

In April 2005, the JPO revised its Examination Guidelines on medicinal inventions. According to this revision, the JPO had started granting patents for medicinal inventions characterised in dosage and administration only if they were described as a product and had a different way of use from a cited invention.[3] This meant that even if medicinal inventions had the inventive step on dosage or administration,

---

1. M. Nakajima, Chizai kōsai heisei 26 nen 12 gatsu 24 nichi hanketsu (heisei 26 nen gyō ke dai 10045 gō) oyobi tōkyō chisai heisei 28 nen 1 gatsu 28 nichi hanketsu (heisei 26 nen wa dai 25013 gō) – yōhō yōryō wo tokuchō to suru iryō hatsumei no tokkyosei oyobi gijutu hanni ni tsuite – *(Patentability and the scope of claim of medicinal inventions characterized in dosage and administration)*, 61-8 AIPPI Journal of the Japanese Group (Japanese edition) 19 (2016).
2. *Id.*, at 19.
3. Chitekizaisan Senryaku Honbu (IP Strategy Headquarter), Sentan iryō bunya ni okeru tokkyo hogo no arikata nitsuite *(About patent protections for the advanced medicinal field)*, 15 (29 May

such inventions could not fulfil the requirement of the novelty since they were made up of the same compounds as a cited invention unless they were attributed to a new group of patients or a different part of a body.[4]

The government of Japan considered the importance of dosage and administration in the medicinal field, the significance of incentivising entities to invest in the research of new dosage and administration, the suitability of protecting inventions characterised in dosage and administration as a product and the negative impact on the medical system.[5] Then, the government proposed that examination guidelines should be revised so that medicinal inventions characterised in dosage and administration could be protected a patents.[6]

According to this proposal, the JPO further revised the Examination Guidelines in November 2009. The new Examination Guidelines[7] provided the following statement regarding methods of judging novelty:

> "Even if compounds etc. of a claimed medicinal invention do not differ from those of a cited invention and there is no difference in the applied disease, the novelty of the claimed invention is not denied when there is a difference between the claimed medicinal invention and the cited invention in medicinal use of applying to a specific disease with a specific dosage and administration based on the attribute of compounds etc. thereof[.]"[8]

And on inventive step:

> "As for a specific disease, in order to solve a problem well known to a person skilled in the art such as the increase of a medicinal effect, the reduction of an adverse effect or the improvement in drug compliance, the optimization of dosage and administration of a medicine is among exercise of ordinary creativity of a person skilled in the art. Accordingly, in the case where the advantageous effect compared with the cited invention can be foreseen by a person skilled in the art, an inventive step is usually denied, even if the claimed medicinal invention is novel compared with the cited invention in that applied disease does not differ but dosage and administration differ from each other ...
>
> However, in the case where there is another reason for inferring the inventive step such that an advantageous effect compared with the cited invention cannot be foreseen by a person skilled in the art from the state of the art, the claimed medicinal invention is considered to involve an inventive step[.]"[9]

2009), available at the website of the Cabinet Secretariat <https://www.kantei.go.jp/jp/singi/titeki2/tyousakai/kyousou/houkoku/090529/090529_tokkyohogo.pdf>

4. *Id.*, at 15.
5. *Id.*, at 17-21.
6. *Id.*, at 21.
7. Currently in the Examination Handbook, not in the Examination Guidelines.
8. Japanese Patent Office, Examination Handbook for Patent and Utility Model in Japan, Annex B, Chapter 3, available at the website of the JPO <https://www.jpo.go.jp/e/system/laws/rule/guideline/patent/handbook_shinsa/document/index/app_b3_e.pdf>.
9. JPO, Examination Handbook for Patent and Utility Model in Japan, Annex B, Chapter 3, available at the website of the JPO <https://www.jpo.go.jp/e/system/laws/rule/guideline/patent/handbook_shinsa/document/index/app_b3_e.pdf>.

Accordingly, inventors need to prove that their inventions have the advantageous effect which cannot be foreseen by a person skilled in the art.[10] This proof is difficult, and therefore, it is burdensome to fulfil the requirement of an inventive step.[11]

As the above are JPO guidelines, the courts may still decide differently.[12]

2. DECISION[13]

a) Facts

1. Procedure before the Japanese Patent Office

On 9 May 2001, the plaintiff filed a patent application for the invention with the title "Use of Zoledronate for Production of Medicine for Treatment of Bone Metabolism Diseases" (patent application No. 2001-585739; priority claim: 19 May 2000, UK; number of claims: 10), and on 24 April 2008 filed an amendment of the claims (number of claims: 14). On 28 October 2011, the plaintiff was notified by the examination department of the JPO of the reasons for rejection. On 9 March 2012, the plaintiff filed a correction of mistranslations for the claims and specification (number of claims: 10), but the examination department on 13 December 2012 decided to reject this. Thus, the plaintiff on 17 April 2013 filed an appeal against the decision of the examination department and on the same day filed an amendment of the claims (number of claims: 10). The appeal board of the JPO handled the case as appeal Case No. 2013-7030, and on 30 September 2013 decided that "the appeal is groundless", and this decision was sent to the plaintiff on 15 October 2013. The plaintiff on 10 February 2014 appealed to the court and requested cancellation of the decision of the JPO.

2. Claim 1 of the patent application

Claim 1 of the patent application after the amendment reads:

> "[Claim 1] Treatment agent which comprises 2-(Imidazol-1-yl)-1-hydroxyethane-1,1-diphosphonic acid (zoledronic acid) or its pharmacologically allowable salt as active ingredient, characterized in that 4 mg of zoledronic acid is administered intravenously for 15 minutes to a patient, for whom bisphosphonate treatment is needed."

3. Summary of the reasoning of the JPO decision

The summary decision of the JPO held that for a person skilled in the art, the invention of the patent application was easy to invent from cited document 1.., and cited document 2.., and cited document 3, and that therefore a patent could not be granted according to sec. 29(2) Patent Act.

10. M. NAKAJIMA, *supra* note 1, at 20.
11. *Id.*, at 21.
12. N. KOIZUMI, Iyakuhin no yōho yōryō no tokkyo hogo *(Patent protections for dosage and administration of medicine)*, 1405 Jurist 98, 102 (2010).
13. Published on the website of the courts <http://www.courts.go.jp/app/files/hanrei_jp/754/084754_hanrei.pdf>

a) Cited Document 1: "Cancer Investigation, Jan 2000, vol. 18, no. suppl. 1, p. 68-69"
b) Cited Document 2: "Cancer, 1997, vol. 80, no. 8 suppl., p. 1699-1701"
c) Cited Document 3: "Endocrine Reviews, 1998, vol. 19, no. 1, p. 80-100".

The decision of the JPO held that document 1 described the following invention:

> "Medicine which comprises zoledronic acid as active ingredient, characterized in that 4 mg of zoledronic acid is administered by drip injection for 5 minutes to a patient with osteolytic disease such as breast cancer or multiple myeloma."

The decision of the JPO determined the common features and different features as follows:

a. Common features

> "Treatment agent which comprises 2-(Imidazol-1-yl)-1-hydroxyethane-1,1-diphosphonic acid (zoledronic acid) or its pharmacologically allowable salt as active ingredient, characterised in that 4 mg of zoledronic acid is administered intravenously for certain minutes to a patient, for whom bisphosphonate treatment is needed."

b. Differences:

The time frame is "5 minutes" in the cited invention 1, but "15 minutes" in the invention of the application at issue.

b) Reasons

3. Mistake in the consideration of inventive step regarding the differences [as alleged by the plaintiff]:

The decision of the JPO considered that a 15 minutes drip injection is very easy to reach by experiment in extending 5 minutes in the cited invention 1, because the cited document 3 describes that slow drip injection of bisphosphonate with a large amount of liquid is desirable because of kidney failure induced by rapid drip injection, and the cited document 2 describes the experiment of 5-30 minutes drip injection of zoledronic acid and the effect of lowering the serum calcium level by the 20 minutes drip injection, on the premise that the cited document 1 is related to a 2nd phase test of zoledronic acid, and side effects which did not occur in the 2nd phase test can possibly occur in the subsequent 3rd phase test, and a person skilled in the art would adjust the normal usage/dosage to avoid such side effects. And the plaintiff argued that (i) a 20 minutes injection of dosage 4 or 8 mg was not clearly disclosed in the cited document 2, (ii) from the beginning, the problem for how to avoid damage to the kidneys was difficult to recognise from the description of the cited document 1, because the cited document 1 assessed the effectiveness and safety for a 5 minutes intravenous injection of 4 mg zoledronic acid, and nephrotoxicity did not occur at this usage/dosage, (iii) the cited document 2 is related to a test for the first clinical phase, the previous stage of the cited document 1, and its purpose was to obtain material in order to consider whether the substance could be advanced to the second test phase, and it describes that the toxicity to kidneys was not observed at a 5 minute injection of a maximum administration dosage of 8 mg. The problem for an improvement of safety to the kidneys in a 5 minute injection of 4 mg was clearly unrecognisable from the description of the cited document 1. (iv) The cited document 3 is related to the first-generation bisphosphonate, the description of the cited document 3 clearly cannot be applied to Zoledronic acid, namely the third generation bisphosphonate which has a remarkably higher activity, and thus the inventions described in the cited documents 1 and 2 do not address any problem of the invention of the patent application at issue. The problem at issue is difficult to recognise by a combination of these inventions, the invention at issue as a solution to the problem is not easy to conceive, and there is no motivation for combining the cited documents 1, 2 and 3. We consider these arguments as follows.

(1) Clinical test

a. From the description of each document, the cited document 2 is a result report of the first phase clinical test of Zoledronic acid to patients of tumour-induced hypercalcemia and osteolytic bone metastasis, the cited document 1 is a subsequently drafted result report of the second phase clinical test of Zoledronic acid to patients of multiple myeloma and breast cancer. And from the evidence, it can be affirmed that the third phase clinical test of zoledronic acid in the medical treatment of skeletal metastasis for patients who had osteolytic lesions of breast cancer or multiple myeloma was made subsequently, and the result of the test was published after the patent application at issue.

b. From the "General Guideline about Clinical Assessment of New Medicine", the notification of the Director of the New Medicine Division of the Pharmaceutical Affairs Bureau of the Ministry of Health at 29 June 1992, the following can be affirmed:

The clinical tests for the purpose of requesting approval of a new medicine for medical treatment are usually advanced in succession, the first phase, the second phase and the third phase.

The first is a test in which an investigational medicine is applied for the first time to humans, and in principle the purpose is to presume the range of a clinical safety dosage or the maximum safety amount regarding the investigational medicine with a small number of healthy male volunteers, and in addition thereto, to make a pharmacokinetic study about absorption, excretion etc., and to obtain material to consider whether the medicine can be advanced to the second test phase.

The second phase is a test to investigate the effectiveness and safety of the investigational medicine in a limited number of patients in an appropriate status of the disease, and to collect information for advancing to the third phase, such as an adaptation disease or adequacy of usage/dosage etc.

The third is a test to collect more clinical test results by comparative clinical tests and general clinical tests, to clarify precisely and objectively the effectiveness and safety of the investigational medicine to the objective indication, and to assess the clinical usefulness of the investigational medicine to the indication.

Still, the first phase test may be made to patients instead of healthy volunteers according to the characteristics of the medicine in cases where the investigational medicine has clearly the possibility to express toxicity to healthy humans or there is a contraindication of a pharmacological nature to healthy humans. Regarding zoledronic acid in this case, as mentioned above, the first phase test was made on patients of tumour-induced hypercalcemia and osteolytic bone metastasis.

In light of the step-by-step character or positioning of the first test phase, the second test phase and the third test phase, even if the safety of the usage/dosage is verified in the first test phase, or the second test phase, it was planned in the third test to collect more clinical test results and to clarify precisely and objectively the effectiveness and safety of the investigational medicine to the objective indication, and to assess the clinical usefulness of the investigational medicine to the indication. So it cannot be denied that there is the possibility that the usage/dosage is considered unsafe and is changed to a safer one, depending on the result.

After all, nephrotoxicity is one of the typical side effects in medicines, and the worsening risk of a kidney dysfunction is known to injection-type bisphosphonate medicinal products. As to the intravenous injection of zoledronic acid, also in this case, after verifying the safety to kidneys in the first test phase (cited document 2), through the second test phase (cited document 1), the medicine was further advanced to the clinical test of the next step, so the possibility of changing the usage/dosage in consideration of a safety to kidneys should be recognised by a person skilled in the art.

(2) Description of the cited documents 1 and 2

From the description of document s1 and 2, zoledronic acid is a third generation bisphosphonate which has strong suppression effects of the functioning of osteoclasts, and it shows a more immediate and persistent effect in lowering serum calcium in the first clinical test phase described in the cited document 2 than other bisphosphonates which were tested until then. Each intravenous drip injection of 0.1 mg, 0.2 mg, 0.4 mg, 0.8 mg, 1.5 mg, 2 mg, 4 mg or 8 mg to 58 patients of osteolytic bone metastasis of normal calcium plasma did not express any symptom of nephrotoxicity. For about the only side effect expressed in 30% of patients, the rise of body temperature, the relationship with zoledronic acid is uncertain, and the safety of a short time drip injection was proposed.

Also in the subsequent second clinical tests described in the cited document 1, each 5 minute drip injection of 0.4 mg, 2.0 mg and 4.0 mg to 280 patients of breast cancer or multiple myeloma showed the safety of a comparable level of 2 hours drip injection of 90 mg of pamidronic acid, and a five minutes drip injection of 4.0 mg of zoledronic acid achieved a prevention effect against osteolytic bone complication of a comparable level of 90 mg of pamidronic acid.

In consideration of the result of the first phase and the second phase tests of zoledronic acid disclosed in the cited documents 1 and 2, it could be understood that zoledronic acid with low dosage of 4 mg achieved a medicinal effect comparable to 90 mg of previously used Pamidronic acid, the safety was ensured by the intravenous drip injection within such short time as five minutes. Therefore, from such result, even taken into consideration the step-by-step character of clinical tests and the possibility that the usage/dosage might be changed to a safer one by a different result about the safety of that usage/dosage in the third phase test, in the cited documents 1 and 2 it is difficult to find a motivation for extending the injection time of 5 minutes of 4 mg Zoledronic acid in the cited invention 1 also from the viewpoint of convenience and reduced burden to patients, because there was no result for doubts about safety in the stages of the first and second clinical tests.

(3) Description of the cited document 3

a. The cited document 3 by citing another reference document describes that care should be taken in respect of the intravenous injection of large amounts of bisphosphonates, because bisphosphonate forms a solid phase in blood, is retained in the kidneys and a short time drip injection induces kidney failure. Harmful events can be avoided by a slow drip injection with a large amount of liquid.

The reference document describes that the function of kidneys should be monitored in the slow injection under 1 mg per day because the injection of etidronate (EHDP) and clodronate (C2MDP) induces kidney failure. This description of the cited document 3 is clearly based on etidronate and clodronate.

...

c. From the description of the above evidence (omitted), it can be affirmed that etidronate and clodronate are first generation bisphosphonates which are used for early clinical tests, and that the slow injection is recommended also to subsequently developed various bisphosphonates, because some deaths due to kidney failure were reported due to the rapid injection of etidronate at early stages when the optimum injection method was not yet established, and that for the second, third generation bisphosphonates, namely namidoronic acid or alendronic acid, which have 100 or 1000 times the medicinal effect of bone absorption suppression, a small dosage is enough, and the rapid injection is investigated in consideration of a convenience for patients. Not only the safety in 1-1.5 mg/minute for pamidronic acid and 10 mg/30 minutes for incadronic acid and alendronic acid was verified, but there is also some report of improvement on the effect of kidney failure in these three medicinal products.

Given the circumstances of the development and the results of the rapid injection of the second and third bisphosphonate on the date of the patent application at issue, it can be affirmed that a person skilled in the art should understand that the knowledge about the harmful events by the rapid injection of the first generation bisphosphonate of the cited document 3 cannot be directly applied to the third generation bisphosphonate zoledronic acid. As described in the cited documents 1 and 2, in consideration that zoledronic acid is a bisphosphonate of a 100 to 8500 times higher activity than pamidronic acid and has a higher bone absorption suppression effect than incadronic acid and alendronic acid, and that a small amount of injection is enough, also from the viewpoint of convenience and reducing the burden for patients, it is difficult to find a motivation for extending the injection time of 5 minutes of 4 mg zoledronic acid of which the safety was verified in the cited inventions 1 and 2 ... for which reason the argument of the plaintiff is well-founded.

3. ANALYSIS

a) Novelty

In this decision, the court did not mention novelty since the decision of the JPO reasoned that the invention did not involve an inventive step, and therefore, the issue before the court was limited invention step in accordance with the Administrative Case Litigation Act.

According to the Examination Handbook, medicinal inventions can be novel "when there is a difference ... in medicinal use of applying to a specific disease with a specific dosage and administration based on the attribute of compounds etc. thereof".[14] The claimed invention in this case is different from the cited invention in the sense that the claimed invention applies a 15 minutes drip injection although the cited invention applies a 5 minutes drip injection. This means that there is a difference between the claimed invention and the cited invention in medicinal use which applies a different administration – a 15 or a 5 minutes drip injection. Therefore, the claimed invention fulfils the requirement of the novelty.

b) Inventive step

(1) Point of the decision

In this case, the parties argued inventive step in two ways: whether the claimed invention was easily arrived at when comparing the difference, and whether the claimed invention had an advantageous effect.

The court decided that the claimed invention could not be easily arrived at and thus set aside the decision of the JPO without examining whether the claimed invention had an advantageous effect.

Yet, according to the Examination Handbook, optimisation of dosage and administration of a medicine involves an inventive step only if the advantageous effect cannot be foreseen by a person skilled in the art in accordance with the rules generally used for inventive step.[15]

In this analysis, I will investigate the reason why the court did not explicitly examine the advantageous effect.

(2) Standard of examination for inventive step

In order to examine the reasons of the court, it is necessary to understand the basis for examining inventive step for medicinal inventions.

The statement of the Examination Guidelines is as follows: "the examiner determines whether the claimed invention involves an inventive step by considering

14. JPO, Examination Handbook for Patent and Utility Model in Japan, Annex B, Chapter 3, available at the website of the JPO <https://www.jpo.go.jp/e/system/laws/rule/guideline/patent/handbook_shinsa/document/index/app_b3_e.pdf>.
15. JPO, Examination Handbook for Patent and Utility Model in Japan, Annex B, Chapter 3, available at the website of the JPO <https://www.jpo.go.jp/e/system/laws/rule/guideline/patent/handbook_shinsa/document/index/app_b3_e.pdf>.

whether or not it could be reasoned that a person skilled in the art easily arrives at the claimed invention based on the prior art."[16] If a claimed invention has an advantageous effects, "the examiner should take these into consideration in determining whether a person skilled in the art would have easily arrived at the claimed invention."[17]

The courts in turn determine whether there is a motivation to arrive at a claimed invention from the prior art.[18] Even if such motivation is found, inventive step can be affirmed where the claimed invention has an advantageous effect which was not predictable from prior art.[19]

(3) Possible reasons

According to this standard, each of the above issues - being easily arrived at or having an advantageous effect - can lead to the conclusion that a claimed invention involves an inventive step.

Another possible explanation is that the court implicitly judged that the claimed invention showed an advantageous effect and therefore determined that the invention involved an inventive step.[20] The court found that the claimed invention solved the problem of renal safety by extending the administration time. Some point out that solving this problem means this invention has an advantageous effect in terms of renal safety which cannot be foreseen by a person skilled in the art.[21]

(4) Analysis

The argument that the court implicitly confirmed the advantageous effect is not convincing because of the reasoning of the decision. The court found that the problem of renal safety was recognised by a person skilled in the art, and such person could consider the possibility of changing dosage and administration. Despite this finding, the court decided that the change of dosage and administration by the claimed invention could not be easily arrived at since the prior art had already sufficiently achieved renal safety, and therefore, a person skilled in the art could not have had a motivation to optimise administration. Accordingly, the decision of the court is based on the finding that the effect of renal safety can be foreseen by a person skilled in the art. The court found an inventive step in the optimisation of administration time, not in the effect of renal safety of the claimed invention.

In this regard, this decision should be interpreted as to what the court explicitly decided. According to this decision, the court considered the difference between the claimed invention and the cited inventions, as the previous decision of the IP High

16. JPO, Examination Guidelines for Patent and Utility Model in Japan, part III, chapter 2, §2, available at the website of the JPO <https://www.jpo.go.jp/e/system/laws/rule/guideline/patent/tukujitu_kijun/document/index/03_0202_e.pdf>.
17. *Id.*.
18. H. Ueda, Shinketsu torikeshi sōshō ni okeru shuchō risshō sekinin *(Burden of claim and proof in litigation rescinding the trial decision)*, *in* Chitekizaisan Saiban Jitsumu Kenkyūkai *(Study Group on Practices in Intellectual Property Litigations)* (eds.), Chitekizaisan soshō no jitsumu *(Practices in Intellectual Property Litigations)*, revised ed. 2014, 273, at 275-276..
19. *Id.*
20. *See* M. Nakajima, *supra* note 1, at 27.
21. *Id.*, at 26-27.

Court stressed the necessity to examine a motivation for the claimed invention.[22] Therefore, although the Examination Handbook stated that such differences are usually foreseen by a person skilled in the art, and advantageous effects are the main requirement for patentability, such differences should be substantially examined. The court, in this case, considerably examined the difference.[23] Furthermore, in the examination of such differences, one should not unconsciously take a solution into account and to analyse whether there is a suggestion for arriving at the solution, as a previous decision of the IP High Court ruled.[24]

4. COMPARATIVE REMARKS

In the **EPO**, before and after the revision of EPC of 2000, which clearly allowed second medical use claims for a known substance,[25] the issue of new dosage regime was left undecided, with conflicting EPO case law.[26] In **G 2/08**, the Enlarged Board of Appeal clearly acknowledged the patentability of new dosage regimes by applying the usual test of novelty and inventive step, stating that Art. 54(5) EPC does not exclude a medicament which is already known to be used to treat an illness be patented for use in a different treatment by therapy of the same illness and such patenting is also not excluded where a dosage regime is the only feature claimed which is not comprised in the state of the art.[27]

In **Germany**, the German Federal Supreme Court decided in 1983 that the second medical use of known substance was not excluded from patentability by itself.[28] Following the above EPO case law, the German Federal Supreme Court further stated that the administration of a medicine for treatment of a disease as such was a therapeutic treatment of human body and excluded from patent protection, while the patentability of a medicine characterised in its dosage regime could be assessed from the point of inventive step.[29]

In the **UK**, the Court of Appeal at first set a high hurdle to inventions of medicine characterised in its dosage regime based on novelty and therapeutic treatment of the

22. IP High Court, 28 Jan. 2009, Case No. 10096 (Gyō-Ke) of 2008, 2043 Hanrei Jihō 117. See, Case No. 5 of this book.
23. M. NAKAJIMA, *supra* note 1, at 26.
24. IP High Court, 28 Jan. 2009, Case No. 10096 (Gyō-Ke) of 2008, 2043 Hanrei Jihō 117. See, Case No. 5 of this book.
25. Before the revision of 2000, which came in force on 13 December 2007, such second use of a known medicine was protected by way of so-called Swiss type claim. See e.g. SCHULTE, Patentgesetz mit EPÜ *(Commentary on the German Patent Act and the EPC)*, 10th ed. 2017, 318.
26. Decision **T 317/95** of 26 February 1999 – *Gastrointestinal compositions/PROCTER & GAMBLE*; Decision of **T 4/98** of 9 August 2001 – *Liposome Compositions/SEQUUS*; Decision of **T 56/97** of 30 August 2001 – *Thiazide diuretics/EURO-CELTIQUE*; Decision **T 584/97** of 5 December 2001 – *Use of nicotine/ELAN CORPORATION*; Decision of **T 1020/03** of 29 October 2004 – *Method of administration of IGF-I/GENENTECH*.
27. Decision **G 2/08** of 19 February 2010 – *Dosage Regime/ABOTT RESPIRATORY.*
28. German Federal Supreme Court, 20 September 1983, GRUR 1983, 729 – *Hydropyridin*.
29. German Federal Supreme Court, 19 December 2006, GRUR 2007, 404 – *Carvedilol II*; German Federal Supreme Court, 25 February 2014, GRUR 2014, 461 – *Kollgenase I*; German Federal Supreme Court, 25 February 2014, GRUR 2014, 464 – *Kollgenase II*.

human body, but later changed its stance on this point towards the assessment of non-obviousness (inventive step) in accordance with the EPO.[30]

The **Swiss** Federal Supreme Court also followed the above EPO case law in a decision of 2011.[31]

On the other hand, even after the EPO decision of 2010, the case law of **France** still showed a negative view on the invention of medicine characterised in dosage regime.[32]

In the **US**, dosage inventions may be claimed as products or medical method claims. In these types of claims, the assessment of novelty and non-obviousness (inventive) step will be made.[33]

30. UK Court of Appeal, *Bristol-Myers Squibb v. Baker Norton*, [2001] RPC 1; UK Court of Appeal, *Actavis v. Merck*, [2008] RPC 26; UK Court of Appeal, *Actavis v. ICOS*, [2017] EWCA Civ 1671.
31. Swiss Federal Supreme Court, 4 March 2011, GRUR Int. 2012, 183 - *Alendronsäure*.
32. Tribunal de Grande Instance Paris *(Paris District Court)*, 28 September 2010 PIBD 2010, 930-IIIB-815; Tribunal de Grande Instance Paris *(Paris District Court)*, 19 June 2015, PIBD 2015, 1036-IIIB-653; Court of Appeal of Paris, 2 March 2018, PIBD 2018, 1092-IIIB-250.
33. US Court of Appeal for the Federal Circuit, *Tyco Healthcare v. Mutual Pharm.*, 642 F.3d 1370 (Fed. Cir. 2011); US Court of Appeal for the Federal Circuit, *Galderma Laboratories v. Tolmar*, 737 F.3d 731 (Fed. Cir. 2013); US Court of Appeal for the Federal Circuit, *Hoffmann-La Roche v. Apotex*, 748 F.3d 1326 (Fed. Cir. 2014); US Court of Appeal for the Federal Circuit, *Acorda Therapeutics v. Roxane Laboratories* (Fed. Cir. 2018). For patent eligibility of the invention related to medical method of dosing, see also US Supreme Court, *Mayo v. Prometheus*, 132 S. Ct. 1289 (2012) = GRUR Int. 2012, 582, in which the US Supreme Court stated that the patent claims at issue, which recited an administering thiopurine drug step, a determining the metabolites level in the blood step, and a suggesting the dosage of the drug step, simply told doctors to engage in well-understood, routine, conventional activity of scientist in light of the natural law, and the steps are not sufficient to transform an unpatentable natural law into a patent eligible application of such a law. (The *Mayo/Alice* test in general, see Case No. 1 of this book.)

Case No. 8

Technical Effect – Late Filed Experimental Results

Ryoko Oshikamo

In order to prove a specific technical effect of an invention, it is permissible to take into consideration experimental results submitted after the filing of the application where the original application contains a statement that allows the skilled person to recognise or presume the effect of the invention.

Intellectual Property High Court, 15 July 2010,
Case No. 10238 (Gyō-Ke) of 2009 – *Sunscreen Compositions*

Procter & Gamble v. Japanese Patent Office

---

1. BACKGROUND

The aim of the patent system is to grant an exclusive patent right over an invention in compensation for the disclosure of the invention in terms of fairness, that is, a balance of the benefits both to the patent holder and third parties. If an applicant can freely submit documents to complement the content of the invention originally filed with incomplete documents under the first-to-file principle of the patent system, this would be to the detriment of third parties' interests. There must be therefore limited opportunities to subsequently submit documents that add to the original filing.

The former Examination Guidelines of the Japanese Patent Office (JPO) for the late filing of experimental results was the following:

> "When a claimed invention is determined to be rejected under sec. 29(2), an office action will be issued to an applicant. The applicant may argue or clarify by submitting an argument or a certificate of experimental results and so on against the office action. When the argument convinces the examiner to the extent that it is unclear that the claimed invention is unpatentable under sec. 29(2), the reason for refusal is withdrawn. Where the examiner does not change their determination by the argument, the application is rejected because of lacking inventive step.[1]"

1. The former Examination Guidelines of the JPO, Part II, Chapter 2, 2.9 Notice of Reasons for Refusal under the provision of Patent Act sec. 29 (2), at the website of the JPO <https://www.jpo.go.jp/system/laws/rule/guideline/patent/tukujitu_kijun/tukujitu_kijun_0930.html>, this former Guidelines were applicable to applications, of which filing dates were before 1 October 2015, and the cited statement was not changed more than 10 years.

In accordance with the above, submitting experimental results as a response to the office action alleging lack of inventive step is allowed even after the filing date of the application.

After the amendment of sec. 36 Patent Act in 1994, the advantageous effect of an invention over prior art no longer needed to be stated in the description of the patent application. However, after this revision of the act, regarding the assessment of inventive step, the Tokyo High Court has decided that even if the structure of an invention can be easily perceived from the prior art, when the real effect of the invention is remarkably significant from the expected effect of the structure of the invention, the invention may involve inventive step.[2] Therefore, the statement of the 'effect of the invention' is still an important factor for examination of inventive step in comparison with the prior art, although such effect does not necessarily have to feature in the description. The Tokyo High Court held in this respect:[3]

> "when an advantageous effect over the prior art is stated in the description, or the effect is not stated in the description but a skilled person can presume the effect from the statement of the description or drawings, an effect, for example, an experimental result, argued or proved in the argument against the office action and so on should be taken into account for the examination of the inventive step of the invention. However, when an effect argued or proved in an argument is not stated in the description, nor, is not presumed from the statement of the description or drawings by those skilled in the art, such the effect should not be taken into account."

This case was cited in the former Examination Guidelines of the JPO for the assessment of inventive step based on the effect of the invention. Based on the case, "when an advantageous effect over the prior art is stated in the description, or the effect is not stated in the description but a skilled person can infer the effect from the statement of the description or drawings," an experimental result can be submitted as evidence against the alleged lack of inventive step.

The question in the decision at issue is therefore whether it is possible to respond with late-filed experimental results to the office action alleging lack of inventive step, and to which extent and detail the effect of the invention had to be stated in order to affirm an advantageous effect over prior art.

---

2. Tokyo High Court, 11 June 2002, Case No. 437 (Gyō-Ke) of 1999, the website of the courts <http://www.courts.go.jp/app/files/hanrei_jp/823/011823_hanrei.pdf>; Tokyo High Court, 22 March 2004, Case No. 409 (Gyō-Ke) of 2003, the website of the courts <http://www.courts.go.jp/app/files/hanrei_jp/443/010443_hanrei.pdf>; Tokyo High Court, 16 April 2004, Case No. 262 (Gyō-Ke) of 2002, the website of the courts <http://www.courts.go.jp/app/files/hanrei_jp/404/010404_hanrei.pdf>.
3. Tokyo High Court, 27 October 1998, Case No. 198 (Gyō-Ke) of 1997, the website of the JPO <https://www.jpo.go.jp/shiryou/kijun/kijun2/tukujitu_kijun/cases/9-1-198.html>.

2. DECISION[4]

a) Facts

1. Procedure before the JPO

The plaintiff filed an international application for an invention relating to "Sunscreen Compositions" (priority date: 30 July 1998 in the United States). This application[5] was rejected on 15 November 2006. The plaintiff filed an appeal (No. 2007-5283) and the board of appeal rejected the appeal on 31 March 2009 and this decision was notified to the plaintiff on 14 April 2009.

2. Claim 1 as amended on 9 May 2005

A composition suitable for use as sunscreen characterised in that the composition comprises:

a) a safe and effective amount of a UVA-absorbing dibenzoylmethane sunscreen active;
b) a safe and effective amount of a stabilising agent having the formula

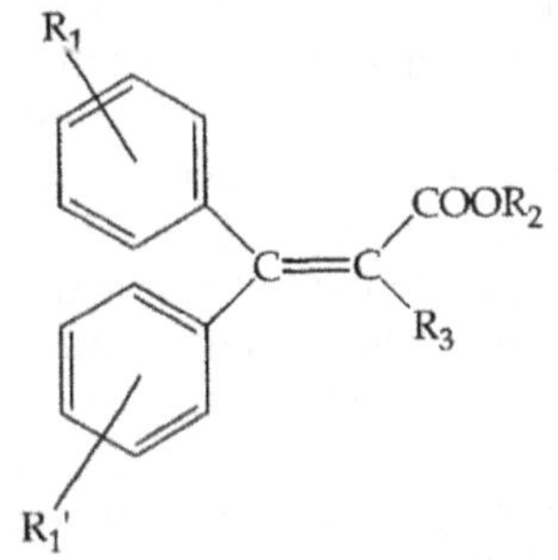

wherein Ri and Ri' are independently in the para or meta position and are independently a hydrogen atom or a straight- or branched chain C1-C8 alkyl radical, R2 is a straight- or branched-chain C2-C12 alkyl radical; and R3 is a hydrogen atom or a -CN radical;
c) a safe and effective amount of a UVB sunscreen which is 0.1-4 weight% of 2-phenyl-benzimidazole-5-sulfonic acid; and
d) a carrier suitable for application to the skin;

wherein the mole ratio of the stabilising agent to the UVA-absorbing dibenzoylmethane sunscreen active is less than 0.8 and wherein the composition is substantially free of benzylidene camphor derivatives.

---

4. Published in 2011 Hanrei Jihō 629 = 1337 Hanrei Times 236 = N. NAKAYAMA et al. (eds.), Tokkyo Hanrei Hyakusen *(Hundred Selected Patent Cases)*, 4th ed. 2012, 36 = English headnote in 44 IIC 100 (2013).
5. JP application No: 2000-561967

b) Reasons

The court decides as follows: (1) the description of the original application can be understood to state the effect of the present invention where the "UV-B filter" is "2-phenyl-benzimidazole-5-sulfonic acid." Regarding the effect of the present invention, since the experimental results filed as a supplement during the appeal procedure can be taken into consideration for determining inventive step, the decision of the JPO was erroneous and should be set aside. (2) Taking into account the experimental results, the present invention demonstrates a significantly remarkable effect which could not be foreseen from the cited prior art, and could not be easily conceived from the cited prior art, thus, the decision of the JPO is also erroneous. The detailed reasons are as follows.

1. Errors of the decision of the JPO board of appeal

(1) The decision of the JPO is based on the lack of inventive step according to sec. 29 (2) Patent Act.

For assessing inventive step, in case of the description of an original patent application without a statement regarding the "effect of the invention," if the applicant could argue or prove such effect by experimental results submitted after the filing date of the application, this is contrary to the aim of the patent system, that under the first-to-file principle grants a patent right, that is, an exclusive right, as compensation for the disclosure of the invention. This is therefore unallowable but for the presence of special circumstances.

While the effect of the invention does not necessarily have to be stated in the patent application, it is an important factor when assessing the inventive step by way of comparison between the invention and the prior art. Determination of the inventive step depends on whether the invention comprises technical subject matter that the skilled person cannot easily reach from the prior art by identifying a problem to be solved in the present invention and its solution. The identification of the problem and the solution closely relate to an "effect of the invention." From this viewpoint, taking into account "experimental results" which are not disclosed in the original application, is not permissible unless in some special circumstances because it compromises the fairness between the applicant and third parties.

In determining inventive step, "the effect of the invention" based on late-filed experimental results is unallowable because of the aim of the patent system and the fairness between the applicant and third parties. Therefore, apart from cases of the description of the original application without a statement of the "effect of the invention," when the description of the original application has a statement that the skilled artisan can recognise or presume the effect of the invention, taking into consideration late-filed experimental results should be allowable within the scope of the description. The allowability [of subsequently late-filed experimental results] should be decided from the perspective of the above-mentioned fairness.

(2) This case is considered from the above-mentioned perspective

...

From the above statement of the description, the person skilled in the art can naturally recognise a further improved UV protection and light stability of the wide range spectrum as effects of the present invention when "2-phenyl-benzimidazole-5-sulfonic acid" is selected as "UV-B filter."

The experimental results demonstrate: (i) SPF and PPD values of the present invention (example 1) correspond to "50 + " and "8 + ," respectively, and compared to the prior art products of comparative examples 1 to 4, the SPF value is remarkably higher, about 3 to10 times, and the PPD value is also about 1.1 to 2 times higher, which means that the present invention has an excellent UV protection effect of wide range spectrum; (ii) the present invention maintains remarkably higher SPF and PPD values after irradiation of UV light and has an excellent light stability. On those points, the present invention has remarkable effects.

The SPF and PPD values as the remarkable effects of the present invention are only indicated in the newly submitted experimental results but not clearly stated in the description of the original application. However, in this case, the person skilled in the art could recognise the effect of the improvement of the UV protection and the light stability of the present invention from the description of the original application. Therefore, the newly submitted experimental results can be taken into account as a basis for affirming inventive step, and this does not undermine the fairness between the applicant and third parties.

3. ANALYSIS

a) Allowability of late-filed experimental results as a response to the office action alleging lack of inventive step

As described above, regarding the assessment of inventive step based on the effect of the invention, the former Examination Guidelines of the Japanese Patent Office (JPO) ruled that experimental results can be submitted as evidence when an advantageous effect over the prior art is already stated in the description, or the effect is not stated in the description but a skilled person can infer the effect from the statement of the description or drawings. According to the above IP High Court decision basically when an effect of the present invention is not stated in the description, experimental results submitted as an argument against an office action alleging lack of inventive step should as a general rule not be taken into account based on the purpose of the patent system and for reasons of fairness, that is, the balance between a patent applicant and society. On the other hand, where the submitted experimental results reinforce the effect of the invention that can be recognised or presumed from the statement of the description of the original application, such newly-submitted experimental results should be taken account for determining inventive step. This approach basically follows the above Examination Guidelines.[6] So, in general, late-filed experimental

6. W. Sugie, Shutsugantōsho meisaisho niha sayōkouka ni tsuite teiseiteki ni kisai sareteiru nomi de atta ga, shutsugango ni sono sayōkouka ni tsuite gutaitekina jikkenkekka ga teishutsu sareta jian ni oite, shinposei wo handan suru zentei tosite sono teishutsu sareta jikkenkekka wo sanshaku surukoto wa yurusareru monotoshi, jikkenkekka wo sanshaku sita kekka, hongan hatumei wa kencho na sayōkouka ga aru mono tosite, shinposei ga koutei sareta jirei *(Case where only qualitative statement on effect was disclosed in the description of the application as filed and specific experimental results on the effect were submitted after filing, it was decided that as premises for examining inventive step, referring the submitted experimental results was allowed,*

results, corroborating the originally disclosed effect, could be taken into account. However, in this case, the JPO board of appeal decided that the effect stated in the description as filed was not concrete, especially regarding the claimed invention at issue, for which reason the late-filed experimental results could not be taken into account. As a result, the invention at issue lacked inventive step, and the late-filed experimental results could not be taken into account in order to remedy this defect.

With respect to the scope of an effect of the invention that can be recognised or presumed from the statement of the description of the original application, there are two earlier decisions that deserve mention.

One of the decisions, the IP High Court decision of 30 July 2007,[7] *Method for Producing Lens* case, considered the significance of late-filed experimental results in response to an office action alleging lack of inventive step. The court held that where the significance of a scope of the numerical range was submitted after filing without supporting embodiments showing a concrete effect for the range in the description of the original application, the late-filed significance of the scope should not be taken into account. This decision is closer to the JPO Boards of Appeal decision of the present case, that the invention does not have inventive step according to sec. 29(2) Patent Act when the mere general and nonconcrete effect was stated in the original description and was presumable.[8] However, the approach of the present *Sunscreen Compositions* decision is different from the above approach since the only information that could be perceived from the application as filed was a superior effect, yet no numerical range was indicated for this effect. Still, the court allowed the subsequent filing of experimental results to demonstrate a superior effect over prior art.[9]

Another decision of the IP High Court of 30 January 2007,[10] *Transportation Load Weight Self-Display Machine* case, considered the effect of an invention that could be inferred from the statement of the description of the original application. It decided that when no effect of the invention was stated in the original description, the effect of the invention is presumed to be the same as in well-known technology having a same constitution as the claimed invention.

The present decision of the IP High Court is different from these two earlier cases because it held that it was sufficient that the effect of the invention could be recognised or presumed from the original description and the late-filed experimental

the inventive step of the invention at issue was affirmed by the consideration of the experimental results), 2111 Hanrei Jihō 180, at 181-2; M. HATTORI, Shinposei handan ni okeru shutsugango ni teishutsu sareta jikkenkekka no sanshaku – chizaikōsai heisei 22 nen 7 gatsu 5 nichi hanketu, heisei 21 nen (Gyō-Ke) 10238 gō [Hiyakedomezai soseibutsu jiken] *(Consideration of experimental results submitted after filing in inventive step examination – IP High Court, 5 July 2010, Case No. 10238 (Gyō-Ke) of 2009 [Sunscreen Composition case])*, 56-5 AIPPI Journal of the Japanese Group (Japanese edition) 2, 282 (2011), at 298; Y. KOMATSU AND M. FUJINO, Atodashi sareta jikkenkekka wo sanshaku sita uede, shinposei wo kouteisita jirei – Hiyakedomezai soseibutsu jiken *(Case where the inventive step was affirmed by considering the results of experiments submitted after filing – Sunscreen Composition case)* 61-3 Chizai Kanri 317 (2011), at 322.

7. Case No. 10094 (Gyō-Ke) of 2006, the website of the courts <http://www.courts.go.jp/app/files/hanrei_jp/011/035011_hanrei.pdf>.
8. W. SUGIE, *supra* note 6, at 182; Y. KOMATSU AND M. FUJINO, *supra* note 6, at 322.
9. W. SUGIE, *supra* note 6, at 182.
10. Case No. 10222 (Gyō-Ke) of 2006, the website of the courts <http://www.courts.go.jp/app/files/hanrei_jp/061/034061_hanrei.pdf>.

results could be taken into account regarding the effect which was only qualitatively stated in the description at filed.[11]

On this point, *Iizuka* states that allowing late-filed experimental results is not an issue of substantive law, but rather an issue of policy-making, namely whether to grant a patent without a clear indication of its technical effect in the original description.[12] *Hattori* also states that this issue is a policy decision as to which kind of criterion is most suitable for the industrial development of Japan.[13]

b) Remarkable effect in the assessment of inventive step

The submitted experimental results in this case indicate a significant effect that was unclearly stated in the description of the original application. The court however decided that the person skilled in the art could however recognise the effect of the invention proven in the subsequently filed experimental results from the description of the original application.

In the assessment of inventive step, the presence of a remarkable effect has been conventionally approached as follows; i) if a claimed invention has a remarkable effect over the prior art, it is assumed that a person skilled in the art could not have easily arrived at the claimed invention (indirect fact theory); and ii) if a claimed invention has a remarkable effect over the prior art, the claimed invention involves an inventive step even if the person skilled in the art could have easily arrived at the claimed invention (independent requirement theory).[14] Though it is unclear which theory the present decision follows, the result would have been the same.[15]

The burden of proof for a remarkable effect is on the patent applicant. Less clear, though, is the scope of the remarkable effect to be proven over the whole range claimed. This problem should arguably be addressed from the viewpoint of the support requirement, in other words whether the scope of the claims is sufficiently supported by the description (for a more detailed analysis of the support requirement, see the following cases 9 and 10 in this book).[16] It was criticised in particular that the present decision did not examine the fundamental issue whether the experimental results showing a remarkable effect carried out after the filing date can be taken into account in the assessment of the inventive step, even when the description of the original application disclosed the effect of the invention merely with qualitative data. The IP High Court however only examined the adequacy of the appeal decision.[17]

---

11. W. Sugie, *supra* note 6, at 182.
12. T. Iizuka and A. Konno, Shinposei youken no handan ni atari shutsugango no jikkendēta no sanshaku ga yurusareru meisaisho no kisai no teido *(Degree of statement in the description, which is required for consideration of experimental data after filing in examination of inventive step requirement)*, 66-3 Patent 21 (2013), at 53.
13. M. Hattori, *supra* note 6, at 299.
14. W. Sugie, *supra* note 6, at 182; M. Hattori, *supra* note 6, at 289-91; K. Miyazaki, Yūrina koukano sanshaku ni tsuite *(Consideration of advantageous effect)*, in N. Nakayama et al. (eds.),, Chizai rikkoku no hatten e *(For development of nation built on IP)*, 2013, 715, at 716.
15. *id.*
16. W. Sugie, *supra* note 6, at 182.
17. K. Miyazaki, *supra* note 14, at 734.

On the other hand, *Hattori* argued that it was for applicant to prove the effect of the invention over the whole range of the claim, and the flexibility shown in the current decision was reasonable from the viewpoint of the international harmonisation.[18]

With respect to the point stated in the present decision that if the applicant could uninhibitedly argue or prove such effect by experimental results submitted after the filing date of the application, this would be contrary to the aim of the patent system under the first-to-file principle, *Iizuka* questioned whether allowing late-filed experimental results was different from allowing the applicant to change the scope of the claims. To him, submitting experimental results after the filing date was irrelevant to issues related to the first-to-file principle.[19]

A practical explanation for this approach is that requiring a quantitative statement of the effect of the invention in the original description unduly burdens an applicant who at the date of the application cannot be sure which kind of data may be required by the Patent Office in the future.

The Examination Guidelines has been revised after the present decision and mentions the approach for advantageous effects[20] and the late-filed experimental results.[21] The Guidelines however does not state to which extent the effect of the invention should be specified with quantitative terms in the original description.

4. COMPARATIVE REMARKS

The issue of post-filed experimental data is discussed in the context of two scenarios: sufficiency of disclosure and inventive step. Both aim at different requirements of patent law: A disclosure is generally considered sufficient if a person skilled in the art can carry out the invention without undue burden, although not necessarily over the whole range claimed. An alleged effect under US law can be speculative,[22] while in Europe, it is not sufficient to allege an unspecified effect.[23] China now allows for post-published evidence backing up what has originally been described.[24]

18. M. Hattori, *supra* note 6, at 292.
19. T. Iizuka and A. Konno, *supra* note 12, at 51.
20. The Examination Guidelines of the JPO, Part III, Chapter 2, Section 2 Inventive step, 3.2 Factor in support of the existence of inventive step, 3.2.1 Advantageous effects, at the website of the JPO < https://www.jpo.go.jp/e/system/laws/rule/guideline/patent/tukujitu_kijun/index.html >.
21. The Examination Guidelines of the JPO, *supra* note 20, Part I, Chapter 2, Section 4 Handling of Written Opinion, Written Amendment, etc., 2.1.1 Handling of written opinion, certificate of experimental results, etc.
22. For US law: US Court of Appeals, Federal Circuit, Atlas Powder v. E.I. Du Pont, 750 F2d 1569 (Fed. Cir. 1984); In re Chu, 66 F.3d 292 (Fed. Cir. 1995).
23. EPO, decision **T 338/10** of 22 January 2015 – Composition anti-allergique/Atlantis; French Supreme Court, decision of 6 December 2017, case B-15-19.726, *Merck Sharp & Dohme v. Teva et al.* – this case concerned the sufficient disclosure of a dosage regime whose only difference to prior art was an allegedly surprising effect of a different dosage. There were no results to back this up, though. UK Patents Court, decision of 19 March 2004, *Glaxo Group Ltd's Patent*, [2004] RPC 43; [2004] EWHC 477 (Pat); UK House of Lords, decision of 9 July 2008, *Conor Medsystems v. Angiotech Pharma* [2008] UKHL 49; UK Patents Court, decision of 19 January 2009, *Laboratorios Almirall v. Boehringer Ingelheim*, [2009] FSR 12; [2009] EWHC 102 (Pat).
24. The 2017 Examination Guidelines for Patent Examination for the first time admit post-filed experimental data, yet in the context of sufficient disclosure: "To evaluate whether the patent description has sufficient disclosure, only the original claims and description shall be considered.

For inventive step, the issue is whether an allegedly advantageous effect over the prior art can be proven by post-published evidence.

a) EPO

The EPO Guidelines require an unexpected technical effect to be described in precise terms rather than in a vague statement.[25]

Experimental results may be submitted as evidence of inventive step against an office action under the EPO procedure. However, new effects submitted can only be taken into account if they are implied by or at least related to the technical problem initially suggested in the originally filed application. Submitting new evidence that shows an unexpected advantage when the skilled person would always contemplate the aspect of the newly-submitted evidence is also allowable.[26]

According to decision **T 440/91**,[27] additional advantages of the invention in support of patentability can be supplied later to the extent that this does not alter the technical problem already specified in the application. Regarding evidence that the claimed solution actually solves the problem and provides the desired effect, post-published evidence may be taken into account if the application already makes credible that the problem is actually solved, but cannot be the only basis for the desired effect.[28] In recent years, the EPO has taken a more restrictive approach towards the subsequent supply of data in support of an inventive step: Decision **T 415/11**[29] held that subsequent data to show a technical effect could not be submitted where the initial application did not clearly state the problem and the solution to which these data referred. In **T 1791/11**,[30] the Board refused to take into account subsequently furnished data due to the fact that the original application mentioned a number of protein variations without however clearly pointing to advantages over the prior art. Finally, in **T 488/16**,[31] the original application contained a generic claim for a group of protein kinases that was subsequently limited to one single combination for which the patentee only supplied data to support its inhibitive effect in opposition.

Examiners shall review experimental data supplemented after the filing date. The technical effect of such post-filing experimental data should be determinable by the skilled person in the art in view of the original disclosure."

25. 10. Unexpected effect in Part G Chapter VII-20 of Guidelines for Examination in the EPO. Examples: "The new compounds have shown unexpectedly good pharmaceutical properties" is too vague and cannot support the presence of inventive step. An overview is provided by EXNER/HÜTTERMANN, Führt das EPA mit Hilfe der "Plausibilität" den Erfindungsbesitz als Patentierungskriterium ein? *(Does the EPO introduce the possession of invention as criteria for patenting with help of "plausibility"?)*, GRUR Int. 2018, 97.
26. Arguments and evidence submitted by the applicant; decision **T 386/89** of 24 March 1992; and decision **T 184/82** of 4 January 1984 – Poly(p-methylstyrene) articles; for example, when the invention relates to a pharmaceutical composition, it is allowable to reformulate the technical problem by including the aspect of toxicity by submitting new evidence showing the claimed composition exhibits an unexpected advantage in terms of low toxicity because pharmaceutical activity and toxicity are related and the skilled person would always contemplate both aspects.
27. Decision **T 440/91** of 22 March 1994 – *Sels mucolytiques/Pharlyse.*
28. Decision **T 1329/04** of of 28 June 2005 – *Factor-9/John Hopkins.*
29. Decision **T 415/11** of 12 January 2012 – *Lyophilized Neisseria meningococcus vaccine/Novartis.*
30. Decision **T 1791/11** of 7 April 2016 – *Subtilase variants/Novozymes.*
31. Decision **T 488/16** of 1 February 2017 – *Dasatinib/Bristol-Myers Squib.*

The Board refused to take these data into account, as the effect for such combination had not been made credible at the filing date and the invention as originally disclosed was rather speculative.

b) US

In a 2014 decision, the judges disagreed as to whether post-published experiments could be taken into account for the purposes of demonstrating inventive step.[32]

c) China

The Supreme People's Court in a ruling of 2012 admitted post-filed experiments in order to prove inventive step under certain circumstances that technical effects were clearly described in original applications.[33]

d) Korea

The Korean Supreme Court also stated in a decision of 2003 about selection invention that an applicant could submit post-filed experimental data to prove doubtful effects of invention, if the effects were clearly described in original application.[34]

32. US Court of Appeals of the Federal Circuit, *Bristol-Myers Squibb v. Teva.*, 752 F.3d 967 (Def. Cir. 2014).
33. Chinese Supreme People's Court, 19 September 2012, in re Takeda, administrative ruling (2012) Zhi Xing Zi No. 41, available at the website of the court <http://www.court.gov.cn/wenshu/xiangqing-7395.html>.
34. Korean Supreme Court, 25 April 2003, *Pfizer Inc. v. KIPO*, Case No. 2740 (Hu) of 2001.

Case No. 9

Enabling Disclosure and Support

Klaus Hinkelmann

---

1. When applying the support requirement provision of sec. 36(6)(i) Patent Act, it is sufficient to decide whether the scope of the claim exceeds the scope of the description. It is unallowable to interpret and decide this provision identical to the requirement of a sufficient enabling disclosure under sec. 36(4)(i).

2. It is not appropriate to hold that a second medical use claim does not fulfil the requirement of sec. 36(6)(i) unless the claimed use is supported by pharmacological data or equivalent.

Intellectual Property High Court, 28 January 2010,
Case No. 10033 (Gyo-Ke) 2009 – *Flibanserin*

Boehringer Ingelheim Pharma v. Japanese Patent Office

---

1. BACKGROUND

The following two provisions in the Patent Act need to be fulfilled in order to obtain a patent, the first of which deals with sufficient disclosure for the invention to be carried out, the second with the sufficient support of the claims by the description.

> Sec. 36
>
> (4) The detailed explanation of the invention in the description under the preceding paragraph (iii) shall comply with the following:
>
> (i) it states the invention, in a manner sufficiently clear and complete for the invention to be carried out by a person having ordinary skill in the art to which the invention pertains, as provided for in an ordinance of the Ministry of Economy, Trade and Industry.
>
> ...
>
> (6) The statement of the patent claim(s) under subsection (2) shall comply with each of the following items:
>
> (i) statements setting forth the invention(s) for which a patent is sought and which is stated in the detailed explanation of the invention."

The requirement under sec. 36(6)(i) Patent Act had been interpreted rather strictly by the Japanese Patent Office for pharmaceutical use inventions. It was also not very clear whether the requirements under the above two provisions were identical or different.

The decision provides in particular some guidance regarding the requirement under sec. 36(6)(i) Patent Act, not least with regard to pharmaceutical use inventions. Moreover, this decision deals with the relationship between the above two provisions.

2. DECISION[1]

a) Facts

1. Procedure before the JPO

The plaintiff filed an international application for the invention with the title "Use of Flibanserin in Medical Treatment of Sex Disorder" (PCT/EP02/11103 on 4 October 2002 (priority claim: 20 October 2001, EP). The corresponding national Japanese part (application No. 2003-537639) was refused by the examination department of the Japanese Patent Office on 4 September 2006. An appeal was filed on 4 December 2006. The board of appeal of the JPO decided on 29 September 2008 that the appeal was ill-founded because there was no statement of pharmacological data or an equivalent statement, which was necessary for the invention of a medicine to fulfil the requirements of sec. 36(6)(i) Patent Act. The plaintiff appealed against the decision of the JPO.

2. Claim 1 of the application after the amendment of 26 December 2005 reads as follows:

> "Use of Flibanserin, which can be in the form of a pharmacologically allowable acid addition salt, for producing a medicine for medical treatment of sexual desire disorder."

b) Reasons

For the following reasons, the court considers that the decision of the JPO is mistaken in requiring that a "statement of pharmacological data or statement equating to it" is necessary to fulfil the requirement of sec. 36(6)(i) Patent Act according to which "the statement of claim shall set forth the invention for which a patent is sought and which is stated in the detailed explanation of the invention." Further, that when interpreting sec. 36(6)(i) Patent Act for an invention which consists of the use of a medicine, claim 1 of the application at issue does not fulfil the requirements of this provision.

---

1. Published in 2073 Hanrei Jihō 105 = 1334 Hanrei Times 152 = N. NAKAYAMA et al. (eds.), Tokkyo Hanrei Hyakusen *(Hundred Selected Patent Cases)*, 4th ed. 2012, 46 = T. ŌBUCHI et al. (eds.), Chitekizaisan hō hanrei shū *(Intellectual Property Law Case Book)*, 2nd ed. 2015, 49

1. Relationship between sec. 36(4)(i) and sec. 36(6)(i) Patent Act

(1) Purpose of sec. 36(4)(i) and sec. 36(6)(i) Patent Act

Sec. 36 Patent Act specifies the requirements for the description of the application upon filing. Here, it must be distinguished: sec. 36(4)(i) requires that the invention shall be stated in "the description" in a manner sufficiently clear and complete for the invention to be carried out, while sec. 36(6)(i) Patent Act refers to "the claims."

Sec. 36(4)(i) thus requires that the description states the "subject matter which is necessary to understand the technical meaning of the invention by a person skilled in the art, such as problem and solution etc." (sec. 24bis Regulations of the Patent Act) "clearly and sufficiently to make the invention work by a person skilled in the art." The patent system is a system in which an exclusive right for a certain period of time is granted to a person who discloses an invention, as a compensation for such disclosure. But when a person who is going to obtain a patent will be granted an exclusive right without disclosing the problem, solution and other subject matter necessary to understand the technical meaning of the invention, or without disclosing the subject matter clearly and sufficiently for making the invention work, the purpose of the patent system that an exclusive right is granted as a compensation for disclosing the invention as a creation of a useful technical idea, might be missed. From such consideration, this provision requires a statement of the above-mentioned subject matter in "the description" of the application.

In contrast thereto, for a "claim" sec. 36(6)(i) requires that the invention to be patented is stated in the description. The purpose of this provision is to give effect to the provisions that a patent owner has an exclusive right to commercially work the patented invention, and that the technical scope of the patented invention must be determined based on "the statement of the claim" (secs. 68, 70(1) Patent Act). If the statement of "the claim" exceeds the scope of the technical subject matter stated/ disclosed in "the description," and if the exclusive right is granted over too broad a scope of the technical subject matter, this deviates from the purpose of the patent system in that the exclusive right is granted only commensurate to the disclosed technical subject matter as a compensation for such disclosure. Any excess when delimiting the claim is unallowable. For example, when it is understood from the statement of "embodiments," etc. in "the description" that only a narrow, limited subject matter is disclosed, but the statement of "the claim" comprises the wide technical scope which exceeds the technical subject matter, such claim is unpatentable because of a breach of this provision.

Thus, the purpose of the provision of sec. 36(6) (i) is to prevent the granting of too broad an exclusive right for the wording of a "claim" compared to the statement of the "description."

(2) Applicability of sec. 36(6)(i) Patent Act

To decide whether "the claim" is consistent with sec. 36(6)(i), i.e. whether "the invention to be patented in the claim is stated in the description," it is necessary to understand what technical subject matter "the description" discloses. Sec. 36(6)(i) requires a statement of "the claim," and the purpose of this provision is to exclude the grant of too wide an exclusive right compared to the technical subject matter disclosed in the description. So the way of understanding the disclosed subject matter of "the description" in order to apply the provision should be in conformity with the consideration of such points. On the other hand, sec. 36(4)(i) independently provides that "the description" states "subject matter which is necessary to understand the technical meaning of the invention by a person skilled in the art, such as the problem and solution, etc.," "clearly enough to make the invention work." So if the application lacks this requirement, by itself the application is as such subject to a ground of rejection or invalidation (sec. 123(1)(iv). So, if we consider and interpret the provision of sec. 36(6)(i) Patent Act in completely the same way as sec. 36(4)(i), apart from the purpose of sec. 36(6)(i) Patent Act "to exclude the grant of too wide an exclusive right compared to the technical subject matter disclosed in the description," we might consider the same concern twice. If we make an interpretation such that the lack of compliance with sec. 36(4)(i) in the description always leads to a lack of compliance with sec. 36(6)(i), we miss the notion that the requirements of patentability under sec. 36(4)(i) and sec. 36(6)(i) are separate and independent of each other.

Therefore, when applying a reasonable method of interpretation for sec. 36(6)(i), it is sufficient to decide whether the scope of the claim exceeds the scope of the description. It is unallowable to interpret and decide this provision identical to sec. 36(4)(i), unless there are some special circumstances, for example, the claim is stated in a special form, or it goes seriously against the purpose of the patent system, or unless "the description" is interpreted under the above mentioned method as a prerequisite for interpreting sec. 36(6)(i).

We consider this case from the above mentioned point of view.

...

3. Reasoning of the decision of the JPO

(1) The decision of the JPO is not based on a comparison between the scopes of disclosure, i.e. whether the scope of "the claim" exceeds the scope of "the description," but based on non-compliance with sec. 36(6)(i) Patent Act only for the reason that there is no statement of the "pharmacological data or statement equating to it, which supports the utility" of Flibanserin as a medicine for medical treatment of sexual desire disorder in "the description." But the decision of the JPO did not indicate a basis for determining why the application did not comply with the requirement of sec. 36(6)(i) Patent Act, unless "the description" stated the "pharmacological data or statement equating to it, which supports the utility."

a. The decision of the JPO indicated that "for an invention about the use of a medicine, the utility of the medicine is generally difficult to predict only from the substance name of the active agent and the chemical structure, and if the effective dosage, administration method and subject matter about medicine formulation are stated to some extent only, the person skilled in the art cannot know the actual utility of the medicine in the use only by these indications. So the utility of the use should be supported by pharmacological data or a statement equating these in the description so that the invention to be patented is stated in the description." In light of the purpose of this provision, we cannot deny that this part may be applicable for considering the requirement under sec. 36(4)(i).

From the perspective that in order to obtain a patent as an exclusive right, it is necessary to disclose to third parties the information necessary to understand the technical meaning of the invention and to offer clear and sufficient information for carrying out the invention, sec. 36(4)(i) provides that the description should state the subject matter to the extent necessary. As under the Japanese patent system inventions of use of medicine are patentable, in many cases the process of objective verification of the utility of the use should be adequately clarified in "the description," and the verification process is clarified most effectively, appropriately and reasonably by corresponding data of the medicine and its use. If such data is not stated, in most cases the description is not clear and insufficient for working the invention.

But for the part of the decision of the JPO that concerns the requirement of sec. 36(6)(i), namely that "the utility of the use should be supported by the pharmacological data or statement equating these in the description," the statement of the pharmacological data or statement equating these cannot be an essential condition (requirement), unless under special circumstances. As mentioned above, the purpose of the provision of sec. 36(6)(i) is to prevent the grant of too wide an exclusive right that exceeds the scope of the description of the "claim" compared to the technical subject matter stated in "description." So in light of the purpose of the provision, for interpreting "the description", it should be necessary and reasonable to consider whether the scope of "the claim" is within the scope of the technical subject matter stated in "the description," and here, a formal understanding of the technical subject matter which is stated/disclosed in embodiment, etc. in "the description" is enough, bar special circumstances.

Therefore the part of the decision of the JPO that holds that the claim does not fulfil the requirement of sec. 36(6)(i) unless "the utility of the use is supported by the pharmacological data or statement equating these" in the description, is generally not appropriate, and bar special circumstances, the decision of the JPO lacks good reasons.

b. The decision of the JPO concluded that taking into account the concrete statement in the description, "there are no pharmacological data or a statement equating these which support the utility of the use of the medicine that is the subject of the invention, in the description of the application at issue," and the application at issue therefore did not fulfil the requirements of sec. 36(6)(i).

The decision of the JPO did not consider the technical subject matter that can be understood through the statement of the description when compared to the claim, but only whether "there are the pharmacological data or a statement equating these." Based thereupon, the JPO decided that the application did not fulfil the requirements of sec. 36(6)(i), because such statement was not in the description. Due to this omission the JPO decided that ... the claim of the application at issue exceeded the technical subject matter stated in the description. And there are no special circumstances in this case such as that "the claim" is stated in a special form that may give rise to concern in that it may hinder the development of industry. ...

3. ANALYSIS

The above IP High Court Decision ("Decision") addresses in principle two issues, namely (a) whether the requirement under sec. 36(6)(i) Patent Act is fulfilled for the present patent application which is an invention directed to a specific pharmaceutical use; and (b) the relationship between the provisions of secs. 36(6)(i) and 36(4)(i) Patent Act.

As regards issue (a), the decision is very clear. The JPO's decision was overturned because the requirement under sec. 36(6)(i) Patent Act was fulfilled even where the detailed explanation of the invention contained in the description of the patent application with regard to the invention relating to the use of a drug does not "include pharmacological data or a statement that can be deemed to be equivalent thereto".

The Decision was made on the basis of a comparison between the statement of the "scope of claims" and the statement of the "detailed explanation of the invention". The IP High Court took a very reasonable, practical stance in that it was obviously decisive for the court that there were statements in the description according to which studies had been found that flibanserin displays sexual desire enhancing properties in male and female patients suffering from sexual dysfunction. The studies were obviously conducted in the form of medical interviews (questionnaires) with patients who had been given flibanserin. There was no established animal or test-tube experiment-based sexual desire rating method before the priority date. Very reasonably, the decision found that a statement based on which a person ordinarily skilled in the art can confirm the usefulness of the use should be considered sufficient. The JPO could not provide any reason as to why this should not be sufficient and as to why pharmacological data should be provided. Indeed, it cannot be seen why further data should be provided in order to fulfil the requirement under sec. 36(6)(i) Patent Act. The Decision is especially reasonable since it cannot be expected from an applicant under these circumstances to await further pharmacological tests before a patent application is filed. The danger of an unintentional disclosure would be too high.

As regards item (b), the Decision appears to be clear at first glance, i.e. from a theoretical standpoint. However, after a closer look it turns out that the comparison of the requirements for the fulfilment of the two provisions is in fact not very clear from a practical point of view.

The IP High Court states that sec. 36(6)(i) Patent Act was established in order to eliminate the granting of an excessively broad exclusive right that exceeds the technical matter disclosed in the detailed explanation of the invention. The court then states that in interpreting the provisions of sec. 36(6)(i) Patent Act, it is sufficient to determine whether the scope of the statement of the scope of claims exceeds that of the statement of the detailed description of the invention by comparing the former with the latter based on a purposive interpretation method.

This statement sounds first of all very vague. The Decision then states that it is not permitted to interpret and determine the compliance with the requirement under sec. 36(6)(i) Patent Act by a method that is the same as that of determining compliance with the requirement under subsection (4), item (i) unless there are special circumstances. But this statement does not provide any clarification; instead it gives rise to the question what methods are to be adopted for the two determinations? A close look at the Decision unfortunately does not provide any guidance in this respect.

Namely as regards the requirement under sec. 36(4)(i) Patent Act, the court states that it is necessary to disclose to third parties the problem to be solved by the invention, means for solving said problem and other matters necessary to understand the technical significance of the invention. To this end, the applicant has to provide information that is clear and sufficient to work the invention in order to obtain an exclusive patent right in the "detailed description of the invention".

According to the Decision, the requirements under secs. 36(6)(i) and 36(4)(i) Patent Act are different. From the Decision the author understands that meeting the requirements under sec. 36(6)(i) Patent Act would not automatically mean that the requirements under sec. 36(4)(i) Patent Act are also fulfilled, and vice versa. This sounds reasonable, but what does it actually mean?

The Decision states that in determining whether the "statement of the scope of claims" complies with sec. 36(6)(i), i.e. to determine whether the "statement of the scope of claims" fulfils the requirement that the "invention for which a patent is sought is stated in the detailed explanation of the invention" it is a necessary prerequisite to understand the technical matter disclosed in the "detailed explanation of the invention".

Upon a closer look at the two provisions, it appears that both require that it is necessary to understand the technical matter disclosed in the "detailed explanation of the invention". Otherwise, neither a comparison with the claimed invention nor a determination as to whether a person skilled in the art could carry out the invention could be made. The decision does not explain why the degree of understanding of the detailed explanation should be different for the requirements of the two provisions.

Moreover, for the application of the two provisions, a comparison of the thus understood detailed explanation of the invention with the statements under sec. 36(6)(i), i.e. the claims, and with the invention mentioned in sec. 36(4)(i) should be made. But what is the "invention" referred to in sec. 36(4)(i)? The invention is in fact defined by the claims. Accordingly, from a practical point of view, the provisions under secs. 36(6)(i) and 36(4)(i) Patent Act would appear to relate to the same comparison. It is thus very difficult to understand the IP High Court's view that both requirements are different and that different methods are required to examine the compliance with the two provisions.

Subsequent case law has not contributed to an understanding of the difference between the two provisions. The IP High Court in its decision of 11 April 2012[2] confirmed its view that the requirements of "enabling disclosure" and "support" are distinct from one other and must be assessed individually. However, the court did not indicate as to how these requirements must be assessed individually. In the specific case at issue, the decision clarified that it is sufficient for the fulfilment of the enabling disclosure requirement under sec. 36(4)(i) Patent Act that a person skilled in the art can manufacture the claimed product based on the description and the state of the art at the time of the application. It would not be necessary to provide a more detailed description of a process for producing a product.

For sec. 36(6)(i), the requirement that the claims must be supported by the description would call for an assessment as to whether or not the invention determined by the scope of the claims was stated in the detailed explanation of the invention and whether a person skilled in the art could recognise this description as solving the problem of the invention either based on the description of the detailed explanation

2. The IP High Court, 11 April 2012, Case Nos. 10146&10467 (Gyō-Ke) of 2011, the website of the courts <http://www.courts.go.jp/app/files/hanrei_jp/189/082189_hanrei.pdf> – *Sawai Pharmaceutical Co., Ltd. vs. Takeda Pharmaceutical.*

of the invention, or based on the state of the art. But what else should this mean but that the description must be enabling. It is clear that in order to solve the problem, the person skilled in the art must be able to produce the product concerned. The description would not be enabling if the problem underlying the invention was not solved, but at the same time a claim directed to such an invention would not be supported by the description. It is thus hoped that the IP High Court will provide a clearer explanation of the differences between the "enablement" requirement and the "support" requirement.

4. COMPARATIVE REMARKS

The above analysis has shown that it is actually very difficult to differentiate between the requirements under secs. 36(4)(i) and 36(6)(i) Patent Act in the way the IP High Court has decided. This is not to say that also other jurisdictions require that both the breadth of the claims is supported by the description and that the latter enables a person skilled in the art to carry out the invention.

a) The EPC

It is especially problematic that sec. 36(6)(i) somehow requires not only to look for and confirm support for claims and claim amendments, but instead requires that the object underlying the invention is identified and supports the claimed subject-matter. Accordingly, the IP High Court interprets sec. 36(6)(i) Patent Act as requiring the fulfilment of both substantive and formal requirements such that it is difficult to see a difference with the requirement under sec. 36(4)(i) Patent Act.

The approach undertaken by the IP High Court is in stark contrast to the practice before the European Patent Office (EPO). Under the European Patent Convention (EPC), the requirements of enabling disclosure (Art. 83 EPC[3]) and clarity/support (Art. 84 EPC[4]) are in the opinion of this author clearly different when the comparison is based on the wording of these provisions. Whether the requirement under Art. 83 EPC is fulfilled is assessed on the basis of the actual technical disclosure which must be enabling. In contrast thereto, the application of Art. 84 EPC is essentially formal. The requirement under Art. 84 EPC means that the subject-matter of the claim must be taken from the description and it is not permissible to claim something which is not described. The claims must be consistent with the description. In decision **T 1020/03**[5] it was noted that a review of the discussions in the various drafts to be found in the preparatory material for the EPC suggests that the requirement for support of the claims was viewed as a formal matter to ensure that the description and claims had the same extent. This formal assessment does however not require an examination of what the problem underlying the invention is and whether this

3. Art. 83 EPC: "The European patent application shall disclose the invention in a manner sufficiently clear and complete for it to be carried out by a person skilled in the art."
4. Art. 84 EPC: "The claims shall define the matter for which protection is sought. They shall be clear and concise and be supported by the description."
5. EPO Boards of Appeal decision **T 1020/03**, Official Journal 2007, 204.

problem has been solved. Such an examination is in fact carried out during the assessment of inventive step (Art. 56 EPC).

Nevertheless, many boards of appeal are of the opinion that the requirement for the claims to be supported by the description should ensure that the extent of protection as defined by the patent claims corresponds to the technical contribution of the disclosed invention to the art such that the skilled person is able to perform the invention over the entire range claimed (see decisions **T 659/93**, **T 94/05**[6]). A purely formal support by the description, i.e. a verbatim repetition of the mention of a claimed feature, cannot meet these requirements (see decision **T 94/05**). This opinion in the view of this author mixes up the separate requirements under Articles 83 and 84 EPC and requires moreover an assessment of what the problem underlying the invention is and whether this problem has been solved. Such an examination is in fact carried out in general during the assessment of inventive step (Art. 56 EPC).

For practical purposes, Articles 83 and 84 EPC can be applied anyway without difficulty. In examination proceedings, the fulfilment of all requirements under the EPC is assessed. An assessment under Art. 83 EPC thus does not require an overlapping assessment under Art. 84 EPC. Moreover, as already mentioned above, the problem underlying the invention and its solution are examined when the existence of an inventive step (Art. 56 EPC) is assessed. And later on, i.e. in opposition proceedings or national invalidation proceedings (Articles 100 and 138 EPC), violations of the provisions under Art. 84 EPC can only be asserted under very specific circumstances since the fulfilment of the requirement under Art. 84 EPC is considered to have been examined in the examination proceedings.

The author is in favour of the handling of the requirements under the EPC and wonders as to why the IP High Court has decided for such a complicate interrelationship between the two provisions.

b) The US

Sec. 112 Patent Act requires that the disclosure supports the scope of the claims, that it allows a person skilled in the art to carry out the invention without undue experimentation and that the applicant provides a description of the best mode how to do so (non-compliance with the latter is no longer a ground for revocation, though):

> "The enablement requirement ensures that the public knowledge is enriched by the patent specification to a degree at least commensurate with the scope of the claims. The scope of the claims must be less or equal to the scope of the enablement. The scope of enablement, in turn, is that which is disclosed in the specification plus the scope of what would be known to one of ordinary skill in the art without undue experimentation."[7]

An application under US law may thus be rejected because, either, the scope of the claims does not correspond to the disclosure, or because the disclosure is non-enabling as such:

6. EPO Boards of Appeal decision **T 659/93** of 7 September 1994; Decision **T 94/05** of 12 July 2007.
7. US CAFC, *Enzo Biochem v. Gen-Probe*, 323 F.3d 956, 982 (Fed. Cir. 2002).

> "The PTO will make a scope of enablement rejection where the written description enables something within the scope of the claims, but the claims are not limited to that scope ... This type of rejection is marked by language stating that the specification does not enable one of ordinary skill to use the invention commensurate with the scope of the claims. On the other hand, if the written description does not enable any subject matter within the scope of the claims, the PTO will make a general enablement rejection, stating that the specification does not teach how to make or use the invention."[8]

8. US CAFC, *In re Cortright*, 165 F.3d 1353, 1356 (Fed. Cir. 1999).

Case No. 10

Support Requirement – Parameter Invention

Masashi Yasui

In order to determine whether the claims are supported by the description, for which the patentee bears the burden of proof, the claim wording must be compared with the description, and the latter must disclose the claimed invention such that it could have been carried out by a person skilled in the art, or alternatively based on common technical knowledge at the filing date.

Intellectual Property High Court, 11 November 2005,
Case No. 10042 (Gyō-Ke) of 2005 – *Method for Producing Polarizing Film*

Nippon Synthetic Chemical Industry Co., Ltd. v. Japanese Patent Office

---

1. BACKGROUND

Japanese Patent Act sec. 36(6)(i)[1] provides that the claimed invention shall be disclosed in the description. It is understood that this corresponds to the requirement that the invention as expressed in the claims is supported by the description. The purpose of this requirement (support requirement) is to prevent a patent from being granted for an invention which is not disclosed to the public.

The provision has its origin in sec. 36(5) of the revised Patent Act of 1965 that stipulated that "only matters that are indispensable for the invention described in the detailed explanation of the invention must be described in the claim". The 1986 revision of the Patent Act of 1965 separated the requirement that "only matters indispensable for the composition of the invention must be described" from the requirement that "the invention to be patented has to be described in the detailed explanation of the invention", which is called "support requirement".

If the exclusive right is granted for a wide technical scope in a case where the claim exceeds the scope of the technical matter disclosed in "detailed explanation of the invention", this is not in line with the purpose of the patent system that

---

1. **Japanese Patent Act Section 36:**

   (6) The statement of the scope of claims as provided in paragraph (2) shall comply with each of the following items:

   (i) the invention for which a patent is sought is stated in the detailed explanation of the invention;

the government grants an exclusive right to the extent that a certain technology is disclosed as compensation for disclosure.

In the present case, the plaintiff owned a patent entitled "Manufacturing Methods of Polarizing Film" (hereinafter "patent at issue") that was revoked in opposition. On appeal, the patentee sought reversal of this decision.[2] The decision by the Patent Office was based on an alleged failure to meet the statutory requirement of a sufficient description ("description" includes "claims" according to the statutory definition before the revision of Law No. 24 of 2002.)

The claimed invention of the patent at issue included an element that was defined by a range limited by a particular mathematical formulation. This mathematical formulation was expressed using two technical parameters, each of which denotes a characteristic of the element of the claimed invention. Thus the present invention was a so-called parameter invention. In the present judicial review, the main issue concerned whether the description sufficiently disclosed the invention as set forth in sec. 36 of the Patent Act so that an exclusive right should be conferred for the invention.

2. DECISION[3]

a) Facts

1. Procedure before the JPO

The plaintiff on 21 October 1993 filed a patent application for an invention with the title "Method of Producing Polarizing Film" (application No.H5-287608). The examination department of the Japanese Patent Office decided to grant the patent that was thus registered as patent No. 3327423. An opposition was filed against the patent, and the JPO decided to revoke the patent on 26 November 2004. This decision was notified to the plaintiff on 18 December 2004.

2. Claim 1 of the application

[Claim 1] Method of producing polariser film by the uniaxial drawing of an original fabric film of a polyvinyl alcohol group, characterised in that the polyvinyl alcohol group film is used as original fabric film of which the thickness is 30-100μm, and the complete dissolution temperature (X) and equilibrium swelling degree (Y) of the original fabric film in hot water are in the range of the following formulas, and the original fabric film is uniaxially drawn 1.2-2 times in a dyeing treatment process, further 2-6 times in a boron compound treatment process:

$$Y > -0.0667X + 6.73 \quad \ldots\ldots \text{(I)}$$
$$X \geq 65 \quad \ldots\ldots\ldots\ldots \text{(II)}$$

2. By the 2003 amendment to the Patent Act, the old opposition system was integrated into the invalidity system, while sec. 2(9) of Appendix provided that the old law should be applied to opposition cases before the entry into force of the amendment.
3. Published in 1911 Hanrei Jihō 48 = 1192 Hanrei Times 164 = N. NAKAYAMA at el. (eds.), Tokkyo Hanrei Hyakusen *(Hundred Selected Patent Cases)*, 4th ed. 2012, 44 = T. ŌBUCHI et al. (eds.) Chitekizaisan hō hanrei shū *(Intellectual Property Law Case Book)*, 2nd ed. 2015, 43.

wherein, X: in hot water complete dissolution temperature of the film piece of 2cm × 2cm (°C), Y: equilibrium swelling degree, when the film piece of 10cm × 10cm is dried 2 hours at 105°C after swelling by 15 minutes dipping, calculated by the formula: weight of the film after the swelling / weight of the film after the drying (weight fraction).

b) Issues

1. With respect to Reason for Revocation 1

A. (Fulfilment of support requirement)

Regarding the invention claimed in the description accompanied with the patent application, which is a so-called "parameter invention", do claim recitations of the application comply with the statutory requirement of the Patent Act, sec. 36(5)(i)? The requirement (hereinafter, "support requirement") was revised by Law No. 116 of 1994 ("patent revision of 1994") to become sec. 36(6)(i) of the Patent Act.

B. (Lawfulness of subsequently adding experimental data to the description)

When the above-specified issue A is not fulfilled, can a patentee-plaintiff comply with the support requirement for the claims by submitting additional experimental data in the course of an opposition procedure for amending the detailed explanation of the description to include data that is not present in the original description?

C. (Legitimacy of ex post facto application of the Guidelines)

In the case that the "Guidelines" (the Examination Guidelines for Patent and Utility Model in Japan) regarding the examination of the statutory requirement have been revised after the filing date of the invention, is it permissible for the Patent Office to apply the Guidelines to the invention?

2. With respect to Reason for Revocation 2

Does the detailed explanation in the description comply with the statutory requirements of the Patent Act, sec. 36 (4) before the patent revision of 1994?

c) Reasons

The Court concludes that the plaintiff's reasons presented in the appeal brief are not persuasive, because, with respect to issue (1), the wording of the claims and description do not comply with the support requirement, and thus it is not necessary to discuss issue (2).

1. With respect to A (Fulfilment of the support requirement of the description)

(1) Whether the wording of the claims fulfil the support requirement or not should be determined by the following scheme: the claim wording is first compared with the detailed description; then it is determined whether the claimed invention is described in the description of the invention such that the claimed invention could have been carried out by a person skilled in the art, or alternatively whether the

claimed invention could have been carried out by a person skilled in the art based on common technical knowledge at the filing date given that the claims were not included nor suggested [in the detailed description]. It is the patentee who has the burden of proof as to the support requirement.

(2) One feature of the present invention is a material that is limited in a range determined by a particular mathematical formula. The mathematical formula includes two technical variables, or parameters, each of which denotes a characteristic of the element. Specifically, the element is a poly-vinyl-alcohol based material film ("PVA film") whose complete salvation temperature, X, and balanced degree of swelling, Y, fall within a range that is denoted by a particular mathematical formula [of X and Y]. Thus, the present invention is a so-called parameter invention. Claims over such inventions meet the support requirement if (i) the detailed explanation in the description discloses a technical teaching for the relationship between the range denoted by the mathematical formula and its effect, or performance, at least in such a way that a person skilled in the art is able to understand it; or (ii) [the detailed explanation] includes the disclosure of examples in a manner that the skilled person can recognise, by consulting the common technical knowledge at the time of filing, that the intended effect, or performance, would have been realised when [X and Y for the claimed invention fall within] the range denoted by the mathematical formula even if particular examples are not included in the description.

(3) The detailed explanation of the present description includes only two examples and two comparative examples for showing the effectiveness of the above structure, as is shown in figure 1. The examples merely show that polarising films with considerable durability and tolerance for high stretch rates are realised by PVA films with specific sets of complete salvation temperature, X, and a balanced degree of swelling, Y; whereas, the comparative examples merely show that polarising films with poor durability and poor tolerance for high stretch rates are realised by PVA films with other specific sets of complete salvation temperature, X, and a balanced degree of swelling, Y. Therefore, such statement does not disclose examples in such a way that a person skilled in the art can recognise, by consulting the common technical knowledge at the time of filing, that the intended effect, or performance, would have been realised when the [numerical values of the characteristics for the PVA films] fall within the range [denoted by the mathematical formula in the claim recitations]. Therefore, the claim recitations do not meet the support requirement.

2. With respect to B (Adding to the description by submitting experimental data after filing)

(1) With respect to so-called parameter invention, notably the present invention, we take into consideration the fact that the detailed explanation neither discloses the examples so specifically that the a person skilled in the art can recognise the problem solved by the present invention, nor discloses [the invention] in such a way that the [disclosure of] the detailed explanation can be expanded or generalised into what is recited in the claims by consulting the technical knowledge on the filing date. Taking into account the objectives of the patent system in which [sufficient] disclosure is assumed for any granted patent, it is not allowed that the [scope of the] detailed description is expanded or generalised to what is recited in the claims for

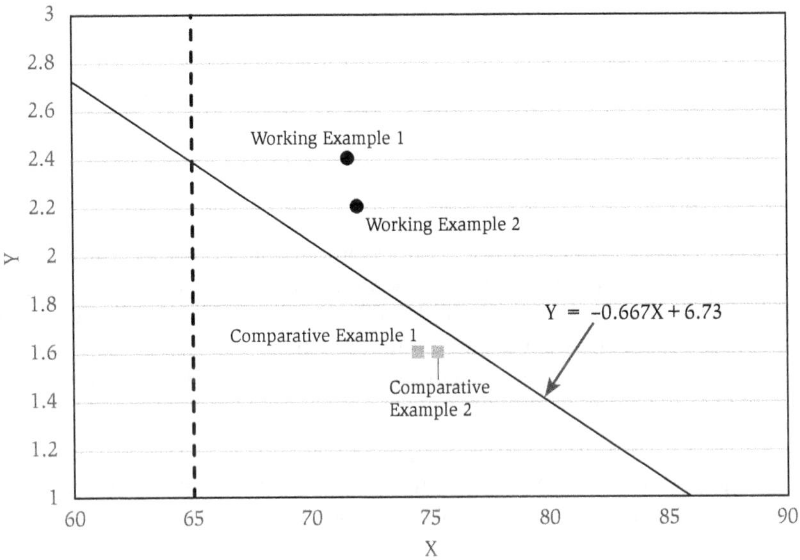

Figure 1. X: complete dissolution temperature (°C), Y: equilibrium swelling degree

the purpose of satisfying the support requirement by submitting experimental data after the filing date, wherein the data amounts to new matter that is not disclosed in the detailed description.

(2) The experimental data that have been filed by the plaintiff during the opposition procedure disclose (i) performance measurement results of polarising film obtained from PVA films of a specific set of [values for] complete salvation temperature X and a balanced degree of swelling Y; and (ii) the relationship between the polariser film performance and the set of [values for] complete salvation temperature X and a balanced degree of swelling Y for PVA films, wherein the relationship is determined based on the measurement results. Both of these have not been specifically disclosed in the detailed description, but were disclosed only after the filing date. Therefore, in light of the above-mentioned (1), [such experimental data] are not allowed to be consulted [as grounds of a sufficient description for the claimed invention] because they introduce new matter to the detailed description.

3. With respect to C (Ex post facto application of the Guidelines)

(1) Whether the wording of the claim meets the support requirement or not should be determined by the meaning of the relevant provisions of the Patent Act. The Guidelines are not a law, but merely an examination standard which has been drafted by the Patent Office for the purpose of ensuring equality and rationality in patent examination as to whether a patent application meets the patentability requirements under the Patent Act. Thus, the holding in 1 (2) is not affected by whether or not the standards set in the Guidelines are applicable to the present invention, and whether these include an interpretation of the above-mentioned provision of the Patent Act.

(2) Since the standard of the Guidelines, which was revised in October 2002, conform with the objective of sec. 36 (5) item 1 of the Patent Act before the 2002 revision (the version as of 1994), there is no contravention of the law even when the standard is retroactively applied in an ex post facto manner to a patent that was filed before the revised standard went into effect.

3. ANALYSIS

In order to determine whether the support requirement is complied with, the Examination Guidelines for Patents and Utility Models compare the claimed invention with the detailed description. In the following cases, the Examination Guidelines regard the support requirement as not complied with:[4]

The following (1) to (4) are types of cases in which the statements in the claims do not satisfy the support requirement.

(1) No statement or implication of claimed elements in the description:
(2) Unclear correspondence between the claimed invention and the statement in the description due to inconsistent use of terms therein
(3) Over-expanded or over-generalised invention claimed
(4) No recitation of elements necessary for the solution of the problem to be solved specified in the description

Prior to the above *Polarizing Film* case, there were some case laws on the support requirement. However, these cases did not clearly distinguish between the enablement requirement and the support requirement. There are few cases where these were considered as separate requirements of patentability.[5]

---

4. The Examination Guideline of the JPO, Part II, Chapter 2, Section 2, at the website of the JPO at <https://www.jpo.go.jp/e/system/laws/rule/guideline/patent/tukujitu_kijun/index.html>.
5. For example, Tokyo High Court, 11 April 2002, Case No. 249 (Gyō-Ke) of 1997, the website of the courts <http://www.courts.go.jp/app/files/hanrei_jp/917/011917_hanrei.pdf>, decided that "According to the above, it is clear that the decision of the Board of Appeal that the present application does not satisfy the requirements of sec. 36(3) and (4) Patent Act [author's note: Provision in its wording between 1985 and 1987] is justified without considering the remaining points". This case did not distinguish between the enablement requirement and the support requirement. In the case of Tokyo High Court, 26 December 2003, Case No. 104 (Gyō-Ke) of 2003, the website of the courts <http://www.courts.go.jp/app/files/hanrei_jp/593/010593_hanrei.pdf>, the enablement requirement, support requirement and clarity requirement were judged together: "[I]n general, it is difficult to predict from the substance itself described as an active ingredient, whether or not it can be used for medical purposes which is the gist of the invention. Therefore, in order to prove that the invention is disclosed to the extent that a person skilled in the art can easily carry it out according to the description, it should be stated that the substance can be used for the specific medical purpose by pharmacological data or a corresponding description. Even taking into account common technical knowledge at the time of filing, a description with the detailed explanation of the invention that does not meet this goal is against the provision of sec. 36(4) [author's note: in 1985] of the revised Patent Act. In addition, on the other hand, it would be reasonable to understand that the description in the claims does not satisfy the requirements stipulated in the Article 36(5)(i) and 36(5)(ii) [author's note: in the version between 1990 and 1994] while the invention described in the scope of claims exceeds the range supported by the detailed description ..." Intellectual Property High Court, 19 October 2005, Case No. 10013 (Gyō-Ke) of 2005, the website of the courts <http://

The current decision stresses the fact that the support requirement should compare the scope of the claims with the contents of the detailed description of the invention, and consider (1) whether or not it is reasonable to assume that a person skilled in the art can recognise the technical problem to be solved by the detailed description of the invention, (2) whether or not it is reasonable to assume that a person skilled in the art can solve the technical problem without the description or suggestion based on the ordinary technical knowledge at the time of filing. This is the general guideline to determine the support requirement applicable to all types of inventions.

In addition, regarding the support requirement in relation to a parameter invention, the court decided that it is necessary that (a) the detailed description of the invention should be explanatory to the extent that a person skilled in the art can understand the technical relationship between the range indicated by the parameter formula and the effect obtained, or that (b) by referring to the ordinary technical knowledge at the time of filing, specific examples should be described to the extent that a person skilled in the art could reasonably believe it possible to obtain the desired effect (performance) within the range indicated by the parameter formula.

On the other hand, interpreting the provision of sec. 36(6)(i) Japanese Patent Act, the *Flibanserin* case[6] stated that the support requirement and the enablement requirement should be distinguished and the support requirement, in principle, should be more formally examined.[7]

In subsequent cases of the Intellectual Property High Court dealing with the support requirement after the *Polarizing Film* case decision, the approach of this case was adopted for almost all technical fields. For example, the *Coated Hard Member* case[8] held that it should be clear for a person skilled in the art that causal relationships or mechanisms which could solve the technical problem were disclosed in the description if the embodiments did cover the whole range of the claims. In the *Lead-Free Solder Alloy* case[9] it was held that after determining the characteristic

---

www.courts.go.jp/app/files/hanrei_jp/324/009324_hanrei.pdf>, decided that "it is important for the description requirement of sec. 36(6)(i) of the Patent Act to determine that the detailed description of the invention supports the scope of the claims, and this and the requirement of a description regarding the earlier version of sec. 36(4), now sec. 36(6)(i), are in both concurrently applicable." Considering both the enablement requirement (sec. 36(4) of the old Patent Act) and the support requirement (sec. 36(6)(i)), the court concluded that none of them were satisfied. Note the expression "support requirement" was not used in the decision.

6. See, Case No. 9 of this book.
7. "[I]t is sufficient to determine whether the scope of the statement of the scope of claims exceeds that of the statement of the detailed explanation of the invention by comparing the former with the latter by a necessary and purposeful interpretation method. It should be said that it is not permitted to interpret and determine compliance with the requirement under said item by a method that is totally the same as that of determining compliance with the requirement under sec. 36 (4) (i) unless there are special circumstances, such as where it significantly goes against the purpose of the patent system not to interpret the "detailed explanation of the invention" by a method as above as a premise for determining sec. 36(6)(i) of the Act because the scope of claims is stated in a unique form."
8. IP High Court, 12 June 2008, Case No. 10308 (Gyō-Ke) of 2007, the website of the courts <http://www.courts.go.jp/app/files/hanrei_jp/439/036439_hanrei.pdf> – *Coated Hard Member*.
9. IP High Court, 29 September 2009, Case No. 10484 (Gyō-Ke) of 2008, the website of the courts <http://www.courts.go.jp/app/files/hanrei_jp/026/038026_hanrei.pdf> – *Lead-Free Solder Alloy*.

part of the invention, it was not necessary to back the invention up with concrete measurement results in the case that the numerical limitations were merely indicative of the desirable numerical range. Also in recent years, the *Polarizing Film* approach was cited in the cases *Composition Containing a Black Ginger Extract*[10] and *Tomato-Containing Beverage.*[11] Thus, while a groundbreaking decision on the support requirement, it will need further case regarding the level and detail that is required in order to claim extensions or generalisations of what has been disclosed in the detailed description, or to what extent a person skilled in the art can carry out the invention as defined in the scope of claims based on the description.

4. COMPARATIVE REMARKS

There are concepts corresponding to the support requirement also in the Europe and the US. The **EPC** has a support requirement stipulated in Article 84[12] and additional guidance for the support requirement is stipulated in "Guidelines for Examination" of the European Patent Office.[13] In the **United States** the "Written Description Requirement" is based on the provisions of 35 U.S.C. sec. 112(a)[14] and MPEP 2163.[15] This requires a written description, enablement and the indication of the best mode

10. IP High Court, 22 February 2017, Case No. 10231 (Gyō-Ke) of 2015, the website of the courts <https://www.jpo.go.jp/e/system/laws/rule/guideline/patent/tukujitu_kijun/index.html> – *Composition Containing a Black Ginger Extract.*
11. IP High Court, 8 June 2017, Case No. 10147 (Gyō-Ke) of 2016, 2364 Hanrei Jihō 63 – *Tomato Drink and Production Method thereof, and Acidity Reduction Method for the Tomato Drink.*
12. *EPC Article 84 Claims* – The claims shall define the matter for which protection is sought. They shall be clear and concise and be supported by the description. The distinction between sufficiency of disclosure and clarity (Art. 83 EPC) is important under the EPC because clarity is not a ground of opposition. In practice, a lack of sufficient disclosure is difficult to prove unless the description lacks indispensable parameters or is so contradictory that even a skilled person with a mind willing to understand cannot make sense of the teaching. In all other cases, case law requires serious doubts, substantiated by verifiable facts, in order to attack sufficiency: decision **T 19/90** of 3 October 1990, OJ EPO 1990, 476 – *Onco Mouse*; it is generally sufficient if the description teaches one way to carry out the invention, and that the invention can be carried out essentially (though not necessarily completely) over the whole range claimed: Decision **T 1727/12** of 1 February 2016. Art. 84 EPC also encompasses the support requirement.
13. Guidelines for Examination in the EPO, Part F – Chapter IV, 6.
14. 35 U.S. Code § 112 – "*Specification*

    (a) In General. – The specification shall contain a written description of the invention, and of the manner and process of making and using it, in such full, clear, concise, and exact terms as to enable any person skilled in the art to which it pertains, or with which it is most nearly connected, to make and use the same, and shall set forth the best mode contemplated by the inventor or joint inventor of carrying out the invention."
15. Manual of Patent Examining Procedure (MPEP), Ninth Edition, Revision 08.2017, Last Revised January 2018. 2163 Guidelines for the Examination of Patent Applications Under the 35 U.S.C. sec. 112(a) or Pre-AIA 35 U.S.C. sec. 112, first paragraph, "Written Description" Requirement [R-08.2017]

how to carry out the invention.[16] [17] In **Germany**, the enablement requirement can be found in section 34(4)[18] of German Patent Act as description requirement. There is no explicit clarity requirement. As the support requirement in the German Patent Act might be considered to require a disclosure "in a way sufficiently clear and complete" for the invention to be carried out, and thus encompass each of clarity, enablement and support.[19]

16. As in other jurisdictions, also the requirement that the claims must be supported by the description over the whole range claimed forms part of this concept: US Supreme Court, *The Incandescent Lamp*, 159 US 465 (1895).
17. The best mode requirement that is unique to US law was particularly problematic for foreign applicants to the extent that they had not disclosed the best mode of carrying out the invention in the priority application (as they did not have to in the country of first filing).The American Invents Act in a reformulation of § 282 makes non-compliance with the best mode requirement no longer a ground for invalidation.
18. *German Patent Act Section 34(4)* – An application shall disclose the invention in a manner sufficiently clear and complete for it to be carried out by a person skilled in the art.
19. MES, Patentgesetz *(German Patent Act)*, 4th ed. 2015, § 34 notes 63 and 74. According to German Federal Supreme Court, 25 February 2010, GRUR 2010, 414 – *Thermoplastische Zusammensetzung*, the support requirement is not complied with once the claims contain too broad or too general indications and thereby exceed the contribution to the state of the art as taught by the description. Insufficient disclosure can be affirmed where the person skilled in the art can arrive at the claimed solution only by trial and error: German Federal Patent Court, 23 October 2010, GRUR 2011, 905 – *Buprenorphinpflaster*.

Case No. 11

Industrial Application – Medical Treatment

Ryōta Shitamichi

The Patent Act must be interpreted so as not to allow the patenting of methods of medical treatment.

Tokyo High Court, 11 April 2002, Case No. 65 (Gyo-Ke) of 2000 – *Method and Apparatus for Optically Displaying Repeatable Surgery*

Surgical Navigation Technologies v. Japanese Patent Office

---

1. BACKGROUND

The Japanese Patent Act, like other many jurisdictions,[1] stipulates "industrial applicability" as one requirement of patentability. Sec. 29(1) Patent Act requires the following condition for patentability:

> **Sec. 29 Conditions of Patentability**
>
> (1) An inventor of an invention that is industrially applicable may be entitled to obtain a patent for said invention, except for one the following cases:
>
> (i) inventions that were publicly known in Japan or a foreign country, prior to the filing of the patent application;
> (ii) inventions that were publicly worked in Japan or a foreign country, prior to the filing of the patent application; or
> (iii) inventions that were described in a distributed publication, or inventions that were made publicly available through an electric telecommunication line in Japan or a foreign country, prior to the filing of the patent application.

Since Japanese courts and the Patent Office (JPO) have interpreted "industrial applicability" with a broad meaning, there are not so many cases where this requirement is at issue. Among these cases, "medical treatments" form a significant category.

If medical treatments were patentable without any exception, patentees could exert their exclusive rights over activities in the area of medicine. The major problem here is related to "humanity" or "ethics". It would certainly be problematic for doctors to be forced to give up using some effective medical treatment because of patent rights.

---

1. See Article 52(1) of the European Patent Convention (EPC).

Medical treatments are, for this reason, excluded from patentability, or, if patented, their scope of protection is restricted in many jurisdictions. In Japan, this issue is discussed in the context of "industrial applicability". One old court ruling of 1970 held that one invention for a process concerning a toothbrush was not patentable because it required a human body as an "essential component".[2]

However, the traditional approach of regarding medical treatment inventions as lacking "industrial applicability" has been exposed to criticism.[3] Meanwhile, the Tokyo High Court, while maintaining this traditional idea in conclusion, could also see some merit in the opposing view and suggested that the issue should be solved by legislation. Yet even more than one decade after the decision, no legislation has been enacted or is planned.

2. DECISION[4]

a) Facts

1. Procedures before Japanese Patent Office

Georg Schlöndorf on 21 May 1988 filed an international application with the title "Method and Apparatus for Optically Displaying a Repeatable Surgical Operation" with a priority claim based on a German patent application dated 27 May 1987. The JPO notified the applicant on 5 August 1998 of the decision to reject the application. Mr. Schlöndorf on 24 November 1998 filed an appeal, case as No. H11-18303. Mr. Schlöndorf on 9 March 1999 transferred the right to the plaintiff, and the plaintiff had the change registered. The JPO after dealing with the appeal decided on 8 October 1999 to reject the appeal because the invention at issue was a "human diagnostic method" i.e. a "medical treatment" which did not belong to the field of "industry" under sec. 29 (1) Patent Act. The decision of the JPO dated 25 October 1999 was notified to the plaintiff. The plaintiff appealed.

b) Reasons

1. Whether or not a "Human diagnostic method" (medical treatment) belongs to the field of "industry"

(1) Sec. 1 Patent Act provides that "the purpose of this Act is to promote inventions and to contribute to industry through the protection and utilisation of inventions", and sec. 29(1) Patent Act stipulates that "who makes an invention that is industrially applicable may be entitled to obtain a patent for said invention, except for one the following cases:..."

---

2. Tokyo High Court, 22 December1970, Case No. 158 (Gyo-Ke) of 1968, 260 Hanrei Times 334.
3. H. Aizawa, Baiotekunōrojī to Tokkyohō (*Biotechnology and Patent Act*), 1994, 78; N. Koizumi, Chiryō Hōhō Hatsumei Hogo no Hōseisaku (*Legal policy on protection of medical treatment invention*), 1227 Jurist 45 (2002); N. Nakayama, Tokkyohō (*Patent Law*), 3rd ed., 2016, 117.
4. Published in 1828 Hanrei Jihō 99 = N. Nakayama et al. (eds.), Tokkyo Hanrei Hyakusen *(Hundred Selected Patent Cases)*, 4th ed. 2012, 18 = T. Ōbuchi et al. (eds.) Chitekizaisan hō hanrei shū (Intellectual Property Law Case Book), 2nd ed. 2015, 11.

If we follow the general meaning of the wording, "industry" means "the work of production, i.e. economic activity which adds the power of man to things of nature and creates the value of utility, and for the enhancement thereof, or which changes the form of things or transfers them: Agriculture, stockbreeding, forestry, fishery, mining, industrial activity, commerce and trade etc."(Kōjien 4th ed.) But, as mentioned above, given that the purpose of the PA is to promote inventions and to contribute to industry, as a rule, there is no first hand reason to interpret "industry" narrowly. The defendant agrees with this point.

The Japanese patent system for a long time has clearly excluded medicines or methods of preparation of medicines as patentable subject matter in addition to food and drink, and under this situation it appeared that this provision expressed the idea that technologies of medical treatment, which are deeply involved with human life or dignity, and the technology which is closely related thereto, were excluded from patent protection. But the law amendment No. 46 of 1975 deleted as unpatentable subject matter medicines, methods of preparation of medicines, food and drink, and clarified that such subject matter was patentable (see sec. 32 Patent Act before and after the law amendment of 1975).

Under such circumstances, the technology related to medicines or medical instruments is clearly understood as an "invention which can be utilised in industry".

There is the argument, as a main basis to deny the patentability of a medical treatment, that the medical treatment is deeply involved with human life or dignity, and should be generally available to all mankind instead of being protected by patents. But such argument is not always particularly convincing. It is clear that a medical treatment is deeply involved with human life or dignity, but it is also reasonable to think that matters which are deeply involved with human life or dignity are not limited to medical treatment, and there exist many such things within the scope of patentable subject matter. Technologies that are so important that they are deeply involved with human life or dignity and should be generally accessible to all mankind should be promoted through patent protection, and such patent protection in the end might contribute more to the public welfare of the human being and be thus in accordance with the purpose of the patent system. At least it would be inconsistent to declare medicines or medical instruments patentable, but medical treatment not.

At present, medical treatment, especially advanced medical treatment greatly depends on medicines or medical instruments, so under this aspect it is difficult to deny that the choice of a medical treatment is in fact dominated by patents, namely for medicines or medical instruments even if the medical treatment as such is unpatentable. Under these circumstances, it is reasonable to ask the question what meaning it should have that only the medical treatment is unpatentable when certain types of the medical treatment strongly depend on specific medicines. Also, how medical treatments can be promoted in case that only medicines and medical instruments are patentable while medical treatments as such not.

Considering the above, the position that after allowing the patenting of technologies related to medicines or medical instruments, not only technologies related to medicines or medical instruments but also medical treatments as such should be patentable as an "invention which can be utilised in the industry", and that there would be no reasons to exclude it from patentability is a legal interpretation that is not without merit.

(2) But in regard of patentability, there is an important difference between medicines/ medical instruments and medical treatment as such.

Even if medicines or medical instruments are patented, this as such does not prevent doctors from applying a medical treatment with the best of their abilities/ means (of course, the medicines or the medical instruments are the most important part thereof) at hand, and they can exercise their profession without any restriction. It is possible that the medicines or the medical instruments which doctors primarily want to use cannot be used because of patent protection with the result that they cannot obtain the medicines or medical instruments. This does not prevent doctors from exercising the best of their abilities/means at hand without any restriction at the time of the medical treatment. Doctors can thereby apply medical treatment without any concern about whether their acts are covered by a patent or not.

Regarding medical treatment, the situation is different. Under a patent system that allows medical treatment to be patentable, for doctors who apply medical treatment there exists at least conceptually a possibility that the medical treatment they apply is patented. Further, in general, whether a conduct is the object of a patent or not is not always immediately and unambiguously clear, and the courts are well aware that claims of injunctive relief etc. against acts which are later found not to infringe patents, are not infrequent. Doctors thereby might always apply a medical treatment with the concern that what they do is patented, and, if they are sued for being liable for patent infringement by engaging in such conduct, what liability they should bear. Under a patent system in which medical treatment as such is patentable, doctors must apply medical treatment under these circumstances unless measures to prevent liability are adopted.

Seen from the nature of medical treatment, a system that puts doctors in such a situation would appear unreasonable, and so it is a reasonable interpretation that the Japanese patent system does not envisage such a result. Given this, and unless appropriate measures to prevent such a result are taken, the Patent Act must be interpreted as not to allow the patenting of methods of medical treatment. When it was stipulated in the Patent Act that medicines and methods for the preparation of medicines, which were hitherto excluded from the list of patentable subject matter together with food and drink, were added to the list of patentable subject matter, for patents related to the preparation of medicines, as a measure it was explicitly provided that the effect of the patent does not cover the "dispensing by prescription of a doctor or a dentist, or a medicine dispensed by prescription of a doctor or a dentist" (sec. 69 (3) Patent Act), while regarding patents related to medical treatment, no such measures are in place.

As mentioned above sec. 1 Patent Act provides that "the purpose of this Act is to promote inventions and to contribute to industry through the protection and utilisation of inventions", and sec. 29(1) Patent Act stipulates that "who invents an invention which can be utilised in industry, other than the following inventions, can be granted a patent to the invention."

But there is no definition of what is understood by "industry" in this respect. And there is no specific provision that medical treatments are generally unpatentable. Therefore, as mentioned above, even if, in general, there should be no reason to interpret "industry" primarily narrowly, there is no interpretation other than that an invention related to medical treatment, which is unpatentable from the above reasons, is not considered an "invention which can be utilised in industry" under the Patent Act.

The argument of the plaintiff that a medical treatment as such should be patentable has a point that should be discussed by legislation, but cannot be affirmed under the current Patent Act that does not provide for any measures that would allow to affirm the patentability of medical treatments as such.

2. Whether the invention at issue is a "human diagnostic method" (medical treatment)

Claim 1 of the application reads as set out in the facts. From the description, it is clear that the invention is a medical treatment which should be unpatentable for the above reasons.

3. ANALYSIS

As the court held, the main reason for introducing some restrictions to the patentability of medical treatments are concerns of "humanity", that is, if medical treatment methods were patentable without any restriction, doctors could be forced to apply a medical treatment with the concern that what they do could be patented, and what liability they should bear if it was. Many Japanese practitioners and scholars seem to understand this point and the necessity of restricting patentability of medical treatments.[5]

One the other hand, there seems to be a growing necessity of granting patents to medical treatments for the following reasons. First, the obscurity of the border between medical devices and medical treatments in the field of cutting-edge medicine accelerated by the advancement of biotechnology. It seems not so easy to distinguish between technical ideas concerning a gene or a cell which are used in gene therapy or regenerative medicine and those concerning the entire process of these cutting-edge treatments.[6] Second, the promotion of research and development (R&D) in medical fields, which is related to the purpose of the Patent Act.[7] R&D in cutting-edge medical technology requires long time and high expenditure, and advancement in this field is mainly supported by venture companies, so it is important to enable them to return their investment by offering patent protection and thereby an incentive[8] to engage in R&D, which is in line with the purpose of the Patent Act.[9] Third, strengthening

5. S. ASAMI, Iryōkōi no Tokkyosei (*Patentability of medical treatment*), 170 Bessatsu Jurist 19 (2004); R. TAKABAYASHI, Hyōjun Tokkyohō (*Standards of Patent Law*), 5th ed., 2014, 46; N. KOIZUMI, *supra* note 3, at 41, 42.
6. S. ASAMI, Wagakuni ni Okeru Baiotekunorojī no Tokkyo Hogo no Genjō to Kadai (*Current situation and problem of patent protection for biotechnology in Japan*) 98, in: CHITEKIZAISANKENKYŪJO (*IIP*) (ed.), Baiotekunorojī no Shinpo to Tokkyo (*Progress of Biotechnology and Patents*), 2002, 89; R. HIRASHIMA, Iryō Kanren Kōi Hatsumei to Sangyōjō no Riyō Kanōsei (*Medicine related act and industrial applicability*), 1246 Jurist 251 (2003).
7. Sec. 1 of the Patent Act
8. There is an intensive debate on the "incentive theory" of the patent system.
9. K. TAKEDA, Tokkyo no Chishiki (*Knowledge of patents*), 7th ed., 2004, 114; N. ONO, Better Than Nothing: Japan's Next Move on Patentability of Medical Methods, 37 IIC 206 (2006); N. KOIZUMI, *supra* note 3, at 45; N, NAKAYAMA, *supra* note 3, at 118; S. ASAMI, *supra* note 5, at 19; S. ASAMI, *supra* note 6, at 98; R. HIRASHIMA, *supra* note 6, at 251.

competitiveness of Japanese business in the medical field.[10] It is sometimes alleged that applicants can obtain patents more easily in the EU or the U.S. than in Japan,[11] although this is difficult to verify.

The issue is, therefore, how to balance the two conflicting needs derived from two rather different concepts, namely "humanity" and "industrial development", and how to reflect this difficult balance within the Japanese patent system.

The court decision above kept this balance and maintained the traditional approach that the medical treatment at issue was not patentable because of a lack of "industrial applicability". However, we must not overlook the underlying "dilemma". The court decision held that "the view that there would be no reasons to exclude medical treatments from patentability is a legal interpretation that is not without merit". "The argument of the plaintiff that the medical treatment as such should be patentable has a point that should be taken up by legislation, but cannot be affirmed under the current Patent Act that does not provide for any measures that would allow us to affirm the patentability of medical treatments as such". In other words, "industrial applicability" is a last resort to meet the needs of "humanity" under the current Patent Act which otherwise does not provide any provisions for balancing the two needs. The Act provides such a solution for the ad hoc mixture of medicines under sec. 69(3), though:

> **Sec. 69 Limitations of Patent Right**
>
> (3) A patent right for the invention of a medicine (refers to a product used for the diagnosis, therapy, treatment or prevention of human diseases, hereinafter the same shall apply in this paragraph) to be manufactured by mixing two or more medicines or for the invention of a process to manufacture a medicine by mixing two or more medicines shall not be effective against the act of preparation of a medicine as is written in a prescription from a physician or a dentist and the medicine prepared as is written in a prescription from a physician or a dentist.

A few people argue that medical treatments are not patentable because the medical field is not included in the definition of "industry" in the context of sec. 29 (1) of the Patent Act,[12] but this argument is not dominant. The reason why this argument does not enjoy much support is that the patentability of medicines or medical devices should lead to the conclusion that "industry" includes the medical field as well.[13]

Accordingly, the court ruling that medical treatments are excluded from patentability because of a lack of "industrial applicability" is, in conclusion, acceptable because it seems the only way to balance the two needs under the current Patent Act, which does not have a provision which specifically excludes medical treatments from patentability, as would be the case under Article 53(c) of the European Patent Convention (EPC),[14] nor a provision which limits the scope of protection of patents

10. N. Nakayama, *supra* note 3, at 117; R. Hirashima, *supra* note 6, at 251.
11. N. Ono, *supra* note 9, at 201.
12. K. Yoshifuji, Tokkyohō Gaisetsu (*Outline of the Patent Act*), 13th ed., 1998, 69.
13. N. Koizumi, *supra* note 3, at 43; R. Takabayashi, *supra* note 5, at 45.
14. See 4. Comparative Remarks.

rights of medical treatments under certain conditions like sec. 287(c) of the U.S. Patent Act.[15]

In order to balance the two needs, "humanity" and "industrial development" in the context of "industrial applicability", the JPO has revised its guidelines[16] several times. The current version describes the "industrial applicability" for medical treatments as follows:

3.1 List of industrially inapplicable inventions

An invention considered as any one of (i) to (iii) shown below does not comply with the industrial applicability requirements. (i) Inventions of methods of surgery, therapy or diagnosis of humans (see 3.1.1) (ii) Commercially inapplicable inventions (see 3.1.2) (iii) Obviously impracticable inventions (see 3.1.3)

3.1.1 Inventions of methods of surgery, therapy or diagnosis of humans

Methods of surgery therapy or diagnosis of humans have been termed "medical activity" and are normally practiced by medical doctors (including those who are directed by medical doctors, hereinafter referred to as "medical doctors"). A method considered as any one of (i) to (iii) shown below is considered as an "invention of methods of surgery, therapy or diagnosis of humans". (i) Methods of surgery of humans (see (1)) (ii) Methods of therapy of humans (see (2)) (iii) Methods of diagnosis of humans (see (3)) The following methods of (a) and (b) are included in "inventions of methods of surgery, therapy or diagnosis of humans". (a) Methods for contraception or delivery (b) Methods for processing samples that have been extracted from a human body (e.g., a method of dialyzing blood) or analysing the samples during the process on the presumption that the samples are to be returned to the same body for therapy (except for the methods described in 3.2.1(4)b)

Even if methods of surgery, therapy or diagnosis are practiced on animals in general, unless it is clear that the methods practiced on humans are explicitly excluded, the methods are deemed as being "inventions of methods of surgery, therapy or diagnosis of humans".

Part III Chapter 1 Eligibility for Patent and Industrial Applicability

(1) Methods of surgery of humans Methods of surgery of humans include the following: (i) Methods for surgical treatment (such as incision, excision, centesis, injection and implant) (ii) Methods of using (e.g., inserting, moving, maintaining, operating and extracting) a medical device (e.g., a catheter or an endoscope) inside the human body (excluding inside the mouth, inside the external nostril, and inside the external ear canal) (iii) Preparatory treatment for surgery (e.g., anaesthetic treatment for surgery and method of disinfecting skin before injection) Cosmetic methods having surgical operations whose purpose is not therapeutic or diagnostic are also considered methods of surgery of humans.

15. See 4. Comparative Remarks.
16. Tokkyo Jitsuyō shin'an shinsa-kijun *(Patent and Utility Model Examination Guidelines)*, available at the website of the JPO <https://www.jpo.go.jp/e/system/laws/rule/guideline/patent/tukujitu_kijun/index.html>.

(2) Methods of therapy of humans Methods of therapy of humans include the followings: (i) Methods of administrating medicine or giving physical treatment to a patient for curing or restraining a disease (ii) Methods of implanting substitute organs such as artificial internal organs or artificial limbs (iii) Methods of preventing a disease (e.g., methods of preventing tooth decay or influenza) Methods of treatment for the maintenance of physical health (e.g., methods of massage or shiatsu therapy) are also considered to be methods of preventing a disease. (iv) Preparatory treatment for therapy (e.g., method for arranging electrodes for electrical therapy) (v) Supplemental methods for improving treatment effects (e.g., rehabilitation methods) (vi) Methods for nursing associated with treatment (e.g., methods to prevent bedsores)

(3) Methods of diagnosis of humans Methods of diagnosis of humans include methods of judging for the medical purposes the physical condition of a human body as indicated in (i) or (ii) below: (i) Physical condition of a human body such as conditions of diseases and physical health or the mental condition of a human body (ii) Prescription or treatment/surgery plans based on the above (i)

Example: Methods of judging whether the patient has had a stroke by observing an image obtained by an MRI scan.

Although we should respect the great efforts of the JPO to balance the two needs by updating their guidelines, there seems a certain limit to achieve this since the wording of "industrial applicability" itself is legally too vague to draw such a concrete border line between patentable subject matter and unpatentable one. In addition, the role of balancing benefits in this field should ultimately be accomplished by legislation, not by guidelines described by an administrative agency.[17] As we saw above, the Tokyo High Court decision has stressed the necessity of legislation.[18] The framework of the Patent Act itself has not changed, despite many discussions conducted at a working group[19] which was established inside the government after the Tokyo High Court decision of 2002.

If the legislator decided to change the Patent Act by abandoning the longstanding idea of dealing with medical treatment inventions in the context of "industrial applicability", what kind of legislation could be introduced? There would be at least three answers to this question. The first answer is to introduce a provision for a special exception of medical treatments like Article 53 (c) EPC.[20] This would be comparatively close to the current practice, and may give some concerns that business cannot be given a sufficient incentive to invest in R&D of cutting-edge medical technology.[21] The second answer is to introduce a provision to restrict patent holders of medical treatments exercising their exclusive rights against doctors who use the medical treatment at issue. This solution would correspond to section 287 (c) of the U.S. Patent

17. Y. Aita & I. Hayashi, Iryōhōhō to Tokkyo (*Medical Methods and Patents*), 25 L&T 28 (2004); R. Takabayashi, *supra* note 5, at 46; S. Asami, *supra* note 6, at 96.
18. The court held: "The argument of the plaintiff that the medical treatment as such should be patentable has a point that should be discussed by legislation".
19. The details of these discussion is introduced in Aita and Hayashi's article (*supra* note 17).
20. N. Koizumi, *supra* note 3, at 45; Y. Aita & I. Hayashi, *supra* note 17, at 30.
21. N. Koizumi, *supra* note 3, at 45.

Act.[22] This solution would more advantageous for medical industry than the first because it allows to obtain patents and to exert the corresponding exclusive rights in other circumstances than in relation to a doctors' direct practice. For instance, patent holders could obtain an injunction against companies manufacturing medicines or devices used in connection with medical treatment methods, as this could constitute indirect infringement.[23] The third solution, and the most pro-patent one, would be to allow patents for methods of medical treatment and even to file a lawsuit seeking damage compensation caused by a doctors' direct practice of a medical treatment. Still, injunctive relief against a doctors' practice should not be available,[24] so that there could not be concerns that doctors are forced to stop patented treatment.

In any case, since there seems to be no imminent intention to introduce legislation to change the status quo, patent applications of this field will be examined in the context of "industrial applicability" according to the JPO Guidelines and any judicial review thereof.

4. COMPARATIVE REMARKS

TRIPs, in general, requires member countries to grant patents to applications in all areas, but leaves to members the freedom to exclude specific subject matter including methods of medical treatment from patentability:

> **Article 27 Patentable Subject Matter**
>
> 1. Subject to the provisions of paragraphs 2 and 3, patents shall be available for any inventions, whether products or processes, in all fields of technology, provided that they are new, involve an inventive step and are capable of industrial application. Subject to paragraph 4 of Article 65, paragraph 8 of Article 70 and paragraph 3 of this Article, patents shall be available and patent rights enjoyable without discrimination as to the place of invention, the field of technology and whether products are imported or locally produced.
>
> 3. Members may also exclude from patentability:
>
> (a) diagnostic, therapeutic and surgical methods for the treatment of humans or animals;

The **EPC** 1973 in Article 52(4) explicitly stipulated that methods of medical treatment were not deemed inventions with industrial applicability, but by the amendment of 2000, one of whose purposes was to keep consistency with the TRIPs provisions, this exception was modified as an independent exception without reference to "industrial applicability":

> **Article 53 Exceptions to patentability**
>
> European patents shall not be granted in respect of:

22. N. Koizumi, *supra* note 3, at 46; N. Nakayama, *supra* note 3, at 119; S. Asami, *supra* note 6, at 97, K. Takeda, *supra* note 9, at 114; Y. Aita & I. Hayashi, *supra* note 17, at 30.
23. Sec. 101 of the Patent Act
24. N. Koizumi, *supra* note 3, at 46.

(c) methods for treatment of the human or animal body by surgery or therapy and diagnostic methods practiced on the human or animal body; this provision shall not apply to products, in particular substances or compositions, for use in any of these methods.

There exists a relatively complicated body of case law related to this exception that in effect covers three different methods: Diagnostic methods,[25] surgery[26] or therapy.[27]

The **US** is almost the sole country which does not distinguish between methods of medical treatment and other technologies at the stage of patentability. Instead, the U.S. Patent Act since 1996 has a provision which restricts the scope of protection for medical treatment patents which has been introduced after one case where a patent holder with a patent concerning a method for surgery filed a lawsuit against a doctor.[28] The provision reads as follows:

Section 287 Limitation on damages and other remedies; marking and notice.

(c)(2) For the purposes of this subsection:

(A) the term "medical activity" means the performance of a medical or surgical procedure on a body, but shall not include (i) the use of a patented machine, manufacture, or composition of matter in violation of such patent, (ii) the practice of a patented use of a composition of matter in violation of such patent, or (iii) the practice of a process in violation of a biotechnology patent.

As discussed above, the current Japanese practice is similar to the previous EPC framework in that medical treatment methods were excluded from patentability because of lack of "industrial applicability", although the Japanese Patent Act does not have an explicit exception for medical treatment methods like the previous version of the EPC. Among the possible three legislative solutions as explained above, the first one would be similar to the current EPC framework and the second one would be similar to the U.S. framework.

---

25. According to the EPO decision **G 1/04** of 16 December 2005 (OJ EPO 2006, 334) to be interpreted narrowly as including the following features: "The diagnosis for curative purposes stricto sensu representing the deductive medical or veterinary decision phase as a purely intellectual exercise; the preceding steps which are constitutive for making that diagnosis, and the specific interactions with the human or animal body which occur when carrying those out among theses preceding steps which are of a technical nature."
26. According to the EPO decision **G 1/07** of 15 February 2015 (OJ 2011, 134) to include all kinds of interventions that form the core activities of a medical doctor and for which doctors have been specifically trained and take responsibility.
27. Therapy covers prophylactic as well as curative treatments (with the exception of purely cosmetic ones) on the human or animal body. It is sufficient that one feature of the claim relates to such activity EPO decision **G 1/08** of 9 December 2010 (OJ EPO 2010, 456).
28. Consent Order in *Pallin v. Singer*, 28 March 1996 36 USPQ 2d 1050 (District Court of Vermont 1996). See also: K. STRANDBURG, Legal but unacceptable: Pallin v. Singer and physician patenting norms, NYU School of Law working papers 12-2014, at the website of the NELLCO Legal Scholarship Repository <https://lsr.nellco.org/cgi/viewcontent.cgi?referer=https://duckduckgo.com/&httpsredir=1&article=1405&context=nyu_lewp>.

Case No. 12

Priority – Added Subject Matter

Kazuo Shibata

Whether or not the invention of a later application is within the technical scope disclosed in the priority application should be decided not by simply comparing the wording of the claims of the later application with the wording of the priority application, but by comparing the essence of the claimed invention of the later application with the technical matter disclosed in the priority application. Even in the case where the wording of the claims of the later application is the same as in the priority application, priority for an added embodiment that affects the essence of the claimed invention, may not be acknowledged.

Tokyo High Court, 8 October 2003,
Case No. 539 (Gyō-Ke) of 2002 – *Artificial Nipple*

Pigeon v. Japanese Patent Office

---

1. BACKGROUND

Sec. 41(2) Patent Act[1] stipulates the effect of the internal priority right in almost same manner as Article 89 EPC. Namely that a filing date is retroactively moved back to the priority date for the purposes of substantive examination.[2] Yet this is questionable where a subsequent application claims internal priority in which all features of the claim (independent claim) of the subsequent application are disclosed in the priority application in terms of wording, but new subject matter in the form of an additional embodiment has been added to the description of the patent application. Such addition used to be called a "complementing embodiment for which priority is claimed" in

---

1. Sec. 41(3) Patent Act stipulates the prior art effect of the priority application which shall be deemed withdrawn when the subsequent application is filed. Some scholars believe that the priority effect in sec. 41(2) and the prior art effect in sec. 41(3) should be determined independently. To this point, see, K. SHIBATA, Kokunai yūsenken seido ni tsuite no ichikousatsu *(A consideration on internal priority system)*, 34 Nihon Kōgyō Shoyūken Hōgakkai Nenpō, 292 (2010); see also K. MATSUDA, Tokkyohō 41 jyō no Kaishyaku jyō no kadai ni tsuite *(Problem of interpretation of sec. 41 Patent Act)*, 52-5 AIPPI Journal of the Japanese Group (Japanese edition) 297 (2007).
2. The Japanese Patent Act does not contain any provisions that independently stipulate the effect of the priority right under the Paris Convention. Therefore, the provisions of the Convention are directly applied to individual international priority applications.

Japanese patent practice. There are two schools of thought concerning the effects of the priority right in such case: (1) Since the claim includes an embodiment that was not disclosed in the priority application, the subsequent application contains added subject matter and the effect of the priority claim is denied; (2) Since the wording of the claim itself can be derived from the priority application although the claim covers additional embodiments, the patent application does not contain added subject matter in the claim, and the effect of the priority claim is acknowledged.

2. DECISION[3]

a) Facts

1. Procedure before the JPO

On 8 October 1999, the plaintiff filed the patent application at issue with the title "Artificial Nipple" (application No. H11-288535, subsequently referred to as "the later application"), claiming priority under sec. 41 Patent Act based on the Japanese patent application dated 20 October 1998 (application No. H10-316899, subsequently referred to as "the priority application"). The later application was rejected by the examining division of the Japanese Patent Office (JPO) on 12 October 2001. The plaintiff appealed against this refusal, and the JPO Board of Appeal rejected the appeal on 12 September 2002 because the later application had added subject matter in the claims, could therefore not rely on the priority application and was not novel over another application.

2. Claims and descriptions in the patent applications

(1) In the priority application:

> [Claim 1] An artificial nipple which comprises a nipple body part and a papilla part which stands out from the nipple body part, wherein at least a part of said papilla part and/or said nipple body part having an extensible part.
>
> [Claim 2] Artificial nipple according to claim 1, wherein a rigid part adjacent to said extensible part is provided.
>
> [Claim 3] Artificial nipple according to claim 2, wherein said extensible part and said rigid part are arranged alternately.
>
> [Claim 4] Artificial nipple according to claim 2 or 3, wherein said artificial nipple consists of silicone rubber, and thickness of the silicone rubber is comparatively thin in said extensible part and comparatively thick in said rigid part.

(2) In the later application after an amendment of 7 August 2001:

> [Claim 1] An artificial nipple which comprises a papilla part having a front end part that can abut on a suckling cavity of an infant, and the papilla part and a

3. Published in the website of the courts <http://www.courts.go.jp/app/files/hanrei_jp/799/010799_hanrei.pdf>

nipple body part having a surface which that can make a tongue move so as to wave when the infant performs peristaltic movement by the tongue, and a base part for being connected with a nursing bottle, characterised in that on the inside of the surface wall of said head part and said body part, wherein an extensible part thinner than a wall surface formed of silicon rubber, of the papilla part and the nipple body part is formed inside the wall surface, and wherein a rigid part thicker than the extensible part is alternately formed adjacently to the extensible part. (subsequently referred to as "the invention 1")

[The explanation of the 4th embodiment (additional embodiment)]

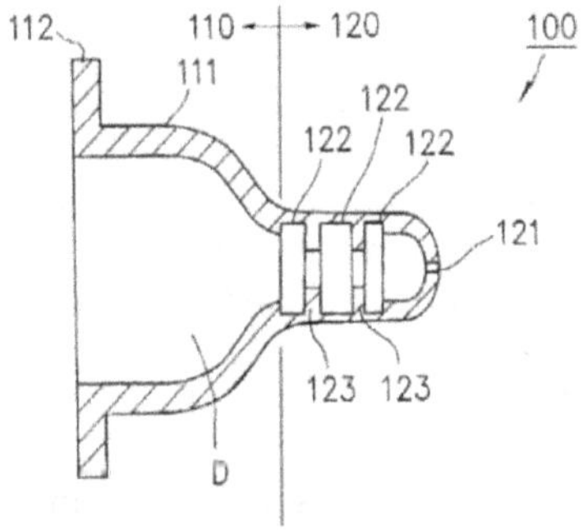

Fig. 1. The first embodiment

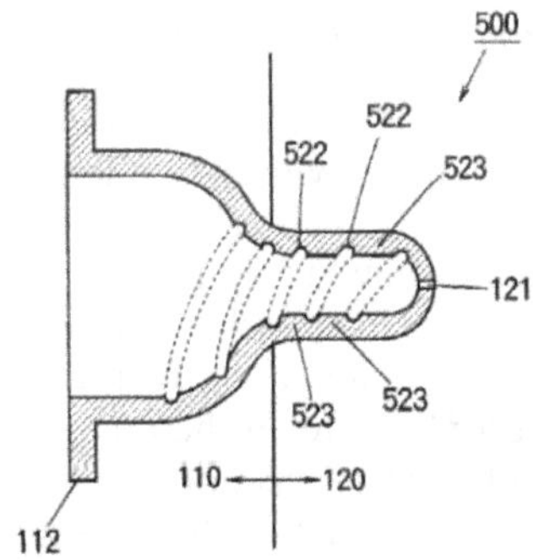

Fig. 11. The fourth embodiment

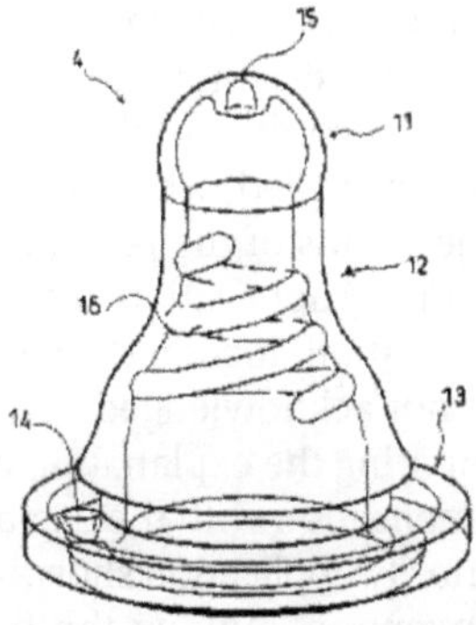

Another intervening application

In Fig. 11, the artificial nipple 500 has the nipple body part 110, the papilla part 120, and the flange part 112, similar to the above-mentioned first embodiment. However, this embodiment is different from the first embodiment in such a point that a thin part 522 that is the extensible part is formed in a spiral shape over the papilla part 120 and the nipple body part 110 of the artificial nipple 500, as shown in Fig. 11. In this way, by forming the thin part 522 in a spiral shape, the artificial nipple 500 becomes more stretched by the sucking movement of the infant 200. Further, at this sucking movement, even when a pressure is added in a lengthwise direction of Fig. 11, a thick part 523 that is the rigid part is always arranged at a position corresponding to the thin part 522 in a lengthwise direction of the artificial nipple 500. Therefore, the artificial nipple 500 is prevented from being flattened, and the sucking movement of the infant 200 is not made difficult. In addition, in this embodiment, because the thin part 522 is formed in a spiral shape as shown in Fig. 11, the artificial nipple 500 formed of silicon rubber is easily removed from a mould at the manufacture, and the manufacture is facilitated.

b) Reasons

1. The applicability of sec. 41(2) PA

(1) Regarding the effect of an internal priority on the applicability of sec. 29bis PA, sec. 41(2) PA provides the following: "Regarding the applicability of sec. 29bis PA to the invention disclosed in the description or figures originally attached to the earlier application on which the priority claim is based, the later application shall be deemed to have been filed at the time when the earlier application was filed." Within these limits, the filing date of the invention in the later application which is disclosed in the description etc. of the priority application, retroactively becomes the filing date of the priority application.

Whether or not the invention of the later application is within a range of matter disclosed in the priority application as filed should be decided not by simply comparing the wording of the claims of the later application with the wording of the description etc. of the priority application as filed, but by comparing the technical matter that is the essence of the invention described in the claims of the later application with the technical matter described in the priority application as filed. Therefore, even in a case where the wording of the claims of the later application is described in the priority application as filed, where subject matter that is the essence of the invention described in the claims of the later application extends beyond the subject matter described in the priority application as filed by including subject matter not described in the priority application, it should be considered that the priority for the part that extends beyond is not acknowledged.

(2) In this case, when comparing the explanation concerning the invention 1 in the description etc. of the later application with the explanation of the description etc. of the priority application, the priority application shows only figure 1 as "embodiment of the artificial nipple of the invention" among the figures, and it is clear that in the later application the embodiment of the figure 11 has been added as "the 4th embodiment of the artificial nipple of the invention," which is not disclosed in the priority application, and the explanation concerning figure 11 has also been added to the description of the later application. As an embodiment of the invention of the priority application, only the ring-shaped extensible part of the artificial nipple was shown in figure 1 of the drawings of the priority application.

In consideration of the description of the later application, it can be affirmed that the artificial nipple of the embodiment of the figure 11 is technical subject matter essential to the invention 1 of the later application, and this corresponds to the embodiment of the invention 1. It also can be affirmed that the artificial nipple of the embodiment of the figure 11 forms a spiral thinner part as an extensible part so that thereby the following characteristic effect of the spiral shape is achieved: the artificial nipple can extend more easily in case of a suckling movement, and even if pressure in a lengthwise direction is applied at the time of the suckling movement, a collapse of the artificial nipple - which makes a suckling movement of an infant difficult - does not occur, the pulling out from the mould during manufacturing becomes easier, and thereby the manufacture is facilitated.

So the artificial nipple of the embodiment of the figure 11 of the later application, in which the thinner part as an extensible part is spirally shaped, is not disclosed in the priority application and in addition achieves the characteristic effect of the spiral shape different from the effect achieved by the embodiment of figure 1 of the priority application, which is actually disclosed in the priority application, and of which the thinner part as an extensible part is ring-shaped.

Accordingly, it is obvious that the technical matter that is the essence of the invention described in the claims of the later application extends beyond the range of the technical matter described in the originally attached description etc. of the priority application by adding the embodiment of the artificial nipple in which the thinner part that is the extensible part is formed in a spiral shape (the embodiment of Fig. 11) to the description of the later application, and therefore, it should be considered that the priority is not acknowledged with respect to the part that is extends beyond.

3. ANALYSIS

The plaintiff argued that acknowledging a right of priority should be examined in the same manner as permitting amendments of claims and explained that in the present case the independent claim was disclosed in an enabling manner in the priority application and did not extend beyond the technical matter disclosed in the description etc. of the priority application. Furthermore, the plaintiff asserted that with regard to "the complementing embodiment for which priority is claimed," in a case where an invention related to claims of the priority application is sufficiently supported by the embodiment(s) of the priority application, even when an embodiment of substantially the same invention is added in the later application, the priority for the claim is not affected by this added embodiment.

When comparing claim 1 of the later application with claims 1-4 of the priority application, it was clear that the special technical feature of the claim 1 of the later application, the alternate arrangement of the extensible part and the rigid part, can be derived from the content of the priority application. However, the claims had changed many times during the examination procedure. There had been claims explicitly describing the spirally shaped arrangement as the special technical feature. At the beginning, only a dependent claim described the spirally shaped arrangement, and after the first notice of reasons for refusal the amended independent claim also described this arrangement. The purpose was to overcome the refusal based on lack of inventive step. The examiner sent the second notice of reasons for refusal because he found an intervening application directed to a spirally shaped artificial nipple. Responding to the second notice, the claims had been amended in order not to describe the spirally shaped arrangement while leaving the embodiment concerning the spirally shaped arrangement remained in the description. During the appeal procedure, the administrative judges urged the plaintiff to delete the embodiment, but the plaintiff argued that the claimed invention was patentable even if the embodiment concerning the spirally shaped arrangement remained in the description.

The Tokyo High Court held that the priority for the added subject matter portion should not be acknowledged because the claim included an embodiment that could not be derived from the content of the priority application. It is clear that the additional embodiment increased the support for the claim, but it is doubtful whether the embodiment broadened the claim. Furthermore, the claim seemed to be sufficiently supported by the examples contained in the priority application. Some criticism has been voiced against this decision.[4] For example, Professor Maeda writes as follows:

> "Because of its definition, the basic invention includes potentially many improvement inventions in the scope of the right, and this case was one of them and became visible by chance. Therefore, even if an improved invention is added, the invention to which the claim was directed was the invention described in the priority application and it can be said that the invention was supported by the description. It is difficult to justify the conclusion of this decision unless the improved invention fundamentally rewrites the functions and effects of the basic invention."[5]

Actually, there is another court decision that took an approach which looks different from the *Artificial Nipple* decision. In the *Rotary Clamp* case, the IP High Court held as follows:

> "In this case, the present inventions 1 and 2 fail to specify the inclination angle for the guide groove, but the present invention 3 specifies the invention with regard to the inclination angle, "the inclination angle is set at a range of 10 to 30 degrees," which was not disclosed in the description (including figures) of the first to third priority applications. Under these circumstances, the present inventions 1 and 2 are not deemed to encompass the above subject matter of the present invention 3. The rationale here would be even clearer if a case is assumed where, for example, claim 3 (the present invention 3) is deleted from the claims. Therefore, in view of the claims of the present inventions 1 and 2 (Claims 1 and 2), there is no way of denying that the patent application was filed based on these inventions described in the description or figures originally attached to "the earlier application as set forth in sec. 41(1) of the former Patent Act" and accordingly the plaintiff can enjoy the effect of the priority claim."[6]

The IP High Court seemed to have judged that the priority for the independent claim (Claim 1) is acknowledged because the wording of the independent claim itself can be derived from the content of the priority application. One question arises whether

4. T. MAEDA, Meisaisho no kaiji ga tokkyohō no nakade hatashiteiru yakuwari ni tsuite *(On the role that the disclosure of the description plays in the Patent Act)*, 66-3 Patent 150 (2013); see also S. KOBAYASHI, Jisshitaiyō wo meisaisho ni tsuikashita kokunai yūsenken shuchō shutsugan niokeru yūsenken no kōka ga mitomerareru hatsumei *(The invention whose priority is acknowledged in a case where an embodiment was added in the description of the later application)*, 63-9 Patent 86 (2010).
5. Ibid, T. MAEDA, at 159.
6. IP High Court, 29 February 2012, Case No. 10127 (Gyō-Ke) of 2011, the website of the courts <http://www.courts.go.jp/app/files/hanrei_jp/044/082044_hanrei.pdf> – *Rotary Clamp*

the theory of the *Rotary Clamp* court was different from the *Artificial Nipple* court, but these cases seem to treat different incidents. First, in the *Rotary Clamp* case the feature of the inclination angle was an add-on feature, but in the *Artificial Nipple* case the feature such as spiral shape was definitely an alternative feature to the ring-shape. Second, in the *Rotary Clamp* case, the dependent claim was corresponding to the additional embodiment. On the other hand, in the *Artificial Nipple* case there was no dependent claim corresponding to the additional embodiment when the appeal was raised.

It seems natural to distinguish between the priority of the independent claim and the priority of the dependent claims when there are dependent claims corresponding to the additional embodiments. Furthermore, if there is no claim corresponding to the additional embodiment, it seems natural to assume that the priority for the independent claim is acknowledged. However, the plaintiff in the *Artificial Nipple* case asserted that he amended the claims so as to restrict the invention described in the priority application, while asserting that the additional embodiment was well supported by the original embodiments. The acceptance of said assertion by the plaintiff would allow the later application to antedate the intervening application concerning the spirally shaped nipple. Thinking that way, the decision of the *Artificial Nipple* court seems to be quite reasonable.

This matter is quite difficult also in Europe. For example, even if a dependent claim in the later application was considered added subject matter, it was not clear whether the effect of a priority claim for the independent claim would be acknowledged or not, see the following decision of the UK High Court:

> "Counsel for Nestec submitted that, even if that was so, the only consequence was that claim 5 was not entitled to priority. He argued that claim 1 would still be entitled to priority, since although claim 1 covered arrangements in which the stop means retained the capsule in an inclined manner relative to the axis of the capsule in the extraction position, they were not disclosed by claim 1. I do not accept this argument. Such arrangements are expressly disclosed in the specification, and the skilled reader would appreciate that claim 1 included them. Thus the invention of claim 1 is not entitled to priority for such arrangements. Counsel for Nestec did not argue that claim 1 was entitled to partial priority in these circumstances. In any event, I do not consider that such arrangements are clearly defined alternatives of the other arrangements covered by claim 1."[7]

In the above case, adding a dependent claim resulted in the loss of priority for the independent claim as well. The same theory can be found in the decision of an EPO technical board.[8] However, this decision was made under the doctrine of toxic priority or poisonous divisionals. In those days, accepting multiple and partial priorities was discussed in the context of the "gold standard" disclosure test. Yet the decision **G 1/15**[9] clarified the conditions for recognising partial priorities for the generic "OR" claim and also made clear that accepting multiple and partial priorities is not the same as

7. UK Patents Court, *Nestec SA & Ors v. Dualit Ltd & Ors* [2013] EWHC 923 (Pat); [2013] RPC 32.
8. European Patent Office decision **T 1496/11** of 12 September 2012.
9. European Patent Office decision **G 1/15** of 29 November 2016.

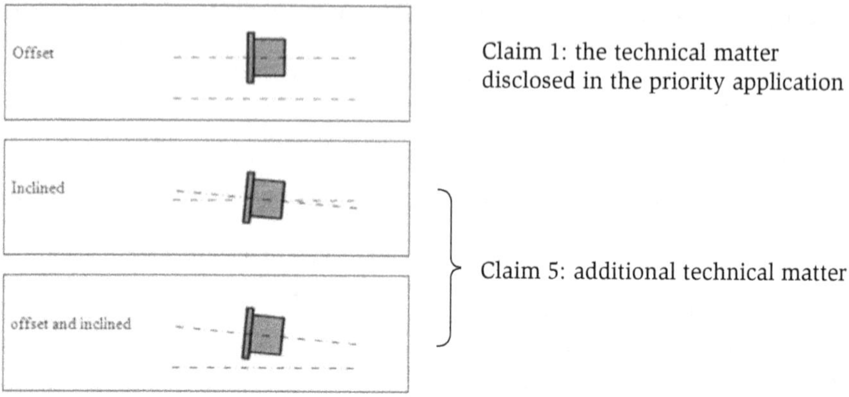

allowing amended claims. Therefore, the theory in which adding a dependent claim results in the loss of priority for the independent claim seems to have been rejected.

Returning to the *Artificial Nipple* decision, it is questionable whether the claim is a generic "OR"-claim. If the claim of the priority application had the expression "ring-shaped extensible parts and ring-shaped stiffness parts are arranged alternately," it would have been possible to hold that the claim of the later application is a generic "OR"-claim. However, the claim of the priority application just contained the expression "extensible parts and stiffness parts are arranged alternately." The Tokyo High Court seems to have judged that the essence of the expression "extensible parts and stiffness parts are arranged alternately" had changed due to the complementing embodiment, perhaps for two reasons. One is the confusion regarding "the complementing embodiment as usage mode of claiming priority" and the other is the effect of the old amendment practice.

The internal priority system was introduced in 1985. The explanation by the Industrial Property Legislation Revision Deliberation Office of the JPO distinguished between different types of claiming priority, "the type of complementing embodiment," "the type of extracting a general concept" and "the type of utilising unity of invention." The second type corresponds to a multiple/partial priority for a generic "OR"-claim. The third type corresponds to the usual way in which multiple/partial priorities are claimed and includes claims that originally existed in the priority application plus additional claims. In order to understand the first type, it is necessary to understand the unity of invention in the old Japanese patent system. Before 1975, Japan had only a single claim system. In 1975, the Patent Act adopted the multiple claim system, but the concept of unity of invention was defined narrowly. Therefore, the meaning of "the type of complementing embodiment" became significant.

With regard to this type, the Industrial Property Legislation Revision Deliberation Office of the JPO gave the following explanation:

> "When an idea is born, it may take considerable time for full enablement. However, under the first-to-file system it is necessary to file an application as soon as possible. In such a case, first of all, the embodiment which is known

> at first is described and an application concerning the idea is filed. As soon as practical embodiments are prepared through verification etc., sequential additions will be made.
>
> When a priority application is subject to examination and the claim is not sufficiently supported by the original embodiment, the claim should be reduced to the extent supported by the original embodiment. However, if a later application claims priority based on a certain priority application, the part corresponding to the original embodiment is entitled to the priority date, and the remaining part complemented by an additional embodiment is entitled to the actual filing date. On the other hand, when examination ascertains that the claim is sufficiently supported by the original embodiment, the entire scope of the claim is entitled to the priority date."[10]

It seems that the plaintiff's assertion that the priority for the claimed invention should be acknowledged if the claimed invention is disclosed in an enabling manner as an original embodiment in the priority application, is based on the above-mentioned second paragraph in the explanation by the Industrial Property Legislation Revision Deliberation Office. Actually, the technical subject matter in which the inside of the surface wall of said head part and said body part, which consist of silicon rubber, out of which extensible parts are formed of which the thickness is thinner than the surface wall, and stiffness parts of which the thickness is thicker than the extensible part, are formed alternately and contiguous to the extensible parts seems to be contained in the original embodiment.

Why did the Tokyo High Court fail to acknowledge the priority for the entire scope of the claim? The reason seems to be the old practice regarding the amendment of the description. Before the reform of the PA of 1993, complementing additional embodiments was not prohibited. For example, adding embodiments by the amendment of the description was permitted provided the claim was left unaltered. However, even when the scope of the claims was not changed, there were some cases where an amendment was not permitted. Permission of the amendment depended on whether a new technical effect was added or not. The Tokyo High court seems to have adopted a similar standard. Especially because in the *Artificial Nipple* case, new effects such as extending more easily with a suckling movement, and easy manufacturing were recognised, the priority of the claim was not partly acknowledged. On the other hand, where an embodiment was added from well-known prior art, priority for the entire scope of the claim was acknowledged in another decision.[11]

The *Artificial Nipple* decision had a significant influence on the JPO's examination practice regarding the acknowledgement of a priority right. Until this decision was rendered, it was believed that if the claim of the later application was adequately supported in the priority application, priority could not be denied on the basis of the additional embodiment. In 2004, the year following this decision, the JPO for the first time published Examination Guidelines related to priority, the basic concepts of which can still be found in the current Examination Guidelines:

---

10. Industrial Property Legislation Revision Deliberation Office of the JPO, Yūsenken seido no dōnyū *(The introduction of priority system)*, 82-9 Hatsumei 32 (1985).
11. Tokyo High Court, 25 January 2005, Case No. 1563 (Ne) of 2004, the website of the courts <http://www.courts.go.jp/app/files/hanrei_jp/812/009812_hanrei.pdf> – *Film with Lens.*

> "In principle, the examiner shall determine the effects of internal priority claim on a claim-by-claim basis. Where matters specifying the invention in one claim are expressed by alternatives, however, the examiner shall determine the effects of an internal priority claim for each invention that is understood based on each alternative. Furthermore, where modes for carrying out the claimed invention are newly added, the examiner shall determine the effects of an internal priority claim for the newly added part within the claimed invention separately from the remaining part."[12]

With regard to a newly added part, there is no examination as to whether a new technical effect was added or not, different from court practice. In the second sentence, the expression that one claim is expressed by alternatives is similar to an explicit "OR"-claim and "a limited number of clearly defined alternatives." The Examination Guidelines seem to have been affected not only by the *Artificial Nipple* decision but also by the EPO **G 2/98**[13] opinion. In addition, it seems that they are also affected by US practice which only recognises priority per claim. According to the current Examination Guidelines, with regard to "the complementing embodiment for which priority is claimed," the priority for the claim shall be determined on a case-by case basis: Priority should be denied if the additional embodiment corresponds to new subject matter.[14] Furthermore, the current Guidelines seem to deny "the type of extracting a general concept," namely the multiple/partial priority for generic "OR"-claims. It seems that this rule is given importance in order to ensure predictability and legal stability.

However, if added subject matter having add-on features in the form of additional embodiments and dependent claims specifying the add-on features are included in the later application, the priority of the independent claim which is identical to the claim in the priority application and does not specify the add-on features at all should not be denied. It is clear that spiral-shape is an alternative of ring-shape, but it is unclear whether spiral-shape is an add-on feature to an "alternately arranged"-form. The *Artificial Nipple* decision should be recognised as a somewhat special case.

For "the type of extracting a general concept," the current Examination Guidelines deny priority, when they are rigidly applied. Even a partial priority for a generic "OR"-claim is not acknowledged. Namely, priority for a generic "OR"-claim shall be determined not by parts, but in case that matter specifying the invention in one claim are expressed by alternatives, priority shall be determined by alternatives. For example, in a case where a claim of a later application includes the concept of "thermoplastic resin" which is a generic concept comprising an unspecified number of concrete embodiments (e.g., polyethylene, polypropylene, etc.) and one of the concrete embodiments (e.g., polyethylene) is disclosed in the priority application, when strictly following the Examination Guidelines of the JPO, partial priority for the

12. Examination Guidelines of the JPO, Part V, Chapter 2, 3.1.2, published in the website of the JPO <https://www.jpo.go.jp/e/system/laws/rule/guideline/patent/tukujitu_kijun/document/index/05_0200_e.pdf>.
13. European Patent Office decision **G 2/98** of 31 May 2001, OJ EPO 2001, 413.
14. After the Examination Guideline regarding priority was first established in 2004, the practice of new matter judgment relating to possibility of correction and amendment in Japan has changed significantly, which may have an impact on the priority right practice. With regard to possibility of correction and amendment, please refer to Case 22 of this book.

polyethylene cannot be acknowledged. This seems to follow the proviso "provided that it gives rise to the claiming of a limited number of clearly defined alternative subject-matters" in point 6.7 of **G 2/98.**[15]

On the other hand, there has been a decision in which the court determined the effect of the right of priority by dividing the claimed invention in parts with regard to a third application claiming a priority under the Paris Convention, which was based on a second application (US continuation-in-part (CIP) application of the first application) including claims that were generic concepts based on the claims of the first application. The Tokyo District Court held as follows:

> "In the patented invention in question, at least for the part using the DC magnetron sputtering system, more than two years and five months have already passed since the first filing date in the United States (8 February 1988) as of the time of the filing of the patent application in question on 18 July 1990, and the period in which a priority under the Paris Convention can be claimed has already lapsed. Therefore, it is obvious that a priority claim for the aforementioned part of the patented invention in question is not recognised."[16]

Different treatment of partial priority between a simple priority claim and a cumulative priority claim seems imbalanced. In Europe, the conceptual approach stipulated in **T 1222/11**[17] led to a referral by Technical Board 3.3.06 to the Enlarged Board, and in **G 1/15,**[18] the Enlarged Board justified partial priority for generic "OR"-claims. In Japan, the revival of "the type of extracting a general concept" is desirable.

4. COMPARATIVE REMARKS

a) US

In the United States, the effects of a priority right are determined only on a claim-by-claim basis. Therefore, multiple/partial priority for a single claim cannot be acknowledged. Of course, there were times when multiple/partial priorities were granted for a single claim. Namely, *In re Ziegler*,[19] partial priority was acknowledged.

15. In Japan, there is no clear case law on this point (in other words, how should the priority be dealt with where first a specific embodiment is claimed, and subsequently a broad category). The above example is based on on a strict interpretation of the Examination Guidelines mandating a rigid claim-by-claim assessment of priority. It should be noted that even if partial priority under the above circumstances is denied, there is no room for an application of the so called-poisonous priority in Japan, because there is no self-collision for usual divisional applications which have different claims. In Japan, for divisional applications which usually have the same application date and same applicants, the whole contents approach under the novelty provision of sec. 29(1) or 29bis PA is not applied. For the novelty assessment in Japan, see also Case No. 3 in this volume.
16. Tokyo District Court, 26 December 2006 Case No. 8811 (Wa) of 2006, the website of the courts <http://www.courts.go.jp/app/files/hanrei_jp/994/033994_hanrei.pdf>
17. European Patent Office decision **T 1222/11** of 4 December 2012.
18. European Patent Office decision **G 1/15** of 29 November 2016.
19. US Court of Customs and Patent Appeals, *In re Ziegler*, 347 F.2d 642, 146 U.S.P.Q. 76 CCPA (1965).

However, the reasoning of *In re Ziegler* was later overruled by *In re Gosteli.*[20] As a reason, the Court of Appeals for the Federal Circuit stated that a priority document must support the entire claim of a subsequent US application prescribed in sec. 119 of 35 USC. The *Gosteli* case concerned Markush type claims, namely "OR"-type claims. The United States does not allow multiple priorities for a single claim even in the Markush type format. However, self-collision does not occur by means of the grace period. *In re Gosteli* affected the **G 3/93**[21] opinion.

b) Europe

For the **EPO**, the early decision **G 3/93**[22] of the Enlarged Board of Appeal (EBoA) held that a document published during the priority interval could constitute prior art against a patent application claiming that priority where the claims of the intervening application contain subject-matter not disclosed in the priority document.

The decision **G 2/98**[23] took the strict approach that "the same invention" for the purpose of claiming priority means that priority of a previous application should be acknowledged only if the skilled person can derive the subject-matter of the claim directly and unambiguously, using common general knowledge, from the previous application as a whole. As cited in the analysis above, this EBoA decision stated in point 6.7 that "[t]he use of a generic term or formula in a claim for which multiple priorities are claimed … is perfectly acceptable under Articles 87(1) and 88(3) EPC, provided that it gives rise to the claiming of a limited number of clearly defined alternative subject-matters" and the standard of "the claiming of a limited number of clearly defined alternative subject-matters" caused the problem of denial of the priority for a generic term claim where the priority application could even be considered prior art for the subsequent application(poisonous priority by self-collision).

The recent decision **G 1/15** (as above) solved the problem after **G 2/98** (as above), clarifying that "entitlement to partial priority may not be refused for a claim encompassing alternative subject-matter by virtue of one or more generic expressions or otherwise (generic "OR"-claim) provided that said alternative subject-matter has been disclosed for the first time, directly, or at least implicitly, unambiguously and in an enabling manner in the priority document."[24]

Of course, there should be supporting embodiments or an enabling disclosure in a previous application for claiming the priority.[25] But how the priority to a patent claim be evaluated that has the same wording supported in the previous application, when adding or complementing an embodiment which falls in the scope of the patent claim? The decision **T 409/90** indicated that "[t]he fact that a claim in a priority document is broad enough to cover specific subject-matter claimed for the

20. US Court of Appeals for the Federal Circuit, *In re Gosteli*, 872 F.2d 1008, 10 U.S.P.Q.2d 1614 Fed. Cir. (1989) = GRUR Int. 1990, 994.
21. European Patent Office decision **G 3/93** of 16 August 1994, OJ EPO 1995, 18– *Priority Interval.*
22. European Patent Office decision **G 3/93** of 16 August 1994, OJ EPO 1995, 18– *Priority Interval.*
23. European Patent Office decision **G 2/98** of 31 May 2001 – *Requirement for claiming priority of the "same invention".*
24. European Patent Office decision **G 1/15** of 29 November 2016.
25. European Patent Office decision **T 81/87** of 24 January 1989 – *Preprorennin*; European Patent Office decision **T 296/93** of 28 July 1994 – *HBV antigen production.*

first time in a European patent application cannot by itself be sufficient evidence that such subject-matter has already been disclosed in the priority document so as to establish identity of invention for the purpose of claiming priority under Article 87 EPC."[26] On the other hand, the decision **T 1080/01** held that the priority of a claim to a product which was sufficiently disclosed in the previous application could be acknowledged even when adding other methods for production.[27] After **G 1/15**, there are cases where the partial priority may be acknowledged for a generic term claim concerning embodiments disclosed in the previous application.[28] In the light of the EPO case law, there may be a possibility to acknowledge priority to the already supported claim with an addition of an embodiment in the description, but this will be decided case by case and the question remains open.

As cited in the analysis above, the **UK** Patents Court denied the priority for the European patent by applying the principle of **G 2/98** where a dependent claim was added and held that adding a dependent claim was not a clearly defined alternative in the independent claim.[29] And the **German** Federal Supreme Court also followed **G 2/98** for a European patent.[30] But in the UK or Germany, there is no concrete case yet for clarifying the specific priority issues after **G 1/15**.

---

26. European Patent Office decision **T 409/90** of 29 January 1991 – *Avalanche photodiodes*;
27. European Patent Office decision **T 1080/01** of 24 October 2003 – *Thermostable enzyme/F. HOFFMANN-LA ROCHE*.
28. European Patent Office decision **T 260/14** of 13 April 2017 – *Polyether-based preparations*; European Patent Office decision **T 1519/15** of 3 August 2017.
29. UK Patents Court, *Nestec SA & Ors v. Dualit Ltd & Ors* [2013] EWHC 923 (Pat); [2013] RPC 32.
30. German Federal Supreme Court, 11 September 2001, GRUR 2002, 146 – *Luftverteiler*; German Federal Supreme Court, 14 October 2003, GRUR 2004, 133 – *Elektoronische Funktionseinheit*; German Federal Supreme Court, 11 February 2014, GRUR 2014, 542 – *Kommunikationskanal*.

Case No. 13

Rights over the Invention – Inventorship

Kengo Sakai

In determining whether an employee had been correctly named as inventor in the patent, only a person involved in the part of the patented invention that actually distinguishes the invention from prior art can be considered an inventor.

Tokyo District Court, 27 August 2002,
Case No. 7196 (Wa) 2001 – *Fine Granule Medicine*

[X] v. Pfizer

---

1. BACKGROUND

There are a number of lawsuits over employee's inventions filed by former managers of R&D departments etc., where the company as defendant argued that these managers were not co-inventors of the invention. This happens because, for one reason, the JPO does not strictly review the correctness of the inventor although the inventor should be named in the patent application document under the Japanese Patent Act (sec. 36(1)(ii)). A company as an applicant in turn simply follows the indication about the inventors from its employees in the R&D department, which may include their manager.[1] Mostly after retirement, such managers initiate a request for compensation with regard to the transfer of his/her right over the invention to the company (sec. 35). This case is a typical example for such kind of dispute.

The amendment of sec. 35 in force since April 2016 allocates the rights over an employee's invention directly the company, while the employee remains the inventor who shall be paid a compensation from the company. Since the company is now able to secure title over the invention, it can be said that there is less motivation for the company to scrutinise the true inventor. Therefore, lawsuits by one of the listed inventors can still be an issue under the current legislation.

---

1. Such practice is said to be changing these days (M. TAKABE, Tokyyo soshō no jitsumu (*Practice in Patent Litigation)*, 1st ed. 2012, 404)

2. DECISION[2]

a) Facts

The plaintiff is a person who is described in the application as co-inventor of the patent at issue, which is owned by the defendant company. The plaintiff argued that the patented invention was an employment invention which was made jointly by the plaintiff as an employee of the defendant company and another employee. As such, the plaintiff should have been remunerated for the transfer of the right to obtain a patent, yet was not fully paid. The plaintiff thus claims proper remuneration based on sec. 35(3) Patent Act.

In 1989, the plaintiff as director of the medicine research division was engaged in the development of fine granule medicine with his staff member B. At the beginning of 1990, the plaintiff found some papers about granulation and handed them over to B. In referring to the papers, B made a document about a method for producing fine granule medicine with low production cost and without using dichloromethane, carried out experiments with the expert engineer E of *Fukae Kōgyō*, and reported the encouraging results to the plaintiff. At the end of August of 1991, the plaintiff proposed to file a patent application over the invention. The plaintiff, B, the person of the patent department C and the patent department director D determined to limit the weight percentage of the crystalline cellulose in the patent claim of the application because of the existence of prior art. With this modification, the defendant company filed on 15 May 1992 a patent application for the invention and named the plaintiff, B and C as co-inventors.

b) Reasons

(1) At first, we consider the content of the invention based on the description of the application and the patent claims 1 to 6.

The description of the invention in the specification of the patent reads as follows: "The main feature of the fine granule cores of the invention is the use of more than 26% crystalline cellulose" (paragraph [0011]), whereby "the invention has the effect of providing the fine granule cores with the principal agent, the granules having a high sphericity and small granularity dispersion, because of comprising the principal agent and at least 26% of the crystalline cellulose and of the average particle size of 80-400μm"(paragraph [0046]). From this description, the special feature of the invention appears to be the point of identifying the effect of providing the fine granule cores with the principal agent, and the fine granule cores having a high sphericity and small granularity dispersion through the use of 26% of the crystalline cellulose.

But the purpose for defining the weight percentage of the crystalline cellulose as "at least 26%" was, in fact, only to avoid a conflict with the known examples and to maximise the scope of the patent. The percentage was determined in theory

2. Published in 1810 Hanrei Jihō 102 = 1117 Hanrei Times 280 = N. NAKAYAMA et al. (eds.), Tokkyo Hanrei Hyakusen *(Hundred Selected Patent Cases)*, 4th ed. 2012, 60 = T. ŌBUCHI et al. (eds.), Chitekizaisan hō hanrei shū *(Intellectual Property Law Case Book)*, 2nd ed. 2015, 19.

and completely lacks technical support by experiment. According to the description, "the cores have a rough surface and can easily wear just as those in prior art if the crystalline cellulose is under 26%. Thereby, it solves problems such as impairing the uniformity of coating, the necessity of a surplus of the coating material, long operation time and bad productivity" (paragraph [0011]). All this has not been verified by experiment but determined, without any basis, as "26 percent" for the above-mentioned reasons, alleging that it had a technical basis.

As mentioned above, the feature "at least comprises crystalline cellulose" (claim 1), and the reason described in the specification is contrary to reality, and actually a fictive parameter without any basis, and so we cannot assess the determination of the percentage as a "creation of a technical idea" (sec. 2(1) PA). Consequently, a person who was only involved in the determination of this parameter is not a co-inventor of the patent. Further, the parameter of "26%" was substantially inserted by the director general D of the patent department and C of the defendant company, and not by the plaintiff.

(2) If we can affirm patentability of the invention, it should be based on the point that "it is especially preferable for the invention to use crystalline cellulose for more than 60 weight%" (paragraph [0012]), i.e. "characterised by the amount of the crystalline cellulose for more than 60 weight%" (patent claim 2). But this point was not the idea of the plaintiff who himself stated in a hearing that the use of such a high amount of the crystalline cellulose was suggested by B who reported that the yield of the fine granules was drastically improved. It is to affirm that the idea of the use of such a high amount of the crystalline cellulose was conceived when the high yield of the high sphericity fine granule cores was obtained in the granulation: 69 weight% of the crystalline cellulose (Avicel), which was remarkably more than in prior art, was prescribed in the *Fukae Kōgyō* experiment. But in fact the use of 69% of the crystalline cellulose and the setting of rotational speed of the agitator and the chopper were both based on an idea of the expert engineer E of *Fukae Kōgyō*.

In consideration of such circumstances, E contributed most to the invention and it can be affirmed that the invention was invented by E or co-invented by E and B, but it cannot be affirmed that the plaintiff contributed to the invention as a co-inventor.

3. ANALYSIS

a) *Venire contra factum proprium*

In the above case, the company needed to proactively prove that the manager was not a co-inventor. This of course begs the question whether the company should indeed be in a position to do so – after all, the company itself filed the patent application indicating the plaintiff as an inventor and even may have made a payment to the plaintiff according to its internal compensation rules for employee inventions (as in the above case), and one can wonder whether the patent applicant can later on contest its own assertions.[3] In fact, there is an IP High Court decision according to which the applicant should be barred from arguing inventorship due to principles of *bona*

3. R. Mimura, Hatsumeisha no igi (*Meaning of the Inventor*), 1236 Kin'yū Shōji Hanrei 124 (2006).

fide unless special circumstances exist, since the applicant itself ascertained that the manager was the inventor.[4] However, there is a view that this limitation should not be strictly applied[5] because of the above-mentioned practice that companies simply follow the report from the R&D department as to who should be named as inventor in the patent application. The background of such practice can be explained by the fact that the nomination of the inventor is not substantially reviewed by the JPO during the application, and also the granted patent is valid so far as the applicant has succeeded in the right to apply for a patent. Thus, the nomination of the plaintiff as inventor may create a rebuttable presumption while allowing the company to prove the contrary, either by positively identifying the true inventor[6] or by demonstrating that the company in its actual practice relied upon the employees' report and generally indicated managers as inventors regardless of the true inventorship.[7]

b) Definition of inventorship

Although there is no definition of "inventor", "invention under the Japanese Patent Act (sec. 2(1))" is defined as "the highly advanced creation of technical ideas utilising the laws of nature". Such creation of a technical idea according to case law,[8] needs to be "completed" in the sense that "the content of such technology shall be understood as consisting as concrete and objective to the extent that a person in the art, the one who has a usual knowledge of such technical field, is able to repeatedly obtain the aimed technical effect". Following such definition of "invention" under the law, the inventor is understood as the one who was actually involved in the inventive process for completing such creation of technical ideas, a definition that is applied in this decision.

In order to determine inventorship, the subsequent step is to decide who was "actually involved with" making the invention. The previous court decisions often adopted both approaches, the negative approach and two steps approach.[9, 10] (i) The negative approach tries to exclude the person who is just an administrator, assistant, sponsor, consignor etc. from the persons "actually involved" in making the invention. For example, a person who only introduced an ordinary subject without any concrete conception or a person who gave general advice or instructions during the inventive

4. 29 March 2007, Case No. 10035 (Ne) of 2006, 1241 Hanrei Times 219.
5. N. Nakayama and N Koizumi (eds.), Shin chūkai tokkyo hō jō (*New Commentary to the Patent Act 1st vol.*), 2011, 367.
6. R. Mimura, *supra* note 3, 124.
7. In the above case, the court determined that as the invention was not going to be filed in the US, the company unreflectedly relied upon the employees' report to describe the manager as inventor. Also, the Tokyo District Court, 13 September 2005, Case No. 14321 (Wa) of 2004, 1214 Hanrei Times 283 = 1916 Hanrei Jihō 133 = 39 IIC 490 (2008) – *Inventor*), denied inventorship of the plaintiff as manager based upon the fact that, although the company made payments to the plaintiff as inventor at the end of the fiscal year for the patent registration under the company's internal employee invention rule, such payment was made to the inventor described in the patent application without any review at all.
8. Supreme Court, 13 October 1977, Case No. 107 (Gyō-Tsu) of 1974, 31-6 Minshū 805.
9. Representative example would be Tokyo District Court, 26 January 2006, Case No. 8496 (Wa) of 2002, 1943 Hanrei Jihō 85
10. K. Yoshifuji and K. Kumagai, Tokkyohō gaisetsu (*Outline of the Patent Act*), 13th ed. 1998, 188.

process should be deemed just an administrator and not an inventor. Also, (ii) the two steps approach analyses the inventive process by dividing it into two steps, namely conception (i.e., conception of a problem or direction for the solution), and reduction to practice. While a person who provided a new conception should be considered an inventor, but such conception should be concrete to some extent.[11] Also the person who reduced such conception to practice should be an inventor unless such reduction is obvious from a person skilled in the art. When there are two or more people "actually involved" in the inventive process, they would be considered co-inventors. Further, it is often discussed that the way to apply the two steps approach should be different for the chemical field since, compared to mechanics, the consequences of reducing to practice are hardly foreseeable at the time of conception. Thus, it is said that in chemistry, experiments would play a greater role in the inventive process and thereby also in determining who should qualify as an inventor.[12]

Inventorship disputes do not only arise in the context of employees' inventions, but also, for example, in litigation between joint R&D partners with regard to the attribution of an invention and the corresponding rights thereto. These disputes may become more frequent as the inventor's right for a transfer of the patent right in cases of misappropriation has been statutorily introduced as of 2011 (sec. 74(1)).

c) Application to the case at issue

Following the above discussion, the court as a starting point defined what should be considered as the inventive contribution, and more generally what should be considered as an "invention" under the Patent Act. The patent claims and the description of the application are referred to for analysis,[13] but a court can scrutinise further. The court judged upon the alleged facts that the weight percentage of the crystalline cellulose as "at least 26%" described in patent claim 1 was a fictive parameter without any experimental support. This led the court to judge that patent claim 1 did not embody the invention probably because the invention should be completed, i.e., able to be repeated and be obvious and concrete for a person in the art as mentioned above. It was also discussed that patent claim 1 could have been denied due to lack of disclosure (Sec. 36(6)(i)).[14] On the other hand, the judgment referred to patent claim 2 and found it patentable, i.e., embodying the invention.

Additionally, when determining the inventor for such invention, the court identified which would be the characteristic part of the invention as a completed creation of a technical idea. This "characteristic part" means the part of the solution

11. N. Nakayama and N. Koizumi (eds.), *supra* note 5, 366. The Tokyo District Court, 26 January 2006, *supra* note 9, argue: "It should be something more than a simple thought come up in mind (*Omoitsuki*)".
12. Also discussed in the Tokyo District Court, 13 September 2005, *supra* note 7.
13. Tokyo District Court, 26 January 2006, *supra* note 9, also discussed the technical idea of the invention should be recognised on the basis of the patent claims.
14. T. Yamane and M. Tokii, Shin no hatsumeisha no nintei – Sairyūkaku jiken – (*Recognition of the True Inventor – Fine Granule Medicine* -), 20 Chitekizaisanhō Seisakugaku Kenkyū 282 (2008). The author also introduced the decision of Tokyo District Court, 9 March 2006, Case No. 27028 (Wa) of 2004, 1948 Hanrei Jihō 136, and discussed that the lack of experimental support can be compensated to some extent by the engineer's knowledge and experience.

to the prior technical problem which is distinct from prior art. The court found claim 2 (but not claim 1) as "patentable", that is, novel and inventive, and thus the basis for determining the relevant contribution to the state of the art.[15] There are also decisions according to which the invention should be identified without any limitation regarding patentability[16] when determining the inventor. Although the Patent Act does not directly link the compensation for an employees' invention (sec. 35(4) to the definition of an invention (sec. 2(1)), it would be appropriate to require patentability because only an inventive solution to a prior technical problem would amount to the substantial value that the Patent Act intends to protect.[17]

After judging that in claim 2, the patentable part of the invention was "characterised by the amount of the crystalline cellulose for more than 60 weight%", the court determined who was actually involved in the inventive process of such part. The court held that the idea of the use of such a high amount of the crystalline cellulose was conceived when the high yield of the high sphericity fine granule cores was obtained in the granulation in the *Fukae Kōgyō* experiment which was carried out upon the idea of E using the amount of crystalline cellulose under certain experimental conditions. It was thus E who foremost contributed to the invention. This is in line with the discussion of the two-step approach in the chemical field in order to give due weight to the experiments rather than the conception. The appeal court in this case also emphasised the importance of the experiments for this invention and mostly upheld the first instance decision.[18]

Separately, the court held that the papers about granulation handed to C by the plaintiff were a starting point for the *Fukae Kōgyō* experiments, but the conception provided by the plaintiff was not sufficiently concrete to qualify as an invention. While determining the appropriate experimental conditions was crucial for the invention, the conception itself only suggested the outline or the direction towards solving the problem. For this reason, the plaintiff could not qualify as an inventor.[19] This could be read in that the plaintiff was just an administrator, but did not perform any inventive activities.

---

15. The Tokyo District Court, 13 September 2005, *supra* note 7, also determined which part of the Invention embodied the inventive step in order to determine the inventor.
16. Osaka District Court, 25 July 2000, Case No. 10432 (Wa) of 1998, the website of the courts: <http://www.courts.go.jp/app/files/hanrei_jp/043/013043_hanrei.pdf>. There is also a decision which admitted the compensation payment to an employee although the invention has been held to lack patentability by the JPO (Osaka District Court, 4 March 1993, Case No. 292 (Wa) of 1991, 26-2 Chiteki zaishū 405).
17. E. TOMIOKA discussed such as a dispute between joint R&D partners with regard to the attribution of the invention, or between inventor and company with regard to the inventor's personal rights. These issues could be decided without having regard to patentability requirements (Hatsumei no chakusō tō gutaika – Sairyukaku jiken – *(Conception and Reduction to Practice of the Invention – Fine Granule Medicine -)*, in: N. NAKAYAMA et al. (eds.), Tokkyo Hanrei Hyakusen *(Hundred Selected Patent Cases)*, 4th ed. 2012, 61.
18. Tokyo High Court, 26 August 2003, Case No. 5077 (Ne) of 2002, the website of the courts: <http://www.courts.go.jp/app/files/hanrei_jp/908/010908_hanrei.pdf>. It held, though, that the primary contributor to the experiments was not E but C.
19. In Tokyo District Court, 13 September 2005, *supra* note 7, the same parties argued with regard to another chemical invention, also focused on the importance of the experiments during the invention process. It judged that the plaintiff was not a co-inventor since he only gave general instructions about the experiments to his team members.

4. COMPARATIVE REMARKS

> "In very recent years, there has been a rash of entitlement cases ... No one really knows why. There was some speculation about an increase in joint ventures, or an increase in the appreciation of the significance of patents. None of them really explain it."[20]

The notion that entitlement cases are on the rise is corroborated by cases from other jurisdictions. There is certainly an enhanced awareness of the value of patents, of the notion that inventive contributions thereto should be appropriately remunerated, and of issues involving technology transfer between research institutions and industry. And yet,

> "Parties to the entitlement disputes should realise that, if fully fought, they could be protracted, very expensive and emotionally draining ... It would often be better to settle early for a smaller share than you think you were entitled to – a small share of a large exploitation was better than a large share of none or little." (Lord Jacob, ibid.)

This refers to the fact that court proceedings with their inevitable delays may not be well-suited to decide upon issues that, depending on the market, might require a speedy solution that does not involve huge sums of money. Lord Jacob's conclusion is thus:

> "This sort of dispute was particularly apt for early mediation ... where a mediator trusted by both sides is given the authority to decide the terms of a binding settlement agreement."

Since in most jurisdictions, ownership follows inventorship (e.g. Art. 60(1) European Patent Convention (EPC) "... the inventor or his successor in title"), determining inventorship under domestic patent law is of paramount importance in order to determine ownership.

a) Inventorship and ownership are issues that are not governed by harmonised community law. Not even the draft **Community Patent Convention** (CPC) made reference thereto, and the issue thus fell under the category where national rules would still apply, Art. 38 CPC. For patents applied before the European Patent Office, Art. 60(1) European Patent Convention (EPC) states that "The European patent shall belong to the inventor or his successor in title." This suggests a uniform interpretation of who should qualify as an inventor.[21] Since however entitlement disputes must be brought before the national authorities (Art. 61), and since the applicant is deemed entitled before the Patent Office (Art. 60(3)), the EPO has rather limited jurisdiction to decide on the position of inventorship. The only conceivable cases are those under Art. 62 (right of the inventor to be mentioned). According to Rule 19, the mention

---

20. Lord Jacob in *University of Southampton Applications*, English Court of Appeal, 2 March 2006, [2006] RPC 567, 578.
21. For the reasons given hereinafter, there is no case law on this point: C. HEATH, Commentary on Art. 60 EPC, Münchener Kommentar zum EPÜ *(Munich Commentary to the EPC)*, 27th supplement 2004.

of an inventor can be corrected at a later stage at the request of the applicant or a third party. This, however, gives the Office no real power to investigate inventorship unless the case may be obvious, eg in cases of a discrepancy between the priority document and the subsequent EPC filing.

b) The courts of the **United Kingdom** have employed a two-step test in order to determine inventorship. The first is an identification of the heart of the invention:

> "What one is normally looking for is 'the heart' of the invention. There may be more than one 'heart' but each claim is not be considered as a separate 'heart' on its own"[22]

What the courts do not particularly look at is thus the claim language, but rather the inventive concept as a whole in comparison with prior art. In the above-mentioned case of the University of Southampton, the court took into consideration the description of the invention in the patent and how the invention is presented there.

The second step is then to identify who in substance came up with the inventive concept.

Interestingly enough, a mere idea may be sufficient to merit (sole) inventorship if the actual application of the invention is a matter of simple routine and experimentation:

> "It is true that he did not know whether his invention would work and it is true that he had not realised that if it did work it would be by adhesion ... Neither of these matters prevents Mr. Metcalfe from being the sole devisor of the invention. For neither or these matters involve the contribution of anything inventive to his idea. So far as finding out whether or not his idea worked that was a matter of simple and routine experimentation – mere verification."[23]

c) The **German** position on co-inventorship is less clear:

> "A joint inventor is anyone who has made a creative contribution to the invention. In contrast, constructive assistance in the implementation of the invention is not sufficient. However, the joint inventor's contribution need not itself be inventive; it is not necessary that it of itself satisfies all the preconditions for a patentable invention. On the other hand, such contributions that have not influenced the overall achievement, i.e., are insubstantial with respect to the solution, and such that have been created on the instructions of the inventor or a third party, do not establish status as a joint inventor."[24]

The court also indicated that the subject matter of the invention should be defined according to the main and the dependant claims.

d) While Art. L. 611-6 **French** Intellectual Property Code rules that the right over an invention shall belong to the inventor, there is hardly any case law on this point.

While ownership of a patent application or a patent is an issue that can be agreed upon, inventorship is not. Thus, there cannot be any contractual regulations

---

22. Lord Jacob, *Markem v. Zipher*, Court of Appeal, [2005] RPC 761.
23. *University of Southampton Applications*, *supra* note 20, 576.
24. German Federal Supreme Court, 16 September 2003, 35 IIC 949 – *Curving Method*.

on who should be considered an inventor.[25] Such stipulations can lead to a wrongful attribution at the most, yet they cannot make a person an inventor who in fact has not substantially contributed to the invention. However, it should be possible to determine by contract which law should determine inventorship.[26] In the case of international research co-operations, there might be an interest in a uniform determination of conditions that make a person an inventor.[27] By subjecting the contract to the laws of one specific country, the laws of that country should then determine the question of inventorship.[28]

25. G. WESTKAMP, Research Agreements and Joint Ownership of Intellectual Property Rights in Private International Law, 37 IIC 638, 641 (2006) and footnote 24 with further references to works by Ginsburg and Fawcett/Torremans.
26. G. WESTKAMP, *supra* note 25, at 658.
27. This can be likened to cases of employees' inventions where it is considered permissible to choose the law applicable to the labour contract, thereby also determining under which law the employees invention and its rights have to be determined: Straus, GRUR 1984, 1, 3. See also the comparative remarks on Case No. 17 *RW Laser Disk*.
28. This issue has been discussed mainly in the context of employees' inventions.

Case No. 14

Rights of Co-Inventors – Action by One Co-Inventor against Revocation

Makoto Hattori

---

1. **Where a patent right is not yet registered, joint owners have to raise an action jointly.**
2. **Once the right is registered, each of the joint owners is allowed to raise an action against a decision that revokes or invalidates such right.**

Supreme Court, 25 March 2002, Case No. 154 (Gyō-Hi) of 2001 – *Pachinko Device*

Nisshō v. Japanese Patent Office

---

1. BACKGROUND

Patent applications and patents can be jointly owned. In the case of joint ownership, the following circumstances beg the question to what extent all owners of the application or the patent have to act jointly:

a) The act of application. Sec. 38 Patent Act (PA) requires common consent in this case;
b) The transfer of a patent application. The courts require common consent also here;[1]
c) The patent application is refused and an appeal against the examiner's decision of rejection is filed. All applicants have to act jointly under sec. 132(1);[2]
d) Where an appeal against the examiner's decision of rejection is dismissed and action is to be taken against this trial decision. Also in this case, the Supreme Court has established that all co-owners have to act jointly;[3]

---

1. Osaka High Court, 10 May 2001, Case No. 2914 (Ne) of 2000, the website of the courts <http://www.courts.go.jp/app/files/hanrei_jp/499/012499_hanrei.pdf>; Abstract of the case in 13 L&T 65 (2001).
2. The provision reads: "Where the joint owners of a patent right or a right to obtain a patent demand a trial concerning the right under joint ownership, the demand shall be made jointly by all the joint owners."
3. Supreme Court, 7 March 1995, Case No. 83 (Gyō-Tsu) of 1994, 1527 Hanrei Jihō 145. German translation in GRUR Int. 1998, 507 with comment by T. IIZUKA – *Magnetic Treatment Device.*

e) Where the patent has been granted and a trial for correction is requested under sec. 126. As this trial is meant to limit the patent right, arguably all patentees have to act jointly under sec. 132(3);[4]
f) License or transfer of the jointly-owned patent. Here, sec. 73(1) and (3) requires common consent;
g) The exploitation of the patent without consent of all joint owners. Here, no common consent is necessary according to sec. 73 (2);
h) Where the patent has been invalidated in invalidation procedures and one of the joint owners brings an action against the Patent Office's decision. According to the Supreme Court, no common consent is required in this case;[5]
i) Only one of the joint owners wants to bring an infringement action against a third party. This is deemed permissible, as each of the joint owners has a right to exclude others from using the invention, sec. 100.

The subject of this case was regarding a situation where the patent was revoked in post-grant opposition procedures, and action was to be taken against the appeal board's decision. The issue was whether one of the joint owners was allowed to act, or whether all owners had to act jointly.

2. DECISION[6] [7]

a) Facts

The appellant was one of joint owners of a patent right which was registered on 19 February 1999. In opposition procedures brought on 5 November 1999 and 10 November 1999 respectively, the Patent Office on 25 October 2000 decided to revoke claim 1 of the patent based on the demand. The appellant independently requested the annulment of the ruling of the Patent Office. The Tokyo High Court dismissed the case on 12 March 2001 reasoning that all patentees have to file the suit jointly.

4. The provision reads: "Where the joint owners of a patent right or a right to obtain a patent demand a trial concerning the right under joint ownership, the demand shall be made jointly by all the joint owners."
5. Supreme Court 22 February 2002, Case No. 142 (Gyō-Hi) of 2001, 56-2 Minshū 348. The case concerned trade marks, yet is also applicable to patents, utility models, and designs.
6. Published in 56-3 Minshū 574 = T. ŌBUCHI et al. (eds.), Chitekizaisan hō hanrei shū *(Intellectual Property Law Case Book)*, 2nd ed. 2015, 89. English translation by M. HATTORI in 35 IIC 686 (2004) w. comment by M. HATTORI.
7. The opposition procedure can be instigated by anyone and is decided by a collegial body of examiners before the Patent Office, merely based on documentary evidence. If the patent is revoked in opposition procedures, an action can be raised against this decision before the Tokyo High Court. The Tokyo High Court can only examine the lawfulness of the decision, but not decide on its own. In case the Tokyo High Court finds the decision faulty, it could remand the case to the Patent Office. By Law No. 47/2003, in force as of 1 January 2004, the opposition procedure was abolished and post-grant invalidation procedures opened to anyone rather than only those with a legal interest. By Law No. 36/2014, however, the opposition procedure was restored as nearly identical to the previous one. Thus, this Supreme Court decision also applies to cases deriving from the current opposition procedure.

b) Reasons

Where the right to obtain a patent is jointly owned, each of the joint owners shall apply for patent together with the others (Patent Act sec. 38). Where the joint owners of a right to obtain a patent demand a trial concerning the right under joint ownership, the demand shall be made jointly by all the joint owners (Patent Act sec. 132(3)). These provisions may require common intent of the joint owners to obtain a patent concerning the right under joint ownership. However, after a patent right is registered, although consent of all joint owners of a patent right is required to dispose of the patent right, including transferring a joint owner's share in the patent right and granting an exclusive licence under the patent right, a joint owner may work the patented invention without the consent of the other joint owners (Patent Act sec. 73). Further, it is provided that where a ruling to revoke a registered patent right is made and no appeal is brought within a given period of time, the patent right shall be deemed never to have existed, and the right to work the patented invention shall retroactively lapse (Patent Act sec. 114(3)). Therefore, where a ruling to revoke a patent right under joint ownership is rendered, one of the joint owners may independently bring an action for annulment of the ruling as an act of preservation (*Hozon-Kōi*) to prevent the extinction of the patent right (*see* Supreme Court, 22 February 2002, 1310 Saibansho Jihō 5). "Where the joint owners of a patent right or a right to obtain a patent demand a trial concerning the right under joint ownership" (Patent Act sec. 132(3)) refers to cases of a trial against the examiner's decision of refusal of the registration of extension of term of a patent right (Patent Act secs. $67^{ter}(1)$, 121), a trial for correction (Patent Act sec. 126) etc. We do not assume that joint owners of a patent right are always required to act jointly. Allowing one of the joint owners to bring an action for annulment of the ruling to revoke the patent is not against the principle of unity of confirmation. Furthermore, when each of the joint owners jointly or separately brings an action for annulment of the ruling to revoke the patent, such an action should be considered to fall into the category of *Ruiji*-necessity joint litigation and should be jointly considered and decided. Thus, the principle of unity of confirmation would be satisfied. Therefore, the original decision that held that this lawsuit was illegal made an error in law, which clearly has an influence to make a decision. The cases of the Supreme Court, 31 August 1961, 15-7 Minshū 2040, the Supreme Court, 18 January 1976, 129 Shūmin 43, and Supreme Court, 7 March 1995, 49-3 Minshū 944, are distinguished from this case and should not be referred to.

3. ANALYSIS

The three Supreme Court decisions, the 1995 Supreme Court decision, the 2002 Supreme Court decision, and this decision seem to express the following principles:

1) Where the right is not yet registered, joint owners have to raise an action jointly, while
2) once the right is registered, each of the joint owners is allowed to raise an action against a decision that revokes or invalidates such right. The correctness of this distinction shall subsequently be examined.

The above distinction made by the Supreme Court between a right already granted and an application finds no particular justification in the law. In addition, it is not endorsed by academic literature[8] that tries to apply other principles in order to arrive at appropriate solutions for the above cases. Both arguments of substantive law and procedure are invoked in order to justify either that all owners have to act jointly or that one can act on his own. Three main trains of thought shall be examined here.

a) Litigation as an act of preservation

The first line of argument is based on substantive law and analyses what type of common property is similar to a jointly owned patent right. The Japanese Civil Code distinguishes between two kinds of common property. The first is common property by ideal shares that requires all to act jointly and does not permit individual acts of one co-owner. This kind of property in Japanese is referred to as *Gōyū* and resembles the German *Gesamthandseigentum*. The reason for such restriction in the case of tangible property is the fact that only in this way can the common purpose of the joint owners be maintained.[9] The corresponding reason under patent law is a different one, however. It lies rather in the preservation of the economic value of the other joint owners' shares that makes consent a sensible legal solution.[10] The prevalence of economic considerations is also apparent in the fact that the working of the patent as such does not require consent of the other co-owners, which is markedly different in the case of property by ideal shares.[11] The other kind of common property is property by fraction shares, *Kyōyū* in Japanese or *Bruchteilseigentum* in German law. Here, sec. 252 Japanese Civil Code and sec. 744(2) German Civil Code would allow one of the co-owners, even in the absence of common consent, to take measures necessary to maintain or preserve the right. Sec. 264 Japanese Civil Code makes the above provision also applicable to rights other than tangible property and thus could apply to patents.[12]

To apply sec. 252 Civil Code to patent rights would require two conditions to be met. First, the necessity of maintaining or preserving the right by the action of one of the joint owners, and, second, the fact that such action is necessarily beneficial to all other joint owners. It is clear that in case a patent right is revoked or invalidated, inaction by the patentees leads to a final loss of such right. Appealing against the Patent Office's decision seems to be a necessary act of preservation or

8. N. Nakayama, Tokkyo hō *(Patent Law)*, 3rd ed. 2016, 293
9. S. Wagatsuma, Minpō kōgi II bukken hō *(Civil law lecture II, Property law)*, 1952, 211.
10. N. Nakayama, Tokkyo hō *(Patent Law)*, 3rd ed. 2016, 288-293.
11. N. Nakayama, Tokkyo wo ukeru kenri no kyōyūsha no hitori ni yoru shinketsu torikeshi soshō no tekikakusei *(Allowability of cancellation lawsuit against a JPO trial decision by one of the co-owners of right to patent)*, in: Chitekizaisan wo meguru shomondai *(Problems around intellectual property)*, 1996, 549 et seq.; E. Takikawa, Jitsuyōshin'an tōroku wo ukeru kenri no kyōyūsha no hitori ga teiki shita shinketsu torikeshi soshō no tekikakusei *(Allowability of cancellation lawsuit against the JPO trial decision by one of co-owners of right to register utility model)*, 46-5 Chizai Kanri 811 (1996); Tokyo High Court, 24 April 1975, Case No. 138 (Gyō-Ke) of 1968, 7-1 Mutaishū 92 (a case on utility models).
12. K. Tamai, Tokkyo hō jō no kyōyū to hitsuyōteki kyōdō soshō *(Co-ownership on the Patent Act and necessary joint lawsuit)*, 21 Tokkyo Kenkyū 67 et seq. (1996).

maintenance. It is also certain that a subsequent decision favourable to the patentee is beneficial to the other co-owners, as the right is upheld for all of them. Yet, there is no agreement to what extent an appeal is *only* beneficial to all co-patentees. If, so the reasoning goes, the co-patentee loses the appeal, the others will equally be bound by this decision under sec. 252 Civil Code. This would be disadvantageous where, e.g., the other joint owners were not properly served with the decision to revoke or invalidate the patent, and could otherwise still appeal. A decision that was binding on such co-patentee would thus be detrimental to his interests. One may regard this from a different angle, though. Both the current Supreme Court decision as well as the previous one of 22 February 2002 take the stance that sec. 32(1) Administrative Litigation Act applies to a favourable decision obtained by one co-patentee regarding the effect of this decision on the other co-patentees. The above provision stipulates a binding effect of a decision on third parties whose rights may be harmed by virtue of the effect of the decision or who should be relieved of obligations for intervention in the first place. Neither is the case here. Where one co-patentee is successful, the rights of the others are not harmed, and since all of them should be served notice on the revocation or invalidation of the patent right, they have a right to independently intervene. The binding effect of a favourable decision on the other co-patentees can be more elegantly explained by other Supreme Court cases concerning requests for repossession of jointly owned land.[13] As to the binding effect of an unfavourable decision, this author takes the stance that such effect does not exist. In the normal course of events, where only one of the co-patentees raises a legal action, the others lose their right to do so because of the time period stipulated to challenge the Patent Office's decision. Thus, if notice of the invalidation or revocation is properly served upon all co-patentees, the (indirectly) binding effect of such decision is triggered by the failure to challenge such decision within the prescribed period of time rather than the decision rendered against the co-patentee actually challenging this decision. Where the Patent Office's decision is not properly served upon one of the co-patentees, the latter will retain the right to raise an action regardless of what decision has been rendered on behalf of the suing co-patentee.[14] In other words, a decision favourable to one co-patentee preserves the right and can be relied upon the other co-patentees. And a decision rendered against the co-patentee is not binding on the others and may be challenged by them if they are still within the time limit (which in the normal course of events they are not).

b) Analogous application of (old) sec. 62 Code of Civil Procedure

The Code of Civil Procedure in force prior to 2001, currently sec. 40, provides that a legal action brought by one of the co-litigants should have an effect on two conditions. First, that there must be a uniform decision vis-à-vis all parties involved, and, second,

13. Supreme Court, 10 May 1956, Case No. 4 of (O) of 1954, 10 Minshū 487; Daishin'in (Imperial Supreme Court), 13 June 1921, Case No. 368 (O) of 1921, 27 Minroku 1155.
14. See M. TAKABE, Shōhyōken no kyōyūsha no hitori ga tōgai shōhyōtōroku no mukō shinketsu ni tsuite tandoku de torikeshi soshō o teiki suru koto no dakuhi *(Allowability of cancellation lawsuit to the JPO trial decision to invalidate by one of co-owners of trade mark)*, 1233 Jurist 123 (2002); M. TAKESHITA, in: H. KANEKO (ed.) Jōkai minjisosōhō (*Code of Civil Procedure Annotated*), 1986, 699.

that the Code of Civil Procedure actually applies. Particularly the latter is doubtful. The argument rests on the assumption that the initial act of joint application "carries through" the whole procedure.[15] Appeals against decisions by the Patent Office go to the Tokyo High Court that does not decide on the subject matter as such, but on the lawfulness of the Patent Office's decision. Thus, there should no longer be room for analogous application of sec. 62 (now sec. 40) Code of Civil Procedure.[16]

c) Necessity of joint litigation

Also this line of reasoning is of procedural nature and argues that the decision regarding the validity of a jointly owned right must be a uniform one vis-à-vis all parties involved.[17] This being so, an action brought by one joint owner should consequently be dismissed. This was basically the argument on which the Supreme Court's decision of 1995 relied. Since there is no continuous procedure between the administrative decisions rendered by the Patent Office and the judicial review by the Tokyo High Court, the latter is only empowered to vacate the trial decision, but not to decide on its own on the merits of granting or denying a patent (Patent Act, sec. 181(1), see also Case No. 26 for further details). While there is no doubt that the court's decision is binding upon the Patent Office (sec. 181(2)), the court's decision cannot and does not replace the one by the Patent Office. Once the case is remanded to the Patent Office, the latter may still uphold its previous decision on different grounds not examined by the Court. Or, to put it differently, *either* the procedure (Patent Office-Tokyo High Court) is regarded as a uniform one with the consequence that sec. 40 Code of Civil Procedure should apply and one of the co-owners would be given standing to sue on behalf of all, *or* the procedures are regarded as different ones (decision on the merits by the Patent Office and judicial review by the Tokyo High Court), with the consequence that there is no necessary joint litigation because the Patent Office rather than the Tokyo High Court decides on the existence of the right as such. The reasoning of the 1995 Supreme Court decision thus cannot be endorsed.

---

15. This is basically argued by T. KIKAWA, Shinpan no tōjisha denai mono no genkoku tekikaku *(Standing to sue of party who was not involved in trial)* in: Tokkyo Hanrei Hyakusen *(Hundred Selected Patent Cases)*, 1st ed. 1966, 108; T. YAMASHITA, Kōsai hanrei kenkyū *(Study of High Court case)*, 159 Hanrei Times 71 et seq. (1964); N. KOMURO, Shinpan tetsuzuki to shinketsu torikeshi soshō tono kankei *(The Relationship Between a trial procedure and an action against a trial decision)*, in: Kyōgyō shoyūken hō no shomondai *(Problems of industrial property law)*, 1972, 293; Y. NUNOI, Jitsuyōshin'an tōroku kyozetsu shinketsu no kyōdō shutsugannin ni yoru torikeshi seikyū *(Cancellation lawsuit to the JPO trial decision to reject utility model registration by co-applicant)*, 83-4 Minshōhō Zasshi 632 (1981).
16. N. NAKAYAMA (*supra* note 14), 549 et seq.; S. YOSHII, Kyōdo shutsugannin no hitori no teiki shita uttae no tekihōsei *(Allowability of lawsuit by one of co-applicant)*, in: T. OOTORI et al. (eds.), Tokkyo Hanrei Hyakusen *(Hundred Selected Patent Cases)*, 2nd ed. 1985, 124; E. TAKIKAWA, Tokkyo soshō tetsuzuki ronkō *(Discussion of the Proceedings of Patent Litigation)*, 1991, 59; E. TAKIKAWA (*supra* note 14), 814.
17. M. UCHIDA, Kyōdo shinpan seikyūnin no sōgo kankei *(Mutual relationship between joint trial requesters)*, in: Tokkyo Hanrei Hyakusen *(Hundred Selected Patent Cases)*, 1st ed. 1966, 84 (this is commentary on the Tokyo High Court decision of Case No. 26 of this book); R. KOSAKA, Tokkyo kankei Shinketsu torikeshi soshō *(An action to revoke a trial decision with regard to a patent right)* in: T. KIGAWA et al. (eds), Shin jitsumu minji soshō kōza 10 *(New practice lectures on civil case 10)*, 1982, 226 et seq.

Nowadays, a good many Japanese companies and organisations conduct joint research and development with each other or with universities or research institutions and patent rights obtained on the basis of such joint research are often jointly owned by the parties. At the same time, it is sometimes difficult to obtain the consent of co-owners of the patent for actions under a jointly owned patent for various reasons. All acts necessary to preserve a right that can be likened to a property right under secs. 252, 264 Japanese Civil Code should be taken by one of the co-owners without the others' consent. This does apply to appeals against the Patent Office's decision to revoke or invalidate an existing patent right in opposition or invalidation proceedings. Given the fact that also the right to apply for a patent and to obtain one is of proprietary nature, the same should apply to the appeal of one of the co-applicants taking legal action against the Patent Office's decision to reject the application. Also from this angle, the 1995 Supreme Court decision cannot be endorsed.

There are no provisions or principles of procedural law that would speak against the above-mentioned solution. It is thus unnecessary and to some extent even incorrect to apply the Administrative Litigation Act to cases of this nature. Should one take the view that the Act applies nonetheless, sec. 9 Administrative Litigation Act gives anyone with a legal interest in the revocation of an administrative measure the right to bring an action against the ruling. Also this would speak in favour rather than against one co-owner or co-applicant bringing an action against an unfavourable decision of the Patent Office without the consent of the others.

4. COMPARATIVE REMARKS

The rules about ownership concern the relationship between different co-owners of patents, their rights vis-a-vis each other and vis-a-vis third parties. Three issues are of particular importance in this respect: Application/maintenance of the right, rights of use, and rights or licensing.

a) Application and maintenance

In the case of several co-applicants of a patent, the question is if one of them should be entitled to apply for a patent and act before the Patent Office or the courts even without consent of the others.

(1) Under the **EPC**, there is no explicit rule on this matter. Yet the rule in Art. 58 EPC is rather general and allows anyone to apply for a patent. Any applicant who is not an inventor according to Art. 81 has to declare how ownership was obtained. The EPO has no means to reject an application that is filed by only one of several co-owners of the invention, and any dispute in this respect has to be brought before the national courts.

In the case of several co-applicants, according to Rule 100, the Office requires one common representative for all. This can be a professional patent attorney, or one of the first applicant mentioned in the application if such applicant would be entitled to act without a patent attorney. This rule may lead to hardships where the applicant being entitled to representation loses interest in the application, and the performance of certain acts is needed to proceed with the application. According to the decision **G 3/99**, an act performed by one of the applicants (here: opponents) who is not entitled to representation is invalid,[18] yet it appears that each co-applicant or co-opponent can at least meet a deadline, and subsequently request a (national) court order against the unwilling representative to act on his behalf (or without his consent).[19] The latter remedy may not be available in all countries, leaving the co-applicant with very little means to proceed with an application or opposition.

(2) In the **United Kingdom**, sec. 7 PA 1977 allows any inventor or co-inventor to file for a patent. Consent of the others is not necessary. In case of disputes in the application phase, any co-applicant under sec. 10 can make an application to the Comptroller on how to proceed:

> "If any dispute arises between joint applicants for a patent whether or in what manner the application should be proceeded with, the comptroller may, on a request made by any of the parties, give such directions as he thinks fit for enabling the application to proceed in the name of one or more of the parties alone or for regulating the manner in which it shall be proceeded with, or for both purposes, according as the case may require."

(3) In **Germany**, there is no provision that would stipulate who of several co-owners could apply for a patent. Sec. 34 Patent Act does not specify who is entitled to apply, not even in cases where the applicant is not the inventor.[20] Thus, the Office cannot reject a request that is made by one of the owners only.[21] German law further applies the rules of partnership to the relationship between co-owners of a patent. Under such rules, one of the co-owner is entitled to all acts that preserve the common right. This would undoubtedly entitle one of the co-owners to act before the Office in order to proceed with an application to oppose a nullity action or an opposition.[22]

(4) In **France**, according to academic writers, applying for a patent requires the consent of all co-owners, although Art. R.612-2 Intellectual Property Code does not seem to require this. A joint application based on common consent carries the presumption that all have equal shares in the invention.[23] For a joint application, all co-inventors have to nominate one representative, who on their behalf will be entitled to conduct all procedures (general power of attorney) with the exception of renouncing the patent, Art. R. 612-2 (2). In cases of disagreement between the co-applicants, the same problems arise as under Rule 100 EPC (see above 1).

---

18. Enlarged Board of Appeal, **G 3/99** of 18 February 2002, OJ 2002, 347.
19. In Germany, the court would order the representative to act, or stipulate that the appellant be entitled to act on behalf of the patent application: Federal Patent Court, 21 April 1988, BlPMZ 1999, 44 – *Gemeinsamer Zustellungsbevollmächtigter.*
20. German Federal Supreme Court, 27 September 2016, GRUR 2016, 1257 – *Beschichtungsverfahren* explicitly left it open whether it was a tort against the other co-inventors where only one of them applied for a patent. However, it is a tort where the applicant does not correctly identify the other co-inventors.
21. German Imperial Supreme Court (*Reichsgericht*), 30 April 1927, RGZ 117, 47, 50.
22. German Imperial Supreme Court, 22 May 1911, RGZ 76, 298, 300.
23. Tribunal de Grande Instance Paris *(Paris District Court)*, 20 December 1968, Gaz.Pal. 1969, 2, Summary 10.

(5) **US** law in section 116 Title 35 requires joint inventors to apply jointly:

> "When an invention is made by two or more persons jointly, they shall apply for patent jointly and each make the required oath ... Inventors may apply for a patent jointly even though (1) they did not physically work together at the same time, (2) each did not make the same type of amount of contribution, or (3) each did not make a contribution to the subject matter of every claim of the patent."

b) Use, licensing and sale of the share in the patent

(1) **UK** law distinguishes between use and licensing. Sec. 36 (2) Patents Act 1977 allows each co-owner the use of the patent without the others' consent and without compensation,[24] which is in line with a House of Lords decision of 1893:

> "The truth is that letters patent do not give the patentee any right to use the invention – they do not confer upon him a right to manufacture according to his invention ... What the letters patent confer is the right to exclude others from manufacturing in a particular way, and using a particular invention. When that is borne in mind, it appears to me to be very clear that it would be impossible to hold, under these circumstances, that where there are several patentees, either of them, if he uses the patent, can be called upon by the others to pay to them a portion of the profits which he takes by that manufacture, because they are all of them entitled, or perhaps any of them is entitled, to prevent the rest of the world from using it".[25]

On the other hand, transfer and licensing[26] of co-owned patents requires consent of all (sec. 36(3) PA 1977). The rationale for each patentee being entitled to exploit the patent without the others' consent was explained in the case *Hughes v. Paxman*:[27]

> "I cannot imagine for a moment that Parliament could have intended it to be possible that exploitation of an invention could be frustrated by a deadlock situation. The whole point of the patent system was and is to encourage innovation and the exploitation of inventions." (para. 13).

According to a subsequent decision, the Comptroller's jurisdiction under sec. 37(1)(c) to determine, upon request, "whether any right ... under the patent should be

24. Sec. 36(5) clarifies that goods marketed by one co-owner should be treated as if marketed by the sole proprietor. This section may be necessary under UK law due to the fact that "common law" exhaustion is the concept of implied consent. Thus, the purchaser of patented goods has the "implied" licence to deal with them as he sees fit. The concept is thus different from the exhaustion doctrine as developed by Josef Kohler that is based on a reward for the first marketing. Under UK law, the other co-owner(s) certainly have not granted any implied licence and in the absence of the above provision could be able to sue for infringement. Similar doctrinal problems come into fore when licensing is concerned, as under traditional common law, a licence is nothing else but a promise not to sue for infringement. Promise by one would, however, not bind the others.
25. *Steers v. Rogers*, (1893) AC 232.
26. Sub-contracting to an agent does not require consent and is interpreted relatively broadly: English Court of Appeal, *Henry Brothers Ltd. Ministry of Defence* [1999] RPC 442, 450.
27. English Court of Appeal, *Hughes v. Paxman*, 23 June 2006, [2007] RPC 34.

... granted" includes the grant of a licence at the request of one co-owner, and the Comptroller given a wide discretion in these matters:[28] In the case at issue, one of the co-owners requested the grant of a licence to a third party. The court held that the Comptroller's power "extended not merely to the grant of licences. The Comptroller could order the sale or lease of the patent too ...[but] must act rationally, fairly, and proportionately and have regard to all the circumstances of the case ... There is no arbitrary power- merely a power to produce a fair commercial solution when co-owners cannot agree." (at 29).

In another case, the Comptroller had ordered that each party would be entitled to grant licences without each other's consent in view of the fact that one party, a research foundation, did not have the means to manufacture the technology itself.[29] No compensation of royalty rates was due to the other co-owner.

(2) As mentioned above, **Germany** applies the rules on partnership to the relationship of co-proprietors. In the absence of a contract, use by one co-proprietor without the others' consent is permissible, even without compensation.[30] Some academic writers have argued that while use without consent is permissible, there should be a proper compensation of the other co-proprietors not using the invention.[31] The question is of particular relevance in cases of industry-university co-operations leading to joint ownership of the right: Here, only the industry partner is in a position to commercially exploit the patent. The Federal Supreme Court grants the co-proprietors the right to demand an internal agreement on how to use the right.[32] In such case, the court may find itself in a similar situation as the British Comptroller of having to accommodate the different interests involved. While each co-owner can transfer his share in the patent without the others' consent and without the obligation to offer the share to the other co-owners, it is generally assumed that a licence can only be granted by common consent or by a majority vote amongst the partners.[33] The request for granting a licence can also be part of the agreement on use that may ultimately be decided by a court.

(3) In **France**, Arts. L 613-29 – 32 CPI provide for relatively detailed rules on joint ownership: Use is allowed against compensation of the non-using co-owners, Art. 613-29 a). Such compensation can be determined by a court. The same holds true for the grant of a non-exclusive licence, Art. 613-29 c). Somewhat unusual are the provisions that apply once one of the co-owners intends to grant a non-exclusive licence. Under the above-mentioned provision, such an offer has to be communicated to the other co-owners *accompanied by an offer to transfer the share at a determined*

28. English Patents Court, 16 Feb. 2006, *Rhone Poulenc v. Yeda* [2006] RPC 24, upheld by Court of Appeal, 31 July 2006, [2007] RPC 167.
29. Comptroller, 12 May 2005, *Elliott and BSP v. Expotech*, Case No. O/132/05.
30. German Federal Supreme Court, 22 March 2005, GRUR 2005, 663 – *Gummielastische Masse II*; German Federal Supreme Court, 16 May 2017, GRUR 2017, 890 – *Sektionaltor II*. The court indicates that for reasons of equity, a co-owner who through no fault of his own cannot exploit the invention may request adequate compensation from the other co-owner(s).
31. R. KRASSER, Patenrecht *(Patent Law)*, 5th ed. 2004, 354.
32. In the course of such agreement, also compensation claims should be settled.
33. R. KRASSER, Patenrecht *(Patent Law)*, 5th ed. 2004, 356 unless the licensor agrees not to use the right himself, as in such case there is multiplication of lawful users.

price. Within three months, anyone of the other co-owners can object to the grant of a licence with the consequence that he is obliged to purchase the share of the other co-owner. Disputes about the proper price of the share may ultimately be settled before the courts. According to one of the leading commentaries of patent law, Chavanne/Burst, "One has to say that the whole procedure is difficult to implement. One does not really understand, why actually there is an obligation for the co-owner who wants to grant a licence to offer his share to the others. It should be sufficient to require an objecting co-owner to state reasons for such refusal and leave it to the courts to decide if such refusal is justified or not".[34]

Granting an exclusive licence requires consent of all co-owners, and in the case one co-owner intends to sell his part, the others have a preferential right of purchase.

(4) Under **US law**:

> "Each co-owner of a United States patent is ordinarily free to make, use, offer to sell and sell the patented invention without regard to the wishes of any co-owner. Each co-owner's ownership rights carry with them the right to license others, a right that also does not require the consent of any co-owner. Thus, unless the co-owner has given up these rights through an "agreement to the contrary", the co-owner may not be prohibited from exploiting its rights in the patent, including the right to grant licenses to third parties on whatever conditions the co-owner chooses".[35]

c) Enforcement against third parties

At least in the case that one co-owner wants to enforce his patent against third parties without the others' consent, there is a certain common understanding between the jurisdictions observed. In the **United Kingdom**, Sec. 66 PA 1977, each co-owner may sue without the others' consent, yet the others have to be made party to the suit either as co-plaintiffs or co-defendants. This makes sure that the decision takes effect in favour of or against all co-owners and excludes subsequent claims by another co-owner based on the same facts. The other two jurisdictions pursue a similar aim. In **Germany**, each co-owner may sue against infringement without the others' consent, but damages have to be paid to all co-proprietors jointly. In contrast thereto, in **France**, Art. 613-29 b) stipulates that each co-owner may sue on his own behalf and expense, but also only for his quota of damages.[36] All three systems thus aim at equitable solutions that do not overburden the infringer nor give the co-proprietor more than his share.

34. CHAVANNE/BURST, Droit de la propriété industrielle, 2nd ed. Paris 1997, 156.
35. US Court of Appeals of the Federal Circuit, *Sheering Corp. v. Roussel-Uclaf sa v. Zeneca Inc.*, 104 F.3d 341-343 (1997); MERGES/LOCKE, Co-ownership of Patents: A Comparative and Economic View, 72 Journal of the Patent and Trademark Office Society 586 (1990). In the case CAFC, *Ethicon v. US Surgical Corporation*, 135 F.3d 1456 (1998), it was even held that a licence could be granted retroactively by one co-inventor who had only contributed to two of the 16 claims of the patent. The latter rule seems questionable.
36. Confirmed by Tribunale de Grande Instance Paris *(Paris District Court)*, 21 February 1994, PIBD 1994, 566-III-255.

For want of exclusive property rights in the patent, one co-owner cannot sue for infringement in the **US**. Rather, all joint owners must sue together.[37]

37. US Court of Appeals, *Willingham v. Lawton*, 555 F2d 1340, 1343 (6th Cir. 1977).

Case No. 15

Rights over the Invention – Transfer of a portion of Patent Right against Misappropriation

Hisayoshi Yokoyama

Where a third party fraudulently obtains a transfer of the patent application to the detriment of the originally mentioned inventor, the latter has a claim against the impostor for a re-transfer even where the patent has already been granted.

Supreme Court, 12 June 2001, Case No. 1918 (O) of 1997 – *Apparatus for Raw Garbage Disposal*

Yugen Kaisha Sunagri v. Itokazu Aomasa

1. BACKGROUND

The Japanese Patent Act stipulates that an inventor is entitled to obtain a patent for his invention, sec. 29(1). Therefore, the right to obtain a patent originally belongs to the inventor, and an application must be filed only by an inventor or his successor in title ("inventor principle"). The application filed by a person who does not have a right to obtain a patent is called a "misappropriated application"[1] of which there are two types: the application filed by an a priori non-titled person, and the application first filed by the legitimate right holder and subsequently misappropriated by a non-entitled person through a change in the name of the applicant.[2]

Since its enactment, the Japanese Patent Act has stipulated that a misappropriated application constitutes a reason for refusal, or, after a patent has been granted, a reason for invalidation, secs. 49(7), 123(1)(vi). The aim of this provision is to prevent those other than the legitimate right holder from obtaining a patent. Therefore, even where a patent has been granted based on a misappropriated application, the legitimate right holder can file a trial for invalidation against the patentee and have the patent revoked in order to freely exploit his invention.

However, a trial for invalidation cannot be an adequate remedy for those who want to obtain a patent over that invention. Certainly, the legitimate right holder

1. A misappropriated application includes an application filed by an inventor who transferred his right to obtain a patent to a third party.
2. T. MATSUYAMA, in: NAKAYAMA/KOIZUMI (eds.), Shin chūkai tokkyohō (*New commentary to the Patent Act*), vol. 2, 2nd ed. 2017, 1427.

can himself file a new application for the same invention, but the application by the legitimate right holder will be refused as the later application, unless the misappropriated application has been waived, withdrawn, dismissed or the decision of refusal for it has become final and binding, sec. 39(6).[3] Besides that, in case the legitimate right holder has filed an application six months after the publication of the misappropriated application, which is often the case, because a misappropriated application will only become known after its publication, the application by the legitimate right holder has to be refused on the ground of lack of novelty.[4] Thus, it is practically difficult for the legitimate right holder to obtain a patent by filing a new application. From here, the question arises whether the legitimate right holder can obtain a patent based on the misappropriated application, either by obtaining the status of the applicant of the misappropriated application or by requesting the transfer of the patent after its registration.

Before the Patent Act amendment of 2011, there was no provision for supporting such remedies. However, as for a remedy before registration of a patent, the lower courts[5] have allowed the legitimate right holder to seek a confirmation that he owns a right to obtain a patent over an invention which is the object of the misappropriated application. On the basis of such a confirmation decision, the legitimate right holder can change the name of the applicant before the Patent Office based on the confirmation decision and become the applicant of the misappropriated application.[6] On the other hand, as for a remedy after registration of a patent, it was generally thought to be impossible for the legitimate right holder to request the transfer of the

3. While the current Patent Act does not deny the status of the prior application of the misappropriated application, the old Patent Act before the law amendment of 2011 denied a status of the prior application of the misappropriated application, and the application by the legitimate rightholder was not refused as the later application. However, it was practically difficult for the examiner to detect a misappropriation, so that the misappropriated application was virtually treated as the prior application, which often led to the refusal of the application by the legitimate rightholder. See, R. TAKABAYASHI, Hyōjun tokkyohō (*Patent Law from the Ground Up*), 6th ed. 2017, 76.
4. With the publication of the misappropriated application, the invention has become known contrary to the will of the legitimate rightholder, in which case the application which he has filed within six months after the publication of the misappropriated application, shall be deemed not to lose the novelty based on that publication, sec. 30(2). In other words, the application which he has filed more than six months after the publication of the misappropriated application, shall be refused on the ground of lack of novelty based on that publication.
5. Tokyo District Court, 5 June 1963, Case No. 5640 (Wa) of 1961, 14-6 Kaminshū 1074 = 146 Hanrei Times 146 – *Powder Volumetric Feeder*; Tokyo District Court, 16 April 1979, Case No. 1107 (Wa) of 1977 & Case No. 1416 (Wa) of 1978, 395 Hanrei Times 155 – *Grain Processing Equipment*; Yokohama District Court 29 March 1985, Case No. 2439 (Wa) of 1980 & Case No. 2049 (Wa) of 1981, 17-1 Mutaishū 166 = 561 Hanrei Times 172 – *Thermoset Forming*; Tokyo District Court, 30 October 1985, Case No. 10654 (Wa) of 1983, 576 Hanrei Times 88 – *Method of Manufacturing Plastic Elements*.
6. The Court has not allowed the legitimate rightholder to request the non-titled applicant to transfer the name of the applicant, because the legitimate rightholder can change the name of the applicant on his own based on the confirmation decision, under sec. 20 of the Patent Registration Ordinance. See, *Powder Volumetric Feeder* case, *supra* note 5; *Thermoset Forming* case, *supra* note 5.

patent,[7] because a patent is a right granted by the Patent Office only to the registered applicant, and the legitimate right holder was not a registered applicant.[8]

Under such circumstances, the Supreme Court upheld a claim of the legitimate right holder for the transfer of the patent, in a case where the patent was registered based on the application first filed by himself. Though this decision is just a case-based judgment, it prompted a vigorous debate about the remedy for the legitimate right holder against misappropriation, which eventually led to the introduction of the "patent transfer registration system" by the Patent Act amendment of 2011.

2. DECISION[9]

a) Facts

Based on an agreement for joint research and development, the plaintiff (appellant before the Supreme Court) and a third party C on 29 October jointly applied for a patent concerning an apparatus for raw garbage disposal. The defendant was employed as a director in the same company as the plaintiff, yet without having been involved in developing the invention. Despite of this fact, the defendant on 29 June 1993 notified the Patent Office of a transfer in that the plaintiff had transferred his share in the patent to the defendant. On behalf of the plaintiff, this document was signed with seal of the representative. For this operation, the seal had been misappropriated. The transfer was duly registered and the patent application published. On 28 March 1996, the patent was granted to both the defendant and party C. The plaintiff while the application was still pending demanded a correction in the name of applicant, and, after registration, amended this claim to a transfer of the defendant's share in the patent. This request was refused in second instance by decision of the Fukuoka High Court dated 31 July 1997. According to the High Court, there was no claim for a (partial) transfer of the patent. As the entitlement for a patent was part of the requirements for grant, and lack of entitlement was a reason for invalidation, a transfer ordered by the court would amount to establishing a reason for invalidation, which was however the exclusive prerogative of the Patent Office. The plaintiff appealed.

b) Reasons

The appealed decision cannot be upheld, and the reasons for this are as follows.

7. T. Matsuyama in: Nakayama/Koizumi (eds.), *supra* note 2, 1428; *Powder Volumetric Feeder* case, *supra* note 5; Fukuoka High Court, 31 July 1997, Case No. 740 (Ne) of 1997, 55-4 Minshū 833 - *Apparatus for Raw Garbage* (second instance of this case).
8. N. Nakayama, Tokkyohō (*Patent Act*), 3rd ed. 2016, 343.
9. Published in 55-4 Minshū 793 = 1753 Hanrei Jihō 119 = 1066 Hanrei Times 217 = N. Nakayama et al. (eds.), Tokkyo Hanrei Hyakusen *(Hundred Selected Patent Cases)*, 4th ed. 2012, 48 = T. Ōbuchi et al. (eds.), Chitekizaisan hō hanrei shū *(Intellectual Property Law Case Book)*, 2nd. ed. 2015, 21. English summary/comment in 34 IIC 671 (2003).

According to the established facts, the patent should rightfully have been granted to the plaintiff and party C, while the defendant is not entitled thereto. The plaintiff thus lost his proprietary interest in the grant of a patent, and correspondingly the defendant owns this interest without legal grounds. Under the above-mentioned factual situation, the patent is registered through prescribed procedures in the Patent Act based on the patent application, and can be seen as having continuity with the right to obtain a patent owned by X and being deformed from it.

Certainly, the plaintiff may initiate nullity proceedings, but after an invalidation of the patent, he is no longer able to apply for a patent over this invention, as the existing patent has already been published and a new application would be rejected. The plaintiff would thus not be able to obtain a patent for his invention, which is clearly unjust. The decision to invalidate the patent would also affect the third party C who is clearly a lawful patent owner and for whom this loss of rights would be even less appropriate. The plaintiff may well claim damages for an unlawful act, namely the impossibility of obtaining a patent right, yet it would be highly difficult in such case to recover the profits which would have been expected had he obtained the patent over the invention. Moreover, the current claim of the plaintiff against the defendant initiated as one to ascertain his share in the right to obtain a patent, and while this request was pending, the patent was granted. Now rejecting this claim as improper, in other words, not to allow an amendment of the claim into one for a transfer of a share in the patent would mean to deny the plaintiff his right and go against procedural economy.

To remedy such inconvenience, instead of invalidating the patent that emerged from the patent application by way of invalidation proceedings, it would be sufficient to transfer the defendant's share of the patent to the plaintiff. For this, it would be sufficient to allow the plaintiff's request to a transfer of his share in the patent, which is ultimately the most direct and simple way.

Still, under patent law, the patent right comes into existence due to a registration by the Patent Office, and the fact that the patent applicant is not the inventor or his successor in title is a ground for refusing the patent application or for invalidating the granted patent, facts which should be determined by the examiner or appeal board member in the first place. However, in the present case it is not in dispute between the parties that the patent at issue is novel and inventive. Rather, the point in dispute is to whom the patent belongs, an issue that can be decided without specific technical knowledge and for which reason there is no justification for a primary jurisdiction of an administrative organ. One can further think of a financial contribution of the defendant for the registration and maintenance of the patent, but a proper compensation of these expenses by the plaintiff to the defendant should be sufficient in no way compromises the plaintiff's claim against the defendant.

For the above considerations and in accordance with the facts of the case, the plaintiff is entitled to demand from the defendant a transfer of the latter's share in the patent.

3. ANALYSIS

a) Meaning of the Supreme Court decision

The Supreme Court affirmed the right of transfer of a patent based on a misappropriated application mainly for three reasons. First, in this case, it was possible to find continuity between the right to obtain a patent owned by the legitimate right holder and the registered patent owned by the non-titled party, because the patent was registered based on the application first filed by the legitimate right holder. Second, the easiest and most efficient remedy for the legitimate right holder in this case was the transfer of the registered patent. Third, this result was not contrary to the intent of the Patent Act which stipulates the misappropriation as a reason for refusal or for invalidation, because in this case only entitlement over an invention was at issue, allowed the court to make a decision without the assistance of the Patent Office.[10] Considering these reasons stated by the Supreme Court, the Supreme Court did not seem to generally affirm the transfer of the patent on the ground of misappropriation, but only under special circumstances, to which these reasons are applicable.[11] In fact, the subsequent lower court decisions[12] unanimously denied the transfer of the patent in the cases where the legitimate right holder had not been involved himself in the filing of the application, because in these cases, different from the Supreme Court case, no continuity could be found between the right to obtain a patent owned by the legitimate right holder and the registered patent owned by the non-titled party. Allowing the transfer of the patent in those cases would mean granting a patent to a person who did not at all file an application, which would conflict with the intent of the Patent Act that adopts the "application system".

However, the aim of the "application system" is to make an invention open to the public and thereby to promote the development of technology. Where the misappropriated application is made public under the laying open system, the invention contributes to the technological development, regardless of whether or not the application was filed by the legitimate right holder himself.[13] Therefore, it can be said that even the legitimate right holder who himself did not file an application

---

10. Today, the third reason has become unpersuasive, because under the current system, the court in a patent infringement litigation can generally determine whether the patent in question should be invalidated in a trial for invalidation, sec. 104ter(1), which presupposes that the court can address technical issues without the aid of the Patent Office.
11. The Supreme Court officer stated that this decision was a case-based judgment based on a specific factual situation, and that it should be carefully determined through further case law under which circumstances the transfer of a right could be affirmed (K. HASEGAWA, Saikōsai hanrei kaisetsu heisei 13 nendo (*Commentary to the Supreme Court Decision of 2001*), vol. 2, 2004, 535).
12. Tokyo District Court, 17 July 2002, Case No. 13678 (Wa) of 2001, 1799 Hanrei Jihō 155 = 1107 Hanrei Times 283 – *Brassiere*; Tokyo District Court, 26 July 2007. Case No. 1623 (Wa) of 2007, the website of the courts <http://www.courts.go.jp/app/files/hanrei_jp/008/035008_hanrei.pdf> – *Granular Transfer Apparatus*; Osaka District Court, 18 November 2010, Case No. 297 (Wa) of 2009, the website of the courts <http://www.courts.go.jp/app/files/hanrei_jp/896/080896_hanrei.pdf> – *Repair Construction Method for the Underside of Edge of Concrete Floor Slab*.
13. See, K. TAMAI, Tokkyohō ni okeru Hatsumeishashugi (1) (*The inventor principle in patent law*), 111-11 Hogaku Kyokai Zasshi (*Journal of the Jurisprudence Association*) 1609 (1994).

deserves being granted a patent for his invention laid open to the public.[14] Based on this reasoning, the Patent Act was reformed in 2011, and the "patent transfer system" was newly introduced.[15]

b) Outline of the patent transfer system

Sec. 74(1) [16] of the Patent Act stipulates that a person who owns a right to obtain a patent may request the patentee to transfer the patent in cases where the patent constitutes the reason for invalidation on the ground of misappropriation. Since the Act no longer requires an application by the legitimate right holder as a requirement for the transfer of a patent, the legitimate right holder who himself did not file an application may request the transfer of the patent according to this provision.[17]

Sec. 74(2) of the Patent Act also stipulates that the patent shall be deemed to originally belong to the legitimate right holder, after the transfer of the right has been registered. By this, exploitation of the invention before registration by the legitimate right holder has become lawful, whereas the patentee who had obtained a patent based on the misappropriated application shall be deemed not to own the patent from the start and his exploitation of the invention retroactively has been unlawful. By this retroactive effect of the transfer of a patent, third parties who had acquired the patent or a licence from that patentee, shall be deemed not to own such rights *ab initio*. That result is appropriate where the third parties knew the fact of misappropriation when acquiring such rights. However, it is not adequate that third parties who were unaware of the fact of misappropriation are forced to stop exploiting an invention, because it is often difficult for outsiders to be aware of the fact of misappropriation, and in general third parties tend to rely on the correctness of the register.[18] Therefore, in order to secure the trust of patent transactions, sec. $79^{bis}(1)$ Patent Act stipulates that a person who owns a patent or a licence and has been exploiting an invention or preparing for the exploitation of an invention at the time of the registration of the transfer of the patent, shall have a non-exclusive statutory licence to the extent that the invention had actually been exploited, while under sec. $79^{bis}(2)$, the patentee shall have a right to receive reasonable consideration from that non-exclusive statutory licensee.

---

14. From this perspective, even prior to the 2011 amendment there was an opinion that generally admitted the transfer of a patent regardless of whether the legitimate right holder himself had been involved in the filing of the application. See, H. YOKOYAMA, *Hatsumeisha no kenri (Right of inventor)*, 322 Hōgaku Kyōshitsu 148 (2007); ŌBUCHI (ed.), Tokkyo soshō *(Patent litigation)* vol. 1, 2012,108.
15. JPO (ed.), Heisei 23 nen tokkyohōtō no ichibu kaisei sangyō zaisankenhō no kaisetsu (*Partial revision of the Patent Act etc in 2011, commentary to the Industrial Property Act*), 2011, 46; T. MATSUYAMA, in NAKAYAMA/KOIZUMI (eds.), *supra* note 2, 1430.
16. This provision also stipulates the transfer of a patent granted in violation of the rights of other co-owners. Where one of the joint owners filed an application only in his own name, and obtained a patent in his single name, the other joint owner may request a partial transfer the patent according to his share, see sec. 40bis of the Patent Law Enforcement Regulation.
17. JPO (ed.), *supra* note 15, 45.
18. JPO (ed.), *supra* note 15, 50-51; T.MATSUYAMA, in: NAKAYAMA/KOIZUMI (eds.), *supra* note 2, 1435, 1509-1510.

The 2011 amendment has also made some partial modifications to the existing provisions, together with the introduction of the patent transfer system, as follows.

Sec. 123(1)(vi) of the Patent Act stipulates that in case the transfer of the patent is registered, the misappropriated application does not constitute a reason for invalidation. As a third party in patent infringement litigation is allowed to raise the estoppel that the patent includes the reason for invalidation on the ground of misappropriation under sec. 104ter(3), the legitimate right holder who had the patent transferred, cannot exercise that patent, unless the reason for invalidation on the ground of misappropriation is resolved.[19]

Sec. 123(2) of the Patent Act stipulates that only a person who owns a right to obtain a patent may request a trial for invalidation on the ground of misappropriation, because otherwise there might be a risk that the patent would be invalidated based on a trial for invalidation which a third party had requested before registration of the transfer of the patent.[20]

Finally, the Patent Act has recognised the status of the prior application of a misappropriated application, which means an application filed by the legitimate right holder after a misappropriated application has to be refused as the later application. This is aimed at avoiding double patenting. If a misappropriated application does not have the status of a prior application, as under the old Patent Act, the legitimate right holder could file a new application subsequent to the misappropriated application and after a successful suit for a patent transfer could have two identical patents in his own name.[21]

c) Remaining issues

(1) Remedies before registration of a patent

The current Patent Act does not stipulate a remedy before registration of a patent. However, since there is no need to distinguish the remedy before and after registration of a patent, it should be interpreted that before registration of a patent, the legitimate right holder may seek the status of an applicant of a misappropriated application, like under the old Patent Act.[22]

(2) Transfer of a patent where the invention has been improved by a third party

The problem still remains, where a third party has somewhat improved an invention and the misappropriated application includes that improvement. In this case, it is not adequate that the legitimate right holder can demand the transfer of the entire patent, because he has a right only of his own invention, not to the improvement made by the third party. Though the Patent Act does not refer to this point, it should be interpreted that the legitimate right holder may demand the transfer of the right

19. JPO (ed.), *supra* note 15, 54; T. MATSUYAMA, in: NAKAYAMA/KOIZUMI (eds.), *supra* note 2, 1436.
20. JPO (ed.), *supra* note 15, 55; T. MATSUYAMA, in: NAKAYAMA/KOIZUMI (eds.), *supra* note 2, 1436.
21. JPO (ed.), *supra* note 15, 58; T. MATSUYAMA, in: NAKAYAMA/KOIZUMI (eds.), *supra* note 2, 1437-1438.
22. M. TAKABE, Bōnin niyoru itentōroku no jitsumu *(Practice of transfer registration on the ground of misappropriation)*, 55 L&T 8 (2012); TAKABAYASHI, *supra* note 3, 78; H. YOKOYAMA, in: SHIMANAMI/UENO/YOKOYAMA Tokkyohō nyūmon *(Introduction to Patent Law)*, 2014, 60-61.

according to his share, which is determined based on the value of his invention in the entire patent.[23]

(3) Burden of allegation and proof of entitlement over an invention

In patent transfer litigation, the legitimate right holder has the burden of proof of entitlement over an invention, which means that he must prove that he owns a right to obtain the patent over the invention which is the object of the registered patent right.[24]

On the other hand, in a trial for invalidation on the ground of misappropriation, the respondent, that is, the patentee has burden of proof of entitlement over an invention, having to allege and prove that he is the inventor or his successor in title,[25] because the current patent system enables only an inventor or his successor in title to obtain a patent.[26] However, this does not mean that the patentee has to prove all details specifically and concretely in any case. Rather, because the fact that the patentee is the first applicant of the invention in question strongly implies that the patentee is an inventor or his successor in title, and the petitioner who alleges misappropriation should proactively disprove that fact.[27] Therefore, the content and level of burden of

---

23. M. Takabe, *supra* note 22, 6; Nakayama, *supra* note 8, 348; Takabayashi, *supra* note 3, 78; H. Yokoyama, in: Shimanami/Ueno/Yokoyama, *supra* note 22, 65-66. There is an opinion that where only one of the claims is an object of misappropriation, the transfer of a patent per each claim should be allowed. See, M. Takeda, Boninshutsugantō ni taisuru shin no kenrisha no kyūsaisochi *(Remedy for the legitimate rightholder against the misappropriated application etc.)*, 54 L&T 47, 48 (2012). In this regard, see also the case IP High Court, 29 June 2009, Case No. 10427 (Gyō-Ke) of 2008 – *Substrate Treatment Equipment* (Case No. 19 in this volume).
24. M. Takabe, *supra* note 22, 6; T. Iimura, Shinketsu torikeshi soshō oyobi tokkyoshingai soshō ni okeru bōnin shutsugan ni kansuru shinri nitsuite (*About proceedings of the misappropriated application in a litigation for revocation of a trial decision and in a litigation for patent infringement*), in Nakayama et al. (ed.), Chizairikkoku no hatten e (Towards the development of IP nation), 2013, 40; E. Takemiya, Hatsumeishasei no risshōsekinin no bunpai (*Division of burden of proof of inventorship*), 59 L&T 27 (2013).
25. IP High Court, 19 January 2006, Case No. 10193 (Gyō-Ke) of 2005, the website of the courts <http://www.courts.go.jp/app/files/hanrei_jp/192/009192_hanrei.pdf> – *Greenery Spraying Material;* IP High Court, 29 June 2009, Case No. 10427 (Gyō-Ke) of 2008, 2104 Hanrei Jihō 101 = 1376 Hanrei Times 205 – *Substrate Treatment Equipment*; IP High Court, 27 April 2010, Case No. 10213 (Gyō-Ke) of 2009, the website of the courts <http://www.courts.go.jp/app/files/hanrei_jp/176/080176_hanrei.pdf> – *Test for Sperm Egg*; IP High Court, 30 November 2010, Case No. 10329 (Gyō-Ke) of 2009, 2116 Hanrei Jihō 107 – *Shellfish Fastener*; IP High Court, 28 March 2013, Case No. 10280 (Gyō-Ke) of 2012, 2200 Hanrei Jihō 125 = 1416 Hanrei Times 116 – *Moving State Management System;* IP High Court, 25 January 2017, Case No. 10230 (Gyō-Ke) of 2015, the website of the courts <http://www.courts.go.jp/app/files/hanrei_jp/479/086479_hanrei.pdf> – *Jetting Nozzle Tube*; IP High Court, 27 March 2017, Case No. 10252 (Gyō-Ke) of 2015, the website of the courts <http://www.courts.go.jp/app/files/hanrei_jp/649/086649_hanrei.pdf> – *Building Method of a Protection Concrete Body for a Septic Tank*; E. Takemiya, *supra* note 24, 25; T. Shōji, Bōninshutsugan/kyōdoshutugan'ihan no shuchōrisshosekinin ni kansuru jitsumuteki kōsatsu (*Practical analysis on the burden of allegation and proof of misappropriated application and violation of joint application*), in: Shitara (ed.) Gendai Chitekizaisanhō Zitsumu to Kadai (*Current Intellectual Property Law Practice and Agenda*), 2015, 429.
26. *Greenery Spraying Material* case, *supra* note 25; *Substrate Treatment Equipment* case, *supra* note 25; *Shellfish Fastener* case, *supra* note 25.
27. *Substrate Treatment Equipment* case, *supra* note 25; *Shellfish Fastener* case, *supra* note 25; *Moving State Management System* case, *supra* note 25; *Jetting Nozzle Tube* case, *supra* note 25;

allegation and proof on the part of the patentee largely depends on the content and level of allegation and proof on the side of the petitioner.[28] Where the petitioner has neither alleged any concrete circumstances suggesting a misappropriated application nor presented any supporting evidence for it, the allegation and proof on the side of the patentee could be relatively simple. On the other hand, where the petitioner has alleged such circumstances concretely and has presented supporting evidence for it, the allegation and proof on the side of the patentee must exceed the one on the side of the petitioner.

Taking these issues into account, although the person who bears the burden of allegation and proof of entitlement is formally different for a patent transfer litigation and for a trial for invalidation, it can be said that in either procedure, a person who will challenge the current ownership, that is, the legitimate right holder in a patent transfer litigation and the petitioner in a trial for invalidation, must substantially allege and prove his entitlement over an invention.[29]

4. COMPARATIVE REMARKS

In **European** countries, there exists a remedy system against misappropriation which, before or after the registration of a patent, enables the legitimate right holder to obtain the patent, regardless of whether or not the true inventor took part in filing the application.[30]

a) Entitlement claims

(1) In Germany, the UK and France, there exists a system whereby the legitimate right holder can demand the transfer of the right to request grant of a patent or the patent, sec. 8 of the German Patent Act, L611-8 of the French IP Act, secs. 8(1) (2)(a), 37(1) (2)(a) of the UK Patent Act. However, this request must be filed within certain period after the publication of grant of a patent, except that the patentee obtained the patent in bad faith (with knowledge of misappropriation).[31] In detail:

Building Method of a Protection Concrete Body for a Septic Tank case, *supra* note 25.

28. *Substrate Treatment Equipment* case, *supra* note 25; *Jetting Nozzle Tube* case, *supra* note 25; *Building Method of a Protection Concrete Body for a Septic Tank* case, *supra* note 25.
29. Additionally, in a trial for invalidation on the ground of violation of joint application, the petitioner bears the burden of allegation and proof. See IP High Court, 13 March 2013, Case No. 10059 (Gyō-Ke) of 2012, 2201 Hanrei Jihō 116 = 1414 Hanrei Times 244 - *Tape for Forming Double Eyelid*; E. TAKEMIYA, *supra* note 24, 24; SHŌJI, *supra* note 25, 429.
30. The main difference between the position in Europe and Japan seems to be that European jurisdictions do not regard the entitlement over an invention as a positive requirement of patentability. According to JOSEF KOHLER, Handbuch des Deutschen Patentrechts *(Handbook of German Patent Law)*, Mannheim 1900, 248, "where an application is filed for an invention, the Patent Office in theory will grant a patent even if the applicant is not the inventor and even if the Patent Office has knowledge that he is not the inventor: The Patent Office grants a right over an invention, subject to later redistribution."
31. This period is two years in Germany and UK, by sec. 8 of the German Patent Act, sec. 37(5) of the UK Patent Act, three years in France, by L 611-8 of the French IP Act. In Japan, such time limitation was discussed in the course of the law amendment of 2011, but was eventually rejected because the non-titled party's expectation that he can keep possessing his right as his own is

(2) In the **UK**, secs. 8, 37 Patent Act 1977 allow any person to question the entitlement of a patent before the Comptroller (before and after grant), or before the courts (after grant).[32] The Comptroller should refer complex cases to the court.[33] Also entitlement related to foreign patents can be ascertained.[34] The action is time-barred after two years from grant, and no new claims may be brought: If the original application is only for a transfer of part of the invention, it cannot later (ie after the two-year period) be broadened to a complete transfer.[35] The plaintiff in an entitlement action needs to show not only that he has contributed to the core concept of the invention, but rather that the current owner on the patent register has committed a breach of law (e.g. breach of a secrecy agreement, theft etc.).[36] In other words, it is not sufficient for the plaintiff to show that he (co-) invented, but that the invention was (partly) misappropriated. After all, the defendant may have made the invention himself in parallel, which would give the plaintiff no claim at all. A plaintiff in entitlement proceedings thus has to show that, first, the defendant broke the law or a contract, and, second, that such breach related to an inventive concept. Finally, ownership disputes may comprise issues of validity if these are clear and unarguable.[37]

(3) In **Germany**, sec. 8 Patent Act allows a civil claim for the transfer of part or the whole of the patent. Sec. 8 requires that the person entitled to the invention raises a claim against a person who is not so entitled. Only an inventor or successor in title is entitled, and the unentitled person must not have an independent claim to the patent (ie a parallel development).[38] However, different from the new case law in the UK, it is not necessary to prove a breach of law or contract. It is sufficient to prove that the defendant obtained his invention from the plaintiff and that the plaintiff did not consent to the application of the patent.[39] The defendant cannot argue that the invention is not patentable.[40] Secs. 7, 8, 21 (1) give the plaintiff the following remedies: Transfer of the whole or part of the patent (or patent application), revocation of the patent and (within one month from the decision) filing a new application that benefits of the initial priority and must not extend beyond the original application. The entitled (co-)inventor may also raise a claim of unjust enrichment and obtain compensation instead.[41] There is a time limit of two years after grant for bringing an

---

not worth a protection, considering that the legitimate right holder can still invalidate the patent through a trial for invalidation, even though the transfer of a patent would be denied based on the time limitation. See, SANGYOKŌZŌSHINGIKAI CHITEKIZAISANSEISAKUBUKAI (*Intellectual Property Committee of Industrial Structure Council*), Tokkyoseido ni kansuru hōseitekina kadai ni tsuite (*About Legal Agenda of the Patent System*), 2011, 64, available at the website of the JPO <https://www.jpo.go.jp/resources/shingikai/sangyo-kouzou/shousai/tokkyo_shoi/document/index/housei_kadai.pdf>

32. English Court of Appeal, 23 June 2006, *Hughes v. Paxman*, [2007] RPC 34.
33. English Court of Appeal, 22 March 2005, *Markem v. Zipher,* [2005] RPC 761.
34. English Court of Appeal, 2 March 2006, *in re University of Southampton Applications*, [2006] RPC 567.
35. English Patents Court, 16 February 2006, *Rhone Poulenc v. Yeda,* [2006] RPC 605.
36. English Court of Appeal, 22 March 2005, *Markem v. Zipher*, [2005] RPC 761.
37. English Court of Appeal, 22 March 2005, *Markem v. Zipher*, [2005] RPC 761.
38. German Federal Supreme Court, 6 October 1981, GRUR 1982, 95 – *Pneumatische Einrichtung.*
39. Appeal Court Düsseldorf, Betriebsberater 1970, 1110.
40. German Federal Supreme Court, 15 May 2001, GRUR 2001, 823 – *Schleppfahrzeug.*
41. Federal Supreme Court, 21 December 2005, 37 IIC 866 [2006] – *Cylinder Pipe.*

action unless the plaintiff can prove bad faith of the unentitled patentee. It seems that German courts would not rule on entitlement proceedings for foreign patents, but only on German and European ones.

(4) In **France**, Art. R 611-18 allows the true inventor (or successor in title) to claim (co-) ownership of the application or invention. Just as before the EPO, grant procedures will be suspended by the request of the person claiming true ownership of the invention. French courts will order the transfer ownership not only of French patents, but also of corresponding foreign ones.[42]

b) Lack of entitlement as an estoppel

Entitlement claims are basically disputes over private rights. The plaintiff can assert such right, and the defendant can deny the plaintiff's entitlement. That much is clear. It becomes more difficult when third parties get involved, as the following examples show.

(1) In the **UK**, it is clear that third party rights cannot be raised as a defence. In the case at issue, a co-owner of the invention had requested the comptroller to order the grant of a licence. The other co-owner was against such request and argued that making such request would contravene a fiduciary duty vis a vis the company both co-owners had jointly founded. The court ruled that breach of such a duty could only be invoked by the company, not by the other co-owner.[43] A request for revocation can only be made by the true inventor, Sec. 72(2) Patent Act.

(2) In entitlement proceedings, it is permissible in **Germany** to argue that the plaintiff (alleged owner of the invention) himself was not entitled to the invention.[44] A request for revocation based on lack of entitlement can only be made by the true inventor, Sec. 81(3) Patent Act.

(3) In **France**, a request for revocation and the estoppel of invalidity can only be raised by the true inventor: "Only [the true inventors] are in a position to contest the right of Wellcome to the disputed European patents. Consequently, Wellcome was deemed to be entitled to exercise the right to the European patent before the European Patent Office. The request of the Apotex companies, which do not claim to be co-inventors, to revoke the patents pursuant to Art. 138(1)(e) of the EPC is therefore unfounded ...".[45]

c) EPC procedures

Under the European Patent Convention, an applicant is deemed to be entitled to exercise a right to obtain a patent in the proceedings before the EPO, Art. 60(3) EPC, which means that the Patent Office is neither required nor competent to settle

42. Paris District Court, 4 May 2006, PIBD No. 835 – III – 527; Paris District Court, 6 April 2006, PIBD Nr. 834 – III – 489; Paris Court of Appeal, 19 May 2006 – *Sofresud*.
43. English Court of Appeal, *Hughes v. Paxman*, 23 June 2006, [2007] RPC 34, 43.
44. German Federal Supreme Court, 30 October 1990, GRUR 1991, 127 – *Objektträger*.
45. Paris Court of Appeal, 15 September 2000, 34 IIC 297 [2003] – *Aids Anti-Virus*.

disputes about entitlement over an invention. Disputes in this respect have to be brought before the national courts, and while such dispute is pending, proceedings before the EPO are interrupted.[46]The procedure envisaged by the EPC is a stay in the application (or opposition (appeal)) procedure once an alleged (co-) owner has given notice of a pending entitlement dispute. Until such notice, the applicant is presumed entitled to the rights over the patent, Art. 60(3) EPC. Suspension is compulsory where an entitlement dispute is pending in one of the EPC Member States, as any decision issued by the competent authorities is automatically recognised by the EPO under the Recognition Protocol. No corresponding rule exists for entitlement disputes in non-member states (e.g. Japan or the US), yet also here, suspension of procedures under Rule 13 would seem appropriate. There is no fixed rule when procedures should be resumed. Certainly after the issuance of a final decision, but perhaps also once a first instance decision dismissing the claim has been issued, or once the defendant can show that the entitlement dispute is a tactical manoeuvre. In such cases, the EPO should go into the merits of the dispute as much as necessary and as little as possible.

Once the national court has made a decision as to entitlement, the legitimate right holder may take an action before the EPO, that is, prosecuting the European patent application as his own application in place of the applicant, filing a new European patent application for the same invention,[47] or requesting that the European patent application should be refused, by Art. 61 EPC.

46. The German Patent Act adopts the same system and deems the patent applicant to be entitled to request grant of a patent in the application procedure in order to avoid delay of substantive examination of a patent application, by sec. 7(1). This system that the application procedure has to determine only whether a patent should be granted, regardless of whether the applicant has entitlement over the invention, has already been advocated by JOSEF KOHLER, Handbuch des Deutschen Patentrechts (*Handbook of German patent law*), Mannheim 1900, 248 on whose ideas Art. 61 EPC is based.
47. The new European patent application shall be deemed to have been filed on the date of filing of the misappropriated application, insofar as it may be filed only in respect of the subject matter which does not extend beyond the content of the misappropriated application, by Art. 61(2), 76(1) EPC.

Case No. 16

Employees' Inventions – Company Rules – Reasonable Remuneration

Anja Petersen-Padberg

1. **An employee can claim additional payment for an invention he has made in the course of employment if the amount of remuneration provided by the employer under the internal company rules is less than reasonable.**
2. **If the company rules contain a payment date for remuneration, additional payment can be claimed as of that date which also triggers the prescription period for such claim.**

Supreme Court, 22 April 2003, Case No. 1256 (Ju) of 2001 – *Olympus*

Tanaka v. Olympus

1. BACKGROUND

According to section 29(1) Japanese Patent Act ("Patent Act"), the right to the patent belongs to the inventor-employee. Sec. 35 Patent Act governs how the employer can obtain the right to the invention from his employee and the employee's right to a "reasonable compensation".

Sec. 35 Patent Act on employees' inventions was originally modelled after German law and was last amended in 2015, becoming effective on 1 April 2016.[1]

The current legal situation is a result of a long history of the right to a compensation for employees' inventions in Japan and in particular the result of the *Olympus* case decided by three court instances.[2]

Since 1921, Japan's Patent Act has provided rules granting an employed inventor the right to a reasonable compensation for transferring the rights over the invention

1. The amendment of the Patent Act was promulgated on 10 July 2015 and became effective on 1 April 2016, see translation of sec. 35 Patent Act below.
2. Tokyo District Court, 16 April 1999, English translation in: 24-6 AIPPI Journal of the Japanese Group (English edition) 255-276 (1999) with comment by K. HINKELMANN; Tokyo High Court, 22 May 2001, 1753 Hanrei Jihō 23; Supreme Court, 22 April 2003, Case No. 1256 (Ju) of 2001, 57-4 Minshū 477 = 1822 Hanrei Jihō 39 = 1121 Hanrei Times 104 = N. NAKAYAMA et al. (eds.), Tokkyo Hanrei Hyakusen *(Hundred Selected Patent Cases)*, 4th ed. 2012, 66 = T. ŌBUCHI et al. (eds.) Chitekizaisan hō hanrei shū *(Intellectual Property Law Case Book)*, 2nd ed. 2015, 33 – *Olympus*.

to the employer.[3] This right was further substantiated in sec. 35 of the Patent Act 1959. Since the 1960ies, many companies established internal rules on employees' inventions not only to fix the amount of remuneration, but also to lay down other rules related to the rights over an employee invention.[4] This is necessary, since different from e.g. German law,[5] there are no laws or guidelines with details on the calculation of the remuneration and the handling of employees' inventions, such as obligation of reporting of inventions, assignment of rights, the point of time of payment, employee's right to objection, the obligation to keep the invention secret, handling of reports on inventions which are not considered as inventions, joint inventions, inventions of retired employees and employees working at other locations, etc.

Remunerations for the assignment of rights over the invention were usually very moderate amounts which were paid by the company to the employee inventor at different points in time ("patent milestones").[6] Due to the (past) traditional life-long employment (and the difficulty of changing jobs) during which employees did not wish to antagonise their employer, employees accepted a few hundred Euros, if at all, for the transfer of the rights over the invention, even for inventions that brought high economic success to the company. Most of them also did not sue their employers after retirement.

A turning point was the High Court decision *Olympus* in May 2001 that confirmed the decision of the Tokyo District Court.[7] Here, the employee inventor had received a moderate remuneration (around USD 1,600 in a lump sum) based on the employer's company rules, while the company gained roughly USD 60 million in royalties for the invention.[8] After retirement, the inventor employee decided to assert that the compensation for his invention was "not reasonable" according to sec. 35 Patent Act and that the employer was required to pay a higher remuneration. The Tokyo High Court decided that despite the existence of fixed amounts to be paid

3. Sec. 14 (3) Patent Act, Law No. 96 of 1921.
4. In 1964, the Japanese Patent Office published model company guidelines. Since that time, particularly large companies have adopted in-house regulations (T. Doi, Patents & Licensing, Vol. 36, No. 5, 2006, 17).
5. German law provides detailed rules in the *Gesetz über Arbeitnehmererfindungen* (AEI, Act on Employees' Inventions) of 25 July 1957 as last amended by Article 7 of law of 31 July 2009 (Federal Gazette 2009 I, 2521). In particular, the calculation of a reasonable remuneration (own use, licensing, sale, no use, etc.) is established in the Guidelines for the remuneration of employees' inventions (*Richtlinien für die Vergütung von Arbeitnehmererfindungen im privaten Dienst*) of 20 July 1959 (BAnz No. 156, 1) as last amended on 1 September 1983 (BAnz No. 169, 9994). The provisions have been interpreted by many court decisions, including a high number of Federal Court of Justice decisions and by a high number of decisions by the Arbitration Board for Employees' Inventions of the German Patent and Trademark Office.
6. In company guidelines, payments are basically made at four different points in time: (1) at the time of application (87.5%), including applications in foreign countries, (2) at the time of patent registration (81.8%), (3) when exploiting the invention (73.3%) and, (4) in the case of another's use of the patent (licensing) (57.5%). According to the survey, more than half of the companies have company guidelines regarding payments at all four points in time (JILPT, Survey 2006, footnote 24 below, 32). The law requires a payment of a reasonable remuneration when making use of the invention. Payments for the application or grant of the patent must therefore be considered as a reward or incentive payment.
7. See *supra* note 2.
8. In 1992, for more details, see below, item 2.

according to the employer's company rules, a court may determine a "reasonable remuneration" pursuant to sec. 35 Patent Act in consideration of the company's profit and the employee's contribution to the invention. The employee should be entitled to an additional remuneration beyond one fixed by company rules if the amount paid was "not reasonable".[9] This decision was later confirmed by the Supreme Court.

After the *Olympus* lower court decisions, Japanese employees became increasingly aware of their rights under sec. 35 Patent Act and the number of similar cases increased. For instance, between 1991 and 2000 only one or two actions, if any at all, were filed each year. In 2001 already four, in 2002 and 2003 five cases were filed.[10] A peak was reached in 2004 when (former) employees went to court in ten cases. Perhaps the best known is the "Blue Diode Case" where the Tokyo District Court granted the extraordinary remuneration of JPY 60 billion (about EUR 600 million) due to the company's high profits made out of the invention of the first high brightness gallium nitride (GaN) LED whose brilliant blue light, when partially converted into yellow by a phosphor coating, is the key to white LED lighting, which went into production in 1993. This sum by far exceeded the payment according to the company rules of the employer.[11] In the second instance, the case was settled for a sum of about EUR 6.1 million.[12]

Concerned about the financial risks under a system in which the courts despite existing company rules would re-evaluate what a reasonable compensation should be, employers in 2004 prompted Japanese Parliament to amend the Patent Act. The 2004 amendment gave company rules priority over the law regarding the determination of a "reasonable remuneration". However, according to the revised law, the employer is now required to disclose and discuss the compensation rules and calculation methods with the employee in advance. The Japanese Patent Office issued "Case Studies" on how to fulfil the new procedural requirements of a company guideline pursuant

9. Tokyo High Court, *supra* note 2. The amount of remuneration determined by the court was about JPY 2.3 million (about EUR 17,000).
10. K. ONISHI/H. OWAN, Incentive Pay or Windfalls: Remuneration for employee inventions in Japan, RIETI (The Research Institute of Economy, Trade and Industry), Discussion Paper Series 10-E-049, published at the website of the RIETI <https://www.rieti.go.jp/en/publications/summary/10100005.html>, 32.
11. The inventor received JPY 20,000 (approx. EUR 150) for his invention according to the company rules of his employer. Tokyo District Court, 30 January 2004, 1852 Hanrei Jihō, 36 – *Blue Diode*, English translation in 35 IIC 941 (2004), German translation in GRUR Int. 2005, 439 *et seq.*, decision commented by A. PETERSEN-PADBERG/P. KLUSMANN, GRUR Int. 2005, 370; T. DOI, Tokyo District Court Awarded 20 Billion yen for Employee's Invention – Is This "Resonable"? – 29-2 AIPPI Journal of the Japanese Group (English edition) 111 *et seq.* (2004).
12. Settlement Agreement in the Second Instance, 11 January 2005, Case No. 962 and 2177 (Ne) of 2004, 30-6 AIPPI Journal of the Japanese Group (English edition) 2005, 311 *et seq.* (2005), commented on by R. SHIMANAMI, The Nichia Corporation Employee Invention Case Settlement – Interpreting the Tokyo High Court's Reasoning, 30-6 AIPPI Journal of the Japanese Group (English edition) 306 *et seq.* (2005). The inventor, *Shuji Nakamura*, complained that he was "forced to settle". *Nakamura* had filed the action after he was sued by his former employer for disclosing trade secrets at his new working place in the US. In 2014, *Shuji Nakamura, Isamu Akasaki* and *Hiroshi Amano* received the Nobel prize in physics "for the invention of efficient blue light-emitting diodes which has enabled bright and energy-saving white light sources".

to sec. 35 Patent Act.[13] If the procedural requirements were observed, in principle, compensation should be considered "reasonable" under sec. 35 and may therefore not be adjusted by the courts anymore. Subsequently, after the amendment of sec. 35 in 2004, the number of employee invention compensation cases decreased. In 2005, there were seven, in 2006 five and in 2007 two cases.[14] However, the revision of 2004 did not fully allay industry's concern that employees would file court actions to claim higher amounts of remuneration compared to the one fixed in the respective company rules. Industry therefore continued to criticise sec. 35 Patent Act and also complained that documenting the information process and calculating a reasonable remuneration was too complex and cumbersome. It was also argued that the current remuneration system prevented teamwork. As a result, sec. 35 Patent Act was newly amended in 2015[15] without a significant change of the existing system, but with a new detailed Guideline of the Ministry of Economy, Trade and Industry ("METI Guideline") explaining the process of setting up a company guideline.[16] Should this Guideline be observed, as a rule, the compensation or "other benefits" fixed by the company should be deemed "reasonable" under sec. 35 Patent Act, meaning that a court action would not have much chance of success. With this Guideline, lawmakers found a compromise between the industry's interest that company rules should have a binding effect and employees' rights to an appropriate compensation. Due to that compromise, sec. 35 Patent Act still permits a court action should the employee consider the amount of remuneration or the economic benefits as "not reasonable" or, if the process to enact the company rules pursuant to sec. 35(5) Patent Act was not observed or company rules were missing at all (sec. 35(7)). However, cases are rare.[17]

---

13. JPO, Shin shokumu hatsumei seido ni okeru tetsuzuki jirei shū *(The Case Studies of the Procedures under the New Employee Inventions System)*, September 2004, published on the website of the JPO <https://www.jpo.go.jp/system/patent/shutugan/shokumu/document/shokumu/zireisyu.pdf>.
14. K. Onishi/H. Owan, *supra* note 10, 32.
15. *Supra* note 1.
16. METI, Kokuji heisei 28 nen dai 131 gō: Tokkyo hō dai 35 jō dai 6 kō ni motozuku hatsumei wo shōrei suru tame no sōtō no kinsen sonota no keizaijō no rieki nit suite sadameru baai ni kōryo subeki shiyōsha tō to jūgyōsha tō tono aida de okonawareru kyōgi no jōkyō tō ni kansuru shishin *(Public Notice No. 131 of 2016: Guideline for Circumstances of Negotiation between Employer and Employee Which Should Be Considered in Determining Reasonable Remuneration or Any Other Economic Benefits for Encouraging Inventions under Section 35, Paragraph (6) of the Patent Act)*, available at the website of the JPO <https://www.jpo.go.jp/system/patent/shutugan/shokumu/shokumu_guideline.html> (hereinafter also called "METI Guideline")
17. Examples of recent court decisions on employees' inventions are the following: IP High Court, 11 July 2013, Case No. 10099 (Ne) of 2012, 2209 Hanrei Jihō 121 – *Nipro* (Remuneration: JPY 734,521, approx. EUR 5,500); IP High Court, 26 June 2014, Case No. 10012 (Ne) of 2014, the website of the courts <http://www.courts.go.jp/app/files/hanrei_jp/308/084308_hanrei.pdf> – *Conglo Engineering* (Remuneration: JPY 9,820,072, approx. EUR 73,600); IP High Court, 26 February 2015, Case No. 10025 (Ne) of 2014, the website of the courts <http://www.courts.go.jp/app/files/hanrei_jp/911/084911_hanrei.pdf> – *Toyota* (Remuneration: JPY 24,015,000, approx. EUR 180,000); IP High Court, 30 September 2015, Case No. 10044 (Ne) of 2015, the website of the courts <http://www.courts.go.jp/app/files/hanrei_jp/645/085645_hanrei.pdf> – *Riken* (Remuneration: JPY 8,014,406, approx. EUR 60,000). T. Okamoto, published a (incomplete) list of recent decisions in: Heisei 27 nen "shokumu hatsumei seido" kaisei ni tsuite no ichikōsatsu *(Some thoughts on the 2015 reform of the employee inventor system)*, 71-6 Patent 11, 16 (2018). According to that list, in 27 of 60 cases, no remuneration at all was granted.

In sum, the amendments in 2015 were the following: **1. Assignment of rights prior to the making of an invention**: Employers can now obtain the right to the invention by publishing respective company rules without an additional act of assignment. **2. Grant of "other economic benefits":** Companies are obliged to pay a reasonable remuneration, but with the new law, they may also grant "other reasonable benefits". They are (relatively) free to fix the amount of payment or the benefits to be granted to the employee in their company rules. **3. METI Guideline:** If the employer has observed the process as described in sec. 35 (5) Patent Act and according to the mentioned METI Guideline, chances are that the employee will not be able to obtain a court decision granting a higher amount of remuneration or a different "reasonable benefit".

The new **sec. 35 Patent Act** reads:[18]

> "(Inventions by Employees)
>
> (1)An employer, a juridical person or a national or local government (hereinafter referred to as "Employer"), where an employee, an officer of the juridical person, or a national or local government employee (hereinafter referred to as "Employee") has obtained a patent for an invention which, by the nature of the said invention, falls within the scope of the business of the said Employer and was achieved by an act(s) categorized as a present or past duty of the said Employee performed for the Employer (hereinafter referred to as "Employee Invention") or where a successor to the right to obtain a patent for the Employee Invention has obtained a patent therefor, shall have a non-exclusive license on the said patent right.
>
> (2) In the case of an invention by an Employee, any provision in any agreement, employment regulation or any other stipulation providing in advance that the right to obtain a patent or that the patent rights for any invention made by an Employee, shall vest in the Employer, or that an exclusive license for the said invention shall be granted to the Employer, shall be null and void unless the said invention is an Employee Invention.
>
> (3) *If an Employee makes an Employee Invention, the right to obtain a patent belongs to the Employer when it occurs, provided that any agreement, employment regulation or any other stipulation made prior to the invention vests the right to the Employer.*
>
> (4) Where the Employee, in accordance with any agreement, employment regulation or any other stipulation, vests the right to obtain a patent or the patent right for an Employee Invention in the Employer, or grants an exclusive license therefor to the Employer, the said Employee shall have the right to receive *reasonable remuneration or other economic benefits (Reasonable Benefits).*
>
> (5) Where an agreement, employment regulation or any other stipulation provides for Reasonable Benefits, the content of the Reasonable Benefits provided

18. The translation is based on "translations of Japanese laws" and the underlined amendments of 2015 by S. OKUYAMA, New Invention Scheme in Japan, Les Nouvelles, Vol. L II, No. 3, June 2017, 111 *et seq.*

in the preceding paragraph, the payment of value in accordance with the said provision(s) *shall not be considered unreasonable* in light of circumstances where a negotiation between the Employer and the Employee had taken place in order to set standards for the determination of the said Reasonable Benefits, the set standards had been disclosed, the opinions of the employee on the content of the Reasonable Benefits had been received and any other relevant circumstances.

(6) *The Minister of Economy, Trade and Industry shall establish and publish guidelines on circumstances to be considered according to the preceding paragraph to promote inventions upon hearing opinions of the Industrial Structure Council.*[19]

(7) Where no provision setting forth Reasonable Benefits as provided in the preceding paragraph exists, or where it is recognized under paragraph 5 that the content of the Reasonable Benefit to be provided in accordance with the relevant provisions is unreasonable, the content of the Reasonable Benefits to be provided according to the paragraph 4, shall be determined by taking into consideration the amount of profit to be received by the Employer from the invention, the Employer's burden, contribution, and treatment of the Employee and any other circumstances relating to the invention."

The JPO[20] and the METI Guideline,[21] provide for the following details on what companies need to do so that the fixed compensation or "other benefits" according to their company guidelines will be considered as "reasonable" under sec. 35(5):[22]

1. Establishing employee invention standards as company rules or in a collective agreement, possibly prior to the completion of an invention. The standards may consider the contribution of the company to the invention, or may depend on expected sales.

2. The standards shall be negotiated, therefore

   a. they need to be disclosed, e.g. by e-mail, via the Intranet or otherwise so that the employee can take notice of them and,
   b. the employees shall get the opportunity to provide their opinion. Employers need not to hear each employee individually, but may organize a gathering of the employees, an electronic conference or a hearing via an Intranet bulletin. However, employees who had no chance to participate need to get another opportunity to provide their opinion. Employers need to respond to employees' questions substantially.
   c. "Negotiation" means "consultation", employer and employee do not have to enter into an agreement.
   d. Employers need to disclose materials and information such as the content of the draft employees' invention rules, the treatment of employees doing

19. See *supra* note 16.
20. *Supra* note 13.
21. *Supra* note 16.
22. Companies may also choose not to establish an employee invention system, but to agree with an inventor individually on a compensation or a reasonable benefit. Such individual agreement without having set any standards in advance will not be considered "unreasonable" from the outset, METI Guideline, *supra* note 16, II.,2. (i).

research and development, profits, expenses and risk related to research and development, etc.

e. Employers should keep records on how the rules were set, minutes of the negotiations, minutes of an explanatory meeting, content of an agreement or materials showing time, date, methods and circumstances of the disclosure, a written notice on the explanations given to an employee, etc.

f. "Reasonable benefits" other than money such as an opportunity to study abroad upon employer's expense, stock options, license rights, promotion accompanied by improvement of monetary treatment, additional paid leave days need to have an economic value, a mere certificate of commendation will not be sufficient.[23]

According to a survey,[24] the establishment of company guidelines for employees' invention is common practice, in particular in Japan's larger companies.[25] 96% of companies with more than 50 employees in R&D departments have enacted company rules on employees' inventions, 93% of the companies surveyed stated that they have provisions stipulating that all rights to inventions are to be assigned to the employer.[26] With regard to companies filing IP rights, no matter which size their R&D division has, 85% of those companies have established some provisions on patent and patent application rights and on remuneration.[27]

After the reform of sec. 35 Patent Act in 2004, Japanese companies began to amend existing rules or to establish new company rules to comply with the required formalities. They could take the JPO interpretation into consideration.[28]

The most significant change, however, was the companies' decision to increase the disclosure of their policies to employees.[29]

A director of the intellectual property rights office of a Japanese electronic machinery manufacturer stated:

> "In 2005 when the law was revised, we held a series of meetings to explain our remuneration policy for employees' inventions to all employees. We were given a roster of all employees and checked their attendance and, if necessary, arranged one-to-one meetings to make sure that everyone received an explanation. Since

23. METI Guideline, *supra* note 16.
24. In view of the amendment of sec. 35 Patent Act in 2004, the Japan Institute for Labour Policy and Training conducted a survey regarding the handling by Japanese companies of employees' inventions, at the end of 2005, Jūgyō-in no hatsumei ni taisuru shogū ni tsuite no chōsa *(Japan Institute for Labour Policy and Training Survey)*, in: JILPT Chōsa Series No. 27, October 2006, published at the website of JILPT <http://www.jil.go.jp/institute/research/2006/027.html> (hereinafter and above: "JILPT, Survey 2006"). The survey is based on the responses of 613 companies made between November 25 and December 15, 2006. With regard to a survey on the handling of employee inventions of 1994, see C. HEATH/M. MŌRI, Employees' Inventions in Japan, 36 IIC 663, 680 (2005).
25. The survey showed that remuneration provisions are usually set out in the company guidelines (79.9%) or are employment instructions (*shūgyō kisoku*) (18.5%). However, almost never are there agreements with a company's labour union (0.8%) or in employment contracts (0.5%) (JILPT, Survey 2006, 31).
26. JILPT, Survey 2006, *supra* note 24, 30.
27. JILPT, Survey 2006, *supra* note 24, 28, 31.
28. *Supra* note 13.
29. K.ONISHI/H. OWAN, *supra* note 10, 2.

> the law requires "consultation" with the employees, we created a special e-mail address to receive their inquiries and comments. Since 2005, we have held an information session for new employees every year including a thirty-page Power Point presentation that explains the Patent Law, describes the legal treatment of employees' inventions, and provides a detailed explanation of the formulae used to determine remuneration levels. Furthermore, all the information including the formal provisions and a two-page summary is available for viewing on our intranet, therefore anyone can see it whenever they want."[30]

Before the amendment, companies did not reveal details of their remuneration policies to employees. Many inventor-employees did not precisely know whether or how much remuneration they would receive prior to developing their inventions.[31]

2. DECISION[32]

a) Facts

The Plaintiff (appellee) was an employee of Defendant from May 1969 to November 1994. The Defendant (appellant), Olympus, is a company, which manufactures and sells optical instruments.

During his work in the R&D division of Defendant, the Plaintiff was engaged in the research and development of videodisc devices and in 1977 created an invention called a "pickup device" to be used in CD or DVD players ("Invention").

Defendant has a set of company rules that apply to employees' inventions. According to those, when an employee transfers his right to obtain a patent for an employee's invention to the company, the company under the rules must pay a remuneration to the employee in three instalments: the first when a patent is filed, the second when the patent is granted, and the third when the invention is actually used and the company makes a profit from it. The third instalment is a lump sum payment of up to a maximum payment of JPY 1,000,000 (approx. EUR 7,635[33]). The Plaintiff, as well as other employees, took an oath to accept any internal rules including those on employee inventions.

Defendant succeeded in the right to obtain a patent for the Invention by the Plaintiff, and obtained patent protection. After October 1990, Defendant had a licence fee income for pickup device patents, including the Invention, from some manufacturing companies amounting to about JPY 7,546 billion (approx. USD 60 million in 1992). According to the above rule, Defendant paid the following remuneration to the Plaintiff: JPY 3,000 for the patent application (on 5 January 1978), JPY 8,000 for the patent grant (on 14 March 1989), and JPY 200,000 in connection with the use

30. K. ONISHI/H. OWAN, *supra* note 10, 2.
31. K. ONISHI/H. OWAN, *supra* note 10, 2.
32. *Supra* note 2, the following facts and reasons are based on the English translation in 35 IIC 1039 (2004) by M. MŌRI and on information on cases, published by the Patent System Subcommittee of the JPO, in: Shokumu hatsumei seido no arikata ni tsuite *(Improvement of employee-invention system)*, December 2003, available at the website of the JPO <https://www.jpo.go.jp/resources/shingikai/sangyo-kouzou/shousai/tokkyo_shoi/document/h15houkokusho/houkoku.pdf>, 10.
33. Conversions Yen – Euro were made for 22 April 2003.

of the Invention owing to the grant of licenses to third parties (on 1 October 1992) in sum about USD 1,600.

The Plaintiff was of the opinion that the amount of remuneration he received was not "reasonable" and claimed (in the second instance) the sum of JPY 200 million (approx. USD 1.6 million in 1999) at the second instance.

The courts of first and second instance sustained the claim, but both of the lower instance courts awarded only JPY 2,289,000 (approx. USD 20,000 which is about EUR 21,300 (in 2001)), since plaintiff was a co-inventor only.[34]

Defendant appealed to the Supreme Court requesting a ruling *inter alia* as to whether the right to claim additional remuneration payment existed when the company had rules for reward and remuneration of employees' inventions, and whether the Plaintiff's claim was time-barred.

b) Reasons

An employer can include a provision in its company rules that it will succeed in the right to obtain a patent or other rules set in advance ("Company Rules"). It is moreover not prohibited to specify the amount of remuneration to be paid for such a transfer or the date of payment, regardless of whether the employee has the intention of transferring the right to obtain a patent for an employee's invention to the employer. However, it is clear that the amount of remuneration cannot be rigidly set before the employee's invention has been made, or before the content and value of the right to be transferred have become specific. To set a certain fixed amount of remuneration is impermissible according to the intent and wording of sec. 35 Patent Act. In other words, the remuneration set by the company rules cannot be deemed to constitute the entire amount of the remuneration under sec. 35(3) and (4), but only a part of it. The amount of remuneration set in advance can be interpreted to constitute the entire amount of reasonable remuneration under sec. 35(3) and (4) only if such an amount of remuneration matches the intent and wording of sec. 35(4). Therefore, it is reasonable to conclude that an employee who transfers the right to obtain a patent for an employee's invention to the employer according to the company rules can claim additional payment under sec. 35 (3) if the amount of remuneration provided by the employer under the company rules is less than the reasonable remuneration determined according to sec. 35(4).

There is no provision in the Patent Act regarding the due date of the remuneration. Therefore, if the company rules specify a payment date, the law prohibits the employee from exercising his right to receive reasonable remuneration before that due date, and the employee cannot claim payment thereof until the payment becomes due under the company rules. If the company rules include a payment date of the remuneration, it is reasonable to conclude that the date of payment shall trigger the prescription period for such reasonable remuneration.

34. Tokyo District Court, 16 April 1999 and Tokyo High Court, 22 May 2001, *supra* note 2.

3. ANALYSIS

The *Olympus* decision of the Supreme Court established and confirmed important principles under the law of employees' inventions in view for transfer of ownership, assessment of company remuneration schemes and the prescription period for claiming remuneration. It is one of the two Supreme Court decisions on employees' inventions in Japan.[35] As mentioned above, the *Olympus* decisions lead to an increase in compensation cases and ultimately resulted in revisions of sec. 35 Patent Act in 2004 and 2015.

a) Transfer of ownership

Olympus confirmed that the employer may unilaterally establish a right to succeed in the employee's rights over the invention,[36] yet needed a separate assignment agreement to this end. Under the new law, such a separate assignment agreement is no longer necessary when so established in company rules or in the employment contract prior to the making of the invention.

b) No maximum amount of remuneration

While the employer may establish a remuneration scheme, the amount of remuneration "cannot be rigidly set before the employee's invention has been made, or before the content and value of the right to be transferred have become specific." This was understood in that it is inadmissible to determine a maximum remuneration sum *ex ante*. Many companies have therefore abolished their payment cap. With the amendment of sec. 35 (3) Patent Act in 2015, this remains unchanged and *Olympus* is still good law.

In the *Olympus* decision, the Supreme Court stated that payments under company rules are "unreasonable" according to (ex-) sec. 35(4), now sec. 35(7) Patent Act, if the employer did not take the profit made by the invention, the employer's contribution, benefits to the employee (granting e.g. additional equipment and further education etc.), and any other circumstances relating to the invention sufficiently into consideration. The new sec. 35(5) as amended in 2004[37] and 2015 made adjustments thereto. According to the new law, as already described above, company rules will be considered "reasonable" if "negotiated" with the employee according to the procedure prescribed in sec. 35(5) and the METI Guideline. However, the observance of formalities cannot prevent that a remuneration (or the grant of "other economic benefits") under a company scheme turns out to be less than reasonable e.g. due to the extraordinary

35. The other Supreme Court decision is the *Hitachi* case (Case No. 17 in this book) of 17 October 2006, Case No. 781 (Ju) of 2004, 60-8 Minshū 2853, English translation available in 39 IIC 733 (2008) w. comment C. Heath, and another translation available at the website of the courts <http://www.courts.go.jp/app/hanrei_en/detail?id=858>.

36. Supreme Court, 22 April 2003, *supra* note 2.

37. Amendment of sec. 35(4) and (5) by the Law on the Partial Reform of the Patent Act to Accelerate Patent Prosecution Proceedings (*Tokkyo shinsa no jinsoku tō no tame no tokkyohō no ichibu wo keiseisuru hōritsu*) No. 79 of June 2004. This law came into force on 1 April 2005.

commercial value of the invention. Therefore, the employee has still a right to claim an additional remuneration pursuant to ex sec. 35(4), now sec. 35(7) Patent Act.

c) Remuneration pursuant to sec. 35(7) Patent Act

The question arises which amount of remuneration must be considered as "unreasonable". So far, courts had a few opportunities to interpret the new sec. 35 Patent Act.[38] Whether this understanding is correct remains to be seen. Courts apply the following calculation method: amount of sales x excess sales (profit of exclusivity) x hypothetical royalty x degree of contribution by the invention.[39]

The calculation methods of Japanese companies usually differ from the calculation methods as applied by the courts. In practice, for instance, an employer's turnover will be taken as a calculation basis rather than the "profit of exclusivity" (i.e. the "profit of a fictitious licensee" or half of the employer's profits). Some companies split the "sources" of the turnover of a patented product into several categories, for instance, equity investment, market potential, technology, etc. As a consequence, only a share of the turnover will be taken as a basis to determine the "relevant" turnover, i.e. the invention-related turnover. Further, the employer's share in the invention is usually calculated as very high (around 99%). Finally, there are various methods of deducting costs from the profits.[40]

d) Statute of limitations

Many claims for additional remuneration were made by retired employees to avoid any disadvantages during their employment term. The question of the statute of limitations of such claims is therefore vital. In "*Olympus*", the Supreme Court held that claims can be raised only after the last payment according to the company's rules has been made. Thereafter, the statute of limitations starts to run, although the Supreme Court did not point out which one.

As there is no specific prescription period indicated in sec. 35 Patent Act, secs. 166(1) and 167(1) Civil Code apply. Pursuant to these provisions, the right to obtain a reasonable remuneration becomes time barred ten years after the date when it became possible to exercise the right (see above). Should there be no company rules, the date of assignment of the right to obtain a patent is relevant.[41] According to a district court decision, the prescription period shall begin when the employee

38. See footnote 17 above.
39. IP High Court, 14 May 2008, Case No. 10008 (Ne) of 2007, the website of the courts <http://www.courts.go.jp/app/files/hanrei_jp/360/036360_hanrei.pdf>, English translation can be accessed at the website of the IP High Court <http://www.ip.courts.go.jp/app/files/hanrei_en/057/000057.pdf>; regarding the calculation method see also Tokyo District Court, 30 January 2004, *supra* note 11.
40. A. PETERSEN-PADBERG, Corporate Remuneration Systems for Employees' Inventions in Japan and Germany, in: B. HANSEN/D. SCHÜSSLER-LANGEHEINE, Patent Practice in Japan and Europe, *Liber Amicorum* for Guntram Rahn, 2011, 757, 770 *et seq.*
41. IP High Court, 31 January 2013, Case No. 10052 (Ne) of 2012, 2180 Hanrei Jihō 104 – *Astellas*, see also Tokyo District Court, 23 December 1983, Case No. 11717 (Wa) of 1969, 1104 Hanrei Jihō 120.

can reasonably exercise his right, i.e. when the employer commences the use of the invention.[42] Further, the IP High Court ruled in *Mitsubishi Chemical* that if the plaintiff claims only a share of his right to remuneration and later enhances his court action, while from the beginning constantly showing that he is willing to enforce the entire claim, in this case, the prescription period of the remaining share was also stayed by the court action.[43]

4. COMPARATIVE REMARKS

Special laws on the rights and obligations regarding employees inventions can be found in a number of European countries such as Germany, Denmark, Finland, Norway, Sweden and Slovenia. Many countries, however, only provide a provision on employee inventions in their patent or IP laws such as, Japan, Great Britain, France, Italy, Luxembourg, the Netherlands, Austria, Portugal, Spain, Hungary, sometimes with additional Regulations, such as in China (see below). Switzerland provides a provision in its Civil Code. In some countries, only contractual agreements and court decisions exist, such as in the US, Canada and Belgium.

a) The US

According to common law, if an employee was "hired to invent", the rights to the patent belong to the entity. Otherwise, the right to apply for a patent belongs to the employed inventor when using employer's resources,[44] while the employer has a right to a royalty-free non-exclusive non-assignable personal license ("shop right").[45] In order to avoid this distinction, both parties can enter into on an assignment agreement. This "one-pager" needs to be submitted to the US PTO when applying for a patent. Increasingly, employment contracts provide that any employee inventions shall belong to the employer. A language to the effect that employee "herewith agrees to assign, and hereby assigns, all inventions made during the course of my employment ..." in the employment agreement transfers ownership rights to the employer without any further assignment becoming necessary.[46] The advantage of a formal separate assignment agreement is that it specifies the invention at issue. The amount of remuneration, which the employer may voluntarily pay, depends on contractual agreements. Typically, the employment contract provides for a "recognition" (to be fixed, e.g. in company rules published e.g. on the company's intranet). While a share in the profits is rare, a variety of awards is more common, e.g. annual and

42. Tokyo District Court, 16 April 1999, *supra* note 2. This approach is shared by C. HEATH/M. MŌRI, *supra* note 24, 36 IIC 676 (2005).
43. IP High Court, 18 April 2013, Case No. 10028&10045 (Ne) of 2012, 2196 Hanrei Jihō 103–*Mitsubishi Chemical*.
44. 35 U.S. Code § 111.
45. According to case law based on equitable principles, e.g. US Supreme Court, *U.S. v. Dubilier Condenser Corp.*, 289 U.S. 178 (1933).
46. 35 U.S. Code § 118, first sentence.

spot bonuses, trophies or plaques, technical stipends, vacations and other financial rewards.[47]

b) China[48]

The Chinese government pushes innovation to become a country not only assembling, but designing products.[49] Incentives are monetary rewards and turnover-shares for inventions and designs. The Patent Act, secs. 2, 6 and 16 and Rules 76-78 of the Implementing Regulations apply to employees' inventions. Special attention must be paid to regional Regulations, such as the Shanghai Regulation. Service inventions belong to the employer if not otherwise agreed, including inventions made one year after termination of the employment (sec. 6 Patent Act). Pursuant to sec. 16 Patent Act, employers shall remunerate inventions, utility models and designs made by employees as follows: (1) a reward, i.e. about EUR 387 for a granted patent and about EUR 129 for a granted utility model or design (Rule 77 Implementing Regulations) and, (2) if the invention or design is used, a turnover-based remuneration of about 2 % of the profits generated by the patented invention or by the granted utility model (Rule 78 Implementing Regulations) and 0.2 % of the profits generated by a patented design. It is, however, possible to agree on a remuneration scheme in a contract or an internal regulation. The agreed payment must be "reasonable" pursuant to sec. 16 Patent Act. Instead of a percentage of the profits, it is also possible to agree on a lump sum or other reward. SIPO's draft on New Regulations on Employees' Inventions as of 31 March 2014 is still under discussion. These Regulations are based on the principle that contractual agreements shall prevail. However, minimal compensation standards are provided in the draft. The draft also provides benefits for inventors when a patent application was not filed, but the invention was maintained as a trade secret and the enterprise has benefited from the invention. By 2017, a third draft of the Employee Invention Regulations has been published.

c) Germany

In Germany, employees' inventions are governed by the Act on Employees' Inventions (AEI) of 1957.[50] The law is accompanied by the "Official Guidelines for the

47. S. Malanowski, Innovation Incentives: How Companies Foster Innovation by September 2007, at the website of Wilson Group <https://www.wilsongroup.com/wp-content/uploads/2011/03/InnovationIncentives.pdf>. This article gives a number of examples how companies in the U.S. reward employee inventions.
48. A recent overview is provided by S. Yang: Service Invention in China – Current Provisions & Proposed Changes, Les Nouvelles, June 2017, 99 *et seq.* and Q. Wie, Draft Regulation on Employee Invention and Innovative Workers Protection in China, Japan Labor Issues, Vol. 1, no. 3, Nov. - Dec. 2017, 14-20 which can be accessed at the website of the JILPT <http://www.jil.go.jp/english/jli/2017/documents/003-03.pdf>.
49. In the first half of 2017, 565,000 invention patent applications were filed (SIPO, Statistics, 20 July 2017).
50. The Act on Employees' Inventions is based on a Regulation of 1942 (*Verordnung über die Behandlung von Erfindungen von Gefolgschaftsmitgliedern*) [Regulation on inventions made by loyalty members] of 12 July 1942, RGBl. 1942, I, 466, its Implementing Regulation of 20 March 1943, RGBl., 1943 I, 257, and the Guidelines on Remuneration (*Richtlinien für die Vergütung*

Remuneration of Employees' Inventions in Private Employment".[51] The Official Guidelines which explain how to calculate the remuneration are not binding, but are applied by the Arbitration Court on Employees' Inventions, civil courts and by most companies. They are therefore of high practical relevance. With the exception of the rules introduced on university inventions in 2002,[52] and a change in 2009 regarding the vest of rights to the invention to the employer, the AEI has not been substantially amended. In particular, the proposal to change from a turnover-based remuneration to a lump sum payment system was rejected in 2000. Since 1957, the law has been interpreted by numerous decisions of the Federal Court of Justice, lower court decisions and court decisions of the arbitration court of employee inventions. It is no exaggeration to say that the German law on employees' inventions including its case law is the most complex in the world. Under German law, it is basically not admissible to assign the right to the patent to the employer before the invention is reported.[53] However, when a report on an invention is made, the invention shall be deemed, as a legal fiction, to have been claimed by the employer unless he expressly releases the invention within the four months following receipt of the report. If the employer obtains the rights to the invention, he will also become responsible for obligations arising therefrom such as the obligation to file a patent application in Germany (if not otherwise agreed upon with the employee), paying a remuneration when using the invention including rendering account, offer the employee the rights to patents abroad in which he is not interested or offer the employee to acquire an IP right before abandonment and a few more. Quite a number of German companies have introduced corporate guidelines on employees' inventions to make an early incentive payment and to pay fixed amounts at different points in time instead of a turnover-based compensation. However, it is against the law to agree on a payment cap. Should the invention be commercially highly successful, the employee must have the right to claim additional payments. Corporate guidelines also help to reduce bureaucratic work. However, the enactment of internal company guidelines fitting the specific needs of a company is complex and must therefore be properly prepared. Quite a variety of company guidelines on employees' inventions in Germany exist.[54] Companies which have taken the effort to enact such a system usually find it satisfactory for both the company and the employees.

von Gefolgschaftserfindungen), Reichsanz. No. 70 of March 25, 1943, No. 271 of 5 December 1944). The history of the AEI is explained by KURZ, GRUR 1991, 422, BARTENBACH/VOLZ, GRUR 1982, 693.

51. *Supra* note 5.
52. Revision of sec. 42 AEI on university inventions by Act of 18 January 2002 as published in the Federal Law Gazette [Bundesgesetzblatt], 2002, I, 4149.
53. An agreement on a transfer of rights to an invention prior to its report is considered as disadvantageous pursuant to sec. 22 Act on Employees' Inventions.
54. Details of different remuneration systems are explained in: A. PETERSEN-PADBERG, *supra* note 40, 784 *et seq.*

Case No. 17

Employees' Inventions – Reasonable Remuneration for Profits made Abroad

Masahito Imai

An equitable remuneration for the transfer of an invention made in the course of employment must take into account the profits made from the invention abroad.

Supreme Court, 17 October 2006, Case No. 781 (Ju) of 2004 – *RW Laser Disk*

Yonezawa v. Hitachi

---

1. BACKGROUND

In light of the Olympus decision[1] (Case No. 16), Japanese companies looked for escape routes when being confronted with claims for equitable remuneration of inventions made by their employees. One approach was to apply the rules stipulated under the Japanese Patent Act only to the Japanese patent application, but not to the corresponding foreign patent applications related to the same invention. The argument used in this respect was territoriality: As the remuneration under Japanese patent law was stipulated by law rather than by contract, the remuneration for foreign applications or granted patents should equally be calculated according to the rules of the place of registration.

On behalf of Hitachi, the case before the Supreme Court was argued by *Wataru Sueyoshi*, one of the leading Japanese IP attorneys. In addition, both parties had asked for and received a number of expert opinions by IP professors,[2] although such opinions are not mentioned in the decisions themselves. Asking for such opinions has become rather common in many IP lawsuits, yet in view of the commercial

---

1. Supreme Court, 22 April 2003, Case No. 1256 (Ju) of 2001, 35 IIC 1039 (2004) – *Olympus*. See Case No. 16 in this volume.
2. On behalf of **Mr. Yonezawa**, the following academics /practitioners submitted opinions: – *Tamura* (professor; unpublished); – *Koizumi* (professor; unpublished); – *Makino/Kimijima* (attorneys; published in Tokkyo News); – *Tamai* (professor; published in Chizai Kanri); – *Kiyonaga* (attorney; unpublished); – *Komtasu* (professor; unpublished); – *Chaen* (professor; unpublished); – *Kidana* (professor; unpublished). On behalf of **Hitachi**, the following academics/practitioners submitted opinions: – *Nakayama* (professor; unpublished); – *Aizawa* (professor; unpublished); – *Ōba* (attorney; published in Chizai Kanri); – *Hanamura* (professor; published in Seiwa Hōgaku Kenkyū) (Information obtained from YOSHIYUKI TAMURA, Hokkaido University).

nature of such opinions, particularly those that go unpublished add preciously little to the academic debate and almost always come out in favour of the party that has asked for such an opinion.

Sec. 35 Patent Act has meanwhile been significantly revised.[3] In preparation of the law amendment, it was discussed whether the provision should explicitly apply to a transfer of the right to obtain a patent abroad;[4] however, no such clarification was made.[5] It is considered that the ruling in the Hitachi case is still applicable to the current sec. 35 Patent Act.

2. DECISION[6]

a) Facts

I. Summary of proceedings so far

The respondent (plaintiff) in this appeal has transferred his rights in an employee's invention to the appellant (defendant), including those rights to take out a patent abroad, and requests an equitable remuneration under sec. 35(3) Patent Act (prior to its amendment by Law No. 79 of 2004).

The previous instance[7] has ascertained the following facts. The appellant is engaged in the development, production and sale of electronic appliances. The respondent was employed by the appellant between November 1969 and November 1996 as a senior researcher in the central research institute. During his employment, the respondent together with other employees made three inventions that will be referred to as "the inventions at issue" and that concern a method and device for the use of laser beams in re-writing information. The inventions were made in the course of the appellant's employment, as it was the respondent's task to make inventions for the appellant. The inventions thus fall within the ambit of sec. 35 (1) Patent Act. The first invention was transferred to the appellant on 13 September 1977, the second on 20 January 1973 and the third on 26 December 1974 under a contract that included

3. See previous Case No. in this volume.
4. Minutes of 8 September 2003, etc. of (Former) Tokkyo Seido Shōinkai (*Patent System Sub-committee*) of Sangyō Kōzō Shingikai Chiteki Zaisan Bunkakai (*Intellectual Property Committee of Industrial Structure Council*) established in the Ministry of Economic, Trade and Industry, available at the website of the JPO <https://www.jpo.go.jp/resources/shingikai/sangyo-kouzou/shousai/tokkyo_shoi/seisakubukai-13-shiryou.html>.
5. In the Intellectual Property Committee, it was considered that if sec. 35 Patent Act was revised so as to explicitly apply to patents abroad, one should still determine under foreign law (1) whether the right to obtain a patent abroad has been transferred to an employer or not, (2) the timing of such transfer, etc.; however, this could cause a major operational problem, and it was concluded that no amendment should be made to sec. 35 Patent Act concerning patents abroad. The concluding report of the Committee is also available at the website of the JPO <http://www.jpo.go.jp/resources/shingikai/sangyo-kouzou/shousai/tokkyo_shoi/h15houkokusho.html>.
6. Published in 60-8 Minshū 2853 = 1951 Hanrei Jihō 35 = 1225 Hanrei Times 190 = N. Nakayama et al. (eds.), Tokkyo Hanrei Hyakusen *(Hundred Selected Patent Cases)*, 4th ed. 2012, 72. English translation w. comment C. Heath in 39 IIC 733 (2008).
7. Tokyo High Court, 29 January 2004, Case No. 6451 (Ne) of 2002, 1848 Hanrei Jihō 25 = 36 IIC 360 (2005) – *Hitachi*.

the rights to take out patents abroad. The appellant apart from applying for and obtaining a domestic patent, took out patents for the first invention in the US, Canada, the UK, France and the Netherlands, and for the second and third inventions in the US, Germany, the UK, France and the Netherlands. The appellant at the time of the transfer contract undertook to pay its inventing employees a fixed amount of money for the registration and grant of the patent, and subsequently a share corresponding to the results of commercially implementing the invention in conformity with the scheme "Guidelines for commendations regarding inventions and proposals". Until June 1991, the inventing employees received a remuneration when patent applications were made domestically and abroad, when registrations were made domestically and abroad, for outstanding economic performance of the patents and in accordance therewith, and when patent licences were granted to third parties on the basis of royalties paid thereupon under the "Rules for obtaining inventions" and "Rules for rewarding inventions" (in the following "Rules"). For the inventions, the appellant both at home and abroad made patent applications, obtained patent registrations and concluded licensing agreements with a substantial number of companies, received licensing fees and derived a profit therefrom. The appellant paid the respondent for each patent according to the Rules, which amounted to JPY 2.31 million for the first invention, JPY 51,400 for the second and JPY 10,700 for the third.[8]

The second instance court held that the appropriate amount to be paid by the appellant to the respondent for the transfer of ownership rights in the patents (considering the remuneration already paid) was JPY 162,846,300 for the first invention, JPY 131,750 for the second and JPY 25,666 for the third. In the amount of JPY 163,003,716, the lower court thus allowed the respondent's claim. In order to determine the problems related to the remuneration for the transfer of the inventions, it is necessary to establish the applicable law with respect to the subject matter of, respectively, the right to obtain a patent Japan, or abroad. The contract was concluded by the appellant as a legal person established under Japanese law, and the Japanese respondent who was resident in Japan and performed his employment duties on behalf of the appellant. The respondent completed his employee's inventions in Japan, and for the conclusion and validity of the transfer contract, the parties were in agreement that the applicable law would be the Japanese one. According to sec. 7(1) Hōrei,[9] the applicable law for the remuneration in consideration of a transfer of the right to take out patents abroad is also Japanese law. Sec. 35(3) mentions "the right to obtain a patent", which does not only mean the right to obtain a patent in Japan, but does include a transfer of the right to obtain a patent abroad, and consequently the request for equitable remuneration under subsections (3) and (4) must take this as a base.

8. As the appellee was paid according to the 1991 Rules, the lower court regarded this as an acknowledgement of obligation and rejected the time-bar estoppel (10 years from the date the obligation was due). The suit at issue was raised in 1998.
9. Hōrei, Law No. 10 of 1898 on the application of laws, since 21 June 2006 the Hō no tekiyō ni kan suru tsūsokuhō *(Act on General Rules for Application of Laws)*, sec. 7 reads: "The formation and effect of legal acts shall be governed by the law of the place chosen by the parties at the time of the act."

b) Reasons

II. The reasons for the appeal as argued by Wataru Sueyoshi *and others (3)*

> "[According to the appellant], the question whether the transferor of a transfer of the right to obtain a patent abroad may request an equitable remuneration from the transferee, and the question about the amount of such remuneration for obtaining a patent cannot be separated from the other rights and obligations between the parties, and must be determined in accordance with the contract and the validity of other legal obligations. This means that according to Art. 7(1) Hōrei, this should be interpreted according to the intention of the parties. Thus, the question of what has been transferred regarding the right to obtain a patent abroad, and how to determine the validity thereof should be separated from the transfer between the parties and the problems related thereto. The applicable law for the former should be determined according to the principle of territoriality according to the law of each country where the right to obtain a patent has manifested in a registration."

There is an agreement between both parties that Japanese law should be the basis of the transfer contract between appellant and appellee. The question whether the appellee can claim a remuneration for the transfer of the right to obtain a patent abroad must be answered on the basis of the transfer contract that gives a right to remuneration for the transfer, and the applicable law is thus Japanese law. The finding of the lower court in this matter are thus correct, and the appellant's point must fail.

III. The reasons for the appeal as argued by Wataru Sueyoshi *and others (4)*

> "It is clear that domestic patent law has no direct provisions on foreign patents or the right to obtain foreign patents (Art. 4bis Paris Convention of 20 March 1883, as amended in Brussels on 14 December 1900, in Washington on 2 June 1911, in the Hague on 6 November 1925, in London on 2 June 1934, in Lisbon on 31 October 1959 and in Stockholm on 14 July 1967). The provision of sec. 35(1) and (2) Patent Act that refers to "the right to obtain a patent" must thus be understood to refer to the right to obtain a domestic patent, and the wording "the right to obtain a patent" in subsection (3) can thus only with considerable difficulty be understood as to comprise the right to obtain a patent abroad. For that reason, subsection (4) of the provision cannot be directly applied to the remuneration for transferring the right to obtain a patent abroad."

However, the provisions of sec. 35(3) and (4) in the case of a disposition over the right of exclusive use have two angles, one concerning employment, the other concerning use. But it is difficult to assume that the employee and the user [the company] trade on equal terms. Therefore, subsection (4) on the one hand determines the scope of remuneration as the profit that should be objectively expected when at the time of the transaction, the user obtains the right for exclusive use, and on the other hand for the employee of said invention provides a certain protection. It is the purpose of patent law to promote and encourage the development of industry, and the argument that with respect to the succession in the right to obtain a patent it would be difficult to take into account the interests of both the employee and the user, there is no difference in the object of the right to obtain a domestic patent or a patent abroad. Of course, the right to obtain a patent will become a different right in every country, yet the underlying invention is the result of one single common technical achievement. The invention of the employee is based on one single employment relationship, and the related right to obtain a patent in every country actually stems from one common achievement and in common understanding should be regarded as such. When the user becomes the employee's successor in title for the right to obtain a patent, often it cannot be determined at the time of transfer if a patent is taken out in a certain country or if the invention is retained as a trade secret, and if a patent application matures to an actual patent. It is thus common that the successor in title to the right to obtain a domestic patent also becomes the successor in title for the right to obtain a patent abroad. It may be true that the interest in obtaining a domestic patent may not always correspond to the interest in obtaining a patent abroad, but even taking this into account, for this invention the user is owner of this invention and between the employee and the user there is one single legal relationship that was transferred in one go, and the parties agreed thereupon. Thus, the provisions of sec. 35(3) and (4) must be understood as also applying to the right to obtain patents abroad. Consequently, once that for an employee's invention under sec. 35(1) the right to obtain patents abroad is transferred to the user, the request for equitable remuneration ensuing therefrom is subject to subsections (3) and (4) of this provision.

In this case, the employee's invention was subject to the provisions on ownership under sec. 35(1) Patent Act, and the right to obtain a patent in the US, the UK, France and the Netherlands was transferred jointly with the right to obtain a patent in Japan. Consequently, the right of remuneration ensuing from the transfer to obtain a patent abroad is governed by the provisions of subsections (3) and (4). The appellee can thus claim from the appellant an appropriate remuneration for the transfer of the right to obtain a patent abroad on the basis of sec. 35(3) and (4) Patent Act.

The reasoning of the lower court being correct in regard of the above-mentioned issues, the appeal cannot succeed.

The decision has been unanimous.

3. ANALYSIS

a) Arguments before the Supreme Court's decision

There were many complicated arguments as to whether sec. 35 Patent Act should be applicable to the right to obtain a patent abroad. These arguments typically considered first which country's laws should govern the right to obtain a patent abroad. If it is found that the Japanese law would govern, the next question would be whether sec. 35 Patent Act was applicable to the right to obtain a patent abroad.

1. The governing law

As to the first question which law governs the right to obtain a patent abroad, there are several views, namely (i) that sec. 35 Patent Act is directly applicable; (ii) that the law of the country where the subsequent patents are registered is applicable;

(iii-1) that the law which governs the employment agreement is applicable; (iii-2); that the law of the country where the labour was provided (i.e. the inventor (employee) worked) is applicable, and (iv) that the law which governs the agreement/arrangement for transferring the right to obtain a patent is applicable.[10] View (i) is based on the understanding that sec. 35 Patent Act is a mandatory provision regardless of the choice of governing law. View (i) is criticised in that there is no clear-cut standard to judge whether a certain law is mandatory.[11] The underlying idea of view (ii) is that the legal requirements for obtaining a patent and the scope of such patent are different in each country with the consequence that the principle of territoriality should apply. According to view (ii), there is no room for sec. 35 Patent Act to apply to the right to obtain a patent abroad. However, this view (ii) is criticised because it requires arrangements for transferring the rights to obtain a patent for each country, which is unrealistic. Views (iii-1) and (iii-2) are based on the idea that an employee's invention is related to an employment relationship. However, the employment relationship is not necessarily relevant in assessing who will be the owner of the right to obtain a patent abroad, whether such a right can be transferred, what will be necessary to effectuate such a transfer, etc..[12] View (iv) assumes that the issue of remuneration under sec. 35 Patent Act is intrinsically linked to the transfer agreement/arrangement. However, this is also criticised indicating that an employee's interest cannot be sufficiently protected because the principle of party disposition is overemphasised.[13]

The Tokyo District Court, 29 November 2002[14] in first instance held that in light of the principle of territoriality, the questions who should be the owner of the right to obtain a patent abroad, whether a transfer of the right to obtain a patent should admissible, whether the employee needs to be remunerated, etc. should be determined by the patent laws of each country. Sec. 35 Patent Act should thus be applicable only to the right of obtaining a patent in Japan. This decision seems to be consistent with view (ii).

The Tokyo High Court, 29 January 2004[15] in second instance held that the transfer agreement of the patent at issue between the employee (a Japanese citizen resident in Japan) and employer (a company incorporated in Japan), which implied that the agreement was governed by Japanese law, and therefore Japanese law was

---

10. N. Takasugi, Gaikoku ni okeru tokkyo wo ukeru kenri ni tsuite no sōtō no taika no seikyū *(Claim of remuneration for the right to patent in abroad)*, in: N. Nakayama et al. (eds.), Tokkyo Hanrei Hyakusen *(Hundred Selected Patent Cases)*, 4th ed. 2012, 72; T. Nakayoshi, Gaikoku no tokkyo wo ukeru kenri no jōto no taika ni kansuru mondai no junkyo hō *(Applicable law for the problem of renumaration for the transfer of the right to patent in abroad)*, in Hōsōkai, Saikō Saibansho Hanrei Kaisetsu Minji-hen -Heisei 18 nendo- ge *(Commentary of the Supreme Court's decisions, civil cases -fiscal year 2006-, vol. 2)*, 2006, 1077-1079.
11. M. Miyawaki, Shokumu hatsumei ni tsuki gaikoku de tokkyo wo ukeru kenri no jōto ni taisuru sōtō taika seikyū *(Claim of equitable remuneration for the transfer of the right to patent in abroad for an employee's invention)*, 57-10 Chizai Kanri 1659 (2007).
12. T. Nakayoshi (above).
13. N. Takasugi (above).
14. Tokyo District Court, 29 November 2002, Cases Nos. 16832 (Wa) of 1998 and 5572 (Wa) of 2000, 1807 Hanrei Jihō 33.
15. Tokyo High Court, 29 January 2004, Case No. 6451 (Ne) of 2002, see note 7.

applicable to the transfer agreement including remuneration for the transfer of the right to obtain patents abroad. This corresponds to view (iv).

Looking into other decisions which were issued before the Supreme Court's decision, the Tokyo District Court, 24 February 2004 (*Ajinomoto "Aspartame"* case[16]) held that Japanese law, which governs the employment agreement according to sec. 7 Hōrei, should govern the establishment and effect of a transfer agreement including the remuneration for such a transfer. This corresponds to view (iii-1) and/or (iii-2).

In Tokyo District Court, 8 September 2006 (*Otsuka Seiyaku*[17]), it was held that the establishment and effect of an agreement about the transfer of the right to obtain a patent and claim for remuneration for such transfer are subject to the law governing such an agreement, which will be determined by sec. 7 Hōrei.[18] The court determined this to be Japanese law in view of the intention of the parties. This decision seems to correspond to view (iv).

2. Whether sec. 35 Patent Act is applicable to patents abroad

Once it is found that Japanese law governs the right to obtain a patent abroad, the next question is whether sec. 35 Patent Act is applicable. This question concerns a construction of sec. 35 Patent Act itself and is different from the first question about determining the governing law. One view is that sec. 35 Patent Act is not applicable to the right to obtain a patent abroad because the term "the right to obtain a patent" is also used in other sections of the Patent Act such as secs. 33, 34 and 38 but it is apparent that the term in these sections does not include the right to obtain a patent abroad, so the same term in sec. 35 Patent Act should be construed in the same manner.[19] Another view is that sec. 35 Patent Act is applicable to the right to obtain

16. Tokyo District Court, 24 February 2004, Case No. 20521 (Wa) of 2002 - *Ajinomoto "Aspartame"*, 1853 Hanrei Jihō 38.
17. Tokyo District Court, 8 September 2006, Case No. 14399 (Wa) of 2005 - *Otsuka Seiyaku*, 1988 Hanrei Jihō 106.
18. In both the *Ajinomoto "Aspartame"* case and the *Otsuka Seiyaku* case, sec. 7 Hōrei was applied. However, it should be noted that the *Ajinomoto "Aspartame"* case relied on the employment agreement, while the *Otsuka Seiyaku* case relied on the agreement about the transfer of the right to obtain a patent. However, the Hō no tekiyō ni kan suru tsūsokuhō *(Act on General Rules for Application of Laws)*, which replaced the Hōrei, now in sec. 12(1) stipulates an exceptional provision for employment agreements setting out that "(e)ven where the applicable law to the formation and effect of a labour agreement as a result of a choice or change under sec. 7 or sec. 9 is a law other than the law of the place with which the labour agreement is most closely connected, if a worker has manifested his/her intention to an employer that a specific mandatory provision from within the law of the place with which the labour agreement is most closely connected should be applied, such mandatory provision shall also apply to the matters stipulated in the mandatory provision with regard to the formation and effect of the labour agreement". As with "the law of the place with which the labour agreement is most closely connected", under sec. 12(2), the law of the place where the work should be provided under the labour agreement shall be presumed to be such most closely connected law. Under sec. 12(3), in the absence of a choice of law with regard to the formation and effect of a labour agreement, the law of the place where the work should be provided under the labour agreement shall be presumed to be the most closely connected law. Thus, if the Hō no tekiyō ni kan suru tsūsokuhō were applied to the *Ajinomoto "Aspartame"* case, the exceptional provision for an employment agreement under sec. 12 would have mattered.
19. T. Nakayoshi (above), at 1084.

a patent abroad. This view is based on the idea of protecting employees' interests and/or innovating inventions and the development of industry,[20] which allows a different construction of the term "the right to obtain a patent" in sec. 35 Patent Act and other sections.

In the second instance "RW Laser Disc" decision and the Tokyo District Court's *Ajinomoto "Aspartame"* case, it was held that sec. 35 Patent Act is applicable to the right to obtain a patent abroad. On the other hand, in the Tokyo District Court's decision *Otsuka Seiyaku*, it was ruled that sec. 35 Patent Act is not applicable to the right to obtain a patent abroad.

3. *The Supreme Court's decision*

This Supreme Court's decision addresses these two questions on how patents abroad should be considered when evaluating remuneration for employees' inventions, specifically, (1) which country's law governs and (2) if the Japanese law is governing law, whether sec. 35 Patent Act concerning remuneration for employees' inventions is applicable to patents abroad in relation to the same invention.

(a) As to the first question, the Supreme Court ruled that a claim for remuneration for transferring the right to obtain a patent abroad is regarding a contractual matter between the parties of the transfer, and therefore, is determined by an intent of the parties under sec. 7(1) Hōrei (then the applicable law regarding conflicts of law). Based on this ruling, the Supreme Court held that the Japanese law should be the governing law in this case.

This is different from the view (iii-1) or (iii-2) above according to which the law which governs a claim for remuneration for transferring the right to obtain a patent abroad should be the one governing the employment agreement because the system of such remuneration under sec. 35 Patent Act is meant to ensure fairness between employee and employer in assessing the amount of remuneration and is related to the employment agreement.[21] However, a claim for remuneration for transferring the right to obtain a patent is not limited to employees, but also directors, etc. of an employer, making this argument doubtful. Fundamentally, a claim for remuneration for transferring the right to obtain a patent is a question relating the rights and obligations between the employee and the employer arising from such transfer.[22] Therefore, as ruled in the Supreme Court's decision, I think that it should be construed as a contractual matter between the parties of the transfer.

It should be noted here that the Supreme Court also held that in assessing how the right to obtain a patent is treated and what effect the right to obtain a patent has, the law of the country in which the patent is to be registered governs in view of the principle of territoriality. In this regard, there are some cases where an employer argued that a patent of an employee's invention was invalid and therefore no remuneration could be claimed. If this is argued for a patent abroad, whether or not the patent is

---

20. T. NAKAYOSHI (above), at 1085.
21. S. WATANABE, Shokumu hatsumei ni yoru gaikoku de tokkyo wo ukeru kenri no iten taika seikyū mondai *(Problem of claim of remuneration for the transfer of the right to patent in abroad for an employee's invention)*, 38 L&T 11 (2008), at 16-17.
22. T. NAKAYOSHI (above), at 1082.

invalid is determined by the laws of the foreign country where the patent is registered, but this is likely to be a complex question from a practical point of view.

While the Hōrei has meanwhile been revised (see above), a claim for remuneration for transferring the right to obtain a patent abroad is treated in the same way, that is, is still governed by Japanese law.[23]

(b) Regarding the second question as to whether sec. 35 Patent Act can be applied to the right to obtain a patent abroad, the Supreme Court held that "the right to obtain a patent" under sec. 35 Patent Act cannot be construed as including the right to obtain a patent abroad; however, sec. 35 Patent Act should be applied "analogously" to the right to obtain a patent abroad considering the purpose of sec. 35 Patent Act, the usual practice of transferring the right to obtain a patent and the normal intent of the parties involved in such a transfer. This finding of the Supreme Court was followed by the lower court decisions such as Intellectual Property High Court, 26 February 2009 – *Canon*[24]).

This reasoning based on an "analogous" construction appears a new approach taken by the Supreme Court,[25] and may seem "drastic".[26] The reasoning and the conclusions were criticised by industry (i.e. employers' sides); however, I agree with this reasoning and the conclusions. As mentioned above in connection with the construction of the term "the right to obtain a patent" in sec. 35 Patent Act, it is unnatural or untenable to construe this term to include also the right to obtain a patent "abroad" considering the consistency with the construction of the same term in other sections of the Patent Act. On the other hand, it is also necessary to consider the employee's interests. If an "analogous" application of sec. 35 Patent Act was not allowed, this would lead to the situation that an employee could claim remuneration if a patent is obtained in Japan while he could not do so if patents were obtained only abroad, which can be unfair. In order to avoid such unfair result as well as an unnatural construction of sec. 35 Patent Act, there is no other way but an "analogous" construction of sec. 35 Patent Act.

4. COMPARATIVE REMARKS

Under the EPC, it seems little disputed that the applicable law regarding remuneration is the law of the country where the invention was made rather than (as was suggested by the appellants in the RW Laser Disk case) the laws of each of the countries where a patent was taken out. For one, issues of international or foreign law do not even occur at this stage – the right to take out a patent in another country is transferred prior to any foreign patent application. Second, it would be rather impracticable having to apply a myriad of different laws with different remuneration schemes. And third,

23. T. Nakayoshi (above), at 1083.
24. Intellectual Property High Court, 26 February 2009, Case No. 10021 (Ne) of 2007 – *Canon*, 2053 Hanrei Jihō 74.
25. T. Nakayoshi (above), at 1087.
26. There is a criticism against the means of "analogous" constriction adopted in the Supreme Court decision. See, M. Miyawaki (above), at 1668.

the close connection with labour law suggests that the law applicable to the labour contract should be the same as the one applicable to the employees' invention.[27]

27. Under the EPC, the issue is discussed by J. STRAUS, Die international-privatrechtliche Beurteilung von Arbeitnehmererfindungen im europäischen Patentrecht *(Consideration with the international private law of employee's invention in the European patent law)*, GRUR Int. 1984, 1.

Case No. 18

Right to be Heard – Addition of Well-Known Prior Art

Nobuyuki Hamanaka

Where the board of appeal interprets an important element of the invention differently from the decision of the examination department and bases its decision on such different interpretation, it is necessary that the board of appeal gives the applicant an opportunity to state his opinion prior to rendering a decision.

Intellectual Property High Court, 16 September 2009,
Case No. 10433 (Gyō-Ke) 2008 – *Purge Method and Purge Apparatus for Exhaust Gas of Internal Combustion Engine*

Honda et al. v. Japanese Patent Office

---

1. BACKGROUND

Sec. 50 Japanese Patent Act (hereinafter "PA") prescribes:

> "[w]here the examiner intends to render an examiner's decision to the effect that an application is to be refused, the examiner shall notify the applicant for the patent of the grounds therefor and give the said applicant an opportunity to submit a written opinion, designating an adequate time limit for such purpose".

This guarantees an applicant an opportunity to submit his comments against the examiner's negative assessment of his application and to make amendments. The underlying rationale behind this provision is that it would be highly detrimental to an applicant if he or she was not given such opportunity when a decision of refusal against the application is rendered, and that it should match to the purpose of PA of protecting patents to accordingly allow an applicant to amend his application to a certain degree, and that examiners may not always be correct in their assessment.[1] This idea to give parties an opportunity to present their comments in case of decision

1. M. Shimizu, Aratana inyōhatsumei to kyozetsuriyūtsūchi no hitsuyōsei *(Newly cited inventions and necessity of notification of grounds for refusal)*, in N. Nakayama at el. (eds.), Tokkyo Hanrei Hyakusen *(Hundred Selected Patent Cases)*, 4th ed. 2012, 80-81. *See also*, N. Nakayama/N. Koizumi (eds.), Shin Chūkai Tokkyohō *(New commentary to the Patent Act)*, 914-915, 2011; K. Yoshifuji/K. Kumagai, Tokkyohō Gaisetsu *(General Analysis of the Patent Act)*, 13th ed. 1998, 419; Tokkyochō *(Japanese Patent Office (hereinafter "JPO"))* (ed.), Kōgyōshoyūkenhō – Sangyōzaisankenhō – Chikujō Kaisetsu *(Commentary to the Industrial Property Acts)*,18th ed. 2010, 428.

unfavourable to them is common in administrative procedures and sec. 50 PA could be seen as a provision which expresses this idea in patent prosecution procedures before the JPO.[2] This opportunity given to an applicant seems to correspond to so called "right to be heard" recognised in other jurisdictions[3] such us under the European Patent Office (hereinafter "EPO").[4] Thus, where an examiner renders a decision of refusal without notifying the applicant of the grounds for refusal beforehand, such decision will constitute a procedural violation and therefore could be reversed in subsequent appeal proceedings.

This principle applies to the appeal procedures before the JPO against an examiner's decision of refusal as well by virtue of sec. 159(2) PA which applies *mutatis mutandis* sec. 50 PA "where a ground for refusal found in appeal against an examiner's decision of refusal is different from the ground(s) of the examiner's decision". Therefore, if a board of appeal finds grounds for refusal which are different from those on which the examiner's decision is based, the board must notify the appellant (the applicant) of the newly found grounds for refusal and would commit a procedural violation if, without such notification, the board were to make a decision of refusal based on those newly found grounds.

However, it is not necessarily an easy task to assess whether or not grounds for refusal of the board's decision are "different" from those of the examiner's decision.[5] In its precedent cases, the courts had decided that a board basically does not commit a procedural violation where a board makes a decision of refusal 1) based on the same prior art documents as those on which the examiner's decision is also based or 2) by adding new prior art documents in its decision in order to show or prove the existence of well-known technologies, because the grounds for refusal in the board's decision are not different from those in the examiner's decision. In the case at issue, the court further clarified that a board of appeal could still contravene sec 159(2) PA and sec. 50 PA applied *mutatis mutandis* therein and therefore constitute a procedural violation even under such circumstances.

2. H. YOSHIDA, Tokkyohō 53 jō 1 kō ni sadameru hoseikyakka shobun no tekihōsei – hoseikyakka ga tekiseitetsuzukiihan to sareta jirei wo tanncho to shite – *(Legality of dismissal of amendments under sec. 53 (1) PA –clues from cases where dismissal of amendments was decided as violation of due process –)*, 55 Tokkyo Kenkyū 71 (2103). *See also*, Y. AOKI and T. ARAGAKI, Shinhan – Tokkyotetsuzukihō *(New edition – Patent procedural law)*, 1981, 20-25.
3. Shinhan – Tokkyotetsuzukihō, *supra* note 2, at 21-25.
4. Art. 113(1) European Patent Convention (hereinafter "EPC"). *See also*, European Patent Office, Case Law of the Boards of Appeal of the European Patent Office, at section III.B. ("Right to be heard") (2016) [hereinafter "EPO Case Law"]; *infra* sec. 4.
5. K. TSUJIMOTO, Shinpanji ni shūchigijutsu ga aratani tekishisareta baai ni okeru saido no kyozetsuriyūtsūchi no yōhi *(Necessity of new notification of grounds for refusal in case well-known technologies are shown in appeal proceedings)*, 183 Chizai Prism 1 (2017). *See also, infra* sec. 3.

2. DECISION[6]

a) Facts

(1) Procedure before the JPO

On 9 December 1997, the plaintiff filed an application for an invention entitled "Purge Method and Purge Apparatus for Exhaust Gas of an Internal Combustion Engine" (application No.H9-339028, publication No.H11-173181), but was notified of the grounds for a likely rejection on 30 January 2004. The plaintiff on 5 April 2004 filed e reply and an amendment of the claims. The examination department of the JPO rejected the application on 19 July 2005. Against this decision, the plaintiff on 25 August 2005 appealed, and on 17 November 2005 filed an amendment. The JPO decided to dismiss the appeal on 7 October 2008 because the invention at issue was easy to conceive from the cited document WO 94/25143 A1 in combination with the well-known technologies of the examples 1, 2 and 3 of JP H7-139340 A, JP H7-332071 A, and JP H6-66129 A. This decision of the board of appeal was notified to the plaintiff on 21 October 2008. The plaintiff appealed.

(2) Claim 1 of the application after the amendment of 5 April 2004

[Claim 1] Exhaust gas purge method in which a NO_x purge catalyst is placed in the exhaust gas flow path, characterised in that the NO_x purge catalyst is a composition which comprises at least an element chosen from alkali metals and alkaline earth metals, at least an element chosen from rare earth metals and at least an element chosen from platinum group metals (so called precious metals), and Titanium (Ti), the NO_x in the exhaust gas is absorptively attached to the surface of the catalyst when the exhaust gas is lean, and the absorptively attached NO_x is reduced to N_2, when the exhaust gas is brought to a stoichiometric or rich state, and the NO_x in the exhaust gas is absorptively attached by the NO_x purge catalyst when the internal combustion engine is in lean operation, and after the absorptive attachment, the status of the exhaust gas is brought to a stoichiometric or rich state during 0.5–4.5 seconds and in the stoichiometric or rich state the depth of the rich status is brought between 13.0–14.7 of an air fuel ratio (A/F) value, and the NO_x absorptively attached by the NO_x purge catalyst is reacted in contact with a reducing agent and reduced to N_2, and thereby the exhaust gas is purged.

b) Reasons

(1) Concerning the meaning of the "absorptive attachment to the surface", the description of the application at issue uses, in the part on "prior art" and "problem to be solved", the expression "absorption" (吸収 *"kyūshū"*), and the expression "absorptive attachment" (吸着 *"kyūchaku"*) in the part of the description that concerns the invention at issue. I.e., the application clearly distinguishes between the "absorption" and the "absorptive attachment". The "embodiment of the invention"

6. Published at the website of the courts <http://www.courts.go.jp/app/files/hanrei_jp/991/037991_hanrei.pdf> = M. SHIMIZU, *supra* note 1, at 80.

describes that "the trapping of NO_x is made mainly by the absorptive attachment to the catalyst surface", "this is based on the fact that the substance moving process accompanying the reduction reaction of the NO_x comprises only the vapor phase diffusion process of the reducing agent or of the generated N_2 and the surface diffusion process of the absorptive attached NO_x, and does not comprise the moving process in the catalyst bulk in which the substance moving resistance is large", "in the NO_x purge catalyst of this embodiment, the rich-shift does not need to be large, because the NO_x purge catalyst does not comprise the moving process in bulk." etc., and clarifies the meaning of the "absorptive attachment to the surface".

On the other hand, the cited invention uses the expression "absorptive attachment", but the description does not distinguish between the "absorptive attachment" and "absorption".

From the understanding that the grounds in the notice of rejection of 30 January 2004 mention the composition of the NO_x purge catalyst in the description of the cited documents 1 and 2, yet without any specific indication to "the absorptive attachment of NO_x to the surface", the plaintiff argued in his reply against the notice dated 5 April 2004 that "the absorptive attachment of NO_x to the surface", cited in the description of the specification of the application at issue was referred to as follows: "in the invention, NO_x is absorbed in the oxidized atmosphere in the lean operation region of the internal combustion engine", "the trapping of NO_x is mainly made through the absorptive attachment to the surface of the catalyst.", and emphasised that the invention at issue was different from the prior art because in the prior art, "the exhaust gas always flows into the NO_x absorbent, and the NO_x is absorbed at the lean phase of the exhaust gas", while in the invention at issue, "the NO_x is mainly absorptively attached to the surface of the catalyst."

In response thereto, the examiner in the decision of rejection dated 19 July 2005 indicated that it was "needless to show examples, as the absorptive attachment of NO_x to the surface of the catalyst was well known before the time of the application."

(2) From the above procedure, although the interpretation of the examiner regarding the feature "the absorptive attachment of NO_x to surface" in claim 1 of the application is not entirely clear because there is no concrete reasoning, the decision of the examination department was written after taking note of the opinion of 5 April 2004, which emphasised that "the absorptive attachment of NO_x to the surface" is the attachment to the surface which is different from internal absorption, and the decision stated that "the absorptive attachment to the surface" is "a well-known technology". Thus, it is natural to infer that the examiner decided with respect to this different feature "the absorptive attachment to the surface" that the invention at issue was easy to conceive based on the cited invention 1 in combination with the well-known technology as taken from the cited invention 2, affirming the interpretation by the plaintiff (applicant) of the meanings of and the relationship between the "absorption" and the "absorptive attachment" in "the absorptive attachment of NO_x to the surface".

On the other hand, in its decision the board of appeal of the JPO, identifying the feature that "NO_x is absorptively attached to the surface of the NO_x purge catalyst" as the difference between the invention at issue and the cited invention, and showing the concrete examples 1 and 2 as a well-known technology, reasoned that the "NO_x purge catalyst the surface of which NO_x is absorptively attached to is well known".

In the examples 1 and 2 of the well-known technology, however, the words "absorptive attachment" are not mentioned and for the word "surface" only the point that "O_2^-, O^{2-} and NO are reacted on the surface of Pt" is mentioned, and it is stated that "it is defused in the absorbent in the form of nitrate ion NO_3^-". So it must be presumed that the decision found that a series of phenomena of the reaction of O_2^-, O^{2-} and NO and the diffusion into the absorbent in the form of nitrate ion NO_3^- as the "absorptive attachment to the surface" phenomenon and that this finding was based on the premise that the "absorptive attachment to the surface" was comprised in "the diffusion (absorption) into the inside of the catalyst with the absorptive attachment to the surface of the catalyst" i.e. that the phenomena "absorptive attachment" and "absorption" occur at the same time.

Thus, it cannot be affirmed that the decisions of the examination department and the board of appeal of the JPO actually reached the same interpretation regarding the "absorptive attachment to the surface". When looking at the interpretation of this term in the decisions of the examination department and the board of appeal of the JPO, the former interpreted the term as "absorptive attachment to the surface", and the latter as a phenomenon which comprises not only absorptive attachment to the surface but also the "absorption". Thus, the decision of the board of appeal was based on grounds different from those given by the examination department.

Based on the interpretation and the premise argued by the plaintiff, the point "absorptive attachment to the surface" is an important part of the invention at issue. From the argument of the plaintiff in the opinion letter or the request for an appeal trial, it can be affirmed that the plaintiff interprets this point differently from the board of appeal and interprets the invention at issue and the cited invention based on a different premise. Therefore, it was necessary that the board of appeal of the JPO gave the applicant an opportunity to state his opinion because the board of appeal considered the element "absorptive attachment to the surface" based on grounds which were different from those of the decision of the examination department.

Even where the board of appeal does not give the plaintiff such opportunity to file an opinion, illegality of the conduct demonstrated by the board of appeal may be denied in the presence of special circumstances, for example where there is a substantive hearing for each point and the plaintiff can state his opinion (see, IP High Court, 21 February 2008[7]). In this case, however, there are no such special circumstances.

(3) Furthermore, the decision of the board of appeal of the JPO cited the well-known technology of the examples 1 and 2 which was not at all indicated in the notice of the grounds for rejection. Yet when not comprised in the grounds of rejection, only a well-known technology can be cited as a prior art invention within the meaning of sec. 29(1), (2) PA, and a reasoning based thereupon.

That is, the decision of the board of appeal noted that "the first difference is well known because the NO_x purge catalyst the surface of which NO_x is absorptively attached to when the exhaust gas is lean is well known (for example, see example 1 and 2 for the well-known technology 1).", and for the second difference it noted that "it is well known to purge the exhaust gas by absorptively attaching NO_x with the NO_x purge catalyst, setting the status of the exhaust gas to the stoichiometric or rich

7. IP High Court, 21 February 2008, Case No. 10538 (Gyō-Ke) of 2006

status after this absorptive attachment and reducing the NO_x absorptively attached by the NO_x purge catalyst to N_2 by contact reaction with a reducing agent when the internal combustion engine is in the lean mode and the time and the depth in the second difference is very easy to determine by taking into account the well-known technology 2 in the examples 1 and 3", and that "the invention at issue is easy to invent by the person skilled in the art based on the cited invention and the well-known technologies 1 and 2." This decision of the board of appeal, however, is in error.

Even if the well-known technologies 1 or 2 may be well known as an invention, as the defendant argued, it is clear from the interpretation of sec. 29(1), (2) and sec. 50 PA that it cannot be said that they can be cited as prior art inventions within the meaning of sec. 29(1), (2) PA even where they are not indicated in the notice of the grounds for refusal, simply because they are well known technologies. Certainly, there are some cases where well-known technologies which are not cited in the notice of the grounds for refusal can be exceptionally cited in order to deny an inventive step under sec. 29(2) PA. However, such cases are limited to those where they are used to give minor modification to the identification of the prior art inventions which constitute the grounds for refusal, or as supplemental considerations in the process of evaluating inventive step, or as knowledge which is well known in the relevant technical fields and constitutes a matter of course or an implicit premise for the understanding of the technology and well-known technologies can be cited as a matter of course even where they are not shown in the notice of the grounds for refusal as long as they are well known. Although it is imaginable that the well-known technologies referred to by the defendant are famous and known to many relevant persons, in view of the fact that they play an important role in the evaluation process concerning inventive step of the invention at issue, citation of them does not fall under the category of a minor change in the identification of the cited invention, a supplemental consideration regarding inventive step or a matter of course or an implicit premise and therefore they cannot serve as determining factors to deny inventive step in this case.

3. ANALYSIS

a) Appeal procedure against an examiner's decision of refusal and right to be heard

An applicant can appeal to the board of appeal of the JPO against an examiner's decision of refusal and not only submit comments against the decision but also make amendments to his application when filing an appeal. This appeal procedure against an examiner's decision of refusal is an *ex parte* procedure and basically proceeds by a written exchange between an appellant and the JPO (sec. 145(2) PA) and in practice oral hearings are not held even where the board makes a decision of refusal.[8] In practice, therefore, an appellant (applicant) will present its opinions and make amendments basically in writing, but not orally in the course of an oral hearing. Whether the board has to hold an oral hearing if the appellant so requires is discussed in Case No. 19 in this volume.

8. Although a board also may, upon a motion by the party or *ex officio*, decide to conduct an oral hearing (sec. 145(2)), an oral hearing is rarely held in practice.

The examination by the board of appeal has the character of a continuation of the previous examination by the examination division and actions conducted in the examination procedure continue to have effect in the procedures of the board of appeal, sec. 158 PA. The board can therefore make a decision of refusal based on the same grounds as those on which the examiner's decision is based, without notifying the appellant (applicant) of those grounds anew.[9] That is, although an applicant is not given any opportunity to state its opinion or make amendments, regardless of in writing or orally, there is still no contravention of sec. 159(2) PA or sec. 50 PA applied *mutatis mutandis* therein and therefore no procedural violation, because the appellant (applicant) has already been notified of such grounds for refusal on which the board's decision is based at the time of the examiner's decision.[10]

On the other hand, as already mentioned, where a board makes a decision of refusal based on grounds different from those on which the examiner's decision is based, the board has to notify the appellant of those grounds. If the board takes the decision of refusal without such notification to the appellant, it contravenes sec. 159(2) PA and sec. 50 PA applied *mutatis mutandis* therein and therefore commits a procedural violation.[11]

In this way, the right of an appellant or applicant to be heard, which is to be inferred from the underlying rationale behind sec. 50 PA, is safeguarded in the appeal procedure even though in practice no oral hearing is held in most cases and an appellant (applicant) seemingly has not been given any opportunity to present its opinion against the grounds of the board's decision or make amendments in some cases.

b) Competence of the board of appeal

A board of appeal has competence to examine *ex officio* whether or not an application should be granted; that is, the board is not bound by the evidence or arguments submitted by the parties (appellant (applicant) in case of appeal against an examiner's decision of refusal) and can freely cite new prior art documents, including well-known technologies, as evidence and even make a decision of refusal based on such newly cited documents, even though these have not been cited and therefore not mentioned as grounds for refusal in the examiner's decision.[12]

---

9. Some court precedents ruled that a board could further make a decision of refusal even based on grounds which are the same as those mentioned in the notification of grounds for refusal but different from those on which the examiner's decision of refusal is based, without notifying the applicant of such grounds before it takes a decision (e.g., Tokyo High Court, 31 March 2003, Case No. 41 (Gyō-Ke) of 2002, the website of the courts <http://www.courts.go.jp/app/files/hanrei_jp/181/011181_hanrei.pdf>). In practice, however, a board of appeal is supposed to notify the appellant of those grounds anew in such cases, taking into account the appellant's expectation that those grounds for refusal do not exist any more at the time of the examiner's decision of refusal (See, 62-06 of TOKKYOCHŌ SHINPANBU *(Trial and Appeal Department of the JPO)*, Shinpan binran *(Manual for Trial and Appeal Proceedings)*, 16th ed., 2015).
10. Shin Chūkai Tokkyohō, *supra* note 1, at 2296.
11. *Id.*
12. N. NAKAYAMA, Tokkyohō *(Patent Law)*, 3rd ed. 2016, 250.

Although the citation of new prior art documents by a board of appeal itself thus does not necessarily constitute an unlawful conduct, the board according to sec. 159(2) PA still has to notify the appellant of the grounds for refusal before it makes a decision of refusal based on these grounds, where those grounds citing new prior art documents are different from those of the examiner's decision.

c) Criteria for "different grounds" within the meaning of sec. 159(2) PA

Where a board of appeal takes the decision of refusal by applying provisions of the PA which are different from those applied in the examiner's decision of refusal, the grounds of the board's decision are apparently "different" from those of the examiner's decision. This is typically the case where a board makes a decision of refusal on the ground of lack of inventive step (sec. 29(2) PA), whereas the examiner refuses the application on the ground of lack of novelty (sec. 29(1)(i)-(iii) PA).[13]

As regards the ground of lack of inventive step, the courts have ruled that, even where both a board of appeal and an examiner decide the refusal of application based on this ground, the grounds of the board's decision may amount to "different ground[s]" within the meaning of sec. 159(2) PA, depending on the cited prior art documents and the established facts on which the decisions are based, and have clarified in which cases the grounds of the board's decision are deemed to be different from those of the examiner's decision. For example, where both a board of appeal and an examiner decided the refusal of an application based on lack of inventive step but the prior art document which the board cited to deny the inventive step are different from those the examiner cited, the grounds of the board's decision should amount to "different grounds" within the meaning of sec. 159(2) PA.[14] As regards cases where both a board of appeal and an examiner decided refusal of an application based on lack of inventive step by citing the same documents, the courts ruled in more recent cases that the grounds of the board's decision should still amount to "different grounds" within the meaning of sec. 159(2) PA, 1) where the identified inventions or technological facts which are cited and derived from those documents and compared with the claimed invention in its decision are different from those identified in the examiner's decision,[15] [16] or 2) where the facts taken into consider-

13. Shin Chūkai Tokkyohō, *supra* note 1, at 917.
14. IP High Court, 4 October 2011, Case No. 10298 (Gyō-Ke) of 2010, 2139 Hanrei Jihō 77; IP High Court, 10 September 2012, Case No. 10315 (Gyō-Ke) of 2011, the website of the courts <http://www.courts.go.jp/app/files/hanrei_jp/548/082548_hanrei.pdf>. *See also*, Shin Chūkai Tokkyohō, *supra* note 1, at 917; M. Shimizu, *supra* note 1, at 81.
15. IP High Court, 21 February 2008, Case No. 10538 (Gyō-Ke) of 2006, the website of the courts <http://www.courts.go.jp/app/files/hanrei_jp/869/035869_hanrei.pdf>; IP High Court, 17 October 2012, Case No. 10056 (Gyō-Ke) of 2012, the website of the courts <http://www.courts.go.jp/app/files/hanrei_jp/689/082689_hanrei.pdf>. In the former case, although the court found a contravention of sec. 50 PA applied *mutatis mutandis* in sec. 159(2) PA, it also found that there had not been any "concrete disadvantage for the appellant" and therefore denied unlawfulness which should lead to revocation of the board's decision, under the concrete circumstance of the case.
16. Tokyo High Court, 20 October 2004, Case No. 11 (Gyō-Ke) of 2002, the website of the courts <http://www.courts.go.jp/app/files/hanrei_jp/994/009994_hanrei.pdf>. *See also*, Shin Chūkai Tokkyohō, *supra* note 1, at 917.

ation in assessment of inventive step, such as well-known facts, in its decision are different.[17]

In the case at issue, which also falls under the category of "grounds of lack of inventive step citing the same documents", the court further decided on a procedural violation where the board takes i) a different interpretation of the claims and ii) cites of new prior art documents for the purpose of adding well-known technologies.

i) Different interpretation of the claim

In the case at issue, where the main prior art document and the findings from this document adopted in both decisions were the same, the court further ruled that the interpretation of the claimed feature of "absorptive attachment to the surface" by the board in its decision of refusal on the ground of lack of inventive step was different from the interpretation of the same feature by the examiner in its decision and therefore the grounds of the board's decision based on such interpretation of the claim that is different from one by the examiner should amount to "different grounds" within the meaning of sec. 159(2) PA.[18] The court further noted that "the point "absorptive attachment to the surface" is an important part of the invention at issue" and "[t]herefore, it was necessary that the board of appeal of the JPO gave the applicant an opportunity to state his opinion".

The above ruling of the court in this case is quite comprehensible and can be agreed to The reason is that the applicant could have amended the claim in such a manner that the feature of "absorptive attachment to the surface" could no longer be interpreted as including "the diffusion (absorption) into the inside of the catalyst", but could be interpreted only as being "absorptive attachment to the surface of the catalyst" itself and thus clearly different from the "a series of phenomena" thereof, unlike the board interpreted the above, and therefore avoided the grounds newly raised by the board, if the appellant had been notified of such interpretation of the claim beforehand and given an opportunity of comments and amendments, and that the conduct of the board in this case which failed to make such notification therefore should be evaluated to have deprived the appellant of such opportunity. This should be the case especially where the interpretation of a claimed feature is an important part of the invention, as in the case at issue.

The ruling of this case also seems to be in line with the recent cases of the courts which have broadened the range of circumstances where a board must notify

17. IP High Court, 28 January 2010, Case No. 10150 (Gyō-Ke) of 2009, the website of the courts <http://www.courts.go.jp/app/files/hanrei_jp/369/038369_hanrei.pdf>. In this case, however, the court finally decided, considering the circumstances of the case, that the board did not need to notify the appellant of the grounds and give the appellant an opportunity to state his opinions against the grounds because it did not impair "procedural fairness" (手続きの公正 *"Tetsuzuki no kōsei"*) even without such notification.

18. The court noted in its decision "[t]hus, it cannot be affirmed that the decisions of the examination department and the board of appeal of the JPO actually reached the same interpretation regarding the "absorptive attachment to the surface". When looking at the interpretation of this term in the decisions of the examination department and the board of appeal of the JPO, the former interpreted the term as "absorptive attachment to the surface", and the latter as a phenomenon which comprises not only absorptive attachment to the surface but also the "absorption". Thus, the decision of the board of appeal was based on grounds different from those given by the examination department." (*See*, *supra* 2. Decision b) (2))

an appellant (applicant) of "different grounds", and further could be said to be appropriate and acceptable in light of the underlying rationale behind sec. 159(2) PA and sec. 50 PA applied *mutatis mutandis* therein, which aims to secure the right to be heard.[19]

ii) Addition of well-known technologies by citation of new prior art documents

As mentioned above, although a board of appeal is competent to examine an application *ex officio* and can freely cite new prior art documents as evidence in deciding refusal of an application based on those newly cited documents which were not cited in the examiner's decision of refusal, the board basically has to notify the appellant (applicant) of the grounds for refusal citing such new documents. However, if the documents newly cited by the board show well-known technologies, it is questionable whether the board still has to notify the appellant. In this regard, the courts have ruled that a board does not have to make a notification anew if such documents show well-known technologies or common knowledge in the technical fields in assessment of inventive step of the claimed invention, because in such cases such citation does not amount to "different grounds".[20] In a few cases, the courts further ruled that where well-known technologies not cited in the examiner's decision are cited not as technologies referred (supplementarily) in a reasoning to deny inventive step but as prior art documents within the meaning of sec. 29(1) and (2) PA, such well-known technologies must have been cited as prior art within the meaning of sec. 29(1) and (2) PA in the ground for refusal by the examiner,[21] and narrowed the range of cases where the new notification to the appellant is not necessary.

In the case at issue the court further limited cases where well-known technologies which are not cited in the grounds for refusal by the examiner can be exceptionally cited in the board's decision in order to deny an inventive step to those where they are used 1) for a minor change in the identification of the cited prior inventions, 2) for a supplemental consideration regarding inventive step or 3) as knowledge which is a matter of course or an implicit premise, and decided that the addition of well-known technologies in the board's decision otherwise contravenes sec. 50 PA applied *mutatis mutandis* in sec. 159(2) PA.

While the above ruling seems to aim at securing the right to be heard and limited the cases where no notification was necessary to only three categories,[22]

19. A similar evaluation of this case is also given in, e.g., M. SHIMIZU, *supra* note 1, at 81.
20. *E.g.*, Tokyo High Court, 26 May 1992, Case No. 228 (Gyō-Ke) of 1990; Tokyo High Court, 8 April 2004, Case No. 133 (Gyō-Ke) of 2001, the website of the courts <http://www.courts.go.jp/app/files/hanrei_jp/402/010402_hanrei.pdf>; Tokyo High Court, 27 January 2004, Case No. 546 (Gyō-Ke) of 2002, the website of the courts <http://www.courts.go.jp/app/files/hanrei_jp/567/010567_hanrei.pdf>. *See also*, Shin Chūkai Tokkyohō, *supra* note 1, at 920-921; H. YOSHIDA, *supra* note 2, at 75.
21. *E.g.*, IP High Court, 26 April 2007, Case No. 10281 (Gyō-Ke) of 2006, the website of the courts <http://www.courts.go.jp/app/files/hanrei_jp/594/034594_hanrei.pdf>. *See also*, IP High Court, 20 December 2006, Case No. 10102 (Gyō-Ke) of 2006, the website of the courts <http://www.courts.go.jp/app/files/hanrei_jp/928/033928_hanrei.pdf>; K. TSUJIMOTO, *supra* note 5, at 2.
22. Actually, each of these three categories could be seen as a factor considered in determination of such cases in precedent cases, e.g., referred in footnotes 18 and 19 and referred in the documents referred in those footnotes, although not necessarily as a norm or criteria for such determination.

there is no argument or justification for these three categories being an exhaustive list or the appropriate criteria. While in some subsequent case the court seems to apply these criteria not all together but only partially in order to determine whether new well-known technologies can be cited by a board of appeal in its decision,[23] in other subsequent cases the court seems to go rather in another direction; in those cases, the court decided on the addition of new well-known technologies without hearing the appellant not by assessing whether the addition of new well-known technologies amounts to "different grounds" within the meaning of sec. 159(2) PA, but rather whether special circumstances exist or not, e.g., whether the procedural fairness and/or appellant's interests are not impaired, considering various factors of the case as a whole.[24] This approach might be evaluated as more flexible and therefore more appropriate, although less predictable, than the application of the criteria ruled in the case at issue.

4. COMPARATIVE REMARKS

a) EPO

The right to be heard under Art. 113 EPC is deemed to be an embodiment of the fundamental principle that "the predictability and verifiability of all state action are indispensable elements of the rule of law and respect for fundamental procedural rights,"[25] and pursuant to Art. 113(1) EPC "[t]he decisions of the [EPO] may only be based on grounds or evidence on which the parties concerned have had an opportunity to present their comments."[26]

On the other hand, Art. 94(3) EPC prescribes that "the examining division shall invite the applicant, as often as necessary, to file his observations and, subject to Art. 123(1) EPC, to amend the application" in case of non-compliance with the requirements of the EPC. The expression "as often as necessary" therein is interpreted as giving the examining division discretion.[27]

---

23. *E.g.*, IP High Court, 27 January 2010, Case No. 10095 (Gyō-Ke) of 2009, the website of the courts <http://www.courts.go.jp/app/files/hanrei_jp/377/038377_hanrei.pdf>; IP High Court, 17 February 2016, Case No. 10272 (Gyō-Ke) of 2014, 2298 Hanrei Jihō 91.
24. *E.g.*, IP High Court, 28 January 2010, Case No. 10150 (Gyō-Ke) of 2009, the website of the courts <http://www.courts.go.jp/app/files/hanrei_jp/369/038369_hanrei.pdf>; IP High Court, 30 November 2010, Case No. 10124 (Gyō-Ke) of 2010, the website of the courts <http://www.courts.go.jp/app/files/hanrei_jp/878/080878_hanrei.pdf>; IP High Court, 21 November 2012, Case No. 10098 (Gyō-Ke) of 2012, the website of the courts <http://www.courts.go.jp/app/files/hanrei_jp/777/082777_hanrei.pdf>.
25. EPO Case Law, *supra* note 4, at 531.
26. Art. 113(1) EPC. And the right to be heard of an applicant is secured as follows: a violation of the right to be heard by the examination department may constitute a "fundamental deficiency" under Art. 11 of Rules of Procedure of the Boards of Appeal (hereinafter "RPBA") that justifies the remittal of the case to the examination department, and a fundamental violation of Art. 113 can be the basis for filling a petition for review to the Enlarged Board of Appeal; a petition for review can also be based on the a failure to arrange a requested oral hearing and to adversely decide on a party's request (EPO Case Law, *supra* note 4, at 531).
27. EPO Case Law, *supra* note 4, at 867.

From those provisions, it is concluded that "if a decision to refuse is taken on the basis of grounds which have not previously been presented to the applicant, then the decision does not comply with the provisions of Art. 113(1) EPC",[28] and "in order to avoid contravening Art. 113(1) EPC 1973 it was "necessary" to issue a further communication".[29]

Following the above it could be said that the basic framework in the procedures before the EPO with regard to the right to be heard is similar to the one in the procedures before the JPO. However, it seems to be not clear from the precedent cases of the EPO's board of appeal whether or not a further communication is necessary to be issued, in case of different interpretation of the claim or addition of well-known technologies in assessment of inventive step in the decision of refusal which have not shown in the grounds for refusal already notified or communicated to the applicant beforehand, as ruled in the Japanese case at issue.

b) Korea

The **Korean** Supreme Court held in 2013 that the KIPO decision was unlawful, when it refused an application or dismissed an appeal on a reason without giving an opportunity to applicant to file a response for the reason, and the KIPO could not argue new reason in later court procedure, but supplement of evidence of well-known or conventional technology to the reason of which the purport was same to the already noticed reason was allowable.[30] After such decision, the Korean Patent Court held also in 2016 that addition of well-known or conventional technology in the KIPO appeal procedure which made substantially new reason beyond simple supplementing the already noticed reason was unlawful when an opportunity to file a response for the new reason was not given.[31]

---

28. *Id.* at 880.
29. *Id.* at 871.
30. Korean Supreme Court, 15 February 2013, Case No. 1439 (Hu) of 2012; Korean Supreme Court, 26 September 2013, Case No. 1054 (Hu) of 2013.
31. Korean Patent Court, 29 September 2016, Case No. 2737 (Heo) of 2016.

Case No. 19

Right to be Heard – Right to Oral Proceedings in Invalidation Trials

Yasuhiko Irinoda

An invalidation trial before the JPO is to be conducted by oral proceedings considering the content and character of the issues involved in the case. An ex officio decision to conduct the trial in writing is deemed inappropriate notwithstanding the discretion enjoyed by the JPO administrative judges in this matter.

Intellectual Property High Court, 29 June 2009,
Case No. 10427, 10428 & 10429 (Gyō-Ke) of 2008 –
Apparatus and Method for Substrate Processing

Tokyo Electron v. Itō

---

1. BACKGROUND

In its decision of 19 January 2006, Case No. 10193 (Gyō-Ke) of 2005,[1] the Intellectual Property High Court had to decide two issues. First, who bears the burden of proof regarding patent ownership or lawful succession from the previous owner. This issue is dealt with in Cases Nos. 15 and 16 of this volume. The second question concerns the right to an oral hearing in proceedings before the Patent Office.

Concerning the principle of the oral proceedings in an invalidation trial, it has been commonly accepted that an *inter partes* trial should in principle be conducted by oral proceedings, especially in cases of misappropriation. An eminent professor of the patent law, *Nobuhiro Nakayama* already referred to this principle of the oral proceedings in his basic textbook prior to this case.[2] However, JPO's trial judges have the tendency to examine only written documents even in cases of *inter partes* trials. There is a divergence between practice and theory even from a practical point of view, as the principle of oral proceedings is significant for unearthing the truth in trial/court procedure particularly in misappropriation cases, seeing that the oral

---

1. Published at the website of the courts <http://www.courts.go.jp/app/files/hanrei_jp/192/009192_hanrei.pdf>.
2. N. Nakayama, Kōgyōshoyūken hō (Industrial Laws) The first volume: Tokkyo hō *(Patent Law)*, The second enlarged ed. version 1993, 261. (The first edition of Tokkyo hō (Patent Law)'s original textbook. The current third edition, which was published in 2016, at the corresponding page 273, cites this case regarding the principle.)

examination of a witness/party testifying against the registered inventor can be a rather effective way to arrive at the truth.

2. DECISION[3]

a) Facts

The defendant is the proprietor of a patent related to a substrate processing apparatus. The application was a divisional application from the original application filed on 27 April 2001. The patent was registered on 29 October 2004.

The plaintiff filed the JPO an invalidation action against the patent on 15 January 2008 because the patent was granted based on an application filed by an individual who was neither the inventor, nor the successor of the right to obtain a patent for aforesaid invention, corresponding to sec. 123(1)(vi) Patent Act.

The written request for invalidation included elaborate grounds and presented compelling evidence. To achieve the inventions disclosed in the original application and the invention of the patent in particular, a large amount of funding for development, large scale facilities and knowledge, experience and inventive ability in this technical field were necessary. However, according to the research conducted by the plaintiff, the defendant did not seem to have sufficient knowledge, experience and inventive ability and technical skills to prepare such an invention. It should be noted that similarities between several of the plaintiff's applications and the application of the patent at issue could be drawn. Moreover, the plaintiff's patent applications were not published at the time of filing the original application of the patent at issue. Taken these into consideration, it must be assumed that a third person, being in a position to access the plaintiff's inventions wrote the patent application at issue, where after the defendant filed the applications on behalf of the aforementioned individual, who – however – opted to go anonymous due to the above circumstances. The defendant submitted a written reply consisting of two pages, arguing that the research by the plaintiff could not prove that the defendant was not being the inventor. On the one hand, the defendant also asked not to hold oral proceedings or to be examined by the other party owing to the concern that personal information should be improperly disclosed thereby; on the other hand, the plaintiff did ask for oral proceedings and the examination of the party/witness. Ultimately, the JPO administrative judges decided to conduct the trial in writing. The administrative judges in the trial decision of 14 October 2008 concluded that the request for invalidation was not well -founded. On the assumption that the plaintiff had the burden of proof for demonstrating that the application had been misappropriated, the decision stated that on the basis of the evidence and grounds provided by the plaintiff, it could not be concluded whether the patent had been misappropriated. On appeal, the court decided that the trial decision should be overturned, because the judgement had been mistaken about the burden of proof, resulting in the dismissal of the request.

3. Published in 2104 Hanrei Jihō 101 = N. Nakayama et al. (eds.), Tokkyo hanrei hyakusen *(Hundred Selected Patent Cases)*, 4th ed. 2012, 84. English translation in 42 IIC 726 (2011).

b) Reasons

Although it is understood that the proprietors have the burden of proof for the fact that the "application was filed by a person who is either the inventor or has succeeded to the right to obtain a patent for the aforesaid invention", the understanding does not necessarily mean that the proprietors are required to prove the precise history of inventions etc. in all cases.

The extent and content of the evidence that proprietors have to provide depends on the concrete facts that suggest the application was misappropriated, and both the extent and content of the proof that a plaintiff in a trial for invalidation has provided. If the plaintiff does not point to any concrete facts that suggest misappropriation and does not submit proof, the burden for the proprietors to prove title to the invention is relatively easy to fulfil. On the other hand, when the plaintiff does point out concrete facts that suggest a misappropriation and has submitted such proof, the proprietors cannot discharge the burden of proof unless they conclusively contradict such allegations. Facts that suggest misappropriation are different in each case, depending on the technical field in question and such like

...

In the trial for invalidation, the defendant as the applicant/proprietor has to prove that he is the rightful inventor of the patent, because the proprietor has the burden of proof that the application has not been misappropriated. In the case at issue, the plaintiff has submitted concrete evidence that suggests misappropriation.

However, the defendant submitted only written replies and did not contradict the claim of the plaintiff in a concrete manner apart from the point that "the application was filed by a person who is the inventor or has succeeded to the right to obtain a patent for said invention."

The trial decision was based on an erroneous interpretation of the burden of proof as to whether the application was misappropriated or not.

...

Sec. 178(1) provides that "[t]he Tokyo High Court shall have exclusive jurisdiction over any action against a trial decision ..." Whereas the trial decision is a type of administrative disposition, the courts of jurisdiction might be basically District Courts by the Administrative Case Litigation Act. But for the following two reasons, the court of jurisdiction shall be the Tokyo High Court omitting the first instance: (α) the trial proceedings before the JPO shall be conducted in strict proceedings similar to the courts and the expeditious resolution of cases prevails over the appropriateness through decisions of district courts, (β) the contents of the cases are technically specialised and the trial proceedings conducted by the JPO with patent expertise can be respected. Also for such reasons, sec. 145(1) Patent Act prescribes that a trial for patent invalidation shall in principle be conducted by oral proceedings.

...

The trial should have been conducted by oral proceedings considering the content and character of the issues involved in this case. The *ex officio* change of proceedings type from oral to documentary was inappropriate in this regard, even though administrative judges have a reasonable discretion in determining the process and method of proceedings. The procedural flaw affected the outcome of the decision, which therefore must be overturned.

3. ANALYSIS

Regarding the principle of a mandatory oral hearing:

(1) The principle of mandatory oral hearing and exceptional examination of written documents

Sec. 145(1) states that the invalidation procedure in principle should be conducted by oral proceedings in the case of an *inter partes* procedure, according to sec. 145(5) in open court. Witnesses and/or of the parties can be heard during oral proceedings, which appears necessary especially for the inter-parties' trial cases, such as cases of misappropriation. However, the JPO board members of first instance rejected the applicant's request for hearing a witness contradicting the defendant party's witness. The JPO trial board decided in a written procedure only, which the IP High Court Found to be a serious violation of sec. 145(1).

> (Procedure of Trial)
>
> Sec. 145(1) A trial for patent invalidation or a trial for invalidation of the registration of extension of the duration of a patent shall be conducted by oral proceedings; provided, however, that the presiding administrative judge may, upon a motion by a party or intervener in the case, or ex officio decide to conduct the trial in writing.

There are two different ideas of trial proceedings before the JPO: the administrative-oriented, "*ex officio* examination" and the civil court-oriented, "*inter partes* civil court procedure". In the case of a patent invalidation trial before the JPO, the question is which of the two is more appropriate: (1) the character of the administrative procedure, or (2) the character of the dispute between the parties with respect to the ownership of the registered patent. Type (1) would allow the JPO to adopt an administrative-oriented procedure without appointing oral proceedings and based on the examination of written documents only. Cases of misappropriation would typically call for civil law type proceedings (2) in order to decide to whom the issued patent should belong to.[4] This is underlined by sec. 151 Patent Act according to which the rules for hearing evidence as set out in sec. 179 of the Code of Civil Procedure should apply *mutatis mutandis*.[5]

(2) Oral proceedings in invalidation trials before the JPO as tatemae*?*

Although the fundamental statutory rule is that trial judges should conduct invalidation trials orally where the subject matter is of a similar character to ordinary civil litigation, JPO trials would sometimes (or often) result in the mere examination of written documents. In fact, the principle of oral hearings becomes a mere formality even in cases where oral proceedings are mandatory.

Considering that the arguments in invalidation trials would often require trial judges to examine technical questions by reviewing the briefs and documentary

4. N. NAKAYAMA (above), at 251
5. T. NAKANO, Chizai shinketsu torikeshi soshō no riron to jitsumu *(Theory and practice of litigation to rescind the JPO decision in IP field)*, 2015, 53.

evidence, the JPO's practice has given trial judges broad discretion and dispense with oral proceeding in favour of an examination of written documents. There are concerns regarding such document-oriented practice and whether trial judges are aware that oral proceedings are mandatory in principle. It would be highly necessary for the trial court's judges to develop appropriate skills for conducting trials orally as do civil court judges.

Against this background, one may appreciate the reasons why the JPO appeal board turned the oral proceeding into a mere examination of written documents and rejected the request for hearing a witness in an oral hearing.[6]

In this connection, one should be aware that already several years before the applicant filed its invalidation trial before the JPO, a legislative proposal had been tabled that was meant to separate ordinary trial matter involving technical questions and not necessitating oral proceedings from those trials where non-technical matters are prevalent, namely entitlement proceedings. The former should remain with the JPO trial boards (with the practice of not holding oral hearings), while the latter should be directly dealt with by the civil courts.[7]

On the other hand, "the trials before the JPO do not need to comply with the fundamental principles of civil litigation because trial judges can rely on their own technical knowledge and experience to reach their conclusions."[8]

4. COMPARATIVE REMARKS

a) EPO

Art. 116(1) EPC provides an absolute procedural right to oral proceedings at each instance of the EPO: "Oral proceedings shall take place either at the instance of the European Patent Office if it considers this to be expedient or at the request of any party to the proceedings." It is considered that this provision is mandatory and there is no room for the discretion of the competent divisions of the EPO in this respect. Decisions that are rendered in disregard of a request for oral proceedings must normally be set aside as null and void.[9]

---

6. N. NAKAYAMA (above): "The invalidation trials shall be conducted by the oral proceedings, especially in the case of misappropriate patent filing. ... In recent years the JPO changed to give importance to the oral proceedings, however, on the other hand, it is necessary to enhance the physical facilities of the trials and the human resources such as the trial judges and clerks for the promotion of oral proceedings in invalidation proceedings."
7. N. NAKAYAMA (above) emphasised this point.
8. T. TAKURA/H. FUTAKI, in: N. NAKAYAMA et al. (eds.), Chūkai tokkyo hō ge (Commentary on Patent Act Volume 2), 3rd ed. 2000, 1474
9. Decision **T 19/87** of 16 April 1987 – *Oral proceedings*; Decision **T 93/88** of 11 August 1988; Decision **T 238/88** of 7 September 1988; Decision **T 560/88** of 19 February 1990; Decision **T 663/90** of 13 August 1991; Decision **T 795/91** of 2 November 1991 – *Oral proceedings/MITSUBISHI*; Decision **T 1048/00** of 18 June 2003; Decision **T 911/04** of 10 February 2005. See also the EPO, Case Law, 8th ed. 2016, 558; SINGER/STAUDER, Europäisches Patentübereinkommen *(Comentary on the European Patent Convention)*, 7th ed. 2016, 1139.

b) Germany

Sec. 82(3) German Patent Act provides mandatory (except as otherwise agreed by the parties) oral proceedings in *inter partes* nullity/invalidation cases, in which there are defendant and plaintiff: "When the defendant files its rebuttal in adequate time, the German Federal Patent Court sends the rebuttal to the plaintiff and sets a date for oral proceedings. With the approval of the parties, oral proceedings may be dispensed with."[10]

c) The US

Sec. 316(a)(10) of 35 USC uses the term "right" to an oral hearing: "The Director shall prescribe regulations ... providing either party with the right to an oral hearing as part of the proceeding ..." And the corresponding regulation sec. 42.70 provides a little more about such request of oral argument: "(a) Request for oral argument. A party may request oral argument on an issue raised in a paper at a time set by the Board. The request must be filed as a separate paper and must specify the issues to be argued. ..."[11]

10. BUSSE/KEUKENSCHRIJVER, Patentgesetz *(Commentary on the German Patent Act)*, 8th ed. 2016, 1626

11. The US Patent Trial and Appeal Board stated in an order of 10 October 2014 in Case No. IPR 2013-00539 *Butamax Advanced Biofuels LLC v. Gevo, Inc.* that either party to an instituted *inter partes review* trial has the right to an oral hearing before the Board. The order is available at the website of law firm *Fish&Richardson* <https://fishpostgrant.com/reports/101714-fish-post-grant-report/>.

Case No. 20

Possibility of Claim Amendment before Grant

Atsuhiro Furuta

To decide whether an amendment is within the scope of the original description, etc., instead of formally comparing added words in the claim with words in the original description, etc., it should be considered whether the added matter has a technical meaning that contributes to the problem and solution of the invention.

Intellectual Property High Court, 28 January 2010, Case No. 10175 (Gyō-Ke) of 2009 – *Heat Storage System*

Enertech v. Japanese Patent Office

---

1. BACKGROUND

Secs. 17 to $17^{\text{quinquies}}$, $120^{\text{quinquies}}$, 126, 134bis and 134ter Japanese Patent Act provides the main requirements for an amendment or correction of claim etc. before or after grant.[1] Sec. 17 provides general requirements of amendment and correction, Sec. 17bis the amendment of claims, specification or figures, Sec. 17ter the amendment of abstracts, Sec. 17^{quater} the amendment of a priority claim document, Sec. $17^{\text{quinquies}}$ corrected claims etc. in a correction request, Sec. $120^{\text{quinquies}}$ the correction request in opposition procedure, Sec. 126 the trial for correction (patentee can request a trial for correction as an independent procedure from opposition or invalidation), Sec. 134bis and Sec. 134ter a correction in invalidation procedure. Such provisions and requirements for the amendment of claims etc. are somewhat complicated in the stipulated form and the situation becomes more complicated as such requirements are often revised by law or guideline amendments.

In the subsequent comment, the historical changes regarding the amendment of claims etc. are analysed in more detail. Two periods can be distinguished: One is period of prohibition of change of essence (up to 1993), and the other is prohibition of addition of new subject matter (until now).

---

1. The Japanese Patent Act uses a different terminology for correction before and after grant. The author uses "amendment" as a translation of "*hosei*" which usually means the correction to claims etc. before grant, and "correction" as that of "*teisei*" which usually means the correction after grant. See also Cases No. 21 and 22 of this book.

By the law amendment of 1993,[2] in force since 1 January 1994, the PA introduced a prohibition of adding new subject matter in Sec. 17bis(2) (currently (3)[3]) as a reason of refusal, as follows:[4]

> "In an amendment under the previous subsection, an applicant may amend the claims, specification or figures within the scope of subject matter of the claims, description or figures originally attached to the application, ..."

The JPO practice regarding amendments was handled very restrictively at first, but the Grand Panel decision of the IP High Court of 30 May 2008 (Case No. 22 of this book) set new criteria as to the introduction of new subject matter and changed the practice of the JPO.

This case is a typical case about the amendment of claims after the above Grand Panel decision. In this case, the JPO also took a somewhat rigid stance on the amendments even after it had changed its practice. Again, the IP High Court did not agree.

2. DECISION[5]

a) Facts

The plaintiff is a proprietor of a patent related to a floor heating system in high heat-insulating and high airtight housing. The application was filed on 2 May 2002 and amended during prosecution. The patent was registered on 19 April 2004.

In the amendment, the plaintiff changed "high heat-insulating and high airtight housing" to "high heat-insulating and high airtight housing, whose heat loss coefficient is between 1.0 to 2.5 $kcal/m^2 \cdot h \cdot °C$" in a claim. The numerical range of the heat loss coefficient, which was newly added, was not written in the original application.

The defendant filed an invalidation action against the patent on 5 November 2008, and the appeal examiners in the trial decision of 19 May 2009 concluded that the patent was to be revoked, because the amendment was not within the scope

2. Law No. 26/1993 of 23 April 1993.
3. By the law amendment of 1994 (Law No. 116/1994 of 14 December 1994), which introduced the amendment of claims etc. based on mistranslation, sec. 17bis (2) was shifted to (3) in amended form.
4. Before the law amendment of 1993, the old secs. 40, 41 and 53 stipulated the prohibition of change of essence for amendments: changes in the essence of the application should be dismissed before the decision of grant, amendments that resulted in a claim extension or reduction in the scope of subject matter stated in the application as filed were deemed to be no change of essence. The application was deemed to be filed at the time of amendment where the amendment of the claim etc. before a decision of grant was recognised to be a change of essence. To determine the difference from a mere comparison of the wording of such provisions before and after the law amendment is a little difficult, but in general, under the old provisions an amendment could be made more freely where there was no change of essence, it being understood that a substantial change in the technical subject matter stated in claim etc., including the possibility of supplementing embodiments, etc. should be considered a change of essence. Also the effect of a breach of the provisions differed, i.e. whether it became a reason of refusal/invalidation/opposition, or not.
5. Translated by T. TADA of the JPO = 2089 Hanrei Jihō 128 = 1329 Hanrei Times 218.

of the subject matter described in the description, scope of claims or drawings originally attached to the application (the original description, etc.) and thereby violated sec. 17[bis](3) Patent Act.

On appeal, the court decided that the amendment that changed the term "high heat-insulating and high airtight housing" to the term "high heat-insulating and high airtight housing, whose heat loss coefficient is between 1.0 to 2.5 kcal/m^2·h·°C" was within the scope of the subject matter described in the original description, etc., and did not violate sec. 17[bis](3) Patent Act.

b) Reasons

Sec. 17[bis](3) was intended to ensure a fair handling and distinction between applications with sufficient disclosure on filing and applications with insufficient disclosure on filing, through encouraging sufficient disclosure of the invention from the onset. Additionally, it prevents any third party who acts based on the scope of the invention as originally disclosed from unforeseen disadvantages.

To decide whether an amendment is within the scope of the original description, etc., instead of formally comparing added words in the claim with words in the original description, etc., it should be considered whether the added matter has a technical meaning that contributes to the problem and solution of the invention.

The invention in the claim is about a heat storage type floor heating system, and uses a unitised sheathed heater in high heat insulating and a high air tight housing to facilitate installation and maintenance after the installation so as to prolong the life of the heater. The invention further describes using the radiant heat from the floor and the convection heat of circulating air in an under floor space and an indoor space through a vent hole using midnight electric power by providing the under floor space between the floor and the heat storage layer and the vent hole penetrating the floor.

Considering the fact that the heat loss coefficient cannot be calculated accurately, the terms before and after the amendment do not include technical matter that relates to the solved problems and the mechanism of the invention, but rather it is reasonable to understand that the elements vaguely indicate subject matter of the solution of the invention.

Even if the amendment is allowed, these purposes of sec. 17[bis](3) above are still fulfilled, for the following reasons.

The amendment in the case merely clarifies the scope of the invention, and does not concern its technical subject matter. It does not contribute to the problem and the means for the solution of the invention. After all, the amendment does not introduce any new technical matter to the technical teaching that can be understood by taking into account all statements in the original description, etc., and it is, therefore, not an unlawful amendment.

Even if the matter added by the amendment is interpreted to include relevant technical content, the added matter can be regarded as matter that was already disclosed in the original description, etc., if no new special meaning can be found in relation to the problem and means for the solutions of the invention.

3. ANALYSIS

Law amendments that concern the amendment of claims etc. have been made frequently until now. As a clarification, the reader is provided with a list of the major changes in chronological order:[6]

	Law Amendment	Examination Guidelines	Relevant Case Law
1959	Establishment of the Current Patent Law Scheme:[7] Change of essence by amendment or correction is prohibited. (came into force on 1 April 1960)		
1972			Decision of the Supreme Court of 14 December 1972 – *Method for Producing Pheno-thiazine Derivative* (Case No. 21)
1975	Introduction of Multi Claim System:[8] Change from one single claim to several claims (came into force on 1 January 1976)		
1985	Introduction of Internal Priority[9] (came into force on 1 November 1985)		

6. The author simplifies this table and only shows principal changes, because there are too many changes on the amendment of claims etc. to describe in one table. For example, there is not enough space to mention the periodical limitation of amendments or corrections in this short analysis. For historical changes on amendments or corrections, see also, H. MORISHITA, Tokkyohō 126 jō 3 kō ni iu kisaishita jiko no han'inai ni oite no kaishaku ni tsuite (1), (2), (3) (*About the interpretation of scope of stated subject matter of Sec. 126 (3) PA (1), (2), (3)*), 1307 Hanrei Times 47 (2009), 1308 Hanrei Times 27 (2009), 1309 Hanrei Times 36 (2010); K. MATSUDA, Tokkyo meisaisho tō no hosei teisei seido no hensen to kadai jō/ge (*Change and problems of the amendment and correction system for patent claims etc. first part and second part*), 48 L&T 43 (2010) and 49 L&T 61 (2010); N TAMAI, Shinkijikō tsuika to naranai hosei wo okonau yūkō na shuhō no kaihatsu (*Development of method of amendments which do not become addition of new matter*), 70-7 Patent 54 (2017).
7. Law No. 121/1959 of 13 April 1959.
8. Law No. 46/1975 of 25 June 1975.
9. Law No. 41/1985 of 28 May 1985.

	Law Amendment	Examination Guidelines	Relevant Case Law
1987	Improved Multi Claim System[10] (came into force on 1 January 1988)		
1993	Introduction of New Provisions about Amendments and Correction:[11] Addition of new subject matter is prohibited. (came into force on 1 January 1994)	Corresponding Guideline to the Law Amendment: Amendment of claims etc. should be derivable directly and unambiguously from application as filed.	
1994	Introduction of Applications Based on Foreign Language and Limitation of Amendment after Last Notice of Reason of Refusal:[12] Amendment or correction of claims etc. based on English becomes possible. Amendment of claims is restricted to limitation of subject matter already stated in the claim before the amendment after the last notice of reason of refusal.		
2003		Relaxation of the Criteria of New Subject Matter[13] Amendments of claims etc. can be made within the scope of subject matter, which is clearly derivable from the application as filed (published on 22 October 2003, applicable to applications filed after 1 January 1994)	Decision of Tokyo High Court of 8 October 2003 – *Artificial Nipple* (Case No. 12)

10. Law No. 27/1987 of 25 May 1987. Before this amendment, plural claims in one application were allowed only in exceptional cases. For a historical overview of the multi claim system, see, N. INOUE, Takōsei sono kigen to hensen (*Multi claim system, its origin and transition*) in N. NAKAYAMA et al. (ed.), Chizai rikkoku no hatten e (*For the development of an IP nation*), 2013, 591.
11. Law No. 26/1993 of 23 April 1993.
12. Law No. 116/1994 of 14 December 1994.
13. For details, see, the JPO documents of 22 October 2003, Meisaisho, tokkyo seikyū no han'i matawa zumen no hosei (shinkijikō) no shinsakijun kaitei ni tsuite (*About revision of the examination guideline of amendments of description, claim or figure (new subject matter)*), available at the website of the JPO <https://www.jpo.go.jp/tetuzuki/t_tokkyo/shinsa/meisai_t_zu_kijyun.htm>

	Law Amendment	Examination Guidelines	Relevant Case Law
2006	Introduction of Prohibition of Shifting Amendments:[14] The invention before and after amendment should fulfil the unity requirement, so that amendments that change the special technical features of the invention are prohibited after receiving the notice of reason of refusal.		
2008			Grand panel decision of the IP High Court of 30 May 2008 – *Solder Resist* (Case No. 22)
2010		Implementation of the Criteria of the Grand Panel's Decision of 2008 as Principles:[15] Amendment are allowed if the technical subject matter is comprehensively derivable from the description as filed, and does not introduce new subject matter. Explanation about clearly derived subject matter still remain a useful method to consider the above criteria. (Published on 1 June 2010 and applicable to the examination from this date)	Decision of the IP High Court of 28 January 2010 (this case)[16]
2014	Introduction of Explicit Provisions about Claims in the Priority Document for Ratification of the Patent Law Treaty[17]		

14. Law No. 55/2006 of 7 June 2006.
15. For detail, see, the JPO documents on 1 June 2010, Meisaisho, tokkyo seikyū no han'i matawa zumen no hosei (shinkijikō) no shinsakijun kaitei ni tsuite (*About revision of the examination guideline of amendment of description, claim or figure (new subject matter))*, available at the website of the JPO <https://www.jpo.go.jp/torikumi/t_torikumi/meisaisyo_shinsa_kaitei.htm>
16. Regarding case law around 2010, see also H. YOHIDA, Tokkyohō ni okeru hosei teisei ni kansuru saibanrei no bunseki to teigen (1)/(2) (*Analysis and proposal about amendment/correction in the patent law*(1)/(2)), 21 Chitekizaisanhō Seisakugaku Kenkyu 31 (2008) and 22 Chitekizaisanhō Seisakugaku Kenkyu 31 (2009); Patent Commitee of JIPA, Hosei teisei tō no shinkijikō tsuika ni kansuru kōsatu (*Condideration about addition of new subject matter in amendment or correction*), 63-11 Chizai Kanri 1729 (2013).
17. Law No. 36/2014 of 8 May 2016.

	Law Amendment	Examination Guidelines	Relevant Case Law
2015		Unification of the Criteria about Amendments of Claim, etc.:[18] An amendment is allowed if it concerns technical subject matter which is comprehensively derivable from the description as filed, and does not introduce new subject matter. (Published on 16 September 2015 and applicable to the examination from 1 October 2015).	

As shown in the above table, at the time of the JPO decision in this case, on 19 May 2009, the practice about amendment was still somewhat little rigid, and the JPO decided that the patent at issue should be invalidated due to the addition of new subject matter because there was no description or suggestion about the "heat loss coefficient between 1.0 to 2.5 kcal/m^2·h·°C" of the high heat-insulating and high airtight housing.

In this case, it is true that there is no description or suggestion about the numerical value of heat loss coefficient between 1.0 to 2.5 kcal/m^2·h·°C in the description of the application, and only the rough indication of an electrical consumption, which is tentatively calculated in the housing of the heat loss coefficient 1.2 kcal/m^2·h·°C in the table 2 of paragraph [0016].

Still, the IP High Court decided that the amendment in this case did not introduce new subject matter because it merely clarified the solution "high heat-insulating and high airtight housing" to a certain extent, because it had no special technical meaning in relation with the problem and the means for the solution of the invention, and the added matter can be regarded as matter that was already disclosed in the original description based on the following facts: (i) table 2 of the original description shows the rough indication of electrical consumption at night in utilising the heater of the invention at issue, and this tentative calculation of electricity consumption in utilising the heater is executed for the housing of the heat loss coefficient 1.2 kcal/m^2·h·°C as an object, (ii) there is no accurate definition of an high heat-insulating and high airtight housing at the time of the application at issue, but it can be understood as a housing whose heat loss coefficient is better than the value defined by the energy saving standard of 1999, (iii) the heat loss coefficient is amount of calorie per 1 hour per 1 m^2 floor space which is lost from the whole housing by 1 °C temperature difference between inside and outside and this is an energy saving index of housing indicating its heat retention performance, (iv) the reference value (lower limit) of the energy saving standard of 1999 is different region by region, but from 1.4 to 2.3 kcal/m^2·h·°C", (v) accuracy of calculation of heat loss coefficient is not high.

18. For details see, the JPO documents on 16 September 2015, Tokkyo jitsuyō shin'an shinsakijun no kaitei ni tsuite (*About revision of the patent/utility model examination guideline)*, available at the website of the JPO <https://www.jpo.go.jp/system/laws/rule/guideline/patent/tukujitu_kijun/kaitei2/h27_kaitei.html>.

The author agrees with the position of the IP High Court in applying of the criteria of the Grand Panel case of 2008 in that an amendment which does not introduce any new technical matter than what can be understood by taking into account all statements in the original description, etc. is a lawful amendment. In assessing the criteria, as in this case the High Court did, common technical knowledge at the time of application should be taken into account. And in this context, only to consider whether the wording of amendment is included in the original description or not, does not lead to a reasonable conclusion.

In general, there are two approaches on amendments: one is rigid and places importance on the original wording in the description etc. of the application as filed, while the other is flexible and takes into consideration the technical meaning of the amendment and the common general knowledge at the time of the application. Prior to the law amendment 1993, the JPO took a rather flexible approach, but this changed after 1993 an became too rigid. In the author's view, the case law of the IP High Court on this point modifies the patent practice in Japan in a correct manner.[19]

This case was further appealed, but the Supreme Court dismissed the appeal, and the decision of the IP High Court became final.

Finally, some decisions are introduced to the reader that concern amendments or corrections.

In the decision of 15 July 2010 – *Mould Motor*,[20] against the JPO decision of refusal on the grounds of added subject matter, the IP High Court indicated that the correction of the claim wording "dented part, which is linked in the inner circumference" of the motor of the invention to "dented part, which is linked with insulating resin in the inner circumference" did not add new subject matter, because it was not disputed that "dented part, which is linked in the inner circumference" included "dented part, which is linked with insulating resin in the inner circumference" and "dented part, which is linked without insulating resin in the inner circumference", and such linking with insulating resin did not affect the technical effect of the invention. This indication of the *Mould Motor* case is a little problematic, because it might have required some further discussion as to whether the two subordinate concepts were included in the broader concept, even though there was no clear disclosure about them. This decision of the IP High Court is similar in approach to the above *Heat Storage System* case.

In the decision of 23 March 2011 – *Method of Producing Anhydrite*,[21] the IP High Court clarified that the above criteria are also applicable to parameters, and the correction of the temperature range of "between 330 and 840 °C" to "between 330 and 500 °C" has no critical meaning and is allowable even where there is no specific embodiment in the range of 500 °C in the original application.

19. For an analysis of this case, see also, K. Nakadaira, Hosei no shinkijikō tsuika eno gaitousei (*Amendment and added new subject matter*), in N. Nakayama et al. (ed.), Chitekizaisanken hōri to teigen *(Intellectual property rights doctrine and proposal*), 2013, 437

20. IP High Court, 15 July 2010, Case No. 10019 (Gyō-Ke) of 2010, 1336 Hanrei Times 261 – *Mould Motor*.

21. IP High Court, 23 March 2011, Case No. 10234 (Gyō-Ke) of 2010, the courts website <http://www.courts.go.jp/app/files/hanrei_jp/181/081181_hanrei.pdf> – *Method of Producing Anhydrite*.

In the decision of 9 October 2014 – *Method of Producing Crystal Oscillator,*[22] the IP High Court indicated that the combination of features which was not clearly disclosed in the original application (but each of them was disclosed individually), could be considered an addition of new subject matter.

Practitioners should therefore pay attention especially in regard of amendments or corrections of claims including combinations or selections which are not clearly disclosed in the original application, yet have some technical meaning for the invention claimed, because such amendments or corrections may be regarded as an addition of new subject matter.

4. COMPARATIVE REMARKS

In the **US**, the USPTO also does not allow the addition of new subject matter by way of amendment and may regard such addition as a reason for rejection. The MPEP states that new matter includes not only the addition of wholly unsupported subject matter, but may also include adding specific percentages or compounds amongst a broader original disclosure, or even the omission of a step from a method.[23]

After the decision of **G 1/93,**[24] the **EPO** has adopted the standard that subject matter "directly" or "unambiguously" derivable from the description is not regarded as new. This standard of the EPO may have influenced the overly rigid practice of the JPO after 1993. But in general, the EPO practice about amendments is more flexible than the initial practice of the JPO after 1993, yet more rigid than the current practice of the JPO. And the EPO examination guidelines explicitly mention that attention should be paid to unallowable intermediate generalisation.[25] An intermediate generalisation is generally unallowable, as it amounts to a new teaching or new technical information when features only disclosed in connection with one specific embodiment are claimed as a general teaching without the other corresponding features of such embodiment.[26] Such generalisation is only allowed where the skilled person can realise that the generalised features do not have a functional or structural relationship with the specific example (decision **T 25/03**, as above).

In **Germany**, the GPTO does not take the same strict approach to the intermediate generalisation as the EPO, and the German patent practice about amendments is similar to the Japanese practice. But recently, the German Federal Supreme Court indicated that there is unallowable intermediate generalisation in the Germany transferred European patent.[27] We have to further regard the trend of Germany.

---

22. IP High Court, 9 October 2014, Case No. 10347 (Gyō-Ke) of 2013, the courts website <http://www.courts.go.jp/app/files/hanrei_jp/550/084550_hanrei.pdf> – *Method of Producing Crystal Oscillator*
23. MPEP, Section 706, at the website of the USPTO <https://www.uspto.gov/web/offices/pac/mpep/s706.html>
24. Decision **G 1/93** of 2 February 1994, OJ EPO 1994, 541.
25. In Japan an intermediate generalisation is usually not regarded as addition of new subject matter. For intermediate generalisation, see, INTERNATIONAL COMMITTEE OF JIPA, ōshū ni okeru chukan ippanka ni kansuru kousatsu (*Analysis on intermediate generalisation in the EPO*), 67-10 Chizai Kanri 1512 (2017).
26. E.g. decision **T 25/03** of 8 February 2005.
27. German Federal Supreme Court, 17 February 2015, GRUR 2015, 573 – *Wundbehandlungsvorrichtung*.

In the **UK**, the UKIPO Guidelines provide that in the case of amendments, subject matter will be added unless such matter is clearly and unambiguously disclosed in the application either explicitly or implicitly so that such matter may be regarded as having been originally disclosed. Matter which is not disclosed but which the skilled reader would find obvious to add is not regarded as having been implicitly disclosed.[28] The Guidelines also address the matter of intermediate generalisation.

China takes very rigid stance to the amendment of claims etc. If the amendment is not clearly stated in the description, or not directly and unambiguously derivable from the original application, it will be rejected.[29]

In **Korea**, KIPO treats amendment almost same as in the JPO.[30]

28. See the Manual of the UKIPO, Section 76, and the cited decisions, at the website of the UK government <https://www.gov.uk/guidance/manual-of-patent-practice-mopp/section-76-amendments-of-applications-and-patents-not-to-include-added-matter>
29. The Examination Guidelines of the SIPO, Part II, Chapter 8, 5.2 Amendments, at the website of CNIPA <http://english.cnipa.gov.cn/docs/20180131104843547234.pdf>. (The Chinese Patent Office, SIPO (State Intellectual Property Office) was renamed to Chinese National Intellectual Property Administration in 2018.)
30. The Examination Guideline of the KIPO, Part IV Chapter 2, at the website of the KIPO <http://www.kipo.go.kr/upload/en/download/patent_examination_guidelines_2013_07.pdf>

Case No. 21

Possibility of Claim Correction after Grant

Hisayoshi Yokoyama

A correction after grant is not permissible when it substantially enlarges or alters the scope of the claims. Whether this is the case must be determined based upon a comparison of the wording of the claims before and after the amendment, and not based on the entire statement of the description.

Supreme Court, 14 December 1972, Case No. 1 (Gyō-Tsu) of 1966 – *Production Method for Phenothiazine Derivatives*

Farben Fabriken Bayer Aktiengesellschaft v. JPO

1. BACKGROUND

A patent becomes effective upon registration of its establishment, sec. 66(1) Patent Act, and the scope of a patent thereby principally becomes fixed upon registration. After the registration has been effected, the scope of claims, the description and drawings are made public through the issuance of a patent gazette, which enables a third party to determine whether the technology used or intended to be used is included in the scope of another's patented invention. Therefore, the modification of these documents should not be easily allowed after registration.

Yet it is often difficult to file a complete application within tight time constraints, and there are more than a few cases where only after registration, the patentee notices that his patent includes reasons for invalidation. Therefore, it cannot be adequate to invalidate the patent without giving the patentee an opportunity to correct the documents. Besides, where the scope of claims or the description includes ambiguous terms, it would be desirable to let the patentee voluntarily modify them, which might help to clarify the scope of a patented invention and thereby avoid unnecessary problems. Thus, sec. 126 of the Patent Act has established a trial for correction.

The Patent Act imposes strict requirements for allowing a correction, so that such act will not unduly harm the interests of third parties who relied on the registration. One of such requirements is that a correction of description, scope of claims, or drawings must not substantially enlarge or alter the scope of claims, as sec. 126(6) stipulates.[1] Since the final and binding trial decision has a retroactive effect by

1. Since the statement of description or drawings might be taken into consideration in interpreting

which the patented invention is deemed to have been filed and registered with the content after the correction (sec. 128), the interests of third parties who relied on the scope of claims before the correction would be unfairly harmed if a correction which substantially broadens or alters the scope of claims was permitted. Therefore, in order to protect the interests of third parties, a correction has to be made within the limit of the scope of the claims as originally registered.[2]

A trial for correction is often requested for the purposes of "correction of errors".[3] According to the Trial Manual,[4] "correction of errors" means correcting the original wording into one whose meaning is obvious from the description, the scope of claims or drawings etc. before that correction, so that the statements of those documents remain the same before and after that correction. Given that, a correction of errors obviously does not substantially broaden or alter the scope of claims. However, in fact, there are cases whether a correction in question should be evaluated merely as modification of errors or as substantially broadening or altering the scope of claims. The issue of this case lies in this point.

2. DECISION[5]

a) Facts

X (plaintiff, appellant) owns a patent with the title of "Production Methods for Phenothiazine Derivative". **X** requested a trial for correction for the purpose of

---

the scope of the claims under sec. 70 (2), a correction which modifies only the description or drawings might be regarded as enlarging or altering the scope of claims. There is in fact a Supreme Court decision that regarded the deletion of the embodiment written only in the description or drawings as a restriction of the scope of claims. See, Supreme Court, 19 March 1991, Case No. 109 (Gyō-Tsu) of 1987, 45-3 Minshū 209 = 1381 Hanrei Jihō 108 = 755 Hanrei Times 101 = N. NAKAYAMA et al. (eds.), Tokkyo Hanrei Hyakusen *(Hundred Selected Patent Cases)*, 4th ed. 2012, 126 – *Clip*. German translation in GRUR Int. 1994, 634 w. comment Y. SOMENO.

2. See, Tokyo High Court, 29 June 1971, Case No. 20 (Gyō-Ke) of 1970, 3-1 Mutaishū 194 = 266 Hanrei Times 194 – *Production Method for Hydrophobic Mono Azo Dye*; IP High Court, 28. October, 2015, Case No. 10109 (Ne) of 2014, the website of the courts <http://www.courts.go.jp/app/files/hanrei_jp/412/085412_hanrei.pdf> – *Transdermal Preparations*; TOKKYOCHŌ (JPO), Kōgyō shoyukenhō chikujō kaisetsu (*Commentary to the Industrial Property Act*), 20th ed. 2017, 265; S. ODA/Y. ISHIKAWA, Shin tokkyohō shōkai *(Detailed commentary to the Patent Act)*, 1971, 420-421; /M. KUROKAWA in: N. NAKAYAMA/N. KOIZUMI (eds.), Shin Chūkai Tokkyohō (*New Commentary to the Patent Act*), 2nd ed. vol. 3, 2017, 2564; M. TAKEDA, Chitekizaisanken soshō yōron (*Commentary to Intellectual Property litigation*), 2012, 512; N. NAKAYAMA, Tokkyohō (*Patent Law*), 3rd ed. 2016, 263; H. YOKOYAMA, in: R. SHIMANAMI/T. UENO/H. YOKOYAMA, Tokkyohō nyūmon (*Introduction to the Patent Act*), 2014, 150.
3. Sec. 126(1) of the Patent Act restricts the purpose of a correction for which a patentee can file a trial to: (i) restriction of the scope of claims, (ii) correction of errors or incorrect translations, (iii) clarification of an ambiguous statement, etc..
4. TOKKYOCHŌ SHINPANBU (*Trial and Appeal Department of the Patent Office*), Shinpan binran (*Manual for Trial and Appeal Proceedings*), 17th ed. 2018, 38-03 3.(1), available at the website of the JPO <https://www.jpo.go.jp/system/trial_appeal/document/sinpan-binran_17/all.pdf>.
5. Published in 26-10 Minshū 1888 = 692 Hanrei Jihō 18 = 297 Hanrei Times 220 = N. NAKAYAMA et al. (eds.), Tokkyo Hanrei Hyakusen *(Hundred Selected Patent Cases)*, 4th ed. 2012, 88 = T. ŌBUCHI et al. (eds.), Chitekizaisan hō hanrei shū *(Intellectual Property Law Case Book)*, 2nd ed. 2015, 55-57.

modifying the statement of the scope of claims, insisting that the statement "A is an alkylene group that has branches" is an obvious error for "A is an alkylene group that may have branches". However, the Patent Office rejected **X**'s request, stating that it substantially broadens the scope of claims, even though it could be said to be modification of an error. **X** filed an action for revocation of that decision, stating that, whether a correction in question substantially broadens or alters the scope of claims should be decided based on the entire statement of the description, and that the requested correction should not be evaluated as substantially broadening the scope of the claim, because the statement "A is an alkylene group that may have branches" is written in the detailed explanation of an invention, and "alkylene groups that do not have any branches" are mainly stated as practical examples. The Tokyo High Court[6] dismissed **X**'s claim. Thus, **X** appealed to the Supreme Court. The Supreme Court dismissed **X**'s appeal for the following reasons:

b) Reasons

Sec. 36(5) Patent Act stipulates that the scope of claims in the description[7] of an application shall state only matters essential to the construction of an invention which is described in the detailed explanation of an invention.[8] And the technical scope of a patented invention shall be determined based upon the statements in the scope of claims attached to an application. Among the statements of the description, the scope of claims is predominantly important, compared with the detailed explanation of an invention and drawings etc. The reason why the scope of claims is a standard for determining the technical scope of a patented invention is that it defines the effective scope of a patent as an absolute right towards third parties. Therefore, a decision as to whether a correction substantially broadens or alters the scope of claims in the sense of sec. 126(2) (sec. 126(6) after law amendment, the same applies hereinafter) must be made based upon the statement of the scope of claims in the description, and **X**'s opinion that a decision should be made according to the entire statement of the description cannot be accepted.

When the decision of a trial for correction has become final and binding, the correction has a retroactive effect by sec. 128 of the Patent Act, and the effect of a patent based on the modified description and drawings will be extended to those skilled in the art and any other unspecified number of third parties. Therefore, a decision as to whether a request for correction is allowed, should be made with particular care. Judging from the facts found by the prior instance, the statement in the scope of claims "A is an alkylene group that has branches" constitutes one of the elements essential for the construction of the patented invention. Certainly, neither of the parties has disputed that it is an error for "A is an alkylene group that may have branches". However, the statement in the chemical formula in the scope

6. Published in 26-10 Minshū 1902 = 185 Hanrei Times 206.
7. At that time, the scope of claims constituted a part of description, but by the law amendment of 2004, the scope of claims has become an independent document separated from the description.
8. This provision was amended in 1994, and the current provision stipulates that the scope of claims shall state all matters necessary to specify the invention for which the applicant requests for the grant of a patent.

of the claims "A is an alkylene group that has branches" is by itself quite clear and its meaning can be easily understood without referring to other statements in the description. Besides, despite that it is erroneous, the purpose and the effect of the invention can be achieved without modifying the statement "A is an alkylene group that has branches", and all of those skilled in the art cannot automatically notice that the statement is an error and that it should be understood in the sense of "A is an alkylene group that may have branches".

Certainly, from the standpoint of X, the statement "A is an alkylene group that has branches" is obviously an error, but the same cannot be said in relation to general third parties. Thus, it should be said that between the statement "A is an alkylene group that has branches" and the statement "A is an alkylene group that does not have branches" written in this detailed explanation of an invention, only the former is stated in this scope of claims.

Based on the above mentioned analysis, we hold that a correction from "A is an alkylene group that has branches" to "A is an alkylene group that may have branches" is not permissible according to sec. 126(2) of the Patent Act, not only because it will formally broaden the scope of claims, but also because it will harm the interests of third parties who rely on the content of the scope of claims, which thereby means that it will substantially broaden the scope of claims.[9]

3. ANALYSIS

a) Meaning of "substantial broadening"

As is confirmed by the Supreme Court, it is undisputable that the correction in question will "formally" broaden the scope of claims, since the scope of claims after the correction "A is an alkylene group that may have branches" includes both "an alkylene group that has branches" and "an alkylene group that does not have branches", whereas the scope of claims before the correction "A is an alkylene group that has branches" obviously does not include "an alkylene group that does not have branches". However, sec. 126(6) of the Patent Act stipulates that a correction shall not "substantially" broaden or alter the scope of claims, which means a correction formally broadening the scope of claims is permissible if it cannot be regarded as "substantially" enlarging it. Therefore, the issue is whether or not the correction in question substantially broadens the scope of claims.

As is mentioned above, since the requirement of prohibition of substantial broadening is intended to protect the interests of third parties who relied on registration, the question of whether a correction substantially broadens the scope of claims should be determined, based on whether the interests of third parties would

9. On the same date of this case, the Supreme Court rendered a similar decision to hold that the correction from "3 to 5 degrees Fahrenheit" to "3 to 5 degrees Celsius" in the description of the scope of claims for an invention of a cubic rice cracker manufacturing method was not allowed, because it substantially altered the claim (14 December 1972, Case No. 46 (Gyō-Tsu) of 1966, 26-10 Minshū 1909 = 692 Hanrei Jihō 23 = 297 Hanrei Times 22 – *Production Method for Cubic Rice Crackers*).

be harmed by allowing that correction.[10] For example, secs 126(1)(i) of the Patent Act permits a correction which restricts the scope of claims, although it obviously formally alters the scope of claims,[11] because the scope of claims after the correction falls within the ambit of the scope of claims before correction, and therefore the interests of third parties who relied on registration will not be harmed by allowing that correction.[12] The same is true of a correction for modification of errors.

Given this interpretation, a correction of errors which formally broadens the scope of claims should be allowed only if such errors are obvious for third parties.[13] In other words, only where third parties getting access to the attached documents can easily notice errors and automatically recognise the correct statement from the erroneous statement, a correction for errors should be interpreted as not broadening the scope of claims, because only in such case is there no risk that technologies which third parties believe to be outside the scope of claims might be included in the scope of claims after correction. As for this case, as the Supreme Court held, the statement in question is not such a clear error, because the statement in question has by itself a clear meaning and indicates an embodiment of the patented invention which can function for its intended purpose. Therefore, the correction in question should be regarded as substantially broadening the scope of claims.

b) Role of the scope of claims for the interpretation of the technical scope of a patented invention

In the reasons for final appeal, X insisted that the entire statement of the description should be taken into consideration when deciding whether a correction substantially broadens the scope of claims. Based on this opinion, X's request for correction might possibly be allowed, because those who read through the entire statement could reasonably notice the inconsistency between the statement of the scope of claims and that of the description, and recognise that the statement in question was an error.[14]

---

10. See M. KUROKAWA, in: N. NAKAYAMA/N. KOIZUMI (eds.) (above), 2565; K. KOJIMA, in: N. NAKAYAMA et al. (eds.), Tokkyo Hanrei Hyakusen (above), 89.
11. The "substantial alteration of the scope of claims" in sec. 126(1) is generally interpreted as not to include a correction for restriction of the scope of claims. See, S. ODA/Y. ISHIKAWA (above), 454; S. CHAEN, Shinpan *(Trial)*, 328 Hōgaku Kyōshitsu 116 (2008).
12. However, there is another requirement in sec. 126(5) that a correction of the description, the scope of claims, or the drawings must remain within the scope disclosed in the description, the scope of claims, or the drawings before correction. Therefore, a correction for restriction of the scope of claims is prohibited if it introduces new technical matter that is not disclosed in the description, the scope of claims, or the drawings before correction.
13. For the same opinion, See, Tokyo High Court, 17 February 2003, Case No. 39 (Gyō-Ke) of 2003, the website of the courts <http://www.courts.go.jp/app/files/hanrei_jp/309/011309_hanrei.pdf> - *Guanidine Derivative*; IP High Court, 27 December 2005, Case No. 10552 (Gyō-Ke) of 2007, the website of the courts <http://www.courts.go.jp/app/files/hanrei_jp/203/009203_hanrei.pdf> - *Electromagnetic Processing Equipment for Magnetic Processing of Associated Molecule*; IP High Court, 28 November 2007, Case No. 10268 (Gyō-Ke) of 2006, the website of the courts <http://www.courts.go.jp/app/files/hanrei_jp/450/035450_hanrei.pdf> - *Powder Detergent Automatic Dishwashing Machine*; S. CHAEN (above), 116; H. YOKOYAMA, in: R. SHIMANAMI/T. UENO/H. YOKOYAMA (above), 151.
14. For a commentary on this case, see M. ŌBA, Tokkyoseikyū no han'i no goki teisei no genkai *(Limit of modification of errors in patent claim)*, 703 Hanrei Jihō 148 (1973)

However, as the Supreme Court held, this interpretation cannot be endorsed because it does not distinguish between the role of the scope of claims and that of the description. The role of the scope of claims is to define the technical scope of a patented invention, sec. 70(1) Patent Act, whereas the role of the description is to enable third parties to understand how to carry out an invention, sec. 36(4)(i). Although the description might be taken into consideration in interpreting the technical scope of an invention, sec. 70(2), it does not by itself provide the standard for interpretation. Therefore, where the meaning of terms in the scope of claims is so clear that third parties can unquestionably understand the content of the patented invention only based on the statement of the scope of claims, it is not permissible to interpret the terms in the scope of claims in a way that modifies it based on the description.[15] Considering the importance of the scope of claims for the interpretation of the technical scope, in case there is an inconsistency between the scope of claims and that of the description and despite such inconsistency, the scope of claims has by itself a clear meaning, it should be assumed that third parties would give priority to the statement of the claims and interpret the technical scope of a patented invention according to the scope of claims, rather than based on the comprehensive understanding of the entire description.[16] In this regard, the Supreme Court rightly denied X's request for correction by focusing on the significance of the role of the scope of claims for the interpretation of the technical scope.[17]

4. COMPARATIVE REMARKS

a) Under Rule 139 of the **EPC**,

> "Linguistic errors, errors of transcription and mistakes in any document filed with the European Patent Office may be corrected on request. However, if the request for such correction concerns the description, claims or drawings, the correction must be obvious in the sense that it is immediately evident that nothing else would have been intended than what is offered as the correction."

The hurdles for such correction are high in particular where claims are concerned. A correction may not contravene Art. 123(2) EPC[18] or Art. 123(3) EPC[19] (see also below).

15. See Case No. 35 of this book – *Ra Lipase*. The Court held that the essence of an invention should be based on the scope of claims attached to the application, unless there are exceptional circumstances that justify references to the description, such as where the technical meaning of the claims is not unambiguously clear or where it is very obvious that the statement is an error when compared to the description.
16. This assumption is verified by the recent Supreme Court Decision (Case No. 40 of this book – *Maxacaltitol*), which held that the doctrine of equivalents cannot be applied to technologies which are not written in the scope of claims but only in the description, because third parties are likely to believe that such technologies are intentionally excluded from the scope of claims.
17. Citing this Supreme Court decision, the IP High Court held that whether or not a correction substantially broadens the scope of claims should be decided based on the description of the scope of claims, not on the entire description considering the interests of third parties that relied on the description of the scope of claims. See, *Electromagnetic Processing Equipment for Magnetic Processing of Associated Molecule* case (above).
18. EPO Decision **G 11/91** of 19 November 1992 (OJ 1993, 125).
19. EPO Decision **T 195/09** of 8 October 2010.

Further, the error must be obvious in the sense that, first, it must be clear that there is an error, and it must be equally clear what the correct information should be. In the case of an inconsistency between the claims and the description, it is insufficient that the inconsistency is clear. Rather, it must also be clear what prevails.[20] Where a claim makes technical sense, there is no room for correction under Rule 139.[21]

> "However, it is always open to a patent proprietor to seek to amend his patent during opposition or limitation proceedings and such an amendment could remove a perceived error. Such an amendment would have to satisfy all the legal requirements for amendments including those of Article 123 EPC."[22]

Claim amendments made after grant in formal proceedings of opposition/appeal (*inter partes*), or in limitation proceedings under Arts. 105a – 105c EPC (*ex parte*) have to comply with the provisions of Art. 123(2) and Art. 123(3) EPC: They may neither be amended "in such a way that it ... extends beyond the contents of the application as filed," nor "in such a way as to extend the protection it confers." Just as held by the Japanese Supreme Court above, the interpretation of a claim that is clear in itself would not allow to refer to the description in order to "adjust" its meaning or give it a meaning that was different from the one as understood by the person skilled in the art:[23]

> "According to Article 69 EPC, the extent of the protection conferred by a European patent shall be determined by the claims. Nevertheless, the description and the drawings shall be used to interpret the claims. It therefore has to be decided whether said interpretation of the claims by the content of the description is limited to cases where the claims are in need of interpretation, e.g. because of functional or unclear features, or whether it also applies to the present case, where a well-known and generally accepted meaning of a term is overthrown and replaced by a new definition given in the description ... The board is of the opinion that the second sentence of Article 69 EPC does not apply to cases where an unambiguous and generally accepted definition of a term figuring in the claims should be superseded by a different definition found in the description. If it is intended that a term which is in no need of any interpretation is given a new meaning, then the definition for this new meaning must be put into the claims. Third parties cannot be expected to check every single term of the claims for a potentially different meaning that might be hidden somewhere in the description."

Under the above constellation of the Japanese Supreme Court case, the patentee did not succeed to amend its claim. Yet the claim as granted would still be sufficiently supported by the description if the alternative "has branches" was disclosed in the application as filed. Otherwise, the patentee under European law may be faced with the quandary that the claims cannot be amended due to Art. 123(3) EPC, yet cannot be left unchanged due to Art. 123(2), either ("inescapable trap"). E.g. in

20. EPO Decision **T 829/05** of 18 July 2007.
21. EPO Decision **T 1702/12** of 8 October 2015.
22. EPO Decision **G 1/10** of 23 July 2012 (OJ 2013, 194).
23. EPO Decision **T 177/08** of 8 April 2011. See also the comparative remarks in Case No. 35 – *Ra Lipase.*

case **T 1772/06,**[24] the claim contained the feature "solvent-free", yet the description and the examples only showed substances with a minimum residue of solvents. According to the Board, the feature "solvent free" was not supported by the description (contravention of Art. 123(2) EPC). As the term had a clear meaning, it could not be read in the light of the description to mean "solvent is removed as far as practicable". Yet the term could not be removed or altered, either, as this would mean a shift in the scope of the claim and thus contravene Art. 123(3) EPC.

b) Under **US** law, typographical errors made in good faith may be corrected on request under 35 USC secs. 254 and 255. In re-issue proceedings under secs. 251 and 252, the patentee may request amendments to the patent that can mean a limitation or a broadening of the claims. The latter is possible within two years from the date of grant. Not only the claims, but also the description may be amended if the invention remains the same. In order to request a reissue, the patentee must hand in its original patent and demonstrate "that the patent is defective or partly inoperative or invalid because of defects in the specification or drawing, or because the patentee has claimed more or less than what he is entitled to ... [and that this] arose through error without deceptive intent."[25] The amended wording of the patent is operative with *ex tunc* effect, that is, retroactively, yet with some safeguards for third parties that relied on the original wording of the patent.

In procedures of *ex parte* re-examination and *inter partes* review (introduced in 2013), the patentee may limit the scope of the claims without having to show "error". Constitutional challenges against re-examination[26] and *inter partes* review[27] have largely failed.

24. EPO Decision **T 1772/06** of 16 October 2007.
25. US CAFC, *In re Wilder*, 736 F2d 1516 (Fed. Cir. 1984).
26. US Supreme Court, *SAS Institute v. Iancu*, USC___(2018).
27. US Supreme Court, *Oil States Energy v. Greene Energy*, USC___ (2018).

Case No. 22

Disclaimer, Correction and Amendment

Atsuhiro Furuta

---

1. A "disclaimer" for the correction of patent claims is admissible in principle insofar as it does not go beyond the content of the application as filed.

2. The use of a trade mark in such a disclaimer is permitted, as far as it is not possible to describe the disclaimed subject matter in any other way.

IP High Court, 30 May 2008, Case No. 10563 (Gyō-Ke) of 2006 – *Solder Resist*

Tamura Kaken v. Taiyō Ink

---

1. BACKGROUND

"Disclaimer", a negative definition excluding some subject matter from scope of patent claim, is sometimes very useful to avoid novelty destroying prior art, etc.[1] But should a disclaimer always be allowable? That is questionable, because such disclaimer cannot always be derived from the original application document in a direct and unambiguous manner. Where the disclaimer is not clearly spelt out in the application as filed, but only introduced later, this becomes the problem of amendment or correction.[2]

In this case, such later introduction of a disclaimer by way of correction became the main issue in this suit because at that time, the JPO practice as stipulated in the Examination Guideline allowed such disclaimers only exceptionally and to the extent necessary for avoiding novelty destroying prior art. In the invalidation trial, the JPO allowed the correction at issue including the disclaimer and decided to maintain the patent in accordance with its practice. The IP High Court also decided

---

1. There are three types of novelty destroying prior art according to the Japanese Patent Act: Published or publicly used inventions, sec. 29(1) PA, inventions disclosed in another prior application (not only in a claim but also in a description etc.) of another applicant or inventor, which is in unpublished at the time of application in question but published later, sec. 29bis (so called extended position of prior application), and While collisions belonging to same applicant or inventor can only relate to identical claims, sec. 39. The author refers all these three types as novelty-destroying prior art.
2. The Japanese Patent Act uses in general different words for correction before and after grant. The author uses "amendment" as a translation of "hosei" which usually refers to a correction to claims etc. before grant, and "correction" as a translation of "teisei" which usually refers to correction after grant. See also Case No. 21 of this book.

to dismiss the case and to uphold the decision of the JPO. But the plaintiff argued that the correction at issue should be considered unallowable in reference to the Examination Guidelines[3] and by this decision the Grand Panel of the IP High Court overturned the old JPO practice about disclaimers and corrections and established new criteria in this regard.[4]

2. DECISION[5]

a) Facts

The plaintiff (original applicant) seeks revocation of the patent held by the defendant (patentee). The Patent Office ordered revocation of the patent as requested. The defendant appealed to the IP High Court and at the same time requested correction of the patent. As a result, the IP High Court reversed the Patent Office's decision and dismissed the request for revocation. The Patent Office allowed the correction and upheld the patent as amended. With its appeal, the plaintiff requested the annulment of the Patent Office's decision which had allowed the correction under sec. 134ter(5) Patent Act, and pursues its request for revocation.

b) Reasons

1. Admissibility of the correction

(1) The correction in the present case is a so-called "disclaimer", which in the opinion of the plaintiff is not "covered by the contents of the application as filed", sec. 134(2) Patent Act before the amendment by Law No 116/1994. The plaintiff further claims that the use of the mark 'TEPIC' in the claim after its correction does not constitute an allowable limitation because the extent of a correction must be technically defined and the correction excludes only part of the combination and the invention actually has the same scope before and after the correction.

...

(2) Meaning of the term "the contents of the application as filed"

a. Purpose and interpretation of the provision

The Patent Act provides that the amendment of claims "must be covered by the contents of the application as filed". This ensures sufficient disclosure of the

3. Of course, the Examination Guidelines are generally applicable to examination procedures and not to trial procedures (there is another Manual for Trial and Appeal Proceedings). But the Examination Guidelines are sometimes referred not only for amendment before grant but also for correction after grant, because the provisions of prohibition of addition of new subject matter are the same before and after grant (Sec. 17bis(3), Sec. 126(5)).
4. In this case the author mainly deals with the disclaimer. For a general history about amendment and correction in Japanese patent practice, see Case No. 21 of this book.
5. Published in 2009 Hanrei Jihō 47 = 1290 Hanrei Times 224 = N. NAKAYAMA et al. (eds.), Tokkyo Hanrei Hyakusen *(Hundred Selected Patent Cases)*, 4th ed. 2012, 90 = T. ŌBUCHI et al. (eds.), Chitekizaisan hō hanrei shū *(Intellectual Property Law Case Book)*, 2nd ed. 2015, 70. German translation in GRUR Int. 2010, 537.

originally filed application, rapid granting of patents and a balance between multiple applications. And it prevents disadvantages to third parties who have adjusted to the originally filed application. In the same way, a correction after grant of the patent ensures sufficient disclosure of the originally filed application and complies with the principle of first filing.

For this reason, the term "the contents of the application as filed" according to sec. 17(2) Patent Act before the amendment by Law No. 116/1994 should be interpreted as follows: The "contents of the application" is disclosed to third parties in the scope of exclusivity of an invention as the meaningful creation of a technical idea, "contents" being the technical object of the invention as disclosed in the application. Thus, an amendment "falls within the scope of the application as filed" if the application does not claim new subject matter in relation to the technical contents which the person skilled in the art will understand from the specification and the drawings.

Sec. 29[bis] Patent Act stipulates that patents are not granted for inventions that have the same content as an earlier published patent application defined by the documents as originally filed. Sometimes, in an action for revocation, patentees seek a correction by way of negative features such as by a so-called "disclaimer", e.g. "... is ruled out" in order to avoid overlaps that may lead to revocation according to secs. 29[bis] and 123(1) Patent Act before the amendment by Law No 26/1993.

Often, a patentee is not aware of the existence of the prior application at the time of his application, and normally there is no concrete description of such an earlier application. But sec. 134(2) Patent Act before the amendment by Law No 116/1994 is also applicable to corrections for articles not specifically described, and such a correction also falls within "the contents of the application as filed", in so far as it does not contain new subject matter in relation to the technical contents disclosed by the application.

...

c. The present case

As held under a. (2), the correction must fall within the scope of "the application as originally filed" in so far as it does not contain any new subject-matter relating to the technical object which the person skilled in the art can understand from the description and drawings. As under b., the correction excludes a particular combination falling within the scope of an earlier application, namely the combination of components (A) - (D) and (A) - (E). After the correction, the invention is also characterised in that hardly any soluble fine particulate epoxy resin is used as a component of duroplast in diluents. Such epoxy resin particles are enveloped by photosensitive prepolymer. This leads to the result that the solubility of photosensitive prepolymers does not decrease, as does the development of low reactivity between epoxy resin and hardener, and that the lithographically exposed portion of the developer is hardly affected and that the lifespan of the fabric is prolonged. The exclusion of combinations that fall within the contents of an earlier application does not change its technical subject matter. Thus, it is clear that the correction does not concern new subject matter in relation to the technical contents which the skilled person will understand from the entire description.

Therefore, the correction falls within "the contents of the application as filed" in accordance with sec. 134(2) Patent Act before the amendment by Law No. 116/1994.

e. The Examination Guidelines of the Patent Office

...

The Examination Guidelines state that a "disclaimer" relating to the contents of the application is only allowed "by way of exception". "Exceptionally" means in relation to the principles otherwise applicable. However, as explained under a., such an approach is inappropriate. That is, an amendment containing negative features, unlike features positively introduced, does not include new technical subject matter insofar as the amendment falls within the scope of the original application and there are no particular circumstances. However, just because the amendment itself is not described in the application does not mean that the amendment per se introduces new technical subject matter.

Therefore, as explained under a., it is decisive for the admissibility of a disclaimer whether or not an amendment contains new technical subject matter when compared to the subject-matter described in the application. A mere "exceptional" admissibility therefore appears unjustified. For this reason, the treatment of "disclaimers" in the Examination Guidelines is inappropriate for a correct interpretation of the Patent Act.

...

(3) "Limitations of claim" and use of a mark

...

b. The correction contained the words "(D) Multifunctional epoxy resin having at least two epoxies in one molecule (TEPIC: trade mark of *Nissan Kagaku Kabushiki Kaisha*)". As in (2) b., the correction is for the purpose of excluding overlapping parts and to avoid revocation of the patent in the light of an earlier application. For example, TEPIC is indicated in the correction as "TEPIC" in example 2 of the application. Although "TEPIC" in the corrected version contained only those products that were so described at the time of the earlier application, the object defined by the mark "TEPIC" is technically not unclear.

...

c. The Implementing Rule 24 before its amendment by the Ministry of International Trade and Industry (Order No. 41/1990) stipulated that "Application documents should be prepared according to template 16". Template 16 states that "trade marks may be used insofar as the description of the object is only possible by reference to that mark. Further, it is necessary to make clear that this is a registered mark". The meaning of this provision is that use of the mark is only exceptionally permissible because under the trade mark system there is no guarantee of conformity between the quality or composition of the object and the mark. The item defined by the registered mark is not unambiguously clear.

As shown under (3) b., the rectification excludes the overlapping part. It defines this part with the negative feature in the form of the so-called "disclaimer", which relates to components (A) – (D) and (A) – (E) of cited example 2 of the earlier application. Only in this way is it possible to exclude neither too much nor too little from the overlapping part. "TEPIC" is one of the elements that define the earlier invention. The use of the mark "TEPIC" for this unclaimed part in the correction does not violate the above rule 24.

3. ANALYSIS

The procedure and history of this case is a little complicated. The plaintiff on 30 June 2005 requested a trial for invalidation of the defendant's patent at issue before the JPO. The JPO on 29 November 2005 decided to invalidate the patent (first JPO decision), and the defendant on 6 January 2006 filed a first lawsuit against the former decision of the JPO. The plaintiff on 30 March 2006 requested a trial for correction, and the IP High Court on 26 April 2006 dismissed the first lawsuit because of the pending correction request and sent the case back to the JPO.[6] The correction of 30 March 2006 was deemed to be filed on 26 April 2006, and the JPO on 28 November 2006 decided to maintain the patent at issue with this correction, which included a disclaimer in the claim, namely "excluding a photosensitive thermosetting resin composition, which comprises (A) 'reaction product, which is produced by reaction of phthalic-anhydride-cresol and epoxy-acrylate, which is produced by reaction of acrylic acid and novolak-epoxy-resin', (B) '2-methyl-anthraquinone' and 'dimethyl-benzyl-ketal', which corresponds to light polymerization initiator, (C) 'penta-erythritol-tetra-acrylate' and 'cellosolve-acetate', and (D) polyfunctional epoxy resin (TEPIC: production of Nissan Chemical, Ltd., registered trade mark), which is 'epoxy compound including at least 2 epoxy groups in a molecule'". The disclaimer at issue was introduced to avoid novelty destroying prior art by another intervening application (Sec. 29bis PA).

The IP High Court agreed with the JPO that such disclaimer was allowable, but heavily criticised the JPO practice at that time.

The Examination Guidelines of the JPO ruled that a disclaimer should be exceptionally allowable for avoiding novelty destroying prior art and to the extent necessary:[7]

> "'Disclaimer', which excludes subject matter stated in the original description, etc. as filed through amendment while leaving the expression of the statement of subject matters stated in claims before amendment, is allowed if the "disclaimer" is within the scope of subject matter stated in the original description, etc. as filed."

The amendment to provide a 'disclaimer' in the following (i) and (ii) is *exceptionally* treated as made in the scope of subject matter stated in the original description, etc. as filed.

---

6. The Japanese Patent Act allowed a correction after filing a lawsuit until the law was amended in 2011.
7. Underlined by the author. See, JPO documents of 22 October 2003, "Meisaisho, tokkyo seikyū no han'i matawa zumen no hosei (shinkijikō)" no shinsakijun kaitei ni tsuite *(About revision of the examination guideline of "amendment of specification, claim or figure (new subject matter)")*, available at the website of the JPO <https://www.jpo.go.jp/tetuzuki/t_tokkyo/shinsa/meisai_t_zu_kijyun.htm>.

(i) The amendment to exclude only the overlap in cases where the claimed invention overlaps the cited invention and is thus likely to lose novelty, etc. (Sec. 29(1)(iii), Sec. 29bis or Sec. 39).
(ii) In the case where the claimed invention includes the term 'human being' and thus does not fulfil the requirement of the main paragraph of sec. 29(1) or falls under the category of unpatentable invention under sec. 32, an amendment which excludes only the term 'human being'."

The IP High Court criticised the above exceptional treatment of the disclaimer, because it found no basis in the PA for such practice, and also in the author's view, the IP High Court reached a reasonable interpretation based on the provisions and the purpose of the PA.

Another minor issue in this case is the treatment of the trade mark in the disclaimer, whether the scope of subject matter specified by the trade mark is clear or not, because the scope of exclusion in the disclaimer should be clear in terms of scope. The IP High Court also reasonably decided that such use of a trade mark was allowable because the trade mark at issue, "TEPIC", comprised all products specified at the time of filing of the application and the use of such trade mark was inevitable for clearly and sufficiently avoiding novelty destroying prior art.

Since then, the IP High Court has applied the above criteria to cases of addition of new subject matter or disclaimers. For example, in the decision of the IP High Court of 31 March 2009 – *Absorptive Agent for Oral Administration,*[8] the court indicated that a disclaimer excluding the consisting part of the invention of the absorptive agent for oral administration, spherical activated carbon, which has an X ray diffraction intensity ratio higher than 1.4 to avoid novelty destroying prior art (sec. 29bis), did not introduce new subject matter and was allowable.

In another case of 11 March 2015 – *Transdermal Absorbent Medicine,*[9] the IP High Court indicated that the technical scope of a disclaimer such as "excluding transdermal absorbent medicine, wherein object material is retained to base agent by sealing in a chamber set in a needle for medical treatment or by holding in vertical hole, and transdermal absorbent medicine, which is held in an instrument providing through-hole able to hold transdermal absorbent medicine, and is introduced by extrusion from the state movable along in the through-hole," was unclear, because the disclaimer specified a method of use that could not clearly define and distinguish the transdermal absorbent medicine in terms of form, structure, composition or physical property, and therefore was unallowable.[10]

8. IP High Court of 31 March 2009, Case No. 10358 (Gyō-Ke) of 2008 – *Absorptive Agent for Oral Administration,* the website of the courts <http://www.courts.go.jp/app/files/hanrei_jp/506/037506_hanrei.pdf>.

9. IP High Court, 11 March 2015, Case No. 10204 (Gyō-Ke) of 2014 – *Transdermal Absorbent Medicine,* the website of the courts <http://www.courts.go.jp/app/files/hanrei_jp/955/084955_hanrei.pdf>.

10. Such indication is same to one of cases of disclaimer before 2008, IP High Court, 20 June 2006, Case No. 10608 (Gyō-Ke) of 2005, the website of the courts <http://www.courts.go.jp/app/files/hanrei_jp/236/033236_hanrei.pdf>.

After the commented decision, the JPO on 1 June 2010 amended the Guidelines,[11] and the current Guidelines of the JPO deleted the word "exceptionally" for the disclaimer:[12]

> "'Disclaimer', which excludes subject matter stated in the original description, etc. as filed through amendment while leaving the expression of the statement of subject matter stated in claims before amendment, is allowed *if the "disclaimer" does not introduce any new technical matter.*
>
> The amendment to provide a 'disclaimer' in the following (i) and (ii) *does not introduce any new technical matter, and the amendment is permitted.*
>
> (i) The amendment to exclude only the overlap in cases where the claimed invention overlaps the cited invention and is thus likely to lose novelty, etc. (sec. 29(1)(iii), sec. 29[bis] or sec. 39) ...
> (ii) In the case where the claimed invention includes the term 'human being' and thus does not fulfil the requirement of the main paragraph of sec. 29(1) or falls under the category of unpatentable invention under sec. 32, an amendment which excludes only the term 'human being'."

Many academics and practitioners appreciated the decision of the IP High Court in this case as establishing new criteria not only for the disclaimer but also as a general rule for amendments and corrections in Japan.[13] The author also shares such common assessment.

Finally, as a reference, the author shows the main requirements for amendments and corrections of the current PA in following table:[14]

11. See, the JPO documents on 1 June 2010, "Meisaisho, tokkyo seikyū no han'i matawa zumen no hosei (shinkijikō)" no shinsakijun kaitei ni tsuite *(About revision of the Examination Guidelines of "amendment of specification, claim or figure (new subject matter)")*, available at <https://www.jpo.go.jp/torikumi/t_torikumi/meisaisyo_shinsa_kaitei.htm>.
12. The JPO translation was slightly modified by the author in this citation for uniformity of terminology as used in this book. And the author underlined the new statement. For details, see, Examination Guidelines for Patent and Utility Model in Japan, Part IV Chapter 2, at <http://www.jpo.go.jp/tetuzuki_e/t_tokkyo_e/1312-002_e.htm>
13. For an analysis of this case, see, for example, A. Tamura, Nozoku kurēmu ni kakaru chizai kōsai daigōgi hanketsu to shinkijikō no shinsakijun *(The decision of grand panel of the IP High Court related to disclaimer and the Examination Guideline about new subject matter)*, in: T. Ōbuchi et al. (ed.) Chitekizaisanhō no atarasii nagare *(New trend of intellectual property law)*, 2010, 395; M. Nanjō, Shiren ni tatsu nozoku kurēmu to suru hosei no tekihōsei yōken *(Requirement of amendment of disclaimer under hardship)*, 64-4 Patent 36 (2011); H. Yoshida, Hosei teisei seido no shushi to daigōgi hanketsu *(Purpose of amendment or correction system and the decision of grand panel of the IP High Court)*, 64-4 Patent 195 (2011); S. Murakami et al., Hosei seigen no hensen to nozoku kurēmu daigōgi hanketsu *(Transition of amendment limitation and the disclaimer decision of grand panel of the IP High Court)*, in: N. Nakayama et al. (ed.), Chizairikkoku no hatten e *(For development of IP nation)*, 2013, 781; S. Shiotsuki, Shinkijikō tsuika kinshi to nozoku kurēmu teisei hosei *(Prohibition of addition of new subject matter and disclaimer amendment or correction)*, 1475 Jurist 32 (2015).
14. The author simplifies the table by showing only the main requirements. A complete list would become too complicated.

	Amendment BEFORE Receiving Notice of Reason of Refusal	*Amendment AFTER Receiving Normal Notice of Reason of Refusal*	*Amendment AFTER Receiving Last Notice of Reason of Refusal*	*Amendment at the time of Appeal against Decision of Refusal*	*Trial for Correction (after Grant)*	*Correction in Invalidation or Opposition Procedure (after Grant)*
Time Limitation	–	Within 2 or 3 months after the receiving of notice of reason of refusal.	Same to left	Amendment should be filed at the same time of appeal	Trial for Correction cannot be requested when the invalidation/ opposition case to the patent is pending at the JPO or the Court.	Within 2 or 3 months after receiving notice of opinion or advance notice of decision
Addition of New Subject Matter	**Prohibited**	**Prohibited**	**Prohibited**	**Prohibited**	**Prohibited**	**Prohibited**
Shift Amendment	No Prohibition	**Prohibited**	**Prohibited** (But usually it is impossible because the scope of claim should be reduced.)	**Prohibited** (But usually it is impossible because the scope of claim should be reduced.)	No Prohibition	No Prohibition
Extension of Scope of Claim	No Prohibition	No Prohibition	**Prohibited**	**Prohibited**	**Prohibited**	**Prohibited**
Limitation in Reduction of Scope of Claim	—	—	**Limitation should be made to already stated subject matter.**	**Limitation should be made to already stated subject matter.**	—	—

	Amendment BEFORE Receiving Notice of Reason of Refusal	*Amendment AFTER Receiving Normal Notice of Reason of Refusal*	*Amendment AFTER Receiving Last Notice of Reason of Refusal*	*Amendment at the time of Appeal against Decision of Refusal*	*Trial for Correction (after Grant)*	*Correction in Invalidation or Opposition Procedure (after Grant)*
Substantial Change or Extension of Claim	—	—	—	—	**The scope of claim should not be extended or changed substantially.**	**The scope of claim should not be extended or changed substantially.**
Allowable Amendment or Correction for Other Purpose	—	—	**Explanation of Unclear Statement/ Rectification of Error in Writing/ Deletion of Claim**	**Explanation of Unclear Statement/ Rectification of Error in Writing/ Deletion of Claim**	**Explanation of Unclear Statement/ Rectification of Error in Writing/ Deletion of Claim/ Resolution of dependency of Claims**	**Explanation of Unclear Statement/ Rectification of Error in Writing/ Deletion of Claim/ Resolution of dependency of Claims**
Independent Patentability	—	—	**Required in the case of limitation of scope of claim**	**Required in the case of limitation of scope of claim**	**Required in the case of limitation of scope of claim**	**Required in the Request for Correction to claims other than claims in question of invalidation or opposition and in the case of limitation of scope of claim**

4. COMPARATIVE REMARKS

In the **US**, a disclaimer can be introduced under special circumstances, because there is a procedure of interference and statutory disclaimer.[15]

Before the **EPO**, the Enlarged Board of Appeal in cases **G 1/03** and **G 2/03**[16] set out the general rules about disclaimers as follows:

> 1. An amendment to a claim by the introduction of a disclaimer may not be refused under Article 123(2) EPC for the sole reason that neither the disclaimer nor the subject-matter excluded by it from the scope of the claim have a basis in the application as filed.
>
> 2. The following criteria are to be applied for assessing the allowability of a disclaimer which is not disclosed in the application as filed:
>
> 2.1 A disclaimer may be allowable in order to:
>
> - restore novelty by delimiting a claim against state of the art under Article 54(3) and (4) EPC;
> - restore novelty by delimiting a claim against an accidental anticipation under Article 54(2) EPC; an anticipation is accidental if it is so unrelated to and remote from the claimed invention that the person skilled in the art would never have taken it into consideration when making the invention; and
> - disclaim subject-matter which, under Articles 52 to 57 EPC, is excluded from patentability for non-technical reasons.
>
> 2.2 A disclaimer should not remove more than is necessary either to restore novelty or to disclaim subject-matter excluded from patentability for non-technical reasons.
>
> 2.3 A disclaimer which is or becomes relevant for the assessment of inventive step or sufficiency of disclosure adds subject-matter contrary to Article 123(2) EPC.
>
> 2.4 A claim containing a disclaimer must meet the requirements of clarity and conciseness of Article 84 EPC.

In the subsequent case **T 2130/11,**[17] the Board of Appeal stated that a disclaimer removing more than strictly necessary to restore novelty would not be in contradiction with the spirit of **G 1/03** if required to satisfy Article 84 EPC and not leading to an arbitrary reshaping of the claims. But the EPO takes a rather rigid approach to the addition of new subject matter and disclaimers, and a disclaimer for avoiding the

15. See, MPEP, Section 706, at the website of the USPTO <https://www.uspto.gov/web/offices/pac/mpep/s706.html>, and Section 1490 at <https://www.uspto.gov/web/offices/pac/mpep/s1490.html>
16. EPO decisions **G 1/03** and **G 2/03** of 8 April 2004, OJ EPO 2004, 413 and 448.
17. EPO decision **T 2130/11** of 2 December 2014.

so-called inescapable trap in which addition of new subject matter is found after grant is unallowable.[18]

The recent decision **G 1/16**[19] of the Enlarged Board of Appeal of 18 December 2017 has clarified that the requirements of **G 1/03** are applicable to both disclosed and undisclosed disclaimers (left open in **G 2/10**[20]).

In **Germany**, the rules for a disclaimer are similar to those of the EPO. Yet in the case of an inescapable trap, the German Federal Supreme Court and the Federal Patent Court allow the patentee to "supplement" the patent claim with a declaration that no rights will be claimed based on the unduly broadened feature and thereby avoid a revocation of the patent.[21]

In the **UK**, as stated in the Manual of Practice, the UKIPO follows the practice of the EPO, and amendments by way of an undisclosed disclaimer can be held to be allowable in principle to limit a claim in the light of conflicting prior art and the disclaimer should not remove more than is necessary either to restore novelty or disclaim excluded subject matter. And a disclaimer is inappropriate for dealing with non-working embodiments, assessment of inventive step or sufficiency of disclosure.[22]

In **China**, the CNIPA (old English name in abbreviation: SIPO) maintains a rather exceptional treatment of disclaimers and ruled that such disclaimer is only allowed for avoiding novelty destroying prior art, lack of inventive step or violation of description requirement for the possibility of carrying out invention.[23] And the Patent Reexamination Board allows amendment/correction after grant only in a

18. Example: The claims as granted contain the feature "solvent free", while the description only discloses a method for removing most solvent, and also in prior art no method of completely removing solvent is known. Here, the feature "solvent free" goes beyond the scope of the application as originally filed and thereby contravenes Art. 123(2) EPC. Yet removing or amending the feature in accordance with the description would broaden (shift) the scope of protection and is equally unallowable under Art. 123(3) EPC. The patentee thereby finds itself in an inescapable trap.
19. EPO decision **G 1/16** of 18 December 2017, OJ EPO 2018, A70.
20. EPO decision **G 2/10** of 30 August 2011, OJ EPO 2012, 376. In the case of G 2/10 the Enlarged Board of Appeal answered to the referred question as follows: 1a. An amendment to a claim by the introduction of a disclaimer disclaiming from it subject-matter disclosed in the application as filed infringes Article 123(2) EPC if the subject-matter remaining in the claim after the introduction of the disclaimer is not, be it explicitly or implicitly, directly and unambiguously disclosed to the skilled person using common general knowledge, in the application as filed; 1b. Determining whether or not that is the case requires a technical assessment of the overall technical circumstances of the individual case under consideration, taking into account the nature and extent of the disclosure in the application as filed, the nature and extent of the disclaimed subject-matter and its relationship with the subject-matter remaining in the claim after the amendment.
21. German Federal Supreme Court, 7 December 1978, GRUR 79, 224 – *Aufhänger*; German Federal Patent Court, 28 June 1988, GRUR 1990, 114.
22. See the Manual of the UKIPO, Section 14, and the cited decisions, at the website of the UK government < https://www.gov.uk/guidance/manual-of-patent-practice-mopp/section-14-the-application > .
23. The Examination Guideline of the SIPO, Part II Chapter 8 5.2.1.1, at the website of CNIPA < http://english.cnipa.gov.cn/docs/20180131104843547234.pdf > . (The Chinese Patent Office, SIPO (State Intellectual Property Office) was renamed to Chinese National Intellectual Property Administration in 2018.)

very narrow and limited way, such as deletion of claims, limitation by statements in claims or correction of clear error.[24]

In **Korea**, as the Examination Guidelines state that a so-called "disclaimer claim" is normally not deemed an addition of subject matter, and allow such disclaimer under similar circumstances as Japan.[25]

24. For the amendment/correction after the revision of the Examination Guidelines of 2017, see the documents at the website of the SIPO < http://www.sipo.gov.cn/zfgg/1097906.htm > and PRB < http://www.sipo-reexam.gov.cn/alzx/scrdzjt/21137.htm > .
25. The Examination Guideline of the KIPO, Part IV Chapter 2, at the website of the KIPO < http://www.kipo.go.kr/upload/en/download/patent_examination_guidelines_2013_07.pdf > .

Case No. 23

Advisory Opinion about the Technical Scope of a Patented Invention

Hisayoshi Yokoyama

An advisory opinion in sec. 71 of the Patent Act does not correspond to an administrative disposition and any other act constituting the exercise of public authority by an administrative agency, and the advisory opinion in question is not subject to an appeal.

Supreme Court, 18 April 1968, Case No. 47 (Gyō-Tsu) of 1967 – *Apparatus for Heat Swelling*

Trustee of Nakajima Zoki v. Japanese Patent Office

---

1. BACKGROUND

The technical scope of a patented invention is often difficult to determine, which accordingly causes disputes between a patentee and a third party. These disputes are ultimately resolved by a court, but it normally requires both time and money. Therefore, it would be beneficial for either party to get an advisory opinion from the Patent Office, because the Patent Office is a technologically specialised public institution and is expected to impartially and reliably determine the scope of a patented invention, which might help to effectively avoid future dispute. In this respect, the Patent Act has introduced the advisory opinion system, under sec. 71 (1).[1]

In the advisory opinion system, the petitioner may request a confirmation of whether or not the subject in question falls under the technical scope of the patented invention. The demandant can request either a positive confirmation to decide that the subject is included in the technical scope, or a negative confirmation to decide that the subject is not included in the technical scope.[2] In its judgment, the doctrine of

---

1. Other Industrial Property Acts also have introduced the advisory opinion system, sec. 26 of the Utility Model Act, sec. 25 of the Design Act, sec. 28 of the Trademark Act.
2. T. Iwatsubo, in: N. Nakayama/N. Koizumi (eds.), Shin chūkai tokkyohō *(New commentary to the Patent Act)*, vol. 2, 2nd ed. 2017, 1331.

equivalence[3] is also taken into account, as long as each party insists on its application.[4] On the other hand, since the object of an advisory opinion is limited to the technical scope of the patented invention in relation to the subject in question, other matters such as whether the patent in question has a reason for invalidation or the subject in question constitutes indirect infringement are not examined.[5]

An advisory opinion can be requested even without a respondent.[6] Where there is a respondent, a duplicate of the written request is sent to the respondent and the latter may submit a written answer, secs. 71(3), 134(1). A decision is made by three trial examiners designated by the Commissioner of the Patent Office, sec. 71(2). In order to make an impartial and adequate decision, provisions on the trial system are applied *mutatis mutandis* to many procedures of an advisory opinion, by sec. 71(3).

The Patent Act does not directly stipulate the legal effect of an advisory opinion, and a problem arises whether either party can appeal against a decision disadvantageous to such party. This is the key issue of this case.

2. DECISION[7]

a) Facts

The non-party company **A** against the non-party **B** as a respondent requested the Patent Office to issue an advisory opinion that the apparatus for heat swelling shown in the drawing and its description was not included in the technical scope of the registered utility model owned by **B**. However, the Patent Office issued an advisory opinion that **A**'s request could not be accepted, because the subject matter was included in the scope of **B**'s registered utility model. **A** filed an objection to this decision with **Y** (the Commissioner of the Patent Office: defendant, appellee) based on the Administrative Appeals Act. Assuming **A**'s objection as a request for review, **Y** dismissed A's request as unlawful, because an advisory opinion did not correspond to a disposition of an administrative agency. Subsequently, **A** fell into receivership, and **X** was appointed as a trustee. **X** (plaintiff, appellant) filed a suit against **Y** for revocation of the award.

The Tokyo District Court[8] dismissed **X**'s claim, reasoning that an advisory opinion on the scope of a patented invention or a registered utility model is just a statement of the Patent Office, which affects neither private rights and duties, nor

---

3. In Japan, the doctrine of equivalence is recognised by case law. See, Case No. 38 of this book - *Ball Spline Bearing III*.
4. TOKKYOCHŌ SHINPANBU *(Trial and Appeal Department of the JPO)*, Shinpan binran *(Manual for Trial and Appeal Proceedings)*, 17th ed. 2018, 58-03 1.(5)(U), available at the website of the JPO <https://www.jpo.go.jp/system/trial_appeal/sinpan-binran_17.html>.
5. TOKKYOCHŌ SHINPANBU (above), 58-03 1.(5)(E) (O).
6. TOKKYOCHŌ SHINPANBU (above), 58-01 2.(2)(I).
7. Published in 22-4 Minshū 936 = 521 Hanrei Jihō 46 = 223 Hanrei Times 159 = N. NAKAYAMA et al. (eds.), Tokkyo Hanrei Hyakusen *(Hundred Selected Patent Cases)*, 4th ed. 2012, 96 = T. ŌBUCHI et al. (eds.), Chitekizaisan hō hanrei shū *(Intellectual Property Law Case Book)*, 2nd ed. 2015, 74.
8. Tokyo District Court, 26 April 1966, Case No. 22 (Gyō-U) of 1965, 17-4 Gyōshū 432 = 466 Hanrei Jihō 19.

their legal position. **X** appealed. The Tokyo High Court[9] dismissed **X**'s appeal for the same reasons. Then, **X** appealed to the Supreme Court. The Supreme Court dismissed **X**'s appeal for the following reasons.

b) Reasons

Since there is no provision in the law about whether an advisory opinion under sec. 71 of the Patent Act as applied *mutatis mutandis* pursuant to sec. 26 of the Utility Model Act is subject to an administrative appeal, there is no way but to solve this problem according to the general principles of administrative disputes. The reason why the Administrative Appeal Act allows an appeal against an administrative disposition and any other act constituting the exercise of public authority by an administrative agency is that such act is directly involved in the rights and duties of individuals and might affect a person's legal interests due to an illegal or unreasonable act. Therefore, an act of an administrative agency which by its nature has no such legal effect should not to be the object of an administrative appeal.

Although an advisory opinion is rendered after a fair hearing in front of three administrative judges with expert knowledge and experience of patent matters, it essentially corresponds to a confirmation act to clarify the technical scope of a patented invention or a registered utility model, which neither amounts to a new grant of a patent or utility model, nor modifies the rights already granted. Besides, there is no provision in the Act that presupposes that an advisory opinion is provided with a certain legal effect, unlike a decision for a trial for confirmation of the scope of a patent under the old Patent Act (Law No. 96 of 1921) or a registered utility model under the old Utility Model Act (Law No. 97 of 1921). Furthermore, the result of an advisory opinion, which might very well be respected in an action for an injunction or damages etc. based on a patent infringement etc., does not have any *res judicata* effect and merely constitutes evidentiary material. In fact, those who are disadvantaged by an advisory opinion can contradict it with other evidence and a court is not precluded from making different factual findings. Considering these issues, an advisory opinion is merely a statement of the Patent Office and should be regarded as an expert opinion.

Therefore, an advisory opinion in sec. 71 of the Patent Act does not correspond to an administrative disposition and any other act constituting the exercise of public authority by an administrative agency, and the advisory opinion in question based on sec. 71 as applied *mutatis mutandis* pursuant to sec. 26 of the Utility Model Act is not subject to an administrative appeal.

3. ANALYSIS

a) Legal nature of an advisory opinion

The problem of this case is the nature of an advisory opinion. Under the old Patent Act, there used to be a trial for confirmation of the scope of a patent. However, the

9. Tokyo High Court, 28 February 1967, Case No. 25 (Gyō-Ko) of 1966, 207 Hanrei Times 148.

nature of this trial was not clear, and there was much argument as to whether or to what extent a trial decision could have a legal effect towards third parties. Therefore, under the current Patent Act, the confirmation trial system has been abolished and instead, the advisory opinion system has been introduced.[10] Although there were some provisions in the old Act that presupposed some binding effect of a trial decision,[11] there is no such provision in the current Act, which makes it obvious that an advisory opinion is just a expert opinion and does not have any legal binding force.[12] The Supreme Court has explicitly confirmed this. There is no dispute on this point.[13] In addition, the 1999 amendment to the Patent Act introduced a system whereby the Patent Office issues an expert opinion upon commission from a court, secs. 71bis, in order for the court to utilise the expertise of the Patent Office in interpreting the technical scope of a patented invention, provided that the court has a final authority on such interpretation. This also makes it obvious that the decision of the Patent Office does not have any legal effect for the court.

However, there is no doubt that the decision of the Patent Office is in fact appreciated as an authoritative opinion when compared to a private expertise.[14] In fact, there is a lower court decision that lifted a temporary injunction based on patent infringement, taking into consideration the negative confirmation of the advisory opinion as one of the reasons for a change in circumstances.[15] As is above mentioned, since the aim of the advisory opinion system is to avoid unnecessary disputes and to

10. About the discussion at the time of enactment of the current Act, see TOKKYOCHŌ (JPO) (ed.), Kōgyō Shoyukenhō Chikujō Kaisetsu *(Commentary to the Industrial Property Act)*, 20th ed. 2017, 268-269, available at the website of the JPO <https://www.jpo.go.jp/system/laws/rule/kaisetu/kogyoshoyu/document/cikujyoukaisetu/all.pdf>.

11. For example, there was a provision that even where the trial decision that held the subject was not included in the technical scope was changed by a retrial, those who, in good faith, exploited the invention or possessed facilities for exploitation of the invention might have a statutory right to exploit the invention to the extent of the invention and the purpose of the business exploited, sec. 126 of the old Patent Act.

12. TOKKYOCHŌ (ed.) (above), 268; T. IWATSUBO (above), 1331. In fact, there are lower court decisions contrary to the result of an advisory opinion. See, Tokyo District Court, 30 July 1970, Case No. 2466 (Ne) of 1966, 253 Hanrei Times 192 – *Structure of a Drying Machine for Rice Bran or Grains*; Tokyo High Court, 19 September 1978, Case No. 2282 (Ne) of 1975 – *Tactile Pressure Magnetic Medical Device.*

13. TOKKYOCHŌ (ed.) (above), 268; T. IWATSUBO (above), 1332; S. ODA/Y. ISHIKAWA, Shin tokkyohō shōkai *(Detailed commentary to the Patent Act)*, 1971, 388; K. YOSHIFUJI/K. KUMAGAI, Tokkyohō gaisetsu *(Manual on the Patent Act)*, 13th ed. 1998, 644-645; T. SHIBUYA, Tokkyohō *(Patent Law)*, 2013, 406; N. NAKAYAMA, Tokkyohō *(Patent Law)*, 3rd ed. 2016, 284; T. UENO, in: R. SHIMANAMI/T. UENO/H. YOKOYAMA, Tokkyohō nyumon *(Introduction to the Patent Act)*, 2014, 403-404.

14. T. KABE, Saikō saibansho hanrei kaisetsu shōwa 43 nendo *(Commentary to the Supreme Court decisions of 1968)*, vol. 1, 1969, 254. Nagoya High Court Kanazawa Branch, 14 June 1967, Case No. 137 (Ne) of 1966, 214 Hanrei Times 160 – *Production Method for Scopolamine Butylbromide* held that the result of an advisory opinion, although an appeal against it is not allowed, should be considered not merely as a private expert opinion, but as a public technical expert decision under an impartial procedure, which must be regarded as one of prima facie authoritative decisions.

15. However, there is an opposition to this decision that it is not adequate for a court to easily rely on the result of an advisory opinion requested by the infringer as a countermeasure to the temporary injunction, because whether or not belonging to the technical scope should be resolved in a principal action of the temporary injunction case. See, T. IWATSUBO (above), 1332.

provide an early conflict resolution at reasonable costs,[16] it would be desirable that the court actively makes use of the result of an advisory opinion,[17] at least regarding technical issues such as the interpretation of technical terms or the existence of prior art at the time of an application.

b) Whether the decision should be subject to an administrative appeal

The object of an appeal under the Administrative Appeal Act is an administrative disposition and any other act constituting the exercise of public authority by an administrative agency, secs. 1(1). Regarding the meaning of "disposition", the Supreme Court[18] held that it does not mean all the acts by an administrative agency based on laws and regulations, but only those acts which legally and directly affect individual rights and duties, or determine their scope.

Given this interpretation, an advisory opinion is obviously not a disposition which is subject to an appeal in the Administrative Appeal Act. A patent is established upon registration as a right which originally has a certain scope of protection, and the result of an advisory opinion, which has no legal binding effect, does not modify the original scope of protection, but just interprets it as it is. In this regard, the Supreme Court held that an advisory opinion is not a disposition against which an appeal can be filed based on the Administrative Appeal Act. This is consistent with previous case law and there is no dispute on this point.[19]

From a legislative perspective, it would certainly be possible to establish an appeal system against the result of an advisory opinion in the Patent Act, regardless of the rules of the Administrative Appeal Act. However, considering that the aim of an advisory opinion is to avoid unnecessary disputes and to provide early dispute resolution, cases which cannot be effectively clarified or resolved by the procedure under the current advisory opinion system, had better be dealt with by the courts.

c) Future of the advisory opinion system

The need to provide an advisory opinion system is sometimes called into question, not least because it is not widely used for dispute resolution as it was intended to

16. The decision can be made in three months at earliest and the fee is 40,000 yen per case. See TOKKYOCHŌ SHINPANBU *(Trial and Appeal Department of the JPO)*, Tokkyochō no hanteiseido ni tsuite *(About the advisory opinion system in the Patent Office)*, 2018, 2, available at the website of the JPO <https://www.jpo.go.jp/system/trial_appeal/shubetu-hantei/document/igi-tebiki/hantei_all.pdf>.
17. K. YOSHIFUJI/K. KUMAGAI (above), 644.
18. Supreme Court, 29 October 1964, Case No. 296 (O) of 1962, 18-8 Minshū 1809 = 395 Hanrei Jihō 20. Although this definition is, strictly speaking, related to the disposition in the Administrative Case Litigation Act, the disposition in the Administrative Appeal Act is generally interpreted as synonymous with the one in the Administrative Case Litigation Act. See, K. SAKURAI/H. HASHIMOTO, Gyōseihō *(Administrative Law)*, 5th ed. 2016, 235.
19. S. ODA/Y. ISHIKAWA (above), 389-390; T. SHIBUYA (above), 406; N. NAKAYAMA (above), 283. After this decision, the Supreme Court reiterated the same interpretation and sustained the prior court decision which denied an appeal against the result of an advisory opinion. See, Supreme Court, 18 September 1990, Case No. 52 (Gyō-Tsu) of 1990 – *Transmission Lever Grip*.

be.[20] In addition, the speed of court proceedings has been rapidly increasing, thus eliminating the need for the Patent Office to provide legal services for a private dispute.[21] However, the advisory opinion system might still be attractive, especially for small companies and universities, because it provides an impartial and reliable dispute resolution at reasonable cost. To promote active use of this system, the Patent Office should make continuous efforts to improve its operations by meeting the needs of the parties and by adopting the results of court cases related to the interpretation of the technical scope of a patent, which in turn might lead the court giving deferrence to the results of an advisory opinion.[22]

4. COMPARATIVE REMARKS

a) In **Korea**, there exists a trial system to confirm the scope of a patent right., sec. 135(1) of the Korean Patent Act,[23] which is very similar to the Japanese advisory opinion system. The aim of a trial for confirmation of scope is to determine the technical scope of a patented invention in relation to a certain technology being used or intended to be used, and thereby to provide an early dispute resolution before or instead of a court action. Just as in Japan, an advisory opinion does not have any binding legal effect, yet under the Korean system an appeal against the trial decision is allowed. The trial system for confirmation in Korea is more widely used than the Japanese advisory opinion system.[24] As to the reasons for this, it is pointed out that an appeal against the decision is allowed and that the courts are inclined to rely on the result of a trial.[25] Recently, the Korean Supreme Court[26] rendered a new decision regarding the trial system. It held that the inventive step of a patented invention cannot be examined and judged in a trial for confirmation, because determining inventive step is beyond the objective of the trial aimed at confirming the scope of a patent. This understanding is the same as in Japan. The Korean Supreme Court in

20. The number of cases from 2008 to 2015 are about 30, but it is notable that the number has increased to 97 in 2016. See TOKKYOCHŌ (ed.), Tokkyo Nenji Hokokusho (Annual Report of Patent) 2017, 9, available at the website of the JPO <https://www.jpo.go.jp/resources/report/nenji/2017/document/index/0107.pdf>. There is an opinion that the low number of positive confirmation decisions is likely to dissuade a patentee from requesting an advisory opinion. See, T. IWATSUBO (above), 1330-1331.
21. N. NAKAYAMA (above), 285.
22. In this respect, it is noteworthy that following the Supreme Court Decision in the *Ball Spline Bearing III* case, the Patent Office has decided to examine the requirements of the doctrine of equivalence, as long as it is necessary for the parties.
23. KIPO (ed.), Understanding the Patent Act of the Republic of Korea, 2007, 178, available at the website of the KIPO <http://www.kipo.go.kr/upload/en/download/Understanding_the_Patent_Act_of_the_Republic_of_Korea.pdf>.
24. According to the KIPO's statistics, the number of requests for a trial for confirmation in 2014 is 385, whereas the number of requests for an advisory opinion in the same year is only 39.
25. S. KIM, Nihon kigyō ga chūisubeki kankoku dokutoku no seido *(The system unique to Korea that Japanese Companies should look out for)*, 56-3 Patent 9 (2003). For comparison between Korean confirmation trial and Japanese advisory opinion systems, there exists a comparative study of patent offices, available at the website of the JPO <https://www.jpo.go.jp/news/kokusai/nityukan/document/nicyukan_shinpan_hikakuken/study_final-en.pdf>.
26. Korean Supreme Court, 20 March 2014, Case No. 4162 (Hu) of 2012 – *Feed Carrier for a Feed Delivery Vehicle.*

2017 indicated that although the inventive step cannot be assessed in the trial for confirmation of the scope, the defence of the free state of the art may be considered even in cases of literal infringement and the invention subject to confirmation should not be included in the scope of a patent right, if it belongs to the free state of the art.[27]

b) In the **UK**, the UKIPO may provide a non-binding opinion by a patent examiner under sec. 74A of the UK Patent Act.[28] The UK opinion system characteristically includes issues about the validity of a patent or a Supplementary Protection Certificate (SPC), sec. 93(6) UK Patent Rules. The UKIPO will be able to start a revocation procedure after an opinion that the patent is invalid, sec. 73(1A). Reviews of opinions can be requested under sec. 74B of the UK Patent Act, and comparable to the Korean system, an appeal against a decision not to set aside an opinion can be filed to the Patents Court.[29] The number of requests for an opinion in the UKIPO between 2014-2017 was in the range of 20 to 30 per year.[30]

27. Korean Supreme Court, 14 November 2017, Case No. 366 (Hu) of 2016 – *High Strength Panel.*
28. The opinion service of the UKIPO started from 2005 and was expanded in 2014, as stated in UKIPO, Expansion of the Patent Opinions Service, available at the website of the UK Government <https://www.gov.uk/government/publications/expansion-of-the-patent-opinions-service-business-guidance/business-guidance-of-the-expansion-of-the-patent-opinions-service>. For the UK opinion system, see also, Opinions manual of the UKIPO, available at the website of the UK Government <https://www.gov.uk/government/publications/opinions-manual/opinions-manual>
29. UK Patents Court, *DLP Ltd, Re UK Intellectual Property Office Decision* [2007] EWHC 2669 (Pat).
30. See, opinion case list, available at the website of the UK Government <https://www.gov.uk/government/collections/requests-for-opinions>.

Case No. 24

Invalidation Trial – Ne Bis In Idem

Makoto Hattori

A request for an invalidation trial (Request A) would not become unlawful even if, after the filing of Request A, a final and binding decision rendered by the JPO to dismiss another request for an invalidation trial (Request B) that is filed on the basis of the same patent, facts and evidence as those cited in Request A, is registered.

Supreme Court, 27 January 2000, Case No. 105 (Gyō-Tsu) of 1995 – *Chromic Acid Pigment and Method of Producing it*

[X] v. [Y]

---

1. BACKGROUND

Sec. 167 of the Patent Act prior to the amendment in 2011 stipulated as follows: "When a final and binding trial decision in a trial for patent invalidation or a trial for invalidation of the registration of extension of the duration has been registered, no one may file a request for a trial on the basis of the same facts and evidence."

There have been three different theories concerning the point in time when "no one may file a request for a trial on the basis of the same facts and evidence." More specifically, there were the following opinions concerning the timing of the decision that a second request for a trial can no longer be pursued: (i) the second request can be pursed if it is filed when a trial decision in another trial has not become final and binding, even if the trial decision in another trial has become final and binding when the second decision is rendered (Theory of the Timing of Trial Request);[1] (ii) the second request cannot be pursed if a trial decision in another trial has become final and binding before the second decision is rendered, even if the trial

---

1. R. Takabayashi, Dōitsu no jujitsu oyobi shōko ni motozuku fukusū no tokkyo mukō shinpan jiken no shinri ga heigō sarete nasareta seikyū fuseiritsu shinketsu ni tsuite shinpan seikyūnin ra no ichibu ga shinketsu torikeshi soshō wo teiki shinakatta baai to tokkyo hō 167 jō -Tokyo kōsai hanketsu heisei 7.2.8- *(Case where a part of petitioners did not file a lawsuit against the JPO decision to dismiss the request in which the JPO conduct jointly proceedings of plural patent invalidation trials based on same acts and proves and sec. 167 Patent Act -Tokyo High Court decision of 8 February 1995-)*, 1594 Harei-Jihō 218 (1997); K. Doi, Tokkyo hō 167 jō no ichiji fusairi kō no tekiyō han'i -Tokyo kōsai hanketsu heisei 7.2.8 hanketsu- *(Applicable scope of ne bis in idem effect of sec. 167 Patent Act -Tokyo High Court decision of 8 February 1995-)*, 47-7 Chizai Kanri 965 (1997).

decision in another trial has not become final and binding when the second request is filed (Theory of the Timing of Rendering the Trial Decision);[2] and (iii) the second request cannot be pursed if a trial decision in another trial has become final and binding before the second decision has become final and binding, even if the trial decision in another trial has not become final and binding when the second decision is rendered (Theory of *res iudicata* of the second Trial Decision).[3]

The Former Supreme Court decision of 19 March 1920[4] adopted the Theory of Rendering the Trial Decision. However, for reasons including the fact that the applicable scope of the provision should not be broadened, the decision was criticised.[5]

The Supreme Court decision of 27 January 2000 clearly stated, as described below, that the Theory of Filing the Trial Request shall be adopted, modifying the above-mentioned Former Supreme Court decision of 19 March 1920.

2. DECISION[6]

a) Facts

Concerning the Patent No. 952065, "Chromic Acid Pigment and Method of Producing it," which is owned by Person Y (Defendant/Appellant), X and two others (Plaintiffs/ Appellees) as well as Company A, which is not a party to the case, respectively filed requests for trials for patent invalidation, each alleging the same facts and producing the same evidence to support the grounds for invalidation. The Japanese Patent Office (JPO) jointly conducted trial proceedings for these requests and determined that the present patent is inventive, and issued a single decision dismissing the requests. X and two others were dissatisfied with the decision and filed an action to seek revocation of the decision, but Company A did not file an action to seek revocation of the decision within the prescribed period for filing an action under sec. 178(3) of the Patent Act.

Consequently, in light of the trial decision dismissing the claim made by Company A, there arises the question of whether or not the filing of a request for a trial for patent invalidation and the pursuit of an action seeking revocation of the trial decision based thereon should be prohibited pursuant to sec. 167.

b) Reasons

Sec. 167 of the Patent Act provides that when a final and binding trial decision rendered by the JPO in response to a request for a trial for the invalidation of a patent

2. H. KANEKO/Y. SOMENO, Kogyō shoyuuken hō kaiteiban *(Industrial Property Law Revised Edition)* 1971 361.
3. M. MIYAKE, Tokkyo Sousyou Zakkan *(Essays on Patent Lawsuit)*, 1970, 289; K. YOSHIFUJI, Tokkyo hō gaisetsu (Outline of Patent Law), 13th ed. 1998, 629.
4. Case No. 811 (O) of 1919, 26 Minroku 371
5. R. TAKABAHASHI (above); K. DOI (above).
6. Published in 54-1 Minshū 69 = 1700 Hanrei Jihō 3 = 1024 Hanrei Times 165 = N. NAKAYAMA et al. (eds.), Tokkyo hanrei hyakusen *(Hundred Selected Patent Cases)*, 4th ed. 2012, 94 = T. ŌBUCHI et al. (eds.) Chitekizaisan hō hanrei shū *(Intellectual Property Law Case Book)*, 2nd ed. 2015, 60.

(hereinafter referred to as a "request for an invalidation trial") has been registered, no one may file a request for an invalidation trial on the basis of the same facts and evidence. The purpose of this provision is as follows. If the trial decision to dismiss the claim in a request for an invalidation trial of a particular patent (hereinafter referred to as a "decision of dismissal") has become final and binding, and such decision is registered, no one is allowed to file another request for an invalidation trial after said registration on the basis of the same facts and evidence. This provision should not be interpreted beyond the meaning stated therein. In other words, if a final and binding decision of dismissal has been registered, it does not mean that any request for an invalidation trial that was already pending before the JPO at the time of such registration would become unlawful. As such, the following interpretation would be appropriate: A request for an invalidation trial (Request A) would not become unlawful even if, after the filing of Request A, a final and binding decision rendered by the JPO to dismiss the claim in another request for an invalidation trial (Request B) that is filed on the basis of the same facts and evidence as those cited in Request A, is registered.

3. ANALYSIS

a) Sec. 167 of the Patent Act

Sec. 167 of the Patent Act was amended as follows by the law amendment of 2011,[7] with effect since 1 April 2012.

Pre-amendment sec. 167 stipulated: "When a final and binding trial decision in a trial for patent invalidation or a trial for invalidation of the registration of extension of the duration has been registered, no one may file a request for a trial on the basis of the same facts and evidence."

Post-amendment sec. 167 stipulates: "Where a final and binding trial decision in an invalidation trial or a trial for invalidation of the registration of extension of the duration has been registered, neither parties nor intervenors may file a request for a trial on the basis of the same facts and evidence."

The decision of 27 January 2000 rendered by the Supreme Court (hereinafter referred to as the "Decision") is based on the provision of the pre-amendment sec. 167. Consequently, as described later, whether or not *res judicata* should still apply to the post-amendment sec. 167 is in question.

b) Conventional judicial precedents and theories concerning the base time

The relevant point in time under sec. 167 of the Patent Act, or in other words, the time at which it becomes no longer permissible to file a new request for a trial is, as described above, disputed, and different theories have been advanced, see above.

In this respect, based on the assumption that the legislative intent of this provision is to prevent contradictory decisions, one could assume that once a final

7. Law No. 63 of 8 June 2011.

and binding trial decision to dismiss Request B has been rendered, currently pending Request A, should become unlawful retroactively. Conventionally, this theory was adopted in judicial precedents.

On the other hand, the Decision stated as follows: "When multiple requests for an invalidation trial are pending before the JPO, and if any of the persons who filed such requests does not appeal against a decision to dismiss his/her request, the procedures conducted so far by the other persons who filed the requests for their own interests would become meaningless and these persons would no longer be able to enjoy their interests. This would be unreasonable." In addition, by taking into consideration that the law provides that "a request for a trial cannot be filed," the Decision stated as follows: "Sec. 167 of the Patent Act aims to ensure a balance between the inalienable interests of a person who files a request for an invalidation trial and the interests residing in the stability of the patent right, and restricts the right of an interested person to file a request for an invalidation trial only under the conditions prescribed in said section. Therefore, the provision of said section should not be interpreted by broadening the scope of cases where it applies. It is appropriate to interpret its text literally," thus modifying the above-mentioned former Supreme Court decision and stating that the relevant point in time at which double jeopardy applies, shall be the filing of Trial Request.

c) 2011 Amendment of the Patent Act

Under the Patent Act, an action for revocation of a granted patent must be instituted by way of a trial for invalidation before the Patent Office, and an action cannot be filed directly with the court (sec. 178(6) of the Patent Act). Accordingly, restricting the inalienable right of a third party to file a request for an invalidation trial bears the risk of violating the right of access to courts, which is one of the fundamental human rights guaranteed under Art. 32 of the Constitution of Japan.

Under the Austrian Patent Act, which was considered to be the law that served as the model for the above provision, the same provision had already been deleted based on a court decision stating that the same provision was in violation of the country's constitution.[8] As such, it has been believed that, other than the Patent Act of Japan, there is no other jurisdiction that provides for the *ne bis in idem* (prohibition of double jeopardy) effect as stipulated in the pre-amendment sec. 167.

In other words, the fundamental rule is that the effect of a court decision in a civil suit extends only to the parties involved, and in order to expand the effect to third parties, there must be a strong need for such expansion as well as a guarantee of due process for the third party. However, the pre-amendment sec. 167 was not sufficient in these respects, and thus it was considered inappropriate to expand the effect of a trial decision to third parties. On the other hand, in the case where a trial decision dismissing a request for an invalidation trial is made final and binding for a certain patent, even if Article 104ter of the Patent Act allows a defendant to use a defence (the invalidity defence) in an infringement suit with regard to the same patent on the basis of the same facts and evidence, no one may file a request for an invalidation trial on the basis of the same facts and evidence as a prior invalidation

8. Austrian Constitutional Court, 17 October 1973, Österreichisches Patent Blatt 1973, 150.

trial. Consequently, if the patent becomes substantially unavailable for use pursuant to the decision given in the infringement suit, it is impossible to invalidate the patent in light of obligations *erga omnes*, and thus the patent remains recorded on the patent registry. As such, it has been pointed out that there may arise problems in light of the public interest. In view of such problems, the effect of a final and binding trial decision against third parties was abolished.

However, since the parties and intervenors in the prior trial were able to establish their claims in the prior trial, it is unreasonable if, after the trial decision is made final and binding, these persons can bring up a dispute based on the same facts and evidence. As such, it was concluded that *ne bis in idem* (prohibition of double jeopardy) shall remain applicable for those parties who were actually involved in the previous invalidation trial.

d) Amendment of the law and the Decision

Pursuant to the purpose of sec. 167 prior to the amendment, the Decision emphasised the inalienable interest of a third party who is not a party to the final and binding trial decision of patent invalidation to file a request for an invalidation trial. The Decision seems to try to ensure a balance between said inalienable interest of the third party and the interests residing in the legal certainty of the patent right by determining that a literal interpretation of the text is appropriate. In such sense, it can be said that the reasons described in the Decision are no longer applicable under the current law, which abolishes the effect against third parties and provides for cases in which a request for a trial is filed by the same party or intervenor.[9]

4. COMPARATIVE REMARKS

a) In **Germany**, a final and binding decision to nullify/invalidate a patent has *ex tunc* effect to the patent and makes a renewal of the case impossible, but there is no provision about the legal effect of the decision to dismiss the request for nullity/invalidation in the German Patent Act. Still, sec. 325(1) of the Code of Civil Procedure is applied *mutatis mutandis* through sec. 99 Patent Act. According to German case law, as the legal effect of the decision the plaintiff in the case cannot file a new request for nullity/invalidation of the same patent based on the same reasons before the German Federal Patent Court even where new evidence is filed.[10]

b) The old **Austrian** Patent Act had the same *ne bis in idem* provision as Japan, which extended the legal effect of decision to third parties outside the case. But the Austrian Constitutional Court decided in 1973 that the legal effect to third parties

9. The same tenor is described in T. MAKINO, Mukō shinketsu no kakutei shinketsu no daisansha kō no haishi *(Abolishment of the effects on third parties of final and conclusive trial decisions in invalidation Trials)*, 52 Tokkyo Kenkyū 17 (2011).
10. German Federal Supreme Court, 19 February 1963, GRUR 1964, 18 – *Konditionierungseinheit*. See also KRASSER/ANN, Patentrecht *(Patent Law)*, 7th ed. 2016, 653. There is critics to this point in Germany, see e.g. A. KEUKENSCHRIJVER, Zur Rechtskraft des klageabweisenden Urteils im Patentnichtigkeitsverfahren *(About the legal effect of the decision to dismiss in the patent nullity procedure)*, GRUR 2009, 281.

was unconstitutional and the provision was deleted in 1977.[11] Currently, in Austria, a final and binding decision to dismiss is effective to parties of the case, but the plaintiff in the case can file a new request with new material.[12]

c) In the **US**, sec. 314(a) of 35 USC gives the Director of the USPTO a discretion not to authorise an *inter partes* review to be instituted when there is no reasonable likelihood that the petitioner would prevail with respect to at least one of the claims challenged in the petition, and sec. 315(e)(1) provides that the petitioner after a final written decision may not request or maintain proceedings before the Office on any ground that the petitioner raised or reasonably could have raised during the review. There is a similar provision for post-grant review in secs. 324(a) and 325(e)(1). Sec. 325(d) provides that the Director may decide to reject the petition or request, etc., taking into account whether the same or substantially the same prior art or arguments which were previously presented to the Office. The parties in the case are estopped to request or maintain further petitions by sec. 325(e),[13] or a second petition by the same petitioner may be denied by sec. 314(a) or 325(d), even with a new prior art material, when the petitioner knew or should have known of it at the time of filing of the first petition.[14]

d) **China** has a *ne bis in idem* provision which extends the legal effect to third parties outside of the case in sec 66(2) Implementing Regulation to the Patent Act. The **Korean** Supreme Court held also in 2012 that a request for invalidation trial did not become unlawful even if the KIPO decision on the same facts and evidences became final and binding after the request, and changed the time to apply the *ne*

11. Austrian Constitutional Court, 17 October 1973, Österreichisches Patent Blatt 1973, 150.
12. It is said that the old Austrian Patent Act of 1897 was base of the introduction the old *ne bis in idem* provision of the old Japanese Patent Act in 1909, which remained to 2011, the purpose of the provision was the stabilisation of patents along with the prohibition of request for invalidation after 5 years, which was introduced after the German Patent Act of 1891 and abolished in 1959, and the abolishment of the *Ne Bis In Idem* provision in Austria influenced the law amendment of Japan of 2011. See e.g. A. Iijima, Tokkyo mukō shinpan ni okeru ichjifusairi *(Ne Bis In Idem in the JPO invalidation trial)*, 16 Chitekizaisan hō Seisakugaku Kenkyū 247 (2007), at 266-267; Sangyōkōzō shingikai Chitekizaisan seisaku bukai *(Intellectual Property Policy Sub-Council under Council for Structure of Industries of the JPO)*, Tokkyo seido ni kansuru hōseiteki na kadai ni tsuite *(About problems of legal system of patent)*, 2011, 41, available at the website of the JPO <https://www.jpo.go.jp/resources/shingikai/sangyo-kouzou/shousai/tokkyo_shoi/document/index/housei_kadai.pdf>.
13. E.g. PTAB, *Kofax v. Uniloc USA* (IPR 2015-1207); PTAB, *IBM v. Intellectual Ventures II* (IPR 2014-01465).
14. E.g. PTAB, *General Plastic Industrial v. Canon* (IPR 2016-01357; 01358; 01359; 01360; 01361); PTAB, *Praxair Distribution v. INO Therapeutics* (IPR 2016-00781). For sec. 325(d), the PTAB can deny a request based on prior art, which was presented during examination and considered by an examiner. See also PTAB, *Unified Patents v. Berman* (IPR 2016-01571); PTAB, *Hospira v. Genentech*, (IPR 2017-00739); PTAB *Cultec, Inc. v. Stormtech*, (IPR 2017-00777). See also S. J. Schwarz et al., Savvy Shaw-Ping: A Strategic Approach to AIA Estoppel, 17 Chicago-Kent Journal of Intellectual Property 67 (2018), available at the website of IIT Chicago-Kent College of Law <https://scholarship.kentlaw.iit.edu/ckjip/vol17/iss3/7>.

bis in idem provision from the time of decision to the time of request as case law, but the provision itself still remains in sec. 163 Patent Act in Korea.[15]

15. Korean Supreme Court, 19 January 2012, Case No. 2234 (Hu) of 2009. For Korean position and critics to the *ne bis in idem* provision, see, e.g., S. KIM, Non Bis In Idem of Finalized IPTAB Decisions, 1 Korean Patent Court IP Law Journal 97 (2014), available at the website of the Korean Patent Court <http://patent.scourt.go.kr/dcboard/new/EngDcNewsListAction.work?gubun=542>.

Case No. 25

Correction Trial – Revocation Proceedings

Hiroaki Kikuchi

Whether in proceedings of patent invalidation and correction, the amendments should to be examined on a claim by claim basis, or as a complete set of claims.

Supreme Court, 10 July 2008, Case No. 318 (Gyō-Hi) of 2007 – *Correction of Patent Claims*

Philips Lumileds Lighting v. Japanese Patent Office

---

1. BACKGROUND

With the Patent Act of 1921, Japan adopted a system that required a single claim in a patent, but when ratifying the PCT in 1975,[1] more than one claim per patent became permissible. However, this multiple claim system was not the same as the Western system that defined the technical scope of the patented invention or the scope of protection of the patent right by a number of independent claims in one application, as the Japanese system merely allowed the addition of dependent claims to a single independent claim for defining further embodiments.

The law amendment of 1987[2] deleted the clause that stipulated the principle of one independent claim for one single application, and introduced an improved multiple claim system that permitted a number of independent claims in one patent.

The law amendment of 1993[3] no longer allowed to file a correction trial during the pendency of an invalidation trial at the Patent Office, but allowed a request for correction in proceedings during an invalidation trial. The law amendment of 1994[4] introduced a system of post-grant opposition and allowed a request for correction in the course of these proceedings. Therefore, the admissibility of partial correction among a number of claims in the case of a request for a correction trial or a request for correction in proceedings of patent invalidation or post-grant opposition became a legal issue.

---

1. Law No. 46/1975 of 25 June 1975
2. Law No. 27/1987 of 25 March 1987
3. Law No. 26/1993 of 23 April 1993
4. Law No. 116/1994 of 14 December 1994

In the case concerning a correction trial of a utility model application, the ruling of the Supreme Court of 1 May 1980[5] prohibited a partial correction, stating that "if a correction substantially influences the scope of the claim, the Patent Office is required to decide on the correction as a whole," and "even if individual parts of the correction were technically not inseparably linked to each other and if a partial correction was to some extent useful for the applicant, the Patent Office cannot decide on this part only." The Patent Office had treated patents as inseparable in case of a request for correction or a request for a correction trial even under the improved multiple claim system, be it before or after this Supreme Court ruling. That is, in case that a correction of one of the claims did not meet the requirements or patentability, the Patent Office dismissed the request as a whole without deciding whether a correction for other claims was admissible or not.

However, the Tokyo High Court on 31 October 2002[6] decided that the admissibility of a correction should be determined for each claim in case of a request of partial correction for each claim, while after the establishment of the IP High Court, rulings on this issue were divided in that the specific division of the IP High Court permitted a partial correction like in accordance with the above Tokyo High Court decision,[7] while other divisions did not allow this avenue.

Therefore, it became necessary for the Supreme Court to decide whether a partial correction of the patent was admissible under the improved multiple claim system.

2. DECISION[8]

a) Facts

1. In the present case, the appellant, who is also the holder of patent No. 3441182, petitions that the ruling of the Patent Office revoking his patent to the extent of claims 1-4 be set aside.

2. The decision at the previous instance rightly determined the following facts:

a) The invention bears the title "Module and light source of a light-emitting diode". The patent was filed on 26 August 1994 on the basis of the priority

5. Supreme Court, 1 May 1980, Case No. 27 (Gyō-Tsu) of 1978, 34-3 Minshū 431 = 967 Hanrei Jihō 49 = 417 Hanrei Times 85.
6. Tokyo High Court, 31 October 2002, Case No. 170 (Gyō-Ke) of 2000, 1821 Hanrei Jihō 117 = 1110 Hanrei Times 102.
7. IP High Court, 20 June 2007, Case No. 10081 (Gyō-Ke) of 2007, 1997 Hanrei Jihō 119 = 1263 Hanrei Times 327; IP High Court, 23 July 2007, Case No. 10099 (Gyō-Ke) of 2007, 1998 Hanrei Jihō 110 = 1266 Hanrei Times 320; IP High Court, 28 December 2007, Case No. 10426 (Gyō-Ke) of 2006, 1999 Hanrei Jihō 102 = 1265 Hanrei Times 326; IP High Court, 12 February 2008, Case No. 10455 (Gyō-Ke) of 2006, 1999 Hanrei Jihō 115 = 1265 Hanrei Times 311.
8. Published in 62-7 Minshū 1905 = 2019 Hanrei Jihō 88 = 1279 Hanrei Times 110 = N. NAKAYAMA et al. (eds.), Tokkyo Hanrei Hyakusen *(Hundred Selected Patent Cases)*, 4th ed. 2012, 92 = T. ŌBUCHI et al. (eds.), Chitekizaisan hō hanrei shū *(Intellectual Property Law Case Book)*, 2nd ed. 2015, 64. English translation in 41 IIC 231 (2010). A provisional translation is also available at the website of the IP High Court <http://www.ip.courts.go.jp/app/files/hanrei_en/669/001669.pdf>.

of an application in the United States of America dated 17 September 1993, and was granted on 20 June 2003. It contains four claims.

b) On 26 December 2003, an opposition was filed against all four claims of the patent. During opposition proceedings No. 2003-73487, the appellant filed a request for the correction of the claims on 7 December 2005 pursuant to sec. 120^{quater}(2) of the Patent Act (old version) before the Act was amended by Law No. 47/2003. Correction a) concerned claim 1, correction b) claim 2, correction c) claim 3 and correction d) claim 4. The appellant is of the opinion that correction a) results in a limitation of the scope of the claim, and correction b) in a clarification of the wording. On the other hand, corrections c) and d) were limited to formal changes of typing errors and the question of their admissibility did not arise in the present revocation proceedings. Claims 1 and 2 before and after the correction are attached to the files. [Attachment omitted]

c) On 22 February 2006, the Patent Office ruled that the request for correction was inadmissible and revoked the patent at issue with all four claims. In summary, the grounds for the ruling were as follows:

(1) Correction b) was intended neither to restrict the patent claim nor to correct errors of typing or translation, or to clarify ambiguous expressions and instead substantially extended the scope of the claim. Thus, the correction contravened sec. 126(1) and (2) of the old version of the Patent Act before the amendment by law No. 16/1994, to which said provision in sec. 120^{quater}(3) of the Patent Act refers *mutatis mutandis*. Correction b) was inadmissible in its entire scope without there being any need to discuss the further corrections.

(2) Before the correction of the claims, moreover, the invention could easily be derived from the state of the art by a person skilled in the art, with the result that it was not patentable under sec. 29(2).

3. In the subsequent judicial proceedings, the previous instance dismissed the appellant's petition for the rescission of the resolution of the Patent Office for the following reasons.

The decision of the Patent Office to refuse the entire correction on the grounds that correction b) did not correspond with the regulations without taking account of all the further corrections was lawful. In case that the request for the correction proceedings and correction amended a number of items in the description or the drawings and if these corrections substantially influenced the scope of the claim, the Patent Office was required to decide on the correction as a whole, unless clearly declaring to correct a specific matter among the multiple matters for correction by taking measures such as amending the matters for correction stated in the written request for correction. Even if individual parts of the correction were technically not inseparably linked to each other and if the acceptance of partial correction was to some extent useful for the applicant, the Patent Office could not only decide on the allowance of this part [ruling of the Supreme Court of 1 May 1980]. This principle was also valid for a system that permitted a number of independent claims in a patent (wording of the claims of sec. 36 (5) of the Patent Act after the amendment by Law

No. 27/1987). The request for correction was not simply for a partial correction, but instead all claims would have to be regarded as inseparably linked.

b) Reasons

4. However, this decision of the previous instance is to be set aside for the following reasons.

(1) The patent right is based on a unitary structure, since the patent is granted in one administrative act for an entire application and not for instance for individual claims. If the application contains a number of claims, the patent is to be granted or refused for the entire application unless a divisional application is submitted. There is no provision for the separate treatment of the individual claims to the effect that a patent is granted for one but is refused for another. This follows from the wording of secs. 49 and 51 of the Patent Act and from the possibility of filing a divisional application. However, if on the other hand the treatment of the patent as an inseparable whole appears inappropriate in the light of a number of the claims, the Patent Act provides for an exception according to which it is possible to assess the individual claims separately. This exception is regulated in sec. 185 of the Patent Act, Sec. 113 of the old version of the Act, according to which "an opposition can be filed against individual claims if the patent contains two or more claims." (The same purpose is pursued by sec. 123(1) with respect to the request for invalidity.)

(2) If against the background of such an underlying structure, the provisions concerning the correction proceedings do not contain regulations that are as clear as in sec. 113 and sec. 123(1) and according to which individual claims can be treated separately. On the contrary, the correction trial proceedings have the character of new proceedings (cf. Patent Act, sec. 126(5) and sec. 128). For this reason, the correction trial proceedings concerning a patent with a number of claims, just like a patent application with a number of claims, is an inseparable entity that must be treated together.

However, pursuant to sec. $120^{quater}(2)$ of the Patent Act, the request for correction was regarded as proceedings that depended on opposition proceedings, and in terms of its position under the Patent Act, it differs from a request for correction trial, which is an independent trial procedure. For instance, a request for correction did not require an independent review of the patent provided that the purpose of the request was to restrict the scope of the claims against which an opposition had been filed (cf. old Patent Act, secs. $120^{quater}(3)$, 126(4)). This view of the correction proceedings means that the correction is not interpreted as a new patent application. The request for correction for the purpose of restricting contested claims is, on the contrary, to be interpreted as a defence against the opposition and can therefore be directed at individual claims. The correction of individual claims by the patent holder appears justified since otherwise the equality of the attack and the defence would be at risk. Accordingly, the opposition against individual patent claims is just as admissible as the restriction of the contested scope of the claim by means of the correction of individual claims, and the restriction of the Patent Office review to the admissibility of the correction of individual claims.

Admittedly, the respondent argues that the invention as set out in its entirety in the description is to be understood as an inseparable whole, but the revision of the Patent Act by Law No. 27 of 1987 abolished the principle according to which one application had to be submitted for each invention and replaced this by the possibility of an application with a number of claims. To this extent, the respondent's argument cannot be endorsed. The ruling of the Supreme Court of 1 May 1980 had admittedly denied the admissibility of partial corrections. However, it concerned a utility model application and related to individual correction matters for one claim. The decision may also be applicable to a number of corrections for one claim, but not to the correction of a number of patent claims.

(3) For the above-mentioned reasons, the Patent Office in the case of a request for correction for the purpose of restricting contested claims should assess whether individually corrected claims are admissible. If only a part of the correction is inadmissible, the Patent Office cannot hold the entire correction to be inadmissible provided that a correction has also been requested for other claims.

(4) In the present case, the appellant has requested the correction of correction a) for the purpose of restricting the patent claims. Correction a) relates to the correction of contested claim 1, which is separable from other claims and whose admissibility should be assessed. The Patent Office, on the other hand, rejected the correction as inadmissible as a whole, since it regarded correction b), which related to claim 2, to be inadmissible without examining correction a) independently. The Patent Office ruling revoking the patent is based solely on the finding that correction b) was inadmissible, determined the scope of the claim and revoked the patent under this condition. The Patent Office ruling and likewise the decision at the previous instance are for this reason faulty. Both are therefore to be set aside on the grounds of a breach of the law.

(5) The grounds submitted by the appellant are well-founded and the part of the previous instance decision that relates to the revocation of the claim 1 is set aside, as is the corresponding part of the Patent Office ruling.

The part of the appeal on the law that concerns the revocation of the other claims on which the Patent Office decided according to the merits of the case is dismissed, since the appeal on the law is not admitted to this extent.

3. ANALYSIS

This decision stated as an *obiter dictum* that the request for a partial correction in the course of a correction trial concerning a patent with a number of claims was inadmissible, since the patent in these proceedings should be treated as an inseparable unit. But this decision also stated that such request was admissible in proceedings of post-grant opposition: these differed from a request for a correction trial which was an independent trial procedure in terms of its position under the Patent Act. As a defensive measure against an opposition request, a claim amendment in these proceedings could be directed at individual claims. The court stressed that the issue of claim amendments in the context of opposition proceedings was outside of the scope of the ruling of the Supreme Court of 1 August 1980.

In addition, post-grant opposition proceedings were abolished and integrated into the proceedings for patent invalidation by amendment by Law No. 47/2003, and the purport of this decision thus also became applicable to the request for correction in the context of a patent invalidation.

In order to implement this decision, the Patent Office changed its practice for patent invalidation trials where patents were now examined on a claim-by-claim basis, yet maintained its practice to treat claims as inseparable in correction trial proceedings. This practice was influenced by the *obiter dictum* of the decision. But such unequal treatment based on this part was harshly criticised. That is, although this decision explained the difference between the request for correction in the proceedings of post-grant opposition and the request for a correction trial, critics took the position that both requests had the same legal nature, substantially functioned as a defensive measure and should not be treated differently.[9]

Moreover, if the ruling of this decision on this point was strictly applied to a case of partial correction of a patent with several claims, the establishment of the patent right would differ on a claim-by-claim basis. Especially where a dependent claim was corrected in the course of a correction trial, the corrected dependent claim and the main claim may no longer correspond and refer to a different description, the main claim to the original description and the dependent claim to the description as supplied in the course of the correction trial. This problem is called "a bundle of descriptions" or "a lack of perspicuity".[10]

As a result of the above mentioned problems, the amendment by Law No. 63/2011 of 8 June 2011 clarified that both in proceedings of patent invalidation and correction, the amendments were to be examined on a claim by claim basis, and in addition provided that dependent claims in a request for correction shall be treated as a group, as follows:

"Where the scope of claims in an application covering two or more claims is corrected, a request may be filed pursuant to paragraph (1) for each claim. In this case, where there is a group of claims, said request shall be filed for the each group of claims." (Sec. 126(3) – request for a correction trial)

> "A request for correction in the preceding paragraph may be filed for each claim in the case where the scope of claims attached to the application covering two or more claims is corrected; provided, however, that a request for correction in said paragraph shall be filed for each claim in the case where a request for

9. R. Mimura, Kaizen takōsei no moto ni okeru kurēmu teisei *(Legal issues on the correction of patent claims under the improved multiple claim system)*, 22 Chitekizaisanhō seisakugaku kenkyuu 1 (2009); R. Mimura, Kaizen takōsei no moto ni okeru tokkyo seikyū o han'i no teisei *(Correction of patent claims under the improved multiple claim system)*, 64-4 Patent 25 (2011); M. Tanaka, Fukusū no seikyūkō ni kakaru teisei seikyū ga sareta baai seikyūkō goto ni dakuhi handan wo subeki mono to shita saikōsai hanketsu *(The Japanese Supreme Court's decision concerning whether the permissibility of correction of a patent should be determined on a claim by claim basis)*, 48 Tokkyo Kenkyū 78 (2009).
10. Y. Yamazaki, Fukusū seikyūkō ni okeru ichibu teisei no dakuhi *(Partial correction in case of multiple claims)*, 32 Chitekizaisanhō seisakugaku kenkyū 249 (2010).

invalidation trial has been filed for each claim." (Sec. $134^{bis}(2)$ – request for a correction in an invalidation trial[11])

"An appeal/trial decision shall become final and binding for each appeal/ trial case; provided, however, that in the cases listed in the following items, an appeal/trial decision shall become final and binding as provided in the corresponding item:

(i) where a request for an invalidation trial has been filed for each claim and a request for correction has been filed under sec. $134^{bis}(1)$ for each group of claims: for the said group of claims;
(ii) where a request for correction trial has been filed for each group of claims: for said group of claims; and,
(iii) where a request for trial has been filed for each claim and a case other than those listed in item (i): for said claim." (Sec. 167bis – scope of res iudicata of an appeal/trial decision)."

4. COMPARATIVE REMARKS

Under the **European Patent Convention** (EPC), in post-grant proceedings of opposition, appeal and limitation, the competent body (opposition division, Boards of Appeal, examining division) only decides upon a set of claims and not individual claims: Even where only one claim in a set of claims does not meet the requirements of patentability, the whole set of claims is refused. This is mitigated by the EPO practice of allowing *auxiliary requests* which are sets of claims that should be considered by the opposition division or Boards of Appeal where the principle request of the patentee (often, but not always the maintenance of the patent as granted) is not allowable. These auxiliary requests may then constitute of combinations of subclaims, or even limitations of claims based on parts of the description. By the possibility of filing auxiliary requests, the patentee can in effect ask the competent body to decide on the patentability of individual subclaims (e.g. where the first auxiliary request consists of a combination of the main claim 1 with subclaim 2, the second auxiliary request of a combination of the main claim with subclaim 3, etc.) without the need to anticipate which of the various sets of claims the opposition division or Board will ultimately find patentable. The possibility of filing auxiliary requests is not mentioned anywhere in the EPC, yet is based on the application of procedural rules recognised in the Member States (Art. 125 EPC). Vice versa, the deciding bodies of the EPC (examining division, opposition division or Boards of Appeal) have no power to grant or uphold the patent in a version that has not been agreed upon by the patentee (Art. 113(2) EPC: "The European Patent Office shall examine, and decide upon, the European patent application or the European Patent only in the text submitted to it, or agreed, by the applicant or proprietor of the patent"; Rule 71a(1) EPC – "and there is agreement as to the text to be granted"). For this reason, a decision cannot uphold only certain claims of a patent unless the patentee has filed them as a separate set of claims that can then be upheld as such. There is no obligation of the opposition

11. Sec. $120^{quinquies}(3)$ provides the same claim by claim basis request for correction in opposition proceedings, which was newly introduced by the Law No. 36/2014 of 14 May 2014.

division or the Boards of Appeal to indicate whether certain claims within a set of claims could be a basis for upholding the patent.

In **German** practice, opposition and appeal proceedings against a granted patent follow the same principles as described for the EPO. They are regarded as a continuation of the grant procedure where only the patentee can decide upon the version in which an application is granted or a patent is upheld. In nullity proceedings before the Federal Patent Court, the latter is bound by the requests of the plaintiff (the person who requests partial or complete revocation of the patent), and can uphold none, certain or all claims of the patent. This can lead to a decision where the patent is upheld with certain claims only, e.g. because the request for revocation only concerned certain claims, or because a dependent claim is considered inventive over the prior art cited, while the main claim is not.[12]

12. BENKHARD, Patentgesetz *(Commentary to the German Patent Act)*, 11th ed. 2015, § 22 notes 22, 23.

Case No. 26

Scope of Appeal Procedure in Court against Decision of Patent Office

Hirotsugu Ishikawa

1. **In appeal proceedings against a revocation decision of the Patent Office, facts that have not been dealt with in the Patent Office procedure cannot be introduced.**
2. **In regard of the lack of novelty as a ground of revocation, different facts invoked against novelty are independent grounds of revocation.**
3. **Previous case law that took a different position no longer applies.**

Supreme Court, 10 March 1976, Grand Panel, Case No. 28 (Gyō-Tsu) of 1967 – *Knitting Machine*

Amiki KK v. Bunji Okumura

1. BACKGROUND

With regard to a patent, utility model right, design right or trade mark right, these rights arise upon registration at the Japan Patent Office. Any person who is dissatisfied with a JPO examiner's decision of refusal or who seeks to invalidate the registration of such rights may, under certain conditions, file a request for a trial with the JPO (*shimpan*). In the case where the JPO makes a decision in such trial, and if the person is dissatisfied with the JPO decision, he/she may file an administrative suit to seek the recession thereof. This is called a suit against an appeal/trial decision made by the JPO (*shinketsu torikeshi soshō*).

Suits against the JPO decisions fall under the exclusive jurisdiction of the Tokyo High Court. These suits would be handled by the Intellectual Property High Court, which is a special branch of the Tokyo High Court. Any person who is dissatisfied with a judgment handed down by the IP High Court may file a final appeal with the Supreme Court.[1]

At the time of the *Knitting Machine* case, the procedure was similar to, but a little different from the above. In those days, any person dissatisfied with a JPO

1. General Secretariat of the Supreme Court of Japan, Chiteki Zaisan Kōtō Saibanshō (Intellectual Property High Court), 10-11 (2017), available at the website of the IP High Court <http://www.ip.courts.go.jp/eng/documents/thesis/141006_setuguusiryo/index.html>.

decision concerning invalidation had to go through another trial before the JPO (*kōkoku shimpan*) before he/she could file a suit against the JPO decision before the Tokyo High Court.[2]

If the court finds a JPO decision incorrect, the decision will be overturned and the case will be remitted to the JPO. For example, if an appeal/trial decision by the JPO reviewing an examiner's decision of refusal is appealed to the court, the court (where appropriate) would only set aside the JPO decision and remit, but would not have the authority to grant a patent.[3]

As mentioned above, suits against JPO decisions are administrative lawsuits. In principle, parties to such suits can claim and prove any new facts regarding the administrative dispositions. However, considering the characteristics of the procedure, one could argue that raising new facts or evidence should be limited in proceedings against the JPO. This is the issue the current decision, as well as the subsequent decision No. 27 are concerned with.

2. DECISION[4]

a) Facts

The defendant in these proceedings is the owner of a patent against which the plaintiff has initiated revocation proceedings based on novelty destroying facts A, B and C. In the quasi-judicial proceedings before the Patent Office Appeal Boards, the patent was revoked based on fact A. The defendant appealed against this decision to the Tokyo High Court. The Tokyo High Court held that fact A was not novelty-destroying, set aside the revocation, and in respect of facts B and C explained the following:

> "These facts have not yet been subject of the proceedings before the Patent Office; for this reason it is not appropriate for this court to determine the correctness of the Patent Office's decision based on these facts."

---

2. This decision of the Supreme Court was based on the old Japanese Patent Act of 1921 (the old PA) which provided another trial/second instance for appeal (*kōkoku shimpan*) in the JPO. Under the old PA, a request for second instance for appeal could be filed in the JPO against a decision of the JPO invalidation trial (*shinketsu*) or a decision of examiner (*satei*). And an appeal could be filed in the Tokyo High Court against a decision of the second instance for appeal (also called *shinketsu*), but as third instance the High Court handled only legal examination (after the High Court, a case could be appealed to the Supreme Court, as in this case). Such Japanese traditional appeal system was abolished by the Japanese Patent Act of 1959. Currently a request of an invalidation trial or an appeal against a decision of examiner can be filed in the JPO and an appeal against a decision made by the JPO Appeal/Trial Board can be filed in the IP High Court. This decision of the Supreme Court should be read in such context, but the general legal principle in this case is considered still applicable to the relationship between the IP High Court and the JPO. For the system under the old PA, see also the comment of G. Rahn in GRUR Int. 1978, 129 and the introduction in this volume.
3. General Secretariat of the Supreme Court of Japan (above), 22-23
4. Published in 30-2 Minshū 79 = 806 Hanrei Jihō 13 = 334 Hanrei Times 113 = N. Nakayama et al. (eds.), Tokkyo Hanrei Hyakusen *(One Hundred Selected Patent Cases)*, 4th ed. 2012,.198 = T. Ōbuchi et al. (eds.) Chitekizaisan hō hanrei shū (Intellectual Property Law Case Book), 2nd ed. 2015,.75 = 88 Tokkyo to Kigyo 15 (April 1976). German translation in GRUR Int. 1976 w. comment *Guntram Rahn.*

On appeal to the Supreme Court, the plaintiff argued that the above opinion of the High Court was not in accordance with the Supreme Court decision of 16 October 1953.

The Grand Chamber of the Supreme Court in this decision no longer followed previous case law and dismissed the appeal.

b) Reasons

In the current case, the old Patent Act (law No. 96 of 1921) applies …

Different from general acts of the administration, for administrative acts concerning patent applications, that is, decisions of grant or refusal, the law requires a quasi-judicial procedure and appeal procedure (in case of decisions of examiners only the appeal procedure) before experienced and technically skilled patent judges. At the same time, the law does not permit an immediate lawsuit against the original grant or refusal, but only against the subsequent decision rendered in the quasi-judicial appeal procedure. Before the courts, subject of the lawsuit is only the lawfulness or unlawfulness of the appealed decision, while the original decision of grant or refusal is only indirectly touched upon … For the quasi-judicial invalidation procedure, the law requires that the ground for invalidation is sufficiently specified and clarified by the parties. This ground is the subject of claim and defence. Further, it is clear that the law envisages a structure of procedure whereby the patent judge in his determination and decision is limited to this ground. This is consistent with sec. 117 Patent Act that provides: "Once a final decision regarding the validity of a patent or a permission under sec. 53 … has been registered, no one is entitled to raise an action of invalidation based on the same facts and evidence". This presupposes a procedural system whereby a final decision in regard of the examined facts is given an effect *inter omnes* and thereby becomes *res iudicata*. To the extent that the law specifies the exclusive jurisdiction of the Tokyo High Court for invalidation suits against the decisions rendered in quasi-judicial appeal proceedings and thereby omits one court instance, this must be understood in that in such quasi-judicial proceedings and appeal proceedings the existence of a ground for nullity has already been sufficiently dealt with due to the interaction of both parties.

When considering the system of legal remedies provided by the law against administrative acts related to patents, and the structure and character of the quasi-judicial procedure, the subject matter of proceedings that challenge the lawfulness of a decision rendered in a quasi-judicial appeal procedure should be limited to what has been raised, discussed and decided in the quasi-judicial proceedings in respect of a certain ground of nullity. According to the purpose of the law, it is not admissible to raise other grounds of nullity in court proceedings in order to argue the unlawfulness of the decision, and to request the court to decide upon these.

In the following, we have to interpret the above-mentioned provision regarding the ground of nullity. Sec. 57(1) Patent Act lists the grounds of nullity in the abstract in each section. As each of these grounds is different in its nature and contents, it is correct to interpret each of them as a specific, individual ground of nullity … yet whether it is sufficient to determine a ground of nullity merely due to its position in the law and its rules of infringement has to be carefully determined in consideration of the legal structure as a whole and especially in context with sec. 117 Patent Act that has the *ne bis in idem* effect for final and incontestable decisions based on the same facts and evidence.

The basic requirement of a patent is that according to sec. 1 Patent Act it concerns "new and industrially applicable inventions". For the question of whether a patent should be granted, or should be invalidated, it is mostly this provision that becomes a problem, specifically as to whether an invention is new. In this respect, sec. 4 Patent Act determines that an invention is not novel if "prior to the patent application it was domestically known or has been domestically used", or if "prior to the patent application it has been described in a domestically distributed publication in such a way that it could have been easily carried out." In other words, whether an invention is "new" (which in the following is referred to as "novelty") must always be determined in comparison with what at that time has been "publicly known or publicly used", or has been described in a publication (in the following "publicly known facts"). Yet such publicly known facts are numerous and diverse, and it is rather difficult to dig up all publicly known facts in respect of a certain invention. Even if such publicly known facts exist, the technical information contained therein is different and varied. For this reason, the question of novelty must be examined and determined for each and every publicly known fact in comparison with the invention in question. It must be assumed that the law provides for the above-mentioned system of examination and quasi-judicial invalidation and appeal system in view of the difficulties and specifics for determining the novelty of an invention. Also the purpose of the above-mentioned section 117 Patent Act can be understood as a recognition that the comparison with the existence - or not - of a publicly known fact and its concrete technical contents must be determined individually. If this is so, also the reason that is the basis for comparison in invalidation proceedings must be concretely defined. The allegation of nullity in comparison with one publicly known fact and the allegation of nullity based on another publicly known facts must be understood as individual reasons, even where both refer to the novelty of the invention.

For this reason, in a judicial appeal against a decision based the comparison with a specific publicly known fact that has not been dealt with in the quasi-judicial appeal procedure, such fact cannot be raised for justifying the lawfulness or unlawfulness of the appealed decision. The previous case law of this court (Supreme Court decisions of 20 December 1960 and 4 April 1968) no longer applies. This is also true for a judicial appeal against a quasi-judicial decision to reject the requested remedy: Reasons for rejection that have not been dealt with in this procedure cannot be invoked in the judicial appeal. For this reason, also the Supreme Court decision of 16 October 1953 no longer applies.

When reviewing the current case based on the above considerations, the facts that the appellants bring forward in their appeal and that the previous instance by error of law has allegedly not dealt with or decided are details that differ from those that have been dealt with and decided as grounds of invalidation in the contested decision. While they all concern an alleged contravention of sec. 1 Patent Act, they relate to publicly known facts that are different from the ones that are mentioned as the basis of the decision. For this reason, it is correct that the previous instance in determining the lawfulness of the decision under appeal did not consider those facts that had not been dealt with and decided and that concerned different grounds of nullity. In view of these considerations, the decision under appeal is correct and the appeal cannot be allowed.

3. ANALYSIS

Before the *Knitting Machine* decision, there were the following decisions of the Supreme Court concerning the scope of lawsuits against appeal/trial decisions made by the JPO:

Supreme Court, 16 October 1953[5] stated that in suits against JPO decisions, parties could bring new facts even though they had not mentioned them in the trial before the JPO.

Supreme Court, 20 December 1960[6] stated that parties could bring new facts as long as they were based on the same provision as the one they had mentioned in the trial with the JPO.

Supreme Court, 4 April 1968[7] stated that parties could claim new facts although there could be a limitation if they claimed them regarding a different provision from one they had mentioned in the trial before the JPO.

In the *Knitting Machine* case, the Supreme Court declared that its own previous case law no longer applied and that in suits against JPO decisions, parties could not invoke new facts that had not been mentioned in the trial before the JPO, even though they related to the novelty of the invention, the same provision as that was cited in the previous proceedings. In other words, in court proceedings challenging a JPO decision, no new documents may be relied upon even if these related to the same ground for invalidation (e.g. lack of novelty) that had been pleaded before the JPO.

This is still one of the most notable decisions in patent procedure because it dealt with a significant issue related to the scope of an appeal against JPO decisions and it has hitherto been the only decision of the Grand Bench of the Supreme Court in the field of intellectual property law.

Under the *Knitting Machine* rule, if a plaintiff claims novelty-destroying facts A, B and C and the JPO revokes the patent based on fact A without referring to facts B and C, the IP High Court can consider only fact A. However, according to Supreme Court, 24 January 1980,[8] the parties can add new evidence to reinforce their attack based on fact A in the appeal against the JPO decision.

If the IP High Court finds that the JPO decision in regard of fact A is incorrect and must be set aside, the procedure will be remitted for a new trial before the JPO, and the JPO will examine facts B and C. In this case, according to Supreme Court, 28 April 1992,[9] the parties can no longer add new evidence about fact A, because the IP High Court decision binds the JPO (sec. 33 Administrative Case Litigation Act).

As the Supreme Court stated, the *Knitting Machine* rule applies both to cases of invalidation and refusal. Although the decision was rendered under the old Patent

5. Supreme Court, 16 October 1953, Case No. 745 (O) of 1951, 10 Shūmin 189.
6. Supreme Court, 20 December 1960, Case No. 567 (O) of 1958, 14-14 Minshū 3103.
7. Supreme Court, 4 April 1968, Case No. 62 (Gyō-Tsu) of 1964, 22-4 Minshū 816.
8. Supreme Court, 24 January 1980, 34-1 Minshū 80.
9. Supreme Court, 28 April 1992, 46-4 Minshū 245.

Act 1921, it applies under the current Patent Act as well.[10] In addition, it seems to apply not only to patent cases, but also to those of utility models, designs and trade marks. Supreme Court, 23 April 1991,[11] which held that a trade mark right owner can claim and prove trade mark use in a suit against a JPO decision even though no such use had been alleged in the trial before the JPO, does not conflict with the *Knitting Machine* decision, because the issue had remained the same throughout both proceedings.[12]

In trials before the JPO and suits against JPO decisions, issues such as the novelty and inventive step have to be examined. Considering that these issues usually include highly technical matters, parties should be given the opportunity to have their case heard both before the JPO and the IP High Court, since the JPO and the IP High Court have different specialties and are expected to examine the issues individually. Concerning those highly technical matters, the JPO should be more specialised than the IP High Court, although the IP High Court has judicial research officials who support judges with specialised knowledge in patent cases. From this point of view, the decision of the Supreme Court in the *Knitting Machine* case can be justified.

However, there are some academics that have criticised the *Knitting Machine* decision and argued that in principle, there should be no limitation on the scope of suits against JPO decisions. They take the view that under the *Knitting Machine* rule, some cases will go up and down between the JPO and the IP High Court (so-called *Catch Ball* phenomenon) and that this is no longer acceptable given that the speed of innovation has dramatically accelerated. [13] In addition, there is no special limitation in general appellate proceedings, so limitation rules are different between general cases and intellectual property cases. Also in this regard, one can argue that the *Knitting Machine* rule is inconsistent.

Therefore, although the *Knitting Machine* decision has been good law for more than forty years, there still remains a possibility that the Supreme Court may change its position, or that legislature may intervene in order to satisfy the need for speedy proceedings.

---

10. T. Shishido, Tokkyo mukō no kōkoku shinpan de shinri handan sarenakatta kōchi giijutsu tono taihi ni okeru tokkyo mukō gen'in wo shinketsu torikeshi soshō ni oite shuchō suru koto no dakuhi *(Allowability of allegation of invalidation ground by comparison to a published fact which is not examined in the JPO trial against invalidation decision in lawsuit to cancel the JPO trial decision)*, at 51-52, in: Saikō Saibansho hanrei kaisetsu minji hen Shōwa 51 nendo *(Explanations of civil decisions of the Supreme Court in 1976)*, 1979, 37
11. Supreme Court, 23 April 1991, Case No. 37 (Gyō-Tsu) of 1988, 45-4 Minshū 538. German translation in GRUR Int. 1992, 927 - *Beweis der Warenzeichenbenutzung*.
12. S. Shiotsuki, Shōhyō tōroku no fushiyō torikeshi shinketsu no torikeshi soshō ni okeru tōgai tōroku shōhyō noshiyō no jijitsu no risshō (Proof of fact of use of the registered trade mark in a lawsuit to cancel to the JPO cancellation trial decision on non-use), at 262, in: Saikō Saibansho hanrei kaisetsu minji hen Heisei 3 nendo *(Explanations of the civil case decisions of the Supreme Court in 1991)*, 1994, 253
13. T. Ōbuchi, Shinketsu torikeshi soshō no shinri han'i *(Scope of patent suits against appeal/trial decisions made by the JPO)*, in: N. Nakayama et al. (eds.), Tokkyo Hanrei Hyakusen *(Hundred Selected Patent Cases)*, 4th ed. 2012, 98-99; T. Ōbuchi, Tokkyo shinketsu torikeshi soshō kihon kōzō ron *(The theory of basic structure of patent suits against appeal/trial decisions made by the JPO)*, 2003, 401-424.

4. COMPARATIVE REMARKS[14]

In the **US**, there is a strict limitation on bringing new issues in general appellate proceedings and therefore parties cannot rely on new facts before the United States Court of Appeals for the Federal Circuit (appellate cases), nor the United States District Court for the District of Columbia (civil action cases).

In **Germany**, there is no such a limitation in general appellate proceedings and therefore parties can freely bring new facts before the Federal Supreme Court (Bundesgerichtshof) (invalidation cases) and the Federal Patent Court (Bundespatentgericht) (refusal cases).

The Boards of Appeal of the **European Patent Office** are given broad powers under Art. 111 EPC. They "may either exercise any power within the competence of the department which was responsible for the decision appealed or remit the case to that department for further prosecution." This must be read in conjunction with Art. 114 EPC that allows an examination of its own motion (paragraph 1), yet disregard facts or evidence not submitted in good time (para. 2). Thereby, the Boards of Appeal have a fairly broad discretion on how to deal with an appeal. In most cases, the case as presented before the Boards is different from the one presented in first instance, be it in *ex parte* proceedings (patent application was refused by the examining division and the applicant appeals) or in *inter partes* proceedings (appeals against the decision of the opposition division): The applicant or patentee may file new claims as a reaction to the decision, be it as a main request or be it as one or more auxiliary requests filed in the event that the main request is not found allowable. Such auxiliary requests, which are not restricted in number, may be combinations of subclaims, or may add subject matter from the description. Often, they are filed for the first time in appeal. Also the opponent may file new documents. A new situation may also arise where the first instance has refused the application, or revoked the patent based on the reasons the Board on appeal finds not convincing (e.g. extension of subject matter; novelty), and the Board needs to decide whether to remit the case for further prosecution, or decide on its own motion even issues (e.g. inventive step) that the first instance did not deal with. All this is essentially an exercise of discretion, as is the question whether the Board allows new facts and issues to be introduced at the appeal stage. The Rules of Procedure of the Boards of Appeal[15] give some guidance in this respect, namely for the remission of a case to the first instance (Art. 11), admittance of late filed facts, evidence or requests (Art. 12(4)), or amendments to a party's case (Art. 13). There are limits to such discretion, though: The Board may not without the patentee's consent introduce new grounds of opposition (the introduction of new documents related to the same objection (e.g. lack of novelty) is not considered a new ground, and lack of novelty and lack of inventive step is essentially treated as the same ground of opposition)[16] or to decide to the detriment of the only appealing party (no *reformatio in peius*).[17]

14. T. Ōbuchi (above note 13), 17-45, 65-104, 409-412.
15. Rules of Procedure of the Boards of Appeal of the European Patent Office, 25 October 2007, CA/D 35/07, published in OJ EPO 2007, 536.
16. EPO Boards of Appeal, decision **G 7/91** of 5 November 1992, OJ EPO 1993, 478.
17. EPO Boards of Appeal, decision **G 2/91** of 29 November 1991, OJ EPO 1992, 206.

Case No. 27

Appeal to the High Court and Inventive Step Assessment

Tetsutaro Yukutake

Even a mistaken inventive step analysis by the JPO trial boards does not lead to a remittal of the case where the outcome is justified by a proper analysis based on the documents that were already before the trial board.

Intellectual Property High Court, 8 February 2012,
Case No. 10164 (Gyō-Ke) of 2011 – *Alarm Apparatus with Battery*

New Cosmos Electronics v. Japanese Patent Office

---

1. BACKGROUND

Who would like to invalidate a patent needs to file a request for a trial which shall include the grounds for the request. According to sec. 131(2) of the Japanese Patent Act, the ground for the request shall specify the facts on which the invalidation of the patent is based and the relationship of each fact that is required to be proven with the relevant evidence:

> Sec. 131(2)
>
> When a request for a trial for patent invalidation is filed, the facts on which the invalidation of the patent are based shall be specified in concrete terms, and the relationship of each fact that is required to be proved with the relevant evidence shall be stated in the grounds for the request as provided in item (iii) of the preceding paragraph [the object and the statement of the claim].

Questions may arise when a party brings a lawsuit to court after the JPO trial decision where the petitioner has challenged the validity of the patent based on a lack of inventive step under sec. 29(2):

> Sec. 29(2)
>
> Where, prior to the filing of the patent application, a person ordinarily skilled in the art of the invention would have been able to easily make the invention based on an invention prescribed in any of the items of the preceding paragraph [inventions that were publicly known, publicly worked, described in a distributed publication, or made publicly available through an electric telecommunication line in Japan or a foreign country, prior to the filing of the patent application], a

patent shall not be granted for such an invention notwithstanding the preceding paragraph.

When reviewing a trial decision, the scope under which the court can make a judgement when determining the inventive step requirement is not always clear. For example, is the court limited to a review of the reasoning of the trial decision and does the court have to remit the case to the JPO if the reasoning in the trial decision has been inappropriate in structure or logic? What does the court do if the invention at issue lacks inventive step based on prior art documents that are in the proceedings, yet for different reasons than those adopted by the JPO? The case at issue gives rise to the questions because the trial decision affirmed an inventive step of the patented invention, but identified differences with prior art that the court disagreed with. Still, the court came to the same conclusion based on the same prior art documents, yet for different reasons.

2. DECISION[1]

a) Facts

(1) On 16 July 2002, the defendant filed an application with the title "Alarm Apparatus with Battery" (application No. 2002-207418) and registered the patent (registration No. 3895646). The plaintiff requested an invalidation trial against the patent (Case No. 2010-800120). The Japanese Patent Office rejected the request of the plaintiff on 6 April 2011 because the patented invention was not easy to invent from the cited invention 1 and the well-known prior art demonstrated by other documents. The decision of the JPO was notified to the plaintiff on 15 April 2011. The plaintiff filed an appeal against the decision of the JPO.

(2) Claims of the patent

[Claim 1] An alarm apparatus with a battery which is powered by the battery and generates an alarm by detecting anomalies in the monitoring field characterised in that the alarm apparatus comprises:

- a voltage monitoring means which monitors whether the voltage of the battery falls under a predetermined voltage or not;
- an indicating light means which lights or blinks to announce the lowering of the voltage when the voltage of the battery is monitored;
- a checking request receiving means which receives a checking request from a user in the said monitoring field to check whether the voltage of said battery falls under the predetermined voltage; and
- a sound output means which outputs a voice message in the monitoring field that indicates to exchange the battery when the voltage of the battery monitored by the voltage monitoring means falls under the predetermined voltage and the checking request means receives the checking request.

1. Published in 2150 Hanrei Jihō 103 = 1391 Hanrei Times 298.

(3) Cited invention 1 (WO 99/08246 A1)

"A detection device which is powered by a battery and generates an alarm with detecting the presence of carbon monoxide and smoke in the atmosphere, comprising:

- a low voltage detection circuitry which checks whether the battery has a sufficient capacity to sustain operation;
- a means which sets a LOW BATTERY flag when the battery has no a sufficient capacity to sustain operation by the low voltage circuitry, and indicates this status to user;
- a test/silence button which can detect whether the battery level is low or not, when the button is pushed by user; and
- a means which turns a yellow LED on, sounds a smoke alarm pattern and subsequently turns a carbon monoxide alarm horn pattern on with simulating the carbon monoxide alarm, when low battery level is detected after pushing the test/silence button by the user."

b) Reasons

(2) Comparison between the invention at issue and the cited invention 1

In comparison with the invention at issue and the cited invention 1, the "test/silence button" corresponds to the "checking request receiving means" of the invention at issue, because the "test/silence button" is a means which receives the "checking request" from the user who is a user in the monitoring field, to check whether the voltage of the battery falls under the predetermined voltage or not.

And the "LED" of the cited invention 1 corresponds to the "indicating light means" of the invention at issue, the "means which sounds the predetermined pattern consisting of a smoke alarm pattern and a carbon monoxide alarm horn pattern" to the "sound output means" of the cited invention 1 at the point that it is the means to indicate the low battery voltage to the user.

These inventions are different in the following respects:

(i) To indicate the low battery voltage to the user and to promote the exchange of the battery by the light or the blinking of the indicating light means and by the sound when operating the checking request, the indicating light means of the invention at issue lights or blinks without waiting for the checking request, but the indicating light means of the cited invention 1 lights or blinks only after operating the checking request.

(ii) To indicate the low battery voltage to the user and to promote the exchange of the battery by the light or the blinking of the indicating light means and by the sound from the sound output means, the means to indicate a low battery voltage by sound is the sound output means which outputs the voice message with the indication to exchange the battery of the invention at issue, in contrast to the "smoke alarm pattern and carbon monoxide horn pattern" which indicates the predetermined pattern.

As mentioned above, the invention at issue promotes the exchange of the battery by the indicating light means which lights or blinks without waiting for the checking request and by the sound output means which outputs the voice message after operating the checking request and does not wait for the checking request for the indicating light means apart from the sound output means to promote the exchange of the battery. On the other hand, the indicating light means of the cited invention 1 indicates the low voltage to the user by the light or blinking after receiving a checking request, and indicates the low voltage to the user by using the smoke or carbon monoxide alarm pattern consisting of sound and light after pushing of the test/silence button by the user, and here, as mentioned above, indicating the low voltage to the user only by light, or indicating the low voltage to the user only by light before sound is not envisaged from the beginning.

(3) Inventive Step

a. As mentioned above, the invention at issue promotes the exchange of the battery by the indicating light means which lights or blinks without waiting for the checking request and by the sound output means which outputs the voice message after operating the checking request, but the indicating light means of the cited invention 1 indicates the low voltage to the user by light or blinking after receiving the checking request, and indicates the low voltage by using the smoke or carbon monoxide alarm pattern consisting of sound and light.

But there is no description about the motivation in the cited document 1 regarding the combination of the need for a user request and the mode of the low voltage indication to the user to promote the exchange of the battery, or about the providing of the low voltage indication means without waiting for the request, other than the indicating light means, to promote the exchange of the battery.

So if the well-known technology – which indicates a status change such as the low voltage by light – is applied to the cited invention 1 which indicates the low voltage to the user by the smoke or carbon monoxide alarm pattern consisting of sound and light after the pushing of the test/silence button by the user and does not plan the indication of the low voltage to the user only by light or the indication of the low voltage to the user only by light before sound from the beginning, this does not make it easy to conceive the feature of the invention at issue that the indicating light means lights or blinks.

b. Taking into account that in the cited invention 1, the indicating light means indicates the low voltage to the user after receiving the checking request, it is incorrect to hold that the feature of the invention at issue that the indicating light means act without receiving the checking request is easy to invent, unless there is a motivation that the exchange of the battery is also promoted by the lighting or blinking of the indicating light means without a checking request through the combination of the necessity of the request from the user and the mode of indication of the low voltage for the user or the providing of additional means which indicate the low voltage without waiting for the request, other than the indicating light means that act only upon the checking request.

There is no description that would provide the above-mentioned motivation, and no other basis for the presence of such motivation. Then, from the other documents, even if the combination of the necessity of the request from the user and the mode of indication of the low voltage for the user to promote the exchange of the battery, or providing the means which indicate the low voltage without waiting for the request other than the indicating light means upon such request, as in the cited invention 1, were found to be well known technology, there is no motivation to apply the well-known technology to the cited invention 1.

c. Therefore, the invention at issue is not easy to invent from the cited invention 1.

(4) The plaintiff's claim

a. The plaintiff argues that the apparatus of the invention does not comprise a means to determine the user's pre-recognition, and thus the user is not limited by the method to use.

Indeed, as mentioned above, the invention at issue is not limited by the method of use, and thus the trial decision based on such limitation includes a mistake when determining similarities and differences.

b. In addition, the trial decision found that the "checking request receiving means" in the invention at issue differs from the "test/silence button" in the cited invention 1 and identified it as a different point 2, but such identification is not based on what is stated in the claim.

c. The plaintiff argues that the phrase "... when ... and ..." merely means the AND operation, and it is incorrect in bringing the element of the timely sequence into the discussion.

In this regard, the claim defines the operation of the "indicating light means" and the "sound output means" when the detected battery voltage by the "voltage monitoring means" is lowered, but it does not define the timely sequence. The word "when" in the phrase "... when ... and ..." specifies the condition and the output condition of the voice message. Therefore, the trial decision based on the understanding that the phrase identifies the timely sequence is not appropriate.

d. The plaintiff argues that even if the invention at issue carries out a checking request on the content of the "indicating light means", the cited invention 1 also adopts the "method to indicate to user" and rechecks by the "test/silence button", so considering such steps, this is a similar point.

As stated above, the "test/silence button" of the cited invention 1 corresponds to the "checking request receiving means" of the invention at issue, and thus the different point 2 identified in the trial decisions is incorrect.

e. As described above, the trial decision includes mistakes in recognising similarities and differences between the invention at issue and the cited invention 1, and we find that the plaintiff's argument includes appropriate reasons in this respect.

However, the statement of the claim for requesting a trial for patent invalidation shall concretely specify the facts which form a basis to invalidate the patent according to sec. 131(2) of Japanese Patent Act. What should be decided when challenging a lack of inventive step under sec. 29(2) of Japanese Patent Act should be whether a person ordinarily skilled in the art of the invention would have been able to easily make the invention based on an invention prescribed in any of the items of sec. 29(1) of Japanese Patent Act (prior art). This is the same for appeals against trial decisions: the purpose of the decision should be whether the invention at issue would have been easy to make by a skilled person based on the prior art identified in the statement of the claim in the request for a trial. This way, it is possible to prevent cases from going back and forth between the court and the Patent Office, and the dispute on the validity of a patent could be solved at once. Thus, mistakes in identifying similarities and differences between the invention at issue and the cited invention should not immediately result in setting aside the trial decision if the outcome remains unaffected.

Although the trial decision in this case included mistakes in identifying the similarities and the differences between the invention at issue and the cited prior art, such mistake did not affect the result (that the invention involved an inventive step over the cited prior art), and there was no reason to set aside the decision under appeal.

3. ANALYSIS

a) The case at issue and relevant case law

Although not explicitly mentioned in the decision, the result seems to be in line with the famous decision by Supreme Court, 10 March 1976, Case No. 28 (Gyō-Tsu) of 1967 – *Knitting Machine*,[2] which held that the grounds for nullity based on a comparison with publicly known facts which have not been considered in trial proceedings cannot be invoked for an appeal against the trial decision.

The *Knitting Machine* decision is applicable until now as leading case law, but there are critics that argue that if strictly applied, a case in which a slight mistake found in the JPO decision may lead to an *a limine* remittal of the case, and a new decision of the JPO could be further appealed to the High Court, and such Catch Ball or Ping Pong game should be avoided for expeditiously resolving a case. In the case at issue, the approach to the *Knitting Machine* case was somewhat flexible because the court could affirm the conclusion of the JP although it differed in the reasoning. After all, the court decided on the same arguments and evidence provided by parties.[3] In the course of such procedure, it seems that the court is also permitted to point out similarities and differences between the invention at issue and the cited prior art that have not been argued in the trial decision provided that the piece of prior art has already been cited in the JPO trial proceedings.[4]

---

2. Case No. 26 of this book.
3. S. Shiotsuki, Shinketsu torikeshi soshō no shinri han'i to kōsokuryoku *(Scope and binding force in a lawsuit against the JPO trial decision)*, 1509 Jurist 34 (2017); S. Shiotsuki, Shinketsu torikeshi soshō ni okeru shinri han'i *(Scope in a lawsuit against the JPO trial decision)*, 64-15 Patent 120 (2011); T. Tsukahara, Shinketsu torikeshi soshō no tetsuzuki kōzō to un'ei ni tsuite *(Procedural structure and operation in a lawsuit against the JPO trial decision)*, in: N. Nakayama et al. (eds.) Chitekizaisanken hōri to teigen *(Intellectual Property Principle and Proposal)*, 2013, 599; T. Tsukahara, Shinketsu torikeshi soshō no shinri no han'i *(Scope in a lawsuit against the JPO trial decision)*, 1236 Kin'yū Shōji Hanrei 100 (2006).
4. M. Takabe, Jitsumu shōsetsu tokkyo kankei soshō *(Practice and Analysis of Patent Related Lawsuits)*, 3rd ed. 2016, 351, citing the case at issue states that even where there is such mistake in the findings of the JPO decision, if the court can correctly identify the cited invention and

The outcome of this case is rather easy to understand. The court stated that the inappropriate identification of the similarities and differences by the trial decision did not affected the final outcome of the decision: the invention at issue involves an inventive step in view of the cited invention in the trial decision because the cited document 1 is silent on the motivation regarding the combination of the need for a user request and the mode of the low voltage indication to the user to promote the exchange of the battery and so on as stated previously, which is theoretically independent from the issue of correctly identifying the similarities and differences.

And there are cases where the courts have affirmed the trial decision even when an inappropriate identification of the similarities and differences did directly affect the arguments for the inventive step analysis:

In IP High Court, 10 July 2007, Case No. 10378 (Gyō-Ke) of 2006,[5] the court affirmed the trial decision stating that the choice of the closest prior art document and the combination document among several prior art documents should be regarded as a matter of the decision-making process, and the differences in such decision-making process cannot be attributed to the differences in the reasoning. A different approach to the identification of the closest prior art and the combination document was thus no reason to set aside the decision under appeal. The court additionally stated that the differences in the passages referred to in the prior art also did not make the inventive step analysis flawed, except for exceptional cases.[6]

In IP High Court, 22 January 2018, Case No. 10055 (Gyō-Ke) of 2017,[7] the court based on the plaintiff's argument recognised an additional difference which had been overlooked by the trial decision, but still affirmed the trial decision (no inventive step) because the additional difference did not contribute to an inventive step. The reasoning can also be stretched to cases where the court bases its decisions on a different assessment of what the closest prior art document should be, and with which

---

the differences with prior art and reach the same conclusion, the JPO decision is correct in its conclusion and no remittal is necessary.

5. Published at the website of the courts <http://www.courts.go.jp/app/files/hanrei_jp/283/035283_hanrei.pdf>.
6. For further comment, there were cases where the inventive step could be considered on well-known prior art brought in the higher stage, for the addition of well-known prior art, see Case No. 19 in this volume. See also K. YAMAGUCHI, Shinketsu torikeshi soshō no shinri no han'i ni kansuru ichi kōsatsu *(An analysis on scope of lawsuit against the JPO decision)*, 58-10 AIPPI Journal of the Japanese Group (Japanese edition) 711 (2013). And, of course, there were cases where the courts found mistakes in the reasoning of the JPO decision and sent cases back to the JPO without further detailed consideration about inventive step, see, as recent examples, IP High Court, 26 December 2016, Case No. 10023 (Gyō-Ke) of 2016, the website of the courts <http://www.courts.go.jp/app/files/hanrei_jp/417/086417_hanrei.pdf>; IP High Court, 26 October 2016, Case No. 10058 (Gyō-Ke) of 2016, the website of the courts <http://www.courts.go.jp/app/files/hanrei_jp/222/086222_hanrei.pdf>; IP High Court, 18 February 2016, Case No. 10051 (Gyō-Ke) of 2015, the website of the courts <http://www.courts.go.jp/app/files/hanrei_jp/712/085712_hanrei.pdf>; IP High Court, 27 January 2016, Case No. 10066 (Gyō-Ke) of 2015, the website of the courts <http://www.courts.go.jp/app/files/hanrei_jp/633/085633_hanrei.pdf>, etc. But in these cases the JPO reversed often the conclusions (to the affirmation of inventive step) after the court's decisions, it seems that the IP High Court carefully considered whether or not mistakes in the JPO decisions leaded different conclusions as result.
7. Published at the website of the courts <http://www.courts.go.jp/app/files/hanrei_jp/403/087403_hanrei.pdf>.

document it may be combined to arrive at the claimed invention, or by referring to passages in a cited document different from those relied upon by the Trial Board.

IP High Court, 17 January 2018, Case No. 10087 (Gyō-Ke) of 2016[8] held that a new argument about similarities and differences or combinations based on the known facts handled in the JPO trial could not be considered in itself to go beyond the comparison made in the JPO trial proceedings. After all, it was not correct that new arguments could never be brought in a lawsuit against a JPO decision, as each party had sufficiently argued the point in this case, and the JPO decision was affirmed (affirmation of inventive step), including the consideration of the cited invention 2 as the closest prior art which was cited as a combination document in the JPO decision.[9]

b) Opinion of the author

It seems that in *inter partes* case, the court may not rely on new facts but may rely on new or different arguments that have not been raised during the trial when discussing whether the invention at issue involves an inventive step. Based on the facts raised by the trial decision, it would be advisable for the parties to consider every possible scenario, including ones that have not been discussed in the trial decision. A party who would like to have the trial decision overturned should not only look for mistakes in the trial decision but should also be cautious to what has not been discussed in the trial decision, yet might lead to the same result. Even the party to whom the trial decision is favourable should consider whether any correctable mistakes exist in the trial decision, because it may be possible for the court to affirm the trial decision if such mistakes would not to lead to a different outcome.

This may seem to be a great burden to the parties. However, since the court is not allowed to rely on new facts, the range of the inventive step analysis is limited. Also, as stated in the court decision, the upside is that such approach prevents cases from going back and forth between the court and the Patent Office. In this sense, allowing new or different arguments but not new facts to the court would provide a balance between the parties' burden and still allow for a timely decision.

4. COMPARATIVE REMARKS

In the system of **European** patents, similar questions to those discussed for the *Alarm Apparatus* case arise for the relationship between examination/opposition and appeal proceedings. Art. 114 EPC stipulates that the European Patent Office shall examine

8. Published at the website of the courts <http://www.courts.go.jp/app/files/hanrei_jp/424/087424_hanrei.pdf>. For commentary of the case, see T. MATSUMOTO, Shinketsu de handan sareteinai shinposei ketsujo no ronrizuke wo shinketsu torikeshi sosh de handan shita jirei *(Case where a reason of lack of inventive step which was not considered in the JPO decision was considered in the lawsuit against the JPO decision)*, 182 Chizai Prism 16 (2017).
9. On the other hand, IP High Court, 19 July 2018, Case No. 10174 (Gyō-Ke) of 2017, the website of the courts <http://www.courts.go.jp/app/files/hanrei_jp/896/087896_hanrei.pdf> stated that the situation where a combination of the cited inventions was not sufficiently argued by parties in the JPO trial and court proceedings differs from the case 17 January 2018, such argument should make a new reason for lack of inventive step, and affirmed the JPO trial decision (affirmation of inventive step) without further consideration of the combination.

the facts of its own motion and shall not be restricted by the parties' submissions, yet may disregard facts or evidence which have not been submitted in due time.[10] While this provision unrestrictedly applies to the examining phase, decisions **G 9/91**[11] and **G 10/91**[12] have clarified that opposition/appeal proceedings are essentially limited to an examination of the case as presented by the opponent. In detail:

In an appeal against the refusal of an application, the applicant/appellant is free to submit new requests even in lieu of grounds why the decision under appeal was wrong.[13] On the other hand, the Appeal Board (that is equal to a court and against whose decision there is no further legal remedy) is not limited to a review of the appealed decision, but may identify different defects in the application. The Board is thus not limited to a review of the decision, but may *ex officio* investigate whether the invention as claimed meets all requirements of patentability.[14]

In opposition-appeal proceedings (*inter partes*), the patentee as appellant is equally free to submit new requests yet with the caveat that these may be (discretionarily) refused admission by the Board if they present a fresh case or could have been submitted earlier.[15] The opponent may equally submit new evidence (e.g. prior art) within the same limits as above. New grounds of opposition may be introduced at this stage only with the patentee's permission. In effect, the Board is thus not limited to a strict review of the decision under appeal, but generally bound to decide within the limits of the parties' submissions. The Board is free to evaluate the facts in a manner different from the opposition division. Where new evidence has been filed or new claims have been submitted, it may decide to remit the case, but can equally decide the case on its own motion, Art. 111 EPC.

10. One should note that the provision does not mention arguments that accordingly can be brought at a later stage: See EPO decision **T 1914/12** of 13 June 2018: "The Boards of Appeal have no power of discretion to refuse late arguments that are based on facts already in the proceedings."
11. EPO decision **G 9/91** of 31 March 1993, OJ EPO 1993, 408.
12. EPO decision **G 10/91** of 31 March 1993, OJ EPO 1993, 420.
13. EPO decision **T 934/02** of 29 April 2004.
14. EPO decision **G 10/93**, of 30 November 1994, OJ EPO 1995, 172.
15. Rules of Procedure of the Boards of Appeal (2007), Arts. 12(4) and 13(1).

Case No. 28

Liability of the Patent Office for Mistakes, e.g. the Omission of Registering a Pledge

Shoichi Okuyama

1. **A person who is unable to obtain an effective pledge because of the negligence of an officer of the JPO can seek reparation from the State.**
2. **The reasonable amount of damages shall be determined based on the entire purport of oral arguments and the result of examination of evidence, even if it is difficult to prove the amount of real damages.**

Supreme Court, 24 January 2006, Case No. 541 (Ju) of 2005 – *Pledge*

Seishin Shinkin Bank v. State of Japan

1. BACKGROUND

Sec. 98 of the Patent Act stipulates that a pledge does not take effect unless it is registered in the Patent Register.[1] The implementing regulations require that the

1. The Patent Act contains a number of provisions on pledges. The following is a non-inclusive list of provisions that are important in forming a framework for pledges on patents.
   - Sec. 33(2): The right to obtain a patent may not be the subject of a pledge.
   - Sec. 73(1): Where a patent right is jointly owned, no joint owner may assign or establish a right of pledge on the said joint owner's own share without the consent of all the other joint owners.
   - Sec. 95: Unless otherwise agreed upon by contract, where a right of pledge is established on a patent right, exclusive license or non-exclusive license, the pledgee may not work the patented invention.
   - Sec. 96: A right of pledge on a patent right, exclusive license or non-exclusive license may be exercised against any consideration to be paid for the patent right, exclusive license or non-exclusive license or any money or goods to be received by the patentee or the exclusive licensee for the working of the patented invention; provided, however, that the pledgee have to attach the consideration, money or goods prior to the payment of money or delivery of goods.
   - Sec. 97(1): Where there is an exclusive licensee, pledgee or non-exclusive licensee as provided in sec. 35(1), 77(4) or 78(1), a patentee may waive the patent right, only where the consent of the said exclusive licensee, pledgee or non-exclusive licensee is obtained.

JPO effects registrations in its Register in the chronological order of receiving the corresponding requests.

2. DECISION[2]

a) Facts

The plaintiff-appellant in this Supreme Court case is a credit union, which is called *Shinyō Kinko* or *Shinkin* for short in Japanese, and it lent JPY 360 million (about EUR 2.8 million at the exchange rate of JPY 127 to EUR 1) to the company *Fujisen Kyōryō Doboku Kabushiki Kaisha* on 1 September 1997. The company *Fujisen* was in the business of building bridges. It was agreed that the appellant would take out a loan on a patent that the company *Fujisen* owned (patent No. 2568987 or "subject patent," which was registered on 3 October 1996). The appellant filed a request to the Japan Patent Office (JPO) to register a pledge ("subject pledge") on 2 September 1997, and the JPO accepted the request, but the registration was not made until 1 December of the same year.

On 31 August 1997, however, the company *Fujisen* transferred the subject patent to the third-party company *Isohata Kensa Kōgyō Kabuhiki Kaisha*. The company *Isohata* filed a request for registering the transfer on 12 September. The transfer was registered on 17 November 1997 in the Patent Register.

In November 1997, the company *Isohata* sold the subject patent with another patent, a pending patent application and the right to file another patent application to the company *Mitsui Bussan Kabushiki Kaisha* for JPY 400 million. The companies *Isohata* and *Mitsui Bussan* filed a request for registering the transfer and the JPO accepted it on 27 November 1997. The transfer of the two patents was registered on 23 February 1998.

In May 1998, the company *Mitsui Bussan* brought a lawsuit before the Tokyo District Court against the appellant to have the registration of the subject pledge cancelled. In July 1998, the court accepted the claim of company *Mitsui Bussan* by a decision of 24 July 1998, which became final and binding, and the registration of the subject pledge was cancelled on 8 October 1998.

The company *Mitsui Bussan*, together with companies *Fujisen* and *Isohata*, tried to commercialise the patented technology. Initially the project looked promising, but by October 2000, the company *Mitsui Bussan* gave it up. The subject patent expired in May 2001 for non-payment of the fifth annuity fee, which was due on 3 October 2000. The company *Fujisen* went bankrupt in March 1998. The company *Isohata* also went bankrupt in November 1998.

In 2000, the plaintiff-appellant brought the lawsuit before the Shizuoka District Court against the State of Japan based on sec. 1(1) of the State Liability Act asking for recovery of damages, JPY 330 million. The plaintiff argued that because an officer of the JPO did not process the registrations in the order of acceptance of the requests, the subject pledge did not take effect and it was impossible to recover the credit. The defendant did not contest the fact that an officer of the JPO was negligent, but

---

2. Published in 219 Minshū 329 = 1926 Hanre Jihō 65 = 1205 Hanrei Times 153.

argued instead that the JPO caused no damages to the plaintiff because the subject patent was economically worthless. On 17 June 2003, the Shizuoka District Court ordered the defendant to pay JPY 180 million to the plaintiff.

The defendant appealed. On 8 December 2004, the Tokyo High Court essentially reversed the original decision and found that no damages actually occurred to the plaintiff because even if the subject pledge had been registered correctly, there was no basis to believe that the plaintiff could have somehow obtained compensation from companies *Isohata* and *Mitsui Bussan*.

The plaintiff appealed before the Supreme Court.

b) Reasons

On 24 January 2006, the Supreme Court reversed and remanded the case back to the Intellectual Property High Court[3] for the determination of damages the appellant suffered, for the following reasons:

(1) Certain transactions related to patents including the establishment of a pledge do not take effects unless they are registered in the Patent Register, which the JPO manages (sec. 27(1)(i) and (ii) and sec. 98(1)(i) and (iii) of the Patent Act). Assume that a patentee X comes into agreement with a party Y to establish a pledge on X's patent for debt, and X simultaneously comes into agreement with another third party for the transfer of the same patent, and also assume the JPO accepts a request for registering the pledge before it accepts a request for registering the transfer, if the JPO registers the transfer earlier, it becomes impossible to register the pledge because the then-current owner of the patent is no longer X. The pledge does not take effect. Therefore, the Patent Registration Order requires that requested registrations shall be made in the order of acceptance of requests (sec. 37(1) of the Order). If an officer of the JPO does not follow this requirement as in the present case and Y is unable to obtain an effective pledge because of negligence of the JPO officer, Y can seek reparation from the State of Japan.

(2) If it becomes impossible to acquire a pledge on a patent due to negligence of an officer in charge at the JPO, the amount of damages incurred shall be the amount of receivables that could have been recovered by enforcing the pledge around the time when the fulfilment of the secured claim falls into arrears, unless any other special circumstances exist.

According to the facts established by the original court, the reference date should be 23 March 1998, when banks suspended business with the company *Fujisen*, and no other special circumstances can be observed. ... Thus, the proper value of the subject patent around March 1998 minus collection costs should be the amount of damages that resulted from the failure to establish the subject pledge.

(3) The proper value of a patent should be determined based on the prospect of profitability of the business that utilises the patent as of the reference date for damages determination. It is clear that, according to facts established by the original court, (α)

3. The four IP divisions of the Tokyo High Court were reorganised as the IP High Court on 1 April 2005.

around March 1996, the company *Fujisen* made the technology in the then-pending patent application public, many newspaper articles about it appeared, and many corporations showed interest in the technology, (β) the company *Isohata*, which became the owner of the subject patent, was able to sell the subject patent and rights to other inventions to the company *Mitsui Bussan* in November 1997 at JPY 400 million, (γ) the company *Mitsui Bussan* worked together with the companies *Fujisen* and *Isohata* for the promotion of the technology, (δ) in 1998, the company *Mitsui Bussan* filed a lawsuit against the plaintiff-appellant and successfully cancelled the registration of the subject pledge, which might become an obstacle to the commercialisation, by a decision of the Shizuoka District Court, (ε) the company *Mitsui Bussan* pursued the commercialisation of the technology until it decided to abandon the project and did not pay for the fifth annuity of the subject patent by October 2000.

Therefore, around March 1998, when banks suspended business with the company *Fujisen*, the subject patent had certain economic values because the patented invention was expected to generate revenues, and it should have been possible to reasonably collect receivables by enforcing the subject pledge.

(4) It is concluded that the plaintiff-appellant suffered damages due to the failure to obtain the subject pledge because of negligence of an officer in charge at the JPO. Thus, the amount of damages shall be determined. Even if it is extremely difficult to prove the amount of damages, the reasonable amount of damages shall be found based on the entire purport of oral arguments and the result of examination of evidence according to sec. 248 of the Code of Civil Procedures. Because the original court denied the existence of any damages as it was difficult, according to the court, to recognise that the appellant could have obtained any amount of compensation for the cancellation of the subject pledge assuming the subject pledge had been properly established. The original decision, therefore, shall be set aside. The case is remanded to the original court for the determination of an award of damages.

3. ANALYSIS

There was no dispute as to the negligence on the part of a JPO officer and as to the loss of a pledge that the appellant relied on for lending due to the negligence.

In its decision, the Supreme Court implicitly supports the theory that it is not possible to give retroactive effect to the registration of a pledge. The Tokyo District Court based its decision of 24 July 1998 on this theory to cancel the registration of the subject pledge made on 1 December 1997. It may have been possible to give more weight to the order of accepting requests than to dates of registration because the Patent Registration Order stipulates that registrations must be made in the order of acceptance of requests for registration and thereby give some relief to the appellant. Apparently, the Supreme Court did not accept this line of argumentation.

On the issue of damages, the IP High Court weighed on the fact that the patent at issue was eventually abandoned without making any actual profits and determined it was objectively worthless. The Supreme Court however noted that as of the effective date of determining receivables, the technology involving the invention of the patent at issue was still alive in a business sense and a prospect for profits still existed.

The present case therefore went back to the IP High Court as Case No. 10008 (Ne) of 2006. The court rendered a decision on 14 January 2009[4] and awarded in the amount of JPY 21.6 million plus interest. The lengthy analysis the court carried out can be summarised as follows: The expert opinion the court relied on arrived at an expected worth of the business covered by the patent at issue as JPY 330 million at the time the company *Fujisen* defaulted. This figure was estimated using the income, market, and cost approaches with risk evaluation. The court accepted this figure and used the general 25% rule for estimating the profit contribution of technology. The resulting figure was JPY 82.5 million. The court verified this figure from different perspectives and divided by four because four items of related rights in total were involved in this case. The court subtracted JPY 2 million as debt collection costs and added JPY 3 million for attorneys' fees.

There is a similar case that involved a delay of more than nine years in renewing a trade mark registration. Formality complications caused a reluctance on the part of the JPO to establish a new practice and resulted in a subsequent delay. The Osaka High Court ordered the State of Japan to pay JPY 0.9 million plus interest to the plaintiff.[5]

The Supreme Court decision is appropriate. The IP High Court took a retrospective approach and found the patent objectively worthless only because at the time of the court proceedings, all parties had abandoned the entire project. As the Supreme Court recognised, the patent at issue had some value and the pledge which was not properly registered also had a corresponding value when the debtor defaulted. The loss of the effective pledge, which was caused by the negligence on the part of a JPO officer, had to be compensated by the State of Japan.

4. COMPARATIVE REMARKS

a) In the **US**, sec. 261 of 35 USC provides that "[a]n interest that constitutes an assignment, grant or conveyance shall be void as against any subsequent purchaser or mortgagee for a valuable consideration, without notice, unless it is recorded in the Patent and Trademark Office within three months from its date or prior to the date of such subsequent purchase or mortgage." And there is a recording of security interest to state, based on Article 9 of the Uniform Commercial Code. Which recording is necessary for perfecting of security interest in what situation remains still a problem of case law in the US,[6] it is often recommended as practice to file both USPTO (federal) and the Secretary of the State recordings.

b) In **Germany**, according to sec. 15 Patent Act a patent as well as a patent application can be made subject to a pledge.[7] A pledge can be contractually agreed and according to sec. 29 of the Order of the German Patent and Trademark Office (GPTO) can be,

4. Published in 2030 Hanrei Jihō 93. English summary of the decision is found in 41 IIC 479 (2010).
5. Osaka High Court, 7 September 1995, Case No. 9&688 (Ne) of 1995, 21-5 AIPPI Journal of the Japanese Group (English edition) 242 – *Maruta K.K. v. State of Japan.*
6. US Court of Appeals for the Ninth Circuit, *In re Cybernetic Servs., Inc.*, 252 F.3d 1039 (9th Cir. 2001); US Court of Appeals for the Federal Circuit, *Rhone-Poulenc Agro, S.A. v. DeKalb Genetics Corp.*, 284 F.3d 1323 (Fed. Cir. 2002).
7. For details, see: H. GANTER, Patentlizenzen in der Insolvenz des Lizenzgebers (*Patent licences in case of insolvency of the patentee*), Neue Zeitschrift für Insolvenzrecht 2011, 833.

but does not have to be registered. The pledge as such does not give the beneficiary of the pledge a right to use the patent or exclude others, in particular licensees.[8] The obligation to pay annuities for the patent remains with the patentee.[9]

Claims against the State for culpable acts in relation to patents can be raised before the ordinary courts based on sec. 839 Civil Code.[10]

8. German Federal Supreme Court, 24 March 1994, GRUR 1994, 602 – *Rotationsbürstenwerkzeug*. See also BENKARD, Patentgesetz *(Commentary on German Patent Act)*, 11th ed. 2015, 692.
9. Karlsruhe High Court, 18 March 2004, GRUR-RR 2005, 68 – *Patentpfändung*.
10. German Federal Patent Court, 20 May 1988, GRUR 1989, 11 – *Amtshaftung*; German Federal Patent Court, 18 December 2012, BeckRS 2013, 02509; German Federal Patent Court, 19 May 2015, BeckRS 2014, 13356.

Case No. 29

Exclusive Rights – Offer for Sale, Manufacture, Export

Shinichiro Tanaka

---

1. The description of patent infringing products in brochures or the homepage in Japan is an "offer for sale" and shall be regarded as working of the patented invention.
2. The assembly for testing the product in Japan is a "production" of the patented invention if the assembled product falls into the patent claim and parts which are added abroad bear no relation to the patent claim.
3. The export of products by parts is a sale of the patented invention if the product is offered in Japan and produced by assembly for the purposes of testing.

Osaka District Court, 22 March 2012, Case No. 15096 (Wa) of 2009 – *Oven Heating Element*

Murata Seisakusho v. OPCC

---

1. BACKGROUND

a) Exclusive right to work the patented invention

Under the Patent Act, a patentee shall have the exclusive right to work the patented invention. Namely, sec. 68 provides as follows:

> "A patentee shall have the exclusive right to commercially work the patented invention; provided, however, that where an exclusive license regarding the patent right is granted to a licensee, this shall not apply to the extent that: the exclusive licensee is licensed to exclusively work the patented invention."

And current sec. 2(3)[1] specifies:

> "Working" of an invention in this Act means the following acts:
>
> (i) in the case of an invention of a product (including a computer program, etc., the same shall apply hereinafter), producing, using, sale, etc. (sale

1. In this translation, "sale" is used for the Japanese word "*jōto.*" But it should be noted that the original Japanese word includes also a transfer without consideration, e.g. as a free gift.

and leasing and, in the case where the product is a computer program, etc., including providing through an electric telecommunication line, the same shall apply hereinafter), exporting or importing, or offering for sale, etc.(including displaying for the purpose of sale, etc., the same shall apply hereinafter) thereof;

(ii) in the case of an invention of a process, the use thereof; and

(iii) in the case of an invention of a process for producing a product, in addition to the action as provided in the preceding item, acts of using, sale, etc., exporting or importing, or offering for sale, etc. the product produced by the process.

b) Territorial limitation

Japanese patent law is effective only in the territory of Japan.[2]

In this connection, for example the Tokyo District Court decision of 20 September 2001[3] held that with respect to the patented invention for a process of producing a product, when one step of the patented process is made outside Japan, a patent infringement cannot be affirmed considering that a Japanese patent right is only effective in the territory of Japan.

c) Issue of this case

The major issues in this case were 1) under what conditions an *"offer for sale"* can be affirmed, and 2) whether and under what conditions a " sale etc. " can be interpreted as a direct or indirect patent infringement in case where all parts of the patented product are exported for assembly outside Japan.

2. DECISION[4]

a) Facts

(1) The plaintiff's patent

a. The plaintiff (*Murata-Seisakusho K.K.*) is the owner of patent No. 319626 that expired on 20 November 2011 and bears the title "Oven Heating Element and Oven for Heat Treatment", applied for on 20 November 1991 and registered on 8 June 2001. The patent claim reads as follows: "Oven for heat treatment in which the oven that contains one side wall and a bottom that closes off the oven form a space for heat treatment whereby several heat elements that are vertically inserted and located parallel to each other contain heating points, and the heat treatment oven is characterised in that the heat heating points are vertically spaced in different locations."

---

2. Supreme Court, decision of 26 September 2002, Minshū Vol. 56, 1251 – *Card Reader*, this volume Case No. 45.
3. Tokyo District Court, Case No. 20503 (Wa) of 2000, 1094 Hanrei Times 245.
4. Published (in a different translation) at the website of the courts <http://www.courts.go.jp/app/files/hanrei_jp/159/082159_hanrei.pdf>. German translation in GRUR Int. 2014, 567.

...

(2) The defendant's acts

a. The defendant (*OPPC K.K.*) between November 2003 and October 2005 has sold 32 devices (ovens). One of these devices was sold to a Japanese enterprise, the others went abroad. Among these, three went to Taiwan and 28 to Korea ...

b) Reasons

3. As to the issue No. 3 (whether the sale abroad can be considered use of the patented invention)

(1) Based on all the evidence and arguments, we can ascertain the following facts in regard of the sales activities for the ovens to the foreign enterprises *Samsung* (Korea) and *Darfon* (Taiwan):

a. The defendants have prepared sales brochures showing the specification and overview of performance data of the same lifting type of the atmospheric heating oven as the defendant's device. On their homepage, the lifting type of the atmospheric heating oven for ceramic condensers were mentioned as their goods with the specification and overview of performance data thereof. In November 2004, their homepage reported that they have actually sold the lifting type of atmospheric heating ovens.

b. The defendants have concluded contracts for sale of the defendant's devices with the customers as mentioned in the list. The transaction with *Samsung* (Korea) was based on the contract between the defendant and a Japanese corporation, *Samsung K.K.* At the time when the contracts were concluded, the defendant's devices did not exist as actual functioning ovens and were planned to be manufactured according to the specifications in the contract (order manufacture).

c. After the conclusion of the contracts with the customers, based on the specification agreed thereby the defendant had the company *Nakamura-Seisakusho* manufacture the oven bodies, lifters etc. in a manufacturing plant in *Ritto*, bought the heating elements from the company *Tokai-Konetsu-Kogyo*, the control from by the company *Kogyo Electrics* to be supplied to the plant in *Ritto*.

Thereafter, the defendant had the devices provisionally assembled, wired and inspected for function test by the company *Nakamura-Seisakusho*. Further, with respect to the provisionally wired devises, test baking steps (operation to remove the binder of heat insulating material by a 700°C air injection, which is necessary for stabilising before actual operation) were sometimes carried out. Every now and then, test baking was carried out after the machines had been supplied to the customers.

Such provisional assembly works in the plant were supervised by the defendant's staff to check whether there were any defective parts.

d. The defendant's devices provisionally assembled in the *Nakamura-Seisakusho* plant in *Ritto* were then disassembled again, packed and upon instructions of the defendant directly exported from the factory. The defendant's devices were re-assembled outside Japan and put into operation. In this process, sometimes new parts prepared outside Japan were added, but such added parts are not related to the features of the patented invention.

(2) Evaluation

a. According to the facts ascertained above, the defendants engaged in acts for the sale of lifting type atmospheric heating ovens by way of brochures or their homepage. In other words, the defendant's devices, namely lifting type atmospheric heating ovens were offered for sale in Japan according to the Patent Act sec. 2(3)(i).

b. Furthermore, after preparing the parts through manufacture or purchase, the defendant had provisionally assembled the defendant's devices, carried out operation tests and further provisionally assembled some devices for baking processes to be tested in the Nakamura-Seisakusho factory. Thereafter, the devices were disassembled, packaged and exported. At reassembly outside Japan, sometimes new parts prepared outside Japan were added, but such added parts are not related to the features of the patented invention. Therefore, it can be ascertained that by the provisional assembly, the defendant's devices were manufactured to an extent that they fulfilled the technical features of the patented invention, although the devices were not yet complete. In this sense, the defendant also engaged in "producing", which means a working of the patented invention according to the Patent Act sec. 2(3)(i).

...

d. After the provisional assembly and the testing of the individual parts, the defendant's devices were disassembled, packaged and exported. But we understand that the provisionally assembled devices were disassembled to parts only for the reason of transportation, because they were not so big to transport even in the state of provisional assembly.

e. Therefore, analysing all of the above, even though it is considered that the defendant's devises were disassembled to parts before export, the defendant's series of acts in Japan related to the sale of the devices cannot be interpreted as anything else but a "sale etc.", in other words a working of the patented invention according to the Patent Act sec. 2(3)(i).

3. ANALYSIS

This decision was issued before the amendment of the patent law of 2016, by which "export" is provided as one of "working" in Sec. 2(3)(i) of the Patent Act. Therefore, this decision considers "export" as one kind of "sale".

a) Offer for sale etc.

An "offer for sale etc." in Patent Act sec. 2(3)(i) is construed as an offer for concrete products with the purpose of sale etc. This decision confirmed that the promotion and advertising of the patented products; i.e. the lifting type atmospheric heating ovens by the distribution of brochures or on a Japanese homepage is an offer for sales etc. as provided in the Patent Act sec. 2(3)(i). Territoriality was no a particular issue, although there is some discussion on this point. The prevailing opinion considers that a sale etc. needs to be made in Japan.[5] Namely, if a "sale etc." is made outside Japan, a Japanese patent with effect only in Japan, cannot be infringed. The same is true for the act of "offering". should be in Japan or not. If a "sale etc." is made in Japan and therefore considered infringing, the author is of the opinion that also an "offer for sale etc." under Patent Act sec. 2(3)(i) has taken place.[6]

b) Export in a disassembled state

aa) This is the first and up to now only decision of a Japanese court that confirms a patent infringement by way of "export" of patented products in a state of parts for assembly outside Japan. But, as mentioned above, this decision confirmed the following: First, before export, the defendant's devices, lifting type atmospheric heating ovens covered by the patented invention were provisionally assembled, which is considered as an act of "production" according to the Patent Act sec. 2(3)(i). Second, even though it is considered that the defendant's devices were disassembled before export, the defendant's series of acts in Japan related to the sale of the devices and thereby to the use of the patented invention according to the Patent Act sec. 2(3)(i). However, it is not so clear whether Japanese courts would confirm a patent infringement when parts in the state easy to assemble are exported for knockdown production outside Japan without a prior provisional assembly in Japan.

The author is of the opinion that export for knockdown production even without such limitation should be considered as working of the patented invention, because, although the final products covered by the patented invention are not assembled in Japan, the patentee's right to exclude others from working the patented invention has already compromised in case of a knockdown production, where all parts are exported for easy assembly outside Japan.[7]

bb) Indirect Infringement

With respect to the export of parts for knockdown production, an indirect infringement has been also discussed. But Japanese courts have not confirmed any indirect infringement of Japanese a patent right when in any jurisdiction outside Japan a product of patented invention is produced or the process of the patented invention is used in that the patented invention is not worked in Japan.[8]

---

5. Judge Takabe's comment in Shogai-Jiken no Arubeki kaiketsu hōhō (Ideal Solution of International Case) MAKIKO TAKABE AND SEIJI OHNO, Patent Vol. 65, No. 3.
6. This is not a problem of the territorial limitation of the Japanese patent right.
7. See commentaries on this case: N. KOIZUMI, Kaigai deno nokkudaun seisan to tokkyo ken shingai *(Knockdown production in oversea and the patent right infringement)*, 1444 Jurist 6 (2012); K. TSUJIMURA, Nokkudaun hōshiki ni yoru bukken no yushutsu to chokusetsu shingai/kansetsu shingai *(Export of product of knockdown type and direct/indirect infringement)*, 62-11 Chizai Kanri 1599 (2012); T. IKUTA/S. MORIMOTO, Nokkudaun seisan ni tsuite tokkyo ken no chokusetsu shingai wo mitometa jirei *(Case where the direct infringement of the patent right is acknowledged to the knockdown prodcution)*, 109-6 Hatsumei 39 (2012); S. CHAEN, Gaikoku ni okeru nokkudaun seisan no tameno buhin no kyōkyū to tokkyo ken shingai *(Supply of parts for the knockdown production in abroad and the patent right infringement)*, 61 L&T 27 (2013).
8. Osaka District Court, 24 October 2000, Case No. 12109 (Wa) of 1996, 1081 Hanrei Times 146; Tokyo District Court, 27 February 2007, 1253 Hanrei Times 241.

4. COMPARATIVE REMARKS

a) In the **US**, sec. 271(f) of 35 USC clearly provides that the export of parts of a patented product may infringe the patent either directly or indirectly:

(1) Whoever without authority supplies or causes to be supplied in or from the United States all or a substantial portion of the components of a patented invention, where such components are uncombined in whole or in part, in such manner as to actively induce the combination of such components outside of the United States in a manner that would infringe the patent if such combination occurred within the United States, shall be liable as an infringer.

(2) Whoever without authority supplies or causes to be supplied in or from the United States any component of a patented invention that is especially made or especially adapted for use in the invention and not a staple article or commodity of commerce suitable for substantial noninfringing use, where such component is uncombined in whole or in part, knowing that such component is so made or adapted and intending that such component will be combined outside of the United States in a manner that would infringe the patent if such combination occurred within the United States, shall be liable as an infringer.

This provision of the US Patent Act was introduced by the law amendment of 1984 to overturn the *Deepsouth* decision of the US Supreme Court, where it was held that the production of easily combinable parts and their export did not constitute the infringement of the patent right.[9]

There are many cases that have applied this provision, including Supreme Court cases: In the *Microsoft v. AT&T* case of 2007, the US Supreme Court held that a tangible copy of software (not abstract software) could qualify as a "component", but the sending of a master copy which should be copied by the foreign recipient was not the supply of "components" from the US. In the *Life Technologies v. Promega* case of 2017, it was held that the sale of a single component in a foreign market did not constitute a "substantial portion" of the component, and in the *WesternGeco v. ION Geophysical* case of 2018, it was held that the award for lost profits was permissible also for infringing acts under sec. 271(f).[10]

b) In **Germany**, a domestic relation of the infringing act is necessary for patent infringement in light of the principle of territoriality. Nevertheless, the production and export of parts easy to assemble into the patented invention is a type of direct patent infringement.[11] There is also the possibility of indirect infringement by the

---

9. US Supreme Court, *Deepsouth Packing Co., Inc. v. Laitram Corp.*, 406 U.S. 518 (1972).
10. US Supreme Court, *Microsoft Corp. v. AT&T Corp.*, 550 U.S. 437 (2007); US Supreme Court, *Life Technologies Corp. v. Promega Corp.*, 580 U.S. ___ (2017); US Supreme Court, *WesternGeco LLC v. ION Geophysical Corp.*, 585 U.S. ___ (2018). For the applicability of sec. 271(f) to method patents, after diverse case, the Federal Circuit decided in 2009 en banc that this provision did not cover method patents: US CAFC, *Cardiac Pacemakers, Inc. v. St. Jude Medical, Inc.*, 576 F.3d 1348 (Fed. Cir. 2009).
11. E.g., German Imperial Supreme Court, 18 September 1897, GRUR 1901, 152 – *exzentrische Klauen*; German Imperial Supreme Court, 30 August 1935, GRUR 1936, 236 – *Stabeisenbiegevorrichtung*; Düsseldorf District Court, 5 February 2004, InstGE 4, 90 – *Infrarot-Messgerät*; Düsseldorf District Court, 6 April 2006, InstGE 6, 130 – *Diffusor*. See also KRASSER/ANN, Patentrecht *(Patent Law)*, 8th ed. 2016, 793; BENKARD, Patentgesetz *(Commentary to the German Patent Act)*, 11th ed.

export of the essential part of the patented invention, if the product is subsequently meant to be imported again to Germany.[12]

As to the question whether an offer for a sale abroad should be considered a domestic patent infringement, such a case was decided in Italy. Here, the defendants from their place of business in Milan had brokered contracts between extra-European makers and extra-European purchasers over products patented in Italy without such products ever being imported to Italy. The court affirmed an infringement, as the act was clearly an "offer for sale" of patented products.[13] Also other comparable cases have been reported.[14] The Italian Supreme Court reasoned that it was the purpose of the Patent Act's provisions "to prevent third parties from all commercial activities related to the patent that may yield an economic or commercial advantage". Also a German academic, *Gerhard Schricker*, has justified this approach as follows:

> "The individual acts of infringement are independent of each other ... The offer for sale is not comprised in the act of first commercial marketing as a mere preparatory act ... In other words, it is irrelevant if the offer for sale implies or prepares an infringing act of marketing or that it relates to a product whose manufacture already qualifies as an infringement. Even the manufacture takes place abroad where no patent right exists, the domestic offer qualifies as an infringement ... In view of the independence of the act of offering for sale, the latter must qualify as an act of infringement even if the supply shall only take place after the patent has expired, as long as the offer as such has been made during the life span of the patent."[15]

One may question, however, whether an offer for sale should be considered infringing when related to products whose actual sale would not infringe. In other words, whether an offer for sale is only infringing if it is an act to prepare an infringing sale.

2015, 458, 478; BUSSE/KEUSCHRIJVER Patentgesetz *(Commentary to the German Patent Act)*, 8th ed. 2016, 389.

12. German Federal Supreme Court, 30 January 2007 – *Funkuhr II*.
13. Italian Supreme Court, 3 April 2003, German translation in GRUR Int. 2003, 876 – *Omeprazole*.
14. Appeal Court Stuttgart, 13 October 1997, GRUR Int. 1997, 806 – *Fender Musikinstrumente* (trade mark law); *Halmar Robicon Group v. Toshiba*, US District Court W D Pennsylvania, 17 November 1999, 53 USPQ 2d 1501 (patent law). In the US, there are also cases to the contrary, however: Listed by P. SIGNORE/P. MICHON, The Impact of US Patents on International Business, Managing IP November 2004, 28, 29.
15. G. SCHRICKER, Anbieten als Verletzungstatbestand im Patent- und Urheberrecht (Offering for sale as an infringing act under patent and copyright law), GRUR Int. 2004, 786.

Case No. 30

Direct and Indirect Infringement

Takuya Iizuka

For a pharmaceutical which is patented as a combination of two ingredients for the treatment of diabetes, prescribing or administering the ingredients individually for patients does not mean producing a combination pharmaceutical that falls within the scope of the patent. Therefore, supply of one of these medicines cannot generally be considered as an act of indirect infringement.

Osaka District Court, 27 September 2012, Case Nos. 7576&7578 (Wa) of 2011 – *Combination Medicine for Diabetes Treatment*

Takeda Pharmaceutical v. Sawai Pharmaceutical et al.

---

1. BACKGROUND

a) Overview and history of the indirect infringement provisions of the Japanese Patent Act

Under the Japanese Patent Act, an act of producing, importing, or assigning, etc. a product, even if said product itself does not fulfil the configuration elements of a patented invention through assignment, etc., which falls under any of the type of acts provided in sec. 101 of the Patent Act is considered an act of indirect infringement of a patent. A person who has conducted any of said acts as a business will be liable for injunctive relief or damages.

Acts of indirect infringement and their requirements provided in each item of sec. 101 are in particular:

(i) Any article to be used *exclusively* for producing of the patented product;
(ii) Any article (excluding those widely and generally distributed within Japan) to be used for producing the patented product and indispensable for the solution of the problem by the said invention knowing that said invention is a patented invention and said article is used for the working of the invention;

Among these types of indirect infringement, type (i) is called exclusive article type indirect infringement. This is a type of indirect infringement that has been on the books since the current Patent Act was enacted in 1959.[1]

The 2003 amendment added item (ii) referred to as "multi-functional article type indirect infringement" which recognised indirect infringement in regard of articles with other, non-infringing uses on certain conditions.

b) Multi-functional article type indirect infringement provisions

The decision commented on is a case where the court was asked to decide whether or not there was a multi-functional article type indirect infringement in connection with a patented invention of a product (a combined pharmaceutical invention in this case) for item (ii) of the types of acts of indirect infringement.

The article that constitutes an act of indirect infringement of item (ii) is any "article to be used for producing" a product belonging to the invention. Different from the exclusive article type indirect infringement of item (i), there is no need for the article to be have no other use than producing the invention.

However, it is required that said article must be "indispensable for the solution of the problem by said invention" and that must not be an article "widely and generally distributed within Japan".

Further, in order for indirect infringement in item (ii) to be established, it is required that, as a subjective requirement of a person who produces, assigns or imports said multi-functional article or a person who offers an assignment, etc. of said article to have knowledge that "the said invention is a patented invention" and that "the said article is used for the working of the invention".

The articles covered by item (ii) include articles that have uses unrelated to patent infringement, and their distribution can thus only be enjoined when supplied for the purposes of patent infringement. Additional safeguards therefore had to be put in place that are however vaguely worded and not easy to interpret.

1. The traditional interpretation of the meaning of "used exclusively", requires that there is no use that is considered under social norms to be economical, commercial, or practical (Tokyo District Court, 25 February 1981, Case No. 9647 (Wa) of 1975, 1007 Hanrei Jihō 72 – *Exchange Lens for Camera*). However, recent court decisions show a broader interpretation of this requirement according to which a product can be regarded as "used exclusively" even if other ways of use exist that do not implement the invention. These decisions only require that continuing to use the product only for the non-infringing use is impractical: Osaka District Court, 24 October 2000, Case No. 12109 (Wa) of 1996, 1081 Hanrei Times 241 – *Breadmaking Machine and Method*, Intellectual Property High Court, 23 June 2011, Case No. 10089 (Ne) of 2010, 2131 Hanrei Jihō 109 – *Device and Method for Food Wrapping and Forming.*

2. DECISION[2]

a) Facts

The plaintiff owns two patents A and B for a combination of pioglitazone, a publicly known medicine for diabetes, and other existing medicines for diabetes, namely "medicine for the prevention/medical treatment of diabetes or diabetic complications, made by a combination" of "pioglitazone or its pharmacologically allowable salt" and other medicines for diabetes (α-glucosidase inhibitor or biguanide), registration Nos. 3148973 and 3973280. After expiry of the plaintiff's (unrelated) patent for pioglitazone alone ("expired patent"), the defendant obtained the approval of the Ministry of Health, Labour and Welfare and now plans to produce and sell pioglitazone medicine which fall into the scope of the expired patent but are not meant to be combined with another active agent (the complementary medicine at issue), as would be the case for patents A and B. The plaintiff claims injunctive relief and damages, etc. against the defendant.

The plaintiff claims that the meaning of "producing" of "medicine made by a combination" includes the act of combining separate preparations of active agents for administering them to the same patient when such active agents were prepared separately.

The defendants argued that the meaning of "medicine" "made by combination" was a combination of active ingredients, which typically meant a combination drug, and that even if said medicine contained separately prepared medicines, this merely referred to a "kit for a package of a fixed prescription which could be deemed equal to a combination drug". It did not include a preparation that had been formulated separately and was subsequently combined for the administration to the same patient.

Further, the defendants argued that pioglitazone was "widely and generally distributed within Japan" and further not an article "indispensable for the solution of the problem by the said invention".

b) Reasons

We consider that there is no indirect infringement under sec. 101 (ii) Patent Act because the medicine of the plaintiff are not, "... [a] article ... to be used for producing said product". For the same reason, direct infringement by the defendant's conduct must be denied. And the patents at issue are all to be invalidated through an invalidation trial.

The detailed reasons are as follows.

1. Whether the medicine of the defendant is, "where a patent has been granted for an invention of a product, ... [a] article ... to be used for the producing of the said product."

The medicine of the defendant is not "... [a] article ... to be used for the producing said product" for the following reasons.

2. Published in 2188 Hanrei Jihō 108 = 1398 Hanrei Times 326 = 38 AIPPI Journal of the Japanese Group (English edition), 260 (2013).

...

In which category of invention the invention at issue falls should be decided by the description of the claim attached to the application (see Supreme Court, 16 July 1999, Case No. 604 (O) of 1998, 53-6 Minshū 957).

...

(b) In consideration of the ordinary meaning of "producing of the said product", "producing of said product" should mean the new making of a product which falls in the technical scope of the patent, and more concretely, the new making of "a product which fulfills all configuration elements of the invention" from "a material which does not fulfill the configuration elements of the invention".

...

(c) The purpose of sec. 101 of the Patent Act is to extend the scope of patent infringement, limited to the producing, assigning, etc. of articles which are highly likely to induce the infringement (working) of the patent, with a view to give effect to the provision, and within a range that is not inadequate considering the effect of the patent.

In addition and taking into account that an indirect patent infringement under sec. 101 of the Patent Act is also a punishable offence (secs. 196bis and 201 Patent Act), an interpretation that renders the extension of the patented scope uncertain should be avoided. Also in the case of indirect infringement, one should consider not to inappropriately extend the effect of the patent and to avoid creating a chilling effect on lawful economic activities ... Under sec. 101 (ii), indirect infringement can be affirmed for the making of articles which are used for "producing said product" within the scope of the patent, but here it is clear that "producing said product" means "producing" as "working of the invention" defined in sec. 2 (3).

...

(2) Considerations in this case

... The patents at issue are inventions related to a medicine, i.e. "product inventions". This is not in dispute between the parties.

Here, "combination" means, as in general, "assembling two or more things", "make" means "emerge with a new form that does not exist before" or "change to another thing/state". So "medicine" "made by combination" is interpreted, in general, to mean a "medicine which is newly made by assembling two or more active agents".

...

There is no dispute between the parties that the products of the defendant are by themselves effective medicines that are not at all meant to be arranged in some way, or used (prescribed, taken) together with other medicine for the prevention/ medical treatment of diabetes or diabetic complications.

Therefore, the defendant's products are not ... "articles which are used for producing said product".

(b) Whether the combination of medicines by prescription of a doctor means "producing said product"

The plaintiff argued that ... the complementary medicine at issue by prescription of a doctor should be interpreted as "producing of the said product" according to the patent.

...

As under above a., "medicine" "made by combination" is interpreted to mean a "medicine which is newly made by assembling two or more active agents". And it cannot be said that a new "product" is newly made by a combination of medicines by prescription.

An invention whose content (technical scope) is the mere combination of two or more medicines should not be the "invention of a product", but rather the "invention of a method" as such ...

Choosing or prescribing medicines is also a medical treatment (sec. 22 Medical Doctor Act), and such conduct itself should not be patentable.

Sec. 69(3) Patent Act provides that a "patent right for the invention of a medicine (refers to a product used for the diagnosis, therapy, treatment or prevention of human diseases, hereinafter the same shall apply in this paragraph) to be manufactured by mixing two or more medicines or for the invention of a process to manufacture a medicine by mixing two or more medicines shall not be effective against the act of preparation of a medicine as is written in a prescription from a physician or a dentist and the medicine prepared as is written in a prescription from a physician or a dentist." This provision should have the same purpose.

Thus, if the technical scope of the patented invention were a combination (combination medicine) using "pioglitazone or the pharmacologically allowable salt" and the complementary medicine at issue, the object of the patent should be a medical treatment itself, and such technical scope of a patent is unpatentable as such under secs. 29(1) and 69(3) Patent Act.

Therefore, the combination prescription by a doctor of "pioglitazone or the pharmacologically allowable salt" and the complementary medicine at issue cannot be the "producing of the said product".

(c) Whether the preparation of medicines by a pharmacist means "producing of the said product"

The plaintiff argues that the sale of the defendant's product in combination with the complementary medicine at issue by a pharmacist means "producing said product". But a pharmacist following the prescription of a doctor to the patient only hands over the two medicines separately, that is, the defendant's product and the complementary medicine at issue. Even if there was some "preparation" of two or more medicines (such as packaging both in one bag), it is difficult to say that this conduct is the "combination (or combined)" of medicines ... [Rather], it is necessary to prepare the ingredient material in some way, but the pharmacist does not prepare the products and the complementary medicine at all.

(d) Whether the combination taken by the patient is a "producing of the said product"

The plaintiff argues that the "product" of the patented invention, i.e. the "medicine" "made by combination", is produced in the human body when a patient takes the product of the defendant and the complementary medicine at issue.

But, as under above a., a "medicine" "made by combination" is interpreted to mean a "medicine which is newly made by assembling two or more active agents". And it cannot be said that a newly assembled medicine, as a concrete, tangible object, is newly created in the body only by taking the products of the defendant and the complementary medicine at issue.

...

(3) Summary

From the above considerations, "producing said product" of the patented invention at issue is not realised by the use of the products of the defendant, and the products of the defendant are not "article[s] to be used for producing said product[s]" of the patented invention.

2. Whether the defendant directly infringes the patents

(1) The plaintiff argues that the defendant steers the conduct of doctors, pharmacists or patients, thereby "producing said product" of the patented invention.

...

From the outset, a direct infringement occurs only in the "working" of the patented invention, and there is no room to interpret instigation as a direct infringement, apart from cases in which the instigator himself is assessed to be the "subject" of the "working".

3. ANALYSIS

a) Tokyo District Court decision[3]

In order to evaluate the Osaka District Court decision of this case, we must look at it together the decision of the Tokyo District Court which was argued about the same time and decided slightly later than the decision.

In the Tokyo case, the main issues were the same as in the Osaka litigation, and so was the result.

The main issues were as follows:

(i) whether "medicine comprised of a combination" includes a combination of combined agents prescribed by a doctor or prepared by a pharmacist, etc., or a medicine administered at the same time or at a different time to a patient;
(ii) whether a combination of medicines or taking a combination of medicines is a production of a product of the invention at issue;
(iii) whether pioglitazone, a publicly known medicine, is an article "indispensable for the solution of the problem by said invention"; and
(iv) whether pioglitazone is an article widely and generally distributed within Japan.

However, the Tokyo District Court's reasons for dismissing the case for indirect infringement were different from those of the Osaka District Court.

The Tokyo District Court upheld the defendant's argument on issue iii), instead of issue ii)[4] and interpreted the meaning of "indispensable for the solution of the problem by said invention" in sec. 101 (ii) of the Patent Act as follows:

3. Tokyo District Court, 28 February 2013, Case Nos. 9435 & 19436 (Wa) of 2011 – *Pioglitazone*, the website of the courts <http://www.courts.go.jp/app/files/hanrei_jp/042/083042_hanrei.pdf>.
4. The Tokyo District Court did not decide on issues i), ii) and iv).

An article "indispensable for the solution of the problem by said invention" is, an article that, by its use, solves the problem of said invention for the first time, in other words, it should be understood that with respect to a characteristic technological method not available in prior art said invention has disclosed a method to solve a problem of prior art. The article must thereby directly provide a unique composition or ingredient which characterises said method ... Therefore, even if said product is *a component or an ingredient, etc., written in the scope of claims, if the product does not directly form a characteristic technological method which said invention has newly disclosed, such product is not an article that is "indispensable for the solution of the problem by said invention".*[5]

Based on this interpretation, the court analysed the description of the scope of claims of the inventions at issue and decided that what the patents at issue newly disclosed as a method to solve the problem of prior art for single uses of individual medicinal drugs was *a certain combination* of pioglitazone and the complementary medicines at issue, and because pioglitazone and the complementary medicines at issue, in themselves, already existed before the priority date of the patent at issue and were products being used for type 2 diabetes, the inventions at issue were not inventions that newly disclosed a composition or ingredients, etc. of pioglitazone and the complementary medicine at issue in themselves.[6]

The court further mentioned the following:

> "In an invention related to a new combination of existing components, if it is interpreted that said existing components that are used not only for combinations related to said invention but also for use as single drugs or for use in existing combinations are considered articles "indispensable for the solution of the problem by said invention", then such interpretation will result in inappropriately extending the effect of the patent related to said invention. In an invention of a patented product related to such combination, the existing components in themselves are merely components of conventional necessity, irrespective of the problems which said invention seeks to solve, and unless there are special circumstances, such as the existing components are produced and sold, etc. for said invention, it is reasonable to understand that the existing components

---

5. This approach essentially identifies the invention's contribution to the prior art and regards as indispensable only elements that embody the advance over prior art. This approach has become mainstream in a number of major jurisdictions: Dutch Supreme Court, 31 October 2003, Blatt for Industriele Ejgendom 2004, 285 – *Coffee Pads* (supply of state-of-the art coffee pads for patented machines where the coffee pad was an element of the claim, yet the inventive contribution concerned the brewing chamber. German Federal Supreme Court, 24 October 2017, Case No. X ZR 55/16 – *Trommeleinheit* (supply of parts of a patented assembly only considered infringing when the effect of the invention is "particularly manifested in the replaced parts"). Even stricter US Supreme Court, *Mercoid Corp. v. MidContent Invest.*, 320 US 661 (1944): "the owner of a patent may not employ it to secure a limited monopoly on an unpatented material used in applying the invention. "
6. A similar issue arose in the decision of the UK House of Lords, 26 November 1995, *Merrel Dow Pharmaceuticals v. H.N. Norton*. Here, the defendant had supplied an off-patent composition that in the human body metabolised into a substance the plaintiff had patented. While the patent was held invalid for inevitable disclosure, also infringement was denied because the defendant had done nothing more than manufacture and sell a composition that was free for all to use.

do not fall under "article indispensable for the solution of the problem by said invention" [7] [8]

Then, the court discussed whether or not "special circumstances" existed for the facts at issue, and because the attached documents for the preparations of the defendants did not recommend a combined dosage with the complementary medicine at issue, or that the preparations of the defendants should be used for a combination with the complementary medicines at issue, the court decided that there were no "special circumstances" to affirm the claim.

b) Evaluation of the Osaka and Tokyo cases

The Osaka and Tokyo district court decisions were the first cases to decide whether or not there was indirect infringement concerning a combined pharmaceutical invention.[9]

As mentioned in the reasoning of the Osaka District Court decision, medical methods are not patentable under sec. 29(1) Patent Act, which is different from the situation in the United States, see Case No. 12 in this book.

With a similar intention, sec. 69(3) denies infringement to an act of preparing a medicine in accordance with a doctor's prescription or a prepared medicine.

Against this background, it is difficult to adopt an interpretation that might result in a de facto prohibition of a medical treatment by a doctor or an act of preparing a medicine, for both of which patent eligibility is denied.

In addition, it is hard to see why an already expired medical patent for treating diabetes should be revived through the backdoor of indirect infringement.

The conclusion reached by the district court in Osaka therefore looks reasonable.

Still, one should discuss whether indirect infringement should be denied based on the concept of producing (Osaka District Court), or an interpretation of

---

7. Tokyo District Court, 23 April 2004, Case No. 6035 (Wa) of 2002, 1892 Hanrei Jihō 89 – *Tool for Plating Printed Circuit Board* and Osaka District Court, 21 February 2013, Case No. 10819 (Wa) of 2008, 2205 Hanrei Jihō 94 – *Hopper for Mixing Machine for Particles* showed a similar view with respect to the meaning of "indispensable for the solution of the problem". R. MIMURA, Hisen'yōhingata kansetsushingaihin no mondaiten (*Issues on Non-Exclusive Article Type Indirect Infringement (Patent Act, Secs. 101(ii) and (v))*), 19 Chitekizaisanhō Seisakugaku Kenkyū 85 (2008) discusses the issue with a similar view.
8. *Yoshiyuki Tamura* opposes the above view and discusses that if a part is indispensable for implementing a patented invention, then this part is "indispensable for the solution of the problem". Y. TAMURA, Takinōgata kansetsushingai seido ni yoru honshitsuteki bubun no hogo no tekihi – kintōron tono seigōsei (*Application or No Application of the Protection of an Essential Part of an Invention by Multi-functional Article Type Indirect Infringement – Consistency with the Doctrine of Equivalents*), 15 Chitekizaisanhō Seisakugaku Kenkyū 209 (2007). *Tamura*'s opinion is problematic, as can be seen from the German case Düsseldorf High Court, 17 November 2005, GRUR-RR, 2006, 39 – *Kaffee-Filterpads* where the court held that to the extent that the coffee pad was a feature of the apparatus claim for a coffee machine, each use of a coffee pad amounted to an act of infringement, and the supply of such pads, although state of the art, amounted to an indirect infringement.
9. Patentability of combined medicine patent was affirmed by an amendment of Patent Examination Guidelines in April 2005.

"indispensable for the solution of the problem" (Tokyo District Court), or on other reasons (such as being an article widely and generally distributed within Japan).

The reasoning of the Osaka District Court (denying the relevance to "producing") looks appropriate in this case, but for situations other than pharmaceutical patents is rather questionable. The scope of the decision as a judicial precedent should be considered as rather narrow,[10] and even to that extent, the author disagrees. Whether or not a certain act is "producing said product" depends on the nature of the invention of a product, and therefore it is unreasonable to define "producing" in a uniform manner in the first place.[11,12] After all, the Patent Act does not give a clear definition of the concept of "producing".[13]

If the concept of "producing" for a pharmaceutical invention is interpreted as strictly as the Osaka District Court would have it, the possibility of establishing indirect infringement for pharmaceutical patents would be extremely limited.[14] For example, where the movement of a (patented) medicine inside the body is controlled by using certain active ingredients which metabolise inside the body after the medicine was administered, there are situations where that medicine was actually produced by its administration to the body. Seen this way, I cannot agree with the reasoning by the Osaka District Court which denied indirect infringement by limiting the concept of producing.

10. There is a lower court decision on exclusive article type indirect infringement where the court took the position that there should be a distinction between use and producing an article and decided that when the coating layer on the surface of a blade was worn as a result of use and the thickness of such coating met the numerical values of the configuration elements of the invention, this was not the producing of a product (Tokyo District Court, 15 May 2002, Case No. 1650 (Wa) of 2001, 1794 Hanrei Jihō 125 – *Doctor Blade*). However, on appeal, the High Court denied infringement for other reasons (Tokyo High Court, 18 July 2003, Case No. 4193 (Ne) of 2002, the website of the courts <http://www.courts.go.jp/app/files/hanrei_jp/939/010939_hanrei.pdf>.
11. For example, if the invention is a radio communication network, when a network is configured by remote control to synchronise communication equipment that constitute a network, this might be understood as the producing of a network.
12. For example, in the decision of the Intellectual Property High Court, 30 September 2005, Case No. 10040 (Ne) of 2005, 1904 Hanrei Jihō 47 = 1188 Hanrei Times 191 = N. NAKAYAMA et al. (eds.), Tokkyo Hanrei Hyakusen *(Hundred Selected Patent Cases)*, 4th ed. 2012, 148 – *Ichitaro Word Processing Software*, the court, with respect to the invention of a product of an information processing equipment with a function that displayed functional explanations of icons on a computer screen, decided that the act of installing the word processing software on a computer was producing of an information processing equipment. It can be said to be self-evident that the court took into consideration the concept of "producing" by taking into account the nature of the information processing equipment.
13. R. HIRASHIMA, Iryō wo chūshin to suru yōto hatsumei no tokkyoken no kōryoku *(Effect of patent of use invention with emphasis on medical related acts)* in: IIP (ed.), Yōto hatsumei – iryō kōi wo chūshin to site *(Use invention – with an emphasis on medical related Acts)*, Yushōdō Shuppan, 2006, 222, comments that there is room for evaluation that a medicine is created through administering a complementary medicine. *See also*, R. HIRASHIMA, Fukusu yakuzai no kumiawase kara naru iyaku tokkyo no kansetsushingai (*Indirect Infringement of a Pharmaceutical Patent Consisting of a Combination of Multiple Dosage – Issues Suggested by the Pioglitazon Cases*), 61 L&T 34 (2013).
14. A case where infringement of a pharmaceutical combination patent is established will be restricted to kits of pharmaceuticals that prepare a plurality of medicines.

In my opinion, the reasoning of the Tokyo District Court is preferable, namely "what does not directly form a characteristic technical means newly disclosed by the invention in order to solve the problem" is not "indispensable for the solution of the problem by said invention".

The Tokyo District Court adopted the above interpretation from the point of view that the scope of establishing multi-functional article type indirect infringement should be limited to some extent,[15] and as mentioned above, the court denied indirect infringement of pioglitazone because the patent at issue newly disclosed a *certain combination* of pioglitazone and the complementary medicine at issue, and because pioglitazone and the complementary medicine at issue already existed prior to the priority date of the patented invention at issue and had been used for treating type 2 diabetes.

However, within such reasoning, the question as to what "the patent has newly disclosed" depends on one's point of view, and is vague as an evaluation standard. I believe that the criteria of denying a multi-functional article type indirect infringement for a product that already existed prior to the priority date, is a clearer starting point: After all, it is a fundamental principle of patent law that a patent should only extend to subject matter that had not previously been in the public domain and should thus take away nothing from the public.

The Tokyo District Court added a reservation to its reasoning, namely "unless there are special circumstances, such as the existing components are produced and sold, etc. for said invention", meaning where the defendant had recommended a co-administration with the complementary medicine at issue or where the preparations of the defendant were for a combination with the complementary medicine at issue.

Although the concern that the criteria lack legal stability cannot be denied, the point that the court has left some room for prior art to still fall under an article "indispensable for the solution of the problem" should be endorsed.[16]

Further, the defendants in Osaka and Tokyo argued that because pioglitazone was a widely available medicine for treating diabetes, it was a widely and generally distributed article within Japan which should be excluded from the subject of indirect infringement; however, both courts did not decide on this matter. The problem is that it is not necessarily clear what an article "widely and generally distributed within Japan" actually is.[17]

Yet considering that a medicine like pioglitazone is a product that is delivered from a pharmaceutical maker to a medical institution where the product is sent through a limited distribution channel by a pharmaceutical wholesaler after receiving an order from a medical institution, and the use of pioglitazone is restricted to the

15. MIMURA, *op. cit.* 8, proposes the above interpretation in the same meaning.
16. On this point, if the reasoning by the Osaka District Court that denied the relevance of the concept of producing is applied, indirect infringement will not be established even if combined use of the product is actively recommended.
17. In the above Intellectual High Court decision *Ichitaro Word Processing Software*, the court mentioned that "it is reasonable to understand that [an article widely and generally distributed within Japan] means, typically, ordinary articles widely used within Japan such as screws, nails, lightbulbs, transistors, etc., in other words, standard articles or popular articles widely available to the public, not custom-made products".

treatment of diabetes, I am hesitant to say that this is an article "widely and generally distributed within Japan".[18]

4. COMPARATIVE REMARKS

The following is a brief comparison[19] of patent laws of Europe and the United States, centring on multi-functional article type indirect infringement of items (ii).

a) Comparison with the Patent Act of several European countries

Although patent law has not yet been harmonised in Europe, the starting point for many domestic patent laws on the issue of indirect infringement is Art. 26 (Draft) Community Patent Convention 1989 (equivalent to Art. 30 Community Patent Convention 1975):

Art. 26 Community Patent Convention (not in force):

> "A Community patent shall also confer on its proprietor the right to prevent all third parties not having his consent from supplying or offering to supply within the territories of the Contracting States a person, other than a party entitled to exploit the patented invention, with means, relating to an essential element of that invention, for putting it into effect therein, when the third party knows, or it is obvious in the circumstances, that these means are suitable and intended for putting that invention into effect."

Correspondingly, sec. 10(1) German Patent Act, sec. 73 Dutch Patent Act or sec. 60(2) UK Patent Act provide corresponding requirements for establishing indirect infringement. At least the thrust of this provision is similar to the requirements for establishing a multi-functional article type indirect infringement under Japanese law.

The meaning of "means relating to an essential element of the invention" was initially interpreted rather broadly as almost every characteristic of the invention except for those that do not make any contribution to resolving a problem of the

18. In some laws, the term "staple product" is used and interpreted as "suitable for use in a variety of applications": Australian High Court, 16 October 2008, *Northern Territory v. Collins*. For a specialised medicine such as pioglitazone, this may not be the case.
19. Comparative writings on indirect infringement include: LOHRAY/BANERJEE/PANIKAR, Contributory Patent Infringement and the Pharmaceutical Industry, 8 Journal of Intellectual Property Rights 302 (2003); KEUKENSCHRIJVER, Flügelradzähler, Kaffeetüte und Drehzahlermittlung – neue Entwicklungen bei der mittelbaren Patentverletzung *(Wing Wheel Counter, Coffee Bag and Rotational Speed Detection – new progress in the indirect infringement)*, Festschrift 50 Jahre VVP 2005, 331; C. HEATH, Repair and Refill as Indirect Patent Infringement, in: HEATH/KAMPERMAN SANDERS (eds.), Spares, Repairs and Intellectual Property Rights, Kluwer Law 2009, 85; C. HEATH, Intellectual Property Liability of Consumers, Facilitators and Intermediaries: The case of Patents, in: HEATH/KAMPERMAN SANDERS (eds.), Intellectual Property Liability of Consumers, Facilitators and Intermediaries, Kluwer Law 2012, 195.

invention.[20] This rather patentee-friendly approach was not upheld in later decisions, and the current position is rather similar to the one taken by the Tokyo District Court.[21]

Further, it can be inferred from sec. 10(3) of the German Patent Act that there is room for indirect infringement even if direct infringement is not established due to other reasons, which is different from the law of the United States (contributory infringement only where there is direct infringement). This point is not yet settled in Japan.

b) Comparison with the Patent Act of the United States

U.S. law distinguishes two kinds of indirect infringement: Inducement and contributory infringement:

"The legislative history of the Patent Act of 1952 indicates that no substantive change in the scope of what constituted "contributory infringement" was intended by the enactment of sec. 271 ... However, the single concept of "contributory infringement" was divided between secs. 271(b) and 271(c) into "active inducement" (a type of direct infringement) and "contributory infringement", respectively. Section 271(c) codified the prohibition against the common type of contributory infringement referred to above, and made clear that only proof of a defendant's knowledge, not intent, that his activity cause infringement was necessary to establish contributory infringement ...[22]

Thus, active inducement as codified in § 271(b) requires a direct infringement and an intent. The latter must be more than mere knowledge and requires, e.g., assistance in preparing instructions for the infringing use:[23]

It must be established that the defendant possessed specific intent to encourage another's infringement and not merely that the defendant had knowledge of the acts alleged to constitute infringement. The plaintiff has the burden of showing that the alleged infringer's actions induced infringing acts and that he knew or should have known his actions would induce actual infringements.[24]

Section 271(c) concerns contributory infringement and was codified in 1952 in accordance with prior case law (see above).

In order to be applicable, the provision requires:

---

20. German Federal Supreme Court, 4 May 2004, GRUR 2004,758 – *Flügelradzähler*; Düsseldorf High Court, 17 November 2005, GRUR-RR, 2006, 39 – *Kaffee-Filterpads* (where each use of a coffee pad for a patented coffee machine was deemed a reconstruction of the machine and thus infringing).
21. Düsseldorf District Court, 16 August 2012, GRUR-Prax 2012, 459 – *Nespresso* (no indirect infringement by furnishing coffee capsules for a protected machine); Federal Supreme Court, 17 July 2012, 44 IIC 612 – *Palettenbehälter II* that makes a more global assessment of technical and economic equations as to what should be considered an "indispensable" part of the invention. Federal Supreme Court, 24 October 2017, X ZR 55/16, GRUR 2018, 170 – *Trommeleinheit* now favours an approach whereby the furnished part must embody the technical effect of the inventive concept in order to be considered infringing. This is in line with the above-mentioned Dutch Supreme Court decision of 31 October 2003, BIE 2004, 285 and the approach taken by the UK courts: UK Court of Appeal, *Schütz v. Werit*, 29 March 2011.
22. US CAFC, *Hewlett Packard Company v. Bausch & Lomb*, 909 F.2d 1464 (Fed. Cir. 1990).
23. US CAFC, *Water Technologies Corp. v. Calco*, 850 F. 2d 660 (Fed. Cir. 1988).
24. US CAFC, *Manville Sales Corp. v. Paramount Systems, Inc.*, 917 F. 2d 544 (Fed. Cir. 1990).

(1) An act of direct infringement:

> "It is plain that sec. 271(c) – a part of the Patent Code enacted in 1952 – made no change in the fundamental precept that there can be no contributory infringement in the absence of a direct infringement. That section defines contributory infringement in terms of direct infringement – namely the sale of a component of a patented combination or machine for use "in an infringement of such patent".[25]

(2) Knowledge of intent to contribute to direct infringement:

Sec. 271(c) does require a showing that the alleged contributory infringer knew that the combination for which his component was especially designed was both patented and infringing.[26]

(3) Not a staple article or commodity of commerce suitable for substantial non-infringing use.

25. US Supreme Court, *Aro Manufacturing Co. Inc. v. Convertible Top Replacement, Inc.*, 365 U.S. 336 (1961).
26. US Supreme Court, *Aro Manufacturing Co. Inc. v. Convertible Top Replacement, Inc.*, 377 U.S. 476 (1964).

Case No. 31

Patent Infringement – Distinction between Repair and Reconstruction

Mineko Mohri

1. Patent rights are not deemed exhausted in regard of products that were modified or where parts were replaced so that as a result the patented product should be considered as newly manufactured.
2. In order to determine whether a patented product was newly manufactured, the entire circumstances, including the attributes of the patented product, the contents of the patented invention, the manner in which the product was modified or its parts were replaced, and the actual conditions of the sales transaction have to be considered.

Supreme Court, 8 November 2007, Case No. 826 (Ju) of 2006 – *Canon Ink Cartridge*

Canon v. Recycle Assist

1. BACKGROUND

Patent law grants the patentee a "right to exclude" others from using, selling or importing the invention for a limited period in the country where the patent is granted.[1] Under the doctrine of domestic exhaustion, the patentee's monopoly effectively ends at the first lawful, unconditional sale of the patented product.[2] Thus, purchasers of patented products may use or resell them without interference from the patentee as the patent right over such product is deemed "consumed" or exhausted. A purchaser's right to "use" includes a right to make "repairs" on a patented product necessary for continued use. Yet, the term "repair" does not include the "reconstruction" of a completely spent or worn-out product. The basic rule of domestic exhaustion seems

1. Such power of the patent right is provided in the US under 35 USC sec. 154(a)(1) (provides grant of the patent right), and sec. 271(a) (defines patent infringement) (1952), in Japan by the Japanese Patent Act sec. 2(3)(i), and sec. 68 (Law No. 121 of 1959, as amended), and under the Germany Patent Act sec. 9(2)(i) (1981 as amended).
2. The patent exhaustion doctrine may not apply to an expressly conditioned sale or license. See Case No. 32.

simple; however, distinguishing between permissible repair and impermissible reconstruction is difficult.

The multitude of commercial activities in the after-sales market ("aftermarket") adds complexities to this issue. Maintenance services, sales of replaceable parts for consumed parts, recycling of used products: these activities could be offered not only by patentees, but also by third parties. Patentees might seek an injunction against third parties' activities in the aftermarket, claiming "impermissible construction" as direct infringement, or asserting the sales of replaceable parts as "indirect infringement".[3]

To what extent patentees can control these activities in the aftermarket has a direct influence upon a patentee's business strategy. Patentees might sell whole patented products at a relatively low profit margin in order to commercialise on the sale of spare parts for the product. Therefore, whether or not the producers of patented products can maximise the turnover of spare parts' sales by invoking patent law is an important issue as their business strategy. In this respect, patentees could simply prohibit recycling so as to boost the sale of new products. For the purposes of clarification, patentees sometimes require special agreements upon the sale of a patented product, such as maintenance agreements or single-use agreements ("post-sales restriction"), in order to prohibit repair or recycling services of third parties, and such restriction triggers competition law issues. The ruling of courts directly affects the interests of patentees, repair business and recycling manufacturers, and it is also of concern to society, namely consumers. Although consumers are rarely subject to patent infringement litigation, their choice between genuine products or third party products in the aftermarket directly affects the profit of patentees.

"Canon ink cartridge" was a controversial case between a major electronic equipment company, the patent owner Canon, and a recycling company, the defendant. The district court, by applying the test of substantive identity, allowed the recycling of ink cartridges, while the Intellectual Property High Court heard the case *en banc* and reversed the decision, applying the "two-exceptions test".[4] The Supreme Court affirmed the appeal court's decision and applied a multi-factor test.

2. DECISION[5]

a) Facts

Canon Inc. (Plaintiff and Appellee, hereinafter referred to only as the "Plaintiff") is one of the leading manufacturers of inkjet printers and suitable ink cartridges for

3. See Case No. 30.
4. IP High Court, 31 January 2006, Case No. 10021 (Ne) of 2005, 1922 Hanrei Jihō 30 = 37 IIC 867 (2006) (English translation). For details about the IP High Court Judgement see e.g. R. Mimura, Patent Exhaustion in Japan, in: Hansen/Schüssler-Langeheine (eds.), Patent Practice in Japan and Europe, 521-526, at 523 et seq.; C. Heath/M. Mōri, Three Recent Decisions on Repair, Refill, and Recycle, in: 23 ZJapanR/J.Japan.L 246 et seq., at 251 et seq. (2007) (summary of the case).
5. Published in 61-8 Minshū 2989 = 1990 Hanrei Jihō 3 = 1258 Hanrei Times 62 = N. Nakayama et al. (eds.), Tokkyo Hanrei Hyakusen *(Hundred Selected Patent Cases)*, 4th ed. 2012, 116 = T. Ōbuchi et al. (eds.), Chitekizaisan hō hanrei shū *(Intellectual Property Law Case Book)*, 2nd. ed. 2015, 99 = 39 IIC 982 (2008) (English translation). Further English translation by C.A. Rakow, in: CASRIP Newsletter (University of Washington, School of Law), Vol. 15, Issue

use with its inkjet printers, selling them worldwide (through affiliated companies). Recycle Assist Co. Ltd. (Defendant and Appellant, hereinafter only referred to as the "Defendant") is a company which has imported to and sold refurbished Canon ink cartridges in Japan and was sued by Plaintiff for patent infringement. Plaintiff raised claims for a permanent injunction to stop Defendant from importing and selling those ink cartridges and for the disposal of Plaintiff's ink cartridges.

Plaintiff sued Defendant on the basis of its Japanese patent JP 3278410 entitled "Liquid Containing Vessel, Manufacture thereof, Package thereof, Ink Jet Head Cartridge Integrated with Vessel and Recording Head, and Liquid Jet Recorder" (hereinafter "the patent"), which relates to a specific type of ink cartridge[6] being sold by Plaintiff as a genuine Canon ink cartridge for certain types of inkjet printers. Claim 1 of the patent pertains to the basic construction of the ink cartridge. The invention seeks to prevent leakage of ink during storage, upon opening of the package, and during installation of the ink cartridge (= the "technical effect" and "object of the invention"). The main features of claim 1 regarding the construction of the patented ink cartridge can be summarised as follows: A liquid containing vessel (i.e. the ink cartridge) with (1) a negative pressure generating member housing chamber housing two negative pressure generating members (i.e. absorptive members of a porous, ink absorbing material) pressing against each other and forming thereby a boundary layer in between, a vent and a liquid supply section (i.e. the ink supply nozzle), and (2) a liquid (in particular ink) containing chamber with a partition wall separating the liquid containing chamber from the negative pressure generating member housing chamber and a passageway that connects both chambers with each other, while the first of the two negative pressure generating members is located closer to the passageway connecting to the liquid containing chamber, and the second closer to the vent, in particular characterised in that:

> "...,
>
> the pressure between the two negative pressure generating members generates a stronger absorption of the boundary layer than the absorption of each of the negative pressure generating members (Limiting Feature H),
>
> the negative pressure generating member housing chamber is filled with a sufficient amount of liquid so that the entirety of the boundary layer can hold liquid regardless of what position the liquid containing vessel may be in (Limiting Feature K)."

This construction has the effect that as long as there is enough ink in contact with the negative pressure generating members, the ink will be absorbed by these members and distributed to the boundary layer with a stronger absorption, thereby creating

1 (Winter/Spring 2008), available at <http://www.law.washington.edu/Casrip/Newsletter/default.aspx?year=2008&article=newsv15i1RecAssist> (with introduction); similar translation with introduction by the same author at <http://usjapanpatentlitigation.files.wordpress.com/2008/04/j-exhaustion_canon-v-recycle-assist-april-7-20081.pdf>), The English translation used here was prepared by *Marc Dernauer* in: Japanese Commercial Law – Cases and Comments, Kluwer Law 2012, 399.

6. Referred to as "ink tank" in the judgement.

an air-proof barrier which entirely blocks the flow of air from the vent into the liquid containing chamber, and thereby holding the ink within the ink cartridge, except for the time when the inkjet printer is in motion and ink is flowing through the ink supply nozzle into the inkjet printer. Thereby, ink leakage is being prevented.

Defendant imported to and sold in Japan refurbished Canon ink cartridges falling within the scope of protection of Plaintiff's patent. Defendant had bought them from a company in Macao. Before that, affiliated companies of this company in Macao had collected used genuine Canon ink cartridges in Japan and other countries and then refurbished them by a process involving the following process steps: (1) opening a hole for cleaning and filling in new ink on the upper surface of the cartridge's liquid containing chamber, (2) cleaning the inside of the cartridge, (3) taking measures to prevent the ink from leaking out of the cartridge's ink supply nozzle, (4) filling ink into the negative pressure generating member housing chamber through the hole on the upper surface of the cartridge's liquid containing chamber until the ink rises above the boundary layer between the two negative pressure generating members in the negative pressure generating member housing chamber and into the entire liquid containing chamber, (5) sealing the hole and the ink supply nozzle, and (6) affixing labels and the like.

The refilled ink cartridges could also have been used again with the suitable Canon inkjet printers without cleaning the interior of the used cartridge. However, the boundary layer would not have been able to hold the ink anymore, and therefore the characteristic technical effect to prevent leakage of ink would no longer have been present. The reason for this is as follows: When the Canon ink cartridges run out of ink after having been fully used and have therefore been removed from the inkjet printer, there always remains a small amount of ink in all parts of the ink cartridge. Within a week to ten days the remaining ink usually dries and hardens. This creates air bubbles and air layers within the spaces of the cartridge, in particular in the small spaces of the porous material of the negative pressure generating members and in the area of the boundary layer, which results in a state where the negative pressure generating members and the boundary layer can no longer hold the new ink, and where especially the function of the boundary layer is extinct. After cleaning and washing away the hardened ink, however, the ability of the boundary layer to create an air-proof barrier is restored and finally its function to prevent leakage is revived after filling in the ink to a point above the boundary layer between the negative pressure generating members.

The Plaintiff warns on its web site, in its user's manual for the genuine ink cartridges and on the packaging that the cartridges should not be refilled with ink and then reused because of technical problems such as reduced printing quality and malfunction of the inkjet printer as a result of dried and hardened old ink in the ink cartridge, but should rather be replaced with new ink cartridges. In addition, Plaintiff indicates that its ink cartridges are intended for single-use only and has established a program to recover used ink cartridges.

The Tokyo District Court held that the importing and selling of the refurbished Canon ink cartridges did not constitute an infringement of Plaintiff's patent because it found that the patent was exhausted in regard of the refurbished ink cartridges.[7] The

7. Tokyo District Court, 8 December 2004, Case No. 8557 (Wa) of 2004, 1889 Hanrei Jihō 110.

judgement, however, was overturned by the IP High Court on appeal by the Plaintiff.[8] The IP High Court established the two-exception test to distinguish reconstruction from permissible repair:

> "However, patentees can enforce their patent rights under one of the following conditions that would be considered reconstruction rather than repair:
>
> 1. The patented product is used or recycled after it has furnished its service along with the lapse of its ordinary life as a product (Type 1: Its use is determined based on the patented product by examining whether the patented product has furnished its service as a product);
> 2. A third party has made modifications or replacements to the whole or part of the components that constitute an essential portion of the patented product (Type 2: It should be determined based on the invention whether any modification or replacement has been made to the whole or part of the components that constitute an essential portion of the patented invention)".

Defendant further appealed to the Supreme Court of Japan (hereinafter: the "Supreme Court").

The Supreme Court dismissed the appeal. Thereby however, the Supreme Court did not adopt the reasoning of the IP High Court, in particular it did not confirm the two exceptions to patent exhaustion which the IP High Court had established. The Supreme Court rather rendered its judgement generally based on the standard that was applied by the Tokyo District Court, with a few modifications, but also took into account some thoughts of the IP High Court[9] about how to decide the case on the merits.[10]

---

8. IP High Court, 31 January 2006, Case No. 10021 (Ne) of 2005, 1922 Hanrei Jihō 30 = 37 IIC 867 (2006) (English translation).
9. For details about the IP High Court Judgement see e.g. R. MIMURA, Patent Exhaustion in Japan, in: HANSEN/SCHÜSSLER-LANGEHEINE (eds.), Patent Practice in Japan and Europe, 521-526, at 523 et seq.; C. HEATH/M. MŌRI, Three Recent Decisions on Repair, Refill, and Recycle, in: 23 ZJapanR/J.Japan.L 246 et seq., at 251 et seq. (2007) (summary of the case).
10. For a summary of the court decisions in all three instances in the *Canon Ink Cartridge* case, see T. YAMADA, Kokunai shōjin *(Domestic Exhaustion)*, in: T. IIMURA/R. SHITARA (eds.), Chiteki zaisan kankei soshō *(Lawsuits Relating to Intellectual Property)*, Vol. 3, Seirin Shoin, 2008, 176 et seq, at 185 et seq. For a comprehensive analysis of the case in Japanese, see e.g. T. NAKAYOSHI, Saikō saibansho hanrei kaisetsu Tokkyokensha matawa tokkyokensha kara kyodaku wo uketa jisshikensha ga wagakuni ni oite tokkyoseihin wo jōto shita baai ni tokkyokensha ga tōgai tokkyoseihin ni tsuki tokkyoken wo kōshi suru kotono kahi *(Analysis of the Supreme Court decision on the allowability of patent enforcement over the patented products which are sold in Japan by patent holder or licensee)*, 62-4 Hōsō Jihō 973 et seq. (2010); T. NAKAYOSHI, Jūyo hanrei kaisetu *(Commentary on important decisions)*, 39 L&T 60-70 (2008); Y. TAMURA, Hishōzumi inkutanku wo saijūten suru kōi to tokkyoken shingai no seihi, jō, ge *(Patent infringement on an act of refilling a spent ink tank part 1, part2)*, 877 NBL 12-23 (2008), 878 NBL 22-34 (2008); H. YOKOYAMA, Tokkyo seihin no risaikuru hin no hanbai ni tokkyoken shingai ga mitomerareta jirei *(Case where patent infringement is acknowledged by the sale of recycled patented products)*, 45 Tokkyo Kenkyū 52-71 (2008).

b) Reasons

In a case where the patentee or its licensee (hereinafter both are referred to as "patentee etc.") has assigned[11] a patented product within Japan, the respective patent has achieved its purpose and is therefore exhausted with respect to this product so that the effect of this patent no longer extends to the use, assignment etc. (here and hereinafter, this means the use, assignment etc., export or import, or offering for assignment etc. as stated in section 2(3)(i) Patent Act.) of this product. When the patentee etc. has assigned a patented product, it is appropriate to conclude that the patentee shall not be permitted [anymore] to enforce its patent right with respect to this specific product.

However, the limitation of the right to enforce a patent because of the exhaustion of the patent applies only to the product actually assigned by the patentee etc. in Japan. Therefore, if the product that was assigned in Japan by the patentee etc. was modified or if part[s] were replaced so that, as a result, one has to acknowledge that the patented product is no longer identical to the assigned one or has been newly manufactured, then the patentee should [still] be permitted to enforce its patent right with regard to this product. Moreover, in order to determine whether a patented product was newly manufactured, it is appropriate to decide this issue by taking into account the entire circumstances, including the attributes of the patented product, the content of the patented invention, the manner in which the product was modified or its parts were replaced, and the actual conditions of the sales transaction, etc. In regard of the issues that have to be considered, it has to be said that the attributes of the patented product include the product's functions, the structure and material[s], the intended use[s], the lifespan, and the manner in which it is used, and that in regard of the manner in which the patented product was modified or its parts were replaced, such consideration shall include the condition of the patented product after it was modified etc., the content and the degree of the modification, the lifespan of the replaced parts, and the technical function and economic value of the replaced parts in the patented product.

In cases where the patentee or one regarded as such in regard of a Japanese patent (hereinafter both are referred to as the "patentee etc." in regard of a Japanese patent) has assigned a patented product outside of Japan, it has to be concluded that the patentee shall not be permitted [anymore] to enforce its patent right in Japan with respect to this specific product against the assignee (unless the patentee etc. agreed with the assignee to exclude Japan from the territory of sale or use in regard of the respective patented product) or against a third party to whom the specific patented product has been [further] assigned or any person who has received the specific product thereafter (unless the patentee etc. reached the aforementioned agreement with the assignee and this is also clearly indicated on the specific patented product). Still, the resulting limitation to enforce the patent only applies to the specific patented

11. Here the term "*jōto*" is used, which literally means "assigned" or "assignment", in particular as a result of the sale of the product. Although "assignment" in the context of patent law is usually considered to mean not only the permanent transfer of a product (of the title to a product), but also the temporary surrender of a product for use (e.g. the letting and lending of an object (cf. section 2(3)(i) Patent Act and N. NAKAYAMA, Chūkai tokkyo-hō *(Commentary to the Patent Act)*, 2000, at sections 2 and 35), here, it can be assumed that it shall not extend to such acts.

product itself that the patentee etc. had assigned. This is no different to the case where the patentee etc. has assigned the patented product in Japan. Therefore, if a patented product that had been assigned by the patentee etc. outside of Japan was modified or if its part[s] were replaced, so that as a result one has to acknowledge that a patented product that is not identical to the assigned one has been newly manufactured, then the patentee should [still] be permitted to enforce its patent right with regard to this patented product in Japan. Moreover, for deciding whether a patented product was newly manufactured in the way stated above, it is appropriate to apply the same standard as in the case where a patented product assigned in Japan was modified or where its part[s] were replaced.

In the present case, the Plaintiff, according to the facts stated above, warned that its products were for single use only and should be replaced with new products because if the ink cartridges were refilled with ink and reused, it had to be feared that problems such as reduced printing quality or malfunction of the printer itself would occur. For this reason, Plaintiff's products did not have a hole for adding ink, and this structure made it necessary to open a hole in the ink cartridge for refilling the ink. The process for the production of Defendant's products also included the opening of a hole on the upper surface of the liquid containing chamber and the plugging of the hole after filling with ink. Such a condition after the modifications etc. have been carried out in the process for the production of Defendant's products is not limited to the simple refilling of consumed ink; it is nothing less than an alteration of the ink cartridge in order to allow the refilling of ink.

Moreover, according to the facts stated above, the ink itself has the function of creating a barrier at the boundary layer of the contact part [where the two negative pressure generating members meet] that prevents the flow of air. Once the ink has been consumed to a certain degree, a part of or the entire boundary layer of the contact part loses its ability to hold the ink. Furthermore, within one week to ten days after the fully used products of the Plaintiff have been removed from the printer, the remaining ink inside hardens. If the ink tanks were refilled in this state, even if the liquid containing chamber and the negative pressure generating member housing chamber were filled with ink to a point above the boundary layer of the contact part, the ink could not perform the function of creating a barrier at the boundary layer of the contact part to prevent the flow of air. In Defendant's products, however, the interior of the ink cartridges at issue was cleaned and the hardened ink was thereby washed away to restore the ability to create the barrier that prevents the flow of air at the boundary layer of the contact part, and the ink was filled in to the same level as Plaintiff's products before they were used. Thereby, the ink cartridge was restored to the state where the boundary layer of the contact part could hold the ink no matter what position the ink cartridge may be in.

Therefore, the condition after the modifications etc. have been carried out in the process of the production of Defendant's products is not limited to the simple refilling of consumed ink. It is a condition where the ink cartridges at issue can be reused after they were [once] fully consumed and where essential features of the invention (Limiting Features H and K) which were once lost are again fulfilled. This has to be evaluated to the effect that the actual value of the invention in this case has been re-created, and the technical effect of the invention, namely the prevention of ink leakage before opening, has been restored anew.

In addition, when considering the overall circumstances of the facts stated above, including the circumstances of the sales transactions with respect to the ink cartridges, it is appropriate to confirm that Defendant's products are newly manufactured ones, not identical to the products of Plaintiff before the modifications etc. Therefore, it has to be said that no limitation to enforce the patent applies here with regard to Defendant's products at issue, which, for their production, made use of fully used ink cartridges that had been previously assigned by the patentee etc. in Japan or by the patentee in regard of a Japanese patent outside of Japan, and Plaintiff as the patentee here can claim, based on the patent, the rendering of a permanent injunction to stop the import and sale etc. of the products as well as their disposal.

3. ANALYSIS

The Supreme Court found infringement based on the doctrine of product "identity". The Supreme Court focused on the "identity" of the original product by analysing the entire circumstances around the patented invention (multifactor test), and established four criteria: "(1) the attributes of a patented product, (2) the subject-matter of a patented invention, (3) the aspect of refurbishment and replacement of parts, (4) in addition to actual conditions of distribution/the sales transactions, etc.". Namely, the court affirmed a reconstruction of "identity" of the product from "a comprehensive standpoint".

The Supreme Court found the "identity of the product" to be the single criterion in deciding patent infringement in the aftermarket. Before this Supreme Court decision, some courts focused on the products that were sold,[12] while others focused on the patented inventions,[13] and still others considered both.[14] The *Canon* decision considered both elements. Based on the "comprehensive standpoint", the court decided whether or not the altered product was "the same product" that the right holder sold on the market.

Since the Supreme Court did not overrule the IP High Court's judgement, the elements of the "two-exception test"[15] became a part of analysis of a "comprehensive standpoint". A judge who had worked at the Supreme Court when the judgement was written explains that the ruling of the Supreme Court allows more flexibility comparing to the criteria of the lower court.[16] For example, in light of the purpose of

12. Osaka District Court, 24 April 1989, Case No. 6851 (Wa) of 1985, 1315 Hanrei Jihō 120 - *Hammer for a sand-making machine,* Tokyo District Court, 6 June 2000, Case No. 22179 (Yo) of 1999, 1712 Hanrei Jihō 175 - *Konica,* Tokyo District Court, 8 Dec. 2004, Case No. 8557 (Wa) of 2004, 1889 Hanrei Jihō 110 - *Canon ink cartridge.*
13. Osaka District Court, 23 July 1992, Case No. 567 (Wa) of 1984, 2399 Hanrei Kōgyō Shoyuken hō (2 ki ban) 263 - *Nori okuri kikou (Nori cutting mechanism).* Tokyo High Court, 29 Nov. 2001, Case No. 959 (Ne) of 2001, 1779 Hanrei Jihō 89 - *Acyclovir.*
14. Tokyo District Court, 24 April 2007, Case Nos. 15327 (Wa) of 2005&26540 (Wa) of 2006, the website of the courts <http://www.courts.go.jp/app/files/hanrei_jp/601/034601_hanrei.pdf> - *Fuji Film.* Osaka District Court, 26 November 2002, Case No. 7271 (Wa) of 2000, the website of the courts <http://www.courts.go.jp/app/files/hanrei_jp/487/011487_hanrei.pdf> - *Step Tool.*
15. IP High Court, 31 January 2006, Case No. 10021 (Ne) of 2005, 1922 Hanrei Jihō 30 = 37 IIC 867 (2006) (English translation).
16. T. NAKAYOSHI (above), 39 L&T 60 (2008), at 68.

patent law, there might be some cases in which the exercise of the patent right is still denied even if the alteration is made to an essential part of the patented invention and such alteration constitutes the type 2 exception under the two-exception test. The lifespan is considered for both the patented product and the replaced part.

Ambiguous "comprehensive standpoint": The Supreme Court's doctrine of product "identity" based on multifactor tests includes almost every aspect around the patented product, such as the attributes of the patented product, the content of the claimed invention, the manner in which the product was modified, and the actual conditions of the transactions made by the patent owner. This might mean that there is a lack of a clear framework and little guidance for patentees, vendors in the aftermarket and consumers.

It might also be a difficult situation for judges, who repeatedly face the issue of "permissible repair and impermissible making". The court might be confident in saying "We can solve the case reasonably, when we hear the case". However, the irony is that, in the *Canon Ink Cartridge* case, the first instance found no infringement and the Supreme Court found infringement based on exactly the same facts, analysing almost the same factors. It revealed the uncertainty of substantive analysis.

The ruling of the IP High Court reflected a different policy in trying to draw a clear scope of exhaustion, so that patentees and vendors would be given a measure of legal certainty. However, this meticulous classification of patent infringement into two types might be too rigorous.

The Supreme Court ruling in *Canon ink cartridge* is convincingly consistent with its ruling in *BBS*.[17] The exhaustion of the right occurs on the basis of the very product that was sold on the market; therefore, the scope of the patent right is determined by whether or not the product is identical to the sold product. Determination should be made based on the totality of circumstances. Lawyers who are only familiar with the *BBS* ruling might reach the same conclusion as *Canon* in the Supreme Court. Still, the predictability of the final ruling on products in the aftermarket remains relatively unstable.

To avoid unforeseeable judgements after time-consuming legal proceedings, patentees might be more interested in making conditional sales, such as single-use agreements ("post-sales restriction"). Although a private agreement may not be able to limit the exhaustion of a patent right, by doing so, patentees could at least give purchasers a contractual obligation not to recycle the patented product. Furthermore, if a patentee reserves a right on the patented product, and leases it to its customer, the patentee can avoid the exhaustion of his patent right completely, just as the Osaka District ruled in 2014 for the *Roll Paper for Enveloping Medicine* case.[18] In this case, the patentee sold the roll paper for enveloping medicine, and the defendant recycled the core roll of the patented product, placed new roll paper around the core roll and sold it as the products of defendant. The Osaka District Court applied the doctrine of product "identity" as developed by the Supreme Court, and found that the defendant was reconstructing the patented product, because the products

17. See Case No. 32.
18. Osaka District Court, 16 January 2014, Case No. 8071 (Wa) of 2012, the website of the courts <http://www.courts.go.jp/app/files/hanrei_jp/881/083881_hanrei.pdf> – *Roll Paper for Enveloping Medicine*.

of defendant were not, socially and economically, identical to the patented product placed in the marked by the patentee.

In addition, concerning the exhaustion of the patent right, the Osaka District Court focused on the fourth criterion of the *Canon* case, "the actual conditions of the transactions", and ruled that "the patented product is as combination of two parts – the core roll and the roll paper. While selling the roll paper, the patentee reserved the ownership of the core roll, and merely leased it to its clients." Therefore, this case lacks the condition of patent exhaustion. Rightly so, during business conversation, the employees of the patentee explicitly explained to their customers/purchasers that the core roll was "on loan free of charge until its clients consume the roll paper", the core roll would be "recollected by the patentee after use", and the core roll "should not be transferred or rent to the third party". These factors gave a solid foundation for the court to find the ownership of the core roll remaining under the patentee's control.

The third criterion of the Canon's multifactor test ruling, "aspect of refurbishment and replacement of parts", can play a vital role in determining permissible repair or impermissible reconstruction. In 2015, the IP High Court heard the *Seaweed Purifying Apparatus* case. Here, the defendant sold supplemental products (a) and offered maintenance services in the aftermarket (b).[19] By applying the four multiple criteria of the *Canon* ruling, the IP High Court affirmed patent infringement by the defendant who had offered the supplemental parts (fixing ring and flat panel) to the users of the patented products because those parts were indispensable elements of the invention, whereby the defendant's products (a) amounted to a "reconstruction" under the Patent Act sec. 2(3)(i). However, concerning the "maintenance" of the patented products offered by the defendant (b), the IP High Court, reversed the lower court's decision and held that the defendant's checking, maintaining, and repairing of patented products merely maintained or improved the function of the patented machine.

4. COMPARATIVE REMARKS

Although the words "repair" and "reconstruction" are not used in statutory patent laws in the UK, the US or Germany, the distinction between permissible repair and impermissible reconstruction is widely made.[20] Drawing a clear conceptual border is not possible, and the scope of the patent exhaustion doctrine needs to be revisited.[21] In the last five years, the highest courts in the UK, the US and the Germany decided

19. IP High Court, 12 November 2015, Case No. 10048&10088 (Ne) of 2015, 1424 Hanrei Times 136 – *Seaweed Purifying Apparatus*.
20. US Court of Appeals for the 1st Circuit, *Goodyear Shoe Mach. Co. v. Jackson*, 112 F. 146 (1st Cir. 1901), at 150. (repair is "restoration to a sound, good, or compete state after decay, injury, dilapidation, or partial destruction". Reconstruction is "the act of constructing again." Reproduction is "repetition," or "the act of reproducing".)
21. For a comparative analysis on the patent exhaustion doctrine, see C. Heath, Exhaustion and Patent Rights, in: Bagley/Okediji, Patent Law in Global Perspective, Oxford University Press 2014, 419-484.

on recycling bases. The case law and mainstream theory concerning repair, recycling or replacement differs in each jurisdiction. Each theory is worth a closer look.[22]

a) In the **UK,** lower courts[23] have traditionally applied the implied license theory. In 2000, however, the House of Lords overruled one of these decisions and held that the act of impermissible refurbishment should be determined according to whether or not the act could be likened to one of manufacturer's "making".[24]

In *United Wire Limited v. Screen Repair Service,*[25] the plaintiff's UK patents aimed at improving the system of a sifting screen used to recycle drilling fluid in the oil industry. The defendant used the original frame of the patented product, refurbished the screen and sold it. The defendant argued that such repair, which prolonged the lifespan of the product, should be covered by an implied license and not be considered a "making" under the Patents Act 1977. The defendant further argued exhaustion of the patent right. The High Court decided for the defendant, but the House of Lords reversed. The court confirmed that the notion of repair and making are mutually exclusive and held that where it was alleged that the defendant had infringed by making the patented product, the concept of an implied license or exhaustion of rights had not part to play. In the Court's view, what could be said to be repair can depend upon the perception of the person answering the question, so the court should focus on whether the act of the defendant amounted to the manufacture of a product rather than whether it could be called repair: The owner's right to repair is not an independent right conferred upon him by license. It is a residual right, forming part of the right to do whatever does not amount to "making" the product. The court found infringement according to the nature of the invention as claimed and the type of refurbishment done by the defendant.

In 2013, a case reached the UK Supreme Court (former House of Lords) after prior two decisions by the Patents Court and the Court of Appeal.

In *Schütz Limited v. Werit Limited,*[26] the newly launched UK Supreme Court (two judges from the former Patent Court) decided on the repair/reconstruction in a case involving replacement of plastic bottles of an intermediate bulk container (IBC). The IBCs consist of a metal case into which a large plastic container (bottle) is fitted. The container has to fit the cage snugly, otherwise the cage will not provide full protection, and the walls of the bottle will not be properly supported. The cage has a significantly longer life expectancy than the bottle; about five or six times as long. The defendant involved with "cross-bottling", namely replacing the (President Lord Neuberger) ruled:

22. M. MOHRI, Maintenance, Replacement and Recycling – Patentees' Rights in the Aftermarkets – Germany, the U.S. and Japan, Herbert Utz Verlag, 2010.
23. English Court of Appeal, *Solar Thomson Engineering Co. Ltd v. Barton* [1997] RPC 537.
24. Under the Patent Act 1977, sec. 60(1)(a). Lord Hoffmann in United Wire case (below) questioned that: "whether, having regard to the nature of the patented article, the defendant could be said to have made it".
25. English House of Lords, *United Wire Ltd v. Screen Repair Service Ltd.* [2001] RPC 439 = [2001] FSR 24.
26. UK Supreme Court, 13 March 2013, *Schütz (UK) Limited v. Werit (UK) Limted,* [2013] UKSC 16. Available at the Court's HP <https://www.supremecourt.uk/cases/docs/uksc-2011-0159-judgment.pdf>.

> "In answering that question, I consider that it is both legitimate and helpful to consider the question of whether the bottle is such a subsidiary part of the patented article that its replacement, when required, does not involve "making" a new article."[27]

In its conclusion, the Supreme Court applied a multi-factor test and denied patent infringement. The Court rejected the simple approach adopted by the Patent Court as the first instance (simply asking whether "when the part in question is removed, what is left embodies the whole of the inventive concept of the claim" as a sole criterion.) The Patent Court's decision of no-infringement, however, was the same as that of the Supreme Court. The Patent Court had considered previous German decisions on repair. Lord Neuberger had given considerable respect, but held that the English courts were not obliged to follow them. The Supreme Court based its decision on the totality of the defendant's activities:

> "78. Deciding whether a particular activity involves "making" the patented article involves, as Lord Bingham said, an exercise in judgment, or, in Lord Hoffmann's words, it is a matter of fact and degree. In some such cases, one can say that the answer is clear; in other cases, one can identify a single clinching factor. However, in this case, it appears to me that it is a classic example of identifying the various factors which apply on the particular facts, and, after weighing them all up, concluding, as a matter of judgment, whether the alleged infringer does or does not "make" the patented article. In the present case, given that (a) the bottle (i) is a freestanding, replaceable component of the patented article, (ii) has no connection with the claimed inventive concept, (iii) has a much shorter life expectancy than the other, inventive, component, (iv) cannot be described as the main component of the article, and (b) apart from replacing it, Delta does no additional work to the article beyond routine repairs, I am of the view that, in carrying out this work, Delta does not "make" the patented article".[28]

b) In **Germany**, the limitation of patent rights in the aftermarket was explained by the exhaustion doctrine.[29] Cases from the last century had established the criteria for distinguishing non-infringing repair from infringing replacement.[30] Under the doctrine of national exhaustion, purchasers are always allowed to act in accordance with the "intended use".[31] Such intended use must be determined from an objective point of view and usual measures for starting operation or maintenance of patented products are included in the intended use. The *Förderrinne* ruling applied another criterion

27. Idem. *Schütz v. Werit*, paragraph 61.
28. Idem. *Schütz v. Werit*, paragraph 78.
29. German Federal Supreme Court, 21 November 1958, 1959 GRUR 232 – *Förderrinne*. German courts often find a reasoning of patent exhaustion once the patentee has recovered the "just profit" based on his patent.
30. German Imperial Supreme Court, 25 October 1924, GRUR 1926, 163 – *Schraubstöpselsicherung*; German Imperial Supreme Court, 5 November 1930, Mitt. 1930, 345 – *Heizkissen*; German Imperial Supreme Court, 9 June 1934, GRUR 1934, 534 – *Diskusschleifrad II*; German Imperial Supreme Court, 4 October 1938, GRUR 1939, 184 – *Gerbsäure*; German Federal Supreme Court, 15 Jun. 1951, GRUR 1951 452 – *Mülltonne II.*
31. *Förderrinne* 1959 GRUR 232, 234. In German "*bestimmungsgemäßer Gebrauch*".

to distinguish permissible repair from impermissible remanufacturing, namely "the normal lifespan of the patented product".

According to the German courts, refill and replacement of consumables, or replacing worn out parts or parts that are intended to be replaced several times during the lifespan of the patented product with new, non-patented parts, are usually permitted. The court will examine if the act of the defendant is within the "intended use" of the patented product, and if it has been done during "the normal lifespan of patented product" judged by the interested circles involved. This approach was confirmed by the German Federal Supreme Court in "*Flügelradzähler*".[32] Furthermore, the Court in *Flügelradzähler* held that when the replacement concerned the essential element of the invention, the court is likely to find an impermissible reconstruction. The ruling thus considers whether or not the alteration by the defendant concerns "the essential part of the patented invention",

> "For, if the replacement of this part implements the technical or commercial benefit of the invention a second time, it cannot be said that the patent holder has already drawn the benefits from the invention as a result of the first putting into circulation of the device as a whole."[33]

Thus, the court first needs to determine whether the part is a "means" under sec. 10(i) German Patent Act and then applies the exhaustion doctrine by evaluating whether such means "embodies the technical effect of the invention" or not.[34]

Exchanging of replaceable parts during the lifespan is permissible. In 2017, the Federal Supreme Court applied these criteria in a case concerning the recyce of Canon's toner cartridges for Canon's printing machines *in Trommeleinheit (Drum Unit)*.[35] *Canon*, the patentee/plaintiff, manufactures and sells printers and toner cartridges which have a photosensitive drum and coupling member. In the spare parts market, recycling companies refurbished *Canon*'s toner cartridges and replaced photosensitive drums by new drums. The Düsseldorf District Court and the High Court found for patent infringement by focusing on the technical function of the replaced part, yet the Federal Supreme Court overruled. The court affirmed the theory established in its precedent cases *Flügelradzähler* and *Palettenbehälter II*,[36] and found that the technical effects of the invention are not reflected in the drum, thus no patent infringement. The Federal Supreme Court confirmed the previous case law focusing on (1) how the commercial public perceives the measure in question given the working life of the protected device, and (2) whether the technical effect of the invention is reflected in the replaced element.

According to the Federal Supreme Court, the first criterion cannot be applied where the patented product is not sold as such, but as a component of a larger product unit. It is, therefore, only important whether or not the technical effects of the invention are reflected in the exchanged part. This the Federal Supreme Court denied.

---

32. German Federal Supreme Court, 4 May 2004, GRUR 2004, 758 = 36 IIC 963 (2005) – *Flügelradzähler/Impeller Flow Meter*.
33. *Flügelradzähler*, 36 IIC 963 (2005), 969-970.
34. Federal Supreme Court, 27 Feb. 2007, Case No. X ZR38/06, 2007 GRUR 769 – *Pipettensystem*.
35. Federal Supreme Court, 24 Oct. 2017, Case No. X.ZR 55/16, 2018 GRUR-Prax 50 – *Trommeleinheit*.
36. Federal Supreme Court, 17 July 2012, Case No. X ZR 97/11 – *Palettenbehälter*.

c) In the **US**, the patent exhaustion doctrine, commonly called the "first sale doctrine" is not codified in the US Patent Act.[37] In 2008, the US Supreme Court issued an eagerly awaited decision in *Quanta Computer Inc. v. LG Electronics, Inc.*,[38] and confirmed the long-standing doctrine of exhaustion, which was established through case law in the mid-19th century.[39] The older cases established the following rules:

i) A purchaser has a right to repair until the whole product is spent. Repair can be done to essential parts as long as the repair does not change the identity of product (*Wilson v. Simpson*).
ii) Upon the sale of a patented product by the patentee or by an authorised person, the patentee loses its monopoly, and the purchaser obtains the right to use (*Bloomer v. McQuewan*).
iii) A satisfactory consideration ("full value") must be paid pursuant to patent law (*Goodyear v. Beverly Rubber, Adam v. Burke*).[40]
iv) Any subsequent controls or restrictions on the ultimate users of patented products are subject to contract law, but not patent law (*Keeler v. Standard Folding Bed Co.*).

The US Supreme Court in *Univis Lens* (1942)[41] expanded the rule above i), ii), and iv) to the case where the patentee sold not the complete patented product, but just a part, which however embodied an essential feature of the patented invention. In such a case, the patentee obtained its reward and the right is exhausted. The final point v) became a heated issue in the 1990s at the Court of Appeals for the Federal Circuit ("CAFC") in the light of contract law and competition law.[42] The Supreme Court in *Quanta* (2008) confirmed the above i) – iv): a patentee loses its right to control the patented product upon lawful sale because it received a consideration (reward).

The US exhaustion doctrine evolved from its relationship with post-sale restrictions, and the US exhaustion doctrine is based on mixed considerations of patent and antitrust law. In the context of US antitrust law, manufacturers' attempts to extend their patent monopoly by prohibiting the act of repair are often denied.

On 30 May 2017, the Supreme Court in *Impression Products, Inc. v. Lexmark International Inc.*[43] helped competition in the aftermarket by reversing the ruling of

---

37. Cf. Copyright Act of 1976m 17 U.S.C. sec. 109(a) provides exhaustion of copyright.
38. *Quanta Computer Inc. v. LG Electronics, Inc.* 553 U.S. 617 (2008).
39. US Supreme Court, *Wilson v. Rousseau*, 45 U.S. 646 (1846); *Wilson v. Simpson*, 50 U.S. 109 (1850); *Bloomer v. McQuewan*, 55 U.S. 539 (1852). These three cases concern *William Woodworth*'s patent on a "planning machine", which was cutting-edge technology at the time and particularly effective in cutting boards for floorboards. His products dominated the market. US Circuit Court for the District of Massachusetts, *Goodyear v. Beverly Rubber* Co., 10 F. Cas. 638 (C.C.D. Mass. 1859); US Supreme Court, *Adams v. Burke*, 84 U.S. 453 (1873); *Morgan Envelope Co. v. Albany Perforated Wrapping Paper Co.*, 152 U.S. 425 (1894); *Keeler v. Standard Folding Bed Co.*, 157 U.S. 659 (1895).
40. *B. Braun Medical Inc. v. Abbott Laboratories*, 124 F. 3d 1419 (1997). In this case, the CAFC explained the exhaustion doctrine by the unconditional sale of the patented device: "the theory behind this rule is that, in such a transaction, the patentee has bargained for, and received, an amount equal to the full value of the goods".
41. *United States v. Univis Lens Co.*, 316 U.S. 241 (1942).
42. *Mallinckrodt, Inc. v. Medipart, Inc.*, 976 F. 2d 700 (Fed. Cir. 1992).
43. US Supreme Court, *Impression Products, Inc. v. Lexmark International Inc.*, 581 U.S. ____ (2017).

the CAFC which favoured the patentee. *Lexmark* designed, manufactured, and sold toner cartridges to consumers and gave them two options: to buy a toner cartridge at full price, with no restrictions, or to buy a toner cartridge at a discount through *Lexmark*'s "Return Program". In the latter case, customers had to sign a contract agreeing to use the cartridge only once and to refrain from transferring the cartridge to anyone but *Lexmark*. A number of refillers acquired empty Lexmark toner cartridges – including Return Program cartridges – from purchasers in the US, as well as from overseas, refilled them with toner, and imported and resold them in the US.

The Supreme court held that

> "*Lexmark* exhausted its patent rights in these cartridges the moment it sold them. The single-use/no-resale restrictions in Lexmark's contracts with customers may have been clear and enforceable under contract law, but they do not entitle *Lexmark* to retain patent right in an item that it has elected to sell."

In its ruling, the Court also affirmed international patent exhaustion (see the comparative remarks in Case No. 32).

Clearly, the US Supreme Court applied the patent exhaustion doctrine equivalent to its first-sale-doctrine under copyright law more explicitly than other jurisdictions such as Germany, the UK or Japan. Which, of course, will have patent owners thoroughly recalculate and reconsider their business plan concerning the "full value" that they have to obtain from the first sale if their patents were to be exhausted afterwards.

The Supreme Court of Japan and the UK both adopt a "multiple-factor test" in deciding "identity" or "making" of the patented products. However, the actual decisions read very differently: one focuses on social norms, and the other decides the case on whether "I/a judge" regard the defendant's activities as "making", or not. While the UK Supreme Court in *Schütz v. Werit* closely examined the criteria established by the German Federal Supreme Court and focuses on the "intended use on the technical effect of the invention", the Japanese approach risks to fall into a tautology, namely: "what is not repair" falls into "making".

The US Supreme Court applies the "first-sale-doctrine" and whether patentees thereby received the "full value" that they had expected.

In comparing cases from different jurisdiction, we should not overlook the importance of understanding character and philosophy of each patent law, judicial systems and case law which have a long history. However, as we saw in *Schütz v. Werit*, the Patent Court of England gave tremendous consideration to German case law. Each theory and ruling can be more objectively analysed once we are aware of other approaches to decide a similar case.

Case No. 32

Limits of Patent Rights – National and International Exhaustion

Christopher Heath

1. **If patented products are sold domestically, either by the patentee or with his consent, the patent in regard of these products is deemed exhausted because it has fulfilled its purpose.**
2. **The importation of products covered by a domestic patent and marketed abroad by the patentee is only infringing if the patentee has clearly excluded such importation.**

Supreme Court, 1 July 1997, Case No. 1988 (O) of 1995 – *BBS Car Wheels III*

BBS v. [Y]

1. BACKGROUND

This case concerns two issues. The first is the issue of limits to the patent right due to *exhaustion*, in other words whether and to what extent the patent can control the further marketing of a patented product that has been put on the market by him or with his consent.

The theories on patent exhaustion, be it the theory of implied licence[1] or the theory of first marketing,[2] are unanimous in that exhaustion applies to a specific product that has been put into the market by the patentee or with his consent, yet cannot have an effect on the marketing of other products that fall under the claims of the same patent. Under the theories supporting patent exhaustion, it is not the "patent right" that exhausts, but the right to use the patent to prohibit the further commercial use of the specific product that has been first marketed. In other words, the exhaustion of the patent right to exclude others from making, marketing, or

1. English High Court, *Betts v. Willmott*, [1871] 6 L.R.Ch. 239, 245; Privy Council, *Nat'l Phonograph Co. of Australia v. Menck*, [1911] 28 R.P.C. 229; English High Court, *Roussel Uclaf S.A. v. Hockley Int'l Ltd.*, [1996] 113 R.P.C. 441.
2. J. KOHLER, Handbuch des Deutschen Patentrechts *(Handbook of the German Patent Law)*, Mannheim 1900) 452. An English translation of *Josef Kohler*'s passages on exhaustion can be found in C. HEATH, Exhaustion and Patent Rights, in: M. BAGLEY/R. OKEDIJI (eds.), Patent Law in Global Perspective, 2014, 419, 424.

further selling the patented products applies only, and is limited to, the specific product at issue.

The second issue of parallel importation arises where the goods in question were marketed by the patentee abroad: "Parallel importation" refers to goods lawfully produced in the country of origin and subsequently imported into another country by a person who is not the original manufacturer or licensee.[3] Where such goods fall within the scope of a patent in the country of importation, already the act of importation (and, of course, subsequent sale) belong to the exclusive scope of the patent granted to the domestic patentee, and the latter could prevent such importation without consent unless the patentee should be barred from exercising his rights.

No legislation in the patent field has been enacted for the primary purpose of dealing with domestic exhaustion or parallel imports. Sec. 68 Patent Act gives the patentee the exclusive right to commercially work the patented invention. Secs. 2(3) (i) and (iii) Patent Act define "working" as including the act of importation. The act is silent on both domestic and international exhaustion, however.

A first decision on the parallel importation of patented goods was rendered by the Osaka District Court in 1969.[4] The case dealt with the import of a second-hand machine from Australia via Hong Kong by the defendant. The plaintiff, a U.S. company that owned a patent for the machine in Japan and Australia, successfully objected to such importation as the Osaka District Court held that the patentee enjoyed the unrestricted right of use within Japan. The court discussed the problem of market separation, but felt bound by "the basic principles of patent law" to protect national patent rights against free competition. For 25 years, this decision was regarded as the precedent of how the parallel importation of patented products should be dealt with.

2. DECISION[5]

a) Facts

The plaintiff, the German manufacturer *BBS*, holds parallel patents for certain car wheels, both in Japan and Germany. The defendant had obtained *BBS* patented car wheels in Germany and subsequently imported them to Japan. No notice was displayed on the car wheels about import restrictions. *BBS* wants to enjoin the defendant from importing the patented product and claims damages. The Tokyo District Court in first instance basically decided along the same lines as the above *Brunswick*

3. Also referred to as 'grey' goods. Yet, as these are goods produced and sold legally, there is nothing 'grey' about them, as the English Patents Court in a decision of 9 October 1995 correctly pointed out: *Roussel Uclaf v. Hockley Int'l*, [1996] R.P.C. 441.
4. Osaka District Court, 9 June 1969, Case No. 3460 (Wa) of 1968, 1 Mutaishū 160 – *Brunswick*.
5. Published in 51-6 Minshū 2299 = 1612 Hanrei Jihō 3 = 951 Hanrei Times 105 = N. NAKAYAMA at el. (eds.), Tokkyo Hanrei Hyakusen *(Hundred Selected Patent Cases)*, 4th ed. 2012, 204 = T. ŌBUCHI et al. (eds.) Chitekizaisan hō hanrei shū *(Intellectual Property Law Case Book)*, 2nd ed. 2015, 518. English translation in 29 IIC 331 (1998); 22-4 AIPPI Journal of the Japanese Group (English edition) 163 (1997), with an annotation by FUJINO; German translation in GRUR Int. 1998, 116.

decision.[6] Already at that stage, some criticism was voiced by academic writers.[7] Still, it came as a considerable surprise when the Tokyo High Court overturned this decision on the grounds of remuneration doctrine:[8]

> "In the following, it shall be examined whether the importation and sale of products manufactured according to the above patent and manufactured and marketed by the patentee or with his consent, and subsequently commercially imported by third parties to Japan (so-called parallel importation of original goods) amounts to an infringement of the Japanese patent, which is held by the Japanese patentee for an identical invention. The question thus lies in determining whether the effect of a Japanese patent with respect to certain patented products, their lawful marketing abroad by the same patentee should be taken into account or not. It has already been mentioned above that when determining the effects of a patent in Japan, taking circumstances abroad into consideration in no way contravenes the principles of independence of patent rights or territoriality. Even in sec. 29(1)(iii) Patent Act, events that have occurred abroad are considered as one of the legal obstacles to obtaining a patent right, i.e. the fact that an invention for which a patent has been applied has already been published abroad. Thus, also in the above-mentioned case, one should examine whether there are significant reasons that should be considered in order to balance the interests of the patentee with those of the general public in economic development. Viewed from this angle, it makes no legal difference whether the patentee markets his products abroad and is able to freely determine the prices for such patented products as a compensation for the publication of his invention, or if this occurs domestically with the consequence of exhaustion. Thus, the possibility of the patentee obtaining a reward for the publication of his invention is limited to one time. Considering this aspect in taking into account the above doctrine of national exhaustion in correspondence with the economic development, it makes no material difference if the first commercial sale occurs domestically or abroad. The fact that borders are crossed are no reasonable grounds for giving the patentee another opportunity to economically profit from the publication of his invention. This is the more so against the background of international trade that has made Japan's economy and trade considerably international and will do so even more in the future."

The decision stirred a lot of controversy and was criticised by a number of eminent academics.[9] The former Managing Director of the Max Planck Institute, Friedrich-Karl Beier, even supplied an expert opinion to the court arguing that international exhaustion contravened the principle of independence of patent rights as laid down in

6. Tokyo District Court, 22 July 1994, Case No. 16565 (Wa) of 1992, 1501 Hanrei Jihō 70 – *BBS Car Wheels I*.
7. Especially T. SHIBUYA, Tokkyohin no heikō yunyū ni tsuite (*The Parallel Importation of Patented Products)*, Tokkyo News, 9 November 1994, 1, and 15 November 1994, 2.
8. Tokyo High Court, 23 March 1995, Case No. 3272 (Ne) of 1994, 1524 Hanrei Jihō 3.
9. E.g. S. ONO, Heikō tokkyo to yunyū (*Parallel Patents and Importation*), in: Chiteki zaisan to kyōsō hō no riron, Writings in Honour of F. K. Beier, Tokyo 1996, 459; N. KOIZUMI, Heikō yunyū wo meguru keizai to hō jō (Economic and law around parallel import part 1), 563 NBL 13 (1995); N. KOIZUMI, Heikō yunyū wo meguru keizai to hō ge (Economics and law around parallel import part 2), 567 NBL 31 (1995).

Art. 4bis (1) Paris Convention.[10] On the other hand, support was voiced for the decision as a prevention of parallel imports under patent law could hardly be justified for legal reasons.[11] The Supreme Court took slightly over two years to reach a decision. It endorsed the High Court's theory of double remuneration in the domestic context, yet rejected it in the international context.

The Tokyo District Court regarded the import of patented products without proper consent of the patentee to be an infringement and upheld the claim (decision of 22 July 1994). The Tokyo High Court allowed the appeal and dismissed the claim, arguing that the patentee was sufficiently rewarded by the act of first sale of the patented product, whether domestically or abroad (decision of 23 March 1995). The plaintiff now appeals to the Supreme Court against this ruling.

b) Reasons

1. The plaintiff is the owner of a Japanese patent for car wheels that was ... registered on 20 December 1991. The patent is subsequently referred to as "the present patent" or "the present invention". The plaintiff is the owner of a corresponding German patent based on an identical invention and ... registered on 22 April 1987, subsequently referred to as "the parallel patent".

At least until August 1992, the defendant had imported BBS, RS, and RSK aluminium wheels. The second defendant had subsequently sold them. Since the defendants had sold said products until that time, there is a certain likelihood that they will also engage in these activities in the future. The products sold by the defendants are subsequently referred to as "the products". The products fall within the scope of the present patent. The products were produced and sold by the plaintiff under his parallel patent in Germany.

2. The defendant has argued that the products protected under the present patent have been marketed by the plaintiff in Germany with the consequence that his right no longer covers these products. Importation and sale of these products by the defendant would not qualify as a patent infringement due to the theory of international patent exhaustion.

According to the Tokyo High Court, producing and marketing the products under the parallel German patent in Germany would give the plaintiff sufficient reward for having made his invention available to the public. Since it was established that compensation could be obtained, the Tokyo High Court did not find any kind of restriction whereby compensation by distribution would have been legally prevented. By having legally marketed products in Germany, the patent right was exhausted with respect to the distributed products, and consequently the plaintiff could no longer invoke his patent right against the defendant for claiming injunctive relief and damages.

10. F. K. Beier, Zur Zulässigkeit von Parallelimporten patentierter Erzeugnisse *(To the jurisdiction of parallel import of patented products)*, GRUR Int. 1996, 1.

11. K. Yoshifuji, Tokkyo hō gaisetsu *(Outline of Patent Law)*, 10th ed. 1994, 349; N. Nakayama, Chūkai tokkyohō (*Patent Law Annotated*), 2nd ed. 1989, 631.

3. This Court agrees with the lower court's findings insofar as, under the present patent right, the plaintiff is not entitled to a claim for damages and injunctive relief. The reasons for this are as follows.

a. According to Art. 4[bis] Stockholm version of the Paris Convention:

> (1) Patents applied for in the various countries of the Union by nationals of countries of the Union shall be independent of patents obtained for the same invention in other countries, whether members of the Union or not.
>
> (2) The foregoing provision is to be understood in an unrestricted sense, in particular, in the sense that patents applied for during the period of priority are independent, both as regards the grounds for nullity and forfeiture, and as regards their normal duration.

The provision denies the interdependency of patents and affirms that patent rights as regards their formation, amendments, and forfeiture are independent of each other in each country. The existence of a patent right does not depend on patent rights being declared void or invalid in another country, or on the duration of the patent right in such country. It is understood that all this does not reciprocally affect patent rights. Having established this, the above provision does not concern the exercise of patent rights by the patentee.

Next, the principle of territoriality with regard to patents means that patent rights in each country are subject to domestic legal provisions insofar as establishment, transfer, and validity are concerned. It means that the patent rights only have effect within the geographical limits of such country. It is only to be determined under domestic patent law as to what constitutes a use of the patent right, and in how far exercise of a patent right can also relate to goods the patentee has circulated outside Japan. This question bears no relation to the principle of territoriality under the Paris Convention, for which reason a violation of the provision of Art. 4(2) Paris Convention cannot be successfully claimed in the present case.

b. According to sec. 68, Japanese Patent Act, a patentee shall have the exclusive right to work the patented invention commercially. In the case of a product invention, "working" means the acts of manufacturing, using, assigning, leasing, importing, or offering for assignment or lease of the product (sec. 2(3)(i) Patent Act). Any person who has purchased products covered by a patented invention, either from the patentee or from a licensee with consent of the patentee, commits an act of use by re-selling these goods to a third party. Equally, such a third party who has obtained the patented products in such a way is, at least formally, working the patented invention when further leasing it, and would thus be liable for patent infringement. However, if patented products are sold domestically, either by the patentee or with his consent, the patent is deemed exhausted because it has fulfilled its purpose. The patent does not give rights to subsequent use of the patented product by acts of transfer or lease. First, patent law has to be understood as balancing the interests of invention protection, and the public benefit of society at large. Next, if a tangible object is transferred, the rights are obtained by the transferee, and the transferee obtains those rights that were originally vested in the transferor. Also insofar as patented products are distributed on the market, the transferee obtains an object from the patentee whose exercising of the right suggests that the right in further acts of re-sale has been transferred as well. If with respect to any acts of marketing patented products, the patentee's consent were necessary each time a transfer occurs, the free movement of goods would be seriously impeded, the smooth distribution of patented products would be hampered and as a result, the interests of the patentee himself would suffer. This would run counter to the purpose of the Patent Act "to encourage inventions by promoting their protection and utilisation so as to contribute to the development of industry" (sec. 1 Patent Act). Finally, by making the invention available to the public, the patentee will have the opportunity to obtain the reward from selling the product or granting a licence for the use of the patent and thereby obtain a licensing fee. In order to protect the financial interests of the patentee who has made his invention public, it would not seem necessary to give the patentee or the licensee rights beyond the first act of marketing, as the patentee would then obtain an unnecessary double reward in the course of further distribution.

c. However, the above considerations are not applicable if the owner of a Japanese patent markets the patented products abroad. For one thing, in the country where the products have been marketed, the patentee may not even hold a parallel patent that corresponds to the one in Japan. But even so, the domestic patent right and the parallel patent right in the country of marketing have to be regarded as separate rights. It cannot be argued that although selling the products under a parallel patent would give a double reward, it may qualify as an act of use of the domestic patent right.

4. Yet some thought should be given to the relationship between the free movement of goods in international trade and the interests of the patentee. In our present day society, international trade and economy affect us very broadly and permit conditions of rapid development. Even in the case that goods are purchased abroad, imported into Japan and put into circulation in the domestic market, there is the need to create conditions for the free distribution of goods, including their importation. Even if economic transactions have been made abroad, as a general principle, the transferee obtains not only the object as such, but also the rights vested therein. In other words, the transferor transfers his rights. To enable such transactions and to set the conditions for international trade in modern day society, it is assumed that the patentee who has transferred the ownership of patented goods abroad has also endowed the transferee or any subsequent purchaser with the right to undertake further transactions with third parties, including the importation to Japan, use in Japan, and transfer of ownership on our domestic market.

Opposed to the above concept, a domestic patentee who markets patented products abroad and wishes to exclude their sale and use in our country by subsequent purchasers, has to make clear his intention of such a restriction when dealing with the transferee, and has to clarify such restriction on the patented goods for the benefit of subsequent purchasers. In the absence thereof, such acts cannot be understood as a use of the patent in Japan. That is to say:

(a) According to the above, if the patented products were marketed abroad, then it can be naturally expected that such goods may be imported into Japan if the patentee puts such goods into circulation abroad without any reservations at the time of transfer. The transferee or any other subsequent purchaser is understood to have purchased the product without any restrictions that might apply to such products in Japan.

(b) On the other hand, if the patentee reserves his rights at the date of transfer with respect to the use in Japan when selling the patented products abroad, at the time of transfer the patentee has agreed with the transferee that sale or use of the patented product should not be allowed in Japan. If clearly indicated on the products, such a restriction is also valid against subsequent purchasers of the patented product along the distribution chain even with a number of intermediaries. Here it is understood that the above products have been sold under certain restrictive conditions, and any purchaser is free if he wants to obtain products bearing such a limitation or not.

(c) In the case where the marketing activities abroad have been undertaken by an affiliated company, a subsidiary or a person with the same standing as the patentee, the case should be treated as if the patentee himself had marketed the patented products.

(d) In view of the fact that the transferee's right of further distribution of the patented products should be maintained, it appears correct to attach no importance to the existence of a parallel patent in the country of marketing.

5. The products were sold by the plaintiff and patentee in the Federal Republic of Germany. When the plaintiff sold the products, no limitation was imposed on the purchaser about any restrictions of sale or use, or even if so, the plaintiff has offered no proof of this fact. For this reason, with regard to the products, the patentee is not entitled to claim an injunction or damages under his patent right.

The decision was unanimous.

3. ANALYSIS

a) Domestic Exhaustion

A very good example of how the above principle is applied is provided by the *Acycrobil* decision.[12] Here, the defendant had obtained marketing approval for a generic drug containing the same active formula as the one described in the plaintiff's (*Glaxo Wellcome*) patent. Marketing approval would expire unless the products were actually brought on the market within six months from the date of marketing approval. The defendant thus purchased the plaintiff's pharmaceuticals containing the active ingredient, distilled the latter and used this basic patented substance for producing the generic drug. As the patentee had received the economic benefits deriving from the patent by the act of first marketing, he could no longer control further acts of commercial exploitation by the purchaser. The action was thus dismissed. The court applied the remuneration doctrine in this case and cited the Supreme Court's decision in this respect.

12. Tokyo District Court, 18 January 2001, Case No. 27944 (Wa) of 1999, 1779 Hanrei Jihō 99, confirmed by Tokyo High Court, 29 November 2001, Case No. 959 (Ne) of 2001, 1779 Hanrei Jihō 89 – *Acycrobil*.

The outcome of the second case was more doubtful in light of the two above-mentioned theories. In the *Tissue Paper* case,[13] the plaintiff and right holder had supplied hospitals with tissue paper in dispensers. The right holder claimed that he had retained title in the tissue paper roll core and under such retention obliged hospitals to have the dispensers refilled with tissue paper only through the patentee. The defendant was a company that had refilled the dispensers with tissue. According to the first instance decision,[14] the plaintiff had validly retained title and refilling by third parties thus amounted to an infringement. The High Court found that the retention of title was invalid (as not clearly expressed) and refilling was permissible under the exhaustion doctrine, as the paper as such was not covered by the rights at issue.

It is easy to see that the court was uncomfortable with this sort of tie-in construction. Yet its legal reasoning is not convincing: A retention of title is nothing other than a failure to pass property. Even if the retention of title was ambiguous or ambiguously expressed, the question must have been to what extent the plaintiff wanted to pass title. If this was not so, property was not transferred even though the purchaser was not aware of this, or may even have a claim for such transfer to be made. In other words: Unless the proprietor wanted to pass title, property did not pass. And in such event, the patented dispensers would still be the property of the patentee. The Osaka District Court's reasoning would be correct if the implied licence doctrine was applied: Where property as such does not pass, there is no assumption that the intellectual property rights would, and the goods could therefore not be deemed exhausted. Their refill by a third party would amount to a commercial use. If exhaustion on the other hand is regarded as a public policy instrument (remuneration doctrine), the Osaka High Court may have reached the correct result: The hospital might have committed a breach of contract, yet in refilling the dispensers third parties merely used an item already exhausted. The result in this case does not depend on the question if property was transferred or not. It would be an additional question to what extent the hospital could be sued for breach of contract, or to what extent the patentee tried to abuse his patent monopoly by imposing additional and unwanted services. Since the hospital was not sued in this case, the question did not require an answer. Neither, however, was the question which of the above-mentioned two theories should prevail in a case of conflict answered.

b) International exhaustion

At the time, BBS was one of the most controversial decisions rendered by a Japanese Court, and perhaps the only one widely cited abroad, with disapproval by the German *Karate* decision,[15] and as a reference by the decision of the Swiss Federal Supreme Court *Kodak II.*[16]

13. Osaka High Court, 1 December 2000, Case No. 728 (Ne) of 2000, 1072 Hanrei Times 234 – *Medicine Envelope Tissue Paper Roll*. This case is related to utility model and design right.
14. Osaka District Court, 3 February 2000, Case No. 11089 (Wa) of 1998, the website of the courts <http://www.courts.go.jp/app/files/hanrei_jp/319/013319_hanrei.pdf> – *Medicine Envelope Tissue Paper Roll*.
15. German Federal Supreme Court, 2000 GRUR Int. 635, 637 – *Karate*.
16. Swiss Supreme Court, 7 December 1999, GRUR Int. 2000, 639 – *Kodak II*.

In the 1990s, Japan became an ever more affluent country, but consumers had the feeling that traditional and opaque distribution structures made it difficult for them to benefit from a strong Yen and actually get hold of cheap (or cheaper) foreign products. In 1991, the Fair Trade Commission had issued new Guidelines on the Distribution System[17] and included a chapter on attempts to prevent the parallel importation of goods. The FTC considered such attempts anti-competitive to the extent that they could not be justified by the exercise of an intellectual property right. After the Parker decision handed down in 1971, it was clear at least that the parallel importation of trade marked goods could not be prevented,[18] while the case for patents had not been seriously tested, see above.[19]

The second instance decision affirming international exhaustion divided Japanese IP experts. Those in favour of the decision were *e.g. Nakayama, Shibuya and Kuwata,*[20] those against e.g. *Koizumi, and Dr. S. Ono.*[21] The Ministry of International Trade (MITI) thought that the diplomatic repercussions of accepting international exhaustion outweighed the benefits for Japanese consumers. *F. K. Beier* wrote an opinion on behalf of the plaintiff BBS (see above), as did *H. Wegner*[22] and *J. Straus.*[23] The Supreme Court entrusted *Ryōichi Mimura,* then an assistant judge on secondment to the Supreme Court, with preparing and drafting the appeal decision, certainly not an easy task especially because no national court outside of Japan had yet adopted such a clear stance in favour of the international exhaustion of patent rights, and most foreign experts had criticised the High Court decision.

In the international arena, the decision of the High Court fell into the time when countries had started to implement the TRIPS Agreement, and intense lobbying efforts were underway by industry to ensure that countries, developed and developing, despite Art. 6 TRIPS Agreement would not pass legislation that allowed for the parallel importation of patented products.[24]

17. FTC, Guidelines on the Distribution System and its Trade Practices, 11 July 1991.
18. Osaka District Court, 27 February 1970, Case No. 7003 (Wa) of 1968, 2 IIC 325 (1971) - *Parker.*
19. Osaka District Court, 9 June 1969, Case No. 3460 (Wa) of 1968, 1 Mutaishū 160 - *Brunswick,* as above.
20. S. KUWATA, Tokkyo seihin no heikō yunyū mondai wo meguru ichikōsatsu (*Thoughts on the parallel importation of patented goods*) in: Chiteki zaisan to kyōsō hō no riron, Writings in Honour of F. K. Beier, Tokyo 1996, 459.
21. Dr. S. ONO in Mutaizaisankenhō Bunken mokuroku *(Bibliography on Intellectual Property)*, vol. 4, 2003, 135 - 141 lists more than 100 articles in Japanese journals on this topic alone.
22. H. WEGNER, Heikō yunyū to tokkyo chiikisei *(Territoriality of Patents and Parallel Imports)*, 41 AIPPI Journal of the Japanese Group (Japanese edition) 6 (1996).
23. J. STRAUS, Implications of the TRIPS Agreement in the Field of Patent Law, in: BEIER/SCHRICKER (eds.), From GATT to TRIPS, Weinheim 1996, 160, 193 ("neglect the principles of territoriality and independence"; "failure to recognize a fundamental principle underlying ... the TRIPS rationale ...").
24. E.g. J. STRAUS, Implications of the TRIPS Agreement in the Field of Patent Law, in: BEIER/SCHRICKER (eds.), From GATT to TRIPS, Weinheim 1996, 160, 192: "... substantive patent law under the TRIPS Agreement amounts to a barrier to international exhaustion." LAUDIEN, Erschöpfung der gewerblichen Schutzrechte aus rechtsvergleichender Sicht: Die Position der forschenden pharmazeutischen Industrie *(Exhaustion of industrial property rights from a comparative view: The position of research-based pharmaceutical industry)*, 2000 GRUR Int. 617.

Rather inconveniently for the plaintiffs in this action, the English Patents Court at the end of 1995 handed down a decision[25] that affirmed the long-standing case law on the doctrine of implied license in cases of parallel importation. As this doctrine was subsequently adopted by the Japanese Supreme Court, a closer look on this concept may be justified.

Under English common law,

> "it is open to the patentee, by virtue of his statutory monopoly, to make a sale sub modo, or accompanied by restrictive conditions which would not apply in the case of ordinary chattels; ... the imposition of these conditions in the case of sale is not presumed, but, on the contrary, a sale having occurred, the presumption is that the full right of ownership was meant to be vested in the purchaser while ... the owner's rights in a patented chattel would be limited, if there is brought home to him the knowledge of conditions imposed, by the patentee or those representing the patentee, upon him at the time of sale."[26]

The case at issue confirmed that "[445] limited licences require that notice be brought to the attention of every person down the chain. That is normally done by putting notice of the licence on the goods ... Once the goods are sold without a limited licence then the purchaser buys them free of any patent restriction."

The Supreme Court might have found the solution appealing for three reasons. First, it could point to international support for this position, second, it provided a compromise between the interests of the patentee and the general public (it would be up to the patentee to prevent parallel importation by an appropriate notice, after all), and, third, in practical terms, the result was an international exhaustion in all but name. The decision was subsequently affirmed in the *Canon Ink Jet* decision (Case No. 31 in this book).

4. COMPARATIVE REMARKS

World-wide, a number of different approaches have been adopted be it by legislation, be it by the courts, to determine whether domestic law should recognise exhaustion in regard of products that were marketed abroad by the domestic patentee or with his consent.[27]

The first approach was already mentioned above: **English** common law makes no distinction between domestic or foreign marketing, as it regards exhaustion as an issue of contract law that allows the patentee to withhold title on condition that this limitation is "brought home" to every purchaser of the product.

The further approaches affirm domestic exhaustion upon the first commercial marketing of the patented products by the patentee or with his consent, but distinguish this from the case of products marketed abroad

25. English Patents Court, 9 October 1995, *Roussel Uclaf v. Hockley*, [1996] RPC 441.
26. Privy Council, 3 February 1911, *National Phonograph Company of Australia Ltd. v. Menck*, [28] R.P.C. 229, 248.
27. For details, see C. HEATH, Exhaustion and Patent Rights, in: BAGLEY/OKEDIJI, Patent Law in Global Perspective, Oxford University Press 2014, 419 – 484

The **German** courts have denied such recognition outright, normally with reference to the territorial nature of patent rights:

> "The appellants' contention that, by marketing his products in a country where he can make use of his patent monopoly, the patentee is already adequately compensated for the advancement of the art brought about by his invention and that a renewed assertion of identical patent rights in another country is not justified, finds no support in German patent law. It also ignores the fact that in every country in which he successfully applies for a patent, the patentee is granted for his invention an independent exclusive right which ends at the borders of such country and that each issuing state grants him an independent claim for compensation for disclosing his invention, which is wholly unrelated to advantages derived from other patents in other countries, even though identical."[28]

And, in a later decision:

> "... the marketing of a patented product by the patentee or with his consent outside the geographical area of the European Union does not entail exhaustion of the German patent or the German part of a European patent. The principle of national exhaustion was already endorsed by the Imperial Supreme Court (references). The Federal Supreme Court has endorsed this in various decisions (references). In addition, this reflects the majority view among academic writings (references). [637] The principle of national exhaustion is further applied in most other Member States of the European Community (references)."[29]

This approach is followed also by a number of other European countries, e.g. **France**.

The **European** Court of Justice has not taken a stance on the domestic patent laws of the EU Member States, yet has prohibited a partitioning of markets based on domestic patent rights and thereby de facto endorsed the principle of regional exhaustion within the EU:

> "The court held, finally, in paragraphs 11 and 13 of Merck that it was for the holder of the patent to decide, in the light of all the circumstances, under what conditions he would market his product, including the possibility of marketing it in a member state where the law did not provide patent protection for the product in question. If he decides to do so, he must then accept the consequences of his choice as regards free movement of the product within the common market. This being a fundamental principle forming part of the legal and economic circumstances which the holder of the patent must take into account in determining how to exercise his exclusive right. Under those conditions, to permit an inventor to invoke a patent held by him in one member state in order to prevent the importation of the product freely marketed by him in another member state where the product was not patentable would cause a partitioning of national markets contrary to the aims of the treaty."[30]

---

28. German Federal Supreme Court, 3 June 1976, 8 IIC 64, 66 (1977) – *Tylosin*.
29. German Federal Supreme Court, 14 December 1999, GRUR 2000, 635 – *Karate*.
30. ECJ, 5 December 1996, *Merck v. Primecrown*, joined cases C-267/95, and ECJ, 5 December 1996, *Beecham v. Europharm*, case C-2668/95, [1996] ECR I-6285.

The ECJ's approach of consented marketing has also been adopted by a number of other countries that permit *international* exhaustion on such condition, for example **Thailand,**[31] **Argentina,**[32] **South Africa**[33] and the **United States.**[34]

One answer to this argument has been given by the **US** Supreme Court:

> "Exhaustion is a separate limit on the patent grant, and does not depend on the patentee receiving some undefined premium for selling the right to access the American market. A purchaser buys an item, not patent rights. And exhaustion is triggered by the patentee's decision to give that item up and receive whatever fee it decides is appropriate. ... The patentee may not be able to command the same amount for its products abroad as it does in the United States. But the Patent Act does not guarantee a particular price, much less the price from selling to American consumers. Instead, the right to exclude just ensures that the patentee receives one reward – of whatever amount the patentee deems to be 'satisfactory compensation,' for every item that passes outside the scope of the patent monopoly."

Whether a regime of national, regional or international exhaustion is compliant with international agreements is also a matter of considerable discussion.[35]

31. Sec. 36(3)(vii) Thai Patent Act as of 27 March 1999.
32. According to Sec. 36 Argentinian Patent Act, "The right granted by any patent shall not have effect against: [...] (c) any person that acquires, uses, imports or commercialises in any way the product patented or obtained by the patented process, *once such product has been lawfully marketed in any country.*" This provision, of course, goes way beyond the above consent rule, as it basically obliges any patentee to obtain patents in all countries of the world to obtain proper protection. In the author's opinion, this is difficult to justify within the framework of TRIPS.
33. The relevant provision cannot be found in South Africa's Patent Act, but in sec. 15C(a) of the Medicines and Related Substances Control Act of 1965, as amended in 1997. The amendment at first did come into force due to lawsuits by several pharmaceutical companies. As these lawsuits were withdrawn in 2002, the amendment could be enacted. For details, see T. KONGOLO, Towards a new fashion of protecting pharmaceutical patents in Africa, 33 IIC 185, 194 (2002).
34. US Supreme Court, *Impression Products v. Lexmark International*, 30 May 2017, 581 US.___ (2017).
35. See C. HEATH, Parallel Imports of Patented Goods, in: HEATH/KAMPERMAN/SANDERS/MOERLAND, Intellectual Property Rights as Obstacles to Legitimate Trade?, Kluwer Law 2018, 21.

Case No. 33

Clinical Trials - Research Exception

Christopher Heath

Clinical trials for generic products undertaken for the purpose of obtaining government approval under Sec. 14 Pharmaceuticals Act do not constitute patent infringement under Sec. 69 Patent Act.

Supreme Court, 16 April 1999, Case No. 153 (Ju) of 1998 - *Clinical Trials III*

[X] v. [Y]

---

1. BACKGROUND

It is a universal concept that patent law is meant to stimulate invention and innovation. A patent can only be granted for an invention which "works". Products which cannot be produced and unworkable processes are not patentable. This rule implicitly mandates an exception to the patent's monopolistic right for the purposes of *experiment*. Everyone must be in a position to verify that the patented substance can indeed be produced or the patented process be carried out as described in the patent. In order to stimulate new inventions, everyone must also be in a position to use the patented invention as a basis of further *research* in order to find an even better way of achieving the same result. For the above reasons, basically all patent laws exempt the working of a patent right by a third party for the purposes of experiment or research. This exception is codified in sec. 69 Japanese Patent Act.

Prior to the marketing of pharmaceuticals, a marketing authorisation of the national health authorities is necessary. In order to obtain such authorisation, in vitro and in vivo studies are necessary in order to demonstrate efficacy and lack of harmful side effects. This can take years. Where pharmaceuticals are protected by a patent, this often means a significant reduction in the period of actual protection. In order to compensate for this loss, many countries have introduced schemes for extending the patent term. These are addressed for cases 59 - 61 in this book. Also producers of generic drugs that wish to market their products after the expiry of the patent need to prove that his substance is identical in its effects to the original one. This is called a bio-equivalency test. The producer of a generic drug does not wish to carry out tests with the purpose of improving the original substance, but with the purpose of demonstrating equivalent effect. Now, can a generic drug producer already carry out clinical trials with the aim of obtaining marketing approval during the patent term? If so, marketing of generic drugs could start from the very day patent protection has expired. If not, marketing would have to be delayed for a couple of years. Clinical trials carried out by generic drug makers during the patent term, certainly mean the use of the patent right. But would these clinical trials, undertaken for the purpose of obtaining government approval, qualify as an exempted research or experiment?

2. DECISION[1]

The appellant in the present proceedings owns a patent for a chemical product, or rather the effective ingredient therein. He claims that the appellee produces and uses a drug identical to the one protected by the patent in substance, dosage, method of use and effect, and requests damages and injunctive relief. The appellee's use relates to clinical trials being carried out under sec. 14 Pharmaceuticals Act necessary to obtain government approval for the drug's manufacture and sale. According to the appellee, his trials are exempt under sec. 69(1) Patent Act as "experiment or research".

A case does not qualify as an infringement where a third party, having the intention of manufacturing and selling a product with the same active ingredient, purpose and use as a patented substance after the life span of the patent, undertakes clinical trials for the purpose of obtaining government approval under sec. 14 Pharmaceuticals Act. Even though the substances so used fall within the technical scope of the patent right, they are exempt by virtue of the purposes of "experiment or research" for the following reasons:

(1) By granting exclusive use of a certain invention for a limited period of time in exchange for a disclosure of the invention, the patent system promotes inventive activity. Yet at the same time, the patent system provides the general public with the opportunity of using these publicly disclosed technologies, thereby contributing to the overall development of industry. It is one of the basic principles of the patent system to allow anyone to exploit freely a new technology after the expiry of the patent term, thereby generating a benefit to society.

(2) For reasons of safety in the production of pharmaceuticals, the Pharmaceuticals Act requires their prior approval by the Ministry of Health and Welfare. The corresponding application must be accompanied by various data obtained from clinical trials, which have to be conducted over a certain period of time, even if the approval relates to a generic product. It is necessary to manufacture and use pharmaceuticals within the scope of the patent right in order to conduct such clinical trials. It stands to reason that if such clinical trials did not qualify as "experiments" under sec. 69(1) Patent Act, they could not be conducted as long as the patent remained in force. As a result, third parties would not be in a position to freely exploit the patented invention for a certain period of time even after the patent had

1. Published in 53-4 Minshū 627 = 1675 Hanrei Jihō 37 = 1002 Hanrei Times 83 = N. Nakayama at el. (eds.), Tokkyo Hanrei Hyakusen *(Hundred Selected Patent Cases)*, 4th ed. 2012, 118 = T. Ōbuchi et al. (eds.) Chitekizaisan hō hanrei shū *(Intellectual Property Law Case Book)*, 2nd ed. 2015, 108. English translation in 30 IIC 448 (1999) – *Clinical Trials III.*

expired. This, in turn, would contradict the basic principles of the patent system as explained above.

(3) However, patent law would not allow third parties to manufacture and use components of a patented pharmaceutical during the life span of a patent beyond what would be required under the Pharmaceuticals Act in order to obtain government approval. Limiting the exemption in this way, the patent owner would still be able to reap the commercial benefit of exclusively exploiting his invention for the life span of the patent right. Extending such protection to also cover clinical trials conducted by generic drug makers and carried out for the purpose of obtaining government approval would effectively prolong the life span of a patent, a benefit that cannot be said to be intended by the Patent Act.

For the reasons explained above, and the facts set out by the lower court, the appellee's acts qualify as "working of the patent right for the purposes of experiment or research" under sec. 69(1) Patent Act. They are not infringing. The lower court's decision can therefore be upheld, and the appellant's particular views on the lower court's findings must be dismissed.

The decision was unanimous.

3. ANALYSIS

a) Case law prior to the Supreme Court decision

In 1987, the Tokyo District Court had decided in a very similar case and found the exemption for experimental research not applicable to cases where experiments were only conducted with the aim of obtaining government approval.[2] Because of the pricing mechanisms of the Japanese Health Ministry, marketing generic drugs in Japan at least in the 1980s when the decision was rendered was not the big business it may have been in other countries. In Japan, generic medicines in the 1990s accounted for about 7–8% of the total pharmaceutical sales, while in Europe and the US the comparable figures amounted to 30–40%.[3] As the market for generic medicines became more lucrative, a new wave of court actions was reported in the mid 1990s, and the first two decisions were decided in favour of originator companies.[4] The reported success of *Synthelabo* in these actions then encouraged other pharmaceutical companies to take on their imitators. Hence it was reported[5] that the UK firm *Glaxo-Wellcome PLC* had taken on the Japanese companies *Kobayashi Kako*, *Fuji Yakuhin*, and *Towa Yakuhin* for an alleged infringement of Glaxo's patents by conducting clinical trials in order to obtain official approval before Glaxo's patents expired. *Glaxo-Wellcome* also sued *Sawai Seiyaku*, *Taiyo Yakuhin Kōgyō* and *Kayaku* on the same grounds. While these cases were filed before the Tokyo District Court,

2. Tokyo District Court, 10 July 1987, Case Nos. 7463&6428 (Wa) of 1985&671 (Wa) of 1986, 20 IIC 91 (1989) – *Monsanto*.
3. Reported in The Nikkei Weekly, 24 June 1996, at p. 9.
4. Nagoya District Court, 6 March 1996, and Nagoya High Court, 18 March 1996, Case No. 4 (Ra) of 1996, 1599 Hanrei Jihō 134, both reported in 28 IIC 398 (1997) – *Synthelabo*.
5. Patents & Licensing, August 1996, at p. 2, 3.

Sandoz Ltd. of Switzerland filed suits both in Tokyo and in Nagoya against nine Japanese companies, *Sagami Kasei Kogyo, Shiono Chemical, Permachem Asia, YIC, Taiyo Yakuhin Kōgyō, MF, Medisa Shinyaku, Taiko Seiyaku* and *Toyo Pharmacy*, on the same grounds of conducting clinical trials with the purpose of obtaining official approval. Short of filing a suit in court, the German-owned *Bayer Yakuhin Ltd.* Sent warning letters to nine Japanese generic drug makers for alleged infringement of its substances by conducting clinical trials in order to obtain official approval prior to the patent expiration date. The nine companies were said to be *Toyama Seiyaku Kōgyō, Ikeda Mohando, Ryukakusan, Taiyo Yakuhin Kōgyō, MF, Maeda Yakuhin Kōgyō, Kyowa Yakuhin Kōgyō, Yoshindo*, and *Fukui Seiyaku*. All the subsequent decisions, however, went in favour of generic manufacturers.[6] The Supreme Court confirmed this approach and put an end to the legal uncertainty in this field.

b) Legal considerations

The arguments for both views are relatively straight-forward.

The strongest argument in favour of patent infringement is the fact that the trials undertaken in order to obtain government approval are done for administrative purposes and not for the purposes of improvement of an existing technology. Only the latter, however, should be exempt under patent law.

Arguments against infringement are three-fold.

First, if trials in order to satisfy the requirements under domestic legislation for health protection were indeed meaningless in terms of their outcome, conducting such trials could not be mandated by law in the first place (because trials on humans must serve the purpose of serving public health and welfare). Accordingly, such trials could not be deemed necessary for public health and welfare on the one hand side, yet be disqualified as not serving the purpose of discovery on the other. Where clinical trials had to be conducted by manufacturers of generic drugs in order to satisfy the requirements under the Pharmaceutical Act, that is, in order to ensure safety and compatibility of these products so as to guarantee public health and well-being, such clinical trials had to be deemed beneficial to research and development in the patented substance and therefore to the overall objective of advancing science. They should thus qualify as "experiments".[7]

---

6. E.g. Tokyo District Court, 18 July 1997, Case No. 7011 (Wa) of 1996, 1616 Hanrei Jihō 34; Tokyo District Court, 29 August 1997, Case No. 10134 (Wa) of 1996, 1616 Hanrei Jihō 34; Nagoya High Court, 14 January 1998, Case No. 59 (Ne) of 1997, 23-2 AIPPI Journal of the Japanese Group (English edition) 57 (1998); Tokyo District Court, 9 February 1998, Case No. 8627 (Wa) of 1996, 1632 Hanrei Jihō 119; Yamagata District Court, 17 March 1998, Case No. 233 (Wa) of 1996, 276 Hanketsu Sokuhō 20 (1998); Osaka District Court, 30 April 1998, Case Nos. 7358 (Wa) of 1996&1811 (Wa) of 1997, 277 Hanketsu Sokuhō 14 (1998); Osaka District Court, 7 May 1998, Case No. 2505 (Wa) of 1996, 277 Hanketsu Sokuhō 15 (1998); Tokyo High Court, 31 March 1998, Case No. 3498 (Ne) of 1997, 39 IIC 454 (1999) – *Procaterole*.
7. Tokyo District Court, 18 July 1997, 1616 Hanrei Jihō 34 = IP Asia 11/2 (February 1998), 11; Tokyo District Court, 29 August 1997, Case No. 10134 (Wa) of 1996, 1616 Hanrei Jihō 34; Tokyo District Court, 6 October 1997, Case Nos. 24181 (Wa) of 1996&2344 (Wa) of 1997, 1630 Hanrei Jihō 127; Tokyo District Court, 9 February 1998, Case No. 8627 (Wa) of 1996, 1632 Hanrei Jihō 119.

Second, clinical trials by generic manufacturers, unless conducted on a huge scale, do not interfere with the exclusive commercial use of a patented invention. In other words, the commercial monopoly of the patentee is not affected by such acts, just as would be the case for classical research.

Third, if such clinical trials were not permissible during the life span of the patent, the patentee could unduly extend his monopoly beyond the patent term. This was the main argument of the Supreme Court. The argument is of course in stronger where the law provides for the possibility of a patent term extension due to the time lost for obtaining marketing approval.

In reaching its decision, the Supreme Court could also draw upon some comparative studies.[8]

4. COMPARATIVE REMARKS

In **Europe** and the **US**, clinical trials with the aim of obtaining marketing approval are not considered infringing, be it based on specific legal provisions or court decisions.

a) The **US** courts have clearly ruled that "limited unauthorised testing of a drug during the term of a patent thereon, with a view to obtaining FDA approval to market the generic version upon expiration of the patent, is infringement. It is excused by neither the experimental purpose doctrine nor the policies of the Food, Drug, and Cosmetic Act".[9] This is in line with the generally narrow construction US Courts have given to the experimental exception: It is fine to do research on, but not research with the patented technology.[10] However, this position for clinical trials was reversed with the Patent Term Restoration Act. The newly introduced sec. 271(e)(1) of Title 35 U.S.C. now clearly states that "it shall not be an act of infringement to make, use, or sell a patented invention solely for uses reasonably related to the development and submission of information under federal law which regulates the manufacture, use, or sale of drugs or veterinary biological products". According to a subsequent decision, "the clear intent of Congress was to create an FDA experimental use exemption for use which *Roche* had held would constitute infringement under sec. 271(a)".[11] In other words, US Congress saw a clear connection between extending the patent term for pharmaceuticals with lengthy approval procedures and putting generic drug makers

8. K. Someno, Shiken kenkyū ni okeru tokkyō hatsumei no jisshi *(Working of a Patented Invention for Experiments or Research)*, 33-3 AIPPI Journal of the Japanese Group (Japanese edition) 5 (1998); S. Maeda and H. Akimoto, The Impact of Public Health Issues on Exclusive Patent Rights, 33-4 AIPPI Journal of the Japanese Group (English edition), 192-195 (2008); A comparative analysis was provided by: W. R. Cornish, Experimental Use of Patented Inventions in European Community States, 29 IIC 735 (1998); C. Heath, The Patent Exemption for "Experimental Use" in Clinical Trials, 22-6 AIPPI Journal of the Japanese Group (English edition) 267 (1997); J. Straus, On the Admissibility of "Biological Equivalence Test" During the Patent Term for Obtaining a Regulatory Approval for Patented Drugs by Third Parties, 23-6 AIPPI Journal of the Japanese Group (English edition) 211 (1998).
9. US CAFC *Roche v. Bollar*, 221 USPQ 1937 (Fed. Cir. 1984).
10. US CAFC, *Madey v. Duke University* (Fed. Cir. 2002): "For amusement, to satisfy idle curiosity, or for strictly philosophical inquiry."
11. US CAFC *Eli Lilly and Co. v. Medronic Inc.*, 873 D 2d 402, 10 USPQ 2d 1304 (Fed. Cir. 1989), affirmed by the Supreme Court, 496 US 661, 110 S.Ct. 2683 (1990).

on the same footing by allowing them to carry out their clinical trials already during the term of the patent right. The statutory exception has been broadly interpreted by the US Supreme Court to "all uses of patented compounds 'reasonably related' to the process of developing information for submission under any federal law regulating the manufacture, use, or distribution of drugs."[12]

b) In **Europe**, there was significant disagreement as to the interpretation of the research exception in cases of obtaining government approval:

The **English** courts regarded such clinical trials as a clear infringement of patent rights: "Trials carried out in order to discover something unknown or to test a hypothesis or even in order to find out whether something which is known to work in specific conditions, e.g., of soil or weather, will work in different conditions can fairly, in my judgement, be regarded as experiments. But trials carried out in order to demonstrate to a third party that a product works or, in order to amass information to satisfy a third party, whether a customer or a body such as the PSPS or ACAS, that the product works as its maker claims are not, in my judgement, to be regarded as acts done 'for experimental purposes'.[13]"

Exactly the opposite position has been taken by the **Italian** courts: "The owner of a patent for a commercial invention cannot oppose the experimental use undertaken by a third party in order to obtain the necessary documents for obtaining the registration of a pharmaceutical with the competent health authorities. The reason for this is if third parties were not allowed to request authorisation from the health authorities in time for putting the products on the market immediately after the expiration of the patent, the term of the exclusive right granted to the patentee would in fact be extended for the time it took to obtain such government approval ... [As the additional protection certificate] is meant to compensate the patentee for the delay incurred due to government approval, it would not seem reasonable to also give the patentee the advantage of the delay incurred by third parties if they were not allowed to request government approval in due time for putting their products on the market immediately upon expiration of the patent term".[14]

A less clear-cut stance has been taken by the **German** courts. In the first Supreme Court Decision on this matter, it was held that "clinical trials on humans with the aim of finding further use of the patented substance fall within the exemption under sec. 11 (2) Patent Act 1981".[15] In its second decision, the Supreme Court further clarified that "the primary purpose of [exempted] clinical trials on humans is the healing or improvement of illnesses, even if such trials are initiated and conducted with certain economic purposes in mind, and if the data obtained therefrom are used to obtain the necessary marketing approval ... This does not mean, however, that experiments of all sorts can be freely conducted. If an experiment does not relate to the [patented] technical solution or if experiments are conducted on such a large scale that cannot be justified, the scope of permissible experimental use has been overstepped. The same holds true for cases in which experiments are conducted with the purpose

12. US Supreme Court, Merck KG v. Integra Lifesciences, 545 US 193 (2005).
13. UK Court of Appeal, 11 June 1985, *Monsanto Co. v. Stauffer Chemical Co.*, 17 IIC 410 [1986].
14. Tribunale di Milano *(Milan District Court)*, 12 June 1995, in Giurisprudenza Annuale del Diritto Industriale, 1995, 1081.
15. German Federal Supreme Court, 11 July 1995, GRUR 1996, 109 – *Klinische Versuche I.*

of interfering with the marketing efforts of the inventor's products. In these cases, experiments do not serve the purpose of technical progress, but are used as a means to pursue competitive interests".[16] It appears from these decisions that clinical trials undertaken *also* but not *only* for the purpose of obtaining government approval are permissible. This was also the position of the French courts.[17]

One would have thought that European legislation attempted to harmonise the different approaches in the regulation introducing the Supplementary Protection Certificate (Regulation 1768/92, now 469/2009), but this was not the case. Rather, an explicit exemption was only introduced by EU Directive 2001/83/EC, subsequently replaced by EU Directive 2004/27/EC, Art. 10(6). This provision excludes from the infringement of patents or SPCs: "Conducting the necessary studies and trials with a view to the application of paragraphs 1, 2, 3 and 4" (in other words, for the purposes of obtaining marketing approval as a generic, quasi generic or biosimilar drug). An interesting case referred to the European Court of Justice concerned the question as to whether in order to benefit from the exception, also third parties could be entrusted with carrying out such trials with the purpose of obtaining marketing approval. Unfortunately, the referral was withdrawn.[18]

c) In **Korea**, the patent exception for experiments and research was given a broad meaning by the courts to include experiments for obtaining marketing approval under the Pharmaceutical Affairs Act.[19] The matter was also clarified by legislation (Act No. 9985 of 28 July 2010).

---

16. German Federal Supreme Court, 17 April 1997, Neue Juristische Wochenschrift 1997, 3092 – *Klinische Versuche II.*
17. Tribunal de Grande Instance Paris *(Paris District Court)*, 20 February 2001, PIBD 2001, 729- III-530.
18. Referring decision: Düsseldorf Appeal Court, 5 December 2013, Case No. I-2 U 68/12, CJEU case C-661/13.
19. Seoul Southern District Court, 16 June 2001, Case No. 1074 (Kahab) of 2001.

Case No. 34

Defence of Prior Use

Kengo Sakai

---

1. "Commercial preparation" as a requirement of the right of prior use should mean that the prior user must not necessarily have arrived at the stage of carrying out the invention, but must have implemented the intention to carry it out immediately to an extent that this is objectively recognisable.
2. The effect of the right of prior use should cover not only the form of working the invention as it was actually worked or prepared by the prior user at the time of the patent application, but also the form of working in which the embodiment does not lose its identity.

Supreme Court, 3 October 1986, Case No. 454 (O) of 1986 – *Walking Beam Furnace*

Midland Ross Corp. and Chugai-ro Kōgyō Kabushiki Kaisha v. Daido Tokushu Kō Kabushikikaisha

---

1. BACKGROUND

Sec. 79 Patent Act ("PA") states the right of prior use as follows: "A person who, without knowledge of the contents of an invention claimed in a patent application, made an invention identical to said invention, or a person who, without knowledge of the contents of an invention claimed in a patent application, learned the invention from a person who made an invention identical to said invention and has been commercially working the invention or preparing for commercially working the invention in Japan at the time of the filing of the patent application, shall have a non-exclusive license for the patent right, within the scope of the invention as commercially worked or prepared." Sec. 26 of the Utility Model Act refers to such provision and sec. 29 of the Design Act and sec. 32 of the Trade mark Act contain a similar provision.

Since the PA of Japan adopts the first filing principle and allows the patentee the exclusive right to commercially work the patented invention (sec. 68 PA), an inventor is not entitled to work the patent invention, in principle, if any other person has filed a corresponding earlier patent application.[1] The right of prior use is thus an exception of such first to file principle which aims to balance the interests of the patentee and the inventor who has been commercially working or preparing to work of the invention at the time of the patent application.[2]

If the requirement for prior use under sec. 79 PA is satisfied for a certain invention, the prior user by law is considered a non-exclusive licensee without obtaining any consent from the patentee. In practice, the right of prior use is raised as a defence to the patentee's infringement claim in most cases.[3] The prior user may also file a lawsuit against the patentee for declaratory judgment of non-infringement, which is the constellation in the case at issue. In line with an ordinary non-exclusive license, however, the prior user is not entitled to claim injunction or compensation of damages against a third party. Further, there is no limit as to how often the invention can be worked. The prior user right is transferable upon transfer of the whole business (sec. 94 PA).

In practice, companies sometimes choose not to file a patent application for an invention but to keep the invention secret as know-how. It is said that an increasing number of those companies prepare for a future defence of prior use as a protection to secure the uninterrupted use of such invention against a future patentee.[4]

The decision at issue is a representative case regarding the right of prior use. The decision is meaningful until now especially in how to interpret the term "preparing for the commercial use of the invention" and for the scope of such right, in regard of which the Supreme Court gave its guidance for the first time.

2. DECISION[5]

a) Facts

On 26 August 1968, the plaintiff company A1 filed a patent application with the title "D" based on the priority of a US patent application dated 26 February 1968. After the application was published on 12 October 1971, the patent at issue was registered on 30 May 1980 (registration No. 999931).

The claim of the patent at issue reads as follows:

> "Walking beam type conveyor for conveying workpieces through a refractory chamber of a furnace, characterised in that the walking beam type conveyor comprises at least two sets of conveyor rails for alternately supporting said workpieces, a carriage for moving at least a set of the conveyor rails relative

1. If such inventor worked or publicly prepared the invention, the patent may be invalid due to a lack of novelty.
2. N. Nakayama and N. Koizumi (eds.), Shin chūkai tokkyo hō jōkan *(New Commentary to the Patent Act, vol. 1)*, 2011, 1247
3. N. Nakayama and N. Koizumi (eds.) (above), at 1247
4. N. Nakayama and N. Koizumi (eds.) (above), at 1248
5. Published in 40-6 Minshū 1068 = 1219 Hanrei Jihō 116 = 627 Hanrei Times 105 = N. Nakayama et al. (eds.), Tokkyo hanrei hyakusen *(Hundred Selected Patent Cases)*, 4th ed. 2012, 158 = T. Ōbuchi et al. (eds.) Chitekizaisan hō hanrei shū (Intellectual Property Law Case Book), 2nd ed. 2015, 178.

to another set of the conveyor rails, each of the conveyor rails having plural workpiece support pads, further a pair of parallel beams extending along the underside of the said carriage, at least four rotatable eccentric rings under said parallel beams for supporting said parallel beams and said carriage, and for vertically reciprocating said carriage, an apparatus for horizontally reciprocating said carriage independently of the vertical reciprocation by the rotatable eccentric rings, and each of said eccentric rings having a freely rotatable peripheral ring bearing for supporting an underside section of said parallel beams."

An exclusive license for the patent at issue was granted on behalf of the plaintiff company A2 on 6 March 1981 and registered on 21 August 1981.

The defendant company received an inquiry for participating in a tender from steel company E for the steel factory F around 20 May 1966. At first, the defendant conceptualised and designed an existing pusher type furnace which had a processing capacity of 100 tons per hour, but from July 1966, with the agreement of the steel company E, it started to conceptualise and design a walking beam type furnace which had a processing capacity of 120 tons per hour with a motorised apparatus for vertical reciprocation. Around 10 August 1966, the defendant completed the plans by focusing its resources because of the inquiry of the steel company E for a motorised walking beam type furnace, and around 31 August 1966 submitted an estimate specification and blueprint.

After that, the defendant company drafted an explanatory document for the walking beam mechanism of the motorised walking beam type furnace, went to the steel factory F, and, as preparation for receiving an order, demanded an estimate from the machinery company G as a subcontractor by showing the drawing of the driving part which included eccentric cams used for the motorised type apparatus for vertical reciprocation. But on 20 September 1966, the steel company E requested a change of the apparatus for vertical reciprocation from the motorised type to an oil pressure type etc., so the defendant submitted the blueprint etc. of an oil pressure type to the steel company E on 27 September 1966.

Finally, around 19 November 1966, it became clear that the defendant would not receive an order from the steel company E, but the defendant maintained the estimate specifications etc. which were made for the bidding process of steel company E. Thereafter, the defendant every year participated in tenders related to requests for walking beam type furnaces from steel companies etc., estimated and designed two oil pressure types each in 1967 and 1968, two motorised types and four oil pressure types in 1969, three motorised types and four oil pressure types in 1970, two oil pressure types in 1971, and succeeded in receiving orders for one oil pressure type in 1967 and 1969, two motorised types in 1970, two motorised types and one oil pressure type in 1970, two oil pressure types in 1973, each one motorised type in 1976 and 1977.

It depends mainly on the preference of users whether for a walking beam type furnace the apparatus for vertical reciprocation is of the motorised type with eccentric cams or of the oil pressure type.

Regarding the motorised walking beam type furnace which was prepared by the defendant by submitting the above mentioned estimate specification etc. to the steel company E around 31 August 1966 in order to be sold, the defendant did not succeed in receiving an order. But had the defendant received it, there was a plan to construct the furnace by fixing a final specification in the course of discussion on details with the factory F, based on the estimate specification etc., and by making a final production drawing.

After the delivery of a product to the steel factory I of the steel company H in May 1971, the defendant company produced and sold several walking type furnaces, henceforth the defendant's "product A". The fundamental structure of the defendant's product A and the product projected earlier is the same and these likewise fall under the technical scope of the patented invention, but there are differences in the following four points: the fixing structure of eccentric rings and eccentric axis for reciprocating the walking beams, the bearing structure of the eccentric rings, the horizontal oscillation prevention structure of the parallel beam for supporting the walking beam and the method of driving the eccentric axis.

b) Reasons

2. An invention is the creation of a technical idea utilising the laws of nature (sec. 2(1) PA) and is completed by such steps as setting a certain technical problem (purpose), adopting a technical means to solve the problem and verifying the effect for achieving the purpose by technical means. In order to complete the invention, the technical means needed must be conceptualised so concretely and objectively that a person skilled in the art can repeatedly work the invention and achieve its effect. No more than this is required (see, Supreme Court, 13 October 1977, Case No. 107 (Gyō-Tsu) of 1974, 31-6 Minshū 805). For the invention of a product, it is not necessary that the product is in fact produced or the final production drawing is made, but it can be said that the invention is completed at the stage that the concrete configuration of the product is shown in a blueprint etc. and the person skilled in the art can make the final production drawing based thereupon, and produce the product.

And "preparing ... for business" as working of the patented invention in sec. 79 PA should mean that a person who does not know the contents of the invention as specified in the application and invents the same, or another person, who knows the invention from the former, not yet in the stage of carrying out the business, but has the intention to carry it out immediately and express the intention to carry it out immediately in this manner, to an extent that it is objectively recognisable.

3. We consider this case.

(1) From the description of the patent claim and its effect, in summary, (i) the problem (purpose) of the patented invention at issue is to produce a simple and robust structure walking beam type conveyor for conveying workpieces through a refractory chamber of a furnace, which can expose the heat uniformly and throughout the whole surface area of a plurality of large steel slabs etc. at once without impairing the surface, and can convey even warped slabs, and can reciprocate in a vertical and horizontal direction either separately or simultaneously, (ii) the problem is solved and the effect of achieving the objected purpose is made through the constitution that the walking beam mechanism is adopted, the fixed beams and the moving beams (two sets of conveyor rails) have plural workpiece support pads, the at least four rotatable eccentric rings (eccentric cams) for vertically reciprocating the moving beams (more correctly, the carriage for moving the moving beams and the

parallel beams extending along the underside of the carriage) and the apparatus for horizontally reciprocating independently of the vertical reciprocation are comprised, and each of said eccentric rings has a freely rotatable peripheral ring bearing for supporting an underside section of said parallel beams.

On the other hand, regarding the products planned by the defendant, the above mentioned estimate specification submitted by the defendant on 31 August 1966 to the steel company E describes: (i) the adoption of the walking beam mechanism, (ii) that the vertical reciprocation of the moving beams is electrically moved, that the vertical reciprocation is made by the rotation of the eccentric plates, that steel slabs are on the fixed beams or the moving beams pendant half cycle, that reheating and uniform temperatures are achieved, (iii) so that the horizontal reciprocation of the moving beams continues even if the steel slabs are not moved by the horizontal stroke, (iv) that the horizontal moving of the moving beams is made by an oil pressure cylinder, (v) that on each of the beams the rails for supporting the steel slabs are placed, (vi) about the apparatus for vertical reciprocating, that the mount is supported at 8 points, the eccentric cams are moved by 2 motors through slowing down the machine and a gear slowing down mechanism that is vertically reciprocated, (vii) for the outer circumference, a ring-type circular roller is placed and this can slide. So taken into account the description, the findings of the previous instance is adequate and can be affirmed, namely that the person skilled in the art can understand the technical problem which at that time the defendant was engaged to resolve, and the structure of the essential parts in the concrete product which should resolve the technical problem.

And the previous instance found and correctly ascertained that actually, the product which the defendant prepared to produce and to sell at that time could be completely produced by the above mentioned estimate specification etc. and the calculation document and drawing as the basis of the estimate specification. So it can be said that the above mentioned estimate specification discloses concretely and objectively the technical means which were adopted for resolving the technical problem in the planned products of the defendant to an extent that the person skilled in the art can repeatedly work and achieve its effect. It can be adequately affirmed that the defendant already completed the invention related to the planned product of the defendant at the time of submitting the estimate specification to the steel company E.

Of course, the previous instance also affirmed the fact that quite a number of drawings should be made to actually produce the planned products of the defendant, and more time would have been necessary. But in the light of the above considerations, this fact does not hinder the above conclusions.

(2) And from the above mentioned facts, the defendant company responded to the inquiry of the steel company E, at first estimated and designed the pusher type furnace, then estimated and designed the motorised type walking beam type furnace, and completed the invention related to the planned product. After that, around 31 August 1966 and thus before the priority date of the patented invention at issue, the defendant submitted the above mentioned estimate specification and blueprint to the steel company E. The defendant had a plan to provide a final production drawing and build a furnace if the steel company E made an order at that time. And the defendant requested an estimate for each part of the apparatus to the subcontracting

company in preparation for receiving an order, and after that, participated every year in tenders for the walking beam type furnace.

And about the walking beam type furnace, the previous instance correctly ascertained that a certain time is needed from inquiry to receiving an order and delivery of the product, further that the product was not a mass production, but only produced after receiving a special order, and parts etc., were not previously bought. Taken into account such special circumstances of industrial furnaces, the defendant had the intention to immediately carry out the business as work of invention related to the planned product, and such intention to immediately carry out was expressed by submitting the estimate specification to the steel company E in a manner and to an extent that it could be objectively recognised. Therefore, it should be understood that the defendant actually prepared for business to work the invention related to the planned product on the date of the priority claim of the patented invention.

(3) The decision of the previous instance in accordance with the above consideration can be affirmed. The decision of the previous instance does not suffer from any defects. The argument of the plaintiff that the decision suffered from legal errors was based on different facts that the previous instance held inadmissible.

The right of prior use provided in sec. 79 PA grants a non-exclusive license for the patent "only to the extent that the invention was commercially worked or prepared". Here, "the extent that the invention … worked or prepared" is not limited to the manner in which the invention has actually been worked or prepared by the prior user at the time of the patent application (date of priority claim), but refers to the scope of the technical idea realised in the form of work, i.e. scope of the invention. Therefore, the effect of the right of prior use should cover not only the form of working the invention as it was actually worked or prepared by the prior user at the time of the patent application (date of priority claim), but also the form of working the invention with amendments within the scope in which the invention as realised does not lose its identity.

The reason for this is that to allow no change whatsoever of what is actually carried out or prepared by the prior user at the time of the patent application (date of priority claim) is too severe and not adequate in light of the main purpose of the prior user right in order to balance the fairness between a patent owner and a prior user, and that to allow a right of prior use within the scope of the invention corresponding in the possession of the prior user is in accordance with the objective of the provision. And where the invention actually carried out corresponds only to a part of the patented invention, the effect of the prior user right is of course limited to that part of the patented invention, but when the scope of the prior use invention corresponds in scope to the patented invention, the effect of the prior user right covers the whole scope of the patented invention.

We consider this point for the case at issue. The product planned by the defendant has a concrete structure as described by the four points above. But considering the state of the art at the time of the patent application at issue (at the date of the priority claim) and the above facts as correctly ascertained by the previous instance, the invention realised in the planned products did not for its special technical meaning set out a concrete structure in detail, but its content was rather a more abstract technical idea, which is not different in the patented invention at issue. The scope of such invention should thus be same as the scope of the patented invention. So the prior user right, which is based on the preparation for business to work the invention related to the envisaged product by the defendant company covers the whole scope of the patented invention at issue. Therefore, the previous instance adequately decided that the effect of the prior user right covered also the products A.

The arguments of the plaintiff, which attacks the decision of the previous instance on a different point of view, therefore cannot be affirmed.

3. ANALYSIS

a) "Preparing for the commercial use of the invention"

Generally, the steps to start commercially working an invention are as follows: (i) research and development, (ii) the completion of an invention (or learning such invention from a third party inventor), (iii) commercial preparation in order to work such invention, and (iv) commercially launching such invention.[6] It was disputed in this case whether the infringer had reached step (iii), since step (iii) or (iv) is required to invoke a prior user right.

The Supreme Court first decided whether the defendant had completed the invention (step (ii)). It ruled that, even without a final production drawing, the invention could be deemed completed at the latest when an actual structure was fixed in the blueprint or other documents and a person skilled in the art was able to provide a final production drawing and produce the product upon those estimate specification etc., even though lots of additional drawings might be needed, which would take a certain time. While the Supreme Court decision of 1977 was cited for a general rule to decide upon completion of an invention, the decision at issue is still meaningful as a precedent to determine completion of an invention in relation to a prior user right for a certain technology.

Regarding step (iii), the Supreme Court held that the submission of the estimate specification to steel company E constituted the commercial preparation of working the invention. For the interpretation of "preparing for commercially working the invention", the expression of intent to immediately carry out commercial working in such manner and to such extent that it can be objectively determined is required. This interpretation was in line with the prevailing view in academic literature.[7] According to this interpretation, such preparation will not be limited to a case where the alleged infringer has the facilities to commercially work the invention (as was the law prior to the PA amendment) but it would be sufficient if such objective expression of intent exists. It excludes cases where such business is only under consideration.[8]

As a background, there is an argument with regard to the purpose or reason for the system of prior use, namely reasons of fairness or economic considerations.

---

6. N. Nakayama and N. Koizumi (eds.) (above), at 1256
7. T. Mizuno, Tokkyohō 79 jō ni iu hatsumei no jisshi dearu jigyō no junbi no igi / senshiyō ni yoru tsujōjisshiken no han'i *(Meaning of preparation for commercially working the invention in sec. 79 Patent Act / scope of non-exclusive license by prior user)*, 881 Jurist 81 (a commentary of this case).
8. Hōsōkai, Saikōsaibansho hanreikaisetsu minjihen shōwa 61 nendo *(Commentary of the Supreme Court's civil law in 1986)*, 1986, 410.

The theory of fairness as a prevailing view argues that the system aims at achieving fairness between the interests of the patentee and the inventor who has worked or prepared to work the invention for business at the time the patent was applied under the first to file principle. The economic theory argues that the system aims at avoiding drawbacks for the national economy which occur by blocking products, facilities etc. in relation to the invention that at the time of the patent application was commercially used without knowledge of the contents of the application.[9] Generally speaking, the theory of fairness allocates a broader right to a prior user than the economic theory[10] since the theory of fairness also focuses on individual interests based on which it interprets the requirement and scope of the right of prior use.

In this regard, the Supreme Court clarified in its decision that it primarily applies the theory of fairness. Upon this theory, "preparing for the commercial working of the invention" should be decided from the perspective of fairness. Thus, whether such preparation is affirmed will be decided by considering the overall situation including but not limited to the contents and character of the invention and also the time, work, and resources spent on the invention by the prior user.[11]

In this regard, it is argued that such preparation can be affirmed where the land and facilities for a factory to manufacture the invention is purchased. If no additional land or facilities or other investment is needed to work the invention, preparations can be affirmed when reaching the phase where blueprints or prototypes are made in order to commercially work the invention, but not earlier.[12]

While previous decisions by lower courts affirmed preparation from the fact of purchase of (or restructure of existing) machinery or other facilities, or based on the order of parts or ingredients, the Supreme Court defined such preparation in this case as an expression of intent to an immediate commercial marketing even in the absence of a purchase or order. Instead, taking into account the characteristics of industrial furnace business (i.e., the production and sales of industrial furnaces at a cost of approx. JPY 1 billion takes a certain time from a customer inquiry to receiving an order and delivery of the product; the product in this case is not mass-produced, but specifically made to order, and parts are not ordered beforehand), the Supreme Court found such intent was manifest at the time the specification etc. was submitted to the steel company E. This is a phase close to the completion of the invention (step (ii)).

The reasons for such finding were as follows: (i) the furnace could be completely produced by the estimate specification etc. and the calculation document and drawings as the basis of the estimate specification, (ii) the defendant had a plan to provide a final production drawing and build a furnace should the steel company E make an order, (iii) the defendant started requesting an estimate for each part of the furnace to the subcontracting company after submitting the estimate specification and blueprint, and (iv) the defendant every year participated in tenders for furnaces afterwards. (ii) to (iv) were needed in addition to the fact of (i), since an intention to immediately implement the invention would be close to a preparation for a commercial implementation. Especially (ii) can be seen as a factor to find such

---

9. Hōsōkai (above) at 407.
10. Hōsōkai (above), at 410.
11. Hōsōkai (above), at 412
12. Hōsōkai (above), at 410 – 411

preparation at the time of submitting the estimate specification which is one of the characteristics of industrial furnace production given that the specification of a furnace also needs a certain time and effort.[13]

This judgment may not be immediately applicable to cases of mass production, but it gives a more flexible interpretation of the condition "preparing for the commercial working of the invention". Until know, the case is meaningful as precedent of the general rule to interpret such preparation in a customised production market.

b) Scope of right of prior use

When the requirements are satisfied, working of the invention under a prior user right is allowed "to the extent that the invention ... is worked or prepared". The scope of the right of prior use should be determined based on its purpose.

The economic theory argues that the scope should be limited by the extent that the invention has actually been prepared, while the theory of fairness argues that the extent of the right should be based on the invention underlying the same technical idea of the invention actually prepared.[14] The Supreme Court clarified in the decision that it adopts the latter as it primarily endorsed the theory of fairness.

The decision determined such invention from the commercial preparation as an actual working of the patented invention, but it did not determine, as arguably it should have, whether the actual embodiment that was alleged as infringement (i.e., "product A") was indeed included in such invention that enjoyed the right of prior use.[15] This is probably because the structure of the patented invention was rather simple and the only working example in the description and drawings of the patent is directly as claimed, i.e., such embodiment would be considered as the technical idea of the patented invention. Also, the invention expressed in the product described in the estimate specification can be recognised as an abstract technical idea at the same level as expressed in the patented invention. Therefore, to the extent that the scope of invention as expressed in the estimate specification is identical to the scope of the patented invention,[16] a more detailed comparison between the invention enjoying the prior use right and the infringing product appeared unnecessary.[17]

In that regard, the decision did not give guidance for cases where the invention by the prior user and the patented invention are not identical, which would be the usual case. In such case, the contents of the invention as commercially used should be determined in order to decide upon the scope of prior use right. Since there is no written description of such invention so as to determine purpose, effect and other factors, it is not easy to determine such contents appropriately without giving an overly narrow or broad scope to such invention.[18]

Generally speaking, the contents and scope of the invention worked by the prior user will normally be decided upon factors such as the technology worked at

13. HŌSŌKAI (above), at 413
14. N. NAKAYAMA and N. KOIZUMI (eds.) (above), at 1267
15. N. NAKAYAMA and N. KOIZUMI (eds.) (above), at 1268
16. HŌSŌKAI (above), at 421
17. The defendant did not argue in this case that product A was within the scope of the patented invention.
18. N. NAKAYAMA and N. KOIZUMI (eds.) (above), at 1268

the time of the patent application, the subsequently altered technology, and also the scope of R&D related thereto (e.g., records, drawings, explanatory documents, materials regarding producing process and prototype). Contents and scope should be determined based on the technological level at the time of the patent application.[19]

In fairness, the exact scope of a prior user right may not need to be determined during litigation where the court has to decide whether the allegedly infringing product falls within the prior user right and/or the patented invention as expressed in the claims. This analysis was also adopted in the subsequent lower court decisions where the courts made a case by case analysis also taking into account the patented invention's description.[20]

4. COMPARATIVE REMARKS

In many countries that have adopted the first-to-file system, there is a right of prior use as an exception to the patent right in order to balance the interests of the patentee who files an invention and a third party who already has already used the invention in secret or prepared to use it. In the first-to-invent system the situation may be different, because in that case the patent might be invalidated by the prior user who has invented the invention before the application date.[21]

a) In **Germany**, sec. 12 Patent Act provides the right of prior use. The right of prior use is considered as a right in itself.[22] Possession of the invention is a requirement, and the German Federal Supreme Court clearly stated that the invention must have been objectively completed from the point of problem and solution, and the prior user must subjectively know the possibility of substantially working the invention.[23] The prior user can continue the business related to the right of prior use, but the right does not extend to the further development by the prior user, which is beyond the scope of the prior use.[24]

b) In **France**, already from the 19th century the right of prior use was acknowledged by case law, and in 1968 by legislation. Current Art. L613-7 of the Code of the Intellectual Property provides the right of prior use. The TGI Paris (Paris District Court)

19. K. MATSUO, Senshiyō ni yoru jisshiken no mitomerareru han'i *(Scope of right to work upon prior use)*, in: Umase Fumio sensei koki kinen – hanrei tokkyo shingai hō *(70th anniversary of Mr. Umase Fumio – patent infringement case book)*, 1983, 672

20. Such way of determination is also discussed among the legal profession. For example, it is discussed which actual facts should be considered: technology level at the time of the patent application, whether the structural difference of the product provided before the application and the infringing product is within the scope of the claim of the patented invention or is related to the effect expected from the patented invention. N. NAKAYAMA and N. KOIZUMI (eds.) (above), at 1269.

21. H. EICHMANN, Kritische Überlegungen zum Vor- und Weiterbenutzungsrecht *(Critical considerations for the right of prior use and continuous use)*, GRUR, 1993, 73.

22. German Federal Supreme Court,, GRUR 1965, 411 – *Lacktränkeinrichtung II.*

23. German Federal Supreme Court, 30 June 1964 GRUR 1964, 673 – *Kasten für Fußabtrittsroste*; German Federal Supreme Court, 28 May 1968, GRUR 1969, 35 – *Europareise*; German Federal Supreme Court, 12 June 2012, GRUR 2012, 895 – *Desmopressin.*

24. German Federal Supreme Court, 13 November 2001, GRUR 2002, 231 – *Biegevorrichtung.*

held that prior possession of the invention should be precise and complete, while a preparation for the purposes of working was not always necessary.[25]

c) In the **UK**, there was no right of prior use under the old Paten Act of 1949, yet prior use was a ground for revocation of the patent. Under the current Patent Act of 1977, which introduced the first-to-file system for the ratification of the Strasburg Convention and the European Patent Convention, sec. 64 provides the right of prior use. Case law requires effective and serious preparation and only possession of prototype or testing of the patented product are not enough.[26]

d) In the **US**, the American Inventors Protection Act of 1999 in sec. 273 of 35 USC provided the defence of prior use in the field of business method inventions because the CAFC in the *State Street Bank* case decided that business methods, which were regarded as unpatentable until that time and usually used as trade secrets were eligible for patent protection. [27] The sudden change of US case law led the US legislation to act especially in relation to patents and trade secrets. Further, the America Invents Act of 2011, introducing a first-to-file like system in the US, also extended the scope of the defence of prior use in sec. 273 to all fields of technology. Sec. 273 of 35 USC requires commercial use at least before the filing date of the claimed invention, etc.

e) In **Australia**, the old Patent Act of 1952 made also a secret use of the invention a ground for revocation of the patent, but after the law amendment of 1990, the current sec. 119 provides for an exception based on prior use.

25. High Court of Paris, 1 July 2003, PIBD 2003, 776-III-587; High Court of Paris, 6 June 2013, PIBD 2013, 992-III-1456.
26. UK Patent Court, *Helitune v. Stewart Hughes* [1991] R.P.C. 78; UK Court of Appeal, *Lubrizol Corporation v. Esso Petroleum Co. Ltd.* [1998] R.P.C. 727.
27. US Court of Appeal for the Federal Circuit, *State Street Bank and Trust Company v. Signature Financial Group, Inc.*, 149 F.3d 1368 (Fed. Cir. 1998).

Case No. 35

Interpretation of Patent Claims – Interpretation with Reference to the Description

Yoshinobu Someno / The Editors

In order to determine inventive step, a claim that in itself is clear cannot be interpreted more restrictedly by referring to the working examples in the description.

Supreme Court, 8 March 1991, Case No. 3 (Gyō-Tsu) of 1987 – *Ra-Lipase*

Boehringer Mannheim GmbH v. Japanese Patent Office

---

1. BACKGROUND

The following case concerns the question whether an unambiguously worded patent claim can be interpreted more narrowly than the claim wording would justify based on the working examples of the description. The court denied this, while *Yoshinobu Someno* in his historical comment does not entirely agree. The editors have added some words on recent developments and comparative remarks.

2. DECISION[1]

a) Facts

The appellee *Boehringer Mannheim GmbH* had applied for a product patent with the Patent Office (appellant). The claim reads as follows:

> "Detection method for the determination of triglycerides, including the enzymatic saponification of triglycerides by lipases, and the determination of glycerol released thereby, wherein the saponification is carried out in the presence of carboxylesterase and an alkali metal or alkaline earth metal alkyl sulfate and wherein the alkyl group contains 10 to 15 carbon atoms."

The Patent Office dismissed the application for lack of inventive step based on a previous patent application by the appellee that was considered prior art. On

1. Published in 1380 Hanrei Jihō 131 = 745 Hanrei Times 141 = 45-3 Minshū 123 = N. Nakayama et al. (eds.), Tokkyo Hanrei Hyakusen *(Hundred Selected Patent Cases)*, 4th ed. 2012, 124. German translation with comment Y. Someno in GRUR Int. 1994, 632.

appeal by the appellee, the Tokyo High Court (decision of 19 October 1986, Case No. 142 (Gyo-Ke) of 1983) reversed and affirmed an inventive step. Although this did not result from the claim itself, it was clear from the embodiments that for the above-mentioned method, not lipases, but Ra-lipases were required, since the process could only be carried out with these. Interpreted this way, this meant an improvement over the prior art.

On appeal by the Patent Office, the Supreme Court overturned the decision of the Tokyo High Court and remanded the case back for further fact finding.

b) Reasons

I ...

II [The decision under appeal reasoned as follows:]...

1. The method described in entry No. (4) of the detailed description of the invention in question is a measurement method for triglycerides produced by enzymatic saponification through a lipase of the type a Rhizopas arrhizus (Ra-lipase), and the glycerol isolated therefrom. This method is indicated in the composition of the invention of the appellee's application (patent application No. S45-130788), that is, within the scope of the claims regarding the measurement method for triglycerides using Ra-lipase. The method is in fact identical regarding the composition of a "quantitative detection method for triglycerides for total enzymatic, and quantitative detection of triglycerides, which are found in solutions, inter alia in conjunction with lipoproteins of the body fluids, as well as protein-free neutral fats whose characteristic is the cleavage of lipoproteins and protein-free neutral fats using the lipase obtained from Rhizopas arrhizus, and also the enzymatic measurement of the glycerol to be obtained from decomposing microorganisms according to a method which is generally known per se." Insofar as one refers to the details of the detailed description of the invention in question, the purpose of the invention is to improve the measuring method given under No. (4). As such, it presupposes the use of Ra-lipase.

2. Since, on the basis of information (4) of the description, it is established that the inventor of the claimed invention recognised that lipases other than Ra-lipase are unable to perform this method as a basic ingredient to completely break down the triglycerides within a given permitted time period, and that s measurement of triglycerides is not suitable because of the isolated glycerol, it was of no importance to the inventor to fully specify the term "lipase" in the patent claims of the claimed invention. Otherwise, in the above-mentioned measurement of the triglycerides also inappropriate lipases would be included.

3. It can be said that the term "lipase" given in the detailed description of the invention means "Ra-lipase".

4. Accordingly, solely the use of Ra-lipase means a technical improvement of the measurement method according to the above-mentioned statement No. (4) based on the detailed description of the invention. Also, in the working examples given in the description, only the use of Ra-lipase is envisaged.

5. Therefore, although not expressly stated, it is appropriate for the term "lipase" set forth in the claims of the invention to be understood as meaning "Ra-lipase" alone.

III. The above reasons cannot be accepted for the following reasons:

Regarding the examination of the patent requirements prescribed in sec. 29(1) and (2) Patent Act, that is novelty and inventive step of the invention for which a patent is claimed, the content of the invention as applied must satisfy the conditions stipulated therein. Unless there are special circumstances, these conditions must be met based on the information from the scope of the claims and from the detailed description attached to the application. As long as one cannot clearly and precisely understand the technical meaning of the information from the scope of the claims, or if there are clear spelling errors, the detailed description can be used to interpret the claim. However, this merely means that it is allowed to take into account the details of the description of the invention for the purposes of claim interpretation. This is based on the provision of sec. 36(4)(ii) Patent Act (previously sec. 36(5) Patent Act that still applies to this patent). This provision stipulates that in the field of claims, only information must be provided which is indispensable for the composition of the invention for which a patent has been sought.

Looking at this in the context of the present case, according to the facts established by the High Court, there is nothing to indicate that the claims are limited to the use of Ra-lipase in the case of the enzymatic isolation of triglycerides. Since there are no such special circumstances as mentioned above, the term "lipase" mentioned in the claims of the invention in question cannot be understood to be limited to "Ra-lipase". Although the first instance has held that the invention in question seeks to improve the measurement method as stated in no. (4), it has also held that only the use of Ra-lipase represents a technical improvement and that the embodiments of the present invention show that only Ra-lipase was used. However, because it does not belong to the general technical knowledge of those familiar with the relevant measurement method that no lipases other than Ra-lipase can be used, the lipase mentioned in the detailed description of the invention cannot be used to interpret the claims. The scope of the claims can therefore not be limited to Ra-lipase only because the working examples describe only the use of Ra-lipase and only the use of Ra-lipase may make technical sense.

IV. It follows that the view taken by the lower court that the term "lipase" mentioned in the claims of the invention in question should be understood as "Ra-lipase", and the enzyme used in the invention in question be limited to Ra-lipase, is legally incorrect and the lower court in so far as it has examined whether the invention shows a sufficient level of inventive step when compared to the prior art misinterpreted the applicable law. As the decision is based on this approach, the decision in this respect is set aside and the case is remitted to the lower court for a further trial in accordance with the legal opinion expressed in this decision. The decision was unanimous.

3. ANALYSIS

a) Case comment by Professor Yoshinobu Someno (1994)

The present decision states that the contents of the claim is determined based on the information given in the application, unless particular circumstances require a different interpretation. Since it was not apparent to a person with average technical knowledge that only Ra-lipases, but not ordinary lipases could be used for the invention, the Supreme Court considered that an interpretation of restricting the claim to Ra-lipases, which were specified solely in the embodiments, as was held by the Tokyo High Court was incorrect. Because the decision was based on this mistake, it had to be set aside and the case remanded.

The principle relied on by the Supreme Court in so far as it considered it necessary to limit the contents of the invention to the scope of the claim is sec. 36(5)(ii) Patent Act. This provision states that the statement of the claim shall be limited to what is explained in the patent description as indispensable for the structure of the invention for which a patent is sought (a violation of this is a ground for rejection under sec. 49(3) Patent Act or, as far as the patent has already been granted, a reason for invalidation pursuant to sec. 123(1)(iii) Patent Act), and to that extent it is the general basis for determining the contents of an invention.

Deviating from this principle and making reference to the detailed description is only allowed if the scope of the claims set forth in the patent is unclear or the application contains an immediately recognisable spelling error.

With regard to the appeal court decision[2] that was based on the above exception, the Supreme Court found that limiting he claim language of "lipases" to "Ra-lipases" was not conceivable because such limitation was not obvious to a person skilled in the art and therefore the ruling of the appeal court was incorrect.

As can be seen, the Supreme Court did not find good reason for referring to the description in this case, although no grounds are spelt out for this. However, the general criteria of interpretation as applied by the Supreme Court are problematic. They are based on the assumption that the contents of the invention can be clearly determined on the basis of the information given in the application. Exceptions apart, this leads to a determination of the contents of the invention which completely disregards the description and drawings appended to the claims.

If one accepts this basis, far-reaching consequences for the interpretation of claims must be taken into account.

(1) If the wording of the claims is unequivocal, even if such wording is extremely broad in relation to the description, (as may well be the intention of the patentee), claim interpretation must be in accordance with such broad wording.

(2) If the wording of the claims is unequivocal, then the determination of the contents of the invention must also be based thereupon even if the wording of the claims does not allow to grasp the meaning of the invention. As a result, the wording of the

2. Tokyo High Court, 29 October 1986, Case No. 142 (Gyo-Ke) of 1983, 45-3 Minshū 145 = Hanrei Kōgyō Shoyūkenhō, vol. 3, 2081-198 (137).

claims has the function of a restriction. This makes the application of the doctrine of equivalents even more difficult.

(3) If the wording of the claims is ambiguous and, for that reason, the description must be included, such an assessment shall be possible only for the purpose of limiting the scope of the claims.

According to the above, the ruling of the Supreme Court seems extremely strict, and there is a particular concern that a very narrow interpretation will become mandatory.

Yoshinobu Someno

b) Postscript by the Editors

The editors appreciate that *Professor Someno*'s dissenting opinion has a certain historical justification, in particular his misgivings about an unduly narrow claim interpretation.

The principle derived from the case at issue is widely accepted nowadays: In examination, a claim shall be interpreted according to its wording as understood by a person skilled in the art, and reference to an interpretation based on a specific embodiment in the description shall be allowed only in exceptional cases where the claim is so unclear that a person skilled in the art would consult the description for such limiting interpretation.[3] This *Ra-Lipase* principle is still applicable today even after the old sec. 36(5)(ii) Patent Act was amended and the indispensability of elements was no longer a requirement of claim drafting.[4] The reason why the greatly inconvenient consequence highlighted in *Someno*'s comment did not occur at a large scale is that his concern about a complete disregard for description and drawings has not happened in practice.[5]

There was admittedly some confusion in the practice of claim interpretation after the *Ra-Lipase* decision and as a consequence sec. 70(2) Patent Act was introduced by the law amendment of 1994:[6]

> **Sec. 70 Technical Scope of Patented Invention**
>
> (1) The technical scope of patented invention shall be determined based on the statement of claims attached to the application.

---

3. See, as commentaries on the case at issue, e.g., H. YOHSHIDA, Hatsumei no yōshi nintei to kurēmu no kisai *(Determination of the scope of invention of an application and the statement of claims)*, in: N. NAKAYAMA et al. (eds.), Tokkyo Hanrei Hyakusen *(Hundred Selected Patent Cases)*, 4th ed. 2012, 124; S. SHIOTSUKI, Tokkyo shutsugan ni kakaru hatsumei no yōshi no nintei *(Determination of the scope of invention of an application)*, in: HŌSŌKAI (ed.), Saikōsai Hanrei Kaisetsu Minjihen Heisei 3 nendo *(Analysis of Supreme Court Civil Cases of 1991)*, 1994, 28; T. IIMURA, Tokkyo shutsugan ni kakaru hatsumei no yōshi nintei to kurēmu kaishaku ni tsuite *(Determination of invention of an application and claim interpretation)*, in: Chitekizaisanhō no atarashii nagare *(New trend in the intellectual property law)*, 2010, 35.
4. There were other minor amendments hereafter, but old sec. 36(5)(ii) Patent Act was amended to the current form of sec. 36(5) by Law No. 116/1994 of 14 December 1994.
5. It should be also considered that his comment was written before the *Kilby* decision of 2000.
6. Law No. 116/1994 of 14 December 1994. Sec. 70(1) has been introduced already by the current Patent Act of 1959.

(2) In the case of paragraph (1), the meaning of terms in the claims is interpreted with regard to the description and drawings.

...

The explanatory notes to this amendment mentioned two different approaches to claim interpretation by infringement courts following the *Ra-lipase* decision: (i) referring to the description and drawings is not allowed even for clarification of terms (this approach considered that the *Ra-lipase* case established new case law at that time), (ii) referring to the description, etc. is allowed for clarification of terms. If the technical subject matter stated in the claim is clear by itself, a further restrictive interpretation of the claim referring to the description, etc. is not allowed. Legislation endorsed clearly the approach (ii),[7] while *Someno* feared that approach (i) could become standard practice.

By the above law amendment of 1994, the determination of the scope of invention in JPO examination/appeal procedure and in infringement cases could be harmonised, but discussions on proper claim interpretation both from a theoretical and practical point of view have been continuing. To the extent that the *Ra-Lipase* principles apply to the JPO procedures and sec. 70(2) to infringement proceedings, these are different standards. Infringement courts have further developed case law on exclusion of known prior art, file wrapper estoppel, equivalents, and specific types of claims.[8]

The *Kilby* decision of 2000 for the first time allowed the abuse of rights defence regarding invalidity of a patent in infringement procedures, and the law amendment of 2004 introduced the *Kilby* principle in sec. 104ter.[9] Thereby, infringement courts are in a position to determine the scope of a patent both for infringement (comparison between the claim and the infringing product) and validity (comparison between the

7. See the explanation document for the law amendment of 1994, JPO, Kurēmu kaishaku ni atatte no hatsumen no shōsai na setsumei no sanshaku *(Referring to the detailed explanation of invention in the interpretation of claims)*, available at the website of the JPO <https://www.jpo.go.jp/system/laws/rule/kaisetu/sangyozaisan/document/sangyou_zaisanhou/h6_kaisei_4.pdf>. There was also criticism that referring to the description for clarification of terms was clear from a practical point of view and the law amendment was not necessary, see, e.g., S. SHIOTSUKI, Hatsumei no yōshi nintei to gijutsuteki han'i kakutei *(Determination of the scope of claim in an application and a patented invention)*, 66-10 Patent 99 (2013).
8. The Examination Guidelines of the JPO were also amended in line with approach (ii) after the *Ra-Lipase* case (June 1993). See JPO (above). For the current version, see, Part I, Chapter 2, Section 1, at the website of the JPO <https://www.jpo.go.jp/e/system/laws/rule/guideline/patent/tukujitu_kijun/document/index/01_0201_e.pdf>. There is no fundamental difference between the practice of the JPO and infringement courts, but is also said that the *Ra-Lipase* case is an examination/appeal procedure case and there is no direct application to infringement cases. See, e.g., T. IWATSUBO, in: N. NAKAYAMA et al. (eds.), Shin Chūkai Tokkyohō *(New Commentary on Japanese Patent Act)*, 2nd ed. 2017, 1209-1212. In Japan, the scope of invention is traditionally called "hatsumei no yōshi" *(essence of an invention)* in the JPO procedure, "tokkyo hatsumei no gijutsuteki han'i" *(technical scope of a patented invention)* in infringement procedure and "kurēmu kaishaku" *(claim interpretation)* in general. These terms are used for distinction in Japanese, but in this postscript the editors do not use such different terms for translation to avoid confusion.
9. For details of the *Kilby* decision, see Case No. 50 in this volume, and for further developments Case No. 51.

claim and the prior art). This makes a different determination of the patent scope less likely and does no longer mandate a restrictive interpretation of claims, because the patentee is forced to apply the same interpretation of claims both for infringement and validity. [10] While there are still some post- *Kilby* decisions that exclude known prior art from the scope of a patented invention, the exclusion of known prior art has become rare.[11]

As to file wrapper estoppel and equivalents, these remain special methods of interpretation for infringement courts, because these are usually not taken into account in the JPO procedure before grant, but used in infringement cases for a fair and balanced assessment of the patent scope beyond the wording of the claims.[12]

The types of claims often referred as specific are so called functional claims or product by process (PBP) claims. For a functional claim, an element which is specified only by its function in a claim is usually considered one which is able to fulfil the function and does not automatically lead to limitation by itself. Therefore, functional claims should be carefully monitored both in JPO and courts procedures as to whether such functional terms make the claim unclear. For a PBP claim, so called "product as such theory" and "process limited product theory" have been discussed and applied in Japan, but the Supreme Court in the *Pravastatin* case of 2015 finally adopted the former theory and has thereby established legal certainty for an interpretation of PBP claims in examination and infringement.[13]

---

10. T. IIMURA, Hatsumei no yōshi no nintei to gijutsuteki han'i no kaishaku sarani kintōron no katsuyō *(Determination of scope of an invention of application and interpretation of technical scope of a patented invention, further utilization of equivalence)*, 64-14 Patent 57 (2011) states that because of sec. 104ter the different treatment in interpretation of claims for infringement and invalidity becomes unnatural and a too restrictive interpretation becomes difficult. See also M. TAKABE, Kurēmu kaishaku no shōrai *(Future of claim interpretation)*, in: Chitekizaisanhō no atarashii nagare *(New trend in intellectual property law)*, 2010, 355; M. TOKII, Kureimu kaishaku no genkyō *(Current status of claim interpretation)*, 40 Chitekizaisan Hōseisakugaku Kenkyū 1 (2012); T. ŌBUCHI et al. kurēmu kaishaku to meisaisho tō *(Claim interpretation and description, etc.)*, 67-14 Patent 152 (2014); Y. ECHI, Hatsumei no yōshi nintei to gijutsuteki han'i kakutei ni okeru kurēmu kaishaku *(Claim interpretation in determination of scope of an invention of application and technical scope of a patented invention)*, in: N. KOIZUMI/Y. TAMURA (eds.), Habataki -20 seiki no chitekizaisanhō- *(Evolution -Intellectual Property Law in 21th century-)*, 2015, 272.
11. T. YOSHIDA (above), states also that after the *Kilby* decision, the interpretation of claims should be unified in infringement and invalidity, but there still remained the use of the exclusion of known prior art with citation of an example case, Tokyo District Court, 28 December 2004, Case No. 19733 (Wa) of 2003, the website of the courts <http://www.courts.go.jp/app/files/hanrei_jp/828/009828_hanrei.pdf> – *Ice Cream Strawberry*.
12. For the file wrapper estoppel in general, see, e.g., the publications in note 10; T. IWATSUBO (above), at 1225-1239; Y. TAMURA, Mukō shinpan ni okeru genteiteki shuchō to hōtai kinhangen *(Restrictive argument in invalidity procedure and file wrapper estoppel)*, in: N. NAKAYAMA et al. (eds.), Tokkyo Hanrei Hyakusen *(Hundred Selected Patent Cases)*, 4th ed. 2012, 124. For details of the doctrine of equivalents, see Cases No. 38, 39 and 40 in this volume.
13. Historically, functional claims were not widely allowed under old sec. 36(5) Patent Act and have been used mainly after the Law amendment of 1994 (Law No. 116/1994). There are cases of functional claims in which courts made some restrictive interpretation such as regarding the scope of enablement or technical idea disclosed in the description, etc. (but even in such cases, the restrictive interpretation was not limited to an embodiment only) because the claims were not clear. But it may be the problem of too broad or unclear claims in general and some special rules for functional claims would be not necessary. In the JPO examination procedure, the

Although the *Ra-Lipase* case had the potential of being misinterpreted, as was highlighted in *Someno*'s comment, the case in fact has clarified that an overly restrictive claim interpretation, e.g. by limiting the claim to an embodiments only stated in the description, should generally be avoided but for exceptional cases.

4. COMPARATIVE REMARKS

The interpretation of patents as technical monopolies always had to accommodate two interests: First, to justify the grant by making sure that the requirements of patentability were met, and second, to allow third parties to clearly determine the area of exclusivity. The first interest was primarily taken into account by the granting authorities, the second by the courts. To do both by referring to the claims is relatively recent. While the **UK** patent system dates back to 1623 (Statute of Monopolies), it only became common to draft a specification and claims after the Patents Act 1852.[14] In the **US**, claims became mandatory with the Patent Act 1836 (§ 5). Only then could the question arise what the function of claims was, what to do in the event of discrepancies between claim and description, and how to make sure that the patent was interpreted in the same way by the granting and enforcing authorities.[15] According to the English House of Lords in a decision of 1938, "if the claims have a plain meaning in themselves, then advantage cannot be taken of the language used in the body of the Specification to make them mean something different."[16] Quite a different path was taken in Germany where the Patent Office determined patentability based on the wording of the claims, while the infringement courts based their assessment on the general inventive concept.[17]

The current approach for all **EPC Member States** is based on Art. 69 EPC according to which the scope of protection shall be determined by the claims, and description and drawings shall be used to interpret them. In this regard, the **German** Federal Supreme Court held that "a working example usually does not permit a

---

problem of too broad or unclear claims is a problem of the claim statement requirement under sec. 36, and in the infringement court procedure, claims may be restrictively interpreted but also dealt with by the invalidity defence under 104ter if the claim is too unclear. For functional claims in general, see, e.g., R. Takabayashi et al. (eds.), Gendai Chitekizaisanhō Kōza II *(Modern Intellectual Property Law Seminer II)*, vol. 2, 2012, 64; T. Iwatsubo (above), at 1291-1303; the papers in note 10. *Ice Cream Strawberry* case (above) is also an example case of restrictive interpretation of a functional claim. For the PBP claim, see Case No. 37 in this volume.

14. H. Laddie, Kirin Amgen – The End of Equivalents in England?, 40 IIC 3, 11 (2009); S. Strobel, The Emergence and Development of the Patent Specification in England, in J. Straus (ed.), Aktuelle Herausforderungen des geistigen Eigentums – Festgabe für F.K. Beier *(Actual Challenges of Intellectual Property – Commemorative Publication for F.K. Beier)*, Köln 1996, 185.
15. "Professor Mario Franzosi likens a patentee to an Angora cat. When validity is challenged, the patentee says his patent is very small: the cat with its fur smoothed down, cuddly and sleepy. But when the patentee goes on the attack, the fur bristles, the cat is twice the size with teeth bared and eyes ablaze." – Lord Jacob in: English Court of Appeal, 19 August 2008, *European Central Bank v. DSS* [2008] EWCA Civ 192.
16. English House of Lords, *Electric and Musical Industries Ltd. V. Lissen Ltd.*, 56 R.P.C. 23 (1938).
17. E. Reimer, Äquivalenz, Erfindungsgegenstand, allgemeiner Erfindungsgedanke in Theorie und Praxis *(Equivalents, object of invention, general concept of invention in theory and practice)*, GRUR 1956, 387.

limiting interpretation of the claim characterising the invention."[18] In particular, "an examination in revocation proceedings cannot be based on an interpretation of a patent claim below its actual meaning."[19] This is also the consistent case law of the **EPO**. According to established jurisprudence, the description can be used as a patent's dictionary and thereby give terms a different meaning than they would ordinarily have.[20] However, if a term in the claim has a clear technical meaning, the description cannot be used to interpret the claim in a different manner: A dictionary is only consulted once the meaning of a word is not clear. If to a person skilled in the art it is, a possibly different definition provided by the description cannot be used for interpretation.[21] EPO case law is thus in line with the approach taken by the Japanese Supreme Court. Yet in all likelihood, the patentee would have been allowed to limit its claim to Ra-lipase, either before the national courts or in a central limitation request under Art. 105a EPC.

In the **US**, claim construction faces its own challenges due to the division of factual and legal issues divided by judge and jury. A number of cases have clarified that the main sources for claim interpretation are the claims themselves, the description and the prosecution history:[22] "First, we look into the claims themselves … second, it is always necessary to review the specification to determine whether the inventor has used any terms inconsistent with their ordinary meaning … third, the court may also consider the prosecution history …".[23] In the case of a discrepancy between a (broader) claim and a (narrower) description, the following should apply: "Absent a special and particular definition created by the patent applicant, terms in a claim are to be given their ordinary and accustomed meaning … Thus, when a claim term is expressed in general descriptive words, we will not ordinarily limit the term to a numerical range that may appear in the written description or in other claims. Nor may we, in the broader situation, add a narrowing modifier before an otherwise general term that stands unmodified in the claim …"[24]

It thus appears that also U.S. law would rather side with the Japanese Supreme Court than with the interpretation as advocated by Professor *Someno*.

The Editors

18. German Federal Supreme Court, 7 September 2004, GRUR 2004, 1023 – *Bodenseitige Vereinzelungsvorrichtung*
19. German Federal Supreme Court, 16 March 2004, GRUR 2004, 579 – *Imprägnieren von Tintenabsorbierungsmitteln.*
20. European Patent Office decision **T 2221/10** of 4 February 2014.
21. European Patent Office decision **T 197/10** of 28 October 2011.
22. US Supreme Court, *Markman v. Westview Instruments*, 517 U.S. 370 (1996), and US CAFC, *Markman v. Westview Instruments*, 52 F.3d 929.
23. US CAFC, *Vitronics Corp. v. Conceptronic, Inc.*, 90 F.3d 1576 (Fed. Cir. 1996).
24. US CAFC, *Renishaw PLC v. Marposs SPA*, 158 F.3d 1243, 1249 (1998).

Case No. 36

Interpretation of Patent Claims – Literal Infringement – Disclaimed Element

Masakazu Kobayashi

A contested product may fall within the scope of a patented invention as a literal infringement even where a disclaimed element is realised.

IP High Court, 7 September 2011, Case No. 10002 (Ne) of 2011 – *Rice Cakes*

Echigo Seika v. Satō Foods

1. BACKGROUND

a) General rules of claim interpretation under Japanese patent law

The major issue in this case is how to determine the technical scope of a patented invention in patent infringement cases, particularly how to interpret and construe a patent claim where a disclaimed element or a negative expression is included.

Under Japanese patent law, (i) claim statements, (ii) the description and drawings, (iii) assertions by patentees during patent prosecution (prosecution history), and (iv) technical level at the filing date are generally taken into consideration to interpret and construe patent claims.

(i) Sec. 70 (1) Patent Act confirms that claim statements define the technical scope of a patented invention as follows:

> "The technical scope of a patented invention shall be determined based upon the statements of claims attached to the description."

Claim language is, therefore, the starting point of claim interpretation and the most significant source to determine the scope of the patent.

(ii) Sec. 70 (2) Patent Act sets forth additional sources as follows:

> "In the case of the preceding paragraph, the meaning of each term used in the claims shall be interpreted in consideration of the description and drawings attached to the application."

Based on this provision, the Japanese patent courts consider description and drawings as additional sources of claim interpretation.[1] For instance, in case a word in a claim could be interpreted in several ways, these additional sources could be used to clarify the most specific meaning in the claim. In some cases, they can be used to interpret the claim language more narrowly than the general meaning found in a dictionary or a glossary. For instance, the effects of the patented invention stated in the description may be taken into consideration for narrowing the scope of the patent before the court.

(iii) Under Japanese patent law, prosecution history, specifically the statements made by applicants in their written statements can be also taken into consideration as an additional source of interpretation: Once a patentee intentionally excludes an element from the technical scope of an invention during patent prosecution, the patentee cannot make assertions that would contradict such an exclusion before the court, because such a contradiction would not be permitted in view of the doctrine of estoppel based on a general principle of civil law or the code of civil procedure (file wrapper estoppel or prosecution history estoppel).[2]

(iv) The state of the art at the filing date is also taken into consideration as an additional source in order to clarify the meaning of a word in a claim and so forth.

The above-mentioned additional sources should be used to clarify or narrowly interpret the claim language, and should not be used to extend the scope of the patented claim beyond its literal wording, except for considerations of infringement under the doctrine of equivalents.

b) All elements rule

An allegedly infringing product or process generally falls within the scope of a patented invention only if it contains all the elements of the patent claim according to the all elements rule present in all major jurisdictions (literal infringement), except for infringement under the doctrine of equivalents.[3] This rule is also true in case of a claim including a disclaimed element or a negative expression.

c) Disclaimed element

Negative expressions such as "not ..." or "except for ..." can be allowed to be used in a claim under Japanese patent practice. However, according to the Examination Guidelines for Patents and Utility Models, in case the scope of an invention becomes unclear because of the use of such negative expressions, the clarity requirement for

1. Supreme Court, 27 May 27 1975, Case No. 54 (O) of 1975, 115 Shūmin 1 = 781 Hanrei Jihō 69 - *Oar*.
2. For example, Osaka District Court, 23 May 1986, Case No. 3515 (Wa) of 1985, 18-2 Mutaishū 133; Tokyo High Court, 1 Feb. 2000, Case No. 5507 (Ne) of 1998, 1712 Hanrei Jihō 167.
3. Supreme Court, 24 February 1998, Case No. 1083 (O) of 1994, 52-1 Minshū 113 - *Ball Spline Bearing III* (Case No. 38 of this book).

claims under sec. 36 (6) (ii) Japanese Patent Act is not satisfied.[4] This requirement was put in issue in this case, although it was not the main issue.

2. DECISION[5]

a) Facts

The plaintiff owns the Japanese patent No. 4111382 for a rice cake (kiri mochi) that was granted on 18 April 2008. Rice cakes are normally rectangular and come as a pre-fabricated food that is then baked in a pan. During baking, the rice cake rises or expands considerably. In order to avoid an uncontrolled expansion, prior art suggests a cross-wise incision either at the top or bottom surface of the cake. The plaintiff's invention however suggests an incision at the lateral sides of the rice cake, which allows the rice cake to rise in a controlled upward movement:

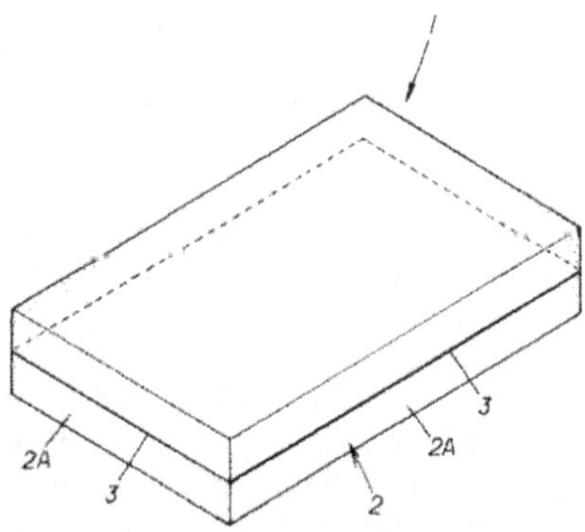

Claim 1 of this patent reads as follows:

> "Rice cake, comprising one or more incision parts or groove parts having length in a peripheral direction at a lateral peripheral surface that is a perpendicular lateral surface of an upper surface part of *kiri-mochi*, the peripheral direction being a direction along a contour edge of the perpendicular lateral surface, and not a lower placement surface or a flat upper surface of the piece of rice cake, which is a piece of rice cake having a rectangular contour shape which is eaten after being placed on a cooking grill and cooked, wherein the incision parts or groove parts are formed in a polygonal ring shape in a continuous circuit in the peripheral direction that is the direction along the perpendicular lateral surface, or are formed at two opposing lateral surfaces of the lateral peripheral surface that is the perpendicular lateral surface, whereby the configuration suppresses external discharge caused by expansion by an upper side of the incision parts or groove parts being raised relative to a lower side during cooking and by expansion-deforming to a state in which expanded content is sandwiched

4. Japan Patent Office, Examination Guidelines for Patent and Utility Model in Japan, English version available at <https://www.jpo.go.jp/tetuzuki_e/t_tokkyo_e/Guidelines/1_1.pdf>.
5. Published in 2144 Hanrei Jihō 121. English translation courtesy of STW Law Offices, Tokyo.

between upper and lower cooking plate-shaped parts similarly to *monaka (Japanese sweet beans paste cake)* or a sandwich."

The effect of the invention is stated to be the following:

"[0032] *Effects of the Invention*

Because the present invention is configured as described above, as a result of the configuration of the incision, it is possible to control the discharge caused by expansion during cooking and also to put the invention into practice without impairing the aesthetic of the toasted rice cake after cooking and, as a result of the configuration of the incision, it is not simply the case that the aesthetic of the cooked rice cake is not impaired due to this incision, but, rather, an innovative toasted shape hitherto unseen is automatically achieved that is extremely easy to eat, stimulates the appetite, and can actually be eaten with full appreciation of flavor; and, moreover, the toasted rice cake can easily be cooked evenly throughout, which has hitherto been thought difficult, and the numbers of rice cakes consumed can be expected to dramatically increase."

The description also mentions the negative aesthetic effects of cross-wise incisions at the top surface:

"[0007] However, while discharge resulting from expansion is suppressed in rice confectionary by providing a number of incisions (line grooves) in the rice cake surface, when, under the same reasoning, a number of incisions or intersecting incisions are provided in the surface of *kiri-mochi* or *maru-mochi (round-mochi)*, although the expansion regions are defined by the incisions and, further, the expansion force is weakened because of the length of the incisions such that it is possible to suppress sudden discharge to the extent of falling and adhering to the cooking grill, the incision regions after cooking have a cooked shape similar to scarring on human skin, resulting in a shape that is actually intolerable, and application thereof to freshly pounded *mochi* that has been packaged as *kiri-mochi* or *maru-mochi* is not ideal."

The defendant produces and sells rice cakes that have incisions both on the top and at the lateral sides:

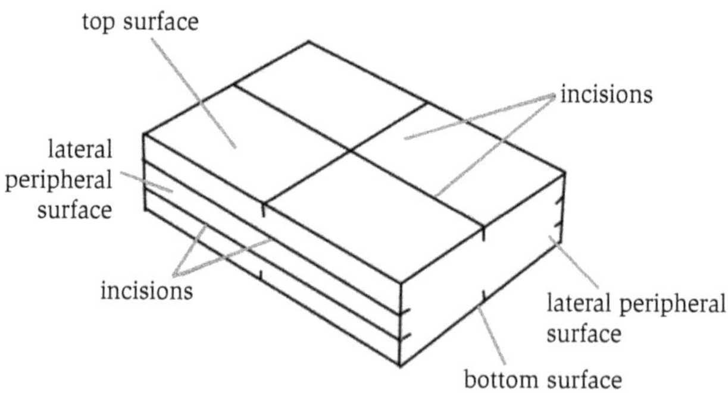

The first instance court (Tokyo District Court, 30 Nov. 2010)[6] denied a literal infringement because it held that incisions at the top of the rice cake had been excluded in the claim.[7] On appeal, the IP High Court affirmed a direct infringement.

b) Reasons

This court finds that the defendant's product falls within the technical scope of the present invention.

Regarding the meaning of "not a lower placement surface or a flat upper surface"

This Court determines that the recitation "not a lower placement surface or a flat upper surface" in configuration requirement B is a recitation for the purpose of clarifying that a "lateral peripheral surface" is meant, and is not a recitation for the purpose of excluding provision of incision parts or groove parts (in the following, also referred to as "incision parts or the like") at a lower placement surface or a flat upper surface.

(i) Recitation of the Scope of the Patent Claims

...

According to ... the scope of the patent claims, the recitation "at a lateral peripheral surface that is a perpendicular lateral surface to the upper side surface part of the body of this piece of rice cake" leads directly on to the recitation "not a lower placement surface or a flat upper surface" without any punctuation added therebetween, and, given this syntax, should naturally be understood such that the recitation "not a lower placement surface or a flat upper surface" modifies the "lateral peripheral surface" together with the recitation "a perpendicular lateral surface to the upper side surface part of the body of this piece of rice cake".

According to the description of the invention above, (1) suppression of a sudden discharge caused by expansion during heating, (2), prevention of an intolerable cooked shape at incision regions (preservation of aesthetic), (3) even cooking throughout, and (4) ease of eating and delicious flavour of the cooked article are indicated as effects of the present invention. Further, it can be understood that in the present invention the above effects (1) to (4) are produced by forming an incision part or the like at a lateral peripheral surface, which is a perpendicular lateral surface of the *kiri-mochi*, and by the upper side being raised during cooking. On the other hand, there is no section in the description of the Invention in which it is explained, for example, that the above effects are not produced when an incision part or the like is provided at a lateral peripheral surface and when an incision part or the like is also provided at a lower placement surface or a flat upper surface ...

---

6. Tokyo District Court, 30 Nov. 2010, Case No. 7718 of 2009, the website of the courts <http://www.courts.go.jp/app/files/hanrei_jp/898/080898_hanrei.pdf>.
7. Before going to court, the plaintiff made a request to the Japanese Patent Office (hereinafter referred to as "JPO") for its advisory (non-binding) opinion on the technical scope of a patented invention (Advisory opinion No. 2009-600006). The panel of the JPO stated the opinion that the defendant's product (having incision parts at a lower and upper surfaces) did not fall within the scope due to lack of the configuration requirement B at issue mentioned later. Despite this opinion, the plaintiff filed this lawsuit against the defendant before the court.

In response, the defendant asserts that with respect to *kiri-mochi*, while the present invention exhibits both an effect of being able to control discharge caused by expansion during cooking (effect 1) and an effect of being able to apply the *kiri-mochi* to practical use without impairing the aesthetic of the toasted rice cake after cooking (effect 2) as a result of the configuration of the incision (paragraph [0032] of the present description), in view of the fact that an intolerable shape results when there is an incision in a flat upper surface or a lower placement surface of the *kiri-mochi* because the cooked state of the incision region after cooking is similar to scarring in human skin (paragraph [0007] of the present description), effect 2 is not exhibited in the present invention.

However, the defendant's assertion cannot be adopted.

That is, the present invention is an invention that utilises the fact that it has an effect of controlling discharge caused by expansion as a result of the incision in a peripheral direction of the lateral peripheral surface of the *kiri-mochi*, and the effect of being able to apply the *kiri-mochi* to practical use without impairing the aesthetic appearance of the toasted rice cake after cooking can be said to a natural consequence thereof. It does not follow that providing an incision at a lower placement surface or a flat upper surface can be understood to be excluded from configuration requirement B simply from the fact that there may be cases when the aesthetic is impaired as a result of an incision part being provided at a lower placement surface or a flat upper surface.

[At one point] the plaintiff, attempting to overcome a reason for rejection, on one occasion submitted an amendment and, on the basis of the features of the invention as amended thereby, declared the opinion that the invention was such that an incision is provided only at a lateral peripheral surface of the *kiri-mochi* and not at a lower placement surface or a flat upper surface that are upper and lower surfaces of the *kiri-mochi*; however, since the examiner determined that this was an addition of new matter, the plaintiff submitted a further amendment and withdrew the above described opinion ... [However], there is no reason for the plaintiff to be restricted by the content of opinions stated by the plaintiff. Rather, if one considers the prosecution history of the application pertaining to the present patent as a whole, excluding the statement of opinion related to the withdrawn amendment, the plaintiff has asserted that it does not matter whether or not there is an incision at a lower placement surface or a flat upper surface that are upper and lower surfaces of the *kiri-mochi* and, in view of these circumstances, the defendant's above assertion cannot be adopted ...

(3) Summary

As per the foregoing, without going as far as to assess the remaining point of contention (whether or not the defendant's product can be said to have an equivalent configuration to the present invention if it does not satisfy configuration requirement B), the defendant's product falls within the technical scope of the present invention.

3. Conclusion

In view of the foregoing, the defendant's product satisfies all of the configuration requirements of the present invention and falls within the technical scope of the present invention, and the present patent is not deemed to warrant invalidation by patent invalidation trial.

3. ANALYSIS

a) Literal claim interpretation

When we try to literally grasp the Japanese meaning of "a lateral peripheral surface ..., and not a lower placement surface or a flat upper surface" in configuration requirement B, this phrase allows one of the two following interpretations:

a) "not" a lower placement surface or a flat upper surface "but" a lateral peripheral surface (only), or
b) a lateral peripheral surface with at least one incision and a lower placement surface or a flat upper surface where there "may or may not" be an incision

Here, according to interpretation (a), the rice cakes with incision parts at an upper or a lower surface are excluded from the scope of the patented invention even if they also have incisions at the lateral side. As a result, they would not constitute a literal infringement. This interpretation is the one which the Tokyo District Court adopted in this case. On the other hand, according to the interpretation (b), if the allegedly infringing products only have incision parts at the lateral surface, regardless of whether they have an incision part at upper or lower side, they would fall within the technical scope of the patented invention. As a result, the products would be considered as having infringed the patent literally. This interpretation is the one which the IP High Court adopted in this case.

With regard to the literal claim interpretation in this case, Prof. *Katō* mentions that only from the viewpoint of claim language itself it would be extremely difficult to find a reason why the disclaimed element "... and not a lower placement surface or a flat upper surface" was added by the applicant (the patentee).[8]

Prof. *Tatsumi*, however, points out that it is possible to find that the disclaimed element was added only for the purpose of putting an emphasis on the characteristic part of the patented invention (incision parts "at the lateral peripheral surface"), and agrees with the interpretation (b) by the IP High Court with an example that when a superior tells a subordinate to "do work A and not work B by tomorrow" the superior focuses on "work A" and requires the subordinate to finish "work A" by tomorrow, which does not mean that the subordinate may not also finish "work B" in addition.[9]

On the other hand, *Takami* mentions that the interpretation (a) adopted by the Tokyo District Court is more correct from a grammatical point of view.[10]

---

8. H. KATŌ, Hanrei Kenkyu tokkyo seikyū no han'i no yōgo no kaishaku ni yotte tokkyo shingai no handan ga sōi shita jirei (*Case study – the case where the decisions of patent infringement varied by the interpretations of the claim*), 6 Nihondaigaku Chizai Journal, 59, 64 (2013)
9. N. TATSUMI, Tokkyo seikyū no han'i ni okeru hatsumei no tokutei to tokkyo hatsumei no gijutsuteki han'I no kakutei *(Identification of the invention in the claims and definition of the technical scope of a patented invention)*, 62-4&5 Kansaidaigaku Hōgaku Ronshū, 593, 657-658 (2013)
10. K. TAKAMI, Tokkyoken shingai soshō saishin hanketsu shōkai *(Review of Recent Patent Infringement Cases in Japan)*, 65-5 Patent 103, 113 (2012).

Also, *Hoshina* points out that in this case, "not A (at an upper or lower surface)" in the claim is unnecessary to define the scope of the invention and it is enough to describe only "B (at a lateral surface)", but that the IP High Court did not find any limitations in the disclaimed element. Therefore, he regards the interpretation (b) by the IP High Court as questionable.[11]

Furthermore, *Iwanaga* takes the example of the sentence "I love Mr. A and not Mr. B or Mr. C" and argues that this phrase naturally means that "I love neither Mr. B nor Mr. C" and that it is unreasonable that Mr. B or Mr. C is referred to just for the purpose of emphasising that "I love Mr. A". Accordingly, he criticises the interpretation (b) by the IP High Court as far-fetched.[12]

b) Statement in the specification

When we interpret and construe the claim, not only the claim language itself (from a literal point of view) but also the statement in the specification (also from technological point of view) are considered. In this case, *Takami* points out that when considering that the "major" effect of the patented invention (effect 1) is to control the discharge caused by expansion during cooking (which is not necessarily related to the incision parts at the upper or lower surface), the IP High Court decision is acceptable because it places great importance on the technical idea (the characteristic part) of the patented invention.[13]

On the other hand, *Hoshina* argues that the person skilled in the art would understand that the patented invention must not have the incision parts at the upper or lower surface, based on (1) the problem of the patented invention (paragraph [0007] and so on), (2) the purpose of the patented invention (suppression of sudden discharge, preservation of aesthetic impression and so on), and also (3) the fact that there is no statement in the specification that an incision part at the upper or lower surface is formed in addition to the ones at the lateral surfaces.[14]

c) Prosecution history

Prof. *Katō* states that the issue whether we should consider the content of opinions by an applicant which was withdrawn later in the prosecution history includes some difficult problems generally, but in this case, he mentions that judging from the statement in the description the patentee does at least not explicitly exclude the element of "a lower placement surface or a flat upper surface".[15]

---

11. T. Hoshina, Kirimochi tokkyo jiken ni miru hatsumei no kowasa (*Risk Inherent in Inventions viewed from the Rice Cake Patent Case*), 70-5 Patent 12, 15-16 (2017).
12. T. Iwanaga, Heisei 23 (Ne) 10002 gō chizai kōsai heiei 23 nen 09 gatsu 07 nichi hanketsu (Case No. 10002 (Ne) of 2011, *The IP High Court decision of 7 September 2011*), The notebook by a lawyer with technical backgrounds (blog), Sep. 9, 2011, available at <http://iwanagalaw.blog.shinobi.jp/%E7%89%B9%E8%A8%B1/%E5%B9%B3%E6%88%9023-%E3%83%8D-10002%E5%8F%B7%EF%BC%88%E7%9F%A5%E8%B2%A1%E9%AB%98%E8%A3%81%E5%B9%B3%E6%88%9023%E5%B9%B409%E6%9C%88>.
13. *Supra note* 10 at 113.
14. T. Hoshina, *supra note* 11, at 12, 16.
15. *Supra note* 8 at 65.

Prof. *Tatsumi* mentioned that the prosecution history should generally not be considered to extend the meaning of the claim and that in this case, it is appropriate that the IP High Court referred to the applicant's assertion during patent prosecution that the claim does not limit the rice cake with "only at a lateral peripheral surface" just to reinforce their own interpretation.[16]

d) Is the decision beyond claim interpretation?

Interestingly, *Kitayama* and *Uematsu*, who disagree with the interpretation (b) adopted by the IP High court, point out that the reason the IP High Court put such a far-fetched interpretation beyond the literal wording in this case and overturned the original decision by the Tokyo District Court might be the defendant's unfaithful conduct before the court concerning the assertion of the public use by the defendant.[17]

e) My own view

In this case, the starting point for a discussion is a literal claim interpretation based on the general meaning of the wording. In the next stage, we should discuss how to consider the description and the prosecution history for the claim interpretation. In other words, we need to find out which literally possible interpretations are more consistent with the statement in the description, and moreover are not contradictory to the manifestation of the applicant's intention indicated in the prosecution history.

With regard to literal claim interpretation, as mentioned before, since the claim language is the most important source to determine the technical scope of the patented invention, each word or phrase in a claim should be regarded as significantly meaningful to determine the scope. Technically, the words in the claim are interpreted as straightforward as possible.[18] Particularly, the disclaimed element (the negative expression) including "not ..." or "except ..." in a claim must have a clear and precise meaning for the purposes of the exclusion. Accordingly, such explicitly disclaimed elements should not be easily disregarded or neglected in the context of the claims.

In this case, when we read the explicitly disclaimed element "and not a lower placement surface or a flat upper surface" in the claim, it is straightforward or natural from the precise meaning of "not" (or the exclusion) that the patented invention should not have any incision parts at "a lower placement surface or a flat upper surface". Since each word or phrase in the claim has the meaning to determine the scope, no elements should be unnecessarily added to patent claims even if this is to put emphasis on a characteristic element. Rather, the explicitly disclaimed element seems to make it almost impossible for the court to reach the interpretation (b) at least from a literal context. In this regard, the absence of a punctuation just before

---

16. *Supra note* 9 at 667-668
17. M. Kitayama and Y. Uematsu, Mochi no tokkyoken ni motozuku shingai sashitome tō seikyū jiken ni oite hikōsonin seihin wa tokkyo hatsumei no gijutsuteki han'i ni zoku suru mono to handan sareta jirei (*Injunction etc. claiming case based on patent of mocha, where the products of appellee were decided to fall within the technical scope of the patented invention*), 2163 Hanrei Jihō 173, 178 (656 Hanrei Hyōron 27, 32).
18. M. Takabe, Tokkyo kankei soshō (*Patent-related litigation*), 3rd ed. 2016, 165.

the element at issue in the original Japanese claim does not necessarily justify interpretation (b) (as the IP High Court argued). Rather, as the Tokyo District Court pointed out, the conjugation of "naku" in Japanese (corresponding to "and not") used in the original Japanese claim seems to indicate the independence of the element, not a mere modifier. Accordingly, in light of the "and not" wording, I agree with the straightforward interpretation (a) of the Tokyo District Court.

Second, although the description should be usually referred to as a source to interpret a literal claim language narrowly, it should not be used to extend the scope of the patented claim beyond the general meaning of a word or a phrase of the claim, for instance by means of "selecting" the effects of the patented invention or by "ranking" the effects as major or minor.

In this case, the incision parts at the lateral side in the claim apparently cause a "suppression of sudden discharge" (effect 1). On the other hand, there is another effect of "preservation of the aesthetic impression" (effect 2) in the description, and the latter is strongly related to the disclaimed element "not a lower placement surface or a flat upper surface". Therefore, the invention without incision parts at a lower or upper side is consistent with and supported by the description. Additionally, as *Hoshina* points out, there seems to be no hint in the description that incision parts at the upper or lower side are formed in addition to the ones at the lateral side.

Accordingly, even if considering the description, the interpretation (b) by the IP High Court cannot be adopted, while the interpretation (a) by the Tokyo District Court is more persuasive.

Finally, the prosecution history should not be used to extend the scope of the patented invention. In this regard, the IP High Court decision is reasonable since it used the prosecution history just for the purpose of supporting its own interpretation (b). However, it cannot be denied that the patentee limited the scope of the claim by using the disclaimed element "not a lower placement surface or a flat upper surface" during examination,[19] even if there was no intention that the claim be limited to having an incision "only at a lateral peripheral surface". The amendments should be regarded as the explicit exclusion of the *kiri-mochi* with incision parts other than at a lateral side. Accordingly, the patentee's assertion that the claim also includes products having incisions at lateral sides is not supported by the prosecution history. Moreover, from my point of view, even the patentee's assertion under the doctrine of equivalents could be denied due to a file wrapper estoppel.

From the viewpoint of the public notice function of patent claims or legal certainty for the public, I would like to point out that the alleged infringers from the claim language "not a lower placement surface or a flat upper surface" would never have foreseen that their rice cake products with incisions on the upper or lower face might infringe the patent. In other words, clarity and conciseness of the meaning of the disclaimed expression would make it much more difficult to predict an infringement than would be the case for doctrine-of-equivalents cases.

19. To be exact, the original claim had the element "not a lower placement surface", but the current disclaimed element "not a lower placement surface or a flat upper surface" was added to the claim by subsequent amendments.

In conclusion, the interpretation of the claim by the IP High Court is unnatural based on a literal meaning of the claims and therefore an unallowably broad interpretation.

Finally, apart from various views of this decision, it can be said that this interlocutory decision by the IP High Court was one of the decisions to show the pro-patent orientation advocated back then by former chief judge *Iimura*. An appeal to the Supreme Court and a motion for the Supreme Court to accept the case were dismissed on 19 September 2012.

4. COMPARATIVE REMARKS

a) Europe

Art. 69(1) European Patent Convention (hereinafter referred to as "EPC") provides the extent of the protection of European patents as follows:

> "The extent of the protection conferred by a European patent or a European patent application shall be determined by the claims. Nevertheless, the description and drawings shall be used to interpret the claims."

Furthermore, Art. 69(1) EPC is supplemented by Art. 1 Protocol on the Interpretation of Art. 69 EPC as a part of the Convention, which gives further guidance particularly for applying the doctrine of equivalents so as to combine

> "a fair protection for the patent proprietor with a reasonable degree of legal certainty for third parties."

For the issue of disclaimers, see case 22 in this book. As the disclaimer in the Rice Cake patent is clearly based on the description, no new teaching was added thereby and from a formal point of view, the disclaimer would be very well allowable under European law.[20]

b) Germany

The legal basis for defining the scope of protection of German patents is provided in Sec. 14 German Patent Act corresponding to Art. 69(1) EPC.

According to German case law, the wording of the claims takes priority over the description and drawings,[21] the use of which may not lead to an extension of the claim's literal meaning.[22] Yet neither should the claims in light of the description

20. Decision **G 2/10** of 30 August 2011, headnotes 1a and 1b.
21. German Federal Supreme Court, 10 May 2011, GRUR 2011, 701 – *Okklusionsvorrichtung (Occlusion Device)*
    'If the description discloses several ways where a particular technical effect can be achieved, but only one was included in the claim, the use of one of the other ways does not, as a general rule, constitute infringement of the patent with equivalent means.'
22. Case Law from the Contracting States to the EPC 2004-2011, Special edition 3 of OJ EPO, 254.
    'Although Art. 69(1), 2nd sentence, EPC provided that the description and drawings were to be used to interpret the claims, such use could not result in an extension of the content or

be interpreted more narrowly than would be suggested by their actual wording.[23]

Under German patent law, the skilled person's knowledge is also used as the basis for interpreting and construing German claims. Omitting a feature of the claim in a contested embodiment may very well lead to a verdict of non-infringement even if the omitted feature appears technically unnecessary.[24]

Unlike Japanese courts, German courts generally disregard prosecution history when they interpret and construe patent claims.[25]

c) The UK

Sec. 125 of the U.K. Patents Act (1977) corresponds to Art. 69(1) EPC and defines the extent of protection conferred by a patent which shall be "taken to be that specified in a claim of the specification of the application or patent, as the case may be, as interpreted by the description and any drawings contained in that specification."

In a few cases, prosecution history was used to interpret the claims.[26] However, the UK courts rarely invoke the prosecution history.

d) The US

According to case law, claim construction must begin with the words of the claim, and a claim term has the meaning that the term would have to a person of ordinary skill in the art, and courts must look at the ordinary meaning in the context of the written description and prosecution history.[27] In other words, "intrinsic evidence" including, in this priority order, claim language, the description, and prosecution history mainly serves as the principle source to interpret and construe the scope of the patent.

Negative limitations may be used which clarify the boundaries of the subject matter for which protection is sought.[28] And while the estoppel of prosecution history is not limited to cases where equivalent infringement is alleged,[29] such history can first and foremost be invoked where the limitation (or disclaimer) was introduced due to a "reason of substantive patentability", which in the above Japanese Rice Cake case was not entirely clear. Even where the amendment is based on reasons that are not clear, it would be a bar to re-claiming such elements.

---

material limitation of the subject-matter as defined by the claim's literal meaning. In the event of a contradiction between the claims and the description, those elements of the description not included in the claims were, as a rule, excluded from the scope of the patent. Accordingly, account could be taken of the description only in so far as it could be read as an explanation of the subject-matter of the claim.'

23. German Federal Supreme Court, 12 December 2006, GRUR 2007, 309 – *Schußfädentransport.*
24. SCHAREN, in: BENKHARD, Patentgesetz *(Commentary to the German Patent Act)*, 15th ed. 2015, sec. 14 note 95.
25. For example, German Federal Supreme Court, 12 March 2002, GRUR 2002, 511 – *Kunststoffrohrteil (Plastic Pipe Part)*.
26. UK High Court, *Furr. v. CD Truline* (Building Products) [1985] FSR 553, 560-4.
27. US CAFC *Phillips v. AWH Corp.*, 415 F.3d 1303 (Fed.Cir.2005) (en banc).
28. US Manual of Patent Examining Procedure (MPEP) 2173.01 Interpreting the Claims [R-07.2015].
29. US Supreme Court, *Warner-Jenkinson v. Hilton Davis*, 520 US 17 (1997).

Case No. 37

Interpretation of Patent Claims – Product by Process Claims

Atsuhiro Furuta

1. **The description of a substance in the claim essentially by its manufacturing process ("Product by Process") is permitted if the determination of the substance by structure or other properties at the time of application is impossible or impractical (especially time-consuming or uneconomic).**
2. **If these conditions are not met, there is a lack of clarity, which constitutes a ground for revocation.**

Supreme Court, 5 June 2015, Case No. 1204&2658 (Ju) of 2012 – *Pravastatin*

Teva v. Kyōwa Hakkō Kirin

1. BACKGROUND

Sec. 2(3) Japanese Patent Act categorises the working of an invention so that the working of a product invention covers the product as such, while a process invention covers the use of the method, and a method of producing a product covers not only the use of the method but also the product which is produced by such method of production.[1] So the invention of a method of production cannot encompass the product which is produced by some other process. Therefore, a product invention has the broadest scope in Japan and many applicants try to obtain patents in the form of the product inventions. But there are cases in which products are very difficult to specify by their quality or structure. Under such circumstances, a "Product by Process" (PBP) claim, in which the product is specified by a production process, is often used in patent practice.[2] But a PBP claim sometimes makes the scope of the claim unclear.

1. The correct Japanese words here are "mono" *(thing)*, "hōhō" *(method)* and "mono wo seisan suru hōhō" *(method of producing a product)*, and the author refers to "product" as translation of "mono" for easier understanding. For clarification, program (software) is comprised in the product category by the law amendment of 2002 (Law No. 24/2002 of 17 April 2002).
2. For clarification, old sec. 36(5)(ii) PA provided that only the subject matter which is essential as an element of the invention to be patented should be described in the claim. This provision was interpreted in that elements of a product invention should be parts of the product and not comprise methods, and it was difficult to specify a product invention with a method. But the

In Japan, there were mainly two theories for the interpretation of the PBP claims: (i) the "product as such" theory, whereby the product as such should fall within the technical scope of the PBP claim even where the product is produced through another process than the process in the claim; and (ii) the "process limited product theory" whereby the product within in the scope of the PBP claim should be limited to the product which is actually produced by the process specified in the claim.

The Japanese Patent Office in examination practice generally adopted the "product as such" theory and rejected an application if there existed some prior art document describing another production process for the same product. Japanese courts interpreted PBP claims in infringement lawsuits by the "product as such" theory or the "process limited product" theory, depending on case.

In this *Pravastatin* infringement case, the main issue was how to interpret a PBP claim.

The first instance, the Tokyo District Court on 31 March 2010 indicated that the PBP claim in this case should be interpreted limitedly so that the product which was produced other process than the process in the claim did not fall in the scope of the claim.

On appeal, the decision of the IP High Court of 27 January 2012[3] indicated new criteria to interpret PBP claims. According to the IP High Court, a PBP claim is generally allowable, but there are two types of the PBP claim, one is a "true" PBP claim (in which the product is impossible or difficult to specify by its structure or characteristics at the time of application), and another is a "non-true" PBP claim (in which that condition is not fulfilled), and the scope of the "true" PBP claim might reach to the product as such, while the "non-true" PBP claim should be limited to the product produced by the process in the claim.

In 2015, the Supreme Court as final instance rejected such criteria of the IP High Court and determined different ones for the interpretation of the PBP claim.

2. DECISION[4]

a) Facts

1. In this case, the plaintiff (*Teva GmbH*) is the patentee of a patent with a so-called "Product by Process" claim, which defines the product according to the invention by a method of production. The plaintiff alleges that manufacturing and placing on the market of the defendant's (*Kyōwa Hakkō Kirin K.K.*) pharmaceuticals infringes its patent, and requests injunction and destruction. The defendant asserts, inter alia, that the product does not fall within the technical scope of the patented invention. Thus, in the present case, it is disputed how to determine the technical scope of a patented invention whose claim defines the product by a method of making it.

---

law amendment of 1994 (Law No. 116/1994 of 14 December 1994) changed this provision and now clearly allows PBP claims or functional claims.

3. IP High Court, 27 January 2012, Case No. 10043 (Ne) of 2010, 2044 Hanrei Jihō 51.
4. Published in 69-4 Minshū 700&904. German Translation in GRUR Int. 2016, 442.

2. Summary of facts established by the lower court

(1) The plaintiff is the owner of a patent entitled "substantially pure pravastatin sodium without pravastatin lactones and epipravastatin and compositions thereof" (registration number 3737801, number of claims 9).

(2) The patented invention

Claim 1 of the patent reads as follows:

Pravastatin sodium containing less than 0.5% by weight of pravastatin lactone and less than 0.2% by weight of epipravastatin produced by a process comprising the following steps:

A) preparation of a concentrated organic solution of pravastatin,
B) precipitation of pravastatin as ammonium salt,
C) purification of the ammonium salt by recrystallisation,
D) conversion of the ammonium salt into pravastatin sodium, and
E) isolation of pravastatin sodium.

(3) The products of the defendant

a. The defendant manufactures and markets the medicine "KH", pravastatin sodium tablet 10 mg (old name: "Merck").

b. The defendant's products contain pravastatin sodium with less than 0.5% by weight pravastatin lactones and less than 0.2% by weight epipravastatin. However, the process of the defendant does not contain step a) "Preparation of a concentrated organic solution of pravastatin" as prescribed in the claim.

3. The lower court dismissed the action for the following reasons:

(1) The technical scope of the patented invention, namely the claim which defines the product by a method of manufacturing it, is limited to the product produced by the method set forth in the claim, as long as there is no indication that the product is impossible to describe by structure or property, or otherwise hard to define.

(2) In the present case, there are no circumstances according to (1), which is why the technical scope of the patented invention is limited to the product produced by the process. The process for preparing the products of the defendant does not contain step a) "preparation of a concentrated organic solution of pravastatin". Therefore, the defendant's products do not fall within the scope of the patented invention.

b) Reasons

4. We cannot agree with the assessment of the lower court as above 3 (2) for the following reasons:

(1) The technical scope of a patented invention is determined by the claims (sec. 70(1) Patent Act). The contents of a pending patent application is also determined by the claims for the purposes of examination (Supreme Court, decision of 8 March 1991 [Case No. 35 in this volume – *Ra Lipase*]). Patents are granted for inventions relating

to a product, process or a method of manufacture. If a product has the same structure, property etc. as the patented product, the effect of the patent extends to this product irrespective of the method of its manufacture.

(2) A claim shall fulfil the conditions according to sec. 36(6)(ii) Patent Act in that "the invention is clearly expressed by the claims". The purpose of the patent system is to protect the invention by granting a patent as an exclusive right for the inventor in return for disclosure of the contents of the invention to third parties so as to promote inventions so that they be used and thereby contribute to the development of the industry (sec. 1 Patent Act). The requirement of clarity of a claim under sec. 36(6)(ii) Patent Act must be interpreted with this purpose in mind. From this point of view, in the case of a "product by process" claim, the determination of the technical scope is such that the effect of the patent should extend to the product as such (structure, property, etc.). This is problematic because it unfairly compromises the interests of third parties. In fact, a claim for a method of manufacture normally does not disclose the structure or characteristic of the product produced, or whether the scope of protection is limited to the product produced by this method. Thus, the reader of the claim cannot clearly understand the contents of the invention in this case and cannot reliably determine the field of exclusive use. This is not appropriate.

On the other hand, a claim for a product normally describes the product directly through clear structures or properties. However, there are cases where it is technically impossible to describe the structure or characteristics of the product by the subject matter, characteristics, etc. at the time of filing, or that their description would be impractical, uneconomical or too time consuming for the patent applicant taking into account the urgency, etc. of a patent application. Therefore, it would not be appropriate to prohibit the definition of products in the claims by way of the process for their preparation. Rather, the interests of third parties are not unduly restricted if the technical field of the patented invention includes the product with the same structure, property, etc., as far as the above circumstances are present.

From the above considerations, we find that the condition in sec. 36(6)(ii) Patent Act that "the invention is clearly expressed" is satisfied in a "product by process" claim only when there are circumstances in which the immediate description of the product by structure or properties is impossible or impractical at the time of the patent application.

5. This interpretation is different from the decision of the first instance court according to which the definition of a product in a claim as a method of manufacture is generally allowed and the technical scope of the patented invention of a product produced by the patented process is in principle limited to that method. This decision is based on this clear legal error. There are therefore reasons to overturn the decision of the lower court. We therefore remand the case to the court of first instance with the order to determine the technical scope of the invention in accordance with our decision and to decide whether in light of the foregoing considerations under 4 (2) the condition that "the invention is clearly expressed" is fulfilled.

3. ANALYSIS

In this case, it is helpful to take a closer look at the decision rendered by the IP High Court (that is, the decision under appeal that was subsequently overturned by the Supreme Court). The IP High Court established new criteria for "true" and "non-true" PBP claims as follows:

> "For the determination of technical scope of patented invention, sec. 70(1) PA provides that 'the technical scope of the patented invention shall be determined by the wording of the claim attached to the application' and sec. 70(2) 'in the case of the previous subsection (1), the wording described in the claim is interpreted in consideration with the specification and the figures attached to the application' etc. So in the case of a lawsuit claiming injunction or damages based on a patent infringement, the basis for the determination of the technical scope of the invention should be the wording of the 'claim'. The wording of the claim should concretely describe the technical scope of the invention, and if some specific 'wording' of the claim had no meaning to limit the technical scope of invention, the trust of third parties who act in accordance with the wording of the claims described in patent gazette might be impaired and legal certainty is compromised. Therefore in a case as this one where the 'method of producing' in the claim refers to a 'product invention', the principle is that the technical scope of such invention should be interpreted/determined as limited to the product which is produced by the method as described in the claim, and it is not allowed to interpret/determine it as comprising methods of producing the product other than the method as described in the claim. In a case of a 'product invention' as this one, the claim should describe and specify the structure or characteristics of the product, but if there are circumstances under which it is impossible or difficult to directly specify the product by its structure or characteristics at the time of application, in the light of sec. 1 Patent Act, which is to promote inventions and to contribute the development of industry, it is allowable to specify the product by the method of manufacture. In such case, the technical scope is interpreted as the 'product as such' without a limitation to the method of manufacture as described in the claim, because the method of manufacture is described for purpose of specifying the product as such."

Thus, the IP High Court adopted the "process limited product theory" in principle and put the burden of proof for a "true" PBP claim, which should be limited to exceptional cases, on the patentee. The decision provoked a lot of reaction amongst academics and practitioners.

On one hand those who criticised the new criteria of the IP High Court,[5] arguing that it would lead to too many "non-true" PBP claims which should be interpreted limitedly, while putting an unnecessary burden on practitioners in order to avoid such result. Further, it made claim interpretation unclear and difficult to foresee,

5. There are many Japanese papers on this topic, for such opinion, see, for example: T. SHIBUYA, Purodakuto bai purosesu kurēmu no kaishaku *(Interpretation of product-by-process claim)*, 117 Chizai Prism 21 (2012); Y. OKADA/S. SAIDO, Purodakuto bai purosesu kurēmu no kaishaku nitsuki handanshita chitekizaisan kōtō saibansho tokubetsubu daigōgi hanketsu *(Intellectual Property High Court Grand Panel's case relating to interpretation of product-by-process claims)*, 54 Tokkyo Kenkyū 38.

because it would be difficult to prove the circumstances for a "true" PBP claim during examination, and many PBP claims should be patented as process-limited at the JPO stage, but there should be no binding indication for such limited interpretation, and patentees could argue them as "true" PBP later at the stage of infringement.

On the other hand those that agreed with the interpretation of the IP High Court.[6] The decision clearly established the "process limited product theory" as a rule, which could be implemented in the examination practice of the JPO, and made a useful option for applicants to obtain patents in process-limited product inventions which obviously have a broader scope than normal method inventions, see Case No. 53 in this volume – *Kallikrein*.

The reaction to the decision was such that after the appeal to the Supreme Court, almost all Japanese patent practitioners and academics eagerly awaited a definite decision of the highest court, while the JPO had to stop the examination of applications which included PBP claims.

The Supreme Court then reversed the interpretation of PBP claims and did not follow the IP High Court. But the Supreme Court also indicated in its decision that a PBP claim becomes unclear in the sense of sec. 36(6)(ii) PA in the absence of circumstances in which it is impossible or impractical to specify the product invention directly by its structure or characteristics of the product at the time of application.

For Japanese patent practice, the decision of the Supreme Court is of great importance to put an end to the various theories of interpreting PBP claims, although there are some problems with the criteria of "impossible" or "impractical" circumstances,[7] inter alia.

The first issue concerns to identify a PBP claim: If only one part of the claim describes a process of producing, should the whole claim be seen as the PBP claim? And the second issue is to identify circumstances where it is "impossible" or "impractical" to otherwise describe the product. Do such circumstances depend on the applicant? Do applicants who are less able to analyse structures or characteristics of products find themselves in a better position to prove such circumstances?

After the decision of the Supreme Court, the JPO, restarting to examine PBP claim applications, published documents to clarify the treatment of PBP claims in the examination process and also revised the Examination Guidelines.[8] Under the

---

6. For such opinion, see, for example: Y. Shiroyama, Purodakuto bai purosesu kurēmu jiken *(Product by process claim case)*, 1475 Jurist 39 (2015); H. Yoshida, Purabasutachin natoriumu purodakuto bai purosesu kurēmu chizai kōsai daigōgi hanketsu *(Pravastatin sodium product-by-process claim IP high court grand panel's case)*, 2160 Hanrei Jihō 164 (2012).
7. The old JPO Examination Guideline indicated also that there were cases in which PBP claims became unclear where concrete products which were produced by the process in the claim could also be produced by taking into consideration common technical knowledge. But this condition of the JPO for lack of clarity was not so strict as the one of the Supreme Court. For the old JPO Guideline, see the JPO documents in Tokkyo jitsuyōshin-an shinsa kijun – shinsa kijun no tsuika kaitei ni tsuite *(Patent and utility model examination guideline – about revision of examination guideline)*, at the website of the JPO <https://www.jpo.go.jp/system/laws/rule/guideline/patent/tukujitu_kijun/kaitei/index.html>.
8. The JPO on 6 July 2015, shortly after the decision of the Supreme Court was rendered, published a notice on: Purodakuto bai purosesu kurēmu ni kansuru tōmen no shinsa/shinpan no toriatsukai tō ni tsuite *(About treatment etc. of product-by-process claims current examination practice)* at <https://www.jpo.go.jp/system/laws/rule/guideline/patent/tukujitu_kijun/product_process/

practice of the JPO, PBP claims at first were very rigidly scrutinised in light of the scope of the claim as determined by the decision of the Supreme Court, and even if only one part of the claim included method-like description, the JPO sent a notice of refusal about a lack of clarity so that the applicant had to come forward with explanations or amendments. More recently, on 30 March 2016, the JPO explained that it no longer objected to a lack of clarity where a method of manufacture was formally included in the claim, while the structure or characteristics of the product were clearly described.[9] The IP High Court in recent decisions seems to have confirmed this practice.[10]

In the author's view, such flexible approach to PBP claims following the Supreme Court decision is quite reasonable. Claims are usually interpreted and determined by the wording of the claim itself, and it is meaningless and too burdensome to require an explanation about "impossible" or "impractical" circumstances where a process is included in the claim and a person skilled in the art can clearly understand the claimed product based on the wording of the claim. By such approach, the problem of burden of proof for the circumstances, in other words, the problem of what are "impossible" or "impractical" circumstances, is no longer of much practical relevancy. The author does not agree with the decision of the IP High Court, but recognises that the step taken by the IP High Court was a bold one in case law development for PBP claims prior to the decision of the Supreme Court of Japan.[11]

C150706.html>. The JPO documents about the PBP claim published to date are assembled in Purodakuto bai purosesu kurēmu ni kansuru shinsa no toriatsukai ni tsuite *(About treatment of product-by-process claim in examination)* at <https://www.jpo.go.jp/system/laws/rule/guideline/patent/tukujitu_kijun/product_process/index.html>.

9. For review of the practice of JPO, see T. Ishihara, PBP kurēmu ni kansuru kentō no keii to shinsa unyō *(Review history and examination practice about PBP claims)*, 106 Chizaiken Forum 3 (2016).
10. For analysis of such decisions, see, K. Fujii, Purodakuto bai purosesu kurēmu to meikakusei yōken *(product process claim and clarity requirement)*, 67-9 Chizai Kanri 14 (2017).
11. There are so many commentaries or analyses of this case or about the PBP claim after the decision of the Supreme Court and there is not enough space to cite all of them, but the author indicates some of them for further reading: N. Nakayama, Tokkyohō *(Patent Law)*, 3rd ed. 2016, 484; R. Shitara, Kisai yōken -jisshikanō yōken to Sapōto yōken tono kankei awasete, purodakuto bai purosesu kurēmu nitsuite - *(Description requirement - relationship between carrying out possibility requirement and support requirement, and also about product-by-process claim)*, 69-2 Patent 93 (2016); R. Iseki, Purodakuto bai purosesu kurēmu no triatsukai *(Treatment of product-by-process claim)*, 70 L&T 1 (2016); Y. Hirai/R. Nishiwaki, Jitsumuka kara mita PBP kurēmu saikōsai hanketsu *(The PBP claim Supreme Court decision from viewpoint of practitioners)*, 70 L&T 19 (2016); E. Kikuchi, Saikōsai Jūyō hanketsu kaisetsu purabasutachin natoriumu purodakuto bai purosesu kurēmu jiken *(Commentary on important decision of the Supreme Court pravastatin sodium product-by-process claim case)*, 69 L&T 91 (2015); K. Maeda, Purodakuto bai purosesu kurēmu no yūkōsei to teisei no kahi *(Validity of product-by-process claim and allowance of correction)*, 60-8 AIPPI 2 (2015).

4. COMPARATIVE REMARKS

In the **US**, the USPTO adopts the product as such theory in examination procedure, and this practice is endorsed by the decision of the CAFC,[12] but infringement courts adopt the process limited product theory along with case law of the CAFC.[13]

The **EPO** adopts the product as such theory in its case law, and the PBP claim should be regarded as unclear if there is no other description in an application for specifying the product as object in the claim.[14]

In **Germany,** the GPTO and infringement courts adopt the product as such theory.[15]

In the **UK**, the UKIPO adopts the product as such theory based on case law,[16] but infringement courts adopt the process limited product theory.[17]

In **China**, the CNIPA (old English name in abbreviation: SIPO) adopts the product as such theory in examination procedure,[18] and there is no clear case law about PBP claims, but there is a decision of 24 November 2010 of the Chinese Supreme Court which limited an extract product invention by its method of manufacture.

In **Korea**, the Korean Supreme Court also adopts the product as such theory for PBP claims both for validity and infringement, as confirmed by two decisions on 22 January 2015 and 12 February 2015.[19]

It can thus be said that many patent offices adopt the product as such theory, because the process limited product theory causes difficulty in usual examination. But stances taken by infringement courts to the PBP claim differ from country to

12. See, MPEP 2113 of the USPTO at the website of the USPTO <https://www.uspto.gov/web/offices/pac/mpep/s2113.html> and cited decision, US CAFC, *In re Thorpe*, 777 F.2d 695, 698, 227 USPQ 964, 966 (Fed. Cir. 1985).
13. US CAFC, *Abbott Laboratories v. Sandoz, Inc.*, 566 F.3d 1282, 90 USPQ 2d 1769 (Fed. Cir. 2009).
14. See, the Examination Guideline of the EPO Part F Chapter IV 4.12 at the website of the EPO <http://www.epo.org/law-practice/legal-texts/html/guidelines/e/f_iv_4_12.htm> and cited cases: European Patent Office, case **T 150/82** of 7 February 1984, OJ EPO 1984, 309. This is established case law, see European Patent Office, case **T 219/83** of 26 November 1985, OJ EPO 1986, 211; European Patent Office, case **T 863/12** of 23 September 2015.
15. German Federal Supreme Court, 6 July 1971, GRUR 1972, 80 – *Trioxan*; German Federal Supreme Court, 19 July 1984, GRUR 1985, 31 – *Acrylfasern*; German Federal Supreme Court, 30 March 1993, GRUR 1993, 651 – *Tetraploide Kamille*; German Federal Supreme Court, 19 June 2001, GRUR 2001, 1129 – *zipfelfreies Strahlband*. See also R. Shitara (above). *R. Shitara* highlights the interesting point that the German Federal Supreme Court for allowing PBP claims uses the words "impossible" and "impractical", which are very similar to the terminology used by the Japanese Supreme Court. But the influence of the German case law is unclear.
16. England House of Lords, *Kirin Amgen v. Hoechst Marion Roussel* [2014] UKHL 46.
17. English High Court, *Hospira v. Genetech* [2014] EWHC 3857.
18. The Examination Guideline of the SIPO, Part II Chapter 3 3.2.5, at the website of CNIPA <http://english.cnipa.gov.cn/docs/20180131104843547234.pdf>. (The Chinese Patent Office, SIPO (State Intellectual Property Office) was renamed to Chinese National Intellectual Property Administration in 2018.)
19. Mentioned in: S. Park, Purodakuto bai purosesu kurēmu ni kansuru saikin no daihōin hanrei no kōsatsu (Comments on recent decision of the Korean Supreme Court about product-by-process claim), 65-10 Chizai Kanri 1405 (2015).

country. Practitioners should thus be careful in claim drafting in consideration of such differences in case law.[20]

20. For treatment of PBP claims in each country, see also, IIP/JPO, Purodakuto bai purosesu kurēmu no shinsa no toriatsukai ni kansuru chōsa kenkyū hōkokusho *(Research report on examination practice of product-by-process claim)*, available at the website of the JPO <https://www.jpo.go.jp/resources/report/sonota/document/zaisanken-seidomondai/2015_13.pdf>; Y. KUROKI, Kakkoku niokeru purodakuto bai purosesu kurēmu *(Product-by-process claim in each country)*, 66-5 Chizai Kanri 584 (2016).

Case No. 38

Interpretation of Patent Claims – Doctrine of Equivalents

Toshiko Takenaka

Whether the contested device infringes a patented invention or not must be determined according to the interpretation of a patent claim under Sec. 70 Patent Act. However, even if the allegedly infringing device partially differs from the wording of the claims, an equivalence can be affirmed if:

i. **the above differences concern an essential part of the claimed invention,**
ii. **the allegedly infringing device despite the replacement still attains the same purpose and result,**
iii. **a person skilled in the art could have easily anticipated the replacement at the time of production,**
iv. **at the time of the patent application the allegedly infringing device did not belong to the state of the art or could have been easily anticipated therefrom, and**
v. **in the course of patent application proceedings, the scope of the patent claims was not meant to exclude the allegedly infringing device.**

Supreme Court, 24 February 1998, Case No. 1083 (O) of 1994 –
Ball Spline Bearing III

Tsubakimoto Seiki v. THK

---

1. BACKGROUND

The *Ball Spline Bearing III* case[1] is the very first case in which the Supreme Court of Japan acknowledged the doctrine of equivalents under the Japanese Patent Act and set forth conditions for applying the doctrine. Patent Act of Japan, sec. 70[2] provides

1. Published in 52-1 Minshū 113 = 1630 Hanrei Jihō 32 = 969 Hanrei Times 105 = N. NAKAYAMA et al. (eds.), Tokkyo Hanrei Hyakusen *(Hundred Selected Patent Cases)*, 4th ed. 2012, 134 = T. ŌBUCHI et al. (eds.), Chitekizaisan hō hanrei shū *(Intellectual Property Law Case Book)*, 2nd ed. 2015, 140. English translation in 30 IIC 443 (1999). Another translation by C. MIZUMOTO & Y. HIRAKI is available at the website of the SOFTIC <https://www.softic.or.jp/en/cases/Tsubakimoto_v_THK.html>
2. Tokkyohō (Patent Act), Law No. 121 of 1959 (Last revised in 2017, Law No. 45 of 2017).

a rule similar to European Patent Convention, Art. 69:[3] The technical scope of patent invention must be decided by the claims.[4] In the past, Japanese courts had developed a theory to limit patent protection to what was disclosed in the application and recognised by the inventor as his/her invention regardless of the language of the claims.[5] This inventor's recognition limitation theory (*Ninshiki gendo ron*) has been a dominant principle for Japanese courts to read limitations from the description into the claims and effectively limit the technical scope to cover only disclosed embodiments. This theory also effectively limits the application of the doctrine of equivalents because contested embodiments whose infringement under the doctrine of equivalents is asserted neither fall within the claim scope nor are disclosed in the description.[6] As a result, the extent of patent protection conferred by a Japanese patent was considered as much less than that conferred by a US patent. This restrictive claim interpretation without the doctrine of equivalents was extensively criticised by the US industry.[7]

Prior to the *Ball Spline Bearing III* cases, there were a small number of lower court decisions that found infringement for embodiments which were not literally covered by the claim scope in citing the facts that the contested embodiments would produce the same effect of the invention even if claim elements were replaced with different features (*chikan kanōsei* - interchangeability) and a person having an ordinary skill in the art of the invention (person skilled in the art) would have easily conceived the interchangeability between the missing claim element and the replaced features in the contested embodiment (*chikan yōi suikōsei* - obviousness of interchangeability).[8] In

3. Convention on the Grant of European Patents, October 5, 1973, 13 I.L.M. 270.
4. The term "technical scope (*gijututeteki han'i*)" is used equivalent to the term "the extent of patent protection" under the European Patent Convention Article 69.
5. T. TAKENAKA, Interpreting Patent Claims: The United States, Germany and Japan, 17 IIC Studies 66-67 (1995).
6. JAPANESE PATENT OFFICE, Sangyō zaisanken hō - Chiteki zaisanken hō - no kaisetsu *(Explanation of Industrial Property Law - Intellectual Property Law, 1994 Industrial Property Law Revision, Law No. 116 of 1994)*, Chapter 4: Claim Interpretation In Light of Detailed Explanation of the Invention 124, available at the website of the JPO <https://www.jpo.go.jp/system/laws/rule/kaisetu/sangyozaisan/document/sangyou_zaisanhou/h6_kaisei_4.pdf>. Another reason for a narrow claim interpretation was the prevailing method of comparing the individual elements of the claim with the allegedly infringing embodiment in disregard of the inventive concept, e.g. Tokyo High Court, 27 March 1969, and Osaka High Court, 28 May 1985, Hanrei Kōgyō Shoyūken hō (HanKō) 2213-278.
7. *E.g.*, DONALD M. SPERO, Patent Protection or Piracy—A CEO Views Japan, 68 Harvard Business Review 58-67 (1990).
8. *E.g.*, Tokyo District Court, 10 July 1987, Case No. 7463 (Wa) of 1985, 20 IIC 91 (1989) - *Monsanto*; Osaka District Court, 31 October 1980, Case Nos. 3925&4016 (Wa) of 1975, 4824 (Wa) of 1979, 12-2 Mutaishū 632; Tokyo District Court 22 Nov. 1966, Case No. 8884 (Wa) of 1962, 17-11&12 Kakyū Minshū 1116; Osaka District Court, 30 July 1974, Case No. 5034 (Wa) of 1970, 6 IIC 81 (1975) - *Lucidril*. For a general discussion on pre- *Ball Spline Bearing III* case law on the doctrine of equivalents, see *supra* note 5, T. TAKENAKA, Claim Interpretation at 248. In the first instance *Lucidril* decision of the Osaka District Court, 30 July 1974, 6 IIC 81 (1975), the presiding judge in this case, judge *Oe*, was a vociferous proponent of both the doctrine of equivalents and the defence of patent invalidity in an infringement suit, both developments that would become mainstream only 30 years later. The relevant part of the decision reads: "Therefore, when in the Patent Gazette the chemical structure, boiling point and so forth of the compound having a novel pharmacologic effect, as well as the detail of the manufacturing process, are disclosed

the *Pulpwood Barking Machine* case (1987), the Supreme Court affirmed one of such lower court decisions: The district court found infringement of a utility model right regarding the contested embodiment involving a replacement of a piston mechanism with a crank mechanism whereby it was well-known to a person skilled in the art to replace a piston.[9] The District Court held that the contested embodiment was an equivalent of the registered device because of the interchangeability between the piston and crank and obviousness of such interchangeability. After the infringement finding was upheld on appeal, the Supreme Court simply affirmed the conclusion of infringement without mentioning the term "equivalent" in its very brief opinion to dismiss the defendant's appeal. Obviously, the Court was not ready to openly endorse infringement under the doctrine of equivalents because leading judges[10] and mainstream scholars strongly supported the inventor's recognition limitation theory and strongly opposed a protection beyond disclosed embodiments.[11]

---

to the public, including those skilled in the art, the patent should be interpreted so that the equivalent techniques satisfying the (inventive) requirements mentioned above are disclosed implicitly by the publication of the invention, because it can be said that those who are skilled in the art should easily conceive of the equivalent techniques, even though the description does not mention them. Then, unless the applicant has expressed his intention that he would disclaim such equivalent process or there are any particular circumstances that the process employing such an equivalent technique is to be interpreted as being excluded from the scope of protection of the patent, it constitutes no more than piracy of the technique of the patented invention to use the process in which such an equivalent technique is employed and it constitutes infringement of the patentee's right." The decision was overturned on appeal, however.

9. Supreme Court of Japan, 29 May 29 1987 (Unreported in Minshū or any other official case reporter). For a case comment, T. HONMA, Kintōron no Tekiyō wo Shijishita Saịkin no Saikōsai Han'ketsu *(Supreme Court Decision Supporting the Application of the Doctrine of Equivalents)*, 903 Jurist 85 (1988); M. SUMIDA, Hanrei shōkai kintōron o tekiyōshite jitsuyō shin'anken no shingai o mitometa genshin no handan o shijishita Saikōsai no hanketsu *(The Supreme Court Judgement Upholding the Second Instance which Found Infringement of a Utility Model Right Invoking the Doctrine of Equivalents)*, 6 Tokkyo Kenkyū 36 (1988); T. TAKENAKA, Claim Interpretation *supra* note 5, at 262.
10. One of the most influential IP judges in the 1980s and 1990s, *Toshiaki Makino*, was an outspoken critic of the equivalents' doctrine.
11. JAPAN PATENT OFFICE & ASIA-PACIFIC INDUSTRIAL PROPERTY CENTER, Intellectual Property High Court of Japan, 2013, 53, available at the website of the JPO <https://www.jpo.go.jp/e/news/kokusai/developing/training/textbook/document/index/Intellectual_Property_High_Court_of_Japan_2013.pdf>. Pre-*Ball Spline* decisions often had no firm doctrinal basis as to why equivalents should be included in the scope of the exclusive right. For example, the well-known decision of Tokyo District Court, 10 July 1987, 20 IIC 91 (1989) – *Monsanto* affirmed infringement outside the literal scope of the claims, but did not use any specific theory for this conclusion: "1. It is found that the above aqueous solution contains glyphosate ion and trimethylsulfonium ion. Hence the defendants' herbicide is the same in constitution as the aqueous solution of the invention. The mole ratio between glyphosate ion and trimethylsulfonium ion in the defendants' herbicide is about 1: 1.13. The mole ratio between glyphosate ion and trimethylsulfonium ion in the above aqueous solution, which is an embodiment of the invention, can be made almost the same as that in the defendants' herbicide by adjusting the amount of trimethylsulfonium hydroxide to be added to glyphosate. 2. The defendants' herbicide has the same composition as that of the above-mentioned aqueous solution, which contains glyphosate as an effective herbicidal ingredient and trimethylsulfonium hydroxide as an adjuvant – an embodiment of the invention. Thus, all the elements of the invention, as defined by the phrase "a herbicide comprising glyphosate as an effective" ingredient, are present. The defendants' herbicide falls within the technical scope of the claimed invention."

In response to criticisms from the US industry, the Japan Patent Office asked its Industrial Property Council to examine whether the conditions for applying the doctrine of equivalents should be codified when the Japanese Patent Act was revised in 1994 for clarifying the rule for claim interpretation in light of the description and drawings.[12] The revision removed the requirement for including only indispensable elements for the invention, which was frequently cited by Japanese courts and legal scholars as a reason to deny infringement if any claim element was missing from the contested embodiment.[13] Although the Council acknowledged the benefit of codifying the doctrine of equivalents, it nevertheless concluded that the time was not ripe for such codification. Accordingly, the Council advised the JPO to continue discussions on selected important issues such as whether the doctrine of equivalents should apply only under exceptional circumstances and an infringement analysis under the doctrine of equivalents should be conducted objectively on an element-by-element basis, although it did not deny the benefits of codification.[14]

Although the doctrine of equivalents has become influential, patent owners were very reluctant to argue for infringement under the doctrine of equivalents because such an argument was viewed as an admission of lack of literal infringement and there was no consensus among judges and legal scholars regarding the conditions for applying the doctrine. As Japan's patent policy shifted towards the so-called pro-patent policy in the 1990s, the Supreme Court took the initiative in clarifying the conditions for applying the doctrine of equivalents.[15]

2. DECISION[16]

a) Facts

The appellee (the plaintiff of the original action) is the owner of a Japanese patent for an endlessly sliding ball spline shaft bearing, which patent was filed on 26 April 1971 and granted on 30 May 1980. The patented claim reads:

---

12. *Supra* note 6, JPO, Explanation of Industrial Property Law at 122.
13. This requirement was included in the pre-1994 Patent Act, Sec. 36(5)(ii). If an element in an allegedly infringing embodiment differed from an element in the claim, equivalence could not be argued because in such case, the element that was replaced could not be called "necessary" (H. NIIHARA, Tokkyohō kaisei – oubeigata kaizen takōsei no dōnyū (*Amendment to the Patent Act – introduction of the improved multiple claims system like Europe/US)*, 888 Jurist 97, 101).
14. *Supra* note 6, JPO, Explanation of Industrial Property Law at 125.
15. H. KIYOKAWA, Wagakunini okeru puropatentoka no hyoka to kongo no kagai – Tokkyo seido wo chushin'ni *(An Evaluation of Pro-Patent Policy Implementation in Japan and future challenges – Focusing on Patent System)*, Keizai Sangyo Journal (April 2007), available at the website of the RIETI <https://www.rieti.go.jp/jp/papers/journal/0704/rr01.html>. For a general discussion on Japan's shift on patent policy, see T. TAKENAKA and I. NAKAYAMA, Will Intellectual Property Policy Save Japan from Recession? Japan's Basic Intellectual Property Law and its Implementation through the Strategic Program, 35 IIC (2004): 877; T. TAKENAKA, Success or Failure? Japan's National Strategy on Intellectual Property and Evaluation of its Impact from the Comparative Law Perspective, 8 Wash. U. Global Studies L. Rev. 379 (2009).
16. Published in 52-1 Minshū 113 = 1630 Hanrei Jihō 32 = 969 Hanrei Times 105 = N. NAKAYAMA et al. (eds.), Tokkyo Hanrei Hyakusen *(Hundred Selected Patent Cases)*, 4th ed. 2012, 134 = T. ŌBUCHI et al. (eds.), Chitekizaisan hō hanrei shū *(Intellectual Property Law Case Book)*, 2nd

> "An endlessly sliding ball spline shaft bearing comprising:
>
> > An outer cylinder having torque transmitting load bearing ball-guiding grooves with a U-shaped cross-section and torque transmitting non-load bearing ball-guiding with the U-shaped cross-section being slightly deeper than that of the load bearing ball-guiding grooves, the load bearing ball-guiding groove and the non-load bearing, ball-guiding groove extending alternately in the axial direction within the cylindrical inner wall, the outer cylinder having an annular circumferentially directed groove at each end with the same depth as that of the deeper groove (Component A);
> >
> > A thin wall portion and the tick wall portion formed respectively in conformity with the torque transmitting load bearing ball-guiding groove and the torque transmitting non-load bearing ball-guiding groove formed in the axial direction within the inner wall of the outer cylinder;
> >
> > A joint portion between the thin wall portion and the thick wall portion having a through-hole;
> >
> > A retainer with an endless track groove for allowing balls to smoothly slide into the non-load ball-guiding groove formed in the thick wall portion (Component B); and
> >
> > A spline shaft provided with a plurality of ribs extending in the axial direction thereof, said ribs being shaped to conform with a plurality of recessed spaces formed by the balls incorporated between the retainer and said outer cylinder (Component C) for engaging the spline shaft with the outer cylinder (Component D)."

The appellee sued the appellant (the defendant of the original action) for infringing its patent. The Tokyo District Court found no infringement because the appellant's device fell outside the scope defined by the claim language and the patentee failed to establish obviousness of interchangeability between the claimed elements and replaced structures in the contested device.[17] On appeal the Tokyo High Court reversed the decision and found that the appellant's device infringed the patented invention under the doctrine of equivalents.[18] The court acknowledged claimed elements were replaced with different structures but found infringement because the replaced structures attained the same technical object and result of the patented invention and PHOSTA would have conceived the replacement. Thus, the court concluded that the appellant's modifications were insignificant and the appellee established that the contested device was equivalent to the patented invention. The appellant appealed.

b) Reasons

III. This Court cannot agree with the lower court's findings for the following reasons.

---

ed. 2015, 140. English translation in 30 IIC 443 (1999). Another translation by C. MIZUMOTO & Y. HIRAKI is available at the website of the SOFTIC <https://www.softic.or.jp/en/cases/Tsubakimoto_v_THK.html>.

17. Tokyo District Court, 19 April 1991, Case No. 12677 (Wa) of 1983, 26-1 Chiteki zaishū 89.
18. Tokyo High Court, 3 February 1994, Case No. 1627 (Ne) of 1991, 26-1 Chiteki zaishū 34; T. TAKENAKA, Case Comment, 26 IIC 683 (1995).

1. Patent Act, Sec. 70 requires courts to determine the technical scope of a patented invention by making reference to the description attached to the asserted claim for deciding whether the contested device or method (contested embodiment) falls within the technical scope. In principle, a contested embodiment falls outside of the technical scope and thus does not infringe the patented invention if there is any difference between the patented invention defined by the claim language and the contested embodiment. However, even if the claimed invention includes elements which are different from the contested embodiment, the contested embodiment should be considered to fall within the technical scope because such embodiment is equivalent to the claimed invention if the following five conditions are met:

i. said different elements do not constitute the essential part of the claimed invention ((1) Non-essential part),
ii. the object of the patented invention can be attained by the contested embodiment even if the claimed elements are replaced with the different structures, and thus the contested embodiment results in having identical functions and effects as the patented invention ((2) Interchangeability),
iii. a person skilled in the art would have easily conceived the replacement at the time of making, selling etc. of the contested embodiment ((3) Obviousness of interchangeability)
iv. the contested embodiment neither formed part of the state of the art nor would have been easily conceived from the state of the art at the time the application for the patented invention was filed ((4) novelty and inventive step of the contested embodiment), and
v. the applicant did not intentionally remove the contested embodiment from the technical scope of the asserted patent claim during the patent prosecution ((5) No disclaimer of the contested embodiment)

The reasons for finding infringement when the above five conditions are met are as follows:

i. At the time an application is filed, it is very difficult for applicants to anticipate all possible infringing embodiments that may occur in the future and draft claims covering all such embodiments. Thus, allowing another party circumventing patent enforcement such as injunction by replacing any element of the patented invention with an interchangeable structure and material that has become known to a person skilled in the art after patent application would diminish incentives for inventions and thereby conflict with the purpose of the Patent Act to encourage inventions by promoting their protection. Moreover, allowing such circumvention would be contrary to social justice and violate the concept of equity.
ii. In view of the above, the substantial value of the patented invention should extend to embodiments which a person skilled in the art would have easily conceived from the claimed invention as being substantially the same as such invention. It is reasonable to assume that anyone should anticipate the scope of claimed invention to cover such embodiments.
iii. On the other hand, embodiments which were known or would have been easily conceived by a person skilled in the art from the state of art at the

time the application for the patent was filed were not patentable. No patent should have been issued on such embodiments, which should have been kept in the public domain.

iv. In addition, the doctrine of estoppel prevents patentees from asserting infringement regarding any embodiment which the applicant intentionally removed from the technical scope of the patented invention during the prosecution by admitting that the embodiment does not fall within the technical scope or engaging an act giving rise to a disclaimer of the embodiment.

2. The above rationales are applied to this case for reviewing the lower court's finding. The lower court found that the contested device fell within the technical scope of the patented invention despite of its finding that some claimed elements in the two components, Components A and B, were replaced with different structures in the contested device because the replacement met the interchangeability and obviousness of interchangeability.

The lower court found the following:

i. The endless sliding ball spline bearings comprising an outer cylinder, a spline shaft, and a retainer were publicly known prior to the application of the asserted patent, and the spline shaft [with citation of all claim elements] of Component C was conventional.

ii. The retainer of the Component B in the patented invention is configured as an integral structure to provide itself the three functions: guiding balls to move in endless circulation; retaining balls when the spline shaft is withdrawn, and forming recessed portions for guiding the rib portions of the spline shaft. In contrast, the retainer of the contested device is configured as a multi-member structure comprising three plate-like members 11, a couple of return caps 31 and the ribs 25, 27 and 29 formed between the load bearing ball-guiding grooves of the outer cylinder. These members cooperate to provide the above functions of the patented invention. However, the retainer of the contested device was disclosed in US Patent 3360308, which was published prior to the application of the asserted patent.

iii. It is obvious to a person skilled in the art that ribs should be provided between the load-bearing ball-guidance grooves of the outer cylinder to retain the balls within the multi-member retainer. Such a multi-member retainer is disclosed in the US Patent 3398999 which was published prior to the application of the asserted patent.

Based on the finding iii, it is likely that the multi-member retainer provided with ribs between the load-bearing ball-guidance grooves of the outer cylinder was already known prior to the application of the asserted patent.

[The Court also acknowledged that the contested device included all claim elements in Components A and C: the circulation of the non-load bearing ball in the circumferential direction and the plural-array type angular contact structure. It concluded that including these elements in an endless ball bearing has been known prior to the application of the asserted patent.]

Given that a ball spline bearing provided with the circulation of the non-load bearing ball in the circumferential direction and the plural-array type angular contact structure were publicly known prior to the application of the asserted patent, the contested device was a mere combination of a ball spline bearing, which was provided with the known circulation of the non-load bearing ball in the circumferential direction and the known plural-array type angular contact structure, and a known multi-member retainer because the lower court held that retainers could not be distinguished by their contacting structures of the balls. If a person skilled in the art would have been able to conceive the combination of the contested device without a disclosure of the patented invention, the contested device should not constitute an equivalent of the claimed invention and thus should fall outside the technical scope of the patented invention.

As discussed above, the claimed invention includes elements which are different from the contested embodiment. The lower court only analysed the difference between the claimed elements and the replaced structures of the contested device with respect to the interchangeability and the obviousness of interchangeability. It concluded that the contested device was equivalent to the claimed invention and thus fell within the technical scope without examining the contested device with respect to the state of the art at the time the application for the asserted patent was filed. Accordingly, the lower court improperly interpreted and applied the Patent Act. It is not necessary to review the lower court's finding with respect to the interchangeability, obviousness of interchangeability and other conditions for applying the doctrine of equivalents.

[The Court vacated the lower court decision and remanded the case to the lower court for further examination regarding the novelty and inventive step of the contested device as well as other conditions for applying the doctrine of equivalents.]

3. ANALYSIS

Within a short period after the decision was issued, the *Ball Spline Bearing III* case had a great impact on how to argue infringement in Japanese courts when the contested embodiment was not disclosed in the description. With the Supreme Court's endorsement of the doctrine of equivalents and clarification of the five conditions, patent owners became more willing to argue infringement under the doctrine of equivalents instead of expansive claim interpretation.[19] In particular, the Supreme Court acknowledged the difficulty of drafting a perfect claim which literally covers all foreseeable equivalents that competitors would develop to circumvent the claim language and suggested a generous application of the doctrine of equivalents to remedy mistakes made by patent drafters. However, patent owners soon found out that the five conditions provided a high hurdle to overcome and began to refrain from asserting infringement under the doctrine of equivalents.[20] Thus, the *Ball Spline*

19. T. TAKENAKA, The Doctrine of Equivalents after the Supreme Court "Ball Spline" Decision, (1999) 5 CASRIP Newsletter (Winter-Spring 1999).
20. Japanese courts refused to apply the doctrine of equivalents in 70 percent of cases involving a failure to meet the essential element test between 1998, after the Ball Spline decision, and 31 December 2006. Trends in K. IIDA, Kin'tō ron ni Kansuru Saikin'no Saiban'rei no Keiko *(Recent Decisions Relating to the Doctrine of Equivalents),"* in T. MAKINO et al. (eds.), Chitekizaisanhō no riron to jitsumu *(Theories and Practice on Intellectual Property Law)*, 2007, vol. I, 177, 184. See also T. TAKENAKA, The Essential Element Test Provides a Big Hurdle to Japanese Doctrine of Equivalents, 7(2) CASRIP Newsletter 13 (Spring 2000).

Bearing III decision did not change the fundamental principle that the claim determines the technical scope of patented invention. The doctrine of equivalents remains as a very limited exception to the principle when the modification in the contested embodiment is evident to a person skilled in the art at the time of infringement.[21] A careful review of *Ball Spline Bearing III* reveals that the Supreme Court denied infringement under the doctrine of equivalents because the contested device was obvious from the state of art, which led to the conclusion that the fourth condition was not met. On remand, the appellee of *Ball Spline Bearing III* case withdrew its appeal and thus the first instance decision of finding no infringement became final.

In the cases following the *Ball Spline Bearing III,* Japanese courts classified the first to third conditions as positive conditions for establishing infringement under the doctrine of equivalents, and the fourth and fifth conditions as negative conditions for limiting infringement under the doctrine of equivalents. They placed the burden of proof on the patentee with respect to the positive conditions and on the accused infringers with respect to the negative conditions.[22] Japanese courts were ready to apply the second to fifth conditions to decide infringement under the doctrine of equivalents because they were familiar with them through the pre- *Ball Spline Bearing III* case law: Lower courts had applied the second and third conditions for affirming infringement for embodiments which did not fall within the literal claim scope regardless of the term used to call such infringement;[23] they applied the fourth and fifth conditions for limiting the literal scope to disclosed embodiments and thus refused to find infringement under the doctrine of equivalents.[24] In contrast, the first condition was new and thus courts and legal scholars engaged extensive debate how to apply the first condition.[25] This debate led to a Supreme Court decision to clarify the definition of the non-essential part.[26] In short, the 2017 tradition to give more weight to the legal certainty rather than the fair reward for inventors dies hard. Because it is difficult to objectively distinguish the essential and non-essential parts of the invention, the first condition gave Japanese courts a lot of flexibility to deny infringement under the doctrine of equivalents.

---

21. For an example of small number of cases in which Japanese courts found infringement under the doctrine of equivalents, see *infra* Case No. 39, IP High Court, 29 June 2009, Case No. 10006 (Ne) of 2009, 2007 Hanrei Times 123 – *Yokohama Rubber v. Yonex – Hollow Golf Club Head*, see *infra* Case No. 39. This case highlights the IP High Court's restrictive claim interpretation and narrow range of the doctrine of equivalents. For more discussion, see T. TAKENAKA et al, Patent Enforcement in the US, Germany and Japan, 2015, 160.
22. *Supra* note 18, K. IIDA, Recent Decisions Relating to the Doctrine of Equivalents at 179.
23. *Supra* note 6, Explanation of Industrial Property Law at 123. Lower courts used terms such as "*tan'naru sekkeijō no bisa* (merely insubstantial differences within the mechanical skills)" or "*sekkei henkō* (mechanical modification)" instead of equivalents.
24. See *supra* note 5, T. TAKENAKA, Claim Interpretation at 277-285. Industrial Property Council examined how these conditions should be incorporated in finding infringement under the doctrine of equivalents. *Supra* note 8, Explanation of Industrial Property Law at 126.
25. JAPAN ASSOCIATION OF INDUSTRIAL PROPERTY LAW, Hatsumei no honshitsuteki bubun no hogo no tekihi (*Appropriateness for protecting the essential part of invention*), JAIPL Annual Report (No. 32), 2009, 8 [JAIPL Annual Report: Essential Part of Invention].
26. See infra Case No. 40, Supreme Court, 24 March 2017, Case No. 1242 (Ju) of 2016 – *DKSH et al. v. Chugai Pharmaceutical – Maxacalcitol.*

4. COMPARATIVE REMARKS

The *Ball Spline Bearing III* case is also significant from a comparative law perspective for bringing the scope of Japanese patent protection more in line with the US and European countries. Through the negotiations to harmonise patent systems, WIPO member states endorsed the scope of patent protection under the doctrine of equivalents. [27] A draft treaty listed as tests for equivalency the way-function-result triple identity test developed by the US Supreme Court[28] and the combination of the interchangeability and the obviousness of interchangeability developed by the Federal Supreme Court of Germany.[29] These two tests were influential for Japan's adoption of the doctrine of equivalents because they were examined by the Industrial Property Council when the JPO charged the Council to examine whether the doctrine of equivalents should be codified.[30]

A couple of years prior to the *Ball Spline Bearing III* case, US influence became significant when the Osaka High Court applied conditions similar to the US triple identity test for finding infringement for an after-arising technology.[31] However, the Supreme Court adopted the German interchangeability and obviousness combination test not only because of the lower courts' application of the test in the pre- *Ball Spline Bearing III* case law, but also because of the tradition of being influenced by German law[32] Nevertheless, the German interchangeability test is substantially similar to the US triple identity test under US case law because both German and US tests focus on the similarity of the function/effect and result.[33] Moreover, the US Supreme Court added the known interchangeability test in the 1997 *Warner-Jenkinson* decision,[34] which test is similar to the German and Japanese obviousness of interchangeability test except for some difference in applying the doctrine: the US test merely requires, either, the triple identity test *or* the known interchangeability being established in

27. The draft of the World Intellectual Property Organization's *Treaty Supplementing the Paris Convention for the Protection of Industrial Property as far as Patents are Concerned* (known as the "Patent Harmonization Treaty")
28. US Supreme Court, *Graver Tank & Mfg. Co. v. Linde Air Products Co.*, 339 U.S. 605, 70 S. Ct. 854, 94 L. Ed. 1097, 85 U.S.P.Q. 328 (1950)
29. German Federal Supreme Court, 29 April 1986, 18 IIC 795 (1987) – *Formstein/Moulded Curbstone.*
30. *Supra* note 6, Explanation of Industrial Property Law 124.
31. Osaka High Court, 29 March 1996, Case No. 3292 (Ne) of 1994, 28-1 Chiteki zaishū 77. T. TAKENAKA, Nihon tokkyo kurēmu kaishaku no shinchoryū *(New Trend of Claim Interpretation in Japan)*, 41 AIPPI Journal of the Japanese Group (Japanese edition) 460 (1996).
32. T. TAKENAKA, Hanrei Hyōron: Tanin no seihin tō ga meisaisho no tokkyo seikyū no han'i ni kisai sareta kōsei to kintō na mono tosite tokkyo hatsumei no gijututeki han'i ni zokusuru to kaisubeki baai *(Case where products etc. of other person are considered to fall in the technical scope of the patented invention as equivalent to the constitution stated in the claim of the description)*, 1688 Hanrei Jihō 232 (1999) (Case Comment on Supreme Court, 24 Feb. 1998, Case No. 1083 (O) of 1994). Judge *Ryōichi Mimura*, who was trained in Germany served as a chōsakan (legal research officer) at the Supreme Court of Japan and assisted the Supreme Court justices to author the *Ball Spline Bearing III* decision. According to the tradition of Japanese courts, judge Mimura later published a case comment on the decision. R. MIMURA, Saikō Saibansho Hanrei Kaisetsu Minji Hen *(Comments on Supreme Court Precedents in Civil Cases)*, 1998, 112.
33. *Supra* note 19, TAKENAKA et al, Patent Enforcement, at 128.
34. US Supreme Court, *Warner-Jenkinson Co. v. Hilton Davis Chem. Co.*, 520 U.S. 17, 117 S. Ct. 1040, 137 L. Ed. 2d 146, 41U.S.P.Q.2d 1865 (1997).

contrast to the Japanese and German tests which require *both* interchangeability and obviousness test being established for showing equivalent.[35] The *Ball Spline Bearing III* case's two negative conditions are similar to the tests that US and German courts developed to limit infringement under the doctrine of equivalents. Both courts refuse to find equivalents if the contested embodiment fails to meet the novelty and inventive step (obviousness).[36] US courts determine a disclaimer by making reference to the specification and the record of prosecution.[37] Although the Federal Supreme Court of Germany refuses to make reference to the record of prosecution in examining infringement under the doctrine of equivalents, the Court in the 2002 *Schneidmesser II* decision adopted a negative test to find a disclaimer by making reference to the description.[38] These developments significantly harmonised the tests applied by courts in the three jurisdictions for deciding infringement under the doctrine of equivalents.[39] For further details, see also the comparative comments for Case Nos. 39 and 40.

In short, the Supreme Court of Japan substantially contributed to this harmonisation by adopting the last four conditions which are a combination of German and US tests of equivalents, yet introduced a minor discord and confusion by adopting the first condition of the non-essential part. European countries adopted similar concepts such as the essence of invention, essential elements of the invention, and the inventive concept in the context of the problem and solution of the invention and have applied these concepts in order to decide not only infringement under the doctrine of equivalents, but also indirect infringement[40] or partial infringement in

35. Compare *Warner-Jenkinson Co.*, 520 U.S. 17 and German Federal Supreme Court, 12 March 2002, GRUR 2002, 515 - *Schneidmesser I;* GRUR 2002, 519—*Schneidmesser II.* Timing to establish an equivalent is also different: Interchangeability must be known or obvious at the time of infringement under the US and Japanese jurisprudence. In contrast, interchangeability must be obvious at the time the application for the asserted patent was filed under German jurisprudence.
36. With respect to Germany, German Federal Supreme Court, 29 April 1986, 18 IIC 795 (1987) -*Formstein/Moulded Curbstone*. and U.S. CAFC, *Wilson Sporting Goods Co. v. David Geoffrey & Associates, 904 F.2d 677, 14 U.S.P.Q. 2d 1942 (Fed. Cir. 1990).*
37. When the contested embodiment is disclosed in the specification but unclaimed, the doctrine of dedication to the public prevents US courts from finding equivalent on the contested embodiment. US CAFC *Johnson & Johnston Associates Inc. v. R.E. Service Co., Inc.*, 285 F.3d 1046, 62 U.S.P.Q. 2d 1046 (Fed. Cir. 2002) (en banc). When the contested embodiment is surrendered during the prosecution through amendments or arguments, the doctrine of prosecution history estoppel prevents courts from finding equivalent on the contested embodiment. US Supreme Court, *Warner-Jenkinson Co., Inc. v. Hilton Davis Chemical Co.*, 520 U.S. 17, 41 U.S.P.Q. 2d 1865 (1997); *Festo Corp. v. Shoketsu Kinzoku Kogyo Kabushiki Co.*, 535 U.S. 722, 740, 122 S. Ct. 1831, 152 L. Ed. 2d 944, 62 U.S.P.Q. 2d 1705 (2002).
38. German Federal Supreme Court, 12 March 2002, GRUR 2002, 519 - *Schneidmesser II.* The Court developed the case law to use this negative test in the manner similar to the doctrine of dedication to the public developed by US courts. Federal Supreme Court of Germany, 10 May 2011, GRUR 2011, 701 -*Okklusionsvorrichtung (Occlusion Device)*; Federal Supreme Court of Germany, 23 August 2016, GRUR 2016, 1254 - *V-förmige Führungsanordnung.* See *supra* note 19, T. TAKENAKA et al, Patent Enforcement at 132.
39. However, German courts are more willing to find infringement under the doctrine of equivalents than US and Japanese courts because they have not adopted the prosecution history estoppel. For a general discussion on the doctrines to limit the doctrine of equivalents, see *supra* note 19, T. TAKENAKA et al, Patent Enforcement at 132.
40. JOCHEN PAGENBERG & WILLIAM CORNISH, Interpretation of Patents in Europe, 2006, 265.

which one or more claim elements were missing from the contested embodiment without any replacement.[41] Until the Supreme Court introduced the non-essential part doctrine in the *Ball-Spline* case, the Japanese legal community was unfamiliar with the distinction between essential and non-essential elements.[42] Japanese legal commentators advocated to expand the applicability of the concept of essential parts to indirect infringement, patent exhaustion and other key requirements of patentability.[43] Japanese courts and the legal community can learn from experiences in Europe, where the rule of EPC Art. 69 substantially diminished the applicability of the essential element concept.[44]

41. *Id.*, at 286.
42. Pre-1994 Revision Patent Act, Sec. 36(5)(ii).
43. R. TAKABAYASHI, Hatsumei no gijutsu shisōni chakumokushita tōitsutekina shingaihandan'no mosaku *(Proposal for Developing a Uniform Approach for Infringement Determination Focusing on the Technical Idea of Invention) supra* note 23, JAIPL Annual Report: Essential Part of Invention at 91; R. MIMURA, Hatsumei no honshitsuteki bubun toiu hassō no igi *(Significance of the Concept of Essential Part of Invention)*, *supra* note 23, JAIPL Annual Report: Essential Part of Invention at 107; A. KAWADA, Hatsumei no honshitsuteki bubun saikō (Reevaluation of Essential Part of Invention), 271 Tokugikon, 61 (2013).
44. *Supra note* 32, PAGENBERG & CORNISH at 286.

Case No. 39

Interpretation of Patent Claims – Doctrine of Equivalents

Wataru Sueyoshi and Yasuhiro Sato

Equivalent infringement can be affirmed for a feature in the defendant's product that although different from the element in the patented invention, has the same purpose and effect as the latter, could have been easily understood as an equivalent of the stitching element in the patent, and could not have been easily conceived on the basis of the prior art at the time of filing. Further, as the replaced feature was not essential for the invention, there are no reasons why protection should be limited thereto.

IP High Court, 29 June 2009, Case No. 10006 (Ne) of 2009 – *Hollow Golf Club Head*

Yokohama Rubber v. Yonex

---

1. BACKGROUND

Even after the doctrine of equivalents was approved and by the *Ball Spline* decision,[1] the actual application of that doctrine in flesh and blood patent infringement cases had been lackluster. In particular, subsequent courts after *Ball Spline* had been rather reluctant to accept the infringement under the doctrine of equivalents, especially by denying the first requirement. That trend probably seemed to be due in part to the rather ambiguous language of the requirements of the equivalent's doctrine expressed by *Ball Spline*.

Against this background, the IP High Court rendered the *Hollow Golf Club Head* decision ("*Golf Club*") in 2009. Once delivered, it soon received considerable attention. Not only did the decision affirm an infringement under the doctrine of equivalents, but also clarified (1) how the first to third requirements of equivalence were related to each other, and (2) how the court should determine whether the first equivalent requirement was met. It is further worth noting that part of the *Golf*

1. Supreme Court, 24 February 1998, Case No. 1083 (O) of 1994, 52-1 Minshū 113. *See* Case No. 38 of this book. The primary literature for *Ball Spline* is R. MIMURA, Saikō saibansho hanrei kaisetsu minji hen *1998 (Civil Law decisions of the Supreme Court)*, 2001, 112. *See* also T. IIMURA, Tokkyoken no kintoshingai no seihi ni kansuru 2, 3 no ronten (*A couple of issues surrounding the doctrine of equivalents for patent rights*), 67-3 Patent 128 (2014).

Club opinion has been followed up by the *Maxacalcitol* decision[2] rendered by the IP High Court Grand Panel in 2016.

2. DECISION[3]

a) Facts

1. The plaintiff owns a patent (Japanese Patent 3725481) for a hollow golf club head. The plaintiff alleged that the golf clubs that the defendant manufactured and sold (the defendant's product) were within the technical scope of the patented invention, and filed a patent infringement lawsuit against the defendant and claimed damages.

The court of first instance dismissed the plaintiff's claim on the grounds that there was no literal infringement, and denied the application of the doctrine of equivalents. The plaintiff appealed. The Intellectual Property High Court rendered an interlocutory judgment in accordance with Section 245 Code of Civil Procedure on the issue of infringement only.

2. The purpose of the patented invention at issue is to increase the bonding strength between the metallic shell member and the fibre reinforced plastic shell member (FRP shell member), which both comprise the main body of the hollow golf club head. The patent claim contains the following elements:

A metallic shell member (11) and an FRP shell member (21) are bonded together, and a through hole (13) is made in said metallic shell member. A stitching member made of FRP (22) is passed through the through hole from the bonded side of the metallic shell member (i.e. the side bonded to the FRP shell member) to the other side of the metallic shell member, binding the FRP shell member and the metallic shell member together. See Figure 1 below:

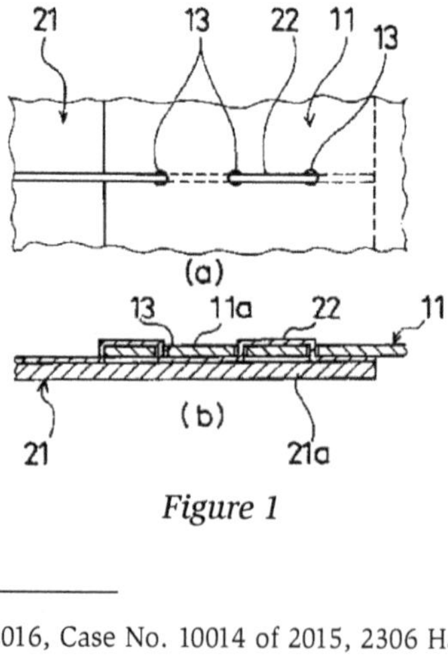

Figure 1

2. IP High Court, 25 March 2016, Case No. 10014 of 2015, 2306 Hanrei Jihō 87. See Case No. 40 of this book.
3. Published in 2077 Hanrei Jihō 123 = N. NAKAYAMA et al. (eds.), Tokkyo Hanrei Hyakusen *(Hundred Selected Patent Cases)*, 4th ed. 2012, 140. English translation in 43 IIC 467 (2012) w. comment OKADA.

The defendant's product has the following structure: Through holes (7) are made in the metallic shell member (5a) and short strips made of carbon fiber (8) are passed through the through holes. Each short strip is passed through one through hole from the upper side of the metallic shell member (which is bonded to the upper FRP shell member (10)) to the lower side of the metallic shell member (which is bonded to the lower FRP shell member (9)). Each short strip is bonded at one point to the upper FRP shell member and to the lower FRP shell member respectively, binding the upper FRP shell member and the metallic shell member together (Figure 2):

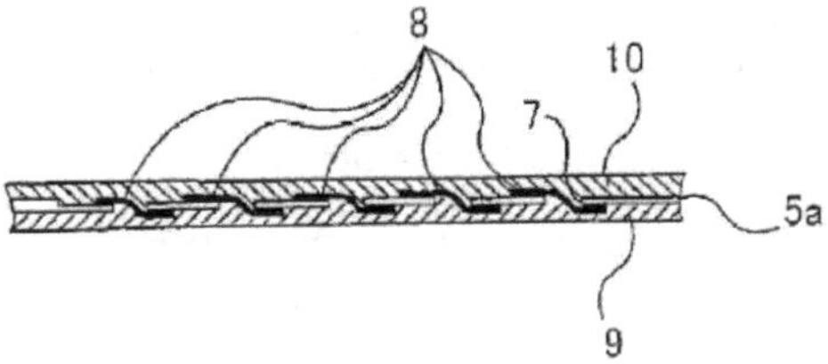

Figure 2

3. With regard to the question of whether the defendant's product fell within the technical scope of the patented invention, the main problem in this case is the interpretation of the word "stitching member", and whether there is an infringement under the doctrine of equivalents. According to the plaintiff, the following steps A – E could be taken in order to arrive from the patented product to the allegedly infringing one:

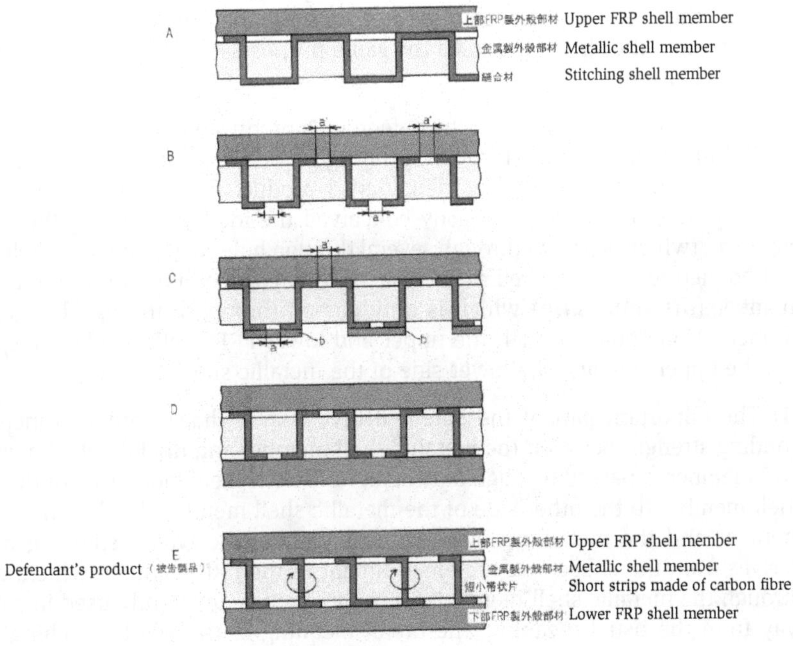

Figure 3

b) Reasons

1. Literal infringement

The meaning of the word "stitching member" should be interpreted as a member that is passed through several (more than two) through holes in the metallic shell member and bonded to the FRP shell member at least at two points. The short strip of the defendant's product (8) is only passed once through a through hole in the metallic shell member, and is bonded at only one point to the upper FRP shell member. The short strip does not therefore satisfy the "stitching member" element of the patented invention, and there is no literal infringement.

2. Infringement under the doctrine of equivalents

(1) In this case, the problem is whether the short strip of the defendant's product (8) is equivalent to the "stitching member" of the patented invention. The difference between the short strip and the "stitching member" is that (1) the short strip is passed through a through hole made in the metallic shell member only once and (2) it is bonded at one point to both the upper and lower FRP shell members respectively (on the upper side and the lower side of the metallic shell member).

(2) According to the specification of the patent, the purpose and advantageous effect of using the "stitching member" is to increase the bonding strength between the metallic shell member and the FRP shell member. By passing the short strip through one through hole and bonding it at one point to both the upper FRP and lower FRP shell members respectively, the short strip also increases the bonding strength between the metallic shell member and the FRP shell member. As the "stitching member" and the short strip have the same purpose and advantageous effect, they are interchangeable.

(3) The patented invention and the defendant's product have a common feature that an FRP member is passed through a through hole that is made in a metallic shell member. At the time when the defendant's product was manufactured, a person skilled in the art could have easily conceived the idea of changing the "stitching member" (which is passed through several through holes of the metallic shell member and bonded to the FRP shell member at least at two points) with the other type of member (the short strip) which is only passed through a through hole once and bonded at one point to both the upper and lower FRP shell members respectively (on the upper side and the lower side of the metallic shell member).

(4) The important part of the patented invention is that in order to increase the bonding strength between the metallic shell member and the FRP shell member, an FRP member is passed through a through hole from the bonded side of the metallic shell member to the other side of the metallic shell member, binding the FRP shell member and the metallic shell member together. The word "stitching member" derives from the shape and the embodiment of the FRP member, which is passed through the metallic shell member. Since the word is apparently used in a different way from the usual meaning, the literal meaning of the word "stitching" should not be emphasised. As such, the "stitching member", which is passed through the through holes, is not regarded as an essential part of the patented invention.

(5) The defendant's product is not the same as the prior art at the time of the patent application and a person skilled in the art could not have conceived the defendant's product from the prior art at the time of the patent application.

(6) The plaintiff did not intentionally exclude the structure of the defendant's product from the patent claim in the prosecution history.

(7) Taking into account all of the above, the defendant's product is the equivalent of the structure of the patented invention. The defendant's product therefore falls within the technical scope of the patented invention.

3. ANALYSIS

a) Analysis of the second and third requirements of equivalence

The first significant point in the *Golf Club* case is that the court has made it clear that the second requirement (*i.e.*, interchangeability) and the third requirement (*i.e.*, obviousness of interchangeability) are central to the analysis of the doctrine of equivalents. For approximately ten years, from the time *Ball Spline* was delivered in 1998 to *Golf Club* in 2009, the first equivalent requirement (*i.e.*, non-essential part) had been considered practically important.[4] It has long been said that the first requirement was the most used by many post-*Ball Spline* decisions in order to deny the infringement under the doctrine of equivalents.[5] The court in *Golf Club*, although not necessarily expressing it in the opinion in itself, did not follow this approach and affirmed the first requirement. This is the first significant holding of the decision, the more so when considering that judicial opposition against the doctrine of equivalents has been rather strong, and according to a study published in 2007,[6] the percentage of judicial precedents affirming equivalent infringement was less than 10%, the reasons of rejection being

- for not meeting the first requirement: more than 70%

4. *See* N. Nakayama, Tokkyohō *(Patent Law)*, 3rd ed., 2016, 473; D. Koo, Comparison of the First Requirement of the Doctrine of Equivalents between Japan and Korea, 44 IIC 178 (2013).
5. *See* T. Shōji, Kureim kaishaku (2): kintōron, kinō teki kureim, purodakuto bai purosesu kureim *(Claim construction (2): doctrine of equivalents, means-plus-function claim, and product-by-process claim)*, published in R. Takabayashi, Gendai chiteki zaisanhō kōza II (*Lectures on Cotemporary Intellectual Property Laws II*), 2012, 47, 52.
6. K. Iida, *Kintōron ni kansuru saikin no saibanrei no keikō ni tsuite (Trends in Judicial Precedents on the Doctrine of Equivalents)* in: T. Makino et al. (eds.), Chitekizaisanhō no riron to jitsumu *(Theory and Practice of Intellectual Property Law)*, vol. 1, Shinnippon-Hoki Publishing Company, 2007, 177, the author provides research performed on more than 150 lower court precedents between 1997 and June 2006. According to a recent study provided by K. Iida, Kintōron ni kansuru kinen no saibanrei no dōkō to kadai ni tsuite (*Recent decisions' trends and challenges regarding the doctrine of equivalents*), 38 Nihon Kogyō shoyūken hōgakkkai Nenpō 77 (2014), the percentage of judicial precedents affirming equivalent infringement between 25 September 2006 to 31 March 2012 was approximately 13%. It also states that the reasons of rejecting the doctrine due to a denial of: (i) the first requirement was approximately 56.7%; (ii) the third requirement was approximately 9.0%; (iii) the fourth requirement was 11.9%; and further, (iv) the fifth requirement was 35.8%.

- for not meeting the second requirement: less than 20%
- for not meeting the third requirement: about 15%
- for not meeting the fourth requirement: about 3%
- for not meeting the fifth requirement: more than 30%

Coinciding with the *Hollow Golf Club* decision, *Tomokatsu Tsukahara*, the former chief justice of the IP High Court, criticised his fellow judges' attitude towards applying the doctrine of equivalents. He writes:

> "... Judges in Japan feel that, basically, they do not want to admit infringement under the doctrine of equivalents. Judges in Japan emphasise consistency with the statement of the claims without showing any substantive, rational grounds. They should not, however, depend solely on grammatical considerations when interpreting the [Ball Spline Bearing] judgment of the Supreme Court with regard to the first requirement [essential element]... Judges in Japan should start understanding the doctrine of equivalents from the original point; they should not start from the wording of the Supreme Court precedent. If judges examine and determine infringement under the doctrine of equivalents based on that idea, they will notice easily that it was wrong that they were relieved in their hearts by denying infringement under the doctrine of equivalents based on the first requirement. With regard to the first requirement, judges in Japan should cease to examine initially and determine the first requirement through comparison with the distinctive matters of the claimed invention as they did in the past. Instead, they should examine and determine infringement under the doctrine of equivalents mainly based on the second and third requirement in almost the same manner as in the United States and Germany ... In order to increase the number of patent lawsuits in Japan, ... the content of the first requirement of the doctrine of equivalents, which has been a source of confusion since the Supreme Court's decision, must be reviewed."[7]

The fact that the *Golf Club* decision has placed more importance on the second and third equivalent requirements becomes even clearer when looking at the sequential order of the doctrine of equivalents analysis in the opinion. Unlike the many pre-*Golf Club* cases, the court started with an analysis of the second and third requirements, and only thereafter analysed the first requirement.[8] In this regard, judge T. Iimura (as he then was) – the author of the *Golf Club* decision – recently wrote: "[a]lthough *Ball Spline* has listed five requirements for the doctrine of equivalents, the interchangeability (the second requirement) and obviousness of interchangeability (the third equivalent requirement) are of the doctrine's very essence[9]". It is therefore clear

---

7. T. TSUKAHARA, Current Situation and Activation of Patent Infringement in Japan, 36 AIPPI Journal of the Japanese Group (English edition), 3 (2011).
8. *See* the legal reasoning described in Section b) 2 (2) through (4) in the main text. *See also* H. IMAI, Saikin ni okeru kintō no saibanrei (*Recent cases dealing with doctrine of equivalents*), 1 L&T Supplement 107, 109 (2015). Also, R. MIMURA (above) 144 states that the doctrine of equivalent analysis should start with the analysis of the second requirement, *see* Tōkyō District Court, decision of 28 January 1999, Case Nos. 14828&14833 (Wa) of 1996, 1664 Hanrei Jihō 109 (starting the doctrine of equivalent analysis with the second requirement; note that the chief judge in this case was R. MIMURA).
9. T. IIMURA, Kintōron (2): Kintōron no kakuyoken to tokuchō (*Each requirement and features of the doctrine of equivalents*), in: T. MAKINO, Chiteki Zaisan Jitsumu Taikei I (*Compendium on*

that the judges of the *Golf Club* decision considered the second and third equivalent requirements to be more important, and hence examined them before turning to the first requirement.

The *Golf Club* approach mentioned above should be considered reasonable. First, in a global landscape, interchangeability and obviousness of interchangeability, rather than non-essential part, have played a more significant role in the analysis of the doctrine of equivalents[10] (see also below 4. for a comparative analysis). Second, the *Golf Club* approach seems to be more consistent with the rationale as set out in the *Ball Spline* decision in order to determine the appropriateness of the doctrine of equivalents. The Supreme Court in the *Ball Spline* decision had specifically emphasised the importance of avoiding an injustice which would arise if another party could easily circumvent patent protection by replacing part of an apparatus or composition with a different arrangement or material.[11] That rationale seems to closely match the relative emphasis on the second and third equivalent requirements as analysed by the *Golf Club* decision.

One additional note with respect to the second and third requirements is that the court in the *Golf Club* decision has demonstrated a rather flexible application of those requirements. Indeed, the court found the second requirement to be met simply because the allegedly infringing products had the same purpose and advantageous effect as specified in the written description of the patent. Even more importantly, the court found the third requirement to be met with little explanation as to why the replaced part could have been easily anticipated. The court here seems to have taken the view that affirming the second requirement would already make a prima facie case for a positive finding on the third requirement.[12] Associating those two requirements with each other can be regarded as a flexible application of the equivalents' doctrine.

b) Analysis of the first requirement of equivalence

The second significant point in the *Golf Club* decision concerns determining whether the elements that are different in the allegedly infringing product concern a non-essential part of the patent claim. Prior to this decision, there were two major schools as to what an "essential part" was. The first argued that an "essential part" should be the key to solve the problem, or a technical idea unique to the patented invention.[13] The second argued that an "essential part" should be a specific element or a selection among various elements or selections of the claim.[14] Although the first view was said

Intellectual Property Practice), 2014, 389, 396.

10. *See* T. Tsukahara, Chizai Kōsai ni okeru Kintō Shingairon no runessansu (*Current Situation and Activation of Patent Infringement in Japan*), 61-12 Chizai Kanri 1777, 784 (2011).
11. *See* the legal reasoning as in Case No. 38.
12. T. Iimura (above) 399 has suggested this understanding. According to T. Iimura, unlike the analysis of obviousness (or inventive step), obviousness of interchangeability should be analysed from a perspective not of whether the composition of the patented invention can easily and actually be changed or arrived at, but whether the patented invention and the allegedly infringing products have a common advantageous effect.
13. *See* R. Mimura (above) 141. This view is the so called "*Kaiketsu Genri Dōitsu Setsu.*"
14. The leading proponent of this view is Y. Nishida, a former judge of the Tōkyō High Court. *See* Shingaisoshō ni okeru kintō no hōri (*Doctrine of equivalents in infringement litigation*), in: T.

to be more prevalent before the *Golf Club* decision, the actual application process of finding an essential part was still uncertain. The court in the *Golf Club* decision adopted the first view, thereby settling the issue for the future judicial practice.

The most interesting feature in the application of the first requirement by *Golf Club* is that the court has found an overarching concept of the claims based on the purpose and advantageous effect of the patented invention, namely that it was important for the composition of the invention to have "a member made of FRP," rather than "a *stitching* member made of FRP" pass through the through hole. The court specifically noted that the language of "*stitching*" was irrelevant for solving the problem unique to the invention. In other words, the *Golf Club* approach in affirming equivalence was essentially to concentrate on whether the allegedly infringing embodiment applied the same principle to solve the problem unique to the patented invention.

Behind the *Golf Club* approach above is probably the court's perception or conviction that the patented invention was a pioneer invention. Indeed, neither the existence of a "through hole" as a means for enhancing the bonding strength, nor the existence of a similar member as the shell member for bonding was described in the prior art. Further, although not mentioned in the analysis of the doctrine of equivalents, but of obviousness (or inventive step), none of the prior art documents submitted to the court by the defendant did disclose having a similar member as the shell member for bonding. Probably considering this, the court may very well have concluded that the contribution of the patented invention to the state of the art was significant.[15] This would have led to a broad interpretation of the patented scope beyond the literal wording of the claims and based on the general inventive concept.

The *Golf Club* approach for the application of the first requirement was further refined by the Grand Panel decision *Maxacalcitol* in 2016 (see Case No. 40 in this volume). There, the Grand Panel dealt with the issue of what the "essential part" was and how it should be determined. The court specifically held that the "essential part" should be the distinctive part of a patent claim that embodied the innovative and unique technical idea of the patented invention; and that the "essential part" (in general) should be determined by a comparison with the prior art described in the specification. The court then noted that if the degree of contribution of a patented invention is significant, the features described in the patent claim should be recognised as part of an overarching inventive concept.[16] In this respect, the *Maxacalcitol* decision confirms the approach taken in the *Golf Club* decision.

MAKINO, Shin Saiban Jitsumu Taikei 4 Chiteki Zaisan Kankei Soshōhō (*New compendium on litigation practice (4): intellectual property litigation laws*) 2001, 182, 192. This view is the so called "*Kōsei Yōken Kubun Setsu*."

15. R. MIMURA had already mentioned the same approach soon after *Ball Spline* opinion was delivered. According to R. MIMURA, in the case of a pioneer invention, it would be difficult for the accused infringer to free itself from the scope of technical idea of the patented invention-at-issue simply by replacing the part of the composition, because the technical idea underlying the pioneer invention is generally considered broad. *See* R. MIMURA (above) 142.
16. *See* 2306 Hanrei Jihō (above) 109.

c) Conclusion

In sum, the *Golf Club* decision is an important milestone in that it can be seen as a revival of the doctrine of equivalents which had been more or less on the verge of extinction at that time,[17] by clarifying that (1) the core requirements of the doctrine of equivalents are not the first but the second and third element, and that (2) the court should examine, in determining the first requirement, the core principle to solve the problem that is unique to the patented invention. Further, its practical impact is significant in it had clearly influenced the later Grand Panel decision *Maxacalcitol* with respect to the first requirement. Last but not least, the court in *Golf Club* has tried to carefully determine the very core of the patented invention by taking into account the specification of the patent from the perspective of a person of ordinary skill in the art. This approach is consistent with the fundamental principles of patent law and should be endorsed.

4. COMPARATIVE REMARKS

a) The US

The doctrine of equivalents has been acknowledged by the US courts for a long time, yet the courts have been better at identifying limitations to the doctrine than a positive definition thereof.[18] Equivalence is affirmed where the differences between the patent claim and the contested embodiment appear insubstantial and where the latter performs substantially the same function, in substantially the same way, to achieve the same result. Just as held by the Ball Spline decision, a modification that was not foreseeable at the priority date of the invention, but at the infringement date, can be an equivalent.[19]

b) EPC Member States

Under the European Patent Convention, claim interpretation is guided by Art. 69 EPC according to which the extent of protection conferred by a European patent … shall by determined by the claims. Nevertheless, the description and drawings shall be used to interpret the claims. The Protocol on the Interpretation of Art. 69 EPC in Art. 2 ("Equivalents") provides that "[f]or the purpose of determining the extent of protection conferred by a European patent, due account shall be taken of any element which is equivalent to an element specified in the claims."

---

17. T. TSUKAHARA (above) 783.
18. The decisions of the US Supreme Court in this respect tend to be rather vague (US Supreme Court, *Hilton Davis Chemical v. Warner-Jenkinson*, 520 US 17, 28 (1997) and *Festo Corp. v. Shōketsu Kinzoku KK*, 535 US 722 (2002), or heavily contested amongst the judges (*Winans v. Denmead*, 56 US 330 (1853) and *Graver Tank v. Linde Air Products*, 399 US 605 (1950)).
19. US CAFC, *Penwalt v. Durand-Wayland*, 883 F2nd 931 (Fed Cir. 1987). This decision requires, however, also a comparison on an element-by-element basis (the plaintiff must show the presence of every element or its substantial equivalent in the accused device"), thereby severely limiting the scope of this doctrine.

(1) **Germany**

The Federal Court of Justice applies a four-step step in order to determine equivalent infringement:

- First, the solution of the alleged infringer must be outside the literal wording of the claim.
- Second, the solution of the alleged infringer has an identical technical effect as the solution described in the patent.
- Third, based on common general knowledge at the priority date, the modifications of the equivalent solution must have been within the reach of the person skilled in the art who would have realised them as a possible alternative.
- Fourth, the equivalent solution needs to solve the same problem as the patented invention and must have been into consideration as technically equivalent by a person skilled in the art on the basis of the teaching of the patent.[20]

However, the German courts handle the principle of equivalents quite restrictively.

Furthermore, if the applicant has included a feature in the claim that a person skilled in the art will understand to be important for the teaching of the patent, its replacement will not lead to an equivalent infringement.

(2) The **UK**

While the courts in the UK have traditionally recognised the doctrine of equivalents,[21] case law has been less consistent in the last 40 years and moved from a "purposive construction"[22] to a denial of equivalents[23] to a relatively generous recognition of the doctrine under the following circumstances:[24]

Whether an item directly infringes a patent is best approached by addressing two questions through the eyes of the notional addressee of the patent, i.e. the person skilled in the relevant art, namely:

1. Does the item infringe any of the claims as a matter of normal interpretation; and if not,
2. Although the item may be characterised as a variant, does it nonetheless infringe because it varies from the invention in a way which is immaterial? This question should be answered as follows:
   a) Notwithstanding that it is not within the literal meaning of the relevant claim(s) of the patent, does the variant achieve substantially the same result in substantially the same way as the invention, i.e. the inventive concept revealed by the patent?

20. German Federal Court of Justice, 12 March 2002, GRUR 2002, 511 – *Kunststroffrohrteil.*
21. H. Laddie, Kirin Amgen – The End of Equivalents in England? 40 IIC 3 (2009).
22. English House of Lords, *Catnic Compnents v. Hill*, [1982] RPC 183.
23. English House of Lords, *Kirin-Amgen v. Hoechst Marrion Russel*, [2004] UKHL 46.
24. English Supreme Court, *Actavis UK Limited and others (Appellants) v. Eli Lilly and Company*, [2017] UKSC 48.

b) Would it be obvious to the person skilled in the art, reading the patent at the priority date, **but knowing that the variant achieves substantially the same result as the invention**, that it does so in substantially the same way as the invention?
c) Would such a reader of the patent have concluded that the patentee nonetheless intended strict compliance with the literal meaning of the relevant claim(s) of the patent was an essential requirement of the invention?

Particularly question 2b) brings the UK doctrine closer to the Japanese and US approach in that it allows hindsight considerations.

c) Korea

Korean courts have adopted practically the same five-step approach to the doctrine of equivalents that was developed in the *Ball Spline Bearing* decision. Prof. *Chaho Jung* writes about the doctrine of equivalents in Korea: "Among 60 Supreme Court cases between 2000 to 2011 whose decision is based on DoE, in 13 cases (21.7%) infringement was affirmed and in 47 cases (78.3%) infringement was denied.[25] Like in other countries, in Korea, (1) the DoE is applied to individual elements of the claim, not to the claimed invention as a whole, (2) the substantial identity of operation and effect (interchangeability), and obviousness of interchangeability are important in determining equivalency, and (3) the prior art defence is available to infringement under DoE. Korea, just as the US, Japan, and China, determines equivalency as of the time of infringement, while the UK does so as of the patent publication date and Germany as of the priority date. Furthermore, Korea, like the US, Japan, and China, takes into account the prosecution history in order to determine the scope of protection,[26] while the UK and Germany do not. Therefore, a scope-narrowing amendment made by the applicant during the prosecution of the patent application may be later used against the patentee when applying the DOE to the patent claims (so-called file wrapper estoppel) ... Equivalence may be found if: (1) the difference in an allegedly infringed article or process does not affect the mechanism or function of the patented invention, and (2) an ordinary person skilled in the art would have recognised the interchangeability thereof from the prior art as of the filing date of the respective patent application.

On recent case law, Professor *Koo*[27] remarks the following:

> "For approximately nine years after the first case (97hu2200) involving the doctrine of equivalents, the Supreme Court of Korea did not interpret the first requirement. In 2007hu3806, the Supreme Court of Korea started to interpret the first requirement of the doctrine of equivalents to mean that an interchanged part is a 'nonessential part' of the patented invention and therefore an allegedly

25. D.J. KIM, *Patent Equivalents Infringement*, (특허균등침해론) Bubmun Press, 2013, p. 292.
26. Korean Supreme Court, 28 July 2000, Case No. 2200 (Hu) of 1997; Patent Court, 7 September 2000, Case No. 9755 (Hu) of 1999.
27. D. KOO, Comparison of the First Requirement of the Doctrine of Equivalents between Korea and Japan, 44 IIC 178, 192 (2013).

> infringing device or process has the same characterizing structure as the patented invention.[28] The Supreme Court of Korea added that the characterizing structure of the patented invention must be defined through practical consideration of the problem-solving principle underlying the specific problem-solving means of the patented invention. This is achieved through a comparison of the disclosure of specifications and the prior art at the time of the patent application."

The first requirement of DoE and the 'essential part' test have played a major role for the court not to apply DoE. With this regard, presumably to enhance the effectiveness of DoE, the Korean Supreme Court in 2014[29] disapplied the 'essential part' test. Due to this change, the DoE could be applied to 'non-essential parts' and could be more often applied than before."[30]

28. Korean Supreme Court, 25 June 2009, Case No. 3806 (Hu) of 2007 (trial to confirm the scope of a patent). The same interpretations are found in the following cases: Korean Supreme Court, 27 May 2010, Case No. 296 (Hu) of 2010; Korean Supreme Court Decision, 24 December 2009, Case No. 66422 (Da) of 2007; Korean Supreme Court, 15 October 2009, Case No. 46712 (Da) of 2009; Korean Supreme Court, 25 June 2009, Case No. 3806 (Hu) of 2007; Korean Patent Court, 19 November 2010, Case No. 4250 (Heo) of 2010; Korean Patent Court, 18 December 2009 Case No. 13299 (Heo) of 2008; Korean Patent Court, 24 July 2009, Case No. 12142 (Heo) of 2008.
29. Korean Supreme Court, 24 July 2014, Case No. 1132 (Hu) of decision 2012.
30. CH. JUNG, Patents, in: B.-I. KIM/C. HEATH, Intellectual Property in Korea, 2nd ed. 2015, 42-44.

Case No. 40

Interpretation of Patent Claims – Doctrine of Equivalents

Kōichi Tanaka

1. **Equivalent infringement shall in principle not be denied for an embodiment that could have been easily conceived at the filling date, yet has not been included in the patent claims.**
2. **Equivalent infringement shall be denied where the applicant objectively or publicly indicated that a feature of the claim could be replaced by a corresponding feature, yet intentionally did not include such feature in the claim.**

Supreme Court, 24 March 2017, Case No. 1242 (Ju) of 2016 – *Maxacalcitol*

DKSH et al. v. Chugai Pharmaceutical

1. BACKGROUND

This Supreme Court decision concerns the fifth requirement of the doctrine of equivalents established by the Ball Spline decision of 24 February 1998.[1] Under the doctrine of equivalents, in a patent infringement case the patentee can make an assertion that the subject product falls within the technical scope of the patented invention due to the equality between the allegedly infringing product with the configuration stated in the claims. The legal problem addressed by this decision is the applicability of the doctrine of equivalents to subject matter that could have been easily conceived at the time of filing, yet was not explicitly claimed. This problem can be divided as follows.

First, for a case where the applicant (patentee) does not specifically mention the configuration of an allegedly infringing product which could be easily conceived at the time of filing the application in the patent claim. Whether only by this fact alone equivalent infringement cannot be asserted due to the special circumstances referred to in the above fifth requirement is a first question.

If the answer to the first question is no (in other words, equivalent infringement can still be affirmed), a second question would be in what kind of situation the above-mentioned special circumstances can be acknowledged.

With regard to the first question, this decision clearly states that it does not adopt the standard of "easy-to-conceive-at-the-time-of-filing", and with regard to

1. See Case No. 38 of this book.

the second question, the decision mentions the following criteria for the "special circumstances" under which the doctrine of equivalents cannot be asserted: "whether the applicant chose to indicate objectively and visibly that he or she intentionally did not list the configuration of the allegedly infringing product in the patent claim". This decision is significant in that the Supreme Court for the first time defined the standard for this point.

2. DECISION[2]

a) Facts

Chugai Pharmaceutical Co., Ltd., (patentee, plaintiff in the first instance, and appellee in the second and the final instance; henceforth referred to as the plaintiff) is one of the joint holders of a patent right over an invention with the title "synthetic intermediate for vitamin D and steroidal derivative and method of producing the intermediate" (Japanese Patent No. 3310301). The scope of an amended claim of the patent, which is broadly defined by the use of a chemical formula, covers a manufacturing process of a drug component, "Maxacalcitol", from the starting material defined as a *cis isomer* of a vitamin D derivative.

DKSH et al., (the defendants in first instance, appellants in the appeal and final appeal proceedings, henceforth referred to as the defendant) are importing and selling a drug that contains "Maxacalcitol" as one of its effective components, which is made from a *trans isomer* of a vitamin D derivative. The only difference between the patented process and the defendant's process is a steric structure of the starting material and intermediate: a *cis isomer* in the patented process and a *trans isomer* in the defendant's process. *Cis-trans isomers* are two different molecules with the same molecular formula but with a different chemical structure (Figure 1, below).

In the claim of the patented process, the starting material of the process is clearly defined as a *cis isomer*. The defendant's process is therefore out of the literal scope of the claim because of the use of a *trans isomer* as a starting material of the process. However, the plaintiff argued patent infringement under the doctrine of equivalents as the patented process and the defendant's process had the same function and result.

An infringement by equivalents under Japanese patent law was first affirmed in the *Ball Spline Bearing* case of the Supreme Court in 1998, in which the court established five requirements for affirming patent infringement under the doctrine of equivalents. Of these, the fifth requirement was disputed in the case at issue.

In order for the **fifth** requirement to be fulfilled, there should be no special circumstances such as a prosecution history estoppel whereby an allegedly infringing product/process was intentionally excluded from the scope of a claim by an applicant during examination. In this case, the plaintiff claimed only a *cis isomer* as a starting material of the process even though a *trans isomer* was known at the filling date and could have been equally claimed. Actually, the process used by the defendant is neither mentioned in the claim nor in the description of the patent at issue. According to the defendant's submission, their process could have been easily conceived by the

2. Published in 2306 Hanrei Jihō 87. English translation in 49 IIC 591 (2018).

plaintiff at the filling date, and accordingly been easily incorporated into the claim. Nevertheless, the plaintiff decided not to claim the process used by the defendant. This way of claim drafting should therefore be recognised as an intentional exclusion of the defendant's process. The courts thus had to decide whether the above circumstances should be considered as a purposive exclusion with the result that the defendant's process could not be considered an equivalent, and this was indeed the main issue before the Supreme Court.

The Tokyo District Court,[3] The IP High Court (grand panel)[4] and the Supreme Court all affirmed infringement by equivalents.

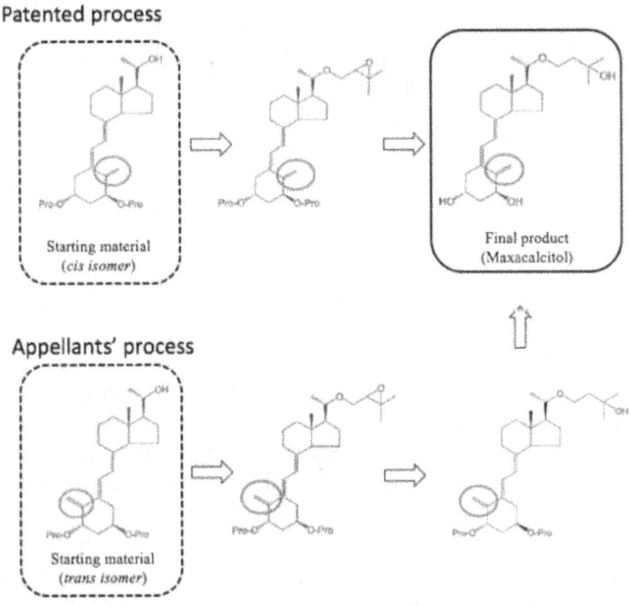

Figure 1

b) Reasons

(1) By granting exclusive rights (patents) to applicants who disclose their inventions, the purpose of the patent system is to encourage inventions and thereby to contribute to the development of industry (sec. 1 Japanese Patent Act). The patent system can protect inventions that patentees have developed. On the other hand, it facilitates the utilisation of inventions by third parties through their disclosure. The technical scope of a patented invention must be determined based upon the wording of the claims attached to the application (sec. 70(1) Patent Act). However, even where the claim

3. Tokyo District Court, 24 December 2014, Case No. 4040 (Wa) of 2013, 2258 Hanrei Jihō 106. English translation is available at the website of the IP High Court <http://www.ip.courts.go.jp/app/files/hanrei_en/004/002004.pdf>.
4. IP High Court, 25 March 2016, Case No. 10014 (Ne) of 2015, 2306 Hanrei Jihō 87. English translation is available at the website of the IP High Court <http://www.ip.courts.go.jp/app/files/hanrei_en/003/002003.pdf>; Another English translation in 47 IIC 994 (2016).

partly differs from the allegedly infringing product/process (hereinafter referred as "the differing feature", and "the allegedly infringing product"), it is valid to consider that an allegedly infringing product falls under the scope of the claim as an equivalent where certain requirements are fulfilled. The concept behind this is that it would go against the purpose of patent system and the principle of equity if a third party can easily circumvent the enforcement of a patent via injunctive relief by replacing one feature of the claim with a different feature which is substantially identical to the claimed feature. One of the requirements for this doctrine of equivalents is the absence of "special circumstances", which means that the doctrine of equivalents should not be applied if there are special circumstances such as the fact that the allegedly infringing product was intentionally excluded from the scope of the claim during patent examination. The reason for this limitation lies in principle of estoppel; i.e. once a patentee concedes that a certain product falls outside of the claim, or a patentee's behaviour could be objectively so perceived, the patentee should not be subsequently allowed to inconsistently ascertain such embodiment.

However, with regard to the differing feature, even where an applicant did not actually include the corresponding feature embodied in the allegedly infringing product in the claim at the time of the patent application in spite of the fact that the applicant could have easily done so, it would not be natural to assume that the patentee had conceded for the product to fall outside the claim, or that the patentee's behaviour objectively gave rise to such perception, namely because the patentee's behaviour is not sufficient for third parties, to whom the patent application is disclosed, to thereby take for granted that the allegedly infringing product is excluded from the scope of the claim. Additionally, it would go against the principle of equity if a court were to reject the application of the doctrine of equivalents in patent infringement litigation only for the reason that the patentee did not actually include the corresponding feature embodied in the allegedly infringing product in the claim at the time of the patent application despite of the fact that the applicant could have easily done so. Under the first-to-file system, it is well-nigh impossible for applicants at the time of the patent application to draft perfect claims that cover all possible types of future infringements. On the other hand, for third parties to whom the patent descriptions are disclosed it would be very easy over time to circumvent the working of the patent by adopting a different feature that is however substantially identical to the claim feature. The court does not find this appropriate.

(2) However, and different from the case of above (1), where an applicant has indicated, objectively or publicly, that one feature of the allegedly infringing product can be replaced with the corresponding feature of the claim, and intentionally has not included this feature in the claim, this may give rise to the assumption that the applicant's behaviour objectively gave rise to such perception that a certain product falls outside of the claim because third parties, to whom the patent application was disclosed, would understand, based on this indication, that the applicant consciously excluded such product from the scope of the claim. One typical example is the case where the applicant in the description of the patent application at the filing date mentioned that the respective feature in the claim could be exchanged with the corresponding feature embodied in the Product [but nonetheless did not claim such feature]. This interpretation of "special circumstances" is consistent with the

purpose of patent system stated above, and strikes a proper balance between the applicants and third parties.

In light of these facts, the court concludes that there are no "special circumstances" in this case because the court cannot affirm the fact that the plaintiff as a patentee had objectively or publicly indicated that one claim feature could be replaced by the corresponding feature of the allegedly infringing product, yet failed to include such feature in the claim.

3. ANALYSIS

a) Theories

(1) The "easy-to-conceive-at-the-time-of-filing" approach (hereafter referred as theory A)

According to theory A, if the applicant does not state the configuration of the allegedly infringing product, which was easy to conceive at the time of filing the application, in the patent claim, this fact alone will qualify as special circumstances, and the doctrine of equivalents cannot apply. This theory basically denies the application of the doctrine of equivalents to an equally effective embodiment at the time of filing, and affirms the application of the doctrine only for equally effective materials that become obvious after the filing date.[5]

This theory puts emphasis on the fact that, when the applicant filed a patent application, he omitted technical solution that could have been easily conceived from the claim. When reading such claim, third parties usually understand that the applicant consciously abandoned such technical subject matter, and therefore this fact alone qualify as special circumstances, and the doctrine of equivalents cannot apply.

Sec. 70(1) of the Patent Act provides that "the technical scope of the patented invention shall be determined based on the statement of the technical scope of the claims attached to the application." From this provision, the principle that "the technical scope of the patented invention is determined by the interpretation of the wording of the configuration stated in the claims" is derived. Although the Supreme Court's Ball Spline decision carved out an important exception to the above principle, there were strong reservations amongst academia and judicial circles, and one can interpret theory A as a cautious stance towards the unlimited application of the doctrine of equivalents.

5. The following academic writings support this theory: R. MIMURA, Saikōsaibansho hanrei kaisetsu minji-hen Heisei 10-nendo jō *(Comments on Supreme Court Precedents in Civil Cases 1998 first volume)*, Hōsōkai, 1998, 156; R. TAKABAYASHI, Hyōjun tokkyo-hō *(Standard Patent Law)*, 5th ed., Yūhikaku, 2014, 154; R. TAKABAYASHI, Kintō-ron wo meguru ronten no seiri to kōsatsu *(Arrangement and discussion of issues on the doctrine of equivalents)*, 38 Kōgyō Shoyūkenhō Gakkai Nenpō 68 (2014); S. ŌNO, Kintō-ron ni okeru honshitsu-teki bubun oyobi ishiki-teki jogai *(Essential parts and intentional exclusion on the doctrine of equivalents)*, 54-9 Chizai Kanri 1345 (2004); Y. AICHI, Shinsa keika kinhangen shutsugan-ji dō kō-zai to kintō-ron – Amerika-hō o sanshō shite – *(Prosecution history estoppel · Same-effective material at the time of filing and the doctrine of equivalents – see the U.S. law)*, 38 Kōgyō Shoyūkenhō Gakkai Nenpō 105 (2014).

(2) *Manifest-intention-display theory (hereafter referred as theory B)*

In a situation where the applicant did not state the configuration of another person's products etc. that could have been easily conceived at the time of patent application in the scope of claim, theory B would not per se affirm special circumstances because of this fact alone.[6] Theory B denies that third parties would normally understand that the applicant consciously excluded the technology. Only when there are further additional circumstances, this theory affirms the above special circumstances. Additional circumstances arise where the applicant has manifested to third parties the following: (a) the applicant recognised that the configuration relating to the allegedly infringing product can replace the structure described in the claims, and (b) the applicant intentionally did not seek protection for such configuration in the claims.

b) Related case law

Most of the decided cases seem to follow theory B, just as the IP High Court decision in this case. In other words, most of the decisions carefully examine the description and determine whether the case contains any special circumstances which bar the assertion of equivalent infringement. The following court cases can be listed as examples:

- IP High Court, 25 September 2006 – *Massage Chair;*[7]
- Nagoya High Court, 27 April 2005 – *Pressure Fluid Cylinder.*[8]

On the other hand, some court decisions have explicitly endorsed theory A, namely:

- IP High Court, 26 September 2012 – *Visual Image Generation Method for Medical Use;*[9]

---

6. The following writings support this theory: R. Shitara, Mukō no kōben dōnyūgo no kurēmu kaishaku to kintō-ron, narabini bōrusupurain sai han no dai 5 yōken to FESTO sai han to no hikaku oyobi shutsugan-ji dō kō-zai-tō ni tsuite (*On the interpretation of claims and the doctrine of equivalents after the introduction of invalid defense, the fifth requirement of the ball spline Supreme Court decision and the comparison with the Festo Supreme Court decision, and same-effective material at the time of filing*), 38 Kōgyō Shoyūkenhō Gakkai Nenpō 270 (2014); N. Nakayama, Tokkyo-hō *(Patent Law)*, 3rd ed., Kōbundō, 2016, 480; Y. Tamura, No. 78 Kintō-ron no meiseki-ka wo hakatta chizaikōsai dai gōgi hanketsu – makisakarushitōru jiken – (*No. 78 Intellectual property high court judgment aiming for clarity of the doctrine of equivalents – Maxacalcitol case* -), West-law Japan HP; T. Iwatsubo, Kurēmuappu sa rezaru gijutsu wa ishiki-teki jogai sa reta ka (*Was the technology that was not claimed up consciously excluded?*) in Gendai chiteki zaisan-hō jitsumu to kadai, Iimura toshiaki sensei taikan kinenronbunshū (*Contemporary Intellectual Property Law Practices and Issues, Iimura Toshiaki's Retirement Commemoration Papers Collection*), 2015, 670.
7. IP High Court, 25 September 2006, Case No. 10047 (Ne) of 2005 – *Massage Chair*. Published at the website of the courts <http://www.courts.go.jp/app/files/hanrei_jp/558/033558_hanrei.pdf>.
8. Nagoya High Court, 27 April 2005, Case Nos. 277&655 (Ne) of 2003 – *Pressure Fluid Cylinder.* Published at the website of the courts <http://www.courts.go.jp/app/files/hanrei_jp/605/009605_hanrei.pdf>.
9. IP High Court, 26 September 2012, Case No. 10035 (Ne) of 2012 – *Visual Image Generation Method for Medical Use.* Published in 2172 Hanrei Jihō 106.

- IP High Court, 25 August 2009 - *Cutting Method*.[10]

In the first case, the allegedly infringing embodiments were disclosed in the specification, and in the second case, the original claim (that would cover the allegedly infringing embodiment) was deleted during examination. Neither of these two cases is thus typical for theory A.

c) Comments on the Supreme Court decision

(1) Relationship with decision under appeal

As stated above, the Supreme Court decision unreservedly endorsed the 1998 Ball Spline decision. And this decision practically approves the decision of the IP High Court under appeal. Comparing the approach of the Supreme Court with that of the IP High Court decision, the former is clearer in that not the subjective "recognition" of the applicant is relevant, but the objective and external "manifestation". In my opinion, however, there is just a subtle difference in expression.

Let us look at this a bit more closely. The Ball Spline decision of 1998 held that it is unjust to easily escape the scope of the patent by replacing a certain element with subject matter or technology that became obvious after the patent application. The decision of 1998 about this point should be read that it is not limited to the same-effect subject matter after the time of filing. Also, the word "conscious exclusion" of the 1998 decision should be understood such that the subjective intention of the applicant is not a requirement that needs to be proven. In my opinion, such understanding seems to be in line with what the 1998 decision wanted to express. Yet why did the Supreme Court instead of dismissing the appeal this time decided to take on the case?

Twenty years have passed since the 1998 decision that clearly affirmed the application of the doctrine of equivalents. Meanwhile, case law has built up and the debate is progressing. Recently, important decisions on the doctrine of equivalents have been rendered in the United States, Germany and others (see below 4). Against this background, further guidance regarding the fifth requirement was sought in Japan. For the Supreme Court, it was thus a useful opportunity to affirm certain principles in accordance with international trends and in line with a majority of academic writers and court decisions.

(2) About the scope of this decision

The factual scope of this decision is that the configuration of the defendant's product (that could have been easily conceived at the time of filing) was not covered by or reflected in the claims. The case of amendment in the examination process or correction after the grant of the patent is different, because these are developments beyond "the time of patent application". Nevertheless, I believe that the rationale

10. IP High Court, 25 August 2009, Case No. 10068 (Ne) of 2008 - *Cutting Method*. Published in 2059 Hanrei Jihō 125.

of this decision will have a certain influence on the way of determining subsequent amendments and corrections. This point will be elaborated later.

In addition, the case where the applicant fails to claim the embodiment of the defendant's product, which could not have been easily conceived at the time of patent application, is also outside the scope of this decision. As such embodiment could not have been easily conceived at the time of filing, there is no reason for allowing any kind of estoppel.

This decision gives some guidance as to whether the applicant manifestly disclaimed certain subject matter in the above situation. If so, the doctrine of equivalents cannot be invoked. Nevertheless, the established interpretation of this decision does not deny that there may also be cases in which special circumstances exist even where plaintiff does not fulfil the above criterion. It is necessary to pay attention to this point.

(3) On the relation with the doctrine of estoppel

The Ball Spline decision of 1998 held that the special circumstances under which the doctrine of equivalents cannot be asserted are rooted in the doctrine of estoppel that derives from the principle of good faith prescribed in sec. 1(2) of the Civil Code. Two situations appear relevant in this context. The first one is the case where the exercise of the right or the assertion of the legal status directly conflicts with a preceding action. This is a type of "conflict with preceding behaviour" (*venire contra factum proprium*). The second one is the case where it is contrary to the trust and expectation based on a preceding act. This is a type of "contrary to induced trust". In these cases, admitting the exercise of the right or the assertion of the legal status is said to be contrary to the principle of good faith.[11]

However, as held in the Ball Spline decision of 1998, the substantial value of the patented invention extends technologies that third parties can readily conceive as substantially the same as the embodiments stated in the claims, and third parties should anticipate this. What should then be the position in a case where the applicant could easily conceive a configuration of the defendant's product at the time of filing the patent application, but nevertheless fails to cover this by the scope of claims?

It is true that the above behaviour may give rise to the understanding that such product is not included in the scope of the claims and that there is no literal or equivalent infringement. Exceptionally, however, it is not always possible for third parties to determine whether the substantial value of a patented invention encompasses other technologies outside the literal scope of the claims. In that situation, it is not sufficient for third parties to infer that the applicant failed to cover such embodiments in the scope of the patent. When the applicant in such a situation later invokes the doctrine of equivalents in a patent infringement litigation, this does not mean that the applicant acts in contradiction to his own previous acts. That is, the above situation does not fall within a type of "conflict with previous behaviour".

11. This point is elaborated by M. YASUNAGA (Professor of Kōbe University), Shinban Chūshaku Minpō No. 1 (Kaiteiban) (*New edition Annotated Civil Code (1) (revised edition)*), vol. 1, 2002, 98.

From this line of argumentation, the decision makes clear that theory A (easy-to-conceive-at-the-time-of-filing) cannot be adopted.[12] Subsequently, the decision analysed in what kind of cases third parties can infer that certain subject matter is disclaimed and where a subsequent application of the equivalents' doctrine would be "contrary to induced trust".

And indeed, this decision focused on whether the applicant had indicated that he or she did not intentionally remove subject matter from the scope of claims, from an objective and external point of view. Because if so, there are special circumstances to bar the invocation of the doctrine of equivalents. Thereby, the decision adopted theory B (as above).

(4) *Relation with amendments during examination process or with corrections after grant of a patent*

The decision does not deal with cases where amendments were made during the examination or in the course of a correction trial. The patentee in such cases may be barred from invoking the doctrine of equivalents because these amendments or corrections in themselves are usually based on the intention of the applicant or patentee. It seems to me, however, that the above decision does not allow an interpretation that the applicant consciously excluded certain subject matter by those amendments or corrections alone. Because even if the defendant's product no longer happens to be included in the scope of claims reduced by amendments or corrections, this fact as such cannot be taken by a third party as an intention that the configuration of the defendant's product has been excluded and such subject matter been abandoned from the scope of the claim. In that sense, I think theory B (the above manifest-intention-display theory) is also applicable to the above situation. The decision however does not allow a clear guidance as to what additional circumstances besides amendments or corrections are needed to meet the above requirement of special circumstances. For instance, in order to meet the requirement, it is said that these amendments and corrections should be made because of meeting patentability requirements, but not the written description requirement. But only future decisions will provide concrete and tangible guidance concerning this matter.

(5) *Relation with the description*

The decision does not give concrete examples of a manifest intention display that could qualify as special circumstances in cases where the description is broader than

12. The fifth requirement of the doctrine of equivalents does not focus on individual circumstances between the parties. It focuses on the particular act of the applicant and a third party in general as a person skilled in the art. The part in this decision that concerns "in the light of" the doctrine of estoppel, implies such meaning. So, it is reasonable to consider the subjectivity of the applicant as long as it can be judged unambiguously by a third party, as it widely affects the public in general. In other words, it is a "manifest intention" that allows a third party to judge whether there are special circumstances that show that the applicant consciously excluded the configuration of the defendant's products from the scope of claims. From this point as well, it is difficult to adopt theory A (easy-to-conceive-at-the-time-of-filing theory at the time), which is based on the subjectivity of "easy to conceive" by the applicant.

the claims. But in my opinion, it can be taken from this decision that only the sentence "geometric isomers include cis isomer and trans isomer" in the description would not be sufficient to infer that where only cis isomers are claimed, all embodiments with trans isomers were disclaimed. Also, in my view, where there is an abstract or general description only, or where only general concepts and effects of the configuration of the defendant's products are stated, these situations do not fall within "manifest-intention-display." On the other hand, if the description would contain a statement regarding the process of converting a trans isomer into a cis isomer, this would have been regarded as "manifest-intention-display." The reason is that a third party would understand from the sentence that the inventor disclosed an invention that made the trans isomer the starting material of the vitamin D structure.

From the point that this decision considers the understanding of third parties' as very significant, the application of the doctrine of equivalent may be barred where a person skilled in the art by reading the claims and the description would normally understand that the particular configuration of the defendant's product was abandoned at the time of application. The person skilled in the art judges the matter by taking the essence of the invention into account, accurately measuring the distance between the concrete statement in the description and the subject matter of the invention, and then comparing it with the distance between the configuration of the defendant's product and the subject matter of the invention.

4. COMPARATIVE REMARKS

It is worthwhile to compare the Japanese Supreme Court case with decisions from the **UK** and **Germany**. The position under US law related to the doctrine of equivalents is mentioned in the comment to Case No. 38 (*Ball Spline Bearing*).

a) In the **UK**, the Supreme Court recently dealt with the alleged equivalent infringement of a patent that claimed the use of pemetrexed disodium in the manufacture of a medicament for use in combination with vitamin B12 for the treatment of cancer.[13] The defendants for their products had exchanged pemetrexed disodium with pemetrexed diacid, pemetrexed ditromethamine, or pemetrexed dipotassium. According to the specification of the patent,

> "(t)he current invention concerns the discovery that administration of a methylmalonic acid lowering agent such as vitamin B12 or a pharmaceutical derivative thereof, in combination with an antifolate drug such as pemetrexed disodium reduces the toxicity of the said antifolate drug."

The court of first instance had ascertained that

> "The only form of pemetrexed which had been shown to be effective and safe to any extent was pemetrexed disodium, which was manufactured by Lilly under the trade mark Alimta".

13. UK Supreme Court, 12 July 2017, *Actavis et al. v. Eli Lilly et al.*, (2017) UKSC 48.

It was not least for this reason that the EPO examiner had insisted that "antifolate" (original filing) was changed not only to "pemetrexed" (first amendment), but rather to "pemetrexed sodium", as only this found a proper basis in the application.

In a major deviation from previous case law,[14] and in referring to an article by Hugh Laddie published in the Max Planck Institute's journal IIC,[15] the Supreme Court affirmed an equivalent infringement. In this context, especially two passages of the decision merit attention. The first concerns the relationship between disclosure in the specification, and the claimed subject matter (and thus the question whether to follow theories A or B, as above):

> "72. More specifically, I do not agree with the Court of Appeal's view that, because the specification referred to "anti-folates" and "anti-folate drugs", the fact that the claims were limited to pemetrexed disodium means that the drafter of the Patent would have been understood to intend that the other pemetrexed compounds would not infringe ...
>
> 73. Further, ... I would have thought that if the specification had not referred to anti-folates but had only referred to pemetrexed disodium, that would have been a more powerful indication that the patentee was intending to limit himself to pemetrexed disodium. The very fact that the specification teaches that there are other anti-folate drugs which have a similar effect to pemetrexed disodium ... highlights (that no) "rational patentee should want to place so narrow a limitation on his invention" as to limit the scope of protection afforded by the Patent to pemetrexed disodium ..."

The second concerns the legal implication of the above claim limitation during examination (which was not addressed in the Japanese Supreme Court decision). After having observed that the courts in Germany and the Netherlands generally discourage the use of the patent office file in aid of construction, Lord Neuberger observes that

> "87. it is appropriate for the UK courts to adopt a sceptical, but not absolutist, attitude to a suggestion that the contents of the prosecution file of a patent should be referred to when considering a question of interpretation or infringement, along substantially the same lines as the German and Dutch courts ... 89. It seems to me clear that the reason why the examiner considered that the claims in the patent should be limited to pemetrexed disodium was because the teaching in the specification did not expressly extend to any other anti-folates ... I do not consider that that consideration can have any bearing on the question whether any pemetrexed salts other than pemetrexed disodium should be within the scope of the patent pursuant to the doctrine of equivalents."

This is certainly a different approach from the one taken by Japanese case law.

b) In **Germany**, the "manifest intention" has been subject to a vivid controversy. Here, two German Supreme Court cases, *Okklusionsvorrichtung (Occlusion Device)*[16] and

14. UK House of Lords, *Kirin Amgen v. Hoechst Marion Roussel*, (2005) RPC 9; UK High Court, *Improver Corp. v. Remington Consumer Products* (1990) FSR 181.
15. H. LADDIE, Kirin-Amgen, The End of Equivalents in England?, 40 IIC 3 (2009).
16. German Federal Supreme Court, 10 May 2011, GRUR 2011, 701 – *Okklusionsvorrichtung*.

Diglycidverbindung (Manufacture of a Reagent)[17] had to deal with a scenario where the patentee in the description had disclosed several ways of implementing the invention, yet claimed only one of them. The defendant had carried out the invention according to one of the ways that was cited in the description, yet not claimed. This scenario is different from the *Macacalcitol* scenario where the patentee could have foreseen the allegedly infringing alternative, yet did neither mention it in the description, nor claim it. It is pretty clear that in the *Maxacalcitol* scenario, the German courts would have found for an equivalent infringement. Both in *Okklusionsvorrichtung* and in *Diglycidverbindung*, the Düsseldorf courts as infringement courts of first and second instance had found in favour of the plaintiff, and in both cases were overturned by the Supreme Court. The headnotes in *Okklusionsvorrichtung* read as follows:

- In the event of contradictions between the patent claims and the description, the elements of the description that are not reflected in the patent claims are, as a matter of principle, not included in the protection afforded by the patent. The description is only to be taken into account to the extent that it can be read as an explanation of the subject matter of the patent claim.
- If the description discloses a number of ways in which a specific technical effect can be achieved, but only one of these ways is included in the patent claim, the use of one of the other ways does not, as a rule, constitute an infringement of the patent with equivalent means.

In the following decision *Diglycidverbindung*, the court further specified this:

> "Where a patent offers several possibilities of how to achieve a certain technical effect, and where only one of these possibilities is actually claimed, an infringement by equivalents can only be affirmed when the modified solution in its specific effects is congruent with the specific effects of the solution that has actually been claimed and in the same way differs from the solution that has been disclosed in the description, but not in the claims."

These decisions were critically commented by *Kühnen*, a presiding judge of the High Court Düsseldorf,[18] and a subsequent decision of the Düsseldorf District Court (*Borreliosekarte*)[19] refused to follow them:

In *Borreliosekarte* case, the patent concerned a so-called "tick card" meant to remove ticks from the skin:

17. German Federal Supreme Court, 13 September 2011, GRUR 2012, 45 – *Diglycidverbindung*.
18. T. KÜHNEN, Die Reichweite des Verzichtsgedankens in der BGH-Rechtsprechung zum Äquivalenzschutz *(The scope of what is renounced in the German Federal Supreme Court case law on equivalent protection)*, GRUR 2013, 1086. *Kühnen* takes the view that equivalent infringement should only be denied where the patentee was forced to limit the claim by objections of prior art rather than out of his own volition.
19. Düsseldorf District Court, 15 September 2011, Case No. 4b O 216/08 – *Borreliosekarte* (unpublished).

Figure 2

The claim was limited to a card that envisages "a corner area designed with a slit for use in removing a tick." The description however also considers other locations for the slit:

> "**[0017]** The disclosed slit or cut-out 36, which may end up in a circular hole, **may** alternatively, or as a supplement, **also be provided at a short side of the card**. The "BorreliaCard" will hereby act as a pre-stressed spring which by itself, after placing under and around the tick, will provide a certain pulling or elevation action on the tick so that it, including mouth parts, will be pulled or lifted off the skin."

The defendant had made use of exactly the embodiment envisaged in paragraph 17 and sold cards with a slit in the middle of the short side of the card, in other words an embodiment that was disclosed, but not claimed. The Düsseldorf District Court found the defendant's embodiment to infringe by equivalent means:

> "Even considering that a guidance according to the patent claim requires not only that the patent claim in all its features is the starting point [for determining infringement], but also the relevant basis for the considerations of the person skilled in the art ..., equivalence can be affirmed according to the previous considerations. This is even so against the background of recent case of law of the Federal Supreme Court on the question of equivalents where the patent claim has made a limiting selection (Federal Supreme Court, 10 May 2011 – "Occlusion Device"). According to this decision, the following applies: Where a description offers several possibilities of how a certain technical effect can be achieved, and only one of these possibilities has actually been claimed, the use of the other alternatives *generally* does not qualify as an infringement by equivalents. However, in the case at issue and in light of paragraph[17], competitors could not in good faith take the view that positioning the slit outside of the corner of the card, and even in the middle between two corner areas, would not amount to an infringement of the patent at issue. Especially due to the advantages disclosed in the above-cited passage, a good-faith reading of the above-mentioned

passage does not give reason to the view that the patentee did not wish to claim protection for cards with slits outside the corner areas."

The Federal Supreme Court revoked the patent and for this reason did not take position on the infringement question. Yet it is clear that the decision of the Düsseldorf District Court argues infringement based on the patentee's contribution to the state of the art rather than, as was mandated by the Federal Supreme Court decisions, the wording of the claim and the patentee's choice not to claim all embodiments that were disclosed.

c) Both the Japanese and the German Supreme Court applied very similar standards in what they considered should exclude an equivalent infringement. They thereby disagreed with more extreme opinions on both ends of the spectrum: *Mimura*[20] would have excluded equivalent infringement already for alternatives the patentee could have foreseen, but did not claim (see above theory A).[21] This is problematic because it essentially leaves no room for equivalent infringement: Either the patentee could have foreseen the alternative at the filing date and subsequently cannot claim it as an equivalent, or the patentee could not have foreseen it, in which case it is an *inventive* rather than an *equivalent* alternative. On the other end, *Kühnen*[22] and the Düsseldorf courts[23] would have affirmed an equivalent infringement even for an alternative that was mentioned in the description, but was not claimed. This is certainly consistent with the notion that a patentee should receive protection commensurate to the contribution to the state of the art, yet difficult to reconcile with the principle that the claims determining the scope of protection are consciously drafted by the patentee and should give third parties certainty also about those features or embodiments that are not claimed and therefore free for all to use. From the cited passages above, it appears that also the UK Supreme Court would now rather side with the Düsseldorf courts than the German Supreme Court: Paragraph 73 of the *Actavis* decision indicates that the broad mention of anti-folates, and the limitation of the claim to pemetrexed disodium is no bar for the patentee to subsequently claim anti-folates beyond the one specifically claimed. The case is different from *Okklusionsvorrichtung* in that the examiner of the Eli Lilly patent thought that there was no support for a broader claim[24] (a view that is backed up by the findings of the *Actavis* first instance decision, but that *Lord Neuberger* thought was wrong). So the limitation was brought about by an objection of insufficient disclosure rather than an objection of prior art or the patentee's own volition.[25] For this reason, the applicant

20. R. Mimura, Saikō saibansho hanrei kaisetsu minji jiken (*Comments on Supreme Court Precedents in Civil Cases)*, 1998, pp. 156
21. This also appears to be the US position in *Wilson Sporting Goods v. David Geoffrey & Ass.*, 904 F.2d 677 (Fed. Cir. 1990).
22. T. Kühnen (above).
23. Düsseldorf District Court, 15 September 2011, Case No. 4b O 216/08 - *Borreliosekarte* (unpublished).
24. Perhaps it would have been wise for the examiner of Eli Lilly's patent to insist on an adaptation of the description, too, in order to have the broader mention of anti-folates deleted and exchanged by what the examiner thought was the inventive contribution, namely pemetrexed disodium.
25. Under US law, it would make no difference for what reason related to patentability a limitation was introduced, as in all cases the patentee would be barred from claiming by equivalents what

of the Eli Lilly patent did not describe subject matter that did exist at the filing date of the invention, because the description in this breadth was non-enabling. Seen this way, Eli Lilly's claim of equivalent infringement under the Japanese doctrine of equivalents might possibly not have fallen at the hurdle of the fifth requirement. The fact that the chemical compounds used by Actavis were non obvious (and even inventive) alternatives at the filing date does not necessarily preclude equivalent infringement, as in Japan, the date for determining obvious interchangeability is the date of infringement rather than the filing date.

It is finally interesting to note that the carefully balanced position of the Japanese Supreme Court whereby the patentee's mere silence cannot be taken as a renouncement is reverberated in *Kühnen*'s article where he writes:

> "Denying that patent protection has been renounced for unmentioned, but obvious alternatives is consistent with the approach under general civil law to which patent law also belongs. There, it is understood that the renunciation of a subjective right (e.g. a claim under the law of obligations, a right that can be exercised or an estoppel) is possible even implicitly and by mere silence. This however requires an intention to renounce by the person entitled to this position."[26]

---

was disclaimed during examination: *Festo Corp v. Shoketsu Kinzoku K.K.*, 234 F.3d 558 (Fed. Cir. 2000).

26. T. KÜHNEN (above), 1089.

Case No. 41

National Jurisdiction – Exclusive Jurisdiction in Patent Matters

Kengo Sakai

The dispute about an exclusive license should be regarded as a lawsuit in connection with the rights of a patent for which the Osaka District Court has exclusive jurisdiction in the Western part, and the Tokyo District Court for the Eastern part of Japan under the Code of Civil Procedure.

Osaka District Court, 21 September 1999, Case No. 5859 (Mo) of 1999 – *Jurisdiction in Patent Matters*

Uemura v. Namu

---

1. BACKGROUND

Under the current law, all the lawsuits in connection with the rights of a patent fall under the exclusive jurisdiction of the Tokyo District Court and Osaka District Court (sec. 6 Code of Civil Procedure[1]). The law provides that any case whose jurisdiction is established under secs. 4 and 5 CCP shall, for the district courts in Eastern Japan, come under the exclusive jurisdiction of the Tokyo District Court, and for the district courts in Western Japan, under the exclusive jurisdiction of the Osaka District Court.

The 1996 revision of the Code of Civil Procedure[2] initially introduced the special jurisdiction over patent-related cases. Before that, all district courts in Japan could have jurisdiction under the general jurisdiction rules of secs. 4 and 5 CCP. For example, for the compensation of damages due to patent infringement where the plaintiff as a patent owner was based in Sapporo and the defendant as an infringer was based in and infringed in Kyoto, the Sapporo District Court and Kyoto District Court had jurisdiction. However, lawsuits in connection with patent rights are of highly technical nature and knowledge of natural science would often be required. In order to achieve prompt proceedings of a high quality, such lawsuit should come under the jurisdiction of a court with sufficient experience and is well organised to

---

1. The jurisdiction of right of utility models, semiconductor circuit layout rights or program copyrights are ruled the same in this sec. 6 CCP. Only the jurisdiction of rights of a patent is focused hereunder.
2. Law No. 109/1996 of 26 June 1996.

handle patent cases. Therefore, the amendment introduced a concurrent, yet not exclusive jurisdiction over such cases to the Tokyo District Court and Osaka District Court. Even before, these courts handled rather more patent cases than others, had patent divisions and were allocated professional court research officials with knowledge of natural sciences.[3] The amendment intended to provide courts with professional knowledge and experience in patent matters without overly restricting the plaintiff's freedom to choose the first instance venue.[4] The decision commented upon is based on this legislative background.

Reflecting the further demand for speedy proceedings, the law amendment of 2003[5] introduced an exclusive jurisdiction for the two above-mentioned courts in first instance, and to the Tokyo High Court on appeal. This amendment was hailed as providing ideal court proceedings judges of professional knowledge and experience in patent disputes, while still maintaining the plaintiff's freedom to choose the venue.[6]

With such exclusive jurisdiction, jurisdiction based on mutual agreement (sec. 11 CCP), by uncontested appearance (sec. 12 CCP) and transfer by consent (sec. 13 CCP)) are no longer applicable in patent cases, just as jurisdiction established by adding a claim (sec. 7 and the first part of sec. 38 CCP). Exceptionally, a transfer to the competent court under the clause for jurisdiction (sec. 4 or 5 CCP) is allowed when there is a necessity to avoid substantial damage or delay in the absence of highly technical matters to be judged (sec. 20bis CCP). Also, if the Tokyo District Court and the Osaka District Court both have an exclusive jurisdiction over the same case, the provisions are still applicable in order to determine jurisdiction between those courts. Separately, a lawsuit for intermediate declaratory judgment (sec. 145(1) proviso CCP) and a counter lawsuit (Clause 1 of sec. 146(1) CCP) related to a patent action can also be raised before the Tokyo District Court or Osaka District Courts even though another court would have exclusive jurisdiction.

In order to avoid undue financial burden, for patent cases with a litigation value of JPY 1.4 million or less, jurisdiction of the Tokyo and Osaka District Courts are concurrent with the small claims courts (Court Act sec. 33(1)(i)).[7] The district court which has jurisdiction over such small claims court will be the appellate court instead of the Tokyo High Court for geographical convenience of the parties.[8]

Under the Act of Establishment of the Intellectual Property High Court, since April 2005 the only appellate court in patent matters is now the Intellectual Property High Court (hereinafter referred as "IPHC"), which is a special branch of the Tokyo High Court. The IPHC also has jurisdiction over appeals against JPO decisions (sec. 178 Patent Act, sec. 2 Act of Establishment of the IPHC). All the patent appeals in Japan now come before the IPHC.

The Japanese judicial system has been reformed as above one by one to achieve a specialised forum for patent disputes. One remaining aspect is the judge's rotation system in Japan whereby judges are assigned to move from one court to another

---

3. M. Akiyama et al., Konmentār Minji soshōhō I *(Commentary to the Code of Civil Procedure I)*, 2nd ed. 2006, 138.
4. M. Itō, Senmonsoshō no yukue *(Future of specialized litigation)*, 1124 Hanrei Times 14 (2003).
5. Law No. 108 of 16 July 2003.
6. M. Itō (above).
7. M. Akiyama et al. (above), 143.
8. M. Akiyama et al. (above), 144

during their career to maintain a generalist knowledge for any kind of cases. This traditional concept of "judge as generalist" was considered on and discussed during the above IPHC reform in a context of introducing the career path of a technical judge. Although it was decided to keep things unchanged, further consideration should be given towards achieving a specialised court for patent disputes.[9]

2. DECISION[10]

a) Facts

The plaintiff is a company with headquarters in Osaka and is the owner of the six patents at issue. The defendant with headquarters in Hiroshima has obtained an exclusive license for said patents.

According to the licensing agreement, the defendant was obliged to work the licensed technology within three years of the conclusion of the licensing agreement, failure of which would allow the licensor to terminate the agreement. The licensee failed to work the patents; the licensor terminated the agreement and now sues the licensee for consenting to delete the already registered exclusive license over the five patents from the patent register, and for confirming that the defendant has no right to work the sixth patent for which the exclusive license had not yet been registered.

The plaintiff brought suit before the Osaka District Court, which would be the competent forum if sec. 6 CCP was applicable. Otherwise, the plaintiff would have to sue before the Hiroshima District Court, as is argued by the defendant. According to the defendant, sec. 6 CCP gives additional jurisdiction to the Tokyo and Osaka District Courts for "suits under rights of a patent or utility model" in order to draw upon their specific technical knowledge in patent matters. Here, the case concerns an issue of contract where no specific expertise in patent matters is necessary.

b) Reasons

2. On the request to transfer the case based on sec. 16 CCP

Sec. 6 CCP provides that for lawsuits in connection with patents, utility models, semiconductor circuit layout rights or program copyrights, the Tokyo District Court has additional jurisdiction for the area of the Nagoya High Court eastwards, and the Osaka District Court for the area of the Osaka High Court westwards. The purpose of this provision is to improve and to promote trials over such disputes through the concurrent jurisdiction of the Tokyo and Osaka District Courts. In these courts, special boards for intellectual property disputes have been established, and court research officials who have technical knowledge have been seconded, because high level technical knowledge is often necessary in such patent etc. related disputes, and a broader range of different know-how and experience than in normal civil cases is needed for guaranteeing an efficient procedure.

9. C. WATANABE, Saiban no Senmonka to Saibankan (Specialisation of litigation and judges), 339/340 Ritsumeikan Hōgaku 662 – 666 (2011).
10. Published in 1785 Hanrei Jihō 78. English summary translation in 35 IIC 324 (2004).

As the defendant pointed out, typical cases where such high-level technical knowledge is needed are lawsuits for injunctive relief or damages based on patent infringement. In such case, it becomes important whether the allegedly infringing product or method falls within the technical scope of the patented invention, and some high-level technical knowledge is necessary for proceeding and deciding such case. A broad range of special know-how and experience of patent infringement is desirable for efficiently handling the procedure. There is a certain necessity of high-level technical knowledge also in other cases closely related to patents, such as related to the existence, attribution etc. of patents or other rights under the Patent Act. For example, as in this case, when it becomes in dispute whether an exclusive licensee produced/sold products according to the licensing contract, the fact should be important that the actually produced/sold products can be assessed to qualify as the working of the patent, and special technical knowledge may be necessary to understand the structure or performance of the actually produced/sold products in addition to the contents of the patented invention.

The time of determining jurisdiction of the courts is the time of filing the lawsuit (sec. 15 CCP). Such jurisdiction cannot be changed depending on the status of the issues in dispute related to the defendant's defences or counterclaims, etc. So the question of jurisdiction cannot be decided by the current status of the case. Whether a court has jurisdiction should be decided by the general character of the case at the time of filing the lawsuit.

According to the above considerations and based on the general notion that there is a possible necessity that high level technical knowledge is required for deciding this case, a "lawsuit in connection with rights of a patent" under sec. 6 CCP should be interpreted as also to comprise a dispute closely related to patents, such as a case related to the existence, attribution etc. of patents or other rights under the Patent Act.

In some of these cases, it might be so that high level technical knowledge for the procedure and determination is not necessary, depending on the concrete situation of the case. But even if jurisdiction for such a case is vested in the Osaka District Court or the Tokyo District Court under sec. 6 CCP, the case can subsequently be transferred under sec. 17 CCP if need be.

As mentioned above, in this case the procedure to get approval for the deletion of an exclusive license and the negative confirmation regarding the existence of a licensed right have been jointly claimed. This case is closely related to patents. Therefore, the Osaka District Court has jurisdiction under sec. 6 CCP. The defendant's argument based on sec. 16(1) CCP is therefore groundless.

3. ANALYSIS

The wording of "lawsuit in connection with rights of a patent" has remained unchanged since this decision was rendered.

As the court judged, jurisdiction shall be decided at the time of filing the lawsuit (sec. 15 CCP) and whether the case falls under the wording of "lawsuit in connection with rights of a patent" should be determined by the general character of the case described in the complaint. Given that the wording of sec. 6 was not "lawsuit based upon rights of a patent" but "lawsuit in connection with rights of a patent", and also the intention of this provision is to concentrate those cases involving highly technical issues before certain courts, sec. 6 CCP should include disputes that based on the claim, appear to involve technical issues.[11] In other words, it should be interpreted to include not only lawsuits based upon rights of a patent such as a lawsuit for injunctive relief, compensation of damages or unjust enrichment as a consequence of patent infringement, but also, among others, lawsuits for declaratory judgment to confirm patent ownership, right to work (prior use of licence), patent registration, payment of remuneration related to an employee invention, or royalty payments under a patent license agreement.[12]

Two types of lawsuits could thus be covered by the provision: (i) a lawsuit relates formally, but not in substance to a patent, (ii) the lawsuit is not formally, but in substance related to a patent.[13]

Type (ii) above would be a lawsuit for compensation of damages based upon tort where the defendant enforced the provisional enforcement order upon a first instance judgment to the plaintiff's real estate due to the alleged patent infringement by the plaintiff although the defendant's patent was invalidated afterwards, or a lawsuit for compensation of damages due to the defendant's notification of false fact under sec. 4 of Unfair Competition Prevention Act where the defendant as patentee notified the plaintiff's customers of an alleged patent infringement which later on proved unfounded. Either case is considered as a "lawsuit in connection with rights of a patent" due to the technical issues involved. Here, sec. 6 CCP prevails since the issue of patent infringement will be the main argument.[14]

Type (i) above would be, among others, a lawsuit for the registration of a patent transfer under a patent purchase agreement where the defendant counter-argues the non-payment by the plaintiff, or a lawsuit for declaratory judgment confirming the ownership of rights of a patent while the actual dispute relates to a succession amongst different heirs. In those cases, the validity or technical scope of the patent is not in dispute. Sec. 6 should equally apply due to the general character of the suit at the time of filing. Still, the case may exceptionally be transferred under section 20bis CCP if appropriate.[15]

The interpretation of the "lawsuit in connection with rights of a patent" above is in line with the court practice before and after the law amendment of 2003. The judgment introduced above concerned a lawsuit for deregistration of an exclusive license due to a cancellation of the contract for cause. This case was deemed a "lawsuit in connection with the rights of a patent" where, in general, highly technical matters may have to be discussed. In another case,[16] compensation of damages due to non-performance - failure to grant a non-exclusive license - was sought because the sub-licensor did not obtain an exclusive license from the licensor since the licence was not registered under an exclusive licensing agreement.[17] Although the actual

11. T. ŌBUCHI, Senmon soshō kōza 6 tokkyo soshō jōkan *(Lecture of professional litigation 6, patent litigation)*, Kabushiki kaisha Minjihō Kenkyūkai, 2012, 533.
12. T. ŌBUCHI (above).
13. T. TSUKAHARA, Chizaikōsai gannen *(1st year of the IP High Court)*, 1236 Kinyū Shojihan'rei 6 (2006).
14. T. ŌBUCHI (above).
15. T. ŌBUCHI (above).
16. IP High Court, 29 January 2009, Case No. 10061 (Ne) of 2008, 1291 Hanrei Times 286.
17. An exclusive license without registration is considered as effective under the law.

issue was not related to technical but rather legal subject matter[18] (in that sense it can be categorised as a lawsuit (i) above), the court determined that such case in connection with non-exclusive and exclusive licensing agreements constitutes a "lawsuit in connection with rights of a patent". It appears that the court also decided from its general character described in the complaint.

4. COMPARATIVE REMARKS

a) In **Germany**, sec. 143 Patent Act provides for the exclusive jurisdiction of certain German district courts (12 district courts at total) as first instance courts in patent matters regardless of the value in dispute. As any forum can be chosen where the defendant has its place of business or where infringing goods can be found, de facto 500 cases per year are filed in Düsseldorf, about 280 in Mannheim and about 170 each in Munich and Hamburg.[19] Due to the German separation of infringement and invalidation actions, all the latter must be filed before the German Federal Patent Court. There are a few exceptional cases which are not regarded as patent matters. The German Supreme Court decided a case in 2011 where the patent attorney's fee was disputed and held that such dispute was not a patent case, indicating that cases where specific aspects of patent law were not in dispute could not be qualified as patent-related cases.[20]

b) In **France**, the law No. 2011-525 of 17 May 2011 in Art. 615-17 Code of the Intellectual Property stipulated the exclusive jurisdiction of high courts (Tribunal de Grande Instance, TGI) in patent related cases. According to Art. D211-6 Code of the Judicial Organization, the TGI Paris should have exclusive jurisdiction. Such patent related cases, which shall be handled exclusively by the TGI Paris, include cases of patent licensing.[21]

c) In the **UK**, there are two special courts to handle patent related cases, the Patents Court (PC), which was established by the Patent Act 1977 in the High Court of Justice, and the Intellectual Property Enterprise Court (IPEC), which since 2013 has been the successor to the Patents Country Court established by the Copyright, Designs and Patent Act 1988. Rule 63.2 of the Civil Procedure Rules provides that any claim under the Patent Act must be commenced in either of them. The IPEC was established to handle lower value cases and Rule 63.17A of the Civil Procedure Rules set a threshold of £500,000. These courts can transfer cases to each other.[22]

---

18. Whether a non-exclusive license can be made by a sub-licensor as a non-registered exclusive licensee.
19. A. OSTERRIETH, Patent Enforcement in Germany, in: C. HEATH (ed.), Patent Enforcement Worldwide, Hart Publishing 2015, note 25.
20. German Federal Supreme Court, 22 February 2011, GRUR 2011, 662 – *Patentstreitsache*. See also German Federal Supreme Court, 20 March 2013, GRUR 2013, 756 – *Patentstreitsache II*. For examples of patent matter cases, see BENKARD, Patentgesetz *(Commentary on German Patent Act)*, 11th ed. 2015, 1934.
21. Court of Appeal of Toulouse, 13 February 2013.
22. UK Patent Country Court, *ALK-Abello v. Meridian Medical Technologies* [2010] EWPCC 14. See also the Intellectual Enterprise Court guide, available at the website of the UK government < https://www.gov.uk/government/publications/intellectual-property-enterprise-court-guide >.

d) **Switzerland** in 2012 set up the Federal Patent Court which has first instance exclusive jurisdiction over patent infringement and validity matters, and also disputes relating to patent licenses may be brought before it.

e) In the **US**, each district court has jurisdiction over patent matters,[23] but at the appeal level, sec. 1295 of 28 USC provides that the Court of Appeals for the Federal Circuit shall have exclusive jurisdiction in any civil action relating to patents, etc.

f) **China** in 2014 established three Intellectual Property Courts in Beijing, Shanghai and Guangzhou which have exclusive jurisdiction over IP matters in each city. The establishment of specialised IP courts at district level courts in Nanjing, etc. has been on the rise after opinion No. 17/2016 of the Chinese Supreme Court which emphasised a common approach to IP related civil, criminal and administrative cases and started its own IP court as appeal court from January 2019 by rule No. 22/2018.

g) In **Korea**, currently five district courts, which are located in the place of the high courts, have exclusive jurisdiction over patent related cases under sec. 24 Code of Civil Procedure, and appeal cases are handled by the Patent Court under sec. 28^{quater} Court Organisation Act. This centralisation of jurisdiction of patent related cases was effected by the law amendment of 2015.[24]

23. US Supreme Court, *TC Heartland v. Kraft Foods Group Brands*, 581 U.S. ___ (2017), ruled that the residence in sec. 1400(b) of 28 USC, which provides the venue on personal jurisdiction in patent infringement cases, refers only to the State of incorporation, as applied to the US domestic corporations. This decision greatly reduced forum shopping, as US domestic corporations now must be sued in their state of incorporation rather than at any place where infringing goods can be found.
24. Law No. 13521&13522 of 1 December 2015. The Korean Supreme Court on 22 December 2017 ordered to transfer patent infringement cases from the Gwangju High Court to the Patent Court because of the exclusive jurisdiction after the law amendment (Case No. 259988 (Da) of 2017).

Case No. 42

International Jurisdiction in Patent Matters

Anja Petersen-Padberg

Where the Japanese Code of Civil Procedure provides a domestic forum (here: the place of domicile of the defendant) for an action for ascertaining non-infringement concerning a foreign patent right, the estoppel of patent invalidity does not constitute "special circumstances" that could lead a Japanese court to deny jurisdiction, since a decision on the invalidity of the foreign patent would have inter partes effect only.

Tokyo District Court, 16 October 2003, Case No. 1943 (Wa) of 2000 – *Coral Sand*

Coral KK v. Marine Bio KK

1. BACKGROUND

The Tokyo District Court had to decide on its international jurisdiction between two Japanese companies concerning defendant's US patent. The plaintiff raised a claim of non-infringement and invalidity of the defendant's US patent at the defendant's place of domicile. The Court followed the Supreme Court's *Card Reader* decision (Case No. 45 in this book) in that Japanese courts may basically exercise their jurisdiction in patent infringement cases even if a foreign patent right is concerned. As a first court in Japan, the Tokyo District Court had to decide not only on infringement, but also on the alleged invalidity of a US patent. The Court decided that the challenge of the validity of the US patent does not negatively affect its jurisdiction at defendant's place of domicile, since, like in domestic cases, the decision on the validity has effect between the parties only (see Case No. 50 – *Kilby*).

2. DECISION[1]

a) Facts

Plaintiff is a company established under Japanese law, which produces fine powder from fossil coral and sells it as an ingredient in health food both in Japan and in the

1. Tokyo District Court, 16 October 2003, Case No. 1943 (Wa) of 2000, 1847 Hanrei Jihō 23 = 1151 Hanrei Times 109 = T. ŌBUCHI et al. (eds.), Chitekizaisan hō hanrei shū *(Intellectual Property Law Case Book)*, 2nd ed. 2015, 505 – *Coral Sand*, 505. English translation in: T. KONO/P. JURCYS,

United States. The Defendant, also a Japanese corporation, is the owner of US patent No 4,540,584 for a composition, which includes coral sand for the promotion of health benefits. Having found that a similar material was being sold in the United States, the Defendant had filed a patent infringement suit in the US and issued warning letters to the Plaintiff and its US distributor, urging them to halt manufacturing and sales activities. The Plaintiff filed a suit at the Tokyo District Court requesting the Court to issue a declaratory judgment that Plaintiff's product is not falling within the technical scope of Defendant's US patent, that the US patent is invalid and that therefore the Defendant has no right to seek an injunction in Japan and to stop Plaintiff's sales in the United States. In response, the Defendant argued that the principle of territoriality of intellectual property rights prevents Japanese courts from exercising international jurisdiction to claims for negative declaratory judgments based on a US patent. Moreover, the Defendant stated that the claims raised by the Plaintiff are unjustified and should therefore be dismissed.

b) Reasons

Regarding its international jurisdiction, the Tokyo District Court decided that "there is no law or well-established customary law regarding international jurisdiction. It is therefore appropriate to decide on the Court's jurisdiction according to *jōri* (reasonableness) under consideration of the principles of fairness between the parties and an appropriate and speedy trial. In light of these principles, it is reasonable to apply the jurisdictional provisions under the Code of Civil Procedure. If the court's jurisdiction can be established according to these rules, it is to assume that the principles of fairness between the parties and an appropriate and speedy trial are fulfilled, unless there are any special circumstances according to which it appears reasonable to deny the court's jurisdiction" (see, Supreme Court, 16 October 1981, Case No. 130 (O) of 1980, 35-7 Minshū 1224– *Malaysia Airlines*; Supreme Court, 24 June 1996, Case No. 764 (O) of 1993, 50-7 Minshū 1451; Supreme Court, 11 November 1997, Case No. 1660 (O) of 1993, 51-10 Minshū 4055).

Since the Defendant has its headquarters in Japan, jurisdiction shall be established based on Defendant's place of business in Japan (sec. 4(4) CCP 1996). There are no special circumstances, which would require the denial of international jurisdiction.

In particular the principle of territoriality of patents does not give rise to decline the court's jurisdiction. "The principle of territoriality of patents means that the grant, transfer, effect etc. of patent rights of a country is governed by the laws of that country. The effects of a patent are to be recognised only within the territory of that country", (see, Supreme Court, 1 July 1997, Case No. 1988 (O) of 1995, 51-6 Minshū 2299 –*BBS* [Case No. 32 in this volume]). The principle of territoriality is a matter of substantive law, but not a matter of international jurisdiction.

General Report, 1, 44 in: T. Kono (ed.), Intellectual Property and Private International Law – International Law – Comparative Perspectives, 2012, 44 and also in: N. Ono, Cross-border Patent Enforcement: Coral Powder Case, Where Japan Court Applies the US Law, ATRIP 2005, Montreal, 13 July 2005, this document can be accessed at the website of ATRIP <http://www.atrip.org/wp-content/uploads/2016/06/Ono.doc>.

A claim for injunction based on a patent is a claim based on person's property rights. Where a dispute relates to a claim based on ordinary private law, it must be decided according to the above-mentioned principles whether Japanese courts have international jurisdiction. Courts shall establish their international jurisdiction, if the defendant's general jurisdiction is in Japan. Regarding patent rights, certainly, their grant, effects etc. are determined by the laws of each country from a viewpoint of economic policy. The limits are subject to political decisions. This should be considered regarding the question of applicable law, but this is no reason to affirm international jurisdiction only for the country where the patent is registered (see, Supreme Court, 26 September 2002, Case No. 580 (Ju) of 2000, 56-7 Minshū 1551 - *Card Reader* [Case No. 45 in this book][2]).

Regarding the grant and the validity of a patent, it is generally recognised that the courts of the country of registration have exclusive jurisdiction. In a number of countries, the patent invalidity defence against the patent owner's claim can be brought against a claim for injunctive relief for alleged patent infringement. Such invalidity defence may be based on substantive law or case law, but even if the defence is well-founded and the injunction claim of the patent owner is rejected, the decision on the patent invalidity takes effect only between the parties as decided in the reasons for rejecting the injunction request, and does not invalidate the patent *erga omnes*. Even if such invalidity defence is made in patent infringement proceedings, it does not hinder litigation in a court outside the country of registration.

In this case, the existence of a right of injunctive relief based on a US patent is disputed, and US law allows explicitly the invalidity defence in patent injunction cases (sec. 282(2) US Patent Act). A decision of patent invalidity in such a case does not render the patent invalid *erga omnes.*

This case concerns a negative declaratory action concerning patent infringement, but the above-mentioned considerations about positive patent infringement cases can be applied in the same way.

Courts both in Japan, in which the main office of the Plaintiff is established, or courts in the US, where the patent is registered and the infringement occurs, can have international jurisdiction over an injunction case once the Defendant files a lawsuit in the US based on the US patent against the sale of the Plaintiff's products in the US. Considering that the Defendant has its head offices in Japan, it is to conclude that Defendant's responding to the action in Japan is no greater inconvenience than filing and continuing an injunction lawsuit in the US. With regard to this point, it is not convincing that the Plaintiff unfairly availed itself of the international jurisdiction of Japan by filing this lawsuit before the Defendant took action in the US.

Based on the above considerations, the general jurisdiction of the Defendant exists in Japan and there are no special circumstances given in terms of fairness

2. Supreme Court, 26 September 2002, Case No. 580 (Ju) of 2000, 56-7 Minshū, 1551 = 1802 Hanrei Jihō 19 = 19 L&T 81 (2003); 16 ZJapanR 251 (2004), comment by Y. NISHITANI; translation also published in 46 Japanese Annual of International Law 168 - *Card Reader*, see also Japan's response to AIPPI Question 174, G. MARUSHIMA/Y. KUMAKURA/K. NORICHIKA/K. KONDO, "Jurisdiction and Applicable Law in the Case of Cross-border Infringement (Infringing Acts) of Intellectual Property Rights", 28 AIPPI Journal of the Japanese Group (English edition) 192, 193 (May 2003).

between the parties and the principle of an appropriate and speedy trial in Japan. Thus, international jurisdiction should be affirmed.

Regarding the question of applicable law, the Law for the Application of laws (*hōrei*) does not provide for any rules concerning infringement matters on foreign patents. The decision must therefore be based on *jōri*. According to *jōri*, the law of the country with the closest connection to the patent shall apply. This shall be the country of registration, i.e. the US, therefore US law shall apply (see Supreme Court in: *Card Reader*[3]).

3. ANALYSIS

The Tokyo District Court had to decide both on a negative declaration claim regarding patent infringement and an invalidity claim concerning a US patent. The parties were both companies with head offices in Japan, but the case must be considered as an "international case", i.e. a case with a "connection to a foreign country", since the subject matter of the case was concerned with a US patent, which takes effect only within the US (principle of territoriality). The Tokyo District Court therefore had to decide on its international jurisdiction in the first place.

When the Tokyo District Court decided this case in 2003, Japanese civil procedure law did not provide for explicit rules on international jurisdiction. Such rules were introduced only in 2011 and came into force in 2012. The new rules would not have changed the result of the Court's decision. So far, parallel to the German Code of Civil Procedure, which originally was the model for the Japanese Code of Civil Procedure, rules on domestic jurisdiction fulfil a "double function" since they apply both for the establishment of the domestic and the international jurisdiction of a court. However, different from German law, when having established international jurisdiction under the rules of the CCP, Japanese courts examine by default whether "special circumstances" are given due to which the court should deny its jurisdiction based on *jōri*, even if a domestic rule on jurisdiction did apply. This can be considered as the "Japanese *forum non conveniens* approach".[4] The "double functionality" of the domestic jurisdiction rules of the CCP plus the "special circumstances according to *jōri*" approach were developed during the 1970ies,[5] became established case law and were finally confirmed by the Supreme Court in the *Malaysia Airlines* case in 1981[6]

3. Footnote 2.
4. *Forum non conveniens* is a (mostly) common law legal doctrine whereby courts may refuse to seize jurisdiction over matters where there is a more appropriate foreign forum available to the parties.
5. By S. IKEHARA/M. HIRATSUKA, Shōgai soshō ni okeru saiban kankatsuken *(Jurisdiction of courts in proceedings with foreign aspects)*, in: A. MIKAZUKI/C. SUZUKI, Jitsumu minji soshō kōza *(Civil Procedure Practice)*, Vol. 6 (1971) 3 *et seq*.
6. Supreme Court, 16 October 1981, Case No. 130 (O) of 1980 - *Malaysia Airlines*, 35-7 Minshū, 1224 = 1020 Hanrei Jihō, 9 = 452 Hanrei Times, 77. See A. PETERSEN-PADBERG, Case No. 66, International Civil Procedure Law - Jurisdiction - Place of Business of Corporations, in: M. BÄLZ, M. DERNAUER, C. HEATH & A. PETERSEN-PADBERG (eds.), Business Law in Japan - Cases and Comments - Intellectual Property, Civil, Commercial and International Private Law, Writings in Honour of Harald Baum, 2012, 727 *et seq*. See also Supreme Court, 11 November 1997, Case No. 1660 (O) of 1993, 51-10 Minshū 4055.

and was then implemented in sec. 3^nonies of the new CCP in 2011.[7] In practice, court decisions show that if a Japanese court has established its jurisdiction according to the domestic jurisdiction rules of the CCP, it will rarely reject jurisdiction according to "special circumstances".[8]

As a result, if the court cannot establish its international jurisdiction according to one of the rules of domestic jurisdiction, it may not exercise its international jurisdiction due to "special circumstances". "Special circumstances" only have the consequence of denying jurisdiction.[9] This is reflected in the wording of the new sec. 3^nonies CCP. Also according to the new rule, "special circumstances" must be tested. The results will probably be similar like in the "old law", i.e. if a court established its jurisdiction according to one of the new rules of international jurisdiction, it will be rarely denied afterwards due to "special circumstances". However, particular broad jurisdiction rules, such as the "place of doing business" (sec. 3ter CCP) could become subject to discussion (e.g. whether each and any "doing business" will

7. In 2011, rules on international jurisdiction including the right to reject jurisdiction due to "special circumstances" were added to the Japanese Code of Civil Procedure (law No. 36 of 2 May 2011 as in force of 1 April 2012). However, the new rules did not change the existing legal practice. See Y. OKUDA, New Provisions on International Jurisdiction of Japanese Courts, 13 Yearbook of Private International Law 367-380 (2011); K. TAKAHASHI, Japan's New Act on International Jurisdiction (17 May 2011), Smashwords, 2011, available at the website of the SSRN <https://ssrn.com/abstract=2189684>; Y. NISHITANI, Einführung in die neuen internationalen Zuständigkeitsregelungen – Die neuen Regelungen über die internationale Zuständigkeit in Zivil- und Handelssachen in Japan (Übersetzung) *(Introduction of the new rules on international jurisdiction – the new rules on international jurisdiction in civil and commercial matters in Japan (translation))*, 33 ZJapanR 197 *et seq.* (2012).
8. In the following cases, courts declined jurisdiction based on *jōri*: No access to evidence caused by the lack of diplomatic relations to Taiwan (Tokyo District Court, 20 June 1986, 31 Japanese Annual of International Law 216 (1988); pending parallel proceedings in a foreign country (Tokyo District Court, 15 February 1984, Case No. 8657 (Wa) of 1983, 28 Japanese Annual of International Law 243 (1985); *ibid*, 29 January 1991, Case No. 9993 (Wa) of 1989, 35 Japanese Annual of International Law 171 (1992). However, as a rule, jurisdiction will not be denied due to prior pending court proceedings in a foreign country between the same parties in an identical or related matter (Tokyo District Court, 19 June 1989, Case No. 4284 (Wa) of 1988, 33 Japanese Annual of International Law 202 (1990) and Supreme Court, footnote 10 – *Ultraman* and Tokyo District Court, footnote 1, *Coral Sand*); a joint defendant had no relations whatsoever to Japan, Tokyo District Court, 23 October 1990, 1398 Hanrei Jihō 87; unpredictability of the "place of performance" in particular since parties have neither agreed on a place of performance nor on the law applicable to the contract (Supreme Court 11, November 1997, Case No. 1660 (O) of 1993, 1626 Hanrei Jihō 74. An English translation is published on the website of the courts <http://www.courts.go.jp/app/hanrei_en/detail?id=329=>; a negative declaratory action at the forum of the property (Tokyo District Court, 28 July 1987, Case No. 1954 (Wa) of 1986, 1275 Hanrei Jihō 77).
9. This is the "special circumstances approach" pursuant to literature and the Supreme Court's *Malaysia Airlines* case (footnote 7), see, Tokyo District Court, 18 November 2002, Case No. 6247 (Wa) of 2002, 1812 Hanrei Jihō, 139 – *Iron Man 28*. Confirmed by Tokyo High Court, 25 February 2004, Case No 1241 (Ne) of 2003, published on the website of the courts: <http://www.courts.go.jp/app/files/hanrei_jp/499/010499_hanrei.pdf>. In this case, jurisdiction with regard to copyright infringement in the US, could not be established since the defendant had no domicile in Japan and also no tortious act was committed in Japan. The fact that plaintiff's court action in the US was also dismissed due to *forum non conveniens* with the effect that he could not enforce his copyright at all was no reason for the Tokyo District Court to assume jurisdiction.

establish jurisdiction). Another broad rule on international jurisdiction, the "place of assets" is already limited by its wording, i.e. it shall not apply, if the asset is of "extraordinary small value".

Jurisdiction in international patent cases can be established based on the following new rules of the CCP of 2012: When the defendant has its domicile, main business office or attachable property in Japan (sec. 3bis CCP), when the place of tort is in Japan (sec. 3ter No. 8 CCP), when the parties have mutually agreed on the jurisdiction of Japanese courts (sec. $3^{septies}$ CCP), when the defendant responds to proceedings without making any objection to the jurisdiction (sec. 3^{octies} CCP) and in case of joint claims (sec. 3^{sexies} CCP) provided that there is a close relationship between the claims.[10] The dismissal of an action due to special circumstances is laid down in sec. 3^{nonies} CCP. Japanese courts have exclusive jurisdiction regarding the registration (and therefore also the *erga omnes* validity) of a patent (sec. $3^{quinquies}$(3) CCP), see also examples of court cases concerning international jurisdiction in IP matters below.

In *Coral Sand*, the Tokyo District Court assumed jurisdiction based on the place of domicile of the defendant in Japan and did not find any special circumstances, which could give reason to deny its international jurisdiction based on *jōri*. The Court followed the decision *Card Reader* (as above) where the Supreme Court also assumed international jurisdiction at the defendant's place of domicile in Japan concerning the alleged infringement of a US patent.[11] In the *Card Reader* case, the plaintiff's claims were based on alleged infringement of a US patent by way of inducement under sec. 271(b) US law which took place in Japan only, where no corresponding patent existed. Import to the US was made by a different legal entity. The Supreme Court dismissed plaintiff's claims, since it denied the application of US patent law on Japanese territory.[12] As a result, Japanese courts may generally exercise jurisdiction at the place of the defendant's domicile with regard to a patent infringement action based on a foreign patent. The Supreme Court had, however, not to decide on the question of whether a Japanese court may assume international jurisdiction with regard to the invalidity claim of a foreign patent.

According to the Tokyo District Court in *Coral Sand*, a Japanese court may even decide on the validity of the foreign patent, since the decision will only take effect among the parties. The registration of the (foreign) patent remains valid. The Court affirming jurisdiction also on the invalidity claim corresponds to domestic law practice, which allows a civil court to decide on the validity in patent infringement cases with effect between the parties only.[13] A decision with an *erga omnes* effect, however, may only be rendered by the Japanese Patent Office.

The Tokyo District Court also discussed whether US courts have exclusive jurisdiction in this case, (which could give reason to assume "special circumstances"

---

10. E.g. Supreme Court 8 June 2001, Case No. 929 (O) of 2000, 55-4 Minshū, 727, 1756 Hanrei Jihō, 55, 1066 Hanrei Times 206 – *Ultraman*, English translation in: 45 Japanese Annual of International Law 151 (2002) and at the website of the courts <http://www.courts.go.jp/app/hanrei_en/detail?id=1526>.
11. Footnote 2.
12. Footnote 2.
13. Sec. 104ter Patent Act, Supreme Court, 11 April 2000, Case No. 364 (O) of 1998, 54-4 Minshū, 1368 – *Texas Instruments v. Fujitsu – Kilby III* (Case No. 50 in this book).

and to decline jurisdiction), but denied it, since the Court's decision on the patent's validity decision will have *inter partes* effect only.

As a result, the Court assumed jurisdiction at the place of Defendant's domicile despite the strong connection of the case to a foreign country (claims are related to a US patent and infringing acts are taking place in the US). The principle of territoriality of patent rights and an earlier pending patent infringement action in the US were no "special circumstances" and therefore not sufficient to deny the Court's international jurisdiction. It shows that Japanese courts affirm "special circumstances" allowing them to reject jurisdiction only in exceptional cases. The place of domicile is therefore a broad venue.

With regard to the applicable law, there are no special rules regarding the infringement of intellectual property rights in the Japanese Act on the General Rules of Application of Laws.[14] The Tokyo District Court in *Coral Sand* followed the Supreme Court decision *Card Reader* and decided that the country of registration has the closest link to the patent and therefore, US law should apply.

In its substantive decision, the Court denied patent infringement and therefore did not have to rule on the issue of validity.

Other cases:

In the following, a brief overview on other recent cases on international jurisdiction in intellectual property matters will be given.

Japanese courts deny international jurisdiction in intellectual property cases when no jurisdiction according to domestic jurisdiction rules can be established. For instance, in the patent infringement case *Ueno Fine Chemicals Industry v. Pharmacia*, the plaintiff, a Japanese company and exclusive licensee of a Japanese patent on "ocular hypotensive agents", filed a patent infringement action against the sales subsidiary Pharmacia Corp. with its place of business in Japan and against its foreign parent company and the affiliated foreign R&D company. International jurisdiction was denied against the foreign parent company and foreign R&D entity, since jurisdiction could not be established under any domestic jurisdiction rule, in particular no evidence of a tortious act in Japan could be shown.[15]

In a copyright case decided by the Tokyo District Court, the plaintiff sued a defendant domiciled in the US seeking injunction and damages based on infringement of its US copyright protecting "*Iron Man 28*". The Court dismissed the action, since the defendant had no place of business in Japan and no tortious act was committed in Japan.[16]

In the copyright case *Ultraman*, the Supreme Court confirmed international jurisdiction of Japanese courts (overruling the lower court decisions), since the defendant, domiciled in Thailand, had issued warning letters to customers in Japan,

---

14. Act on the General Rules of Application of Laws, *Hō no tekiyō ni kansuru tsūsokuhō*, Law No. 10 of 1898 (as newly titled and amended on 21 June 2006).
15. Tokyo District Court, 14 May 2001, Case No. 16175 (Wa) of 1999, 1754 Hanrei Jihō 148 - *Ueno Pharm. KK v. Pharmacia et al.*
16. Tokyo District Court, 18 November 2002, Case No. 6247 (Wa) of 2002, 1812 Hanrei Jihō 139 - *Iron Man 28*. Confirmed by Tokyo High Court, 25 February 2004, Case No. 1241 (Ne) of 2003, published on the website of the courts <http://www.courts.go.jp/app/files/hanrei_jp/499/010499_hanrei.pdf>.

thereby hindering plaintiff's business operations. The warning letters were considered as tortious acts, which gave a forum at the "place of tort". The fact that parallel proceedings were pending in Thailand were no "special circumstances" and therefore no reason for the Supreme Court to decline international jurisdiction.[17]

According to the IP High Court decision *Nidec v. Samsung*, (Case No. 43 in this volume), an advertisement of patent infringing goods on a website, explicitly for sale in Japan, published in English, with information on sales contacts in Japan and allowing "inquiries about the sale" was considered as a patent infringing "offer" and therefore a tortious act in Japan. The IP High Court assumed international jurisdiction at the place of tort (sec. $3^{ter}(8)$ CCP) against the defendant, a Korean company. The Court denied "special circumstances", since due to the explicit offering on the Japanese market, the defendant could have foreseen litigation in Japan. Further, the defendant was a large Korean company, having sales subsidiaries all over the world including Japan. It was therefore not burdensome for the defendant to respond to the court action in Japan.[18]

In the Tokyo District Court case *Fujitsu v. CCI* concerning the infringement of a Japanese patent entitled "data transmission method" related to ADSL modem chipsets, the Court established international jurisdiction at the "place of tort". assuming a "joint tortious act" of a US based company CCI (Defendant) which sold its products in the US, but two Japanese companies (Sumitomo and NEC) sold them in Japan ("Importer"). The Court affirmed joint patent infringement, since it was clear also for the Defendant that its goods would be sold on the Japanese market given that CCI had a close cooperation with the Importer based not only on business contacts but also on mutual R&D agreements. Another consulting agreement which was related to the relevant technology (and which was needed by the Importers' customer) was entered into by the Defendant and a Japanese sub-supplier of the Importers' main customer. This close co-operation between the US company with Japanese companies to supply one main Japanese customer established sufficient contacts in Japan in order to assume a jointly committed tortious act in Japan and therefore jurisdiction at "the place of tort".[19]

A joint tortuous act however was denied by the Tokyo District Court in the case *Solvay v. Jiangsu Yangnong*. Defendant had sold a pharmaceutical ingredient to a third company, which imported this to Japan, thereby infringing a Japanese patent. The Court decided that such a transaction "is common in international trade" and should not to be considered a tortious act and therefore jurisdiction of Japanese courts

17. Supreme Court, 8 June 2001 – *Ultraman*, footnote 10.
18. IP High Court, 15 September 2010, Case No. 10001&10002&10003 (Ne) of 2010, 1340 Hanrei Times 265 – *Motor* – *Nidec v. Samsung* (Case No. 43 in this volume). English translation is available at the website of the IP High Court < http://www.ip.courts.go.jp/app/files/hanrei_en/531/000531.pdf >. Another translation in 35 AIPPI Journal of the Japanese Group (English edition) 353 *et seq.* (November 2010), comments by D. YOKOMIZU, Intellectual Property Infringement on the Internet and Conflict of Laws, 36 AIPPI Journal of the Japanese Group (English edition) 104, 105 et seq. (May 2011). Previous instance: Osaka District Court, 26 November 2009, Case No. 9732&9736&9742 (Wa) of 2008, 1326 Hanrei Times 267.
19. Tokyo District Court, 28 November 2007, Case No. 2004 (Wa) 10667 – *Fujitsu v. CCI*, 33 AIPPI Journal of the Japanese Group (English edition) 299 *et seq.* (September 2008) with comments by M. HANAI.

had to be declined.[20] It can be said that the collaboration between the manufacturer and the importer was not as close as in the above-mentioned case *Fujitsu v. CCI*.

As a result, Japanese courts will most likely assume jurisdiction in cases related to a foreign IP rights where the defendant has a place of business in Japan. This applies both to positive patent infringement actions and declaratory actions of non-infringement. Japanese courts will also decide on the validity of the foreign patent with *inter partes* effect only. Courts can, however, reject international jurisdiction due to "special circumstances", which they do only reluctantly. With regard to an infringement of a Japanese patent, a foreign company can be sued in Japan if it has committed a (joint) tortious act in Japan.

4. COMPARATIVE REMARKS

a) German law including EU law ("Brussels Regulation")

With regard to patent infringement matters, German domestic law does not provide for any special rules on international jurisdiction. Domestic jurisdiction rules of the CCP (Code of Civil Procedure) fulfil a "double function", they establish both domestic and international jurisdiction of a Court. However, with regard to European infringement cases, which are not purely domestic, i.e. whenever the defendant has its place of business in Europe, the jurisdiction rules of the "Brussels Regulation" shall apply.[21] Jurisdiction in patent matters can be established at the place of domicile of the defendant (secs. 13, 17 CCP, Art. 4 (1) Brussels Regulation, according to Art. 63 Brussels Regulation a company is domiciled at the place where it has its statutory seat, or its central administration, or its principle place of business). Infringement needs to be examined according to the applicable foreign patent law.[22] At the place of domicile, the competent court may also decide on the infringement with regard to a foreign patent. However, should the defendant raise a nullity claim, under the Brussels Regulation the court has to deny its jurisdiction not only regarding the nullity claim, but also regarding the infringement claim, no matter at which point of time and no matter whether the claim has *inter partes* or *erga omnes* effect.[23]With regard to a declaration of non-infringement action combined with a nullity claim regarding a foreign patent, a court cannot establish its international jurisdiction at the defendant's place of domicile.[24] The loss of jurisdiction due to a nullity claim

20. Tokyo District Court, 28 April 2015, Case No. 5011 (Wa) of 2014 – *Method for Producing Epichlorohidrine*.
21. Regulation (EU) No. 1215/2012 of the European Parliament and of the Council of 12 December 2012 on jurisdiction and the recognition and enforcement of judgments in civil and commercial matters ("Brussels Regulation", "BR") repealing Regulation (EU) No 44/2001 (however no replacement with regard to UK and DK). Regulation 44/2001 had replaced the European Jurisdiction and Enforcement Convention of 1968. Both Regulation 44/2001 and the Convention have quite similar rules to Regulation (EU) No. 1215/2012, court decisions with regard to these laws are therefore still of relevance.
22. Düsseldorf District Court, 1 February 1994, Entscheidungen 1998, 1 – *Kettenbandförderer III*.
23. ECJ, 13 July 2006, Case C-4/03, ECR 2006, 6509 – *GAT v. LuK*, Marginal Note 30.
24. ECJ, 13 July 2006, Case C-4/03, ECR 2006, 6509 – *GAT v. LuK*, Marginal Note 30. T. KÜHNEN, Handbuch der Patentverletzung *(Handbook of the Patent Infringement)*, 9th Ed. 2016, 352 *et seq.*

does not apply for provisional injunction proceedings, since no final decision on the patent validity will be issued.[25]

In patent matters, jurisdiction of the courts at the place of tort is of importance (sec. 32 CCP, Art. 7 No. 2 Brussels Regulation, hereinafter "BR", both provisions provide for the principle of strict liability regarding the tortious act). According to sec. 32 CPA, "the court in the jurisdiction in which the tortious act was committed" and, according to Art. 7 No. 2 BR, "the courts for the place where the harmful event occurred or may occur" shall have jurisdiction. According to this wording, Art. 7 No. 2 BR also provides jurisdiction for a preventive injunction claim in case of a risk of first infringement.[26] Also a preventive negative declaration of non-infringement can be filed at the place of tort according to Art. 7 No. 2 BR,[27] however, only with regard to the part of the European patent of the country of the seized court (for other parts, the place of domicile must be chosen[28]). At the place "where the harmful event occurred", the place of purely financial damage affecting the plaintiff's assets at its place of business shall not establish jurisdiction.[29] Jurisdiction can be also established against joint tortfeasors (against the same national patent or the same national part of an EP) at the place of business of one of the joint tortfeasors (Art. 8 BR). With regard to sec. 32 CCP, the same principles apply.[30]

If the jurisdiction is based on the place of tort, the court may also establish jurisdiction for the nullity claim, since it is the country of registration of the national patent or the relevant country part of the European patent. Art. 24 No. 4 BR reads: "in proceedings concerned with the registration or validity of patents, trade marks, designs, or other similar rights required to be deposited or registered, irrespective of whether the issue is raised by way of an action or as a defence, the courts of the Member State in which the deposit or registration has been applied for, has taken place or is under the terms of an instrument of the Union or an international convention deemed to have taken place." These courts have exclusive jurisdiction for proceedings concerning the grant or validity of a patent including positive and negative declaratory actions.[31] However, patent infringement actions do not fall under the scope of Art. 22, but rather general rules of jurisdiction apply (Art. 2, 5 No. 3 Brussels Regulation or national CPA rules). Neither the CPA nor the Brussels Regulation provide for "*forum non conveniens* rules".

Outside the scope of the Brussels Regulation, the ordinary rules of jurisdiction under the German Code of Civil Procedure apply. In other words, claims related to

---

25. CJEU, 12 July 2012, Case C-616/10 – *Solvay*, see the website of the Kluwer Patent Blog: <http://patentblog.kluweriplaw.com/2012/07/22/court-of-justice-of-the-european-union-strengthens-the-protection-of-holders-of-european-patents-in-solvay-case-c-61610/>.
26. T. KÜHNEN, footnote 25, 356.
27. CJEU of 25 October 2012, C-133/11, ECR 2012, 664 – *Folien Fischer*.
28. Düsseldorf High Court, 12 May 2005, Case No. I-2 U 67/03, the case can be accessed at <https://openjur.de/u/108376.html>.
29. Düsseldorf District Court, InstGE 3, 153 – *WC Erfrischer*, since the ECJ has limited Art. 7 No. 2 to the place where the harmful event occurred, ECJ, 19 September 1995, Case C-364/93, ECR 1995, I-2719 – *Marinari* and ECJ, 10 June 2004, Case C-168/02, ECR 2004 I, 6009 – *Kronhofer*.
30. T. KÜHNEN, footnote 24, 357.
31. Munich High Court, 15 May 2003, IPRax 2004, 346, 347 *et seq.* It is of no relevance whether the declaratory judgment has effect *erga omnes* or only *inter partes*, ECJ, ECR 2006, 6509, Note 30 – *GAT v. LuK*.

the (non)infringement of (non-EU) foreign intellectual property rights could be raised at the domicile of the defendant, and a German court could thus decide a *Coral Sand* type suit including an *inter partes* assessment of validity.[32]

b) The US

In the leading US decision on this matter, the US Court of Appeals for the Federal Circuit adopted the view that the rule of international intellectual property law treaties that sets the principle of independence of national patents, when combined with the treaties' silence on foreign patent adjudication, should be interpreted to mean that courts "should not determine the validity and infringement of foreign patents."[33] The majority of the panel also identified comity and the local action doctrine as reasons for not adjudicating cases involving foreign patents.

32. Düsseldorf District Court, 1 February 1994, Entscheidungen 1998, 1 – *Kettenbandförderer III*; Düsseldorf District Court, 31 May 2001, Case No. 4 O 128/00 – *GaT v. LuK*. M. ZIGANN, Entscheidungen inländischer Gerichte über ausländische gewerbliche Schutzrechte und Urheberrechte *(Decisions of domestic courts over foreign industrial property rights and copyrights)*, München 2002.
33. US CAFC, *Jan K. Voda v. Cordis Corporation*, 476 F.3d 887, 899 (Fed. Cir. 2007).

Case No. 43

International Jurisdiction in Patent Matters – Offer on the Internet

Hisayoshi Yokoyama

In an action for an injunction and damages based on the infringement of a Japanese patent against a foreign defendant, international jurisdiction of Japanese courts based on the place of tort can be affirmed where the defendant operates a website on which a Japanese consumer can purchase the defendant's allegedly infringing products.

Intellectual Property High Court, 15 September 2010,
Case No. 10001&10002&10003 (Ne) of 2010 – *Motor*

Nidec v. Samsung

1. BACKGROUND

With the globalisation of the economy and the development of IT technology, international disputes are gradually increasing, and there are a number of cases over patent matters between Japanese and foreign companies. In such cases, international jurisdiction of Japanese courts often becomes an issue.

For the legislative background or international jurisdiction, see the previous case 42 – *Coral Sand*. Even in a case where a foreign company in a foreign country commits an act relating to infringement in Japan, international jurisdiction of Japanese courts over an action relating to a tort could be affirmed, sec. $3^{ter}(8)$. However, as mentioned in the previous case, international jurisdiction of Japanese courts shall be denied under special circumstances when conducting a trial in Japan is contrary to the equality between the parties and the idea of a fair and speedy trial, sec. 3^{nonies}.

The issue of the present case is whether international jurisdiction of Japanese courts could be affirmed based on the rule of an action relating to a tort. Since the Code of Civil Procedure had not been amended at the time of the conclusion of the oral arguments, the present court made a decision based on the prior judicial doctrine, under which the application of sec. 5(9) Code of Civil Procedure, the provision concerning domestic territorial jurisdiction based on the place of tort, became an issue. However, the interpretation of the previous provision is not much different from the current law[1] on which this comment is based.

2. DECISION[2]

a) Facts

X (plaintiff, appellant) is a Japanese company and owns a patent named "Motor". Y (defendant, appellee) is a Korean company. On Y's website, available from Japan at the time of the present lawsuit, there are pages in English that introduce a group of products "Slim ODD Motor" including allegedly infringing products, pages in English that introduce sales offices located in Japan (Tokyo and Osaka), and also pages in Japanese that present an inquiry form.

X filed an action for patent infringement against Y with the Osaka District Court, insisting that Y has made an offer to sell infringing products in the course of business in Japan, and sought for an injunction prohibiting Y from making an offer to sell its products and for damages in the amount equivalent to the attorney's fees. Y opposed international jurisdiction of the Japanese courts.

The court of first instance[3] denied international jurisdiction based on Sec. 5 (9) and dismissed the case, holding that X did not sufficiently prove that Y has conducted or is likely to conduct an offer to sell in Japan. X appealed.

The present court affirmed international jurisdiction based on sec. 5(9), revoked the earlier decision and remanded the case to the first instance court.

b) Reasons

The existence or absence of international jurisdiction of Japanese courts over a case with international implications such as the present case should be decided according to a rule of reason derived from the equality between the parties and the idea of a fair and speedy trial at the present time, given there is neither a Japanese statute nor an international common law concerning this matter. The content of the rule of reason is that the defendant shall be principally subject to jurisdiction of a Japanese court over an action filed with the Japanese court if one of the domestic venues stipulated in the Code of Civil Procedure is within Japan, while international jurisdiction of a Japanese court shall be denied if there are special circumstances because of which

---

1. Sec. 3[ter](8) of Code of Civil Procedure differs from sec. 5(9) in that it explicitly excludes the case where the the result of a wrongful act committed in a foreign country occurred in Japan and the occurrence of the result in Japan was ordinarily unforeseeable. However, even under the prior judicial doctrine, if the occurrence of the result in Japan was unforeseeable, international jurisdiction of Japanese courts based on sec. 5(9) would normally be denied because of the existence of special circumstances. T. SATO/Y. KOBAYASHI, Ichimon Itto Heisei 23 Nen Minji soshōhō tō kaisei *(Exchange of Questions and Answers: The Amendment of Code of Civil Procedure etc. of 2011)*, 2012,70.
2. Published in 1340 Hanrei Times 265. English translation in IIC 2013, 99.
3. Osaka District Court, 26 November 2009, Case No. 9732 (Wa) of 2008, 2081 Hanei Jihō 131 = 1326 Hanrei Times 267.

conducting a trial in Japan is contrary to the equality between the parties and the idea of a fair and speedy trial.

The present action is a claim for an injunction based on a patent and a claim for damages based on a tort, both of which are an action based on a property right. The relationship between these claims and the Sec. 5 Code of Civil Procedure is as follows: It is obvious that a claim for damages based on a tort literally falls into an action relating to a tort in sec. 5(9) Code of Civil Procedure. An injunction based on a patent is sought on the ground that the plaintiff's right or interest has been or is likely to be injured by the defendant's wrongful infringing act and the substance of the dispute is not different in case of a claim for a tort. Thus, an action for an injunction should be included in an action relating to a tort in sec. 5(9) Code of Civil Procedure.

As for an application under sec. 5(9) Code of Civil Procedure, based on which the existence or absence of international jurisdiction over the present case shall be decided, the place of jurisdiction over an action relating to a tort shall be the place where the tort has taken place, which should be interpreted to include both the place where the wrongful act was committed and the place where the result occurred. Since the right that X insisted was infringed in the present action is a Japanese patent and the act that X insisted constitutes a tort is Y's offer to sell, the presence or absence of international jurisdiction of Japanese courts should be decided according to whether an act of sending an offer or the result of receiving it took place as an objective factual relationship in Japan.

In the present case, the following facts can be ascertained: First, Y set up a website in English, posts one of the Y's allegedly infringing products as a product, lists "Japan" as sales inquiry, and indicates a Japanese address, phone and fax number of a base in Japan as "Sales Headquarters". Second, Y also operates a website in Japanese with pages for the introduction of the "Slim ODD Motor", which enables a customer who selects an item of "Inquiry to purchase" to make an inquiry form about the sale of the "Slim ODD Motor". Third, X's sales manager stated in the written statement that Y's sales people have been doing business in the sales of the "Slim ODD Motor" in Japan and Y's allegedly infringing products are objects of evaluation as to whether to be installed in the products (ODD). Fourth, A, Y's management consultant, makes and uses a name card with his title, Y's company name and his address in Minato Ward, Tokyo. Finally, it is highly probable that DVD multi-drives on which one of Y's allegedly infringing products are installed, have been made and sold by Japanese companies and have been distributed in Japan. Based on the comprehensive consideration of these facts, it would be appropriate to affirm that, as for the offer to sell Y's infringing products which X insisted amounts to a tort, either Y's act of sending an offer or the result of receiving it occurred in Japan.

The content of the present claim is that X, a Japanese company located in Japan, requests an injunction prohibiting Y from offering to sell Y's infringing products and damages, based on the present patent, a Japanese patent, as an exercise of right of access to the court. The law applicable to the present case would be a law of the country where the present patent is registered, that is, the Japanese Patent Act. Therefore, it would be consistent with the idea of of a fair and speedy trial for the Japanese court to consider and decide the present case, while, considering the facts found mentioned above, even though X files an action for an injunction etc. in Korea, where Y's head office is located, the possibility that the Korean courts will affirm international jurisdiction would not be necessarily high. On the other hand, since Y has set up a sales base in the Tokyo Prefecture, has disclosed that fact on its website, has introduced the allegedly infringing products on its website in English, and has not only recognised that its products are also distributed in Japan, but also enables sales inquiries about the ODD motors including Y's infringing products, it could be within Y's predictable range that an action for infringement etc. relating to the Y's products will be filed in Japan. Furthermore, Y is a company which belongs to the Samsung Group, one of the largest global corporations in Korea, and Y itself has a lot of branches overseas.

Considering these circumstances, it would not be contrary to the equality between the parties and the idea of a fair and speedy trial to request Y to respond to the present claim in Japanese courts, and, also seen from a viewpoint of distribution of judicial power in the international society, there is a legal connection sufficient to justify an exercise of jurisdiction of Japanese courts. Thus, we hold that there are no special circumstances whereby international jurisdiction of Japanese courts should be denied.

3. ANALYSIS

a) International jurisdiction over an action for an injunction

The first issue is whether an action for an injunction based on patent infringement can be filed with the Japanese court as an action relating to a tort.

As the present court held, it is unquestionable that an action for damages based on patent infringement relates to a tort, but there would be room for argument as to whether an action for an injunction should be included in an action relating to a tort, because the legal character of an injunction and damages are different: an injunction derives from the effect of a patent as an exclusive right, while damages aim to compensate for the past loss incurred by the patentee based on the concept of justice and fairness.[4] In fact, the court of first instance in the present case had found the ground for jurisdiction over an action for an injunction in a rule of reason, without referring to the jurisdiction on the place of tort.

However, since a right to seek an injunction only exists when the plaintiff's patent has been or is likely to be infringed by the defendant, an action for an injunction can be literally interpreted as an action relating to a tort. The "tort" in the provision of international jurisdiction does not need to be strictly limited to a "tort" in the substantive provisions of domestic law.[5] In addition, the reason for jurisdiction in the

---

4. In this respect, the Supreme Court interpreted the applicable law to each claim differently: The law applicable to a claim for an injunction based on a patent is the law of the country where the patent is registered, while a claim for damages based on patent infringement is the law of the country where an infringement action was committed and the result of patent infringement occurred. Supreme Court, 26 September 2002, Case No. 580 (Ju) of 2000, 56-7 Minshū 1551 = 1802 Hanei Jihō 19 = 1107 Hanrei Times 80 – *Card Reader* (Case No. 45 in this volume).
5. H. SANO, Fuhōkōichi no Kankatsuken *(Jurisdiction based on the place of tort)*, in: A. TAKAKUWA/ M. DOGAUCHI, Shin Saiban Jitsumu Taikei 3 Kokusai Minji Soshōhō (*New court practice Compendium No. 3 International Civil Procedure)*, 2002, 93 states that the question of which range of actions are included in "an action relating to a tort" should be rationally decided from

place of tort is that (1) means of evidence relating to a tort is normally concentrated in the place of tort, which is convenient for a trial, (2) it would be beneficial for the victim to file an action with a court in the place of tort, while it would be within the range of the defendant's expectation to respond to an action in the place of tort, and (3) an action relating to a tort is concerned with the public policy of the country where the tort took place, etc..[6] As the present court stated, since the substance of dispute in an action for an injunction is substantially not different from that in an action for damages, the above-mentioned reason for jurisdiction in the place of tort also applies for an action for an injunction. Thus, an action for an injunction should be regarded as an action relating to tort in the context of international jurisdiction.[7]

In this respect, the Supreme Court,[8] when deciding domestic territorial jurisdiction based on sec. 5(9) Code of Civil Procedure, held that an action for an injunction should be regarded as an action relating to a tort, considering the purpose of the provision to facilitate the proof of the parties. The same is true of international jurisdiction. Therefore, it is appropriate that the present court, citing the above-mentioned Supreme Court decision, interpreted an action for an injunction as an action relating to a tort under sec. 5(9) Code of Civil Procedure.[9] Thereafter, the Supreme Court[10] which addressed indirect jurisdiction[11] of the foreign court, referring to the above-mentioned Supreme Court Decision, held that an action for a tort under sec. 3[ter](8) Code of Civil Procedure, like an action for a tort under sec. 5(9) Code of Civil Procedure, includes not only an action for a tort stipulated in the Code Civil, but also an action for an injunction filed by those whose interests has been or are likely to be infringed by the wrongful act. This judgment would also apply to direct jurisdiction.[12]

---

a standpoint of our international civil procedure, considering the purpose of international jurisdiction on the place of tort.

6. H. Sano (above), 91; T. Sato/Y. Kobayashi (above), 68.
7. T. Sato/Y. Kobayashi (above), 69.
8. Supreme Court, 8 April 2004, Case No. 44 (Kyo) of 2003, 58-4 Minshū 825 = 1860 Hanei Jihō 62 = 1151 Hanrei Times 297 - *Pioneer Trading Company.*
9. As to academic literature on the present decision, see: S.Shimizu, Kokusai saiban kankatsu *(International Jurisdiction in Patent Infringement Litigation)*, 50 L &T 48 (2011); S. Teramoto, in: N. Nakayama et al. (eds.), Tokkyo Hanrei Hyakusen *(Hundred Selected Patent Cases)*, 4th ed. 2012, 203 (2012); T. Yamauchi/Y. Ujiike, Uebusaito no kisai tō wo konkyo ni wagakuni no kokusai saiban kankatsu ga mitomerareta jirei *(Case where the international jurisdiction is acknowledged in Japan on the ground of the statement in the website)*, 88 Chizaiken Forum 69-70 (2002).
10. Supreme Court, 24 April 2014, Case No. 1781 (Ju) of 2011, 68-4 Minshū 329 = 2221 Hanei Jihō 35 = 1401 Hanrei Times 157 - *Brow Treatment.*
11. The issue of international jurisdiction has two dimensions: One is whether, as in the present case, domestic courts shall have jurisdiction, and the other is whether foreign courts shall have jurisdiction as a requirement for recognition and enforcement of their judgments by domestic courts. The former is referred to as direct jurisdiction and the latter as indirect jurisdiction.
12. K. Nakamura/S. Sakugi, Kokusaitekina Chizaifunso no Kaiketsu ni tsuite *(About the resolution of international IP dispute)*, 69-6 Patent 119 (2016).

b) The object and extent of proof

The second issue is what facts need to be proven and up to what level in order to affirm the existence of a tort at the stage of jurisdiction.

The "place of tort" includes both the place where the wrongful act was committed and the place where the result occurred.[13] The present court, based on this principle, clarified that in a case where an "offer for sale" allegedly constitutes a tort, the place where the act of sending an offer or the result of receiving it took place was regarded as the place of tort.

As for jurisdiction in the place of tort, a decision on jurisdiction and a decision on cause of action overlap, because the existence or absence of a tort is to be decided in both cases. Since it is not appropriate to request the plaintiff to prove the same facts at the stage of jurisdiction as in a trial, the problem arises at the stage of jurisdiction what facts should be proven and to what extent in order to affirm the existence of a tort. In this respect, the Supreme Court,[14] which addressed international jurisdiction of Japanese courts over an action for damages based on the tort of business interference, held that in order to affirm international jurisdiction of Japanese courts, it is principally enough for the plaintiff to prove an objective factual relationship that the defendant's act in Japan caused damage to the plaintiff's legal interests, because if these facts exist, there are generally reasonable grounds to request the defendant to respond to the action, and, seen from a perspective of distribution of judicial function in the international society, there could be a sufficient legal connection to justify the exercise of jurisdiction by the Japanese courts ("objective factual relationship theory"). The Supreme Court limited the range of facts required to prove at the stage of jurisdiction to the facts consisting of an objective factual relationship. Thus, among the necessary facts for the right to seek damages, the plaintiff has normally only to prove (1) the existence of the plaintiff's infringed interest, (2) the defendant's act against the infringed interest, (3) the occurrence of damages, (4) a factual causality between (2) and (3).[15]

This standard would also apply to an action for patent infringement. However, because the necessary facts for patent infringement are different from those for a general tort, it is necessary to consider what kind of facts should be proven as an "objective factual relationship" in order to affirm the existence of a patent infringement.[16] In this regard, there are mainly two remarkable points in the present decision.

---

13. H. Sano (above), 92; T. Sato/Y. Kobayashi (above), 69.
14. 55-4 Minshū 727 = 1756 Hanei Jihō 55 = 1066 Hanrei Times 206 - *Tsuburaya*55-4 Minshū 727 = 1756 Hanei Jihō 55 = 1066 Hanrei Times 206 - *Tsuburaya Pro.*
15. M. Takabe, Saikō saibanshō Hanrei Kaisetsu Minjihen *(Commentary of the Supreme Court Decision Civil Affairs Volume)*, vol. 2, 2004, 494-495. Before this Supreme Court decision, there had also been an influential opinion called "prima facie proof theory", according to which international jurisdiction based on a tort can be affirmed when prima facie examination of evidence has been carried out to the extent necessary for a decision on jurisdiction, and the existence of the tort could be affirmed with more than a certain level of certainty. However, the Supreme Court explicitly refused this theory, holding that the standard for the degree of proof is so ambiguous that decisions might vary from court to court and it would be extremely difficult for the defendant in a foreign country to predict the result.
16. Since the content of an objective factual relationship stated by the Supreme Court is just a principle, the facts required to prove as an objective factual relationship could differ according to a

First, although the plaintiff in the present case claimed not only an injunction but also damages, the present court did not refer to the occurrence of damages.[17] It means that in an action for damages based on patent infringement, different from an action for damages based on a general tort, the occurrence of damages does not necessarily need to be proven for the assessment of international jurisdiction. This would be derived from the legal nature of a patent. The Patent Act stipulates a number of different forms of use that are the object of an exclusive right. Since all the forms of use as stipulated by the Patent Act are closely related to the ordinary use of an invention by the patentee, each unauthorised use causes damage to the patentee. Therefore, every patent infringement is likely to cause damage.[18] Thus, the specific occurrence of damages does not need to be proven at the stage of jurisdiction. The concrete existence and amount of damages should be considered and identified in a trial.[19]

Second, in spite of an action for patent infringement, the present court does not address the issue of the technical scope of X's patented invention. This implies that the issue of the technical scope should not be considered and judged at the stage of jurisdiction. Needless to say, the issue of technical scope is normally the main issue in patent infringement litigation. However, the issue of technical scope is usually very complicated and time-consuming. Besides, it sometimes requires normative considerations such as estoppel and doctrine of equivalence. The aim of the *"objective factual relationship theory"* is to limit the scope of proof and judgment at the stage of jurisdiction and thereby to enable a prompt judgment as to whether there is a sufficient legal relationship between the action and the place of forum to justify jurisdiction of the present court. It is obviously contrary to this aim to address the

---

type of tort and it is necessary to consider what kind of facts should consist of an objective factual relationship for such special type of tort as patent infringement. See, S. SHIMIZU (above), 47. There are opinions questioning that the present court adopted the "objective factual relationship theory", because the present court neither referred to all of the requirements established by the Supreme Court nor cited the Supreme Court. D. YOKOMIZO, Tokkyoken higi shingai seihin no website e no keisai to kokusai saiban kankatsu [chizai kōsai heisei 22.9.15 hanketsu] *(Posting of the patent infringing products in the website and international jurisdiction [IP High Court decision on 15 September 2010])*, 1417 Jurist 173-174 (2011); M. SHIN, Nihon tokkyoken shingai sashitome/songaibaishō ni tsuki higi shingai seihin ga website ni keisai sareteita tō no jijō kara fuhō kōichi ni motozuku wagakuni saibansho no kokusai saiban kankatsu wo kōtei shita chizai kōsai hanketsu *(Case Regarding International Jurisdiction over Foreign Company for Japanese Patent Infringement in Light of Website Contents and Other Considerations)*, 52 Tokkyo Kenkyū 53, 2011. However, since the present court used the term "objective factual relationship" to list the facts required to prove at the stage of jurisdiction, the present court would also be based on the "objective factual relationship theory". See, T. YAMAUCHI/Y. UJIIKE (above), 68-69.

17. If the plaintiff only claims an injunction, it is natural that the occurrence of damages does not need to be proven, S. SHIMIZU (above), 48.
18. M. SHIN (above), 52.
19. The Supreme Court officer stated that "occurrence of damages" means the result which could be evaluated as an infringement of legal interests, that is, the fact that might cause the occurrence of damages, not the occurrence of concretely specified monetary damages. M. TAKABE (above), 495. Based on this understanding, the "occurrence of damages" could automatically be affirmed in an action for patent infringement, if the occurrence of infringement could be affirmed. See, M. SHIN (above), 57 (note 28).

issue of technical scope at the stage of jurisdiction.[20] Based on the above-mentioned aim of the *"objective factual relationship theory"*, it would be enough to prove such facts as would indicate that the defendant's product or method has some degree of resemblance to the patented invention and can accomplish the same effect and function as the patented invention, and that the defendant has committed or is likely to commit deemed infringing acts under the present Patent Act.[21] In this regard, it would be appropriate that in a case where an offer for sale allegedly constitutes a patent infringement, the present court requested the plaintiff only to prove either of the act of sending an offer or the result of receiving it as an objective factual relationship.

Under the "objective factual relationship theory", the facts consisting of an objective factual relationship need to be proven to the same extent as in a trial. Therefore, the present court carefully evaluated the defendant's offer to sell in Japan based not only on the contents of the defendant's website, but also on the comprehensive consideration of all the relevant facts, such as the statement of the plaintiff's sales manager, the business of the defendant's sales consultant in Japan, the probability of distribution of Y's allegedly infringing products in Japan, etc. An "offer for sale" under the Patent Act is an act to motivate the consumer to purchase a patented product. Thus, in order to affirm the occurrence of an "offer for sale" in Japan, Y's allegedly infringing act must objectively be directed to purchases by the Japanese consumer.[22] All the facts established by the present court confirmed this point. Thus, it would be appropriate for the present court to affirm the occurrence of an offer for sale in Japan.[23]

c) Interpretation of "special circumstances" that deny international jurisdiction

The third issue is how to judge the "special circumstances" in order to deny international jurisdiction.

---

20. There are many opinions according to which the issue of technical scope should not be addressed at the stage of jurisdiction. See, D. YOKOMIZO (above), 173-174; S. SHIMIZU (above), 49; M. SHIN (above), 53. Other than the present court, there is a decision that affirmed international jurisdiction without addressing the issue of technical scope. Tokyo District Court, 28 November 2007, Case No. 10667 (Wa) of 2004 the website of the courts <http://www.courts.go.jp/app/files/hanrei_jp/446/035446_hanrei.pdf> - *Data Transfer Mode.*
21. S. SHIMIZU (above), 49.
22. D. YOKOMIZO (above), 174-175; S. TERAMOTO (above), 203.
23. Since the contents on a website can be seen around the world, it would not be appropriate to regard the operation of a website in itself as an offer for sale, just because the Japanese consumer can get access to it and possibly purchase a patented product. However, in the present case, as the present court implies, there would be room for evaluating the operation of the Y's website itself as an offer for sale in Japan, because considering the form and description of the Y's website, it could be said that Y expects and enables the purchase by Japanese consumers proactively. See, H. YOKOYAMA, "Jisshi" Gainen wo tooshitemiru "Jōto no Mōshide" Gainen no Igi *(The Meaning of the Concept "offer to sell" seen through an Analysis of the Concept "Exploitation of an Invention")*, in: N. NAKAYAMA/H. SAITO/T. IIMURA (eds.), Chitekizaisanken Hōri to Teigen " Gainen wo tooshitemiru "Jōto no Mōshide" Gainen no Igi *(The Meaning of the Concept "offer to sell" seen through an Analyse of the Concept "Exploitation of an Invention")*, in: N. NAKAYAMA/H. SAITO/T. IIMURA (eds.), Chitekizaisanken Hōri to Teigen *(IP Right, Doctrine and Proposal)*, 2012, 204.

Sec. 3[nonies] Code of Civil Procedure stipulates that the court may decline jurisdiction if there are special circumstances due to which the court finds that conducting a trial in Japan is contrary to the principle of the equality between the parties and the idea of a fair and speedy trial, considering the nature of the case, the defendant's degree of proof, and the location of evidence and other circumstances.[24] This provision is derived from prior jurisprudence,[25] and remains unchanged.

As is clear from the gist of the provision, the existence or absence of special circumstances shall be decided based on a balancing of private interests between the parties and public interest for a fair and speedy trial. The judgment of the present court was also based on this perspective: It denied the existence of special circumstances, holding that conducting a trial in Japan conforms with the idea of a fair and speedy trial,

- because the applicable law to the present case would be the Japanese Patent Act *(from a perspective of public interest)*, and that considering the facts found,
- the necessity for the plaintiff to file the case before a Japanese court is high, because the plaintiff cannot possibly file an action with the Korean court, while conducting a trial in Japan would not impose an excessive burden on the defendant, since it would be within the range of the defendant's expectation and the defendant is one of the largest international cooperations in Korea *(from a perspective of balancing the interests between the parties)*.

d) International jurisdiction in an action based on joint patent infringement or inducement or accessory

Last, although unrelated to the present case, the case of joint patent infringement or joint tort such as inducement or accessory will be mentioned here.[26]

Since joint patent infringement or inducement and accessory constitutes a joint tort under the Civil Code, an action based on joint patent infringement or inducement and accessory can be considered a tort under sec. 3[ter](8).[27]

In the case *Method for Producing Epichlorohidrine*, the defendant, a Chinese company, which made and sold the allegedly infringing products to a Japanese trading company which imported and sold them in Japan, was sued as one of the joint tortfeasors. The court denied international jurisdiction of the Japanese courts, holding that neither concerted action, nor inducement or accessory could be proven.

24. The "other circumstances" in this provision mean the existence or absence of jurisdiction of a foreign country over the present action and the pending of the same or related action in a foreign court. T. SATO/Y. KOBAYASHI (above), 158-159.
25. Supreme Court, 11 November 1997, Case No. 1660 (O) of 1993, 51-10 Minshū 4055 = 1626 Hanrei Jihō 74 = 960 Hanrei Times 102 - *Claim of Deposit*.
26. Joint patent infringement is an infringement action which was conducted jointly by two or more actors and all the actors are regarded as infringers, whereas inducement or accessory is not in itself an infringement, but an action which promotes and contributes to the infringer's wrongful act and is regarded as a tort.
27. *Data Transfer Mode* case (above); Tokyo District Court, 28 April 2015, Case No. 5011 (Wa) of 2014, 2264 Hanrei Jihō 59 - *Method for Producing Epichlorohidrine*. On the other hand, it would not be necessary to prove the subjective elements, such as intentional connection between the parties. See, W. SUZUKI (above), 261.

The mere knowledge of importation to Japan and the promise to hold the importer harmless did not exceed the scope of general international business between a manufacturer and a trading company. On the other hand, in the *Data Transfer Mode* case, the defendant, while recognising that its allegedly infringing products would be sold in Japan, was presumably engaged in the sales activities of the Japanese importers, for which reason either concerted relationship relating to the tort committed by the Japanese companies could be affirmed, or the defendant's act could be regarded as an act of inducement or accessory for the tort committed by the Japanese companies and the court affirmed international jurisdiction of the Japanese courts.

4. COMPARATIVE REMARKS

For the international jurisdiction in general, see Case No. 42 in this volume. Here, we focus on the international jurisdiction and patent infringement in relation to offers on the Internet. For offers for sale as patent infringement, see Case No. 29.

a) In **Germany**, it is considered that the allegation of domestic infringement is enough for a court to assume international jurisdiction of the German courts under Art. 5(3) Brussels Regulation, while the offer in a foreign website is not in itself infringing a patent right only because it is accessible in Germany. Rather, a relationship to the domestic market is considered necessary, namely that the offer on the website is directed to Germany.[28] For infringement by an offer for sale, see the comparative remarks for Case No. 29. For patent infringement in relation to an offer on the internet, the Düsseldorf District Court granted interim relief in the 2008 decision *Geogitter* where the starting site was in Czech but the infringing product description appeared in the English version through a link: English could be understood in the relevant market, the defendant was active in Germany in relation to the products offered existed in Germany and the infringing products were offered on the German market by the website.[29]

b) In **France**, there is also a case where the Paris District Court affirmed jurisdiction for the alleged infringement through a website because the website was accessible to the French public.[30]

---

28. German Federal Supreme Court, 13 October 2004, GRUR 2005, 431 – *Hotel Maritime*; German Federal Supreme Court, 30 March 2006, GRUR 2006, 513 – *Arzneimittelwerbung im Internet*; German Federal Supreme Court, 12 December 2013, GRUR 2014, 60 – *englischsprachige Pressemitteilung*. These are trade mark, unfair competition, etc. cases. For copyright cases: ECJ, 3 October 2013, Case C-170/12, – *Peter Pinckney v. KDG Mediatech AG*; ECJ, 22 January 2015, Case C-441/13 – *Pez Hejduk v. EnergieAgentur*. In these cases, to the copyright infringement through the Internet sites, the ECJ held by the interpretation of Art. 5(3) Brussels Regulation that courts have jurisdiction only to determine the damage caused in the Member State within which it is situated.
29. Düsseldorf District Court, 16 December 2008, InstGE 10, 193 – *Geogitter*. See also Düsseldorf High Court, 21 December 2006, GRUR-RR 2007, 259 – *Thermocycler*; Karlsruhe High Court, 14 January 2009, InstGE 11, 15 – *SMD-Widerstand*. In these cases, the links to the infringing product websites of foreign related companies were deemed to be an infringing offer under the Patent Act.
30. Tribunal de Grand Instance Paris *(Paris District Court)*, 14 September 2005, Case No. 03/17767.

Case No. 44

Arbitration Law – Separability and Arbitrability – Estoppel of Invalidity

*Christopher Heath and Luke Nottage**

1. Where a licensing agreement contains an arbitration clause, the ordinary courts have no jurisdiction over any civil disputes arising from this agreement, even if it has been terminated.
2. Termination of the licensing agreement ordinarily does not affect the arbitration agreement.
3. Patent invalidation procedures are not "civil disputes" that can be made subject to arbitration.

Intellectual Property High Court, 28 February 2006,
Case No. 10120 (Ne) of 2005 –
Arbitration Clause in Patent License Agreement

Taiyō Ink Mfg. Co. Ltd. v. Tamura Kaken Corporation

1. BACKGROUND

Traditionally, arbitration has been little used within Japan to resolve commercial disputes. Some commentators have viewed this phenomenon as simply reflecting "pre-modern" Japanese culture, particularly an unwillingness to subject disputes to binding "black and white" decisions.[1] But the reality was never that straightforward and certainly is not so nowadays.[2]

* This chapter includes research for the project, "Fostering a Common Culture in Cross-Border Dispute Resolution: Australia, Japan and the Asia-Pacific", supported by the Australian Commonwealth through the Australia-Japan Foundation which is part of the Department of Foreign Affairs and Trade. The authors thank Professor Tatsuya Nakamura for helpful information, although all views expressed remain our own.

1. T. KAWASHIMA, Dispute Resolution in Contemporary Japan, in: VON MEHREN (ed.), Law in Japan: The Legal Order in a Changing Society, Harvard 1963, 41. See generally E. FELDMAN, Law, Culture, and Conflict: Dispute Resolution in Postwar Japan, in: D. FOOTE (ed.), Law in Japan: A Turning Point, Seattle 2007, 50-79.
2. L. NOTTAGE, Japan's New Arbitration Law: Domestication Reinforcing Internationalisation?, 7 International Arbitration Law Review 54-60 (2004); C. TSENG, Factors Affecting the Choice of Dispute Resolution Methods in Japan (with an Emphasis on Arbitration), 24 Journal of

Domestically, private or commercially-supplied arbitration services have been unattractive partly because of the advantages of other more well-established, trusted and cost-effective dispute resolution processes. One category comprises government-supported processes, mostly involving mediation services, although a scheme established after World War II to resolve construction disputes involves some arbitration as well as mostly mediation cases.[3] A second category comprises court processes, which of course enjoy financial support from taxpayer funds as well. These processes also benefit from the flexibility that Japanese judges have to encourage settlement during proceedings (even through "caucusing" or private meetings with each party), or to encourage or order parties to refer their disputes to court-annexed mediation panels under the Civil Conciliation Act (Law No. 222/1951).[4] Of course, both categories may reflect some underlying *cultural* preferences in Japan, but they also developed in particular *political* contexts.[5] In addition, in the (unlikely) event that these state-supported dispute resolution procedures were significantly wound back, cost and time savings potentially available in arbitration procedures would probably make the latter much more widely used.

2. DECISION[6]

a) Facts

The Plaintiff (patentee of two patents on printing ink) and the Defendant in 2002 entered into a non-exclusive licensing agreement, under which Defendant or any of its sub-licensees was to pay a running royalty of 160 Yen for every kilo of the patented printing ink. Two years later, Defendant got in arrears with its payments. In the case of any dispute between the parties, Clause 15 of the licensing agreement envisaged an amicable settlement between the parties. If no such settlement could be reached within a reasonable period of time, the dispute was to be brought before the International Chamber of Commerce (ICC) to be settled according to its Rules of Arbitration. The licensing agreement was terminated in 2005. Subsequently, Y brought two actions for revocation of the patents before the Patent Office. X requested the Tokyo District Court to order payment of the outstanding royalties. Invoking the arbitration clause, Defendant sought dismissal of the action for lack of jurisdiction

International Arbitration 211-230 (2007) (based on a 2003 survey of companies belonging to the Japan Shipping Exchange). Compare also generally now T. TANASE, Community and the Law: A Critical Reassessment of American Liberalism and Japanese Modernity, Cheltenham 2010.

3. T. NAKAMURA, Arbitration, in: L. NOTTAGE (ed.), Business Law in Japan, Tokyo 2008, 441-59, 444.
4. Y. SATO, Commercial Dispute Processing and Japan, The Hague et al. 2001; R. NISHIKAWA, Judges and ADR in Japan, 18 Journal of International Arbitration 361-9 (2001); K. ISHIDA and Y. TAMURA, Introduction to Code of Civil Procedure, in: L. NOTTAGE (ed.), Business Law in Japan, Tokyo 2008, 323-47, 346-7.
5. See generally J. HALEY, The Myth of the Reluctant Litigant, 4 Journal of Japanese Studies 359-90 (1978); F. UPHAM, Law and Social Change in Post-War Japan, Cambridge, Mass. 1987.
6. Published in 1926 Hanrei Jihō 127 = LEX/DB28110611. English translation of the decision of the Tokyo District Court in 38 IIC 841 (2007) w. comment C. HEATH.

of the ordinary courts. The Court dismissed Plaintiff's claim, as did the Intellectual Property High Court on appeal.

b) Reasons

In dismissing the appeal, the Intellectual Property High Court gave the same reasons as those given in the ruling of the court at first instance, except for the following additional points.

1. Plaintiff asserted that, since Defendant did not apply for arbitration within 40 days of receipt of the relevant cancellation notice in accordance with Clause 12(2) of the contract, Plaintiff's claim in this suit was no longer subject to the arbitration clause prescribed in Clause 15 of the contract. Clause 12(2) of the contract prescribed, however, that cancellation of the contract would be invalidated if default in an obligation was rectified within 40 days of the written notice from one party to the other regarding the other party's default in that obligation. Also, the proviso to the same Clause merely provided that, if an application was made for arbitration during this time period, time did not run during the arbitration proceedings. It followed that even if Y did not apply for arbitration within 40 days of receipt of the cancellation notice, disputes such as whether or not there had been default in an obligation, or regarding the demand for performance of an obligation, were not excluded from the coverage of the arbitration clause.

2. Plaintiff asserted that Defendant breached the relevant agreement by not itself applying for arbitration, and that it was against the "clean hands" principle, and principles such as those of fairness and balance, for Defendant to demand the dismissal of Plaintiff's claim in this suit. However, the relevant agreement was only to "refer to arbitration in accordance with the rules of the ICC, where a dispute, argument or difference in opinion cannot be resolved within a reasonable period of time", and could not be understood to impose an obligation to proactively apply for arbitration on either party.

The District Court had ruled as follows: "... The applicable law for the contract was Japanese law, and the seat of arbitration was Tokyo. According to the Guidelines issued by the ICC on 1 January 2000, international as well as domestic disputes can be made subject to arbitration [under ICC Rules]. Only if the parties have reached an arbitration agreement can arbitral proceedings be instigated. In the case at issue, the parties agreed that current or future civil disputes that bore a legal relation to the contract for their interpretation should be brought before one or more arbitrators. In other words, an agreement in this matter can be interpreted as an agreement in accordance with sec. 2(1) of the Arbitration Act. Such an arbitration clause can be regarded as covering a civil dispute between the parties that can be settled by arbitration, and the clause is binding according to sec. 13(1) of the Arbitration Act. As it is clear that the clause related to civil disputes, and none of the grounds listed in sec. 14(1) Arbitration Act apply, there is no reason to deny validity of the clause under those exceptions.

Plaintiff alleged that the licensing agreement was terminated due to arrears in the payment of the running royalty, and that this termination meant that the arbitration clause had lost its validity. However, Y does not dispute the validity of the arbitration clause, and, to begin with, it is not clear if the default in payments led to a termination of the agreement in the first place. Even if Plaintiff were correct and the agreement was terminated due to arrears in the payment of the running royalty, and Plaintiff had given proper notice of termination, sec. 13(6) of the Arbitration Act states that: "In the event that certain provisions of an agreement that contains an arbitration clause are void, have been terminated or are invalid for other reasons, the validity of the arbitration clause remains generally unaffected". Thus, the termination of the licensing agreement does not affect the validity of the arbitration clause, which does not become void. Plaintiff therefore fails on this point.

Plaintiff further argues that Defendant has lodged two cases of patent invalidity. In this respect, Clause 6(2) the licensing agreement bars Defendant from asserting patent invalidity for the duration of the contract, for which reason the current actions of Defendant cannot be interpreted as a breach of this agreement. In addition, where there is a ground for patent invalidity in an action for revocation of the patent, the patent will be declared void by an administrative order, and this does not constitute a "civil dispute between the parties that can be settled by arbitration". By bringing a case of patent invalidity, Y has thus not breached Clause 15 of the licensing agreement. Even if Y's actions were regarded as a breach of Clause 15 of the licensing agreement, this would simply mean that the requests for patent invalidity were unlawful, but this would be insufficient to call into question the validity of the arbitration clause. For the dispute at issue, it would certainly not qualify as a ground under sec. 14(1) of the Arbitration Act, and thus Plaintiff must fail on this point as well."

3. ANALYSIS

a) Arbitration legislation, case law development and practice

The present case is remarkable as it arose in a purely domestic setting, and also because the parties escalated the dispute (seeking binding outcomes from third parties: the Tokyo District Court, the Patent Office, and potentially the arbitral tribunal). Even more unusually, they specified the ICC to administer the arbitration, even though it mostly resolves international disputes (between companies having the place of business in different countries) and the most popular institution for (non-maritime) commercial arbitrations in Japan is the Japan Commercial Arbitration Association (JCAA). Perhaps the parties agreed to arbitration to resolve their civil disputes because of familiarity with ICC arbitration from other international dealings. This case also provides a rare instance where a Japanese court was faced with an application contesting the validity and effect of the arbitration agreement, which it upheld and so declined to itself resolve the dispute – opening the way for the plaintiff instead to commence arbitral proceedings. Such applications, and other cases where parties to the courts to uphold and support the arbitral process are much more infrequent than applications to enforce awards generated by proceedings with the seat abroad.[7]

7. For example, 14 enforcement decisions were rendered by Japanese courts between March 2004 and July 2006; but there was only one case each for appointment of an arbitrator, service of an award and service of a document. See H. TEZUKA & A. HIRONAKA, Recent Trends in International Arbitration in Japan, in: The Asia-Pacific Arbitration Review 2007, 45-7 (2007).

This is usually done pursuant to sec. V of the 1958 New York Convention on the Recognition and Enforcement of Foreign Arbitral Awards, signed by Japan as early as 1959 and which Japanese courts have applied very faithfully.[8]

The judgment therefore should be welcomed by those who have been worried about the persistently low uptake of arbitration especially within Japan. Concerns were highlighted regarding domestic as well as international dispute resolution particularly in the deliberations led by the Justice System Reform Council (JSRC, 1999-2001). As part of the JSRC's suite of recommendations to reorient Japan away from a reliance on ex ante government regulation, towards more indirect socio-economic ordering through ex post relief provided primarily through the legal system at private initiative, the JSRC urged improvements in the regime for privately-supplied Alternative Dispute Resolution (ADR) as well as in court proceedings.[9]

A framework for certification and promotion of ADR services (but expressly excluding arbitration services) was duly enacted in 2004 and may now be achieving some modest success.[10] The Arbitration Act was also enacted (Law No. 138/2003), with effect from 1 March 2004, based on the 1985 UNCITRAL Model Law on International Commercial Arbitration (ML). It extended coverage to domestic as well as international arbitration agreements and proceedings, and thus was applicable to the present case;[11] but it also added some extra provisions aimed at balancing different public interests related solely to domestic settings. In particular, arbitration agreements purporting to govern individual labour related disputes are null and void, and consumers are entitled to cancel arbitration agreements with businesses "for the time being, until otherwise enacted" in order to protect the weaker party (Arts 3 and 4 of the Supplementary Provisions). By contrast, the Arbitration Act did not expressly specify whether or not disputes involving the validity of intellectual property rights, such as the patent rights at issue in this case, were "arbitrable". There is also limited statutory or case law guidance on what other matters may not be capable of resolution through arbitration, but one commentary adds: other intellectual property rights issued by the government (utility models and trademarks), anti-trust law matters, shareholders' suits against resolutions of general shareholders'

---

8. T. Tateishi, Recent Japanese Case Law in Relation to International Arbitration, 17 Journal of International Arbitration 63-75 (2000); T. Nakamura, above n. 3; T. Nakamura & L. Nottage, Japan, in: T. Ginsburg & S. Ali (eds.), Arbitration in Asia, New York 3rd ed. 2013.
9. D. Foote, Introduction and Overview: Japanese Law at a Turning Point, in: D. Foote (ed.), Law in Japan: A Turning Point, Seattle 2007, xix-xxxix; T. Kitagawa and L. Nottage, above n. 6.
10. A. Yamada, A.D.R. In Japan: Does the New Law Liberalize A.D.R. From Historical Shackles or Legalize It?, 2 Contemporary Asia Arbitration Journal 1-23 (2009); L. Nottage, New Legislative Agendas, Legal Professionals and Dispute Resolution in Australia and Japan: 2009-2010, 28 Ritsumeikan Law Review 33-85, 66-9 (2011). But see H. Irie, An Overview on the Current Status of Japanese Private Dispute Resolution – Small Impact of the ADR Act and It's Still at the Early Stage, 25 JCAA Newsletter 1 (2010), available at the website of the JCAA <http://www.jcaa.or.jp/e/arbitration/docs/news25.pdf>.
11. By contrast, many of Australia's recent revisions to the *International Arbitration Act (Cth)* probably do not apply to agreements specifying Australia as the seat, which were concluded before 6 July 2010. See L. Nottage & R. Garnett, The 2010 Amendments to the International Arbitration Act: A New Dawn for Australia?, 7 Asian International Arbitration Journal 29-53 (2011), available at the website of the SSRN <http://papers.ssrn.com/sol3/papers.cfm?abstract_id=1676604>.

meetings, administrative decisions of government agencies, and insolvency and civil enforcement procedural decisions.[12]

Japanese experts in international civil procedure and arbitration law had long urged enactment of a new statute, based primarily on the ML, to replace the quite serviceable but occasionally unusual and certainly venerable, provisions in the German-influenced Code of Civil Procedure (Law No. 29/1890).[13] The Arbitration Act did get rid of the previous possibility of ending up with two arbitrators, for example, and validated arbitral agreements concluded by exchanging "data messages" (anticipating 2006 revisions to the ML, which also liberalised "writing" requirements). More importantly, the Act provided for court decisions related to arbitral proceedings to be made by more informal and faster rulings (*kettei*) rather than judgments (*hanketsu*), allowing only one appeal from a ruling.[14] Another innovation was to clarify that arbitrators should not attempt settlement unless the parties provided consent in writing, unless they dispensed with that requirement. There had been persistent remarks, particularly on the part of jurists from common law jurisdictions since the late 1980s, that some Japanese arbitrators – rather like some Japanese judges – had tended to press for settlement relatively aggressively.[15]

However, over-enthusiastic use of "Arb-Med" had already diminished by the late 1990s.[16] In addition, in several important respects the ML-based Act is not too dissimilar to the old statute, or the Act is consistent with influential Japanese case law. For example, sec. 13(6) – quoted above and applied in this case – states that the arbitration agreement on dispute resolution and any other underlying substantive contract (like licensing) are in principle "separable"; but the Supreme Court had already established this point in 1975.[17] This help explain why the Arbitration Act could be enacted relatively quickly – some two years – after the JSRC recommendations

12. Y. Furuta & N. Iguchi, Japan, in: Global Legal Group (ed.), The International Comparative Legal Guide to International Arbitration 2008, London 2008, 55-61, 56. Other countries are also not very helpful in clarifying which matters are or are not arbitrable: see, e.g., L. Nottage & R. Garnett, The Top 20 Things to Change in or around Australia's International Arbitration Act, in: L. Nottage & R. Garnett (eds.), International Arbitration in Australia, Sydney 2010, 149-90, 152-6.
13. See, e.g., H. Ogawa, Proposed Draft of Japan's New Arbitration Law, 7 Journal of International Arbitration 33-41 (1990). The Code's arbitration provisions were left unchanged when it was otherwise comprehensively reformed in 1996. They were retained in the original 1890 Code, which was then renamed the "Law concerning Procedure for General Pressing Notice and Arbitration Procedure", accessible at the website of the Kyushu University <http://www.tomeika.jur.kyushu-u.ac.jp/arbitration/legislation.html>.
14. H. Tezuka & A. Hironaka, above n. 7.
15. C. Ragan, Arbitration in Japan: Caveat Foreign Drafter and Other Lessons, 7 Arbitration International 93-11 (1991)3; R. Thirgood, A Critique of Foreign Arbitration in Japan, 18 Journal of International Arbitration 177-89 (2001).
16. T. Nakamura, Continuing Misconceptions of International Commercial Arbitration in Japan, 18 Journal of International Arbitration 641-7 (2001). Anyway, Arb-Med is increasingly acknowledged world-wide as having a role to play in international arbitration, provided it is carried out carefully and with the participant's informed consent. See L. Nottage and R. Garnett, above n. 12, 179-84; and 'Arb-Med and New International Commercial Mediation Rules in Japan' (21 July 2010) at the blogs of the University of Sydney <http://blogs.usyd.edu.au/japaneselaw/2009/07/arbmed_and_new_international_c_1.html> (also in: L. Nottage, above n. 10, 73-7).
17. Supreme Court, 15 July 1975, Case No. 103 (Ne) of 1974, 29-6 Minshū, 1061 – *Kokusan Kinzoku Kogyo KK v. Guardlife Corp.*

were issued in 2001. Other contributing factors were that the enactment was part of a high-profile set of civil justice reforms; and the emergence of "competing" regional arbitration venues, often supported by newly-enacted ML-based legislation (such as Korea's Arbitration Act of 1999). Another possible impetus may have been the impending inauguration (from 2004) of the option for full profit-sharing partnerships for international law firms in Japan, which also triggered the consolidation and expansion of large Japanese law firms.[18]

However, precisely because Japan's Arbitration Act does not represent a large departure from earlier legislation and mainly just brings the country up to the (ML-based) "global standard", there have not yet been large quantitative changes in arbitral activity and related court proceedings. The surge in commentary on Japanese arbitration law published over 2003-6[19] has not been associated with any dramatic increase in cases filed with the JCAA, for example. This contrasts with the ongoing growth in caseloads reported by other regional venues, consolidating their "first mover" advantages.[20] Nonetheless, perhaps as in other legal fields, the Japanese courts seem to have taken the enactment as a signal to do their bit in trying to make arbitration - even within Japan - a more attractive dispute resolution option. The decisions in the present case, insisting that the parties should abide by their decision to have civil disputes heard only through the agreed arbitral procedure, represent one recent example among several.[21] This is in conformity with international practice: One of the main issues of dispute between the parties may be precisely the validity of the

18. See generally K.-W. CHAN, The Emergence of Large Law Firms in Japan: Impact on Legal Professional Ethics, 11 Legal Ethics 154-180 (2009).
19. Just in English, see L. NOTTAGE, above n. 2; D. A. LIVDAHL, Cultural and Structural Aspects of International Commercial Arbitration in Japan, 20 Journal of International Arbitration 375-386 (2003); N. T. BRASLOW, Contractual Stipulation for Judicial Review and Discovery in United States-Japan Arbitration Contracts, 27 Seattle University Law Review 659-720 (2004); M. KONDO et al., Arbitration Law of Japan, Tokyo 2004; G. MCALINN & L. NOTTAGE, Changing the (JCAA) Rules: Improving International Commercial Arbitration in Japan, 18 ZJapanR/J.Japan.L 23-36 (2004); S. NAKANO, International Commercial Arbitration under the New Arbitration Law of Japan., 20 Japanese Annual of International Law 96-118 (2004); R. NISHIKAWA, Arbitration Law Reform in Japan, 21 Journal of International Arbitration 303-308 (2004); H. ODA, Arbitration Law Reform in Japan, 18 ZJapanR/J.Japan.L 5-22 (2004); D. ROUGHTON, A Brief Review of the Japanese Arbitration Law, 1 Asian International Arbitration Journal 127-140 (2005); Y. SATO, The New Arbitration Law in Japan: Will It Cause Changes in Japanese Conciliatory Arbitration Practices?, 22 Journal of International Arbitration 141-148 (2005); A. TAKAKUWA, Arbitration, in: Y. TANIGUCHI et al. (eds.), Civil Procedure in Japan, New York 2005, chapter 12; Y. TANIGUCHI & T. NAKAMURA, Japan, in: INTERNATIONAL COUNCIL ON COMMERCIAL ARBITRATION. ARBITRATION (ed.), International Handbook on Commercial Arbitration, The Hague 2005, 1-38 (updated 2010); K. IWASAKI, Key Features of New Japanese Arbitration Law, 2 Asian International Arbitration Journal 76-88 (2006).
20. L. NOTTAGE & R. GARNETT, above n. 11, 10-11 and 32-33. Australia is also still struggling to attract more than a handful of international commercial arbitration cases each year, despite adopting the ML in 1989 and revising its legislative framework further in 2010.
21. T. NAKAMURA, above n. 3; Y. TANIGUCHI & T. NAKAMURA, Japan, in: M. MOSER et al. (eds.), Arbitration in Asia, New York 2008, JAP-1-30; and the case notes at the website of the Kyushu University <http://www.tomeika.jur.kyushu-u.ac.jp/arbitration/courtcases.html>.

licensing agreement.[22] For that reason, arbitration clause and licensing agreement are regarded as two separate agreements.

b) Arbitrability of patent validity claims

Admittedly, the Courts might have gone further, to hold that disputes over patent validity were instead arbitrable. They could have reasoned that:

a) the parties probably intended the arbitrators to resolve such disputes, closely linked with the fundamental question of whether the licensee should have to pay royalties related to the licensor's patents, rather than having a costly and public separate proceeding on validity disputes (through the Patent Office, and indeed possibly the Japanese courts[23]); and
b) there exist sufficient public interests to interpret "civil dispute" expansively in secs. 2 and 13 of the Arbitration Act (namely, cost-efficiency in dispute resolution, funded more from private parties than through taxpayers' funds, and the potential to promote ADR more generally – in line with JSRC recommendations and subsequent government policy).

However, this would have pushed the boundaries of statutory interpretation, and the public interests involved are difficult to assess.[24] That is why different countries continue to adopt different approaches to the question of arbitrability of claims about the validity of intellectual property rights.[25] Leaving the issue to be revisited by the

22. For Germany: SCHWAB/WALTER, Schiedsgerichtsbarkeit *(Arbitration)*, 7th ed. Munich 2005, chapter 4 marginal note 17.
23. See Japanese Supreme Court, 11 April 2000, Case No. 364 (O) of 1998 – *Kilby III*, in this volume Case No. 50.
24. For various views expressed among Japanese commentators on this point, see also T. NAKAMURA & L. NOTTAGE, above n. 8.
25. See e.g. L. BOO, Arbitrability of Intellectual Property Disputes, in: Proceedings of 4th AIPPI Forum in Singapore, 4 – 6 October 2007, available at the website of the AIPPI <https://www.aippi.org/?sel=meetings&cf=4forumsingapore> (with further references comparing especially the situation in Singapore, Switzerland and the United States); G. BORN, International Commercial Arbitration, Vol. 1, Alphen aan den Rijn 2009, 805-8. See also recently *Larkden Pty Limited v. Lloyd Energy Systems Pty Limited* [2011] NSWSC 268 (1 April 2011), available at the website of the Australasian Legal Information Institute <http://www.austlii.edu.au/au/cases/nsw/NSWSC/2011/268.html>. The Supreme Court of New South Wales dismissed the licensor's claim and confirmed that the arbitrator in a domestic arbitral proceeding retained jurisdiction to make a declaratory decision regarding interpretation of a licencing agreement, Hammerschlag J. stated that:

    "[66] The powers to grant a patent, to make a declaration of eligibility and to decide the case where the grant of a standard patent is opposed, are powers conferred by the provisions of the Patents Act on, and only on, the Commissioner of Patents or the Federal Court on appeal from the Commissioner. These statutory powers cannot, by private arrangement, be conferred by parties on an arbitrator. [67] There is, however, no impediment to the parties investing in the arbitrator power to resolve a dispute as between themselves as to their rights in and entitlements to a patent application, or for that matter an invention."

    The outcome, reasoning and situation show remarkable similarities to the Japanese case law, although in *Larkden* the licensee had not (yet) applied to the authorities or Federal Court to determine the validity of the patents giving rise to dispute with the licensor.

legislature is understandable, particularly given that the Japanese government has agendas not just to expand ADR, but also to improve the formal court system as well as to develop an integrated intellectual property policy program.[26]

This case instead takes the view that while issues of infringement, damages and injunctive relief may be brought within the ambit of an arbitration clause, this is not so for patent invalidation actions, as these are considered administrative in nature. In Japan, these disputes have to be brought before the Patent Office that has exclusive jurisdiction over matters of invalidation. As a consequence of the *Kilby* decision, the courts may refuse the enforcement of a patent held revocable (sec. 104[bis] Patent Act), a provision that applies to civil litigation before the courts that in order to determine revocability are assisted by personnel from the Patent Office. Yet the *Kilby* ruling in expressing a general principle of equity (it is an abuse to enforce obviously voidable patents) should also be applicable in arbitration proceedings. Thus, while it is permissible to insert a clause that prevents the licensee from challenging the patent,[27] bringing an invalidation action before the Patent Office may be a breach of the non-challenge clause, allowing for a court injunction preventing such action. But an action for invalidity does not breach the arbitration clause, as this is not considered a matter that may be subjected to arbitration.

While arbitration clauses may be useful in a number of ways, not least because ready enforceability of arbitral arbitration awards under the New York Convention or (largely equivalent) provisions in sec. 45 of the Arbitration Act, they may also have drawbacks – quite apart from the inconvenience of the arbitrators not being able to determine any issues raised about the validity of Japanese patents. For one thing, court procedures in Japan have become so efficient that a first-instance decision in intellectual property matters is now handed down in about 14 months.[28] In addition, arbitration clauses can benefit a recalcitrant party unless drafted rather clearly. In one case, it was agreed that in case of a dispute, each party should nominate one

26. See generally e.g. SECRETARIAT OF INTELLECTUAL PROPERTY STRATEGY HEADQUARTERS, Overview of "Intellectual Property Strategic Program 2010", 35 AIPPI Journal of the Japanese Group (English Edition) 255 (2010); R. TAPLIN, Intellectual Property and the New Global Japanese Economy, London et al. 2009; S. MATSUI, The Intellectual Property High Court of Japan, in: A. HARDING & P. NICHOLSON (eds.), New Courts in Asia, London 2009, 83-100; P. GANEA & S. NAGAOKA, Japan, in: P. GOLDSTEIN et al. (eds.), Intellectual Property in Asia – Law, Economics, History and Politics, Berlin 2009, 129-153.
27. However, no-challenge clauses may give rise to antitrust concerns. The Japan Fair Trade Commission's *Guidelines for the Use of Intellectual Property under the Antimonopoly Act*, Tokyo 2007 (as amended in 2016), state the following in this respect (<https://www.jftc.go.jp/en/legislation_gls/imonopoly_guidelines_files/IPGL_Frand.pdf>

    "(vii) No-contest obligation

    Imposing an obligation by a licensor on its licensees not to contest the validity of rights for licensed technology (Note 14) is recognized to have aspects to promote competition by facilitating technology transactions and is unlikely to reduce competition directly. However, it may constitute an unfair trade practices when it is found to tend to impede fair competition by continuing rights that should be invalidated and by restricting the use of the technology associated with the said rights. (Paragraph (13) of the General Designation) In principle, stipulating termination right of the agreement for the technology with any licensee that challenges the validity of rights may not constitute unfair trade practices."
28. R. TOKUNAGA, The Reform of Japanese Judicial System to make an IP-based Nation, in: HANSEN/SCHÜSSLER (eds.), Patent Practice in Japan and Europe, Kluwer Law 2011, 61.

arbitrator. As the Defendant failed to do so, the Plaintiff sued. The court – perhaps correctly – held that in such case, the Plaintiff was not entitled to nominate both arbitrators, and thus only ordered the Defendant to select an arbitrator as was stipulated in the arbitration agreement.[29] This, however, makes the whole process extremely cumbersome.

4. COMPARATIVE REMARKS

In the international dispute resolution arena, specific government-supported schemes or court processes become inapplicable or relatively unattractive. Unsurprisingly, therefore, we find that Japanese companies have long been prepared to agree to arbitration clauses in cross-border contracts, and to fight out disputes in arbitral proceedings – and even litigation related to such proceedings or arbitration agreements.[30] The distinctive feature here, though, is that this has predominantly involved arbitration with the seat outside Japan. Originally this involved "core" Western venues such as the London (especially for maritime disputes), New York, Geneva and Paris (main venues for arbitrations administered the ICC). Nowadays Japanese companies increasingly agree to having the arbitral seat in regional centres such as Beijing (or other parts of China), Seoul, Hong Kong and (to a lesser extent) Singapore.[31] These venues, and more recently Seoul, have seen rising caseloads especially over the last decade. This partly reflects the growth of regional economic activity, but it also

29. Tokyo District Court, 25 January 1958, Case No. 3730 (Wa) of 1957, 142 Hanrei Jihō, 22. See also P. GODWIN, "Finger-Pointing" Arbitration Clauses – Don't Use Them!, in: Herbert Smith – Dispute Avoidance Newsletter 43 (March 2006), available at the website of the law firm Herbert Smith <http://www.herbertsmith.com/NR/rdonlyres/F5762A87-D8B7-40BF-92A8-A6C68B9C1CE6/1894/Newsletter43 EnglishMarch2006.pdf>.

30. L. NOTTAGE, Educating Transnational Commercial Lawyers for the 21st Century: Towards the Vis Arbitration Moot in 2000: Part Two, 66-3 Hosei Kenkyū [Kyushu University] F1-F32 (1999); C. TSENG, above n. 2; T. KITAGAWA & L. NOTTAGE, Globalization of Japanese Corporations and the Development of Corporate Legal Departments: Problems and Prospects, in: W. ALFORD (ed.), Raising the Bar, Cambridge, Mass. 2007, 201-85. However, some empirical research suggests that Japanese parties are somewhat more likely to be respondents than claimants, overall across major venues surveyed over 2005-7, in international arbitration proceedings. See WHITE & CASE, "Evolving Japanese Attitudes to International Arbitration and Litigation for Dispute Resolution", ABA International Legal Exchange Program seminar, Temple University, Tokyo, 9 July 2008 (topics listed at the Temple University of Japan <http://www.tuj.ac.jp/newsite/main/law/news/event20080709.html>, Powerpoint presentation on file with the authors).

31. This can be inferred from the WHITE & CASE survey (*ibid.*), assuming that cases administered by regional arbitration centres have the seat in their respective states. Out of around 100 arbitration cases involving Japanese companies reported each year over 2005-7, 15% were administered by CIETAC (which only administers arbitrations with the seat in China), 3% by HKIAC and 5% by (Seoul-based) KCAB. Six cases involving Japanese firms were administered by (Singapore-based) SIAC over 2002-4, but none over 2005-7. Around 43% were administered by the (US-based) AAA-ICDR, 2% by the (London-based) LCIA, and 20% by the (Paris-based) ICC – some of which probably had the seat in Asia, rather than the US or Europe. See also, e.g., Supreme Court of Victoria at Melbourne, 20 December 2000, *Toyo Engineering Corporation v. John Holland Pty Ltd.* [2000] VSC 553 (involving arbitration with the seat in Singapore); Yokohama District Court, 25 August 1999, Case No. 3851 (Wa) of 1998, 1707 Hanrei Jihō 146 (one of several CIETAC awards from China enforced in Japan).

undermines some earlier broader assertions that the "Asian way" is fundamentally averse to resolving disputes through binding decisions based on legal considerations.[32]

Nonetheless, while the willingness of Japanese corporations to agree to international arbitration is steadily increasing, they still seem to place relatively low priority on securing the "home court advantage" by pressing hard for Japan to be the seat. Japanese corporations are more likely to believe that they will be the subject of claims, rather than having to initiate them, which is why we still often see "finger-pointing" clauses whereby each party agrees to commence proceedings in the other party's jurisdiction.[33] That attitude may also be related to the lower profile of legal departments and outside lawyers in corporate activity in Japan, although this has gradually expanded over the last two decades.[34] Again, all this could be seen as a persistently "cultural" trait[35] – indeed, one stronger than in several other Asian countries nowadays – but it could also represent a plausible cost-benefit assessment. After all, international arbitration has become increasingly expensive and time-consuming, in tandem with the rise of large law firms active in the field which increasingly adopt a "billable-hours" or "time-charge" approach.[36] Actually initiating arbitration to resolve a dispute could well involve "throwing good money after bad". Using the arbitral clause as leverage for a negotiated settlement, better preserving the business relationship in the expectation of recouping losses over the longer term, can make good sense even in today's more competitive business environment both within and outside Japan.[37]

It is notable that despite a number of attempts to make forms of alternative dispute resolution such as arbitration or mediation more attractive in the last 20 years or so, success has been rather limited. For mediation, it has been observed that the "critical deficiency in mediation as prescribed by law and carried out by the

32. L. NOTTAGE & R. GARNETT, Introduction, in: L. NOTTAGE & R. GARNETT (eds.), International Arbitration in Australia, Sydney 2010, 1, 6-11; S. GREENBERG et al., International Commercial Arbitration: An Asia-Pacific Perspective, Cambridge; New York 2011, 33-53.

33. See e.g. P. GODWIN, "Finger-Pointing" Arbitration Clauses – Don't Use Them!, in: Herbert Smith – Dispute Avoidance Newsletter 43 (March 2006), available at the website of the law firm Herbert Smith <http://www.herbertsmith.com/NR/rdonlyres/F5762A87-D8B7-40BF-92A8-A6C68B9C1CE6/1894/Newsletter43 EnglishMarch2006.pdf>, noting a sample 'finger-pointing' clause at the website of JCAA <http://www.jcaa.or.jp/arbitration-j/jyoukou/clause.html>.

34. T. KITAGAWA & L. NOTTAGE, above n. 30.

35. Cf. generally T. COLE, Commercial Arbitration in Japan: Contributions to the Debate on "Japanese Non-Litigiousness", 40 New York University Journal of International Law and Politics 29-114 (2007).

36. L. NOTTAGE, Addressing International Arbitration's Ambivalence: Hard Lessons from Australia, in: K. BHATIA et al. (eds.), Arbitration Practice and Discourse: Issues, Challenges and Prospects, Dartmouth 2012.

37. This is even more plausible for cross-border investment contracts, which may explain the paucity of direct and even indirect investor-state arbitration claims by Japanese firms despite the arbitration rights increasingly available through investment treaties. See S. HAMAMOTO, A Passive Player in International Investment Law: Typically Japanese?, in: V. BATH & L. NOTTAGE (eds.), Investment Law and Dispute Resolution Law and Practice in Asia, London 2011, 53-67. Asian parties, especially Asian investor claimants, are generally under-represented in investor-state arbitration filings and awards; but this too may be changing as "institutional barriers" to contesting claims begin to come down. See L. NOTTAGE & J. R. WEERAMANTRY, Investment Arbitration in Asia: Five Perspectives on Law and Practice, in: V. BATH & L. NOTTAGE (eds.), Foreign Investment and Dispute Resolution Law and Practice in Asia, London 2011, 25-52.

institutional mechanisms in the field of intellectual property is the lack of accessibility. Although much effort has been made to promote mediation at every level, any visible success is yet to be confirmed."[38] It is also questionable whether governments should actively engage in the promotion of alternative forms of dispute resolution given their (intended) lack of transparency, their incomplete institutional guarantees of judicial independence and their limited jurisdiction over issues of validity.

38. A. WECHS HATANAKA, Optimising Mediation of Intellectual Property Law, 49 IIC 384, 405.

Case No. 45

Infringement of a US Patent and Applicable Law

Yuko Nishitani

---

1. **A claim for injunctive relief and destruction of infringing goods is related to the effects of a patent and governed by the law of the registration country. Adjudication of such claim would run counter to the principle of territoriality.**
2. **A damage claim based on the infringement of a US patent is considered an act of tort governed by US law. While Japanese law is cumulatively applicable thereto, it is no tort to actively induce a patent infringement outside the country of registration.**

Supreme Court, 26 September 2002 – Case No. 580 (Ju) of 2000 – *Card Reader*

Fujimoto v. Neuron Co. Ltd.

---

1. BACKGROUND

A cross-border patent infringement, where preparatory or inducing acts take place outside the country of registration, causes a difficult question of how to determine the international jurisdiction to adjudicate, as well as the law governing the patent infringement. The underlying case concerned a US patent infringement, whereby the originating acts of producing and exporting the products took place in Japan. While the international jurisdiction of Japanese courts was taken for granted, the Supreme Court for the first time tackled with the issues of designating the applicable law. Interestingly enough, it distinguished between claims for injunction and destruction of products, and the claim for damages.

For the purpose of conflict of laws, the Supreme Court namely characterised the claim for injunction and destruction of products as a matter of the effects of patent to be governed by US law. There are no written rules in this respect, but the Court relied on the characteristics and specificities of patents. Sec. 271(b) and sec. 284 of the US Patent Act enjoin preparatory or inducing conducts of a US patent infringement, including those taking place outside the US territory. The question was whether such an extraterritorial application of the US patent law was admissible in light of public policy of Japan under ex-sec. 33 *Hōrei*.

On the other hand, the Supreme Court characterised the claim for damages concerning the infringement of the US patent as a matter of tort. Pursuant to ex-sec. 11(1) *Hōrei*, the Court held US law to be applicable. However, due to the "double actionability" principle under ex-sec. 11(2) *Hōrei*, Japanese law was cumulatively applied. The question was whether the preparatory or inducing acts by the parent company in Japan could be held unlawful pursuant to secs. 709 and 719(2) Civil Code, while the actual infringing acts by selling the products on the US territory were committed by the US subsidiary that was not involved in this suit.

Secs. 11 and 33 *Hōrei*:[1]

Sec. 11 *Hōrei*[2]

(1) The formation and effect of claims arising from agency by necessity (negotiorum gestio), unjust enrichment, and tort shall be governed by the law of the place where the events causing the claims occurred.

(2) The preceding paragraph shall not apply where the events that comprise the tort occurred abroad and do not constitute a tort under Japanese law.

(3) Even where the events that occurred abroad constitute a tort under Japanese law, the injured person may not demand recovery of damages or any other remedy not available under Japanese law.

Sec. 33 *Hōrei*[3]

Where a case shall be governed by a foreign law but application of those rules would be contrary to public policy (ordre public), those rules shall not apply.

---

1. Translation by K.ANDERSON AND YASUHIRO OKUDA, Horei, Act on the Application of Laws, Law No. 10 of 1898 (as amended 2001), available at the website of the University of Hawaii <http://blog.hawaii.edu/aplpj/files/2011/11/APLPJ_03.1_okuda.pdf> (last visited on 25 August 2018).
2. Now secs. 17 (with modifications) and 22(1), (2) of the Act on General Rules for Application of Laws ("AGRAL"), Law No. 78 of 2006. For the translation below, *see* M. DOGAUCHI *et al.*, Act on General Rules for Application of Laws, 50 Japanese Annual of International Law 87 ff. (2007); *see also* K. ANDERSON/Y. OKUDA, Translation of Japan's Private International Law: Act on the General Rules of Application of Laws, 8 Yearbook of Private International Law (2006), 427 ff.; 23 ZJapanR/J.Japan.L. 227 ff. (2007) = 8-1 Asian-Pacific Law & Policy Journal 138 ff. (2006); Y. SAKURADA/Y. NISHITANI/E. SCHWITTEK, Gesetz über allgemeinen Regeln über die Anwendung von Gesetzen (Rechtsanwendungsgesetz) *(Act on general rules for application of laws)*, 22 ZJapanR/J.Japan.L. (2006), 269 ff. = IPRax 2007, 560 ff. = 34 ZfRV 227 ff. (2006); Y. OKUDA/N. TOUBKIN, Loi sur les règles générales d'application des lois *(Act on general rules for application of laws)*, 134 Journal du droit international (Clunet) 921 ff. (2007).

   Sec. 17 [Torts]:

   The formation and effect of claims arising from a tort shall be governed by the law of the place where the results of the infringing act are produced. However, if it was not foreseeable under normal circumstances that the results would be produced at that place, the law of the place where the infringing act occurred shall apply.

   Sec. 22 [Limitation on Torts by Public Policy (Ordre public)]:

   (1) If the rights and obligations relating to a tort shall be governed by a foreign law, claims for damages or any other remedies under that law may not be claimed if the actions causing the tort are not unlawful under Japanese law.

   (2) If the rights and obligations relating to a tort shall be governed by a foreign law, even if the actions causing the tort are unlawful both under that foreign law and Japanese law, the victim may not claim any greater recovery of damages or any other remedies than those available under Japanese law.
3. Now sec. 42 AGRAL.

Secs. 709 and 719 Civil Code:[4]

Sec. 709 (Damages in Torts)

A person who has intentionally or negligently infringed any right of others, or legally protected interest of others, shall be liable to compensate any damages resulting in consequence.

Sec. 719 (Liability of Joint Tortfeasors)

(1) If more than one person has inflicted damages on others by their joint tortious acts, each of them shall be jointly and severally liable to compensate for those damages. The same shall apply if it cannot be ascertained which of the joint tortfeasors inflicted the damages.

(2) The provisions of the preceding paragraph shall apply to any person who incited or was an accessory to the perpetrator, by deeming him/her to be one of the joint tortfeasors.

2. DECISION[5]

a) Facts

In 1985, a Japanese national residing in Japan (the Plaintiff) obtained a US patent for an invention named "FM Signal Demodulating Apparatus". A Japanese company (the Defendant), with its principal place of business in Japan, owned the parallel Japanese patent. From approximately 1986 to 1991, the Defendant produced in Japan "Card Reader No. 1" and later, from 1992 on, "Card Reader No. 2". These products were exported to the US and sold there by the Defendant's wholly-owned US subsidiary.

Card Reader No. 1 was within the technical scope of the Plaintiff's invention protected by his US patent. The Plaintiff argued that Card Reader No. 2 was also within this scope, and that the Defendant induced the infringement of his US patent pursuant to sec. 271(b) of the US Patent Act. He filed a claim against the Defendant seeking the following remedies: (a) an injunction against the production of Card Reader No. 2 for the purpose of export to the US, export of Card Reader No. 2 to the US, and inducement of the Defendant's US subsidiary to import and sell them in the US; (b) the destruction of the Defendant's products in her possession in Japan; (c) compensatory damages.

---

4. Civil Code, Law No. 89 of 1898 (as amended); *see* the website of the Japanese Law Translation provided by the Ministry of Justice <http://www.japaneselawtranslation.go.jp/> (last visited on 25 August 2018).
5. Published in 56-7 Minshū 1551 = 1802 Hanrei Jihō 19 = 1107 Hanrei Times 80. English translation in 46 Japanese Annual of International Law 168 (2003). On this decision, see also Y. NISHITANI, Cross-Border Patent Infringement in Japan – Comment on the Supreme Court's Decision of September 26, 2002 ["Card Reader" case] –, 16 ZJapanR/J.Japan.L. 251 ff. (2004); *idem*, Infringement of a US Patent – Patent Law – Applicable Law (Supreme Court, 26 September 2002 – 'Card Reader' with comment), in: M. BÄLZ et al. (eds.), Business Law in Japan — Cases and Comments: Intellectual Property, Civil, Commercial and International Private Law: Writings in Honour of Harald Baum, Alphen aan den Rijn 2012, 679 ff.

Both the Tokyo District Court (1999)[6] and the Tokyo High Court (2000)[7] dismissed the Plaintiff's claim on the merits. The Plaintiff appealed to the Supreme Court.

b) Reasons

(1) The appellant's claim seeking (a) injunction against infringing acts and (b) destruction of products is based on the property right of a private person. It concerns a Japanese national domiciled in Japan and a Japanese company whose principal place of business is in Japan, and the latter party's activities in Japan are being questioned. However, because this claim draws upon a property right that is granted under US patent law, it includes a foreign element and therefore requires the determination of applicable law.

The "principle of territoriality" of patent law means that the formation, transfer and effects of each country's patents are determined by each country's laws, and that the effects of patents do not extend beyond the border of the country concerned.[8] In other words, every country regulates, based on its own industrial policy, in which procedure what kind of effects shall be conferred on an invention. The effects of a Japanese patent are restricted to the territory of Japan. However, this does not exempt the judge from determining the applicable law pursuant to *Hōrei*[9] when a dispute arises concerning a foreign patent between private persons.

The claims for (a) injunction and (b) destruction of products pursuant to a US patent draw upon its exclusive effects. These claims are different from a tort action that seeks, in light of justice or fairness, (c) compensation for damages caused to the victim in the past. They should, therefore, be characterised as a matter of the effects of patent. Since neither the *Hōrei* nor other statutes contain any legal provisions governing the effects of patent, the law concerned should, as a matter of *jōri* (reasonableness), be the law of the country of registration, namely the law of the country that has the closest connection to the patent. Hence, the law governing the (a) injunction and (b) destruction of products based on the US patent is US law.

Sec. 271(b) of the US Patent Act stipulates that someone who actively induces infringement of a patent shall be liable as an infringer. This provision is interpreted as also covering an active inducement committed outside the US territory, so long as the directly infringing conduct takes place within the US borders. Furthermore, Sec. 283 of the US Patent Act provides that courts can order an injunction as a remedy. It is construed as allowing courts to order the destruction of the products infringing the patent as well. However, issuing a court order that enjoins certain conducts in Japan

---

6. Tokyo District Court, 22 April 1999, Case No. 23109 (Wa) of 1997, 56-7 Minshū 1575 = 1691 Hanrei Jihō 131.
7. Tokyo High Court, 27 January 2000, Case No. 3059 (Ne) of 1999, 56-7 Minshū 1600 = 1711 Hanrei Jihō 131.
8. The judgment quotes Supreme Court 1 July 1997, Case No. 1988 (O) of 1995, 51-6 Minshū 2299 – *BBS*. (Case No. 32 in this volume.)
9. *Hōrei* (Law No. 10 of 21 June 1898) has been substituted by the AGRAL (*supra* note 2 and 3); for the background of the reform, *see, inter alia,* Y. NISHITANI, Internationales Privat- und Zivilverfahrensrecht *(International private and civil procedure law)*, in: BAUM/BÄLZ (eds.), Handbuch Japanisches Handels- und Wirtschaftsrecht (*Compedium on Japanese Business and Commercial Law*), Köln 2011, para. 7 (with further reference).

based on the US patent would mean extending the effects of US patent extraterritorially to Japan. This would run counter to the principle of territoriality. In addition, Japan and the US have not signed a treaty that provides for mutual recognition of patents. Thus, granting these remedies pursuant to US patent law would be incompatible with the fundamental principles of Japanese patent law and violate Japan's public policy under sec. 33 *Hōrei*. The appellant's claim for injunction and destruction of products is to be dismissed.

(2) The appellant's claim for (c) compensatory damages based on the infringement of the US patent is not a specific question of patent law, but concerns a civil remedy for the infringement of property right. This claim should therefore be characterised as tort. It is governed by the law designated by sec. 11(1) *Hōrei*.

With regard to the claim for damages, the place of tort in the sense of sec. 11(1) *Hōrei* should be interpreted as indicating the US, in which the directly infringing act was committed and its result was felt. This is because (i) the result of the appellee's conduct in Japan to actively induce the infringement of the US patent occurred in the US, and (ii) the application of the US law does not run counter to the appellee's foreseeability, so long as the appellee had intended to have its products imported and sold in the US by its US subsidiary.

Sec. 284 of the US Patent Law provides for compensatory damages as a civil remedy. Those who have actively induced infringement of a US patent in Japan could therefore be considered as liable pursuant to sec. 271(b) and sec. 284 of the US Patent Act. However, Japanese law is cumulatively applicable, according to sec. 11(2) *Hōrei*. The question is whether the appellee's active inducement of patent infringement, effectuated outside the country of registration, constitutes a tort under Japanese patent and civil law. Unlike sec. 271(b) of the US Patent Act, Japanese law lacks a provision that enables to extend the effects of Japanese patent to an extraterritorial active inducement of infringement. So long as there is no legislation or treaty in this sense, such an act cannot be regarded as illegal or constitute a tort. Since the appellee's conduct is "not unlawful according to Japanese law" in the sense of sec. 11(2) *Hōrei*, the appellant's claim for damages is to be dismissed.

(3) Hence, the majority of the Supreme Court Justices affirmed the judgment of the Tokyo High Court and dismissed the appellant's claims. Judge *Ijima* delivered a supplementary opinion and Justice *Machida* an opinion. On the other hand, Judge *Fujii* delivered a dissenting opinion concerning the claim for damages as follows:

In applying Japanese law cumulatively pursuant to sec. 11(2) *Hōrei*, the existence of the US patent is taken for granted. We should examine whether the infringement of an equivalent right in Japan would be regarded as a tort. According to secs. 709 and sec. 719(2) Civil Code, an active inducement of patent infringement is a solicitation or assistance of a wrongful act. The one who committed the act is regarded as a joint tortfeasor and is liable for damages together with the direct infringer. Thus, the appellee's conduct fulfilled the requirements of tort under Japanese law. This consideration does not contravene the principle of territoriality, as it does not extend the effects of the US patent to conducts effectuated outside the country of registration. It only recognises the appellee's joint liability with the direct infringer for the direct infringement taking place in the country of registration. Even if we were to imagine an equivalent case in which active inducement of the infringement of a Japanese patent took place outside Japan, it would constitute a tort under Japanese law as an act of joint tortfeasor. The judgment of the Tokyo High Court contains obvious violations of law. It should therefore be reversed and remanded.

3. ANALYSIS

a) Jurisdictional rules in Japan

(1) General principles

The international adjudicatory jurisdiction of Japan was first developed by case law. In 1981, the Supreme Court held[10] that there were no general rules on international jurisdiction in national laws, treaties or established international law. It should therefore be determined based on *jōri* (reason) in light of the balance of interests between the parties, as well as due and expeditious process. So far as a specific court in Japan had the territorial jurisdiction pursuant to national jurisdictional rules, the international jurisdiction was presupposed (doctrine of "reverse presumption"). Lower courts introduced an exception to this rule, allowing judges to decline jurisdiction under "special circumstances" to avoid exorbitant jurisdiction, which was eventually confirmed by the Supreme Court in 1997.[11]

This general framework has been upheld in the 2011 "Act for the Amendment of the Code of Civil Procedure (CCP) and Civil Provisional Remedies Act"[12] that adopted rules on international jurisdiction in civil and commercial matters. The general jurisdiction is based on the domicile or principal place of business of the Defendant (sec. 3bis (1) and (3) CCP). Special jurisdiction is conferred on the basis of, inter alia, the place of performance of the contractual obligation (sec. 3ter Item (i) CCP), the location of the object of the claim or, in the case of monetary claim, the location of the asset to be seized (Item (iii)), branch office for claims concerning

10. Supreme Court, 16 October 1981, Case No. 130 (O) of 1980, 35-7 Minshū 1224 – *Malaysian Airlines*.
11. Supreme Court, 11 November 1997, Case No. 1660 (O) of 1993, 51-10 Minshū 4055 – *Family;* for an overview, Y. NISHITANI, *supra* note 9, para. 111 ff.; A. PETERSEN, Das internationale Zivilprozessrecht in Japan *(International Civil Procedure Law in Japan)*, Köln 2003, 41 ff.
12. Law No. 36 of 2011; for translation, *see* M. DOGAUCHI, Act for Partial Revision of Code of Civil Procedure and Civil Provisional Remedies Act, 12 Japanese Yearbook of Private International Law 225 ff. (2010) = 54 Japanese Yearbook of International Law (2011) 723 ff.; Y. OKUDA, New Provisions on International Jurisdiction of Japanese Courts, 13 Yearbook of Private International Law 369 ff. (2011); Y. NISHITANI, Neue Regelungen über die internationale Zuständigkeit in Zivil- und Handelssachen in Japan *(New legislation on international jurisdiction in civil and commercial matters in Japan)*, IPRax 2013, 298 ff. = 33 ZJapanR/J.Japan.L. 205 ff. (2012); for an overview of the reform, *see, inter alia,* the contributions in 54/55 Japanese Yearbook of International Law (2011/12); *also* Y. NISHITANI, International Jurisdiction of Japanese Courts in Comparative Perspective, 60 Netherlands International Law Review 251 ff. (2013) (with further reference); *idem*, Die internationale Zuständigkeit Japans in Zivil- und Handelssachen *(The international jurisdiction of Japan in civil and commercial matters)*, IPRax 2013, 289 ff.; *idem*, Wann sind die Gerichte in Japan zuständig? – Einführung zu den neuen internationalen Zuständigkeitsregelungen – *(When do the courts in Japan have jurisdiction? – Introduction to the new rules on international jurisdiction)*, 33 ZJapanR/J.Japan.L. 197 ff. (2012).

its activities (Item (iv)), engagement in business in Japan (Item (v)), and the place of tort (Item (viii)). Furthermore, in addition to special rules on consumers and employees (sec. 3quater CCP), exclusive jurisdiction (sec. 3quinquies CPC), objective joinder of claims (sec. 3sexies CCP), choice of court agreement (sec. 3septies CCP) and general appearance (sec. 3octies CCP) are provided for. On the other hand, jurisdiction can exceptionally be declined absent an exclusive choice of court agreement, when exercising jurisdiction would run counter to the balance of the parties' interests or hinder due and expeditious proceedings (sec. 3nonies CCP).

(2) Adjudicatory jurisdiction of patent infringement

A patent is an intellectual property right that is conferred by the authority of a country and presupposes registration. The registration or validity of patents is subject to the exclusive jurisdiction of the country of registration pursuant to sec. 3quinquies(3) CCP, the same as Article 24(4) of the Brussels Ibis Regulation.[13] On the other hand, patent infringement is a dispute where the right holder seeks remedies from the infringer. Unlike the revocation or invalidation of patent that involves administrative acts and has *erga omnes* effects, it is a litigation between private parties seeking remedies. It therefore falls within the category of tort.[14] From a practical viewpoint, granting jurisdiction at the Defendant's domicile enables an efficient implementation of remedies and consolidation of infringement disputes over parallel patents.[15] In this particular case, the judges in all instances implicitly affirmed the jurisdiction of Japan by deciding on the merits, presumably due to the Defendant's domicile in Japan. Subjecting infringement disputes to general jurisdictional rules was in line with the previous case law as well.[16]

13. Council Regulation (EC) No 1215/2012 of the European Parliament and of the Council of 12 December 2012 on jurisdiction and the recognition and enforcement of judgments in civil and commercial matters (recast), *O.J.* 2012, L 351/1.
14. Sec. 2:202 of the "CLIP Principles"; *see* EUROPEAN MAX PLANCK GROUP ON CONFLICT OF LAWS IN INTELLECTUAL PROPERTY (CLIP) (ed.), Conflict of Laws in Intellectual Property: The CLIP Principles and Commentary (Oxford 2013), para. 2:202.C01 ff.; *also* sec. 204(1), (2) of the "ALI Principles"; *see* AMERICAN LAW INSTITUTE (ed.), Intellectual Property: Principles Governing Jurisdiction, Choice of Law, and Judgments in Transnational Disputes (St. Paul/MN 2008), 47 ff.; sec. 105 of the Transparency Proposal on Jurisdiction, Choice of Law, Recognition and Enforcement of Foreign Judgments in Intellectual Property (2009); *see* J. BASEDOW et al. (ed.), Intellectual Property in the Global Arena, Tübingen 2010, 395; Art. 203 of the "Kidana Principes"; *see* S. KIDANA (ed.), Chitekizaisan no Kokusaishihō Gensoku Kenkyū – Higashi Asia kara no Nikkan Kyōdō Teian *(Studies on Principles of Private International Law on Intellectual Property Rights – A Japanese-Korean Joint Proposal from East Asian Points of View)*, Tokyo 2012, 138 f. (principles and comments in English).
15. See S. CHAEN, Gaikoku Tokkyo Shingai Jiken no Kokusai Saiban Kankatsu *(International Jurisdiction with regard to foreign patent infringement cases)*, 21 Nihon Kōgyō Shoyūken-hō Gakkai Nenpō, 59 ff., 73 ff. (1998).
16. Tokyo District Court, 12 June 1953, Case No. 314 (Wa) of 1939, 4-6 Kaminshū 847 – *Manchurian Patent*; Tokyo District Court, 14 May 2001, Case No. 16175 (Wa) of 1999, 1754 Hanrei Jihō 148 – *Ueno Seiyaku*; Tokyo District Court, 16 October 2003, Case No. 1943 (Wa) of 2000, 1874 Hanrei Jihō 23 – *Coral Sand* (Case No. 42 in this volume); in this sense, also the case law (*infra* note 18); *see* S. CHAEN/T. KONO/D. YOKOMIZO, Jurisdiction in Intellectual Property Cases: The Transparency Proposal, in: BASEDOW et al. (ed.), *supra* note 14, 94 ff.; Y. HONMA/S. NAKANO/H.

Also under the current statute, jurisdiction in infringement disputes is conferred on the Defendant's domicile (sec. 3bis CCP) and place of tort. The place of tort covers both *locus damni* and *locus delicti commissi* (sec. 3ter, Item (viii) CCP).[17] *Locus damni* is the country of registration in which patent is effective and damage is felt. Pursuant to this provision, the *locus damni*-jurisdiction is exceptionally denied if it was unforeseeable under normal circumstances that the results of the wrongful act would come into effect at that place. *Locus delicti commissi* should be interpreted as the place where the tortfeasor acted or induced the infringement, including acts taken outside the country of registration. So far as the infringing result occurs in the country of registration, granting jurisdiction at the place of extraterritorial preparatory or contributory acts serves for effective remedies, especially injunctions.[18]

An objective joinder of claims between the same parties is possible when the claims are closely related to each other (sec. 3sexies CCP). Furthermore, recent doctrine and case law had started to permit the joinder of Plaintiffs or Defendants so far as the object and legal basis of the dispute are common among parties,[19] which found its way to the statutory rule in 2011 (sec. 3sexies CCP). In light of these rules, the consolidation of claims should be approved in parallel patent infringement, including those caused by a parent company and its subsidiaries in different countries ("spider in the web" doctrine).[20] In Japan, an exorbitant jurisdiction can be avoided by exceptionally declining jurisdiction based on "special circumstances" (sec. 3nonies CCP).

An important question is whether courts having jurisdiction over the infringement of a foreign patent can incidentally decide on the validity issue when raised as a defence. The European Court of Justice denied this in 2006, maintaining that the

---

SAKAI, Kokusai Minji Tetsuzukihō *(International Civil Procedure Law)*, 2nd ed. Tokyo 2012, 65; S. KIDANA (ed.), *supra* note 14, 138 f.; *idem*, Kokusai chitekizaisanhō *(International Intellectual Property Law)*, Tokyo 2009, 343 ff.; Y. NISHITANI, Intellectual Property in Japanese Private International Law, 48 Japanese Annual of International Law 87 ff. (2005).

17. *See* T. SATO/Y. KOBAYASHI (ed.), Heisei 23nen Minji Soshōhō tō Kaisei: Kokusai Saiban Kankatsu Hōsei no Seibi *(2011 Reform of the CCP etc.: Legislation on International Jurisdiction)*, Tokyo 2012, 69; HŌMUSHŌ MINJIKYOKU SANJIKAN-SHITSU *(Ministry of Justice Civil Affairs Bureau, Legal Affairs Bureau)*, Kokusai Saiban Kankatsu Hōsei ni kansuru Chūkan Shian Hosoku Setsumei *(Explanatory Report on the Interim Proposal on the new Legislation on International Adjudicatory Jurisdiction)*, Tokyo 2009, 21.
18. In this sense, *also* Tokyo District Court, Case No. 5011 (Wa) of 2014, 28 April 2015, 2264 Hanrei Jiho 59; Tokyo District Court, 27 July 2017, Case No. 25969 (Wa) of 2016, the website of the courts <http://www.courts.go.jp/app/files/hanrei_jp/012/087012_hanrei.pdf>; *also* previous case law, Tokyo District Court, 28 November 2007, the website of the courts <http://www.courts.go.jp/app/files/hanrei_jp/446/035446_hanrei.pdf>; IP High Court, 15 September 2010, Case No. 10001&10002&10003 (Ne) of 2010, 1340 Hanrei Times 265 – *Motor* (Case No. 43 in this volume); in this sense, also sec. 204 (1), (2) ALI Principles. However, Article 2:202 CLIP Principles denies jurisdiction of the *locus delicti commissi* for conducts taken outside the country of registration, on the ground that they do not constitute an infringement as such due to the principle of territoriality. See C. HEINZE, A Framework for International Enforcement of Territorial Rights, in: BASEDOW et al. (ed.), *supra* note 14, 62 ff.; CLIP (ed.), *supra* note 14, para. 2:202. C04.
19. Y. SAKURADA, Shukan-teki heigō ni yoru kankatsu-ken *(Jurisdiction based on Joinder of Parties)*, in: TAKAKUWA/DOGAUCHI (ed.), Kokusai Minji Soshōhō *(International Civil Procedure Law)*, Tokyo 2002, 127 ff.; for further indication, *see* Y. NISHITANI, *supra* note 9, para. 140.
20. The European Court of Justice decided differently on 13 July 2006 in *Roche Nederland et al. v. Primus and Goldenberg* – Case C-539/03, [2006] ECR I-6535.

invalidity defence of the patent falls within the exclusive jurisdiction of its country of registration.[21] This means, however, that right holders, who typically hold parallel patents in different countries, have to seek remedies in each country of registration. This is not only cumbersome, but could also result in contradictory decisions for parallel patents. Making jurisdiction depend on a later plea of invalidity by the Defendant also contradicts the established procedural rules.[22] The infringer may even strategically raise an invalidity defence to hamper the infringement suit, without bringing an invalidation claim in the country of registration.[23] For the sake of effective remedies, Japanese courts should be allowed to incidentally decide on the validity of foreign patents with *inter partes* effects, insofar as the applicable substantive rules provide for this.[24] This would be in line with Japanese national rule that permits an incidental validity decision in infringement suit (sec. 104[ter] Patent Act),[25] independent of the invalidation by the Patent Office with *erga omnes* effects (sec. 123 Patent Act).

b) Applicable law

(1) Characterisation

In the present case, the appellant's claims for (a) injunction against production, export and inducement of infringement, as well as (b) destruction of the products were characterised as "effects of patent", whereas the claim for (c) compensatory damages was characterised as "tort". As a result, US law was applicable to (a) and (b) in the capacity of *lex loci protectionis* based on *jōri* (reasonableness), and to (c) as the law of the place of tort pursuant to sec. 11(1) *Hōrei*.

Arguably, the rationale of this distinctive characterisation lay in Japanese substantive law that subjects injunction and prevention of infringing acts as *actio negatoria* to patent law (sec. 100(1), (2) Patent Act), and damages to compensate a loss sustained in the past to tort law (sec. 709 Civil Code).[26] Such an approach, however,

21. European Court of Justice 13 July 2006, *GAT v. LuK* – Case C-4/03 [2006] ECR I-6509; *also Roche Nederland* case (*supra* note 20). This principle has been confirmed in Article 24 No. 4 Brussels I[bis] Regulation and Article 22 No. 4 of the revised Lugano Convention (Convention on jurisdiction and the recognition and enforcement of judgments in civil and commercial matters, concluded at Lugano on 30 October 2007, *O.J.* 2007, L 339/3).
22. HEINZE, *supra* note 18, 56, 60 ff.
23. In this respect, Handelsgericht des Kantons Zürich *(Commercial Court of Zürich)*, 13 October 2006, GRUR 2007, 285, rightly set a time frame for the defendant to bring an invalidation suit.
24. For the substantive law solution, SATO/KOBAYASHI (ed.), *supra* note 17, 69, 111 ff.; for granting jurisdiction without regard to the applicable substantive law, HONMA/NAKANO/SAKAI, *supra* note 16, 65 f.
25. *See* Case No. 57 in this volume.
26. *See* comments of the clerk, M. TAKABE, Saikō Saibansho Hanrei Kaisetsu Minjihen *(Commentary on Supreme Court Decisions – Civil Matters)*, vol. 2, 2002, 716 ff.; *also* R. KOJIMA/R. SHIMANAMI/M. NAGATA, Applicable Law to Exploitation of Intellectual Property Rights in the Transparency Proposal, in: BASEDOW et al. (ed.), *supra* note 14, 183. The second instance held that claims (a) and (b) concerning the effects of patent be deemed as a matter of public law without giving rise to a conflict of laws question, and claim (c) as a tort (*also* M. DOGAUCHI, Tokkyo ken shingai ni motozuku seikyū ken no junkyohō hoka *(Applicable law to the claim based on the patent infringement, etc.)*, 1246 Jurist 279 ff. (2003)). However, once granted and registered, patents can be licensed, assigned or laid in pledge as an intangible property right. Its infringement as a

contradicts the generally recognised principle that the criteria of characterisation be found in the conflict of laws itself, independent of any substantive laws.[27] While it is a matter of substantive law to design the remedies available, patent infringement as such constitutes one legal phenomenon. Besides, the distinctive characterisation runs the risk that the claims may be subject to different applicable laws that lead to a contradictory result. Also pursuant to Article 8 and 15 of the Rome II Regulation,[28] all the remedies for patent infringement, i.e., injunction and prevention of infringement as well as damages, are governed by one single applicable law. The same as in matters concerning adjudicatory jurisdiction, patent infringement should have been uniformly characterised as a tort in relation to applicable law.[29]

(2) Law governing tort

Concerning the claim (c) for damages, the Supreme Court regarded the US as the place of tort in the sense of sec. 11(1) *Hōrei*, on the grounds that the directly infringing act took place and the damage was felt there, and that the application of US law did not violate the appellee's foreseeability. On the other hand, the first and second instance held, just as Judge *Machida*'s opinion, that the place of tort was Japan, considering that the Defendant's allegedly wrongful acts were all performed in Japan.[30] These diverging results stemmed from the reasoning that the underlying patent infringement was a complex tort. Arguably, the lower courts followed the then prevailing interpretation of sec. 11(1) *Hōrei*, according to which a tort based on negligence was subject to the *lex loci delicti commissi* to control the conducts of the tortfeaser, while a tort based on strict liability was subject to the *lex loci damni* aiming at the compensation of the victim.[31]

However, a patent right has specific characteristics as the entitlement to an exclusive exploitation of invention. Since the effects of a patent right do not go beyond the border of the country of registration, its infringement always takes place in that country, even if part of the infringing acts is committed outside of it. So long as the conduct of the alleged tortfeasor does not affect the country of registration, infringement must be denied. Thus, patent infringement should not be subject to the general conflicts rules applicable to complex tort, but always governed by the law of

---

dispute between private persons is independent of the administrative procedure of conferring a patent and should therefore be subject to conflicts rules.

27. *See* Y. NISHITANI, *supra* note 9, para. 13 ff.
28. Regulation (EC) No 864/2007 of the European Parliament and of the Council of 11 July 2007 on the law applicable to non-contractual obligations (Rome II), *O.J.* 2007, L 199/40.
29. S. KIDANA, Hanrei hihyō: Tokkyo ken no kōryoku no junkyohō *(Case note: Law applicable to the effects of patent, etc.)* 129-1 Minshōhō Zasshi 118 (2003); R. KOJIMA/R. SHIMANAMI/M. NAGATA, *supra* note 26, 186.
30. Supported by K. ISHIGURO, 21 Shihō Hanrei Remarks 153 (2000).
31. Y. ORIMO, Kokusaishihō Kakuron (*Private International Law – Special Part*), 2nd ed. Tokyo 1972, 180; S. IKEHARA, Kokusaishihō, Keiei Hōgaku Zenshū: Kokusai Torihiki-hō *(Private International Law – Series on Business Law: International Business Law)*, Tokyo 1967, 377. Other authors, however, have criticised this opinion for lack of clear-cut criteria and supported the principle of *lex loci damni*. Y. TAMEIKE, Kokusaishihō Kōgi (*Lectures on Private International Law*), 3rd ed. Tokyo 2005, 396.

the country of registration.[32] The Supreme Court rightly decided to designate the U.S. law as applicable concerning the claim (c) for damages, apart from its superfluous reference to the appellee's foreseeability.

After *Hōrei* was substituted by the AGRAL in 2006,[33] detailed conflicts rules on tort in general were adopted (secs. 17 to 22 AGRAL). It left out, however, the envisaged special rule on the infringement of intellectual property rights pointing to the country of protection for lack of unanimous understanding on this connecting factor.[34] Under the AGRAL, the general conflicts rule on tort (sec. 17)[35] and the escape clause (sec. 20) focus on a close connection with the parties, and party autonomy (sec. 21) aims at realising their private interests. These conflict rules are not adequate to determine the law governing the infringement of intellectual property rights, which always occurs in the country of protection as a violation of territorially exclusive rights geared to the economic and industrial policy of the country concerned. *De lege lata*, therefore, the law of the country of protection should be applied based on *jōri* (reason) to the exclusion of secs. 17, 20 and 21 AGRAL.[36]

(3) The application of governing law and double actionability

Sec. 11(2) and (3) *Hōrei* stipulated the so-called "double actionability" principle, providing for the cumulative application of Japanese law in relation to the existence and remedies of tort. Despite criticism by academics, these rules have been maintained in sec. 22(1) and (2) AGRAL.[37]

In the Manchurian patent case (1953),[38] the Plaintiff, a Japanese company owned a Japanese and Manchurian patent for vacuum tubes. The Defendant, also a Japanese company, bought the products from the Plaintiff's licensee in Japan, made radio receivers by using them in Japan and sold its end products in Manchuria. The Tokyo District Court regarded Manchuria as the place of tort pursuant to sec. 11(1)

32. Also § 3:601 CLIP Principles; *see* A. METZGER, Applicable Law under the CLIP Principles: A Pragmatic Revaluation of Territoriality, in: BASEDOW et al. (ed.), *supra* note 14, 171 ff.; CLIP (ed.), *supra* note 14, para. 3:601.C01 ff.; comparatively, M. PERTEGÁS SENDER, Cross-Border Enforcement of Patent Rights, London 2002, 209 ff.
33. *Supra* note 5.
34. *See* K. KOIDE (ed.), Chikujō Kaisetsu: Hō no Tekiyō ni kansuru Tsūsokuhō (*Commentary on the AGRAL*), 1st (revised) ed. Tokyo 2014, 229 ff.; *see also* HŌMUSHŌ MINJIKYOKU SANJIKAN-SHITSU (Ministry of Justice Civil Affairs Bureau, Legal Affairs Bureau), Kokusaishihō no Gendaika ni kansuru Yōkō Chūkan Shian Hosoku Setsumei (*Explanatory Report on the Interim Proposal on the Legislation concerning Modernization of Private International Law*), in: Bessatsu NBL Henshū-bu (ed.), Hō no Tekiyō ni kansuru Tsūsoku-hō Kankei Shiryō to Kaisetsu (*Materials and Explanation on the AGRAL*), Tokyo 2006, 201; Y. NISHITANI, Die Reform des internationalen Privatrechts in Japan *(The reform of private international law in Japan)*, IPRax 2007, 556 (note 46).
35. Sec. 17 AGRAL subjects a wrongful act to the *lex loci damni* in principle and, in the absence of foreseeability by the tortfeasor, to the *lex loci delicti commissi*.
36. *Also* Article 8(1), (3) Rome II; *cfr.* Secs. 301(1)(a) and 302(1) ALI Principles; Article 3: 601(1) CLIP Principles; Y. NISHITANI, Fuhōkōi no Junkyo-hō *(Law applicable to torts)*, in: SUAMI/DOGAUCHI (ed.), Kokusai Business to Hō: Business Hōmu Taikei *(International Business and Law: System of Business Law)*, vol. 4, Tokyo 2009, 176 ff.
37. Y. NISHITANI, *supra* note 34, 556.
38. *See* Tokyo District Court, *supra* note 16.

Hōrei. It dismissed the Plaintiff's claim for damages, however, on the grounds that the Defendant's conducts did not constitute tort under Japanese law (sec. 11(2) *Hōrei*), because the effects of the Manchurian patent did not extend to Japan. This decision was rightly criticised by academics, because an "equivalent act" committed in Japan would have constituted, by all means, infringement of a Japanese patent.[39]

In the current case, the appellee's acts were completed in Japan and solely induced a patent infringement through its US subsidiary in the US. The Supreme Court did apply the "equivalent act" test under sec. 11(2) *Hōrei*. It denied, though, the existence of tort, holding that the inducement of a Japanese patent infringement committed outside of Japan would be legal, as the effects of a Japanese patent would not extend extraterritorially in default of a provision corresponding to sec. 271(b) of the US Patent Act. It should, however, be pointed out that sec. 11(2) *Hōrei* solely concerns the unlawfulness of a conduct, not the territorial scope of application of patent law. In this respect, it would have sufficed to ascertain that an active inducement of patent infringement establishes joint liability as a solicitation or assistance under Japanese law (secs. 709 and 719(2) Civil Code). Even if one considers a parallel case in which an active inducement of patent infringement in Japan was committed outside of Japan, the result would be the same so long as the directly infringing act took place in Japan. In this regard, Justice *Fujii* delivered a convincing dissenting opinion.[40]

The Supreme Court was certainly hesitant to apply US law extraterritorially to the appellee's conducts in Japan. Indeed, the appellant could not claim the appellee's production of the products in Japan to be unlawful because he did not have a corresponding patent in Japan. It could not have been enjoined from production or for destruction of the products pursuant to US patent law. However, considering that the appellee purposefully induced the infringement of the appellant's US patent through its US subsidiary, said appellee could have been held liable for its conducts that affected the US market. In this respect, the appellant's claim could have been granted to the extent of damages, as well as the injunction against the inducement of the patent infringement in the US.[41]

4. COMPARATIVE REMARKS[42]

a) EU countries

(1) The **EU rules on jurisdiction** are provided for in the 2011 Brussels I^{bis} Regulation.[43] It governs the case, in principle, insofar as the defendant is domiciled in one of the EU Member States (except Denmark).[44] A parallel instrument has been adopted by

39. Y. Orimo, *supra* note 31, 187 (note 4); R. Yamada, Kokusaishihō no Kenkyū *(Studies on Private International Law)*, Tokyo 1969, 150 ff.
40. Also S. Kidana, *supra* note 29, 122 *et seq.*; as a result, *also* M. Dogauchi, *supra* note 26, 280.
41. Y. Nishitani, *supra* note 36, 178.
42. For details, see M. Trimble, The Extraterritorial Enforcement of Patent Rights, in: C. Heath (ed.), Patent Enforcement Worldwide, 3rd ed. 2015, 569.
43. *Supra* note 13.
44. Art. 5(1) Brussels I^{bis} Regulation.

the 2007 revision of the Lugano Convention, so that principally the same rules apply in relation to the **EEA Countries** (Switzerland, Norway and Iceland) as well.[45]

As for patent infringement, the so-called Brussels/Lugano system characterises it as a tort and subjects it to the general jurisdiction rules as in Japan. However, compared to Japanese jurisdiction rules, there are several differences.

(i) The jurisdiction grounds in Japan are in principle broader. As objective grounds for jurisdiction, the Japanese CCP provides for not only for the defendant's domicile, the branch office and the place of tort as under the Brussels I[bis] Regulation,[46] but also the jurisdiction of the location of the defendant's assets, business engagement, as well as a broad joinder of claims and parties. This enables Japanese courts, unlike the EU and EEA countries,[47] to adopt the so-called "spider in the web" doctrine. This means that, in parallel patent infringement cases committed by the parent company and its subsidiaries in different countries, claims can be consolidated at the seat of the parent company.

(ii) The exercise of jurisdiction can also be broader in Japan, as the courts are allowed to hear the foreign patent infringement case even where the defendant raises the invalidity defence. In contrast, the EU and EEA countries always subject the decision of the patent validity to the exclusive jurisdiction of the country of registration, even if it has been raised as an incidental question within the patent infringement proceedings.[48] If the estoppel of invalidity is not raised, a domestic court may adjudicate the issue of non-infringement even if foreign patents are involved.[49]

(iii) On the other hand, unlike the Brussels/Lugano system, the Japanese jurisdiction rules provide for, under exceptional circumstances, a partial or whole dismissal of the claim when exercising jurisdiction appears to be inappropriate in light of balancing the parties' interests or assuring due and expeditious proceedings. This enables Japanese judges to strike a balance in a flexible way between the broad jurisdiction grounds and the need to avoid exorbitant jurisdiction.

(2) As for the **law governing patent infringement in the EU**, the Rome II Regulation[50] designates the law of the country of registration in relation to all remedies, i.e., injunction and prevention of infringement as well as damages. This is in clear contrast to the underlying Card Reader decision of the Japanese Supreme Court, which adopted two different conflicts rules depending on the nature of the claim. In addition, the Rome II Regulation does not provide for the double actionability principle, unlike the Japanese conflict of laws rules.

45. *Supra* note 21. It ought to be noted, however, that the Brussels I[bis] Regulation has introduced some deviating provisions in 2011.
46. Art. 4(1), Art. 7 No. 2 and 5 Brussels I[bis] Regulation.
47. *See* the 2006 *Roche* case (*supra* note 20).
48. *See supra* note 21.
49. The English High Court in *Actavis v. Ely Lilly*, 15 May 2014, [2014] EWHC 1511 assumed jurisdiction over declarations of non-infringement regarding the UK, German, French, Italian and Spanish parts of a European patent.
50. *See supra* note 28.

b) The US

(1) In what can be considered the leading case on the question of **adjudicating foreign patents**, the US Court of Appeal of the Federal Circuit took the view that the principle of independence of national patents combined with the absence of any domestic rules on adjudicating foreign patents, should lead to the result that US courts "should not determine the validity and infringement of foreign patents".[51]

(2) As to the issue of **extraterritorial application**, it has already been mentioned that US law under sec. 271(f) US Patent Act allows an extraterritorial application to acts of supply or cause to supply a component in or from the United States meant to be assembled into a device that would infringe a US patent.

51. US CAFC, *Jan Voda v. Cordis Corporation*, 476 F3d. 887 (Fed. Cir. 2007).

Case No. 46

International Civil Procedure, Recognition of Foreign Judgements, Punitive Damages

Toshiyuki Kōno

---

1. **The recognition and enforcement of a foreign decision awarding punitive damages is contrary to public policy and must therefore be declined.**
2. **Interest in an average foreign damage award including legal costs and fees is enforceable.**

Supreme Court of 11 July 1997, Cases Nos. 1761&1762 (O) of 1993 – *Punitive Damages*

Northcon I, Oregon Partnership v. Mansei Kyogyo Co. Ltd and Yoshitaka Katayama

---

1. BACKGROUND

If a party to legal action taking place before a foreign court succeeds against a party which has assets in Japan, the question is whether this title can be recognised and enforced in Japan as well. Prerequisites for this are recognition of the foreign decision as well as the issue of an exequatur (a title of execution) through a Japanese court, because sec. 24(2) Civil Execution Act requires that the foreign decision meets the preconditions of sec. 118 Code of Civil Procedure, formerly sec. 200. In line with sec. 118(3) Code of Civil Procedure, foreign judgements must not contravene the Japanese *public policy*. Not only the Code of Civil Procedure, but also the Japanese Act on the Rules of Application of Laws (the Code of Private International Law in Japan),[1] and the *Minpō*, the Japanese Civil Code, use the term "public policy" in order to protect fundamental legal values of Japanese law. The protection provided by the *public policy* in the Code of Civil Procedure and the Act on Applicable Law is, however, of a different kind than that of the Civil Code. The Japanese Court must examine *ex officio* whether a foreign judgement breaches the Japanese *public policy*. In doing so, the court must consider as the basis of its *ratio decidendi* not only the operative provisions of foreign decisions, but also the facts upon which they are based. A *révision au fond* is, however, prohibited. In practice, it is often difficult to make a clear distinction between the examination of the *public policy* and a *révision au fond*.

1. Hō no tekiyō ni kansuru tsūsokuhō (*Act on the general Rules of Application of Laws*), Law no. 10 of 1898 as newly titled and amended on 21 June 2006.

Sec. 118 Code of Civil Procedure differs from the previous sec. 200(3) Code of Civil Procedure in that neither the contents nor the *proceedings* of a foreign judgement may be allowed to breach the *public policy* of Japan. This was already the prevailing opinion in literature at the time of the old Code of Civil Procedure, and in an *obiter dictum* the Supreme Court had expressed a similar view.[2]

2. DECISION[3]

a) Facts

The plaintiff, a company based in California, on 19 May 1982, was awarded compensatory damages in the amount of USD 425,251 plus costs in the amount of USD 40,104.71 by the California District Court. In addition, the court awarded punitive damages in the amount of USD 1,125,000. The defendant was ordered to pay 7% interest on the above amount until 30 June 1983, thereafter 10%. The decision was confirmed by the California Appeals Court on 12 May 1987. In 1989, the plaintiff requested the Tokyo District Court to have the above California decision recognised and enforced in Japan. Both the Tokyo District Court (18 February 1991, 760 Hanrei Times 250) and the Tokyo High Court (28 June 1993, 823 Hanrei Times 126) held the part on compensatory damages plus interest as enforceable, but declined enforcement of the punitive damages. Both parties appealed without success.

b) Reasons

Foreign judgements can be enforced in Japan unless, *inter alia,* they contravene the *ordre public,* sec. 200(3) Code of Civil Procedure. The system of punitive damages under Californian civil law provides not only compensation for actual loss, but in the case of wilfulness acts as a deterrent to the infringer to desist from committing the infringing act in the future. From the purpose it is clear that under our system, punitive damages would belong to criminal law, while on the basis of our tort law, damages can only be awarded up to the amount of actual damages suffered ... The purpose for awarding punitive damages against the infringer is thus different from our system ... that compensates for actual damages suffered. ... Accordingly, different from the amount of compensatory damages plus legal costs, the part of the decision awarding punitive damages is against public order in our country and can therefore not be recognised.

In principle, enforcement of monetary awards is limited to those parts of a foreign decision which were clearly spelt out. This is not the case with the interest awarded. ... However, the awarded interest is based on California law and ensues from the damage award. It can therefore also be executed insofar as the interests refer to the compensatory damages and legal costs incurred by the plaintiff.

---

2. Supreme Court, 7 June 1983, Case No. 2217 (Ne) of 1979, 37-5 Minshū 611.
3. 51-6 Minshū 2530 and 51-6 Minshu 2573 = 1199 Saibansho Jihō 3 = 1624 Hanrei Jihō 90 = 958 Hanrei Times 93 = 1039 Kinyū Shōji Hanrei 28 = 163 Shiryōban Shōji Hōmu 278. English translation in 30 IIC 480 (1999) w. comment C. HEATH.

3. ANALYSIS

a) A much-discussed issue regarding the recognition of foreign decisions in Japan is the question of recognition of US-American court decisions which award punitive damages. The question is a particularly explosive one, not least because of the tendency of these types of decisions to order the defendant to pay extensive damages – a punishment intended to act as a deterrent to future perpetration of incriminatory behaviour on the part of the liable party itself, as well as others.

b) Japanese domestic law follows the principle that damages are only meant as compensation for loss and cannot serve another purpose such as punishment of the infringer, deterrent against future recurrences or education of the general public. In that respect, sec. 416 Civil Code reads as follows:

> "(1) A demand for damages shall be for compensation for such damages as would ordinarily arise from the non-performance of an obligation or duty.
>
> (2) The person obliged may also recover damages which have arisen from special circumstances if these could have been foreseen by both parties."

Apart from this general provision, the general tort provision of Sec. 709 also obliges the tortfeasor to "compensate for damages arising" from certain violations. In certain cases, the law facilitates the *calculation* of damages, e.g., in cases of intellectual property rights infringement. Here, the right owner may statutorily request the infringer's profits or an appropriate licensing fee as a basis of damage calculation. Apart from this, however, attempts in Japan to introduce damages beyond what could be considered compensatory have failed.[4] More modest proposals have advocated for a greater flexibility on the part of the courts in assessing damages.[5] These more modest proposals finally led to an amendment of sec. 102 Patent Act, which now

4. The introduction of a system of treble damages for patent infringement was publicly advocated by the report of 21 SEIKI NO CHITEKIZAISANKEN WO KANGAERU KONDANKAI (the JPO Commissioner's Commission on IP Rights in the 21st Century), Korekara wa nihon mo chiteki sōzō jidai (*Towards the era of intellectual creation*), 7 April 1997. After this report, the idea of treble damages was deliberated in Kōgyōshōyken Shingikai Songaibaishōtō Shōiinkai *(Subcommittee on Damages of Industrial Property Council)* of the JPO, the final report of the Subcommittee of 25 November 1997 led to an improvement in the presumption of damages in the law amendment of 1998, but no treble damages. It was also deliberated in Shihōseido Kaikaku Shingikai *(Judicial Reform Council)* of the Cabinet from 2000 to 2001, but no conclusion was reached. There was also a deliberation on treble damages for copyright infringement in Bunka Shingikai Chosakuken Bunkakai Shihōkyūsaiseido Shōiinkai *(Judicial Remedy Subcommittee of Copyright Committee of Cultural Council)* of the Agency for Cultural Affairs from 2002 to 2003. The issue was also proposed in Chitekizaisan Seisaku Suishin Honbu *(Headquarter of Intellectual Property Strategy)*, e.g., in a recent report of March 2016 of Chizaifunsōshori Sisutemu Kentōiinkai *(Committee on IP Judicial Resolution)* or a most recent report of February 2019 of Tokkyo Shōiinkai (*Patent Subcommittee*) at <https://www.jpo.go.jp/resources/shingikai/sangyo-kouzou/shousai/tokkyo_shoi/190215_tokkyo_houkoku.html> which gave no positive view on the introduction of treble damages. The discussion and attempts to introduce treble damages have been continuing over 20 years in Japan, but up to now without success.
5. E.g., the proposals of the Second Reform Committee for Patent Matters of the Japan Intellectual Property Association: TOKKYO IINKAI DAI 2 SHŌIINAI *(Second Subcommittee, Patent Committee)*, Tokkyoken tō no shingai ni taisuru kyūsai – songai baishō seikyū seido no arikata ni tsuite no

gives the judge more discretion in determining the appropriate licensing fee, the most common form of calculation in patent infringement cases.

c) In respect of the problem of recognition it is important to differentiate between two questions. First, it must be clarified whether judgements with punitive damages may be classified as "civil judgements" at all. If the answer to this question is in the negative, then recognition is automatically rendered impossible. However, if the answer is positive, the second question arises; namely, whether recognition of this kind of foreign decision, i.e. with punitive damages, breaches the Japanese *public policy*. In Japanese scholarly opinion, there are two different views concerning this matter. According to the first, recognition should be categorically ruled out.[6] The second opinion, however, holds that punitive-damages decisions should be capable of achieving recognition under certain conditions.[7] An absolute repudiation is rejected in favour of analysis of the function of that part of the judgement which awards punitive damages in individual cases. What becomes problematic, however, is the fact that this approach can in essence lead, in a given case, to the necessity to undertake a prohibited *révision au fond*. The first-instance decision of the Tokyo District Court[8] in the present case makes clear this difficulty. The court has also been criticised for having gone beyond the admissible analysis in its review.

The Tokyo High Court seems to concur in the stance which negates the civil-law character of punitive-damages judgements and, in doing so, fundamentally rules out the possibility of recognition.[9] The Supreme Court has not disclosed its stance on the issue. However, it too emphasises the penal character of punitive damages and that they are, as a legal principal, alien to Japanese law.[10] This being the case, it can probably be assumed that the discussed part-recognition of punitive-damages judgements, concerning at least *similar* case configurations, could not be endorsed.

d) This rigid attitude can have grim consequences for the injured party in individual cases. One only has to think of the circumstances where the refusal of even part-recognition of punitive damages cases could lead to the injured party receiving only a minimal amount of compensation. This can occur when, for example, compensation

---

ichi kōsatsu – (*Remedy for patent infringement – a consideration about damages claim system* –), 47-10 Chizai Kanri 1465-1484 (1997).

6. E.g., M. DŌGAUCHI, Amerika no songai baishō hanketsu ni tsuite chōbatsuteki baishō no bubun no nihon deno shikkō wo mitomenakatta jirei *(Case where the enforcement of punitive damages part in the damages decision of US was not acknowledged in Japan)*, 1388 Hanrei Jihō 202 (1996).
7. So argued by Y. FUJITA, Shōgai minji jiken no jitsumu to mondaiten (*Practice and problem of international civil case)*, 31-11 Jiyū to Seigi 18 (1980).
8. Tokyo District Court, 18 February 1991, Case No. 1447 (Wa) of 1989, 1376 Hanrei Jihō 79 = 760 Hanrei Times 250 = 882 Kinyū Shōji Hanrei 31 = 85 Shiryōban Shōji Hōmu 104.
9. Tokyo High Court, 28 June 1993, Case Nos. 703&722 (Ne) of 1991, 1471 Hanrei Jihō 89 = 823 Hanrei Times 126 = 927 Kinyū Shōji Hanrei 3 = 112 Shiryōban Shōji Hōmu 112.
10. Worth mention is the decision of 28 April 1998 (Case No. 1838 (O) of 1994, 52-3 Minshū 853) where the Supreme Court recognised a judgment rendered in Hong Kong which applied the so-called Indemnity Basis standard to determine the litigation costs to be borne by defendant. The Court acknowledged the punitive character of the standard. In this judgment, what seems decisive is the fact that the costs to be borne by the defendant as the result of the Indemnity Basis standard did not exceed the amount of the actual expenses.

for immaterial damage is calculated not as part of the compensatory damages, but as part of the punitive damages instead.

4. COMPARATIVE REMARKS

Interesting parallels can be drawn between the above decision and a more detailed, yet similarly worded decision of the **German** Federal Supreme Court.[11] As in the case of the Japanese decision, the German Federal Supreme Court had to consider recognition and enforceability of a Californian decision awarding the plaintiff not only actual and future damages, but also exemplary and punitive ones. In addition, the German Federal Supreme Court had to consider a number of additional issues which were not touched upon in the Japanese case, yet might be an interesting guideline for Japanese courts having to deal with recognition and enforcement of US decisions in the future.

Taking the same approach as Japanese courts would under sec. 118 Japanese Code of Civil Procedure (as above), the German Federal Supreme Court examined to what extent the basic rules of due process were adhered to. First of all, this would require proper notice to the defendant. This is often problematic in cases where US attorneys decide to directly serve notice without using the proper diplomatic channels under the Hague Service Convention[12] of 15 November 1965, to which Germany, Japan and the US are members.

An interesting aspect discussed in the German decision concerns the pre-trial discovery procedures very common to US law. The court held that in accordance with German academic writings, "procedures aimed at obtaining evidence between the date of filing a claim and the oral hearing ('trial') conducted mostly by the parties themselves in the US gives no cause for a contravention against the *ordre public* according to sec. 328(1)4 German Code of Civil Procedure".

In considering the recognition of the damage award, the German Federal Supreme Court dealt with four different positions:

(1) An award for future medical expenses regardless of the fact that the plaintiff might not actually undergo medical treatment;
(2) A contingency fee for the attorney amounting to 40% of the damage award;
(3) A lump sum punitive damage award; and
(4) A damage award for pain and suffering disproportionately high by German standards.

As to the first point, "it is true that German tort law in cases of personal injury do not allow the victim any discretion in the manner in which they are permitted to use the money awarded for medical treatment in order to avoid 'fictitious' medical expenses (German Federal Supreme Court, 14 January 1986, BGHZ 97, 14). Yet, this in itself does not prevent a recognition of the Superior Court's decision ... After all, the Superior Court has awarded expenses for medical treatment that in similar circumstances could have been awarded under German law, too."

11. German Federal Supreme Court, 4 June 1992, ZIP 1992, 1256 = NJW 1992, 3096.
12. Convention on the Service Abroad of Judicial and Extrajudicial documents in Civil and Commercial Matters.

As to item two, "while under German legal tradition, an agreement according to which 40% of all incoming damages would have to be paid to the attorney as a contingency fee would be null and void, for German attorneys this principle is not so important according to German ideas of justice that it would require worldwide recognition. ... Even if the compensatory damages awarded to the plaintiff have been estimated generously in order to account for the costs of legal proceedings, this as such is no untenable result from a German point of view. Even when sued for damages in Germany, the defendant would have had to pay the plaintiff's legal expenses under sec. 91 German Code of Civil Procedure. The domestic *ordre public* would not have difficulties in awarding the tort victim compensation for the costs of legal proceedings in addition to complete compensation for damages suffered."

It should be noted here that a Japanese court may well have decided differently due to the fact that Japanese law in principle does not recognise compensation for attorneys' fees incurred by the successful party of a lawsuit that are therefore only awarded in exceptional cases.

Concerning item three, "a foreign decision that awards punitive damages in a substantive amount in addition to material and immaterial damages is generally unenforceable in Germany ... The lower court has correctly affirmed that an order for the payment of punitive damages is not a criminal penalty which in principle could not be enforced under secs. 722, 723 German Code of Civil Procedure ... Yet, the execution of a US American decision that obliges the defendant to pay punitive damages would be barred by German *ordre public* ..., as the modern German system of civil law establishes the system of compensation for torturous acts, but not the enrichment of the victim ... A different approach may only be taken if the punitive damages are meant to compensate for economic disadvantages not otherwise accounted for or difficult to prove, or are meant to disgorge the profits obtained by the infringer through his torturous act."

These considerations by the court may well be a precedent also for other civil law jurisdictions, particularly in Asia. Only in rare cases and under US pressure have these jurisdictions introduced statutory punitive or treble damages, as has been the case with the Taiwanese Trade Secrets Act of 17 January 1996. This Act in sec. 13(2) gives the judge discretion to award up to the treble amount of damages in case of wilful infringement. Taiwanese Patent Act of 11 June 2013 has also the treble damages provision in sec. 97(2) (For the Taiwanese Patent Act, the multiple damages were at first introduced as double damages in 1994, changed up to treble in 2001, abolished in 2011, and reintroduced in 2013). Most recently Korean Diet passed in December 2018 a bill which introduces sec. 128(8) and (9) for the treble damages (Law No. 16208 of 8 January 2019. It will be set in force in July 2019). In China, a bill including multiple damages for patent infringement is sent to the Congress in December 2018.

As to the fourth item of additional damages for pain and suffering, "these might come close to the German equivalent of damages for pain and suffering according to sec. 847 German Civil Code, even though the Superior Court's award may surpass an award that would be in conformity with German ideas by far. Accordingly, this amount can be recognised".

Refusing the recognition of punitive damage awards may also be justifiable on different grounds. In contrast to the US, systems such as Japan and Germany do not as easily allow an asset stripping of a defendant facing a damage award against him.

Case No. 47

Discovery – Order of Documents – Defence of Secrecy

Motoyuki Nakashima

---

1. For a court order to present documents according to sec. 105(1) Patent Act, such documents must on the one hand side be necessary in order to prove infringement or the amount of damages, and on the other hand there must not be a legitimate interest to withhold such documents.

2. In order to avoid abusive or exploratory requests for obtaining information about a competitor's business, an applicant who requests the delivery of documents need not conclusively prove infringement, but must make a prima facie case that makes an infringement credible.

IP High Court, 28 March 2016 – *In camera proceedings/FOMA*

NTT Docomo KK v. IPCom GmbH & Co. KG

---

1. BACKGROUND

Japan introduced the substantive protection of trade secrets only in 1990,[1] while the courts were traditionally reluctant to order to the production of documents that allegedly contained secret information.[2] Effective as of 1 January 1998, the revised Code of Civil Procedure now allows the court to grant more broad-based requests for the production of documents (sec. 222, 223 Code of Civil Procedure[3]), and seal those

1. The 1934 Unfair Competition Prevention Act was amended in 1990 in order to provide for the protection of trade secrets outside contractual relationships: Law no. 66/1990. Prior to this amendment, the courts refused to grant protection of trade secrets under tort law: Tokyo High Court, 5 September 1966, Case No. 381 (Ra) of 1966, 199 Hanrei Times = Doi Digest 1971, 92 – *Waukesha*.
2. While discovery orders were completely unknown, only concretely identified documents from the other side could be requested, sec. 223 Code of Civil Procedure. Yet until the decision Tokyo High Court, Case No. 605 (Ra) of 1997, 20 May 1997, 40 IIC 452 (1999) = 1601 Hanrei Jihō 143 – *Sale of Pharmaceuticals – Solvay v. Kissei Pharmaceutical* and Osaka District Court, 4 December 2001, Case Nos. 12225 (Wa) of 1998&143 (Wa) of 2001, 44 IIC 203 (2003), the defendants could withhold any such documents alleging that they contained trade secrets. The court in these decisions held that this was no good reason for not producing the documents, highlighting the need for legislative intervention in this field.
3. Of interest is particularly sec. 222 that no longer requires the applicant to precisely identify the document to be produced.

parts of the court records of proceedings which concern trade secrets (sec. 92 Code of Civil Procedure). Parts of a decision that describe the trade secret will thus be made illegible by the court.[4] Complementary to these general provisions, the discretionary powers of the courts in patent infringement proceedings were strengthened for, both, to order the production of documents, and to conduct the hearing *in camera*.

(a) Sec. 105(1) Patent Act now allows the court to order the production of documents "necessary for the proof of alleged infringement",[5] or the inspection of devices (sec. 105(4)). Such order is under the caveat that the respondent has no "legitimate interest" to withhold these documents, namely where these documents contain trade secrets. In order to strike a proper balance, the law provides for a three-step procedure: First, the applicant must make a prima facie case to show that the production of documents related to a certain issue are necessary in order to prove infringement. Where they are not, because they either do not relate to the issue of infringement, or infringement can be proven by other means, the court should not make an order. Second, where the court deems these documents necessary, sec. 105(2) Patent Act allows the court to order their production *in camera* only in the presence of the respondent, that is, the person in possession of the documents. It is this step that deviates from proceedings in, for example, France or Germany, where no such *ex parte in camera* procedure is foreseen. The purpose of this step is for the court to ascertain whether the documents indeed contain trade secrets, and whether production of the documents is necessary for the applicant to prove infringement.[6] Thereafter, or alternatively, the court under sec. 105(3) Patent Act may conduct the *in camera* proceedings *inter partes*, in the presence of the other "party, advocate or assistant." Here, as in the case of the protective order, it is the applicant who must indicate to the court who should be present in such hearing. Negotiations between the parties about this issue are not uncommon.[7]

A court order for producing documents also has the nature of a ruling on the taking of evidence by accepting a request for admission of the relevant document as evidence. Hence a court shall also apply sec. 181 Japanese Civil Procedure Act to the necessity as an evidence regarding documents which is produced by sec. 105(1) Japanese Patent Act.

4. This of course is no help where the other party to the lawsuit is a competitor: M. TAKABE, Intellectual Property Litigation: Future Issues (3), 33 AIPPI Journal of the Japanese Group (English edition) 143 (2008): "This restriction simply prevents third parties from inspecting and copying the record of litigation, and such protection is not available to the other party to the proceedings".
5. As a rather general rule, sec. 181 Japanese Code of Civil Procedure provides that "the court shall not be required to examine evidence offered by a party that the court considers to be unnecessary."
6. Where documents are not produced despite a judicial order and without any good reason, the court can assume that the applicant's allegations in regard of the contents of the documents are proven, sec. 224 Code of Civil Procedure.
7. T. MAKINO, Himitsu hoji meirei oyobi himitsu hoji meirei torikeshi no jitsumu (*Practice on secrecy orders and the repeal of secrecy orders*), 55 AIPPI Journal of the Japanese Group (Japanese edition) 606, 612 (2010). In the current case, the court mentions the existence of a secrecy agreement between the parties, but was not convinced that this would adequately protect the interests of the respondent (plaintiff in the action).

This decision has a significant meaning for determining the criteria on interpreting both provisions regarding a court order for producing documents.

2. DECISION[8]

a) Facts

1. In the case at issue, the plaintiff (respondent in appeal) a company that provides third generation mobile telephone communication of the W-CDMA type "FOMA", requests the court to ascertain that the services it provides with the method for operating a telecommunication network by way of an access control through a random access channel do not infringe the defendant's patent No. 4696179 (registration date 4 March 2011), and that no damages or claims are unjust enrichment are due in this respect.

The first instance Tokyo District Court allowed the request because the plaintiff's services did not fall within the scope of the defendant's patent. The defendant appealed. One contentious issue was the defendant's request that the court under sec. 105(1) Patent Act should order the plaintiff to produce certain documents. The first instance court dismissed this request without any *in camera* hearing provided in sec. 105(2) Patent Act, as the defendant by way of evidence had only presented two experiments that however supported the plaintiff's allegations of non-infringement. The defendant has not raised a counter-claim for damages or unjust enrichment. As can be deduced from the file, the District Court held the defendant's request for the production of evidence so as to prove infringement to be unsubstantiated and vexatious. Although the IP High Court dismissed the appeal due to a lack of infringement, it held *in camera* proceedings according to sec. 105(2) Patent Act for ascertaining whether the requested documents should be produced. Thereafter, the request for the production of such documents was refused.

(1) The parties

The plaintiff is a limited company on shares that offers telecommunication services for mobile phones.

The defendant is a German company that commercially buys and licences patents in the area of telecommunications.

(2) The defendant's patent

The defendant is the owner of the following patent:

- Registration number: 49696179
- Filing date: 17 September 2010 (Application number: 2010-209728)
- Date of registration: 4 March 2011

Title of the invention: Method for the allocation of access rights to a participating station of a telecommunication network, participating station, method for the

8. English translation in 48 IIC 980 (2017) w. comment C. Heath.

operation of a telecommunication network consisting of participating stations and a telecommunication system.

...

b) Reasons

On appeal, this court decides to affirm the first instance decision. The appeal is unfounded. The reasons for our decision are the following:

...

4. On the request for the production of documents

(1) Under sec. 105(1) Patent Act, the defendant has requested that the court should order the production of those documents that concern the source code of the application program related to the processing of incoming calls in the defendant's transmitting and receiving base station (BTS), the BTS manual, source code and manual for the radio network coordination (RNC), and the source code and manual of the data related to the station. This request is almost identical to the request for the production of documents made before the first instance, which the latter refused.

The order for the production of documents under sec. 105(1) Patent Act hinges on two requirements, the necessity for producing such documents in order to prove infringement, and the absence of legitimate reasons for not submitting such documents. We consider both requirements.

(2) On the determination which documents should be produced:

The production of documents first mentioned in the defendant's request of 3 April 2015 with the additional explanations of the plaintiff can be defined as follows: (α) (omission) manual, (β) (omission) manual (omission), (γ) (omission) manual, (δ) technical data regarding the technical conditions of RNC and BTS in the plaintiff's system to manufacturers, (ε) all source codes related to the application programs of processing calls that use BTS or are based thereupon, (ζ) all program source codes that use RNC and have been produced thereupon.

(3) On the necessity for producing such documents

The necessity for making an order to produce documents must be determined under sec. 181(1) Code of Civil Procedure. In procedures that concern proof of patent infringement, it is frequently the case that documents are in the possession of the opposing party, or that in the case of a method patent there is no evidence which method the opposing party actually makes use of. On the other hand, in such cases both parties are often in competition with each other and the object of proof contains a trade secret. In such cases, the opposing party is severely disadvantaged as in reaction to an order for the production of documents it is required to give access to such information even if the request is vexatious or exploratory. In order to prevent requests that are vexatious or exploratory, the right owner who makes such request for the production of documents should furnish prima facie evidence that make a reasonable case for affirming an infringement. The order for the production of documents must be understood as a measure for the necessary collection of evidence in order for the requesting party to prove infringement. For this reason, the order for the production of documents must be interpreted such that the prima facie evidence does not require ultimate proof of infringement, yet that thereupon a reasonable assumption for affirming infringement can be made that can dispel any suspicion that the request is made vexatiously or as an exploratory mission. This standard of prima facie evidence should be determined in considering the necessity for examining the documents, the difficulty of proving infringement in the case at issue, and the question whether there is a different route of proving infringement or whether there are alternatives to the production of such documents.

The court thus considers the request in the light of the above considerations. The request concerns experiments of the plaintiff, experiments of the defendant and the evidence submitted in this regard. As far as we can see, N (omission) is the method used by the plaintiff, just as ASC (omission) and AC-to-ASC mapping. Other results have not been submitted.

Given the importance of the feature "access threshold" for the allegations of the defendant, the latter has to prove whether the method used by the plaintiff has a structure that allows it to send N (omission). The main point of the defendant's auxiliary argumentation is the proof whether an AC has a structure on the system that (omission) allows it to indeed send a correspondingly configured AC-to-ASC mapping. The evidence as furnished above only demonstrates the state of the signals SIB5 and SIB7 as covered by the experiments. The timely collection of the sequence by way of experiment is not easy when the method used by the plaintiff shows a structure that generates N (omission) only under certain circumstances. Yet the structure of the method used by the plaintiff is the subject matter that needs to be proven. The evidence for this is exclusively in the hands of the plaintiff. The above outcome is in line with the allegations of the plaintiff, yet the plaintiff has not proven N (omission) or ASC (omission). Therefore, we cannot deny that there is a necessity for examining the requested evidence, as the plaintiff's attempts to prove the contrary are not sufficiently convincing.

The services of the plaintiff follow the 3GPP standard. The 3GPP standard requires a method for the control of capacity overload, and when applying such method, all features of the claim are actually used. On the other hand, not all features are used when (omission).

In considering the evidence furnished by the defendant so as to prove infringement, we cannot deny the necessity of examining the requested evidence, as there is a sufficient indication for an infringement.

However, document (δ) bears no relation to the conditions for using the "AC-to-ASC mapping", and there is no necessity for examining the value N. The request for supplying documents in this respect must be refused, as the evidence bears no relation to the infringement.

(4) On the legitimate reasons for not obeying the order for the submission of documents

The plaintiff has alleged that the documents to be submitted to the court are trade secrets of the plaintiff's and there is thus a legitimate reason for refusing to submit them. Whether there is a legitimate reason must be determined in balancing the disadvantage to the owner of the documents if the documents were submitted (degree of protection as a trade secret) and the disadvantage to the applicant if the documents were not submitted (necessity for proving infringement). A legitimate reason must be affirmed where the degree of protection as a trade secret outweighs, namely where the documents clearly relate to the use of a technical teaching that is different from the patented invention of the applicant, yet must be denied where the degree of trade secret protection does not outweigh and the teaching used by the opposing party clearly falls within the technical scope of the applicant's patent. Thus, the necessity of such a balancing of interests will be used as an indication as to whether infringement can be proven thereby. And in determining whether the trade secret merits such protection, the following must be taken into account: The character and presumed disadvantage when submitting the documents, the order for secrecy under sec. $105^{quarter}$ Patent Act, the scope and object of the order, the existence, if any, of a secrecy agreement between the parties, etc..

Accordingly, the court when conducting the *in camera* hearing has determined the existence of a legitimate reason as follows:

In considering the difficulty for determining a legitimate reason for refusing to submit the documents, namely to find a balance between the necessity to protect a trade secret on the one hand side, and the necessity of submitting the requested documents in order to prove infringement, the court for part of the documents regarded it necessary to inspect them and according to sec. 105 (2) Patent Act ordered an *in camera* hearing in the presence of the attorneys and employees of the respondent (plaintiff). As a result of this hearing, the court is convinced that the contents of the documents are a trade secret of the plaintiff's. Yet there is nothing in these documents to indicate that their submission could serve as evidence for proving infringement of the access control and method of the defendant. Even in regard of the secrecy agreement between the parties the court thus determines that the interest in keeping the information secret outweighs the necessity of submitting them as evidence.

Apart from that, for a part of these documents the information mentioned in the defendant's request on the conditions of using the "AC-to-ASC Mapping" can be supplied in a manner that does not touch upon any trade secrets. The court has thus suggested the plaintiff a submission in such a manner. The plaintiff has submitted this part as "information on the 'Arrangement to Access Service Class' directed to manufacturers."

(5) On the other documents

The source code of documents (ε) and (ζ) contains a trade secret that highly merits protection and it is clear that the submission of these documents in order for the defendant to analyse them would seriously disadvantage the plaintiff. The document (γ) is a manual actually used by the plaintiff and by looking at the contents of the document we can confirm its character as a trade secret. But it cannot be assumed that a necessity of providing this document as evidence on the day of the last oral proceedings outweighs the interest in keeping the document secret. Concerning the above documents, we have not considered it necessary to conduct *in camera* proceedings, but then the determination as to whether it is necessary to order the production of documents is within the discretion of the court, sec. 181 Code of Civil Procedure. The court in the course of the proceedings can determine about this matter, and in light of the evidence submitted in the course of these proceedings, the court at the end of the oral hearing has decided without an *in camera* procedure that the plaintiff has a legitimate reason for not submitting the documents.

(6) For the above reasons, we decide that the plaintiff has a legitimate reason not to submit documents (α) to (γ), while the submission of documents (δ), (ε) and (ζ), as well as parts of document (δ) does not appear necessary for proving infringement. Thus, the defendant's request for the submission of these documents is ill-founded and the court refuses the request on the last day of the oral hearing.

3. ANALYSIS

a) First, this decision presents the criteria for when the court should order the production of evidence, thus taking into consideration the recent criticism that requests for evidence might be abused for fishing exhibitions.[9] To prevent these abusive or inquiring motions, a petitioner who requests an order to produce a document is required to make a prima facie case to prove a reasonable case of infringement.

b) The decision then identifies the criteria for what should be considered legitimate reasons for withholding documents and thereby addresses the concerns that had been voiced against the decision of the Tokyo High Court on 20 May 1997[10] (see above 1.) that did not consider the mere existence of trade secrets to be sufficient for withholding documents.

Whether or not there is a reasonable ground to refuse submission of a document shall be determined in light of the balancing between disadvantage of a document possessor by disclosing the document (the necessity to protect trade secret) and disadvantage of a petitioner for the document not being submitted as evidence (the value as evidence).

In this balancing, when the document clarifies that a respondent uses structures different from patented invention, the necessity to protect trade secret becomes relatively high, but when the document clarifies that a respondent uses structures within the technical scope of patented invention, the necessity to protect trade secret becomes relatively low, therefore, the value as evidence which may prove infringement act shall be appraised in consideration of necessity to protect trade secret. While determining the necessity to protect trade secret, issuance of protective order (Article 105^{quater} et seq. Patent Act), scope of subjects of the protective order, a conclusion

9. The improvement of evidence collection methods was discussed also under the Judicial System Reform under the former prime minister Koizumi in the early 2000s and thereafter law amendments were made in this point. Still, there has always been a conflict in Japan between those that fear a potential abuse and those that advocate more effective remedies. For a recent discussion and opinion from a comparative view, see, e.g., T. TAKENAKA, Amerika no disukabarī seido no gaiyō to nihon no shōko shūshū tetsuduki kaizen teian no hikakuhōteki bunseki *(Comparative analysis on the discovery system of US and proposal of improvement of evidence collection procedure in Japan)*, 71-4 Patent 45 (2018); H. KOBAYASHI, Chitekizaisanken soshō ni okeru shōko shūshū *(Evidence collection in intellectual property lawsuit)*, 71-4 Patent 1 (2018); R. MIMURA, Chitekizaisan funsō ni okeru shōko shūshū tetsuzuki ni tsuite *(Evidence collection procedure in intellectual property dispute)*, 1499 Jurist 37 (2016). The discussion on this point continues also at governmental level in 2019. See the documents of the Patent Subcommittee under the JPO at the website of the JPO <https://www.jpo.go.jp/resources/shingikai/sangyo-kouzou/shousai/tokkyo_shoi/index.html>.

10. Tokyo High Court, 20 May 1997, Case No. 605 (Ra) of 1997, 40 IIC 452 (1999) = 1601 Hanrei Jihō 143 – *Solvay v. Kissei Pharmaceutical – Sale of Pharmaceuticals.*

of non-disclosure agreement, scope of assenters of it, and its effectiveness shall be taken into consideration in addition to content and nature of the trade secret and presumed disadvantage by disclosing the trade secret.

c) As this decision indicates, the procedure regarding a court order for producing documents consists of four steps.

- Is the documentary evidence necessary? As of yet, this cannot be determined *in camera*, yet a revision of the Patent Act passed the Diet in 2018 (in force on 1 July 2019) that allows to adopt *in camera* proceedings in this respect as well.[11]
- If so, the documents will be submitted for the court to examine legitimate reasons for withholding them. This determination can be made *in camera*.
- The court will then decide whether or not to grant the protective order. Here, an attorney of the petitioner (who has requested to inspect the documents) has the opportunity to argue against the claim for secrecy by the attorney of the respondent. The court prior to such discussion can issue a protective order to the attorney of the petitioner in order to protect the trade secrets in question, and, if the attorney is accompanied by an employee of the petitioner, also to such employee.
- Based on an evaluation of the previous steps, the court will decide whether there is a legitimate reason for the respondent to refuse the submission of documents, and, if the court decides that there is no legitimate reason, the court will issue a protective order, so as to assure the right of appeal against this decision, also to the person who is responsible for the management of the petitioner.

d) The IP High Court of Japan conducted the procedure for producing documents in a mock trial dated 31st October 2017 during the Judicial Symposium on Intellectual Property/Tokyo 2017, where the court adopted the *in camera* proceedings and then issued the order for producing document as well as a protective order.[12] The decision of this mock trial has added substantially new insights regarding the production of documents on the basis of the criteria of this decision.[13]

e) A new bill drafted by the Japanese Government in March 2019 and possibly enacted possibly in 2019, will introduce an inspection for evidence collection by a neutral expert in new sec. 105bis etc. If the new bill is enacted, the inspection can be conducted by experts by a court order at the patentee's request, while the respondent can request the court to seal trade secrets in the expert's opinion and the court can

11. Law No. 33/2018 of 30 May 2018. The documents about the law amendment of 2018 are available at the website of the JPO <https://www.jpo.go.jp/system/laws/rule/hokaisei/sangyozaisan/fuseikyousou_h300530.html>. For the explanation of the law amendment, see M. TAKABE, Shōko shūshū wo meguru tokkyohō kaisei *(The Patent Act amendment for evidence collection)*, 1525 Jurist 45 (2018).
12. Results of Mock Trials held in Judicial Symposium on Intellectual Property/Tokyo 2017 are available at the website of the courts <http://www.jp.courts.go.jp/eng/documents/thesis/2017_sympo_kaijyo/index.html>.
13. M. SHIMIZU & M. NAKASHIMA, Kokusai sihō shinpojiumu 2017 no gaiyō hōkoku *(Results of Mock Trials in Judicial Symposium on IP 2017)*, 1444 Hanrei Times 5 (2018).

conduct a hearing *in camera* to decide whether or not to seal certain information (sec. 105$^{bis\text{-}6}$ in the new bill). This is an approach very close to the German-type inspection although in Japan it can only be requested in the course of an infringement procedure and not before the infringement case is filed.[14]

4. COMPARATIVE REMARKS

a) **Community (EU) law.** There are two legal instruments at Community level that apply to the disclosure of documents in infringement litigation, and the protection of trade secrets. First, the Enforcement Directive[15] in Article 6 ("Evidence") provides that

> "1. Member States shall ensure that, on application by a party which has presented reasonably available evidence sufficient to support its claims, and has, in substantiating those claims, specified evidence which lies in the control of the opposing party, the competent judicial authorities may order that such evidence be presented by the opposing party, subject to the protection of confidential information. For the purposes of this paragraph, Member States may provide that a reasonable sample of a substantial number of copies of a work or any other protected object be considered by the competent judicial authorities to constitute reasonable evidence."

Second, the Trade Secrets Directive[16] specifies in its preamble that

> (24) ... "it is necessary to establish, subject to appropriate safeguards ensuring the right to an effective remedy and to a fair trial, specific requirements aimed at protecting the confidentiality of the litigated trade secret in the course of legal proceedings instituted for its defence. Such protection should remain in force after the legal proceedings have ended and for as long as the information constituting the trade secret is not in the public domain".

Further, (25) that these

> "requirements should include, as a minimum, the possibility of restricting the circle of persons entitled to have access to evidence or hearings, bearing in mind that all such persons should be subject to the confidentiality requirements set out in this Directive, and of publishing only the non-confidential elements of judicial decisions ... The restricted circle of persons should therefore consist of at least one natural person from each of the parties as well as the respective lawyers of the parties."

---

14. For the bill, see the documents at the website of the METI <http://www.meti.go.jp/press/2018/03/20190301004/20190301004.html>. For the background, see the report of February 2019 of the Patent Subcommittee of the JPO at the website of the JPO <https://www.jpo.go.jp/resources/shingikai/sangyo-kouzou/shousai/tokkyo_shoi/190215_tokkyo_houkoku.html>.
15. Directive 2004/48/EC of the European Parliament and of the Council of 29 April 2004 on the Enforcement of Intellectual Property Rights.
16. Directive (Eu) 2016/943 of the European Parliament and of the Council of 8 June 2016 on the Protection of Undisclosed Know-How and Business Information (Trade Secrets) Against their Unlawful Acquisition, Use And Disclosure.

These principles essentially follow the case law of the European Court of Justice:[17]

> 49 The Court of Justice has, moreover, acknowledged that the protection of business secrets is a general principle (see Case 53/85 AKZO Chemie and AKZO Chemie UK v Commission [1986] ECR 1965, paragraph 28, and Case C-36/92 P SEP v Commission [1994] ECR I-1911, paragraph 37).
>
> 52 The principle of the protection of confidential information and of business secrets must be observed in such a way as to reconcile it with the requirements of effective legal protection and the rights of defence of the parties to the dispute (see, by analogy, Case C-438/04 Mobistar [2006] ECR I-6675, paragraph 40) and, in the case of judicial review or a review by another body which is a court or tribunal within the meaning of Article 234 EC, in such a way as to ensure that the proceedings as a whole accord with the right to a fair trial.

In the case at issue, the court deduced from these principles the following:

> 47 The adversarial principle means, as a rule, that the parties have a right to a process of inspecting and commenting on the evidence and observations submitted to the court. However, in some cases it may be necessary for certain information to be withheld from the parties in order to preserve the fundamental rights of a third party or to safeguard an important public interest (see Rowe and Davis v The United Kingdom [GC] no 28901/95, §61, ECHR 2000-II, and V v Finland no 40412/98, §75, ECHR 2007-…).

b) **The UK.** The guiding principle under UK law is the enormous flexibility and discretionary power that courts in enjoy in issuing order tailor-made to the case at issue. For the balancing or interests between the production of documents, and the protection of trade secrets, the leading case is *Warner-Lambert v. Glaxo*[18] where the Court of Appeal held as follows:

> 1. Where the alleged infringer claimed secrecy in an alleged infringing process, the governing principle was that the court should resolve the conflict of interests of the parties by ordering a controlled measure of discovery to selected individuals upon terms ensuring that there should neither be use nor further disclosure of the confidential information to the prejudice of the defendants and yet so that the plaintiffs would have a free full degree of disclosure as would be consistent with adequate protection of any trade secret of the alleged infringer; that the authorities did not purport to lay down a form of universal order in such circumstances nor did they indicate that the court might not in appropriate circumstances at a later stage in the action, direct disclosure to a wider class of persons or on a different basis; that the court must in each case decide what measure of disclosure was appropriate, to whom it should be made and on what terms that disclosure should be given.
>
> 2. Although parties to litigation were generally entitled fully to know what had been disclosed to their legal and technical advisers so as to be able to make

17. European Court of Justice, 14 February 2008, case C-450/06.
18. English Court of Appeal, 7 May 1975, *Warner-Lambert Co. v. Glaxo Laboratories Ltd.* [1975] R.P.C.354.

judgments of their own, this principle must be subject to modification if trade secrets are to be protected and in appropriate circumstances the court may even be justified in wholly excluding disclosure of secret material from a particular party.

The current Civil Procedure Rules (CPR) now specify in para. 31.22 ("Subsequent use of disclosed documents and completed Electronic Documents Questionnaires") that

(1) A party to whom a document has been disclosed may use the document only for the purpose of the proceedings in which it is disclosed, except where –
   (a) the document has been read to or by the court, or referred to, at a hearing which has been held in public;
   (b) the court gives permission; or
   (c) the party who disclosed the document and the person to whom the document belongs agree.
(2) The court may make an order restricting or prohibiting the use of a document which has been disclosed, even where the document has been read to or by the court, or referred to, at a hearing which has been held in public.

c) **Germany.** Already back in 1889, Josef Kohler had suggested protective measures when trade secrets were the subject of civil proceedings.[19] His suggestions – inspection of the secret process by an expert, but not the opponent, undertakings of the opposing party not to use or disclose the secret, and making the hearing and parts of the decision non-public – were not followed up until the EU Enforcement Directive[20] forced a new debate on this issue,[21] not least because prior to the implementation of this Directive, the courts were most restrictive in granting inspection orders in the first place.[22] The basis and requirements for such orders has now been clarified in sec. 140 c Patent Act that reads:

> "(1) The right owner or another entitled person can request from someone who with a certain likelihood has used a patented invention contrary to secs. 9–13 the production of a document or the inspection of a device in its possession, or the inspection of a process that is subject to the patent where this is necessary for the substantiation of the claim. Where the sufficient likelihood concerns an infringement of commercial scale, the claim also covers the production of bank-related, finance-related or trade-related documents. To the extent that the presumed infringer claims that the documents concern secret information, the court takes the necessary steps to provide protection in the case at issue.

19. J. Kohler, Prozeßrechtliche Forschungen *(Studies on procedural law)*, Berlin 1889, 83-88.
20. EU Directive 2004/48/EC.
21. A. Stadler, Geheimnisschutz im Zivilprozeß aus deutscher Sicht *(Secrecy protection in civil procedure from a German point of view)*, 123 Zeitschrift für Zivilprozeß 261 (2010).
22. Although a right of inspection of devices was already contained in sec. 809 Civil Code (1900), the courts refused to properly apply the provision: German Federal Supreme Court, 8 January 1985, GRUR 1985, 512 – *Druckbalken*, with critical comment by Stauder. Different only German Federal Supreme Court, 2 May 2002, 41 IIC 331 (2003) – *Fax Card*. For the situation prior to 1990, the reader is referred to H. Marshall, Der Besichtigungsanspruch *(The Right of Inspection)*, in: Festschrift Albert Preu *(Writings in the Honour of Albert Preu)*, München 1988, 151.

> (2) There is no claim under paragraph 1 if the request would be disproportionate in the case at issue.
>
> (3) The obligation to produce a document or to allow inspection of a device can also be granted in the course of interim proceedings according to secs. 935 – 945 Code of Civil Procedure. The court takes the necessary measures in order to guarantee the protection of confidential information. This applies in particular here the interim order is granted without hearing the other side."

The applicant in a case of interim measures needs to demonstrate a high likelihood of infringement,[23] yet is not required to describe the trade secret in all detail.[24] Normally, the applicant makes the request for inspection together with a request for an interim injunction.

For carrying out the inspection or the production of documents, the District Court Düsseldorf (the main forum for litigating patents in Germany) has developed the following procedure:[25] During the inspection, only the respondent and a technical (or commercial) expert will be present. The petitioner may be represented, but is not allowed to be present in person. The petitioner's representative by way of an undertaking can be obliged to secrecy also towards his client:

> "Where an expert opinion has been drafted in the course of a procedure for obtaining evidence concerning an alleged patent infringement, the secrecy interests of the alleged infringer can be accommodated in a manner that the expert opinion is made available only to the right owner's attorney or representative, while these would then obliged to secrecy.
>
> The expert opinion may not be made available to the right owner in person until the alleged infringer had an opportunity to voice his concerns in keeping the report secret. In order to do so, he has to specify which of the information contained in the expertise contains matters to be kept secret, namely trade secrets, and what disadvantage would result in the making available of such information to the applicant."[26]

Based on the expertise, and hearing the other side, the judge would then determine whether protectable interests of the defendant are at stake, and, if so, to what extent the expertise should be made available to the applicant. The latter is the case where the expertise affirms a high likelihood of infringement. Otherwise, the expertise would not be made available to the applicant.

The judge in granting the request for inspection would thus require the appellant to agree with such a procedure, or else refuse the request for inspection. Thereby, the judge has a sufficient degree of leeway in order to balance the differing interests.

In the main proceedings, the public can be excluded from hearings, and the decision may be rendered in a non-public session as well, sec. 172 Act for the Constitution of Courts (GVG). The court can further order those that are present in

23. Appeal Court Frankfurt, 4 May 2011, GRUR-RR 2012, 10149.
24. German Federal Supreme Court, 13 December 2007, GRUR 2008, 727 – *Schweißmodulgenerator*.
25. T. KÜHNEN, Eine Besichtigung im Patentrecht *(An Inspection under Patent Law)*, GRUR 2005, 185.
26. German Federal Supreme Court, 16 November 2009, GRUR 2010, 318 – *Lichtbogenschnürung*.

a non-public hearing to maintain secrecy about information they have obtained in the course of such hearing, sec. 174 Act for the Constitution of Courts (GVG). This is deemed insufficient in cases where the other party is a competitor, as secs. 172, 174 only refer to the general public, not the parties to the suit.

Thus, to the extent that the above-mentioned expertise is made available to the appellant (trade secrets of the respondent/defendant), or to the extent that the appellant/plaintiff needs to elaborate its trade secrets in the main proceedings (trade secrets of the appellant/plaintiff), no particular safeguards are currently in place to prevent the trade secret being subsequently used by the other party to the proceedings. In addition, one should be aware that sec. 140c Patent Act only applies to cases of patent infringement (and thus not to cases where the right invoked by the plaintiff is a trade secret that allegedly has been misappropriated), and that the above-mentioned Düsseldorf procedure may not necessarily be applied in the same manner by other courts, namely the labour courts that generally hear cases on the misappropriation of trade secrets by former employees.

d) **France.** The facts underlying a recent Supreme Court decision[27] illustrate the conflict of interests rather well: In order to ascertain whether there was an infringement, the petitioner requested the court to allow a seizure (*saisie contrefaçon*), a request that under French law does not require the petitioner to show a likelihood of infringement.[28] The order was granted *ex parte* and subsequently carried out. The respondent objected to the handing over of certain documents to the petitioner, claiming that such documents contained trade secrets. The judge overseeing the seizure thus went through the documents together with the respondent, and decided that certain documents should not be handed over. The petitioner disagreed with this procedure as it should have had a chance to be heard prior to this decision. On appeal, the court decided that the decision on which documents to withhold should be made in the presence of the petitioner's attorney, while the latter should not be allowed to communicate the contents of the discussion to his client: A compromise solution that allows the petitioner to be heard, yet also protects the respondent's trade secrets. For the court of appeal, the legal basis for this approach was sec. 145 Code of Civil Procedure that reads as follows:

> "Where there are legitimate grounds to preserve or to present the evidence of facts upon which the outcome of a suit could depend, the lawfully available measures for the investigation may be ordered either at the request of an interested party, or ex officio."

In an earlier decision, the French Supreme Court held that the existence of a trade secret as such was no reason why presentation of certain documents could not be

27. French Supreme Court, 25 February 2016, 48 IIC 977 – *KCM v. Viel.*
28. The measure is clearly exploratory and may serve to remove the petitioner's doubt as to whether there is infringement or not. The measure is further granted *ex parte*, and for patents does not even require a granted right, but merely a published patent application. It is thus obvious that there is ample room for abuse.

ordered, yet that in such case the judge should take appropriate measures for the protection of the trade secret.[29]

In the case at issue, the Supreme Court held that all communication between an attorney and his client, and between attorneys were privileged, and the attorney had a corresponding obligation of secrecy. The same however was not true for communication between the attorney and third parties, namely the adverse party in a court action.[30] Based on this precedent, the Supreme Court held in the above decision that no secrecy obligation could be construed (or, so it seems, imposed) on an attorney not to communicate information from the other party (the respondent to the action of *saisie contrefaçon*) to his client. It thus appears that legislature needs to step in to fill this gap.

While the legislative and/or judiciary responses to the challenges of providing both an acceptable level of enforcement and trade secret protection may not by perfect in all cases, the comparison above shows that in the last decade, considerable efforts for improvement have been made.

29. French Supreme Court (CC 2nd chambre civile), 8 December 2009, case 08-21225, and 19 March 2013, case 12-13880.
30. So held also by French Supreme Court (CC 1st chambre civile), 31 January 2008, case 06-14.303.

Case No. 48

Interim Procedures and Protective Orders

Makoto Hattori

In view of the purpose of a secrecy order, sec. 105^{quater}(1) of the Patent Act has to be interpreted such that cases of an interlocutory injunction are considered "disputes concerning the infringement of a patent" and such that a secrecy order can also be requested in that context.

Supreme Court, 27 January 2009, Case No. 26 (Kyo) of 1999 – *Liquid Crystal Monitor*

Kōno K.K. v. Nagashima et al.

---

1. BACKGROUND

Judicial remedies available to a person whose patent right has been infringed, especially as a means of seeking an injunction against the infringing act, include interim procedures (sec. 23 of the Civil Provisional Remedies Act) as well as litigation on the merits. A remedy granted in litigation on the merits may not be executed until the judgment becomes final and binding; however, a provisional disposition order may be executed immediately upon issuance, and it can be a very powerful weapon for the patentee.

Sec. 105^{quater} of the Japanese Patent Act stipulates protective orders. A protective order, issued in patent right infringement litigation, bans (i) the use of briefs and evidence containing trade secrets for purposes not related to the conduct of the suit and (ii) their disclosure to persons other than the addressee of the protective order. This legal system came into force in April 2005.[1]

Issues in the present case include determining whether a protective order can be sought in interim procedures rather than litigation on the merits, and whether a case of provisional disposition seeking an injunction against the infringement of a patent right or exclusive license constitutes "litigation concerning the infringement of a patent right or exclusive license" prescribed in the main clause of the main paragraph of sec. 105^{quater}(1) of the Patent Act. See the previous case for details on the interpretation of this provision.

---

1. Law No. 120/2004 of 18 June 2004. Please see Case No. 47 in this volume for the details of a protective order.

The Supreme Court's judgment reversed the original judgment by the Intellectual Property High Court on the grounds that the purpose of the protective order system also applies to interim procedures and held that a petition for a protective order should be permitted in provisional disposition cases as well.

2. DECISION[2]

a) Facts

1. It is disputed in the present case whether a motion for the classification of certain facts introduced into the proceedings as secrets can be raised in cases of interlocutory protection pursuant to sec. $105^{quater}(1)$ of the Patent Act.

2. From the Facts:

(1) The petitioner sued the respondent and appellant [hereinafter: the appellant] in proceedings for an interlocutory injunction for cease and desist of the patent infringement committed through the importation, sale, etc. of the LCD televisions and LCD monitors in dispute. The court had held a hearing at which the appellant was present as the respondent.

(2) The appellant, who at the hearing produced documents containing trade secrets, had filed for a secrecy order with regard to the petitioner's representative, on the basis of sec. $105^{quater}(1)$ of the Patent Act.

3. The previous instances had rejected the motion because the claim for issuance of a secrecy order under sec. $105^{quater}(1)$ of the Patent Act only applied to "disputes concerning the infringement of a patent," which was not understood to include proceedings for an interlocutory injunction.

b) Reasons

4. The impugned decision of the appeal court is to be set aside on the following grounds:

If the documents or evidence to be submitted contain trade secrets, then the party submitting them would like to have their use by the opponent restricted to the purpose of the proceedings and prevent their disclosure to third parties, in order to avoid adverse effects on business. To this end patent law permits issuance of a secrecy order (sec. 105^{quater} – sec. 105^{sexies}, sec. 200bis and sec. 201 of the Patent Act). These provisions punish the use of such trade secrets by third parties and by the opponent insofar as such use is not restricted to the purpose of the proceedings.

Proceedings for interlocutory injunctions concern disputes that are different to normal proceedings insofar as the necessity of the interlocutory injunction has to be examined. However, there are no differences regarding other aspects, and the

2. Published in 63-1 Minshū 271 = 2035 Hanei Jihō 127 = 1292 Hanrei Times 154 = N. NAKAYAMA et al. (eds.), Tokkyo Hanrei Hyakusen *(Hundred Selected Patent Cases)*, 4th ed. 2012, 184 = T. ŌBUCHI et al. (eds.), Chitekizaisan hō hanrei shū *(Intellectual Property Law Case Book)*, 2nd ed. 2015, 209. English translation in 41 IIC 858 (2010).

above-mentioned conflict [between the production of documents and their classified nature] can arise for a party in the present context. Hence the instrument of a secrecy order cannot be handled or interpreted as if it were inapplicable in the present context. The necessity of expediting matters that is inherent to proceedings for an interlocutory injunction does not conflict with a secrecy order.

In patent law the term "dispute" is used, as the case may be, not only for regular patent proceedings, but also for civil matters in general (sec. 54(2), sec. 168(2) of the Patent Act). In view of the purpose of a secrecy order, sec. $105^{quater}(1)$ of the Patent Act has to be interpreted such that cases of an interlocutory injunction be considered "disputes concerning the infringement of a patent" and such that a claim for issuance of a secrecy order can also accrue in that context.

5. Consequently, the decision of the appeal court is evidently based on a legal error. The judgment of the appeal court therefore has to be set aside, as does the judgment of the district court. The case is remanded back to the district court for continuation of the proceedings. The decision was unanimous.

3. ANALYSIS

a) Introduction

Judicial means by which a patentee may seek an injunction against a patent infringement in Japan include the initiation of litigation on the merits and the filing of a petition for a provisional disposition.

A provisional disposition enjoining patent infringement is one that determines a provisional status that temporarily gives rise to the final realisation of a right (satisfactory provisional disposition; sec. 23 of the Civil Provisional Remedies Act), so the contents of a decision upholding the petition are almost the same as a decision in litigation on the merits, and a provisional decision may be immediately executed upon notification (in the case of litigation on the merits, the judgment of the first instance may not be immediately executed if the respondent appeals the case). Moreover, a petition for a provisional disposition is rather cost-effective (2,000 yen per petition) and may be withdrawn unilaterally by the petitioner (without the consent of the respondent). For these reasons, a provisional disposition enjoining patent infringement is often sought as a means of achieving the prompt resolution of patent infringement disputes in Japan.

The following sections give an overview of the interim procedures for enjoining patent infringement, and then examine what the petitioner and the respondent should take heed of in these procedures.

b) An overview of the interim procedures for enjoining patent infringement in Japan

(1) Jurisdiction

Provisional proceedings enjoining patent infringement fall within the exclusive jurisdiction of the court that has jurisdiction over the merits (sec. 12(2) of the Civil

Provisional Remedies Act); pursuant to sec. 6(1) of the Code of Civil Procedure, the case will be heard before the Tokyo or Osaka District Court, which both have an intellectual property division.

(2) Requirements for the issuance of a provisional remedy order

In order for a petition for a provisional disposition enjoining patent infringement to be upheld, there must be prima facie evidence of the existence of a right to be preserved and the necessity of a provisional remedy, as is the case with ordinary provisional disposition cases (sec. 13(1) and (2) of the Civil Provisional Remedies Act). In general, under the Code of Civil Procedure, the term "proof" (*shōmei*) refers to an item that is sufficient to convince the judge, while the term "prima facie evidence" (*somei*) refers to an issue that is not proven but is sufficient to make the judge presume that the allegation is probable. In addition, in the case of prima facie evidence, the only permitted evidence is "evidence that can be examined immediately" on the appointed date (sec. 13(2) of the Civil Provisional Remedies Act and sec. 188 of the Code of Civil Procedure). Satisfactory provisional dispositions, including provisional dispositions enjoining patent right infringement, temporarily give rise to the final realisation of a right; therefore, in practice, prima facie evidence in the sense set forth above is not sufficient, and "a higher level of prima facie evidence" (in which the judge's determination is very unlikely to be reversed even when the respondent in the provisional disposition case presents rebutting evidence) is required.[3]

For clarification, damages may not be sought in interim procedures because such remedy may be granted at a later date through procedures on the merits, so the "necessity of a provisional remedy" is deemed to be absent. In order to make that claim before the court, one needs to initiate litigation on the merits.

i) Existence of a right to be preserved

The allocation of the burden of prima facie evidence in a provisional disposition case can be considered in the same way as the allocation of the burden of proof;[4] therefore, the contents of allegations and prima facie evidence concerning a right to be preserved (sec. 13(2) of the Civil Provisional Remedies Act) can be considered almost in the same way as in the case of procedures on the merits. The respondent can claim the invalidity of the patent or prior use as a defence. However, the only permitted evidence is "evidence that can be examined immediately" on the appointed date (sec. 13(2) of the Civil Provisional Remedies Act and sec. 188 of the Code of Civil Procedure), while document production orders (sec. 223 of the Code of Civil Procedure) and witness examinations that require summoning (sec. 185 of the Code of Civil Procedure) are unavailable. With regard to the question of whether the protective order, introduced in the 2004 revision of the Patent Act, can be used in interim procedures, its possibility is not expressly excluded by the provisions of the

3. M. Takeda, Chitekizaisanken shingai yōron [tokkyo/ishō/shōhyō] *(A Summary of Intellectual Property Right Infringement [Patents/Designs/Trademarks])*, 4th ed., Hatumei Kyōkai, 2003, 294.
4. T. Kikui and T. Muramatsu, Zentei minji soshōhō, *(Fully Revised Lectures on the Code of Civil Procedure)*, vol. 2, Nippon Hyoron Sha, 1989, 447.

Patent Act (sec. 105^{quater} *et seq.*). Thus, the author is of the opinion that the above Supreme Court decision was appropriate.

ii) The necessity of a provisional remedy

In provisional disposition cases concerning patent right infringement, the necessity of a provisional remedy is acknowledged if (i) actual or threatened infringement is acknowledged and is expected to continue into the future and (ii) the right has been commercially worked by the right holder. With regard to (ii), the question of whether the term "commercially worked" here includes cases where a company has granted a license to another company without working itself was answered affirmatively by the Tokyo District Court:[5] "Generally speaking, the holder of a utility model right, when granting a non-exclusive license, usually makes the decision in the light of the prospective licensee's production capacity or selling capability, ... the holder will be placed in a difficult position in its relationship with the licensee if the infringer's act is left unaddressed. Furthermore, its social status as the developer or manager of industrial property rights could possibly be endangered." The Osaka District Court also affirmed the necessity of a provisional remedy on 22 October 1991[6] on the grounds that a product embodying the patent at issue was competing with the alleged infringing product.

(3) *Petition and hearing*

The court can only issue an interim injunction after the appointed date of an oral argument or a hearing that the respondent can attend (cases requiring hearings; sec. 23(4) of the Civil Provisional Remedies Act). In practice, it is common for the first *ex parte* hearing to be held about two to four weeks after the filing of the petition, and for the hearing to be attended by both the petitioner and the respondent to be held about one month later (however, the intervals may be shorter in urgent cases). Other than that, there is hardly any difference to ordinary proceedings. What makes Japan different from foreign countries is that there is little difference between interim procedures and merits procedures in terms of the parties' burden of making preparations for substantiating their allegations, and the actual duration of examining allegations on the alleged infringement and invalidity.

(4) *A provisional decision and its execution*

If a court renders an affirmative decision on a petition, the decision is issued after security has been provided by the petitioner or subject to the condition of it being provided by the petitioner at a later date. This security is intended to cover any damage that may result if the final and binding judgment on the merits turns out to be different (sec. 14 of the Civil Provisional Remedies Act). In practice, in the case of a provisional disposition enjoining patent right infringement, prior to the issuance of a provisional disposition order, the court requires the petitioner to

5. Tokyo District Court, 16 February 1990, Case No. 7011 (Mo) of 1989, 22-1 Mutaishū 1.
6. Osaka District Court, 22 October 1991, Case No. 548 (Yo) of 1988, the website of the courts <http://www.courts.go.jp/app/files/hanrei_jp/692/014692_hanrei.pdf>.

deposit with an official depository the amount of money determined by referencing the damages expected to be incurred by the respondent as a result of the order. The amount of the security may be, for example, sufficient to cover the profits that the respondent is expected to lose over a period of six to 12 months; however, in the author's experience this amount varies from one case to another because one of the considerations seems to be the chances of the provisional disposition decision being reversed in the subsequent litigation on the merits.

A provisional disposition order becomes enforceable immediately upon notification, and the provisional disposition can be executed with the original copy of the provisional disposition order as a title of obligation (sec. 52(2) of the Civil Provisional Remedies Act) and simultaneously with the service of the provisional remedy order to the respondent because of the required secrecy of the execution of the provisional remedy (sec. 52 (1) and sec. 43(3) of the Civil Provisional Remedies Act). It should be noted that the provisional remedy order must be executed within two weeks from its issuance (sec. 43(2) of the Civil Provisional Remedies Act).

In addition, there are few actual cases in which petitions for the stay of execution set forth below (sec. 27 of the Civil Provisional Remedies Act) are approved, so if an upholding decision is issued, the respondent's manufacture and sale will most likely be enjoined. Hence, most cases will reach settlement agreements and withdraw their petitions before court decisions are issued in order to avoid actual injunctions.

With regard to the means of provisional disposition, unlike the procedures on the merits, seizure by a court execution officer may be requested as a "necessary disposition" (sec. 24 of the Civil Provisional Remedies Act) for the preservation of injunction and disposal purposes. In some cases, seizure by a court execution officer was permitted not only for the infringing goods themselves, but also the semi-finished goods or associated manufacturing machines.[7]

(5) Appeal against a provisional remedy order

i) Procedures for the respondent

If an order upholding the petition is issued, the respondent may file an objection to the provisional remedy or petition for its revocation with the court that issued the order (sec. 26 *et seq.* and sec. 37 *et seq.* of the Civil Provisional Remedies Act). A party (including the petitioner) who has a complaint regarding a provisional remedy may file an appeal before the appeal court within an unextendible period of two weeks from the date of receipt of service thereof (sec. 41(1) and (2) of the Civil Provisional Remedies Act). No further appeal may be filed against a judicial decision on an appeal concerning a provisional remedy (sec. 41(3) of the Civil Provisional Remedies Act).

a. Objection to a provisional remedy

Once a decision upholding a petition for a provisional remedy order is issued, the respondent may file a petition for the revocation or modification of the order with the court that issued the order (sec. 38 *et seq.* of the Civil Provisional Remedies Act).

7. Hirosaki Branch, Aomori District Court, 22 May 1972, Case No. 2 (Yo) of 1971, 4-1 Mutaishū 313; Tokyo District Court, 6 June 2000, Case No. 22179 (Yo) of 1999, 1034 Hanrei Times 235.

The nature of this system is described as a petition for the renewed examination of the provisional remedy order in terms of whether there is an actual right to be preserved and its necessity through oral arguments or through a hearing that both parties may attend as if the examination had taken place immediately before the issuance of the provisional order;[8] However, in the case of a provisional disposition enjoining patent right infringement, a careful examination has already been made during the interim procedures as discussed above, so the petitioner cannot usually expect that the court will revoke its decision in response to the objection to the provisional remedy.

b. Revocation of a provisional remedy

A provisional remedy is revoked upon the respondent's request if (i) litigation on the merits is not instituted (sec. 37 of the Civil Provisional Remedies Act), (ii) the circumstances have changed (sec. 38 of the Civil Provisional Remedies Act), and (iii) there are special circumstances (sec. 39 of the Civil Provisional Remedies Act).

With regard to (i), the provisional remedy order is revoked upon the respondent's petition if the petitioner does not institute litigation on the merits and submit a written document to that effect within the specified period of time.

With regard to (ii), if the right to be preserved or the necessity of a provisional remedy ceases to exist or the circumstances have otherwise changed, the provisional remedy is revoked upon the respondent's petition. "Changes in the circumstances" include, for example, a case in which a judgment against the plaintiff is rendered in litigation on the merits and becomes final and binding, and a case in which a trial decision declaring the invalidity of the patent at issue is rendered and becomes final and binding. (However, the Osaka District Court on 1 February 2002[9] held that a provisional remedy may be revoked before an invalidation decision becomes final and binding on the grounds of changes in the circumstances.)

With regard to (iii), the provisional disposition order is revoked when the order appears likely to cause irreparable damage or there are any other special circumstances, subject to the condition that security be provided by the respondent; however, this raises the question of exactly what circumstances are "special." In this respect, the Osaka District Court on 20 September 1984[10]approved the revocation of a provisional disposition due to special circumstances considering the fact that the damage that would be caused to the petitioner by a provisional decision was without doubt far greater than the damage that would be caused to the respondent by the revocation of the provisional disposition, and considering the circumstances that gave a prima facie evidence that the utility model right at issue will most likely be invalidated by the Patent Office.

---

8. I. NAKAYAMA, Hozen igi no mōshitate *(Filing an Objection to a Provisional Remedy)*, in: H. SEGI et al. (eds.) (complied under the supervision of U. YAMAZAKI), Chūshaku minji hozen hō *(The Civil Provisional Remedies Act Annotated)*, Vol. 1, Kinzai, 1999, 370.
9. Osaka District Court on 1 February 2002, Case No. 59032 (Mo) of 2001.
10. Osaka District Court, 20 September 1984, Case No. 2907 (Mo) of 1984, 16-3 Mutaishū 613.

c. A petition for the stay in the execution of a provisional remedy

An objection to a provisional remedy or petition for the revocation of a provisional remedy alone, or an appeal against a decision to revoke a provisional remedy order alone does not have the effect of staying the execution of the provisional remedy; therefore, if a stay of execution is sought, a separate petition must be filed (secs. 27, 40, and 42 of the Civil Provisional Remedies Act; a petition for the stay of execution is not allowed in the case of revocation due to the non-initiation of litigation on the merits (sec. 37 of the Civil Provisional Remedies Act)). However, the stay of execution is subject to strict requirements: "Only when a prima facie case is made for the presence of circumstances that clearly provide grounds for the revocation of the provisional remedy order and for the likelihood of irreparable damage resulting from the execution of the provisional remedy." Once a provisional decision is issued, the respondent must expect that the act at issue will be enjoined unless the respondent can give specific and convincing explanations that it has voluntarily stopped the act or a settlement agreement has been reached between the parties.

ii) Procedures for the petitioner

If a decision dismissing the petition for a provisional disposition order is issued, the petitioner may file an immediate appeal within a non-extendable period of two weeks from the date of receipt of notification (sec. 19(1) of the Civil Provisional Remedies Act). If the appeal is allowed by the court in charge of the appeal as a result of the immediate appeal, the respondent may file an objection to the provisional remedy or petition for its revocation with that court; however, if the appeal is dismissed, the petitioner may not make a re-appeal (sec. 19(2) of the Civil Provisional Remedies Act).

(6) Unjust provisional disposition and compensation for damage

If a provisional disposition order is revoked after execution, the question arises whether the petitioner is subject to tortious liability for having obtained and executed the provisional disposition order.

In this respect, the Osaka High Court on 15 October 2004[11] affirmed the existence of negligence as follows "Generally speaking, if a provisional disposition order is revoked in objection or appeal procedures, or a decision against the petitioner is rendered in litigation on the merits and becomes final and binding, negligence on the part of the petitioner should be presumed unless there are special circumstances that indicate otherwise; however, if there was a good reason for the petitioner to take such action, such revocation alone should not be taken as inevitably implying negligence on the part of the petitioner (see Supreme Court, 24 December 1968, Case No. 260 (O) of 1968, 22-13 Minshū 3428)."[12] "It stands to reason that this also holds true in a case where, after a provisional disposition order was issued and executed with regard to the right to claim an injunction based on a patent right, which is claimed to be preserved, a trial decision declaring the invalidity of the patent becomes final and binding ... if a provisional disposition to enjoin manufacturing

11. Osaka High Court, 15 October 2004, Case No. 648 (Ne) of 2004, 1188 Hanrei Times 313.
12. Supreme Court, 24 December 1968, Case No. 260 (O) of 1968, 22-13 Minshū 3428.

and sales is executed, it is not rare for the respondent to suffer very serious damage or consequences to its business and credibility ... given this, denying negligence on the part of the petitioner by mentioning in general, abstract terms that patent rights were established and registered after examinations and decisions by Patent Office examiners or that an inventive step is often a difficult and subtle issue to be clear on, is to disregard equity between the parties and is not reasonable ... judging whether there was a good reason why the defendant filed a petition for the present provisional disposition order and obtained and executed the order ... should come after examining whether the defendant knew about or could have easily learned about prior art before filing the petition for the present provisional disposition order and then examining whether there were reasonable grounds for the defendant to believe that the patented invention at issue was an inventive step based on the prior art that the defendant already knew about or could have easily learned about." Other cases of a similar nature in which negligence on the part of the petitioner was confirmed include a decision by the Tokyo District Court of 17 December 2002 and a decision by the Osaka District Court of 13 April 1995.[13]

Given the petitioner's ability to foresee that the respondent will face serious economic consequences by the provisional decision and that there can be a controversy as to the validity of the right at issue, it seems reasonable to hold the petitioner liable for making compensation for the damage from the perspective of equity, in principle, and the author agrees with the court precedents mentioned above.

(7) Relationship with litigation on the merits

It is possible to initiate interim proceedings and litigation on the merits at the same time. In practice, litigation on the merits is initiated to enjoin an infringing act and obtain compensation for damage and, at the same time, interim proceedings are commenced for a provisional disposition in order to promptly obtain a judgment on the former point and put pressure on the adverse party. If litigation on the merits is raised and a petition for a provisional disposition is filed simultaneously, more often than not, the case will be handled by the same division of the court; a hearing and an oral argument on the alleged infringement and invalidity will be scheduled for the same date and time; and each party will present completely the same arguments and evidence for both. In addition, if the court forms a decision that the patent is infringed and valid, a provisional decision will be rendered first, followed by an examination of the alleged damage in litigation on the merits. One practical strategy may be to initiate litigation on the merits first, and file a petition for a provisional disposition at the time when the court's determination on the alleged infringement is found to be in favour of the plaintiff.

13. Tokyo District Court, 17 December 2002, Case No. 22452 (Wa) of 2001, the website of the courts <http://www.courts.go.jp/app/files/hanrei_jp/435/011435_hanrei.pdf>; Osaka District Court, 13 April 1995, Case No. 2996 (Wa) of 1993, 27-3 Chizaishū 930.

4. COMPARATIVE REMARKS

While the issuance of protective orders for the protection of trade secrets is addressed in the comparative remarks of Case No. 47 in this volume, a closer look should be given to interim or provisional measures in general. In many jurisdictions, these are of major importance both for obtaining evidence as well as for enjoining the alleged infringer.

a) The **US** *discovery* is available in all sorts of proceedings and requires the other party to supply a myriad of documents. While the discovery is meant as a preparation for trial, it is not a surprise measure, and it takes place without the intervention of a bailiff. The scope of permissible discovery is broad and allows a party to seek from its opponent or a non-party any information that is not protected by a recognised privilege and is either relevant to an issue in the case or appears 'reasonably calculated' to lead to admissible relevant evidence.

On the other hand, the *preliminary injunction* is considered an extraordinary remedy, to be granted only when monetary damages cannot make a patent owner whole. To obtain a preliminary injunction, the patent owner must show: '[1] that he is likely to succeed on the merits, [2] that he is likely to suffer irreparable harm in the absence of preliminary relief, [3] that the balance of equities tips in his favour, and [4] that an injunction is in the public interest'.[14] Interim injunctions are granted only in a minority of cases in which they are sought, as the showing required for injunctive relief is often difficult to make at an early stage of the proceeding before liability is established.

b) In the **UK**, the *Anton Piller order* (now *seizure order*) was developed particularly for IP cases and consisted essentially of an *ex parte* court order to give the other party access to the defendant's premises so as to inspect the defendant's premises and seize, copy or photograph material demonstrating the alleged infringement; to deliver up infringing goods, and keep infringing stock or incriminating papers; and in many cases, to require answers to questions concerning sources of supply or the subsequent destination of illicit material.

To obtain such order, the petitioner must satisfy the court that there is an extremely strong prima facie case of infringement, that the damage is likely to be very serious, and that the defendant possesses incriminating articles or documents which otherwise may be destroyed or removed before any application *inter partes* can be made. A cross-undertaking in damages must be given. The procedure was rightly tightened up in 1994,[15] notably by requiring that an independent supervising solicitor accompany the inspection party and serve the order on the defendant. That of course has increased the costs of search orders considerably, with the possibly beneficial effect that they are less frequently used.

Procedures before either the Patents Court or the Intellectual Property Enterprise Court are now so fast that requests for *interim injunctions* have become less frequent. A typical case for the principles applied to interim injunctions is *SmithKline*

14. US CAFC, *Titan Tire Corp v. Case New Holland, Inc*, 566 F.3d 1372, 1375–76 (Fed. Cir. 2009) (quoting US Supreme Court, *Winter v. Nat Res Def Council, Inc*, 129 S. Ct. 365, 374 (2008)).
15. English Court of Appeal, 8 July 1992, *Universal Thermosensors v. Hibben* [1992] 1 WLR 840.

Beecham v. Generics.[16] Here, the injunction was granted because the plaintiff had a good arguable case and damages would not be an adequate remedy at trial. Owing to the complexity of the matter, the Court held that it was impossible to determine the relative strengths of the parties' contentions. However, given the well-known fact that once exposed to competition, the price of a patented drug would spiral down very quickly, damages were unable to compensate the plaintiff for loss of market share from which it would be unable to recover. The Court also concluded that the defendant's damages would be unquantifiable if the injunction was granted and that the order of damage to the claimant was likely to be a good deal greater than that to the defendant.

c) In **Germany**, a claim for *inspection* under sec. 140c Patent Act requires that there is a reasonable likelihood of infringement. This likelihood must be demonstrated by the plaintiff.

There are different ways how to enforce such claim for inspection. The claim for inspection based on a specific patent may be granted in *preliminary injunction proceedings* (see below) upon request of the patentee. By issuing a preliminary injunction, the court may order the potentially infringing defendant to allow a court-appointed expert and claimant's attorneys to enter the defendant's premises and inspect a device. The court may further order the defendant that specific documents must be presented to the expert.[17]

Cases of *interim relief* in patent actions are infrequent owing to the difficulty of showing a good case in technically complicated matters. The requirement of urgency is strictly interpreted and requires the IP owner to act quickly, according to some courts within one month's time limit.[18] A successful request requires a clear infringement - though not necessarily a simple technology - and a confirmation of the patent's validity beyond the mere act of granting the patent. This is typically the case once the patent has successfully survived opposition or nullity proceedings and has thereby proven to be solid, even if such decisions are subject to appeal or new validity attacks could be launched.[19] Thus, one should be aware that although the estoppel of invalidity cannot be raised in ordinary proceedings, consideration to this aspect is given in interim proceedings. In order to avoid an *ex parte* interim injunction, defendants can submit a 'protective letter' ('*Schutzschrift*') to the court where such request is likely to be made (there are four courts where patent cases are frequently litigated in Germany), which is a kind of anticipated defence and which may persuade the court to set an *inter partes* hearing instead of granting the injunction *ex parte*.

d) In **France**, the *saisie-contrefaçon* was first introduced in the Patent Act 1844 and is an interim order available *ex parte*. It is different from the UK and Italian discovery orders because the patentee is not required to furnish prima facie evidence

16. English Patents Court, 23 October 2001, *SmithKline Beecham v. Generics* [2001] EWHC 563 (Pat).
17. BUSSE-KEUKENSCHRIJVER/KAESS, *Patentgesetz (Commentary to the German Patent Act)*, 8th ed. 2016, § 140c recitals 21 *et seq*.
18. Which would be the case for Munich and Düsseldorf.
19. T. KÜHNEN, Handbuch der Patentverletzung *(Handbook of the Patent Infringement)*, 7th ed. Heymanns 2014, recitals 2029 and 2037.

of infringement to get the *saisie contrefaçon* order.[20] The inspection is carried out by a bailiff, and the party requesting the *saisie* must not be present. Depending on the scope of the order, the bailiff may either only inspect, or also take samples. In **Italy**, inspection orders (*descrizione*) require a showing of likely infringement.

Interim injunctions can be requested under Article 615-3 of the Industrial Property Code (in the new version as of 2007), yet seem to be rarely granted. In judging the balance of probabilities, the judge would have to take into account the likelihood of infringement, the strength of the underlying IP right, and the defences by the alleged infringer. **Italy** has comparable rules. France has a special expedited *inter partes* procedure in order to accommodate the interests of both parties: An excellent example of how to balance competing interests for an alleged infringement occurring 17 days before the expiry of the patent is the French *Valsartan* decision.[21] Here, the Court held that even such a short period of time allowed for an *inter partes* hearing: "it should not be forgotten that there exists an urgent *inter partes* procedure that even in a brief interval allows for the other party to be heard. The courts are able to set dates for oral hearings in such cases even on weekends and bank holidays, and that school holidays do not compromise this at all, in particular in the month of November when there are no court holidays."

e) The **Dutch** *kort geding* comes closer to a pre-emptive decision on the merits and is carried out according to a very strict timetable, normally within two to three months. Although urgency is also required here, the courts do not interpret this too strictly, and even in patent cases, about half of all cases are decided by *kort geding* procedures.[22]

20. This principle has been pointed out by the Douai Appeal Court, 4 February 2002, 2002 Annales de la propriété industrielle 17.
21. Appeal Court Paris, 11 December 2012, 45 IIC 945 (2014) – *Valsartan*. The decision was upheld by the French Supreme Court, 16 September 2014, PIBD 2014, 1016-III-836.
22. *Kort geding* procedures have become less popular with IP owners after the courts have started to give more consideration to the defendant's interests: Hague Court of Appeal, 12 September 1996, *Hoffman-Laroche v. Orgonen*, 1996 Intellectuelle Eigendom en Reclamerecht 237.

Case No. 49

Defence of Invalidity

Asayo Ohyori and Christopher Heath

Even if a device was publicly known or used, and should not have been granted utility model protection, a utility model right does not lose its effect until a final and binding decision of the Japanese Patent Office invalidates the registration of the utility model.

Imperial Supreme Court ("*Daishin'in*"), 23 April 1917,
Case No. 1033 (O) of 1916 –
Apparatus for Producing Bracelets

Ōi Tokujiō v. Yamane Tomokazu

1. BACKGROUND

a) Imperial Supreme Court decisions

An invention lacks patentability if it does not fulfil the requirements specified under the Patent Act. If a patent was nevertheless granted for such an invention, a request for a trial on patent invalidation may be filed with the Patent Office (Patent Act, sec. 123(1)), and once a decision to invalidate a patent in that trial has become final and binding, the patent right is deemed never to have existed (Patent Act, sec. 125).

The question is how then the court should react if a claim of patent infringement was based on a patent which was granted to an invention which lacks patentability, but has not yet been invalidated by a decision of an invalidation trial. In Japan, it had been a longstanding and widely accepted doctrine since the Meiji Period that the Patent Office has exclusive jurisdiction over grant and extinction (invalidation, revocation etc.) of a patent, and that such matters are outside the courts' jurisdiction which only have power over issues of infringement.

Imperial Supreme Court decision of 15 September 1904[1] is the first judgment which clarified such doctrine: "A patent granted by the Patent Office continues to exist unless held invalid by an administrative decision of the Patent Office, and it is appropriate to construe that ordinary courts can decide neither on the correctness of a patent nor on the existence or non-existence of the effect of a patent ... a person accused of infringing a patent right in civil or criminal courts cannot escape civil or

1. Case No. 2662 (Re) of 1903, 10 Keiroku 1679 (a criminal case on breach of patent law).

criminal responsibilities by claiming and proving to the court that the patent is invalid. That person must file a request for a trial before the Patent Office and invalidate the patent". The judgment also stated that a court should stay the proceedings of a patent infringement case if a request for invalidity of the patent was filed before the Patent Office.

A similar reasoning was adopted in decisions of the Imperial Supreme Court of 23 April 1917 (as explained in detail below in 2); 4 December 1922;[2] and 22 March 1940,[3] thereby making it established case law that invalidity of a patent (or any other intellectual property right registered with the Patent Office) could not be argued as a defence within an infringement case.

b) Supreme Court's decision in *Kilby* case

This fundamental doctrine which dominated the court practice for nearly 100 years was overturned to a certain extent when the Supreme Court changed its attitude and handed down the landmark *Kilby* judgment on 11 April 2000.[4] It held that a court considering a claim of patent infringement is *capable* of judging whether or not there exists a clear reason to invalidate the patent even prior to the issuance of a final decision by the Patent Office to invalidate the patent. The judgment did not change the traditional idea that the findings of an infringement court does not have the power to invalidate the patent per se; but it concluded that "a claim for injunction, damages or other claims based on a patent will be treated as *beyond the scope of the patent's right*, except in special circumstances, when there exists a clear reason to invalidate the said patent, and therefore in such a case, the claim will not be allowed" (emphasis added. Generally referred to as the "Abuse of Right Defence"). Prior decisions handed down by the Imperial Supreme Court were thus reversed to the extent contrary to the explanation given in the above *Kilby* judgment.

2. DECISION[5]

a) Facts

The plaintiff was the owner of the utility model right registration No. 32543 with the title "Apparatus for producing bracelets", and the registered scope of the utility model covered the "Structure of apparatus for producing bracelets in which a rolling shaft is rotated over a furnace by a gear shaft combination as shown in the figures and the description". The defendant argued that it was publicly known and publicly used that a combination of two big and small gears were used to allow a higher rotation of the rolling shaft, and there was no infringement of the utility model. The Osaka Court of Appeal (*Kōsoin*) on 30 September 1916 confirmed the scope of the plaintiff's utility

2. Case No. 178 (O) of 1922, 1 Minshū 697.
3. Case No. 10 (Re) of 1940, 29 Hōritsu Hyōron 290 (in the part of Shohō *(diverse law)*).
4. Supreme Court, 11 April 2000, Case No. 364 (O) of 1998, 54-4 Minshū 1368 – *Kilby III*. Case No. 50 in this volume.
5. Published in 23 Minroku 654.

model right as registered and affirmed infringement. The defendant filed an appeal to the Imperial Supreme Court against this decision.

b) Reasons

The arguments of the defendant were as follows: there was absolutely no doubt in the interpretation of the Utility Model Act that everyone could use and produce products which were publicly known and publicly used, and because of this, even if the plaintiff has registered such products as a utility model, there was no change in the nature of the publicly known and publicly used products and no obstruction to the right of the defendant should be affirmed. This was confirmed by the decision of this court about a patent invalidation, Case No. 240 (O) of 1911. The former instance should thus consider whether the products produced and used by the defendant were publicly known and publicly used or not, because the defendant argued that the products were publicly known and publicly used, and the Court of Appeal should affirm the defence and reject the claim of the plaintiff if the products were publicly known and publicly used.

Nevertheless, the utility model was registered as a new industrial device.[6] So even if the device was publicly known or used, and should not have been granted utility model protection, the utility model right does not lose its effect as of right until a final and binding decision of the Japanese Patent Office invalidates the registration of the utility model. So it is adequate that the former instance decided that "clearly, the act of the defendant infringed the right as of law, given that the utility model right of the plaintiff clearly existed and the structure of the defendant's apparatus is similar to the structure of the plaintiff's, and the defence of the defendant's attorney has no basis". There is no conflict between this explanation and the judgment cited by the defendant, which only stated that even if a new product is granted a patent by an addition of a new idea to publicly known and used parts, there was no obstruction to producing these publicly known or used parts as such. Thus, the plaintiff has no grounds for appeal.

3. ANALYSIS

a) Ideas behind the Imperial Supreme Court decisions and difficulties posed

The decisions of the Imperial Supreme Court are said to have derived from the following legal theories: binding effect of administrative acts, and distribution of power between the Patent Office and the courts.[7] It was said that since granting a patent is an administrative act, a new administrative act (namely, an administrative decision by the Patent Office) is necessary to overturn and invalidate a patent; and it was thought that

6. The current Utility Model Act allows registration without screening the novelty or non-obviousness of the device (cf. Utility Model Act, sec. 6-2), but this was only after the amendment in 1993.
7. M. TAKABE, Mukō riyū ga sonzai suru koto ga akirakana tokkyoken ni motozuku sashitome tō no seikyū to kenri no ranyō *(Injunction claim based on a patent which has clear ground of invalidity and abuse of right)*, in: Hōsōkai (ed.), Saikōsai Hanrei Kaisetsu Minjihen Heisei 12 nendo jō *(Analysis of Supreme Court Civil Cases of 2000, vol. 1)*, 2003, 418, at 427. Also Tokyo High Court, 18 May 1995, Case No. 3375 (Ne) of 1994, 27-2 Chiteki zaishū 443.

an invalidation of a patent, like a grant of a patent, must primarily pass the scrutiny of administrative judges with specialised technical knowledge, and that it was appropriate for the judiciary to focus on reviewing the lawfulness of administrative decisions.

However, the refusal of the court to consider the existence of invalidity completely within an infringement case mainly poses two difficulties. One is the problem of unjust result. As mentioned earlier in 1, an invention which lacks patentability should not be granted a patent, and even if it happens to be granted, there is no substantive reason to allow an owner of such a patent to exercise exclusive power over others. For example, in the Imperial Supreme Courts' decision of 1917 introduced above, the court reasoned that a utility model granted to a publicly known or used device is still completely effective, and rejected the need to determine what is publicly known and used. This would result in giving power to a patentee to prohibit the production of publicly known and used devices (even if temporarily[8]), and to profit exclusively from what should be the common property of the public. It could be said that by refusing to consider the issue of publicly known and used device at all, the 1917 decision applied the traditional doctrine too rigidly and failed to strike the right balance between the patentee and the public interest.

On the other hand, if a court considering a claim of patent infringement stays the proceedings (Patent Act, sec. 168(2)) to wait for a decision of an invalidation trial to become final and binding, it will inevitably delay the court proceedings and lead to the other problem of litigation efficiency and speed. Generally, it takes a certain time for an administrative decision in an invalidation trial to become final and binding.[9] In addition, unlike the defences argued within an infringement case, which will be controlled under certain timeframe set by the judge, there is no time limit to file of a request for an invalidation trial and a party can file as many such requests as desired as long as they are based on different facts or evidence.[10] Speedy resolution is essential for patent infringement disputes, and it has even been said that "justice delayed is justice denied".[11]

---

8. If the court ignored invalidity issues and judged in favour of a patentee, and the patent was later found to be invalid in an invalidation trial after the infringement judgment has become final and binding, it was possible for the losing party to file a retrial under sec. 338(1)(viii) of the Code of Civil Procedure 1996 (before the 2011 amendment to the Patent Act mentioned in Case No. 57) and rescind the judgment. However, the injustice done to the alleged infringer in the meantime is clear. See Case No. 57 for further details.
9. Even if a patent is found invalid at an invalidation trial, the losing party can file an action asking to rescind the decision to the High Court (possibly further appeal to the Supreme Court) before the decision to be finalised. If such action succeeds, the administrative judges must re-open the invalidation trial, and issue a decision again. There are also chances for the patentee to request the correction of the patent claim (Patent Act, sec. 134[bis]. Article on procedure and time limit for correction was amended several times and differs depending on point of time), which will result in further delays.
10. The current sec. 167 of the Patent Act states "When a final and binding trial decision in a trial for patent invalidation ... has been registered, the parties ... may not file a request for a trial on the basis of the same facts and evidence". For details, see Case No. 25 in this volume.
11. N. Nakayama, Kōchi-gijyutsu no kōben no kyohi *(Allowability of defence of publicly known prior art)*, in: R. Murabayashi et al. (eds.), Hanrei Tokkyo Shingaihō *(Patent Infringement Case Law)*, 1983, 305, at 308.

b) Methods taken to overcome the above difficulties

A method the Supreme Court has taken later to mitigate such difficulties was to allow consideration of publicly known and used art in the area of claim construction. Supreme Court decision on 4 August 1964[12] held: "When determining the scope of a utility model which includes a device publicly known and used at the time of application, such publicly known and used device should be excluded and the extent of the new device should be clarified".

However, this method was insufficient for cases in which the whole of the invention/device registered was publicly known or used. It did also lead to an unnatural construction of the claim, departing from its actual wording and written description, and carried the danger of inviting inconsistency with the claim construction of the same patent in invalidation trials due to the different standard.

Another possible solution would have been to adopt the "Defence of Publicly Known Art" (a defence to limit the effect of a patent if the alleged product/skill is a publicly known or used art) as did a couple of the lower courts, but this, too, would have been insufficient for cases based on patents with a reason for invalidation other than to do with publicly known or used art.

Under such circumstances, the defence of Abuse of Right as admitted by the Supreme Court in *Kilby* (see the following Case No. 50) can be appreciated as overcoming the aforementioned difficulties while avoiding a head-to-head collision with the traditional theories of the "distribution of powers" and the "effect of administrative acts".

4. COMPARATIVE REMARKS

As the above case goes far back in history, it may be appropriate to look into the issue of bifurcation from a historical perspective. When looking at the time of the above decision, from the major patent countries only **Germany** had a system of strict bifurcation: Neither could the civil courts in the course of an infringement action invalidate a patent, nor could they take into account reasons of invalidity by way of estoppel. This position, already stipulated when the first German Patent Act came into force in 1877, is still good law today. The reasons owe as much to historical coincidences as to doctrinal considerations.

Back in 1877, civil courts were exclusively state courts, while the Federal Patent Office was a federal institution. It was seen as undesirable that any state should have jurisdiction to revoke a federally granted title. Mostly because due to the technical nature of patents, it was feared that standards for determining validity would be highly divergent.[13]

The solution originally envisaged was to set up a "Patent Court" alongside the Patent Office. The court was to operate with technically and legally trained judges and with jurisdiction over cases of (isolated) invalidation and cases of infringement where

12. Case No. 871 (O) of 1962, 18-7 Minshū 1319. The decision also cites decision of Supreme Court, 7 December 1962, Case No. 464 (O) of 1961, 16-12 Minshū 2321, which held that when determining the scope of an invention which has been granted, it is inevitable to consider the state of the art at the time.
13. C. Dresel, Das Trennungsprinzip im Patentrecht *(The principle of bifurcation in patent law)*, Europäische Hochschulschriften vol. 5801, 2015, 138.

validity was contested. Only infringement cases where validity of the patent was not contested should be argued before the civil courts. Owing to various historical factors, this Patent Court never came into existence. Yet within the Patent Office, a special invalidation division was set up as a "judicial division". It operated with technical and legal members, and its decisions could be directly appealed to the Imperial Supreme Court that in this case could also review the facts rather than only the law. The separation thereby did not lead to a bar for the Imperial Supreme Court to look at new facts or take into account new arguments, and to render a final decision itself (e.g. to revoke the patent) rather than remit the case back to the Patent Office even where facts or evidence were presented before the court for the first time,[14] which is much different from the deference given to Patent Office decisions by the courts in Japan (see Cases Nos. 26 and 27) where only a strict review of the Patent Office decision is allowed.

Numerous attempts were made to revive the idea of a Patent Court in the discussions about revisions of the German Patent Act in 1891 and 1936. Back in 1891, arguments against setting up such court were the relatively low number of patent infringement cases (200 per year; back then, most cases where handled by the criminal courts) and the fact that the 1879 Code of Civil Procedure would have to be changed in such event. However, the invalidation divisions were restructured to operate more like a court with regular oral proceedings (for Japan, see the discussion in Case No. 19), and with boards deciding in a composition of two legal and three technical members. The discussions preceding the Patent Act 1936 concerned mostly the limitation of patent infringement jurisdiction to a small number of courts, and the possibility of the civil courts to hear a technical expert from the Patent Office in patent infringement cases.

When the judicial review of Patent Office decisions had to be reformed due to a decision of the Federal Administrative Court of 13 June 1959,[15] the newly established Federal Patent Court became the successor to the Patent Office's invalidation divisions. Endowing this court with jurisdiction over infringement matters was vetoed by the German federal states, however.[16]

Although the infringement courts can stay proceedings while an invalidation action is pending (then and now sec. 148 German of Code of Civil Procedure),[17] initially it was not even foreseen to re-open procedures once the patent was revoked after the infringement action had become final.[18] Today, it is accepted that retroactive invalidation of a patent allows for a retrial (see the comparative remarks for Case No. 57).

---

14. H. ISAY, Patentgesetz *(German Patent Act)*, 6th ed. 1932, § 33 note 4. This corresponds to the powers of the Boards of Appeal of the European Patent Office that also act as a first (and final) instance court in appeals against the decision of the EPO.
15. German Federal Administrative Court, 13 June 1959, BVerwGE 8, 350 = GRUR 1959, 435.
16. A. KRIEGER, Das Bundespatentgericht als "Bundesgericht für Angelegenheiten des gewerblichen Rechtsschutzes" *(The German Federal Patent Court as "federal court for industrial property cases")*, GRUR 1977, 343, 346.
17. This is discretionary and thus rather uncertain for the defendant. In German Federal Supreme Court, 8 July 2014, 46 IIC 249 (2015) – *Nicht zu ersetzender Nachteil*, the court refused a stay in the execution of a decision where the patent had been revoked in parallel invalidation proceedings, yet without this decision having become final.
18. German Imperial Supreme Court, 4 March 1901, Reichsgericht in Zivilsachen 48, 384. Different J. KOHLER, Handbuch des Deutschen Patentrechts *(Handbook of the German patent law)*, Mannheim 1900, 365.

The above history can only incompletely explain the vehemence with which German courts have stonewalled any attempts to allow the defendant an estoppel of invalidity, either based on general principles of trust and good faith[19] (Treu und Glauben; the equivalent of sec. 1 Japanese Civil Code on which the *Kilby* decision based the estoppel), or the estoppel that the allegedly infringing embodiment etc. is part of the prior art[20] (estoppel of the free state of the art; *Einwand des freien Standes der Technik*). Academic literature was much more equivocal on these issues.[21] Particularly *Ohl*, himself a judge, in 1969 made a powerful case for the estoppel of the free state of the art[22] – to no avail. However, the courts allowed the estoppel of invalidity in certain cases where the patentee sought protection beyond the literal wording of the claims, namely where protection was based on the general inventive concept (rather than the claims).[23] The estoppel of the free state of the art was allowed in the case of an equivalent infringement where the allegedly infringing embodiment was state of the art[24] or equivalent thereto – this later became known as the *Formstein* defence.[25] Also in interim proceedings, the validity of a patent can be called into question by the respondent.[26]

While particularly Asian countries such as Japan, Korea, China and Taiwan (but also Austria, Poland and Brazil) adopted the bifurcation system (see the comparative remarks in the following Case No. 50), most other countries did not. This stands to reason in countries with no or with only an incomplete system of substantive examination (**France**;[27] **Italy**[28]), but has also been so in countries with an examination system, namely the **UK**[29] and the **United States**.[30]

---

19. Denied by German Imperial Supreme Court, 29 March 1930, Marke und Wettbewerb 1930, 372.
20. Denied by German Imperial Supreme Court, 3 February 1915, Reichsgericht in Zivilsachen (RGZ) 86, 197.
21. A. OSTERRIETH, Materielles Recht und formelles Recht im Patentrecht *(Substantive and formal law under patent law)* GRUR 1913, 189, 197 thought it was imperative to allow the courts to taken into account the free state oft he art as a defence to infringement.
22. A. OHL, Der Einwand des freien Standes der Technik im Patentverletzungsstreit *(The estoppel of the free state of the art in the patent infringement dispute)*, GRUR 1969, 1. Also E. REIMER, Patentgesetz *(German Patent Act)*, 2nd ed. 1958, § 6 note 42.
23. German Federal Supreme Court, 28 October 1952, GRUR 1953, 112 – *Feueranzünder*.
24. German Federal Supreme Court, 24 June 1952, GRUR 1953, 29 – *Plattenspieler.*
25. German Federal Supreme Court, 29 April 1986, GRUR 1986, 803 = 28 IIC 795 (1987) – *Formstein/ Moulded curbstone.*
26. T. KÜHNEN, Handbuch der Patentverletzung *(Handbook of the patent infringement)*, 7th ed. 2014, recital 2029. The probability that the patent is invalid must be very low.
27. In France, the invalidity defence can be raised both as an estoppel (*inter partes*) or as a counterclaim: ROMET/MÉTIER/TALVARD, Patent Enforcement in France, in: C. HEATH (ed.), Patent Enforcement Worldwide, Hart Publishing 2015, note 179.
28. In Italy, even patent applications are a valid title for enforcement, and enjoy a presumption of validity: G. CASUCCI, Patent Enforcement in Italy, in: C. HEATH (ed.) Patent Enforcement Worldwide, Hart Publishing 2015, notes 98, 102.
29. E.g. sec. 77 UK Patent Act 1977.
30. 35 U.S.C § 282. "The validity of the patent can also be raised as a defence and must be proven by a more difficult clear and convincing standard of proof ... If the prior art offered by the challenger is not materially different from that considered by the PTO during examination of the patent, the challenger will have a difficult time showing that the patent is not valid." T. MALONEY, Patent Enforcement in the United States, in: C. HEATH (ed.) Patent Enforcement Worldwide, Hart Publishing 2015, notes 158, 159. The strong presumption of validity even applies when prior art is introduced that has not been reviewed by the USPTO: US CAFC, *Sciele Pharma Inc. v. Andrx Corporation*, 684 F.3d 1253 (Fed. Cir. 2012).

Case No. 50

Patent Infringement – Defence of Invalidity

Christopher Heath

---

1. The court that examines a case of patent infringement may judge whether or not the patent is valid, even before a patent annulment decision of the Japanese Patent Office becomes final.
2. If it is found that there are obvious reasons for holding the patent invalid as a result of the court hearing, a claim for injunction, damages, etc., based on the patent is deemed an abuse of rights.

Supreme Court 11 April 2000 – Case No. 364 (O) of 1998 – *Kilby III*

Texas Instruments v. Fujitsu

---

1. BACKGROUND

It has always been clear that only the Japanese Patent Office has jurisdiction over invalidating a registered IP right, either by request of an interested party (patent law) or the public at large (trade marks). In the case of trade marks, the courts have long refused enforcement in cases where the trade mark should not have been registered in the first place[1] or was prone to cancellation.[2] Things were far more complicated for patents. Here, decisions of the Imperial Supreme Court of 1904 and 1917 had held that the estoppel of patent invalidity would give the court discretion to stay procedures, yet not to regard the patent invalid (see the previous Case No. 49).[3] Invalidation procedures before the Patent Office were not only slow, but both parties

1. E.g., Kobe District Court, 21 December 1982, Case No. 1264 (Wa) of 1978, 14-3 Mutaishū 813 - *Dorothee Bis*. Here, a former distributor of the French fashion designer *Dorothee Bis* had registered the mark while still distributing *Dorothee Bis* goods. The court held that the goodwill rested only in the French fashion undertaking, not the registered trade mark owner, and thus refused enforcement of the mark.
2. Supreme Court, 20 July 1990, Case No. 1576 (O) of 1985, 25 IIC 118 (1994) – *Popeye Scarves III*. Here, the Supreme Court held that the registered mark even at the time of registration conflicted with an existing copyright and should thus be cancelled. Cancellation procedures at the Patent Office seemed to take forever as the Patent Office apparently was unable to make up its mind about the cancellation request already filed years earlier.
3. Old Supreme Court, 23 April 1917, Case No. 1033 (O) of 1916, 23 Minroku 654: "If a new commercial model has been registered as a utility model ..., it is not permissible to deny the validity unless the right has been declared null and void in nullity procedure". See Case No. 49.

could even supply the Tokyo High Court with completely new facts on appeal.[4] In circumstances where the patent was presumably invalid, the courts sometimes tried to narrow the patent's scope,[5] or grant the defendant a prior user right.[6] This somewhat unsatisfactory state of affairs was changed only in this decision.

2. DECISION[7]

a) Facts

Fujitsu Ltd. (the Plaintiff), one of the leading Japanese manufacturers of semiconductors, had a cross-licence agreement with *Texas Instruments Inc.* (the Defendant).

The Defendant *Texas Instruments*, a leading U.S. manufacturer of semiconductors, holds a Japanese patent called the *Kilby* Patent after its inventor Dr. Kilby ("*Kilby* Patent", Registration No. 320275) concerning a semiconductor integrated circuit. The application of the *Kilby* Patent, filed on 21 December 1971, was a divisional from the patent application No. 4689/1964 filed on 30 January 1964 which in turn was a divisional from the invention filed on 6 February 1960 ("grandparent application" No. 3745/1960). These applications, grandparent application, parent application and the *Kilby* application, were based on the priority of two U.S. patents filed in the U.S. on 6 and 12 February 1959. Under the old 1921 Patent Act that applied to applications filed on or before 31 March 1960, an application could include only a single claim in one application. In order to obtain a comparable scope of protection, TI selected one grandparent application and filed divisional applications. The grandparent patent expired on 26 June 1980, 15 years from the date of publication, as was the law under the old 1921 Patent Act. The parent application was rejected by the Japanese Patent Office on 21 June 1967 and the rejection was finalised on 26 April 1984, because the parent invention lacked an inventive step.

There were nine parent applications divided from the grandparent application and two applications divided from these parent applications including the *Kilby* Patent. All of them, except the *Kilby* Patent, were finally rejected by the Japanese Patent Office. The *Kilby* Patent application was published on 27 November 1986,

4. Supreme Court, 4 April 1968, Case No. 62 (Gyō-Tsu) of 1964, 22-4 Minshū 816. The invalidation procedure has two further disadvantages. First, the Patent Office and the courts would only examine the reason of invalidation as argued by the petitioner, rather than make a general assessment of patentability (Supreme Court, 10 March 1976, Case No. 28 (Gyō-Tsu) of 1967, 30-2 Minshū 79 – *Knitting Machine*, see Case No. 26). Second, the patentee can almost endlessly prolong invalidation procedure by requesting an amendment of the patent before the end of the invalidation trial, as this trial would then have to be repeated in light of the amended patent (Supreme Court, 9 March 1999, No. 204 (Gyō-Tsu) of 1995, 53-3 Minshū 303 – *Rectangular Steel Pipe*, and Supreme Court, 22 April 1999, Case No. 81 (Gyō-Tsu) of 1998, 1675 Hanrei Jihō 115 – *Calendar*). Should the amendment not be accepted, the patentee can of course appeal against this decision, too. These complications are further explained in Case No. 51 – *Knife*.
5. E.g., Osaka District Court, 25 March 1993, Patent 11/1994, 121.
6. E.g., Nagoya District Court, 31 July 1991, 15 Tokkyo Kenkyū 3.
7. Published in 54-4 Minshū 1368 = 1710 Hanrei Jihō 68 = 1032 Hanrei Times 120 = N. NAKAYAMA et al. (eds.), Tokkyo Hanrei Hyakusen *(Hundred Selected Patent Cases)*, 4th ed. 2012, 150 = T. ŌBUCHI et al. (eds.), Chitekizaisan hō hanrei shū *(Intellectual Property Law Case Book)*, 2nd ed. 2015, 163. English translation in 35 IIC 91 (2004) by M. MŌRI.

and the *Kilby* Patent was registered on 20 October 1989. Its expiration date would have been 27 November 2001, 15 years from the date of publication, under the old 1921 Patent Act that governed the grandparent patent application.

The Defendant had entered into cross-licence agreements with many leading Japanese semiconductor manufacturers and those agreements were going to expire at the end of 1990. After the defendant was granted the *Kilby* Patent in 1989, it strongly demanded that Japanese manufacturers renew these agreements at a higher royalty rate, insisting that the *Kilby* Patent was the basic patent for manufacturing semiconductors, and most of the semiconductors manufactured in Japan fell within the scope of the *Kilby* Patent. Most Japanese manufacturers accepted the defendant's proposal and renewed their licensing agreements. However, the plaintiff rejected the defendant's demand and brought a lawsuit to the Tokyo District Court requesting a declaratory judgment that: 1) the defendant was abusing its right as the *Kilby* Patent was unlawfully filed and should be revoked, and 2) the plaintiff's products did not infringe the *Kilby* Patent.

The Tokyo District Court under a very narrow and literal construction of the claim held that the plaintiff's products did not infringe the *Kilby* Patent. The defendant appealed to the Tokyo High Court that dismissed the appeal based on the notion of an abuse of rights. The defendant then appealed to the Supreme Court.

The Supreme Court also held that the defendant abused its right and dismissed the appeal.

b) Reasons

Certainly, the Patent Act provides that if a patent contains a reason for annulment, the patent shall be examined and judged by the Patent Office's Appeal Board which has the special knowledge and experience necessary to invalidate a patent (secs. 123(1), 178(6) Patent Act). Such patent shall be deemed nonexistent from the beginning once an annulment decision becomes final (sec. 125 Patent Act). Therefore, the patent remains lawful and valid, and is not deemed invalid by any third party until an annulment decision becomes final.

However, in case of a patent such as the one in this case, where there are obviously grounds for annulment and where it may be that the patent will be annulled once a patent annulment trial before the Japan Patent Office has been initiated and such decision becomes final, it is appropriate to disallow a claim for injunction, damages, etc., based on such patent for the following reasons:

(i) if a claim for injunction and damages arising out of any act of using the invention based on such patent was accepted, this would give unreasonable advantages to the patent owner and unreasonable disadvantages to any person using the invention. This is contrary to the spirit of equity;

(ii) it is desirable to settle a dispute as quickly as possible in one proceeding. In the case of an infringement claim based on the above patent, the defendant should be allowed to argue the existence of the reason for annulment as a measure for defending itself against the existence of the patent right, even before a patent annulment trial is initiated before the Patent Office and an annulment decision has become final. Otherwise even a defendant who does not intend to seek patent annulment also on behalf of any third party would be forced to initiate proceedings for an annulment trial. This is against the economy of legal procedures; and

(iii) sec. 168(2) Patent Act may not be interpreted to provide that legal procedures shall be suspended even in cases where the patent obviously contains a reason for annulment, and it can be predicted that the patent will be annulled with certainty as stated above.

Therefore, it must be understood that the court that examines a case of patent infringement may judge whether the patent has an obvious reason for annulment or not, even before a patent invalidation decision becomes final. If it is found that the patent is obviously invalid as a result of the court hearing, it is reasonable that a claim for injunction, damages, etc., based on the patent is considered an abuse of rights unless there are special circumstances to the contrary. It cannot be held that this interpretation is against the spirit of the patent system. Precedents given by this Court including the judgment dated 15 September 1904 on Case No. 2662 (Re) of 1903 (10 Keiroku 1679), the judgment dated 23 April 1917 on Case No. 1033 (O) of 1916 (23 Minroku 654), etc., which are contrary to the above opinion, shall not be upheld to the extent that they are in conflict with the above opinion.

The judgment of the Tokyo High Court held that the patent was obviously invalid and that there were no recognisable special circumstances, including, for instance, an application for corrective trial. A claim for damages based on such patent should be considered an abuse of right, and therefore, the appeal should be dismissed. This Court holds such judgment as appropriate and lawful. The judgment of the Tokyo High Court is not in conflict with the precedents quoted by the appellant, and is lawful.

3. ANALYSIS

The significance of this decision is to give the courts the ability to enforce patents more flexibly in a time-saving manner, rather than oblige the parties to proceed both with a nullity procedure before the JPO and an infringement case at the court. It also ensures a speedy court hearing of the infringement action. In retrospect, it is perhaps the most important patent decision rendered by the Japanese courts in the last decades.

a) "Obvious" invalidity and the TI case history

Even from the facts, the case is one of the most complicated in Japanese patent litigation history. The patent application was still governed by the 1921 Patent Act, in disuse since 1 April 1960. While the original US application contained 25 claims, these had to be packed into one single claim in Japan, as multiple claims were not permitted. For that reason, the patent application was divided several times, permissible under sec. 9 of the 1921 Patent Act. The last divisional application of 1971 was examined and laid open in 1986. It took the Patent Office three years to decide about the 12 oppositions that were raised by basically all major Japanese producers of semiconductors. Three of these oppositions also raised the issue of nullity due to an impermissible division for a lack of an independent inventive object. The Patent Office thus dealt with a broad range of possible grounds for nullity and eventually granted the patent in 1989. It is fair to say that the patented technology was crucial to the production of semiconductor chips for all Japanese semiconductor producers. The defendant, *Texas Instruments*, was willing to license its technology and concluded agreements with all major Japanese producers. Only the plaintiff *Fujitsu* decided to fight the case and requested a declaratory decision of non-infringement by the Tokyo District Court. The latter granted the claim in 1994, based on the reasoning that *Fujitsu*'s semiconductors did not fall within the scope of the patent claims.[8] *Texas Instruments* appealed. As the Tokyo High Court had just rendered a decision confirming a relatively broad doctrine of equivalents,[9] the Tokyo District Court's opinion could not be affirmed on the grounds of claim interpretation. The Tokyo High Court thus focussed on the divisional application of 1971 and its differences to the divisional application of 1964. A divisional application may not claim subject matter not claimed in the original application, may use the same priority date and must not be identical to the original application. Thus, there is a bar of double patenting. The issue of double patenting is of course of particular relevance where the patent protection period is calculated from the date of grant rather than of application, as was the case in the old US Patent law (15 years from the date of grant) and the old Japanese Patent Act 1921 (15 years from the date of publication after substantive examination). Otherwise, the patentee could extend the life span of his patent without adding any new subject matter. The divisional application thus may (and often does) contain subject matter similar to the parent application, yet not identical. The Tokyo High Court compared the claim language of the 1971 divisional application with the parent and grandparent applications. The only difference between the subject matter of the latter and the former was claim (e) that was contained in the divisional application, yet not in the parent patent application. The Tokyo High Court held that

> "The inventions that were stated in specification of the US patent applications filed on 6 and 12 February 1959 on which the parent application and the grandparent application were based, the revised specification of the grandparent patent and the original specification and the specification of the *Kilby* Patent all basically contained structures technically identical to claim (e) ... Thus, claim (e) that describes a semiconductor integrated circuit that is placed on a plain surface is the summary of the structure based on the other claims and, consequently, claim (e) does not contain any particular technical meaning, making the current *Kilby* Patent in suit virtually identical to the parent patent."

According to the court, the Japanese Patent Office had erred in only making a literal comparison between the parent application and the *Kilby* Patent, rather than comparing their technical substance.

The interpretation of the Tokyo High Court is open to question, however. First, the double patenting bar relates only to identical, but not to similar or obvious

8. Tokyo District Court, 31 August 1994, Case No. 9782 (Wa) of 1991, 29-3 Chizaishū 875 = 1510 Hanrei Jihō 35.
9. Tokyo High Court, 3 February 1994, Case No. 1627 (Ne) of 1991, 26 IIC 683 (1995) with comment by T. Takenaka – *Ball Spline Bearing II*, reversed by Supreme Court, 24 February 1998, Case No. 1083 (O) of 1994, 30 IIC 443 (1999) – *Ball Spline Bearing III*. See Case No. 38 in this volume.

modifications. However, the court has "examined obvious modifications of the original subject matter of the invention, as an examination for identity under Japanese law equals an examination of novelty. When examining novelty, the question whether two inventions are substantially identical is checked. This examination does not always clearly distinguish between novelty and inventive step. In addition, the court impermissibly used the defendant's parent and grandparent application as prior art, although a divisional application relates to the same priority date. The court thus had better compared the inventive concept of the 1971 application with the one of 1964."[10] Also other academics have voiced concern that the Tokyo High Court in essence examined not identity, but inventive step.[11]

Even without taking a position on the above-mentioned issues, it is fair to say that the case was far from clear. To hold under these circumstances that invalidity was "obvious" is difficult to justify. It would therefore have been preferable to develop and apply the doctrine of obvious invalidity in a less complicated case where the Patent Office had not previously confirmed validity in opposition or invalidation procedures. The wrong case for the right reasons.

It should be added that after the Tokyo High Court's decision, the Patent Office decided that the patent was invalid indeed,[12] a decision subsequently affirmed by the Tokyo High Court,[13] and the Supreme Court.[14]

b) Subsequent developments

Subsequent decisions affirmed that the grounds for holding a patent invalid could relate to a lack of novelty[15] or inventive step,[16] insufficient disclosure[17] or misappropriation[18] even where invalidity was not "obvious". The new approach towards invalidity may have speeded up procedures, but it is not necessarily beneficial to the patentee. According to statistics, the patentee's success rate in infringement procedures was a mere 24% of the 70 cases where the estoppel of invalidity was raised after the Supreme Court's decision.[19] According to information supplied to the authors by former presiding Judge Mimura, alleged invalidity was affirmed by the courts in about half of the infringement cases after the *Kilby* decision was rendered. This also had repercussions on the Patent Office's handling of nullity procedures.

10. Takenaka, CASRIP Newletter Autumn 1997, available at. http://www.law.washington.edu/casrip/newletter/newsv7i2jp1.pdf.
11. Y. Tamura, Tokkyo shingai soshō ni okeru mukō no shuchō wo mitometa hanketsu *(Decision which acknowledged the invalidity defence in the patent infringement case)*, 50-12 Chizai Kanri 1847 (2000), at 1858.
12. Decision of the Patent Office of 19 November 1997.
13. Decision of Tokyo High Court, 28 March 2001.
14. Supreme Court, 26 October 2001.
15. Tokyo District Court, 14 July 2000 (unreported); Osaka District Court, 5 September 2000 (unreported).
16. Tokyo District Court, 27 September 2000 (unreported).
17. Tokyo District Court, 25 April 2001 (unreported).
18. Tokyo District Court, 30 January 2001 (unreported).
19. 111 Japan Patents and Trademarks 12 [February 2002].

While between 1997 and 1999 nullity actions had a success rate of 10-15%, this escalated in 2001 to almost 50%.[20]

In a legislative change of 2005, the power of the courts to hold patents unenforceable has been clearly expressed in sec. 104ter Patent Act:

> "(1) In a litigation that concerns a patent or an exclusive license thereof, the patentee or the exclusive licensee is barred from exercising the patent right if the latter is likely to be invalidated in a nullity action.
>
> (2) If an estoppel or an attack under the preceding subsection has been raised in order to cause unreasonable delay, the court is entitled to disregard it."

4. COMPARATIVE REMARKS

Problems and rationale of bifurcation have been explained in the previous case comment. Subsequent to the *Kilby* decision, also Korea and Taiwan, countries with a traditionally bifurcated system, have changed their practice:

In **Korea**, In the case of *Shindo Mulsan Co., Ltd. v. Hanmi Silup Co., Ltd.*[21] the Supreme Court held that if every single inventive element constituting a patented invention had been in the public domain prior to the filing date of the patent application, then such a patent is inherently defective due to lack of novelty, and therefore the Court, without declaring the patent invalid, can refuse to enforce the patent and dismiss the infringement action. This unanimous judgement reversed the Court's previous decisions. The impact of the above decision was somewhat mitigated by the later case *F. Hoffmann La-Roche v. Cheil Sugar.*[22] Here, the alleged infringer tried to extend the scope of the above ruling to the case where a patented invention allegedly lacked inventive step rather than novelty. The Supreme Court rejected this argument, holding that the said exception should be strictly applied to cases of lack of novelty; in all other cases, the court should hear the infringement action with the presumption that the patent is valid even if the patented invention could have been easily conceived over the prior art. Korea thereby applies the *Kilby* doctrine rather literally.

In **Taiwan**, in 2007, the Legislative Yuan passed the Intellectual Property Court Organisation Act and the Intellectual Property Case Adjudication Act that set up a specialised IP Court that began its operation on 1 July 2008. Before the implementation of the IP Adjudication Act, it was rare to see a defendant raise the invalidity defence in patent infringement litigation. Under the bifurcation system of Taiwan, patent validity was an administrative issue governed by administrative proceedings. However, after the implementation of the IP Adjudication Act, it has become more and more common to see the parties raise the invalidity defence in patent infringement litigation based

20. 1997: 184 invalidation requests, upheld in 22 cases; 1998: 252 invalidation requests, upheld in 46 cases; 1999: 293 requests for invalidation, upheld in 27 cases; 2000: 296 requests for invalidation, upheld in 77 cases; 2001: 283 requests for invalidation, upheld in 138 cases. Source: Tokkyo Chō, Tokkyo gyōsei nenji hōkokusho (Annual Report on Patent Administration), Tokyo 2002, 183.
21. Korean Supreme Court, 81 Hu 56 (26 July 1983).
22. Korean Supreme Court, 91 Ma 540 (2 June 1992).

on Sec. 16 IP Adjudication Act.[23] Under Sec. 16(1) "when a party claims or asserts that an IPR shall be cancelled or revoked, the court shall decide based on the merits of the case, and the Code of Civil Procedure, Code of Administrative Litigation Procedure, Trade mark Act, Patent Act, Species of Plants and Seedling Act, or other applicable laws concerning the stay of an action shall not apply." Therefore, the civil court handling a patent infringement case is entitled to decide whether the patent right at issue is valid without having to wait for the decision of the administrative authorities. This is due to Sec. 16(2) of the IP Adjudication Act which states that "under the circumstances in the preceding paragraph, the holder of the IPR shall not claim any rights during a civil action against the opposing party where the court has recognised a ground for cancellation or revocation of the IPR." In the first years of the court's existence, more than 50% of all litigated patents were held invalid by the court.[24] The position of Taiwan thus comes rather close to the one in Japan.

23. By contrast, if the invalidity of the patent right is not contested by either party, a civil court is strictly prohibited from adjudicating on whether such a right is valid or not.
24. M.-Y. Shien and S.-H. Lee, Patent Enforcement in Taiwan, in: K.-C. Liu/R. Hilty (eds.), The Enforcement of Patents, Berlin: Springer Verlag 2012, 180-182.

Case No. 51

Defence of Invalidity – Correction of Patent Claim – Late Filing

Christopher Heath and Atsuhiro Furuta

A patentee whose patent has been regarded as invalid by the courts can only be heard with the argument that such patent was successfully upheld in amended form in a correction trial before the Patent Office where such trial was conducted without unreasonable delay.

Supreme Court, 24 April 2008, Case No. 1772 (Ju) of 2006 – *Knife Processing Device*

Laserck v. Ideon

---

1. BACKGROUND

The *Kilby* decision of 2000 (this book Case No. 50) brought an end to the bifurcation system in Japan whereby only the Patent Office could determine the validity of patents and the courts in infringement proceedings had no power to hold the patent invalid.[1] This new jurisprudence was subsequently reflected in sec. 104ter Patent Act by the law amendment of 2004. Sec. 104ter(2) also allowed the courts to disregard the estoppel of invalidity if raised unreasonably late in the proceedings:[2]

> "(2) If an estoppel or an attack under the preceding subsection has been raised in order to cause unreasonable delay, the court is entitled to disregard it."

This provision was in line with the general rules on late-filed submissions, but was incomplete: it still allowed the defendant to raise an invalidation action before the Patent Office, and after a successful invalidation trial to notify the infringement court of this result (where infringement proceedings were still pending), or to request a retrial based on sec. 338(1)(viii) Code of Civil Procedure (CCP) where a decision in infringement proceedings had become final and conclusive. This was considered problematic both for defeating the purpose of sec. 104ter(2) Patent Act and for legal certainty in general. As a consequence, also the rules for retrials were amended, see Case No. 57 in this book.

---

1. See Case No. 50 in this volume.
2. Law No. 120/2004 of 18 June 2004 which was set in force on 1 April 2005.

Under the current law, the courts can hold the patent invalid *inter partes*, and the Patent Office can invalidate the patent *erga omnes*. Invalidation and infringement proceedings may be conducted concurrently, subsequent to each other or in isolation, creating all sorts of legal problems. As if this was not enough, the patentee can request *ex parte* limitation proceedings before the Patent Office, often in response to the court holding the patent invalid *inter partes*. Different from many other jurisdictions, the courts in Japan still cannot declare the patent invalid in the course of infringement proceedings, and they cannot limit the scope of the patent by request of the patentee. In correction (limitation) proceedings, the patentee has the advantage of dealing with the Patent Office in the absence of any third party, but is significantly inconvenienced by the fact that the Patent Office in such proceedings does not accept auxiliary requests.[3] Correction (limitation) proceedings cannot be instigated where an invalidation action is already pending.

In the case at issue, at the fifth attempt, the patentee had arrived at a limitation the Patent Office found acceptable, while the infringement proceedings had meanwhile reached the Supreme Court.[4] As a result (sec. 128 Patent Act, corresponding to Art. 68 EPC), the patented scope had changed *ex tunc*, that is, retroactively from the date of grant. This in turn had the consequence that the appeal court's decision was based on a patent deemed never to have existed in the form decided upon, and the version that was deemed to have existed had not been before the court. Thus, facts had occurred after the appeal decision was rendered that made the latter look incorrect. The question was whether the amended facts should still be taken into account, or whether the courts should have the power to apply sec. 104ter(2) analogously to issues raised by the patentee. The Supreme Court held that the court could disregard the counter-defence of patent claim limitation brought by the patentee at this stage of procedure.

2. DECISION[5]

a) Facts

This somewhat lengthy and complicated litigation concerns the relationship between a pending infringement action, and parallel actions before the Patent Office in order

3. For correction (limitation) proceedings after grant ("*teisei*"), see Cases Nos. 21 and 25 in this volume.
4. The number of five limitation proceedings in the case at issue is less surprising when seen in this light – after all, five auxiliary requests in *ex parte* appeal or limitation proceedings before the European Patent Office are nothing out of the ordinary. Greater procedural flexibility in this respect would benefit all those involved in concurrent infringement procedures: The patentee, the defendant and the court. But even if auxiliary requests were allowed, patentees would perhaps be reluctant to use them, as such requests could be seen as an acknowledgement that the main request will not succeed.
5. Published in 62-5 Minshū 1262 = 2068 Hanrei Jihō 142 = 1317 Hanrei Times 130 = N. NAKAYAMA et al. (eds.), Tokkyo Hanrei Hyakusen *(Hundred Selected Patent Cases)*, 4th ed. 2012, 154 = T. ŌBUCHI et al. (eds.), Chitekizaisan hō hanrei shū *(Intellectual Property Law Case Book)*, 2nd ed. 2015, 163. English translation in 40 IIC 721 (2009) w. comment C. HEATH.

to limit the patent to a scope that avoids a nullity declaration by the courts, yet is still broad enough to cover the allegedly infringing embodiment.

In September 2001, the plaintiff raised a patent infringement action before the Osaka District Court against the defendant, claiming injunctive relief. The suit was essentially based on an alleged infringement of independent claim 1. The defendant pleaded invalidity of claim 1 before the court, and concurrently filed an invalidation action before the Patent Office. On 30 January 2004, the Patent Office invalidated claim 1, whereupon the plaintiff added a pleading for infringement also of claim 5 before the District Court. The latter in a decision of 21 October 2004 also held claim 5 invalid and dismissed the action. The plaintiff appealed and simultaneously requested a limitation of the patent before the Patent Office by way of a correction trial under sec. 126 Patent Act. After two requests for limitation were rejected by the Patent Office, the patentee on 18 April 2006 filed the third request. On 31 May 2006 the Osaka High Court affirmed the first instance decision that claim 5 was invalid. The patentee appealed to the Supreme Court and made two further attempts before the Patent Office to limit the patent to an acceptable scope. Based on the fifth request for limitation, the Patent Office on 29 August 2006 held the limitation allowable, a decision that became final.

The plaintiff now argues before the Supreme Court that the appeal court erroneously held the patent invalid - as the subsequent Patent Office decision demonstrated -, that the appeal court decision was based on such error and for that reason should be set aside.

b) Reasons

[*By the majority*] ... The limitation that has an *ex tunc* effect was made in order to restrict the scope of the claims, and the grounds for invalidating the patent cited by the appeal court may have been overcome. If this is so, and while the allegedly infringing products still fall within the scope of the patent after such limitation, the appellant may be entitled to injunction and damages. These may constitute grounds for a retrial under sec. 338(1)(viii) Code of Civil Procedure.

Even so, the appellant in relying on the final and binding decision of the Patent Office is causing an unreasonable delay in bringing this patent litigation to a close. In light of sec. 104ter Patent Act, this must be considered as inequitable conduct. According to sec. $104^{ter}(1)$ Patent Act, it is not a proper exercise of rights to rely on a patent likely to be invalidated by the Patent Office. The court does not have to wait for the Patent Office to actually invalidate such right, and the provision thereby helps to promptly solve patent litigation. Also to this end, sec. $104^{ter}(2)$ Patent Act allows the court to dismiss the estoppel of invalidity if raised only in order to unreasonably delay proceedings ... When interpreted according to its purpose, the provision allows the court not only to dismiss the estoppel of invalidity, but also any argument or allegation raised as a defence thereto, even if based on a successful trial for limitation ...

Any defence against the estoppel of invalidity could have been brought by the plaintiff before the first instance infringement court. Under sec. 104ter Patent Act, the plaintiff should have brought this defence at least at the appeal stage after the first instance court held the patent invalid. When looking at the contents of the limitation trial and the fact that the plaintiff filed and withdrew two requests for limitation at the appeal stage, there is no justification why the defence of validity based on the limitation proceedings was not raised in the phase of oral hearings before the appeal court. Relying on the defence of validity based on the successful outcome of the correction trial at this late stage means that the plaintiff now invokes a defence that should have been raised at the stage of oral hearings before the appeal court. To entertain this defence at this stage would mean but an unreasonable delay in concluding this litigation, and this cannot be reconciled with sec. 104ter(2) Patent Act ...

[*By judge Izumi*] I agree with the majority, but for different reasons ... In my view, a final decision by the Patent Office in a correction trial cannot be a ground for a retrial under sec. 338(1)(viii) Code of Civil Procedure ... After all, for the defendant to raise the estoppel of invalidity, no invalidation decision by the Patent Office is necessary. The estoppel can be successfully raised once the patent is likely to be invalidated by the Patent Office. Vice versa, a defence against such estoppel does not require a final decision of validity by the Patent Office. Rather, it is sufficient to convince the infringement court that the patent could be successfully restricted in a limitation action, while the defendant's products would still fall within the scope of the patent ... Thus, in determining the estoppel of invalidity under sec. 104ter Patent Act, the infringement court not only scrutinises the Patent Office's decision to grant the patent, but also the likelihood that a request for limitation will be successful ... A final and conclusive decision of the Patent Office based on a request for limitation therefore cannot be regarded as a change of the administrative act on which the court's decision is based ... If the plaintiff in patent infringement procedures does not argue that a request for correction before the Patent Office would in most likelihood succeed, the court cannot rule on this point, and the plaintiff is barred from raising this issue at a later stage in proceedings. But to say that a request for limitation has been successful is equal to the argument that such a request, if made, would succeed ...

3. ANALYSIS

a) Late filing and retrial

The Supreme Court at some length dealt with sec. 338 Code of Civil Procedure that the appellant put forward in order to justify its appeal. Based on the version of sec. 338(1)(viii) CCP then in force, this is indeed a relevant consideration: What sense should it make for a court to disregard an amended patent as late-filed if after final and conclusive proceedings, the plaintiff would be entitled to file a retrial based on the fact that the legal basis for the decision (that is, the patent in the version as considered by the courts) had subsequently changed. Such possibility of a retrial is typical for bifurcation systems where the infringement court has to accept a patent as valid, yet would be exceptional for cases where the courts can also deal with validity issues in infringement procedures. As Japan after *Kilby* had moved to a hybrid system, the situation was not clear, as is also reflected in the different opinions taken by the Supreme Court judges: Judge *Iizumi*'s view is based on the perception that courts have jurisdiction over the issue of validity, while the other judges saw this differently. Yet the majority still came to the same conclusion and argued that sec. 338 CCP should not limit the judicial discretion to disregard facts or arguments as late-filed. In other words, a retrial could only be requested if best efforts had been made to raise all relevant arguments at the previous stage of procedure.[6]

Presumably as a result of the above decision, the 2011 amendment to the Patent Act[7] introduced sec. 104^{quater} Patent Act that in a situation where the patent is subsequently invalidated or corrected no longer allows parties to rely on a retrial in order to undo the outcome of a final decision finding infringement. In other words, a final decision on infringement can no longer be re-opened even if the infringed patent is subsequently revoked or corrected with *ex tunc* effect. Thus, sec. 104^{quater} Patent Act prevents the defendant (alleged infringer) from requesting a retrial in a case where the patent was deemed valid by the infringement courts, while the patent subsequently became invalid through a invalidation trial before the JPO, and the plaintiff (patentee) from requesting a retrial in a case where the patent was deemed invalid by the infringement courts, but subsequently maintained in a limited version by a trial before the Patent Office.

b) Infringement, correction and invalidation proceedings

In addition to the issue of a possible retrial, complications arose where during infringement proceedings, the defendant before the Patent Office requested an invalidation trial, and the patentee (plaintiff) concurrently with the filing of a lawsuit

6. For a commentary to the case at issue, see, e.g., T. Iwatsubo, Teisei kyoka shinketsu to shingai soshō ni okeru saishin jiyū no seihi *(Correction decision of the JPO and allowability of a retrial in infringement case)*, 888 NBL 22 (2008); R. Wakabayashi, Saikō saibansho heisei 20 nen 4 gatsu 24 nichi hanketsu ni motozuku teisei no shuchō to tokkyo hō 104 jō no 3 oyobi saishin jiyū *(Counterclaim of correction, sec. 104ter Patent Act and grounds for a retrial based on the Supreme Court decision of 24 April 2008)*, 43 L&T 109 (2009); T. Shigetomi, Tokkyo ken shingai shoshō ni okeru daburu torakku genshō to hanketsu kō *(Double-track phenomenon and effect of decision in infringement case)*, 1292 Hanrei Times 36 (2009); G. Kondō, Tokkyo hō 104 jō no 3 ni yoru seikyū kikyaku hanketsu to jōkoku shin keizoku chū ni tōgai tokkyo ken ni tsuite kakutei shita teisei shinpan to no kankei *(Relation of the decision based on sec. 104ter Patent Act to dismiss the claim to the correction decision of the JPO which became final and binding while the infringement case was pending at the Supreme Court)*, 27 Chitekizaisan Hōseisakugaku Kenkyū 187 (2010); M. Wakuda, Tokkyo hō 104 jō no 3 dai 1 kō ni motoduku mukō shuchō wo saiyō shite tokkyo kenn o shingai wo riyū to suru songai baishō tō no seikyū wo kikyaku subeki mono to suru kōso shin hanketsu ga sareta ato ni tokkyo seikyū no han'i no gensshuku wo mokuteki to suru teisei shinketsu ga kautei shita baai ni oite dō shinketsu ga kakutei shita tame minso hō 338 jō 1 kō 8 gō no saishin jiyū ga zonsuru tosite kōso shin no handan wo arasou koto ga tokkyo hō 104 jō no 3 no kitei no shushi ni terashi yurusarenai to sareta jirei *(Case where it was not allowed by the provision of sec. 104ter Patent Act to dispute the decision of the appeal court on grounds of retrial in sec. 338(1)(viii) Code of Civil Procedure, when the correction decision of the JPO of which purpose was to limit the patent claim became final and binding after the decision of the appeal court was rendered to dismiss the claims of damages, etc. for the patent infringement by acknowledging the counterclaim of invalidity based on sec. 104ter(1))*, in: Hōsōkai, Saikō saibansho hanrei kaisetsu minji hen -heisei 20 nendo- *(The Supreme Court case analysis -fiscal year 2010-)*, 2011, 248.
7. Law no. 63/2011 of 8 June 2011. For sec. 104^{quater} Patent Act which was introduced by the law amendment of 2011, see Case No. 57 in this volume.

for the cancellation of the invalidation decision of the JPO[8] requested a correction trial. If the correction trial was successful, the invalidation case before the court had to be sent back to the JPO, and the patentee could request another correction trial unless this was unreasonable. This ping pong game between the JPO and the courts made patent infringement proceedings longer and more complicated. The patent law amendment of 2011 also addressed this point in that it limited the possibility of the patent owner to request a correction while invalidation proceedings were pending not only before the JPO, but also before courts. Sec. 126(2) Patent Act now reads:[9]

> "A request for correction trial may not be filed from the time the relevant opposition to a granted patent or invalidation trial has become pending before the Patent Office to the time the ruling on the opposition or the trial decision has become final and conclusive."

This at least ensures that for any given patent, only one procedure for correction (invalidation/correction trial) can be pending before the Patent Office or the courts at any given time.

The current legal framework thus allows the patentee to request a correction (limitation) trial in order to account for an invalidity defence before the infringement court. However, a correction trial cannot be requested in cases where the defendant (or a third party) has already requested an invalidation trial. Also in an invalidation trial, the patentee can defend its patent in a more limited version, yet again such that this version cannot be freely changed in the course of proceedings before the JPO, and that auxiliary requests cannot be filed.

c) Further development of case law

After the *Knife* decision and the law amendment of 2011, the question remained, whether or not an actual request for correction was necessary for a counter-defence of correction (limitation). After all, there were now cases where such request might be barred by the concurrent pendency of an invalidation action.

According to judge *Izumi* in the *Knife* case, the patentee should present the court with a version of the patent that could become the subject of correction (limitation) proceedings, and the court should thereupon rule on the question if such limitation could overcome the invalidity estoppel.

8. By the law amendment of 1993 (Law No. 26/1993 of 23 April 1993), the independent correction trial could not be requested while an invalidation trial was pending before the JPO yet a correction could be made where the outcome of the invalidation trial was contested before the courts (because in such case the case was pending before the court and not before the JPO). By the patent law amendment of 2003 (Law No. 47/2003 of 23 May 2003), the period for requesting a correction trial was limited to 90 days after the filing of a lawsuit for cancellation of the invalidation decision taken by the JPO.
9. Later patent law amendment (Law No. 36/2014 of 14 May 2014) introduced the new opposition system that is slightly different from the old opposition system (the old system was abolished by the patent law amendment of 2003 (Law No. 47/2003 of 23 May 2003)). But the timing for the opposition request is limited to six months after the publication of the patent grant in the patent gazette (sec. 113 Patent Act). Due to these strict time limits, the defendant (alleged infringer) in an infringement case will usually revert to an invalidation trial.

On the other hand, some previous decisions of the IP High Court had indicated that in order to raise the counter-defence of limitation in the course of infringement proceedings, the patentee should actually be required to request a correction before the Patent Office.[10] Academic writings on this point were divided: One opinion argued that an actual request for correction was rigidly necessary for invoking such counter-defence, and the counter-defence without an actual request should be dismissed even if an actual request could not be made by law. Another opinion argued that an actual request for correction was not necessary in every case.[11]

The question was finally answered by the Supreme Court in the *Sheet Cutter* case of 2017 in which the patentee could not respond to the estoppel of invalidity by requesting a correction trial or a correction because of a pending invalidation action. According to the Supreme Court, where the patentee is barred by law (secs. 126(2), 134bis(1) Patent Act) from requesting a correction, it should be possible to file a limiting version of the patent before the infringement court and ask the court to base its validity assessment on this version. This would allow the patentee to invoke the counter-defence of limitation while at the same time not unreasonably delay proceedings.[12]

4. COMPARATIVE REMARKS

From a comparative perspective, it is worthwhile to take look at the situation in EPC Member States: Here, the EPC 2000 introduced limitation proceedings in Arts. 105a EPC:

> (1) At the request of the proprietor, the European patent may be revoked or be limited by an amendment of the claims. The request shall be filed with the European Patent Office in accordance with the Implementing Regulations. It

10. IP High Court, 25 August 2009, Case No. 10068 (Ne) of 2008, 2059 Hanrei Jihō 125; IP High Court, 27 April 2010, Case No. 10023 (Ne) of 2009, the website of the courts <http://www.courts.go.jp/app/files/hanrei_jp/155/080155_hanrei.pdf>, Summary in 43 IIC 230 (2012); IP High Court, 17 September 2014, Case No. 10090 (Ne) of 2013, 2247 Hanrei Jihō 103. There are many comments for the last case published in journals, for example, J. Mimura, Teisei no saikōben no shuchō ni saishi kore ni taiō shita teisei seikyū matawa teisei shinpan seikyū wo okonau koto ga kanō dearu baai niwa gensoku toshite kore wo okonatta ue de saikōben wo okonau hitsuyō ga aru to handan shita jirei *(Case where it was held that a request should be filed for counterdefence of correction in principle, when the corresponding request of correction or correction trial could be filed)* 2274 Hanrei Jihō 168 (2016); K Tosaki/T Nakano, Teisei no saikōben no shuchō suru ni atatte no teisei seikyū matawa teisei shinpan seikyū no yōhi *(Necessity of request of correction or correction trial for counterdefence of correction)*, 100 Chizaiken Forum 30 (2014).
11. For theories in this point, see, e.g., M Takabe, Heisei 23 nen tokkyohō kaiseigo no saiban jitsumu *(Court practice after the patent law amendment of 2011)*, 53 L&T 20 (2011); R. Mimura, Heisei 23 nen tokkyohō kaisei sekōgo ni okeru tokkyo kankei soshō no genjō to ryūiten *(Present situation and remarks on patent related litigation after the 2011 amendment to the Patent Act)*, 60 L&T 21 (2013); M. Shimizu, Mukō no kōben to teisei no saikōben no shinri oyobi mondaiten ni tsuite *(About proceedings and problems concerning the defence of invalidity and the counter-defence of correction)*, 69-3 Patent 80 (2016).
12. Supreme Court, 10 July 2017, Case No. 632 (Ju) of 2016, 49 IIC 237 (2018) - *Sheet Cutter* w. comment A. Furuta.

> shall not be deemed to have been filed until the limitation or revocation fee has been paid.

Further, Art. 138(3) EPC was added:

> In proceedings before the competent court or authority relating to the validity of the European patent, the proprietor of the patent shall have the right to limit the patent by amending the claims. The patent as thus limited shall form the basis for the proceedings.

Neither the central limitation procedure under Art. 105a EPC, nor the domestic one under Art. 138(3) EPC has any time limits and is therefore allowed at any point in time. A patentee in Europe could therefore do the same as in the case at issue: Limit the patent at the appeal stage, and then ask the court to rule on infringement and validity of the patent in its newly amended form. Whether this course of action is allowable depends on the domestic rules of civil procedure.

Two **English** cases are instructive in this respect. In the first case, the Court of Appeal[13] held as follows:

> "As a result, if the central amendment applications were to be allowed, there would be no basis upon which this court could find the amended claims valid and infringed, and so set aside the judge's order for revocation and grant the relief which Samsung now seeks. The action would therefore have to be remitted for retrial on the amended claims. That, [the defendant] argued, would constitute an abuse of the process of the court because Apple should not now be put to the trouble and jeopardy of a second trial ... we do not consider it to be an abuse of the process of this court for Samsung to make and pursue its central amendment applications ... they do not involve the exercise by the EPO of any discretion. If the requirements of the Implementing Regulations are met, the amendments will be allowed. Further, and again unlike an application made in this jurisdiction for amendment of a UK designation, the amendments will take effect in relation to the patents in every designated state ... we nevertheless have no doubt that the English courts do retain the power to control their own proceedings and to prevent activities which would amount to an abuse of process ..."

A subsequent case before the Patents Court was concerned with a domestic limitation under Art. 138 (3) EPC.[14] Here, the judge refused to acknowledge the limitation for the following reasons:

> "Article 138(3) is not concerned with procedural fairness in litigation ... I therefore conclude that, if the amendment application was permitted to proceed, it would necessitate a second trial with respect to the validity of claim 3 as proposed to be amended. Furthermore, I agree with counsel for Actavis that, as the preceding discussion shows, the second trial would be likely to involve a substantial dispute as to the extent to which it was permissible for either side to challenge the findings made in *Warner-Lambert V* ... I consider that the application to amend claim 3 is an abuse of process because it could and should

13. UK Court of Appeal, *Samsung v. Apple*, [2014] EWCA Civ 250.
14. UK Patents Court, *Generics (UK) Ltd (t/a Mylan) v. Warner-Lambert Company LLC* [2015] EWHC 3370 (Pat) (25 November 2015).

have been made prior to trial. Warner-Lambert not only had ample opportunity to make a conditional application to amend prior to trial … If the amendment application was allowed to proceed, it could not be determined fairly without a second trial on validity. Furthermore, there is a risk that such a second trial would delay the overall resolution of the dispute. Accordingly, in my view, the amendment application amounts to unjust harassment …"

The English Court of Appeal in the above case *Apple v. Samsung* also cited a Dutch case where the patentee had made a limitation during infringement:

> "The Supreme Court of the **Netherlands** (First Chamber) in Case No. C07.085HR *Boston Scientific Scimed Inc v. Medinol Ltd* given on 6 March 2009 in which precisely this issue did arise. In that case Scimed sued Medinol for patent infringement. Medinol contested the claim and, by way of counterclaim, sought revocation of the patent. The District Court of the Hague rejected the claim and revoked the patent, a decision which was upheld by the Court of Appeal. After the decision of the Court of Appeal, Scimed filed a central amendment application at the EPO seeking to limit the claims. The application was allowed in a matter of months and shortly thereafter, Scimed's appeal to the Supreme Court came on for hearing. On that further appeal, Scimed argued that the amendment operated retrospectively and invited the Supreme Court to allow the appeal and remit the case for rehearing. The Supreme Court, having reviewed the provisions of the EPC and the central amendment procedure, agreed. It held that it was required to consider the patent in its amended form and duly remitted the case to the Court of Appeal."[15]

In **Italy**, it was discussed whether courts in domestic proceedings under Art. 138(3) EPC should allow auxiliary requests. This was denied in two cases.[16]

On the other hand, in a traditionally split system such as **Germany**, validity of a patent will not be examined in infringement proceedings, invalidation claims can be filed at any time before the Federal Patent Court (bar pending opposition/appeal proceedings before the EPO) where the patentee can then request a limitation also by way of auxiliary requests, and a subsequent invalidation or patent amendment must either be taken into account by the infringement court (when proceedings are still pending, regardless at which stage), by the execution authorities (estoppel against the execution of a decision), or afterwards in the course of a retrial (see Case No. 57 in this book).

In sum, some sort of preclusion of late-filed amendments may become necessary in order to avoid a dragging-out of proceedings. Otherwise, limitation procedures under the EPC could become a strategic torpedo in the hands of the patentee that may turn a successful estoppel of invalidity in first instance into a pyrrhic victory. Such preclusion in most countries cannot be circumvented by a retrial, as the possibility of re-opening infringement proceedings after a final decision is not available. For a comparative overview, see Case No. 57 in this book.

15. Dutch Supreme Court, 6 March 2009, https://uitspraken.rechtspraak.nl/inziendocument?id=ECLI:NL:HR:2009:BG7412
16. Court of Milan, 27 November 2017, *Raimondi v. FIRP*; Court of Milan, 5 July 2017, *Advachem v. Sadean Chimica*) as reported in http://patentblog.kluweriplaw.com/2018/06/22/auxiliary-requests-admitted-italian-patent-validity-proceedings/

Case No. 52

Injunctive Relief – Exception for Standard Essential Patents

Miki Gotō and Yūsuke Ichikawa

An injunction cannot be claimed against a willing licensee under FRAND terms of a standard essential patent (SEP), because such injunction would confer an excessive leverage to the SEP owners, stymie a wide range of exploitation of the patented technology and hinder the development of industry which is the purpose of the Patent Act.

Intellectual Property High Court, 16 May 2014, Case Nos. 10007&10008 (Ra) of 2013 – *FRAND Declaration*

Samsung v. Apple

---

1. BACKGROUND

The present cases are the cases of the Intellectual Property High Court (the "IPHC") regarding the effects of a FRAND declaration (a declaration by the patentee to grant third parties a licence based on fair, reasonable and non-discriminatory terms) in connection with standard essential patents ("SEPs"). In these cases, it was essentially disputed how and to what extent a FRAND declaration shall affect the enforceability of SEPs in terms of injunctive relief against the infringer of the patent. The cases were part of the worldwide disputes between Samsung Electronics Co., Ltd ("Samsung") and Apple Japan, Inc. ("Apple"), and decided by the Grand Panel[1] of IPHC.

Sec. 100(1) of the Patent Act of Japan essentially provides that a patentee or exclusive licensee may demand infringers of the patent to stop or prevent such infringement. Accordingly, if the court finds that a patent is infringed by the defendant, the court shall, in principle, order an injunction against the defendant without additional requirements when such injunctive order is requested by the patentee.

In respect of SEPs, patentees usually participate in the relevant Standard Setting Organisations ("SSOs") to set standards for a certain technology, wherein the SSOs usually require the participating patentees to disclose the relevant SEPs and to make a declaration to the effect that the patentees are willing to grant licenses to anyone who wishes to use SEPs on fair, reasonable and non-discriminatory terms ("FRAND"

1. At the IP High Court, cases are usually decided by a panel of three judges, yet when cases involve important legal issues and it is appropriate to provide unified opinions of the court, a Grand Panel comprising of five judges decides a case.

terms). The question here is how and to what extent such FRAND declaration affects patentee's rights to seek an injunction under the Patent Act of Japan as mentioned above.

2. DECISION[2]

a) Facts

In the case at issue, the plaintiff (Samsung Inc.) has requested interim measures against the defendant (Apple Limited), namely injunctive relief against the production, sale and importation of the defendant's products, seizure of which is also requested. According to the plaintiff, the acts of the defendant infringe the plaintiff's patent no. 4642898 with the title "Process and device for sending and receiving certain package data with predetermined length indication in a system of mobile communication" (subsequently referred to as "the patent").

The first instance court dismissed the request and regarded the plaintiff's request as an abuse of rights, even though the defendant's products fell into the scope of the plaintiff's patent. The plaintiff now appeals against this decision.

...

(1) Parties to the dispute

a. The defendant is a limited liability company whose purpose is the sale of personal computers, hardware, software and additional appliances for computers. It has been established as a successor to Apple Inc. Japan, an affiliate of Apple Inc. US, on 30 October 2011.

b. The plaintiff is a Korean company whose purpose is the manufacture and sale of electronic machinery, communication devices and devices and components related thereto.

b) Reasons

...

2. On the estoppel of abuse of rights

We have to consider the plaintiff's argument that the estoppel of abuse of rights should not be recognised in respect of the claim for injunctive relief based on the patent concerning the manufacture, sale etc. We hold that the claim for injunctive relief based on the patent cannot be granted. The reasons for this are the following:

(1) Jurisdiction

2. Published in 2224 Hanrei Jihō 89 = 1402 Hanrei Times 226 = T. Ōbuchi et al. (eds.), Chitekizaisan hō hanrei shū *(Intellectual Property Law Case Book)*, 2nd ed. 2015, 182. English translation in 46 IIC 124 (2015). German translation in GRUR Int. 2015, 142.

First of all we have to examine our jurisdiction as a prerequisite of the action. Competent for a claim for injunctive relief are the courts of the country in which the patent has been registered, Supreme Court, 26 September 2002. In the case at issue, this is Japan.

(2) On the claim for injunctive relief in the case of a FRAND declaration

a. Facts ascertained by the court

From the facts, documents, and arguments in these proceedings, the following facts can be ascertained:

...

(b) Circumstances of the FRAND declaration

α. The plaintiff on 14 December 1998 declared to ETSI that it was willing to license its intellectual property pertaining to the UTMS standard of the W-CDMA technology according to the ETSI IPR Policy para. 6.1 under "fair, reasonable and non-discriminatory" terms (FRAND terms).

β. The plaintiff on 4 May 2005 filed a patent application in Korea, and based on this priority (priority number 10-2005-003774 filed the patent. Between 9 May 2005 and 13 May 2005, the plaintiff participated in a working group on 3GPPs and made a proposal for amendment. Subsequently, this proposal was accepted and the interpretation of the replacement E-bit became part of the standard. The plaintiff filed that application for the patent on 4 May 2006, and the patent was registered on 10 December 2010.

γ. On 7 August 2007, the plaintiff supplied ETSI with a document entitled "declaration on information and licenses for intellectual property" according to ETSI IPR Policy para. 4.1 and declared that the priority patent and the patent (PCT/KR2006/001699) etc. were or would be essential intellectual property for the UTMS Standard (TS 25.322 etc.) and that such intellectual property would be irrevocably licensed under the terms of IPR Policy para. 6.1 (FRAND terms) as a standard in an essential sector (FRAND declaration).

(c) Importance of the patent

The patent is an essential and thus inevitable patent for the manufacture, sale etc. of the products and for the use of the process for "interpretation of replacement E-Bits" as mentioned in technical specification V6.9.0 of the UTMS Standards.

In general, there are rules in associations on how to treat intellectual property rights in standards, e.g. the ETSI IPR Policy, whereby the members are required to publish the patent information and make a declaration on licensing according to FRAND or RAND terms ("reasonable and non-discriminatory") should such patents be intended for an essential standard.

b. FRAND declaration and injunctive relief

(a) The unconditional claim for injunctive relief based on an essential patent undermines the trust of third parties that implement the standard, leads to an overly broad scope of the patent, hinders the development of industry that is the purpose of the

Patent Act (sec. 1) by a delayed diffusion of the patented technology in society, and is contrary to common sense. The reasons for this are the following:

Someone who plans to manufacture and sell products according to the standard and subsequently invests, manufactures and sells, and has looked at the rules of associations on the use of intellectual property rights that are parts of a standard, must feel reassured that the rules on FRAND declarations for essential patents oblige the members to grant licences under FRAND terms also for the future. If injunctive relief could be requested for essential patents, this would undermine the trust of those that had counted on obtaining a licence under FRAND terms when investing in the manufacture and sale of standard products. The owners of essential patents declare that their patents can be used on condition that a license under FRAND terms has been obtained. On this, potential licensees of standard patents should be able to rely. As long as the owners of essential patents can obtain a remuneration based on FRAND terms, there is no comparable necessity to protect the patent monopoly by way of injunctive relief. Under these circumstances, a claim for injunctive relief against third parties that are willing to obtain a license under FRAND terms would lead to an unduly broad protection for the owners of substantial patents and hinder the development of industry as a purpose of the Patent Act (sec. 1) due to delays in the development of parallel technologies.

(b) Application of the above principles to the case at issue:

Someone who intends to manufacture or sell products in which the UTMS standard is embedded, recognises that the information on essential patents for the manufacture and sale of such products, or at least the patents of ETSI members, has been published together with the IPR Policy para. 4.1, and that para. 6.1 etc. of this policy requires a FRAND declaration. A third party thus relies on the fact that in the future, it will be able to obtain a licence under FRAND terms through negotiations with the patentee. Such expectation should be protected. For this reason, the unconditional possibility of obtaining injunctive relief based on a patent with a FRAND declaration goes against the expectation of those that in the above expectation produce and sell products that use the UTMS standard.

The interests of proprietors of essential patents are safeguarded by the fact that they can expect from the users of UTMS standards that their patents, including the patent at issue, will be used by many companies all around the world and will yield licensing fees that could not have been obtained without making the patents part of the UTMS standard. Who makes a FRAND declaration, as the patent proprietor, irrevocably offers licences on FRAND terms. As long as remuneration according to FRAND terms is paid, the patent proprietor is not entitled to injunctive relief based on the monopoly. The necessity for such claim for injunctive relief based on the monopoly cannot be rated particularly high in such case.

Those, including the defendant, that intend to manufacture and sell products implementing the UTMS standard have no other possibility but to use the patent if they want to carry out the standard. And there is no possibility of using other technologies or of changing the configuration. In order to avoid claims for injunctive relief, third parties would have to agree to high licensing fees or detrimental licensing terms beyond the FRAND terms, or abandon their commercial endeavours altogether should injunctive relief based on the patent be allowed unconditionally. Many companies have put quite a number of patents in a UTMS standard (more than 50 companies have declared more than 1800 patent families as essential patents). Therefore, we take the view that is too difficult to negotiate licenses for such a number of patents of different companies in advance and one at a time, and that an unfettered right of injunctive relief would make the application of a UTMS standard impossible. Such circumstances would impede the diffusion of a UTMS standard and contradict the purpose of the ETSI IPR Policy for the harmonisation and diffusion of communication standards. Under such circumstances, the harmonisation and diffusion of communication standards would be of no benefit to society.

Allowing a request for injunctive relief based on an essential patent with a FRAND declaration against third parties who are willing to obtain a licence under FRAND terms is not appropriate.

(c) On the other hand, injunctive relief can be obtained against those third parties that manufacture and sell products that implement a UMTS standard, but that have no intention to conclude a licensing agreement according to FRAND terms. After all, third parties that have no intention to conclude a licensing agreement on FRAND terms and do not rely on FRAND terms and do not observe the standard do not deserve protection. If the claim for injunctive relief against such third parties was hindered, the protection of patent proprietors would be curtailed. Thus, it must be carefully ascertained whether third parties have the intention to conclude a licensing agreement on FRAND terms, because this has repercussions on the enforcement of a claim for injunctive relief.

(d) Based on the above considerations, the claim for injunctive relief is an impermissible abuse of rights (sec. 1 Civil Code) if the defendant can successfully prove that the plaintiff made a FRAND declaration and that the defendant had the intention to obtain a licence on FRAND terms.

(3) Intention to obtain a licence on FRAND terms

Both the defendant and Apple Inc. have claimed that they were willing licensees. We consider this point:

a. Considerations

Based on all documents and arguments, the following can be ascertained: (a) The plaintiff in a letter to Apple Inc. dated 25 July 2011 demanded concrete licensing fees for the use of its essential patent portfolio. (b) Apple Inc. suggested a cap on licensing fees in a letter dated 18 August 2011 and in a letter dated 3 March 2012 suggested a licensing fee of 1% or less as a cap, and further made a concrete proposal for a mutual licensing agreement in a letter dated 7 September 2012, (c) the plaintiff demanded a concrete proposal only to the extent that Apple Inc. did not agree with its proposals, (d) the plaintiff in a letter dated 14 September suggested a different cap for the calculation of a licensing fee, (e) in a letter dated 12 December 2012, the plaintiff demanded less than half of the original sum, (f) Apple Inc. and the plaintiff met on 12 December 2012, 17 December 2012 and 18 December 2012, and during these meetings the plaintiff suggested a huge lump as licensing fee, and Apple Inc. proposed an agreement on the portfolio of essential patents in the UTMS standard, (g) Apple Inc. and the plaintiff met again on 14 January 2013, where Apple Inc.

proposed a licensing agreement without any licensing fees, (h) both companies worked out a licensing agreement during their encounter on 7 February 2013, (i) thereafter, several negotiations between the plaintiff and Apple Inc. took place, eg on arbitration clauses.

As can be appreciated from the above facts, Apple Inc. in its letter dated 18 August 2011 suggested a cap on the licensing fee, and several times proposed concrete figures as a basis for calculating licensing fees, and has met several times with the plaintiff in order to conduct intensive negotiations. Therefore, it can be ascertained that Apple Inc. and the defendant had the intention to conclude a licensing agreement under FRAND terms. However, for a very long time there were differences between the plaintiff and Apple Inc. on the amount of the licensing fee. The two companies as licensee and licensor have substantial conflicts of interest with one another. And there is no clear guideline as to which licensing fee would be appropriate under FRAND terms. Different ways of calculation are possible in respect of necessity, importance, etc. of one single patent in the UTMS standard, and the appropriate licensing fee can change in this respect. To that extent, the proposals made by Apple Inc. are justified to a certain extent. Furthermore, it can be ascertained that the conduct of the plaintiff was not conducive to a licensing agreement with Apple Inc.. But this does not prevent our finding that Apple Inc. and the defendant had the intention to conclude a licence on FRAND terms, even if for a long time there were differences in opinion between the two companies.

b. Against these findings the plaintiff has alleged that Apple Inc. did not precisely identify any patents, that its proposals every time favoured only Apple Inc., that every time, Apple refused the terms offered by the plaintiff in light of the FRAND terms, and that it purposefully torpedoed any conclusion of a licensing agreement, for which reason Apple had no intention to conclude a licensing agreement on FRAND terms. But in light of the purpose and significance of developing standards it must be checked very carefully whether there was an intention to conclude a licensing agreement. Against the background of the negotiations Apple Inc. and the plaintiff, it must be held that the defendant had the intention to conclude a licensing agreement on FRAND terms, and the allegation of the plaintiff must be rejected.

(4) Result

The request for injunctive relief based on the patent must be dismissed as an abuse of rights (sec. 1 Civil Code).

3. ANALYSIS

a) Injunctive relief

Prior to this decision, several legal solutions had been proposed as a basis to constrain claims for injunctive relief based on SEPs, including the theories of contracting commitments and abuse of rights.[3] In another related IP High Court case between

3. K. Yamagami, FRAND sengen sareta hyōjun hissu tokkyo no kenri kōshi wo seigen suru konkyo ni tsuite *(About the grounds to constrain enforcement of FRAND declared SEPs)*, in: N. Koizumi

the same parties,[4] while the contracting commitments theory was alleged as a basis to deny injunctive relief along with the abuse of rights theory, the IP High Court in the case at issue did not apply the contractual commitment theory to the case for the reason that the FRAND declaration made by Samsung could not be construed as an offer to form a valid license agreement under the applicable law (here: French law) taking account of a tentative nuance of the language of the FRAND declaration at issue and lack of any conditions regarding the licensing in the FRAND declaration.

In view of the significant importance of the legal issue in the present case, the IP High Court, for the first time in its history, made an attempt to collect public opinions through the parties. In its judgment, the court noted that the majority of the collected opinions supported the distinction between "a willing licensee" and "an unwilling licensee" as the criterion to deny injunctive relief, although such opinions were divided over the definition of a "willing licensee".

Although the theory of abuse of rights is case specific and thus generally tends to lack foreseeability, commentators have observed that the court decision in the present case has increased foreseeability by clarifying the requirements to apply the theory of abuse of rights to constrain an injunctive relief based on a FRAND-declared SEP:[5] 1) the patentee declared FRAND and 2) the alleged infringer is a willing licensee under FRAND terms, and the burden of proof thereof is on the alleged infringer. Under this framework, those who wish to use FRAND-declared SEPs ("Implementers") are readily expected to avoid an injunction as far as they pursue license negotiations as willing licensees, which would prevent a reverse hold and encourage licensing negotiations.[6]

The practically important question would be under what circumstances licensees can be considered "willing". While the court did not provide for a clear definition of willing licensees, it is noted that the court mentioned that a finding of non-willingness should be exceptional. Some researchers also suggest that only in exceptional cases such as for a reckless infringer without any intent to pay licensing fees should fall outside the definition of "willing" licensees.[7]

Under such strict standard, licensees might be still considered to be "willing" licensees even when they take actions not affirmative for the SEPs at issue. For example, even when users challenge the validity of the SEPs or make an argument that they do not actually use the SEP, as long as they conduct negotiations with the

---

et al. (eds.), Habataki – 21 seiki no chitekizaisanhō *(Advancement – Intellectual Property Law of 21th Century)*, Kōbundō, 2015, 403.

4. IP High Court, 16 May 2014, Case No. 10043 (Ne) of 2013, 2224 Hanrei Jihō 146 = 1402 Hanrei Times 166. English translation in 46 IIC 116 (2015). German translation in GRUR Int. 2015, 144.
5. T. IIMURA, Kokusaiteki chizaifunsou to chitekizaisan kōtō saibansho no hatasu yakuwari *(International Intellectual Property Disputes and the Role of Intellectual Property High Court)*, 68-12 Hōritsu no Hiroba 25 (2015); Y. TAMURA, FRAND sengen wo nashita tokkyoken ni motozuku kenri kōshi to kenri ranyou no seihi 5 *(Enforcement of FRAND declared patents with and determination of abuse of right part 5)*, 1033 NBL 37 (2014); M. SUZUKI, FRAND sengen ga nasareta hyōjun kikaku hissu tokkyo ni motozuku kenri kōshi *(Enforcement of FRAND declared SEPs)*, 65 Law and Technology 60 (2014).
6. Y. ECHI, Tokkyoken kōshi no seigenhōri *(Constraint doctrine of the Patent Enforcement)*, Shōji-hōmu, 2015, 289.
7. Y. TAMURA (above), 40; M. SUZUKI (above), 61.

FRAND-declared patentee to obtain licenses, as Apple did in the present cases, such users might be considered to be willing licensees.

On the other hand, in terms of burden of proof, there is the concern that the imposition of a burden of proof on the side of the user would practically lead to a "hold-up" situation, particularly when a proposed licensing rate of the patentee and the user differ to a large extent.[8] To see whether such concerns are correct, we would need to watch how the courts in subsequent cases will apply the court's standard to negate an injunctive relief taking account of specific factual circumstances of each case related to the relevant negotiation history between the patentee and the user.

As a reference for the court's application of the court's standard, there is a case of the Tokyo District Court in 2015,[9] in which it was disputed whether the patentee of a standard patent related to Blue Ray Discs should be able to obtain injunctive relief against an alleged infringer although the patentee made a FRAND declaration for the patent. The District Court denied injunctive relief based on the finding that the alleged infringer qualifies as a "willing" licensee in consideration of the following factual circumstances:

1) In a letter on 25 June 2012, the patentee proposed a licensing rate by making a notice of a license program on its website to the alleged infringer.
2) In a letter on 4 September 2012, the alleged infringer declared that he expects to pay, and is willing to pay, a fair and reasonable license fee, and proposed a specific royalty rate of 3.5 % of cost of goods sold to the patentee. The alleged infringer also requested the patentee to provide grounds of the patentee's proposal.
3) In a letter on 11 September 2012, the patentee answered that an individual negotiation was not an option and not possible, and did not show any grounds of the royalty rate proposed by the patentee.
4) In a letter on 26 September 2012, the alleged infringer requested the patentee to provide grounds of the "fair" rate.
5) In a letter on 11 April 2013, the patentee proposed a license agreement based on the license rate proposed by the patentee.
6) In a letter 9 May 2013, the alleged infringer answered that he was prepared to discuss the "fair and reasonable" license rate with the patentee.

b) Damages

In another related lawsuit between Samsung and Apple,[10] it was disputed whether and to what extent the patentee (Samsung) should be entitled to damage compensation based on an infringement of the FRAND-declared patent. The court held essentially that Samsung's claim for damages constituted an abuse of rights as the amount thereof exceeded a FRAND royalty. Yet a claim for damages should not be precluded as long as the amount thereof was within a FRAND royalty.

8. M. SUZUKI (above), at 61.
9. Tokyo District Court, 18 February 2015, Case No. 21383 (Wa) of 2013, 1412 Hanrei Times 265. German translation in GRUR Int. 2016, 375 – *Blue Ray Disk*.
10. IP High Court, 16 May 2014, Case No. 10043 (Ne) of 2014 (above).

In determining the amount of a FRAND royalty, the court applied the so-called top-down approach, which seems similar to the one adopted in a US case.[11] The top-down approach has the benefit of preventing royalty-stacking by setting a ceiling on the contribution of all SEPs to the whole product value.[12] On the other hand, under such an approach, the damage awarded is to be limited to a compensation for past infringement, which is pointed out to be different from the compensation for the future infringement, such as ongoing royalty in the U.S. system.[13]

Since the IP High Court did not explicitly rule out other possible approaches to calculate FRAND rates, it is still not clear whether the Japanese courts in future cases may apply other approaches such as the so-called "comparable license" approach. On this point, it is noted that the court in the aforementioned case[14] did not force the patentee to disclose relevant licenses with third parties, holding that such licenses with third parties are not necessarily relevant in determining the license terms between Samsung and Apple because such other licenses with third parties would have been executed on the basis of the relative strength of patent portfolios between the patentee and third parties, which would be different from those between Samsung and Apple.

4. COMPARATIVE REMARKS

a) Injunctive relief

While the constraint on an injunctive relief based on SEPs as such seems to be a world-wide trend, the specific criteria to be applied vary depending on the jurisdiction and even on cases within the same jurisdiction.

In the **US**, the Court of Appeals for the Federal Circuit ("CAFC")[15] denied the so-called *per se* rule that injunctions are unavailable for SEPs, and clarified that the *eBay* case's four factors standard should be applied, stating that "we see no reason to create, ... a separate rule or analytical framework for addressing injunctions for FRAND-committed patents." The CAFC further noted that, while a patentee who made FRAND commitments may have difficulties establishing irreparable harm, an injunction may be justified where an infringer unilaterally refuses a FRAND royalty or unreasonably delays negotiations to the same effect. It is noted that in another case of the Northern District Court of California, the court held that it was a breach

11. U.S. District Court for the Northern District of Illinois, *In re Innovatio IP Ventures, LLC*, 956 F. Supp. 2d 925 (N.D. Ill. 2013).
12. T. Tamura (above), at 48
13. R. Takabayashi, FRAND sengen ga sareta hyoujunka hissu tokkyo ni motoduku sashidome songai baishou no seigen *(Constraint on injunctive and damages relief based on SEPs declared FRAND)*, 1479 Jurist 273 (2015); R. Shimanami, Chitekizaisanken shingai no sashitome ni kawaru kinsenteki baishō *(Monetary damages in lieu of injunction on intellectual property infringement)*, in: T. Ōbuchi et al. (eds.), Chitekizaisan hō no atarashii nagare, 2010, 669; Y. Echi (above), at 271-272.
14. IP High Court, 16 May 2014, Case No. 10043 (Ne) of 2014 (above).
15. US CAFC, *Apple Inc. v. Motorola, Inc.*, 757 F.3d 1286 (Fed. Cir. 2014).

of contractual obligations under FRAND terms for the patentee to seek an injunctive relief before making a FRAND offer.[16]

On the other hand, the International Trade Commission ("ITC") is not required to apply the eBay test.[17] In one case,[18] the ITC issued a limited exclusion order and a cease and desist order based on an SEP, which was, however, subsequently disapproved by the US Trade Representative.[19]

In the **European** Union ("EU"), more specific procedural and substantive standards for the enforcements of SEPs have been developed in terms of negotiations between FRAND-declared patentees and users. The basic legal framework was provided by the Court of Justice of the European Union (CJEU)[20] ruling on questions referred from Düsseldorf High Court regarding *Huawei v. ZTE* case:[21] 1) the patentee must notify the user of the patents, 2) the user must show a willingness to license, 3) the patentee must offer a license under FRAND terms, and 4) the user must show acceptance of the offer, or provide security and a counteroffer if he rejects it, and 5) if no agreement is reached under the FRAND terms, the parties may request that the amount of the license fee be determined by an independent third party.[22]

In **Germany**, there are many SEP related cases. Before the CJEU case, the German Federal Supreme Court (GFSC) took position in the *Orange Book Standard* case of 2009 that in that a defence of compulsory license under competition law was available against a claim for injunctive relief in an SEP case.[23] The conditions for this defence as developed in the *Orange Book Standard* case are more restrictive than those of the *Huawei v. ZTE* case of CJEU. German courts are now applying the conditions as set forth by the CJEU.[24]

16. US District Court for the Northern District of California, *Realtek Semiconductor Corp. v. LSI Corp.*, 946 F. Supp. 2d 998, 1003 (N. D. Cal. 2013).
17. US CAFC, *Spansion, Inc. v. ITC*, 629 F.3d 1331, 1358 (Fed. Cir. 2010).
18. US ITC, *Certain Electronic Devices, Including Wireless Communication Devices, Portable Music and Data Processing Devices, And Tablet Computers*, Inv. No. 337-TA-794, Final Det. (2013).
19. Letter from Ambassador *Michael B. G. Froman*, US Trade Representative (USTR), Executive Office of the President, to Honorable *Irving A. Williamson*, Chairman, US International Trade Commission (3 August 2013), available at the website of the USTR <https://ustr.gov/sites/default/files/08032013%20Letter_1.PDF>.
20. CJEU, 16 July 2015, case C-170/13, 61, 63, 66-68.
21. Düsseldorf District Court, 21 March 2013, Case No. 4b O 104/12 – *Huawei Technologies Co. Ltd v. ZTE Corp.*.
22. The European Commission (EC) in November 2017 released the communication "Setting out the EU approach to Standard Essential Patents", available at the website of EC <https://ec.europa.eu/docsroom/documents/26583>. The discussion around SEPs is still continuing in the EC. The JPO in June 2018 also released the "Guide to Licensing Negotiations involving Standard Essential Patents", including world-wide SEP case law, available at the website of the JPO <https://www.jpo.go.jp/e/system/laws/rule/guideline/patent/seps-tebiki.html>.
23. German Federal Supreme Court, 6 May 2009, GRUR 2009, 694 – *Orange-Book-Standard*.
24. E.g., Düsseldorf High Court, 9 May 2015, Case No. I-15 U 36/16 – *St. Lawrence v. Vodafone*; Karlsruhe High Court, 31 May 2016, Case No. 6 U 55/16 – *Pioneer v. Acer*; Düsseldorf High Court, 30 March 2017, Case No. I-15 U 66/15 – *Sisvel v. Haier* (this case is appealed and pending before the German Federal Supreme Court). For SEP related cases in Germany, see also, SCHULTE, Patentgesetz mit EPÜ *(Commentary on the German Patent Act and the EPC)*, 10th ed. 2017, 707.

In the **UK**, apart from applying the above CJEU criteria, an injunction can be ordered based on FRAND-declared patents that can later be "discharged if the defendant enters into the FRAND license", see *Unwired-planet v. Huawei.*[25]

b) Damages

Two major methodologies to calculate the FRAND rate have been established by the courts around the world. One is the aforementioned top-down approach, and the other is the comparable license approach.[26]

While the *Innovation* case in the **US** referred solely to the top-down approach in calculating the FRAND rate, the *Unwired-Planet v. Huawei* case[27] in the **UK** and the *TCL v. Ericsson* case[28] in the **US** calculated FRAND rates referring to both the top-down approach and the comparable approach and adopted the rate that appeared more reasonable.

In **Germany**, the Düsseldorf High Court in the 2017 *Sisvel v. Haier* case held that the damages were limited to the amount as calculated by "license analogy" based on FRAND license rates, while damages based on the "patentee's lost profits" or "profits of the infringer" could not be applied as long as the willing licensee could benefit from the FRAND scheme.[29]

25. English Patents Court, *Unwired Planet International Ltd v. Huawei Technologies Co. Ltd.* [2017] EWHC 1304 (Pat), 20, 70. The appeal in this case was dismissed by the UK Court of Appeal, [2018] EWCA Civ 2344.
26. In US, the comparable license approach is applied within the framework of the modified Georgia-Pacific Factors. For the US case law to the FRAND rate, see also, US District Court for the Western District of Washington, *Microsoft Corp. v. Motorola Mobility, Inc.*, 2013 WL 2111217 (W.D. Was. April 25, 2013) (Findings of Fact and Conclusions of Law); US CAFC, *CSIRO v. Cisco Systems, Inc.*, 809 F. 3d 1295 (Fed. Cir. 2015).
27. English Patents Court, *Unwired Planet International Ltd v. Huawei Technologies Co. Ltd.* [2017] EWHC 711 (pat).
28. US District Court in the Central District of California, *TCL Communication Technology Holdings, Ltd. v. Ericsson Inc.*, Case No. 14-CV-341 (C.D. Cal. 2017).
29. Düsseldorf High Court, 30 March 2017, Case No. I-15 U 66/15 - *Sisvel v. Haier.* German courts decides often on infringement and obligation to pay damages without determination of amount, the parties in the case can set damages amount by themselves after the court decision or further process can be filed in the court to determine the amount. For damages calculation/presumption in general, see Case No. 55 in this volume.

Case No. 53

Scope of Injunctive Relief – Process Patent

Takuya Iiizuka

Where an invention over a process for measuring the qualities of a product has been infringed, remedies for injunctive relief, destruction etc. do not extend to the products subjected to such process.

Supreme Court, 16 July 1999, Case No. 604 (O) of 1998 – *Kallikrein*

Nippon Zoki Pharmaceutical v. Fujimoto Diagnostics

---

1. BACKGROUND

Section 100(1) of the Japanese Patent Act provides that a patentee or exclusive licensee has a right to demand injunctive relief against a person who works or is likely to work the patented invention without authorisation from the patentee or exclusive licensee, and sec. 100(2) provides further remedies as a secondary claim of relief:[1]

> (1) A patentee or exclusive licensee may demand a person who infringes or is likely to infringe the patent right or exclusive license to stop or prevent such infringement.
>
> (2) In making a demand under the preceding paragraph, the patentee or exclusive licensee may demand measures necessary for the prevention of such infringement including the disposal of products constituting such act of infringement (including, in the case of a patented invention of a process of producing products, products produced by the act of infringement; the same shall apply in [section] 102 (1)) and the removal of facilities used for the act of infringement.

Further, the Japanese Patent Act divides inventions into product and method (or process) inventions, while the latter can be methods of producing a product and other methods (for example measuring the quality of a product, as in the case at issue), and sec. 2(3) provides which acts constitute a "[w]orking" of an invention for each of the three categories of inventions:

---

1. English translation from the website of the Japanese Law Translation which is provided by the Ministry of Justice <http://www.japaneselawtranslation.go.jp/law/detail/?ft=1&re=01&dn=1&co=01&ia=03&x=69&y=20&ky=%E7%89%B9%E8%A8%B1%E6%B3%95&page=27> (tentative translation). The same translation used hereafter.

(3) "Working" of an invention in this Act means the following acts:

(i) in the case of an invention of a product (including a computer program, etc., the same shall apply hereinafter), producing, using, assigning, etc. (assigning and leasing and, in the case where the product is a computer program, etc., including providing through an electric telecommunication line, the same shall apply hereinafter), exporting or importing, or offering for assignment, etc. (including displaying for the purpose of assignment, etc., the same shall apply hereinafter) thereof;
(ii) in the case of an invention of a process, the use thereof; and
(iii) in the case of an invention of a process for producing a product, in addition to the action as provided in the preceding item, acts of using, assigning, etc., exporting or importing, or offering for assignment, etc. the product produced by the process.

An act of direct infringement of a patented invention is the unauthorised working of a patent according to one of the above categories against which injunctive relief can be requested.

In the present case, one of the major issues was the analogous application of remedies available for production methods (namely the destruction of products directly obtained from a patented production method) to a measurement method that was necessarily applied to products in order to market them. The Supreme Court denied such analogous application due to the fact that patent infringement also constitutes a criminal offence, and under criminal law, analogous applications that may broaden responsibility are not appropriate.

Sec. 100(2) of the Patent Act allows a patentee or an exclusive licensee to make a joint claim against the infringer when demanding an injunction, so as to prevent an act of patent infringement such as (i) disposal of a product that constitutes such act of infringement (including, products produced by the act of infringement for a patented invention of a method to produce a product), and (ii) removal of facilities used for the act of infringement; however, these are examples and the details of the demand is not limited to them, and with respect to what kind of demand is possible, the provision does not provide a standard that is more detailed than "measures necessary for the prevention of such infringement".

In the present case, as a measure for preventing infringement of a patented invention of a testing method, the second instance court ordered the destruction of the defendant's medicine and withdrawal of its listing from the drug price standard which is the standard for determining prices to medical institutions. Whether this order was within the scope of sec. 100(2) also became an issue before the Supreme Court.

2. DECISION[2]

a) Facts

The plaintiff is owner of the patent No. 1725747 entitled "Method for Measuring a Physiologically Active Substance".

Claim 1 of the patent at issue reads as follows:

> Method for measuring Kallikrein inhibitory capacity of a substance, characterized in that a solution composed of animal plasma, blood coagulation XIIth factor activator and the substance to be measured is mixed and reacted, and next, an inhibitor, which has no substantial influence to generate Kallikrein activity but inhibits specifically only active blood coagulation XIIth factor is added in time, in which a linear relationship between the generation of Kallikrein and the reaction time exists, and the quantity of generated Kallikrein is measured.

The defendant produced and sold an extract liquid and medicine with the sales name "Rose Morgen", which comprised the extract liquid as an active ingredient that was approved as a drug based on the Pharmaceutical Affairs Act (PAA). The medicines at issue are listed in the drug price standard based on the Health Insurance Act (HIA).

The Osaka High Court, the court of original judgment, found that the defendant used the method at issue as a verification test for a Kallikrein like substance productive activity for verification of a quality standard in the production of the medicines at issue.

The plaintiff in the present case requested (1) an injunction against the production, sale and advertisement/publicity of the medicines at issue, (2) the destruction of the medicines at issue, (3) withdrawal of the request of the listing in the drug price standard, based on the HIA, and (4) the withdrawal of the obtained approval for the production, based on the PAA, and the prohibition of transfer of the status obtained through the approval to third parties, because the production of medicines at issue by using the method at issue and selling them infringed the patent.

The previous instance, the Osaka High Court, affirmed infringement and granted injunctive relief against (1) the production, sale and advertisement/publicity of the medicines at issue, ordered (2) the destruction of the medicines at issue, and (3) the withdrawal of the request of listing in the drug price standard, dismissing the other claims. It held that as the method at issue fell in the technical scope of the patent, and the method of the patent could be substantially seen as a method of producing a product, the patent could be invoked against the sale of the products which were produced by using the method of the patent.

b) Reasons

The decision of the previous instance cannot be affirmed from the following reasons.

2. Published in 53-6 Minshū 957 = 1686 Hanrei Jihō 104 = 1010 Hanrei Times 245 = N. Nakayama et al. (eds.), Tokkyo Hanrei Hyakusen *(Hundred Selected Patent Cases)*, 4th ed. 2012, 162 = T. Ōbuchi et al. (eds.) Chitekizaisan hō hanrei shū *(Intellectual Property Law Case Book)*, 2nd ed. 2015, 93, 195.

1. The patent owner can claim injunctive relief against anyone who infringes the patent or is likely to do so (sec. 100(1) Patent Act). The patent owner has the exclusive right to commercially work the patent (sec. 68), and therefore the commercial working of the patent by a third party infringes the patent. And the working of a method patent consists of using the method (sec. 2(3)(ii)), so that the patent owner can claim an injunction against whoever uses the method of the patented invention. On the other hand, where the invention concerns the production of products, the working of the patent is defined as using, selling renting or importing, or offering for sale or renting of the products which are produced by the method, in addition to the use of the method (sec. 2(3)(iii)), and the patent owner can claim injunctive relief against anyone who engages in such conduct.

2. The invention of a working method and the invention of production method are distinguished by clear provisions, and the effects of the patents are clearly different. The invention of a working method and the invention for producing products cannot be regarded as the same, and the patent related to an invention for producing products does not have the same effect as a patent related to the invention of a working method. And to which type of invention an invention belongs to in the first place must be decided by the wording of the patent claim attached to its application (sec. 70(1) Patent Act).

We consider the above points in the present case. Here, claim 1 of the patent describes a method for measuring Kallikrein inhibitory capacity, so it is clear that the invention at issue is not the invention of a method for producing products, but the invention of a working method. Even if the method at issue is integrated into the production process of the medicines at issue, it is impossible to say that the invention at issue is an invention for producing products, and it is difficult to affirm the same effect as for an invention of a method for producing products.

3. Because the method at issue falls within the technical scope of the patent, the use of the method in the production process infringes the patent. So the plaintiff can claim an injunction against the use of the method based on sec. 100(1) of the Patent Act. But the invention at issue is not an invention for a production method, and even if the defendant uses the method at issue as a verification test for quality standards in the production of the medicines at issue, the production and sale after that is not an infringement of the patent. Therefore, request (1) of the plaintiff for an injunction against the production of the medicines at issue, etc. cannot be granted (and in consideration of the subject matter of the dispute, request (1) cannot be understood as a request for an injunction against the use of the method at issue).

4. Because sec. 100(2) allows, by way of example, the destruction of objects which are related to the infringing conduct (which comprises products produced by the infringing conduct where the invention relates the manufacture of products), and the removal of facilities used for the infringing conduct as a necessary means for preventing further infringement. The patent owner can claim these remedies together with the request for injunctive relief. The "necessary acts for preventing infringement" must be reasonably interpreted so as to make the injunction effective in light of the patented invention, the modalities of existing and potential infringement, and the necessary scope for actually realising injunctive relief.

In the present case, the medicine of the defendant is neither a facility used for the infringing conduct nor an object which embodies the infringing conduct. The invention at issue is an invention of a method, and the infringement is the use of the method at issue, for which reason the patent owner can only claim injunctive relief against the use of the method at issue, while the destruction of the medicine of the defendant and the withdrawal of the request for de-listing of the medicine in the drug price standard clearly exceeds the necessary scope for the realisation of the injunction. Therefore, requests (2) and (3) against the defendant must also fail.

3. ANALYSIS

a) Reasons

The reasoning of the Supreme Court decision can be summarised as follows:

(1) Demanding an injunction to enjoin the production and sales of a product for which the quality standard has been measured by using a patented method is not allowed;
(2) The "measures necessary for the prevention of such infringement" under sec. 100 (2) of the Patent Act are only those that are indeed necessary and adequate to prevent further acts of infringement and to remove infringing products, or products directly obtained by the patented method, from the channels of commerce;
(3) Yet, the destruction of products beyond the scope under (2), and the withdrawal of the application for the listing in the pricing standards of pharmaceutical products are not "measures necessary for the prevention of such infringement".

Each of the reasons above is simple and easy to understand; however, with respect to points (1) and (2), which were seldom discussed in the past, it is important to be very clear in what the Supreme Court has actually held, as its decision is frequently cited in later cases.

b) Plaintiff's claim

The defendant's pharmaceutical medicine is an analgesic and a generic drug of the plaintiff's pharmaceutical medicine "Neurotropin" which the plaintiff manufactures and sells; however, the active ingredients of the defendant's pharmaceutical medicine are unknown and the medicine's standard cannot be determined by its contents. The patented method in the present case is a measuring method concerning whereby the quantity of the product is determined from its effectiveness in order to see whether or not the product meets the standard provided by the plaintiff.

Specifically, the patent relates to a method to determine the quantity of the effect of inhibiting the increase of an enzyme that causes pain and inflammation called Kallikrein, which is generated in blood plasma, and functions by mixing an active agent that produces Kallikrein with a test substance in animal plasma, and after producing Kallikrein for a certain period of time, it stops generating Kallikrein by deactivating the active agent only, and then measure the amount of Kallikrein produced within such period of time.

Because this testing method has been adopted as a testing standard for the plaintiff's product, and the approval of the plaintiff's product refers to this method, the plaintiff assumed that the defendant, the producer of the generic drug, was likely to have adopted the same method.

Although the patent right exercised by the plaintiff in the present case is a testing method, the patentee requested that the defendant be enjoined from the production and sales of the defendant's pharmaceutical drug, that the drugs already produced by destroyed and the defendant's product be de-listed from the pricing standard. There was no request for an injunction against the use of the patented invention, perhaps because it would be difficult to determine directly whether or not the defendant kept using the measuring method even after an injunction, and the plaintiff thus thought that it would be difficult to enforce any decision in this respect.

The defendant denied the use of the patented method but did not make clear what kind of method it actually did use. However, the Osaka District Court, the court of first instance, held that it could not deny the possibility of the defendant using a method other than the patented method and dismissed the plaintiff's claims (Osaka District Court, 29 July 1995[3]).

On appeal, the Osaka High Court found the defendant liable for patent infringement because the defendant's product was a generic drug of the plaintiff's product and it was difficult to imagine that the defendant had adopted a different inspection test, and because the test was inseparably incorporated into the production process of the defendant's pharmaceutical medicine. The Osaka High Court thus ordered injunction against the production and sales of the defendant's pharmaceutical medicine under sec. 100(1) of the Patent Act, and ordered the disposal of already produced pharmaceutical medicines and the de-listing for the pricing standards of pharmaceutical products under the health insurance system under sec. 100(2).

c) The standard of classification of an invention

As mentioned above, there was no dispute that the invention at issue was an invention of a measuring method. With respect to the distinction between an invention of a method and an invention of a product, it is understood that an invention of a method must include a process feature, and any invention that does not include such element is not deemed to be an invention of a method, but an invention of a product, Tokyo High Court, 21 May 1957.[4]

With respect to an invention of a method, there is a decision of the Imperial Supreme Court (*Daishin'in)* on the distinction between an invention for producing a product and an invention for a "simple" (or working) method, where the court held that the latter "is an invention of a method of use where the invention does no more than simply use the product without changing the product itself in any way,

3. Osaka District Court, 29 July 1995, Case No. 7157 (Wa) of 1992, 53-6 Minshū 1008.
4. Tokyo High Court, 21 May 1957, Case No. 18 (Gyō-Na) of 1956, 8-8 Gyosaishū 1463.

and is unaccompanied by the production of a product" (28 April 1943, Case No. 556 (O) of 1942, 22-9 (Daishin'in) Minshū 315).[5]

In a Tokyo High Court case, the court was asked to decide whether a construction method for paving asphalt on a road while cutting out its manhole part was a method of producing a product, or a working method, and the court decided that the method in question was not "an invention of a method of producing a product" because the method was not a method aimed at making a change to a product.[6]

The patented invention at issue does not change the characteristics of the product and is a working method to measure the quantity of inhibitory capacity of generated Kallikrein through a plurality of steps, and is therefore a typical invention of a working method.

d) The decision to deny injunctive relief

The Osaka High Court, while affirming that the invention was a working method, focused on the fact that the invention was inseparably connected with the production process of the defendant's product and granted injunctive relief against the production and sales of the product because it was substantially an invention of a method of production. The court presumably focused on the fact that the defendant's product could not be sold without going through the inspection test and by way of analogy tried to apply the right to demand injunctive relief regarding the production of the final product as if the method was one of production.

In contrast, the Supreme Court emphasised that the Patent Act clearly distinguishes the scope of injunctive relief according to the categories of patented inventions, and denied an analogous application for working methods. While application by analogy is widely adopted in the area of private law in Japan, an act of patent infringement is followed by criminal punishment. As a corollary of the criminal law principle that there should be no punishment without law, the application of criminal provisions by analogy is prohibited, and thus, it is likely that the Supreme Court took this into account when denying an analogous application.

This approach of not allowing an application by analogy in interpreting the Patent Act has influenced the outcome of disputes related to the interpretation of patent infringement, and is referred to in other court cases when interpreting the concept of working a patent or interpreting the requirements for an act deemed to be a patent infringement.

For instance, in a case of indirect infringement, (sec. 101(ii) of the Patent Act), the Osaka District Court quoted from the above decision and mentioned that "under the text of the law, 'invention of a product', 'invention of a method' and 'an invention of a method for producing a product' are clearly distinguished from each other and the extent of the effect of such patent right is clearly different from each other" and then held that for "producing a product", it is necessary to apply some treatment

5. Imperial Supreme Court, 28 April 1943, Case No. 556 (O) of 1942, 22-9 (Daishin'in) Minshū 315.
6. Tokyo High Court, 24 February 2005, Case No. 4518 (Ne) of 2004, the website of the courts <http://www.courts.go.jp/app/files/hanrei_jp/746/009746_hanrei.pdf> – *Cutting Overlay Method*.

to the material that is supplied, while an act of merely using a material according to its originally intended purpose does not qualify as "producing a product", and decided that the act of prescribing a plurality of pharmaceutical medicines and their medication to a patient did not amount to producing a combined pharmaceutical (Osaka District Court, 27 September 2012).[7]

As such, the above Supreme Court decision in *Kallikrein* is understood as a case where the court in interpreting and applying the Patent Act applied an abstract criterion for interpreting the Act, namely that an extensive or analogous interpretation beyond the literal wording of the law is undesirable in a situation where the court must decide whether a certain act qualifies as a patent infringement.

e) Measures necessary for the prevention of infringement

As a result of affirming the plaintiff's request for injunctive relief against acts of infringing the plaintiff's patent right to acts of production and sales of the product, the Osaka High Court decision ordered disposal of the products constituting such act of infringement and de-listing of the medicine in the drug price standard under sec. 100(2).

As the Supreme Court denied the request for injunctive relief regarding the production and sale of the products subject to the measuring method, it also set aside the other measures related to the products.

Nevertheless, the Supreme Court gave an indication on how to determine the scope of the "measures necessary for the prevention of such infringement" under sec. 100(2) so as to prevent lower courts from making excessive orders for measures to prevent infringement.

Typical examples of "measures necessary for the prevention of such infringement" are the disposal of "products constituting such act of infringement" and the "removal of facilities used for the act of infringement" listed in the provisions of the Patent Act.

A "product constituting such act of infringement" is a product within the scope of a product patent, or a product produced by a patented method of production. Because it is difficult to conceptualise a "product constituting infringement" in an invention of a working method, removal of tools or equipment to carry out such method can be claimed as a "removal of facilities used for the act of infringement". Of course, production equipment, etc. supplied for the invention of the product or working the invention to manufacture the product can be subject to demand such removal as well.

Where a court finds infringement of a patented production method, would this be enough for a court to affirm a claim to withdraw an application for including a pharmaceutical medicine in a drug price list under the health insurance system? In the past, a lower court has affirmed a claim for injunction against a contract to test the effects of a herbicide and an application for agricultural chemical registration.[8]

---

7. Osaka District Court, 27 September 2012, Case Nos. 7576&7578 (Wa) of 2011, 2188 Hanrei Jihō 108 – *Combination Medicine for Diabate Treatment*. See Case No. 30 in this volume.
8. Tokyo District Court, 10 July 1987, Case Nos. 7463&6428 (Wa) of 1985, 671 (Wa) of 1986, 655 Hanrei Times 233.

Although this lower court decision was rendered before the present Supreme Court decision, there may be a situation where such claim is necessary as a claim for measures to prevent an act of sale. On the other hand, a decision of 23 March 1998 by the Tokyo District Court[9] ruled that there was no need for discontinuing an approval procedure for the production of a generic drug, or a free assignment to the patentee. This ruling is appropriate.

The standard to determine the necessity for preventive measures mentioned by the Supreme Court is frequently used in later lower court decisions.

For instance, in the Intellectual Property High Court (IP High Court) decision of 12 November 2015,[10] the court quoted from the Supreme Court decision and then decided that even if the act of exchanging a certain part of a machine could qualify as a method for "producing a product" and an injunction could be granted, a demand for an inspection of the machine itself and the request to stop the maintenance of the said machine as a prior step before the exchange of equipment exceeded the necessary scope of appropriate measures against the act of manufacture, and was therefore dismissed.

Further, the Supreme Court decision is sometimes referred to by courts when they apply other laws with similar provisions to demand measures to prevent infringement.

For example, although an obiter dictum, a decision of the IP High Court[11] referred to the Supreme Court decision in connection with a demand for an injunction against an act of unfair use of a trade secret; the court mentioned that if the defendant had obtained a trade secret of the plaintiff's, and a demand for injunction against such act of use was possible, a further injunction to enjoin the defendant from engaging in such business or from working as a director or an employee of the defendant company exceeded the scope necessary to protect the plaintiff against the unfair use of trade secret, and therefore, did not fall under "an act necessary to stop or to prevent infringement" provided in sec. 3(2) Unfair Competition Prevention Act.

Further, with respect to the Copyright Act, in a case where a demand for injunction was granted against an act of distributing photo posters, the court,[12] upon deciding on the ancillary demand to seek a recall of photo posters that were already distributed, referred to the Supreme Court decision and mentioned that "equipment necessary to prevent infringement" in sec. 112(2) of the Copyright Act requires that measures to be within the scope necessary to enforce the right for injunctive relief, while a recall of the photo posters at issue that were already distributed exceeded the necessary scope and was therefore refused.[13]

9. Tokyo District Court, 23 March 1998, Case No. 18040 (Wa) of 1997, the website of the courts <http://www.courts.go.jp/app/files/hanrei_jp/902/009902_hanrei.pdf>.
10. IP High Court, decision of 12 November 2015, Case No. 10048 (Ne) of 2015, 2287 Hanrei Jihō 91 – *Equipment to Prevent Simultaneous Rotation on a Machine for Removing Foreign Substances in Raw Laver.*
11. IP High Court, order of 26 May 2010, Case No. 10006 (Ra) of 2010, 2108 Hanrei Jihō 65.
12. Tokyo High Court, decision of 29 November 2004, Case No. 1464 (Ne) of 2003), the website of the courts <http://www.courts.go.jp/app/files/hanrei_jp/902/009902_hanrei.pdf>.
13. Website of the courts <http://www.courts.go.jp/app/files/hanrei_jp/902/009902_hanrei.pdf>.

4. COMPARATIVE REMARKS

The same distinction between methods for the manufacture of a product and working methods that is contained in the Japanese Patent Act can be found in **German** jurisprudence: Already the Imperial Supreme Court held that a wooden table that was subjected to a patented polishing procedure could not be interpreted as a product directly obtained from such procedure.[14] The same was held for measuring methods.[15] The German Federal Supreme Court maintained this distinction: Only where the product without an application of the method had no commercial value whatsoever could the method be interpreted as one of production.[16] The distinction between method of production and measuring method was confirmed by a 2016 Federal Supreme Court decision:[17] Here, the plaintiff was the owner of patent EP 0959132 that relates to a process for determining tumour markers, namely the use of a certain nucleic acid molecule that can be used in order to act as a marker for diagnosing leukaemia. The defendant in Germany offered certain genetic analyses, receives tissue probes from patients and extracts certain nucleic acids from the cell probes. These were then sent to the Czech Republic where the patented diagnostic process was carried out on the probes and the results sent back to Germany. While the patented process was only carried out abroad (where it was not patented), it was disputed whether the results of the process as transmitted to Germany were "products directly obtained from a patented process". The Federal Supreme Court denied this, holding that the patented process was diagnostic and the results of the process contained of information only. In order to qualify for a directly obtained product, the result of such process either had to be a (second) product different from the original product, or the original product had to be changed by the process. Neither was the case, though. In the case at issue, the process was applied to an object that as such remained unchanged, typical for a process of diagnosis or measurement.

Consequently, the effect of a patent over a working method does not extend to the products that were made subject to this method (as would be the case for methods of production under sec, 9(1)(iii) Patent Act), and neither to any claims for the destruction or otherwise of such products, sec. 140a(3) second sentence. German law would thus arrive at the same result as the Japanese Supreme Court.

14. German Imperial Supreme Court, 15 October 1912, RGSt 46, 262 – *Treibriemen*.
15. German Imperial Supreme Court, MuW 1939, 177.
16. German Supreme Court, 16 February 1951, GRUR 1951, 314 = BGHZ 1, 194 – *Motorblock*.
17. German Federal Supreme Court, 27 September 2016, 49 IIC 231 – *Receptor Tyrosin Kynase II*.

Case No. 54

Damage Calculation – Presumption of Damages

Hisayoshi Yokoyama

---

1. When calculating the patentee's damages based on the presumption that the number of infringing products sold equal lost sales (sec. 102(1) Patent Act), the patentee's sales capacity, the existence of competing products on the market, the infringer's advertising efforts, his branding power and his sales capacity, and the low sales price of the infringing products, shall be taken into account and may lead to a disapplication of the presumption.
2. The patentee cannot cumulatively request an adequate licensing fee for that part of the products for which the court have denied causality between the infringement action and the patentee's lost sales.

IP High Court, 25 September 2006, Case No. 10047 (Ne) of 2005 – *Massage Chair*

Toshiba Tec v. Family

---

1. BACKGROUND

Damages for patent infringement have its basis in the provision of a tort in sec. 709 Civil Code.[1] Since the Japanese Civil Code only admits compensation for actual damages,[2] the nature of damages based on patent infringement is generally interpreted as the same, neither punitive nor preventive, but compensatory.

According to sec. 709 Civil Code, the patentee bears a burden of proof for the sum of damages and a causal link between his losses and the infringer's action. Although the main damages based on patent infringement is the patentee's lost profits such as the patentee's lost sales due to the sales of the infringing goods, it is often difficult for the patentee to directly prove the sum of damages and a causal link between his lost profits and an infringement. Thus, in order to alleviate the burden of proof on the patentee, the Patent Act provides special calculation methods.

There are three calculation methods: First, the patentee's loss is presumed to be the number of sales of infringing products multiplied by the patentee's profits

---

1. K. IIDA, in: N. NAKAYAMA/N. KOIZUMI, Shin Chūkai Tokkyohō (*New Commentary to the Patent Act*), vol. 2, 2nd ed. 2017, 1775.
2. Supreme Court, 11 July 1997, Case No. 1762 (O) of 1993, 51-6 Minshū 2573 = 1624 Hanrei Jihō 90 = 958 Hanrei Times 93 – *Punitive Damages*, see Case No. 46 in this volume.

per each item, as long as the patentee had the capacity for selling the same number of products sec. 102(1). Second, the infringer's profits, sec. 102(2), and, third, an adequate licencing fee for the infringing products, sec. 102(3). The first calculation method was newly introduced by the Patent Act amendment of 1999, while the second and third one had already existed before.[3]

Even before the 1999 amendment, the patentee could claim damages for lost sales based on sec. 709 Civil Code. However, since the courts requested proof of causality, damages could be affirmed only in such case, where the plaintiff obviously could have sold the same number of products as the infringer. That the patentee's sales were more or less reduced due to the defendant's infringement was not good enough.[4] Proper damages could not be obtained, which is why the special calculation method for the patentee's lost sales was introduced into the Patent Act.[5]

Sec. 102(1) stipulates that the number of sales of the infringing products, multiplied by the patentee's profits per each item shall be presumed to the patentee's sales loss as long as the patentee had the capacity for selling the same number of products, and that if there are circumstances because of which the patentee could not have sold all or a part of the infringing products, the court shall deduct from the above-mentioned presumed damages the amount calculated based on the number of the products corresponding to the above mentioned circumstances. It is generally interpreted that the patentee must prove the former part, while the infringer must prove the latter part.[6] By such a shift of burden of proof, sec. 102(1) enables the patentee to obtain damages even in cases where it would be difficult for him to prove that he could have sold the same number of products in the absence of infringement.[7] In addition, since the presumed damages could be reduced on a proportional basis

3. By the amendment of the Patent Act in 1999, the wording of sec. 102(3) was partially modified: Before the amendment, the Patent Act provided that the patentee can claim an ordinary licensing fee for the infringer's exploitation of the patented invention, but the term "ordinary", which was often said to have been the cause of low damages, was deleted by the amendment.
4. For example, the courts refused a claim for lost sales just because there were competing or substituting products other than the infringing products on the market. See, Tokyo District Court, 21 September 1963, Case No. 8888 (Wa) of 1960 and Case No. 2253 (Wa) of 1962, 152 Hanrei Times 177 – *Vinylcan*; Tokyo District Court, 26 June 1972, Case No. 8785 (Wa) of 1966, 282 Hanrei Times 267 – *Table Lamp*; Tokyo District Court, 20 December 1984, Case No. 7035 (Wa) of 1982, 1138 Hanrei Jihō 137 = 543 Hanrei Times 304 – *Hairbrush*; Osaka District Court, 26 August 1987, Case No. 5141 (Wa) of 1986 – *Mortar Injector*. These decisions were criticised as an "all or nothing approach". See, Y. TAMURA, Chiteki zaisanken to Songaibaishō *(Intellectual Property Rights and Damages)*, 2nd ed. 2004, 2-6; S. CHAEN, Tokkyoken shingai ni yoru Songaibaishō *(Damages for Patent Infringement)*, 1162 Jurist 50 (1999).
5. TOKKYOCHŌ (JPO) (ed.), Kōgyōshoyukenhō Chikujōkaisetsu (*Commentary to the Industrial Property Act*), 20th ed. 2017, 325. However, it is notable that just before the amendment, a decision was rendered that anticipated the amendment: Tokyo District Court, 12 October 1998, Case No. 11876 (Wa) of 1993, 1653 Hanrei Jihō1 54 = 986 Hanrei Times 144 = 30 IIC 457 [1999] – *Cimetidine*. Like sec. 102(1) after the amendment, the court calculated the patentee's lost sales based on the infringer's amount of sales, multiplied by the exclusive licencee's profits per each item, on the premise that the exclusive licencee's sales would have been reduced by the sales of the infringing products, and affirmed damages in the amount of 3 billion yen.
6. K. IIDA(above),1823-1824.
7. TOKKYOCHŌ (above), 325.

to the extent of the infringer's proof, the court can calculate the damages flexibly and adequately.[8]

However, several interpretation issues concerning sec. 102(1) remain, two of which are addressed in the present case. The first issue is which circumstances should be taken into account as "circumstances because of which the patentee could not have sold all or a part of the infringing products" in the proviso of sec. 102(1), and the second issue is whether the patentee can request damages for an adequate licensing fee based on sec. 102(3) for part of the infringing products for which damages are not be awarded based on sec. 102(1).

2. DECISION[9]

a) Facts

X (the plaintiff, appellee) sued Y (the defendant, appellant) for damages under sec. 102(1), insisting that Y makes and sells massage chairs that infringe the claims (from No. 1 to No. 5) of the X's patent. The court of the first instance[10] held that Y infringed the claims of the X's patent, and calculated damages to be 1.52 billion yen. Y appealed. Since the claims (from No. 1 to No. 4) had been revoked during the pendency of the present case, the present court only affirmed infringement of the claim No. 5. As for damages, Y argued that sec. 102(1) should not be applied to the present case, because there were substituting products other than the Y's massage chairs in the market and X could not have sold the same number of the infringing products. On the other hand, X argued in the auxiliary that X can obtain an adequate licensing fee based on sec. 102(3) for the part of the infringing products to which sec. 102(1) cannot be applied.

The present court affirmed the application of the proviso of sec. 102(1) to the present case and eventually calculated damages to be about 11.5 million, while refusing to apply sec. 102(3) to the infringing product, to which sec. 102(1) are not applied.

8. For example, IP High Court, 19 November 2015, Case No. 10051 (Ne) of 2013, 1425 Hanrei Times 179 - *Offset Rotary Press Plate Cylinder* held that the aim of the sec. 102(1) is to shift the burden of proof for the decrease in the sales amount which has causality with an infringement action and thereby to flexibly determine the decrease in the sales amount in order to overcome the all or nothing approach of the past. N. NAKAYAMA, Tokkyohō *(Patent Law)*, 3rd ed. 2016, 380 also stated that with this amendment, the prior all or nothing phenomenon would disappear and the amount of damages is expected to become adequate through a proportional calculation.
9. Published at the website of the courts <http://www.courts.go.jp/app/files/hanrei_jp/558/033558_hanrei.pdf> = N. NAKAYAMA et al. (eds.), Tokkyo Hanrei Hyakusen *(Hundred Selected Patent Cases)*, 4th ed. 2012, 170. English translation in IIC 2011, 858.
10. Tokyo District Court, 26 March 2003, Case No. 3485 (Wa) of 2001, 1837 Hanrei Jihō 101 = 1135 Hanrei Times 262 = IIC 2006- *Massage Chair*.

b) Reasons

(1) Meaning of the circumstances, because of which the patentee could not have sold in the proviso of sec. 102(1) Patent Act

The main clause of sec. 102(1) Patent Act stipulates a calculation method for lost profits based on sec. 709 Civil Code, and should be interpreted to presume that the number of products the infringer actually sold, multiplied by the patentee's profits per each item shall be damages to the extent of the patentee's marketing capacity. The proviso of sec. 102(1) stipulates that if the infringer could prove the circumstances, because of which the presumption based on the main clause of the provision would be overturned, the amount of damages could be reduced to that extent. Such "circumstances, because of which the patentee could not have sold" are not limited to those peculiar to the products that the patentee could have sold, but the existence of competing or substituting products in the market, the infringer's own advertising efforts, his branding power and his sales capacity, other features (design or function etc.) of the infringing products, that would motivate consumers' purchase, and low sales price of the infringing products, should be able to be taken into account.

The essential feature of the present invention No. 5 is the stretch or massage effect brought by the well-devised timing of dilation of seat bags and leg bags. On the other hand, the following circumstances can be found in the present case: First, the function of the present invention No. 5 only comes out, after a part of modes operation of Y's product are chosen. Second, the effect of the present invention No. 5 is ancillary for massage chair's effect, and the effect is limited. Third, the effect concerning the present invention No. 5 is barely introduced in both the X's and Y's pamphlets. Fourth, at the time of the registration of the present patent No. 5, X's market share was only a small percent, and there are big competitors in the market of massage chairs. Fifth, Y's product contains such characteristic features unrelated to the present invention No. 5 as combine massage with massage balls and massage with air-bags and automatically search the pressure points of the body through a light censor, because of which consumers had presumably chosen Y's product. Sixth, X's product uses a massage method with air-bags, which competitive power is not necessarily strong, and X's sales power was limited. Based on a comprehensive consideration of all these matters, among the number of the products that Y has actually sold, the number after deducting the number of products that X could not have sold should be assessed to be one percent of the above-mentioned number of sales.

(2) Cumulative application of sec. 102(1) and sec. 102(3) Patent Act

X argued that even if the proviso of sec. 102(1) Patent Act is applied, considering the presence of competing products in the market, 5% of the sales of the products that the court found X could not have sold (thus, 99%) should be recognised as damages for an adequate licensing fee in sec. 102(3). However, sec. 102(1) calculates lost profits as if the infringement had not occurred, while sec. 102(3) regards an adequate amount of fee for the exploitation of the patented invention. Thus, these are two separate types of calculation methods based on different premise. In addition, under the interpretation that the patentee can request an adequate licensing fee for the products that he could not have sold, the patentee would be allowed to obtain compensation beyond the range of his lost profits that the patentee can originally request as damages for the infringement action. However, It is difficult to find a reason why the patentee should be compensated beyond his lost profits. Therefore, X's request in this regard must fail.

3. ANALYSIS

a) Meaning of the circumstances, because of which the patentee could not have sold in the proviso of sec. 102(1) Patent Act

The first issue is what kind of circumstances should be taken into account as circumstances because of which the patentee could not have sold all or a part of the infringing products in the proviso of sec. 102(1). This issue relates to how to understand the legal character of sec. 102, and there are mainly two opinions in this respect: "lost profits theory" and "constructive supplementary relationship theory".

The "lost profits theory" argues that sec. 102(1) is just a provision which presumes the patentee's lost profits based on the number of infringing products, the aim of which is to reduce the patentee's burden of proof.[11] According to this understanding, sec. 102(1) can be applied even to a case where the products that the patentee actually sold were not patented products, but merely products in competition with the infringing products, because, even in such a case, the patentee might have incurred lost sales of his own products due to an infringement action.[12] Besides, the

11. As mentioned above, this is an original legislator's intention. See, TOKKYOCHŌ (above), 325.
12. Tokyo High Court, 15 June 1999, Case No. 2249 (Ne) of 1998, 1069 (Ne) of 1999, 1697 Hanrei Jihō 96 -*Heatbank System*; IP High Court, 24 January 2012, Case No. 10032 (Ne) of 2010, 10041(Ne) of 2010 - *Solid Golf Ball*; IP High Court, 1 June 2016, Case No. 10091(Ne) of 2015, 2322 Hanrei Jihō 106 = 1433 Hanrei Times 142 - *Device for Breakage Package and its driving Method*; Y. TAMURA (above), 313-314; Y. KOIKE, Tokkyohō 102 Jō no Kaishaku ni kansuru Jitsumu no Dōkō (*Practical Movement concerning interpretation of Sec. 102 Patent Act*), Chizai Nenpō (*I.P. Annual Report*) 2007, 280; H. KOJŌ, Songai 1 Tokkyohō 102 Jō 1 Kō ni motozuku Seikyū ni tsuite *(Damages 1 About a claim based on Sec. 102(1) Patent Act)*, in: T. MAKINO/T. IIMURA/R. MIMURA/W. SUEYOSHI/S. ONO (eds.), Chitekizaisanhō no Riron to Jitsumu (*The theory and practice of IP Law*), vol. 2, 2007, 256; H. YOKOYAMA, in: T. OBUCHI/T. TSUKAHARA/S. KUMAKURA/R. MIMURA/E. TOMIOKA (eds.), Tokkyo Soshō (*Patent Litigation*), vol. 1, 2012, 362-363; K. YOSHIDA, Songai Baishō (*Damages*), in: R. TAKABAYASHI/R. MIMURA=T. TAKENAKA (eds.), Gendai Chitekizaisanhō Kōza II Chitekizaisanhō no jitsumuteki Hatten *(IP Law Lecture II: The practical development of IP Law)*, 2012, 164; T. MAKINO/N. ISODA, Songai Baishō (Damages), in: T. MAKINO/T. IIMURA/M. TAKABE/Y. KOMATSU/T. IHARA (eds.), Chitekizaisansoshō Jitsumutaikei (*Practical Structure of IP lawsuit*), vol. 2 2014, 39; K. IIDA (above), 1833. In the *Heatbank System* case, the patentee held patents A and B, made its turnover by exploiting patent A, while the infringer used the technology of patent B, which then led to a drop in sales of the patentee's products using technology A. The case resembles a similar US case (*Rite-Hite Corporation v. Kelley Corporation*, 56 F3d 1538 (Fed. Cir. 1995) and is open to question: First, the result would doubtlessly be different if patents A and B were held by different owners. Second, if the Patent Act aims at patents being exploited, why should strategic non-exploitation be rewarded. Third, a patent is meant to protect the monopolistic rewards obtained for products that could have been sold within the patented scope, because only such scope is exclusively allocated to the patentee. In other words, the scope of damages cannot exceed the scope of protection.

presumption under the main clause must be wholly or partially overturned, to the extent that it is clarified that there are circumstances that wholly or partially deny a causal link between the infringement action and the sales number of the infringing products. For example, if the reason for the sales of the infringing products lies not in the use of a patented invention but other factors, such as other excellent features of the infringing products, the infringer's own advertisement efforts or his marketing power, low sales price of the infringing products etc., the patentee could not have sold the same number of the infringing products even in the absence of infringement. Likewise, if there were strong competitors other than the infringer in the same market and they also sold competing or substituting products, the patentee could not have sold the same number of the infringing products, because other competitors could also have sold their products in place of the infringing products. Thus, these circumstances should be broadly recognised as the circumstances that the patentee could not have sold in the proviso of Sec. 102(1).[13]

On the other hand, the "constructive supplementary relationship theory" argues that sec. 102(1) is a provision which establishes a legal fiction that the infringing products have a supplementary relationship with the patentee's products, because a patent is an exclusive right for an invention and a product using the invention is only allowed to be sold by the patentee.[14] Therefore, the sale of the infringing products which deprive the patentee of an opportunity to sell products using an invention, should in principle be identified as equivalent to the patentee's lost sales.[15] Given this understanding, sec. 102(1) can only be applied to a case where the patentee himself sold patented products, because otherwise, there is no supplementary relationship between the infringing products and the patentee's products, which will make the presumption under sec. 102(1) inoperative.[16] Besides, the damage

13. *Heatbank System* case (above); Osaka High Court, 10 April 2002, Case No. 257 (Ne) of 2001, 343 (Ne) of 2001 - *Double Tire*; Osaka District Court, 10 February 2005, Case No. 4726 (Wa) of 2003, 1909 Hanrei Jihō 78 - *Tray for Preparation of Histopathological Diagnosis Specimen*; Osaka District Court, 19 April 2007, Case No. 12207 (Wa) of 2005, 1983 Hanrei Jihō 126 - *Goggle*; *Solid Golf Ball* case (above); Tokyo District Court, 28 June 2013, Case No. 14955 (Wa) of 2008, 43334 (Wa) of 2009, 2146 (Wa) of 2010 - *Roof Base Sheet*; *Offset Rotary Press Plate Cylinder* case (above); *Device for Breakage Package and its driving Method* case (above); Osaka District Court, 17 March 2016, Case No. 4916 (Wa) of 2014 - *Pad for supporting feet*; Y. TAMURA (above), 318; Y. KOIKE (above), 278; H. KOJŌ (above), 261; H. YOKOYAMA (above), 366-367; K. YOSHIDA (above), 166-167; T. UENO, in: R. SHIMANAMI/T. UENO/H. YOKOYAMA, Tokkyohō Nyūmon (*Introduction to the Patent Law*), 2014, 382; T. MAKINO/N. ISODA (above), 39; H. KATSUHISA, in: S. CHAEN (ed.), Tokkyohō (*Patent Law*), 2nd ed. 2017, 302; K. IIDA (above), 1863.
14. R. MIMURA, Songai No. 1 - Tokkyohō 102 Jō 1Kō *(Damages – sec. 102(1))*, in: T. MAKINO/T. IIMURA (eds.), Shin Saiban Jitsumu Taikei 4 Chitekizaisankankeisoshōhō *(New Court Practice Compendium 4: IP related Procedure Law)*, 2001, 296-297; N. NAKAYAMA (above), 382.
15. R. MIMURA (above), 296-297.
16. R. MIMURA (above), 300. Tokyo District Court, 19 March 2002, Case No. 23945 (Wa) of 1999, 1803 Hanrei Jihō 78 = 1119 Hanrei Times 222 - *Pachinko Slot Machine I*; Tokyo District Court, 19 March 2002, Case No. 13360 (Wa) of 1999, 1803 Hanrei Jihō 99 = 1119 Hanrei Times 244 - *Pachinko Slot Machine II*; Tokyo District Court, 16 April 2002, Case No. 8456 (Wa) of 2000, 19476 (Wa) of 2000 - *Hook Device*; Tokyo District Court, 25 April 2002, Case No. 14954 (Wa) of 2001 - *Cracking and Removal Device for tampered dried laver Seaweed I*; Tokyo District Court, 27 June 2002, Case No. 14499 (Wa) of 2000 - *Cracking and Removal Device for tampered dried laver Seaweed II*; Tokyo District Court, 27 February 2003, Case No. 19329 (Wa) of 1999 - *Welding Endtab I*; Tokyo High Court, 29 October 2003, Case No. 1901 (Ne) of 2003 - *Welding Endtab II.*

presumption under the main clause should not be disapplied just on the grounds of such circumstances as: excellent features of the infringing products; the existence of other strong competitors, etc., because sec. 102(1) had ignored such circumstances when creating a constructive supplementary relationship between the patentee's products and the infringing products.[17] According to the *"constructive supplementary relationship theory"*, the presumption under the main clause can only be overturned in exceptional cases, where, even on the premise of a constructive supplementary relationship between the infringing products and the patentee's products, it is impossible to determine that the patentee lost an opportunity to sell products, e.g. where the infringing products will be or need to be consumed only within a limited time during which the patentee could not have sold its patented products.[18]

While just after the introduction of sec. 102(1), there were some decisions that adopted the "constructive supplementary relationship theory", the "lost profits theory" is dominant in current court practice. The present decision which also adopted the "lost profits theory", deducted 99 % from the total number of infringing products and thereby almost wholly denied the presumption under the main clause due to the existence of competing products other than the infringing products, the existence of other features of the infringing products that would motivate consumer purchase, low contribution of the patented invention to the purchase of the infringing products etc.

The author supports the *"lost profits theory"*. Certainly, like the *"constructive supplementary relationship theory"* insisted, the presumption under sec. 102(1) is based on a kind of legal fiction that, in the absence of infringement, the patentee could have sold the same number of products, because the infringing products could only be sold by the patentee.[19] However, as long as damages for patent infringement have their basis in the provision of tort law in sec. 709 Civil Code, sec. 102(1) should be construed as a provision for calculating the patentee's lost profits, and therefore, the presumption under the main clause must be overturned to the extent that the infringer can prove that the actual damages incurred by the patentee fall below the presumed damages. According to the "constructive supplementary relationship theory", the patentee can obtain damages beyond the range of the actually lost sales, which is obviously contradictory to the legislator's intention to reduce the patentee's burden of proof within the framework of the current tort law.[20]

---

17. R. MIMURA (above), 297-298. *Pachinko Slot Machine I* case (above); *Pachinko Slot Machine II* case (above); *Cracking and Removal Device for tampered dried laver Seaweed I* case (above); *Cracking and Removal Device for tampered dried laver Seaweed II* case (above). N. NAKAYAMA (above), 383 also states that we should be cautious about allowing a decrease in the amount of damages based on the proviso of sec. 102(1).
18. For example, *Pachinko Slot Machine I–II* cases (above) admitted the existence of the circumstances in the proviso of sec. 102 (1), in the case where some of the infringing products had been purchased at the time of regular replacement with new products, during which the patentee could not have sold patented products, and therefore, even in the absence of infringement, not the patentee's products but third parties' products would have been sold based on the schedule for regular replacement.
19. *Roof Base Sheet* case (above); R. TAKABAYASHI, Hyōjun tokkyohō *(Patent Law from the Ground Up)*, 6th ed. 2017, 283.
20. K. YOSHIDA, 163; T. MAKINO/N. ISODA, 39. In this regard, N. NAKAYAMA (above), 382 states that considering that sec. 102(1) was newly introduced, despite that there is no such empirical rule that the sales of the infringing products are equivalent to the patentee's lost sales, this provision

A similar interpretation could be applied to sec. 102(2). sec. 102(2) stipulates that the infringer's interest obtained from an infringement action is presumed to be the patentee's damages. This presumption, like sec. 102(1), would be based on a kind of legal fiction that, in the absence of infringement, the patentee could have obtained the same amount of profits, because the profits arising from the use of a patented invention can only be obtained by the patentee. However, like sec. 102(1), as long as damages for patent infringement have its basis in the provision of tort law in sec. 709 Civil Code, sec. 102(2) should also be construed as the provision for calculating the patentee's lost profits.[21] Based on this understanding, in a case where the patentee and the infringer sold competing products on the same market and the infringer's profits is calculated based on the infringer's amount of sales, multiplied by the infringer's profits per each item, the presumption under sec. 102(2) should be overturned on a proportional basis, like in case of sec. 102(1), to the extent that the infringer could prove that the patentee could not have sold all or a part of the infringing products. Thus, the circumstances in the proviso of sec. 102(1) should also be taken into account as circumstances which wholly or partially overturn the presumption under sec. 102(2).[22]

b) Cumulative application of sec. 102(1) and sec. 102(3) Patent Act

The second issue is whether the patentee can cumulatively request an adequate licensing fee for the part of the products to which sec. 102(1) could not be applied.

---

aims not only to compensate for lost profits but also to take a step forward into the domain of normative damages, although it might deviate from the legislator' s intention to construe this provision within the framework of tort law. Seen from a legislative standpoint, the concept of normative damages beyond the framework of tort law mentioned by Prof. *Nakayama* could be adopted.

21. Therefore, just like in case of sec. 102(1), it is generally interpreted that the patentee can request damages based on sec. 102(2) even in cases where the patentee did not sell patented products, but merely products in competition with the infringing products, as long as the sales of the patentee's products were reduced due to the infringement. See, K. IIDA(above), 1920ff. In this regard, recent courts held that sec. 102(2) should be applied to cases where in the absence of infringement, the patentee could have obtained comparable profits. See, Tokyo District Court, 8 October 2009, Case No. 3493 (Wa) of 2007, 42 IIC 869 - *Kyucal*; IP High Court, 1 February 2013, Case No. 10015 (Ne) of 2014, 2179 Hanrei Jihō 36 = 1388 Hanrei Times 77 - *Container for Disposing Paper Diaper* (Case No. 56 in this volume).

22. H. TAKAMATSU, Songai 2 - Tokkyohō 102 Jō 2 Kō-3 Kō *(Damages - sec. 102(2)-(3))*, in: T. MAKINO/T. IIMURA, Shin Saiban Jitsumu Taikei 4 Chiteki zaisan kankei soshōhō *(New Court Practice Compendium 4: IP related Procedure Law)*, 2001, 317-319; S. SANO, Songai 2 - Tokkyohō 102 Jō 2 Kō-3 Kō - *(Damages 2 - sec. 102(2),(3)* -, in: T. IIMURA/R. SHITARA (eds.), Chiteki zaisan Kankei soshō *(IP related Lawsuits)*, 2008, 219-220; M. TAKABE, Jitsumu Shōsetsu Tokkyo Kankei Soshō *(Detailed Practice on Patent related Lawsuits)*, vol. 3, 2016, 265. For example, Tokyo District Court, 16 July 1999 - *Tool for Escape out of a Rough Road*, Case No. 6636 (Wa) of 1996, 1698 Hanrei Jihō 132 = 1017 Hanrei Times 245 - *Tool for Escape out of a Rough Road* partially overturned the presumption under sec. 102(2), considering the fact that the patentee could not have sold all of the infringing products, because the patentee gave a non-exclusive license to the third party, and both of the patentee and the third party sold the patented products.

Opinions are divided into "positive theory"[23] and "negative theory".[24] Although decisions in the early days adopted the "positive theory",[25] the present decision first adopted the "negative theory", and since then, the "negative theory" has become dominant in current court practice.[26]

The main reason for the "positive theory" lies in a balance theory that in a case where the claim for damages based on sec. 102(1) is thoroughly denied, the patentee can still request damages for the remainder of the infringing products based on sec. 102(3).

On the other hand, the main reason for the "negative theory" is that, as the present decision stated, each calculation methods stipulated in sec. 102 separately calculates the patentee's lost profits based on a different premise: sec. 102(1) calculates damages as if the infringement had not occurred, whereas sec. 102(3) calculates damages because the infringer used the patented invention. Thus, the cumulative application of these provisions is contradictory. Besides, because both sec. 102(1) and sec. 102(3) are self-contained calculation methods for assessing the patentee's lost profits, the amount of damages calculated under sec. 102(1) reflects the result of evaluation for all the patentee's lost profits including a case where the patentee's claim was partially denied. Thus, under the interpretation that the patentee can request damages for a part of the infringing products to which sec. 102(1) could not be applied based on Sec. 102(3), the patentee would be allowed to obtain compensation beyond his lost profits, the result of which is not adequate within the framework of the current damages system. In this regard, supporters of the *"positive theory"*consider that among the whole patentee's damages, the damages calculated based on sec. 102(1) reflects only the lost profits caused by a decrease in sales of the patentee's products, and therefore, even though the patentee is allowed

---

23. Y. TAMURA (above), 317; M. ICHIKAWA, Songai 1 - Tokkyohō 102 Jō 1 Kō - *(damages 1 - sec. 102(1) -)* in: T. IIMURA/R. SHITARA (eds.), in: Chitekizaisan Kankei soshō*(IP related Lawsuit)*, 2008, 215; S. SANO (above), 238-239; S. CHAEN, Tokkyoken Shingai ni taisuru Kyusai 1 *(Remedy for patent infringement 1)*, 348 Hōgaku Kyōshitsu 99 (2009); H. YOKOYAMA (above), 383-384; K. TOSHIYA, Tokkyoken shigai ni yoru Songai no Futatsu no omona Toraekata *(Two major understanding of damages for the patent infringement)*, in: N. KOIZUMI/Y. TAMURA (eds.), Habataki -21 seiki no chiteki zaisanhō *(Flying up- IP Law in the 21st Century)*, 2015, 453-454; K. IIDA (above), 1887-1888.
24. Y. KOIKE (above), 284-285; M. TAKABE (above), 259-260. There is also an *"intermediate theory"* which allows cumulative application of sec. 102(1) and sec. 102(3) based on the reason why sec. 102(1) could not be applied to a part of the infringing products. For example, there are opinions that exceptionally admit cumulative application in cases where sec. 102(1) cannot be applied to a part of the infringing products due to the lack of the patentee's marketing ability, or because the patentee's products and the infringing products are substantially not on the same market due to their different consumer segments or their different sales prices. See, H. KOJŌ (above) 272-273; K. YOSHIDA (above), 188.
25. *Heatbank System* case (above); *Double Tire* case (above); *Tray for Preparation of Histopathological Diagnosis Specimen* case (above).
26. *Goggle* case (above); *Solid Golf Ball* case (above); IP High Court, 22 December 2011, Case No. 10091 (Ne) of 2010, 2152 Hanrei Jihō 69 = 1399 Hanrei Times 181 - *Processing of Heavy Metal Immobilization*; *Roof Base Sheet* case (above). Tokyo District Court, 26 February 2010, Case No. 26473 (Wa) of 2005, *Solid Golf Ball* case adopted an *"intermediate theory"* and held that the cumulative application might exceptionally be affirmed in a case where sec. 102(1) cannot be applied to a part of the infringing products, due to the lack of the patentee's marketing capacity.

to request damages for a part of the infringing products to which sec. 102(1) could not be applied, based on Sec. 102(3), the total sum of damages would not exceed the patentee's lost profits.[27]

The author supports the "positive theory". Since the patentee has an exclusive right to use a patented invention, the patentee can freely determine and carry out the way to maximise the profits arising from an invention.[28] For example, in a case where the patentee intends to sell the patented products, but his business scale is not big enough to meet the entire market demand for patented products, or his products and another company's products not entirely in competition because of their different price ranges, their different consumer segments etc., the patentee who, while selling patented products by himself, gives a licence to others, could obtain more profits than when exclusively the selling patented products. The infringer deprives the patentee of an opportunity to decide how to use an invention and how to maximise his profits. Thus, it would be fair to award the patentee damages for his maximum lost profits by supposing that among the entire sales number of the infringing products, sec. 102(1) should be applied to the number of the products that could have been sold due to the use of the patented invention, as long as the patentee had capacity to sell that number, because that number shows the maximum the patentee who sells patented products ideally could have sold, while sec. 102(3) should be applied to the rest number of the products, just like in the case where the patentee, while selling his own patented products, gave a license to a third party and obtains royalties from him.[29]

However, in a case where sec. 102(1) and sec. 102(3) are cumulatively applied, only the infringing products that the patentee could not have sold are objects of damages based on sec. 102(3), and therefore, the sum of damages per each unit under sec. 102(3) would be generally lower than in a case where all the infringing products are objects of damages based on Sec. 102(3).[30] For example, in the present case, where sec. 102(1) could not be applied to 99% of the infringing products, because of low contribution of the patented invention to the purchase of the infringing products, the sum of damages per each unit based on sec. 102(3) would be extremely low, if permitted.

There is also a similar argument between sec. 102(2) and sec. 102(3). As mentioned above, in a case where the patentee and the infringer sold competing products on the same market and the infringer's profits are calculated based on the infringer's amount of sales, multiplied by the infringer's profits per each item, the presumption under sec. 102(2) should be overturned on a proportional basis, like in case of sec. 102(1), to the extent that the infringer could prove that the patentee could not have sold the same number of the products. In that case, the problem arises whether sec. 102(3) can be cumulatively applied to the products which are not an

27. K. Toshiya, in: N. Nakayama et al. (eds.), Tokkyo Hanrei Hyakusen *(Hundred Selected Patent Cases)*, 4th ed. 2012, 171.

28. In this regard, Y. Tamura (above), 213 states that the Patent Act gives a patentee an exclusive right on the use of a market opportunity for the demand of the patented invention and thereby adopts a system where profits expected to be obtained from the exploitation of a patented invention will flow back to him in a way chosen by him.

29. H. Yokoyama (above), 383-384.

30. See, K. Toshiya (above), 454.

object of calculation based on sec. 102(2), and opinions are divided into "positive theory"[31] and "negative theory".[32] Just like in case of 102(1), the "positive theory" should be supported.

A new bill submitted by the Japanese Government in March 2019 and sent to the Diet and possibly enacted in 2019, clearly endorses the "positive theory" approach.[33]

4. COMPARATIVE REMARKS[34]

a) In the **US**, there are two types of damages calculation/presumption: patentee's lost profit ("damages adequate to compensate for the infringement") and reasonable royalty ("in no event less than a reasonable royalty for the use made of the invention by the infringer").[35] In the patentee's lost profit type, the patentee has to prove (the *Panduit* test for determining "but for" causation): 1) demand for the patented products, 2) absence of acceptable non-infringing substitutes, 3) his manufacturing and marketing capability to exploit the demand, 4) the amount of profit that he would have made.[36] In the reasonable royalty type, the *Georgia Pacific* factors which increase or decrease the amount of the license are taken into account.[37] The US Court of Appeals for the Federal Circuit states that a patentee may obtain lost profit damages for that portion of the infringer's sales for which the patentee can demonstrate "but for" causation and reasonable royalties for any remaining infringing items.[38]

31. Tokyo District Court, 19 September 2007, Case No. 1599 (Wa) of 2005 – *Pin Tumbler Rock*; S. CHAEN, Tokkyoken Shingai ni taisuru Kyusai 2 *(Remedy for patent infringement 2)*, 349 Hōgaku Kyōshitsu 126 (2009); H.YOKOYAMA (above), 384; S. SANO, in: T. OBUCHI/T. TSUKAHARA/S. KUMAKURA/R. MIMURA (eds.), Tokkyo Soshō, Senmon Soshō Kōza 6 *(Technical Lawsuit Lecture 6)*, vol. 2 2012,1199; K. IIDA (above), 1983-1984.
32. Tokyo District Court, 14 February 2014, Case No. 16885 (Wa) of 2011 – *Zoom Lense*; R. MIMURA, Tokkyoken Shingai to Songaigaku no Santei *(Patent Infringement and Damage Calculation)*, in: N. NAKAYAMA (ed.), Chitekizaisan, Computer to Hō *(IP, Computer and Law)*, 2016, 450.
33. For the bill, see the documents at the website of the METI <http://www.meti.go.jp/press/2018/03/20190301004/20190301004.html>. For the background, see the report of February 2019 of the Patent Subcommittee of the JPO at the website of the JPO <https://www.jpo.go.jp/resources/shingikai/sangyo-kouzou/shousai/tokkyo_shoi/190215_tokkyo_houkoku.html>.
34. A comparative study has recently been published by C. JUNG, Patent Damages Determination in Korea, 2018 IIC 267 with an analysis of the practice in the US, Germany, Japan, Korea, the UK and France.
35. Sec. 55 of the old US Patent Act of 1870 provided also infringer's profits as damages ("the claimant shall be entitled to recover, in addition to the profits to be accounted for by the defendant, the damages the complainant has sustained thereby"), but such type was abolished by the law amendment of 1946. On the other hand, for design patents, sec. 289 still provides infringer's profits as damages. For sec. 289, see e.g., US Supreme Court, *Systems Inc. v. Nordock, Inc.*, 137 S. Ct. 589 (2016); US Supreme Court, *Samsung Electronics Co. v. Apple Inc.*, 137 S. Ct. 429 (2016). In the same *Nordock* case, before the 2016 decision of the Supreme Court, the CAFC, *Nordock, Inc. v. Systems Inc.*, 803 F.3d 1344 (Fed. Cir. 2015) stated: "Only where § 289 damages are not sought, or are less than would be recoverable under § 284, is an award of § 284 damages appropriate."
36. US Court of Appeals, *Panduit Corp. v. Stahlin Bros. Fibre Works*, 575 F.2d 1152 (6th Cir. 1978).
37. US Courts, *Georgia-Pacific Corp. v. United States Plywood Corp.*, 318 F. Supp. 1116 (S.D.N.Y. 1970), modified and affirmed, 446 F.2d 295 (2d Cir. 1971), certiorari denied, 404 U.S. 870 (1971).
38. See, e.g., US CAFC, *Crystal Semiconductor Corp. v. Tritech Microelectronics International Inc.*, 246 F.3d 1336 (Fed. Cir. 2001). US CAFC, *Asetek Danmark A/S v. CMI USA Inc.*, 852 F.3d 1352

b) In the **UK**, the same calculation methods as in the US are provided, yet cases are few and far in between. The most important modern case on lost profits awards is *Gerber Garment Technology v. Lectra Systems*,[39] in which the court states as a general principle that the right holder is entitled to recover any reasonably foreseeable loss caused by the infringement and not otherwise precluded by public policy. In principle, such losses may include not only lost profits on lost sales, but also damages for price erosion and so-called springboard damages.[40]

c) In **Germany**, there are also three types of calculation methods/presumptions: patentee's lost profit (secs. 249 – 252 Civil Code), infringer's profit (2nd sentence of sec. 139(2) Patent Act) and license analogy (3rd sentence of sec. 139(2) Patent Act). The infringer's profit and license analogy types were acknowledged by German case law from around 140 years ago, and only in 2008 codified in the German Patent Act.[41] In each type, the causality between infringing act and patentee's lost profit or infringer's profit,[42] or various factors to make license higher or lower, such as importance of patent, etc.,[43] is taken into account. The German case law clearly states that these three types cannot be combined.[44]

d) The same calculation methods are also included in Art. 13 the **EU** Enforcement Directive of 2004 and can be used in Europe-wide.[45]

e) The **Korean** Patent Act in sec. 128 contains a provision that closely resembles sec. 102 Japanese Patent Act. *Chaho Jung* in his comparative study[46] mentions similar discussions in Korea about causation and limited production capacity when determining lost profits. It is unclear whether for the same act of infringement, a mixed calculation of lost profits (within the limits of the patentee's marketing capacity) and a reasonable royalty (for further items sold) can be applied.

(Fed. Cir. 2017) states also that a patent owner, having prevailed on liability, may receive a reasonable royalty or lost profits, but not both for the same infringing units. Here is not the place to discuss the point, but under US case law, the Entire Market Value (EMV) rule or the Smallest Salable Patent Practicing Unit (SSPPU) rule is quite often discussed as a calculating base for damages, see, e.g., for recent cases, US CAFC, *Exmark Manufacturing Co. v. Briggs & Stratton Power Products Group, LLC,* 879 F.3d 1332 (Fed. Cir. 2018); US CAFC, *Power Integrations, Inc. v. Fairchild Semiconductor International, Inc.*, 894 F.3d 1258 (Fed. Cir. 2018).

39. English Court of Appeal, *Gerber Garment Technology v. Lectra Systems* [1997] R.P.C. 443, 452–56.
40. English Patents Court, *Ultraframe (UK) Ltd. v. Eurocell Bldg. Plastics Ltd.*, [2006] EWHC (Pat) 1344.
41. KRASSER/ANN, Patentrecht *(Patent Law)*, 8th ed. 2016, 899.
42. For the causality in the infringer's profit type, see e.g., German Federal Supreme Court, 24 July 2012, GRUR 2012, 1226 – *Flaschenträger*.
43. For the factors to increase or decrease a license, see e.g., German Federal Supreme Court, 30 May 1995, GRUR 1995, 578 – *Steuerrinrichtung II*; SCHULTE, Patentgesetz mit EPÜ *(Commentary on the German Patent Act and the EPC)*, 10th ed. 2017, 1982; H. OSTEN, Schadensersatz im Patentrecht *(Damages in Patent Law)*, Mitteilungen der deutschen Patentanwälte 2000, 95.
44. German Federal Supreme Court, 29 May 1962, GRUR 1962, 509 – *Dia-Rähmchen II*; German Federal Supreme Court, 18 February 1977, GRUR 1977, 539 – *Prozessrechner*; German Federal Supreme Court, 6 March 1980, GRUR 1980, 841 – *Tolbutamid*. See also KRASSER/ANN, Patentrecht *(Patent Law)*, 8th ed. 2016, 901.
45. Directive 2004/48/EC of the European Parliament and of the Council of 29 April 2004 on the enforcement of intellectual property rights.
46. C. JUNG, Patent Damages Determination in Korea, 2018 IIC 267.

Case No. 55

Damage Calculation – Presumption of Damages

Masahito Imai

Sec. 102(2) Patent Act should be understood in that the patentee can claim the infringer's profits even without working the patented invention himself.

IP High Court, 1 February 2013, Case No. 10015 (Ne) of 2012 –
Container for Disposing Paper Diapers

Sangenic v. Aplica

---

1. BACKGROUND

As mentioned in the previous case comment, sec. 102 Patent Act was introduced to reduce the patentee's burden of proving the amount of damages caused by patent infringement. Sec. 102(2) Patent Act provides that the amount of the infringer's profits obtained by infringing the patent shall be presumed to be the amount of damages caused by patent infringement. Because unlike for sec. 102(1) Patent Act (lost profits), the patentee does not need to disclose its profit margins for relying on sec. 102(2) Patent Act, and the amount of damages may be much greater than the amount of damages calculated on a royalty basis under sec. 102(3) Patent Act, It is thus advantageous for a patentee to claim damages based on sec. 102(2) Patent Act, and indeed, there are many cases where damages calculated based on sec. 102(2) Patent Act are claimed.[1]

---

1. Examples of recent decisions where more than 100 million Japanese Yen were awarded based on sec. 102(2) Patent Act are as follows: Tokyo District Court, 1 March 2018, Case Nos. 24571 (Wa) of 2017&16435 (Wa) of 2014, the website of the courts <http://www.courts.go.jp/app/files/hanrei_jp/633/087633_hanrei.pdf>; Osaka District Court, 28 June 2018, Case No. 4292 (Wa) of 2015, the website of the courts <http://www.courts.go.jp/app/files/hanrei_jp/963/087963_hanrei.pdf>; Tokyo District Court, 10 April 2015, Case No. 12351 (Wa) of 2012, the website of the courts <http://www.courts.go.jp/app/files/hanrei_jp/042/085042_hanrei.pdf>; IP High Court, 22 March 2012, Case No. 10002 (Ne) of 2011, the website of the courts <http://www.courts.go.jp/app/files/hanrei_jp/175/082175_hanrei.pdf>; Osaka District Court, 28 January 2010, Case No. 2076 (Wa) of 2007, 2094 Hanrei Jihō 103; Tokyo District Court, 27 August 2009, Case No. 3494 (Wa) of 2007, the website of the courts <http://www.courts.go.jp/app/files/hanrei_jp/145/038145_hanrei.pdf>, etc.

However, one unsolved issue regarding the application of sec. 102(2) Patent Act is whether or not a patentee needs to work its patent in order to use the calculation method stipulated there.

If so, the further unresolved issue is whether the working of the patent by a licensee is considered a working of the patent by the patentee with the consequence that the latter can rely on the calculation method of sec. 102(2) Patent Act.

2. DECISION[2]

a) Facts

In the case at issue, the plaintiff (*Sangenic International Limited*) alleges that the diaper disposal containers (in the following: infringing goods) imported and sold by the defendant (*Aplica Children's Products Ltd.*) infringe the plaintiff's patents and design rights, in particular JP registered patent No. 4402165 (diaper disposal and container for disposing paper diapers), and breach the former agency agreement between plaintiff and defendant according to which the defendant pledges not to infringe the plaintiff's intellectual property rights.

The plaintiff has requested injunctive relief against the importation of the infringing goods on the basis of sec. 100(1) Patent Act, sec. 37(1) Design Act and contractual rights, destruction of the infringing goods on the basis of sec. 100(2) Patent Act, sec. 37(2) Design Act, as well as damages in the amount of 206,739,983 Yen based on Patent Act sec. 102(2) and (3), Design Act sec. 39(2) and (3), and sec. 709 Civil Code, as well as interest in the amount of 5%. The defendant has counterclaimed damages in the amount of 75,274,696 Yen based on sec. 4 Unfair Competition Prevention Act (UCPA) and secs. 709,710 Civil Code plus interest in the amount of 5% due to damages to business reputation (sec. 2(2)(xiv) UCPA), as the plaintiff sent warning letters to the defendant's customers incorrectly alleging patent infringement and thereby spreading false facts.

The first instance court to a large part allowed the claim and dismissed the counterclaim. In regard of the damage claim, the first instance court denied the application of sec. 102(2) Patent Act (infringer's profits), as the plaintiff had not used the patent in Japan. This, however, was a requirement for claiming damages in the form of infringer's profits. Thus, the patentee could only be awarded damages on the basis of a licensing fee, sec. 102(3) Patent Act in the amount of 18,139,152 Yen, plus legal fees in the amount of 3,000,000 Yen. The first instance court dismissed claims based on design rights due to the difference in appearance. Both parties have appealed, and the main issue before this court was the application of sec. 102(2) Patent Act.

---

2. Published in 2179 Hanrei Jihō 36 = 1388 Hanrei Times 77 = T. Ōbuchi et al. (eds.), Chitekizaisan hō hanrei shū *(Intellectual Property Law Case Book)*, 2nd. ed. 2015, 203. German translation in GRUR Int. 2015, 237.

b) Reasons

1. On the infringement claim

...

(2) On the claim for damages

a. As described above, the defendant has infringed the plaintiff's patent by the importation, sale and offer for sale of the infringing products and is thus liable to pay damages.

b. On the calculation of damages based on sec. 102(2) Patent Act

The plaintiff has requested that damages be calculated on the basis of sec. 102(2) Patent Act. The defendant has contested this, as this provision could not be applied where the patentee had not used the invention. This fact did not allow for the application of the presumption stipulated in sec. 102(2) Patent Act. However, we decide that the defendant's allegations must be rejected and that there are no circumstances that speak against the application of sec. 102(2) Patent Act. The reasons are the following:

(a) On the application of sec. 102(2) Patent Act

Sec. 102(2) Patent Act has the following wording: "Where the patentee demands damages from the infringer, the profits of an intentional or negligent infringer derived from the infringement are presumed to be the damages incurred." The purpose of sec. 102(2) Patent Act is to facilitate the proof of damages by the presumption that the infringer's profits correspond to the damages incurred. Applying the principles as stipulated in the Civil Code, the patentee in the case of a patent infringement has difficulties to furnish proof for the occurrence of damages, the amount of damages and the causality between these two, for which reason the patentee often ends up in obtaining an inadequate amount of damages. In this respect, sec. 102(2) Patent Act is meant to facilitate proof of infringement. It is a presumption, and there are no reasons for a narrow interpretation when applying this provision.

For this reason, sec. 102(2) Patent Act is applicable where there are circumstances according to which the patentee could have obtained a profit but for the patent infringement. Differences in marketing between the patentee and the infringer are reasons not to apply the presumption at face value. As we will explain in the following, the use of the patented invention by the patentee is not a necessary requirement for the application of sec. 102(2) Patent Act. On this basis we analyse the application of sec. 102(2) in the case at issue.

(b) Ascertained facts

From the fact and arguments in this case we can determine the following facts:

(1) The plaintiff and *Combi Ltd.* have concluded an "Agency contract for the disposal of baby diapers".
(2) This contract contains the following provisions ...
(3) The plaintiff exports (sells) the containers that it produces in the UK to *Combi Ltd.*, and *Combi Ltd.* sells these containers in Japan to consumers.

(4) The plaintiff on a regular basis, once or twice a month, and at management level once a year, meets up with *Combi Ltd.* in order to discuss sales figures of the products and to determine the future plans, activities and sales increases, and supports *Combi Ltd.* in its sales activities.
(5) The defendant had imported the infringing goods from China and sold them in Japan between 30 July 2009 and 31 December 2011.
(6) As held above, importation and sales of the infringing goods infringe the patent.

(c) Evaluation

As held above, the plaintiff had concluded an agency agreement with *Combi Ltd.* Thereby, *Combi Ltd.* is the sales agent for the plaintiff in Japan. And the plaintiff sells (exports) the goods made in the UK to *Combi Ltd.*, and *Combi Ltd.* sells these goods to consumers in Japan. Thereby, we can say that the plaintiff sells the goods in Japan through *Combi*. By the importation and sale of the infringing waste containers in Japan the defendant is in competition with *Combi* and also the plaintiff. The turnover of the plaintiff's goods is diminished by the patent infringement of the defendant due to the sale of the allegedly infringing goods.

From the above facts there are circumstances according to which the plaintiff could have obtained higher profits but for the defendant's patent infringement. Therefore, there are no reasons why the application of sec. 102 Patent Act should be denied in order to calculate the plaintiff's damages.

Against this, the defendant has argued that in order to apply sec. 102(2) Patent Act, the "working" of the invention according to sec. 2(3) Patent Act should be undertaken by the plaintiff, as otherwise the presumption could not be applied. This followed from the principle of territoriality. The defendant alleges that it is not the plaintiff that sells the goods in Japan and for this reason sec. 102(2) Patent Act could not be applied.

But we do not share this argumentation. The wording of sec. 102(2) Patent Act gives no indication that the working of the patented invention must be undertaken by the patentee himself. Also in view of the purpose of sec. 102(2) Patent Act, namely to facilitate proof when calculating damages, there are no specific requirements when applying the provision. Applying the provision does not require that the invention is worked by the patentee himself. From the above, sec. 102(2) Patent Act should be understood in that the patentee can claim the infringer's profits even without working the patented invention himself. Therefore, it is immaterial whether in the case at issue that patentee has been working the invention according to sec. 2(3) Patent Act. This interpretation does not mean an extraterritorial broadening of the effect of the patent and does not contravene the principle of territoriality.

According to the above, we cannot agree with the defendant's allegations that sec. 102(2) Patent Act could not be applied in order to calculate the damages in this case.

(d) Damage calculation on the basis of sec. 102(2) Patent Act

a. From the facts ascertained above the amount of sales of the allegedly infringing goods are 509,583 pieces with a complete turnover of 215,043,189 Yen starting from 6 November 2009, the date the patent was registered, until 31 December 2011.

b. The plaintiff has alleged that the profit per infringing item amounted to 356 Yen. This has been admitted by the defendant....Yet the details regarding the sales expenses do not appear do be very clear in this case, and to us, pure profits in the amount of 62.6% appear more appropriate...For this reason, the infringer's profits are presumed to be in the amount of 134,617,022 Yen.

(3) Regarding the allegations as to a diminution of profits

The defendant has invoked four grounds (a) – (d) why the above amount should be diminished and the presumption under sec. 102(2) Patent Act should be modified. We do not concur with these grounds for the following reasons.

(a) First, the defendant alleges that it was *Combi Ltd.* that made the profits with the plaintiff's products in Japan, rather than the plaintiff. The defendant alleges in this respect that the contract between the plaintiff and *Combi* required a minimum sales target for the latter, for which reason the plaintiff was not damaged by lessened sales. We do not agree.

As mentioned above, the plaintiff has concluded as sales agency contract with *Combi* according to which *Combi* acts as a sales agent and sells the goods manufactured by the plaintiff in the UK and subsequently exported to Japan. *Combi* sells the products in Japan to consumers, and as a result the plaintiff sells the containers in Japan through *Combi*. For this reason, not only *Combi*, but also the plaintiff profit from such sales in Japan. And there is no sufficient evidence to affirm the allegation of minimum sales or a penalty for selling less than a minimum target. In addition, the defendant has not furnished proof for its allegations, and therefore we cannot regard the presumption of damages as rebutted by the fact that the patented products are sold by *Combi*.

(b) The defendant further alleges that for those products most often sold by the plaintiff, *"Mark II"*, the effect of the patent does not occur, for which reason the products *"Mark II"* should not feature in the calculation. We do not concur ...

(c) The defendant further argues that the sales price of the plaintiff's containers was 500 Yen higher than the price for the defendant's product. It was therefore highly unclear whether the defendant's customers had otherwise bought the plaintiff's products. Further, any customers bought the defendant's products due to the trade mark *"Aplica"*, and it was not clear whether they would otherwise have bought the plaintiff's product. Further, the defendant in light of the current patent dispute had subsequently marketed other, non-infringing products, and there were also products from other manufacturers on the market. Finally, there were modifications in the manner of sales that had equally influenced the sale of the plaintiff's products. For all these reasons it would not be adequate to calculate damages based on the infringer's profits.

We do not concur.

The allegedly infringing products of the defendant, just as the products of the plaintiff (waste containers) are normally sold together with the plaintiff's main product, buckets for diapers, and only used in this combination. The difference in price between the plaintiff's product and the infringing products or the defendant are 500 Yen per pack (three items), and *Combi* presumably sells under a trade mark that is as popular as *"Aplica"*. From this, and from all other arguments there is the presumption that the plaintiff's lost sales of its containers amount to what the defendant has sold. The presumption of damages is not weakened by the attraction of the trade mark *"Aplica"*, the fact that competing products for the disposal of diapers exist or that there were problems with the plaintiff's buckets.

(d) From the above it is clear that we so not share the arguments advanced by the defendant. The plaintiff has lost profits due to the defendant's infringement, and there are no cogent reasons that would speak in favour of disapplying, or only applying with modifications, the presumption of damages under sec. 102(2) Patent Act.

3. ANALYSIS

a) Damage calculation under sec. 102(2) Patent Act: Infringer's profits

The framework of calculating damages based on sec. 102(2) Patent Act is the following:

The infringer's profit under sec. 102(2) Patent Act is calculated by multiplying the amount of the sales of the infringer's products by the gross profit ratio.[3] It is generally considered that the infringer's profit under sec. 102(2) Patent Act means its marginal profit, which is generally calculated by deducting actual costs such as costs for manufacturing and selling products (e.g. material costs, transportation costs for the infringer's products) from the amount of sales.

In calculating damages based on 102(2) Patent Act, in addition to the infringer's profits, it is necessary to consider whether the presumption that the infringer's profits correspond to the damages incurred is rebuttable or not. While the court seemed to affirm that such a rebuttal was possible in principle, none of the assertions by the defendant in order to totally or partially rebut the presumption under sec. 102(2) Patent Act was actually accepted by the IP High Court. Whether such allegations are accepted depends on each case, yet the following factors can be taken into account: the difference in business between a patentee and an infringer, the existence of competitive products, the marketing efforts of the infringer (strength of brand, advertisement, the performance of the infringer's products, e.g. characteristics other than the patented invention such as function and design of the infringer's products), the existence of licenses, the existence of other infringing products, and the difference in territories of sales.[4]

Before the decision *Paper Diaper (Aplica)* case, the common view was that a patentee needs to work its patent in order to claim damages based on sec. 102(2)

3. The infringer's profit is established by the infringer's documents necessary for calculating the infringer's profit such as account books, and the infringer usually submits them voluntarily if the court has found infringement and the plaintiff seeks damages based on sec. 102(2) Patent Act. If the infringer refuses to submit them voluntarily, the court can issue an order to submit them under sec. 105 Patent Act.
4. M. Takabe, Tokkyo Kankei Soshō *(Lawsuits concerning patents)*, 3rd ed. 2016, 265; H. Takamatsu, in: T. Makino/T. Iimura (eds.), Chiteki Zaisan Kankei Soshōhō *(Procedural laws concerning intellectual properties)*, 2001, 318-319.

Patent Act.[5] One of the reasons for this view is the following consideration: sec. 102(2) Patent Act is only a presumption for the *amount* of damages, but not for the *occurrence* of damages *as such*. As no damages are caused by the infringement of a patent that the patentee commercially works, the presumption under sec. 102(2) cannot help, either. A patentee therefore needs to commercially work its patent in order to prove the occurrence of damages in the first place. Only then can the damage claim be based on sec. 102(2) Patent Act. Many court cases have endorsed this view.[6]

In contrast, the opposite view[7] argues that damages based on sec. 102(2) Patent Act can also be claimed by a patentee who does not work its patent. According to this view, it suffices that a patentee manufactures and sells products which compete to products which constitute infringement of the patent.[8]

Thus, there have been two views which sharply conflict in regard of the question whether a patentee needs to work its patent or not in claiming damages based on sec. 102(2) Patent Act. Considering the importance of this question, the *Aplica* case was decided the Grand Panel of the IP High Court which consists of five judges (usually, a case brought to the IP High Court is decided by three judges). This decision is notable for providing an answer to this important question on sec. 102(2) Patent Act

The court ruled that the act of working the patented invention by the patentee may not be regarded as a requirement for the application of sec. 102(2) Patent Act and it suffices that the patentee could have gained a profit but for the infringement. In this decision, considering that the plaintiff (the patentee) can be said to sell its products to consumers in Japan via *Combi*, that the defendant (the infringer) is a competitor not only of *Combi* but also of the plaintiff in the sale of the infringing products, and that the sale of the plaintiff's product is decreasing due to the defendant's infringement, the court found the above circumstances sufficient to hold that the plaintiff could have gained a profit if the defendant had not infringed the plaintiff's patent. The court thus allowed the plaintiff to claim damages based on sec. 102(2) Patent Act.

---

5. I. Yoshikawa, in: T. Makino et al. (eds.), Chiteki Zaisanhō no Riron to Jitsumu *(Theory and practice concerning intellectual property laws)*, 2007, 279; K. Iida, Gomi chozōki jiken tizai kōsai toku han heisei 25 nen 2 gatsu 1 nitchi to tokkyo hō 102 jō 2 kō no tekiyō han'i *(Paper diaper case, IP High Court, 1 February 2013, and scope of application of sec. 102(2) Patent Act)*, 70-14 Patent 10 (2017), at 18 etc.; Arguments on this point are analysed and disused in detail by K. Iida, in N. Nakayama et al. (eds.), Shin Chūkai Tokkyohō *(New Commentary to the Patent Act)*, 2nd ed. 2017, 1913-1934.
6. Tokyo High Court, 15 June 1999, Case Nos. 2249 (Ne) of 1998&1069 (Ne) of 1999, 1697 Hanrei Jihō 96 – *Heat Storage Material*; Tokyo District Court, 31 October 2001, Case No. 15912 (Wa) of 2000, the website of the courts <http://www.courts.go.jp/app/files/hanrei_jp/215/012215_hanrei.pdf> = 15 L&T 92 (2002); Osaka District Court, 29 October 2009, Case No. 13513 (Wa) of 2007 the website of the courts <http://www.courts.go.jp/app/files/hanrei_jp/170/038170_hanrei.pdf>; Tokyo District Court, 23 May 2012, Case No. 26341 (Wa) of 2010, the website of the courts <http://www.courts.go.jp/app/files/hanrei_jp/335/082335_hanrei.pdf> – *Compositions for Cleansing*.
7. H. Takamatsu (above), 310, etc.
8. There were some court cases where this view was adopted, e.g. Tokyo District Court, 8 October 2009, Case No. 3493 (Wa) of 2007, the website of the courts <http://www.courts.go.jp/app/files/hanrei_jp/141/038141_hanrei.pdf>.

b) Use by a licensee

Whether use by a licensee is considered use by the patentee was addressed in a trade mark case back in 1993.[9] In this case, not the plaintiff who was the owner of the trade mark concerned, but an affiliate sold the trade marked products in Japan. This situation is similar to the *Sangenic v. Aplica* case, and it was an issue whether sec. 38(1) Trade Mark Act (which is currently sec. 38(2) Trade Mark Act and corresponds to sec. 102(2) Patent Act) required actual use of the mark by the trade mark owner in order to claim the infringer's profits. The Tokyo District Court denied the application of then sec. 38(1) Trade mark Act for the reason that the plaintiff (trade mark owner) did not sell products in Japan using the trade mark. Following the IP High Court's ruling in the *Sangenic v. Aplica* case, the Tokyo District Court may have needed to consider whether the trade mark owner could have obtained (more) profits in the absence of infringement. Apart from this, the decision seems incorrect bearing in mind that "use" in sec. 50(1) Trade mark Act explicitly includes use by the exclusive or non-exclusive licensee.

c) Own opinion

The findings of this decision have been accepted by some academics[10] and I agree with this decision for the following reasons. First, the purpose of sec. 102(2) Patent Act is to reduce the plaintiff's burden to prove the amount of damages caused by patent infringement and it is not appropriate to limit the scope of applying sec. 102(2) Patent Act by requiring that a patentee should work the patent by himself, which among other things is not clearly provided in sec. 102(2) Patent Act. Secondly, in case of patent infringement by the sale of infringing products, a scenario where a patentee manufactures and sells products which are within the scope of the patent and a scenario where the patentee manufactures and sells products which lack only a minor element of the patent (and therefore, the patentee does not work the patent) are not so different from the viewpoint of the patentee's damages caused by the patent infringement. However, the view requiring the patentee's working its patent leads to totally different conclusions in these two scenarios: sec. 102(2) Patent Act is applicable in the former scenario while it is not applicable at all in the latter scenario. Thirdly, sec. 102(2) Patent Act only "presumes" that the amount of damages is equivalent to an infringer's profit gained by patent infringement, so the amount of damages for which an infringer is liable does not become excessive by proving factors which undermine this presumption. One should further bear in mind that "use" of a patented invention can take all forms as listed in sec. 2(3)(i) Patent Act: Working by way of manufacture, importation or offer for sale. Sec. 78 explicitly recognises the non-exclusive licensee as an authorised user. Even if use of

---

9. Tokyo District Court, 24 March 1993, Case No. 7534 (Wa) of 1991, 26 IIC 566 – 569 (1995) w. comment C. Heath – *Chanel No. 5 Type*.

10. N. Nakayama, Tokkyohō *(Patent Law)*, 3rd ed. 2016, 387-388; K. Iida, in : Shin Chūkai Tokkyohō (above), 1916-1918; N. Ōtomo, Tokkyo hō 102 jō 2 kō no tekiyō yōken -gomi chozōki jiken chizai kōsai daigōgi hanketsu- *(Requirement for application of sec. 102(2) Patent Act -paper diaper case, IP High Court Grand Panel decision-)*, 67 Tokkyo Kenkyū 56 (2013), etc.

the patented invention is required for a damage claim in the form of infringer's profits, every use by an authorised user should qualify as such. Also the use requirement in Art. 5A of the Paris Convention and in domestic rules that concern compulsory licensing only attaches importance to the question whether authorised goods are on the market, not by whom.

4. COMPARATIVE REMARKS

a) The **US**, while providing IP owners with the possibility of obtaining multiple damages in cases of wilful infringement, the US system has also significant limits to damage awards in that it does not allow the owner of a patent to claim the infringer's profits.[11]

b) In **Germany,** the infringer's profits can be claimed based on the assumption that the infringer engaged in a business that only the right owner could have lawfully conducted, and for that reason should surrender to the right owner all the profits made from such business.[12] According to some precedents, the infringer's profits cannot be claimed where the right owner would definitely not have used the right at all, while it is insufficient that the right was not actually used.[13] Obviously, the claim for the infringer's profits fails if the infringer has not actually made a profit, a fact that can be ascertained by an inspection of the relevant commercial documents prior to raising such claim. However, the infringer's profits can only be claimed to the extent that such profit was actually made from using the infringed right. Other factors such as adroit advertising, quality, size of the distribution system, reputation of the selling enterprise, special commercial relationships or other factors unrelated to the infringed right bear no conditional relationship to the infringed right and thus cannot be claimed as profits by the plaintiff.[14] Profits made from articles unrelated to the patent infringement can only be claimed under exceptional circumstances. In one case, a patent for slide frames was infringed, and the infringer distributed the slide frames as a free gift together with his cameras. The Court held that part of the profit made from such cameras could count as the infringer's profits.[15] Awards of infringer's profits appear to have taken on additional importance following the Federal Supreme Court *Gemeinkostenanteil* decision,[16] holding that the infringer normally is not entitled to deduct any portion of its overhead that would have been incurred even in the absence of infringement.[17]

11. Design patent owners may obtain this remedy, however, see 35 U.S.C. § 289, as can owners of copyrights trade marks, and trade secrets under certain circumstances.
12. E.g. German Imperial Supreme Court, 22 October 1930, RGZ 130, 108; German Federal Supreme Court, 29 May 1962, GRUR 1962, 509 - *Dia-Rähmchen II.*
13. German Imperial Supreme Court, 22 October 1930, RGZ 130, 108. For a more recent discussion of whether awards of an infringer's profits are or should be available to non-practising entities, see WALZ, Patentverletzungen im Lichte des Kartellrechts: In Sachen Europäische Kommission gegen Orange-Book *(Patent infringement in the light of competition law: In the case European Commission against Orange-Book)*, GRUR Int. 2013, 718.
14. Cologne Appeal Court, 16 March 1990, GRUR 1991, 60 - *Rolex-Imitation.*
15. *Dia-Rähmchen II*, above.
16. German Federal Supreme Court, 2 November 2000, 33 IIC 900 - *Gemeinkostenanteil.*
17. German Federal Supreme Court, 2 November 2000, 33 IIC 900 - *Gemeinkostenanteil.*

Characteristic for the German method of damage calculation is the necessity of exact calculation mandated by the proportional reimbursement of attorneys' fees: a right owner who claims more than he actually receives in the end partially loses his case and thus has to reimburse the other party for part of the attorneys' fees proportional to the percentage to which the claim is upheld. While the courts are given a significant amount of leeway in the calculation of damages, punitive elements of calculation can only be found in copyright cases.

c) As to the claim for account of profits by the infringer in the **UK**, this is an equitable remedy at the discretion of the court. Until recently, such an account has rarely been requested owing to the difficulty in computation and the possibility that such computation would show little or no profits by the infringer, thereby making any recovery impossible. Nevertheless, the claim has been used more frequently since the Patents Court's 1998 decision in *Celanese Int'l Corp v. BP Chemicals Ltd.*[18] Although the Court concluded that it could not take into account the defendant's ability to earn a comparable profit from the use of a non-infringing alternative, the court awarded the patent owner £567,840 (only 0.3 per cent of the amount it sought) based on its conclusion that the defendant earned no profit from the production occurring at one of its plants, and that only 0.6 per cent of the gross profit earned at the other plant was attributable to the patented process. In a more recent decision involving an account of profits for trade mark infringement, the Court of Appeal (like the German Federal Supreme Court in *Gemeinkostenanteil*) held that for purposes of calculating the defendant's profit there should be no deduction of allocable overheads; rather, the defendant must show that the deducted costs are properly attributable to the production of the infringing merchandise.[19]

d) The **French** Intellectual Property Code's provision on patent damages has been amended twice in recent years, first following the 2004 Enforcement Directive and again in early 2014. The current law permits the court, in assessing damages and interest, to take into account 'loss of profit and the loss sustained by the injured party'; 'the moral prejudice incurred by the latter'; and 'the profits realised by the infringer, including the savings of intellectual, material, and promotional investments which the later has derived from the infringement'

Under the new law, the court may make awards of infringer's profits - which French law prior to the Directive did not allow, and the availability of which since then has resulted in conflicting decisions - more common.[20]

e) In **Korea**, sec. 128(4) Patent Act provides a presumption of damages based on the infringer's profit, and the Seoul High Court in 2009 also held that the patentee's

18. UK Patents Court, 26 October 1998, *Celanese Int'l Corp v. BP Chemicals Ltd.* [1999] RPC 203.
19. English Court of Appeal, 9 November 2012, *Hollister Inc v. Medik Ostomy Supplies Ltd* [2012] EWCA Civ 1419.
20. Buffet Delmas d'Autane & Fabre, Nouveautés, clarifications, carences et incertitudes du dispositif de lutte contre la contrefaçon tel que renforcé par la loi no 2014-315 du 11 mars 2014 *(Novelty, clarification, deficiency and uncertainty of the desposition of fight against the counterfeit strengthened by the Law No. 2014-315 of 11 March 2014)*, 2014-5 *Propriété Industrielle* 10 (May 2014).

working of a patented invention was no requirement for the application of the damages presumption based on the infringer's profit.[21]

21. Seoul High Court, 3 February 2009, Case No. 17757 (Na) of 2009. In this case, the appeal was dismissed by the Korean Supreme Court. On the other hand, for trade marks, the Korean Supreme Court, 29 October 2009, Case Nos. 22514&22521 (Da) of 2009 stated that the right holder's commercial use of the registered trade mark was necessary for the application of the provision of damages presumption based on the infringer's profit in the Trade Mark Act.

Case No. 56

Threats – Warning Letter alleging Patent Infringement – Standard of Liability

Christopher Heath

Where the infringement of a patent is alleged vis-à-vis third parties, and the patent is subsequently invalidated, unlawfulness of such allegation depends on whether the allegation can be regarded as the lawful exercise of the patent right. This depends on the time and contents of the allegation, the search efforts of the right owner, the addressee of the allegation and the latter's capacity to react adequately.

Tokyo High Court, 29 August 2002, Case No. 5555 (Ne) of 2001 – *Magnetic Powder*

Dowa Kōgyō v. Bayer Aktiengesellschaft

1. BACKGROUND

a) Primary infringers, secondary infringers and third parties

The case deals with threats (warning letters)[1] to customers of a competitor alleging that the competitor infringed that the sender's patent.

Warning letters in general serve a legitimate function if they are used to notify a potential infringer that infringement proceedings may be initiated unless the alleged infringing activities stop. In some countries, warning letters are required in order to (subsequently) recover the costs of the litigation from the infringer, or in order to recover damages or interest. Different from counterfeiting or piracy where warning letters may alert fly-by-night infringers, warning letters in the case of patent infringement proceedings may assist in an amicable settlement, or may prepare a

1. Recent literature regarding threats under Japanese law: M. TAKABE, Chiteki zaisanken wo shingai suru mune no kokuchi to fusei kyōsō kōi no seihi *(Unfair competition and a notice of intellectual property infringement)*, 1290 Jurist 88 (2005); T. HIROSE, Chiteki zaisanken shingai ni kan suru keikoku *(Warning letters for intellectual property infringement)*, 57 Chizai Kanri 929 (2007); Y. KOMADA, Riyū no nai tokkyo ken shingai keikoku to fusei kyōsō bōshi hō *(Unjustified warning letters for patent infringement and unfair competition law)*, 66 Tokkyo Kenkyū 5 (2018). Literature in English: C. HEATH, Unfair Competition Prevention in Japan, London 2001, 179 – 180; C. HEATH, Wrongful Patent Enforcement, 39 IIC 307 (2008); S. MURATA, Sending out Warning Letters for Patent Infringement, 40 AIPPI Journal of the Japanese Group (English edition) 20 (2015).

court action. A warning enables the alleged infringer to make an assessment as to whether he wishes to test the validity of the right or the non-infringing freedom to operate in court. This is especially true if the communication is addressed to a primary infringer (e.g. a manufacturer or importer) who knows the field of technology or trade. A primary infringer will typically be engaged in acts of manufacture, distribution, storage or offer for sale of infringing items.

In the case at issue, the warning letter alleging infringement was sent to a 'secondary infringer', meaning someone involved in the downstream distribution or use of the allegedly infringing items (e.g. distributors, retailers, exporters, etc.), or in the upstream value chain (i.e. component part manufacturers and suppliers). Liability for secondary infringers can arise based on inducement, or contributory infringement. Putting secondary infringers on notice may serve the purpose of establishing infringement, e.g. by constructive knowledge of the use of supplied items. The threat to alleged secondary infringers may also serve the purpose of locating the primary infringer who directly infringes on account of acts of importation or manufacture. The difference between a warning letter to primary and secondary infringers is important for the purposes of liability, however: A warning letter to secondary infringers spreads information possibly detrimental to third parties, as it alleges that the primary infringer engages in acts of patent infringement. This is relevant in that liability for threats is based on the spreading of false information detrimental to the business reputation.

Where warning letters are sent to consumers or others that are neither primary nor secondary infringers, legitimacy is dwindling fast: Such letter cannot serve the purpose of preventing infringement or establishing liability, but merely of tarnishing reputation and preventing those informed from purchasing allegedly infringing products.

b) The law

Starting with international law, the Paris Convention in Art. 10bis requires members of the union to prohibit 'any acts of competition contrary to honest practices in industrial or commercial matters', which under Article 10bis(3)(ii) includes "false allegations, in the course of trade, which are of such a nature as to discredit the establishment, the goods or the industrial or commercial activities of a competitor" as part of the overall goodwill of a business.[2]

The corresponding provision in Japanese law can be found in sec. 2(1)(xxi)[3] Unfair Competition Prevention Act (UCA) that prohibits "acts of making or circulating false allegations injurious to another's business reputation in a competitive relationship".

The plaintiff in cases based on sec. 2(1)(xxi) UCA is thus the person injured by such false allegations, typically the manufacturer or importer of the allegedly

2. S. LADAS, Patents Trade Marks and Related Rights – National and International Protection, 1975, Harvard University Press 1975, at 1725-27.
3. The provision of sec. 2(1)(xiii) as mentioned in the decision later became sec. 2(1)(xv) and after the law amendment of 2018 (Law No. 33/2018 of 30 May 2018) in force since 1 July 2019, became sec. 2(1)(xxi)

infringing goods. In the case at issue, the allegations sent to customers of the alleged infringer were incorrect: The patent on which the sender relied was held invalid. Thereby, the question of liability arose.

2. DECISION[4]

a) Facts

The plaintiff is a manufacturer and a distributor of metallic powder for the recording of magnetic signals. The defendant, who has its head office Germany, is a world-leading company in the chemical industry, and a patentee of metallic powder for the recording of magnetic signals (Patent No. 1733787).

In this case, the plaintiff asserted that the warning letter sent by defendant to a customer of the plaintiff's claiming the infringement of the defendant's patent contained untrue facts, and thus such warning by the defendant fell within one of the acts listed in the Unfair Competition Prevention Act sec. 2(1)(xiii) [current paragraph (1)(xxi)], namely "the spreading of untrue facts".

The defendant filed the patent application for its invention in 17 February 1988, and the patent was granted in 17 February 1993. Around 26 May 1993, the plaintiff received a letter from the defendant; the letter stated that the defendant determined that plaintiff's product, metallic powder, infringes the defendant's patents granted in Japan, US and Europe. Several letters (four times each) were exchanged between both parties from August to December in 1993. In March 1994, the defendant sent a warning letter to *SONY Corporation* ("*SONY*"), a Japanese corporation and a customer of the plaintiff's that buys metallic powder from the plaintiff and manufactures and sells video tape recorders as its products. In the warning letter, the defendant asserted a patent infringement in regard of the plaintiff's products.

Later, on 9 January 1995, the defendant brought a lawsuit asserting patent infringement against *SONY Electronics Inc.*, an American corporation and an affiliated company of *SONY*, with the Delaware District Court in US, and n 8 July 1997 also brought the same infringement lawsuit against SONY and the plaintiff before the same court.

On 16 February 1996, in Japan, the plaintiff brought a lawsuit against the defendant seeking a declaration of non-infringement of the defendant's patent before the Tokyo District Court. On 25 January 2000, the Court held that the metallic powder as manufactured by the plaintiff and used by *SONY* for the manufacture of videotape did not infringe the defendant's Japanese patent and declared that the defendant was not entitled to an injunction and damages against the plaintiff (this decision became final by the withdrawal of the appeal by the defendant). Also the Tokyo High Court decision declaring the defendant's Japanese patent invalid became final on 17 August 2000.

4. Published in 1807 Hanrei Jihō 128. English translation in 37 IIC 758 (2006) – *Warning Letter/ Metallic Powder*. The decision of the previous instance (Tokyo District Court, 20 September 2001, Case No. 11657 (Wa) of 2000) is published in 1801 Hanrei Jihō 113.

The Tokyo District Court determined that the warning of the defendant is not "the spreading of untrue facts" and rejected the claim of the plaintiff (20 September 2001, Case No. 11657 (Wa) of 2000). The plaintiff appealed. The Tokyo High Court upheld.

b) Reasons

When a patentee warns customers of a competitor stating that the competitor's product infringes patentee's patent, and when (i) the invalidation decision for the patent becomes final, or (ii) the decision that declares non-infringement afterwards becomes final and conclusive, such warning by the patentee is a prima facie unfair competition act as "the spreading of untrue facts" However, in certain cases, such warning can be regarded as the lawful exercise of patentee's patent right and is considered a legitimate conduct …

When a patentee is so bold as to warn in spite of knowing that there are no factual grounds or no legal basis for the allegation, or when a patentee could have easily concluded that the warning was groundless by examining the facts and doing legal research necessary for commencing a patent infringement suit, the warning should be regarded as unlawful and should be considered the spreading of untrue facts injuring a competitor's business reputation. Where the above precautions are taken, the warning should be regarded as a legitimate conduct, because it is a part of the legal exercise of the patentee's patent rights. When the notice to customers of a competitor at first sight looks like the lawful exercise of a patent right, but in contents or style goes beyond what can be considered adequate, in other words, when the right is substantially exercised for the purpose of injuring a competitor's business reputation vis-à-vis its customers, thus threatening the competitor's relationship with customers or competition in the market as such, it is obvious that such notice cannot be regarded as a legitimate conduct and constitutes an act of unfair competition. The patentee in such case is liable for the competitor's damage.

It must thus be determined whether the warning letter directed at customers of the competitor was part of the exercise of the patent right or rather beyond what was necessary according to common sense. Whether such letter was part of the exercise of the patent right or only formally complied with such exercise should also be determined by looking at the synthesis of the negotiation process with the competitor until the warning, the timing and the distribution of the warning letter, the number and range of customers the letter was distributed to, the size and type of business concerned, the relationship and the style of dealing with the competitor, the allegedly infringing products, the way a patent infringement can be dealt with at the level of customers supplied with the allegedly infringing goods, the reaction to the distribution of the warning letter, the conduct of the patentee and the customers after the distribution, and other circumstances.

3. ANALYSIS

Judging by the surprisingly high number of Japanese decisions in this field,[5] the sending out of (often groundless) warning letters does not seem to be completely uncommon.

a) Definition of "warning letter" (threat)

For the definition of a threat or warning letter alleging infringement, the courts take into account how such letter is perceived by the addressee:

> "[1.] This court for the following reasons holds that the circular in its contents, form, particulars and circumstances prior to its dispatch by the members of the business association receiving the circular was understood in the sense that making use of the allegedly infringing device amounted to a patent infringement, and thus had the appearance of a warning letter. First, the circular in the beginning explicitly mentions the plaintiff's product by name (sawayakasan) in connection with the patent, and that the plaintiff's technology of using humus for treating waste water fell within the scope of the defendant's patent. In this connection, the phrase '... please advise your department's that these are using the contents of the patent' deserves mention. Second, the circular was sent as a letter with registered contents. Third, the addressees of the letter, that is the local water boards that used the allegedly infringing devices were members of the study group, and it was made clear to the participating persons reading the circular that in using the devices, they would infringe the patent at issue. Thus, the circular can be understood as a warning letter not to use the patent at issue, and this is indeed the ordinary meaning the letter should be given ..."[6]

b) Warning letters sent to primary infringers

To the extent that the warning letter or allegation of infringement is targeted at the manufacturer or importer ("primary infringer"), this cannot be considered an act of tarnishing, as the allegation of infringement is not sent to third parties. One could only think of a general tort of harming business, yet the courts have refused to acknowledge a "right of business",[7] and have explicitly held that (unfounded) requests for border detention[8] or unwarranted lawsuits[9] are no unlawful acts unless they are "inequitable". There are no known cases where the sending of a warning letter to the manufacturer or importer was regarded as unlawful, regardless of the later outcome of a lawsuit, since

> "It is a justified exercise of the patent right and the right to avail oneself to the courts where the patentee upon infringement of his patent requests an interim

---

5. M. TAKABE in her article (above) lists 20 decisions, C. HEATH (above) 21 between 1972 and 1995.
6. Tokyo District Court, 15 March 2004, Case No. 20812 (Wa) of 2002, 39 IIC 247 (2008) – *Water Pellets.*
7. Osaka District Court, 27 February 1970, Case No. 7003 (Wa) of 1968, 2 IIC 325 (1971) with comment by S. KUWATA – *Parker.*
8. Osaka District Court, 27 February 1970, Case No. 7003 (Wa) of 1968, 2 IIC 325 (1971) – *Parker.*
9. Tokyo High Court, 19 October 2004, Case No. 3324 (Ne) of 2004, 39 IIC 121 (2008) – *Kojima/ Yamada* w. comment by C. HEATH.

> injunction or raises a lawsuit against a competitor's distributors, and such act lacks unlawfulness (Supreme Court, 26 January 1988[10])."[11]

c) Warning letters sent to commercial customers and suppliers

Different from a communication to the primary infringer, targeting secondary infringers with warning letters alleging the primary infringer's act of infringement amounts to a "spreading of facts" under the UCA, and in the case that the allegation is wrong, to a spreading of false facts:

> "The patentee's act of exercising its right by sending a warning letter where in the end of the day it turned out that there was no infringement, be it for the invalidity of the patent at issue, be it because the allegedly infringing act falls outside the scope of the right, amounts to the publication or circulation of false facts under the UCA ..."[12]

As sending out warning letters to customers seems a convenient way of avoiding a lawsuit and still achieve the result of blocking the manufacturer's sales channels for good,[13] the Japanese courts prior to 2002 regarded such warning letters as unlawful *per se* if it later turned out that there was no infringement,[14] an approach criticised by some academics.[15] The standard of practically no-fault liability changed with the above *Metallic Powder* decision where the court made unlawfulness dependent upon on "the contents and timing of the warning letter, the search efforts of the right owner, the addressee, and the latter's possibilities of dealing with such allegation."

This standard has been followed by subsequent decisions[16] that absolved the patentee from liability even where no detailed enquiries about the patent's validity were made, but determining validity was rather unclear.[17] These decisions are clearly

10. Supreme Court, 26 January 1988, Case No. 122 (O) of 1985, 42-1 Minshū 1.
11. Tokyo District Court, 6 July 2006, Case No. 10073 (Wa) of 2005, 39 IIC 374 (2008) – *Powdered Fish Food.*
12. Tokyo District Court, 6 July 2006, Case No. 10073 (Wa) of 2005, 39 IIC 374 (2008) – *Powdered Fish Food.*
13. Typical examples: Tokyo District Court, 1 July 1995, Case No. 4948 (Wa) of 1993, 27 IIC 570 (1996) – *Beauty and the Beast*, where instead of the importer of films, cinemas were informed of the infringing copies (in the end, this allegation was true), Tokyo District Court, 15 March 2004, Case No. 20812 (Wa) of 2002, 39 IIC 247 (2008) – *Water Pellets*, where allegations of infringement were circulated to public water boards that used the allegedly infringing technology.
14. E.g. Osaka District Court, 29 June 1979, Case No. 4683 (Wa) of 1977, Tokkyo Kanri Bessatsu 554 (1979): "Unless there are specific facts, the defendant in stating that there is an infringement is presumed to have acted negligently".
15. K. DOHI, Eigyō hibō kōi toshite no kenri shingai keikoku *(Infringement claims as slander)*, 5 Kōgyō Shoyūken Hōgakkai Nempō 56 (1982).
16. Tokyo District Court, 15 March 2004, Case No. 20812 (Wa) of 2002, 39 IIC 247 (2008) – *Water Pellets*; Tokyo District Court, 31 March 2004, Case No. 8180 (Wa) of 2003, the website of the courts <http://www.courts.go.jp/app/files/hanrei_jp/407/010407_hanrei.pdf> – *School Bags*; Tokyo District Court, 6 July 2006, Case No. 10073 (Wa) of 2005, 39 IIC 374 (2008) – *Powdered Fish Food.*
17. Tokyo District Court, 8 August 2006, Case No. 3056 (Wa) of 2005, the website of the courts <http://www.courts.go.jp/app/files/hanrei_jp/423/033423_hanrei.pdf> – *Coat Hanger Clip.* The court found the preparations of the patent attorney when drafting the application as sufficient. Tokyo District Court, 6 July 2006, Case No. 10073 (Wa) of 2005, 39 IIC 374 (2008) – *Powdered*

based on an *ex-ante* analysis at the time of sending the letter rather than the previous ex-post standard based on the outcome of whether there is infringement or not:

> "The act of alleging a patent infringement by way of sending a warning letter first of all is the announcement of an actual or future enforcement. Under these circumstances, the duty of care requires an exhaustive enquiry of the facts and a close scrutiny whether there is infringement or not. Only if on that basis an infringement can be affirmed should a warning letter be sent. If such duty of care has not been exhaustively observed, or if the warning letter contains factual errors, the sender acts negligently."[18]

A different standard of liability is applied for (unexamined) utility models that can only be enforced based on a prior assessment report. If this is negative, negligence is assumed: Osaka District Court, 31 October 2000[19] and Osaka District Court, 26 March 2015.[20] *Okuyama* in his comment to Case No. 66 in this book is rather critical towards this approach and argues that where warning letters are sent to business people, these will be very well able to deal with such threats, for which reason liability should not be overstretched. This author begs to differ.

Things have become even less clear on the basis of a 2013 decision that generally denied the application of the Unfair Competition Act for warning letters directed at an upstream manufacturer that supplied parts of the allegedly infringing goods, as this would not be "injurious" to the business reputation of the supplier of the allegedly infringing parts.[21]

In a decision of 2015, the defendant (patentee) had communicated to the plaintiff's customers that blue ray disks sold by the plaintiff were infringing and the defendant could enjoin such distribution and sale. While it was true that the blue ray disks were using the defendant's patent, the latter had no right to injunctive relief due to the fact that it had to grant a licence to the plaintiff under FRAND conditions. The court held that the defendant was liable for spreading false facts, yet denied a claim for damages due to uncertain position of the courts regarding FRAND licences.[22]

Fish Food concerned a warning letter sent while the patent had already been revoked in first instance and an appeal was pending. Negligence was affirmed because there were no rational reasons why the first instance decision was incorrect and the appeal should succeed.

18. Tokyo District Court, 15 March 2004, Case No. 20812 (Wa) of 2002, 39 IIC 247 (2008) – *Water Pellets*.
19. Osaka District Court, 31 October 2000, Case No. 5090 (Wa) of 1998, the website of the courts <http://www.courts.go.jp/app/files/hanrei_jp/874/012874_hanrei.pdf>.
20. Osaka District Court, 26 March 2015, Case No. 5064 (Wa) of 2014, the website of the courts <http://www.courts.go.jp/app/files/hanrei_jp/080/085080_hanrei.pdf>.
21. IP High Court, 25 March 2013, Case No. 10059 (Ne) of 2012, 40 AIPPI Journal of the Japanese Group (English edition) 20 (2015). Here, allegedly infringing parts were supplied to a manufacturer who was the addressee of the warning letters in question, while the plaintiff whose business reputation had suffered was the supplier of allegedly infringing parts that were used in the manufacture of a device. The court reasoned that warning letters against primary infringers were not acts of denigration under the UCA. That seems to be correct also given the fact that both supplier (plaintiff) and manufacturer coordinated their activities for having the defendant's patent revoked. The case rather seems to indicate that the plaintiff was a subcontractor of the manufacturer.
22. Tokyo District Court, 18 February 2015, Case No. 21383 (Wa) of 2013, German translation in GRUR Int. 2016, 375 – *Blue Ray Disc*.

d) There seem to be no cases where warning letters were sent to non-infringing customers or consumers at large.

e) The question crucial for determining whether a threat is an act of unfair competition is the **standard of liability**. Two approaches are conceivable that may be termed the "unfair competition approach" and the "intellectual property approach".[23]

(1) The "**IP approach**" applies a standard of liability that is a mirror image to the standard of liability for IP infringement: If in the case of IP infringement, there is a presumption of negligence, and making thorough efforts to clarify the factual and legal situation is no excuse to liability for injunctive relief and damages, then the same should apply to an action for disparagement by way of an allegation of infringement. In other words: Where domestic law privileges the infringer having made thorough investigations, e.g. by limitations of the damage claim or by flexibilising the remedy of injunctive relief, the same would be appropriate for the circumspect IP owner who sends warning letters. Where domestic law does not distinguish between reckless and prudent infringers, no such distinction should be made for threats, either. Liability would thus depend only on the question of infringement,[24] which is an *ex post* standard that is determined with certainty only after the warning letter has been sent. This line was taken by the old German and French cases, was statutory in the UK prior to the 2004 amendment, and may still be good law in France (for a comparative overview, see below). In effect, this means justification for threats (whether sent to secondary infringers or third parties) that are factually correct, and strict liability where they are not.

(2) The "**unfair competition**" approach refrains from such *ex post facto* analysis and looks at the way threats are made and presented: If the right owner had acted prudently and presented the warning letters in an appropriate manner, then this does not amount to an act of "unfair" competition. This ex ante approach is more in line with the standards of liability applied to other competition cases, yet begs two questions: First, should it matter whether it was necessary to send out threats to customers in the first place (the manufacturer or importer could be contacted easily), and, second, even if made recklessly, can the correctness of the allegation (there was infringement, and the patent was valid) be invoked as justification. In this respect, the provisions in the UK law and the case law in France seem to indicate that allegations vis-à-vis a competitor's customers are regarded as unnecessary.[25] Different from lawsuits, such threats are not suitable for determining if there was

23. A similar distinction is used by Y. KOMADA, Riyū no nai tokkyo ken shingai keikoku to fusei kyōsō bōshi hō *(Unjustified warning letters for patent infringement and unfair competition law)*, 66 Tokkyo Kenkyū 5 (2018).

24. This position was taken by J. KOHLER, Lehrbuch des Patentrechts (*Handbook of Patent Law*), Mannheim 1908, 232: "Gross negligence must be required as a standard [for liability for threats], with regard to the fact that in the reverse, also patent infringement only leads to a liability for damages in cases of gross negligence and the reasons for both are the same."

25. The Japanese *Powdered Fish Food* decision makes a distinction between the announcement (to customers) of a prevised court action against the manufacturer (this is supposed to be a true fact), and an allegation of infringement.

infringement or not.[26] This would indicate that a distinction between suits and threats as argued by the German Supreme Court (see below) is correct: The primary objective of threats vis-à-vis customers of a competitor would seem a disparagement, the primary objective of a suit to ascertain infringement, and it may well be argued that threats vis-à-vis secondary infringers, different from infringement suits, are unlawful per se.[27] If true, they must be allowable, though, as in such case no "false" facts have been spread.

It therefore seems that under both of the above approaches, threats vis-à-vis secondary infringers (and, *a fortiori*, third non-infringing parties) appear presumptively unlawful even if well-researched, as they destroy the competitor's market without helping to clarify the issue of infringement. After all, it should be borne in mind that the purpose of a warning letter should be clarify whether there is infringement, ultimately through the courts. Warning letters should not become instruments of private enforcement in itself. Yet who takes the law in his own hands instead of using the channels as provided by the law enforcement authorities, knows that this is risky business.

It thus appears that the recent trend towards the standard of the reasonably circumspect patentee, as introduced in the UK legislation and as decided in more recent decisions by the Japanese courts is *not* the preferable approach: Issuing threats against a multitude of alleged secondary infringers is not what a reasonably circumspect patentee would do in order to clarify the question of infringement. It is thus not enough to simply look at the search efforts of the patentee – diligence must also manifest itself in the choice of the addressee(s) as potential defendants in light of the (justified) aim of clarifying whether there is infringement.

4. COMPARATIVE REMARKS[28]

a) In the **UK**,[29] warning letters are not actionable under a claim for libel and slander even if the warning turns out to be wrong, as this would require a malicious attempt in the knowledge that the threat was without any foundation.[30] Abusive attempts

26. This aspect is mentioned by HORN, Die unberechtigte Verwarnung aus gewerblichen Schutzrechten *(Unjustified threats based on industrial property rights)*, Munich 1971, 205/206: "The question of infringement must primarily be clarified vis-à-vis the primary infringer". In fact, the 1907 UK Patents and Designs Act in Sec. 32 made threats unlawful "provided that this section shall not apply if the person making such threats with due diligence *commences and prosecutes an action for infringement of his patent.*"
27. With certain exceptions: The primary infringer is domiciled abroad or otherwise unavailable.
28. An in-depth international comparison and analysis is provided by A. KAMPERMAN SANDERS, Unjustified threats and the repression of unfair competition, in: HEATH/KAMPERMAN SANDERS/MOERLAND (eds.), Intellectual Property Rights as Obstacles to Legitimate Trade, Kluwer Law 2018, 181; C. HEATH, Wrongful Patent Enforcement, 39 IIC 307 (2008).
29. Literature: H.-P. BRACK, Patent Infringement Warnings in a Common Law versus a Civil Law Jurisdiction – An Actionable Threat? 37 IIC 1 (2007); Terrell on the Law of Patents, 15th ed. 2000, § 16; I. DAVIES/T. SCOURFIELD, Threats: Is the Current Regime Still Justified? EIPR 2007, 259; E. NETTLETON/B. CORDERY, Walking the groundless threats minefield, 1 Journal of Intellectual Property Law 51 (2005).
30. English High Court, 11 March 1932, *Farr v. Weatherhead*, 49 RPC 262 [1932] for patents; English High Court, 21 February 1977, *Redwood Music v. Francis, Day & Hunter*, [1978] RPC 429 for

to enforce steam engine patents led to the introduction of specific provisions in the Patent Act that made threats against secondary infringers actionable under certain circumstances. The provisions were revised in 1977, in 2004,[31] and, most importantly, by the UK's Intellectual Property (Unjustified Threats) Act 2017, which came into effect in October 2017. The latter includes threats based on pending industrial property applications, and Unified Patent Court actions.[32]

Actionable under sec. 70 Patents Act are threats (in contrast to enquiries or factual information as mentioned in sec. 70(5))[33] against secondary (but not primary) infringers (excluded are those who make or import, even if in addition they also distribute or sell, sec. 70(4)) by the patentee or a lawyer – the latter liability having been removed by the 2017 legislation.[34] Although the threat action allows the aggrieved person to seize the initiative, e.g. to choose the most suitable forum, it may also be used as a tactical counterclaim in an infringement action.[35] The aggrieved person is entitled to injunctive relief and damages unless the threat was justified (i.e. there was infringement), or the patentee can prove that the allegedly infringing acts fall inside the scope of the patent and the patentee had no reason to suspect invalidity of the patent. Liability relates to the damage done by the threats, but not by a subsequent infringement action.[36] Absolving professional representatives from liability by the 2017 did not go uncontested: Sir *Robin Jacob*[37] thought such liability 'a healthy restraint on cowboy (and other) legal advisers – of whom there are lots out there'.[38] His comment on the Bill has also been included in the Law Commission report:

> "I consider [the Bill] extraordinarily elaborate and complicated. It is not the right solution and in its present form should be dropped. I remain of the opinion that something much simpler – along the nature of 'abusive communication'

copyrights. Judging by the latter case, it would appear that reckless allegations or those not well-researched may well qualify as acts of slander. It may thus rather be the difficulty to prove recklessness that acts as a counter-incentive to such suits.

31. Patents Act 2004 as of 22 July 2004.
32. UK LAW COMMISSION, Patents, Trade Marks and Designs: Unjustified Threats, Law Com No. 360 (2015, HMSO), available at the website of the UK government <https:// www.gov.uk/government/publications>.
33. The distinction is often difficult to make. A threat may be implicit when so understood by the recipient (English High Court, 4 May 1990, *Bowden v. Acco Cable Controls*, [1990] RPC 427), or even where the primary object is just to close a manufacturer's channel of commerce: English High Court, 13 October 2006, *Quads 4 Kids v. Campbell*, [2006] EWHC 2482, regarded the notification of an alleged infringement to eBay as a threat and granted relief. "Without prejudice" communication are normally not considered threats: UK Court of Appeal, 28 October 1999, *Unilever v. Procter & Gamble*, [1999] EWCA Civ 3027. General warnings are not threats: English High Court, 22 July 1887, *Challender v. Boyle*, 4 RPC 363 [1887].
34. It is particular to the UK that also the solicitor who wrote the warning letter can be sued: English High Court, 23 January 1964, *H.V.E. v. Cufflin Holdings*, [1964] W.L.R. 378.
35. In English High Court, 3 February 2004, *Reckitt Benkiser v. Home Pairfum*, [2004] FSR 774, the counterclaim also included the solicitors as defendants.
36. English High Court, 7 March 1996, *Carflow Products v. Linwood Securities*, [1996] FSR 424, where previous threats had been ignored.
37. The full consultation response can be found at the website of the UK Law Commission <https:// www.lawcom.gov.uk/project/patents-trade-marks-and-designs-unjustified-threats/>.
38. UK LAW COMMISSION, Patents, Trade Marks and Designs: Unjustified Threats, Law Com No. 360 (2015, HMSO), para 1.45, p. 11.

would be enough. Tinkering with this will serve no useful purpose. There is no hurry – threats of IP infringement proceedings are far from top of the problems in the IP world. I am saying this now so no one ever thinks I thought it was a good idea."[39]

Specific to the UK are thus the statutory basis of the action and the limitation to primary infringers.

b) In **Germany**,[40] liability for unjustified threats from the very start went beyond damages to reputation and also covered threats directed at the primary infringer and damages ensuing from the latter's decision to stop production.[41] To this end, the Imperial Supreme Court invented the "right to an established and working business" and subsequently broadened liability also to cover unjustified infringement suits,[42] although this is no longer pursued.[43] The courts initially applied what came close to a no-fault liability – if the warning turned out to be unjustified, the right owner had to pay all damages that ensued therefrom,[44] and later limited this standard of liability to threats against secondary infringers and to unexamined rights.[45] Claims based on unfair competition law were unsuccessful because threats were not perceived as the spreading of false *facts*,[46] or because they were no wilful distortions of another's business.[47] As mentioned above, German decisions make a distinction between warning letters and suits. The latter are "privileged", which may also find its justification in the allocation of costs. The losing party pays all expenses of the winning party, thereby making an infringement suit far more risky than a warning letter. On the other hand, sending out threats in Germany has the additional incentive that the costs thereof can be recovered if the addressee undertakes to stop the allegedly infringing behaviour. **Specific to Germany** are thus the liability also

39. UK Law Commission, Patents, Trade Marks and Designs: Unjustified Threats, Law Com No. 360 (2015, HMSO), para 1.46, p. 12.
40. Literature: H.-P. Brack, Patent Infringement Warnings in a Common Law versus a Civil Law Jurisdiction – An Actionable Threat? 37 IIC 1 (2007); O. Teplitzky, Zur Frage der Rechtmäßigkeit unbegründeter Schutzrechtsverwarnungen *(About the question of lawfulness of unjustified threats)*, GRUR 2005, 9; *id.*, Die prozessualen Folgen der Entscheidung des Großen Senats für Zivilsachen zur unberechtigten Schutzrechtsverwarnung *(The procedual consequences of the decision of the Grand Panel regarding unjustified threats)*, wrp 2005, 1433; R. Sack, Die Haftung für unbegründete Schutzrechtsverwarnungen *(The liability for unjustified threats)*, wrp 2005, 253; *id.*, Unbegründete Schutzrechtsverwarnungen *(Unjustified threats)*, Cologne 2006; P. Meier-Beck, Die Verwarnung aus Schutzrechten – mehr als nur eine Meinungsäußerung! *(Threats – more than a simple expression of opinion!)*, GRUR 2005, 535; *id.*, Die unberechtigte Schutzrechtsverwarnung als Eingriff in das Recht am Gewerbebetrieb *(Unjustified threatsas an infringement of the right to business)*, wrp 2006, 790. W. Horn, Die unberechtigte Verwarnung aus gewerblichen Schutzrechten *(Unjustified threats based on industrial property rights)*, Munich 1971.
41. German Imperial Supreme Court, 27 February 1904, RGZ 58, 24 – *Juteartikel*.
42. German Imperial Supreme Court, 6 March 1931, GRUR 1931, 640 – *Schwatten Dorfs*.
43. German Federal Supreme Court, 17 July 2005, GRUR 2005, 882 – *Warning Letter* speaks of a "privilege" for lawsuits.
44. German Federal Supreme Court, 5 November 1962, GRUR 1963, 260 – *Kindernähmaschinen*.
45. German Federal Supreme Court, 19 January 1979, GRUR 1979, 33 – *Brombeerleuchte*.
46. German Imperial Supreme Court, 17 October 1916, RGZ 88, 437 – *Rohrkrümmer*.
47. German Supreme Court, 8 February 1963, WRP 1965, 97 – *Kaugummikugeln*.

vis-à-vis primary infringers, the rather flexible way that liability is ascertained, and the financial incentive of lawyers to send out warning letters.

c) In **France**,[48] warning letters against primary infringers are not actionable,[49] as the law against threats is based on an action for denigration under the general tort clause of Sec. 1382 Civil Code. French courts view the court action as the appropriate form and forum of making allegations of infringement to secondary infringers, while warning letters are considered improper regardless if the allegation of infringement is well-founded or not,[50] although such action may be justified if done in an inoffensive and discrete manner.[51] Not only warning letters, but also information about a pending lawsuit against the manufacturer may give rise to an action for denigration.[52]

d) Finally, in the **US**, warning letters are regarded as the appropriate manner of initiating proceedings for infringement.[53] Actions based on unfair competition law against abusive communication are considered to be pre-empted by federal IP legislation unless false facts are spread intentionally - a rather high threshold.[54]

48. Literature: A. Bertrand, Le dénigrement par la publicité donnée à une action en justice (*The denigration by publicity given to an action in justice)*, 72 Revue de Droit de la Propriété Intellectuelle 9 (1997).
49. French Supreme Court, 13 May 1964, Annales 1964, 266.
50. French Supreme Court, 2 March 1965, Annales 1966, 1 with comment by Mathély. French Supreme Court, 12 June 2007, 39 IIC 354 (2008) - *False Ceiling*, even upheld damages based on denigration where the patent was revoked after the (successful) infringement action had become final.
51. Tribunal de la Seine, 18 March 1932, Annales 1933, 14.
52. French Supreme Court, 12 May 2004, Case No. 02-16623.
53. US CAFC, 29 August 2008, *800 Adept, Inc. v. Murex Securities, Inc.*, 505 F. Supp. 2d 1327 (M.D. Fla. 2007).
54. Section 772 of the Restatement (Second) of Torts, '[o]ne who intentionally causes a third person not to perform a contract or not to enter into a prospective contractual relation with another does not interfere improperly with the other's contractual relation, by giving the third person ... truthful information.

Case No. 57

Retrial due to Revocation after Successful Infringement Suit

Christopher Heath

Pre-2012, a defendant could request a retrial after a being convicted of patent infringement in the case where the patent was subsequently invalidated by the Patent Office after the defendant had filed numerous requests for invalidation.

IP High Court, 14 July 2008, Case No. 10002 (Mu) of 2006&10003 (Mu) of 2007 – *Seaweed Purifying Apparatus*

Furuta Denki v. Shinwa Seisakushō

---

1. BACKGROUND

Problems arise where the patentee obtains a favourable decision on infringement, executes it, the decision becomes final, and the patent is later revoked or reduced in scope. After all, such invalidation or reduction in scope has retroactive effect, secs. 114(3), 125bis(1)(iv), 128, 134bis(9) Japanese Patent Act. This scenario then begs two questions: First, can the defendant have the initial decision confirming infringement overturned, and second, if so, would the plaintiff/patentee be liable for any damages, and by what standard. Where the validity of patents can be challenged in court, this is a less common situation. Where there are separate proceedings for nullity and infringement, as there are e.g. in China, Germany and Austria, but also in all Member States of the European Patent Convention where opposition or appeal proceedings are pending, such cases may, and in fact do, occur with a certain frequency. Japan in this respect is a hybrid system in that the courts since the *Kilby* decision (Case No. 50 in this book) can determine whether a patent should be held invalid, yet cannot invalidate the patent.

Sec. 338 (1) No. 8 Code of Civil Procedure 1996 allowed for a retrial:

> "where a civil or criminal decision, any other decision or an administrative act on which the decision [at issue] is based, has been modified by a subsequent decision or a subsequent administrative act."

Both the grant and the revocation of a patent being administrative acts, the Tokyo[1] and Osaka courts[2] in the past allowed a retrial once the revocation of the patent had become final and conclusive. However, this rather far-reaching possibility of unwinding a final decision by way of retrial was considered inequitable given the fact that invalidity could be argued in infringement proceedings following the *Kilby* decision (as above), the more so since sec. 104ter(2) had introduced a rule whereby the defence of invalidity could be ignored if filed too late[3] (see Case No. 51 - *Knife* - in this book). Still, at the time the decision in the case at issue was rendered, neither the Code of Civil Procedure nor the Patent Act had been amended and the court despite some misgivings had to allow the retrial. A legislative intervention only came when the 2012 amendment to the Patent Act[4] introduced **sec. 104^{quater} Patent Act** that in a situation where the patent is subsequently invalidated no longer allows a convicted infringer to rely on a retrial in order to undo the outcome of a final decision finding infringement:

> **Sec. 104^{quater} Limitation to the Assertion of Invalidity**
>
> Where one of the following decisions (i) - (iii) has become final and conclusive after a final and binding judgment regarding the infringement of a patent right or an exclusive license ..., a person who was a party to said infringement litigation may not invoke such final and binding administrative decision in proceedings for a retrial of such final judgment (including proceedings for claiming damages in case of a provisional seizure order or proceedings for claiming compensation for damages or unjust enrichment incurred due to provisional measures):
>
> (i) an administrative decision to the effect that the litigated patent is revoked or invalidated;
> (ii) an administrative decision to the effect that the registration of extension of the term of the litigated patent is invalidated;
> (iii) an administrative decision as provided by Cabinet Order to the effect that the description, scope of claims or drawings attached the application for the said patent is corrected.

This provision is far-reaching in that it does not only limit the restitution of damages already paid for an alleged infringement, but also bars the infringer (but not third parties) from challenging the effects of the injunctive order or asserting that

1. Tokyo High Court, 31 January 2005, Case No. 2722 (Ne) of 2004, the website of the courts <http://www.courts.go.jp/app/files/hanrei_jp/790/009790_hanrei.pdf> = 135 Chizai Kenkyū 15 - 20. English translation in 39 IIC 359 (2008).
2. Osaka High Court, 15 October 2004 and 29 March 2005, Case No. 648 (Ne) of 2004, 1912 Hanrei Jihō 106 - 118. English translation in 39 IIC 228 (2008).
3. As is explained in an analysis by the Patent Office (JPO): Tokkyo seido ni kan suru hōseiteki na kadai ni tsuite *(Several Legal Problems related to the Patent System)*, at the website of the JPO <https://www.jpo.go.jp/resources/shingikai/sangyo-kouzou/shousai/tokkyo_shoi/document/index/housei_kadai.pdf>.
4. Law no. 63/2011 of 8 June 2011.Background and motives for the legislative change from the perspective of the Japanese Patent Office are described in the document, Saishin no arasoi tō ni okeru shuchō no seigen *(Limiting the system of retrial litigation)*, at the website of the JPO <https://www.jpo.go.jp/system/laws/rule/kaisetu/h23/document/tokkyo_kaisei23_63/04syou.pdf>.

provisional measures were wrongly imposed (on condition that these have become final and conclusive, though).

2. DECISION[5]

a) Facts

Both the Tokyo District Court and the Tokyo High Court had affirmed infringement of a patent for an apparatus to purify seaweed, and ordered an injunction against the defendant. The latter had raised the estoppel of invalidity in the infringement action, yet in both instances the courts held that the patent was valid. After the decision concerning infringement had become final and conclusive, the patent was invalidated by the Patent Office after the defendant had filed numerous requests for invalidation.

b) Reasons

[If such retrial was allowed], confidence of the parties to the previous final decision would be compromised. Thus, there is some merit in the defendant's arguments against allowing such retrial. Nevertheless, the thrust of such arguments is to stress the blocking effect of a final and conclusive decision due to the principle of *res iudicata*. Yet, there is no such effect once the decision that allows such a retrial to be initiated [in other words, the decision to revoke the patent] has become final, for which reasons the defendant's arguments have to be rejected ... Even after the *Kilby* decision, the court hearing a patent infringement proceeds on the assumption that the patent is valid when determining whether there are reasons that make the exercise of the patent an abuse of rights. The court does not determine the validity of the patent. The defence against an abuse of rights as set out in the *Kilby* decision is one thing and the action based on the revocation of a right due to a final and conclusive decision is another. There is no time limit for an invalidation request, and it can be filed by anyone. The same party may file an invalidation request several times within the limits of sec. 167 Patent Act, namely that a new request may not be filed by a third party based on the same facts or evidence. Against this background, the fact that the plaintiff has filed several invalidation requests as such is no reason to hold that the dispute over the validity of the patent at issue has been conclusively resolved ...

3. ANALYSIS

a) Late filing, *res iudicata* and retrial

A retrial is a remedy under the law of civil procedure. Its appropriateness and availability should therefore be determined not only by the fact that a patent invalidation has retroactive effect (which of course would speak in favour of a retrial), but also in the context of procedural rights, remedies and obligations. This becomes particularly

5. Published in 2050 Hanrei Jihō 137 = N. NAKAYAMA et al. (eds.), Tokkyo Hanrei Hyakusen *(Hundred Selected Patent Cases)*, 4th ed. 2012, 86 w. comment M. TANOUE.

clear when looking at Case No. 51 – *Knife*[6] and the underlying notion that the court must have the power to disregard new submissions as late-filed: As judge *Izumi* noted in his votum in the *Knife* decision, makes little sense to give courts the power to disregard late-filed facts (be it that the patent has been revoked, or upheld in limited form), attacks (a newly filed estoppel of invalidity) or defences (the patent was after all upheld in amended form) where an amended or invalidated patent can afterwards lead to the possibility of retrial: Where the court deems the introduction of new facts or evidence as belated due to the specific stage of procedure or an abusive behaviour by the parties, there should not be an occasion to introduce such facts etc. at a later instance or in a retrial. The interplay between substantive patent amendment and procedural economy has been explained in Case No. 51 – *Knife* both for Japan and for the EPC Member States.

Even where submissions are not refused as late filed, they can only be taken into account until a case is closed: Once a decision has become *res iudicata*, new facts cannot be filed in the same proceedings any more. When a decision becomes *res iudicata* is an issue of domestic law and, in patent matters, also the way in which patent infringement proceedings are conducted. In Japan,[7] and in the US,[8] an infringement case is pending until all issues have been decided both as to liability and damages, even though these may be different phases of procedure. In Germany[9] and the UK,[10] liability and account of damages are two distinct phases and the first can very well become final and conclusive before the second is started.

b) Patent invalidation and retrial

The question whether to allow a retrial once a patent has been revoked with retroactive effect is ultimately a political one. Different interests have to be balanced: A revocation with retroactive effect means that the patent should never have been granted, and thus could never have been infringed. This is the strongest argument

6. Supreme Court, 24 April 2008, English translation in 40 IIC 721 (2009).
7. In the *Massage Chair* case (IP High Court, 25 September 2006, 42 IIC 858 (2006), Case No. 54 in this book), both the issues of infringement and damages were highly contested, yet dealt with in one single decision. There is some discussion as to whether a formalised two-step procedure should be introduced whereby the first step (decision on infringement) can become separately appealable: The PATENT COMMISSION OF THE JPO published a report on this issue, yet no firm conclusions were reached: Report of 15 February 2019, pp. 24-27:
   <https://www.jpo.go.jp/resources/shingikai/sangyo-kouzou/shousai/tokkyo_shoi/document/190215_tokkyo_houkoku/01.pdf>
   <https://www.jpo.go.jp/resources/shingikai/sangyo-kouzou/shousai/tokkyo_shoi/190215_tokkyo_houkoku.html>
8. In US CAFC, *Fresenius USA, Inc. v. Baxter International, Inc.*, No. 12-1334 (Fed. Cir. 2013), the decision of invalidation came right at the end of a several-phase litigation where only the quantum of damages was still in litigation. Still, the court held that this was enough to prevent the case from becoming *res iudicata*.
9. It is customary in Germany that a (separately contestable) interim decision about liability is rendered, and only once this decision has become final would the parties commence further litigation about the quantum of damages (or, as in most cases, settle).
10. After a successful litigation on infringement, the plaintiff can request an account of profits in separate proceedings. See, e.g., English Supreme Court, 3 July 2013, *Virgin Atlantic Airways Ltd v. Zodiac Seats UK Ltd* [2013] UKSC 46.

in favour of a retrial, and a complete restoration of the status quo. On the other hand, the possibility of re-opening final proceedings creates uncertainty, and there may be justice in leaving things as they are. A comparison (below 4.) shows that the decision as to which principle should be given precedence very much depends on the procedural setting: Where invalidity cannot be argued in infringement proceedings (Germany; Austria), a retrial must be possible, as otherwise the relative speed of infringement and revocation proceedings would decide on the final outcome. The same is true in the EPC countries where bifurcation of infringement proceedings before national courts and invalidation proceedings before the opposition division or the Boards of Appeal may also lead to the conclusion of infringement proceedings before invalidity has been finally decided upon. On the other hand, where invalidity can be argued by way of counterclaim or estoppel, there is less reason to protect the convicted infringer by way of a retrial. Italy and France take a middle ground in that they do not allow for the restitution of damages already paid, yet permit the alleged infringer after revocation of the patent to withhold payments not yet made, and to ignore the injunctive order.

c) Japanese legislation on retrial

The Japanese provision of sec. 104^{quater} Patent Act is problematic in five respects:[11]

First, the provision makes a special case for patents that are thereby shielded from the general effects of sec. 338 Code of Civil Procedure. As sec. 338 CCP remains unamended, a retrial is still possible, yet sec. 104ter Patent Act no longer allows the alleged infringer to rely on the outcome of such retrial. This is questionable not only because the grant of a patent is an administrative act like all others, but also because in practice, patents are probably the acts of administration most often overturned and invalidated.

Second, the provision does not distinguish between provisional and final decisions. This is questionable because in provisional proceedings, the estoppel of invalidity can be argued to a limited extent only. In addition, the provision is in conflict with Art. 50(7) TRIPS Agreement whereby judicial authorities shall have the possibility of offering compensation to the respondent of an interim measure where it is subsequently found that there was no infringement.

Third, the provision does not distinguish between judicial orders that have already been complied with by the alleged infringer, and those that have not. If the

11. For an explanation of this provision, see TOKKYOCHŌ *(Japanese Patent Office)* (ed.), Kōgyōshoyūkenhō Chikujō Kaisetsu *(Commentary to the Patent Act)*, 2017, 335, available at the website of the JPO <https://www.jpo.go.jp/system/laws/rule/kaisetu/kogyoshoyu/document/cikujyoukaisetu/all.pdf>; N. NAKAYAMA, Tokkyohō *(Patent Law)*, 3rd ed. 2016, 450; M. SHIMIZU, Saishin no arasoi ni kan suru tokkyohō kaisei *(Amendment to the Patent Act regarding Retrial)*, 1436 Jurist 60 (2012); see also ZADANKAI *(discussion group)*, Tokkyohō kaisei no igi to kadai *(Significance and problem of the Patent Act amendment)*, 1436 Jurist 26 with some remarks by T. IIMURA; T. IIMURA, Heisei nijusannendō tokkyohōtō kaisei ga minjisosho jitsumu ni kaeru eikyō ni tsuite *(On the influence of the Patent Act Amendment 2011 over the realities of civil litigation)*, 59 Minshōhō Zasshi (2013), 89; R. MIMURA, Heisei 23nen tokkyohō kaisei go ni okeru tokkyo kanren soshō no ryūiten *(Remarks about patent related litigation after the 2011 Amendment to the Patent Act)*, 60 L&T 21 (2013).

reason for enacting the provision is simplification, the provision should distinguish between those orders that have already been carried out at the time the patent was revoked (e.g. damages already paid), and those that have not (e.g. damages not yet paid). Particularly for the latter, there is some good reason why payments should no longer be due once the patent has been revoked.[12]

Fourth, the provision does not distinguish between damages and injunctive relief. Thereby, the alleged infringer is apparently meant to comply with an order for injunctive relief even after the patent has been invalidated, and although third parties would now be free to use the patented technology.[13]

Fifth and last, the provision obviously complements sec. 104ter Patent Act that requires the estoppel that the patent should be revoked to be raised in good time, and allows the court to disregard it otherwise. A defendant who has raised the estoppel too late in the proceedings should not be able to rely on invalidity by way of a retrial. Yet the provision does not distinguish between a subsequent invalidation by the defendant in the infringement action, or a third party. After all, the subsequent invalidation may be due to a prior use the defendant of the infringement action could not have known, and the late filing of the request for revocation may not be attributable to him.

All in all, it is doubtful whether the above provision strikes the right balance. At the time of writing, there was no decision that would put this new provision to the test.

4. COMPARATIVE REMARKS

a) The **UK** decision *Unilin Beheer v. Berry Floor et al.*[14] concerned a (successful) infringement claim that became final before the patent on which it was based was invalidated by the European Patent Office. The court flatly denied any remedy by the defendant in the absence of a statutory provision that would allow a retrial or even the estoppel of unenforceability. This decision is no longer good law in view of a later Supreme Court decision *Virgin Atlantic Airways Ltd v. Zodiac Seats UK Ltd,*[15] 3 July 2013, [2013] UKSC 46 that came to the opposite conclusion:

> "Absent special factors, principle, fairness and commercial sense support the view that the fact that the patent in issue had been revoked was a point which the alleged infringer should have been entitled to rely on in the assessment. It was a new, centrally important, uncontroversial fact, and to deny the alleged infringer the ability to raise it would be to give effect to a monopoly right which the patentee never should have had."

12. This is discussed by R. Mimura (above), 25.
13. This result is considered inequitable in Japanese literature. N. Nakayama (above) wants to give the alleged infringer an estoppel against the continued enforcement of an injunctive order, while R. Mimura (above, p. 26) argues that an order of injunctive relief is always conditional upon the existence of the patent.
14. English High Court, 25 April 2007, *Unilin Beheer v. Berry Floor* [2007] EWCA Civ. 364. The decision is commented by Cohen/Davies, [2007] E.I.P.R. 466.
15. English Supreme Court, 3 July 2013, *Virgin Atlantic Airways Ltd v. Zodiac Seats UK Ltd* [2013] UKSC 46.

However, it is important to note that in this case, only the infringement phase had become final, but not yet the assessment of damages. Had damages been assessed, and had the convicted infringer already paid, a retrial might not have been on the cards. The court expressed strong reservations as to whether a restitution claim could be allowed in such circumstances.[16]

b) The situation in the **US** seems to be comparable: The defence of invalidity can be raised until the last part of the infringement litigation (e.g. assessment of damages) has become final and conclusive,[17] but not beyond.[18]

c) In **Germany**, there is two-fold defence of the convicted infringer: An estoppel against the execution of the decision under sec. 767 Code of Civil Procedure (CCP) for facts that only came to light after the proceedings were brought to an end,[19] and a retrial under sec. 580 No. 6 CCP. The latter provision allows for a retrial if a previous "decision of an ordinary court, an extraordinary court of an administrative court, on which the [current] decision [at issue] is based has been overturned." The difficulty with the wording of this provision is the fact that a patent is ordinarily granted by an act of the administration rather than the court, and the provision is thus not directly applicable.[20] Where the patent is initially refused, the patent may be granted on appeal by the Federal Patent Court, though, and the same is true on a European level when the order to grant a patent is made by the EPO's Boards of Appeal, a quasi-court. Yet a distinction between patents granted by the Patent Office and those granted by the courts would make little sense for the question at issue. Perhaps also for this reason, it is now established law that revocation of the patent allows for a retrial.[21] The Düsseldorf Appeal Court in its 2006 decision on an analogous application of sec. 580 No. 6 CCP gives weight to the fact that the infringement court is bound to hold the patent valid and has no powers to deny its validity or order its revocation. From this reasoning, it appears that the court would accept the English *res judicata* approach had it jurisdiction over the question of validity as well. A retrial cannot be requested where in subsequent proceedings the patent is not revoked or limited

---

16. English Supreme Court, 3 July 2013, *Virgin Atlantic Airways Ltd v. Zodiac Seats UK Ltd* [2013] UKSC 46, para. 67.
17. US CAFC, *Fresenius USA, Inc. v. Baxter International, Inc.*, No. 12-1334 (Fed. Cir. 2013).
18. US Supreme Court, *Moffitt v. Garr*, 66 U.S. 273, 283 (1861).
19. There seems to be no case-law on this point, but academic writings favour the application of sec. 767 CCP to this case: HORN, Patentverletzungsprozeß und Nichtigkeitsverfahren *(Patent Enforcement Procedure and Nullity)*, GRUR 1969, 169, 174; KRASSER, Patentrecht (Patent Law), 5th ed. Munich 2004, 916; BENKARDT-ROGGE/GRABINSKI, Patentgesetz *(Commentary on the Patent Act)*, 6th ed. Munich 2005, sec. 139 marginal note 149.
20. For which reason the (pre-war) Imperial Supreme Court denied the possibility of a retrial: Imperial Supreme Court, 4 March 1901, Reichsgericht in Zivilsachen (RGZ) 48, 384.
21. Düsseldorf District Court, 24 June 1986, GRUR 1987, 628 – *Restitutionsklage*; Düsseldorf Appeal Court, 11 May 2006, Case No. 2 U 86/05, available at the archive site of the University of Düsseldorf <https://www3.hhu.de/duesseldorfer-archiv/?p=5317> = 39 IIC 355 (2008) – *Restitutionsklage II*. The latter decision also seems to require that the defendant tried to obtain a stay in proceedings in view of a pending nullity action, but it is uncertain what weight the court gives to this issue.

in scope, but given a certain interpretation that would have absolved the defendant from liability in the previous proceedings.[22]

d) In **France**, once a decision on infringement has become final and conclusive, there is no possibility of getting this decision set aside even though the relevant patent is subsequently revoked.[23] This is different where proceedings for the quantum of damages are still pending when the patent was revoked. as the Supreme Court has clarified.[24] The Supreme Court held that the damage claim could not be carried any further due to such revocation, while the defendant could claim damages for denigration in view of previous threats made to suppliers.

e) The **Italian** position is regulated by statute under Sec. 77 Industrial Property Code that stipulates "The declaration of nullity of a patent has a retroactive effect, yet does not affect: a) Measures already carried out for the enforcement of final decisions in infringement matters ..." This corresponds to the French position, yet on a statutory basis.

In summing up, only in Germany would a wrongly convicted infringer be allowed a true retrial after the patent was invalidated. Other countries would give an infringer a defence up until the infringement litigation (including the assessment of damages) has become final and conclusive.

---

22. Düsseldorf Appeal Court, 9 August 2007, Case No. 2 U 49/06 = 39 IIC 357 (2008) – *Spundfass II*. In this case, the patentee in order to avoid the revocation of the patent agreed to a certain (limited) interpretation of the claim in nullity proceedings.
23. Paris Appeal Court, 29 September 1995, PIBD 1995, 600-III-10. Affirmed by Cour de Cassation *(French Supreme Court)*, 27 January 1998, PIBD 653 (1988), III, 237. Cour de Cassation, 28 January 2003, Case No. 00-12149. Doubts have been voiced only by P. MATHÉLY, Le nouveau droit français des brevets d'invention *(The new French law on patents)*, 390, as in such case two contradictory decisions would exist.
24. French Cour de Cassation *(French Supreme Court)*, 12 June 2007, 39 IIC 354 (2008) – *False Ceiling*.

Case No. 58

Requirements for a Patent Term Extension of Pharmaceutical Patents

Marc Dernauer

A prior marketing approval for a medicinal product with the same active ingredients, efficacy and effect cannot be held against a patent extension for a subsequent product where the former product is not within the technical scope of the claims of the patent for which extension is sought.

Supreme Court, 28 April 2011, Case No. 326 (Gyō-Hi) of 2009 – *Pacif Capsule 30mg*

Takeda Pharmaceutical v. Japanese Patent Office

---

1. BACKGROUND

The regular term for a Japanese patent is twenty years, calculated from the filing date of the patent application (sec. 67(1) Patent Act). Secs. 67(2), 67ter(1)(i) Patent Act allow an application for a patent term extension (hereinafter: "PTE") of up to five years in cases where a specific approval or other disposition was necessary to work (i.e. to commercially use and exploit) the invention and where the proceedings to obtain such an approval or disposition caused a delay (a loss of time) in working the invention ("the invention could not be worked [*hatsumei no jisshi wo suru koto ga dekinai*]"), which eventually resulted in a reduced period of patent protection. The PTE has to be filed at the JPO.

However, not all kinds of approvals or dispositions necessary for working the invention are eligible for a PTE. Sec. 67(2) Patent Act stipulates that only approvals or dispositions which (1) are explicitly prescribed by legal provisions, (2) have the purpose of ensuring the safety of the product that embodies the invention (and similar purposes), and (3) are designated as such by cabinet ordinance can constitute a basis for the application of a PTE. The relevant designations by cabinet ordinance in this respect can be found in sec. 2 of the Implementing Ordinance Referring to the Patent Act[1] (hereinafter: "Implementing Ordinance"). Sec. 2 of the Implementing Ordinance designates the following approvals or dispositions as relevant in this

1. Tokkyo-hō sekōrei, Cabinet Ordinance No. 16/1960, last amended by Cabinet Ordinance No. 5/2017.

regard: an approval for the manufacture, sale, and/or import of medicinal products (*iyaku-hin*) according to sec. 14(1), 14(9) or 19bis(1) Act for Ensuring the Quality, Efficacy and Safety of Medicinal Products and Medical Devices[2] (hereinafter: "Medical Products' Act" - short "MPA" - or referred to by the former name "Pharmaceutical Affairs Act" (*Yakuji-hō*) - short "PAA")), an approval for the manufacture, sale, and/or import of medicinal products for diagnostics to be applied outside of the body (*taigai shindan-yō iyaku-hin*) according to sec. $23^{\text{bis-5}}$(1), $23^{\text{bis-5}}$(11) or $23^{\text{bis-17}}$(1) MPA, a certification issued by a registered certification body for the manufacture, sale and/or import of medicinal products for diagnostics to be applied outside of the body according to sec. $23^{\text{bis-23}}$(1) or $23^{\text{bis-23}}$(6) MPA, an approval for the manufacture, sale and/or import of regenerative medical products (*saisei iryō-tō seihin*) according to section $23^{\text{quinqiesvicies}}$(1), $23^{\text{quinqiesvicies}}$(9) and/or $23^{\text{septiestricies}}$(1) MPA, and a registration required for the manufacture, processing, and/or import of plant protection products and fertilisers (*nōyaku*) according to secs. 2(1), 6bis(1) or 15bis(1) of the Act on the Regulation of Chemicals Used in Agriculture[3].[4]

Moreover, in view of secs. 67(2), 67bis, $67^{\text{bis-2}}$, and 67ter Patent Act, the following further requirements have to be met in order to obtain a PTE: (1) the patentee or registered exclusive or non-exclusive licensee must have actually obtained the respective approval, certification or registration, (2) the requested term of the PTE may not exceed a period corresponding to the loss of time actually suffered by the proceedings for obtaining the approval, certification or registration, (3) the patentee must file the application for the PTE, (4) in case of a jointly owned patent, all joint owners together must file the application, (5) the application for a PTE must be filed no later than three months after having obtained the respective approval, certification or registration, and (6) if the approval, certification or registration is unlikely to be obtained until a date six months prior to the expiry of the patent, the patentee must notify the JPO at least six months prior to the expiry of the patent that an application for an approval, certification or registration is still pending and that a PTE application will be filed after the grant of the approval, certification or registration.[5]

The PTE shall compensate the patentee (and possible licensees) for the time lost due to the proceedings for obtaining the approval or disposition. If the conduct of specific tests is necessary for obtaining the approval or disposition, the starting point for calculating the possible term of extension is either the day on which the basic patent was registered or the day on which the necessary tests for obtaining the approval or disposition have commenced, whichever is later; the endpoint is the day that precedes the day on which the applicant has received the respective marketing approval.[6] In practice, the day on which the applicant's notice of commencement

2. Iyakuhin, iyaku kigu-tō no hinshitsu, yūkō-sei oyobi anzen-sei no kakuho-tō ni kansuru hōritsu, Law No. 145/1960.
3. Nōyaku torishimari-hō, Law No. 82/1948, last amended by Law No. 69/2014.
4. For details cf. M. DERNAUER, Patent Term Extension in Japan, in: HANSEN/SCHÜSSLER-LANGEHEINE (eds.), Patent Practice in Japan and Europe, Liber Amicorum for Guntram Rahn, Alphen aan den Rijn 2011, 589, 593–596.
5. For details cf. M. DERNAUER (supra note 4), 592–600.
6. Supreme Court, 22 October 1999, Case No. 102 (Gyō-Ke) of 1997, 1693 Hanrei Jihō 133 - *New Sort of Polypeptides*; IP High Court, 28 October 2009, Case No. 10486 (Gyō-Ke) of 2008, 2058 Hanrei Jihō 101 - *Levofloxacin*.

of the necessary tests is received by the competent authority is usually taken as the relevant starting point for the calculation.[7] Not relevant for calculating the allowable extension time is the period of time the applicant has spent on searching for the appropriate test facility or similar preparatory acts.[8] Medical tests carried out in foreign countries can be sufficient for obtaining a marketing approval for medicaments in Japan. If the results of those tests in fact provided the necessary basis for fulfilling the requirements of obtaining the marketing approval in Japan, the test and the time spent on those tests would be deemed necessary for obtaining the marketing approval and could be taken into account when calculating the specific extension period. However, if medical tests were carried out in a foreign country for the purpose of obtaining an additional marketing approval for a medicament in Japan intended to widen a previously obtained marketing approval for a medicament, although previous medical tests for obtaining the previous marketing approval had already produced data likely sufficient for obtaining also the additional marketing approval, the additional medical tests and the time spent on them will not be deemed necessary for obtaining the additional marketing approval. Such period of time therefore will not be taken into account when calculating the actual term of the allowable patent extension.[9] More generally speaking, time spent on tests carried out for the purpose of obtaining an approval or disposition will not be deemed necessary for obtaining the respective approval or disposition if the necessary data for that purpose were already produced by previous similar tests.

In Japan, the system of PTE was introduced in 1987 by a revision of the Patent Act. This is, one the one hand side, only a few years after a similar patent term extension was made available in the United States under the Drug Price Competition and Patent Restoration Act of 1984,[10] also known as the Hatch-Waxman Act, and, on the other hand side, shortly before the EU established a similar system of additional protection by supplementary protection certificates (SPCs) in 1992 for medicinal products[11] and in 1996 for plant protection products.[12]

7. IP High Court, 28 October 2009, Case No. 10486 (Gyō-Ke) of 2008, 2058 Hanrei Jihō 101 - *Levofloxacin*.
8. IP High Court, 28 October 2009, Case No. 10486 (Gyō-Ke) of 2008, 2058 Hanrei Jihō 101 - *Levofloxacin*.
9. IP High Court, 28 October 2009, Case No. 10486 (Gyō-Ke) of 2008, 2058 Hanrei Jihō 101 - *Levofloxacin*.
10. Public Law 98-417; the patent term extension now provided for by 35 U.S.C. §156 (2011).
11. Council Regulation (EEC) No. 1768/92 of 18 June 1992 concerning the creation of a supplementary protection certificate for medicinal products; now replaced by Regulation (EC) No. 469/2009 of the European Parliament and of the Council of 6 May 2009 concerning the supplementary protection certificate for medicinal products.
12. Regulation (EC) No. 1610/96 of the European Parliament and of the Council of 23 July 1996 concerning the creation of a supplementary protection certificate for plant protection products.

2. DECISION[13]

a) Facts

This is an appeal filed by the Japanese Patent Office (hereinafter: the "Appellant") against the decision of the IP High Court of 29 May 2009 overturning a decision to deny the extension of a patent.[14] The Supreme Court rejects the appeal, but gives somewhat different reasons than the IP High Court.

b) Reasons

Regarding the arguments of the Appellant, represented by *Sudō Noriaki* and others,

1. The case concerns an appeal filed by the Appellee to this suit, who is a patent holder of the Japanese patent No. 3134187 (hereinafter "the patent in suit", and the right based on this patent, "the patent right in suit"), challenging the decision of the Patent Office which rejected the application for patent term extension based on the patent right in suit.

2. The facts correctly confirmed by the original ruling are as follows:

(1) The patent in suit (with 22 claims) is for an invention entitled "composition for controlled release." The patent application was filed on 6 March 1997, and the patent grant was registered on 1 December 2000.

The invention claimed in the patent in suit is related to a controlled release composition comprising a core containing a drug coated with a water insoluble substance, a coating agent with a certain hydrophilic substance or a cross-linked acrylic acid polymer.

(2) The Appellee has received an approval for manufacturing and sales (hereinafter "disposition in suit") according to sec. 14(1) of the Pharmaceutical Affairs Act (PAA)[15] on 30 September 2005, for a medicinal product marketed as "Pacif Capsule 30mg" (hereinafter "medicinal product in suit"). The medicinal product in suit has hydrochloride morphine as the active ingredient and its effect and efficacy relate to an analgesic for medium to high grade cancerous pain.

(3) There was a prior manufacturing and sales approval according to sec. 14(1) PAA, (hereinafter "prior disposition in suit") issued for a medicinal product marketed as "Opso Oral Solution Internal 5mg, 10mg" with the same active ingredient, efficacy and effects, (hereinafter "prior medicinal product in suit"), predating the disposition

13. Published in 65-3 Minshū 1654 = 2115 Hanrei Jihō 32 = 1348 Hanrei Times 102 = N. NAKAYAMA et al. (eds.), Tokkyo Hanrei Hyakusen *(Hundred Selected Patent Cases)*, 4th ed. 2012, 120 = = T. ŌBUCHI et al. (eds.) Chitekizaisan hō hanrei shū *(Intellectual Property Law Case Book)*, 2nd. ed. 2015, 110. English translation by N. LEE in 42 IIC 972 (2011) and in BÄLZ/DERNAUER/HEATH/PETERSEN-PADBERG (eds.), Business Law in Japan – Cases and Comments, Alphen aan den Rijn, 2012, 422–423.
14. Case No. 10460 (Gyō-Ke) of 2008.
15. Yakuji-hō, Law No. 145/1960, last amended by Law No. 85/2006.

in suit. The prior medicinal product is not within the technical scope of the patented invention as claimed in the patent in suit.

(4) The Appellee has filed a patent term extension application on 16 December 2005, as there was a period during which time the patented invention based on the patent in suit could have not been worked, as it was necessary to obtain the disposition in suit. This application was rejected and the Appellee requested a trial to set aside the decision rejecting the patent term extension based on the patent in suit.

(5) The Japanese Patent Office has denied the above request (hereinafter, "Decision in suit") on 21 October 2008, because there was the prior disposition in suit for the prior medicinal product in suit with the same active ingredient, efficacy and effect as the medicinal product in suit, and because the disposition in suit was not deemed necessary.

3. Even when there is a prior marketing approval based on sec. 14(1) PAA (hereinafter "prior disposition") for a medicinal product with the same active ingredient, efficacy and effect (hereinafter "prior medicinal product") as the subsequent medicinal product (hereinafter "subsequent medicinal product"), predating a subsequent marketing approval according to sec. 14(1) PAA (hereinafter "subsequent disposition") for which the application for patent term extension is based on, it is not possible to hold that the prior disposition makes the subsequent disposition unnecessary in case the prior medicinal product is not within the technical scope of the claims of the patent which patent term extension application is based on. This is because the patent term extension system aims to restore the period during which time the working of patented invention is not possible, due to the disposition according to the regulation provided in sec. 67(2) Patent Act. Even when there is a prior disposition for a prior medicinal product with the same active ingredient, efficacy and effect, as long as the prior medicinal product does not fall within the technical scope of the claims of the patented invention which the patent term extension of the right is sought for, the patented invention as claimed, nevertheless could not be worked for the subsequent medicinal product. Moreover, when the prior medicinal product is not within the technical scope of the patented invention, the conclusion above cannot be decided by considering the effect of the prior disposition on the scope of protection for the patent whose term is extended (sec. 68bis Patent Act).

The prior medicinal product in suit is not within the technical scope of the claimed invention of the patent in suit and thus, based on the prior disposition in suit, it is not possible to deny that the disposition in the suit was necessary to practice the patented invention.

4. As reviewed in the above, the original ruling which held the decision in suit unlawful and which held that the presence of the prior disposition could not form the ground to deny the necessity of the marketing approval according to sec. 14(1) PAA is correct subject to the above reasons.

The decision has been rendered unanimously.

3. ANALYSIS

a) Explanation of the decision

This Supreme Court decision in the *Pacif Capsule 30mg* case clarified certain requirements for the extension of pharmaceutical patents based on secs. 67(2), 67bis, 67^{bis-2}, 67ter, and 68bis Patent Act and had an enormous impact on the prior practice of the Japanese Patent Office (JPO) in deciding on applications for (the registration of) a patent term extension. Moreover, the decision is of tremendous importance for the pharmaceutical industry on the whole, with significant economic implications.[16]

Briefly summarised, in this case the Supreme Court held that a previous marketing approval for a medicinal product with the same active ingredient, efficacy and effect cannot be held against a patent extension for a subsequent product based on a subsequent and different marketing approval where the former product is not within the technical scope of the claims of the patent for which extension is sought.

The case concerned an application by Takeda Pharmaceutical Company Limited (*Takeda Yakuhin Kōgyō Kabushiki Kaisha)* for a PTE of a patent relating to a controlled-release-type microcapsule capable of carrying inter alia morphine hydrochloride as an active ingredient. The application was based on a marketing approval according to sec. 14(1) PPA (now sec. 14(1) MPA) for the medicament (= medicinal product) "Pacif Capsule 30mg (*Pashiifu Kapuseru 30mg*)", which pertained to a controlled-release-type microcapsule with the active ingredient morphine hydrochloride in a concentration of 30mg for pain treatment in cancer patients. However, a prior marketing approval had already been obtained and was held by a competitor of Takeda, Dainippon Sumitomo Pharma Co., Ltd. (*Dainippon Sumitomo Seiyaku Kabushiki Kaisha*), for the medicament "Opso Liquid for Oral Administration 5mg/10mg" (or "Opso Oral Solution Internal 5mg, 10mg") that related to a medicament with the same active ingredient ("morphine hydrochloride") and for the same medicinal application ("pain treatment of cancer patients") as the medicament "Pacif Capsule 30mg". However, in contrast to the medicament "Pacif Capsule 30mg", this medicament was a solution and thus different in its dosage form and, moreover, comprised the active ingredient in a lower concentration. The existence of the prior marketing approval for the medicament "Opso Liquid for Oral Administration 5mg/10mg" was the only reason why the JPO rejected the PTE application of Takeda. Takeda appealed to the IP High Court and the appeal was successful.[17] The JPO decision was set aside. The JPO then filed the appeal with the Supreme Court, which rejected the appeal and upheld the decision of the IP High Court to quash the JPO decision.

The Supreme Court argued that the prior marketing approval for the medicament "Opso Liquid for Oral Administration 5mg/10mg" was not a justified reason to reject the application for a PTE regarding a patent with a technical scope as applied for by Takeda, i.e. with technical features corresponding to the features of the medicament "Pacif Capsule 30mg", because the previously approved medicament "Opso Liquid for

16. For an earlier comment on this case cf. M. DERNAUER, Case No. 39, in: BÄLZ/DERNAUER/HEATH/PETERSEN-PADBERG (supra note 8).
17. See supra note 9.

Oral Administration 5mg/10mg" did not fall into the technical scope of the claims of the patent for which extension was sought, and the subsequent marketing approval obtained by Takeda was thus also necessary for working the patented invention in the form of the PTE applied for by Takeda. In other more general words, the Supreme Court held that if a (subsequent) marketing approval for a medicament features the same active ingredient and medicinal application (referred to by the Supreme Court by the attributes "efficacy [*kōnō*]" and "effect [*kōka*]" of the medicament) as a prior marketing approval for a different medicament, but differs in further features from the prior marketing approval (such as the dosage form and the concentration of the active ingredient), the subsequent marketing approval is deemed to be necessary for working the patented invention identified by the scope of the patent for which the PTE was requested, and, at the same time, the prior medicament identified by the prior marketing approval is not covered by the technical scope of the patent for which the PTE was claimed. Hence, the PTE for the patent has to be granted in such cases.[18]

This conclusion is based on the legal requirement that the medicament as the object of a marketing approval and the technical scope of the patent for which a PTE is requested must be identical to grant the requested PTE. According to section 68bis Patent Act, the extended patent shall only cover the patented invention to the extent identified by the marketing approval that forms the basis for the PTE application, i.e. in regard of the "object" of the marketing approval. As a result of the Supreme Court decision in the present case, a prior marketing approval for a medicament is no longer an obstacle to obtaining a PTE for a patent with a technical scope equal to the attributes of a subsequent marketing approval, if the prior marketing approval and the subsequent marketing approval both refer to the same active ingredient and the same medicinal application, but if they differ from each other in regard of further attributes, such as the dosage form or the concentration of the active ingredient. Of course, the technical scope of the original patent always has to include the technical scope of the patent in the form for which a PTE is sought, i.e. in the form of the medicament identified by the marketing approval that forms the basis for the respective PTE application. The technical scope of the patent for which the PTE is requested is always a limited part of the technical scope of the originally granted patent, i.e. it is limited to the object of the relevant marketing approval. It is not possible to apply for a PTE for a medicament that does not fall within the claims of the originally granted patent.

18. For further comments on this case see T. TAKENAKA, A Change of Leadership in Patent Policy and Law Development? The Active Role Played by Japanese Courts in Japan's Patent Term Extension Reform, in: HALEY/TAKENAKA (eds.), Legal Innovations in Asia: Judicial Lawmaking and the Influence of Comparative Law, Cheltenham/Northampton 2014, 293–311; T. IIMURA, Patent Term Extension in Japan: Focusing on the Pacif Capsule Decision, in: DREXL/LEE (eds.), Pharmaceutical Innovation, Competition and Patent Law: A Trilateral Perspective, Cheltenham/Northampton 2013, 220–239; R. ISEKI, Iyaku-hin no fukusū shōnin to tokkyo-ken no sonzoku kikan enchō tōroku – pashiifu kapuseru 30mg jiken Saikō-sai hanketsu *(Multitude of Approvals for the Manufacturing of Medicinal Products and the Registration of the Extension of Patent Rights)*, 56-9 AIPPI Journal of the Japanese Group (Japanese edition) 596 (2011); M. DERNAUER, Japan – Oberster Gerichtshof entscheidet über Voraussetzungen der Verlängerung von Pharmapatenten *(Japan – Supreme Court Decides on the Requirements for the Extension of Pharmaceutical Patents)*, GRUR Int. 2011, 657–659.

The decision of the Supreme Court (and of the IP High Court) in the *Pacif Capsule 30mg* case is fully convincing. Sec. 67(2) Patent Act refers to necessary marketing approvals for commercially using the invention. There is no doubt that the subsequent marketing approval was necessary for Takeda to put the medicament Pacif Capsule 30mg" on the market. The prior marketing approval was not sufficient in this regard. Even if the prior marketing approval had been granted to Takeda, it would not have been sufficient because the medicament "Opso Liquid for Oral Administration 5mg/10mg" is different from the medicament "Pacif Capsule 30mg" in terms of its dosage form and in its concentration of the active ingredient. As was correctly stated by the IP High Court, as the trial court, in its judgment, a marketing approval under the PAA (now MPA) is not only characterised by the active ingredient and the intended application, but also by several other specifications such as e.g. the dosage form and the concentration of the active ingredient as set out in sec. 14 PAA (now MPA). The IP High Court further stated that each marketing approval was actually quite narrow and did not extend to similar medicaments with the same active ingredient and for the treatment of the same disease, if they differ in any other relevant feature set out by sec. 14 PAA (now MPA). For the manufacture and sale of such similar medicaments, a new marketing approval is necessary. The IP High Court also took into consideration the fact that Drug Delivery Systems (DDS) and similar technologies are growing in relevance in medicine.[19] The decision of the IP High Court in the present *Pacif Capsule II* case, and thus also the decision of the Supreme Court, which upheld the decision of the IP High Court, has been widely welcomed by legal practitioners and scholars alike.[20]

b) The previous practice of the JPO and the former case law

According to the former practice of the JPO and the established case law of the courts, in particular the case law of the IP High Court, before the IP High Court decision in this case, the object of the marketing approval as stated in section 68bis Patent Act was only deemed to be characterised by the contained "active ingredient" and the "medicinal application". The medicinal application, i.e. the disease which the medicament is designed to treat, was usually referred to as the "effect" and "efficacy" of the medicament. Whenever there was a prior marketing approval for a medicament which was identical to another subsequent marketing approval in regard of the contained active ingredient and the intended medicinal application, the subsequently granted marketing approval was generally not accepted as a basis for a PTE. It was of no relevance whether the prior marketing authorisation was held by the patentee and holder of the second marketing authorisation or by another party. The other features in which the two marketing approvals differed, such as e.g. the

19. T. IIMURA (supra note 18) 229–230, 236; T. IIMURA, Patent Term Extension in Japan, manuscript of a presentation at the Munich Intellectual Property Law Center (MIPLC) in May 2010, slide 5 (on file with the author).
20. Cf. for example Y. SONODA, Controversy over Patent Term Extensions, Asia-Pacific & Middle East IP Focus 2009, 51–53; R. ISEKI, Case Revoking the JPO Decision which Refused Application for Patent Term Extension Based on the Previous Marketing Approval for the Same Active Ingredient and Indication of Another Drug, 35-1, AIPPI Journal of the Japanese Group (English edition) 3–20, at 17 (2010).

dosage form (capsule, tablet, solution for oral, nasal, or ophthalmic administration, solution for injection, etc.), the concentration or amount of the active ingredient, the existence of a further active ingredient (i.e. a combination of active ingredients) or whether the intended treatment concerned adults or children, were also not deemed to be relevant at all. Moreover, it did not matter whether the patent for which the PTE was filed referred to a specific active ingredient and medicinal application or rather to the form of the medicament itself. Furthermore, it was not relevant whether the application for the PTE was a first application in regard of a patent or whether it was a second application for a PTE of the same patent, for which one PTE had been already granted based on a prior marketing approval.[21] In all such cases, it was always decided that a PTE could not be granted. The JPO and the courts in such cases stated that the patented invention could already be worked after the first marketing approval, at least partly.

c) Decisions in similar PTE cases

Takeda has also filed an appeal against the JPO decision in several other, but similar PTE cases. In five of these cases the IP High Court also rendered a judgment in favour of Takeda,[22] and in two of these cases, the judgment of the IP High Court was

---

21. R. ISEKI, Registration of Patent Term Extension and Marketing Approval under the Pharmaceutical Affairs Law, 34-3 AIPPI Journal of the Japanese Group (English edition) 107 (2009); S. MATSUI, Yakuji-hō no kōsaku suru tokkyo-ken sonzoku kikan enchō seido no mondai-ten *(The Problematic Issues Regarding Complicated Cases in Pharmaceutical Law with Respect to the Patent Term Extension System)*, 52 AIPPI Journal of the Japanese Group (Japanese edition) 690–703, at 693 et seq. (2007); M. DERNAUER (supra note 4) 602. Cf. for example: Tokyo High Court, 5 March 1998, Case No. 155 (Gyō-Ke) of 1995, 1650 Hanrei Jihō 137 – *Ketitofen Fumarate*; Tokyo High Court, 10 February 2000, Case No. 361 (Gyō-Ke) of 1998, 1719 Hanrei Jihō 133 – *Ondansetrone Hydrochloride*; IP High Court, 30 May 2005, Case No. 10012 (Gyō-Ke) of 2005, 1919 Hanrei Jihō 137 – *Lamivudine and Zidovudine* (see also a partial translation of the judgment by M. MŌRI, in: 40 IIC 872 (2009)); IP High Court, 18 January 2007, Case No. 10724 (Gyō-Ke) of 2005, the website of the courts <http://www.courts.go.jp/app/files/hanrei_jp/015/034015_hanrei.pdf> – *Microencapsulation of Water Soluble Polypeptides*; IP High Court, 11 October 2005, Case No. 10345 (Gyō-Ke) of 2005, the website of the courts <http://www.courts.go.jp/app/files/hanrei_jp/015/034015_hanrei.pdf> – *Microcapsule with Hormonally Active Water-Soluble Polypeptide*; IP High Court, 16 November 2005, Case No. 10184 (Gyō-Ke) of 2005, 1208 Hanrei Times 292 – *Eye Perfusion and Cleansing Solution Packaged Container*; IP High Court, 19 July 2007, Case No. 10311 (Gyō-Ke) of 2006, 1980 Hanrei Jihō 133 – *Long-Term Sustained Release Type of a Microcapsule*; IP High Court, 27 September 2007, Case No. 10016 (Gyō-Ke) of 2007, the website of the courts <http://www.courts.go.jp/app/files/hanrei_jp/186/035186_hanrei.pdf> – *Beclomethasone Aerosol Medicament*.
22. IP High Court, 29 May 2009, Case No. 10458 (Gyō-Ke) of 2008 – *Pacif Capsule I* (or *Morphin Hydrochloride I*) [in contrast to the *Pacif Capsule 30mg* case, which sometimes is being referred to as *Pacif Capsule II* or *Morphin Hydrochloride II* case, because it was filed later than the *Pacif Capsule I* case], 2047 Hanrei Jihō 11 (English translation of N. LEE, in: 42 IIC 478 (2011)); IP High Court, 29 May 2009, Case No. 10459 (Gyō-Ke) of 2008, the website of the courts <http://www.courts.go.jp/app/files/hanrei_jp/656/037656_hanrei.pdf> – *Leuplin* (or *Leuprorelin Acetate*); IP High Court, 27 May 2009, Case No. 10476 (Gyō-Ke) of 2008, the website of the courts <http://www.courts.go.jp/app/files/hanrei_jp/636/037636_hanrei.pdf> – *Takepron I* (or *Lansoprazole I*); IP High Court, 27 May 2009, Case No. 10477 (Gyō-Ke) of 2008, the website of the courts <http://www.courts.go.jp/app/files/hanrei_jp/635/037635_hanrei.pdf> – *Takepron II* (or

also finally upheld by the Supreme Court by judgments of the same day as in the *Pacif Capsule 30mg* case (i.e. the 28 April 2011), with almost the same reasoning.[23] In the three remaining cases, the JPO has also filed an appeal at the Supreme Court against the decisions of the IP High Court. These appeals, however, seem to have been withdrawn by the JPO after the Supreme Court decisions of 28 April 2011 had been rendered.

d) Consequences, remaining issues, and subsequent developments

The JPO quickly reacted to the new precedents set by the Supreme Court in the *Pacif Capsule 30mg* case and the other similar cases. Only around one month after the respective Supreme Court judgments were rendered, the JPO announced on 26 May 2011 that "Part VI: Patent Term Extension (PTE)" of the then applicable Examination Guidelines for patents would be revised and that the examination of applications for the registration of a PTE would be suspended until the establishment of the new guideline. The revised JPO guideline took into account the Supreme Court decisions of 2011 and became applicable as of 28 December 2011.[24]

In the *Pacif Capsule 30mg* case, the patent in suit related to a specific form of a medicament (dosage form) which was able to carry, for instance, the active ingredient identified by the marketing approval at issue, i.e. morphine hydrochloride. Therefore, the respective patent was not a patent relating to the active ingredient itself. Hence, the Supreme Court had not to decide on and left it therefore open whether the same reasoning can be applied in a case relating to a patent for an active ingredient or, more broadly formulated, a medicinal substance. In two further decisions of the IP High Court, however, following the IP High Court decision in the *Pacif Capsule 30mg* case (but issued before the Supreme Court decision), the IP High Court confirmed its new case law by allowing a PTE also for a patent relating to a combination medicament (tablet) for the treatment of an HIV infection containing abacavir sulfate and lamivudine as active ingredients (i.e. two active ingredients) on the basis of a marketing approval for a corresponding medicament, and this even though there was a prior marketing approval for a medicament containing one of these active ingredients and another one for a combination treatment with two medicaments, each containing one of these active ingredients for a treatment of the same disease.[25]

Lansoprazole II); IP High Court, 27 May 2009, Case No. 10478 (Gyō-Ke) of 2008, the website of the courts <http://www.courts.go.jp/app/files/hanrei_jp/634/037634_hanrei.pdf> – *Takepron III* (or *Lansoprazole III*). For a discussion of the IP High Court decisions in these cases, see N. LEE, Patent Term Extension in Japan in Light of the Pacif Capsule Decision, 42 IIC 442 (2011).

23. R. ISEKI (supra note 18) 607, in footnote 1. Supreme Court, 28 April 2011, Case No. 324 (Gyō-Hi) of 2009 (corresponding to IP High Court, 29 May 2009, Case No. 10458 (Gyō-Ke) of 2008); Supreme Court, 28 April 2011, Case No. 325 (Gyō-Hi) of 2009 (corresponding to IP High Court, 29 May 2009, Case No. 10459 (Gyō-Ke) of 2008).
24. Cf. the website of the JPO <https://www.jpo.go.jp/e/news/public/feedback/patent_term_rev.html>, the revised Examination Guidelines are also available there. However, thereafter, the Examination Guidelines were again revised several times. The effective Examination Guidelines are always retrievable on the website of the JPO.
25. IP High Court, 28 March 2011, Case No. 10178 (Gyō-Ke) of 2010, the website of the courts <http://www.courts.go.jp/app/files/hanrei_jp/191/081191_hanrei.pdf> – *Lamivudine and Abacavir*;

In another judgment, the IP High Court allowed a PTE for a substance patent covering a specific antibody antagonist for treatment of cancer tumours in a specific concentration based on a corresponding marketing approval, even though the applicant held a prior marketing approval for the same kind of antibody antagonist for the treatment of cancer, where the second marketing approval (based on section 14(9) MPA) was intended to modify and supersede the first marketing approval (based on section 14(1) MPA), because the applicant wanted to market the pertaining medicament in a different concentration of the substance for a different period of application.[26] This judgment was also upheld by the Supreme Court in appeal proceedings[27] (*Bevacizumab* case; see also Case No. 59 (*Bevacizumab*) in this book).[28] Therefore, the subsequent case law confirmed that the reasoning of the Supreme Court decision in the *Pacif Capsule 30mg* case is also applicable for the evaluation of PTE applications in regard of substance patents.

The Supreme Court decision in the *Bevacizumab* case also clarified a further question that the *Pacif Capsule 30mg* decision had left open. That is, whether it is possible to obtain a second PTE for the *same* patent on the basis of a subsequent different marketing approval. It is imaginable, for instance, that a patent for a specific active ingredient was first extended based on a marketing approval for a medicament (e.g. a film coated tablet) with an amount of 5mg of the active ingredient, and that afterwards the patentee obtained a second marketing approval for a medicament with the same active ingredient, but with an amount of 10mg, and maybe also in another dosage form (e.g. a solution for oral administration). In such a case, the patentee would probably like to obtain a further PTE for the same patent, limited of course to the object of the second marketing approval. In practice, the JPO has often granted such second PTEs of the same patent, and this legal possibility, in theory, can be also derived from the reasoning of the Supreme Court and the IP High Court in the *Pacif Capsule 30mg* case. In the *Bevacizumab* case, the patentee had already obtained a first PTE based on the first marketing approval before he filed the second PTE application for the same patent based on the second marketing approval, the actual matter in dispute. The Supreme Court as well as the IP High Court saw no problem in granting the PTE as a second PTE for one and the same patent.[29] Therefore, in principle, multiple PTE applications for one patent are possible.

Another issue is how the technical scope (i.e. the scope of protection) of the extended patent has to be interpreted in infringement proceedings. The *Pacif Capsule 30mg* case was no patent infringement case, and Japanese courts apparently never had to decide on an infringement case relating to a patent whose term had been extended before the *Pacif Capsule 30mg* case,[30] and also not for a while thereafter.

---

and Case No. 10177 (Gyō-Ke) of 2010 of the same day, the website of the courts <http://www.courts.go.jp/app/files/hanrei_jp/190/081190_hanrei.pdf>

26. IP High Court, 30 May 2014, Case No. 10196 (Gyō-Ke) of 2013, 69-7 Minshū 1952 – *Bevacizumab* (or *Avastin*).
27. Supreme Court, 17 November 2015, Case No. 356 (Gyō-Hi) of 2014, 69-7 Minshū 1912 = 2309 Hanrei Jihō 127 = 1427 Hanrei Times 73 – *Bevacizumab* (or *Avastin*).
28. For a comment on the case from a different perspective see also R. ISEKI, "Abasuchin (bebashizumabu)" jiken *(The "Avastin (Bevacizumab)" Case)*, 1475 Jurist 62 (2015).
29. Supra note 25 and 26.
30. R. ISEKI (supra note 20) 17.

For a long time, most commentators believed that the technical scope of an extended pharmaceutical patent would also extend to similar medicaments, for example to a medicament for the treatment of a disease substantially the same, to a medicament with a different concentration/amount of the same active ingredient or to a medicament with a different dosage form, if only the active ingredient was the same.[31] After the decision in the *Pacif Capsule 30mg* case, it seemed that the technical scope of an extended patent must be interpreted very narrowly, i.e. limited to its literal scope (and identical to the scope of the underlying marketing approval) with hardly any leeway for arguing equivalent infringement. In a subsequent decision in the *Bevacizumab* case, however, the IP High Court took a position similar to the previous common understanding among scholars and practitioners in Japan. Although there was no need for the IP High Court to decide about the scope of protection of extended patents in that case, the court took the opportunity to express its view on this matter in an obiter dictum. The IP High Court in that case argued that in view of the purpose of the PTE system the scope of protection of an extended patent could be broader than the scope of the marketing approval, and thus would also include the use of medicaments similar to the substance of the medicament, which is the object of the extended patent, and also to equivalent medicaments in general.[32] Nonetheless, the issue remained in dispute.

In the *Oxaliplatinum* case (See Case No. 60 (*Oxaliplatinum*) in this book) the IP High Court had its first opportunity to decide on this issue in a patent infringement case, and rendered its judgement on 20 January 2017.[33] The IP High Court here confirmed its view on the issue expressed in the earlier case. The court stated that, in principle, the scope of protection of an extended patent would cover not only objects defined by its literal scope (medicaments identical to those defined by the marketing approval), but also to products that are substantially identical. Such broader scope of protection should be in particular considered in cases where the protected medicament relates to an active ingredient and where the protected medicament and the allegedly infringing medicament differ in its active ingredient, in the concentration (amount/quantity) of the active ingredient, the dosage form of the medicament or the medicinal application. In other cases, such considerations were also possible, but this would afford a much more comprehensive and thorough medical analysis. In the specific case, the IP High Court held that the allegedly infringing product was not a substantially identical medicament because it included a further additive not present in the protected medicament, and would therefore not fall into the scope of protection of the extended patent.

31. Cf. for example H. Aoyama, Tokkyo-hō (Patent Law), 10th ed., Hōgaku Shoin, 2008, 205.
32. Cf. supra note 21.
33. IP High Court, 20 January 2017, Case No. 10046 (Ne) of 2016, 2361 Hanrei Jihō 73 – *Oxalipratinum*. For a comment on the case see also R. Iseki, Enchō tōroku wo uketa tokkyo-ken no kōryoku *(The Scope of Protection of a Patent for which a Patent Term Extension was Granted)*, 1509 Jurist 46 (2017).

4. COMPARATIVE REMARKS

When explaining the background of the Japanese PTE system it was already pointed out that the **United States** and the **European Union** have a similar system for extending the protection of patented medical and agrochemical inventions. "Similar", however, does not mean fully harmonised. The legal instrument being used, the requirements for the grant of a PTE, and the effects of the extended protection in Japan, in the U.S. and in the EU countries remain significantly different.[34] While Japan and the U.S. use a PTE system, the European Union has created a system where an extension of patent protection is granted by issuing a supplementary protection certificate, which is a different intellectual property right. Moreover, while U.S. law and EU law limit a patent term extension to only one extension per patent and to patents that protect an active ingredient/substance or a combination of active ingredients/substances, in particular of a medicinal product, the Japanese PTE system does not contain such limitations. In Japan, one and the same patent on medicinal products may be extended several times. A patent protecting an active ingredient of a medicament may be extended for each marketing authorisation regarding the use of the active ingredient in a specific concentration (amount/quantity), in a specific dosage form, and for a specific medicinal application of the active ingredient. Even for patents that do not specifically protect an active ingredient, but rather the dosage form, the combination of or the medicinal application of known active ingredients, patent term extension may be obtained. This makes the Japanese PTE system more brand-name drug manufacturer friendly than the corresponding systems in the U.S. and the EU.[35]

34. For details see e.g. T. TAKENAKA (supra note 18) 308–311.
35. T. TAKENAKA (supra note 18) 309.

Case No. 59

Requirements for a Patent Term Extension of Pharmaceutical Patents – Second Marketing Approval for the Same Patent

Hirotaka Nonaka

---

1. **The extension of the patent term is possible where the manufacture or marketing of a patented medicinal product can only take place after obtaining marketing authorisation.**
2. **A second authorisation for the working of the patented invention can be the basis of a further request for extending the patent term of the same patent where the manufacture or marketing of the precisely identified medicinal product has not become possible already on the basis of the first marketing authorisation.**

Supreme Court, 17 November 2015, Case No. 356 (Gyō-Hi) of 2014 – *Bevacizumab*

Genentech v. Japanese Patent Office

---

1. BACKGROUND

Sec. 68(2) Japanese Patent Act prescribes that where there is a period during which the patented invention cannot be worked because of obtaining a marketing authorisation, the patent term may be extended by a period not exceeding 5 years.

However, since the scope of the patented invention is broad, it is possible that one patent includes several drugs and accordingly results in several authorisations. The issue here is whether a patent term extension can be applied for each authorisation or not.

The first authorisation (referred to as "previous authorisation") was granted on 18 April 2007 in response to the plaintiff's request for the manufacturing and marketing approval of a new drug specified by the generic name "Bevacizumab (transgene)." The plaintiff filed an application for a patent term extension and obtained the extension of 4 years, 2 months and 3 days.

The second authorisation was granted in response to the plaintiff's request for approval on a partly changed contents when compared to the first authorisation. The (only) difference between the first and second authorisation was the way of application and the dosage (See table 1).

Table 1.

	The first authorisation	The second authorisation
Generic name	Bevacizumab (transgene)	
Substance	hVEGF antagonist	
Efficacy and effect	Advanced or recurring inoperable colon cancer	
Way of application and dosage	Intravenous infusion of Bevacizumab, dosage 5mg/kg or 10mg/kg (per body weight), once daily for an adult, in intervals of at least two weeks, in combination with other anti-tumour drugs for advanced or recurring inoperable colon cancer.	Intravenous infusion of Bevacizumab, dosage 7.5 mg/kg (body weight) once a day for an adult, in intervals of at least three weeks, in combination with other tumour-inhibiting drugs for advanced or recurring inoperable colon cancer.

The plaintiff filed another request for a patent extension of five years because a new authorisation was necessary for the working of a new drug.

The Japanese Patent Office rejected this application, and the IP High Court in its composition as a grand panel overturned the JPO's decision.[1] The JPO appealed before the Supreme Court.

2. DECISION[2]

a) Facts

1. Proceedings before the Patent Office

(1) The plaintiff is the owner of the patent entitled "vascular endothelial cell with growth factor antagonist" (registration number 3398382, number of claims 11, date of application 28 October 1992, date of registration 14 February 2003). The plaintiff has requested a patent extension for five years, as an authorisation as specified by Patent Regulation is necessary in order to use the patented invention. The Patent Office with date of 6 January 2011 refused the request for extension. On 18 April 2011, the plaintiff filed an appeal against this decision (appeal no. 2011-8105). This appeal was dismissed on 5 March 2013 and served on the plaintiff on 15 March 2013.

1. IP High Court, 30 May 2014, Case No. 10195-10198 (Gyo-Ke) of 2013, 2232 Hanrei Jihō 3. English translation is available at the website of the IP High Court <http://www.ip.courts.go.jp/app/files/hanrei_en/135/001135.pdf> (10195), <http://www.ip.courts.go.jp/app/files/hanrei_en/136/001136.pdf> (10196), <http://www.ip.courts.go.jp/app/files/hanrei_en/137/001137.pdf> (10197), <http://www.ip.courts.go.jp/app/files/hanrei_en/138/001138.pd> (10198).
2. Published in 69-7 Minshū 1912 = 2309 Hanrei Jihō 127. German translation in GRUR Int. 2016, 345

(2) Subject of the authorisation

a. The request for marketing authorisation as a reason for extending the patent: Request under sec. 14(9) Pharmaceuticals Act.
b. Number of authorisation: 21900AMX00910000.
c. Subject of authorisation: Sale of "Abastin for the intravenous infusion 100mg/mL", generic name "Bevacizumab (transgene)".
d. Medical application: "Intravenous infusion of Bevacizumab, dosage 7.5 mg/kg (body weight) once a day for an adult, in intervals of at least three weeks, in combination with other tumour-inhibiting drugs for advanced or recurring inoperable colon cancer."
e. Day of authorisation: 18 September 2009.
f. Relation between pharmaceutical and patent claims: The anti-hVEGF antibody mentioned in claim 1 is Bevacizumab (transgene) as subject of the authorisation.

...

(3) For this pharmaceutical product, there exists a previous authorisation for the manufacture and sale dated 18 April 2007.

a. Legal basis: sec. 14(1) Pharmaceuticals Act.
b. Number of authorisation: 21900AMX00910000
c. Efficacy or effect: "advanced or recurring inoperable colon cancer".
d. Way of application, dosage: Intravenous infusion of Bevacizumab, dosage 5mg/kg or 10mg/kg (per body weight), once daily for an adult, in intervals of at least two weeks, in combination with other anti-tumour drugs for advanced or recurring inoperable colon cancer.

The authorisation in question is an authorisation to amend the previously granted authorisation. Reason for the amendment is the addition of a new way of application and dosage.

2. On the patent claims

The patent has the following claims:

Claim 1: Combination for the treatment of cancer that contains the anti-VEGF antibody as an hVEGF antagonist in sufficient quantity.

...

The Japanese Patent Office concluded the following: (a) The pharmaceutical as the object of an authorisation is determined by the description contained in the authorisation. On the other hand, the patented invention is determined by the "object" of the patented invention as the creation of a technical idea. And both are different. (b) For this reason, sec. 67ter(1)(i) Patent Act does not apply to the "working of the patented invention" (the manufacture or sale of the pharmaceutical as such), but rather the manufacture etc. of the pharmaceutical that is defined as the "object" of the patented invention in the authorisation. (c) Where there exists an earlier authorisation for the pharmaceutical with a corresponding "object", the patentee within the scope of such "object" that is determined by the patented invention could work the invention due to the earlier application. For this reason, the request for an extension of the patent term according to sec. 67ter(1)(i) should be refused.

On appeal by the patentee, the IP High Court in a decision dated 30 Mai 2014 overturned the decision of the Patent Office and granted the request for patent extension. It reasoned that an extension could be requested where the first and second authorisation differed in the way of application and dosage. Further, that the scope of the extended patent for a composition as a medication was determined by the scope of the marketing authorisation that in turn defined the scope within which the otherwise prohibited manufacture and marketing could be allowed. The authorisation was defined by the "substance", "efficacy or effect", and "way of application, dosage" as stated in the marketing authorisation.

The defendant appealed to the Supreme Court. The latter upheld the decision of the IP High Court on slightly different grounds, yet did not take position on the scope of such an extended patent.

b) Reasons

3. The reason for extending the patent term is a compensation for the period of time within which the patented invention cannot be worked in the absence of a marketing authorisation. The wording of sec. $63^{ter}(1)(i)$ (request for patent extension) reflects this in that the necessity of an authorisation for working the patented invention is clearly stated as a requirement. In light of the purpose and wording of the provision, there is no need for a further authorisation for working the patented invention where the first authorisation allows the manufacture and marketing of the pharmaceutical, and the request for another extension for manufacture and marketing of the pharmaceutical is already contained in the first authorisation. In order to determine the necessity for a subsequent authorisation in order to carry out the patented invention, not the mere wording of the patent claims should be considered, but rather a comparison between the first and subsequent authorisation.

Only an authorisation under the Pharmaceuticals Act allows the manufacture and sale of a pharmaceutical that is determined by its "name, substance, quantity, way of application, dosage, efficacy, effect, side effects and other criteria related to the quality, efficacy and safety", sec. 14(2)(iii) Pharmaceuticals Act. In conformity with the purpose of the patent term extension, for an examination thereof it is not appropriate to use criteria that bear no relationship to the objective identity of the pharmaceutical in regard of type or object of the patent, as in order to examine the extension of the patent term it need only be examined whether the working of the patented invention has previously been possible or not. Whether a previous authorisation allows the manufacture or marketing of a pharmaceutical does not depend on a formal comparison of the respective criteria, but rather on a comparison of those criteria that bear a direct relation to the objective identity of the medicament in relation to the type or object of the patent.

4. In the case at issue, the patented invention relates to a combination for the treatment of cancer that contains an inhibitor for the growth factor for vascular endothelial cells in an effective quantity. The invention concerns a substance that as its object has a pharmaceutical. For the invention of a substance that has a pharmaceutical as its object, the criteria for examining [the request for an extension of the patent term] are those that bear a direct relation to its objective identity, namely substance, quantity,

way of application, dosage, efficacy and effect of the medicine. A comparison between the previous authorisation and the current one shows that the way of application and dosage of the first authorisation concerned "intravenous infusion of Bevacizumab, dosage 5mg/kg or 10mg/kg (per body weight), once daily for an adult, in intervals of at least two weeks, in combination with other anti-tumour medicines", while the subsequent authorisation relates to "intravenous infusion of Bevacizumab, dosage 7.5mg/kg (per body weight) once daily for an adult, in intervals of at least three weeks, in combination with other anti-tumour medicines". Also a mixed treatment of XELOX (a treatment in intervals of at least three weeks with oral application and intravenous infusion for two hours) and Bevacizumab was only permitted by the subsequent authorisation, and not by the first. From these circumstances it cannot be inferred that the manufacture and marketing of the medicine based on the first authorisation would comprise such acts as authorised in the second authorisation.

5. From the above considerations, the appeal court (IP High Court) has concluded without error that the decision of the Japanese Patent Office according to which the subsequent authorisation was not necessary in order to carry out the patented invention, was erroneous. The arguments raised by the defendant against this decision are not convincing. The decision has been unanimous.

3. ANALYSIS

a) Issue in this case

In this case, (i) the plaintiff filed a patent application for a new drug and obtained a registration, (ii) the first authorisation was granted for the drug, (iii) the plaintiff filed an application for a patent term extension and obtained the extension based on the first authorisation (ii), (iv) the second authorisation was granted for a new drug with a different way of application and dosage, yet within the range of the same patent. The issue was thus whether the patent term extension based on the second authorisation (iv) could be granted or not.

b) Relevant provision sec. 67ter(1)(i)

The reasons for rejecting an application for a patent term extension are listed in sec. 67ter(1). Sec. 67ter(1)(i) prescribes as the following. "Where an application for the registration of extension of the duration of a patent right falls under any of the following items, the examiner shall render a decision to the effect that the application is to be refused: (i) where the disposition designated by Cabinet Order under sec. 67(2) is not deemed to have been necessary for the working of the patented invention."

c) Traditional interpretation

The traditional way of interpreting sec. 67ter(1)(i) was in line with sec. 68bis which prescribes the scope of a patent with extended term in connection with its substance, efficacy and effect. As a result, the application of a patent term extension was only allowed for a new drug with a marketing authorisation for a new substance, efficacy and effect. In other words, a patent term extension was not allowed in the case of a first and second authorisation where the second authorisation was granted for a drug with the same substance, efficacy and effect.

However, this interpretation has been criticised because of the following reasons; (a) It is not in line with the literal meaning of sec. $67^{ter}(1)(i)$,[3] (b): Just as drugs characterised by features other than substance, efficacy and effect[4] are becoming more common, applications for a patent term extension should equally be allowed.

The Supreme Court in the *Pacif Capsule* decision (Case No. 58 in this book)[5] did not follow this interpretation and held that there was no inevitable link between secs. $67^{ter}(1)(i)$ and 68bis. The courts subsequently applied this ruling, see the comment for Case No. 58 in this book. What was left open, however, was the question whether the decoupling of secs. $67^{ter}(1)(i)$ and 68bis should also apply to cases where both authorisations were related to the same patent, in other words whether the same patent could be the subject of two extensions. In the *Pacif Capsule*, the first authorisation was for an active ingredient that was outside the scope of the patent at issue, and the second authorisation was for a patented dosage form of this medicament. While the Supreme Court held that two authorisations could justify two extensions, it did not have to decide whether this would also apply if both authorisations related to one single patent.

d) Gist of the Supreme Court's judgment

In the *Bevacizumab* case, upholding the IP High Court decision,[6] the Supreme Court held that the application for a patent term extension should be rejected under sec. $67^{ter}(1)(i)$ if the manufacturing and marketing of the drug as the subject of the first authorisation included the subject matter of the second authorisation. In determining the existence of the relationship between the first and the second authorisation, the court clarified that it was necessary to compare both in view of the issues which directly related to a substantial identity of pharmaceutical products in consideration of the type or the subject of the patented invention.

On the other hand, the Supreme Court did not clarify the meaning of "the working of the patented invention" in Article $67^{ter}(1)(i)$.[7] This issue has not been

---

3. R. Iseki, Abasuchin [Bebashizumabu] jiken *(Avastin [Bevacizumab] case)*, 1475 Jurist 62 (2015).
4. A typical example is a drug characterised by a drug delivery system (DDS).
5. IP High Court, 29 May 2009, 2008 Case No. 10458-10460 (Gyo-Ke) of 2008, 2047 Hanrei Jihō 11 = 1305 Hanrei Times 80. English translation is available at the website of the IP High Court < http://www.ip.courts.go.jp/app/files/hanrei_en/140/000140.pdf >. Supreme Court, 28 April 2011, Case No. 326 (Gyō-Hi) of 2009 – *Pacif Capsule 30mg –Takeda Pharmaceutical v. JPO*. Published in 65-3 Minshū 1654 = 2115 Hanrei Jihō 32 = 1348 Hanrei Times 102 = N. Nakayama et al. (eds.), Tokkyo Hanrei Hyakusen *(Hundred Selected Patent Cases)*, 4th ed. 2012, 120 = T. Ōbuchi et al. (eds.), Chitekizaisan hō hanrei shū *(Intellectual Property Law Case Book)*, 2nd ed. 2015, 110. English translation by N. Lee in 42 IIC 972 (2011) and in Bälz/Dernauer/Heath/Petersen-Padberg (eds.), Business Law in Japan – Cases and Comments, Alphen aan den Rijn 2012, 422–423.
6. See note 1.
7. N. Koizumi, Abasuchin [Bebashizumabu] jiken jōkokushin *(Avastin [Bevacizumab] case of the Supreme Court)*, 1490 Jurist 8 (2016).

sufficiently discussed by scholars and practitioners, and therefore it was hoped that the Supreme Court would provide a clear interpretation.[8]

e) The Examination Guidelines revised

After the Supreme Court's decision, the Japanese Patent Office revised the Examination Guidelines on patent term extension in line with the Supreme Court's decision.[9] The Examination Guidelines further explain in detail the relationship between two authorisations[10] and the issues which directly relate to the substantial identity of pharmaceutical products.[11]

According to the explanation in the Examination Guidelines, examples which directly relate to the substantial identity in case of the authorisation for manufacturing and marketing a pharmaceutical product are listed in Table 2.

Table 2

Type of the patented invention	Issues which directly relate to a substantial identity
a drug	substance, quantity, way of application, dosage, efficacy and effect.
a process for manufacturing a drug	matters on the process in addition to the above 5 factors.
a drug formulation	matters on the drug formulation in addition to the above 5 factors.

After the revision of the Examination Guidelines, many pharmaceutical companies nowadays obtain patent term extensions for the second authorisation.[12]

4. COMPARATIVE REMARKS

While the basic features of patent extension schemes in the US and Europe have been addressed in the previous case comment (Case No. 58 – *Pacif Capsule*), there are some details that merit attention.

---

8. R. ISEKI, Tokkyoken no sonzokukikan no enchō *(Patent term extension)*, in: N. NAKAYAMA et al. (eds.), Tokkyo Hanrei Hyakusen *(Hundred Selected Patent Cases)*, 4th ed. 2012, 120.
9. Part IX Extension of Patent Term, in the Examination Guidelines of the JPO. English translation is available at the website of the JPO <https://www.jpo.go.jp/e/system/laws/rule/guideline/patent/tukujitu_kijun/document/index/09_0100_e.pdf>.
10. The Examination Guidelines clarified that a partly overlapping relationship is one aspect of the inclusion relationship. See 3.1.1.b. in the Examination Guidelines.
11. See 3.1.1.c. in the Examination Guidelines.
12. Y. SHIROYAMA, Enchōtōroku no yōken oyobi kōryoku *(Requirements and scope of patent term extension)*, 1499 Jurist 56 (2016).

a) In the **EU** (and Switzerland), a pre-condition for the grant of a supplementary protection certificate (SPC) is that the product has not already been the subject of an SPC, Arts. 3(c) and 1(d) of Regulation 469/2009, and that the product on which the request for extension is based is the first authorisation to place the product on the market as a medicinal product. According to case law by the CJEU, while it may be possible to obtain the extension of several patents where the marketing authorisation relates to a product covered by several patents,[13] and for different products or product combinations protected with the same patent[14] on condition that the active ingredients are different, the wording of the Regulation makes clear that a second SPC cannot be granted where the same active ingredient was already the subject of an earlier SPC. It appears however possible to obtain a second SPC for the human use of an active ingredient that had already been the subject of an SPC for veterinary use.[15] Whether this translates into a general recognition of several SPCs for different usages of the same active ingredient covered by different patents (*Pacif Capsule*) or even the same patent (*Bevacizumab*) remains to be seen.

b) In the **US**, 35 USC sec. 156(a) allows for the extension of a patent term also in regard of "a method using a product", yet explicitly provides under (2) that the term of the patent must never have been extended before. In other words, there cannot be several extensions for one and the same patent, a reading that is confirmed by a 1996 decision of the Federal Circuit:[16] "If the term of the patent has received such an extension, the patent may not be given another restauration extension even for another drug covered by the patent whose marketing also is delayed by reasons of FDA procedures."

13. CJEU, 23 January 1997, case C-181/95 – *Biogen Inc. v. SmithKline Beecham Biologicals.*
14. CFEU, 12 December 2013, case C-443/12 – *Actavis Group v. Sanofi.*
15. CFEU, 18 April 2013, case C-103/11 – *Neurim Pharmaceuticals v. Comptroller of Patents.*
16. US CAFC, *Merck et al. v. Kessler et al.*, 80 F.3d 1543 (1996).

Case No. 60

Scope of Extended Patent

Hirotaka Nonaka

---

1. The scope of a patent with an extended term shall not only cover a product (a drug) which is specified by the criteria of marketing authorisation (component, quantity, usage, dosage, efficacy and effect), but also products with only superficial differences ("substantially identical products").

2. "Substantially identical products" are considered those with (1) simple additions/replacements of a non-effective component, (2) minor modifications in composition while maintaining the same technical feature and effect, (3) meaningless modifications in quantity, usage and dosage, and (4) a different quantity, yet being considered as the same in consideration of usage and dosage.

Intellectual Property High Court, 20 January 2017, Case No. 10046 (Ne) of 2016 – *Oxaliplatinum*

Debiopharm International S.A. v. Towa Pharmaceutical Co. Ltd.

---

1. BACKGROUND

The preceding decisions *Pacif Capsule*[1] and *Bevacizumab*[2] clarified the conditions under which the term of a patent could be extended in cases where a lack of marketing authorisation prevented the patentee from marketing the product. These decisions concerned the conditions for extension, yet not the scope of such extended patent, in particular whether the rules developed for determining the scope of ordinary patents also applied to extended patents. *Oxaliplatinum* is the first decision to elaborate on this issue. As it was rendered by the IP Court's Grand Panel, the decision carries particular weight.

---

1. Supreme Court, 28 April 2011, Case No. 326 (Gyō-Hi) of 2009 – *Pacif Capsule*, this book Case No. 58.
2. Supreme Court, 17 November 2015, Case No. 356 (Gyō-Hi) of 2014 – *Bevacizumab*, this book Case No. 59.

2. DECISION[3]

a) Facts

The plaintiff *Debiopharm International S.A.*, an originator pharmaceutical company, holds a patent right over an invention with the title "Pharmaceutically Stable Oxaliplatinum Preparation" (Japanese Patent No. 3547755), and markets an anti-cancer drug as one embodiment of the patented invention. The term of the patent was extended because delays in the marketing authorisation procedure for the drug did not allow the plaintiff to work the patented invention for a certain period of time during the ordinary patent term.

The defendant, a manufacturer of generic pharmaceuticals, *Towa Pharmaceutical Co. Ltd.*, started to manufacture and market a similar generic drug during the extended term of the patent. The only difference between the two drugs was one component (concentrated glycerine), which was added to the generic drug as a non-effective component (stabiliser).

After marketing of the generic drug, the originator pharmaceutical company filed a patent infringement lawsuit based on the patent with an extended term. The defendant won in first instance, and the plaintiff appealed to the IP High Court, which decided to hear the case before the grand panel due to the importance. The main issue was whether or not the scope of a patent with an extended term should cover a product which was not identical but quite similar to the original drug.

b) Reasons

1. Sec. 68[bis] Japanese Patent Act

Section 68[bis] Japanese Patent Act reads: "Where the duration of a patent right is extended [...], such patent right shall not be effective against any act other than the working of the patented invention for the product which was the subject of the disposition designated by Cabinet Order under sec. 67(2) which constituted the reason for the registration of the extension (where the specific usage of the product is prescribed by the disposition, the product used for that usage)."

The purpose of the patent term extension system is to restore a patent term which was shortened because the patentee could not work the patented invention due to a marketing authorisation procedure (see the Supreme Court decision *Bevacizumab*[4]). Taking this into consideration, sec. 68[bis] prescribes that the scope of a patent with an extended term shall not cover the whole range of the patented invention, but shall cover the working of the patented invention only with regard to the product which was the subject of the disposition designated by Cabinet Order (where the specific usage of the product is prescribed by the disposition, and the product used for that usage).

3. Published in 2361 Hanrei Jihō 73, English translation in 49 IIC 858 (2018).

4. Supreme Court, 17 November 2015, Case No. 356 (Gyō-Hi) of 2014 – *Bevacizumab*, this book Case No. 59.

The relevant law[5] prescribes that "A person who intends to market pharmaceuticals [...] shall obtain an approval from the Minister of Health, Labour and Welfare for each such item.",[6] and the issues to be examined are "the name, component, quantity, dosage, efficacy, effect, side effect and other matters related to quality, efficacy and safety".[7]

Therefore, in case of a patented invention on components of a drug, it is reasonable to interpret that the scope of a patent with an extended term shall cover the working of the product specified by "the component, quantity, usage, dosage, efficacy, and effect". Needless to say, if the specific usage imposes further restrictions upon "the usage, dosage, efficacy, and effect", these factors should be restricted by the specific usage when interpreting the scope (same as below).

According to the above, when an allegedly infringing product is different in terms of "the component, quantity, usage, dosage, efficacy and effect", it seems to be impossible to claim that the allegedly infringing product falls under the scope of the patent. However, if a third party could easily circumvent a patent with an extended term by adopting minor changes in terms of the above factors, it would be not only against the purpose of the patent term extension, but also out of line with the principle of equity. From this point of view, the scope of a patent with an extended term shall cover not only the product which is specified by "the component, quantity, usage, dosage, efficacy and effect", but also cover a substantially identical product as a drug. In relation to this, a third party thus should take this interpretation into consideration.

Therefore, even if an allegedly infringing product differs in one of the factors above, it is reasonable to interpret that the allegedly infringing product would fall under the scope of the patent with an extended term as a substantially identical product in case the differing part is very minor or only superficial as a whole.

With regard to the criteria for deciding what should be considered as substantially identical, we first hold that in a limited situation where a feature of a patent lies in a component of a drug, and there are one or several differences in "component", "quantity" or "usage and dosage", and no other differences. The process of determining whether an allegedly infringing product is substantially identical or not (i) should be made on the premise that what is the content of the patented invention (i.e.; whether the feature of the patented invention lies only in the components of a drug, or in its stability or in the form of a drug using a known effective component), whereby technical features and effects are to be considered as well, (ii) should involve a comparison of the identity of technical features and effects between the allegedly infringing product and the product specified by "the component, quantity, dosage, usage, efficacy and effect" and (iii) should take into account the common general technological knowledge of a person skilled in the art.

---

5. Law on Securing Quality, Efficacy and Safety of Products Including Pharmaceuticals and Medical devices. English translation is available at the website provided by the Ministry of Justice <http://www.japaneselawtranslation.go.jp/law/detail/?vm=04&re=01&id=2766>.
6. Sec. 14(1).
7. Sec. 14(2), (9).

Under the limited situation stated above, the types of drugs acknowledged as substantially identical to the products specified by "the component, quantity, dosage, usage, efficacy and effects" are indicated as follows:

(1) In case that the principal feature of the patented invention only lies in its components, and where an allegedly infringing product, based on well-known or commonly used technology, partially replaces a non-effective component by a different non-effective component, or adds a different non-effective component, it should be considered a substantially identical product.
(2) In case that the principal feature of the patented invention lies in its stability or the form of a drug using a known effective component, and where an allegedly infringing product partially replaces a component by a different component, or adds a different component, it should be considered a substantially identical product as long as it has the same technical features and effects in light of the content of the patented invention.
(3) In case that an allegedly infringing product shows a difference in "quantity" or "usage and dosage", if those quantitative differences are meaningless, it should be considered as a substantially identical product.
(4) In case that an allegedly infringing product shows a difference in "quantity", yet is considered to be identical when taking into account the features "usage and dosage", it should be considered as a substantially identical product.

On the other hand, in situations other than the limited situation stated above where an allegedly infringing product shows a difference in "the component, quantity, usage, dosage, efficacy and effect", it is necessary to take different approaches. Like the relationship between a spray drug and an injection drug, in case that there is a difference in "usage and dosage" beyond the quantitative difference, it is necessary to examine the substantial identity from different angles in accordance with the content of the concrete difference. In addition, in case that there is a difference in "efficacy and effects" because the targeted diseases are different, it is important to examine the substantial identity from a medical point of view such as the similarity of diseases.

Finally, it is also an issue whether or not the doctrine of equivalents would be applied when deciding the scope of substantial identity under sec. 68bis. While equivalence concerns the technical scope of a patented invention, sec. 68bis is based on the concrete marketing authorisation. Therefore, since the doctrine of equivalents and the substantial identity under sec. 68bis apply to different situations, the doctrine of equivalents should not be considered when examining the scope of a patent with an extended term.

3. ANALYSIS

a) The scope of "the product" or "the product used for that usage" in sec. 68bis

The Grand Panel in the IP High Court took into consideration both the purpose of the patent term extension and the principle of equity between the patentee and third parties, and held that the scope of a patent with an extended term should cover not only the product (a drug) which is specified by "component, quantity, usage, dosage, efficacy and effects" in marketing authorisation, but also substantially identical products. The significance of this decision lies in providing the clear-cut criteria based on the purpose of the patent term extension and the principle of equity, while denying the concept of "equivalents".[8]

On this doctrinal foundation, the IP High Court rejected the plaintiff's appeal, holding that the allegedly infringing product containing concentrated glycerine should not be considered a substantially identical product because one of the features of the patented invention was not to include any additives. Although the plaintiff appealed the IP High Court decision, the Supreme Court dismissed the appeal.

b) History leading up to the IP High Court decision

Before the IP High Court for the first time determined how "the product" or "the product used for that usage" in sec. 68bis should be interpreted in an infringement situation, the issue was discussed as *obiter dicta* in appeals against trial decisions.[9] The reason for this was that a dispute[10] as to whether or not the interpretation of sec. $67^{ter}(1)$, which establishes the requirements for patent term extension, should be linked to the interpretation of sec. 68bis.

In litigation to cancel trial decisions, the courts, being in a position to link the interpretation of sec. $67^{ter}(1)$ to that of sec. 68bis, interpreted "the product" and "the usage" as "effective component" and "efficacy and effect" respectively, and if effective component, efficacy and effect were identical, the scope of a patent with an extended term should cover also products with a different quantity, dosage, dosage form and manufacturing method and so on. However, the IP High Court decision *Pacif Capsule*[11] changed this direction and held that in light of the normal interpretation of the technical scope of a patent with an extended term included equivalents or substantially identical products.

8. K. SHINOHARA, Enchōtōroku wo uketa tokkyoken no kōryoku *(The scope of a patent with an extended term)*, 1509 Jurist 53 (2017).
9. See R. ISEKI, in: N. NAKAYAMA et al. (eds.), Shin Chūkai Tokkyohō *(New Commentary on Japanese Patent Act)*, vol. 2, 2nd ed. 2017, 1169.
10. Articles which support the linkage of the interpretation between sec. 68bis and sec. $67^{ter}(1)$: R. ISEKI, Tokkyoken no sonzoku kikan no enchō *(Patent term extension)*, in: N. NAKAYAMA et al. (eds.), Tokkyo Hanrei Hyakusen *(Hundred Selected Patent Cases)*, 4th ed. 2012, 120; T. MAEDA, Senkō shobun ga sonzai suru baai ni tokkyoken sonzoku kikan no enchōtōroku ga mitomerareru yōken oyobi enchōsareta tokkyoken no kōryoku ni tsuite *(Requirement for patent term extension and effect of the extended patent in case where a prior disposition existed)*, 57-3 AIPPI Journal of the Japanese Group (Japanese edition) 162-163 (2012); Y. SHIROYAMA, Enchōtōroku no yōken oyobi kōka *(The requirement and effect of the patent term extension)*, 1499 Jurist 56 (2016). Articles which do not support the linkage: Y. TAMURA, Tokkyoken no sonyoku kikan enchōtōroku seido no yōken to enchō go no tokkyoken no hogo han'i ni tsuite *(Requirement of the patent term extension system and the scope of protection of a patent after extension*, 57-3 AIPPI Journal of the Japanese Group (Japanese edition) 60-3 AIPPI Journal of the Japanese Group (Japanese edition) 21-23 (2015); S. MATSUI, Tokkyoken enchōtōrokuseido no gaiyō *(An overview of the patent term extension system)*, 32-7 AIPPI Journal of the Japanese Group (Japanese edition) 21-23 (1987); R. HIRASHIMA, Tokkyoken enchō tōrokuseido ni kakaru kitei no gōriteki kaisyaku *(A reasonable interpretation of the patent term extension system)*, 46 L&T 52 (2010).
11. IP High Court, 29 May 2009, Case No. 10460 (Gyō-Ke) of 2008. For the *Pacif Capsule* case, see Case No. 58 of this book.

The Grand Panel of the IP High Court basically followed the approach taken in the *Pacif Capsule* decision and for the first time determined in infringement litigation how to interpret "the product" or "the product used for that usage" in sec. 68bis as described above.

4. COMPARATIVE REMARKS

a) In the **EU,** the Regulation on Supplementary Protection Certificates[12] states in Recital 10 that "the protection granted should furthermore be strictly confined to the product which obtained authorisation to be placed in the market as a medicinal product", a principle that is then specifically addressed in Articles 4 and 5. Art. 4 specifies that "the protection conferred by a certificate shall extend only to the product covered by the authorisation to place the corresponding medicinal product on the market and for any use of the product as a medicinal product that has been authorised ...", while Art. 5 clarifies that "the certificate is to confer the same rights as conferred by the basic patent and to be subject to the same limitations and the same obligations".[13] These provisions particularly apply in the case of infringement[14] and seem to imply a double limitation: An SPC can only be infringed if the basic patent would have been infringed (Art. 5), *and* the allegedly infringing product would fall within the scope of the authorisation (Art. 4 and Recital 10). However, the CJEU ignored the plain meaning of the statute and conferred protection in a case where the marketing authorisation covered Valsartan as a sole active ingredient, while the allegedly infringing product contained Valsartan with another active ingredient.[15]

b) In the **US,** under 35 USC sec. 156(b), the patent as a whole is deemed to be extended, although the actual scope of the extended patent is tied to the approved uses of the product and can never be broader than the scope of the original patent. Where the extension relates to the active ingredient, also salts and esters appear to be covered.[16]

12. Regulation 469/2009 corresponding essentially to the old Regulation 1768/92.
13. Which seems to imply that also Art. 69 EPC can be invoked in order to claim equivalents, although this provision is clearly extraneous to the Regulation and even EU law in general.
14. CJEU, decision of 12 December 2013, case C-484/12 *Georgetown University v. Octrooicentrum Nederland.*
15. CJEU, decision of 9 December 2012, case C-442/11, *Novartis v. Actavis UK.* The result is strange because the patentee may not even have been able to obtain an SPC for the combination of Valsartan with another active ingredient.
16. US CAFC, *Pfizer v. Dr. Reddy's*, 359 F.3d 1361 (Fed. Cir.2004).

Case No. 61

Exclusive Registered Licensee – Standing to Sue

Miki Gotō and Yumiko Shirahase

A patentee shall retain the right to seek injunctive relief even when he has granted an exclusive, registered licence to a third party.

Supreme Court, 17 June 2005, Case No. 997 (Ju) of 2004 – *FlexX*

IMMD v. Sumisho Electronics

1. BACKGROUND

In the matter of *FlexX IMMD v. Sumisho Electronics*, it was disputed whether a patentee is qualified to seek an injunctive relief against an infringer even when the patentee had granted an exclusive license to a licensee. It may thus be helpful to briefly outline the basics of patent licensing in Japan.

a) Types of patent licenses under Japanese Patent Act

Under the Japanese Patent Act ("Patent Act"), there are essentially two types of licenses which a patentee may grant to a third party; the *"sen'yō jisshiken"* license, which is an exclusive, registered license (henceforth referred to "registered exclusive license"), and the *"tsūjō jisshi-ken"* license, a non-exclusive license. A registered exclusive license (*"sen'yō jisshiken"*) confers an exclusive right to work the patented invention, while a non-exclusive license (*"tsūjō jisshi-ken"*) does not. A provisional exclusive license (*"kari sen'yō jisshiken"*) can also be granted for a patent application, Sec. 34bis Patent Act.

In order to validate a registered exclusive license, it is necessary to register it with the Patent Office. After registration, the patentee can neither use the licensed patented invention nor grant other licensed rights to any other parties to the extent that such use/grant overlaps with the exclusive right of the licensee. The previous distinction between registered and unregistered non-exclusive licences has been abolished as of 1 April 2012,[1] and now non-exclusive licences can no longer be registered at all.

According to sec. 100 Patent Act, the registered, exclusive licensee is entitled to sue for injunctive relief:

1. Amendment of the Patent Act by Law No 63/2011 of 8 June 2011, in force since April 2012.

(1) The patentee or exclusive licensee may request a person who infringes or is likely to infringe the patent right or exclusive license to stop or prevent such infringement.

(2) In making a request under the preceding subsection, the patentee or exclusive licensee may request measures necessary for the prevention of such infringement ...

2. DECISION[2]

a) Facts

The plaintiff (appellant, appellee) is the owner of a patent involving a method of searching for the structure of the stability complex of ligand molecules and a biopolymer (Pat. No. 2621842). The patentee granted an exclusive license for the territory of Japan over the complete period of the patent term to a third party. The defendant (appellee, appellant) imported and distributed CD-ROMs containing a program called "FlexX" that is in effect a molecule modelling system software.

The plaintiff asserted that the program falls within the scope of the above-mentioned process patent. More specifically, the plaintiff argued that the defendant's acts of importing and distributing "the program" and the "CD-ROM" constitutes an infringement of their process patent and sought an injunction against the importation and distribution of the "CD-ROM" and the "program".

The Tokyo District Court (6 February 2003, Case No. 21278 (Wa) of 2001) dismissed the plaintiff's claim, holding that the patentee lacked standing to sue for an injunctive relief against an infringer:

> "Sec. 77(2) provides that an exclusive licensee shall have the exclusive right to commercially work the patented invention in accordance with the scope of the license agreement, while sec. 68 provides that a patentee shall have an exclusive right to commercially work the patented invention. However, this right of the patentee shall not be exercised to the extent that the exclusive licensee has a right to work the patented invention under the exclusive license.
>
> Thus, when a patentee has granted an exclusive license, only an exclusive licensee has the right to seek injunctive relief over the scope of the licensed patent, and the patentee no longer has a corresponding right to seek an injunction. The right to seek injunction (sec. 100 Patent Act) is designed to secure the right to work the patented invention. A patentee therefore cannot claim such a right where the corresponding right to work the patented invention has been ceded to the exclusive licensee, and there are no specific needs to allow the patentee to exercise such right for claiming injunctive relief."

On appeal, the Tokyo High Court (27 February 2004, Case No. 1223 (Ne) of 2003) reversed the Tokyo District Court's decision:

2. Published in 59-5 Minshū 1074 = 1900 Hanrei jihō 139 = 1183 Hanrei Times 208 = N. NAKAYAMA et al. (eds.), Tokkyo hanrei hyakusen *(Hundred Selected Patent Cases)*, 4th ed. (2012), 196 = T. ŌBUCHI et al. (eds.), Chitekizaisan hō hanrei shū *(Intellectual Property Law Case Book)*, 2nd ed. (2015), 217. English translation by M. MŌRI in 37 IIC 221 (2006).

"Sec. 100 of Patent Act provides that a patentee or exclusive licensee shall have the right to request a person who is infringing or likely to infringe the patent or exclusive licensee to discontinue or refrain from such infringement ...

Even when a patentee has granted an exclusive license, a patentee needs to seek injunctive relief against infringement where he receives a licensing fee based on the exclusive licensee's sales turnover. The same holds true where the patentee under an exclusive license agreement is obliged to request the discontinuance of infringing acts against third parties. Also here, such patentee is in need of exercising the right to claim injunctive relief. Even when the patentee is under no such duty, it is necessary for him to preserve his right by claiming injunctive relief in case an exclusive license is terminated or is abandoned by the licensee."

The defendant (appellee) appealed to the Supreme Court, and the Supreme Court affirmed the Tokyo High Court judgment.

b) Reasons

We determine that a patentee has standing to sue for seeking injunctive relief even where the patentee has granted an exclusive license to a third party.

A patentee has a right to seek injunctive relief in order to have others discontinue or refrain from infringement (sec. 100(1)). When a patentee grants an exclusive license to a licensee, his exclusive right to commercially work the patented invention shall not be exercised to the extent that the exclusive licensee has a right to work the patented invention (sec. 68). Thus, the issue here is whether a patentee's right to seek injunctive relief is also restricted by this provision.

Judging from the wording of sec. 100(1) of the Patent Act, there is no room for the interpretation that the patentee's right to seek injunctive relief is restricted. Also on substantive grounds, it is necessary to protect the patentee's right to seek discontinuance of an infringement so as to protect the patentee's licensing income in cases where the amount of licensing fee is based on the turnover of an exclusive licensee's sales. In addition thereto, it is generally necessary to allow patentees to exercise their right to seek injunctive relief, because a patentee might suffer a loss when an exclusive license is terminated for some reason and the patentee is in need of exercising his patent right.

From above reasons, we conclude that a patentee shall not lose his right to seek injunctive relief even when the patentee has granted an exclusive license to a licensee.

3. ANALYSIS

Sec. 100 of the Patent Act is clear in that a registered exclusive licensee can sue for *injunctive relief*, while non-exclusive licensees cannot do so even if authorised by the patentee. A non-exclusive licensee can neither sue for *damages* nor for injunctive relief.[3] An exclusive but unregistered licensee may sue for damages out of his own

3. Osaka District Court, 26 April 1984, Case No. 3453 (Wa) of 1983, 536 Hanrei Times 379. An agent who is empowered to grant licences on behalf of the right owner has no independent

right.[4] There are further some indications by some court cases[5,6] that also exclusive but unregistered licensees are entitled to sue for injunctive relief by the licensor's subrogation right, although some court cases denied this.[7] Some academic literature also favours standing for the exclusive but unregistered licensee to sue for injunctive relief.[8] There is also a similar discussion in the field of unfair competition.[9]

In the case at issue, the courts had to determine whether a patentee may seek an injunction against an infringing third party even if an exclusive license for this patent had been granted.

Pertaining to this topic, there have been three theories prior to *FlexX*: a negative theory, an affirmative theory and an intermediate theory. The negative theory denied the patentee the right to demand an injunction; the affirmative theory allowed the patentee to seek injunctive relief, and the intermediate theory allowed the patentee to seek injunctive relief under certain circumstances. The affirmative theory enjoyed most support among the lower court decisions on this issue.[10]

a) Negative theory

The first instance decision in this case held that the patentee did not have a right to seek injunctive relief.

The negative theory[11] argues as follows:

First, it is in conformity with the wording of secs. 68 and 77(2) of the Patent Act. The patentee has the exclusive right to commercially work the patented invention (sec. 68). However, to the extent that an exclusive licensee is entitled to

---

standing to sue for injunctive relief: Tokyo District Court, 31 January 2002, Case No. 12516 (Wa) of 2001, 35 IIC 1110 (2004) - *Tonttu.*

4. Osaka High Court, 20 June 1986, Case No. 2592&2648 (Ne) of 1984, 18-2 Mutaishū 15 - *Permabrush.*
5. Tokyo District Court, 31 August 1965, Case No. 9862 (Wa) of 1962, 185 Hanrei Times 209 - *Cum instrument*
6. Tokyo District Court, 3 October 2002, Case No. 17298 (Wa) of 2000, the website of the court <http://www.courts.go.jp/app/files/hanrei_jp/593/011593_hanrei.pdf>.
7. The exclusive but unregistered licensee cannot sue for injunctive relief even by the licensor's subrogation right: Osaka District Court, 26 April 1984, Case No. 3453 (Wa) of 1983, 16-1 Mutaishū 271; Osaka District Court, 20 December 1984, Case No. 7035 (Wa) of 1982, 16-3 Mutaishū 803 - *Permabrush.*
8. M. TAKEDA, Chiteki Zaisanken Shingai Yōron *(Theory of Intellectual Property Rights Infringement)*, 5th ed. 2007, 278; N. NAKAYAMA, Tokkyo hō *(Patent Law)*, 2010, 435; T. TOSHIAKI, Tokkyoshingai soshō ni okeru sashitome seikyu oyobi songaibaishō no yōken jijitsu *(Case requirement of an injunction request and claim for damage in patent-infringement lawsuit)*, in: T. MAKINO/T. IIMURA (eds.), Shin Saiban Jitsumu Taikei - chiteki zaisankankei soshō hō *(New practice of court system,* 201 ce on *intellectual property - related procedure law)*, 2001, 55; Y. TAMURA, Chiteki zaisan hō *(Intellectual Property Law)*, 5th ed. 2010, 341; S. MUTO, Hōsōyōsei to saibanjitsumu *(Nurturing the Legal Profession and practice of court system)*, 2006, 569.
9. *Obiter dictum* in the above *Tonttu* decision, and Osaka District Court, 26 July 2004, Case No. 8501(2) (Wa) of 2003, 37 IIC 480 (2006) - *NuBra*; M. TAKABE, Eigyō jō no rieki *(Interest on commerce)*, in: Shin Saiban Jitsumu Taikei (above), 433.
10. Yamaguchi District Court, 28 February 1963, Case No. 250 (Wa) of 1959, 142 Hanrei Times 184; Tokyo District Court, 18 March 1964, Case No. 5836 (Wa) of 1961, 377 Hanrei Jihō 63.
11. H. KANEKO and Y. SOMENO, Kōgyō Shoyūken hō *(Intellectual Property Law)*, revised ed. 1968, 251.

the exclusive right (sec. 77(2)), the patentee shall lose the right to do so (sec. 68 proviso). Therefore, it is understood that by this provision, the patentee not only loses the right to commercially work the patented invention, but also the right to demand an injunction: the patentee's rights become an empty shell.

In addition, from the view of the negative theory, it is possible to interpret sec. 100(1) to the effect that "or" in "the patentee or exclusive licensee" is alternative rather than cumulative. If so, when the exclusive licensee has the right to demand injunctive relief, the patentee does not.

Also from a substantial point of view, it is argued that there is no real benefit to allow the patentee the exercise of claiming injunctive relief although he does not have the right to commercially work the patented invention. In other words, the right to commercially work the patent (positive right) corresponds to the right to prevent others from doing so (negative right).

b) Affirmative theory[12]

The High Court and the Supreme Court decision allowed the patentee to seek an injunction even where the patentee had granted an exclusive license. Therefore it is basically understood that those decisions applied the affirmative theory. The reasons for this theory are as follows:

First of all, with regard to the provisions of the Patent Act, it can be interpreted that the proviso of sec. 68 focuses on the commercial working of the patented invention, while the right to demand cessation is a separate right. In other words, there is no reason to interpret sec. 68 to eliminate the patentee's right to enjoin a third party from infringing its patent since there is no mention of the right of injunction in sec. 68.[13]

In addition, regarding the phrase "or" in sec. 100(1), generally the phrase of "A or B" in legal terms cannot always be interpreted as an alternative relationship between either A or B.[14] Therefore, it is difficult to derive a negative theory only from a literal interpretation of sec. 100(1).

Rather, sec. 77(4) can be cited as the basis for the affirmative theory. This provision stipulates that even an exclusive licensee cannot grant a non-exclusive license to a third party without obtaining permission from the patentee. Therefore,

12. N. NAKAYAMA Chūkai Tokkyo hō *(Patent Law)*, 3rd ed. 2000, 665; N. MONYA, Sen'yō jisshi ken settei go no tokkyo kesha no tokkyo ken ni motozuku sashitome seikyū ken no umu *(Allowability of injunction claim by the patentee after the registration of the exclusive license)* [A commentary on the case of the Yamaguchi District Court case in note 10], 349 Jurist 112 (1966); Y. KOMATSU, Baio tekunorojī kanren gijutu no tokkyo ken ni tsuite sen'yō jissi ken wo setteishita tokkyo kensha ni sashitome seikyū wo mitometa jirei *(A case where injunction is acknowledged for the patentee who grants the exclusive license for a biotechnology related patent)* [A commentary on this case], 55-10 Chizai Kanri 1457 (2005); R. TAKABAYASHI, Hyojun Tokkyo hō *(Standard Patent Law)*, 1st ed. 2002, 161.
13. N. MATSUMOTO, Sen'yō jisshiken wo settei shita tokkyo kensha no sashitome seikyū ken *(Injunction claim by the patentee who grants the exclusive license)* [A commentary on this case], 1215 Hanrei Times 184 (2006), at 185.
14. M. MIYASAKA, Sen'yō jisshiken wo settei shita tokkyo kensha ga sono tokkyo ken ni motozuku sashitome seikyū wo suru koto no kahi *(Allowability of injunction claim by the patentee who grants the exclusive license)* [A commentary on this case], 59-10 Hōsō Jihō 3518 (2007), at 3526.

it is understood that the patentee must be able to enjoin a third party who receives a non-exclusive license from the exclusive licensee without the patentee's consent. If so, as a matter of course, the patentee can also demand an injunction against those who commercially work the patented invention without the permission from the exclusive licensee.[15] Otherwise, sec. 77(4) would become a toothless tiger since the patentee could in effect do nothing to prevent the exclusive licensee from granting a non-exclusive license to someone without the patentee's permission.

Further, from a substantive perspective, it is necessary to allow the patentee to exercise an injunctive right, because there is a benefit for the patentee to eliminate infringement in the case where the amount of royalties is determined by sales amount, since in such case, the patentee can increase the licensing fee by eliminating other sellers (i.e. infringers) and thereby increasing the sales of the exclusive licensee. Also, in the event that the exclusive license is terminated, the patentee can implement the patented invention again, therefore, in such a case, an infringement could disadvantage the patentee. To avoid such situation, the patentee needs to exercise an injunctive right and stop an infringement before the exclusive license is terminated.

c) Intermediate theory

The intermediate theory[16] argues that in principle, the right to demand injunctive relief should be exercised by the exclusive licensee only, yet in exceptional cases (i.e. if the exclusive licensee does not exercise such right), the patentee should be entitled to exercise this right where otherwise the patentee's interest in receiving royalties etc. is affected. In other words, the right to demand cessation only exists where the exclusive licensee's failure to act prejudices the patentee's position.

There is still an opinion based on the intermediate theory after that the Supreme Court's decision at issue. It is said that the result might be different in a case where it is difficult to find a practical necessity for admitting the patentee's standing to sue, e.g. the royalty has been paid as an initial lump sum and the licensing period is unlimited, and in another case where e.g. the licensing period is limited.[17]

The intermediate theory has been subject to some criticism based on an analysis of the court case at issue.[18] Namely, in those articles, it is said that the intermediate theory does not have a basis in the wording of the law. Thus, the Patent Act does not make any distinction for the patentee's right to seek an injunction. Also in practical

15. Y. TAMURA, Chitekizaisan hō *(Intellectual Property Law)*, 5th ed. 2010, 344.
16. K. YOSHIDA, Sen'yō jisshiken settei to tokkyo ken ni yoru shingai sashitomeseikyu *(injunction claim by patent right and setting an exclusive right)*, 33-11 Patent 29 (1980).
17. Y. KOMADA, Sen'yō jisshiken wo settei shita tokkyo kensha no sashitome seikyū *(Injunction claim by a patentee who grants the exclusive license)*, 120 Bessatsu NBL 228 (2007).
18. Sen'yō jisshiken wo settei shita tokkyo kensha ga sono tokkyo ken ni motozuku sashitome seikyū wo suru koto no kahi *(Allowability of injunction claim by the patentee who grants the exclusive license)* [A unnamed commentary on this case], 1232 Kinyu-Shoji Hanrei 37 (2006). See also commentaries on this case (above); M. SUZUKI, in: N. NAKAYAMA et al. (eds.), Shin Chūkai Tokkyohō (*New Commentary to the Patent Act*), 2nd ed. 2017, 1149-1154; T. IMAMURA, Sen'yō jisshiken wo settei shita tokkyo kensha ni yoru sashitome seikyū no kahi *(Allowability of injunction claim by the patentee who grants the exclusive license)*, in: N. NAKAYAMA et al. (eds.), Tokkyo hanrei hyakusen *(Hundred Selected Patent Cases)*, 4th ed. 2012, 196.

terms it is not appropriate to make the exercise of injunctive relief depend on the relationship between patentee and exclusive licensee, because, if so, the patentee's right would be subject to change even for ongoing disputes.

4. COMPARATIVE REMARKS

a) European countries

In the **UK**, infringement proceedings may be instituted by the patentee or by an exclusive licensee, UK Patents Act secs. 61, 66 and 67. If a proprietor refuses to join an action raised by the exclusive licensee as a joint plaintiff, the licensee must make him a joint defendant so as to ensure that the patentee is party to the proceedings.

In **Germany**, the matter is mostly resolved by contract: Even a non-exclusive licensee can sue for injunctive relief if so empowered by the patentee (e.g. by way of a clause in the licensing agreement).[19] Even in the absence of any contractual provision, the exclusive licensee (no requirement of registration) can sue for injunctive relief to the extent that his position is affected by the infringement.[20] The patentee may still be able to sue even upon granting an exclusive license.[21]

In **France**, under Intellectual Property Code Art. L-615-2, the exclusive licensee (registration no longer required) may institute infringement proceedings if, after being placed on notice, the patentee does not institute such proceedings. The patentee is entitled to join ongoing proceedings instituted by the exclusive licensee.

In **Italy**, the position is identical to the one in France.

In **Switzerland**, sec. 75 Patent Act allows the exclusive licensee (no registration required) to bring an action for infringement independent from the patentee.

b) The US

In the **US**, a licensee may only sue in its own name for patent infringement if it owns all substantive rights in the patent, such that the licence operates as a virtual assignment. Otherwise, a licensee may have standing to sue as a co-plaintiff.[22] In order to determine whether an agreement vests all substantive rights in the licensee, the courts analyse the contractual intentions of the parties. A provision that confers standing to the sue to the licensee as such is not sufficient.[23]

19. German Federal Supreme Court, 29 September 2011, MDR 2012, 182.
20. German Federal Supreme Court, 20 December 1994, GRUR 1995, 338 – *Kleiderbügel*.
21. KÜHNEN, Handbuch der Patentverletzung *(Handbook of Patent Infringement)*, 7th ed. (2014), note 994.
22. U.S. CAFC, *Enzo APA & Sons v. Geapag AG*, 134 F.3d 1090 (Fed Cir 1998).
23. U.S. CAFC, *Textile Products v. Mead Corp.*, 134 F.3d 1481 (Fed Cir. 1998).

Case No. 62

Licensing Agreement - Patent Subsequently Reduced in Scope

Kumiko Katsumata

---

1. Where a licensing agreement over a patent application defines the scope of the licensed right as that of the underlying right, grant of the patent in limited form also reduces the scope of the contract. For products that no longer fall under the patent as granted, no royalties are due.
2. Where royalties have already been paid and the contract provides a no refund clause in such case, royalties cannot be claimed back by the licensee even if they would not have been due.

Intellectual Property High Court, 31 March 2010, Case No. 10033 (Ne) of 2009 - *Silicon Gum Compound*

Panasonic Denkō v. Fuji Kōbunshi Kōgyō

---

1. BACKGROUND

Under the principle of freedom of contract, parties may select any kinds of intellectual property as an object of license, be it a patent, know-how, trade mark, copyright and so on. It occasionally happens that parties enter into the patent licensing agreement even before the patent is granted in order to avoid the risk of being faced with claims for injunctive relief (sec. 100 Patent Act, only available after patent grant), or compensation according to sec. 65(1) of Patent Act after publication of the patent application. Therefore, the licensee is sometimes willing to enter into a contract with the licensor even before the registration of the patent.

Sec. 65(1) Patent Act[1]

After the laying open of a patent application, where the applicant for the patent has given warning with documents stating the contents of the invention claimed in the patent application, the applicant may claim compensation against a person

---

1. All English translations of Japanese law in this paper is from the website of Japanese Law Translation which is provided by the Ministry of Justice < http://www.japaneselawtranslation.go.jp >

> who has worked the invention as a business after the warning and prior to the registration establishing a patent right, and the amount of compensation shall be equivalent to the amount the applicant would be entitled to receive for the working of the invention if the invention were patented. Even where the said warning has not been given, the same shall apply to a person who knowingly commercially worked an invention claimed in a laid open patent application, prior to the registration establishing a patent right.

However, the patent is not always granted with the same technical scope as in the patent application or the time when the contract was concluded. Patent applicants are often required to amend of the claim for the patent to be granted, and some amendments may cause the licensee's products no longer to fall under the scope of the patent. Furthermore, patent applications may be refused. When the scope of the patent becomes narrower than what the parties expected at the time of the contract, or the granted right can be invalidated, arguments about the scope and validity of the contract may arise between the parties.

In such cases, the licensee often insists that the contract is no longer in effective due to an "error" under sec. 95 of Civil Code:

> **Sec. 95 Civil Code**
>
> Manifestation of intention has no effect when there is an error in any element of the juristic act in question; provided, however, that the person who made the manifestation of intention may not assert such nullity by himself/herself if he/she was grossly negligent.

According to sec. 95, a contract signed by the person who misunderstood an *element of the juristic act in question* without being grossly negligent takes no effect. Thus, if the licensee misunderstood that its act (such as manufacture of a certain product or use of a certain process) infringes the licensor's patent right, and "the fact that said act infringes the right" is deemed *an element of the juristic act in question*, the contract may have no effect, unless the licensee in its perception was *grossly negligent*.

Generally, contracts need to be interpreted. If the object of a license is not a patent but a certain technology, the scope of the licensor's patent may not have any influence on the validity of the contract. However, if the object of the license is the patent, the scope of the patent or its validity might have a huge influence on the effectiveness of the contract, and whether the licensee can claim back the royalties from the licensor in the event that the contract is later deemed to be void.

2. DECISION[2]

a) Facts

The plaintiff is the owner of a patent application with the title "Heat Conducting Silicon Gum Compound" that was non-exclusively licensed to the defendant for the

2. Published in 2128 Hanrei Jihō 84. The first instance decision (Osaka District Court, 7 April 2009) is published in 2065 Hanrei Jihō 115. English translation in 43 IIC 97 (2012) w. comment C. Heath.

latter to produce, use and sell the licensed goods. The licensing agreement defined the licensed right as the patent application, or the patent right ensuing therefrom, and the licensed goods as those falling within the scope of the patent right. Under the agreement, the licensee was not entitled to claim back any money even in case the patent should not be granted or be invalidated. The contract envisaged an initial period of three years from 1 October 2000 to 1 October 2003, and subsequently an extension of one year unless terminated three months prior to the expiration date.

As the patent application was initially refused, the plaintiff amended the patent, and the latter was granted on 22 March 2002 in a reduced scope when compared to the application. The defendant initially was unaware of these developments, but once it received knowledge thereof, noticed that the manufactured products no longer fell within the patented scope. The defendant refused further payments and challenged the contract due to a substantial error.

The plaintiff now demands unpaid licensing fees (18 million Yen) for those licensed products produced prior to the termination of the agreement, damages (104 million Yen) in regard of those products manufactured thereafter, and injunctive relief to enjoin further production. According to the defendant, (1) the contract was void to a substantial error, which should lead to a restitution of all moneys paid due to unjust enrichment, in the auxiliary, (2) the reduction in the scope of the right should also lead to the conclusion that the licensing fees were paid without any legal basis (as the licensed goods were not covered by the amended right), further in the auxiliary, (3) a reduction in the scope of the right should generally lead to a cause of unjust enrichment in part, as was held in the decision of the Supreme Court, 19 Oct. 1993, Case No. 364 (O) of 1992, and, finally, (4) the licensor had a good faith obligation to inform the licensee of the reduction in scope. Failure to inform should lead to a claim for damages.

The Osaka District Court held that some of the defendant's products even after the amendment still fell into the scope of the patent right, found that none of the above reasons prejudiced the continued validity of the agreement and ordered the defendant to pay the outstanding royalties plus damages. The first instance court reasoned as follows:

- a provision in case of a refusal of the application, or its amendment or limitation with the consequence that the scope of the patent application would change, was not contained in the agreement;
- the risk that a patent application should subsequently be reduced or limited in scope should fall on the licensee, because in this contract the amount of royalties before grant was set comparatively low (only 1 %) compared to the amount after grant (3 %);
- the question whether the licensing agreement has been retroactively limited is an issue of interpretation of contracts; in general, where a patent application due to a limiting amendment has been reduced in scope, this does not retroactively limit the scope of the corresponding licensing agreement;
- when the licensor limits the scope of the patent application, it is possible for the licensee to check the scope of the patent by asking to the licensor or referring to the patent gazette, etc.

The IP High Court held that the defendant's products did not fall within the scope of the patent right as granted by interpreting the patented claim in the light of the description and the purpose of the amendment.

b) Reasons

The obligation to pay the unpaid royalties, 18 million Yen, is based on the licensing agreement. Whether the defendant is under an obligation to pay and how much to pay depends basically on how the contract stipulates the licensee's obligation. The provision 2(2) of the agreement defined that "the licensed goods are heat radiation sheets consisting of heat conducting silicon gum compound which falls under the scope of the licensed patent right." So the plaintiff can claim royalties only when the defendant's products actually fall under the scope of the patent right. However, as mentioned above, all of the defendant's products do not fall under the scope of the patent right. Therefore, the plaintiff does not have a right to claim the unpaid royalties.

Nevertheless, the defendant cannot claim back royalties that were actually paid, 7,295,377 Yen, because the provision 4(2) of the agreement stipulates that "the licensee is not entitled to claim back any money, which is paid to the licenser by this agreement, on any grounds whatsoever even in case the patent should be invalidated or the agreement is cancelled, etc.", as the first instant held.

3. ANALYSIS

a) This case

Whether the obligation under a contract is effective or not depends on how the contract stipulates the matter. In this case, the licensing agreement stipulated that the licensed goods should fall within the scope of the patent right in order to create an obligation for the payment of royalties. This means that the licensee does not have any obligation to pay royalties when the products do not infringe the patent right. The IP High Court found that the defendant's products did not fall within the scope of the patent right, and thus concluded that the defendant had no obligation to pay royalties. Though the IP High Court did not express its view about the validity of the contract, the decision rests on the assumption that the contract is valid, because the decision held that the licensee could not claim back paid royalties as stipulated in the agreement. So in this case, though the contract is valid, the licensee does not have to pay outstanding royalties because its products no longer fall within the scope of the patent and thereby also outside the scope the contract.

In my opinion, the court's decision is reasonable because the licensing agreement in this case clearly stipulated that the licensed goods were falling within the scope of the patent right, and therefore it was natural to find that the licensee had no obligation to pay royalties if the products did not infringe the patent. And the licensee who desired to start its business by using the patent should have realised that it was certainly possible that the scope of the patent application could be reduced or the patent could be invalidated, and should have calculated carefully the value of the license when entering into the contract. The more so in view of the provision of the agreement stipulating that the licensee was not entitled to claim back any money even if the patent was not granted or invalidated.

The court of first instance held that some of the defendant's products infringed the plaintiff's patent by interpreting the claim of the patent differently from IP High Court. It further held that the contract was effective,[3] see above. The first instance court thus found no "error" under sec. 95 Civil Code and pointed out that when the parties entered into the agreement, the patent was still in the application phase and therefore both parties concluded the contract in the knowledge that the patent application could to be rejected or reduced in scope and because of this agreed on a low royalty rate (1%) that after grant should be raised to 3%. Though the interpretation of the claim was reversed by the IP High Court, the rest of the decision of the first instance seems to be reasonable and instructive.

In this connection, the defendant relied on the Supreme Court decision of 19 Oct. 1993,[4] where the court held that the scope of the licensing agreement was reduced when the patent was granted in a reduced scope. When said agreement was concluded, the patent was in the application phase and the parties agreed that the licensee could produce the apparatus using the patent pending. The Supreme Court held that the parties when they entered into the contract had the intention that the scope of the agreement should correspond to the scope of the patent after grant by interpreting contract. This Supreme Court Case is consistent with this IP High Court Decision, though the IP High Court did not mention the Supreme Court Case.

b) Other cases

Now, I would like to introduce other cases related to the licensing or sale of patents.

(1) IP High Court, 28 January 2009 – *Stone Bath Device*[5]

The defendant owned a patent for a "Stone Bath Device" and granted an exclusive license to the plaintiff for a certain part of Japan (Gifu and Nagano prefectures). The plaintiff granted a sub-license to a third party Z. Several months later, Z alleged that the patent was invalid and terminated the sub-license agreement. Thereafter, Z filed an invalidation trial before the JPO, and the patent was invalidated. The plaintiff claimed that the licensing agreement with the defendant was void on the grounds of an "error" under Sec. 95 Civil Code and the royalties should be reimbursed.

The IP High Court held that there is no element of error because (a) the exclusive licensee could make exclusive use of the patented device at least before the patent was invalidated (the licensee could even receive royalties from a sub-licensee), and (b) the purpose of the licensing agreement was for a joint enterprise and thus both parties should carefully examine the patent, including its scope, likelihood of

---

3. See 43 IIC 97 (2012). This decision was reversed by the IP High Court as explained above.
4. Supreme Court, 19 October 1993, Case No. 364 (O) of 1992, 170 Shūmin 31 = 844 Hanrei Times 84. German translation in GRUR Int. 1995, 341 – *Bohraushubmaschine*. See also, a commentary of the case, O. TAKURA, Gijutsu matawa burando kyōyo to fusakui gimu *(Technology or brand licensing and omission obligation)*, 91-3 Hatsumei 105 (1994).
5. IP High Court, 28 January 2009, Case No. 10070 (Ne) of 2009, published in 1303 Hanrei Times 77 (2009); also see 41 IIC 977 (2010) – *Stone Bath Device*.

revocation, the usefulness of the patent to the business and so on, before entering into the contract. So in this case, the court held that the invalidity of the patent had no influence on the patent licensing agreement.

(2) IP High Court, 27 September 2017 – *Flocculants Manufacturing Process*[6]

The plaintiff owned a patent on "Flocculants and its Manufacturing Process" and had sold the patent to the defendant on the assumption that the defendant would start the business of using the manufacturing process of the patented flocculants. According to the sales contract, the plaintiff under the sales agreement had an additional obligation to provide the technology of the flocculants manufacturing process to the defendant. However, the technology provided by the defendant did not fall within the scope of the patent. Therefore, the defendant claimed that the sales contract was void on the grounds of "error" under sec. 95 Civil Code.

The IP High Court held that the sales contract was void because (a) the defendant believed that the manufacturing process provided by the plaintiff fell under the scope of the patent, and that the defendant could use the manufacturing process only when purchasing the patent, (b) the defendant did not have any experience or knowledge of manufacturing and flocculants, (c) the purpose of the sales contract was not only a transfer of the patent right, but also to provide the technology for manufacturing flocculants. However, the manufacturing technology provided by the plaintiff was not covered by the patent, and thus the defendant could not obtain the monopolistic profits that the patent could confer. Considering this, the court held that the sales contract was void on the grounds of "error" under sec. 95 Civil Code.

c) Theory

According to common accepted theory about this issue in Japan,[7] the validity of the contract is determined by interpreting the agreement in the event that the licensee's products are no longer considered to infringe the patent.

In general, there are two ways to stipulate the object of a licence in the written agreement, one is so-called an "overall license" and the other is so-called an "if-used license". Under the "overall license" agreement, the licensee should pay royalties based on the amount of the sales of a certain product, regardless of whether the product falls within the scope of the patent or not, and there is no possibility of the contract being void on the grounds of "error" under sec. 95 Civil Code. On the other hand, under the "if-used licence" agreement, the licensee should pay royalties based on the amount of the sales only if the products fall under the scope of the patent, and the contract might be void under certain circumstances on the ground of a material error.

---

6. IP High Court, 27 September 2017, Case No. 10056 (Ne) of 2017, published at the website of the courts <http://www.courts.go.jp/app/files/hanrei_jp/136/087136_hanrei.pdf>. See also the decision of the first instance (Osaka District Court) at the website of the courts <http://www.courts.go.jp/app/files/hanrei_jp/599/086599_hanrei.pdf>
7. E. KATAYAMA and M. HATTORI, Raisense keiyaku to sakugo mukou (*License agreement and nullity due toerror*), in: T. MAKINO et al. (eds.), Chiteki zaisan soshō jitsumu taikei II (*System of intellectual property litigation practice II*), 2014, 115; M. TAKABE, Tokkyo soshō no jitsumu (*Practice of patent litigation*), 2012, 507.

If the amount of royalties is fixed in the licensing agreement, the contract would not become void on the ground of an error even if the licensee's products falls under the scope of the patent, because in that situation, it is immaterial for the licensee's obligation whether the licensee works the patent or not. On the other hand, if the contract has been agreed on the assumption that the licensee's designated products fall under the scope of the patent, the contract might be void on the ground of a material error in the event that the patent is invalid or the products do not infringe the patent.

d) Conclusion

According to the cases and theories mentioned above, it can be said that the validity of the contract is basically determined by interpreting the agreement in the event that the licensee's products become no longer infringe the patent. The license agreement in the *Silicon Gum Compound* case can be categorised as an "if-used license" agreement and thus the licensee does not have to pay royalties when the products do not fall within the scope of the patent.

In the *Flocculants Manufacturing Process* case, the court found that the contract was void on the grounds of an error under sec. 95 Civil Code because the licensee did not to have enough knowledge about the manufacture of flocculants. However, when the licensee is a professional on the area where the patent belongs to, both parties should have enough knowledge and be able to carefully examine the patent including the possibility of subsequent invalidation or modification. In such case, it seems to be difficult for the licensee to escape from the obligation to pay royalties by claiming a material error.

Note that in the *Silicon Gum Compound* case, the plaintiff claimed royalties after the amendment of the patent claim, which the IP High Court denied, as it held that the licensee does not have to pay royalties after the scope of patent as amended. This result was based on the interpretation of the contract and was no general statement that in general, licensing agreements should be so interpreted.

4. COMPARATIVE REMARKS

The approach taken by the IP High Court is similar to the stance courts would take in Europe, but not necessarily in the US.

German law recognises the primacy of any contractual stipulation and only in the absence of an agreement has developed the following principles in the case of a subsequent limitation or revocation of a licensed patent:[8] First, this would not lead to a claim of the licensee for modifying the agreement or its automatic invalidation due to a change in material circumstances. Second, the licensee in such case can neither claim damages nor restitution of royalties already paid,[9] as the licensee up to the actual revocation enjoyed the benefits of using the licensed right without the risk of being sued for infringement.[10]

8. Düsseldorf District Court, 12 August 2008, BeckRS 2009, 08738 – *Münzpfandschloß*.
9. German Imperial Supreme Court, 17 December 1886, Rep. II 251/86 – *Cellulose*.
10. German Federal Supreme Court, 28 September 1976, GRUR 1977, 107 – *Werbespiegel*.

Under **EU** competition law, two referrals were made to the European Court of Justice in order to determine whether a licensee could be obliged to pay royalties even after the licensed IP right had expired,[11] or where a court had decided that the licensed right was not used by the licensee (because the products did not fall within the scope of the right, or where the IP right was retroactively invalidated).[12]

As to the first question, the court found such obligation not necessarily anti-competitive where the agreement was concluded prior to the grant of the patent and where the licensee was entitled to terminate the agreement. A further obligation not to manufacture and sell the licensed products after termination of the agreement could be, but was not necessarily anti-competitive.

As to the second question, the Court decided that EU competition law does not prohibit the obligation to pay royalty for the use of technology, even where such use does not give rise to an infringement, or the technology is deemed never to have been protected in the event of retroactive revocation of the patent. Article 101(1) TFEU does not preclude the imposition on the licensee, of a requirement to pay a royalty for the use of a patented technology for the entire period in which that agreement was in effect even in the event of the revocation or non-infringement of a licensed patent, provided that the licensee could freely to terminate that agreement by giving reasonable notice. It seems that the conclusion is similar to the cases in Japan, though the applicable law is not same.

The above issues are less clear under **US** law. On the one hand side, a 1964 Supreme Court decision[13] prohibited as anti-competitive an obligation of the licensee to pay royalties after the expiration of a patent (a decision that also had its critics[14]). This was affirmed in a highly contested Supreme Court decision in 2015[15] where the court held that the prohibition was not based on antitrust considerations, but on the patent misuse doctrine. On the other hand, the Supreme Court affirmed the obligation to continuously pay royalties under a licensing agreement over a patent application that was ultimately refused and no patent was ever granted.[16] The latter approach would be closer to Japanese and European law.

11. ECJ, 12 May 1989 case 320/87 in re *Ottung* (OJ EU:C:1989:195),
12. CJEU, 7 July 2016, Case C-567/14, *Genentech Inc. v. Hoechst GmbH* and *Sanofi-Aventis Deutschland GmbH.*
13. US Supreme Court, *Brulotte v, Thys,* 379 US 29 (1964).
14. E.g. in the decision of the 7th Federal Circuit *Schreiber v. Dolby,* 293 F3d 1014 (7th Cir. 2002).
15. US Supreme Court, *Kimble et al. v. Marvel Entertainment, LLC, successor to Marvel Enterprises, Inc.,* 576 U.S. ___ (2015).
16. US Supreme Court, *Aronson v. Quick Point Pencil,* 440 US 257 (1979).

Case No. 63

Licensing Agreement over Foreign Patent – Royalties not Taxable in Japan

Jinzō Fujino

Whether past and future royalties by a Japanese exporter paid for a US patent under a settlement agreement are taxable in Japan (source jurisdiction) or not (residence state jurisdiction)

Supreme Court, 24 June 2004, Case No. 44 (*Gyō-Hi*) of 1999 – *Daisy Wheel Printer*

Higashi Murayama Tax Bureau v. Silver Seikō

1. BACKGROUND

Each sovereign state has the right to tax any income arising in its territory and has its own tax law to assure tax payments on domestic income. In Japan, the Japanese Income Tax Act defines domestic income as profits, dividends, interests and royalties in sec. 161. Accordingly, patent royalties are taxable so far as they arise based on and in connection with domestic business in Japan. More specifically, sec. 161(7)(i) sets forth in part as follows:

> Royalties include compensations for the use of industrial property rights and other technologies or for the use of methods for production. The term royalties also include remuneration for the assignment of industrial property rights and technologies.

Japan and the US amended their bilateral income tax treaty in 1971 ("old treaty") to set the upper limit of the withholding tax in the source country at 10%. Under the old treaty, the Japanese licensee was required to deduct a 10% tax on the royalties to be paid to the US licensor. The 10% tax thus deducted was ought to be paid to the tax authority. However, the old treaty was extensively revised in November 2003. The revised treaty which became effective in July 2004 ("new treaty") sets forth in sec. 12(1) and (2) the following:

> 1. Royalties arising in a Contracting State and beneficially owned by a resident of the other Contracting State may be taxed only in that other Contracting State.
> 2. The term "royalties" as used in this Article means payments of any kind received as a consideration for the use of, or the right to use, ..., any patent,

> trade mark, design or model, plan, or secret formula or process, or for information concerning industrial, commercial or scientific experience.

The new treaty obviously exempts the licensee from the withholding tax in the source country, provided that a set of necessary documentation has been filed with the tax authority on behalf of the foreign licensor.

The case discussed below was brought to the Tokyo District Court in 1988 when the old treaty was effective. This case was appealed to the Supreme Court which upheld the lower court's decision in June 2004 when the source theory on the withholding tax had been waived under the new treaty.

2. DECISION[1]

a) Facts

Higashi Murayama Tax Bureau was the appellant before the Tokyo High Court and is the petitioner before the Supreme Court ("Petitioner"). *Silver Seiko K.K.* is a Japanese company engaging in the manufacture and sale of business machines and equipment ("Respondent").

The Respondent developed new technologies and installed them in its rotary wheel impact printers and electronic typewriters. Since around 1982, these printers and typewriters had been imported into the United States of America through a Respondent's US subsidiary. Thus imported products were distributed in North, Central and South America.

Qume Corporation, a third party to this case, was a California-based company engaging in the manufacture of printers for office use. *Qume* made an invention relating to a daisy wheel type printer and filed a patent application in the US, Japan and other countries. The patent application was granted in the US in 1976 as US Patent 4,118,129 ("'129 patent") and in Japan in 1988. Several corresponding patents were granted in other countries.

In June 1983, *Qume* filed a series of Section 337 complaints under the Tariff Act of 1930 with the US International Trade Commission. The complaints were filed against several Japanese printer manufacturers including the Respondent. *Qume* alleged, among other things, unfair practices in connection with the importation of printer-related products and sought investigations under Section 337 of the 1930 Tariff Act.

The Respondent decided to settle the patent dispute in connection with the '129 patent and entered into a settlement agreement in November 1983. In return for the payment of settlement fees, *Qume* agreed to withdraw the Section 337 complaint against the Respondent and agreed not to enforce the '129 patent against the Respondent. *Qume*'s major concern was to keep the market share of its printers on the US market and to assure profits under the '129 patent. During negotiations for the settlement agreement, no specific reference was made with respect to the treatment of the corresponding patents abroad, including the Japanese patent.

1. Translation in 2006 IIC 967 w. comment J. FUJINO = 1872 Hanrei Jihō 46 = 1163 Hanrei Times 136 = M. NAKAZATO et al. (eds.) Sozei Hanrei Hyakusen *(Hundred Selected Tax Cases)*, 6th ed. 2016, 132

The settlement agreement between the Respondent and *Qume* included the following provisions:

i) A covenant not to sue the Respondent.
ii) A world-wide non-exclusive license for the Respondent to make and have (licensed products) made under the '129 patent, and to use or sell them in the US. Sales volume was limited to a half million units for printers, but there was no limitation on the sales volume of typewriters.
iii) The Respondent was to pay *Qume* USD 190,000 as royalty to clear the past infringement and USD 570,000 for the future sale.
iv) These payments were defined as "settlement fees" to be paid in advance. The payments should be made in the full amount without deducting the withholding tax. Under the agreement, the Respondent paid USD 400,000 in December 1983 and USD 360,000 in April 1984 without deducting any withholding tax.

In June 1985, Petitioner *Higashi Murayama Tax Bureau* sent an official notice and a determination to the Respondent that the Respondent had failed to deduct the withholding tax with respect to its payments (i.e., USD 760,000 in total) and that the Respondent should pay the national income tax with overdue penalties. Although the recipient of the payments was the licensor *Qume*, Japanese law obliges the paying person in such cases to deduct the withholding tax from its payments and submit the deducted amount to the tax authorities.

In 1988, the Respondent filed a complaint with the Tokyo District Court seeking a declaratory judgment that the Tax Bureau's determination was void on the grounds that the national tax law was inapplicable to the settlement fees in this case.

In 1992, the Tokyo District Court decided in favour of the Respondent, concluding that the payments made by the Respondent were exempted from the application of withholding tax under the Income Tax Act because they related to a US patent. In determining the US as the source country where the taxable income was generated, the Tokyo District Court emphasised the territoriality of the '129 patent (Tokyo District Court, 27 October 1992, 1058 Jurist 124, German summary in 1995 GRUR Int. 988).

The Tax Bureau appealed the District Court's decision to the Tokyo High Court. On appeal, the Tokyo High Court affirmed the district court's decision in 1999 (unreported). The Tax Bureau further appealed to the Supreme Court.

b) Reasons

[Majority Opinion]

> "The Income Tax Act defines, as domestic source income, a royalty payable by a person doing business in Japan in connection with intellectual property rights and other technology-related rights (Income Tax Act, sec. 161(7)(i)). It sets forth that a foreign legal institution who receives such royalty has a duty to pay an income tax under the law (sec. 5(4)) prior to the amendment by Law No. 96 of 1987).
>
> According to the facts discussed above, ..., the purpose of this agreement was to enable the Respondent to resolve disputes under the subject US patent

(which is valid only in the US) and to assure that it would be able to continue the exportation of its products to US. The agreement includes provisions that: i) Company B [the name '*Qume*' was withheld in the court decision] grants to the Respondent and its related company (The Respondent's US subsidiary falls into this category) a limited right and license under the subject US patent for the sale of licensed products in the US, and Company B covenants not to sue the Respondent or its related company on the ground that the subject US patent was infringed by the sale of products manufactured by the Respondents prior to the effective date of this Agreement; and ii) the Respondent pays to Company B the royalties with respect to the products sold by the Respondent or its related company in the US prior to and on or after the effective date of the agreement. ...

There are other provisions in the license agreement. For example, the Respondent pays to Company B the settlement fees as stipulated in the agreement and in return of such payment, Company B grants to the Respondent and its related company a world-wide, non-exclusive license under the subject US patent to manufacture licensed products and have them made (Article 2). Such fees are for the dismissal of the [Section 337] complaint and the settlement of the outstanding disputes between the Respondent and Company B (Article 6(a)). However, these provisions are subordinates to the above-mentioned main provisions of the license agreement and nothing in these [subordinate] provisions adversely affects the Court's interpretation that the settlement fees were made as royalties [for sale] in US under the subject US patent. The covenant-not-to-sue provision (Article 5(a)) relates to the foreign patents corresponding to the subject US patent owned or controlled by Company B and its affiliates and trades off the covenant-not-to-sue offered in Article 5(b) under the patents owned and controlled by the Respondent and its related company. These provisions would not affect the interpretation of this court.

The Respondent was not engaging in the importation into and the sale in the US of licensed products, thus being free from liability of infringement under the subject US patent. However, its subsidiary would be economically damaged if the sale of the licensed products was banned in the US. Therefore, the Respondent had willingly entered into the agreement in order for its US subsidiary to continue its business in the US. There is nothing wrong with this kind of arrangement.

As discussed above, the fees paid under the settlement agreement amounted to the royalties with respect to the sale in the US of licensed products, and they were not for the manufacture and the sale in Japan. The fees therefore do not fall into the class of taxable income under the Income Tax Act, Sec. 161 (7)(i)). Company B has no liability as a tax payer with regard to the settlement fees, which, in turn, exempts the Respondent from withholding the income tax on the settlement fees. The judgment of the lower court denying that the Respondent had a duty to withhold the income tax and dismissing the determination of the Petitioner for taxation purposes was appropriate ..."

[Dissenting Opinion]

"We [two judges of a 5-judge panel] disagree with the majority opinion that the settlement fees in this case did not amount to the royalty as defined in the Income Tax Act, Sec. 161(7-1) for the following reasons:

1. Facts established by the lower court show that the Respondent manufactured its own products in Japan and sold them to its US subsidiary, an independent business entity. Licensed products thus sold were imported into the US for sale in the US. The Respondent's business was therefore to manufacture and sell the licensed products in Japan. It was the US subsidiary that had to assume a liability of direct infringement of the subject US patent, but not the Respondent.
2. The settlement agreement aimed at resolving all of the outstanding disputes existing between the Respondent and Company B (Preamble F of the agreement). Several provisions are directed to the resolution of the outstanding disputes. For example, Article 2 provides a non-exclusive license under which the Respondent and its related company are allowed to manufacture, or have made licensed products under the subject US patent, and sell them directly or indirectly in the US in return for payments of the stipulated royalties. Article 4 sanctions any past infringements by the Respondent and its related company prior to the effective date of the agreement by waiving any legal action with regard to products manufactured or sold in the US prior to the agreement. In Article 5(a), Company B promises not to sue under the foreign patents corresponding to the subject US patent. Article 6(a) defines the payments made under the agreement as a consideration for the settlement of the outstanding disputes. From these provisions, it is clear that the resolution of the outstanding disputes between the Respondent and Company B was not only the direct infringement of the US patent by the sale of products in the US, but also possible infringements in other parts of the world, including the manufacture of licensed products outside the US and their possible re-sale in the US. ... Therefore, an appropriate interpretation should be that the dispute was not limited to the direct infringement of the subject US patent, but concerned all disputes arising in connection with the use of the invention and technology constituting the subject US patent.
3. -omitted-
4. Under the factual background as discussed above (Para. 1 through 3), the Respondent manufactured its own products in Japan and sold them to its US subsidiary for exportation to the US. The Respondent was not in a position to be liable for the direct infringement of the US patent. The royalties stipulated in the agreement were calculated in accordance with the sales price and the volume of such products at the time the Respondent sold them to its US subsidiary. Such royalties were required to be paid before their actual sale in the US. Thus, the royalties not only pertained to the license under the US patent and the sale of licensed products, but also to the license for the invention and technology constituting the subject US patent enabling the Respondent to manufacture the products in Japan and sell them. With the payment of such royalties, the Respondent obtained a waiver under Articles 2 and 4 of the agreement for infringement claims against its US subsidiary that was selling the licensed products in the US.
5. ... The royalties paid by the Respondent under the agreement can be considered as payments for the industrial property rights and other technology-based rights ... as provided for in the Income Tax Act, sec. 161(7)(i). The Respondent was engaging in the manufacture and sale of licensed products in Japan. Such royalties should be construed as domestic source income."

3. ANALYSIS

Simply stated, arguments in this case were whether the fees paid under the settlement agreement amounted to royalties for the US patent or foreign counterparts. The majority opinion regarded them as the royalty paid under the US patent while the dissenting opinion regarded as one under the foreign counterparts. The factor that affected the majority opinion was the territoriality of the US patent while it was the package license including foreign counterparts in the dissenting opinion.

Following the principle of source jurisdiction, the tax authority argued that the fees were taxable as domestic source income because of the place of production. This argument was based on the facts that a corresponding Japanese patent was included in the settlement agreement and that the products in question were manufactured and sold in Japan. This argumentation relied on the existence of patent license under the corresponding Japanese patent although it was not mentioned in the settlement agreement. The dissenting opinion supported this argumentation. The Respondent counter-argued, however, that the settlement fees are payments for the deal to settle the past infringement and trade off future royalties under the US patent at issue. As was noted above, the majority opinion supported this argument.

The deduction by the licensee of the withholding tax from the royalty to be paid to the licensor had been an established practice under the old treaty between Japan and the US. The courts had accumulated a case law which regarded the royalty as the domestic source income. There were four reported cases dealing with this issue. Three out of the four were from the courts,[2] and the remaining one was from the tax tribunal.[3]

Among the three court cases, the *Compressor* case of 1985[4] is a landmark decision in which the Tokyo District Court put more weight on the place of manufacture than the place of sale and use in determining the source country for taxation. As no appeal was made in the case, the District Court's decision became a precedent for tax practice.

In the present case, however, the majority opinion deviated from the decision in the *Compressor* case in view of the territoriality of US Patent. Although there was no specific reference in the decision, it can be reasonably presumed that the Supreme Court was aware of the forthcoming change of the withholding tax practice under the new Japan-US treaty. The Court seems to have sought compliance with the new treaty which adopts the principle of residence state jurisdiction rather than the source country jurisdiction. The fact that the decision in this case was delivered in June 2004, a month earlier than the effective date of the new Japan-US tax treaty, may witness the correctness of such presumption.

---

2. This *Daisy Wheel Printer* case, the *Compressor* case and Tokyo High Court, 25 September 1997, Case No. 69 (Gyō-Ko) of 1994, 48-9 Gyōseijiken Saihanreishū 661
3. Tax Tribunal, 13 May 2010, Saiketsujireishthū No. 79, the website of the Tax Tribunal <http://www.kfs.go.jp/service/JP/79/20/index.html>
4. Tokyo District Court, 13 May 1985, Case No. 3128 (Wa) of 1982, 577 Hanrei Times 79 = H. Kaneko et al. (eds.) Sozei Hanrei Hyakusen *(Hundred Selected Tax Cases)*, 3rd ed. 1992, 96 – *Compressor*.

4. COMPARATIVE REMARKS

In the 1990's when this case was pending, it was an international norm at least among the economically advanced countries that the avoidance of double taxation should be based on the principle of residence state jurisdiction. A quick review of international conventions would suffice to verify this fact.

a) Model conventions recommend residence state jurisdiction

In 1992, the Organisation for Economic Cooperation and Development (OECD) proposed a comprehensively modified version of the model convention. It is known that the OECD's model convention adopted the principle of residence state jurisdiction (Art. 12 OECD Model Tax Convention). The US government also announced a draft model income tax convention in 1996. The US model convention states in Article 12 that royalties arising in a contracting state and beneficially owned by a resident of the other contracting state may be taxed only in that other state. It is also known that the US initially proposed this model convention for negotiations of bilateral tax treaties. The Japan-US tax treaty is no exception.

b) Shift from source jurisdiction to resident state jurisdiction

Both the OECD Model Tax Convention and the US model convention adopted the principle of residence state jurisdiction. Given an adherence to source jurisdiction by the tax authority, the Japanese government was obliged to change its position toward residence state jurisdiction. In the new Japan-US tax treaty agreed upon in 2003, the Japanese government made a concession so as to exempt from the taxes on income within the source country subject to the submission of a set of documents to be filed by the beneficiary owner. This was the first tax treaty in which Japan waived the principle of source jurisdiction.

Many countries that in principle follow the OECD model still require the licensee to notify domestic tax authorities of the payments and require the licensee to pay a certain percentage to the national authorities (for example in Germany: 15,825%) that can subsequently be reclaimed by the licensor upon proof that taxes on the royalties have been paid in the country of residence.

Case No. 64

Antimonopoly Act – Patent Licensing Agreement – Vertical Restraints – Maximum Output Restriction

Jinzō Fujino

A scheme whereby a patent licensee is allowed to produce the patented products for free up to the amount of 75% of the estimated annual demand of each municipality divided by the number of licensed bidders, while the remainder must be purchased from the licensor that sells such products to the licensee under the latter's brand at a price that includes a royalty (maximum output limitation), qualifies as a lawful exercise of the patent right and is not anti-competitive.

Intellectual Property High Court, 20 July 2006, Case No. 10015 (Ne) of 2006 – *Manhole Cover*

Hinode Suidō Kiki v. Roppō Sangyō

---

1. BACKGROUND

The Antimonopoly Act (AMA), enacted in 1947, aims at promoting fair and free competition by prohibiting private monopolisation, unreasonable restraint of trade and unfair trade practices. The AMA exempts, however, the enforcement of intellectual property rights from its application. The AMA sets forth in sec. 21 as follows:

> The provisions of this Act do not apply to acts found to constitute an exercise of rights under the Copyright Act, Patent Act, Utility Model Act, Design Act or Trademark Act.

Given the statutory exemption, however, it was not clear what acts would cause the violation of the AMA. To answer this question, the authority of competition policy, the Japan Fair Trade Commission (JFTC), announced the Guidelines relating to Know How and Patent License Agreements in 1999 ("Old Guidelines"). The Old Guidelines were extensively revised in 2006 and partly in 2016.

The Old Guidelines showed examples of clauses which might be considered to cause a violation of the AMA. The following four types of restrictions were considered to be "grey" under the AMA:

1) Restrictions on the scope of the license (e.g., territories and/or durations);
2) Restrictions and obligations on the license (e.g., restrictions imposed in connection with activities for research and development);

3) Restrictions and obligations with regard to the manufacture of licensed products (e.g., upper limits and minimum requirements of production); and
4) Restrictions and obligations on the sale with regard to the sale of licensed products (e.g., upper limits and minimum requirements of marketing)

In the case discussed below, arguments were made as to whether the numerical output limitation amounted to the restriction to violate the AMA.

2. DECISION[1]

a) Facts

The plaintiff is the owner of a patent that relates to covers for manholes. The defendant is its non-exclusive licensee. These patented manhole covers for most of the municipalities in the northern Kyushu area have become a de-facto standard in that they have to be used in public work constructions for sewage systems. The plaintiff has agreed to grant licences to all successful bidders of public construction tenders.

The licensing agreement in question contains a maximum output limitation for the licensee that the latter is alleged to have been in breach of. The plaintiff now sues for damages.

The contractual terms of the licensing agreement stipulated the following:

(1) A numerical output limitation arrived at the following formula: 75% of the estimated demand of each municipality for manhole covers divided by the number of registered bidders for this area.
(2) Should there be a demand exceeding this limit, the licensor should produce this amount and furnish it to the licensee under the latter's brand (OEM).
(3) The licensee should furnish the licensor with quarterly sales figures, and should immediately inform the licensor if the output limit was reached.
(4) The licensor would not request a licensing fee for those manhole covers produced within the numerical limit.

It turned out that at a certain point, the licensee exceeded the above production quota without informing the licensor.

The agreement was part of a number of licensing agreements the licensor concluded with registered construction companies that could take part in bids for public works. All of these got the agreements and the same conditions, that is, 75% of their estimated market share could be produced by themselves, while the rest would be furnished by the licensor under the licensee's brand, and sold through the licensee. As the price of these 25% was not fixed, the licensor could charge an amount that could comfortably cover the royalties also for the first 75%. In addition, the agreements could well throttle a licensee who was more successful than the others in obtaining public bids, as the fixed amount for production would in this case cover much less than 75% of its total output.

1. Translation in IIC 2009, 617 = T. Kanai et al. (eds.), Keizaihō Hanrei Shinketsu Hyakusen *(Hundred Selected Competition Cases)*, 2nd ed. 2017, 186

The Osaka District Court (decision of 16 January 2006, 1947 *Hanrei Jihō* 108) found the above output restriction in compliance with sec. 21 of the Antimonopoly Act and awarded damages to the plaintiff in the amount of 8.2 million Yen. The defendant's appeal was dismissed.

b) Reasons

According to sec. 21 of the Antimonopoly Act, the provisions of this Act shall not apply to acts that qualify as the exercise of rights under the Copyright Act, the Patent Act, the Utility Model Act, the Design Act or the Trade Mark Act. In the case of patent rights, this refers to sec. 68 of the Patent Act that grants an exclusive right over the exercise of the patented invention, and the same holds true for utility models under sec. 16 of the Utility Model Act and Designs under sec. 23 of the Design Act. That means that cases that qualify as the exercise of the patent right are exempt from the application of the Antimonopoly Act with the purpose of promoting inventions, models and the creation of designs in order to foster progress in industry, sec. 1 of the Patent Act, sec. 1 of the Utility Model Act, sec. 1 of the Design Act. Yet acts that do not comply with this overall purpose qualify as an unlawful exercise of the patent right and are thus not exempt from the application of the Antimonopoly Act. According to the findings of the first instance court, Art. 4(1) of the licensing agreement provides that for the period of the agreement, the manufacture and sale of the patented products was limited to a certain amount. Art. 4(2) required in the case that production or sale exceeded this limit for the licensor to supply to the licensee with those goods exceeding the limit for the licensee to sell these goods as supplied by the licensor under the licensee's brand (OEM manufacture). Art 6 of the agreement provides that the licensor will not ask for a licensing fee where the licensee stays within the numerical limit for the production and sale of the patented products. Thus, according to this contractual provision, the licensor would allow the licensee the free exploitation of the patent right until the agreed number of goods was reached, while for the number exceeding this limit, the licensee would receive the goods from the licensor in trust and the licensing fee for the use of the patent right be included in the commercial price of the entrusted products.

According to the facts as ascertained, the limit for production and sale was based on the licensor's calculation of the annual demand of municipal governments for iron covers, and set at 75% thereof, divided approximately equally by the number of the registered undertakings. Beyond such limit, products would be sold by the licensor to the licensee with a profit meant to cover the licensing fee. The licensor had also concluded patent licensing agreements with other suppliers of covers that contained a corresponding clause.

Thus, in respect of the relevant patent, the licensor agreed to a sale and production up until the numerical limit free of charge, while for any production of a number exceeding this limit, it would be the licensee's obligation to entrust it to the licensor. There is nothing unreasonable in itself about such a formula for concluding non-exclusive licensing agreement with these contents. In addition, the limitation up to which the products can be produced free of charge is calculated according to the demand of local governments, and hereby taking into account the market share of other registered construction companies is not unreasonable, either.

According to the defendant, as the municipal governments have specified that manhole covers for the sewage system should be built according to the *Hinode Suidō Kiki* [the plaintiff] standard, by granting such non-exclusive licenses the licensor aims at a market control, and the numerical limits are imposed with the prospect of such market control in view of the actual demand. According to the evidence, the patent right may not be exercised in order to obtain an undue profit, and the numerical limit may give rise to problems under the Antimonopoly Act. However, in the case at issue, the non-exclusive licensing agreement stipulates a royalty-free production of the goods up to a numerical limit that is calculated according to the set demand by the municipal governments (in this respect, there is no basis to conclude that the set demand in itself is unreasonable because calculated as too low) and set as an average of 75% thereof, while there is the obligation for the licensee to obtain the amount exceeding this number from the licensor. On the evidence submitted, there is no proof that the result of such scheme has in fact the effect of distorting supply and demand or impeding fair competition between entrepreneurs in the market for manhole covers in municipalities, and the numerical limit as stipulated in the agreement does not amount to an undue exercise of the patent right and thus no contravention of the Antimonopoly Act.

According to the defendant, the obligation that products exceeding the stipulated amount under Art. 4 of the agreement should be purchased from the licensor on an exclusive basis would mean a coordination of prices and as a result lead to a price monopolisation. However, the fact that under the free licence, goods can be produced and sold up to the stipulated number, while for any number in excess thereof, goods have to purchased from the licensor in order to allow the licensor to obtain a royalty-equivalent remuneration for the patent in question through a profit from such OEM, in itself is not an undue exercise of the patent right, and there is no evidence that this amounts to any price fixing for iron covers by the plaintiff.

Furthermore, and regarding the numerical limitation under Art. 4 of the agreement, the defendant alleges that other registered traders but for a significant drop in manufacturing prices would not be in a position to undercut the plaintiff's bid, resulting in a factual restraint of competition. After all, the plaintiff despite maintaining high prices between 22 December 2004 and 13 December 2005 won all 14 public tenders in the area of Fukuoka. However, even if for the 14 public tenders in the district of Fukuoka the plaintiff was the successful bidder in all of these, this says nothing about who in the year 2005 was successful in public tenders in other municipalities. Furthermore, as to the bidding price in a tender, the possibility of successful bidding depends on the intention and the market regarding each bidder, and when the patentee in comparison to a bidder without a corresponding patent right from the point of view of the price offers a more viable position, then this does not amount to unfair trading … If, as a result, the plaintiff successfully made 14 tender offers (the timing of which does not correspond to the period of the licensing agreement in this case), and when only taking into account the plaintiff's bidding price, it cannot be established that the clause in the licensing agreement limiting the production has led to an undue increase in prices …

3. ANALYSIS

a) This case and the Guidelines

The exercise of an intellectual property right is statutorily exempt from the application of the Antimonopoly Act (AMA). Partly for this reason, cases on this issue have rarely been brought to the courts. But this does not necessarily mean that there were no arguments on this issue. In the case of patent infringements or a breach of a licensing agreement, for example, defendants often raise the defence that the plaintiff's exercise of its intellectual property rights violates the AMA.

One of the grounds on which defendants often sought to justify their defence was the arrangement of multiple licenses by the plaintiff. However, the Old Guidelines of 1999 gave a perspicacious message that a non-exclusive license for a plurality of licensees or multiple licensees should not be considered a violation of the AMA so far as the terms and conditions of the non-exclusive license were fair and equal to each licensee. Only exception, according to the Guidelines, was a situation where the license included discriminatory or restrictive terms and conditions against (multiple) licensees.

In the present case, however, the licensing agreement had a clause to impose an output limitation on the licensee. Under the agreement, the licensee was also required to purchase the licensed products from the licensor in addition to the output limitation. Singling these restrictions out, the defendant argued that a combination of the output limitation and the purchase requirement would amount to a restraint which might constitute a violation of the AMA. However, this argument was not successful. Rejecting the argument of the defendant, the Intellectual Property High Court affirmed the decision of the Osaka District Court which found no AMA violation.

The Old Guidelines included, as an example of AMA violations, a concerted-price fixation for manhole covers which were produced by seven manufacturers including the plaintiff to this case.[2] Being aware of the reputation of *Hinode Suido Kiki* in the region, the defendant might have expected that its arguments for defence would have a psychological support in the proceedings, but this was not so.

The Old Guidelines were extensively revised in 2007. It should be noted that the revised text of the new Guidelines no longer regard the clause to limit the production volume by the licensee as a *per se* violation of the AMA.[3] When the case was decided by the High Court in 2006, the JFTC had already changed its basis for determination of the AMA violation from the *per se* rule to the rule of reason.

In this case, it was not argued before the court whether the plaintiff would have had any obligation to refrain from enforcing its patent against the defendant as the plaintiff had agreed that the patented technology had been adopted in the design specification of the manhole covers. This is a more contemporary argument based on the licensor's duty to offer a fair, reasonable and non-discriminatory (FRAND)

---

2. See, JFTC, Decision of 10 September 1993, Case No. 2 (Han) of 1991, 40 Kōseitorihiki Iinkai Shinketsushū 3 = T. KANAI et al. (eds.), Keizaihō Hanrei Shinketsu Hyakusen *(Hundred Selected Competition Cases)*, 2nd ed. 2017, 184
3. The Guidelines for the Use of Intellectual Property under the Antimonopoly Act of 2007, revised 2016

license as the holder of a standard-essential patent. In order to deal with the FRAND issue, a few paragraphs were added to the text of the new Guidelines in 2016. Under patent law, this issue is further discussed in Case No. 52.

b) Related case law

There are a limited number of cases in Japan where the JFTC determined that the exercise of intellectual property rights caused the violation of the AMA, including the *Paramount Bed* case[4] and the *Pachinko Slot Machine* case.[5] The latter is discussed in detail in Case No. 65.

In the *Paramount Bed* case, the Tokyo metropolitan government sought a bid for hospital beds specifying design specifications for the bed. The design specifications included features which were covered by patents and utility models owned by the *Paramount Bed*. The existence of the patented features turned out to exclude other companies from participating in the bid opened by the metropolitan government. The patented features, according to the evidence, were introduced in the design specification by the metropolitan government following advice given in bad faith by a sales person of the *Paramount Bed*.

In the *Pachinko Slot Machine* case, a consortium of major patent holders formed patent pool arrangement with the intent to exclude new comers in the market by way of refusing licenses to the non-members. A license under the patent pool arrangement was denied even to a member when and if they merged with a non-member company. The management of the consortium was handled by representatives of the member companies. These facts caused the JFTC to conclude that the consortium violated the AMA by way of restrictive licensing policies to exclude others. For details, see Case No. 65.

In these cases, the JFTC found the intent of private monopolisation by way of excluding others under the patent.

4. COMPARATIVE REMARKS

a) US Guidelines and EU Guidelines

Historically, the **US** antitrust authority regarded output limitations as per se illegal. However, in the early 1980s, the Antitrust Division began to question the theory underlying the Nine No-No's, focusing on the principle that unconstrained patent licensing increases the value of patents and encourages licensing and innovation. In 1988, the Antitrust Division formalised the "Antitrust Enforcement Guidelines for International Operations" which adopted a "rule-of-reason" approach to patent

---

4. JFTC, Decision of 31 March 1998, Case No. 3 (Kan) of 1998, 44 Kōseitorihiki Iinkai Shinketsushū 362 = T. KANAI et al. (eds.), Keizaihō Hanrei Shinketsu Hyakusen *(Hundred Selected Competition Cases)*, 2nd ed. 2017, 32 – *Paramount Bed*.
5. JFTC, Decision of 6 August 1997, Case No. 5 (Kan) of 1997, 44 Kōseitorihiki Iinkai Shinketsushū 238 = T. KANAI et al. (eds.), Keizaihō Hanrei Shinketsu Hyakusen *(Hundred Selected Competition Cases)*, 2nd ed. 2017, 22 – *Pachinko Slot Machine*.

licensing that allowed for a balancing of the pro-competitive effects of licensing against possible anticompetitive effects in related markets.

In 1995, the Department of Justice and the Federal Trade Commission (FTC) released the new "Antitrust Guidelines for the Licensing of Intellectual Property" (IP guidelines). The IP guidelines shared the core principle expressed in the 1988 guidelines: An explicit recognition of the generally pro-competitive nature of licensing arrangements; a clear rejection of any presumption that intellectual property necessarily creates market power in the antitrust context; and an endorsement of the validity of applying the same general antitrust approach to the analysis of conduct involving intellectual property that the agencies apply to conduct involving other forms of tangible or intangible property. Under the IP guidelines, antitrust concerns in licensing arrangements including output limitation normally will be evaluated under the rule of reason.

In the **EU**, the latest Technology Transfer Block Regulation was published in 2014.[6] The Regulation covers licensing agreements in relation to most intellectual property rights. Anti-trust concerns are tagged to a minimum market share in addition to specific clauses that are perceived anti-competitive.[7] Output restrictions are one of the hardcore restrictions in Art. 2 generally deemed anti-competitive:

> "1. Where the undertakings party to the agreement are competing undertakings, the exemption provided for in Article 2 shall not apply to agreements which, directly or indirectly, in isolation or in combination with other factors under the control of the parties, have as their object any of the following:
>
> ...
>
> (b) the limitation of output, except limitations on the output of contract products imposed on the licensee in a non-reciprocal agreement or imposed on only one of the licensees in a reciprocal agreement;"

In the Japanese case at issue, the output limitation was non-reciprocal.

From these, it appears that the case would be in conformity with the guidelines of the US and EU.

6. Commission Regulation (EU) No 316/2014 of 21 March 2014 on the application of Article 101(3) of the Treaty on the Functioning of the European Union to categories of technology transfer agreements Text with EEA relevance, https://eur-lex.europa.eu/legal-content/EN/TXT/HTML/?uri=CELEX:32014R0316&from=EN. The Regulation takes a generally positive stance towards licensing: "Such agreements will usually improve economic efficiency and be pro-competitive as they can reduce duplication of research and development, strengthen the incentive for the initial research and development, spur incremental innovation, facilitate diffusion and generate product market competition."
7. Preamble 11: "For technology transfer agreements between non-competitors it can be presumed that, where the individual share of the relevant markets accounted for by each of the parties does not exceed 30% and the agreements do not contain certain severely anti-competitive restrictions, they generally lead to an improvement in production or distribution and allow consumers a fair share of the resulting benefits."

Case No. 65

Patent Pools, Refusal to License and Abuse of a Dominant Position

Christopher Heath

The refusal of a licensing request of another slot machine manufacturer by the pachinko patent pool group prevents competition in the field of manufacturing pachinko machines in Japan, is no exercise of the rights under the patent or utility model laws within the exception of the Anti Monopoly Act, and contravenes the prohibition of private monopolisation.

Japanese Fair Trade Commission, 20 June 1997 – *Pachinko Patent Pool*

In re Sanyo K.K. et al.

---

1. BACKGROUND

a) This case concerns the abuse of a dominant marketing position by a patent pool in a very typical Japanese entertainment industry: Pachinko.

> "As of 2002, there were 16,504 pachinko parlours throughout the country, and the number of pachinko machines and pachinko slot machines totalled 4.83 million. This number should be surprising when compared to the 600,000 slot machines in the U.S., which has a population twice the size of Japan."[1]

Although the pachinko industry has shrunk in recent years, "the Wall Street Journal reported in 2012 that the pachinko market is five times the size of the Las Vegas gambling industry."[2]

b) Sec. 21 Japanese Anti Monopoly Act (hereinafter AMA) (formerly sec. 23) in its present wording reads as follows:

---

1. K. HIRANO/K. TAKAHASHI, Trends of Japan's Giant Leisure Industry: Pachinko, available at the website of the repository of the University of Nevada <http://digitalscholarship.unlv.edu/cgi/viewcontent.cgi?article=1184&context=grrj>.
2. M. SCHULZ, Japan is the largest slot-machine market, available at the website http://casino.sportsinteraction.com/articles/land-based/japan-is-the-worlds-largest-slot-machine-market-10613/ (accessed June 2018).

Sec. 21 (Intellectual property rights)

The provisions of this Act shall not apply to acts that qualify as the exercise of rights under the Copyright Act, the Patent Act, the Utility Model Act, the Design Act, or the Trade Mark Act.

Sec. 21 was renumbered in 2000 in an amendment to the AMA, and literature prior to 2000 refers to the section as sec. 23. The wording, however, remained completely unchanged.

2. DECISION[3]

a) Facts

The ten businesses in question employ a total of 3,584 employees and manufacture pachinko machines. They hold a market share for these machines of 90% and in 1995 had a total turnover of 550 billion Yen from manufacturing and selling about 3.5 million pachinko machines. For some time, the ten businesses have had a superior capacity in developing pachinko machines. They own a significant number of patents and utility models for the manufacturing of pachinko machines. The businesses empowered the Society for Administering Japanese Pachinko Patents ("Society") to decide about granting non-exclusive licences, about entering into licensing agreements with a duration of one year, the issuing of certificates and the collection of licensing fees, yet the businesses also took part in the decision of whether or not to grant licences. The ten businesses directly or indirectly hold a majority stake in the Society and nominate a significant number of its directors.

In 1961, the above Society was founded by the manufacturers of pachinko machines organised in the Pachinko Association of Japan ("Association") with the purpose of carrying out all business related to the granting and obtaining of licences for intellectual property rights (IPR) related to the manufacture of pachinko slot machines. Since its foundation, the Society has granted licences with one-year durations to all of its members. Since 1979, the Society has been empowered to identify those patents and utility models owned by one of its ten members that were open to be licensed, and to administrate these rights. Without the use of those patents and utility models that are administered by the Society it is virtually impossible to manufacture pachinko slot machines in conformity with the safety regulations under the Restaurant Act. All 19 members of the Association, that is, essentially all manufacturers of pachinko slot machines in Japan, have obtained licences for the manufacture of pachinko slot machines.

Competition in the field of selling pachinko slot machines to the about 18,000 pachinko parlours has always been rather limited. As early as 1987, the maximum number of machines to be certified by way of a security check introduced by the Society for each of the 19 businesses was set. Since about 1989, the pricing policies of

3. Published in 44 Kōsei Torihiki Iinkai Shinketsushū 238. (Hereafter Kōsei Torihiki Iinkai Shinketsushū is referred as KTIS.)

each of the ca. 650 dealers that sell pachinko machines alongside the manufacturers have been limited.

With an eye on benefitting the members of the Association, the Society has never granted licences to non-members and even introduced a termination clause to licensing agreements with members in case of changes to the business, the name, the representatives and directors, and significant changes in the economic performance of the company. With the introduction of the "Fiibaa" (*fever*) pachinko slot machine in spring 1983 [a sort of combination of pachinko and slot machines], the market for pachinko machines expanded. During this time, large manufacturers of other slot machines tried to obtain access to the production of pachinko machines by way of purchasing the stock of pachinko machine manufacturers. Of the ten businesses, nine who were the owners of important patents in the field of pachinko machine production, as well as the Society, started in 1983 to include clauses in their licensing agreements to the effect that any intended change in ownership of the licensee had to be notified and, unless permission to such change was granted by the licensor, the licensing agreement would automatically be terminated. At that time, no licences were granted outside the group, and competition intensified. Due to this, fewer patents were administered by the Society. It thereby became possible to manufacture pachinko machines without licences from the Society. The system of limiting price competition set up by the Society was disbanded and led to concerns by the manufacturers of pachinko machines about their profits.

Against this background, nine pachinko machine manufacturers and the Society agreed on a new scheme in order to exclude outsiders and to limit price competition. Until 1985, the termination clauses that related to termination in case of takeover in the licensing agreements for those patents and utility models administered by the Society were to be enforced in order to increase the entry barriers for outsiders. No licences were to be granted to outsiders. Subsequently, this led to the exclusion of outsiders. The tenth company joined the agreement in the fiscal year of 1994.

The ten businesses and the Society succeeded in preventing the market entry of several outsiders by acting according to the agreement in the following two cases:

1. In 1985, a large manufacturer of slot machines that was not a member of the Society wanted to gain access to the pachinko machine market by purchasing the majority of stock of one of the members to the Society. In response to this, nine members and the Society refused an extension to the licensing agreements beyond May 1985 on the ground that the market entry would have a significant impact on other manufacturers and would seriously affect their interests.
2. In September 1995 the above ten businesses and the Society refused a licensing request of a former member of the Association and another major manufacturer of slot machines that intended to jointly manufacture pachinko machines.

Other companies that were interested in the manufacture and sale of pachinko machines also desisted from requesting a licence because they understood that they would not receive such licence.

b) Reasons

According to the above facts, the ten businesses and the Society jointly, prevented competition in the field of manufacturing pachinko machines in Japan. This is contrary to the public interest, it does not exercise the rights under the patent or utility model laws and contravenes the prohibition of private monopolisation (sec. 3(i), 2(5) AMA). Therefore, the JFTC makes the following order:

1. Sankyo et al. are to cease and desist from jointly excluding others from the market of making pachinko machines.
2. Sankyo et al, are to repeal the before-mentioned measures concerned with the grant or refusal of non-exclusive licences.
3. a) The Society in managing the licensing agreements is prohibited from inserting a contractual clause that would require the consent of the Society (or would otherwise lead to the cancellation of the contract) when the licensee changes its trade name, mark, representative, or board members.
   b) Sankyo et al. in drafting the contracts related to the manufacture of pachinko machines are prohibited from requiring permission whenever the licensee changes the set-up of its company or business situation, or from inserting such clause in the contract, or from terminating the contract in such case.
4. Sankyo et al. are to bring the following to the attention of third parties who manufacture or intend to manufacture pachinko machines:
   a) The orders under above 1. - 3.
   b) Joint measures that prevent the exclusion by mutual or collusive acts of those who in the future seek a licensing agreement for the manufacture of the above machines from the owners or managers of these rights.

   As to the method of making this completely known, this will have to be agreed beforehand with the JFTC.
5. Sankyo et al. are not to refuse the licence of patents or utility models and prevent entry into the field of manufacture of pachinko machines.
6. Sankyo et al are to swiftly notify the JFTC of measures taken in order to comply with the orders 1. - 4. as above.

3. ANALYSIS

a) The *Pachinko Patent Pool* decision was instrumental in defining Japanese Fair Trade Commission (JFTC) position towards horizontal restraints. It held that a refusal to license amounts to an unlawful attempt at monopolisation (AMA secs. 3, 23) in a situation where several patent holders have pooled their patents in the same technical field in which they hold a market share of 90% and license exclusively amongst themselves, and where market entry is possible only by obtaining a licence. The JFTC did not order the society administering the patent pool to grant a licence to a specific third party, but ordered the society to cease their anti-competitive behaviour, i.e. the refusal of licences to non-members. The decision was upheld by a decision of the Tokyo High Court on 4 June 2003,[4] and the JFTC has taken the same approach in a decision on 27 February 2009 against the collecting society *JASRAC*, which calculated copyright levies on an across-the-board price rather than based on actual use, thereby effectively preventing other collecting societies from entering the market.[5] The latter decision was overturned by the Appeal Board of the JFTC on 12 June 2012, yet confirmed on appeal by the Tokyo High Court (decision on 1 November 2013) and the Supreme Court on 28 April 2015.[6]

b) It took the JFTC a long time to explicitly state its opinion on the relationship between sec. 23 and the application of the AMA. One would have expected such a statement in the first guidelines on patent and know-how licensing agreements of 1968. However, these guidelines were based on sec. 6 AMA, the prohibition of unfair business practices in international agreements. The guidelines were thus less concerned with IPRs as such than with restrictions imposed on the (presumably weaker) Japanese licensee. Only the subsequent 1999 guidelines make explicit mention of the relationship between IPRs and the AMA:

> "... For instance, even if an act is, on its face, considered to be an exercise of rights under the Patent Act, etc., if the said act is conducted under the pretext of exercising rights but in reality is considered to be employed as part of a series of acts that constitute an unreasonable restraint of trade or private monopolisation, the said act is considered to deviate from or to run counter to the purposes of the IPR system to, among other things, encourage innovation and, for this reason, the said act is no longer deemed an 'act recognisable as the exercise of rights' under the Patent Act, etc., and is subject to the Antimonopoly Act ..."[7]

Subsequently the JFTC issued a decision that concerned restrictions on the sale and distribution of software. The copyright owner and defendant, Sony Computer Entertainment, had requested retailers and wholesalers to strictly comply with the policy of no discount, no second-hand sales and no under-the-counter sales of PlayStation software. In its decision the FTC held that

> "In this case the act of prohibiting the sale of second-hand goods was carried out in connection with the act of fixing the retail price, and worked as an additional fortification thereof. However, the act of fixing retail prices including the act of prohibiting the sale of second-hand articles is detrimental to fair competition. Therefore, even if, as argued by the defendant, the PlayStation software is considered a cinematographic work which is given additional distribution rights, and if the act of prohibiting the sale of second-hand articles is within the scope

4. Tokyo High Court, 4 June 2003, Case No. 4085 (Ne) of 2002 – *Pachinko Patent Pool – Arze v. Samy*.
5. English press release on the JFTC's homepage. German summary in 2011 GRUR Int. 276.
6. Supreme Court, 28 April 2015, Case No. 75 (Gyō-Hi) of 2014, 69-3 Minshū 518. German translation in GRUR Int. 2016, 78.
7. Guidelines for Patent and Know-how Licensing Agreements, Fair Trade Commission, July 1999. The summary is accessible in the annual report of 1999 at the website of the JFTC <https://www.jftc.go.jp/info/nenpou/h11/11top00001.html>. The revised version, Chitekizsaisan no riyō ni kansuru dokusen kinshihō jō no shishin *(Guidelines of Anti Monopoly Act for Use of Intellectual Property)* is available at the website of JFTC <https://www.jftc.go.jp/dk/guideline/unyoukijun/chitekizaisan.html>.

of such distribution rights, such act would still deviate from or run counter to the purpose of the IP protection system."[8]

The underlying considerations of the FTC when issuing the Guidelines on Patent and Know How Agreements of 1968, 1989 and 1999, and the latest Guidelines for the Use of Intellectual Property Rights under the Anti-Monopoly Act of 28 September 2007 were basically the following:

(1) Clauses imposed on the licensee that were unenforceable;
(2) Restrictions on the licensee's research capacity; and
(3) Leverage of the IPR to impose other restrictions that are deemed anti-competitive.

Cases of (1) can best be exemplified by the JFTC's *Nihon Record II* decision.[9] Here, certain manufacturers of audio discs had tried to prevent shops from renting out these discs to customers. Since the Copyright Act at that time did not provide for any specific rights of rental and lending, the obligation was unenforceable. It was anti-competitive to try to enforce the restriction by way of boycotting these shops.

Case (2) concerns limits imposed on the licensee in further developing the licensed technology, or unilateral grant-back clauses without due remuneration.[10]

Case (3) concerns other restrictions imposed on the licensee, e.g. tie-in sales[11] or resale price maintenance schemes.[12] The issue of maximum output restrictions remains unclear.[13]

c) While the JFTC has been very active in pursuing vertical restraints in technology transfer agreements, horizontal restraints ("undue restraint of trade" under sec. 3

8. JFTC, 1 August 2001, 612 Kōsei Torihiki 64 (2001) w. comment by SUWAZONO - *Sony Computer Entertainment.*
9. JFTC, 15 December 1983, 389 Kōsei Torihiki 34 - *Nihon Record II.*
10. Between 1969 and 1996, the JFTC found a contravention against this prohibition in no less than 1,986 contracts: H. IYORI/A. UESUGI, Chiteki shoyū ken to dokusen kinshihō *(Intellectual Property and Anti Monopoly Act)*, 52 Bessatsu NBL 25/26 (1998).
11. JFTC, 14 December 1998, 30 IIC 478 (1999) - *Microsoft*: "The licensing of a computer program to manufacturers of personal computers with the obligation to license also other programs of the same software maker with a significant market share constitutes an unfair trade practice and is unlawful". The case concerned the bundling of the programs "Word" and "Excel"
12. JFTC, 13 September 1965, 13 KTIS 72 - *Yakult*: resale price maintenance scheme for imported patented products.
13. See the rather inconclusive decision Tokyo High Court, 20 June 2006, Case No. 10015 (Ne) of 2006, 40 IIC 617 (2009) - *Manhole Cover* (Case No. 64 in this volume): "A scheme whereby a patent licensee is allowed to produce the patented products for free up to the amount of 75% of the estimated annual demand of each municipality divided by the number of licensed bidders, while the remainder must be purchased from the licensor, which sells such products to the licensee under the latter's brand at a price that includes a royalty (maximum output limitation), qualifies as a lawful exercise of the patent right and is not anti-competitive."

AMA)[14] or attempts of private monopolisation (also, sec. 3 AMA)[15] have rarely been subject to the JFTC's scrutiny.

In its Guideline on Joint Research and Development of 20 April 1993, the JFTC addressed the problem of undue restraints of trade in the course of technical cooperation agreements. It particularly identified restrictions regarding research activities, either outside the field of common research, or beyond the contractual period of time as unlawful. The same applies to restraints in research and development (R&D) for the jointly-developed technology, restraints in the grant-back for improvement inventions, and restraints in the sale of the developed products in terms of territory, suppliers, or retail price maintenance.

Restrictions in joint venture agreements may be objectionable when limiting competition between the partners. In one instructive case, a foreign company and a domestic company founded a joint venture meant to produce "power shovels" with technology obtained from the foreign partner. The domestic enterprise agreed not to compete with the products developed by the joint venture and not to export certain products to a number of Asian markets. The FTC qualified this as an abuse of a superior bargaining position (unfair trade practice).[16]

In the 1999 Guidelines for Patent and Know-how Licensing Agreements, the FTC, for the first time, offered a systematic approach on how to deal with private monopolisation and undue restraints of trade in connection with IPRs. This approach has essentially been repeated in the Guidelines for the Use of Intellectual Property Rights under the Anti-Monopoly Act of 28 September 2007.

According to the Guidelines, acts of prohibited private monopolisation are:

(1) Forming patent pools or cross-licensing agreements and refusing to grant licences without justifiable reasons to new entrants or existing businesses, or taking other measures that have the effect of impeding the market entry of other businesses;
(2) Acquiring patents and behaving as described in above (1); and
(3) Using licensing terms aimed at the exclusion of outsiders.

When cross-licensing agreements, open licensing schemes or patent pools are used in a manner contrary to the purposes of the system to stimulate innovation, they may also become prohibited acts of private monopolisation. The FTC would regard it as an act of private monopolisation when a cross-licensing scheme is set up for the purpose of accumulating all future improvement inventions made by members

14. JFTC, 23 April 1982, 381 Kōsei Torihiki 21 – *Fujisawa*: the parties to a lawsuit used a settlement to agree on a licensing agreement that obliged the licensee not to sell below a certain price. The JFTC viewed this as an unlawful restraint of trade, which it is not: it is rather a vertical restriction between licensor and licensee, and thus an unfair trade practice (resale price restriction): H. Iyori/A. Uesugi, Chiteki shoyū ken to dokusen kinshihō (above), 40. JFTC, 10 September 1993, 40 KTIS 3 – *Fukuoka Sewage System* concerned a joint activity of seven sewage companies, one the patentee, the others licensees, to agree on certain margins for bid-rigging schemes.
15. JFTC, 19 September 1951, 3 KTIS 166 – *Toho Subaru*: one market-dominating cinema tried to bully others out of the market by using its distribution rights for film works.
16. JFTC, 26 October 1981, 28 KTIS 79 – *Komatsu/Bicycrus*. Yet one might well argue that since the restrictions had not been imposed on the recipient of the licensed technology, it should have been classified as a case of undue restraint of trade between two potential competitors, H. Iyori/A. Uesugi, Chiteki shoyū ken to dokusen kinshihō (above), 39.

and when the scheme is meant to deny licensing of the jointly held patents to new market entrants without justifiable reason.[17] Also the strategic accumulation of patents in order to prevent others from entering the market could be regarded as an act of private monopolisation. Restrictive clauses in licensing agreements concluded by a licensor holding a patent that has become a market standard would also be regarded as an act of private monopolisation. Private monopolisation refers to specific markets, not specific technologies. For this reason, patents as "monopolies" that allow the exclusion of others rarely qualify as market monopolies. They may do so if pooled to an extent that they allow a control of market entry. Due to the rapidly changing technology markets, this is often difficult to ascertain.

Undue restraints of trade in connection with IPRs can occur if several enterprises in a cross-licensing or patent pool agreement impose a mutual restriction on the manufacturing volume, sales volume, sales price, sales outlets, sales territories, or other aspects of the patented products. It would be immaterial if these restrictions were directly agreed upon, agreed through a trade association (this would make sec. 8 AMA[18] applicable), or established in a joint venture agreement, as long as the result is an undue restraint.

Particular attention is given to the frequent Japanese practice of cross-licensing, granting several non-exclusive licences, and of patent pools. In the case of cross-licences, any additional restrictions on sales prices, quantities of production or sale, and territory would be interpreted as undue restraints of trade if this had a negative effect on the market. The same would be assumed for limitations on R&D. In the case of licensing the patent to several licensees, the agreement on mutual restrictions between the licensor and several licensees on sales prices, quantity of production, etc., would be considered as an undue restraint of trade. Patent pools per se are not regarded as restricting competition, as they may have pro-competitive effect. However, when the members of the patent pool agree on mutual restrictions of sales prices, quantities of production, R&D, this may amount to an undue restraint of trade.

d) A number of academics both specialised in intellectual property and in anti-trust have published their opinions on the interpretation of sec. 23/21 AMA, and with varying degrees of approval concur that a proper balance must be found between the lawful exercise of intellectual property rights, e.g. *Toyosaki*,[19] *Monya*,[20] *Kawaguchi*,[21] *Shōda*,[22]

17. The example given in the Guidelines shows that the JFTC does not regard the grant of a compulsory licence in such cases as a factor that would eliminate an anti-trust violation or that should be given precedence over any measures taken under the AMA.
18. Sec. 8 AMA prohibits trade associations from engaging in anti-competitive conduct.
19. K. TOYOSAKI, Kōgyō shoyūkenhō *(Industrial Property Law)*, Tokyo 1956, 273 *et seq.*
20. N. MONYA, Tokkyo ken, nouhau to dokusen kinshi seisaku *(Patent Law, Know-how and Anti-trust Policy)*, in: Dokusen kinshihō kōsu II *(Course on the Anti-trust Law II)*, Tokyo 1976, 293 *et seq.*
21. H. KAWAGUCHI, Tokkyo ken tō no kōshi to dokusen kinshihō no kankei *(The Exercise of Patent Rights, etc., and Its Relation to the Antimopoly Act)*, 21 Keizaihō 23 *et seq.* (1978).
22. A. SHŌDA, Zentei dokusen kinshihō I *(Commentary on the Antimonopoly Act, Vol. 1)*, Tokyo 1981, 223 *et seq.*; also idem, Patentlizenzverträge im japanischen Antimonopolgesetz *(Patent license in the Japanese Anti Monopoly Act)*, GRUR Int. 1997, 206 *et seq.*

Negishi,[23] *Nakayama*,[24] *Hienuki*[25] and *Shibuya*.[26]

It is interesting to note that despite differences in the details, specialists in both intellectual property and antitrust are of the unanimous opinion that sec. 23 does not justify restrictive clauses in licensing agreements. The application of the AMA to restrictive clauses in licensing agreements has consequently been the primary focus in the JFTC's practice.

e) It should further be mentioned that also the Japanese Patent Act foresees the possibility of granting a compulsory license. Sec. 83 Patent Act requires in this case that "a patented invention has not been sufficiently and continuously worked during a period of three years or more in Japan". The provision thereby follows Art. 5A(4) Paris Convention, and yet does not make use of the possibility provided for in Art. 5A(2) Paris Convention to grant compulsory licences also for types of abuse other than non-use. Not a single compulsory licence has been granted in Japan under this provision.[27] For the de-facto grant of a compulsory licence in the case of FRAND patents, see Case No. 52 – *FRAND Licence / Apple Samsung*.

4. COMPARATIVE REMARKS

In the **EU**, anti-trust aspects of patent pools have been addressed by the 2014 EU Guidelines on Technology Transfer.[28] The Guidelines take a rather critical view on patent pools being set up by a limited group of patent owners that is not open for all interested parties to join (para. 249). Where the inclusion of patents leads to collective bundling, the danger of price fixing, and, in the case of standard patents, the exclusion of outsiders, this is viewed as a breach of Art. 101 TFEU. In a case on the pooling of (all) patents related to stereo television by two German institutions, the Commission objected to the practice that only German manufacturers were licensed and all foreign manufacturers were excluded.[29] It found a restriction of competition "where the exercise of the patent rights thus acquired has the object and effect of excluding from the relevant market firms not belonging to the group ... This case in fact involved the joint acquiring and exercise of certain patents with

23. A. Negishi, Chiteki zaisan kenhō to dokusen kinshihō *(Intellectual Property Rights and the Antimonopoly Act)*, 15 Nihon Kōgyōshoyūken Hōgakkai Nenpō 65 (1991).
24. N. Nakayama, Kōgyō shoyū kenhō I *(Industrial Property Rights, Vol. I)*, Tokyo 1994, 38 *et seq.*
25. T. Hienuki, Chiteki zaisan to dokusen kinshihō *(Intellectual Property and the Antimonopoly Act)*, Tokyo 1994. Particularly interesting are Hienuki's views on cases of patent pools, cross-licensing agreements and patents in co-ownership where several patentees practise a joint licensing policy. The discrimination of one member in a group should be considered an act of domination by the majority of members and thus a case of private monopolisation. The exclusion of an outside entrepreneur from membership in a patent pool or cross-licensing agreement without just cause should also be considered an act of private monopolisation.
26. T. Shibuya, Tokkyo hō to dokusen kinshihō *(Patent Law and Anti-monopoly Law)*, N. Kokusaika, Kokusaika Jidai no dokusen kinshihō no kadai *(The Task of the Antimonopoly Act in an Era of Internationalisation)*, Writings in Honour of Akira Shōda, Tokyo 1993, 578 et seq.
27. N. Nakayama, Tokkyo hō *(Patent Law)*, 2nd. ed. Tokyo 2012, 483.
28. Guidelines on the application of Article 101 of the Treaty on the Functioning of the European Union to technology transfer agreements of 28 March 2014, OJ C 89 28.3.2014, 3.
29. Case *IGR Stereo Television*, reported in Eleventh Report on Competition Policy, Brussels 1981, 63.

a view to controlling the market in stereo television sets." A termination clause whereby participants of the patent pool lost all access to the licensed patent rights, but were still obliged to honour their licensing obligations towards the continuing members of the pool was found to be anti-competitive in a 1978 decision on video recording technology.[30]

In the **US**, The US Guidelines for Intellectual Property 2007 in chapter 3[31] address concerns for the exclusion of outsiders and restraints of trade by way of patent pools and cite the following case:

> "The Summit-VISX Pool
>
> In 1998, the FTC challenged a pool formed by Summit Technology, Inc. and VISX, Inc. that contained patents relating to the manufacture and use of lasers employed in performing photo-refractive keratectomy ("PRK"), which is a form of vision-correcting eye surgery. At the time, Summit and VISX were the only firms whose laser equipment had received marketing approval from the U.S. Food and Drug Administration for performing PRK. Through the pool, Summit and VISX relinquished the right to license their patents unilaterally, but each received the right to prohibit the pool from licensing any third party. The pool issued no third-party licenses over its six year existence. In addition, the pool agreement required ... The FTC alleged that the pool eliminated competition between Summit and VISX in the sale or leasing of PRK equipment, and in the licensing of technology related to PRK."[32]

Although in the US, a patent owner has no duty to practice his invention[33] or to licence it, a patent pool with a selective licensing policy to the participants of a patent portfolio firm, but not to outsiders, may be anti-competitive.[34]

30. *In re Video Cassette Recorders*, 1978 OJ L 47/42.
31. Chapter 3: Antitrust Analysis Of Portfolio Cross-Licensing Agreements And Patent Pools
32. Decision and Order, *In re VISX, Inc.*, 127 F.T.C. 236 (1999) (No. 9286); Complaint, *Summit*, 127 F.T.C. at 208 (No. 9286).
33. US Supreme Court, *Continental Paper Bag v. Eastern Paper Bag*, 210 U.S. 405 (1908).
34. US Supreme Court, *Hartford-Empire Co. v. United States*, 323 U.S. 386 (1945) for a cartel in the glass industry.

Case No. 66

Utility Model – Technical Assessment Report

Shoichi Okuyama

The Technical Assessment Report prescribed in sec. 12 of the Utility Model Act does not directly affect scope or validity of the utility model right, and therefore the appeal against such Report to the court based on the Administrative Litigation Act is inadmissible. The validity of a utility model right can only be determined by way of invalidity proceedings.

Tokyo High Court, 17 May 2000, Case No. 22 (Gyō-Ko) of 2000 –
Dental Mirror with Lighting Device

[X] v. Japanese Patent Office

---

1. BACKGROUND

It may be helpful at this stage to give a brief introduction to the system of utility model rights in Japan both before and after the 1993 revision.

The main features of the 1959 Utility Model Act were as follows:

(1) Protection could be sought for "innovations relating to the shape or structure of an article or combination of articles";
(2) Novelty remained confined to Japan except for printed publications;
(3) Rejected patent and registered design applications could still be converted into applications for utility models within 30 days;
(4) Examination and grant of utility models closely followed the rules for patent applications.

Some further amendments of utility model legislation were made in 1971 and 1987. On both occasions, the changes were in fact related to the patent system which also extended to utility models. In 1971, it was decided that all applications had to be open for public inspection after 18 months from the filing date. As of 1987, it became possible to file more than one independent claim per utility model application on condition that the unity of invention was maintained.

For a number of reasons, in 1993 the utility model system was substantially revised.[1] By the late 1980s, the number of patent applications had exceeded those of

---

1. Law No. 26/1993 of 23 April 1993.

utility models. In addition, there had been complaints that the process of substantive examination for utility models was too slow and should be scrapped. To compensate for the ensuing legal uncertainty, the protection period should be substantially shortened. To some academics, these changes sounded the death knell of the whole utility model system.[2]

The main features of the current utility model system are the following:

(1) protection for all kinds of inventions, except for processes, compositions of matter, chemical substances and computer programs;[3]
(2) grant of rights upon registration without substantive examination;
(3) protection period of ten years from the filing date (originally six years, extended to ten years in 2004);
(4) compulsory search carried out by the Japanese Patent Office (JPO); search report necessary before raising an infringement action.

By the 2004 amendment, it also became possible to amend claims for registered utility models. Prior to this change, only the deletion of claims was possible. It also became possible to convert a registered utility model into a patent application within three years from the filing date.

The two drawbacks of the current system are, first, that the value of utility models with regard to technology transfer is limited because the rights are unexamined and their substantive validity is thus unclear; and second, that there is little chance of succeeding in a claim for injunctive relief within the protection period of ten years.

By 1980, 185,455 utility model applications were filed and 44,600 rights granted. By 1990, however, the utility model system was past its prime. Applications peaked at over 200,000 a year in the mid 1980s, but by 1990 they were down to 138,294, with 44,290 grants. In 1993, immediately before the revision of the system, 77,101 utility models were applied for. By 1995, this figure had dropped to 14,886 and has meanwhile further dropped to a steady level of 7.000 applications per year.[4]

When the owner of the registration wishes to enforce the utility model right, it is necessary to obtain a "Utility Model Technical Assessment Report" on substantive requirements from the JPO. The alleged infringer has to be furnished with a copy of this Report. If the registration is found invalid during enforcement, the registrant may be held liable for damages that the enforcement caused to the alleged infringer

---

2. K. TAMAI, Tokkyo ni okeru mushinsa shugi no fukuken? (*Rehabilitation of the Principle of Unexamined Patents*), 1005 Jurist 55 [1992]; IDEM, Mushinsa tokkyo toshite no saisei ka kanman na shi ka (*Revival or Slow Death of Unexamined Patents?*), 1007 Jurist 63 (1992). On the revision process and its reasons, see also K. KOBASHI, Jitsuyo shin'anjhō kaisei no eikyō (*Influence of the Utility Model Act's revision*), 16 Kōgyō Shoyūken Hōgakkai Nenpō 151 (1992); K. KUMAGAI, Jitsuyo shin'an seido no minaoshi ni tsuite (*Perspectives of the Utility Model System*), 16 Kōgyō Shoyūken Hōgakkai Nenpō 135 (1992); F. ŌTSUKA, Revision des japanischen Gebrauchsmusterrechts (*Revision of the Japanese Utility Model Act*), 1993 Mitteilungen der deutschen Patentanwälte 132.
3. In the 1993 amendment, statutory language as to registrable subject matter remained unchanged. Only inventions relating to "the shape or structure of an article or combination of articles" are registrable.
4. See the JPO annual or status reports, available at the website of the JPO <http://www.jpo.go.jp/resources/report/nenji/index.html> or <https://www.jpo.go.jp/e/resources/report/statusreport/index.html>.

unless the registrant has received a positive assessment report from the JPO or a positive opinion from a patent attorney. Once registered, possibilities of amendment are very limited compared to pending patent applications.

The utility model technical assessment report, which any person may request, is a search report prepared by a JPO examiner with any one of the following six categories of assessment indicated for each claim:

1: Lack of novelty;
2: Lack of inventive step;
3: Lack of novelty over secret prior art;
4: Not patentable due to double patenting;
5: Existence of a conflicting (double patent) application, etc., filed on the same day;
6: No prior art found (including cases in which claims are indefinite and a meaningful search is not possible).

These categorical assessments are meant to indicate a likelihood. To invalidate a utility model registration, it is necessary to obtain an *inter partes* trial decision of invalidation before the Trial and Appeal Department of the JPO. Such decision has to become final and conclusive.

Also, it is possible for the registrant to amend the description and/or utility model claims within two months from the receipt of the first technical assessment report while possible types of amendments are limited.[5] After amendment, the registrant may request a second report.

As a matter of fact, it is not prohibited, but practically difficult to enforce a utility model right unless the registrant receives a report with assessment "6" (no prior art found), because the court may find the owner liable for damages caused

5. The relevant provisions on allowable amendments (called "corrections" to distinguish them from amendments made prior to grant) are found in sec. 14bis of the Utility Model Act.

Sec. 14bis Except for the following cases, a holder of utility model right may correct the description, scope of claims, or drawings attached to the application only once.

(i) where two months have lapsed from the date when the first Utility Model Technical Assessment Report of sec. 13(3) was served; and

(ii) where the time limit initially designated under Article 39(1) for a trial for invalidation of utility model registration has expired.

(2) The correction under the preceding paragraph shall be limited to those for the following purposes:

(i) restriction of the scope of claims;

(ii) correction of errors;

(iii) clarification of an ambiguous statement; and

(iv) changing the statement of claims, which cite other claims, into the statement, which do not cite the other claims.

(3) Any correction under paragraph (1) shall be made within the scope of the matters described in the description, scope of claims or drawings attached to the application (in the case of correction for the purpose of item (ii) of the preceding paragraph, the description, scope of claims or drawings originally attached to the application).

(4) The correction under paragraph (1) shall not substantially enlarge or alter the scope of claims.

...

to the alleged infringer by the enforcement of a utility model registration that has any of assessments "1" to "5." It is also possible for the alleged infringer to ask the JPO to invalidate the registration in addition to arguing invalidity before the infringement court.

2. DECISION[6]

a) Facts

In the present case, the plaintiff filed a utility model application on 30 April 1998 which was registered on 2 June 1999 as Registration No. 3060298. On 30 April 1998, the plaintiff asked for a Utility Model Technical Assessment (the Assessment) before the JPO. The JPO sent a report on 6 July 1999. In the report, claim 1 was found to belong to assessment "1" (lack of novelty) and claim 2 assessment "2" (lack of inventive step). The plaintiff filed a complaint before the Tokyo District Court and appealed before the Tokyo High Court, seeking cancellation of the Assessment.

The plaintiff's arguments involved legal and non-technical issues regarding such Assessment. The plaintiff argued that the Assessment is a disposition under sec. 3(2) of the Administrative Litigation Act and can be cancelled by the court for the following reasons: (a) while a utility model registration is deemed valid unless invalidated as a result of a trial for invalidation before the Japan Patent Office, if the utility model is assessed any of "1" to "5," the registration is substantially invalidated as the substantive requirements are not satisfied, and any of assessments "1" to "5" has a de facto binding effect with respect to the utility model registration, (b) because the utility model holder is required to show a Utility Model Technical Assessment Report at the time of warning, any of assessments "1" to "6" has legal effects, and (c) the proviso of sec. $29^{ter}(1)$ of the Utility Model Act stipulates that even if the JPO trial decision of invalidating the registration becomes final and conclusive, if the enforcement was done relying on assessment "6", the right holder will not be held liable for damages the enforcement caused to the opposing party unless special circumstances exist such as knowledge of existence of prior art that would invalidate the registration, and therefore, assessment "6" has legal effects.

b) Reasons

In the decision, the Tokyo High Court commented on the two new arguments the plaintiff presented on appeal, but otherwise relied on the judgement and reasoning of the Tokyo District Court without any substantial changes. The following are excerpts from the Tokyo District Court decision:

(1) The "disposition" mentioned in sec. 3(2) of the Administrative Litigation Act is understood to mean an act that directly forms the right and obligation of a citizen

---

6. Published at the website of the courts <http://www.courts.go.jp/app/files/hanrei_jp/151/013151_hanrei.pdf> = N. NAKAYAMA et al. (eds.), Tokkyo hanrei hyakusen *(Hundred Selected Patent Cases)*, 4th ed. 2012, 208 = T. ŌBUCHI et al. (eds.) Chitekizaisan hō hanrei shū *(Intellectual Property Law Case Book)*, 2nd ed. 2015, 222.

or defines their scope under the provisions of statutory laws among acts conducted by the state or a local government which is an entity that exercises public power.

(2) The Utility Model Act adapts the so-called non-examination registration system which registers a utility model right without examining substantive requirements for utility model registration. The question of whether the registered utility model right satisfies the substantive requirements or not is left for parties to decide, but such judgement requires technical skills and special expertise.

Thus, the Utility Model Act has provisions concerning "utility model technical assessment" and provides that: "With regard to an application for a utility model registration or a utility model registration, any person may file with the Commissioner of the Patent Office a request for a 'Utility Model Technical Assessment' as to the application of the registered utility model ... In this case, in respect of applications or registered utility models that contain two or more claims, such request may be filed for each claim" (sec. 12(1)), and "When a request under paragraph (1) is filed, the Commissioner of the Patent Office shall direct an examiner to prepare a written report containing a Utility Model Technical Assessment (hereinafter referred to as 'Utility Model Technical Assessment Report')" (sec. 12(2)[7]). The examiner prepares a technical assessment report to provide prior art documents and his or her evaluation of the validity to each claim of the right in view of such prior art documents.

The technical assessment according to sec. 12 of the Utility Model Act is to provide objective information for deciding on the validity of the utility model right that was registered without examination of substantive requirements, and it does not conclusively determine the validity or invalidity of the registered right and does not affect the strength of the right.

(3) The owner, etc. of the utility model right is required to show the technical assessment report at the time of warning when wishing to enforce the right (sec. 29bis Utility Model Act). With any of assessments "1" to "6," the owner, etc. is by no means prevented from enforcement. The technical assessment report according to sec. 12 Utility Model Act does not have any legally binding effect that affects the possibility of enforcement.

(4) Sec. 29ter(1) of the Utility Model Act stipulates that: "If a trial decision to the effect that the utility model registration is invalidated ... has become final and binding after the holder of utility model right or exclusive licensee exercised his/her right against, or gave warning thereof to, an infringer, etc., the holder or exclusive licensee shall be held liable to compensate damage sustained by the infringer, etc. as a result of the exercise of his/her right or the warning, with the proviso that this shall not apply where the holder or exclusive licensee exercised his/her right or gave warning thereof, based on the technical assessment stated in the technical assessment report (excluding those to the effect that the object claimed in the application for a utility model registration or the registered utility model cannot be registered ...), or using other due care."

The above provisions exist because the utility model right is registered without carrying out an examination of the substantive requirements. In order to prevent

7. Currently, the same provision appears under sec. 12(4).

abusive use of a defective right, the utility model right holder, etc. will be held liable unless he or she can prove that due care has been taken in the enforcement, etc. of the right.

As discussed earlier, the proviso in that paragraph is understood to mean that the main text of the same paragraph is not applicable if the enforcement was done replying to a technical assessment in a technical assessment report (excluding one providing an assessment that the registration cannot be sustained) because the technical assessment report is to provide objective information in determining the validity of the right. It is understood that the proviso does not provide that the right holder is positively exempted from liability for damages, and if the opposing party who was accused of infringement based on a defective right can prove that due care has not been paid in the enforcement, the right holder will be held liable for damages even if an affirmative technical assessment is involved.

Therefore, from the proviso in the same paragraph, it cannot be said that the technical assessment prescribed in sec. 12 of the Utility Model Act has the legal effect of directly determining the existence or nonexistence of liability for damages against the utility model owner or the like.

(5) As discussed above, the technical assessment prescribed in sec. 12 of the Utility Model Act neither directly confers rights and obligations for anyone nor defines their scope under the above legal provisions, and therefore, the assessment at issue is not a "disposition" under sec. 3(2) of the Administrative Litigation Act.

(6) Thus, the present lawsuit demanding the cancellation of the assessment at issue ... is therefore rejected ...

3. ANALYSIS

a) Discussion of this case

The decisions made by the Tokyo District and High Courts follow the statutory provisions of the Utility Model Act and are correct within the existing legal framework of the Utility Model Act. This is because the technical assessment report has the status of a non-binding opinion provided by the Japan Patent Office. Even if we look at the historical discussions made towards the 1993 amendments to the Utility Model Act, this is appropriate.[8]

One question, however, is the requirement of having and showing a technical assessment report issued by the JPO at the point of warning and enforcement. Almost all disputes related to patents or utility models are addressed to businesses, i.e., manufacturers and retailers. It may be argued that businesses do not have to be overly protected from possibly abusive accusations of utility model owners. In fact, the plaintiff's arguments seem to have some merit for future consideration because, in fact, the requirement of a technical assessment has weakened the effectiveness and utility of utility model registrations. When it was decided that substantive

8. See Japanese Patent Office (ed.), Kaisei Tokkyohō Jitsuyoshinanhō Kaisetsu (*Commentary on the amendments to the Patent and Utility Model Acts*), Yūhikaku 1994, 70-99 (third printing with revisions on 20 March 1994).

examination should be abandoned prior to utility model registration at the peak of utility model filings (200,000 a year), public sentiment was overly cautious about the enforceability of utility model rights. Now that we have less than 7,000 utility model applications per year, it may be useful to make some changes if we are not going to abandon the utility model system in its entirety.

The German Utility Model Act, for example, does not contain any provisions as to the requirement of a search report provided by the patent office at the time of warning or enforcement. The Chinese Utility Model Act does not provide for substantive examination prior to registration, but currently a simplified substantive examination is carried out. It also does not have any provisions as to the requirement of a search report.

b) Related cases

There are only a few utility model infringement cases in Japan. There are, however, some notable court decisions.

(1) Osaka District Court, 27 April 2006[9] and Osaka District Court, 19 November 2007[10]

These decisions dealt with the presumption of negligence prior to a warning letter sent by the owner of the utility model registration. In the former case, negligence was denied on the part of the alleged infringer prior to the warning sent by the plaintiff with a copy of the technical assessment report, although the plaintiff argued that a general warning was given without showing the report. Also in the latter case, no negligence was found prior to the warning sent with a copy of the technical assessment report. These decisions indicate a clear difference between utility models and patents for which negligence is presumed on the part of an alleged infringer.

(2) Osaka District Court, 17 March 2016[11]

This decision affirmed an infringement of a utility model right under the doctrine of equivalents and awarded the plaintiff damages in the amount of JPY 163 million (or about USD 1.5 million).

(3) Osaka District Court, 31 October 2000[12] and Osaka District Court, 26 March 2015[13]

In the former case, the right holder obtained a negative assessment in the technical assessment report for its utility model registration, but also had two positive opinions from patent attorneys. The right holder sent a warning to the alleged infringer showing the negative technical assessment report. The right holder was held liable for acts of

9. Osaka District Court, 27 April 2006, Case No. 13028 (Wa) of 2003, the website of the courts <http://www.courts.go.jp/app/files/hanrei_jp/961/032961_hanrei.pdf>.
10. Osaka District Court, 19 November 2007, Case Nos. 6536&12229 (Wa) of 2006, the website of the courts <http://www.courts.go.jp/app/files/hanrei_jp/408/035408_hanrei.pdf>.
11. Osaka District Court, 17 March 2016, Case No. 4916 (Wa) of 2014, the website of the courts <http://www.courts.go.jp/app/files/hanrei_jp/907/085907_hanrei.pdf>.
12. Osaka District Court, 31 October 2000, Case No. 5090 (Wa) of 1998, the website of the courts <http://www.courts.go.jp/app/files/hanrei_jp/874/012874_hanrei.pdf>.
13. Osaka District Court, 26 March 2015, Case No. 5064 (Wa) of 2014, the website of the courts <http://www.courts.go.jp/app/files/hanrei_jp/080/085080_hanrei.pdf>.

unfair competition by making public announcements of alleged infringement of the utility model. The announcements mentioned the existence of a negative technical assessment report, but stated that the registration was valid. Later the utility model registration was invalidated. In the latter case, the right holder was held liable for acts of unfair competition and violation of the Utility Model Act as it had warned a potential infringer and its dealers without showing the negative assessment of its utility model it had obtained.

4. COMPARATIVE REMARKS

Currently, the WIPO website lists more than 50 countries and two international organisations, which have introduced a utility model system,[14] which is a considerable number. Even if the Paris Convention mentions utility models as one category of industrial property and there exist constant efforts for the international harmonisation of intellectual property rights, until now no treaty or agreement has addressed utility model rights.[15] Utility models are said to be "small (or petty) patents" and the protection conferred is generally not as broad as for patents. Yet protection period, protected subject matter, requirements of substantive examination for registration or enforcement, etc. depend on domestic law.

a) In **Europe**, the European Commission proposed a harmonisation of the utility model system, but reached no agreement.[16] In an EC study published in 2013, the economic impact of utility model legislation was assessed. The study listed Belgium, the Netherlands, the UK and Sweden as countries with no utility model system, on the other hand Germany, etc. which have a utility model system. Many countries in Europe have a system with no substantive examination before grant, yet Poland makes a substantive examination as to novelty. The study shows that the systems are very different also in the EU.[17]

Germany was the first country in the world that introduced a utility model system back in 1891.[18] From the beginning, Germany opted for a registration right without substantive examination, yet excluded certain subject matter, namely processes: A limitation that still exists today. The validity of utility models is either decided by way of invalidation procedures before the German Patent and Trademark

14. Website of the WIPO <http://www.wipo.int/sme/en/ip_business/utility_models/where.htm>. There is also a comparison table of utility model systems in the world made by the JPO, which lists more than 80 countries, available at the website of the JPO <https://www.jpo.go.jp/news/kokusai/sangyouzasisankenhou_itiran.html>.
15. A legal and economic analysis of utility models is provided by U. SUTHERSANEN, The Economic Efficacy of Utility Model Protection, in: HEATH/KAMPERMAN SANDERS, Industrial Property in the Bio-medical Age, 2003, 231.
16. See the website of the EC <https://ec.europa.eu/growth/industry/intellectual-property/patents/utility-models_en>. It is interesting that the EC proposal included also the obligation of seeking a search report before enforcement.
17. Available at the website of the EC <https://publications.europa.eu/en/publication-detail/-/publication/830fedd7-a1cf-46bd-a460-ba4a9eb01e63>.
18. For the history of the law amendments in Germany, see KRASSER/ANN, Patentrecht *(Patent Law)*, 7th ed. 2016, 71; KRASSER, Developments in Utility Model Law, 26 IIC 950 (1995); KRASSER, Harmonisation of Utility Model Law in Europe, 31 IIC 797 (2000).

Office (GPTO) with an appeal to the German Federal Patent Court and the German Federal Supreme Court (current secs. 15 to 18 Utility Model Act), or assessed by the courts in infringement proceedings, sec. 19 (with an *inter partes* effect only). The law amendment of 1986 introduced a prior art search report (sec. 7 UMA).

A utility right holder can claim the injunction and damages against an infringer (sec. 24 UMA). Sec. 24(2) stipulates that who intentionally and negligently infringes shall be liable for damages.[19] Negligence may be denied when there are reasons for the invalidity of the right. Yet in such case, financial compensation based on unjust enrichment can be claimed.[20] On the other hand, the right holder should carefully assess the validity of the utility model right before enforcement e.g. by warning alleged infringers or else might be liable for unjustified threats.[21] Utility models are granted for a period of ten years from the date of filing.

In **France**, the utility model (*certificat d'utilité*) system was introduced by the law of 1968. Different to national, European or PCT patents in France, a utility model is only examined as to formalities by the Institut National de la Propriété Industrielle (INPI) and registered (Art. L611-2 Code of Intellectual Property (CPI: Code de la Propriété Intellectuelle)).[22] The utility model right holder is required to request a search report made by INPI (Art. L615-6 CPI).[23]

b) In **East Asia**, countries including Japan, Cambodia, China, Indonesia, Korea, Laos, Malaysia, Philippine, Thailand,[24] Vietnam, etc. introduced utility model systems. In many of them, there is no substantive examination, but some countries such as Indonesia, Korea, Malaysia make a substantive examination as to novelty.

In **China**, the utility model system was introduced in 1984 at the same time of the patent system.[25] In China, a utility model is registered without substantial examination (sec. 40 Patent Act). A search report is not regarded as a requirement for enforcement of the utility right, but an infringement court demands the right holder to request a search report of the utility model by the Patent Office and to file it as evidence (sec. 61 PA), or the right holder by himself/herself requests a search

19. This sec. 24(2) corresponds to sec. 139(2) Patent Act. There is no clear provision to supposition of negligence in the PA in Germany as sec. 103 PA in PA, but it is in normal patent case acknowledged by German case law. See, e.g., BENKARD, Patentgesetz *(Commentary on German Patent Act)*, 11th ed. 2015, 1753.
20. German Federal Supreme Court, 30 November 1976, GRUR 1977, 250 – *Kunststoffhohlprofil*; German Federal Supreme Court, 24 November 1981, GRUR 1982, 301 – *Kunststoffhohlprofil II*.
21. German Federal Supreme Court, 13 December 1962, GRUR 1963, 255 – *Kindernähmaschinen*; German Federal Supreme Court, 11 December 1973, GRUR 1974, 290 – *maschenfester Strumpf*.
22. The INPI examines novelty of French national patent applications, though (but only novelty and not inventive step).
23. Such utility model systems in Germany and France influenced the law amendment of 1993 in Japan. See, e,g,, K. KUMAGAI, Jitsuyō Shin'an Seido no minaoshi ni tsuite (About the reform of utility model system), 16 Nihon Kōgyōshōyuken Hōgakkai Nenpō 135 (1992).
24. W. WERAWORAWIT, Utility Models in Thailand, in: HEATH/KAMPERMAN SANDERS, Industrial Property in the Bio-medical Age, 2003, 269.
25. In China, utility model right is a type of exclusive right (Zhuanli quan), which encompass also patent and design right. Here the Patent Act is used for the translation of the name of the Chinese Patent, Utility Model and Design Act in the correct meaning. For a history. See Y. LI, Utility Models in China, in: HEATH/KAMPERMAN SANDERS, Industrial Property in the Bio-medical Age, 2003, 257.

report (sec. 57 Regulation of PA).[26] The search report by the Patent Office has no legally binding force and appeal against it is impossible. The validity of a utility model right shall be finally examined by the invalidation trial by the Patent Office (secs. 45 to 47 PA). The Chinese Supreme Court by the legal interpretation No. 29 of 2009 (sec. 18) clarified that the warned party may file a counter lawsuit against the right holder who has warned but not filed an infringement lawsuit after the warning.

In **Korea**, utility model applications were registered after substantive examination just as the old system of Japan, but by the law amendment of 1999, Korea adopted almost the same system as in Japan, namely a non-examined registration and a required search report before enforcement. However, by the law amendment of 2006, Korea reverted to the substantial examination system for utility models (secs. 12, etc. Utility Model Act).[27]

26. It is said that there is a clear difference on the inventive step assessment in China between patents and utility models. The Chinese Supreme Court stated in a case of utility model (Chinese Supreme Court, 19 January 2012, Case No. 19 (Zhixing zi) of 2011) stated that in principle, only the prior art which belongs to the same technical field should be taken into account in the assessment of the inventive step of the utility model.
27. H. Ahn/N. Lee, Utility Models, in: Kim/Heath, Intellectual Property Law in Korea, 2nd ed. 2015, 79.

Index of Japanese Decisions in Chronological Order

Bold numbers refer to the leading cases commented in this book.

30 November 2010, IP High Court - *Shellfish Fastener*: 15/25; 15/26; 15/27.

30 November 2010, IP High Court: 18/24.

30 Nov 2010, Tokyo District Court: 36/6.

8 March 2011, IP High Court - *Aluminium Foil*: **6**; 6/3.

23 March 2011, IP High Court - *Method of Producing Anhydrite*: 20/21.

28 March 2011, IP High Court - *Lamivudine and Abacavir*: 58/25.

28 April 2011, Supreme Court - *Pacif Capsule 30mg*: **58**; 58/13; 59/5; 60/1; 60/11.

23 June 2011, IP High Court - *Device and Method for Food Wrapping and Forming*: 30/1.

7 September 2011, IP High Court - *Rice Cakes*: **36**; 36/5.

4 October 2011, IP High Court: 18/14.

22 December 2011, IP High Court - *Processing of Heavy Metal Immobilization*: 54/26.

24 January 2012, IP High Court - *Solid Golf Ball*: 54/12; 54/13; 54/25.

27 January 2012, IP High Court: 37/3.

31 January 2012, IP High Court - *Method for Producing Semiconductor Device*: 6/9.

8 February 2012, IP High Court - *Alarm Apparatus with Battery*: **27**; 27/1.

29 February 2012, IP High Court - *Rotary Clamp*: 12/6.

22 March 2012, Osaka District Court - *Oven Heating Element*: **29**; 29/4.

22 March 2012, IP High Court: 55/1.

11 April 2012, IP High Court: 9/2.

23 May 2012, Tokyo District Court - *Compositions for Cleansing*: 55/6.

10 September 2012, IP High Court: 18/14.

26 September 2012, IP High Court - *Visual Image Generation Method for Medical Use*: 40/9.

27 September 2012, Osaka District Court - *Combination Medicine for Diabetes* Treatment: I/48; **30**; 30/2; 31/3; 53/7.

17 October 2012, IP High Court: 18/15.

21 November 2012, IP High Court: 18/24.

5 December 2012, IP High Court - *Ecology Action Sheet*: 1/5.

31 January 2013, IP High Court: 16/41.

1 February 2013, IP High Court - *Container for Disposing Paper*: I/53; 54/21; **55**; 55/2; 55/5.

21 February 2013, Osaka District Court - *Hopper for Mixing Machine for Particles showed a similar view with respect to the meaning of "indispensable for the solution of the problem"*: 30/7.

28 February 2013, Tokyo District Court - *Pioglitazone*: 30/3.

Alphabetical Keyword Index

MAX PLANCK SERIES ON ASIAN INTELLECTUAL PROPERTY LAW

1. Christopher Heath & Kung-Chung Liu (eds), *The Protection of Well-Known Marks in Asia,* 2000 (ISBN 90-411-9705-2).
2. Christoph Antons, *Intellectual Property Law in Indonesia,* 2000 (ISBN 90-411-9803-2).
3. Christopher Heath,*The System of Unfair Competition Prevention in Japan,* 2001 (ISBN 90-411-9837-7).
4. Christopher Heath & Kung-Chung Liu (eds), *Legal Rules of Technology Transfer in Asia,* 2002 (ISBN 90-411-9883-0).
5. Christopher Heath (ed.), *Intellectual Property Law in Asia,* 2002 (ISBN 90-411-9894-6).
6. Byung-Il Kim & Christopher Heath (eds), *Intellectual Property Law in Korea,* (2nd Edition), 2015 (ISBN978-90-411-5831-4).
7. Christopher Heath (ed.), *Intellectual Property Law in Taiwan,* 2003 (ISBN 90-411-9920-9).
8. Christopher Heath & Anselm Kamperman Sanders (eds), *Industrial Property in the Bio-Medical Age,* 2003 (ISBN 90-411-9926-8).
9. Christopher Heath (ed.), *Parallel Imports in Asia,* 2004 (ISBN 90-411-2114-5).
10. Christoph Antons, Michael Blakeney & Christopher Heath (eds), *Intellectual Property Harmonisation within ASEAN and APEC,* 2004 (ISBN 90-411-2292-3).
11. Peter Ganea, Thomas Pattloch & Christopher Heath (eds), *Intellectual Property Law in China,* 2005 (ISBN 90-411-2340-7).
12. Peter Ganea, Christopher Heath & Hiroshi Saitô (eds), *Japanese Copyright Law: Writings in Honour of Gerhard Schricker,* 2005 (ISBN 90-411-2393-8).
13. Shan Hailing, *The Protection of Trade Secrets in China* (2nd Edition Rev.), 2012 (ISBN978-90-411-3893-4).
14. Christoph Antons (ed.), *Traditional Knowledge, Traditional Cultural Expressions and Intellectual Property Law in the Asia-Pacific Region,* 2009 (ISBN 978-90-411-2721-1).
15. Christoph Antons (ed.), *The Enforcement of Intellectual Property Rights: Comparative Perspectives from the Asia-Pacific Region,* 2011 (ISBN 978-90-411-3219-2).
16. Kung-Chung Liu & Reto M. Hilty (eds), *The Enforcement of Patents,* 2011 (ISBN 978-90-411-3527-8).
17. Christopher Heath & Atsuhiro Furuta (eds), *Japanese Patent Law – Cases and Comments*, 2019 (ISBN 978-90-411-9419-0)

www.ingramcontent.com/pod-product-compliance
Lightning Source LLC
LaVergne TN
LVHW020649300926
849161LV00004B/871